England in
LITERATURE

AMERICA READS   **CLASSIC EDITION**

AMERICA READS

CLASSIC EDITION

BEGINNINGS IN LITERATURE
Alan L. Madsen
Sarah Durand Wood
Philip M. Connors

DISCOVERIES IN LITERATURE
L. Jane Christensen
Edmund J. Farrell

EXPLORATIONS IN LITERATURE
Nancy C. Millett
Raymond J. Rodrigues

PATTERNS IN LITERATURE
Edmund J. Farrell
Ouida H. Clapp
Karen J. Kuehner

TRADITIONS IN LITERATURE
Helen McDonnell
James E. Miller, Jr.
Russell J. Hogan

THE UNITED STATES IN LITERATURE
The Red Badge of Courage Edition
Three Long Stories Edition
James E. Miller, Jr.
Kerry M. Wood
Carlota Cárdenas de Dwyer

ENGLAND IN LITERATURE
Macbeth edition
Hamlet edition
John Pfordresher
Gladys V. Veidemanis
Helen McDonnell

CLASSICS IN WORLD LITERATURE
Kerry M. Wood
Helen McDonnell
John Pfordresher
Mary Alice Fite
Paul Lankford

The authors and editors wish to thank the following consultants for reading and teaching editorial material and proposed selections for America Reads.
■ Barbara E. Anderson, Junior Level Coordinator and Teacher, James B. Conant High School, Hoffman Estates, Illinois
■ Anita Arnold, Chairman, English Department, Thomas Jefferson High School, San Antonio, Texas
■ Pat Dudley, Principal, Jane Long Elementary School, Abilene ISD, Abilene, Texas
■ Dr. V. Pauline Hodges-McLain, Coordinator, Language Arts, Jefferson County Public Schools, Golden, Colorado
■ Rance Howe, English/Language Arts Consultant K–12, Anoka-Hennepin ISD 11, Coon Rapids, Minnesota
■ Lisbeth Johnson, English Teacher, Capital High School, Olympia, Washington
■ Daniel Lane, Supervisor of Humanities, Holmdel Twp. Public Schools, Holmdel, New Jersey
■ May Lee, English Teacher, Baldwin Senior High School, Baldwin, New York
■ Richard T. Martin, English Department Chairman, Burrillville Junior-Senior High School, Harrisville, Rhode Island
■ Barbara McCormick, Systemwide Chairman of English, Greenville Public Schools, Greenville, Mississippi
■ James McCullough, English Teacher, Carmel High School, Mundelein, Illinois
■ Cathy Nufer, Teacher, Grade 6, Elm School, Hinsdale, Illinois
■ Marlyn Payne, Teacher, Grade 7, Nichols Middle School, Evanston, Illinois
■ Sally P. Pfeifer, English Department Chair, Lewis and Clark High School, Spokane, Washington
■ James B. Phillips, Instructor in English and Reading, Norwood Senior High School, Norwood, Massachusetts
■ John Pratt, Language Arts Chairperson, Edison High School, Stockton, California
■ Cora Wolfe, English Department Chairperson, Antelope Union High School, Wellton, Arizona

England in LITERATURE

AMERICA READS　　　　　　　**CLASSIC EDITION**

John Pfordresher
Gladys V. Veidemanis
Helen McDonnell

S C O T T ,　 F O R E S M A N

Scott, Foresman and Company　　　Editorial Offices: Glenview, Illinois
Regional Offices:
Sunnyvale, California　　Tucker, Georgia　　Glenview, Illinois　　Oakland, New Jersey　　Dallas, Texas

John Pfordresher

Professor of English Literature, Georgetown University, Washington, D.C. Editor of *Variorum Edition of the Idylls of the King* and coauthor of *Matthew Arnold, Prose Writings: The Critical Heritage.* Author of articles in the *English Journal, Studies in Short Fiction,* and *Studies in Bibliography.* Currently a member of the National Council of Teachers of English Commission on Literature.

Gladys V. Veidemanis

Chairman of the Department of English at North High School, Oshkosh, Wisconsin. Wisconsin High-School Teacher of the Year (1983–1984). Member of the National Advisory Panel for the British Broadcasting Corporation's *The Shakespeare Plays.* Director, National Council of Teachers of English Commission on Literature.

Helen McDonnell

Professor of English (adjunct faculty) at Manatee Community College, South Campus, Venice, Florida. Formerly: English Supervisor of the Ocean Township Junior and Senior High Schools, Oakhurst, New Jersey; member of the Commission on Literature, National Council of Teachers of English. Member and former chairman of the Committee on Comparative and World Literature, NCTE. Coeditor, *Teacher's Guide to World Short Stories,* NCTE.

Cover: *The Opening of Tower Bridge* (detail) by William Lionel Wyllie, 1894. *Guildhall Art Gallery, City of London.* Bridgeman Art Library/Art Resource, NY.

Pronunciation key and dictionary entries are from *Scott, Foresman Advanced Dictionary* by E. L. Thorndike and Clarence L. Barnhart. Copyright © 1988 Scott, Foresman and Company.

ISBN: 0-673-29384-X (*Macbeth* edition)
ISBN: 0-673-29383-1 (*Hamlet* edition)

CONTENTS

UNIT 1   THE ANGLO-SAXONS   *450–1066*

THINKING CRITICALLY ABOUT LITERATURE

George Herbert *286*	**Easter Wings** *287*	
	Virtue *287*	
Andrew Marvell *288*	**To His Coy Mistress** *289*	
John Milton *292*	**On His Having Arrived at the Age of Twenty-Three** *293*	
	On His Blindness *293*	*Apply metonymy*
	from **Paradise Lost, Book I** *294*	*Apply blank verse*
The King James Bible *302*	**Genesis, Chapters 1–3** *302*	

THINKING CRITICALLY ABOUT LITERATURE

CONCEPT REVIEW	*309*	
William Shakespeare	**Sonnet 73** *309*	
CONTENT REVIEW	*310*	
COMPOSITION REVIEW	*311*	

UNIT 4 THE AGE OF REASON *1660–1780*

	Time Line *312*	
	Preview *314*	
	Background *315*	
John Dryden *320*	*from* **Absalom and Achitophel** *321*	*Apply heroic couplet*
	from **Mac Flecknoe** *322*	
Samuel Pepys *324*	*from* **The Diary** *325*	
Jonathan Swift *333*	**A Satirical Elegy on the Death of a Late Famous General** *334*	*Apply satire*
	A Description of a City Shower *335*	
	A Modest Proposal *337*	*Review irony*
	A Voyage to Brobdingnag, *from* **Gulliver's Travels** *344*	*Apply point of view*
Sir Richard Steele *358*	**The Spectator Club** *358*	*Apply tone*
Joseph Addison *365*	**Will Wimble** *365*	
	Party Patches *367*	
Daniel Defoe *372*	**The Education of Women** *372*	

Apply epigram

Apply setting

THINKING CRITICALLY ABOUT LITERATURE

UNIT 5   THE ROMANTICS   *1780–1830*

Apply repetition

Review rhythm

(Handwritten notes: identify author, matching. (bank) multiple choice)

(Handwritten note: mock epic)

(Handwritten note: attitude)

(Handwritten note: popular lines)

(Handwritten note: essay. & what is it about. Social problems in certian stories. what the problem is & how it is addressed.)

THINKING CRITICALLY ABOUT LITERATURE

UNIT 6   THE VICTORIANS   *1830–1880*

THINKING CRITICALLY ABOUT LITERATURE

UNIT 7   NEW DIRECTIONS   *1880–1915*

THINKING CRITICALLY ABOUT LITERATURE

UNIT 8   THE TWENTIETH CENTURY   *1915–*

THINKING CRITICALLY ABOUT LITERATURE

READING LITERATURE

COMMENTS

READER'S NOTES

THEMES IN ENGLISH LITERATURE

THE CHANGING ENGLISH LANGUAGE

HANDBOOK OF LITERARY TERMS

WRITER'S HANDBOOK   *933*

GLOSSARY OF LITERARY TERMS   *968*

PREVIEW

★*England in Literature* has eight chronological units presenting a survey of major British writers from the beginning until the present time. Alternate editions offer *Hamlet* or *Macbeth* by William Shakespeare.

UNIT ORGANIZATION

Every unit begins with a time line showing major events from world history, the English monarchs, and landmarks in English literature. A unit preview follows. Next, a background article provides political and social history, so that the works of literature can be read in a more meaningful context.

Author biographies precede each selection or group of selections. Often, these contain some discussion of why that author is considered important. Generally, authors appear in order of their birthdates.

Most selections contain **footnotes** or **sidenotes** to define and pronounce words or to help clarify passages. A **date** on the right following a selection indicates the publication of the work. If there is a date on the left, it indicates the year the author wrote the book. *Circa* (or its abbreviation, *c.*) with a date means "approximate."

Think and Discuss questions follow each selection or group of selections. They are divided into three levels: *Understanding, Analyzing,* and *Extending.* You may find it helpful to study the questions as a guide before you read a selection.

Many selections are preceded by a **handbook reference** that directs you to an article in the Handbook of Literary Terms at the back of

the text. There you will learn about or review an essential literary term before you read the selection. Then, following the selection, **Applying/Reviewing** questions about that literary term help ensure your understanding of the literary techniques involved. After a term has been introduced, it may appear in boldface type in the editorial material accompanying subsequent selections.

Vocabulary exercises focus on selected words in a piece of writing and help you learn or review techniques for determining the meanings of unfamiliar words as well as for increasing your vocabulary. You may be tested on the words in these exercises.

Thinking Skills exercises will help you learn to think about literature in new ways by *classifying, generalizing, synthesizing* (putting together parts and elements to form new ideas), and *evaluating.*

Composition assignments and ideas follow most selections. You can refer to the Writer's Handbook at the back of this text for more help with some of these assignments.

Enrichment sections occasionally provide ideas for class projects, research, and speaking and listening activities.

OTHER FEATURES

Five types of articles occur from time to time throughout this text.

Comment articles provide interesting sidelights on a work, an author, or a period. (See, for example, "The Treasure of Sutton Hoo" on page 42.)

Reader's Note articles provide help in reading certain works, or present a critical insight into an author's technique or style. (See, for example, "Dover Beach" on page 415.)

A **Themes in English Literature** article in each unit explores the major themes in the writings of the different periods. (See, for example, "The Inner Life" on page 847.)

The Changing English Language articles, also appearing in each unit, discuss the development of the language and provide useful insights about why we speak as we do. (See, for example, page 147.)

A **Reading Literature** article in each unit gives you some helpful hints on reading various types of literature. (See, for example, "Reading Shakespearean Drama" on page 190.) **Reading Literature Skillfully** exercises follow the selections to which these articles apply, to give you further practice in exercising certain reading skills.

UNIT REVIEWS

Each unit ends with a review entitled **Thinking Critically About Literature.** It is divided into three parts.

In the **Concept Review** appears a new, short work typical of the period, accompanied by sidenotes to guide your reading. Questions then measure your understanding of the work and review applicable literary terms that you have studied in the unit.

In the **Content Review,** classifying, generalizing, synthesizing, and evaluating questions help you review the selections in the unit.

A **Composition Review** provides topics for writing about the period or the literary genres you have studied.

END-OF-BOOK MATERIAL

The **Handbook of Literary Terms** contains brief lessons about the important terms you need in order to understand and discuss the literature. Handbook references preceding selected writings refer you to specific articles, to be studied before reading the selections.

The **Writer's Handbook** contains lessons on the writing process and on writing about various types of literature. You will be referred to these lessons from time to time.

A **Glossary of Literary Terms** provides definitions and examples of many more terms than are taught in the Handbook.

A dictionary-type **Glossary** contains all words featured in Vocabulary exercises, plus other words you will encounter in your reading.

The various types of literature included in this text have been written over more than twelve centuries by a wide variety of authors. An understanding of this vast heritage of literature in English provides insights into the culture that profoundly influenced the founding and development of the United States. We continue to read these works, however, not only for what they can teach us about ourselves—where we have come from and where we are going—but for the very real enjoyments they continue to offer.

HE ANGLO-SAXONS 450–1066

450	550	650	750

HISTORY AND THE ARTS

- Roman withdrawal begins
  - St. Patrick converts Irish
    - Anglo-Saxon invasion begins
      - Mayan culture (Mexico)
        - King Arthur (?)
- Mohammed born (Arabia)
  - St. Augustine converts English
    - T'ang Dynasty (China)
      - Lindisfarne founded
        - Sutton Hoo ship burial
- Iona monastery founded
- Synod of Whitby
- Jarrow founded

MONARCHS AND HOUSES

SEPARATE KINGDOMS

ENGLISH LITERATURE

- Lindisfarne Gospels
  - *Beowulf* transcribed

Gorgon's head from Roman temple at Bath, England.

St. Patrick stained glass window by J. Henry Dearle.

Illuminated page from the Book of Lindisfarne.

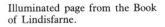

UNIT 1

850	950	1050

- Vikings invade Lindisfarne
  - Charlemagne's Holy Roman Empire
    - Battle of Edington

- Ericson explores North America (?)

Battle of Hastings

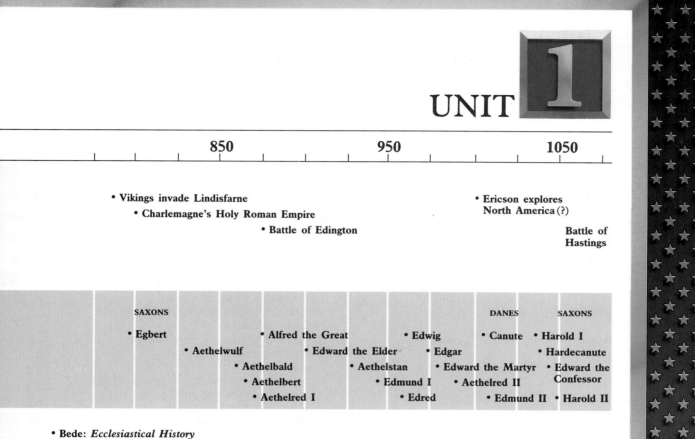

| | SAXONS | | | | DANES | SAXONS |

- Egbert
  - Alfred the Great • Edwig
  - Aethelwulf • Edward the Elder • Edgar
    - Aethelbald • Aethelstan
    - Aethelbert • Edmund I
    - Aethelred I • Edred
- Canute • Harold I
  - Hardecanute
- Edward the Martyr • Edward the Confessor
- Aethelred II
  - Edmund II • Harold II

- Bede: *Ecclesiastical History*
  - Book of Kells
  - Book of Durrow
  - *Anglo-Saxon Chronicle* begun
  - Exeter Book

Reliquary bust of Charlemagne, Cathedral Treasury, Aachen.

Silver coin depicting a Viking longship. 9th century.

Manuscript illumination depicting Alfred the Great.

1

PREVIEW

UNIT 1   THE ANGLO-SAXONS   450–1066

Authors
The *Beowulf*-poet
The Exeter Book
Bede
Celtic Literature

Features
Reading an Epic Poem
Comment: The Nature of Grendel
Reader's Note: The Poetry of Beowulf
Reader's Note: Translating Beowulf
Comment: Heroic Morality
Comment: The Treasure of Sutton Hoo
Themes in English Literature:
    The Violent Face of Nature
The Changing English Language

Application of Literary Terms
alliteration
metaphor
foreshadowing
elegy
personification
theme

Reading Literature Skillfully
comparison/contrast

Vocabulary
etymology
context
antonyms

Thinking Skills
classifying
generalizing
evaluating

Composition
Writing an Anglo-Saxon Letter
Explaining Beowulf's Motives
Describing a Monster's Lair
Writing a Persuasive Essay
Defining Beowulf's Heroism
Explaining Wiglaf's Role in *Beowulf*
Describing a City in Ruins
Analyzing an Elegy
Explaining How Riddles Reflect Daily Life
Analyzing How a Riddle Works
Explaining a Literary Comparison
Analyzing Bede's Theme
Describing a Change of Seasons
Narrating the Fall of Trenn

Enrichment
Researching a Reference

Thinking Critically About Literature
Concept Review
Content Review
Composition Review

BACKGROUND

THE ANGLO-SAXONS 450–1066

For the first eleven hundred years of its recorded history, the island of Britain suffered a series of invasions. The southern part of the island, warmed by the waters of the Gulf Stream, was inviting to outsiders with its mild climate and rich, easily-tilled soil. The long, irregular coastline, broken frequently by bays and rivers, provided safe anchorage for invading fleets, which then followed the rivers to penetrate deep into the island's interior. Each successive invasion brought bloodshed and sorrow, but each also brought a new people with a new culture. Through conflict and amalgamation these different peoples created a nation.

Cave dwellers lived on the island 250,000 years ago. Invaders from the Iberian peninsula (modern Spain and Portugal) overcame their fragile culture about 2000 B.C., creating a society sophisticated enough to erect Stonehenge—the circle of huge upright stones called *megaliths*—on Salisbury Plain. Then a new group appeared, the Celts. Migrating from further east, the Celtic peoples spread throughout Europe before reaching the British Isles around 600 B.C. The Celts built walled farms and hut villages. They used bronze and, later, iron tools and grew crops. Separate Celtic tribes, each with its own king, warred with each other, erecting timber and stone fortresses and riding to battle in two-wheeled chariots. Their priests—called *druids*—conducted sacrifices in forest shrines.

ROMAN BRITAIN

In 55 B.C. Rome, already dominating the Mediterranean world, first tried to conquer Britain. The Roman general Julius Caesar raided the land to punish the Britons for helping the Continental Celts in their struggle with the Romans. The account he later wrote of his raids begins the recorded history of Britain. Nearly a hundred years later, in A.D. 43, the Roman emperor Claudius successfully invaded the island. Despite the rebellion led a few years later by Boadicea (bō′ad i sē′ə), queen of one of the British tribes, the Romans eventually subdued most of Britain, driving the defeated tribes into the highlands of Wales and Scotland. To keep them there, the Romans garrisoned the province of Britannia with three legions, and early in the second century the emperor Hadrian built a wall seventy-three miles long to protect the northern border.

Roman Britain became a prosperous colony with a population of three to four million people. Over one hundred towns served as administrative centers. Some of these had large buildings—meeting halls, law courts, temples, amphitheaters, and public baths—as well as elaborate sanitation systems. Straight, well-made Roman roads connected the towns. But Roman Britain was primarily a rural society. The sites of over six hundred large country villas have been discovered; there may have been as many as eight hundred.

The Romans ruled Britain for nearly four

Stonehenge, in Salisbury Plain, is a circle of huge rocks, or megaliths.

hundred years, but with the decline of Rome itself after the year 300, life in the province became more troubled. Warriors from Ireland, Scotland, and Germany periodically raided the British coast, looking for plunder and taking slaves. (St. Patrick, a Briton, first reached Ireland as the captive of a group of these raiders.) In 410 the city of Rome fell to an army of German barbarians, and the emperor Honorius sent a letter to the Roman Britons announcing that they must now see to their own defense.

After the Roman withdrawal, some Britons continued to think of themselves as citizens of the empire; they still spoke Latin and tried to keep up the old forms of provincial economic and political life. But soon towns were being abandoned, manufacturing declined, and tribal warfare reappeared. The Celtic language, with some words adapted from Latin, became once again the dominant tongue. Weak and divided, Britain stood open to foreign aggression.

To the east, across a relatively short span of sea, lay the coast of the European mainland, inhabited by a number of Germanic tribes, including the Angles, Saxons, and Jutes (see map). Germanic tribesmen were vigorous warriors and skilled seamen, but their low-lying homelands, which had poor soil and were subject to frequent flooding from the North Sea, were inadequate for a growing population. By 441 they had a firm foothold at the mouth of the Thames River, and groups of Angles, Saxons, and Jutes were spreading throughout eastern, central, and southern Britain, driving the Celtic inhabitants before them and settling their own people on the conquered land. As had happened during the Roman occupation, the defeated fled west into the highlands of Wales. It is among these people that the legend of King Arthur and his Round Table arose. (The earliest known reference to King Arthur appears some 500 years later; see page 66.)

In some areas of the northeast, the Anglo-Saxon peoples may have managed, after conquest, to coexist with the Britons, but in the southeast they evidently expelled the former inhabitants altogether. By the middle of the sixth century most of the southern lowland part of the island was under the control of a people we now call—after the Angles—the English.

ANGLO-SAXON ENGLAND

The culture of these Germanic settlers, during their first decades in England, seems to be faithfully recorded in the heroic poem *Beowulf*. This was a tribal society, ruled by warrior kings who led their men into battle. Defeat and capture meant death. Even in peacetime one's position was never secure. There were always rival warriors within the tribe seeking to take power, and neighboring tribes posed a constant threat.

To protect himself and his lands, a king gathered around him a retinue of fighting men called *thanes*. By oath they pledged to defend him. Defeat in battle for a thane meant death or slavery at the hands of the victors, so battle was fierce and unyielding. The king rewarded faithful service with treasure: rings, gold, and especially weapons. These gifts were a form of honor due to faithful thanes. The wealth given by a king usually came from robbing someone else, however. Bloodshed was common. Any offense to one thane had to be avenged, and his king and fellow thanes had to come to his aid. Hence there were endless feuds both between individuals and between tribes.

The royal living quarters were a small cluster of wooden buildings surrounded by a stockade fence. (Castles built of stone did not appear until later.) The main structure was the mead-hall. *Mead* (mēd) is a fermented drink made from water, honey, malt, and yeast. Modern archaeologists have found the remains of one mead-hall that is eighty feet long and forty feet wide, its walls made of wooden planks over five inches thick, sunk eight feet into the ground. Here the king, thanes, wives, and servants gathered together, and here the warriors slept after the king retired to a smaller outbuilding. While the king and his court feasted, they were entertained by a singing poet called a *scop*. He composed his poetry extemporaneously—recounting both past history and present events. The scop was more than an entertainer. Fame and honor mattered greatly to these people, and it was the scop who preserved a record of their achievements for later generations.

These relatively primitive warrior bands now spread over much of England and took over some of the old Roman towns and governmental procedures, such as taxing, conscripting men for

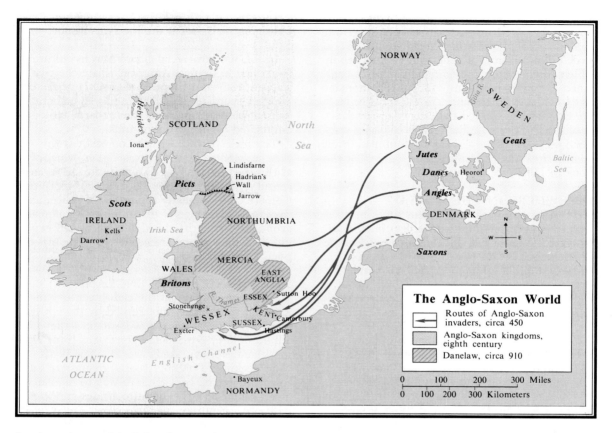

The Anglo-Saxon World

Routes of Anglo-Saxon invaders, circa 450

Anglo-Saxon kingdoms, eighth century

Danelaw, circa 910

local armies, and building long defensive walls. The country was divided into a number of petty kingdoms. Soon, more ambitious kings began to assert an authority over other rulers, each claiming to be a ruling king, or *bretwalda*. The first of them, Aethelbert, who ruled from 560 to 616, seems already to have dreamed of a nationwide confederation of tribes that would bring unity and a measure of peace to the land.

These efforts at achieving unity and peace found aid in the developing power and influence of the Christian church. Even in Roman days there had been Christian communities in Britain, though the invasion of pagan Germanic tribes nearly destroyed them. St. Patrick began converting Celtic Ireland to Christianity in the 430s. With time the Irish church spread as far as the remote Scottish islands called the Hebrides, where it established the celebrated monastery of Iona in 563. But Anglo-Saxon Britain remained pagan until 597, when St. Augustine, sent from Rome to convert England, established the first archbishopric at Canterbury. During the next forty years missionaries were able, despite setbacks, to convert most of the Anglo-Saxon kings and their people to Christianity.

The spread of Christianity was crucial for the development of Anglo-Saxon culture. The Church brought contact with the distant and ancient Mediterranean world. To the illiterate Germanic tribes it brought the essential skill for advanced culture—writing. Soon Anglo-Saxon monasteries were copying books from Rome and beginning to produce the illuminated manuscripts for which they are so famous. The Church also served as an early force for unity and peace, trying to teach new values to these warrior-kings—compassion and cooperation, instead of arrogance and violence.

Anglo-Saxon culture reached a peak during the rule of the Mercian *bretwaldas* of the eighth century. From this era come most of the 30,000 lines of Anglo-Saxon poetry that have survived, as well as important works in prose such as Bede's Latin history of England. It is an era in which Anglo-Saxon and Christian cultures combined to form a new synthesis. This is dramatically evident, for instance, in the transfer of the complex, interlaced patterns of ornament, once used to decorate the regalia of pagan warrior-kings (see pages 42–43), to illuminate Bible manuscripts like the Lindisfarne Gospels or the Book of Durrow.

ELSEWHERE IN THE WORLD

Cultures may peak at different times in different countries. While the Mercian *bretwaldas* struggled to unite England, in northern Europe Charlemagne (742–814), king of the Franks, embarked on an effort to expand his nation's power, taking northern Italy, northern Spain, and parts of Germany. In 800 he declared himself the Emperor of the West and instituted what he hoped would be a renewal of the reign of the Caesars, the Holy Roman Empire.

In Arabia the prophet Mohammed (570?–632) founded the new religion of Islam. His followers, carrying with them the collection of his sayings called the *Koran*, spread throughout northern Africa into Spain and India, establishing their new faith and a rich Arabic culture that achieved striking advances in mathematics, built richly ornamented cities, and sponsored poets and philosophers. Islam also came into conflict with developing western cultures; in 778 Charlemagne defeated the Moslems in northern Spain.

In the Western Hemisphere Mayan culture flourished in Central America, where the city states of the "Old Empire" (317–987) perfected a highly accurate calendar, employed elaborate hieroglyphic writing, and erected large cities dominated by massive pyramids.

The most powerful nation on earth at this time in history, however, was China, which was at the crest of the T'ang Dynasty in the seventh century. Under emperor Taizong (627–650) the Chinese enjoyed nearly fifty years of peace, and they took advantage of this tranquility to create economic prosperity through wide-spread exportation of their goods, and to develop the arts of poetry and painting.

THE VIKING ERA IN ENGLAND

The achievements of the eighth century in England were finally interrupted by the appearance of yet another wave of invaders—the Vikings. They crossed the North Sea from Denmark and Norway. At first only a few boats came seeking to plunder coastal monasteries and towns. These early raids gave way to regular attacks after 835. Then entire armies appeared, with fleets of up to 250 ships commanded by Danish kings. Between 867 and 877 the Vikings invaded and took over most of the northeast and central portions of England. Part or all of the Anglo-Saxon kingdoms of Northumbria, East Anglia, Mercia, and Essex were absorbed

Hay-making and plowing are depicted in this page from an *Anglo-Saxon Calendar*. 11th century. *British Library, London*

into the Danelaw (see map, page 5), a region where Danish rather than Anglo-Saxon law was in force. (The restless Vikings continued their explorations; one of their leaders, Leif Ericson, probably landed in North America around the year 1000.)

The most successful English opponent of the Vikings was Alfred the Great (849–899). He ruled the one surviving Anglo-Saxon kingdom, Wessex, in southern England. To prevent the Vikings from seizing Wessex the way they had the Danelaw, he built what was essentially the first English navy, a fleet of longboats, each manned by sixty oarsmen. To repel unexpected attacks, he constructed fortified towns—*burhs* (bergs)—in a grid pattern throughout Wessex, manned by standing garrisons. After a series of setbacks, Alfred decisively defeated the Vikings at Edington in 878, forcing them to retire within the Danelaw. In the uneasy peace that followed, Alfred was able to foster a second great era of Anglo-Saxon literary culture at his court, where along with the scholars he had invited from the continent, he studied and translated Latin works, including Bede's history of England, into Anglo-Saxon. About 891 the *Anglo-Saxon Chronicle* was begun. A year-by-year account of happenings in the kingdom, it remains our greatest single source of information about this historical period.

Alfred's successors were able to contain the Vikings, but essentially the England of the tenth century was divided between Scandinavian peoples in the north and east, and the surviving Anglo-Saxon peoples in the southeast and south. The struggle for control of this severed land was only halted for good by another invasion, the last one, that of the French-Norman, William the Conqueror.

The Anglo-Saxons dominated the history of England for 600 years. Over that period, so full of strife and confusion, this hardy people nevertheless managed to build some of the foundations for the culture of their land. They provided its language; they began its literature; and they established traditions in law, government, and religion. They were the first English people.

THINKING ABOUT GRAPHIC AIDS
Using the Time Line

The time line on pages xx–1 shows the chronological sequence of the historic and literary events discussed in Unit 1. Keep in mind that although events happen at the same time or follow each other, they do not necessarily share a cause-effect relationship. For example, both the Battle of Edington and the beginning of the *Anglo-Saxon Chronicle* occurred during the reign of Alfred the Great. Edington was a major victory for Alfred, but there is no evidence that he was connected to the writing of the *Chronicle*. Use the time line to answer these questions:

1. About how long after the Roman withdrawal did England remain separate kingdoms?
2. Who is considered the first king of all England?
3. Could Aethelred II have been the son of Aethelred I?
4. About how old was Christianity when Mohammed, founder of Islam, was born?
5. For about how many years was England ruled by Danish kings?
6. Could Bede have included Edward the Martyr in his *Ecclesiastical History?* Could he have included St. Patrick?

Using the Map

The map on page 5 shows the geographical area discussed in the Background to Unit 1. Use the map to answer these questions:

1. About how many miles did the Saxons have to sail to reach Kent?
2. What made East Anglia especially vulnerable to invasion?
3. What about the position of Wales made it a logical place for the defeated to flee?
4. Roughly what percent of the entire island did the Danelaw cover?

Many of the world's great literatures begin with the appearance of a long verse narrative describing the adventures and achievements of a hero from the distant past—an **epic poem.** These records of heroic deeds served warrior cultures by boosting tribal pride and by helping to teach later generations a code of values.

It may be difficult for you, as a twentieth-century reader, to project yourself completely into the thoughts and feelings of an Anglo-Saxon audience. Still, by understanding why the *Beowulf*-poet wrote certain speeches, actions, and scenes in certain ways, you can understand a great deal about the poet's world. Here are some guidelines for reading the poem.

Understand the nature of the epic hero. The heroic actions described—perilous journeys, battles with monsters, and so on—may be familiar to you; however, concepts of heroes differ from culture to culture. As you read *Beowulf,* look for clues that tell what *this* hero is like. Winning always matters, but the epic focus is more on *how* the hero fights. Read to learn what weapons and strategies Beowulf uses and how he responds to unforseen challenges. You will soon notice that the hero, like everything else in the poem, is definitely larger-than-life.

Appreciate the pageantry. Ceremony plays an important part in Anglo-Saxon life. After Beowulf has killed the monster Grendel, for example, King Hrothgar delivers a speech and formally presents the hero with gifts, which the poet meticulously lists. The oratory and the rewards define what the poet considers the most important values in life: honor, loyalty, perseverance, and measured good sense.

Understand the purpose and nature of dialogue. Characters in epics rarely make casual conversation. Instead, they communicate through formal speeches, boasting of their own accomplishments, challenging hostile rivals, advising each other about how to act, and philoso-phizing about human destiny. As part of this formal style, characters use elaborate forms of address with each other. Thus, Beowulf addresses King Hrothgar in this way:

> "Prince of the Danes, protector of Scyldings,
> Lord of nations, and leader of men,
> I beg one favor . . . ."

Compare and contrast parallelisms. The poem begins with the story of the King Scyld, who does not play any part in what follows. Anglo-Saxon audiences understood, however, that Scyld is mentioned because his story will parallel, or be similar to, the story of Beowulf. You will find not only parallel events, but parallel characteristics, like heroism and leadership, as well. The comparison of people and events from different times is meant to add to the stature of the hero, by seeing him as part of a long heroic tradition. Characters further this comparison by frequently recalling their own and each other's family histories.

Look for symbolic descriptions. The *Beowulf*-poet does not spend much time in describing the appearance of people and places, but when he does describe something, it is for a purpose. He dwells upon the beauty of Hrothgar's mead-hall because it represents certain goals: order, security, human closeness. Similarly, the details of the forest lair where Grendel's mother hides suggest the dangers she represents. Much description occurs in the form of *epithets*—descriptive phrases that may be repeated over and over. Frequently, several epithets are used in the same sentence, as in the speech quoted above.

Examine the sentence structure. To suggest the effect of the original, the translator uses long, involved sentences. Read these poetic sentences as you would prose ones, looking for the subject and the verb. Recognize also that many phrases are simply repetitions of what has just been said, added for greater emphasis.

The *Beowulf*-Poet

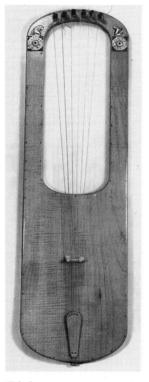

This lyre was reconstructed from pieces found in the Sutton Hoo ship-burial (see pages 42–43). 7th century. *British Museum, London*

Beowulf (bā′ō wŭlf) is the first masterpiece in English literature. But who wrote it and when? For what audience was it written and for what purpose? These are questions for which there will probably never be conclusive answers. Even a close study of the poem, along with a more general consideration of the culture it comes from, still leaves questions.

Although written in England, *Beowulf* describes the adventures of a hero who came from the southern part of what is now Sweden, to aid a people living in what is now Denmark (see map on page 5). The poem contains scarcely a reference to England. However, it does name a known historical figure, a Swedish king, Hygelac (hij′ə lak), who died in battle in 521. It must be that the stories *Beowulf* tells were a part of a culture that some Germanic tribe brought with them when they invaded and then settled in England, perhaps after Hygelac's death.

Around 725, according to the best modern estimates, someone took the folk epic of Beowulf as it had been orally transmitted by the Germanic tribes, and wrote it down in Anglo-Saxon. The *Beowulf*-poet has an absolute knowledge of the customs, the traditions, and the values of Anglo-Saxon society. But he is far more learned than the earlier *scops*, since he also knows something about the Hebrew scriptures (referring to the story of Cain and Abel). He may also have known something of Latin literature, since his poem seems to echo some passages from Virgil's *Aeneid*.

Modern readers debate the *Beowulf*-poet's relationship to Christianity. The poem certainly does come from a Christianized culture. Yet, oddly, the poem never names either the pagan gods or Jesus. At Beowulf's death his most faithful follower simply says, " ' . . . long he shall lie/In the kindly care of the Lord of all' " (lines 1827–1828). But is this a reference to the Christian Lord, or to the Northern god Odin?

The Old English scholar J. R. R. Tolkien argues that the *Beowulf*-poet was writing an intentionally *archaic* poem—that he knew about Christianity, and consequently would no longer name the heathen gods, but that because he was writing about the past he did not introduce any explicit references to the New Testament, even though its spirit helps to shape the way he thinks about life and death.

By simply examining what the *Beowulf*-poet wrote, it is possible to reach some conclusions. First, he is a writer in love with words and language. The poetry of *Beowulf* is densely packed, vigorous, full of sound. Further, the story it tells touches the receptive reader at the deepest levels. While the tales he narrates deal with heroic adventures somewhat akin to those in fairy tales, with their fire-breathing dragons, the *Beowulf*-poet is ultimately interested in the problems that trouble us most: the nature of success, true friendship, the final value to be found in life and in death. This poet has distinct, serious, and persuasive conclusions about these topics, which grow out of a story as richly suggestive as some of the greatest myths.

HLT See ALLITERATION in the Handbook of Literary Terms, page 926.

from Beowulf

translated by **Charles W. Kennedy**

The tale of Beowulf's adventures begins with the legendary Scyld, founder of the Danish royal line. Sailing alone over the sea, the child Scyld mysteriously comes to the Danish people. As a young man he leads them through a series of battles in which they capture the mead-halls of surrounding tribes, subduing them and forcing them to pay tribute to the Danes. Thus Scyld establishes a pattern for success as a ruler. At his death the Danes return him to his mysterious source, setting his body, amid a heap of the treasures he has won, adrift at sea.

The Danish Court and the Raids of Grendel

Lo! we have listened to many a lay
Of the Spear-Danes'[1] fame, their splendor
   of old,
Their mighty princes, and martial deeds!
Many a mead-hall Scyld, son of Sceaf,[2]
5 Snatched from the forces of savage foes.
From a friendless foundling, feeble and
   wretched,
He grew to a terror as time brought change.
He throve under heaven in power and pride
Till alien peoples beyond the ocean
10 Paid toll and tribute. A good king he! . . .
'Tis by earning honor a man must rise
In every state. Then his hour struck,
And Scyld passed on to the peace of God.
   As their leader had bidden, whose word
     was law
15 In the Scylding realm[3] which he long had
   ruled,
His loving comrades carried him down
To the shore of ocean; a ring-prowed ship,
Straining at anchor and sheeted with ice,
Rode in the harbor, a prince's pride.

20 Therein they laid him, their well-loved lord,
Their ring-bestower, in the ship's embrace,
The mighty prince at the foot of the mast
Amid much treasure and many a gem
From far-off lands. No lordlier ship
25 Have I ever heard of, with weapons heaped,
With battle-armor, with bills and byrnies.[4]
On the ruler's breast lay a royal treasure
As the ship put out on the unknown deep.
With no less adornment they dressed him
   round

---

1. Spear-Danes. The poet supplies the Danish people with various epithets (descriptive names) in the course of the poem, partly to help his lines alliterate, and perhaps partly as an attempt at characterization. In addition to "Spear-Danes," he calls them "Ring-Danes" and "Bright-Danes," as well as "South-," "East-," and "West-Danes."
2. Scyld (shĭld), **son of Sceaf** (shāf), founder of the Danish line of kings, the *Scyldingas*, "descendants of Scyld." The Danish people are also referred to as "Scyldings." Scyld's name means "Shield, son of Sheaf," or perhaps "Shield with a sheaf."
3. Scylding realm, Denmark.
4. bills and byrnies, swords and shirts of chain mail.

30 Or gift of treasure, than once they gave
Who launched him first on the lonely sea
While still but a child. A golden standard
They raised above him, high over head,
Let the wave take him on trackless seas.
35 Mournful their mood and heavy their hearts;
Nor wise man nor warrior knows for a truth
Unto what haven that cargo came. . . .

In the next lines, omitted here, the
poet traces the subsequent line of Danish kings, descended from Scyld: first his
son Beowulf (not the hero of this poem,
but a warrior of more ancient times); then
his grandson Healfdene (hā′alf den ə).
In time one of Healfdene's four children,
Hrothgar (hrōth′gär), takes command of
the kingdom. Following the young Scyld's
earlier example, he begins by gathering
about him a band of warriors.

To Hrothgar was granted glory in war,
Success in battle; retainers bold
40 Obeyed him gladly; his band increased
To a mighty host. Then his mind was moved
To have men fashion a high-built hall,
A mightier mead-hall than man had known,
Wherein to portion to old and young
45 All goodly treasure that God had given,
Save only the folk-land,[5] and lives of men.
His word was published to many a people
Far and wide o'er the ways of earth
To rear a folk-stead richly adorned;
50 The task was speeded, the time soon came
That the famous mead-hall was finished and
done.
To distant nations its name was known,
The Hall of the Hart;[6] and the king kept well
His pledge and promise to deal out gifts,
55 Rings at the banquet. The great hall rose
High and horn-gabled,[7] holding its
place. . . .
Then an evil spirit who dwelt in the
darkness
Endured it ill that he heard each day

(margin: alliteration (m))
(margin: Grendel) (arrow)
(margin: happiness (doesn't like it))

The din of revelry ring through the hall,
60 The sound of the harp, and the scop's sweet
song. . . .[8]
They called him Grendel, a demon grim
Haunting the fen-lands, holding the moors,
Ranging the wastes, where the wretched wight
Made his lair with the monster kin;
65 He bore the curse of the seed of Cain[9]
Whereby God punished the grievous guilt
Of Abel's murder. Nor ever had Cain
Cause to boast of that deed of blood;
God banished him far from the fields of men;
70 Of his blood was begotten an evil brood,
Marauding monsters and menacing trolls,
Goblins and giants who battled with God
A long time. Grimly He gave them reward!
Then at the nightfall the fiend drew near
75 Where the timbered mead-hall towered on
high,
To spy how the Danes fared after the feast.
Within the wine-hall he found the warriors
Fast in slumber, forgetting grief,
Forgetting the woe of the world of men.
80 Grim and greedy the gruesome monster,
Fierce and furious, launched attack,
Slew thirty spearmen asleep in the hall,
Sped away gloating, gripping the spoil,
Dragging the dead men home to his den.
85 Then in the dawn with the coming of
daybreak

(margin: alliteration (2))
(margin: alliteration (3))
(margin: alliteration (6))
(margin: dead bodies)

---

5. *folk-land*, common land (the public land owned by the
community). Germanic tribal law reserved this land for
grazing.
6. *Hall of the Hart*, *Héorot* (hā′ə rot), Hrothgar's mead-
hall. The hart (or stag) was a symbol of Germanic kingship.
The head of the scepter found at Sutton Hoo (see pages
42-43) was a stag.
7. *horn-gabled*, perhaps with roof ornaments carved to
resemble a stag's antlers, or perhaps simply "wide-gabled."
8. *scop's sweet song*. The scop (skop) was the tribe's sto-
ryteller, chanting his tales to the sound of the harp.
9. *seed of Cain*. In Genesis, Cain murders his brother
Abel and is driven into the wilderness by God. According
to legend his offspring included a variety of monsters. The
poet mentions *eotenas*, "etans" (cannibal giants like trolls),
ylfe "elves," (beautiful but evil), and *orc-nēas*, "goblins"
(animated corpses like zombies). Grendel may have been a
creature of this last type (see Comment on page 12).

The war-might of Grendel was widely
   known.
Mirth was stilled by the sound of weeping;
The wail of the mourner awoke with day.
And the peerless hero, the honored prince,[10]
90 Weighed down with woe and heavy of heart,
Sat sorely grieving for slaughtered thanes,[11]
As they traced the track of the cursed
   monster.
From that day onward the deadly feud
Was a long-enduring and loathsome strife. *(battle)*
95   Not longer was it than one night later
The fiend returning renewed attack
With heart firm-fixed in the hateful war,
Feeling no rue for the grievous wrong.
'Twas easy thereafter to mark the men
100 Who sought their slumber elsewhere afar,
Found beds in the bowers, since Grendel's
   hate
(alliteration) Was so baldly blazoned in baleful signs.
He held himself at a safer distance
Who escaped the clutch of the demon's claw.
105 So Grendel raided and ravaged the realm,
One against all, in an evil war

Till the best of buildings was empty and still.
'Twas a weary while! Twelve winters' time
The lord of the Scyldings had suffered woe,
110 Sore affliction and deep distress.
And the malice of Grendel, in mournful lays,
Was widely sung by the sons of men,
The hateful feud that he fought with
   Hrothgar—
Year after year of struggle and strife,
115 An endless scourging, a scorning of peace
With any man of the Danish might.
No strength could move him to stay his
   hand,
Or pay for his murders;[12] the wise knew well

---

10. *honored prince*, Hrothgar.
11. *thanes*, warriors. A thane ranked between an earl (a
nobleman) and an ordinary freeman.
12. *murders.* The poet here ironically refers to the Danes'
inability to force Grendel to pay *wergild* ("man-payment"),
or compensation, to the families of the warriors he has
murdered. In Anglo-Saxon and Germanic law, a fixed price
in money was placed on the life of every individual in the
tribe, from the churl (the lowest-ranking freeman) to the
king. This money was paid by the killer's family to that of
the victim to avoid blood feud.

Comment

The Nature of Grendel

   Grendel's nature is, of course, diabolical from
a Christian point of view: he is a member of
the race of Cain, from whom all misshapen and
unnatural beings were spawned, such as ogres
and elves. He is a creature dwelling in the outer
darkness, a giant, a cannibal. When he crawls off
to die, he is said to join the rout of devils in Hell.
However, he also appears to have roots in Scandinavian folklore. In Old Norse literature, monsters of his type make their appearance chiefly as
draugar,[1] or animated corpses. They are ordinary
folk who have been buried upright in cairns,[2]
according to Norse custom, but if they harbor
a grievance after death they will refuse to stay
put and will roam about at night wreaking aimless vengeance. They are articulate and usually
angry, in contrast to the silent zombies of Haiti.
A *draugr* is supernaturally strong and invulnerable (being already dead) and will often have a
mother called a *ketta*, or "she-cat," who is even
more monstrous than he. Grendel, then, appears
to be a blend of the *draugr* figure and a devilish
monster from the world of Christian folklore.

---

1. *draugar* (drou'gär), plural of *draugr* (drou'gər).
2. *cairns* (kernz, karnz). A cairn is a pile of stones serving
as a memorial, tomb, or landmark.

From *Beowulf: A Dual-Language Edition*, translated by
Howell D. Chickering, Jr. Garden City: Anchor Books, 1977.

They could hope for no halting of savage
    assault.
120 Like a dark death-shadow the ravaging
    demon,
Nightlong prowling the misty moors,
Ensnared the warriors, wary or weak.
No man can say how these shades of hell
Come and go on their grisly rounds. . . .
125   The son of Healfdene was heavy-hearted,
Sorrowfully brooding in sore distress,
Finding no help in a hopeless strife;
Too bitter the struggle that stunned the
    people,
The long oppression, loathsome and grim.

The Geats (yā′əts) lived in southwestern
Sweden. Hygelac, their king as the story
begins, is historical. He was famous for
his unusual height. ("Even when he was
twelve years old, no horse could carry
him," claims an eighth-century *Book of
Monsters*.) He died in battle while raiding
the European mainland in 521. Beowulf,
as Hygelac's thane, owes the king obedience. But hearing of Grendel's attacks on
the neighboring Danes, he decides to go to
their rescue, sailing from the valley of the
Göta river in Sweden to the Danish island
of Zealand, where Hrothgar has erected
his mead-hall, Heorot (see map, page 5).

The Coming of Beowulf

130   Then tales of the terrible deeds of Grendel
Reached Hygelac's thane in his home with
    the Geats;
Of living strong men he was the strongest,
Fearless and gallant and great of heart.
He gave command for a goodly vessel
135 Fitted and furnished; he fain would sail
Over the swan-road to seek the king
Who suffered so sorely for need of men.
And his bold retainers found little to blame

In his daring venture, dear though he was;
140 They viewed the omens, and urged him on.
Brave was the band he had gathered about
    him,
Fourteen stalwarts seasoned and bold,
Seeking the shore where the ship lay waiting,
A sea-skilled mariner sighting the land-
    marks.
145 Came the hour of boarding; the boat was
    riding
The waves of the harbor under the hill.
The eager mariners mounted the prow;
Billows were breaking, sea against sand.
In the ship's hold snugly they stowed their
    trappings,
150 Gleaming armor and battle-gear;
Launched the vessel, the well-braced bark,
Seaward bound on a joyous journey.
Over breaking billows, with bellying sail
And foamy beak, like a flying bird
155 The ship sped on, till the next day's sun
Showed sea-cliffs shining, towering hills
And stretching headlands. The sea was
    crossed,
The voyage ended, the vessel moored.
And the Weder people[13] waded ashore
160 With clatter of trappings and coats of mail;
Gave thanks to God that His grace had
    granted
Sea-paths safe for their ocean-journey.
    Then the Scylding coast guard watched
    from the sea-cliff
Warriors bearing their shining shields,
165 Their gleaming war-gear, ashore from the
    ship.
His mind was puzzled, he wondered much
What men they were. On his good horse
    mounted,
Hrothgar's thane made haste to the beach,
Boldly brandished his mighty spear
170 With manful challenge: "What men are
    you,

---

13. *Weder* people, *Weder-Gēatas*, "Storm-Geats," an epithet for Beowulf's people.

Carrying weapons and clad in steel,
Who thus come driving across the deep
On the ocean-lanes in your lofty ship?
Long have I served as the Scylding outpost,
175 Held watch and ward at the ocean's edge
Lest foreign foemen with hostile fleet
Should come to harry our Danish home,
And never more openly sailed to these shores
Men without password, or leave to land.
180 I have never laid eyes upon earl on earth
More stalwart and sturdy than one of your
troop,
A hero in armor; no hall-thane he
Tricked out with weapons, unless looks belie
him
And noble bearing. But now I must know
185 Your birth and breeding, nor may you come
In cunning stealth upon Danish soil.
You distant-dwellers, you far seafarers,
Hearken, and ponder words that are plain:
'Tis best you hasten to have me know
190 Who your kindred and whence you come."
        The lord of the seamen gave swift reply,
The prince of the Weders unlocked his word-
hoard:
"We are sprung of a strain of the Geatish
stock,
Hygelac's comrades and hearth-companions.
195 My father was famous in many a folk-land,
A leader noble, Ecgtheow[14] his name! . . .
With loyal purpose we seek your lord,
The prince of your people, great Healfdene's
son. . . .
You know if it's true, as we've heard it told,
200 That among the Scyldings some secret
scather,
Some stealthy demon in dead of night,
With grisly horror and fiendish hate
Is spreading unheard-of havoc and death.
Mayhap I can counsel the good, old king
205 What way he can master the merciless fiend,
If his coil of evil is ever to end
And feverish care grow cooler and fade—
Or else ever after his doom shall be
Distress and sorrow while still there stands

210 This best of halls on its lofty height."
        Then from the saddle the coast guard
spoke,
The fearless sentry: "A seasoned warrior
Must know the difference between words and
deeds,
If his wits are with him. I take your word
215 That your band is loyal to the lord of the
Scyldings.
Now go your way with your weapons and
armor,
And I will guide you; I'll give command
That my good retainers may guard your
ship, . . ."
        Then the Geats marched on; behind at her
mooring,
220 Fastened at anchor, their broad-beamed
boat
Safely rode on her swinging cable.
Boar-heads[15] glittered on glistening helmets
Above their cheek-guards, gleaming with
gold;
Bright and fire-hardened the boar held watch
225 Over the column of marching men.
Onward they hurried in eager haste
Till their eyes caught sight of the high-built
hall,
Splendid with gold, the seat of the king,
Most stately of structures under the sun;
230 Its light shone out over many a land.
The coast guard showed them the shining
hall,
The home of heroes; made plain the path;
Turned his horse; gave tongue to words:
"It is time to leave you! The mighty Lord
235 In His mercy shield you and hold you safe
In your bold adventure. I'll back to the sea
And hold my watch against hostile horde."

---

14. *Ecgtheow*, (edj'thä ō).
15. *Boar-heads*. Germanic tribesmen regularly used the
boar's head as a magical decoration for their helmets. The
boar, sacred to the Norse god Frey, is a desperate fighter
when cornered.

Reader's Note

The Poetry of *Beowulf*

To celebrate Beowulf's victory over Grendel, one of Hrothgar's thanes steps forward,

A minstrel mindful of saga and lay.
He wove his words in a winsome pattern,
Hymning the burden of Beowulf's feat,
Clothing the story in skillful verse.

This is the way the Anglo-Saxon minstrel, or *scop*, composed poetry—spontaneously, in oral form, before an audience. The audience usually knew the story already and, as the poet says, the scop's art was to "clothe" it in "skillful verse," shaping the words and the details of the story to fit the occasion. The *Beowulf*-poet could read and write, but he worked in the traditions of this older oral poetry, as did the writers of the other Anglo-Saxon poetry that survives.

How were the scops able to stand in front of a crowd and compose acceptable poetry for hours at a time? First, they knew intimately a body of stories they had heard from earlier scops—the history and legends of their tribe. Probably they knew long passages of these earlier tellings by memory.

Second, they used a form of verse that is simple, direct, and relatively flexible, admirably fitted to oral composition. Printed above are a few lines from *Beowulf*[1] that serve to illustrate how Anglo-Saxon verse works. The symbol ð , called *edh* (eth), stands for the *th* sound.

Each line, as you can see, breaks in the middle. This pause is called a *caesura* (si zhùr′ə, si zyùr′ə). Thus each line of verse divides into two half-lines, the basic building-blocks of Anglo-Saxon poetry. Each half-line contains two stressed syllables and any number of unstressed syllables; thus there are four strong beats to each line. Note the absence of rhyming. In Anglo-Saxon poetry a different type of repetition is used—the repetition of initial sounds called *alliteration*. Normally, alliterating consonants appear in the stressed syllables, one or two in the first half-line, and one in the second. Vowels in this scheme can also alliterate. (Any vowel

Alliterating words are in red.

Fyrst forð ġewāt;	flota wæs on ȳðum,
bāt under beorge.	Beornas ġearwe
on stefn stigon, —	strēamas wundon,
sund wið sande;	

Caesura — Half line

was considered as alliterating with any other.) Read a few lines aloud to yourself and you will begin to get a feel for its rhythm.

Another device that helped the scop to compose on the spot was what Anglo-Saxons called a *word-hoard*, a great store of words to choose from. Their language was rich in synonyms: *beorn, freca,* and *wiga* all mean "warrior," but with different connotations, derived from their original meanings as terms for "bear," "wolf," and "fighter." In addition, the scops had developed a special vocabulary for poetry over the centuries, words and phrases that fit neatly together. Alternate forms were available to fit a particular context. For example, if the scop began a line with a stressed syllable starting with an *h* sound, he could say "on the sea" by the phrase *on hranrāde* ("on the whale-road"); whereas if he began with an *s* sound, he could use *on seglrāde* ("on the sail-road").

Most of the compound words used in *Beowulf,* like "shield-bearer," are easily understood. But sometimes a more farfetched, riddling kind of descriptive comparison appears, for instance in the phrase "candle of heaven" (line 1060), used to describe the sun. This is a *kenning,* two or more words that name something by a metaphor. There are many of them in Anglo-Saxon poetry: "whale-road" for ocean, "peace-weaver" for woman, "light of battle" for sword.

---

1. A literal translation is: "Time forth went; floater was on waves,/boat under cliff. Warriors eager/on prow climbed; streams eddied,/sea against sand . . ." See lines 145–148 in your text.

Beowulf's Welcome at Hrothgar's Court

The street had paving of colored stone;
The path was plain to the marching men.
240 Bright were their byrnies, hard and hand-
    linked;
In their shining armor the chain mail sang
As the troop in their war-gear tramped to the
    hall.
The sea-weary sailors set down their shields,
Their wide, bright bucklers along the wall,
245 And sank to the bench. Their byrnies rang.
Their stout spears stood in a stack together
Shod with iron and shaped of ash.
'Twas a well-armed troop! Then a stately
    warrior
Questioned the strangers about their kin:
250 "Whence come you bearing your burnished
    shields,
Your steel-gray harness and visored helms,
Your heap of spears? I am Hrothgar's herald,
His servant-thane. I have never seen
    strangers,
So great a number, of nobler mien.
255 Not exiles, I ween, but high-minded heroes
In greatness of heart have you sought out
    Hrothgar."
Then bold under helmet the hero made
    answer,
Mighty of heart: "We are Hygelac's men,
His board-companions; Beowulf is my
    name.
260 I will state my mission to Healfdene's son,
The noble leader, your lordly prince,
If he will grant approach to his gracious
    presence."
And Wulfgar answered, the Wendel prince,[16]
Renowned for merit in many a land,
265 For war-might and wisdom: "I will learn
    the wish
Of the Scylding leader, the lord of the
    Danes,
Our honored ruler and giver of rings,
Concerning your mission, and soon report
The answer our leader thinks good to give."
270   He swiftly strode to where Hrothgar sat
Old and gray with his earls[17] about him;

Crossed the floor and stood face to face
With the Danish king; he knew courtly
    custom.
Wulfgar saluted his lord and friend:
275 "Men from afar have fared to our land
Over ocean's margin—men of the Geats,
Their leader called Beowulf—seeking a boon,
The holding of parley, my prince, with thee.
O gracious Hrothgar, refuse not the favor!
280 In their splendid war-gear they merit well
The esteem of earls; he's a stalwart leader
Who led this troop to the land of the Danes."
  Hrothgar spoke, the lord of the Scyldings:
"Their leader I knew when he still was a
    lad. . . .
285 Seafaring men who have voyaged to
    Geatland
With gifts of treasure as token of peace,
Say that his hand-grip has thirty men's
    strength.
God, in His mercy, has sent him to save us—
So springs my hope—from Grendel's
    assaults.
290 For his gallant courage I'll load him with
    gifts!
Make haste now, marshal the men to the hall,
And give them welcome to Danish ground."
  Then to the door went the well-known
    warrior,
Spoke from the threshold welcoming words:
295 "The Danish leader, my lord, declares
That he knows your kinship; right welcome
    you come,
You stout sea-rovers, to Danish soil.
Enter now, in your shining armor
And vizored helmets, to Hrothgar's hall.
300 But leave your shields and the shafts of
    slaughter
To wait the issue and weighing of words."
  Then the bold one rose with his band
    around him,

---

16. *Wulfgar . . . the Wendel prince.* Hrothgar's herald
may have been one of the Vandals, a Germanic tribe living
south of the Baltic Sea (see map, page 5).
17. *earls,* his chief men.

Viking ships are shown in this scene from the Bayeux Tapestry. circa 1077. *Museum of Queen Matilda, Bayeux, France*

A splendid massing of mighty thanes;
A few stood guard as the Geat gave bidding
305 Over the weapons stacked by the wall.
They followed in haste on the heels of their
leader
Under Heorot's roof. Full ready and bold
The helmeted warrior strode to the hearth;
Beowulf spoke; his byrny glittered,
310 His war-net woven by cunning of smith:
"Hail! King Hrothgar! I am Hygelac's thane,
Hygelac's kinsman. Many a deed
Of honor and daring I've done in my youth.
This business of Grendel was brought to my
ears
315 On my native soil. The seafarers say
This best of buildings, this boasted hall,
Stands dark and deserted when sun is set,
When darkening shadows gather with dusk.
The best of my people, prudent and brave,
320 Urged me, King Hrothgar, to seek you out;
They had in remembrance my courage and
might.
Many had seen me come safe from the
conflict,
Bloody from battle; five foes I bound
Of the giant kindred, and crushed their clan.
325 Hard-driven in danger and darkness of night
I slew the nicors[18] that swam the sea,

Avenged the woe they had caused the
Weders,
And ended their evil—they needed the
lesson!
And now with Grendel, the fearful fiend,
330 Single-handed I'll settle the strife!
Prince of the Danes, protector of Scyldings,
Lord of nations, and leader of men,
I beg one favor—refuse me not,
Since I come thus faring from far-off lands—
335 That I may alone with my loyal earls,
With this hardy company, cleanse Hart-
Hall.
I have heard that the demon in proud disdain
Spurns all weapons; and I too scorn—
May Hygelac's heart have joy of the deed—
340 To bear my sword, or sheltering shield,
Or yellow buckler, to battle the fiend.
With hand-grip only I'll grapple with
Grendel;
Foe against foe I'll fight to the death,
And the one who is taken must trust to God's
grace! . . .
345 If death shall call me, he'll carry away
My gory flesh to his fen-retreat →
To gorge at leisure and gulp me down,

---

18. *nicors*, water demons, animal in shape.

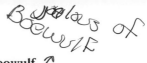

Soiling the marshes with stains of blood.
There'll be little need longer to care for my
    body!
350 If the battle slays me, to Hygelac send
This best of corselets that covers my
    breast, . . .
Finest of byrnies. Fate goes as Fate must!"
    Hrothgar spoke, the lord of the Scyldings:
"Deed of daring and dream of honor
355 Bring you, friend Beowulf, knowing our
    need! . . .
It is sorrow sore to recite to another
The wrongs that Grendel has wrought in the
    hall,
His savage hatred and sudden assaults.
My war-troop is weakened, my hall-band is
    wasted;
360 Fate swept them away into Grendel's grip.
But God may easily bring to an end
The ruinous deeds of the ravaging foe.
Full often my warriors over their ale-cups
Boldly boasted, when drunk with beer,
365 They would bide in the beer-hall the coming
    of battle,
The fury of Grendel, with flashing swords.
Then in the dawn, when the daylight
    strengthened,
The hall stood reddened and reeking with
    — gore,
Bench-boards wet with the blood of battle;
370 And I had the fewer of faithful fighters,
Beloved retainers, whom Death had taken.
Sit now at the banquet, unbend your mood,
Speak of great deeds as your heart may spur
    you!"
    Then in the beer-hall were benches made
    ready
375 For the Geatish heroes. Noble of heart,
Proud and stalwart, they sat them down
And a beer-thane served them; bore in his
    hands
The patterned ale-cup, pouring the mead,
While the scop's sweet singing was heard in
    the hall.
380 There was joy of heroes, a host at ease,
A welcome meeting of Weder and Dane.

Unferth Taunts Beowulf

    Then out spoke Unferth, Ecglaf's son,[19]
Who sat at the feet of the Scylding lord,
Picking a quarrel—for Beowulf's quest,
385 His bold sea-voyaging, irked him sore;
He bore it ill that any man other
In all the earth should ever achieve
More fame under heaven than he himself:
"Are you the Beowulf that strove with
    Breca[20]
390 In a swimming match in the open sea,
Both of you wantonly tempting the waves,
Risking your lives on the lonely deep
For a silly boast? No man could dissuade you,
Nor friend nor foe, from the foolhardy
    venture
395 Of ocean-swimming; with outstretched arms
You clasped the sea-stream, measured her
    streets,
With plowing shoulders parted the waves.
The sea-flood boiled with its wintry surges,
Seven nights you toiled in the tossing sea;
400 His strength was the greater, his swimming
    the stronger! . . .
Therefore, I ween, worse fate shall befall,
Stout as you are in the struggle of war,
In deeds of battle, if you dare to abide
Encounter with Grendel at coming of night."
405   Beowulf spoke, the son of Ecgtheow:
"My good friend Unferth, addled with beer
Much have you made of the deeds of Breca!
I count it true that I had more courage,
More strength in swimming than any other
    man.
410 In our youth we boasted—we were both of
    us boys—
We would risk our lives in the raging sea.
And we made it good! We gripped in our
    hands
Naked swords, as we swam in the waves,

---

19. Unferth, Ecglaf's (edj'lafs) **son.** Unferth's name can
be interpreted as "Peacebreaker." His role is a familiar one
in heroic poetry, that of the king's rude retainer whose
mockery provokes the hero to reveal himself. Something
very like the Unferth episode occurs in Book VIII of the
Odyssey.
20. Breca (brek'ə).

Guarding us well from the whales' assault.
415 In the breaking seas he could not outstrip
me,
Nor would I leave him. For five nights long
Side by side we strove in the waters
Till racing combers wrenched us apart,
Freezing squalls, and the falling night,
420 And a bitter north wind's icy blast.
Rough were the waves; the wrath of the sea-
fish
Was fiercely roused; but my firm-linked
byrny,
The gold-adorned corselet that covered my
breast,
Gave firm defense from the clutching foe.
425 Down to the bottom a savage sea-beast
Fiercely dragged me and held me fast
In a deadly grip; none the less it was granted
me
To pierce the monster with point of steel.
Death swept it away with the swing of my
sword.
430   The grisly sea-beasts again and again
Beset me sore; but I served them home
With my faithful blade as was well-befitting.
They failed of their pleasure to feast their fill
Crowding round my corpse on the ocean-
bottom!
435 Bloody with wounds, at the break of day,
They lay on the sea-bench slain with the
sword.
No more would they cumber the mariner's
course
On the ocean deep. From the east came the
sun,
Bright beacon of God, and the seas subsided;
440 I beheld the headlands, the windy walls.
Fate often delivers an undoomed earl
If his spirit be gallant! And so I was granted
To slay with the sword-edge nine of the
nicors.
I have never heard tell of more terrible strife
445 Under dome of heaven in darkness of night,
Nor of man harder pressed on the paths of
ocean.
But I freed my life from the grip of the foe

Though spent with the struggle. The billows
bore me,
The swirling currents and surging seas,
450 To the land of the Finns.[21] And little I've
heard
Of any such valiant adventures from you!
Neither Breca nor you in the press of battle
Ever showed such daring with dripping
swords—
Though I boast not of it! But you stained
your blade
455 With blood of your brothers, your closest of
kin;
And for that you'll endure damnation in hell,
Sharp as you are! I say for a truth,
Son of Ecglaf, never had Grendel
Wrought such havoc and woe in the hall,
460 That horrid demon so harried your king,
If your heart were as brave as you'd have men
think!
But Grendel has found that he never need
fear
Revenge from your people, or valiant attack
From the Victor-Scyldings; he takes his toll,
465 Sparing none of the Danish stock.
He slays and slaughters and works his will
Fearing no hurt at the hands of the Danes!
But soon will I show him the stuff of the
Geats,
Their courage in battle and strength in the
strife;
470 Then let him who may go bold to the mead-
hall
When the next day dawns on the dwellings of
men,
And the sun in splendor shines warm from
the south."
Glad of heart was the giver of treasure,[22]
Hoary-headed and hardy in war;
475 The lordly leader had hope of help
As he listened to Beowulf's bold resolve.

---

21. **Finns,** probably the Lapps, inhabitants of Finmarken,
around the North Cape in the northern extremity of Norway and considerably above the Arctic Circle.
22. **giver of treasure,** Hrothgar.

There was revel of heroes and high carouse,
Their speech was happy; and Hrothgar's queen,
Of gentle manners, in jewelled splendor
480 Gave courtly greeting to all the guests. . . .

Beowulf Slays Grendel

In the hall as of old were brave words spoken,
There was noise of revel; happy the host
Till the son of Healfdene would go to his rest.
He knew that the monster would meet in the hall
485 Relentless struggle when light of the sun
Was dusky with gloom of the gathering night,
And shadow-shapes crept in the covering dark,
Dim under heaven. The host arose.
Hrothgar graciously greeted his guest,
490 Gave rule of the wine-hall, and wished him well,
Praised the warrior in parting words:
"Never to any man, early or late,
Since first I could brandish buckler and sword,
Have I trusted this ale-hall save only to you!
495 Be mindful of glory, show forth your strength,
Keep watch against foe! No wish of your heart
Shall go unfulfilled if you live through the fight."
Then Hrothgar withdrew with his host of retainers, . . .
The Geatish hero put all his hope
500 In his fearless might and the mercy of God!
He stripped from his shoulders the byrny of steel,
Doffed helmet from head; into hand of thane
Gave inlaid iron, the best of blades;
Bade him keep well the weapons of war.
505 Beowulf uttered a gallant boast,

The stalwart Geat, ere he sought his bed:
"I count myself nowise weaker in war
Or grapple of battle than Grendel himself.
Therefore I scorn to slay him with sword,
510 Deal deadly wound, as I well might do!
Nothing he knows of a noble fighting,
Of thrusting and hewing and hacking of shield,
Fierce as he is in the fury of war.
In the shades of darkness we'll spurn the sword
515 If he dares without weapon to do or to die.
And God in His wisdom shall glory assign,
The ruling Lord, as He deems it right."
Then the bold in battle bowed down to his rest,
Cheek pressed pillow; the peerless thanes
520 Were stretched in slumber around their lord.
Not one had hope of return to his home,
To the stronghold or land where he lived as a boy.
For they knew how death had befallen the Danes,
How many were slain as they slept in the wine-hall. . . .
525 Then through the shades of enshrouding night
The fiend came stealing; the archers slept
Whose duty was holding the horn-decked hall—
Though one was watching—full well they knew
No evil demon could drag them down
530 To shades under ground if God were not willing.
But the hero watched awaiting the foe,
Abiding in anger the issue of war.
From the stretching moors, from the misty hollows,
Grendel came creeping, accursed of God,
535 A murderous ravager minded to snare
Spoil of heroes in high-built hall.
Under clouded heavens he held his way
Till there rose before him the high-roofed house,
Wine-hall of warriors gleaming with gold.

540 Nor was it the first of his fierce assaults
   On the home of Hrothgar; but never before
   Had he found worse fate or hardier hall-
      thanes!
   Storming the building he burst the portal,
   Though fastened of iron, with fiendish
      strength;
545 Forced open the entrance in savage fury
   And rushed in rage o'er the shining floor.
   A baleful glare from his eyes was gleaming
   Most like to a flame. He found in the hall
   Many a warrior sealed in slumber,
550 A host of kinsmen. His heart rejoiced;
   The savage monster was minded to sever
   Lives from bodies ere break of day,
   To feast his fill of the flesh of men.
   But he was not fated to glut his greed
555 With more of mankind when the night was
      ended!
      The hardy kinsman of Hygelac waited
   To see how the monster would make his
      attack.
   The demon delayed not, but quickly
      clutched
   A sleeping thane in his swift assault,
560 Tore him in pieces, bit through the bones,
   Gulped the blood, and gobbled the flesh,
   Greedily gorged on the lifeless corpse,
   The hands and the feet. Then the fiend
      stepped nearer,
   Sprang on the Sea-Geat lying outstretched,
565 Clasping him close with his monstrous claw.
   But Beowulf grappled and gripped him hard,
67 Struggled up on his elbow; the shepherd of
      sins
   Soon found that never before had he felt
   In any man other in all the earth
570 A mightier hand-grip; his mood was
      humbled,
   His courage fled; but he found no escape!
   He was fain to be gone; he would flee to the
      darkness,
   The fellowship of devils. Far different his
      fate
   From that which befell him in former days!
575 The hardy hero, Hygelac's kinsman,

   Remembered the boast he had made at the
      banquet;
   He sprang to his feet, clutched Grendel fast,
   Though fingers were cracking, the fiend
      pulling free.
   The earl pressed after; the monster was
      minded
580 To win his freedom and flee to the fens.
   He knew that his fingers were fast in the grip
   Of a savage foe. Sorry the venture,
   The raid that the ravager made on the hall.
      There was din in Heorot. For all the
      Danes,
585 The city-dwellers, the stalwart Scyldings,
   That was a bitter spilling of beer!
   The walls resounded, the fight was fierce,
   Savage the strife as the warriors struggled.
   The wonder was that the lofty wine-hall
590 Withstood the struggle, nor crashed to earth,
   The house so fair; it was firmly fastened
   Within and without with iron bands
   Cunningly smithied; though men have said
   That many a mead-bench gleaming with gold
595 Sprang from its sill as the warriors strove.
   The Scylding wise men had never weened
   That any ravage could wreck the building,
   Firmly fashioned and finished with bone,
   Or any cunning compass its fall,
600 Till the time when the swelter and surge of
      fire
   Should swallow it up in a swirl of flame.[23]
      Continuous tumult filled the hall;
   A terror fell on the Danish folk
   As they heard through the wall the horrible
      wailing,
605 The groans of Grendel, the foe of God
   Howling his hideous hymn of pain,
   The hell-thane shrieking in sore defeat.
   He was fast in the grip of the man who was
      greatest
   Of mortal men in the strength of his might,
610 Who would never rest while the wretch was
      living,

---

23. *swirl of flame.* This is one of a number of references
in the poem to the later burning of Heorot.

Counting his life-days a menace to man.
Many an earl of Beowulf brandished
His ancient iron to guard his lord,
To shelter safely the peerless prince.
615 They had no knowledge, those daring thanes,
When they drew their weapons to hack and hew,
To thrust to the heart, that the sharpest sword,
The choicest iron in all the world,
Could work no harm to the hideous foe.
620 On every sword he had laid a spell,
On every blade; but a bitter death
Was to be his fate; far was the journey
The monster made to the home of fiends.
Then he who had wrought such wrong to men,
625 With grim delight as he warred with God,
Soon found that his strength was feeble and failing
In the crushing hold of Hygelac's thane.
Each loathed the other while life should last!
There Grendel suffered a grievous hurt,
630 A wound in the shoulder, gaping and wide;
Sinews snapped and bone-joints broke,
And Beowulf gained the glory of battle.
Grendel, fated, fled to the fens,
To his joyless dwelling, sick unto death.
635 He knew in his heart that his hours were numbered,
His days at an end. For all the Danes
Their wish was fulfilled in the fall of Grendel.
The stranger from far, the stalwart and strong,
Had purged of evil the hall of Hrothgar,
640 And cleansed of crime; the heart of the hero
Joyed in the deed his daring had done.
The lord of the Geats made good to the East-Danes
The boast he had uttered; he ended their ill,
And all the sorrow they suffered long
645 And needs must suffer—a foul offense.
The token was clear when the bold in battle
Laid down the shoulder and dripping claw—
Grendel's arm—in the gabled hall!

The Joy of the Danes
When morning came, as they tell the tale,
650 Many a warrior hastened to hall,
Folk-leaders faring from far and near
Over wide-running ways, to gaze at the wonder,
The trail of the demon. Nor seemed his death
A matter of sorrow to any man
655 Who viewed the tracks of the vanquished monster
As he slunk weary-hearted away from the hall,
Doomed and defeated and marking his flight
With bloody prints to the nicors' pool.
The crimson currents bubbled and heaved
660 In eddying reaches reddened with gore;
The surges boiled with the fiery blood.
But the monster had sunk from the sight of men.
In that fenny covert the cursed fiend
Not long thereafter laid down his life,
665 His heathen spirit; and hell received him.
Then all the comrades, the old and young,
The brave of heart, in a blithesome band
Came riding their horses home from the mere.
Beowulf's prowess was praised in song;
670 And many men stated that south or north,
Over all the world, or between the seas,
Or under the heaven, no hero was greater.
Then spoke Hrothgar; hasting to hall
He stood at the steps, stared up at the roof
675 High and gold-gleaming; saw Grendel's hand:
"Thanks be to God for this glorious sight!
I have suffered much evil, much outrage from Grendel,
But the God of glory works wonder on wonder.
I had no hope of a haven from sorrow
680 While this best of houses stood badged with blood,
A woe far-reaching for all the wise
Who weened that they never could hold the hall

Against the assaults of devils and demons.
But now with God's help this hero has compassed

Alit. A deed our cunning could no way contrive.
I will keep you, Beowulf, close to my heart
In firm affection; as son to father
Hold fast henceforth to this foster-kinship.
You shall know not want of treasure or wealth
690 Or goodly gift that your wish may crave,
While I have power. For poorer deeds
I have granted guerdon,[24] and graced with honor
Weaker warriors, feebler in fight.
You have done such deeds that your fame shall flourish
695 Through all the ages! God grant you still
All goodly grace as He gave before."
    Beowulf spoke, the son of Ecgtheow:
"By favor of God we won the fight,
Did the deed of valor, and boldly dared
700 The might of the monster. I would you could see
The fiend himself lying dead before you!
I thought to grip him in stubborn grasp
And bind him down on the bed of death,
There to lie straining in struggle for life,
705 While I gripped him fast lest he vanish away.
But I might not hold him or hinder his going
For God did not grant it, my fingers failed.
Too savage the strain of his fiendish strength!
To save his life he left shoulder and claw,
710 The arm of the monster, to mark his track,
But he bought no comfort; no whit thereby
Shall the wretched ravager racked with sin,
The loathsome spoiler, prolong his life.
A deep wound holds him in deadly grip,
715 In baleful bondage; and black with crime
The demon shall wait for the day of doom
When the God of glory shall give decree."
    Then slower of speech was the son of
    Ecglaf, → *Unferth.*
More wary of boasting of warlike deeds,
720 While the nobles gazed at the grisly claw,
The fiend's hand fastened by hero's might
On the lofty roof. Most like to steel

Were the hardened nails, the heathen's hand-spurs,
Horrible, monstrous; and many men said
725 No tempered sword, no excellent iron,
Could have harmed the monster or hacked away
The demon's battle-claw dripping with blood.

The Feast
    In joyful haste was Heorot decked
And a willing host of women and men
730 Gaily dressed and adorned the guest-hall.
Splendid hangings with sheen of gold
Shone on the walls, a glorious sight
To eyes that delight to behold such wonders.
The shining building was wholly shattered
735 Though braced and fastened with iron bands;
Hinges were riven; the roof alone
Remained unharmed when the horrid monster,
Foul with evil, slunk off in flight. . . .
    Soon was the time when the son of Healfdene
740 Went to the wine-hall; he fain would join
With happy heart in the joy of feasting.
I never have heard of a mightier muster
Of proud retainers around their prince. . . .
Upon Beowulf, then, as a token of triumph,
745 Hrothgar bestowed a standard of gold,
A banner embroidered, a byrny and helm.
In sight of many, a costly sword
Before the hero was borne on high; . . .
On the crest of the helmet a crowning wreath,
750 Woven of wire-work, warded the head — *Alit.*
Lest tempered swordblade, sharp from the file,
Deal deadly wound when the shielded warrior
Went forth to battle against the foe.
Eight horses also with plated headstalls
755 The lord of heroes bade lead into hall;

---

24. *guerdon* (gėrd'n), reward.

This torque (or *torc*) was designed to be worn as an ornament around the neck. Found at Snettisham, in Norfolk, it is fashioned from electrum, an alloy of gold and silver. 1st century B.C. *British Museum.*

On one was a saddle skillfully fashioned
And set with jewels, the battle-seat
Of the king himself, when the son of
    Healfdene
Would fain take part in the play of swords;
760 Never in fray had his valor failed,
His kingly courage, when corpses were
    falling. . . .
   Then on the ale-bench to each of the earls
Who embarked with Beowulf, sailing the
    sea-paths,
The lord of princes dealt ancient heirlooms,
765 Gift of treasure, and guerdon of gold
To requite his slaughter whom Grendel slew,
As he would have slain others, but all-wise
    God
And the hero's courage had conquered
    Fate. . . .

overcame Fate [handwritten annotation]

Stewards poured wine from wondrous
    vessels;
770 And Wealhtheow,[25] wearing a golden crown,
Came forth in state where the two were
    sitting,
Courteous comrades, uncle and nephew,[26]

Each true to the other in ties of peace. . . .
Wealhtheow spoke to the warrior host:
775 "Take, dear Beowulf, collar and corselet,
Wear these treasures with right good will!
Thrive and prosper and prove your might!
Befriend my boys with your kindly counsel;
I will remember and I will repay.
780 You have earned the undying honor of
    heroes
In regions reaching as far and wide
As the windy walls that the sea encircles.
May Fate show favor while life shall last!
I wish you wealth to your heart's content;
785 In your days of glory be good to my sons!
Here each hero is true to other,
Gentle of spirit, loyal to lord,
Friendly thanes and a folk united,
Wine-cheered warriors who do my will."
790 Then she went to her seat. . . .

---

25. **Wealhtheow** (wā′al thā ō), Hrothgar's wife, the queen of the Danes.
26. **uncle and nephew**, Hrothgar and Hrothulf, the son of Hrothgar's younger brother Halga.

THINK AND DISCUSS

Understanding

1. Explain the process by which Hrothgar wins power and fame.
2. What kind of monster is Grendel? Describe his appearance, the way he lives, and his methods of attack.
3. Before Beowulf fights Grendel, he defeats Unferth in a battle of words (lines 406–472). What arguments does he use?
4. Why does Beowulf insist upon fighting Grendel without weapons? How does he kill the monster?
5. In what ways does Hrothgar reward Beowulf?

Analyzing

6. What achievements of Hrothgar and Beowulf does the poet choose to describe? What do his choices tell you about what matters most to people in his society?
7. What are Beowulf's motives in aiding Hrothgar? Explain how they suggest an Anglo-Saxon idea of heroism.

Extending

8. Beowulf repeatedly makes the kind of speech that the poet calls "a gallant boast" (line 505). How does his audience respond? How do you respond?
9. Is Grendel evil? Explain your answer.

APPLYING: Alliteration HΤ
See Handbook of Literary Terms, p. 926

Alliteration is the repetition of sounds, usually consonants, at the beginning of words or accented syllables:

> Their *s*tout *s*pears *s*tood in a *s*tack together.

In Anglo-Saxon verse, alliteration is used rather than rhyme to provide verbal music and to underscore rhythms.

1. Which words alliterate in lines 629–632? in lines 659–662?
2. Read these two examples aloud, putting most stress on the syllables that alliterate. How many beats do you hear in each line?

COMPOSITION
Writing an Anglo-Saxon Letter

Imagine that you are a thane in Hrothgar's court on a night when Grendel attacks. Write a letter to a distant friend about what happens. Begin by looking over the first part of *Beowulf* for ideas or details. Brainstorm for other details to make your narrative interesting. Plan your letter to run at least four paragraphs. In the first you might describe the mead-hall during the evening meal. In the second explain how you feel as you prepare for sleep. In the third narrate, from your point of view, what happens when Grendel attacks. In your final paragraph, tell of your reactions the next morning.

Explaining Beowulf's Motives

Explain to someone who has not read the poem why Beowulf would risk a hazardous ocean voyage to battle an unknown beast for a distant king. In outlining your paper, plan for at least three paragraphs, one each devoted to Beowulf's ideas about honor, fame, and courage. Scan his speeches in the first part of the poem to find what he has to say about these values, and use short quotations from the text to illustrate your explanation. See "The Writing Process" in the Composition Handbook.

ENRICHMENT
Researching a Reference

Look up the original story of Cain and Abel in a Bible (Genesis 4:1–16). Read it aloud to your classmates, and then as a group discuss why the *Beowulf*-poet calls Grendel "the seed of Cain" in line 65. Be sure to consider where Grendel lives, how he treats others, and how they deal with him.

Reader's Note

Translating *Beowulf*

At first glance, most modern readers of English would think that a passage from *Beowulf*, like that below, is in a foreign language. A closer look, however, suggests something a little different. In the first line is the word *lond*, in the second *wulf*, in the third *strēam*. A little guesswork will suggest modern English equivalents for these words. The lines below are translated by Charles Kennedy on page 29 (lines 868–884). Four other translations of this same passage appear on page 27. Notice how these five translations differ.

Hīe dȳgel lond
warigeað, wulf-hleoþu,   windige næssas,
frēcne fen-gelād,   ðær fyrgen-strēam
under næssa genipu   niþer gewīteð,
flōd under foldan.   Nis þæt feor heonon
mīl-gemearces,   þæt se mere stan[d]eð
ofer þæm hongiað   hrinde bearwas,
wudu wyrtum fæst   wæter oferhelmað.
Þær mæg nihta gehwæm   nīð-wundor sēon,
fȳr on flōde.   Nō þæs frōd leofað
gumena bearna   þæt þone grund wite.
Ðēah þe hæð-stapa   hundum geswenced,
heorot hornum trum   holt-wudu sēce,
feorran geflȳmed,   ær hē feorh seleð,
aldor on ōfre,   ær hē in wille,
hafelan [hȳdan].   Nis þæt hēoru stōw!

In line 12 of the Anglo-Saxon, the poet uses the kenning *hæ -stapa* to describe a male deer. Both Spaeth and Kennedy choose a very literal, only slightly modernized version of the original words: "heather-stepper." Crossley-Holland uses a slightly different form: "moor-stalker." These odd phrases can puzzle some readers, so to make it easier Alexander stretches the kenning out until it becomes a whole image: "The hart that roams the heath . . ." Now its meaning may be clearer, but the translation doesn't sound very much like the original. Raffel avoids the difficulty, and the poetic force, of the kenning altogether—in his version it becomes just "A deer."

At the beginning of line 10 in the Anglo-Saxon is the phrase *fȳr on flōde*, part of a description of the frightful lake where Grendel and his mother live. The word *on* can be translated in various ways, and so, depending upon whose translation you turn to, the fire is "beneath" (Spaeth), "in" (Kennedy and Alexander), or "on" (Crossley-Holland) the water. Again Raffel ingeniously turns to a different solution: "At night that lake/Burns like a torch."

As the irregular line lengths suggest, all these translators try not only to convey the ideas, but also the quality of the poetry in *Beowulf*. While you may not be able to understand the third line of the Anglo-Saxon here, it is easy enough to notice the alliteration created by the repeated initial *f* sound, as well as the caesura, the gap in the middle of the line that indicates a pause. Now the question is, can the translators somehow imitate these sounds and rhythms in a form the modern reader can understand? Alexander's translation is very close to the order and the literal meaning of the original words: "and treacherous fen-paths: a torrent of water." There are four *t* sounds here, but only two in stressed syllables. There is alliteration, then, but it is not very pronounced. Spaeth employs a different solution, intertwining the repetition of the *m* and *s* sounds: "Ledges of mist, where mountain torrents . . ."

Every good translation makes a statement of some kind about the text it translates. For example, when Raffel uses a plain word like "deer" he emphasizes fact and action; when Kennedy uses "hart" he suggests a more elevated and remote world. Spaeth's "To die on the brink ere he brave the plunge" is certainly different from Alexander's "will die there/ sooner than swim"; the one echoes an older tradition of poetic speech, while the other sounds almost like slang.

translated by **J. Duncan Spaeth** (1921)

Lonely and waste is the land they inhabit,
Wolf-cliffs wild and windy headlands,
Ledges of mist, where mountain torrents
Downward plunge to dark abysses,
5 And flow unseen. Not far from here
O'er the moorland in miles, a mere expands.
Spray-frosted trees o'erspread it, and hang
O'er the water with roots fast wedged in the rocks.
There nightly is seen, beneath the flood,
10 A marvelous light. There lives not the man
Has fathomed the depth of the dismal mere.
Though the heather-stepper, the strong-horned
    stag,
Seek this cover, forspent with the chase,
Tracked by the hounds, he will turn at bay,
15 To die on the brink ere he brave the plunge,
Hide his head in the haunted pool.

translated by **Kevin Crossley-Holland** (1968)

                    . . . These two live
in a little-known country, wolf-slopes,
    windswept headlands,
perilous paths across the boggy moors, where
    a mountain stream
plunges under the mist-covered cliffs,
5 rushes through a fissure. It is not far from here,
if measured in miles, that the lake stands
shadowed by trees stiff with hoar-frost.
A wood, firmly-rooted, frowns over the water.
There, night after night, a fearful wonder may
    be seen—
10 fire on the water; no man alive
is so wise as to know the nature of its depths.
Although the moor-stalker, the stag with
    strong horns,
when harried by hounds will make for the wood,
pursued from afar, he will succumb
15 to the hounds on the brink, rather than
    plunge in
and save his head. That is not a pleasant place.

translated by **Burton Raffel** (1963)

They live in secret places, windy
Cliffs, wolf-dens where water pours
From the rocks, then runs underground, where
    mist
Steams like black clouds, and the groves of trees
5 Growing out over their lake are all covered
With frozen spray, and wind down snakelike
Roots that reach as far as the water
And help keep it dark. At night that lake
Burns like a torch. No one knows its bottom,
10 No wisdom reaches such depths. A deer,
Hunted through the woods by packs of hounds,
A stag with great horns, though driven through
    the forest
From faraway places, prefers to die
On those shores, refuses to save its life
15 In that water. It isn't far, nor is it
A pleasant spot!

translated by **Michael Alexander** (1973)

                    Mysterious is the region
they live in—of wolf-fells, wind-picked moors
and treacherous fen-paths: a torrent of water
pours down dark cliffs and plunges into the
    earth,
5 an underground flood. It is not far from here,
in terms of miles, that the Mere lies,
overcast with dark, crag-rooted trees
that hang in groves hoary with frost.
An uncanny sight may be seen at night there
10 —the fire in the water! The wit of living men
is not enough to know its bottom.
The hart that roams the heath, when hounds
    have pressed him
long and hard, may hide in the forest
his antlered head; but the hart will die there
15 sooner than swim and save his life;
he will sell it on the brink there, for it is not
    a safe place.

The Troll-Wife Avenges Grendel

790   . . . At the fairest of feasts
Men drank of the wine-cup, knowing not Fate,
Nor the fearful doom that befell the earls
When darkness gathered, and gracious Hrothgar
Sought his dwelling and sank to rest.
795 A host of heroes guarded the hall
As they oft had done in the days of old.
They stripped the benches and spread the floor
With beds and bolsters. But one of the beer-thanes
Bowed to his hall-rest doomed to death.
800 They set at their heads their shining shields,
Their battle-bucklers; and there on the bench
Above each hero his towering helmet,
His spear and corselet hung close at hand.
It was ever their wont to be ready for war
805 At home or in field, as it ever befell
That their lord had need. 'Twas a noble race!
    Then they sank to slumber. But one paid dear
For his evening rest, as had often happened
When Grendel haunted the lordly hall
810 And wrought such ruin, till his end was come,
Death for his sins; it was easily seen,
Though the monster was slain, an avenger survived
Prolonging the feud, though the fiend had perished.
The mother of Grendel, a monstrous hag,
815 Brooded over her misery, doomed to dwell
In evil waters and icy streams. . . .
But rabid and raging his mother resolved
On a dreadful revenge for the death of her son!

She stole to the hall where the Danes were sleeping,
820 And horror fell on the host of earls
When the dam[1] of Grendel burst in the door.
But the terror was less as the war-craft is weaker,
A woman's strength, than the might of a man . . .
As soon as discovered, the hag was in haste
825 To fly to the open, to flee for her life.
One of the warriors she swiftly seized,
Clutched him fast and made off to the fens.
He was of heroes the dearest to Hrothgar,
The best of comrades between two seas;
830 The warrior brave, the stouthearted spearman,
She slew in his sleep. Nor was Beowulf there;
But after the banquet another abode
Had been assigned to the glorious Geat.
There was tumult in Heorot. She tore from its place
835 The bloodstained claw. Care was renewed!
It was no good bargain when both in turn
Must pay the price with the lives of friends!
    Then the white-haired warrior, the aged king,
Was numb with sorrow, knowing his thane
840 No longer was living, his dearest man dead.
Beowulf, the brave, was speedily summoned.
    . . .
The hero came tramping into the hall
With his chosen band—the boards resounded—
Greeted the leader, the Ingwine[2] lord,
845 And asked if the night had been peaceful and pleasant.

---

1. *dam,* mother.
2. *Ingwine* (ing'wi nə), literally, "friends of Ing," an epithet for the Danes. Ing was an epithet of the Norse god Frey.

Hrothgar spoke, the lord of the Scyldings:
"Ask not of pleasure; pain is renewed
For the Danish people. Æschere[3] is
    dead! . . .
He was my comrade, closest of counsellors,
850 My shoulder-companion as side by side
We fought for our lives in the welter of war,
In the shock of battle when boar-helms
    crashed.
As an earl should be, a prince without peer,
Such was Æschere, slain in the hall
855 By the wandering demon! I know not
    whither
She fled to shelter, proud of her spoil,
Gorged to the full. She avenged the
    feud. . . .
    Oft in the hall I have heard my people,
Comrades and counsellors, telling a tale
860 Of evil spirits their eyes have sighted,
Two mighty marauders who haunt the
    moors.
One shape, as clearly as men could see,
Seemed woman's likeness, and one seemed
    man,
An outcast wretch of another world,
865 And huger far than a human form.
Grendel my countrymen called him, not
    knowing
What monster-brood spawned him, what
    sire begot.
Wild and lonely the land they live in,
Windswept ridges and wolf-retreats,
870 Dread tracts of fen where the falling torrent
Downward dips into gloom and shadow
Under the dusk of the darkening cliff.
Not far in miles lies the lonely mere
Where trees firm-rooted and hung with frost
875 Overshroud the wave with shadowing
    gloom.
And there a portent appears each night,
A flame in the water; no man so wise
Who knows the bound of its bottomless
    depth.
The heather-stepper, the horned stag,
880 The antlered hart hard driven by hounds,
Invading that forest in flight from afar

Will turn at bay and die on the brink
Ere ever he'll plunge in that haunted pool.
'Tis an eerie spot! Its tossing spray
885 Mounts dark to heaven when high winds stir
The driving storm, and the sky is murky,
And with foul weather the heavens weep.
On your arm only rests all our hope!
Not yet have you tempted those terrible
    reaches,
890 The region that shelters that sinful wight.
Go if you dare! I will give requital — payback
With ancient treasure and twisted gold,
As I formerly gave in guerdon of battle,
If out of that combat you come alive."
895   Beowulf spoke, the son of Ecgtheow:
"Sorrow not, brave one! Better for man
To avenge a friend than much to mourn.
All men must die; let him who may
Win glory ere death. That guerdon is best
900 For the noble man when his name survives
    him.
Then let us rise up, O ward of the realm,
And haste us forth to behold the track
Of Grendel's dam. And I give you pledge
She shall not in safety escape to cover,
905 To earthy cavern, or forest fastness,
Or gulf of ocean, go where she may.
This day with patience endure the burden
Of every woe, as I know you will."
Up sprang the ancient, gave thanks to God
910 For the heartening words the hero had
    spoken.

Beowulf Slays the Troll-Wife
    Quickly a horse was bridled for Hrothgar,
A mettlesome charger with braided mane;
In royal splendor the king rode forth
Mid the trampling tread of a troop of → alib
    shieldmen.
915 The tracks lay clear where the fiend had
    fared
Over plain and bottom and woodland path,

---

3. *Æschere* (ash'her ə).

carrying the body the back.

Through murky moorland making her way
With the lifeless body, the best of thanes
Who of old with Hrothgar had guarded the
    hall.
920 By a narrow path the king pressed on.
Through rocky upland and rugged ravine,
A lonely journey, past looming headlands,
The lair of monster and lurking troll.

going with some people

Tried retainers, a trusty few,
925 Advanced with Hrothgar to view the ground.
Sudden they came on a dismal covert
Of trees that hung over hoary stone,
Over churning water and bloodstained wave.
Then for the Danes was the woe the deeper,
930 The sorrow sharper for Scylding earls,
When they first caught sight, on the rocky
    sea-cliff,
Of slaughtered Æschere's severed head.
The water boiled in a bloody swirling
With seething gore as the spearmen gazed.
935 The trumpet sounded a martial strain;
The shield-troop halted. Their eyes beheld
The swimming forms of strange sea-
    dragons,
Dim serpent shapes in the watery depths,
Sea-beasts sunning on headland slopes;
940 Snakelike monsters that oft at sunrise
On evil errands scour the sea.
Startled by tumult and trumpet's blare,
Enraged and savage, they swam away;

hear noise swim away

But one the lord of the Geats brought low,
945 Stripped of his sea-strength, despoiled of
    life,

Beowulf

As the bitter bow-bolt pierced his heart.
His watery-speed grew slower, and ceased,
And he floated, caught in the clutch of death.
Then they hauled him in with sharp-hooked
    boar-spears,
950 By sheer strength grappled and dragged him
    ashore,
A wondrous wave-beast; and all the array

all

Gathered to gaze at the grisly guest.
    Beowulf donned his armor for battle,
Heeded not danger; the hand-braided byrny,

put on armour

955 Broad of shoulder and richly bedecked,
Must stand the ordeal of the watery depths.

Well could that corselet defend the frame
Lest hostile thrust should pierce to the heart.
Or blows of battle beat down the life.
960 A gleaming helmet guarded his head
As he planned his plunge to the depths of
    the pool
Through the heaving waters—a helm adorned
With lavish inlay and lordly chains,
Ancient work of the weapon-smith
965 Skillfully fashioned, beset with the boar,
That no blade of battle might bite it through.
Not the least or the worst of his war-
    equipment

(made up w/ Beowulf) → Unferth

Was the sword the herald of Hrothgar loaned
In his hour of need—Hrunting[4] its name—

name of the sword

970 An ancient heirloom, trusty and tried;
Its blade was iron, with etched design,
Tempered in blood of many a battle.
Never in fight had it failed the hand
That drew it daring the perils of war,
975 The rush of the foe. Not the first time then
That its edge must venture on valiant
    deeds. . . .
Beowulf spoke, the son of Ecgtheow:
"O gracious ruler, gold-giver to men,
As I now set forth to attempt this feat,
980 Great son of Healfdene, hold well in mind
The solemn pledge we plighted of old,
That if doing your service I meet my death
You will mark my fall with a father's love.
Protect my kinsmen, my trusty comrades,
985 If battle take me. And all the treasure
You have heaped on me bestow upon

give to my king

    Hygelac. . . ."
    After these words the prince of the Weders
Awaited no answer, but turned to the task,
Straightway plunged in the swirling pool.
990 Nigh unto a day he endured the depths
Ere he first had view of the vast sea-bottom.
Soon she found, who had haunted the flood,
A ravening hag, for a hundred half-years,
Greedy and grim, that a man was groping

---

4. **herald of Hrothgar . . . Hrunting** (hrŭn'ting).
Hrothgar's herald here is Unferth, now reconciled to
Beowulf. *Hrunting* may mean "Thruster."

995 In daring search through the sea-troll's
        home.
    Swift she grappled and grasped the warrior
    With horrid grip, but could work no harm,
    No hurt to his body; the ring-locked byrny
    Cloaked his life from her clutching claw;
1000 Nor could she tear through the tempered
        mail
    With her savage fingers. The she-wolf bore
    The ring-prince down through the watery
        depths
    To her den at the bottom; nor could Beowulf
        draw
    His blade for battle, though brave his mood.
1005 Many a sea-beast, strange sea-monsters,
    Tasked him hard with their menacing tusks,
    Broke his byrny and smote him sore.
        Then he found himself in a fearsome hall
    Where water came not to work him hurt,
1010 But the flood was stayed by the sheltering
        roof.
    There in the glow of firelight gleaming
    The hero had view of the huge sea-troll. *(mother)*
    He swung his war-sword with all his
        strength,
    Withheld not the blow, and the savage blade
1015 Sang on her head its hymn of hate.
    But the bold one found that the battle-flasher
    Would bite no longer, nor harm her life. *(sword*
    The sword-edge failed at his sorest need. *doesn't*
    Often of old with ease it had suffered *work)*
1020 The clash of battle, cleaving the helm,
    The fated warrior's woven mail.
    That time was first for the treasured blade
    That its glory failed in the press of the fray.
    But fixed of purpose and firm of mood
1025 Hygelac's earl was mindful of honor;
    In wrath, undaunted, he dashed to earth
    The jewelled sword with its scrolled design,
    The blade of steel; staked all on strength,
    On the might of his hand, as a man must do
1030 Who thinks to win in the welter of battle
    Enduring glory; he fears not death.
    The Geat-prince joyed in the straining
        struggle,
    Stalwart-hearted and stirred to wrath,

    Gripped the shoulder of Grendel's dam
1035 And headlong hurled the hag to the ground.
    But she quickly clutched him and drew him
        close,
    Countered the onset with savage claw.
    The warrior staggered, for all his strength,
    Dismayed and shaken and borne to earth.
1040 She knelt upon him and drew her dagger,
    With broad bright blade, to avenge her son,
    Her only issue. But the corselet's steel
    Shielded his breast and sheltered his life
    Withstanding entrance of point and
        edge. . . .
1045   Swift the hero sprang to his feet;
    Saw mid the war-gear a stately sword,
    An ancient war-brand of biting edge,
    Choicest of weapons worthy and strong,
    The work of giants, a warrior's joy,
1050 So heavy no hand but his own could hold it,
    Bear to battle or wield in war.
    Then the Scylding warrior, savage and grim,
    Seized the ring-hilt and swung the sword,
    Struck with fury, despairing of life,
1055 Thrust at the throat, broke through the bone-
        rings; *(in neck)*
    The stout blade stabbed through her fated
        flesh.
    She sank in death; the sword was bloody;
    The hero joyed in the work of his hand.
    The gleaming radiance shimmered and
        shone
1060 As the candle of heaven shines clear from
        the sky. *(sun, moon. god overtaking evil.)*
    Wrathful and resolute Hygelac's thane
    Surveyed the span of the spacious hall;
    Grimly gripping the hilted sword
    With upraised weapon he turned to the
        wall. . . .
1065 And there before him bereft of life
    He saw the broken body of Grendel
    Stilled in battle, and stretched in death,
    As the struggle in Heorot smote him down.
    The corpse sprang wide as he struck the
        blow,
1070 The hard sword-stroke that severed the
        head.

Then the tried retainers, who there with
Hrothgar
Watched the face of the foaming pool,
Saw that the churning reaches were
reddened,
The eddying surges stained with blood.
1075 And the gray, old spearmen spoke of the
hero,
Having no hope he would ever return
Crowned with triumph and cheered with
spoil.
Many were sure that the savage sea-wolf
Had slain their leader. At last came noon.
1080 The stalwart Scyldings forsook the
headland;

— Their proud gold-giver departed home.
But the Geats sat grieving and sick in spirit,
Stared at the water with longing eyes,
Having no hope they would ever behold
1085 Their gracious leader and lord again.
Then the great sword, eaten with blood of
battle,
Began to soften and waste away
In iron icicles, wonder of wonders,
Melting away most like to ice

1090 When the Father looses the fetters of frost,
Slackens the bondage that binds the wave,
Strong in power of times and seasons;
He is true God! Of the goodly treasures
From the sea-cave Beowulf took but two,
1095 The monster's head and the precious hilt
Blazing with gems; but the blade had
melted,
The sword dissolved, in the deadly heat,
The venomous blood of the fallen fiend. . . .

Beowulf Returns to Heorot
With sturdy strokes the lord of the seamen
1100 To land came swimming, rejoiced in his
spoil,
Had joy of the burden he brought from the
depths.
And his mighty thanes came forward to meet
him,
Gave thanks to God they were granted to see
Their well-loved leader both sound and safe.

1105 From the stalwart hero his helmet and byrny
Were quickly loosened; the lake lay still,
Its motionless reaches reddened with
blood. . . .
From the sea-cliff's brim the warriors bore
The head of Grendel, with heavy toil;
1110 Four of the stoutest, with all their strength,
Could hardly carry on swaying spear
Grendel's head to the gold-decked hall.
Swift they strode, the daring and dauntless,
Fourteen Geats, to the Hall of the Hart;
1115 And proud in the midst of his marching men
Their leader measured the path to the mead-
hall.
The hero entered, the hardy in battle,
The great in glory, to greet the king;
And Grendel's head by the hair was carried
1120 Across the floor where the feasters drank—
A terrible sight for lord and for lady—
A gruesome vision whereon men gazed!
Beowulf spoke, the son of Ecgtheow:
"O son of Healfdene, lord of the Scyldings!
1125 This sea-spoil wondrous, whereon you stare,
We joyously bring you in token of triumph!
Barely with life surviving the battle,
The war under water, I wrought the deed
Weary and spent; and death had been swift
1130 Had God not granted His sheltering
strength.
My strong-edged Hrunting, stoutest of
blades,
Availed me nothing. But God revealed—
Often His arm has aided the friendless—
The fairest of weapons hanging on wall,
1135 An ancient broadsword; I seized the blade,
Slew in the struggle, as fortune availed,
The cavern-warders. But the war-brand old,
The battle-blade with its scrolled design,
Dissolved in the gush of the venomous gore;
1140 The hilt alone I brought from the battle.
The record of ruin, and slaughter of Danes,
These wrongs I avenged, as was fitting and
right.
Now I can promise you, prince of the
Scyldings,
Henceforth in Heorot rest without rue

1145 For you and your nobles; nor need you dread
     Slaughter of follower, stalwart or stripling,
     Or death of earl, as of old you did."
     Into the hand of the aged leader,
     The gray-haired hero, he gave the hilt,
1150 The work of giants, the wonder of gold. . . .
        Hrothgar spoke, beholding the hilt,
     The ancient relic whereon was etched
     An olden record of struggle and strife,
     The flood[5] that ravaged the giant race,
1155 The rushing deluge of ruin and death.
     That evil kindred were alien to God,
     But the Ruler avenged with the wrath of the
        deep! . . .
     Then out spoke Hrothgar, Healfdene's son,
     And all the retainers were silent and still:
1160 "Well may he say, whose judgment is just,
     Recalling to memory men of the past,
     That this earl was born of a better stock!
     Your fame, friend Beowulf, is blazoned
        abroad
     Over all wide ways, and to every people.
1165 In manful fashion have you showed your
        strength,
     Your might and wisdom. My word I will
        keep,
     The plighted friendship we formerly
        pledged.
     Long shall you stand as a stay to your
        people. . . .
        'Tis a wondrous marvel how mighty God
1170 In gracious spirit bestows on men
     The gift of wisdom, and goodly lands,
     And princely power! He rules over all!
     He suffers a man of lordly line
     To set his heart on his own desires,
1175 Awards him fullness of worldly joy,
     A fair homeland, and the sway of cities,
     The wide dominion of many a realm,
     An ample kingdom, till, cursed with folly,
     The thoughts of his heart take no heed of his
        end.
1180 He lives in luxury, knowing not want,
     Knowing no shadow of sickness or age;
     No haunting sorrow darkens his spirit,
     No hatred or discord deepens to war;

The world is sweet, to his every desire,
1185 And evil assails not—until in his heart
     Pride overpowering gathers and grows!
     The warder slumbers, the guard of his spirit;
     Too sound is that sleep, too sluggish the
        weight
     Of worldly affairs, too pressing the Foe,
1190 The Archer who looses the arrows of sin.
        Then is his heart pierced, under his helm,
     His soul in his bosom, with bitter dart.
     He has no defense for the fierce assaults
     Of the loathsome Fiend. What he long has
        cherished
1195 Seems all too little! In anger and greed
     He gives no guerdon of plated rings.
     Since God has granted him glory and wealth
     He forgets the future, unmindful of Fate.
     But it comes to pass in the day appointed
1200 His feeble body withers and fails;
     Death descends, and another seizes
     His hoarded riches and rashly spends
     The princely treasure, imprudent of heart.
     Beloved Beowulf, best of warriors,
1205 Avoid such evil and seek the good,
     The heavenly wisdom. Beware of pride!
     Now for a time you shall feel the fullness
     And know the glory of strength, but soon
     Sickness or sword shall strip you of might,
1210 Or clutch of fire, or clasp of flood,
     Or flight of arrow, or bite of blade,
     Or relentless age; or the light of the eye
     Shall darken and dim, and death on a
        sudden,
     O lordly ruler, shall lay you low.
1215   A hundred half-years I've been head of the
        Ring-Danes,
     Defending the folk against many a tribe
     With spear-point and sword in the surges of
        battle
     Till not one was hostile 'neath heaven's
        expanse.
     But a loathsome change swept over the land,
1220 Grief after gladness, when Grendel came,

---

5. *flood*, Noah's flood, which also destroyed the giant race
mentioned in Genesis 6:4.

That evil invader, that ancient foe!
Great sorrow of soul from his malice I
   suffered;
But thanks be to God who has spared me to
   see
His bloody head at the battle's end!
1225 Join now in the banquet; have joy of the
   feast,
   O mightly in battle! And the morrow shall
      bring
   Exchange of treasure in ample store."
      Happy of heart the Geat leader hastened,
   Took seat at the board as the good king bade.
1230 Once more, as of old, brave heroes made
   merry
   And tumult of revelry rose in the hall.
      Then dark over men the night shadows
         deepened;
   The host all arose, for Hrothgar was minded,
   The gray, old Scylding, to go to his rest.
1235 On Beowulf too, after labor of battle,
   Came limitless longing and craving for sleep.
   A hall-thane graciously guided the hero,
   Weary and worn, to the place prepared,
   Serving his wishes and every want
1240 As befitted a mariner come from afar.
   The stout-hearted warrior sank to his rest;
   The lofty building, splendid and spacious,
   Towered above him. His sleep was sound
   Till the black-coated raven, blithesome of
      spirit,
1245 Hailed the coming of Heaven's bliss.

The Parting of Beowulf and Hrothgar

      Then over the shadows uprose the sun.
   The Geats were in haste, and eager of heart
   To depart to their people. Beowulf longed
   To embark in his boat, to set sail for his
      home.
1250 The hero tendered the good sword Hrunting
   To the son of Ecglaf, bidding him bear
   The lovely blade; gave thanks for the loan,
   Called it a faithful friend in the fray,
   Bitter in battle. The greathearted hero
1255 Spoke no word in blame of the blade!
   Arrayed in war-gear, and ready for sea,

The warriors bestirred them; and, dear to the
   Danes,
   Beowulf sought the high seat of the king.
   The gallant in war gave greeting to Hrothgar;
1260 Beowulf spoke, the son of Ecgtheow:
   "It is time at last to tell of our longing!
   Our homes are far, and our hearts are fain
   To seek again Hygelac over the sea.
   You have welcomed us royally, harbored us
      well
1265 As a man could wish; if I ever can win
   Your affection more fully, O leader of
      heroes,
   Swift shall you find me to serve you again!"
      Hrothgar addressed him, uttered his
         answer:
   "Truly, these words has the Lord of wisdom
1270 Set in your heart, for I never have hearkened
   To speech so sage from a man so young.
   You have strength, and prudence, and
      wisdom of word! . . .
   The Sea-Geats could have no happier choice
   If you would be willing to rule the realm,
1275 As king to hold guard o'er the hoard and the
      heroes.
   The longer I know you, the better I like you,
   Beloved Beowulf! You have brought it to
      pass
   That between our peoples a lasting peace
   Shall bind the Geats to the Danish-born;
1280 And strife shall vanish, and war shall cease,
   And former feuds, while I rule this realm."
      Then the son of Healfdene, shelter of earls,
   Bestowed twelve gifts on the hero in hall,
   Bade him in safety with bounty of treasure
1285 Seek his dear people, and soon return.
   The peerless leader, the Scylding lord,
   Kissed the good thane and clasped to his
      bosom
   While tears welled fast from the old man's
      eyes.
   Both chances he weighed in his wise, old
      heart,
1290 But greatly doubted if ever again
   They should meet at council or drinking of
      mead.

Nor could Hrothgar master—so dear was the
    man—
His swelling sorrow; a yearning love
For the dauntless hero, deep in his heart,
1295 Burned through his blood. Beowulf, the
    brave,
Prizing his treasure and proud of the gold,

Turned away, treading the grassy plain.
The ring-stemmed sea-goer, riding at anchor,
Awaited her lord. There was loud acclaim
1300 Of Hrothgar's gifts, as they went their way.
He was a king without failing or fault,
Till old age, master of all mankind,
Stripped him of power and pride of strength.

THINK AND DISCUSS
Understanding
1. Describe the lair of Grendel's mother.
2. How does Beowulf defeat this enemy?
3. What trophies does Beowulf take from his victory in the cavern?

Analyzing
4. The battle scenes in *Beowulf* are full of specific, sometimes grisly, detail. What do you think is the attitude of the poet toward the violent actions he portrays?
5. List the sounds that create **alliteration** in lines 1032–1037.
6. What warning does Hrothgar give Beowulf right after the hero's victory (lines 1206–1214)? Why does he do so?
7. What examples of human affection appear in *Beowulf*?

Extending
8. Compare Beowulf's fight with Grendel and his fight with Grendel's mother. Which seems more dangerous from these accounts?
9. Why do you suppose fictional encounters with monsters—both ancient and modern—so often take place in caves or underground spaces?

APPLYING: Metaphor H7
See Handbook of Literary Terms, p. 906
A **metaphor** is a figure of speech that makes a comparison between two basically unlike things that have something in common. This comparison may be stated or implied, but contains no connectives such as *like* or *as*. For example, in lines 1087–1088, Beowulf's sword "Began to soften and waste away/In iron icicles . . . ." Here the metal of the sword is compared to ice.

1. " . . . From the east came the sun,/Bright beacon of God . . . " (lines 438–439). What is the sun compared to? Why is the comparison appropriate?
2. "I thought to grip him in stubborn grasp/And bind him down on the bed of death,/There to lie straining in struggle for life . . . " (lines 702–704). Why is *bed* more appropriate than *chair, floor,* or *ground*?
3. "Called it [the sword] a faithful friend in the fray . . . " (line 1253). What does the sword have in common with a friend?

COMPOSITION
Describing a Monster's Lair
Lines 868–887 describe where Grendel's mother lives. Write a description of an appropriate lair for a modern monster. To begin, review the scene in *Beowulf*, noting the important details. Then, using your imagination, translate those details into modern terms. For example, the hidden cave might become a sewer pipe or an underground garage. Organize your description in the form of a journey, the first paragraph picturing the surrounding countryside, the second the means of entering the hiding place, the

third what the lair itself looks like, and the last the kinds of things one finds there. Assume that your classmates will be your audience and write to capture their interest.

Writing a Persuasive Essay

In several speeches Beowulf talks about his achievements. Write an essay of at least five paragraphs directed to your classmates in which you take a side on the question: Is Beowulf a braggart? First review Beowulf's speeches, listing statements that seem to you excessively boastful, or, by contrast, appropriate for the situation. Next outline your argument. Your first paragraph should define *brag;* you may use a dictionary definition or write your own. In the second, third, and fourth paragraphs, examine your text examples to determine whether they are or are not brags. Finally, in a concluding paragraph, sum up your ideas about the way this hero talks. See "Writing to Persuade an Audience" in the Writer's Handbook.

H/T   See FORESHADOWING in the Handbook of Literary Terms, page 908.

Beowulf Returns to Geatland

Then down to the sea came the band of the brave,
1305 The host of young heroes in harness of war,
In their woven mail; and the coast-warden viewed
The heroes' return, as he heeded their coming!
No uncivil greeting he gave from the sea-cliff
As they strode to ship in their glistening steel;
1310 But rode toward them and called their return
A welcome sight for their Weder kin.
There on the sand the ring-stemmed ship,
The broad-bosomed bark, was loaded with war-gear,
With horses and treasure; the mast towered high
1315 Over the riches of Hrothgar's hoard.
A battle-sword Beowulf gave to the boat-warden
Hilted with gold; and thereafter in hall
He had the more honor because of the heirloom,
The shining treasure. The ship was launched.
1320 Cleaving the combers of open sea

They dropped the shoreline of Denmark astern.
A stretching sea-cloth, a bellying sail,
Was bent on the mast; there was groaning of timbers;
A gale was blowing; the boat drove on.
1325 The foamy-necked plunger plowed through the billows,
The ring-stemmed ship through the breaking seas,
Till at last they sighted the sea-cliffs of Geatland,
The well-known headlands; and, whipped by the wind,
The boat drove shoreward and beached on the sand. . . .
1330 Then the hero strode with his stalwart band
Across the stretches of sandy beach,
The wide sea-shingle. The world-candle shone,
The hot sun hasting on high from the south.
Marching together they made their way
1335 To where in his stronghold the stout young king, . . .
Dispensed his treasure. Soon Hygelac heard
Of the landing of Beowulf, bulwark of men,

36 *The Anglo-Saxons*

That his shoulder-companion had come to
    his court
Sound and safe from the strife of battle.
1340   The hall was prepared, as the prince gave
    bidding,
Places made ready for much travelled men.
And he who came safe from the surges of
    battle
Sat by the side of the king himself, . . .
In friendly fashion in high-built hall
1345 Hygelac questioned his comrade and thane;
For an eager longing burned in his breast
To hear from the Sea-Geats the tale of their
    travels. . . .

Beowulf now tells the king of his battles with
Grendel and Grendel's mother, and of the rewards his victory has won. He concludes:

"These riches I bring you ruler of heroes,
And warmly tender with right good will.
1350 Save for you, king Hygelac, few are my
    kinsmen,
Few are the favors but come from you."
    Then he bade men bring the boar-crested
    headpiece,
The towering helmet, and steel-gray sark,[1]
The splendid war-sword, and spoke this
    word:
1355 "The good king Hrothgar gave me this gift,
This battle-armor, and first to you
Bade tell the tale of his friendly favor. . . .
Well may you wear it! Have joy of it
    all.". . .
    Then the battle-bold king, the bulwark
    of heroes,
1360 Bade bring a battle-sword banded with gold,
The heirloom of Hrethel;[2] no sharper steel,
No lovelier treasure, belonged to the Geats.
He laid the war-blade on Beowulf's lap,
Gave him a hall and a stately seat
1365 And hides[3] seven thousand. Inherited lands
Both held by birth-fee, home and estate.
But one held rule o'er the spacious realm,
And higher therein his order and rank.

This carved wooden face ornaments the end of a cross-
piece supporting the body of a Viking cart. 7th century.
University Museum of Antiquities, Oslo, Norway

The Fire-Dragon and the Treasure
    It later befell in the years that followed
1370 After Hygelac sank in the surges of war, . . .
That the kingdom came into Beowulf's
    hand.
For fifty winters he governed it well,
Aged and wise with the wisdom of years,
Till a fire-drake[4] flying in darkness of night
1375 Began to ravage and work his will.
On the upland heath he guarded a hoard,
A stone barrow lofty. Under it lay
A path concealed from the sight of men.
There a thief broke in on the heathen
    treasure,
1380 Laid hand on a flagon all fretted with gold,
As the dragon discovered, though cozened in
    sleep
By the pilferer's cunning. The people soon
    found

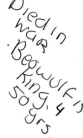

Died in war Beowulf is king 50 yrs.

---

1. *sark*, shirt (here, of mail).
2. *Hrethel* (hreth'əl), king of the Geats, father of Hygelac,
grandfather of Beowulf.
3. *hides*. The *hide* (roughly, as much land as could be
worked by one plow in a single year) varied from 40 to
120 acres. Seven thousand hides is a huge piece of land.
4. *fire-drake*, a fire-breathing dragon.

That the mood of the dragon was roused to
    wrath! . . .
  For three hundred winters this waster of
    peoples
1385 Held the huge treasure-hall under the earth
Till the robber aroused him to anger and
    rage,
Stole the rich beaker and bore to his master,
Imploring his lord for a compact of peace.
So the hoard was robbed and its riches
    plundered;
1390 To the wretch was granted the boon that he
    begged;
And his liege-lord first had view of the
    treasure,
The ancient work of the men of old.
Then the worm awakened and war was
    kindled,
The rush of the monster along the rock,
1395 When the fierce one found the tracks of the
    foe; . . .
Swiftly the fire-drake sought through the
    plain
The man who wrought him this wrong in his
    sleep.
Inflamed and savage he circled the mound,
But the waste was deserted—no man was in
    sight.
1400 The worm's mood was kindled to battle and
    war;
Time and again he returned to the barrow
Seeking the treasure-cup. Soon he was sure
That a man had plundered the precious gold.
Enraged and restless the hoard-warden
    waited
1405 The gloom of evening. The guard of the
    mound
Was swollen with anger; the fierce one
    resolved
To requite with fire the theft of the cup.
Then the day was sped as the worm desired;
Lurking no longer within his wall
1410 He sallied forth surrounded with fire,
Encircled with flame. For the folk of the land
The beginning was dread as the ending was
    grievous

That came so quickly upon their lord.
  Then the baleful stranger belched fire and
    flame,
1415 Burned the bright dwellings—the glow of the
    blaze
Filled hearts with horror. The hostile flier
Was minded to leave there nothing alive.
From near and from far the war of the
    dragon,
The might of the monster, was widely
    revealed
1420 So that all could see how the ravaging scather
Hated and humbled the Geatish folk.
Then he hastened back ere the break of dawn
To his secret den and the spoil of gold.
He had compassed the land with a flame of
    fire,
1425 A blaze of burning; he trusted the wall,
The sheltering mound, and the strength of
    his might—
But his trust betrayed him! The terrible news
Was brought to Beowulf, told for a truth,
That his home was consumed in the surges
    of fire. . . .
1430 Dark thoughts stirred in his surging bosom,
Welled in his breast, as was not his wont.
The flame of the dragon had levelled the
    fortress,
The people's stronghold washed by the
    wave.
But the king of warriors, prince of the
    Weders,
1435 Exacted an ample revenge for it all.
The lord of warriors and leader of earls
Bade work him of iron a wondrous shield,
Knowing full well that wood could not serve
    him
Nor linden[5] defend him against the flame.
1440 The stalwart hero was doomed to suffer
The destined end of his days on earth;
Likewise the worm, though for many a
    winter
He had held his watch o'er the wealth of the
    hoard.

---

5. *linden,* a shield of linden wood.

Comment

Heroic Morality

In his *Germania,* the Roman historian Tacitus (A.D. 55?–120?) gave a detailed and generally reliable account of the customs of the Germanic tribes from among whom came the Anglo-Saxon peoples that would later populate England:

"On the field of battle it is a disgrace to a chief to be surpassed in courage by his followers, and to the followers not to equal the courage of their chief. And to leave a battle alive after their chief has fallen means lifelong infamy and shame. To defend and protect him, and to let him get the credit for their own acts of heroism, are the most solemn obligations of their allegiance. The chiefs fight for victory, the followers for their chief. Many noble youths, if the land of their birth is stagnating in a long period of peace and inactivity, deliberately seek out other tribes which have some war in hand. For the Germans have no taste for peace; renown is more easily won among perils, and a large body of retainers cannot be kept together except by means of violence and war. They are always making demands on the generosity of their chief, asking for a coveted war horse or a spear stained with the blood of a defeated enemy. Their meals, for which plentiful if homely fare is provided, count in lieu of pay. The wherewithal for this openhandedness comes from war and plunder. A German is not so easily prevailed upon to plough the land and wait patiently for harvest as to challenge a foe and earn wounds for his reward. He thinks it tame and spiritless to accumulate slowly by the sweat of his brow what can be got quickly by the loss of a little blood."

From *The Agricola and The Germania* of Tacitus, translated by H. Mattingly, revised by S. A. Handford. New York: Penguin Books, 1948, 1970.

The ring-prince scorned to assault the
   dragon
1445 With a mighty army, or host of men.
He feared not the combat, nor counted of
   worth
The might of the worm, his courage and
   craft,
Since often aforetime, beset in the fray,
He had safely issued from many an onset,
1450 Many a combat and, crowned with success,
Purged of evil the hall of Hrothgar
And crushed out Grendel's loathsome
   kin. . . .
With eleven comrades, kindled to rage
The Geat lord went to gaze on the dragon.
1455 Full well he knew how the feud arose,
The fearful affliction; for into his hold
From hand of finder the flagon had come.
The thirteenth man in the hurrying throng
Was the sorrowful captive who caused the
   feud.

1460 With woeful spirit and all unwilling
Needs must he guide them, for he only knew
Where the earth-hall stood near the breaking
   billows
Filled with jewels and beaten gold.
The monstrous warden, waiting for battle,
1465 Watched and guarded the hoarded wealth.
No easy bargain for any of men
To seize that treasure! The stalwart king,
Gold-friend of Geats, took seat on the
   headland,
Hailed his comrades and wished them well.
1470 Sad was his spirit, restless and ready,
And the march of Fate immeasurably near;
Fate that would strike, seek his soul's
   treasure,
And deal asunder the spirit and flesh.
Not long was his life encased in the body!
1475 Beowulf spoke, the son of Ecgtheow:
"Many an ordeal I endured in youth,
And many a battle. I remember it all. . . ."

Beowulf 39

For all the rich gifts that Hygelac gave me
I repaid him in battle with shining sword,
1480 As chance was given. He granted me land,
A gracious dwelling and goodly estate. . . .
I was always before him alone in the van.
So shall I bear me while life-days last,
While the sword holds out that has served
    me well, . . .
1485 With hand and hard blade, I must fight for
    the treasure," . . .

Beowulf and Wiglaf Slay the Dragon

The king for the last time greeted his
    comrades,
Bold helmet-bearers and faithful friends:
"I would bear no sword nor weapon to battle
With the evil worm, if I knew how else
1490 I could close with the fiend, as I grappled
    with Grendel.
From the worm I look for a welling of fire,
A belching of venom, and therefore I bear
Shield and byrny. Not one foot's space
Will I flee from the monster, the ward of the
    mound.
1495 It shall fare with us both in the fight at the
    wall
As Fate shall allot, the lord of mankind.
Though bold in spirit, I make no boast
As I go to fight with the flying serpent.
Clad in your corselets and trappings of war,
1500 By the side of the barrow abide you to see
Which of us twain may best after battle
Survive his wounds. Not yours the
    adventure,
Nor the mission of any, save mine alone,
To measure his strength with the monstrous
    dragon
1505 And play the part of a valiant earl.
By deeds of daring I'll gain the gold
Or death in battle shall break your lord."
Then the stalwart rose with his shield upon
    him,
Bold under helmet, bearing his sark
1510 Under the stone-cliff; he trusted the strength
Of his single might. Not so does a coward!
He who survived through many a struggle,

Many a combat and crashing of troops,
Saw where a stone-arch stood by the wall
1515 And a gushing stream broke out from the
    barrow.
Hot with fire was the flow of its surge,
Nor could any abide near the hoard
    unburned,
Nor endure its depths, for the flame of the
    dragon.
Then the lord of the Geats in the grip of his
    fury
1520 Gave shout of defiance; the strong-heart
    stormed.
His voice rang out with the rage of battle,
Resounding under the hoary stone.
Hate was aroused; the hoard-warden knew
'Twas the voice of a man. No more was there
    time
1525 To sue for peace; the breath of the serpent,
A blast of venom, burst from the rock.
The ground resounded; the lord of the Geats
Under the barrow swung up his shield
To face the dragon; the coiling foe
1530 Was gathered to strike in the deadly strife.
The stalwart hero had drawn his sword,
His ancient heirloom of tempered edge;
In the heart of each was fear of the other!
The shelter of kinsmen stood stout of heart
1535 Under towering shield as the great worm
    coiled;
Clad in his war-gear he waited the rush.
In twisting folds the flame-breathing dragon
Sped to its fate. The shield of the prince
For a lesser while guarded his life and his
    body
1540 Than heart had hoped. For the first time
    then
It was not his portion to prosper in war;
Fate did not grant him glory in battle!
Then lifted his arm the lord of the Geats
And smote the worm with his ancient sword
1545 But the brown edge failed as it fell on bone,
And cut less deep than the king had need
In his sore distress. Savage in mood
The ward of the barrow countered the blow
With a blast of fire; wide sprang the flame. . . .

1550 Not long was the lull. Swiftly the battlers
    Renewed their grapple. The guard of the
        hoard
    Grew fiercer in fury. His venomous breath
    Beat in his breast. Enveloped in flame
    The folk-leader suffered a sore distress.
1555 No succoring band of shoulder-companions,
    No sons of warriors aided him then
    By valor in battle. They fled to the forest
    To save their lives; but a sorrowful spirit
    Welled in the breast of one of the band.
1560 The call of kinship can never be stilled
    In the heart of a man who is trusty and
        true.
      His name was Wiglaf, Weohstan's son,
    A prince of the Scylfings, a peerless thane,
    Ælfhere's kinsman;[6] he saw his king
1565 Under his helmet smitten with heat.
    He thought of the gifts which his lord had
        given,
    The wealth and the land of the
        Wægmunding line
    And all the folk-rights his father had owned;
    Nor could he hold back, but snatched up his
        buckler,
1570 His linden shield and his ancient sword. . . .
      Wiglaf spoke in sorrow of soul,
    With bitter reproach rebuking his comrades:
    "I remember the time, as we drank in the
        mead-hall,
    When we swore to our lord who bestowed
        these rings
1575 That we would repay for the war-gear and
        armor,
    The hard swords and helmets, if need like
        this
    Should ever befall him. He chose us out
    From all the host for this high adventure.

        . . .

    Now is the day that our lord has need
1580 Of the strength and courage of stalwart men.
    Let us haste to succor his sore distress
    In the horrible heat and the merciless flame.
    God knows I had rather the fire should enfold
    My body and limbs with my gold-friend and
        lord. . . .

1585 One helmet and sword, one byrny and
        shield,
    Shall serve for us both in the storm of strife."
    Then Wiglaf dashed through the deadly reek
    In his battle-helmet to help his lord.
    Brief were his words: "Beloved Beowulf,
1590 Summon your strength, remember the vow
    You made of old in the years of youth
    Not to allow your glory to lessen
    As long as you lived. With resolute heart,
    And dauntless daring, defend your life
1595 With all your force. I fight at your side!"
    Once again the worm, when the words
        were spoken,
    The hideous foe in a horror of flame,
    Rushed in rage at the hated men.
    Wiglaf's buckler was burned to the boss
1600 In the billows of fire; his byrny of mail
    Gave the young hero no help or defense.
    But he stoutly pressed on under shield of his
        kinsman
    When his own was consumed in the
        scorching flame.
    Then the king once more was mindful of
        glory,
1605 Swung his great sword-blade with all his
        might
    And drove it home on the dragon's head.
    But Nægling[7] broke, it failed in the battle,
    The blade of Beowulf, ancient and
        gray. . . .
      A third time then the terrible scather,
1610 The monstrous dragon inflamed with the
        feud,
    Rushed on the king when the opening
        offered,
    Fierce and flaming; fastened its fangs

---

6. **Wiglaf . . . kinsman.** Wiglaf's father Weohstan (wā'ō-stan) was apparently both a prince of the Scylfings (shil'fings), the ruling family among the Swedes, and a member of the Wægmunding (wäg'mŭn ding) family (see lines 1567-1568), the Geatish clan to which Beowulf belonged. Weohstan may have been a Swedish exile in Geatland (as the result of a blood feud) who had settled on Wægmunding lands. Ælfhere (alf'her rə) is not otherwise known.

7. **Nægling** (nag'ling). The name of Beowulf's sword is related to *nægl*, "nail."

In Beowulf's throat; he was bloodied with
    gore;
His lifeblood streamed from the welling
    wound.
1615   As they tell the tale, in the king's sore need
His shoulder-companion showed forth his
    valor,
His craft and courage, and native strength.
To the head of the dragon he paid no heed,
Though his hand was burned as he helped
    his king.
1620 A little lower the stalwart struck

At the evil beast, and his blade drove home
Plated and gleaming. The fire began
To lessen and wane. The king of the Weders
Summoned his wits; he drew the dagger
1625 He wore on his corselet, cutting and keen,
And slit asunder the worm with the blow.
So they felled the foe and wrought their
    revenge;
The kinsmen together had killed the dragon.
So a man should be when the need is bitter!
1630 That was the last fight Beowulf fought;
That was the end of his work in the world.

Comment

The Treasure of Sutton Hoo

In the late spring of 1939, archaeologists began excavating a large burial mound on an estate called Sutton Hoo, on the east coast of England in the area once known as East Anglia (see map, page 5). The mound was the largest in a group of earth mounds or barrows that lay on a steep hundred-foot slope overlooking the inlet where the River Deben flows into the North Sea. As the painstaking work continued, the diggers realized they had uncovered the richest hoard of early Anglo-Saxon objects ever found. A jeweled sword, a richly decorated shield and helmet, gold coins, silver bowls, and, above all, nineteen pieces of magnificently wrought gold jewelry set with thousands of elaborately cut garnets—these objects must have been the treasure of a mighty king. The great gold buckle alone weighs over fourteen ounces. With these objects were found an iron standard-frame and a two-foot carved whetstone, the symbols of sovereignty of an East Anglian king.

The treasure, scattered and corroded by time, lay within the hull of what had once been an eighty-nine-foot wooden ship. Only the iron bolts and nails remained, but the outline of the ship was plainly visible in the sand. No trace of a body was found; the ship was evidently a cenotaph or memorial to a king[1] whose bones lay elsewhere. From the evidence offered by the coins placed with the hoard —perhaps intended as payment for the ghostly oarsmen who were to convey the king to the next world—it is thought that the burial must have been made between the years A.D. 625 and 660. Ship burials were fairly numerous among the pagan Vikings of Europe at a later period, but rare in Anglo-Saxon England. The Sutton Hoo find was hailed as the most exciting archaeological discovery of the century in Britain.

In August 1939 a local Coroner's Jury was called upon to decide the legal status of the Sutton Hoo finds—whether they should be considered as treasure-trove and therefore the property of the Crown, or whether they belonged to Mrs. Pretty, the owner of the Sutton Hoo estate. If the artifacts had been secretly hidden, with the intent of recovering them later, they would become Crown property. But if it could be shown that they had been publicly buried

---

1. Some scholars think the king may have been Redwald, mentioned by Bede in his story of the conversion of King Edwin (see page 60). Redwald had been converted to Christianity, but lapsed into pagan practices. This would account for the combination of Christian and pagan elements in the cenotaph.

with no intention of ever recovering them, they would remain the property of Mrs. Pretty.

The evidence presented to the jury consisted of the description in *Beowulf* of Scyld Sceafing's ship-passing and the story of the final disposal of the dragon's hoard in the account of Beowulf's funeral. The jury easily concluded on the basis of this evidence that the Sutton Hoo treasures must have been buried at a public ceremony and been intended to remain forever undisturbed. Thus they became the property of Mrs. Pretty, who then generously presented them to the British Museum, where they are now on public display.

The opening section of *Beowulf* is said to be the earliest existing documentary evidence of a ship funeral. But the description of the rich treasures that were placed in the ship had generally been looked upon as poetic fancy. The find at Sutton Hoo confirmed the historical accuracy of the *Beowulf* description of a heroic society rich in gold and other beautifully wrought objects.

Beowulf may have been composed at a time when the spectacular Sutton Hoo ship burial was still remembered. Some scholars even think the poem may have been intended as a compliment to a king of East Anglia; there is evidence pointing to the possibility that an ancestor of the East Anglian royal line was a member of the Geatish or South Swedish tribe to which Beowulf belonged.

The articles found at Sutton Hoo indicate not only that Anglo-Saxon culture of the seventh century was far more advanced than had previously been imagined, but also that the Anglo-Saxons traded widely. Found on the site were a Swedish helmet and shield, the blade of a sword probably forged in the Rhineland, silver bowls and spoons from the Near East, and gold coins from France.

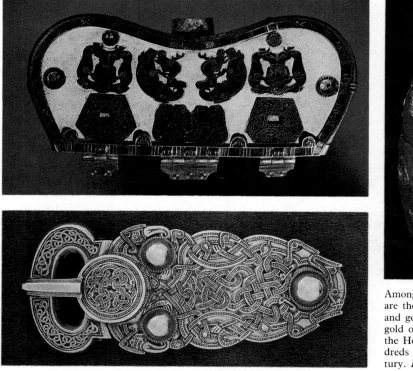

Among the objects found at Sutton Hoo are the Purse-lid, decorated with garnets and gold; the Buckle (the heaviest solid gold object ever found in England); and the Helmet, here reconstructed from hundreds of corroded iron fragments. 7th century. *British Museum*

Beowulf's Death

The wound which the dragon had dealt
    him began
To swell and burn; and soon he could feel
The baneful venom inflaming his breast.
1635 The wise, old warrior sank down by the wall
And stared at the work of the giants of old,
The arches of stone and the standing
    columns
Upholding the ancient earth-hall within.
His loyal thane, the kindest of comrades,
1640 Saw Beowulf bloody and broken in war;
In his hands bore water and bathed his
    leader,
And loosened the helm from his dear lord's
    head.
    Beowulf spoke, though his hurt was sore,
The wounds of battle grievous and grim.
1645 Full well he weened that his life was ended,
And all the joy of his years on earth;
That his days were done, and Death most
    near:
"My armor and sword I would leave to my
    son
Had Fate but granted, born of my body,
1650 An heir to follow me after I'm gone.
For fifty winters I've ruled this realm,
And never a lord of a neighboring land
Dared strike with terror or seek with sword.
In my life I abode by the lot assigned,
1655 Kept well what was mine, courted no
    quarrels,
Swore no false oaths. And now for all this
Though my hurt is grievous, my heart is
    glad.
When life leaves body, the Lord of mankind
Cannot lay to my charge the killing of
    kinsmen!
1660 Go quickly, dear Wiglaf, to gaze on the gold
Beneath the hoar stone. The dragon lies still
In the slumber of death, despoiled of his
    hoard.
Make haste that my eyes may behold the
    treasure,
The gleaming jewels, the goodly store,
1665 And, glad of the gold, more peacefully leave

The life and the realm I have ruled so long."
    Then Weohstan's son, as they tell the tale,
Clad in his corselet and trappings of war,
Hearkened at once to his wounded lord.
1670 Under roof of the barrow he broke his way.
Proud in triumph he stood by the seat,
Saw glittering jewels and gold on the ground,
The den of the dragon, the old dawn-flier,
And all the wonders along the walls.
1675 Great bowls and flagons of bygone men
Lay all unburnished and barren of gems,
Many a helmet ancient and rusted,
Many an arm-ring cunningly wrought.
Treasure and gold, though hid in the
    ground,
1680 Override man's wishes, hide them who will!
High o'er the hoard he beheld a banner,
Greatest of wonders, woven with skill,
All wrought of gold; its radiance lighted
The vasty ground and the glittering
    gems. . . .
1685 As I've heard the tale, the hero unaided
Rifled those riches of giants of old,
The hoard in the barrow, and heaped in his
    arms
Beakers and platters, picked what he would
And took the banner, the brightest of
    signs. . . .
1690 In haste returning enriched with spoil.
He feared, and wondered if still he would
    find
The lord of the Weders alive on the plain,
Broken and weary and smitten with wounds.
With his freight of treasure he found the
    prince,
1695 His dear lord, bloody and nigh unto death.
With water he bathed him till words broke
    forth
From the hoard of his heart and, aged and
    sad,
Beowulf spoke, as he gazed on the gold:
"For this goodly treasure whereon I gaze
1700 I give my thanks to the Lord of all,
To the Prince of glory, Eternal God,
Who granted me grace to gain for my people
Such dower of riches before my death.

I gave my life for this golden hoard.
1705 Heed well the wants, the need of my people;
My hour is come, and my end is near.
Bid warriors build, when they burn my
body,
A stately barrow on the headland's height.
It shall be for remembrance among my
people
1710 As it towers high on the Cape of the Whale,
And sailors shall know it as Beowulf's
Barrow,
Seafaring mariners driving their ships
Through fogs of ocean from far countries."
Then the great-hearted king unclasped from
his throat
1715 A collar of gold, and gave to his thane;
Gave the young hero his gold-decked helmet,
His ring and his byrny, and wished him well.
"You are the last of the Wægmunding line.
All my kinsmen, earls in their glory,
1720 Fate has sent to their final doom,
And I must follow." These words were the
last
The old king spoke ere the pyre received
him,
The leaping flames of the funeral blaze,
And his breath went forth from his bosom,
his soul
1725 Went forth from the flesh, to the joys of the
just. . . .
Not long was it then till the laggards in
battle
Came forth from the forest, ten craven in
fight,
Who had dared not face the attack of the foe
In their lord's great need. The shirkers in
shame
1730 Came wearing their bucklers and trappings of
war
Where the old man lay. They looked upon
Wiglaf.
Weary he sat by the side of his leader
Attempting with water to waken his lord.
It availed him little; the wish was vain! . . .
1735 He reproached the cowards whose courage
had failed: . . .

"Lo! he may say who would speak the truth
That the lord who gave you these goodly
rings,
This warlike armor wherein you stand—
When oft on the ale-bench he dealt to his
hall-men
1740 Helmet and byrny, endowing his thanes
With the fairest he found from near or from
far—
That he grievously wasted these trappings of
war
When battle befell him. The king of the folk
Had no need to boast of his friends in the
fight.
1745 But the God of victory granted him strength
To avenge himself with the edge of the sword
When he needed valor. Of little avail
The help I brought in the bitter battle!
Yet still I strove, though beyond my
strength,
1750 To aid my kinsman. And ever the weaker
The savage foe when I struck with my sword;
Ever the weaker the welling flame!
Too few defenders surrounded our ruler
When the hour of evil and terror befell.
1755 Now granting of treasure and giving of
swords,
Inherited land-right and joy of the home,
Shall cease from your kindred. And each of
your clan
Shall fail of his birthright when men from
afar
Hear tell of your flight and your dastardly
deed.
1760 Death is better for every earl
Than life besmirched with the brand of
shame!"

**The Messenger Foretells the Doom
of the Geats**

Then Wiglaf bade tell the tidings of battle
Up over the cliff in the camp of the host
Where the linden-bearers all morning long
1765 Sat wretched in spirit, and ready for both,
The return, or the death, of their dear-loved
lord.

Not long did he hide, who rode up the
    headland,
The news of their sorrow, but spoke before
    all:
"Our leader lies low, the lord of the Weders,
1770 The king of the Geats, on the couch of death.
He sleeps his last sleep by the deeds of the
    worm.
The dreadful dragon is stretched beside him
Slain with dagger-wounds. Not by the sword
Could he quell the monster or lay him
    low. . . .
1775 Let us go quickly to look on the king
Who brought us treasure, and bear his
    corpse
To the funeral pyre. The precious hoard
Shall burn with the hero. There lies the heap
Of untold treasure so grimly gained,
1780 Jewels and gems he bought with his blood
At the end of life. All these at the last
The flames shall veil and the brands devour.
No man for remembrance shall take from the
    treasure,
Nor beauteous maiden adorn her breast
1785 With gleaming jewel; bereft of gold
And tragic-hearted many shall tread
A foreign soil, now their lord has ceased
From laughter and revel and rapture of joy.
Many a spear in the cold of morning
1790 Shall be borne in hand uplifted on high.
No sound of harp shall waken the warrior,
But the dusky raven despoiling the dead
Shall clamor and cry and call to the eagle
What fare he found at the carrion-feast
1795 The while with the wolf he worried the
    corpses." . . .
They went with tears to behold the wonder.
They found the friend, who had dealt them
    treasure
In former days, on the bed of death,
Stretched out lifeless upon the sand. . . .
1800 They had sighted first, where it lay
    outstretched,
The monstrous wonder, the loathsome
    worm,
The horrible fire-drake, hideous-hued,

Scorched with the flame. The spread of its
    length
Was fifty foot-measures! Oft in the night
1805 It sported in air, then sinking to earth
Returned to its den. Now moveless in death
It had seen the last of its earthly lair.
Beside the dragon were bowls and beakers,
Platters lying, and precious swords
1810 Eaten with rust, where the hoard had rested
A thousand winters in the womb of
    earth. . . .
    Then spoke Wiglaf, Weohstan's son:
"Often for one man many must sorrow
As has now befallen the folk of the Geats.
1815 We could not persuade the king by our
    counsel,
Our well-loved leader, to shun assault
On the dreadful dragon guarding the gold;
To let him lie where he long had lurked
In his secret lair till the world shall end.
1820 But Beowulf, dauntless, pressed to his
    doom. . . .
Let us haste once more to behold the
    treasure,
The gleaming wonders beneath the wall.
I will show the way that you all may see
And closely scan the rings and the gold.
1825 Let the bier be ready, the pyre prepared,
When we come again to carry our lord,
Our leader beloved, where long he shall lie
In the kindly care of the Lord of all."

Beowulf's Funeral
    Then the son of Weohstan, stalwart in war,
1830 Bade send command to the heads of homes
To bring from afar the wood for the burning
Where the good king lay: "Now glede[8] shall
    devour,
As dark flame waxes, the warrior prince
Who has often withstood the shower of steel
1835 When the storm of arrows, sped from the
    string,
Broke over shield, and shaft did service,

---

8. *glede* (glēd), glowing coal, ember.

With feather-fittings guiding the barb."
  Then the wise son of Weohstan chose from
    the host
Seven thanes of the king, the best of the
    band;
1840 Eight heroes together they hied to the barrow
In under the roof of the fearful foe;
One of the warriors leading the way
Bore in his hand a burning brand.
They cast no lots who should loot the
    treasure
1845 When they saw unguarded the gold in the
    hall
Lying there useless; little they scrupled
As quickly they plundered the precious
    store.
Over the sea-cliff into the ocean
They tumbled the dragon, the deadly worm,
1850 Let the sea-tide swallow the guarder of gold.

Then a wagon was loaded with well-wrought
    treasure,
A countless number of every kind;
And the aged warrior, the white-haired king,
Was borne on high to the Cape of the Whale.
1855   The Geat folk fashioned a peerless pyre
Hung round with helmets and battle-boards,
With gleaming byrnies as Beowulf bade.
In sorrow of soul they laid on the pyre
Their mighty leader, their well-loved lord.
1860 The warriors kindled the bale on the barrow,
Wakened the greatest of funeral fires.
Dark o'er the blaze the wood-smoke
    mounted;
The winds were still, and the sound of
    weeping
Rose with the roar of the surging flame
1865 Till the heat of the fire had broken the body.

Dragon in classic Ringerike style, a tombstone from St. Paul's Cathedral churchyard,
London. 11th century.

With hearts that were heavy they chanted
    their sorrow,
Singing a dirge for the death of their lord;
And an aged woman with upbound locks
Lamented for Beowulf, wailing in woe.
1870 Over and over she uttered her dread
    Of sorrow to come, of bloodshed and
        slaughter,
Terror of battle, and bondage, and shame.
The smoke of the bale-fire rose to the sky!
  The men of the Weder folk fashioned a
    mound
1875 Broad and high on the brow of the cliff,
Seen from afar by seafaring men.
Ten days they worked on the warrior's
    barrow
Inclosing the ash of the funeral flame
With a wall as worthy as wisdom could
    shape.
1880 They bore to the barrow the rings and the
    gems,

The wealth of the hoard the heroes had
    plundered.
The olden treasure they gave to the earth,
The gold to the ground, where it still remains
As useless to men as it was of yore.
1885 Then round the mound rode the brave in
    battle,
The sons of warriors, twelve in a band,
Bemoaning their sorrow and mourning their
    king.
They sang their dirge and spoke of the hero
Vaunting his valor and venturous deeds.
1890 So is it proper a man should praise
His friendly lord with a loving heart,
When his soul must forth from the fleeting
    flesh.
So the folk of the Geats, the friends of his
    hearth,
Bemoaned the fall of their mighty lord;
1895 Said he was kindest of worldly kings,
Mildest, most gentle, most eager for fame.
circa 725

THINK AND DISCUSS
Understanding
1. What further honors come to Beowulf?
2. For how many years does he govern his kingdom before the dragon appears?
3. How does Beowulf kill this enemy? In what way does Wiglaf help?
4. What punishment awaits the men who fail to stay by Beowulf during the fight?

Analyzing
5. Beowulf has survived wounds before. Why does he die from this one?
6. Why is Beowulf, even as he is dying, so eager to see the dragon's treasure?
7. What does his death mean for the Geats?
8. How does Beowulf's funeral reflect the feelings and the fears of his people?

9. Explain the **metaphors** in lines 1834–1836 and line 1850.

Extending
10. Do you think Beowulf's struggle against his three foes is meant to be interpreted on a larger, more universal level? Explain.

APPLYING: Foreshadowing HT
See Handbook of Literary Terms, p. 908
    When hints or clues in a narrative suggest events that will occur later, the author is using the technique of **foreshadowing**. For example, when the dragon first attacks Beowulf's people, the narrator comments:

                For the folk of the land
The beginning was dread as the ending was
    grievous
That came so quickly upon their lord.

The obscure reference to a "grievous" ending foreshadows Beowulf's death, though exactly how the hero will end is not clear. Here foreshadowing darkens the account of Beowulf preparing for battle, since the reader now knows the hero will die.

1. Lines 1470–1474 describe Beowulf's state of mind as he plans the fight with the fire-dragon. Explain how these lines foreshadow the ending.
2. Find further examples of foreshadowing in the last part of the epic.

READING LITERATURE SKILLFULLY
Comparison/Contrast

The *Beowulf*-poet frequently creates parallels between characters, actions, even whole scenes. By comparing and contrasting these elements, you can understand the poem much more fully.

1. Beowulf engages in three major battles. What characteristics do these battles share?
2. How do Beowulf's enemies differ?
3. Compare the ways Beowulf rises to each of these challenges. What does this comparison reveal about Beowulf's heroism?
4. What do people today consider a hero to be? Compare and contrast modern concepts of a hero with Anglo-Saxon concepts, as exemplified by Beowulf.

VOCABULARY
Etymology

An etymology is the derivation of a word, an account of the word's origin and history. In the Glossary (page 978), etymologies are given in brackets at the ends of entries. The symbol < means "derived from." Use your Glossary to determine the etymologies of the following words from *Beowulf*. On separate paper, write a brief explanation for each.

martial (line 3)	boon (line 277)
blazon (line 102)	guerdon (line 692)
stalwart (line 142)	besmirched (line 1761)
brandish (line 169)	dirge (line 1867)

THINKING SKILLS
Classifying

To classify things is to arrange them into categories or groups according to some system. For example, writings can be classified as prose or poetry, and poetry can be further classified as epic, dramatic, lyric, and so on.

1. Scan *Beowulf* to find what kinds of personal possessions are mentioned and classify them according to purpose (clothing, adornment, weapons, and so on.)
2. Classify the characters mentioned by name in the poem. Devise your own classifications.

COMPOSITION
Defining Beowulf's Heroism

Beowulf is obviously the hero of this poem, but what makes him a hero? To answer this question, write an essay of at least four paragraphs in which you define for your fellow students what makes an Anglo-Saxon hero and why Beowulf qualifies as one. Begin by listing what you think are Beowulf's most significant traits, and then skim through the poem to find examples of them. Next outline your essay, devoting the first paragraph to defining heroism and subsequent paragraphs to describing different heroic characteristics. Support your ideas with quotes from the poem. See "Writing About Characters" in the Writer's Handbook.

Explaining Wiglaf's Role in *Beowulf*

Quite late in his epic, the *Beowulf*-poet introduces Wiglaf, a new and important character. Write an essay of at least four paragraphs in which you explain to other students why Wiglaf is included. First clarify your understanding of Wiglaf's role by going over the scenes in which he appears, imagining how each would be different if he were absent. Try to figure out why he is not mentioned earlier. Next outline your essay, devoting the first paragraph to Wiglaf's first appearance and subsequent paragraphs to what he does at specific, important moments. In your concluding paragraph, determine what impact this character has on the entire poem.

Poems from the Exeter Book

Around the year 1070, Loefric, the first bishop of Exeter, presented to the cathedral library an old manuscript that the library catalogue described as "a big English book about every sort of thing, wrought in song-wise." Onto its 122 pages a single scribe had copied, around A.D. 975, a wide-ranging collection of Anglo-Saxon poems, including "The Wife's Lament," "The Ruin," and ninety-five verse riddles.

Because Exeter is inland (see map, page 5), it escaped the destructive Danish raids on coastal areas. However, the events of a thousand years had their effects. The front cover of the book served at one time as a cutting-board and as a beer mat, and the back fourteen pages, containing the last riddles, were burned through with a firebrand. Nevertheless, the book survived, becoming the source for most of the Anglo-Saxon lyric poetry we still possess. *Lyric poetry* differs from epic poetry in that it is usually short and is highly personal, expressing a basic emotion or state of mind rather than telling a story.

The poems found in the Exeter book have no titles; modern editors have named them for convenience. But "The Wife's Lament" seems appropriate enough as the title for a poem that is the utterance of a woman who has been deserted, and who now lives in enforced solitude, uncertain of her future.

This is one of the three surviving Anglo-Saxon love lyrics. Why are there so few? Perhaps the scribes who compiled books were not very interested in such poems. Or, it may be that the warrior culture of these Germanic tribes did not produce many. Whatever the reason, for the modern reader interested in poetry speaking of human love, these texts are the more valuable because they are so rare.

This shoulder brooch, of gold inlaid with glass and decorated with cloisonné enamel, was among the items found at the Sutton Hoo ship-burial. 7th century. *British Museum*

H⊤ See ELEGY in the Handbook of Literary Terms, page 904.

The Wife's Lament

Wife is a little crazy.

translated by **Charles W. Kennedy**

A song I sing of sorrow unceasing,
The tale of my trouble, the weight of my woe,
Woe of the present, and woe of the past, *she is*
Woe never-ending of exile and grief, *very young*
5 But never since girlhood greater than now. *when*
First, the pang when my lord departed, *married.*
Far from his people, beyond the sea;
Bitter the heartache at break of dawn,
The longing for rumor in what far land
10 So weary a time my loved one tarried.
Far I wandered then, friendless and
    homeless,
Seeking for help in my heavy need.
    With secret plotting his <u>kinsmen purposed</u>
<u>To wedge us apart</u>, wide worlds between,
15 And bitter hate. I was sick at heart.
Harshly my lord bade lodge me here.
In all this land I had few to love me,
Few that were loyal, few that were friends.
Wherefore my spirit is heavy with sorrow
20 To learn my beloved, my dear man and mate
Bowed by ill-fortune and bitter in heart,
Is masking his purpose and planning a wrong.
With blithe hearts often of old we boasted
That nought should part us save death alone;
25 All that has failed and our former love *→ he once*
Is now as if it had never been! *loved her.*
Far or near where I fly there follows
The hate of him who was once so dear.
    In this forest-grove they have fixed my abode
30 Under an oak in a cavern of earth,
An old cave-dwelling of ancient days,
Where my heart is crushed by the weight of
    my woe.

Gloomy its depths and the cliffs that
    o'erhang it,
Grim are its confines with thorns
    overgrown—
35 A joyless dwelling where daily the longing
For an absent loved one brings anguish of heart.
    Lovers there are who may live their love,
Joyously keeping the couch of bliss,
While I in my earth-cave under the oak
40 Pace to and fro in the lonely dawn.
Here must I sit through the summer-long day,
Here must I weep in affliction and woe;
Yet never, indeed, shall my heart know rest
From all its anguish, and all its ache,
45 Wherewith life's burdens have brought me low.
    Ever man's years are subject to sorrow,
His heart's thoughts bitter, though his bearing
    be blithe;
Troubled his spirit, beset with distress—
Whether all wealth of the world be his lot,
50 Or hunted by Fate in a far country
My beloved is sitting soul-weary and sad,
Swept by the storm, and stiff with the frost,
In a wretched cell under rocky cliffs
By severing waters encircled about—
55 Sharpest of sorrows my lover must suffer
Remembering always a happier home.
Woeful his fate whose doom is to wait
With longing heart for an absent love.

8th century

From *An Anthology of Old English Poetry,* translated by Charles W. Kennedy. Copyright © 1960 by Oxford University Press, Inc. Reprinted by permission.

The Ruin

translated by **Michael Alexander**

Picture an Anglo-Saxon warrior meditating on the wreckage of an ancient city. The Anglo-Saxons, who did not build in stone, usually referred to Roman ruins as "the work of the Giants." Once, the speaker imagines, this city was well-fortified, with mead-halls, a prosperous citizenry, and hot baths for relaxation. But, using the Anglo Saxon word for fate, he notes that "*Wierds* broke it." Destiny has destroyed the city.

The only surviving copy of this poem was found on two pages of the Exeter Book. It had been badly scarred by fire, and parts of some of its lines are lost. The translator has tried to restore what he could, but notes that "my attempts to translate the defective lines, wherever it was possible, should not be taken as more than guesses."

Well-wrought this wall: Wierds[1] broke it.
The stronghold burst. . . .

Snapped rooftrees, towers fallen,
the work of the Giants, the stonesmiths,
5 mouldereth.
   Rime scoureth gatetowers
   rime on mortar.

Shattered the showershields, roofs ruined,
age under-ate them.
    And the wielders & wrights?
Earthgrip holds them—gone, long gone,
10 fast in gravesgrasp while fifty fathers
and sons have passed.
    Wall stood,
grey lichen, red stone, kings fell often,
stood under storms, high arch crashed—
stands yet the wallstone, hacked by weapons,
15 by files grim-ground . . .
 . . . shone the old skilled work
 . . . sank to loam-crust.

Mood quickened mind, and a man of wit,
cunning in rings, bound bravely the wallbase
20 with iron, a wonder.

Bright were the buildings, halls where springs
  ran,
high, horngabled,[2] much throng-noise;
these many meadhalls men filled
with loud cheerfulness: Wierd changed that.

25 Came days of pestilence, on all sides men fell
  dead,
death fetched off the flower of the people;
where they stood to fight, waste places
and on the acropolis, ruins.
    Hosts who would build again
shrank to the earth. Therefore are these courts
  dreary
30 and that red arch twisteth tiles.
wryeth from roof-ridge, reacheth groundwards.

 . . .
Broken blocks. . . .

---

1. *Wierds*, the powers that rule man's destiny; the Fates.
2. *horngabled*. The hall-gables were often made to appear more fearsome by means of animal horns mounted as decorations.

"The Ruin" from *The Earliest English Poems*, translated by Michael Alexander. Copyright © 1966, 1967, 1969 by Michael Alexander. Reprinted by permission of Penguin Books Ltd.

There once many a man
mood-glad, goldbright, of gleams garnished,
flushed with wine-pride, flashing war-gear,
35 gazed on wrought gemstones, on gold, on
    silver,
on wealth held and hoarded, on light-filled
    amber,
on this bright burg of broad dominion.

Stood stone houses; wide streams welled
hot from source, and a wall all caught
40 in its bright bosom, that the baths were
hot at hall's hearth; that was fitting . . . .

Thence hot streams, loosed, ran over hoar
    stone
unto the ring-tank . . . .
    . . . It is a kingly thing
45   . . . city . . . .

8th century

THINK AND DISCUSS
THE WIFE'S LAMENT
Understanding
1. In the speaker's view, who are her enemies?
2. Describe her daily life.

Analyzing
3. What does the speaker imagine her husband is doing? How do her imaginings reflect her own solitary life?
4. List the statements that the speaker makes about her husband's departure. Do they suggest hope that he will return?

Extending
5. What rights would you guess women held in Anglo-Saxon society?

THE RUIN
Understanding
1. Describe the principal features of this city before its destruction.
2. What prevented its inhabitants from repairing it?

Analyzing
3. How did *wierd* contribute to the downfall of such a powerful city?

Extending
4. How does the condition of the parchment copy of the poem itself illustrate the power of *wierd*?
5. Compare the description here with that of the dragon's lair in *Beowulf* (lines 1635–1638 and 1671–1690). Explain how they share an attitude toward the past.

APPLYING: Elegy HT
See Handbook of Literary Terms, p. 904
An **elegy** is a mournful or melancholy poem that reflects upon death or other serious subjects. Expressions of sorrow are central to Anglo-Saxon poetry. For example, grief for a lost leader overshadows parts of the epic poem *Beowulf*. In addition, "The Wife's Lament" and "The Ruin" view life as harsh, and happiness as passing swiftly.

1. What is the speaker in "The Wife's Lament" sorrowful about? In what way is this elegiac?
2. The wife concludes that "Ever [always] man's years are subject to sorrow . . . " (line 46). How does "The Ruin" illustrate this generalization?

THINKING SKILLS
Evaluating
To evaluate is to make a judgment based on some sort of standard. For example, a critic sees a play and writes a review that includes judgments about how well written, directed,

and acted it is, compared to all other plays he or she has seen.

1. How effective is "The Ruin" as a poem?
2. How worthwhile is it for anyone to read a poem that is so old—and only a fragment, at that?

VOCABULARY
Context

When you encounter a word whose exact meaning you may be unsure of, you often can make a useful guess about its meaning from its context, the way it is used in a sentence. Reread the sentence in "The Wife's Lament" in which each of the following words appears, and then write your own definitions for them using context to guide you. When you have finished, measure your accuracy by looking the words up in the Glossary.

> tarried (line 10)
> blithe (line 23)
> nought (line 24)
> abode (line 29)
> affliction (line 42)

COMPOSITION
Describing a City in Ruins

Imagine that some calamity has hit the area where you live, and that after some time you have returned to see what has happened. Write a journal entry in which you describe what you see. Organize your journal chronologically and divide it into paragraphs according to the places you visit. For example, you might want to devote a paragraph to what your school looks like. Include specific details to create a vivid word picture. Use your last paragraph to make some generalizations about the nature of human life.

Analyzing an Elegy

Write an essay for your school literary magazine in which you explain what makes "The Wife's Lament" an **elegy**. Begin by reviewing the term in the Handbook of Literary Terms. Then skim through the poem, listing all the things the wife laments. Next organize this list under at least three different topic headings; for example, her "absent love," where she must live, and so on. Decide on the order you wish to present these topics and develop a topic outline before beginning to write.

H🖊 See **PERSONIFICATION** in the Handbook of Literary Terms, page 906.

Anglo-Saxon Riddles

translated by **J. Duncan Spaeth and Michael Alexander**

Among the contents of the Exeter Book (see page 50) are ninety-five verse riddles. This playful form of expression, found worldwide, is based on making comparisons between different things, and thus has an unexpected connection with both poetry and myth-making. For example, imagine an Anglo-Saxon poet getting the idea that the sun is like a candle. If he were to use this comparison in fashioning a myth, he might invent a creation tale in which a god burns a giant candle to light the earth. In writing a poem, he might use this same comparison as a **metaphor:** "the sun, god's shining candle in the sky." This readily condenses into an actual Anglo-Saxon kenning, "world-candle."

But the poet could also create a riddle by simply omitting any direct reference to part of the comparison (in this case, the sun) and putting what is left in the form of a question: "What is the world's candle?" Riddle 68 is a good example of this process at work.

Beowulf gives us the world of the Anglo-Saxon hero. The **elegies** share profound human emotion. In the riddles we find the details of everyday life, more than a thousand years ago. The manuscript containing these riddles offers no solutions for them. Once you have tried finding your own, compare them with guesses made by other modern readers printed upside down at the bottom of page 56.

Riddle 5

Wounded I am, and weary with fighting;
Gashed by the iron, gored by the point of it,
Sick of battle-work, battered and scarred.
Many a fearful fight have I seen, when
5 Hope there was none, or help in the thick of it,
Ere I was down and fordone in the fray.
Offspring of hammers, hardest of
    battle-blades,
Smithied in forges, fell on me savagely,
Doomed to bear the brunt and the shock of it,
10 Fierce encounter of clashing foes.
Leech[1] cannot heal my hurts with his simples,[2]
Salves for my sores have I sought in vain.
Blade-cuts dolorous, deep in the side of me,
Daily and nightly redouble my wounds.

Riddle 16

I war with the wind, with the waves I wrestle;
I must battle with both when the bottom I seek,
My strange habitation by surges o'er-roofed.
I am strong in the strife, while still I remain;
5 As soon as I stir, they are stronger than I.
They wrench and they wrest, till I run from
    my foes;
What was put in my keeping they carry away.

If my back be not broken, I baffle them still;
The rocks are my helpers, when hard I am
    pressed;
10 Grimly I grip them. Guess what I'm called.

Riddle 21

My beak is below, I burrow and nose
Under the ground. I go as I'm guided
By my master the farmer, old foe of the forest;
Bent and bowed, at my back he walks,
5 Forward pushing me over the field;
Sows on my path where I've passed along.
I came from the wood, a wagon carried me;
I was fitted with skill, I am full of wonders.
As grubbing I go, there's green on one side,
10 But black on the other my path is seen.
A curious prong pierces my back;
Beneath me in front, another grows down
And forward pointing is fixed to my head.
I tear and gash the ground with my teeth,
15 If my master steer me with skill from behind.

---

1. *Leech*, an archaic term for "doctor."
2. *simples*, plants or herbs used in medicine.

Riddle 47

bookworm

I heard of a wonder, of words moth-eaten;
that is a strange thing, I thought, weird
that a man's song be swallowed by a worm,
his binded sentences, his bedside stand-by
5 rustled in the night—and the robber-guest
not one whit the wiser for the words he had
      mumbled.

The symbol of St. Matthew is a man. This illustration is from the Book of Durrow. 7th century. *Trinity College, Dublin, Ireland*

Riddle 68

ice

The wave, over the wave, a weird thing I saw,
through-wrought, and wonderfully ornate:
a wonder on the wave—water became bone.

Riddle 80

weathervane

I am puff-breasted, proud-crested,
a head I have, and a high tail,
eyes & ears and one foot,
both my sides, a back that's hollow,
5 a very stout beak, a steeple neck
and a home above men.
                Harsh are my sufferings
when that which makes the forest tremble
    takes and shakes me.
Here I stand under streaming rain
and blinding sleet, stoned by hail;
10 freezes the frost and falls the snow
on me stuck-bellied. And I stick it all out
for I cannot change the chance that made me.

8th–10th century

Riddles 47, 68, and 80 from *The Earliest English Poems*, translated by Michael Alexander (Penguin Classics, Second Edition, 1977). Copyright © 1966, 1977 by Michael Alexander. Reprinted by permission of Penguin Books Ltd.

THINK AND DISCUSS
RIDDLE 5
Understanding
1. What sort of life does the speaker lead?

Analyzing
2. What kind of attitude does the speaker have about battle?

Extending
3. How does this riddle demonstrate Anglo-Saxon melancholy?

Answers: 5. a shield; 16. an anchor; 21. a plow; 47. a bookworm; 68. ice; 80. a weathercock.

RIDDLE 16

Understanding

1. Describe the speaker's "strange habitation" (line 3).

Analyzing

2. When is the speaker strong? when helpless?

RIDDLE 21

Understanding

1. Who is the speaker's master?

Analyzing

2. Why is the speaker's path "green on one side,/But black on the other" (lines 9–10)?

Extending

3. Using information from this riddle, describe farming in Anglo-Saxon times.

RIDDLE 47

Understanding

1. Where are the words of the song located before being "swallowed by a worm"?

Analyzing

2. Why is the robber-guest "not one whit the wiser"?

Extending

3. Describe modern versions of this threat.

RIDDLE 68

Understanding

1. Explain how water can become hard as bone.

Analyzing

2. What sound is most insistently **alliterated**?

Extending

3. What view of nature do the words *weird*, *wonderfully*, and *wonder* suggest?

RIDDLE 80

Understanding

1. What kinds of weather are emphasized?

Analyzing

2. What is the speaker's "home above men" (line 6)?

3. What "makes the forest tremble" (line 7)? What does it do to the speaker?

APPLYING: Personification H7

See Handbook of Literary Terms, p. 906

Personification is a form of figurative language in which human characteristics, such as the power of speech, are given to things not human—animals, inanimate objects, even ideas. In these riddles, for example, the objects refer to themselves as "I" and speak of being weary, of battling with wind and waves, and of being "full of wonders."

1. What human traits does the object in Riddle 5 express?

2. How does the object personified in Riddle 80 demonstrate the Anglo-Saxon attitude toward fate?

COMPOSITION

Explaining How Riddles Reflect Daily Life

Anglo-Saxon riddles are full of the small details of everyday experience: a ship's anchor caught among rocks, a plow furrowing the ground, a weathercock in the rain. Write an essay in which you explain to an uninformed reader how one can use these riddles to guess at what life was like for these ancient people. Begin by making lists of the details in these poems. Cluster them under headings like *farming*, *sailing*, and *soldiering*. Then write an essay in which you devote a paragraph to each topic, describing Anglo-Saxon life and explaining how the details provide a basis for your description. In your concluding paragraph, express your own opinion about Anglo-Saxon times: would you like to have lived then?

Analyzing How a Riddle Works

The art of these riddles comes in developing a **personification** as far as possible. To show how these riddles work, select one for careful analysis and write an essay for your classmates in which you go through the riddle line by line, explaining how each statement fits the speaker (the solution to the riddle). For example, if you were discussing Riddle 16 you would explain why the waves are stronger than the speaker as soon as he moves (line 5). Organize your paper according to the development of the poem and provide a paragraph break each time the riddle starts on a different aspect of its subject.

The Violent Face of Nature

A riddle from the Exeter Book describes nature in this way:

Here I stand under streaming rain
and blinding sleet, stoned by hail;
freezes the frost and falls the snow
on me stuck-bellied. And I stick it all out
for I cannot change the chance that made me.

The attitude is characteristic: nature is an adversary. The wisest response is mute endurance. After all, fate has made things as they are, and there is little one can do about it.

In "The Ruin" these ideas reappear in the picture of what, just a few centuries before, had been an impressive, bustling city. But "Wierd changed that." The fate that determines all things has intervened, and the forces of nature have succeeded in destroying what people so cunningly made: "Snapped rooftrees, towers fallen,/the work of the Giants, the stonesmiths,/mouldereth." In the struggle against natural forces, human effort has once again lost out.

For twentieth-century readers such an attitude may seem surprising. So many people now inhabit the earth, and human technology has made such striking inroads, that today nature often seems a victim of human activity in the forms of pollution, exhaustion of resources, and endangering of species.

In Anglo-Saxon times, however, tiny, scattered tribes lived in a forest wilderness. Cities and roads left by the Romans were run-down or in ruins. Everything about their world illustrated how vulnerable people were to wild beasts, bad weather, and failed harvests. Travel was usually on sea lanes, in small wooden vessels that frequently sank. The weapons and tools available to fight back against natural enemies and to carve out places to live seemed pitifully inadequate to the challenge (although the plow in Riddle 21 can tear and gash the ground when guided by his master, "old foe of the forest").

Anglo-Saxon literature contains repeated examples of the efforts made to fashion small, safe, human centers for life and for happiness. The *Beowulf*-poet celebrates Hrothgar's mead-hall, Heorot, because it is a triumph of human skill and ingenuity over the forces of nature: "Its light shone out over many a land." In Bede's *History*, one of Edwin's counselors describes a mead-hall in this way: "Inside there is a comforting fire to warm the room; outside, the wintry storms of snow and rain are raging." He then compares life to a mead-hall; the storms outside represent the unknown—what went on before this life and what follows after death. To the wary pagan mind, the hall seems the only place of comfort. Outside there is a dark and terrifying wilderness, where dwell the wicked, the outcast, the monstrous.

Grendel, who comes to assault Heorot, is a creature of that wilderness, "Haunting the fenlands, holding the moors,/Ranging the wastes. . . ." And so the poet associates Grendel with the first murderer, Cain, who was also "banished . . . far from the fields of men . . . ."

The speaker in "The Wife's Lament," exiled to a cavern under an oak, sorely misses the relative safety and comfort of human society, and she describes her retreat in this way:

Gloomy its depths and the cliffs that
o'erhang it,
Grim are its confines with thorns overgrown—
A joyless dwelling . . . .

In subsequent centuries, as human effort ordered and controlled at least some aspects of nature, people became more comfortable with it. By the eighteenth century, Thomas Gray (page 408) finds peace in solitude and companionship in nature. A half century later, William Wordsworth (page 449) turns to nature as "The anchor of my purest thoughts, the nurse,/The guide, the guardian of my heart, and soul/Of all my moral being." To the Anglo-Saxons, this attitude would have seemed incomprehensible.

Bede, author of the most important history of early England, was born in the Anglo-Saxon kingdom of Northumbria (see map, page 5) in 673. Bede was apparently orphaned early; when he was seven, his relatives put him under the supervision of the monks at Wearmouth Abbey. Two years later, in 682, he transferred to the newly built abbey of Jarrow, where he was to spend the rest of his life.

Jarrow was the creation of Benedict Biscop (628–690), an ambitious, aristocratic abbot who traveled to Rome and throughout western Europe acquiring manuscripts, pictures, and sacred vestments for his monastery. When he returned he brought, along with these treasures, skilled stone-cutters and makers of stained glass, to build and ornament his new abbey and train native craftsmen. But it was through supporting Bede that he made his greatest contribution in English culture.

From boyhood Bede studied in the library Benedict created at Jarrow. Then in 703, the year of his ordination to the priesthood, Bede began to write. During the ensuing 28 years he completed forty books: commentaries on the Bible; lives of abbots, martyrs, and saints; books on philosophy and poetry—a literary achievement unequaled in European literature since the days of Augustine (354–430).

Bede's masterpiece, completed in 731, when he was 51 years old, is his *Ecclesiastical History of the English People,* describing the growth of the Christian church in England from the attack of Julius Caesar in 55 B.C. to Bede's own day. He used modern historical methods. He examined past records of events, securing copies, for example, of official letters on file in Canterbury and Rome. He gathered eyewitness accounts from churchmen all over England and at the beginning of his book carefully listed all of his sources. Modern research has tended to verify the accuracy of his account. Bede's *History* is the most important work of its kind to be written between classical times and the Renaissance.

It is written in Latin, the language he habitually spoke, wrote, and taught in; his prose is natural and direct. Late in the ninth century, scholars at the court of King Alfred translated it into Anglo-Saxon. Already the *History* seemed to them one of the central works of their culture, worthy of reproduction into a language more people could read. That high estimate has remained into our own day.

As this passage begins Paulinus, a Christian missionary, is trying to convert the pagan Edwin, King of Northumbria. Paulinus has not been able, in Bede's words, "to bring the king's proud mind to accept the humility of the way of salvation." Then one day Edwin recalls a peculiar experience from his youth, when fleeing the persecution of his predecessor, King Ethelfrid, he had taken refuge in the court of Redwald, King of East Anglia (see note, page 42).

from The Ecclesiastical History of the English People

translated by **Leo Sherley-Price**

The Conversion of Edwin

When his predecessor was persecuting him, Edwin wandered as an unknown fugitive for many years through many lands and kingdoms, until at length he came to Redwald, and asked him for protection against the plots of his powerful enemy. Redwald gave him a ready welcome, and promised to do everything he asked, but as soon as Ethelfrid heard that he had arrived in that province, and that he and his companions were living at the king's court as his friends, he sent messengers to offer Redwald a large sum of money to murder him. Obtaining no satisfaction, he sent a second and third time, offering even heavier bribes, and threatening war if his demand were refused. At length Redwald, either intimidated by his threats or corrupted by his bribes, agreed to his demand and promised either to kill Edwin, or to surrender him to Ethelfrid's messengers. This plot was discovered by a loyal friend of Edwin, who went to his room early one night when he was about to retire, and calling him out, warned him of the king's wicked intentions, adding: "If you are willing, I will act as your guide out of this province, and take you immediately to some place where neither Redwald nor Ethelfrid can find you." Edwin replied: "Thank you for your goodwill, but I cannot act as you suggest. I cannot break the agreement that I have made with so great a king, who has so far done me no harm, nor showed any hostility towards me. If I must die, I would rather die by his hand than by an hand less noble. For what refuge remains for me, who have already wandered for so many years in every corner of Britain, trying to escape the hatred of my enemies?" When his friend had left, Edwin remained, sitting sadly alone outside the palace, burdened with many gloomy thoughts, and not knowing what to do, or where to turn.

He had remained a considerable time in silence, grieving and desperate, when suddenly, at dead of night, he saw a man approaching whose face and clothes were strange to him, and whose unexpected arrival caused him considerable alarm. But the stranger came up and greeted him, asking why he was sitting sadly on a stone, watchful and alone, at an hour when everyone else was asleep. Edwin asked what concern it might be of his whether he passed the night indoors or outside. In reply, the man said: "Don't think that I am unaware why you are sad and sleepless and why you are keeping watch alone. I know very well who you are, what your troubles are, and what coming evils you dread. But tell me this: what reward will you give the man who can deliver you from your troubles, and persuade Redwald not to harm you or betray you to death at the hands of your enemies?" Edwin answered that he would give any reward in his power in return for such

From *Bede: A History of the English Church and People*, translated by Leo Sherley-Price. Reprinted by permission of Penguin Books Ltd.

This illustration is from a Canon Table in the Book of Kells, an Irish illuminated manuscript. A canon table is a numerical table for drawing up concordances between the four Gospels. circa 800. *Trinity College, Dublin, Ireland*

an outstanding service. Then the other went on: "And what if he also promised that you should become king, defeat your enemies, and enjoy greater power than any of your predecessors who have ever ruled the English nation?" Heartened by these enquiries, Edwin readily promised that, in return for such blessings, he would give ample proofs of his gratitude. The stranger then asked a third question. "If the man who can truthfully foretell such good fortune can also give you better and wiser guidance for your life and salvation than anything known to your parents and kinsfolk, will you promise to obey and follow his salutary advice?" Edwin at once promised that he would faithfully follow the guidance of anyone who could save him out of so many troubles and raise him to a throne. On his assurance, the man who addressed him laid his right hand on Edwin's head,

saying: "When you receive this sign, remember this occasion and our conversation, and do not delay the fulfilment of your promise." Hereupon, it is said, he vanished, and Edwin realized that it was not a man but a spirit who had appeared to him.

The young prince was still sitting there alone, greatly heartened by what he had heard, and puzzling over the identity and origin of the being who had talked with him, when his loyal friend approached with a cheerful greeting, and said: "Get up and come inside. You can now sleep without fear, for the king has had a change of heart. He now intends you no harm, and will keep the promise that he made you. For when he privately told the queen of his intention to deal with you as I warned, she dissuaded him, saying that it was unworthy in a great king to sell his best friend for gold, and worse still to sacrifice his royal honor, the most valuable of all possessions, for love of money." In brief, the king did as she advised, and not only refused to surrender the exiled prince to the envoys of his enemy, but assisted him to recover his kingdom. As soon as the envoys had left, he raised a great army to make war on Ethelfrid, who met him with a much smaller force—Redwald allowing him no time to summon his full strength—and was killed in Mercian territory on the east bank of the river Idle. In this battle Regnhere, son of Redwald, was killed. So Edwin, as his vision had foretold, not only escaped the plots of his enemy, but succeeded to his throne at his death.

While King Edwin hesitated to accept the word of God at Paulinus's preaching, he used to sit alone for hours, deliberating what he should do, and what religion he should follow. On one of these occasions, the man of God came to him, and laying his right hand on his head, enquired whether he remembered this sign. The king trembled, and would have fallen at his feet, but Paulinus raised him, and said in a friendly voice: "God has helped you to escape from the hands of the enemies whom you feared, and it is through His bounty that you have received the kingdom that you desired. Remember the third promise that you made, and hesitate no longer. Accept the Faith and keep the commands of Him who has delivered you from all your earthly troubles, and raised you to the glory of an earthly kingdom. If you will henceforward obey His will, which he reveals to you through me, he will save you from the everlasting doom of the wicked, and give you a place in His eternal kingdom in heaven."

When Paulinus had spoken, the king answered that he was both willing and obliged to accept the Faith which he taught, but said that he must discuss the matter with his principal advisers and friends, so that if they were in agreement, they might all be cleansed together in Christ the Fount of Life. Paulinus agreed, and the king kept his promise. He summoned a council of the wise men, and asked each in turn his opinion of this new faith and new God being proclaimed.

Coifi,[1] the High Priest, replied without hesitation: "Your Majesty, let us give careful consideration to this new teaching, for I frankly admit that, in my experience, the religion that we have hitherto professed seems valueless and powerless. None of your subjects has been more devoted to the service of the gods than myself, yet there are many to whom you show greater favor, who receive greater honors, and who are more successful in all their undertakings. Now, if the gods had any power, they would surely have favored myself, who have been more zealous in their service. Therefore, if on examination these new teachings are found to be better and more effectual, let us not hesitate to accept them."

Another of the king's chief men signified his agreement with this prudent argument, and went on to say: "Your Majesty, when we compare the present life of man with that time of which we have no knowledge, it seems to me like the swift flight of a lone sparrow through the banqueting-hall where you sit in the winter months to dine with your thanes and counselors. Inside there is a comforting fire to warm the room; outside, the wintry storms of snow and rain are raging. This sparrow flies swiftly in through one door of the hall, and out through another. While he is inside, he is safe from the winter storms; but after a few moments of comfort, he vanishes from sight into the darkness whence he came. Similarly, man appears on earth for a little while, but we know nothing of what went before this life, and what follows. Therefore if this new teaching can reveal any more certain knowledge, it seems only right that we should follow it." The other elders and counselors of the king, under God's guidance, gave the same advice.

Coifi then added that he wished to hear Paulinus's teaching about God in greater detail; and when, at the king's bidding, this had been given, the High Priest said: "I have long realized that there is nothing in what we worshipped, for the more diligently I sought after truth in our religion, the less I found. I

---

1. *Coifi* (kō′ə fē).

now publicly confess that this teaching clearly reveals truths that will afford us the blessings of life, salvation, and eternal happiness. Therefore, Your Majesty, I submit that the temples and altars that we have dedicated to no advantage be immediately desecrated and burned." In short, the king granted blessed Paulinus full permission to preach, renounced idolatry, and professed his acceptance of the Faith of Christ. And when he asked the High Priest who should be the first to profane the altars and shrines of the idols, together with the enclosures that surrounded them, Coifi replied: "I will do this myself, for now the true God has granted me knowledge, who more suitably than I can set a public example, and destroy the idols that I worshipped in ignorance?" So he formally renounced his empty superstitions, and asked the king to give him arms and a stallion—for hitherto it had not been lawful for the High Priest to carry arms, or to ride anything but a mare—and, thus equipped, he set out to destroy the idols. Girded with a sword and with a spear in his hand, he mounted the king's stallion and rode up to the idols. When the crowd saw him, they thought he had gone mad, but without hesitation, as soon as he reached the temple, he cast a spear into it and profaned it. Then, full of joy at his knowledge of the worship of the true God, he told his companions to set fire to the temple and its enclosures and destroy them. The site where these idols once stood is still shown, not far east of York, beyond the river Derwent, and is known as Goodmanham. Here it was that the High Priest, inspired by the true God, desecrated and destroyed the altars that he had himself dedicated.

So King Edwin, with all the nobility and a large number of humbler folk, accepted the Faith and were washed in the cleansing waters of Baptism in the eleventh year of his reign, which was the year 627, and about one hundred and eighty years after the first arrival of the English in Britain.[2]

731

---

2. *first arrival . . . Britain,* traditionally dated A.D. 449.

THINK AND DISCUSS
Understanding
1. What is life like for Edwin before the visit of the mysterious messenger?
2. What three questions does the stranger ask? What promises does Edwin make?
3. Who—or what—does Edwin realize the stranger is?
4. How does Edwin become king?

Analyzing
5. What is the significance of the sign, or gesture, used by the stranger and Paulinus?
6. How does Paulinus use Edwin's success to argue for conversion?
7. What role does Coifi play in the conversion of the Northumbrian kingdom? Why do you think Bede gives him so much emphasis?

Extending
8. What attitude toward the human condition is illustrated by the comparison of a sparrow flying through a banqueting-hall with "the present life of man"? How does this attitude compare with present-day attitudes toward life?

APPLYING: Theme HŻ
See Handbook of Literary Terms, p. 931
Theme is the underlying meaning of a literary work. A theme may be directly stated, but more often it is implied. For example, one theme in the **elegies** is that life is short and uncertain.

Bede's history of England is more than just that, for Bede was a priest, and his history is an *ecclesiastical* one—having to do with the church. To discern what theme or meaning Bede finds in his materials, consider the episodes he chooses and the way he reports them.

1. "Edwin realized that it was not a man but a spirit who had appeared to him." What does

Bede's simple, factual reporting of this incident suggest about his own beliefs?

2. What meaning is expressed by the sign that is used by two different men?

3. In what ways does the manner in which Bede reports the destruction of the temples express his theme? If the same events were reported instead by a pagan priest, how might the theme be different?

VOCABULARY
Antonyms

An antonym is a word that means the opposite of another word. For example, Bede speaks of "agreement with this *prudent* argument." *Prudent* means "careful; sensible." Antonyms to *prudent* are *foolish* and *rash*. Find antonyms for the following terms. Use your Glossary if necessary.

salutary	zealous
heartened	profane
dissuaded	desecrate

THINKING SKILLS
Generalizing

To generalize is to draw a general conclusion from particular information. For example, a scholar examines all the kinds of writing available from a particular culture and generalizes about why or how these people wrote.

1. What picture of Anglo-Saxon politics is suggested by Edwin's progress from fugitive to king?

2. From the behavior of both nobles and commoners, as described by Bede, explain the relationship of church and state in Anglo-Saxon England.

COMPOSITION
Explaining a Literary Comparison

One of Edwin's advisors compares life to "the swift flight of a lone sparrow through the banqueting-hall." Write a four-paragraph essay for a literary journal in which you analyze this curious comparison. In your first paragraph, explain the context of the speech and restate the comparison so that it is clear to the ordinary reader. In your second and third paragraphs, compare and contrast experience in and outside of the banqueting-hall, and discuss what these two locations represent. In your final paragraph, consider how effective this comparison is and why it was used instead of another.

Analyzing Bede's Theme

Bede gives a detailed account of how and why a pagan priest rebels against his gods. Write an essay of at least three paragraphs in which you explain to your classmates how Bede describes this dramatic personal transformation and the lesson he draws from it. First review the selection, jotting down details of language and description to make your writing vivid and credible. Outline your essay according to the stages of the story. Show how Bede stresses Coifi's doubts about the old gods, illustrates the priest's evaluation of the new religion, and demonstrates his commitment through his actions after converting. In a concluding paragraph, discuss how Bede uses this story to illustrate the changes Christianity brought to Anglo-Saxon culture. See "Writing About Theme" in the Writer's Handbook.

Celtic Literature in Wales and Ireland

After the retreat of the Roman legions, Celtic Britons struggled to defend their land against Anglo-Saxon tribes. During the sixth century, driven north and west, they fought a series of ultimately futile battles with the invaders. Their poets subsequently recorded, in clusters of three-line stanzas, the names of the heroes who died then. These "Stanzas of the Graves" served primarily as mnemonic devices—to aid the bards in recalling names that otherwise might be forgotten. They are probably the oldest surviving Welsh poems. Some of the names they record subsequently became the heroes of Arthurian legend: Bedwyr—Bedivere; Gwalchmai—Gawain; March—King Mark; and Arthur himself. This reference to Arthur is the earliest now known, but already it seems to suggest the growth of legend and mystery around him. His grave is "The world's enigma."

With the ultimate success of the Anglo-Saxon conquerors, surviving Britons fled south and west, carrying with them vivid memories of their past defeats. In Wales their bards now began to compose heroic tales about the past. Unlike the Anglo-Saxon story of *Beowulf,* these were a mixture of prose narrative and lyric reflection. The prose narratives have disappeared, but some of the lyrics survive. They express intense emotion—usually tragic grief at loss and death. The "Eagle of Pengwern" comes from a longer work composed about 850 which describes a disaster suffered two hundred years earlier. In this poem the woman Heledd laments the death of her brother Cynddylan and the destruction of their town Trenn, luckless in defeat but "shining" from the fame of Cynddylan's heroism.

Because of the early and rapid spread of Christianity in Ireland, Latin was already in use there by the fifth century, and poetry in the vernacular Irish language from the sixth century still survives—the oldest vernacular literature in western Europe. Like the Welsh, Irish bards created narratives in prose and verse recording the exploits of national heroes. The greatest of these, the *Tain* (tôn), celebrating the battles of the hero Cuchulain (kə hul'ən), may have been orally composed between A.D. 500 and 700. From the seventh century comes a new sort of poetry, short lyrics with regular meter and end rhyme—probably derived from Latin models, but already speaking in an authentically Irish voice.

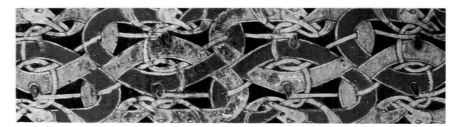

from The Stanzas of the Graves

translated by **Gwyn Jones**

Stanza 1
The graves the rain makes wet and sleek,
Not men who turned the other cheek,
Cerwyd, and Cywryd, and Caw.

Stanza 4
Siawn's grave is on Hirerw Mound,
5 Between the earth and his oaken shroud,
A treacherous smiler, bitter, proud.

Stanza 9
Whose grave is this? [. . .]
Crazed as a wild boar in mortal strife,
He'd smile on you as he spilled your life.

Stanza 10
10 At Camlan[1] the grave of Osfran's son,
After many a bloody fight.
Bedwyr's grave's on Tryfan height.

Stanza 11
Gwalchmai is in Perydon ground,
His grave reproaches all mankind;
15 Cynon in Llanbadarn find.

Stanza 12
A grave for March, a grave for Gwythur,
A grave for Gwgawn Red-glaive;[2]
The world's enigma, Arthur's grave.

9th–10th century

---

1. *Camlan*, site of Arthur's last battle.
2. *glaive* (glāv), sword.

Eagle of Pengwern

translated by **Gwyn Williams**

Eagle of Pengwern, grey-crested, tonight
    its shriek is high,
  eager for flesh I loved.
Eagle of Pengwern, grey-crested, tonight
5   its call is high,
  eager for Cynddylan's flesh.
Eagle of Pengwern, grey-crested, tonight
    its claw is high,
  eager for flesh I love.
10 Eagle of Pengwern, it called far tonight,
    it kept watch on men's blood;
  Trenn shall be called a luckless town.
Eagle of Pengwern, it calls far tonight,
    it feasts on men's blood;
15 Trenn shall be called a shining town.

circa 850

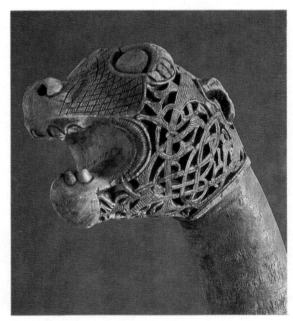

The anonymous sculptor of this Viking post head has been nicknamed "the Academician." 7th century. *University Museum of Antiquities, Oslo, Norway*

Pangur Ban

translated by **Robin Flower**

I and Pangur Ban, my cat,
'Tis a like task we are at;
Hunting mice is his delight,
Hunting words I sit all night.

5 Better far than praise of men
'Tis to sit with book and pen;
Pangur bears me no ill will,
He too plies his simple skill.

'Tis a merry thing to see
10 At our tasks how glad are we,
When at home we sit and find
Entertainment to our mind.

Oftentimes a mouse will stray
In the hero Pangur's way;
15 Oftentimes my keen thought set
Takes a meaning in its net.

'Gainst the wall he sets his eye
Full and fierce and sharp and sly;
'Gainst the wall of knowledge I
20 All my little wisdom try.

When a mouse darts from its den,
O how glad is Pangur then!
O what gladness do I prove
When I solve the doubts I love!

25 So in peace our tasks we ply,
Pangur Ban, my cat, and I;
In our arts we find our bliss,
I have mine and he has his.

Practice every day has made
30 Pangur perfect in his trade;
I get wisdom day and night
Turning darkness into light.

9th century

Summer Is Gone

translated by **Kuno Meyer**

My tidings for you: the stag bells,
Winter snows, summer is gone.

Wind high and cold, low the sun,
Short his course, sea running high.

5 Deep-red the bracken, its shape all gone—
The wild-goose has raised his wonted cry.

Cold has caught the wings of birds;
Season of ice—these are my tidings.

9th century

The Viking Terror

translated by **Frank O'Connor**

Since tonight the wind is high,
The sea's white mane a fury,
I need not fear the hordes of hell
Coursing the Irish Channel.

9th century

"Pangur Ban" translated by Robin Flower from *1000 Years of Irish Poetry*, ed. by Kathleen Hoagland. Copyright 1947 by the Devin-Adair Company, renewed 1975. Reprinted by permission. "Summer Is Gone" and "The Viking Terror" from *A Book of Ireland* edited by Frank O'Connor. Copyright © 1959 William Collins Sons and Company Limited. Reprinted by permission.

THINK AND DISCUSS

THE STANZAS OF THE GRAVES

Understanding

1. What function do these stanzas serve?

Analyzing

2. What sort of qualities do they celebrate?

EAGLE OF PENGWERN

Understanding

1. What has happened at Trenn?

Analyzing

2. The poem employs both repetition and variation. What effect does the repetition have? What effect does the variation have?

Extending

3. In what ways do the attributes of the eagle fit the scene this poem evokes?

PANGUR BAN

Understanding

1. What occupies the speaker's evenings?

Analyzing

2. Explain the parallel between the speaker and his cat.
3. Why does Pangur's success delight his master?

Extending

4. How do you think the speaker regards himself and his work?

SUMMER IS GONE

Understanding

1. What signs of winter are mentioned?

Analyzing

2. What seems to be the speaker's reaction to the coming of winter?

THE VIKING TERROR

Understanding

1. Who are the "hordes of hell"? Why need the speaker not fear them?"

Analyzing

2. Explain the **metaphor** in line 2.

Extending

3. How does this little Irish poem echo the Anglo Saxon **elegies**?

COMPOSITION

Describing a Change of Seasons

The phrase "My tidings to you" in "Summer is Gone" imply that it is a letter. Write a letter of at least three paragraphs to a friend or relative, listing signs familiar to you both that tell of the changing of seasons. Try to be as specific in describing particular details as the Irish poet is. You might suggest your personal reaction to the coming season by choosing details—negative or positive—that reflect your feelings.

Narrating the Fall of Trenn

The Welsh lyric "Eagle of Pengwern" is the lament of Heledd after the death of her brother and the destruction of her town. Using the small amount of information available in the poem as a starting point, imagine what may have led up to the moment when she speaks, and then write a narrative describing the fall of Trenn. You may find it useful to recall details of weaponry and fighting from *Beowulf* and images of a fallen city from "The Ruin." Use these and your own imaginative details in your fictional reconstruction.

The English language has developed and continues to evolve as the people who speak it have been affected by social conditions, political events, and contacts with other cultures. This series of articles will explore the nature of the changes that our language has undergone, and the events and forces that have brought about those changes.

The first inhabitants of the British Isles whose language we know about were the Celts. Beginning in 55 B.C., the Roman general Julius Caesar led a series of unsuccessful attacks on the British Celts. About a hundred years later, in A.D. 43, Romans began settling in Britain. For the next four hundred years, Britain was part of the Roman Empire, and camps of the Latin-speaking Roman legions dotted the countryside. Their influence can still be seen in the names of such English towns as Lancaster, Manchester, and Worcester, the suffixes -caster, -chester, and -cester being derived from castrum, the Latin word for "camp."

Early in the fifth century, when the Roman Empire began to disintegrate, the Romans were forced to withdraw their troops from Britain. Left without the defenses of the Roman legions, the Celts were soon attacked by Germanic tribes from across the North Sea—Jutes, Angles, and Saxons—whose homelands were along the Danish peninsula and the northwest coast of Germany. The invaders drove some of the Celts to Brittany across the sea and many others into what are now Wales and Cornwall. The Celtic language survives today as Welsh, the language of Wales; Irish, the Celtic language of Ireland; Scots Gaelic, the ancient tongue of the Highlands; and Breton, the Celtic language still spoken in Brittany.

The invading tribes of Germanic people spoke dialects of the language now called Old English or sometimes Anglo-Saxon. The largest group, the Angles, settled the lands from the Thames River to the north of England. It is from this group that the names England (Angleland) and English (Anglisc) are derived, although most of the literature written in the dialect of this northern area has been lost. The Saxons, who lived south of the Thames, spoke the variety of Old English in which most of the surviving documents of the period are written. In Kent were the Jutes; only a very few texts in the Kentish dialect have been preserved.

In 597, Augustine and other missionaries arrived from Rome, bringing Christianity and initiating the introduction of Latin words into Old English. The largest number of such words were those related to the new religion; among them were *altar, candle, hymn, organ, pope, priest,* and *temple,* which today differ only slightly from their Old English forms. Contact with the Roman church also led to the adoption of words describing clothing (e.g., our modern *sock, cap*), foods (*beet, pear*), plants and trees (*pine, lily*), and words related to education (*school, Latin, verse, meter*), as well as many others.

Beginning in the eighth century, Old English was further modified by contact with the Scandinavian languages. The inhabitants of the Scandinavian peninsula and Denmark, once close neighbors of the early Anglo-Saxons and similar to them both in blood and in language, began a series of raids on England that culminated in the eleventh century when Cnut, king of Denmark, conquered all of England and seized the English throne. For the next twenty-five years, Danish kings ruled England.

During the nearly three hundred years of Scandinavian attacks, a considerable number of Scandinavians also settled peacefully in England, especially in the northern and eastern sections. Evidence of the extent of such settlement survives in place names. A map today shows more than six hundred names such as Grimsby, Rugby, and Derby, formed from the Danish word *byr,* meaning "farm" or "town." There are also names like Thistlethwaite and Braithwaite from *thveit,* meaning "isolated piece of land."

The first page of the Beowulf manuscript.
10th century. *British Library*

Since Old English and the language of the invaders were quite similar, there was a ready intermingling of forms of speech. In some cases, when the languages had different words to describe the same thing, the English word survived. In other cases, such Scandinavian words as *egg* and *systir* (sister) replaced their Old English equivalents. The Scandinavian pronouns *they*, *their*, and *them* were substituted for the Old English equivalents *hie*, *hiera*, and *him*. Occasionally, Old English words that had fallen into disuse were revived because of Scandinavian parallels.

You saw a brief passage in Old English in the note on the poetry of *Beowulf*. Another passage appears in the note on translating *Beowulf*, followed by a variety of translations. You may recognize a few words of the Anglo-Saxon; still, we who speak modern English must constantly remind ourselves when we see Old English that this was not a truly foreign language but the not-far-removed ancestor of our own tongue.

Our difficulty in reading Old English becomes more understandable when we realize that it was quite different in grammatical structure from the English we speak and write today. Modern English depends heavily upon the arrangement of words in a sentence to give meaning; it relies only slightly on word endings to indicate number, gender, and case (e.g., whether a noun is the object of a verb or its subject). For example, when we read

1. The king greeted the foreigner.
2. The foreigner greeted the king.

we know that in the first sentence, *king* is the subject of the verb *greeted*, and in the second sentence, *king* is the object of the verb, even though there is no change in the spelling of *king* as the function of the word changes. In Old English, "the king," when used as the grammatical subject (as in sentence 1) would be written as *se cyning;* as the object (as in sentence 2), it would be *þǣm cyninge*. Old English was what linguists call a highly inflected language, which means that the meaning of a sentence depended on changes in the spelling of nouns, pronouns, adjectives, and verbs. Although modern English still makes use of inflections, there are far fewer inflected forms than there were in Anglo-Saxon times.

Old English verbs were of two types: "strong" and "weak." In strong verbs, the vowels changed in the principal part, as they do in modern *sing, sang, sung;* weak verbs indicated change of time by adding *d* or *t*, as do the majority of verbs today (*look, looked, looked*).

Apart from grammatical differences, some of the strangeness that Old English presents to a modern reader is due to differences in spelling and vocabulary. Old English used two characters, þ and ð, to represent the sound *th*, so that *wiþ* is our modern word *with*, and *ða* is the equivalent of *then*. The sound *sh* was represented in Old English by *sc*, and the sound of *k* was represented by *c*. Words like *scip, bæð, nacod*, and *þæt*, which look strange to us, were most likely pronounced in Anglo-Saxon times almost as we pronounce them today: *ship, bath, naked*, and *that*.

Fewer than a fourth of the words in modern English are derived from Old English, but among those are the most commonly used nouns, pronouns, verbs, connectives, and articles.

Why don't we still speak Anglo-Saxon? What forces made English take the form it has today? Later articles in this book will trace the political and social forces that influenced—and continue to influence—the evolution of the English language.

THINKING CRITICALLY
ABOUT LITERATURE

UNIT 1   THE ANGLO-SAXONS   450–1066

■ CONCEPT REVIEW

At the end of each unit in *England in Literature* is a selection that contains many of the important ideas and literary terms found in the period you have just studied. It also contains notes and questions designed to help you think critically about your reading. Page numbers in the notes refer to an application. A more extensive discussion of these terms is in the Handbook of Literary Terms.

"The Seafarer" comes from the *Exeter Book* (see page 50).

The Seafarer

translated by **Burton Raffel**

This tale is true, and mine. It tells
How the sea took me, swept me back
And forth in sorrow and fear and pain,
Showed me suffering in a hundred ships,
5 In a thousand ports, and in me. It tells
Of smashing surf when I sweated in the cold
Of an anxious watch, perched in the bow
As it dashed under cliffs. My feet were cast
In icy bands, bound with frost,
10 With frozen chains, and hardship groaned
Around my heart. Hunger tore
At my sea-weary soul. No man sheltered
On the quiet fairness of earth can feel
How wretched I was, drifting through winter
15 On an ice-cold sea, whirled in sorrow,
Alone in a world blown clear of love,

■ As you read, look for details that characterize the speaker.

■ **Alliteration** (page 25): Note how the repeated *s* sound in line 6 suggests the sound of surf.
■ **watch:** assigned duty period.
■ **Metaphor** (page 35): Note the *bands* and *chains* of ice.

■ Note what hardships and difficulties the speaker dwells on throughout.

Hung with icicles. The hailstorms flew.
The only sound was the roaring sea,
The freezing waves. The song of the swan
20 Might serve for pleasure, the cry of the sea-fowl,
The death-noise of birds instead of laughter,
The mewing of gulls instead of mead.
Storms beat on the rocky cliffs and were echoed
By icy-feathered terns and the eagle's screams;
25 No kinsman could offer comfort there,
To a soul left drowning in desolation.
    And who could believe, knowing but
The passion of cities, swelled proud with wine
And no taste of misfortune, how often, how wearily,
30 I put myself back on the paths of the sea.
Night would blacken; it would snow from the north;
Frost bound the earth and hail would fall,
The coldest seeds. And how my heart
Would begin to beat, knowing once more
35 The salt waves tossing and the towering sea!
The time for journeys would come and my soul
Called me eagerly out, sent me over
The horizon, seeking foreigners' homes.
    But there isn't a man on earth so proud,
40 So born to greatness, so bold with his youth,
Grown so brave, or so graced by God,
That he feels no fear as the sails unfurl,
Wondering what Fate has willed and will do.
No harps ring in his heart, no rewards,
45 No passion for women, no worldly pleasures,
Nothing, only the ocean's heave;
But longing wraps itself around him.
Orchards blossom, the towns bloom,
Fields grow lovely as the world springs fresh,
50 And all these admonish that willing mind
Leaping to journeys, always set
In thoughts travelling on a quickening tide.
So summer's sentinel, the cuckoo, sings
In his murmuring voice, and our hearts mourn
55 As he urges. Who could understand,
In ignorant ease, what we others suffer
As the paths of exile stretch endlessly on?
    And yet my heart wanders away,
My soul roams with the sea, the whales'
60 Home, wandering to the widest corners
Of the world, returning ravenous with desire,
Flying solitary, screaming, exciting me

■ **And who . . . sea:** No city-dweller, who has not known misfortune, could understand his returning to the sea.

■ **Personification** (page 57): His soul challenges him to go on yet another perilous journey.

■ **sentinel:** watch or guard.

■ Note how the *kenning* "whale's home" connects land and sea travel.
■ **ravenous:** very hungry; greedy.

To the open ocean, breaking oaths
On the curve of a wave.
                         Thus the joys of God
65 Are fervent with life, where life itself
Fades quickly into the earth. The wealth
Of the world neither reaches to Heaven nor remains.
No man has ever faced the dawn
Certain which of Fate's three threats
70 Would fall: illness, or age, or an enemy's
Sword, snatching the life from his soul.
The praise the living pour on the dead
Flowers from reputation: plant
An earthly life of profit reaped
75 Even from hatred and rancor, of bravery
Flung in the devil's face, and death
Can only bring you earthly praise
And a song to celebrate a place
With the angels, life eternally blessed
80 In the hosts of Heaven.
                         The days are gone
When the kingdoms of earth flourished in glory;
Now there are no rulers, no emperors,
No givers of gold, as once there were,
When wonderful things were worked among them
85 And they lived in lordly magnificence.
Those powers have vanished, those pleasures are dead,
The weakest survives and the world continues,
Kept spinning by toil. All glory is tarnished,
The world's honor ages and shrinks,
90 Bent like the men who mold it. Their faces
Blanch as time advances, their beards
Wither and they mourn the memory of friends,
The sons of princes, sown in the dust.
The soul stripped of its flesh knows nothing
95 Of sweetness or sour, feels no pain,
Bends neither its hand nor its brain. A brother
Opens his palms and pours down gold
On his kinsman's grave, strewing his coffin
With treasures intended for Heaven, but nothing
100 Golden shakes the wrath of God
For a soul overflowing with sin, and nothing
Hidden on earth rises to Heaven.
    We all fear God. He turns the earth,
He set it swinging firmly in space,
105 Gave life to the world and light to the sky.
Death leaps at the fools who forget their God.

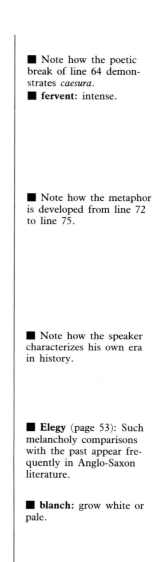

■ Note how the poetic break of line 64 demonstrates *caesura*.

■ **fervent**: intense.

■ Note how the metaphor is developed from line 72 to line 75.

■ Note how the speaker characterizes his own era in history.

■ **Elegy** (page 53): Such melancholy comparisons with the past appear frequently in Anglo-Saxon literature.

■ **blanch**: grow white or pale.

He who lives humbly has angels from Heaven
To carry him courage and strength and belief.
A man must conquer pride, not kill it,
110 Be firm with his fellows, chaste for himself,
Treat all the world as the world deserves,
With love or with hate but never with harm,
Though an enemy seek to scorch him in hell,
Or set the flames of a funeral pyre
115 Under his lord. Fate is stronger
And God mightier than any man's mind.
Our thoughts should turn to where our home is,
Consider the ways of coming there,
Then strive for sure permission for us
120 To rise to that eternal joy,
That life born in the love of God
And the hope of Heaven. Praise the Holy
Grace of He who honored us,
Eternal, unchanging creator of earth. Amen.

8th century

■ **Theme** (page 63): *Fate* is a constantly recurring term in Anglo-Saxon literature, retained by Christian writers from their pagan traditions.

THINK AND DISCUSS

Understanding
1. Who is the speaker? What details tell you?
2. What are some of the hardships and difficulties the speaker has known in his years at sea?
3. Point out lines in which the speaker mentions the joys of seafaring.

Analyzing
4. What is it that keeps luring the speaker back to the sea?
5. How does he characterize his own era in history?
6. Distinguish the two different forms of reward after death in lines 72–80.
7. The speaker mentions both Fate and God in the same sentence (lines 115–116) and again several times in the poem. Which does the speaker seem to feel controls his life more?

Extending
8. Do you agree with the speaker's statement that "A man must conquer pride, not kill it . . ."? Explain.
9. Name some other situations in life that people say they hate but cannot stay away from.

REVIEWING LITERARY TERMS

Alliteration
1. Identify the principal alliterated sounds in lines 17–22 and 42–43.
2. What rhythm do these alliterations create?

Personification
3. How does the poet personify his soul in lines 59–64?
4. How does personification intensify the poet's description of death in line 106?

Metaphor
5. Explain the metaphor in line 33.
6. Note the metaphor established in lines 72–73. Write a phrase to describe something that death might bring that would be consistent with this metaphor.

Elegy
7. How do lines 64–71 connect this poem with the elegiac tradition?

Theme

8. Given the speaker's depiction of his world, what thematic conclusions does he reach about human life?

■ CONTENT REVIEW

THINKING SKILLS

Classifying

1. List the places where people in this unit live. Classify them according to status, or importance of the dwellers.

2. Make a chart with the selection titles down the side and these heads across the top: *Religion, Warfare, Travel, Occupations.* For each selection, place a check mark under each head that describes information contained in the selection.

Generalizing

3. What types of journeys do Anglo-Saxon writers describe? What purposes do they find in them?

4. Discuss the various sorts of adversity that characters in Anglo-Saxon literature face. What virtue(s) do these adversities demand of individuals?

5. What emotional bonds exist between people depicted in Anglo-Saxon literature?

Evaluating

6. The words *fate* and *wierd* appear frequently in these selections. To what extent do the writings prove the contention that fate controls all human destiny?

7. The translators of these selections have used various literary devices in an attempt to capture the feel of the original Anglo-Saxon verse. Do you prefer translations that do this, or would you prefer prose retellings? Why?

■ COMPOSITION REVIEW

Describing an Anglo-Saxon

In the selections in Unit 1 you have read about a variety of men and women with full lives and deep emotions. Choose one of them as the subject of an essay describing that character in detail. First reread parts of the selection for details. Organize your essay so that the first paragraph defines your character's function in the work, and so that subsequent paragraphs describe details of that character's physical appearance, significant actions, and value system. If the selection has little or nothing to say about some of these matters, make reasonable guesses.

Explaining Anglo-Saxon Loyalty

In Anglo-Saxon culture, one was expected to demonstrate loyalty to rulers, family members, friends, and to one's own promises. Write an essay for a reader familiar with Unit 1 in which you survey the various examples of loyalty found in the selections and explain how this particular standard of conduct helped to hold Anglo-Saxon society together. Prepare by reviewing instances of loyal or disloyal conduct. Take notes on details and quotations you can use to illustrate your essay. Devote your introductory paragraph to what loyalty meant and how it held together the members of a society; then devote three or four subsequent paragraphs to particular examples derived from literary works.

Analyzing Happy Moments

There are plenty of cold rain storms and violent deaths in Anglo-Saxon literature, but there are also moments of happiness and fulfillment. Write an essay in which you analyze the kinds of happiness such moments depict. Begin by reviewing the selections in Unit 1 and listing what the selections describe as pleasing and fulfilling. Organize them under general topic headings such as *victory in battle, parties, respect and love,* and so on. Use these to organize your paragraphs, and then within each paragraph discuss the specific examples that illustrate each kind of happiness.

THE MEDIEVAL PERIOD

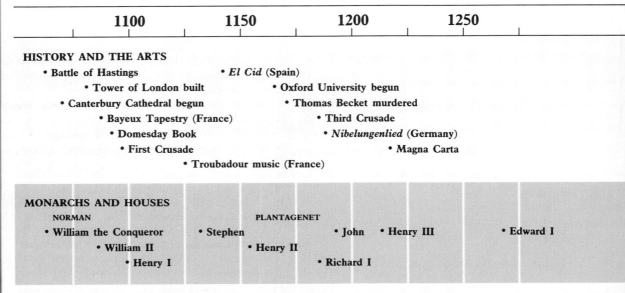

	1100	1150	1200	1250

HISTORY AND THE ARTS

- Battle of Hastings
- *El Cid* (Spain)
- Tower of London built
- Oxford University begun
- Canterbury Cathedral begun
- Thomas Becket murdered
- Bayeux Tapestry (France)
- Third Crusade
- Domesday Book
- *Nibelungenlied* (Germany)
- First Crusade
- Magna Carta
- Troubadour music (France)

MONARCHS AND HOUSES

NORMAN   PLANTAGENET

- William the Conqueror
- Stephen
- John
- Henry III
- Edward I
- William II
- Henry II
- Henry I
- Richard I

ENGLISH LITERATURE

- Earliest record of a miracle play
- Geoffrey: *History of the Kings of Britain*
- Folk ballads composed

The Tower of London, from Visscher's map of London. 1616.

English soldiers in the Battle of Hastings. Bayeux Tapestry.

Henry II at Canterbury. 13th century stained glass window.

1350	1400	1450	1500

- First Parliament
  - Giotto paints frescoes (Italy)
    - Dante: *Divine Comedy* (Italy)
      - Hundred Years' War begins
        - Black Death in England
          - Boccaccio: *Decameron* (Italy)
            - Peasants' Revolt
- Battle of Agincourt
  - Joan of Arc executed
    - Gutenberg's Bible (Germany)
      - Wars of the Roses begin
        - Caxton's printing press
          - Battle of Bosworth Field
            - Columbus explores America
- da Vinci paints *The Last Supper* (Italy)

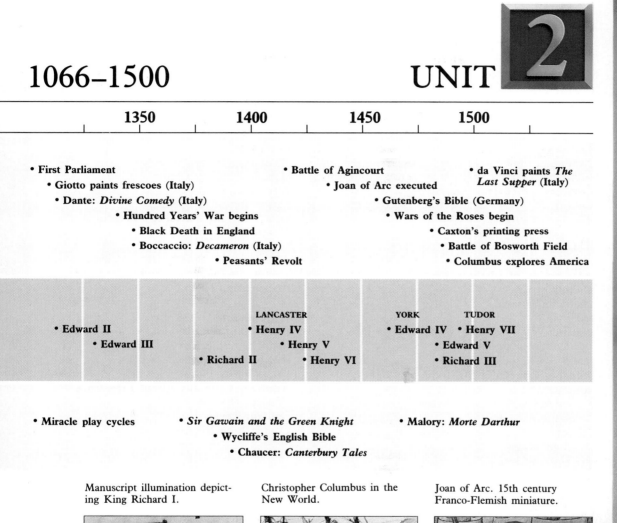

	LANCASTER	YORK	TUDOR

- Edward II
  - Edward III
    - Richard II
- Henry IV
  - Henry V
    - Henry VI
- Edward IV
  - Edward V
    - Richard III
- Henry VII

- Miracle play cycles
  - *Sir Gawain and the Green Knight*
    - Wycliffe's English Bible
      - Chaucer: *Canterbury Tales*
- Malory: *Morte Darthur*

Manuscript illumination depicting King Richard I.

Christopher Columbus in the New World.

Joan of Arc. 15th century Franco-Flemish miniature.

PREVIEW

UNIT 2   THE MEDIEVAL PERIOD   1066–1500

Authors
Geoffrey Chaucer
Sir Thomas Malory
Folk Ballads

Features
Reading a Folk Ballad
Comment: The Ballad: An Enduring Art Form
Comment: Medieval Tourists
Comment: A Fifteenth-Century Valentine
Themes in English Literature:
    The Medieval Romance
The Changing English Language

Application of Literary Terms
rhythm
characterization
irony
allusion
protagonist/antagonist

Reading Literature Skillfully
summarizing

Vocabulary Skills
context
word analogies
prefixes and roots

Thinking Skills
generalizing
synthesizing
evaluating

Composition
Writing a Newspaper Story
Writing About a Theme
Writing an Interview
Explaining the Pilgrimage
Describing the Pardoner's Preaching
Writing to Persuade
Composing a Link
Analyzing the Wife of Bath's Views
Telling Sir Bedivere's Story
Interpreting Theme

Enrichment
Performing Ballads
Readers Theater
Researching Arthurian Stories

Thinking Critically About Literature
Concept Review
Content Review
Composition Review

THE MEDIEVAL PERIOD   1066–1500

For some time, ties had existed between the court of England and that of the Duchy of Normandy in northern France. In 1002 King Aethelred of England married Emma, daughter of the duke of Normandy. Their son, Edward the Confessor, was half Norman in blood but wholly Norman in outlook. Before becoming king of England in 1042, he had spent thirty years at the Norman court, learning the French language and customs and making French friends. As king he welcomed Norman courtiers and churchmen; his court even adopted the Norman style of dress.

When Edward died without an heir in January, 1066, his throne was claimed by both Harold Godwinson of England and William, Duke of Normandy. Godwinson was the choice of the Witan, the king's council, but William maintained, apparently with justification, that Edward had declared him heir to the English throne. After a hasty coronation Harold marched north to battle the Viking army of another claimant, King Harold Hardrada (the Ruthless) of Norway, whom he defeated and killed near York on September 25. Three days later William landed at Pevesney Bay on England's southeastern coast with an army estimated at between 4,000 and 7,000 men, the sons of the Norman nobility and other well-born adventurers from throughout Europe. According to a contemporary chronicle, "As soon as his men were fit for service, they constructed a castle at Hastings. When King Harold was informed of this, he gathered together a great host, and came to oppose [William] at the gray apple tree, and William came upon him unexpectedly, before his army was set in order. Nevertheless the king fought against him most resolutely with those men who wished to stand by him, and there was great slaughter on both sides. King Harold was slain, and Leofwine, his brother, and Earl Gurth, his brother, and many good men. The French had possession of the place of slaughter." The famous Bayeaux tapestry commemorates this Norman Conquest.

Norman England

Although Harold was dead, England was not subdued without a lengthy struggle, during which most of the Angle-Saxon nobility was wiped out. Claiming that every bit of England belonged to him, William proceeded to redistribute lands belonging to 4,000-5,000 Anglo-Saxon nobles among some 180 of his followers, in exchange for a solemn oath of loyalty to him and the promise of military service. Under this system, known as *feudalism*, all the landowners in England became vassals (tenants) of the king.

Almost immediately after being crowned in 1066, William initiated work on the Tower of London, designed to protect that city. Just four years later, in 1070, construction began on Canterbury Cathedral, one of the first buildings to utilize the new Norman style of architecture.

In order to set up an efficient system of taxation, in 1086 William carried out a survey of his entire kingdom, arousing great resentment among his English subjects. William's agents recorded most of the land in England, together with the name of the person who owned it, its size, its value, the number and type of workers employed on it, and so on. "So thoroughly did [William] have the enquiry carried out," complains the *Anglo-Saxon Chronicle*, "that there was not a single hide (120 acres) of land . . . not even one ox, nor one cow, nor one pig which escaped notice in his survey." This survey, offi-

French soldiers on horseback defeat the English at Hastings in 1066. Detail of Bayeux Tapestry. Circa 1077. *Queen Matilda Museum, Bayeux, France*

cially referred to as "the description of England," was popularly called "Domesday (Doomsday) Book," because there was no appeal from its judgment. The Domesday Book is still valuable today as a source for genealogical studies as well as for insights into medieval life.

William's policy for consolidating governmental power in the kingship was continued during the reigns of his two sons, William II and Henry I. But when Henry died without a male heir, the throne was contested by his daughter Matilda and his nephew, Stephen of Blois. With the support of the Church, Stephen became king, but his mild rule soon led to anarchy. "For every great man built castles and held them against the King," says a contemporary chronicle, ". . . and when the castles were built, they filled them with devils and wicked men. By night and by day they seized those whom they believed to have any wealth, whether they were men or women; and in order to get their gold and silver, they put them into prison and tortured them with unspeakable tortures." Things grew worse throughout the nineteen years of Stephen's reign

and were only remedied during that of his successor, Matilda's brilliant son Henry II.

England became involved in the First Crusade in 1095. Inspired by religious fervor, nobles and commoners alike undertook the long and dangerous journey to Palestine to fight the Moslem Turks, who had held Christian shrines there since 1071. Also taking part in these expeditions was another Norman innovation—the knight, the mounted warrior who became the chief symbol of the code of chivalry. Far more than merely etiquette, chivalry was more nearly an aristocratic world-view. Its ideals affected the whole conduct of the lives of the nobility. That those ideals were more often professed than practiced did not lessen their influence. Chivalry did soften some of the harshness of medieval life. It bound the often lawless warrior by a code, the violation of which meant loss of honor. In combination with a wave of devotion to the Virgin Mary that swept across Europe late in the eleventh century, it raised the status of women and gained them a larger role both in life and in literature.

Higher education also had its beginning in England under the Normans. As early as 1117, documents mention a school at Oxford, and by 1133 its size and reputation had grown sufficiently for a theologian, Robert Pullen, to travel there from Paris to lecture. Cambridge University had its origins just a few years later.

In 1136 Geoffrey of Monmouth finished *The History of the Kings of Britain*, including the first complete account of the rise and fall of the legendary King Arthur, thus contributing to the great body of Arthurian legend (see page 146). Both in the original Latin version and in a French translation, Geoffrey's book was enormously popular, so that toward the end of the twelfth century one writer exclaims, "Whither has not flying fame spread and familiarized the name of Arthur the Briton, even as far as Christendom extends."

England Under the Plantagenets

Henry II (called "Plantagenet" from the French name for the broom plant, his father's heraldic emblem) took the throne in 1154. His first task was to subdue the great feudal lords of England and Normandy, who had grown so powerful during Stephen's weak reign. He immediately raised an army and re-established the power of the monarchy. A brilliant and tireless administrator, he reformed the judicial system and ran the operations of government so efficiently that at his death he left a surplus in the treasury (the last English king for over 300 years to do so). The latter part of Henry's reign was darkened, however, by conflict with his wife, Eleanor of Aquitaine, and his friend, Thomas Becket, the Archbishop of Canterbury. The long and bitter struggle between Henry and Becket over the issue of the legal rights of the clergy reached its climax on December 30, 1170, when Becket was killed by four of Henry's knights, but apparently without the king's knowledge. Becket's death was a disaster for Henry, both personally and politically. England was horrified by the murder of its leading priest, who was immediately acclaimed a martyr. Excommunicated by an outraged Church, Henry attempted reconciliation by restoring clerical rights, and even went as a pilgrim to Becket's shrine at Canterbury.

Henry's son Richard Coeur de Lion (the Lionheart) spent most of his reign outside of England. Having fought against the brilliant Moslem leader Saladin in the Third Crusade, he was captured on his return home and held for ransom by the Holy Roman Emperor. While Richard was absent, his brother John tried unsuccessfully to seize the throne. John did finally attain the throne after his brother's death in 1199, whereupon he managed to alienate his nobles, the clergy, his late ally the king of France, and the Pope. His autocratic rule, his personal excesses, and his heavy taxation finally led the nobles to rise against him. On June 15, 1215, he was forced to sign Magna Carta, "the Great Charter," that limits the power of the king and is the foundation of the representative English government. Among other reforms, it defined and safeguarded the basic rights of nobles, clergy, and freemen; it established *habeas corpus* (a protection against unjust imprisonment) and trial by jury; and it gave the general council (the forerunner of Parliament) power over expenditures.

It was in 1295 that Edward I summoned the first English Parliament to include, in addition to the nobility and the clergy, two representatives "from every city, borough, and leading town." The appearance of members of the middle class in Parliament was an indication of the growing wealth and power of English cities like London and Norwich.

In 1337 England became involved in the Hundred Years' War with France. The issue was English control of large parts of France, the English king holding possessions extending from the English Channel to the Pyrenees. The early battles of the war were all great English victories, and the heroic Battle of Agincourt in 1415 made Henry V effective ruler of both England and France. But eventually the French recovered, partly due to the inspiration of Joan of Arc (1412–1431). The fighting dragged on until 1453, when the French were finally victorious, and England lost all her French possessions except the Channel port of Calais.

New weapons like the crossbow (and, more importantly, cannon) weakened feudalism by lessening the military importance of the mounted knight and, later, of the castle. Another factor hastening feudalism's decline was the appearance of the Black Death, or bubonic plague, which in 1348 and 1349 devastated England, killing perhaps a third of the population. In the disorder that resulted, many serfs escaped their feudal bondage by running away to London and other population centers. Wages rose dramatically, despite government attempts to freeze them. Later, desperate for money to continue the endless war with France, the government tried to impose a poll tax (a fixed tax levied on every adult, regardless of income). This led to riots in the cities and eventually to a major rebellion, the Peasants' Revolt in 1381. The principal leader was Wat Tyler, an eloquent adventurer who had served in the French wars. When the rioters reached London, killing, burning, and pillaging along the way, they seemed on the point of enforcing their demands, which included the abolition of serfdom. But Tyler was killed, and the revolt collapsed.

Feudalism was not the only major institution to be weakened in the fourteenth century. The authority of the Church suffered when a quarrel over the papal succession in 1378 led to the division in the Church known as the Great Schism, which lasted until 1417. During this period there were two and, briefly, even three rival popes. A further blow to Church authority occurred in 1381, when John Wycliffe's English translation of the Bible appeared. The Church had always opposed translating the Latin of the Scriptures into the vernacular (the language of the people), fearing the spread of heresy. Wycliffe's defiance is regarded as one of the first steps toward the Reformation of the fifteenth century.

Literature did well under the Plantagenets. The upper classes began to adopt English as their language. Chaucer's *Canterbury Tales* (see page 96) and the Arthurian romances (see page 146) did much to legitimize English as a literary language. The common people had been developing their own oral literature for centuries. Now they added ballads (see page 84) about the adventures of a hero of their own, Robin Hood. The **alliterative** verse form of the Anglo-Saxons had largely disappeared, replaced by the French system of end rhyme.

Drama had begun its modern evolution as early as A.D. 900, with the inclusion of a brief bit of dialogue in the liturgy of the Easter mass. As time passed, this brief dialogue was expanded, and similar dialogues appeared in other liturgies. Eventually attendance became so large that the dramas were moved outside the church itself and into the churchyard, where secular elements began to be introduced. To playlets dealing with the life of Christ were added others, often with more characters and of a greater length, presenting episodes from the Bible and the lives of the saints. These plays were called *miracle* or *mystery plays*. The earliest recorded date for a miracle play is 1110; gradually they evolved into cycles of plays presented from about 1300–1500 in large towns like Coventry and York on the feast of Corpus Christi.

Elsewhere in the World

Popular forms of literature such as epics and songs seemed to develop almost spontaneously in several cultures at once. The early twelfth century saw the beginning of troubadour music, recognized as the first cultivated lyric poetry in the vernacular, in Provence in the southern part of France. Famed troubadours traveled throughout Europe spreading their new music and the code of courtly love.

In Spain, about 1140, the great national epic *El Cid* was written, and in Germany the *Nibelungenlied* was composed about 1190. A heroic epic that tells the story of Siegfried and Brunhilde, it later furnished the basis for a cycle of operas by Richard Wagner (1813–1883).

In Italy there began very gradually the movement known as the Renaissance that would spread to France and other European countries, reaching England near the end of the fifteenth century. In 1305 Giotto, the most influential artist of the century, was painting frescoes in Florence. In 1307 Dante began *The Divine Comedy*, and in 1348 Boccaccio wrote *The Decameron*. Leonardo da Vinci painted his masterpiece, *The Last Supper*, in 1497.

In 1453 in Germany, there occurred a momentous event: the Gutenberg Bible, the first book to be printed by means of movable type, came off the press of Johann Gutenberg in Mainz. Gutenberg's achievement, making multiple copies of books without painstaking hand copying, made it possible for the new learning of the

As he threatens young King Richard II, Wat Tyler is killed by one of Richard's men. From a 15th century copy of Froissart's *Chronicles. British Library*

Renaissance to reach all people who could read —and eventually contributed to the increase of literacy. Printing reached England in 1476, when William Caxton set up his press in London.

In 1492, as a result of the spirit of adventure and exploration that accompanied the Renaissance, Christopher Columbus made his first voyage to America.

The Wars of the Roses

The end of the Hundred Years' War in 1415 brought only a brief peace. In 1455 began the Wars of the Roses, the bloody, thirty-year dynastic struggle between the Houses (family lines) of Lancaster and York, supporters of rival claimants to the English throne. (The conflict derives its name from the heraldic emblems of the two Houses, the red rose of Lancaster and the white rose of York.) In 1485 the Yorkist king, Richard III, faced his Lancastrian rival, Henry Tudor, Earl of Richmond, at the battle of Bosworth Field. Richard was defeated and killed, and the victor, crowned Henry VII, married Elizabeth of York, uniting the two Houses and establishing the Tudor dynasty that ruled for the next century.

THINKING ABOUT GRAPHIC AIDS
Using the Time Line

Use the timeline on pages 76–77 to answer these questions.

1. Under what monarch was the Domesday Book compiled?
2. Which Houses, or family lines, could Geoffrey of Monmouth not have included in his *History of the Kings of Britain?*
3. About how long did it take the printing press to reach England after Gutenberg first used movable type to print his Bible?
4. Which of these monarchs was involved in war of some sort: William the Conqueror, Richard I, Richard II, Henry IV, Henry VI, Edward IV?
5. This time line encompasses fewer years than the Unit 1 time line (page 1) but shows more events. What reasons can you give for this?

A **ballad** is a narrative poem that was originally composed to be sung or recited. Exactly when and how they originated and developed is unknown, but most ballads were probably composed by anonymous musicians or entertainers and then passed along from generation to generation before they were actually written down. Coming from centuries of oral tradition in this way, the ballads have come to be considered folk literature.

By the time they were collected and written, some ballads had acquired many different versions. "Lord Randal," for example, is known in dozens of countries from Italy to Iceland. But most of them have certain characteristics in common. Here are some guidelines for reading the ballads that follow.

Understand the dialogue.   Most ballads rely on dialogue rather than narration to advance the plot. In "Lord Randal," for example, the first two lines in each stanza are spoken by Lord Randal's mother and the last two by Lord Randal himself. These two characters alternate in this way throughout the poem—the mother questioning, the son answering—and the story is told solely through their dialogue.

Study the notes.   The language in this printed version of "Lord Randal" reflects the original dialect in which it was composed—that of the border region between Scotland and England. The symbol ° after a word tells you to look in the margin for a modern translation. Also in the margin you will find various kinds of explanatory notes.

Summarize the plot.   Often you can aid your understanding of a work of literature by making note of the main actions or events and then putting them together in a summary. For example, the story line of "Lord Randal" can be summarized as follows: *Lord Randal meets his true-love in the greenwood, where she poisons him with eels. Later he tells his mother of his bequests to his family and curses his true-love.* Such a summary can help you understand how all parts of a work fit together; it can also free your mind from what happens and let you concentrate on how it happens.

Appreciate the form.   "Lord Randal" is about a murder, and, indeed, most ballads tend to be tragic, ending in death by accident, murder, or suicide, or with the return of the dead. Many of the ballads seem to have been based on true stories or composed to commemorate events of importance to particular communities. Early audiences were probably familiar with the stories they were hearing; at any rate listeners were more interested in rapid and dramatic action than in characters or setting. As a rule, background material is sketched in briefly, and the action moves swiftly to its climax. Often this practice results in gaps in the plot or fails to provide for character motivation. In "Lord Randal," the listener never does discover why Lord Randal's true love has poisoned him.

Note the symbolism.   Another characteristic is the use of a kind of symbolic reference familiar to its original audiences but not to modern audiences. For example, a request to make a bed, especially a narrow one, usually meant that someone was sick unto death, and feeding someone eels was as sure a sign of poisoning as cyanide is today.

"Lord Randal" illustrates another characteristic that appears in a number of ballads. Variously referred to as "the legacies" or "the testaments," it involves the addition of stanzas in which the dying character leaves appropriate bequests for family and loved ones. Such legacies symbolically reflect feelings and relationships. Sometimes the suspense of the ballad is not resolved until the last legacy is revealed. "Edward," on page 87, provides an excellent example of this technique.

Let the repetition have its effect. The repetition of words, phrases, or lines is employed for melodic effect, to provide emphasis, and to heighten emotion. *Incremental repetition*, or the repetition in succeeding stanzas of lines containing some small addition, or increment, is used to build to a climax. In "Lord Randal," notice how the first three lines of each stanza are repeated, with incremental changes. For example, the mother's question changes from "O where ha you been?" in line 1 to "An wha met ye there?" in line 5. "Lord Randal"—like many of the oldest ballads—also has a *refrain*, the repetition of one or two lines, usually at the end of a stanza. Notice how Lord Randal's refrain also changes from "For I'm wearied wi hunting" in line 4 to "For I'm sick at the heart" in line 24. For the repetition to have its greatest effect, the ballads should be sung or read aloud.

Lord Randal

"O where ha° you been, Lord Randal, my son?
And where ha you been, my handsome young man?"
"I ha been at the greenwood; Mother, mak° my bed soon,
For I'm wearied wi huntin, and fain wad lie down."°

5 "An wha° met ye there, Lord Randal, my son?
An wha met you there, my handsome young man?"
"O I met wi my true-love; Mother, mak my bed soon,
For I'm wearied wi huntin, and fain wad lie down."

"And what did she give you, Lord Randal, my son?
10 And what did she give you, my handsome young man?"
"Eels fried in a pan;° Mother, mak my bed soon,
For I'm wearied wi huntin, and fain wad lie down."

"And wha gat your leavins,° Lord Randal, my son?
And wha gat your leavins, my handsome young man?"
15 "My hawks and my hounds; Mother, mak my bed soon,
For I'm wearied wi huntin, and fain wad lie down."

"And what becam° of them, Lord Randal, my son?
And what becam of them, my handsome young man?"
"They stretched their legs out an died; Mother, mak my bed soon,
20 For I'm wearied wi huntin, and fain wad lie down."

"O I fear you are poisoned, Lord Randal, my son!
I fear you are poisoned, my handsome young man!"

ha, have.

mak, make.
wearied . . . down, wearied with hunting, and need to lie down. *Down* is pronounced in the Scottish manner (dūn) to rhyme with *soon*.
wha, who.

Eels . . . pan, a method of poisoning that appears in many old ballads.

wha . . . leavins, who ate the food you didn't eat?

becam, became.

English and Scottish Popular Ballads. Helen Child Sargent and George Lymann Kittredge, eds. Boston: Houghton Mifflin Company, 1904, 1932.

"O yes, I am poisoned; Mother, mak my bed soon,
For I'm sick at the heart, and I fain wad lie down."

25 "What d'ye leave to your mother, Lord Randal, my son?
What d'ye leave to your mother, my handsome young man?"
"Four and twenty milk kye;° Mother, mak my bed soon,
For I'm sick at the heart, and I fain wad lie down."

"What d'ye leave to your sister, Lord Randal, my son?
30 What d'ye leave to your sister, my handsome young man?"
"My gold and my silver; Mother, mak my bed soon,
For I'm sick at the heart, and I fain wad lie down."

"What d'ye leave to your brother, Lord Randal, my son?
What d'ye leave to your brother, my handsome young man?"
35 "My houses and my lands; Mother, mak my bed soon.
For I'm sick at the heart, and I fain wad lie down."

"What d'ye leave to your true-love, Lord Randal, my son?
What d'ye leave to your true-love, my handsome young man?"
"I leave her hell and fire; Mother, mak my bed soon,
40 For I'm sick at the heart, and I fain wad lie down."

kye, (line 27) cows.

Balladeer, from an illuminated
manuscript. *British Library*

H𝕬 **See RHYTHM in the Handbook of Literary Terms, page 921.**

Bonny Barbara Allan

It was in and about the Martinmas time,°
  When the green leaves were a falling,
That Sir John Graeme, in the West Country,
  Fell in love with Barbara Allan.

5 He sent his men down through the town,
  To the place where she was dwelling:
"O haste and come to my master dear,
  Gin ye be° Barbara Allan."

O hooly,° hooly rose she up
10 To the place where he was lying,

Martinmas time, Martinmas is the
feast of St. Martin, November 11.

Gin ye be, if you are.

Hooly, slowly; reluctantly.

And when she drew the curtain by,
  "Young man, I think you're dying."

"O it's I'm sick, and very, very sick,
  And 't is a'° for Barbara Allan."
15 "O the better for me ye's never be,°
  Tho° your heart's blood were a spilling.

"O dinna ye mind,° young man," said she,
  "When ye was in the tavern a drinking,
That ye made the healths gae° round and round,
20   And slighted Barbara Allan?"

He turned his face unto the wall,
  And death was with him dealing:
"Adieu,° adieu, my dear friends all,
  And be kind to Barbara Allan."

25 And slowly, slowly raise she up,
  And slowly, slowly left him,
And sighing said, she coud° not stay,
  Since death of life had reft him.°

She had not gane a mile but twa,°
30   When she heard the dead-bell ringing,
And every jow that the dead-bell geid,°
  It cry'd, Woe to Barbara Allan!

"O mother, mother, make my bed.
  O make it saft° and narrow.
35 Since my love died for me to-day,
  I'll die for him to-morrow."

't is a', it is all.
ye's never be, if you didn't exist.
Tho, though.

dinna ye mind, don't you remember.

healths gae, toasts go.

Adieu (e dü', ə dyü'), good-by.
[French]

coud, could.
death . . . him, death had robbed or deprived him of life.
gane . . . twa, gone a mile or two.

jow . . . geid, toll that the dead-bell gave.

saft, soft.

Edward

"Why dois your brand sae drap wi bluid,°
    Edward, Edward,
Why dois your brand sae drap wi bluid,
  And why sae sad gang yee° O?"
5 "O I hae killed my hauke sae guid,°
    Mither,° mither,
O I hae killed my hauke sae guid,
  And I had nae mair bot hee° O."

dois . . . bluid, does your sword so drip with blood.

gang yee, go you.
hae . . . guid, have killed my hawk so good.
Mither, Mother.

nae . . . hee, no more but him.

"Your haukis bluid was nevir sae reid,°
        Edward, Edward,
Your haukis bluid was nevir sae reid,
    My deir° son I tell thee O."
"O I hae killed my reid-roan steid,°
        Mither, mither,
O I hae killed my reid-roan steid,
    That erst was sae fair and frie° O."

"Your steid was auld,° and ye hae gat mair,
        Edward, Edward,
Your steid was auld, and ye hae gat mair,
    Sum other dule ye drie° O."
"O I hae killed my fadir° deir,
        Mither, mither,
O I hae killed my fadir deir,
Alas, and wae° is mee O!"

"And whatten penance° wul ye drie for that,
        Edward, Edward,
And whatten penance wul ye drie for that?
    My deir son, now tell me O."
"Ile set my feit° in yonder boat,
        Mither, mither,
Ile set my feit in yonder boat,
    And Ile fare ovir° the sea O."

"And what wul ye doe wi your towirs and your ha,°
        Edward, Edward,
And what wul ye doe wi your towirs and your ha,
    That were sae fair to see O?"
"Ile let thame stand tul they doun fa,°
        Mither, mither,
Ile let thame stand tul they doun fa,
    For here nevir mair maun° I bee O."
"And what wul ye leive to your bairns° and your wife,
        Edward, Edward,
And what wul ye leive to your bairns and your wife,
    Whan ye gang ovir the sea O?"
"The warldis room, late them beg thrae life,°
        Mither, mither,
The warldis room, late them beg thrae life,
    For thame nevir mair wul I see O."
"And what wul ye leive to your ain° mither deir,
        Edward, Edward,
And what wul ye leive to your ain mither deir?

haukis . . . reid, hawk's blood was never so red.

deir, dear.
reid-roan steid, red-roan horse. "Red-roan" means a red coat mottled with white or gray.

erst . . . frie, once was so fair and free.
auld, old.

Sum . . . drie, some other sorrow you suffer.
fadir, father.

wae, woe.

whatten penance, what kind of penance. A penance is a punishment borne to show sorrow for wrongdoing.

Ile . . . feit, I'll set my feet.

fare ovir, go over.

doe . . . ha, do with your towers and your hall.

thame . . . fa, them stand till they fall down.

maun, must.
leive . . . bairns, leave to your children.

warldis . . . life, world is room (large enough); let them beg through life.

ain, own.

My deir son, now tell me O."
"The curse of hell frae me sall ye beir,°
    Mither, mither,
55 The curse of hell frae me sall ye beir,
    Sic counseils° ye gave to me O."

from _Reliques of Ancient English Poetry_, 1765

Sir Patrick Spence

Although no mention of Sir Patrick Spence can be found in old Scottish or English records, most authorities agree that this ballad records an actual event. While there is disagreement as to what event the ballad commemorates, evidence points toward the ill-fated return voyage of the ship that in 1281 had carried Margaret, daughter of King Alexander III of Scotland, to Norway, to marry Eric, King of Norway.

The king sits in Dumferling toune,°
    Drinking the blude-reid° wine:
"O whar° will I get guid sailor,
    To sail this schip° of mine?"

5 Up and spak an eldern knicht,°
    Sat at the kings richt kne:°
"Sir Patrick Spence is the best sailor
    That sails upon the se."

The king has written a braid letter,°
10   And signed it wi his hand,
And sent it to Sir Patrick Spence,
    Was walking on the sand.

The first line that Sir Patrick red,
    A loud lauch° lauched he;
15 The next line that Sir Patrick red,
    The teir blinded his ee.°

"O wha is this has don this deid,°
    This ill deid don to me,
To send me out this time o' the yeir,°
20   To sail upon the se!

"Mak haste, mak haste, my mirry° men all,
    Our guid schip sails the morne."
"O say na sae,° my master deir,
    For I feir° a deadlie storme.

25 "Late late yestreen° I saw the new moone,
    Wi the auld moone in hir arme,°
And I feir, I feir, my deir master,
    That we will cum to harme."

O our Scots nobles wer richt laith°
30   To weet their cork-heild schoone;°
But lang owre a'° the play wer playd,
    Their hats they swam aboone.°

O lang,° lang may their ladies sit,
    Wi their fans into their hand,
35 Or eir° they se Sir Patrick Spence
    Cum sailing to the land.

O lang, lang may the ladies stand,
    Wi their gold kems° in their hair,
Waiting for thair ain deir lords,
40   For they'll se thame na mair.°

Haf owre, haf owre to Aberdour,°
    It's fiftie fadom deip,°
And thair° lies guid Sir Patrick Spence,
    Wi the Scots lords at his feit.

from *Reliques of Ancient English Poetry*, 1765

mirry, merry.

na sae, not so.
feir, fear.

yestreen, last evening.
new moone . . . arme. The semi-luminous surface of the moon was visible between the horns of the new moon. The bad omen lay in the fact that the new moon was seen *late* in the evening.
wer . . . laith, were right loath (very unwilling).
weet . . . schoone, wet their cork-heeled shoes.
lang owre a', long ere (before) all.
aboone, above. Either the shoes were *aboone* (because their wearers were floating head downward), or the hats were *aboone* (floating on the surface of the water).
lang, long.
Or eir, Before.

kems, combs.

na mair, no more.

Haf owre . . . Aberdour. Aberdour is a port on the north shore of the Firth of Forth, some ten miles from Dunfermline. "Haf owre" means halfway over, halfway home on the sea voyage from Norway.
fadom deip, fathoms deep.
thair, there.

Manuscript illumination of ships (detail). c. 1415. *Walters Art Gallery, Baltimore*

Comment

The Ballad: An Enduring Art Form

Since the dawn of civilization people have sung to entertain themselves and others. Almost surely, the people who developed the ballad were not consciously inventing an art form. Their creations survived, however, to be passed down from one generation to another.

The English and Scottish folk ballads were sung for centuries before they were written down. From references in old documents and the character of the ballads themselves, it seems that most were composed in the Scottish border region in the late Middle Ages. At least some of the ballads were probably composed to commemorate events of importance to particular communities. As generations of singers passed the songs on, words or lines were changed here and there, stanzas were omitted or added, and differing versions of the same ballad often appeared. Ballads originating in England and Scotland crossed the Atlantic with the first settlers and went on developing in the New World. In the state of Virginia alone 51 of these ballads survived in 650 versions.

The first important collection of ballads was made by Bishop Thomas Percy (1729–1811). As a young man he had found a manuscript collection of poetry dating from about 1650. Though it was damaged (servants had torn out leaves to use in lighting fires), 191 poems survived. This became the chief source for Percy's *Reliques of Ancient English Poetry* (1765). Inspired by Percy's *Reliques*, the novelist Sir Walter Scott (1771–1832) published ten years of ballad-collecting as *Minstrelsy of the Scottish Border* (1802).

The attitude of writers toward the ballads has altered over the centuries. Sir Philip Sidney (see page 181), in his *Apology for Poetry* (1595), feels he must apologize for his preference: "Certainly I must confess my own barbarousness, I never heard the old song of Percy and Douglas [the ballad of *Chevy Chase*] that I found not my heart moved more than with a trumpet, and yet is sung by some blind crowder (fiddler), with no rougher voice than rude style."

Joseph Addison (see page 365), writing in *The Spectator* (1711), sees his liking for the ballads as a universal one: ". . . it is impossible that anything [like the ballads] should be universally tasted and approved by a multitude. . . which hath not in it some peculiar aptness to please and gratify the mind of man."

Listeners have continued to be pleased and gratified. The early 1900s saw yet another resurgence of interest in ballads, from a scholarly point of view. But ballads continue to be performed, not just collected to be read. In the 1950s and 1960s, many solo artists and groups performed these old ballads before audiences of growing numbers, and today it is possible to hear most of them on various recordings.

Get Up and Bar the Door

It fell about the Martinmas time,
   And a gay time it was then,
When our goodwife got puddings° to make,
   And she's boild them in the pan.

5 The wind sae cauld° blew south and north,
   And blew into the floor;
Quoth our goodman to our goodwife,
   "Gae° out and bar the door."

puddings, sausages.

cauld, cold.

Gae, Go.

"My hand is in my hussyfskap,°
10 Goodman, as ye may see;
An it shoud nae° be barrd this hundred year,
It's no be barrd for° me."

They made a paction tween them twa,°
They made it firm and sure,
15 That the first word whaeer° shoud speak,
Shoud rise and bar the door.

Then by there came two gentlemen,
At twelve o clock at night,
And they could neither see house nor hall,
20 Nor coal nor candlelight.

"Now whether is this a rich man's house,
Or whether is it a poor?"
But neer a word wad ane° o them speak,
For barring of the door.

25 And first they° ate the white puddings,
And then they ate the black;
Tho muckle° thought the goodwife to hersel,
Yet neer a word she spake.

Then said the one unto the other,
30 "Here, man, tak ye my knife;
Do ye tak aff° the auld man's beard,
And I'll kiss the goodwife."

hussyfskap (hùs'if skap), housewife's
work.

An . . . nae, If it should not.
no . . . for, not going to be barred
by.

paction . . . twa, agreement
between the two of them.
whaeer, whoever.

neer . . . ane, never a word would
any.

they, that is, the "two gentlemen."

Tho muckle, though much.

aff, off.

"But there's nae water in the house,
　　And what shall we do than?"
35 "What ails ye at the pudding-broo,°
　　That boils into the pan?"

O up then started our goodman,
　　An angry man was he:
"Will ye kiss my wife before my een,°
40 　And scad° me wi pudding-bree?"

Then up and started our goodwife,
　　Gied° three skips on the floor:
"Goodman, you've spoken the foremost word,
　　Get up and bar the door."

from *The Ancient and Modern Scots Songs*, 1769

pudding-broo, the hot broth in which the sausages are cooking.

een, eyes.

scad, scald.

Gied, gave.

THINK AND DISCUSS
BONNY BARBARA ALLAN
Understanding
1. What three characters' speeches are quoted? Identify the lines spoken by each.
2. Why does John say he has sent for Barbara?
3. How does Barbara treat him when she arrives? What reason does she give?

Analyzing
4. How does John's last speech affect her? Why?
5. What does the bell signify to Barbara?
6. Why does she ask her mother to make her bed?

Extending
7. Does Barbara's reason for her treatment of John seem sufficient to you? Explain.
8. Devise an earlier scene between Barbara and John that would account for their behavior.

EDWARD
Understanding
1. Identify the speakers and their speeches.

2. There is one surprising revelation in the middle and another at the end. What are these revelations?

Analyzing
3. Why does Edward not admit outright what he has done?
4. What does Edward accuse his mother of in the last stanza? What do you think he means by this?

Extending
5. In your opinion, who is more at fault, Edward or his mother? Explain.
6. If this story were told today, how might it differ? Would today's audiences be satisfied with the "sic counseils" hint?

SIR PATRICK SPENCE
Understanding
1. What happens to Sir Patrick Spence?

Analyzing
2. Why does Patrick think that an "ill deid" has been done to him (lines 17–18)?

3. Why does he go anyway?
4. How is the tragic end **foreshadowed?**
5. What is the effect of shifting the focus from the ship to the ladies in lines 33–40?

Extending
6. Discuss whether Patrick had any other options.

GET UP AND BAR THE DOOR
Understanding
1. What is the argument between the goodwife and the goodman?
2. Who wins the argument? How do you know?

Analyzing
3. Why do you think it is the goodman and not the goodwife who first breaks the silence?

Extending
4. Is the humor in this ballad out of date, or can it be appreciated by modern readers? Why?

APPLYING: Rhythm HT
See Handbook of Literary Terms, p. 921

Rhythm is the arrangement of stressed and unstressed syllables in speech or writing. To *scan* poetry, or examine its *scansion*, is to note how many of what kind of feet are used in each line. Most folk ballads are written in *ballad stanzas*, alternating lines of iambic tetrameter and iambic trimeter, like this:

$$\smile \,' / \smile \,' / \smile \,' / \smile \,'$$
$$\smile \,' / \smile \,' / \smile \,'$$
$$\smile \,' / \smile \,' / \smile \,' / \smile \,'$$
$$\smile \,' / \smile \,' / \smile \,'$$

Variations in this basic pattern are permitted and are plentiful, to allow for various kinds of repetition and the fact that folk ballads were, first of all, an oral literature.

1. Scan the ballads you have read to find at least one example of a "perfect" ballad stanza, as shown above.
2. Describe the ways in which "Edward" departs from the ballad stanza. What causes these variations?

READING LITERATURE SKILLFULLY
Summarizing

Often you can aid your understanding of a work of literature by summarizing the plot. Such a summary should include only main actions or events.

1. In one sentence, summarize the plot of "Edward."
2. Find the stanza in "Get Up and Bar the Door" that summarizes the agreement between the goodman and the goodwife and the reason for it.

COMPOSITION
Writing a Newspaper Story

Many of the old ballads were apparently based on real current events. Select one ballad and use it as the basis for a newspaper story of three to five paragraphs. Write for your school newspaper, using the standard news-story format of presenting important facts first and then going on to less important details. Make up details as necessary; you may even wish to make up interviews to quote from.

Writing About a Theme

Many folk ballads deal with the relationship between the sexes. Write a three-to-five paragraph essay in which you compare and contrast the ballads you have read that deal with this theme. To begin, reread the ballads and take notes on how the male and female characters relate to each other; then organize your notes into a working outline before you start to write. See "Writing About Theme" in the Writer's Handbook.

ENRICHMENT
Speaking and Listening

All the ballads were written to be sung, and they lend themselves well to dramatic reading. They can be read by one person, or by several people narrating and taking different parts. A guitar makes an appropriate accompaniment. (Because so many ballads use the standard ballad stanza, the words of one will often fit the melody of another.) Perform them in class or else tape record them to exchange with other classes. You might want to find other ballads not included here to expand your program.

Although the exact birth date of Geoffrey Chaucer is uncertain, we do know a surprising amount about his life and public career. In fact, over 300 references to him and to his family have been found in the official records of the time. Chaucer's father was a prosperous London wine merchant who had been in Flanders in 1338 with the retinue of King Edward III. In 1357 Geoffrey was listed as a page in the household of the wife of Prince Lionel, a son of Edward III. His service in that household indicates that his family had sufficient social status for him to receive a courtly education. Throughout the rest of his lifetime, Chaucer was in some way connected with members of the royal family.

Sometime in or before 1366, Chaucer married Philippa Roet, a lady-in-waiting to the Queen. Chaucer rose socially through his marriage. In 1368 he became one of the King's esquires, which in those days meant that he worked in the administrative department of the King's government. One of his duties was to act as a government envoy on foreign diplomatic missions, carrying on such work as that performed by embassies of our day.

Chaucer's diplomatic missions took him first to France and later to Italy. While in France he came in contact with French literature, and from his very earliest writings through 1370 a French influence is noticeable. To the French period can be assigned his translation of *The Romance of the Rose* (a long, allegorical poem written in French about a century earlier).

In 1372 Chaucer was sent to Genoa to arrange a commercial treaty. As he became acquainted with Italian life and culture, he discovered that a new interest in the learning of the past, in the literature of Greece and Rome, was sweeping over the Italian towns—the Renaissance had begun. Chaucer became acquainted with the classical authors and with the newer Italian works of Dante and Petrarch, perhaps with the tales of Boccaccio. In Chaucer's own writing the French models of his earlier years gave way to this Italian influence. To the Italian period can be assigned *The House of Fame*, *The Legend of Good Women*, and *The Parliament of Fowls*.

After his return to London, Chaucer became a customs official at the port of London. As one of the benefits of this position the government provided him with free lodgings above Aldgate, one of the gates in the wall around London. There he liked to retire "as an hermyte," he says, after his working day was done, to write or read or to look down upon the colorful throng that passed through the gateway beneath him.

Chaucer lost or gave up his job in 1386—the year in which it is believed he began composing *The Canterbury Tales*, his unfinished masterpiece. His move may have been occasioned by the illness and death of Philippa, in 1386 or 1387. He retired to live in Kent, serving as justice of the peace for the shire and later representing it in Parliament. When he died in 1400, he was buried in Westminster Abbey in a section which later became established as the Poets' Corner.

from The Canterbury Tales

Geoffrey Chaucer   *translated by* **Nevill Coghill**

More than ten years in the writing, *The Canterbury Tales* is an
ingenious concoction of character sketches, conversations, and stories—all
set within the *frame*, or larger narrative, of a pilgrimage to the shrine of
St. Thomas Becket in Canterbury, undertaken by twenty-nine intrepid
pilgrims (and Chaucer).

Representing a cross section of the population of fourteenth-century
England, the pilgrims range in rank from a knight to a poor plowman. Only
the very highest and lowest ranks—the nobility and the serfs—are missing.
En route to Canterbury, the pilgrims eat, drink, sightsee, and talk—more
than anything else they talk, and in so doing reveal more than they realize about themselves. Chaucer introduces each of his pilgrims in *The Prologue*, and then he lets us know still more about them through the stories
they tell, which range from sermons and courtly romances to scurrilous
fabliaux (brief stories, usually humorous, often off-color), and through the
"links"—the conversations and squabbles they engage in between stories.

Chaucer planned to include 120 stories (two told by each pilgrim each
way on their journey), but he managed only twenty-four, some of these
incomplete, before his death. The passage below is the opening of the
Prologue in Chaucer's English.

Whan that Aprille with his shoures soote
The droghte of March hath perced to the roote,
And bathed every veyne in swich licour
Of which vertu engendred is the flour;
5 Whan Zephirus eek with his sweete breeth
Inspired hath in every holt and heeth
The tendre croppes, and the yonge sonne
Hath in the Ram his halve cours yronne,
And smale foweles maken melodye,
10 That slepen al the nyght with open ye
(So priketh hem nature in hir corages);
Thanne longen folk to goon on pilgrimages,
And palmeres for to seken straunge strondes,
To ferne halwes, kowthe in sondry londes;
15 And specially from every shires ende
Of Engelond to Caunterbury they wende,
The hooly blisful martir for to seke,
That hem hath holpen whan that they were seke.

Pilgrim's badge from
Canterbury Cathe-
dral, showing Thomas
Becket as an arch-
bishop, riding in tri-
umph. Pilgrims wore
badges like this
around the neck or
pinned to a hat.
Museum of London

HLT See **CHARACTERIZATION** in the Handbook of Literary Terms, page 898.

The Prologue

Geoffrey Chaucer

When in April the sweet showers fall
And pierce the drought of March to the root,
    and all
The veins are bathed in liquor of such power
As brings about the engendering of the
    flower,
When also Zephyrus[1] with his sweet breath
Exhales an air in every grove and heath
Upon the tender shoots, and the young sun
His half-course in the sign of the *Ram* has
    run,[2]
And the small fowl are making melody
10 That sleep away the night with open eye
(So nature pricks them and their heart
    engages)
Then people long to go on pilgrimages
And palmers[3] long to seek the stranger
    strands
Of far-off saints, hallowed in sundry lands,
15 And specially, from every shire's end
Of England, down to Canterbury they wend
To seek the holy blissful martyr,[4] quick
To give his help to them when they were
    sick.
    It happened in that season that one day
20 In Southwark, at *The Tabard*,[5] as I lay
Ready to go on pilgrimage and start
For Canterbury, most devout at heart,
At night there came into that hostelry
Some nine and twenty in a company
25 Of sundry folk happening then to fall
In fellowship, and they were pilgrims all
That towards Canterbury meant to ride.
The rooms and stables of the inn were wide;
They made us easy, all was of the best.
30 And, briefly, when the sun had gone to rest,

I'd spoken to them all upon the trip
And was soon one with them in fellowship,
Pledged to rise early and to take the way
To Canterbury, as you heard me say.
35   But none the less, while I have time and
        space,
Before my story takes a further pace,
It seems a reasonable thing to say
What their condition was, the full array
Of each of them, as it appeared to me,
40 According to profession and degree,
And what apparel they were riding in;
And at a Knight I therefore will begin.

There was a *Knight*, a most distinguished man,
Who from the day on which he first began
45 To ride abroad had followed chivalry,
Truth, honor, generousness, and courtesy.
He had done nobly in his sovereign's war
And ridden into battle, no man more,
As well in Christian as in heathen places,
50 And ever honored for his noble graces.

---

1. Zephyrus, the west wind.
2. young sun . . . has run. Since the Ram, the first sign of the Zodiac, begins its run about March 21, Chaucer dates the pilgrimage in early April.
3. palmers, pilgrims to the Holy Land wore the image of crossed palm leaves as their emblem.
4. martyr, St. Thomas Becket, murdered in Canterbury Cathedral in 1170. His tomb was a favorite destination for medieval English pilgrims.
5. Southwark, at The Tabard. The Tabard was a famous inn at the beginning of the road from London to Canterbury, located in a suburb south of London.

When we took Alexandria,[6] he was there.
He often sat at table in the chair
Of honor, above all nations, when in Prussia.
In Lithuania he had ridden, and Russia,
55 No Christian man so often, of his rank.
When, in Granada, Algeciras sank
Under assault, he had been there, and in
North Africa, raiding Benamarin;
In Anatolia he had been as well
60 And fought when Ayas and Attalia fell,
For all along the Mediterranean coast
He had embarked with many a noble host.
In fifteen mortal battles he had been
And jousted for our faith at Tramissene
65 Thrice in the lists, and always killed his man.
This same distinguished knight had led the van
Once with the Bey of Balat,[7] doing work
For him against another heathen Turk;
He was of sovereign value in all eyes.
70 And though so much distinguished, he was
    wise
And in his bearing modest as a maid.
He never yet a boorish thing had said
In all his life to any, come what might;
He was a true, a perfect gentle-knight.
75   Speaking of his equipment, he possessed
Fine horses, but he was not gaily dressed.
He wore a fustian tunic stained and dark
With smudges where his armor had left mark;
Just home from service, he had joined our
    ranks
80 To do his pilgrimage and render thanks.

He had his son with him, a fine young
    Squire,[8]
A lover and cadet, a lad of fire
With locks as curly as if they had been
    pressed.
He was some twenty years of age, I guessed.
85 In stature he was of a moderate length,
With wonderful agility and strength.
He'd seen some service with the cavalry
In Flanders and Artois and Picardy[9]
And had done valiantly in little space
90 Of time, in hope to win his lady's grace.
He was embroidered like a meadow bright

The Squire, from the Ellesmere Chaucer. Circa 1410.

And full of freshest flowers, red and white.
Singing he was, or fluting all the day;
He was as fresh as is the month of May.
95 Short was his gown, the sleeves were long
    and wide;
He knew the way to sit a horse and ride.
He could make songs and poems and recite,
Knew how to joust and dance, to draw and
    write.
He loved so hotly that till dawn grew pale
100 He slept as little as a nightingale.
Courteous he was, lowly and serviceable,
And carved to serve his father at the table.

6. *Alexandria.* Here and in the following lines the narrator refers to battles against the major non-Christian enemies of Chaucer's era.
7. *Bey of Balat.* A bey was a governor of a province or district in the Ottoman Empire.
8. *Squire,* a young man learning to be a knight through service.
9. *Flanders and Artois and Picardy,* battles much closer to home than those the Knight has seen.

There was a *Yeoman*[10] with him at his side,
No other servant; so he chose to ride.
105 This Yeoman wore a coat and hood of green,
And peacock-feathered arrows, bright and
   keen
And neatly sheathed, hung at his belt the
   while
—For he could dress his gear in yeoman
   style,
His arrows never drooped their feathers
   low—
110 And in his hand he bore a mighty bow.
His head was like a nut, his face was brown.
He knew the whole of woodcraft up and
   down.
A saucy brace was on his arm to ward
It from the bowstring, and a shield and
   sword
115 Hung at one side, and at the other slipped
A jaunty dirk, spear-sharp and well-
   equipped.
A medal of St. Christopher[11] he wore
Of shining silver on his breast, and bore
A hunting-horn, well slung and burnished
   clean,
120 That dangled from a baldrick of bright green.
He was a proper forester, I guess.

    There also was a *Nun*, a Prioress,[12]
Her way of smiling very simple and coy.
Her greatest oath was only "By St. Loy!"[13]
125 And she was known as Madam Eglantyne.[14]
And well she sang a service, with a fine
Intoning through her nose, as was most
   seemly,
And she spoke daintily in French,
   extremely,
After the school of Stratford-atte-Bowe;[15]
130 French in the Paris style she did not know.
At meat her manners were well taught
   withal;
No morsel from her lips did she let fall,
Nor dipped her fingers in the sauce too deep;
But she could carry a morsel up and keep
135 The smallest drop from falling on her breast.
For courtliness she had a special zest,

The Prioress, from the Ellesmere Chaucer.

And she would wipe her upper lip so clean
That not a trace of grease was to be seen
Upon the cup when she had drunk; to eat,
140 She reached a hand sedately for the meat.
She certainly was very entertaining,
Pleasant and friendly in her ways, and straining
To counterfeit a courtly kind of grace,
A stately bearing fitting to her place,
145 And to seem dignified in all her dealings.
As for her sympathies and tender feelings,
She was so charitably solicitous
She used to weep if she but saw a mouse
Caught in a trap, if it were dead or bleeding.

---

10. *Yeoman,* a freeman and a commoner, servant to the
Knight.
11. *St. Christopher,* patron of travelers and foresters.
12. *Prioress,* religious woman who runs a convent.
13. *St. Loy.* This saint refused to swear on sacred relics.
To swear by him was to swear mildly or not at all.
14. *Eglantyne* (eg'lən tīn'), sweet briar.
15. *daintily . . . Stratford-atte-Bowe,* inferior French
learned in an English convent. (See "Medieval Tourists,"
page 112.)

150 And she had little dogs she would be feeding
With roasted flesh, or milk, or fine white bread.
And bitterly she wept if one were dead
Or someone took a stick and made it smart;
She was all sentiment and tender heart.
155 Her veil was gathered in a seemly way,
Her nose was elegant, her eyes glass-gray;
Her mouth was very small, but soft and red,
Her forehead, certainly, was fair of spread,
Almost a span across the brows, I own;
160 She was indeed by no means undergrown.
Her cloak, I noticed, had a graceful charm.
She wore a coral trinket on her arm,
A set of beads, the gaudies tricked in green,[16]
Whence hung a golden brooch of brightest
    sheen
165 On which there first was graven a crowned A,
And lower, *Amor vincit omnia.*[17]
    Another *Nun,* the secretary at her cell,
Was riding with her, and *three Priests*[18] as well.

A *Monk* there was, one of the finest sort
170 Who rode the country; hunting was his sport.
A manly man, to be an Abbot[19] able;
Many a dainty horse he had in stable.
His bridle, when he rode, a man might hear
Jingling in a whistling wind as clear,
175 Aye, and as loud as does the chapel bell
Where my lord Monk was Prior of the cell.[20]
The Rule of good St. Benet or St. Maur[21]
As old and strict he tended to ignore;
He let go by the things of yesterday
180 And took the modern world's more spacious
    way.
He did not rate that text at a plucked hen
Which says that hunters are not holy men
And that a monk uncloistered is a mere
Fish out of water, flapping on the pier,
185 That is to say a monk out of his cloister.
That was a text he held not worth an oyster;
And I agreed and said his views were sound;
Was he to study till his head went round
Poring over books in cloisters? Must he toil
190 As Austin[22] bade and till the very soil?
Was he to leave the world upon the shelf?
Let Austin have his labor to himself.

This Monk was therefore a good man to
    horse;
Greyhounds he had, as swift as birds, to
    course.
195 Hunting a hare or riding at a fence
Was all his fun, he spared for no expense.
I saw his sleeves were garnished at the hand
With fine gray fur, the finest in the land,
And on his hood, to fasten it at his chin
200 He had a wrought-gold cunningly fashioned
    pin;
Into a lover's knot it seemed to pass.
His head was bald and shone like looking
    glass;
So did his face, as if it had been greased.
He was a fat and personable priest;
205 His prominent eyeballs never seemed to
    settle.
They glittered like the flames beneath a
    kettle;
Supple his boots, his horse in fine condition.
He was a prelate fit for exhibition,
He was not pale like a tormented soul.
210 He liked a fat swan best, and roasted whole.
His palfrey was as brown as is a berry.

There was a *Friar,* a wanton one and
    merry,
A Limiter,[23] a very festive fellow.

---

16. A set . . . green, coral rosary beads with every larger tenth bead ("gaudies") made from a green stone.
17. Amor . . . omnia. "Love overcomes all." The phrase might be used for sacred or secular love. [Latin]
18. three Priests. Since the addition of three priests would bring the total of the pilgrims up to thirty-one (instead of the twenty-nine mentioned in line 24), their appearance here is probably a result of an error made in copying Chaucer's manuscript. Moreover, it is improbable that even a distinguished churchwoman like the Prioress would have been accompanied by so large a party. So the probability is that Chaucer intended only *one* priest.
19. Abbot, director of a monastery.
20. Prior of the cell, head of a subordinate monastery.
21. The Rule . . . St. Maur, ancient laws governing the life of a monk, first established by St. Benedict and his disciple St. Maur.
22. Austin. St. Augustine (A.D. 354-430) advised monks to engage in manual labor.
23. Limiter. Within a specific district ("limitatio") such a friar would beg for donations, preach, and bury the dead.

In all Four Orders[24] there was none so
    mellow,
215 So glib with gallant phrase and well-turned
    speech.
He'd fixed up many a marriage, giving each
Of his young women what he could afford
    her.[25]
He was a noble pillar to his Order:
Highly beloved and intimate was he
220 With County folk[26] within his boundary,
And city dames of honor and possessions;
For he was qualified to hear confessions,
Or so he said, with more than priestly scope;
He had a special licence from the Pope.
225 Sweetly he heard his penitents at shrift[27]
With pleasant absolution, for a gift.
He was an easy man in penance-giving
Where he could hope to make a decent
    living;
It's a sure sign whenever gifts are given
230 To a poor Order that a man's well shriven,
And should he give enough he knew in verity
The penitent repented in sincerity.
For many a fellow is so hard of heart
He cannot weep, for all his inward smart.
235 Therefore instead of weeping and of prayer
One should give silver for a poor Friar's care.
He kept his tippet[28] stuffed with pins for
    curls,
And pocketknives, to give to pretty girls.
And certainly his voice was gay and sturdy,
240 For he sang well and played the hurdy-
    gurdy.[29]
At singsongs he was champion of the hour.
His neck was whiter than a lily flower
But strong enough to butt a bruiser down.
He knew the taverns well in every town
245 And every innkeeper and barmaid too
Better than lepers, beggars and that crew,
For in so eminent a man as he
It was not fitting with the dignity
Of his position, dealing with a scum
250 Of wretched lepers; nothing good can come
Of commerce with such slum-and-gutter
    dwellers,
But only with the rich and victual-sellers.

But anywhere a profit might accrue
Courteous he was and lowly of service too.
255 Natural gifts like his were hard to match.
He was the finest beggar of his batch,
And, for his begging-district, paid a rent;
His brethren did no poaching where he
    went.
For though a widow mightn't have a shoe,
260 So pleasant was his holy how-d'ye-do
He got his farthing from her just the same
Before he left, and so his income came
To more than he laid out. And how he
    romped,
Just like a puppy! He was ever prompt
265 To arbitrate disputes on settling days[30]
(For a small fee) in many helpful ways,
Not then appearing as your cloistered
    scholar
With threadbare habit hardly worth a dollar,
But much more like a Doctor[31] or a Pope.
270 Of double-worsted was the semi-cope[32]
Upon his shoulders, and the swelling fold
About him, like a bell about its mold
When it is casting, rounded out his dress.
He lisped a little out of wantonness
275 To make his English sweet upon his tongue.
When he had played his harp, or having
    sung,
His eyes would twinkle in his head as bright
As any star upon a frosty night.
This worthy's name was Hubert, it appeared.

---

24. Four Orders, the four groups of begging friars were
Dominicans, Franciscans, Carmelites, Augustinians.
25. He'd fixed . . . afford her. He found husbands,
and perhaps dowries, for women whom he had himself
seduced.
26. County folk, the local gentry, the socially prominent
and well-to-do.
27. shrift, confession of sins.
28. tippet, a narrow part of hood or sleeve used as a
pocket.
29. hurdy-gurdy. Chaucer's term, "rote," refers to a
stringed instrument.
30. settling days, days on which disputes could be settled
by independent negotiators out of court. Friars often acted
in this capacity and received "gifts" for their services. In
Chaucer's day this was officially forbidden.
31. Doctor, a university professor.
32. semi-cope, a short cope. A cope was a type of cloak,
intended to be worn out-of-doors.

280   There was a *Merchant* with a forking beard
And motley[33] dress; high on his horse he sat,
Upon his head a Flemish beaver hat
And on his feet daintily buckled boots.
He told of his opinions and pursuits
285 In solemn tones, he harped on his increase
Of capital; there should be sea-police
(He thought) upon the Harwich-Holland
    ranges;[34]
He was expert at dabbling in exchanges.
This estimable Merchant so had set
290 His wits to work, none knew he was in debt,
He was so stately in administration,
In loans and bargains and negotiation.
He was an excellent fellow all the same;
To tell the truth I do not know his name.

295   An *Oxford Cleric*,[35] still a student though,
One who had taken logic long ago,
Was there; his horse was thinner than a rake,
And he was not too fat, I undertake,
But had a hollow look, a sober stare;
300 The thread upon his overcoat was bare.
He had found no preferment in the church
And he was too unworldly to make search
For secular employment. By his bed
He preferred having twenty books in red
305 And black, of Aristotle's philosophy,[36]
Than costly clothes, fiddle or psaltery.[37]
Though a philosopher, as I have told,
He had not found the stone for making gold.[38]
Whatever money from his friends he took
310 He spent on learning or another book
And prayed for them most earnestly,
    returning
Thanks to them thus for paying for his
    learning.
His only care was study, and indeed
He never spoke a word more than was need,
315 Formal at that, respectful in the extreme,
Short, to the point, and lofty in his theme.
A tone of moral virtue filled his speech
And gladly would he learn, and gladly teach.

    A *Sergeant at the Law*[39] who paid his calls,
320 Wary and wise, for clients at St. Paul's[40]

There also was, of noted excellence.
Discreet he was, a man to reverence,
Or so he seemed, his sayings were so wise.
He often had been Justice of Assize
325 By letters patent,[41] and in full commission.
His fame and learning and his high position
Had won him many a robe and many a fee.
There was no such conveyancer[42] as he;
All was fee-simple[43] to his strong digestion,
330 Not one conveyance could be called in
    question.
Though there was nowhere one so busy as
    he,
He was less busy than he seemed to be.
He knew of every judgment, case and crime
Ever recorded since King William's time.[44]
335 He could dictate defences or draft deeds;
No one could pinch a comma from his
    screeds[45]
And he knew every statute off by rote.
He wore a homely parti-colored coat.

---

33. motley, here, cloth woven with a figured design.
34. sea-police . . . Harwich-Holland ranges. He wants
ships sailing the England-to-Holland route protected at any
cost.
35. Cleric, any divinity student; not necessarily a priest.
36. twenty books . . . Aristotle's philosophy. Aristotle
(384-322 B.C.) was a Greek philosopher whose works had
a great influence on medieval thought. Private libraries of
the size possessed by the Cleric were extremely uncommon
in Chaucer's day; it is not surprising that his expenditures
on books left him little for food or clothing.
37. psaltery, stringed instrument played with the hand.
38. stone for making gold. In alchemy the philosopher's
stone was supposed to turn ordinary metals into gold. No
one ever found it.
39. Sergeant at the Law, one of the king's legal servants.
There were only twenty such men in Chaucer's day. They
were chosen from lawyers with over 16 years' experience,
and sat as judges both in London and in the traveling
courts, the assizes (line 324) which met at various country
towns.
40. St. Paul's, Old St. Paul's Cathedral (destroyed by the
Fire of London in 1666). During the afternoon, when the
courts were closed, lawyers would meet clients on church
porches to discuss business.
41. letters patent, official documents from the king
empowering an individual to act as Judge of the Assize.
42. conveyancer. The Sergeant is an expert on real-estate
law.
43. fee-simple, land owned outright. The Sergeant is
obtaining as much of this as he can.
44. King William's time, era of William the Conqueror
(1066-1087), when systematic legal records were first kept.
45. screeds, writing.

The Franklin, from the Ellesmere Chaucer.

He kept fat partridges in coops, beyond,
360 Many a bream and pike were in his pond.
Woe to the cook unless the sauce was hot
And sharp, or if he wasn't on the spot!
And in his hall a table stood arrayed
And ready all day long, with places laid.
365 As Justice at the Sessions none stood higher;[49]
He often had been Member for the Shire.[50]
A dagger and a little purse of silk
Hung at his girdle, white as morning milk.
As Sheriff[51] he checked audit, every entry.
370 He was a model among landed gentry.

A *Haberdasher*, a *Dyer*, a *Carpenter*,
A *Weaver*, and a *Carpet-maker* were
Among our ranks, all in the livery
Of one impressive guild-fraternity.[52]
375 They were so trim and fresh their gear would
        pass
For new. Their knives were not tricked out
        with brass
But wrought with purest silver, which
        avouches
A like display on girdles and on pouches.
Each seemed a worthy burgess, fit to grace
380 A guild-hall with a seat upon the dais.[53]
Their wisdom would have justified a plan
To make each one of them an alderman;[54]
They had the capital and revenue,
Besides their wives declared it was their due.
385 And if they did not think so, then they
        ought;

Girt with a silken belt of pinstripe stuff;
340 Of his appearance I have said enough.

There was a *Franklin*[46] with him, it
        appeared;
White as a daisy petal was his beard.
A sanguine man, high-colored and benign,
He loved a morning sop of cake in wine.
345 He lived for pleasure and had always done,
For he was Epicurus'[47] very son,
In whose opinion sensual delight
Was the one true felicity in sight.
As noted as St. Julian[48] was for bounty
350 He made his household free to all the
        County.
His bread, his ale were finest of the fine
And no one had a better stock of wine.
His house was never short of bakemeat pies,
Of fish and flesh, and these in such supplies
355 It positively snowed with meat and drink
And all the dainties that a man could think.
According to the seasons of the year
Changes of dish were ordered to appear.

---

46. *Franklin*. Literally the term means "free man." Here we have a wealthy landowner.
47. *Epicurus*, Greek philosopher (342?-270 B.C.) whose ideas seemed to urge pursuit of pleasure.
48. *St. Julian*, patron of hospitality.
49. *Justice . . . higher*. When the Justices of the Peace sat in session, he presided.
50. *Member . . . Shire*, member of Parliament for his county.
51. *Sheriff*, royal administrator who collected taxes and delivered them to the king's exchequer.
52. *guild-fraternity*. Since these men came from different trades, this probably refers to a social or religious guild to which they all belonged.
53. *guild-hall . . . dais*, worthy to preside at meetings of the guild.
54. *alderman*, leading member of a town council.

To be called "*Madam*" is a glorious thought,
And so is going to church and being seen
Having your mantle carried, like a queen.

They had a *Cook* with them who stood alone
390 For boiling chicken with a marrowbone,
Sharp flavoring-powder and a spice for savor.
He could distinguish London ale by flavor,
And he could roast and seethe and broil and fry,
Make good thick soup and bake a tasty pie.
395 But what a pity—so it seemed to me,
That he should have an ulcer on his knee.
As for blancmange,[55] he made it with the best.

There was a *Skipper* hailing from far west;
He came from Dartmouth, so I understood.
400 He rode a farmer's horse as best he could,
In a woolen gown that reached his knee.
A dagger on a lanyard falling free
Hung from his neck under his arm and down.
The summer heat had tanned his color brown,
405 And certainly he was an excellent fellow.
Many a draught of vintage, red and yellow,
He'd drawn at Bordeaux,[56] while the trader snored.
The nicer rules of conscience he ignored.
If, when he fought, the enemy vessel sank,
410 He sent his prisoners home; they walked the plank.
As for his skill in reckoning his tides,
Currents and many another risk besides,
Moons, harbors, pilots, he had such dispatch
That none from Hull to Carthage[57] was his match.
415 Hardy he was, prudent in undertaking;
His beard in many a tempest had its shaking,
And he knew all the havens as they were
· From Gottland to the Cape of Finisterre,[58]
And every creek in Brittany and Spain;
420 The barge he owned was called *The Maudelayne*.[59]

A *Doctor* too emerged as we proceeded;
No one alive could talk as well as he did
On points of medicine and surgery,
For, being grounded in astronomy,[60]
425 He watched his patient closely for the hours
When, by his horoscope, he knew the powers
Of favorable planets, then ascendent,
Worked on the images for his dependent.[61]
The cause of every malady you'd got
430 He knew, and whether dry, cold, moist or hot;[62]
He knew their seat, their humor and condition.
He was a perfect practicing physician.
These causes being known for what they were,
He gave the man his medicine then and there.
435 All his apothecaries in a tribe
Were ready with the drugs he would prescribe
And each made money from the other's guile;
They had been friendly for a goodish while.
He was well-versed in Aesculapius[63] too
440 And what Hippocrates and Rufus knew
And Dioscorides, now dead and gone,
Galen and Rhazes, Hali, Serapion,

---

55. *blancmange* (ble mänzh'). In Chaucer's day, this referred to a kind of chicken stew.
56. *Bordeaux* (bôr dō'), a seaport in southwestern France. The region near Bordeaux is famous for both its red and white wines.
57. *Hull to Carthage.* These and subsequent references indicate how widely the skipper has traveled.
58. *Gottland . . . Finisterre.* Gottland is an island in the Baltic Sea off Sweden; the Cape of Finisterre is part of Brittany, in northwestern France.
59. *The Maudelayne.* A real ship of this name from Dartmouth paid customs duties in 1379 and 1391, and Chaucer may have had its master in mind in creating the Skipper.
60. *astronomy.* Here, astrology. It was believed that the position of the planets determined the best time to treat a patient.
61. *images . . . dependent.* These "images" may have been wax figures of the dependent (the patient) such as those used in witchcraft, or charms inscribed with astrological symbols.
62. *dry . . . hot.* In the Middle Ages people thought the human body was composed of the four elements: earth, air, fire, and water. Sickness came from too much of any one element. Character traits, too, could be explained by a slight excess of an element: too much fire produced a hot temper, etc. Such traits were called *humors* (line 431).
63. *Aesculapius.* This and the names that follow belong to eminent medical authorities from ancient times to Chaucer's day. The Doctor was well-read in his profession.

Averroes, Avicenna, Constantine,
Scotch Bernard, John of Gaddesden,
     Gilbertine.
445 In his own diet he observed some measure;
There were no superfluities for pleasure,
Only digestives, nutritives, and such.
He did not read the Bible very much.[64]
In blood-red garments, slashed with bluish
     gray
450 And lined with taffeta, he rode his way;
Yet he was rather close as to expenses
And kept the gold he won in pestilences.[65]
Gold stimulates the heart, or so we're told.
He therefore had a special love of gold.

455   A worthy *woman* from beside *Bath* city
Was with us, somewhat deaf, which was a
     pity.
In making cloth she showed so great a bent
She bettered those of Ypres and Ghent.[66]
In all the parish not a dame dared stir
460 Towards the altar steps in front of her,
And if indeed they did, so wrath was she
As to be quite put out of charity.
Her kerchiefs were of finely woven ground;
I dared have sworn they weighed a good ten
     pound,
465 The ones she wore on Sunday, on her head.
Her hose were of the finest scarlet red
And gartered tight; her shoes were soft and
     new.
Bold was her face, handsome, and red in hue.
A worthy woman all her life, what's more
470 She'd had five husbands, all at the church
     door,[67]
Apart from other company in youth;
No need just now to speak of that, forsooth.
And she had thrice been to Jerusalem,
Seen many strange rivers and passed over
     them;
475 She'd been to Rome and also to Boulogne,
St. James of Compostella and Cologne,[68]
And she was skilled in wandering by the way.
She had gap-teeth, set widely, truth to say.
Easily on an ambling horse she sat
480 Well wimpled up,[69] and on her head a hat

As broad as is a buckler or a shield;
She had a flowing mantle that concealed
Large hips, her heels spurred sharply under
     that.
In company she liked to laugh and chat
485 And knew the remedies for love's mischances,
An art in which she knew the oldest dances.

    A holy-minded man of good renown
There was, and poor, the *Parson* to a town,
Yet he was rich in holy thought and work.
490 He also was a learned man, a clerk.
Who truly knew Christ's gospel and would
     preach it
Devoutly to parishioners, and teach it.
Benign and wonderfully diligent,
And patient when adversity was sent
495 (For so he proved in much adversity)
He hated cursing to extort a fee,
Nay rather he preferred beyond a doubt
Giving to poor parishioners round about
Both from church offerings and his property;
500 He could in little find sufficiency.
Wide was his parish, with houses far asunder,
Yet he neglected not in rain or thunder,
In sickness or in grief, to pay a call
On the remotest, whether great or small,
505 Upon his feet, and in his hand a stave.
This noble example to his sheep he gave
That first he wrought, and afterwards he
     taught;
And it was from the Gospel he had caught
Those words, and he would add this figure
     too,
510 That if gold rust, what then will iron do?
For if a priest be foul in whom we trust

---

64. read . . . much. Doctors had a reputation for free-thinking and impiety.
65. pestilences, plagues.
66. Ypres . . . Ghent, Flemish cities famous for their weavers and markets for the wool trade.
67. at the church door. In Chaucer's day marriage services were held at the church door, and the subsequent nuptial Mass was held inside.
68. Rome . . . Cologne. The Wife has visited most of the important shrines in Italy, France, Spain, and Germany.
69. well wimpled up. A linen garment covers her head, neck, and the sides of her face.

No wonder that a common man should
    rust; . . .
The true example that a priest should give
Is one of cleanness, how the sheep should
    live.
515 He did not set his benefice[70] to hire
And leave his sheep encumbered in the mire
Or run to London to earn easy bread
By singing masses for the wealthy dead,
Or find some Brotherhood and get
    enrolled.[71]
520 He stayed at home and watched over his fold
So that no wolf should make the sheep
    miscarry.
He was a shepherd and no mercenary.[72]
Holy and virtuous he was, but then
Never contemptuous of sinful men,
525 Never disdainful, never too proud or fine,
But was discreet in teaching and benign.
His business was to show a fair behavior
And draw men thus to Heaven and their
    Savior,
Unless indeed a man were obstinate;
530 And such, whether of high or low estate,
He put to sharp rebuke, to say the least.
I think there never was a better priest.
He sought no pomp or glory in his dealings,
No scrupulosity had spiced his feelings.
535 Christ and His Twelve Apostles and their lore
He taught, but followed it himself before.

There was a *Plowman* with him there, his
    brother;
Many a load of dung one time or other
He must have carted through the morning
    dew.
540 He was an honest worker, good and true,
Living in peace and perfect charity,
And, as the gospel bade him, so did he,
Loving God best with all his heart and mind
And then his neighbor as himself, repined
545 At no misfortune, slacked for no content,
For steadily about his work he went
To thrash his corn, to dig or to manure
Or make a ditch; and he would help the poor
For love of Christ and never take a penny

The Miller, from the Ellesmere Chaucer.

550 If he could help it, and, as prompt as any,
He paid his tithes in full when they were due
On what he owned, and on his earnings too.
He wore a tabard smock and rode a mare.

There was a *Reeve*, also a *Miller*, there,
555 A College *Manciple* from the Inns of Court,
A papal *Pardoner* and, in close consort,
A Church-Court *Summoner*, riding at a trot,
And finally myself—that was the lot.

The *Miller* was a chap of sixteen stone,[73]
560 A great stout fellow big in brawn and bone.
He did well out of them, for he could go
And win the ram at any wrestling show.
Broad, knotty and short-shouldered, he
    would boast

70. *benefice,* a Church office and its income.
71. *find . . . enrolled.* The Parson refuses the easy work
of the paid chaplain for a London guild.
72. *shepherd . . . mercenary.* The reference here is to
Jesus' parable of the hireling shepherd (John 10:12-13).
73. *sixteen stone,* two hundred twenty-four pounds.

Chaucer, from the Ellesmere Chaucer.

He could heave any door off hinge and post,
565 Or take a run and break it with his head.
His beard, like any sow or fox, was red
And broad as well, as though it were a spade;
And, at its very tip, his nose displayed
A wart on which there stood a tuft of hair
570 Red as the bristles in an old sow's ear.
His nostrils were as black as they were wide.
He had a sword and buckler at his side,
His mighty mouth was like a furnace door.
A wrangler and buffoon, he had a store
575 Of tavern stories, filthy in the main.
He was a master-hand at stealing grain.
He felt it with his thumb and thus he knew
Its quality and took three times his due—
A thumb of gold,[74] by God, to gauge an oat!
580 He wore a hood of blue and a white coat.
He liked to play his bagpipes up and down
And that was how he brought us out of town.

The *Manciple* came from the Inner Temple;[75]
All caterers might follow his example
585 In buying victuals; he was never rash

Whether he bought on credit or paid cash.
He used to watch the market most precisely
And got in first, and so he did quite nicely.
Now isn't it a marvel of God's grace
590 That an illiterate fellow can outpace
The wisdom of a heap of learned men?
His masters—he had more than thirty then—
All versed in the abstrusest legal knowledge,
Could have produced a dozen from their
        College
595 Fit to be stewards in land and rents and game
To any Peer in England you could name,
And show him how to live on what he had
Debt-free (unless of course the Peer were
        mad)
Or be as frugal as he might desire,
600 And make them fit to help about the Shire
In any legal case there was to try;
And yet this Manciple could wipe their eye.[76]

The *Reeve*[77] was old and choleric and thin;
His beard was shaven closely to the skin,
605 His shorn hair came abruptly to a stop
Above his ears, and he was docked on top
Just like a priest in front; his legs were lean,
Like sticks they were, no calf was to be seen.
He kept his bins and garners very trim;
610 No auditor could gain a point on him.
And he could judge by watching drought and
        rain
The yield he might expect from seed and
        grain.
His master's sheep, his animals and hens,
Pigs, horses, dairies, stores and cattle-pens
615 Were wholly trusted to his government.
He had been under contract to present

---

74. *thumb of gold.* Unscrupulous millers would secretly press their thumbs down on their scales when weighing grain to take a larger cut for themselves.
75. *Manciple . . . from the Inner Temple.* London lawyers formed themselves into societies which inhabited buildings once owned by the ancient society of Knights of the Temple. They hired administrators, called manciples, to purchase food for their meals.
76. *wipe their eye,* knock the conceit out of them.
77. *Reeve,* a minor official on a country estate who served as an intermediary between the lord of the manor and his serfs.

The accounts, right from his master's
    earliest years.
No one had ever caught him in arrears.
No bailiff,[78] serf or herdsman dared to kick,
620 He knew their dodges, knew their every
    trick;
Feared like the plague he was, by those
    beneath.
He had a lovely dwelling on a heath,
Shadowed in green by trees above the sward.
A better hand at bargains than his lord,
625 He had grown rich and had a store of treasure
Well tucked away, yet out it came to pleasure
His lord with subtle loans or gifts of goods,
To earn his thanks and even coats and hoods.
When young he'd learnt a useful trade and
    still
630 He was a carpenter of first-rate skill.
The stallion-cob he rode at a slow trot
Was dapple-gray and bore the name of Scot.
He wore an overcoat of bluish shade
And rather long; he had a rusty blade
635 Slung at his side. He came, as I heard tell,
From Norfolk, near a place called ⁻
    Baldeswell.
His coat was tucked under his belt and
    splayed.
He rode the hindmost of our cavalcade.

    There was a *Summoner*[79] with us at that
    Inn,
640 His face on fire, like a cherubin,[80]
For he had carbuncles.[81] His eyes were
    narrow,
He was as hot and lecherous as a sparrow.
Black scabby brows he had, and a thin beard.
Children were afraid when he appeared.
645 No quicksilver, lead ointment, tartar
    creams,
No brimstone, no boracic, so it seems,
Could make a salve that had the power to
    bite,
Clean up or cure his whelks[82] of knobby
    white
Or purge the pimples sitting on his cheeks.
650 Garlic he loved, and onions too, and leeks,

And drinking strong red wine till all was
    hazy.
Then he would shout and jabber as if crazy,
And wouldn't speak a word except in Latin
When he was drunk, such tags as he was pat
    in;
655 He only had a few, say two or three,
That he had mugged up out of some decree;
No wonder, for he heard them every day.
And, as you know, a man can teach a jay
To call out "Walter" better than the Pope.
660 But had you tried to test his wits and grope
For more, you'd have found nothing in the
    bag.
Then *"Questio quid juris"*[83] was his tag.
He was a noble varlet and a kind one,
You'd meet none better if you went to find
    one.
665 Why, he'd allow—just for a quart of wine—
Any good lad to keep a concubine
A twelvemonth and dispense him altogether!
And he had finches of his own to feather.[84]
And if he found some rascal with a maid
670 He would instruct him not to be afraid
In such a case of the Archdeacon's curse
(Unless the rascal's soul were in his purse)
For in his purse the punishment should be.
"Purse is the good Archdeacon's Hell," said
    he.
675 But well I know he lied in what he said;
A curse should put a guilty man in dread,
For curses kill, as shriving brings, salvation.
We should beware of excommunication.

---

78. *bailiff,* a servant of the lord of the manor whose job
was to help direct the maintenance of farms; traditionally
a superior to the reeve.
79. *Summoner,* a paid messenger who summoned
"sinners" to appear before an ecclesiastical court.
80. *cherubin,* a member of one of the nine orders of
angels. In medieval art the cherubim are generally depicted
with flame-colored faces.
81. *carbuncles,* swellings like boils.
82. *whelks,* pimples.
83. *"Questio quid juris."* "The question is, what part of
the law applies?" [Latin]
84. *And . . . feather.* The Summoner indulged in the
same sins he is just said to have excused in others.

Thus, as he pleased, the man could bring
    duress
680 On any young fellow in the diocese.
He knew their secrets, they did what he said.
He wore a garland set upon his head
Large as the holly-bush upon a stake
Outside an ale-house,[85] and he had a cake,
685 A round one, which it was his joke to wield
As if it were intended for a shield.

    He and a gentle *Pardoner*[86] rode together,
A bird from Charing Cross[87] of the same
    feather,
Just back from visiting the Court of Rome.
690 He loudly sang, *"Come hither, love, come
    home!"*
The Summoner sang deep seconds to this
    song,
No trumpet ever sounded half so strong.
This Pardoner had hair as yellow as wax,
Hanging down smoothly like a hank of flax.
695 In driblets fell his locks behind his head
Down to his shoulders which they
    overspread;
Thinly they fell, like rat-tails, one by one.
He wore no hood upon his head, for fun;
The hood inside his wallet[88] had been
    stowed.
700 He aimed at riding in the latest mode;
But for a little cap his head was bare
And he had bulging eyeballs, like a hare.
He'd sewed a holy relic on his cap;
His wallet lay before him on his lap,
705 Brimful of pardons come from Rome, all
    hot.
He had the same small voice a goat has got.
His chin no beard had harbored, nor would
    harbor,
Smoother than ever chin was left by barber.
I judge he was a gelding, or a mare.
710 As to his trade, from Berwick down to Ware
There was no pardoner of equal grace,
For in his trunk he had a pillow-case
Which he asserted was Our Lady's veil.
He said he had a gobbet[89] of the sail
715 Saint Peter had the time when he made bold

Tavern scene, from *De Septem Vitiis*. Italian, late 14th century. *British Library*

85. *Large . . . ale-house* A tavern was customarily identified by such a bush on a stake.
86. *Pardoner.* In the Middle Ages sinners under sentence of an extended penance could purchase a remittance of their penance duties from official pardoners. This soon led to corrupt practices, the ignorant believing they could buy complete forgiveness for a sin. Fake pardoners were only too willing to exploit such people.
87. *Charing Cross,* district of London in which was located the hospital of the Blessed Mary of Rouncivalle. In Chaucer's time unauthorized pardons were sold by persons claiming they were collecting money for the hospital, and Pardoners of Rouncivalle were often satirized.
88. *wallet,* pack.
89. *gobbet,* piece.

To walk the waves, till Jesu Christ took hold.
He had a cross of metal set with stones
And, in a glass, a rubble of pigs' bones.
And with these relics, any time he found
720 Some poor upcountry parson to astound,
In one short day, in money down, he drew
More than the parson in a month or two,
And by his flatteries and prevarication
Made monkeys of the priest and
congregation.
725 But still to do him justice first and last
In church he was a noble ecclesiast.
How well he read a lesson or told a story!
But best of all he sang an Offertory,[90]
For well he knew that when that song was
sung
730 He'd have to preach and tune his honey-
tongue
And (well he could) win silver from the
crowd.
That's why he sang so merrily and loud.

Now I have told you shortly, in a clause,
The rank, the array, the number and the
cause
735 Of our assembly in this company
In Southwark, at that high-class hostelry
Known as *The Tabard*, close beside *The Bell*.
And now the time has come for me to tell
How we behaved that evening; I'll begin
740 After we had alighted at the Inn,
Then I'll report our journey, stage by stage,
All the remainder of our pilgrimage.
But first I beg of you, in courtesy,
Not to condemn me as unmannerly
745 If I speak plainly and with no concealings
And give account of all their words and
dealings,
Using their very phrases as they fell.
For certainly, as you all know so well,
He who repeats a tale after a man
750 Is bound to say, as nearly as he can,
Each single word, if he remembers it,
However rudely spoken or unfit,
Or else the tale he tells will be untrue,

The things pretended and the phrases new.
755 He may not flinch although it were his
brother,
He may as well say one word as another.
And Christ Himself spoke broad in Holy
Writ,
Yet there is no scurrility in it,
And Plato says, for those with power to read,
760 "The word should be as cousin to the
deed."[91]
Further I beg you to forgive it me
If I neglect the order and degree
And what is due to rank in what I've
planned.
I'm short of wit as you will understand.

765 Our *Host* gave us great welcome; everyone
Was given a place and supper was begun.
He served the finest victuals you could think,
The wine was strong and we were glad to
drink.
A very striking man our Host withal,
770 And fit to be a marshal in a hall.
His eyes were bright, his girth a little wide;
There is no finer burgess in Cheapside.[92]
Bold in his speech, yet wise and full of tact,
There was no manly attribute he lacked,
775 What's more he was a merry-hearted man.
After our meal he jokingly began
To talk of sport, and, among other things
After we'd settled up our reckonings,
He said as follows: "Truly, gentlemen,
780 You're very welcome and I can't think when
—Upon my word I'm telling you no lie—
I've seen a gathering here that looked so
spry,
No, not this year, as in this tavern now.
I'd think you up some fun if I knew how.
785 And, as it happens, a thought has just
occurred

---

90. *Offertory*, a portion of the liturgy of the Mass.
91. *Plato . . . deed.* The reference here is to a passage in the *Timaeus*, one of the dialogues of the Greek philosopher Plato (427?-347? B.C.).
92. *burgess in Cheapside*, citizen of a district in London.

To please you, costing nothing, on my word.
You're off to Canterbury—well, God speed!
Blessed St. Thomas answer to your need!
And I don't doubt, before the journey's done
790 You mean to while the time in tales and fun.
Indeed, there's little pleasure for your bones
Riding along and all as dumb as stones.
So let me then propose for your enjoyment,
Just as I said, a suitable employment.
795 And if my notion suits and you agree
And promise to submit yourselves to me
Playing your parts exactly as I say
Tomorrow as you ride along the way,
Then by my father's soul (and he is dead)
800 If you don't like it you can have my head!
Hold up your hands, and not another word."
   Well, our opinion was not long deferred,
It seemed not worth a serious debate;
We all agreed to it at any rate
805 And bade him issue what commands he
      would.
   "My lords," he said, "now listen for your
      good,
And please don't treat my notion with
      disdain.
This is the point. I'll make it short and plain.
Each one of you shall help to make things
      slip
810 By telling two stories on the outward trip
To Canterbury, that's what I intend,
And, on the homeward way to journey's end
Another two, tales from the days of old;
And then the man whose story is best told,
815 That is to say who gives the fullest measure
Of good morality and general pleasure,
He shall be given a supper, paid by all,
Here in this tavern, in this very hall,
When we come back again from Canterbury.
820 And in the hope to keep you bright and
      merry
I'll go along with you myself and ride
All at my own expense and serve as guide.
I'll be the judge, and those who won't obey
Shall pay for what we spend upon the way.
825 Now if you all agree to what you've heard

Tell me at once without another word,
And I will make arrangements early for it."
   Of course we all agreed, in fact we swore
      it
Delightedly, and made entreaty too
830 That he should act as he proposed to do,
Become our Governor in short, and be
Judge of our tales and general referee,
And set the supper at a certain price.
We promised to be ruled by his advice
835 Come high, come low; unanimously thus
We set him up in judgment over us.
More wine was fetched, the business being
      done;
We drank it off and up went everyone
To bed without a moment of delay.
840   Early next morning at the spring of day
Up rose our Host and roused us like a cock,
Gathering us together in a flock,
And off we rode at slightly faster pace
Than walking to St. Thomas's watering
      place;[93]
845 And there our Host drew up, began to ease
His horse, and said, "Now, listen if you
      please,
My lords! Remember what you promised
      me.
If evensong and matins will agree[94]
Let's see who shall be first to tell a tale.
850 And as I hope to drink good wine and ale
I'll be your judge. The rebel who disobeys,
However much the journey costs, he pays.
Now draw for cut and then we can depart;
The man who draws the shortest cut shall
      start. . . ."

---

93. *St. Thomas's watering-place,* a brook on the
pilgrimage route to Canterbury.
94. *If evensong . . . agree.* If you feel in the morning
(matins) as you did the night before (evensong).

Comment

Medieval Tourists

By Chaucer's time, as can be seen from his remark about the Prioress (who spoke her French "after the school of Stratford-atte-Bowe"), French had become, even for the well-born, a foreign language. It was no longer learned at home, but had to be taught. According to historian Paul Johnson, "From the late fourteenth century we get the first French-conversation manuals for the use of English travelers. One, entitled *La Maniere de language qui t'enseignera bien a droit parler et escrire doulx françois [A Manual of Language That Will Teach You to Speak French Correctly and Write It Smoothly]*, and dating from 1396, tells the Englishman what to say while on the road or at an inn. It unconsciously gives the English racial view of the French: how to instruct lazy, incompetent, and venal [greedy] French hostlers [stablemen] in their duties; how to tell French innkeepers to clean up their filthy and vermin-ridden bedrooms, and to serve food which is wholesome and not messed about. . . . It differs only in detail—certainly not in fundamental attitudes—from the phrase books supplied to the English Grand Tourists in the eighteenth century."

Paul Johnson, *The Offshore Islanders*, New York: Holt, Rinehart and Winston, 1972, page 110.

THINK AND DISCUSS
Understanding
1. What causes this group of people to gather at the Tabard Inn?
2. What agreement does the group reach about telling stories?
3. Who does not have to tell any stories? Why?
4. How does Chaucer the narrator spend the evening? with what result?

Analyzing
5. The Knight and the Squire both belong to the age of chivalry; yet they present very different pictures. Compare and contrast the Knight and the Squire as representatives of chivalry.
6. Discuss the extent to which these church people exhibit worldly qualities: The Prioress, the Monk, the Friar, the Pardoner, and the Summoner.
7. Chaucer calls the Parson "a holy-minded man of good renown." What do you think Chaucer considered the best ways for a religious person to behave?
8. In what ways are the Merchant, Oxford Cleric, Sergeant at the Law, and Doctor typical of their professions?
9. What might have been Chaucer's reason for his disclaimer, "I'm short of wit as you will understand" (line 764)?

Extending
10. Scholars have discovered that there was a real-life host of an inn called the Tabard in Southwark. His name was Harry Bailly, the name Chaucer assigns to his Host in *The Cook's Prologue*. This discovery has led to the belief that some of the other pilgrims had real-life originals. Select one for whom you think this may be true, and explain why you think so.
11. In lines 743–764 Chaucer disclaims responsibility for anything offensive in what he is about to present. How do you feel about his statement that an author "is bound to say, as nearly as he can,/Each single word if he remembers it,/However rudely spoken or unfit"?

APPLYING: Characterization H⅂Z
See Handbook of Literary Terms, p. 898

Characterization is the process by which an author acquaints a reader with his or her characters. An author may describe a character's appearance and personality, speech and behavior, thoughts and feelings, and/or interactions with other characters.

1. Which details in the description of the Monk (lines 169–211) indicate that he has expensive tastes? Which details indicate that he is not spending his time in study and contemplation?
2. One of Chaucer's tricks of characterization is to make a statement about a character and then present details that hint at the opposite. For example, he calls the Friar "a noble pillar to his Order." Find details about the Friar that suggest the opposite.
3. Chaucer claims that after one evening's conversation with all the pilgrims he was "one with them in fellowship." Find examples of personal details that seem unlikely for anyone to disclose to a stranger on such short acquaintance. How do you account for the narrator Chaucer's knowing these things?

THINKING SKILLS
Generalizing

To generalize is to draw a general conclusion from particular data. For example, a reader notes all the things a writer says about a topic and makes a general statement about how that writer regards the topic.

1. Given the examples of some of the less honest pilgrims, would you say that Chaucer believed he lived in a particularly corrupt age?
2. Would you call Chaucer's age more corrupt than ours? Explain.

COMPOSITION ◄━━━━
Writing an Interview

Assume that television existed in Chaucer's day and that you were the host of a talk show. Write an interview with one of the pilgrims for your national TV audience. Using question-and-answer form, talk about that pilgrim's life and journey to Canterbury. Try to write questions that will allow you to create interesting and revealing responses for your chosen pilgrim.

Explaining the Pilgrimage

Chaucer uses the narrative device of a frame— the pilgrimage itself—to provide a reason for all these characters to get together and tell their stories. Write an essay explaining their pilgrimage to classmates who are unfamiliar with *The Canterbury Tales*. First, review what is said about Canterbury and the pilgrimage in the Background (page 79), the introduction (page 96), and the *Prologue*, and take notes on what you find. Devote a paragraph of your essay to explaining what Canterbury is and where it is located and another paragraph to explaining why people went there on pilgrimages. Then explain how Chaucer uses this pilgrimage as a frame for his various tales and how effective you think his use of this literary device is. See "Writing Notes and Summaries" in the Writer's Handbook.

VOCABULARY
Context

Use context to help get the meaning of the italicized word in each of the following passages. You may use your Glossary if you need help.

1. "At night there came into that *hostelry*/Some nine and twenty in a company. . . ." (lines 23–24)
2. "Our Host gave us great welcome; everyone/Was given a place and supper was begun./He served the finest *victuals* you could think. . . ." (lines 765–767)
3. "For in so *eminent* a man as he/It was not fitting with the dignity/Of his position, dealing with a scum. . . ." (lines 247–249)
4. "I saw his sleeves were *garnished* at the hand/With fine gray fur, the finest in the land. . . ." (lines 197–198)

ENRICHMENT
Readers Theater

Participate in a Readers Theater presentation of *The Prologue*. First decide how many speaking parts you will have. For example, one student could play Chaucer and narrate; another student could play the Prioress; and a third student could play all five Guildsmen (lines 371–388). Rehearse together, so that your reading is fluent. You could present your reading live or record it on tape.

The Pardoner's Prologue

Geoffrey Chaucer

"My lords," he said, "in churches where I
    preach
I cultivate a haughty kind of speech
And ring it out as roundly as a bell;
I've got it all by heart, the tale I tell.
5 I have a text, it always is the same
And always has been, since I learnt the game,
Old as the hills and fresher than the grass,
Radix malorum est cupiditas.[1]
    "But first I make pronouncement whence
      I come,
10 Show them my bulls[2] in detail and in sum,
And flaunt the papal seal for their inspection
As warrant for my bodily protection,
That none may have the impudence to irk
Or hinder me in Christ's most holy work.
15 Then I tell stories, as occasion calls,
Showing forth bulls from popes and
    cardinals,
From patriarchs and bishops; as I do,
I speak some words in Latin—just a few—
To put a saffron tinge[3] upon my preaching
20 And stir devotion with a spice of teaching.
Then I bring all my long glass bottles out
Cram-full of bones and ragged bits of clout,[4]
Relics they are, at least for such are known.
Then, cased in metal, I've a shoulder bone,
25 Belonging to a sheep, a holy Jew's.[5]
'Good men,' I say, 'take heed, for here is
    news.
Take but this bone and dip it in a well;
If cow or calf, if sheep or ox should swell
From eating snakes or that a snake has stung,
30 Take water from that well and wash its
    tongue,
And it will then recover. Furthermore,

Where there is pox or scab or other sore,
All animals that water at that well
Are cured at once. Take note of what I tell.
35 If the good man—the owner of the stock—
Goes once a week, before the crow of cock,
Fasting, and takes a draught of water too,
Why then, according to that holy Jew,
He'll find his cattle multiply and sell.
40   " 'And it's a cure for jealousy as well;
For though a man be given to jealous wrath,
Use but this water when you make his broth,
And never again will he mistrust his wife,
Though he knew all about her sinful life,
45 Though two or three clergy had enjoyed her
    love.
  " 'Now look; I have a mitten here, a
    glove.
Whoever wears this mitten on his hand
Will multiply his grain. He sows his land
And up will come abundant wheat or oats,
50 Providing that he offers pence or groats.
  " 'Good men and women, here's a word
    of warning;
If there is anyone in church this morning
Guilty of sin, so far beyond expression
Horrible, that he dare not make confession,
55 Or any woman, whether young or old,
That's cuckolded her husband, be she told
That such as she shall have no power or grace

---

1. *Radix . . . cupiditas.* "Avarice is the root of all evil."
[Latin]
2. *bulls,* important papal documents or letters.
3. *saffron tinge.* The yellow spice saffron is used to color
and flavor food.
4. *clout,* cloth.
5. *a holy Jew's,* presumably some Old Testament figure,
possibly the patriarch Jacob.

To offer to my relics in this place.
But those who can acquit themselves of blame
60 Can all come up and offer in God's name,
And I will shrive them by the authority
Committed in this papal bull to me.'
    "That trick's been worth a hundred marks[6] a year
Since I became a Pardoner, never fear.
65 Then, priestlike in my pulpit, with a frown,
I stand, and when the yokels have sat down,
I preach, as you have heard me say before,
And tell a hundred lying mockeries more.
I take great pains, and stretching out my neck
70 To east and west I crane about and peck
Just like a pigeon sitting on a barn.
My hands and tongue together spin the yarn
And all my antics are a joy to see.
The curse of avarice and cupidity
75 Is all my sermon, for it frees the pelf.
Out come the pence, and specially for myself,
For my exclusive purpose is to win
And not at all to castigate their sin.
Once dead what matter how their souls may fare?
80 They can go blackberrying,[7] for all I care! . . .
    "But let me briefly make my purpose plain;
I preach for nothing but for greed of gain
And use the same old text, as bold as brass,
Radix malorum est cupiditas.
85 And thus I preach against the very vice
I make my living out of—avarice.
And yet however guilty of that sin
Myself, with others I have power to win
Them from it, I can bring them to repent;
90 But that is not my principal intent.
Covetousness is both the root and stuff
Of all I preach. That ought to be enough.
    "Well, then I give examples thick and fast
From bygone times, old stories from the past;
95 A yokel mind loves stories from of old,

The Pardoner, from the Ellesmere Chaucer.

Being the kind it can repeat and hold.
What! Do you think, as long as I can preach
And get their silver for the things I teach,
That I will live in poverty, from choice?
100 That's not the counsel of my inner voice!
No! Let me preach and beg from kirk[8] to kirk
And never do an honest job of work,
No, nor make baskets, like St. Paul,[9] to gain
A livelihood. I do not preach in vain.
105 There's no apostle I would counterfeit;
I mean to have money, wool and cheese and wheat

---

6. *marks.* The mark was worth 13 shillings and fourpence, or two-thirds of a pound sterling. In Chaucer's time, the purchasing value of money was at least thirty times what it is today.
7. *They . . . blackberrying,* go wandering at large.
8. *kirk,* church.
9. *make baskets . . . St. Paul.* The reference is not to St. Paul the Apostle, but to St. Paul the Hermit, who spent most of his very long life in the Egyptian desert. He died around A.D. 347 and is traditionally regarded as the first Christian hermit.

Though it were given me by the poorest lad
Or poorest village widow, though she had
A string of starving children, all agape.
110 No, let me drink the liquor of the grape
And keep a jolly wench in every town!
   "But listen, gentlemen; to bring things down
To a conclusion, would you like a tale?

Now as I've drunk a draught of corn-ripe ale,
115 By God it stands to reason I can strike
On some good story that you all will like.
For though I am a wholly vicious man
Don't think I can't tell moral tales. I can!
Here's one I often preach when out for winning;
120 Now please be quiet. Here is the beginning."

The Pardoner's Tale

Geoffrey Chaucer

. . . It's of three rioters I have to tell
Who, long before the morning service bell,
Were sitting in a tavern for a drink.
And as they sat, they heard the hand-bell clink
5 Before a coffin going to the grave;
One of them called the little tavern-knave[1]
And said "Go and find out at once—look spry!—
Whose corpse is in that coffin passing by;
And see you get the name correctly too."
10 "Sir," said the boy, "no need, I promise you;
Two hours before you came here I was told.
He was a friend of yours in days of old,
And suddenly, last night, the man was slain,
Upon his bench, face up, dead drunk again.
15 There came a privy thief, they call him Death,
Who kills us all round here, and in a breath
He speared him through the heart, he never stirred.
And then Death went his way without a word.
He's killed a thousand in the present plague,
20 And, sir, it doesn't do to be too vague
If you should meet him; you had best be wary.
Be on your guard with such an adversary,

Be primed to meet him everywhere you go,
That's what my mother said. It's all I know."
25 The publican joined in with, "By St. Mary,
What the child says is right; you'd best be wary,
This very year he killed, in a large village
A mile away, man, woman, serf at tillage,
Page in the household, children—all there were.
30 Yes, I imagine that he lives round there.
It's well to be prepared in these alarms,
He might do you dishonor!" "Huh, God's arms!"
The rioter said, "Is he so fierce to meet?
I'll search for him, by Jesus, street by street.
35 God's blessed bones! I'll register a vow!
Here, chaps! The three of us together now,
Hold up your hands, like me, and we'll be brothers
In this affair, and each defend the others,
And we will kill this traitor Death, I say!
40 Away with him as he has made away
With all our friends. God's dignity! Tonight!"
   They made their bargain, swore with appetite,

---

1. *knave*, servant.

These three, to live and die for one another
As brother-born might swear to his born
    brother.
45 And up they started in their drunken rage
And made towards this village which the
    page
And publican had spoken of before.
Many and grisly were the oaths they swore,
Tearing Christ's blessed body to a shred;
50 "If we can only catch him, Death is dead!"
    When they had gone not fully half a mile,
Just as they were about to cross a stile,
They came upon a very poor old man
Who humbly greeted them and thus began,
55 "God look to you, my lords, and give you
    quiet!"
To which the proudest of these men of riot
Gave back the answer, "What, old fool?
    Give place!
Why are you all wrapped up except your
    face?
Why live so long? Isn't it time to die?"
60   The old, old fellow looked him in the eye
And said, "Because I never yet have found,
Though I have walked to India, searching
    round
Village and city on my pilgrimage,
One who would change his youth to have my
    age.
65 And so my age is mine and must be still
Upon me, for such time as God may will.
    "Not even Death, alas, will take my life;
So, like a wretched prisoner at strife
Within himself, I walk alone and wait
70 About the earth, which is my mother's gate,[2]
Knock-knocking with my staff from night to
    noon
And crying, 'Mother, open to me soon!
Look at me, mother, won't you let me in?
See how I wither, flesh and blood and skin!
75 Alas! When will these bones be laid to rest?
Mother, I would exchange—for that were
    best—
The wardrobe in my chamber, standing
    there
So long, for yours! Aye, for a shirt of hair[3]

To wrap me in!' She has refused her grace,
80 Whence comes the pallor of my withered
    face.
    "But it dishonored you when you began
To speak so roughly, sir, to an old man,
Unless he had injured you in word or deed.
It says in holy writ, as you may read,
85 'Thou shalt rise up before the hoary head
And honor it.' And therefore be it said
'Do no more harm to an old man than you,
Being now young, would have another do
When you are old'—if you should live till
    then.
90 And so may God be with you, gentlemen,
For I must go whither I have to go."
    "By God," the gambler said, "you shan't
    do so,
You don't get off so easy, by St. John!
I heard you mention, just a moment gone,
95 A certain traitor Death who singles out
And kills the fine young fellows hereabout.
And you're his spy, by God! You wait a bit.
Say where he is or you shall pay for it,
By God and by the Holy Sacrament!
100 I say you've joined together by consent
To kill us younger folk, you thieving swine!"
    "Well, sirs," he said, "if it be your design
To find out Death, turn up this crooked way
Towards that grove. I left him there today
105 Under a tree, and there you'll find him
    waiting.
He isn't one to hide for all your prating.
You see that oak? He won't be far to find.
And God protect you that redeemed
    mankind,
Aye, and amend you!" Thus that ancient
    man.
110   At once the three young rioters began
To run, and reached the tree, and there they
    found
A pile of golden florins[4] on the ground,

---

2. *mother's gate,* the grave, the entrance to "mother
earth."
3. *shirt of hair,* a garment worn by penitents.
4. *florins,* coins worth a third of a pound sterling.

New-coined, eight bushels of them as they
    thought.
No longer was it Death those fellows sought,
115 For they were all so thrilled to see the sight,
The florins were so beautiful and bright,
That down they sat beside the precious pile.
The wickedest spoke first after a while.
"Brothers," he said, "you listen to what I
    say.
120 I'm pretty sharp although I joke away.
It's clear that Fortune has bestowed this
    treasure
To let us live in jollity and pleasure.
Light come, light go! We'll spend it as we
    ought.
God's precious dignity! Who would have
    thought
125 This morning was to be our lucky day?
    "If one could only get the gold away,
Back to my house, or else to yours,
    perhaps—
For as you know, the gold is ours, chaps—
We'd all be at the top of fortune, hey?
130 But certainly it can't be done by day.
People would call us robbers—a strong gang,
So our own property would make us hang.
No, we must bring this treasure back by
    night
Some prudent way, and keep it out of sight.
135 And so as a solution I propose
We draw for lots and see the way it goes.
The one who draws the longest, lucky man,
Shall run to town as quickly as he can
To fetch us bread and wine—but keep things
    dark—
140 While two remain in hiding here to mark
Our heap of treasure. If there's no delay,
When night comes down we'll carry it away,
All three of us, wherever we have planned."
    He gathered lots and hid them in his hand
145 Bidding them draw for where the luck
    should fall.
It fell upon the youngest of them all,
And off he ran at once towards the town.
    As soon as he had gone the first sat down
And thus began a parley with the other:

150 "You know that you can trust me as a
    brother;
Now let me tell you where your profit lies;
You know our friend has gone to get supplies
And here's a lot of gold that is to be
Divided equally amongst us three.
155 Nevertheless, if I could shape things thus
So that we shared it out—the two of us—
Wouldn't you take it as a friendly act?"
    "But how?" the other said. "He knows
    the fact
That all the gold was left with me and you;
160 What can we tell him? What are we to do?"
    "Is it a bargain," said the first, "or no?
For I can tell you in a word or so
What's to be done to bring the thing about."
"Trust me," the other said, "you needn't
    doubt
165 My word. I won't betray you, I'll be true."
    "Well," said his friend, "you see that we
    are two,
And two are twice as powerful as one.
Now look; when he comes back, get up in
    fun
To have a wrestle; then, as you attack,
170 I'll up and put my dagger through his back
While you and he are struggling, as in game;
Then draw your dagger too and do the same.
Then all this money will be ours to spend,
Divided equally of course, dear friend.
175 Then we can gratify our lusts and fill
The day with dicing at our own sweet will."
Thus these two miscreants agreed to slay
The third and youngest, as you heard me say.
    The youngest, as he ran towards the town,
180 Kept turning over, rolling up and down
Within his heart the beauty of those bright
New florins, saying, "Lord, to think I might
Have all that treasure to myself alone!
Could there be anyone beneath the throne
185 Of God so happy as I then should be?"
    And so the Fiend, our common enemy,
Was given power to put it in his thought
That there was always poison to be bought,
And that with poison he could kill his
    friends.

The Buying of the Poison and the Death of the Youngest Rioter. English wood-relief, circa 1400. *Museum of London*

190 To men in such a state the Devil sends
Thoughts of this kind, and has a full
permission
To lure them on to sorrow and perdition;
For this young man was utterly content
To kill them both and never to repent.
195 And on he ran, he had no thought to tarry,
Came to the town, found an apothecary
And said, "Sell me some poison if you will,
I have a lot of rats I want to kill
And there's a polecat too about my yard
200 That takes my chickens and it hits me hard;
But I'll get even, as is only right,
With vermin that destroy a man by night."
   The chemist answered, "I've a preparation
Which you shall have, and by my soul's
salvation
205 If any living creature eat or drink
A mouthful, ere he has the time to think,
Though he took less than makes a grain of
wheat,
You'll see him fall down dying at your feet;
Yes, die he must, and in so short a while
210 You'd hardly have the time to walk a mile,

The poison is so strong, you understand."
   This cursed fellow grabbed into his hand
The box of poison and away he ran
Into a neighboring street, and found a man
215 Who lent him three large bottles. He
withdrew
And deftly poured the poison into two.
He kept the third one clean, as well he might,
For his own drink, meaning to work all night
Stacking the gold and carrying it away.
220 And when this rioter, this devil's clay,
Had filled his bottles up with wine, all three,
Back to rejoin his comrades sauntered he.
   Why make a sermon of it? Why waste
breath?
Exactly in the way they'd planned his death
225 They fell on him and slew him, two to one.
Then said the first of them when this was
done,
"Now for a drink. Sit down and let's be
merry,
For later on there'll be the corpse to bury."
And, as it happened, reaching for a sup,
230 He took a bottle full of poison up

And drank; and his companion, nothing loth,
Drank from it also, and they perished both.
    There is, in Avicenna's long relation[5]
Concerning poison and its operation,
235 Trust me, no ghastlier section to transcend
What these two wretches suffered at their end.
Thus these two murderers received their due,
So did the treacherous young poisoner too.

    "O cursed sin! O blackguardly excess!
240 O treacherous homicide! O wickedness!
O gluttony that lusted on and diced!
O blasphemy that took the name of Christ
With habit-hardened oaths that pride began!
Alas, how comes it that a mortal man,
245 That thou, to thy Creator, Him that wrought
        thee,
That paid His precious blood for thee and
        bought thee,
Art so unnatural and false within?
    Dearly beloved, God forgive your sin
And keep you from the vice of avarice!
250 My holy pardon frees you all of this,
Provided that you make the right approaches,
That is with sterling, rings, or silver brooches.
Bow down your heads under this holy bull!
Come on, you women, offer up your wool!
255 I'll write your name into my ledger; so!
Into the bliss of Heaven you shall go.
For I'll absolve you by my holy power,
You that make offering, clean as at the hour
When you were born. . . . That, sirs, is
        how I preach
260 And Jesu Christ, soul's healer, aye, the leech
Of every soul, grant pardon and relieve you
Of sin, for that is best, I won't deceive you.
    One thing I should have mentioned in my
        tale,
Dear people. I've some relics in my bale
265 And pardons too, as full and fine, I hope,
As any in England, given me by the Pope.
If there be one among you that is willing
To have my absolution for a shilling
Devoutly given, come! and do not harden
270 Your hearts but kneel in humbleness for
        pardon;

Or else, receive my pardon as we go.
You can renew it every town or so
Always provided that you still renew
Each time, and in good money, what is due.
275 It is an honor to you to have found
A pardoner with his credentials sound
Who can absolve you as you ply the spur
In any accident that may occur.
For instance—we are all at Fortune's beck—
280 Your horse may throw you down and break
        your neck.
What a security it is to all
To have me here among you and at call
With pardon for the lowly and the great
When soul leaves body for the future state!
285 And I advise our Host here to begin,
The most enveloped of you all in sin.
Come forward, Host, you shall be first to
        pay,
And kiss my holy relics right away.
Only a groat. Come on, unbuckle your
        purse!"
290 "No, no," said he, "not I, and may the curse
Of Christ descend upon me if I do!
You'll have me kissing your old breeches too
And swear they were the relic of a
        saint. . . . "
    The Pardoner said nothing, not a word;
295 He was so angry that he couldn't speak.
"Well," said our Host, "if you're for
        showing pique,
I'll joke no more, not with an angry man."
    The worthy Knight immediately began,
Seeing the fun was getting rather rough,
300 And said, "No more, we've all had quite
        enough.
Now, Master Pardoner, perk up, look
        cheerly!
And you, Sir Host, whom I esteem so dearly,
I beg of you to kiss the Pardoner.
    "Come, Pardoner, draw nearer, my dear sir.
305 Let's laugh again and keep the ball in play."
They kissed, and we continued on our way.

---

5. *Avicenna's long relation,* a work on medicine by an
Arabian physician (A.D. 980-1037).

THINK AND DISCUSS

Understanding
1. How does the Pardoner earn his living?
2. Whom do the three rioters go in search of? Why?
3. What happens to the youngest rioter? to the other two?

Analyzing
4. How sound is the psychology used by the Pardoner to extort money? See, for example, lines 51–63 of his *Prologue*, describing the trick "worth a hundred marks a year" to him.
5. In the *Tale*, how is Death **personified**? If the old man is also a personification, what do you think he might represent?
6. How do the actions of the rioters prove the Pardoners' moral?
7. After revealing all his tricks to the other pilgrims and relating his tale, the Pardoner offers to sell them the same pardon he has already admitted is worthless. How do you account for this?

Extending
8. *The Pardoner's Tale* has been called one of the greatest short stories ever written. Explain why you agree or disagree.

APPLYING: Irony H🖋
See Handbook of Literary Terms, p. 912
Irony is a term used to describe the contrast between what appears to be and what really is. Different types of irony include verbal, dramatic, and situational, in which something occurs contrary to what is expected or intended.

1. In his *Prologue*, the Pardoner admits that he always uses the same text or moral in his sermon. What is ironic about his use of this particular text?
2. In the *Tale*, the old man tells the three rioters that they will find Death under a tree in a nearby grove. When they get there what do they find? What is the irony in this situation?
3. What is ironic about the deaths of the three rioters?

VOCABULARY
Word Analogies
An analogy is a similarity. Many standardized tests include word analogies, in which the same relationship exists between two sets of paired words. For example: *cup* is to *gallon* as *inch* is to *foot*. That is, a cup is a part of a gallon in the same way that an inch is a part of a foot; furthermore, they are all units of measure. Complete each of these sentences by filling in the appropriate word. You will not use all the words.

avarice	florins	pique
castigate	miscreant	publican

1. *Church* is to *minister* as *inn* is to _____.
2. *Pride* is to *peacock* as _____ is to *miser*.
3. _____ is to *insult* as *pleasure* is to *compliment*.
4. *Saint* is to *virtue* as _____ is to *sin*.
5. *Hunger* is to *food* as *poverty* is to _____.

COMPOSITION ◄━●
Describing the Pardoner's Preaching
Imagine that you are listening to the Pardoner preach. You can be either a person who believes the Pardoner to be a holy and honorable man, or a person who sees through his tricks. With your classmates as your audience, write a description of at least three paragraphs. In your first paragraph, describe his general appearance and how he behaves when preaching; in your second, describe his sermon and how the listeners react; in your third, summarize your own reactions. See "Writing About Characters" in the Writer's Handbook.

Writing to Persuade
F. N. Robinson, a distinguished editor of Chaucer, wrote: "In spite of his contemptible nature, physical and moral, the Pardoner is one of the most intellectual figures among the pilgrims and his performance is worthy of his powers." React to this comment in a composition of from three to five paragraphs. First, make clear whether you agree or disagree; then explain why you feel as you do, providing supporting details.

The Wife of Bath's Prologue

Geoffrey Chaucer

"If there were no authority on earth
Except experience, mine, for what it's
worth,
And that's enough for me, all goes to show
That marriage is a misery and a woe;
5 For let me say, if I may make so bold,
My lords, since when I was but twelve years
old,
Thanks be to God Eternal evermore,
Five husbands have I had at the church door;
Yes, it's a fact that I have had so many,
10 All worthy in their way, as good as any. . . .
Welcome the sixth, whenever he appears.
I can't keep continent for years and years.
No sooner than one husband's dead and gone
Some other Christian man shall take me on,
15 For then, so says the Apostle,[1] I am free
To wed, o' God's name, where it pleases me.
Wedding's no sin, so far as I can learn.
Better it is to marry than to burn. . . .
Show me a time or text where God
disparages,
20 Or sets a prohibition upon marriages
Expressly, let me have it! Show it me!
And where did He command virginity?
I know as well as you do, never doubt it,
All the Apostle Paul has said about it;
25 He said that as for precepts he had none.
One may advise a woman to be one;[2]
Advice is no commandment in my view.
He left it in our judgment what to do. . . .
And as for being married, he lets me do it
30 Out of indulgence, so there's nothing to it
In marrying me, suppose my husband dead;
There's nothing bigamous in such a
bed. . . .

"I grant it you. I'll never say a word
Decrying maidenhood although preferred
35 To frequent marriage; there are those who
mean
To live in their virginity, as clean
In body as in soul, and never mate.
I'll make no boast about my own estate.
As in a noble household, we are told,
40 Not every dish and vessel's made of gold,
Some are of wood, yet earn their master's
praise,
God calls His folk to Him in many ways.
To each of them God gave His proper gift,
Some this, some that, and left them to make
shift.
45 Virginity is indeed a great perfection,
And married continence, for God's
dilection,
But Christ, who of perfection is the well,
Bade not that everyone should go and sell
All that he had and give it to the poor
50 To follow in His footsteps, that is sure.
He spoke to those that would live perfectly,
And by your leave, my lords, that's not for
me.
I will bestow the flower of life, the honey,
Upon the acts and fruit of matrimony.
55 ". . . I'll have a husband yet
Who shall be both my debtor and my slave
And bear his tribulation to the grave
Upon his flesh, as long as I'm his wife.
For mine shall be the power all his life

---

1. Apostle, St. Paul. In the passages that follow, the Wife quotes scripture freely—but not always accurately—to support her arguments.
2. one, that is, a virgin.

60 Over his proper body, and not he,
Thus the Apostle Paul has told it me,
And bade our husbands they should love us
     well;
There's a command on which I like to
     dwell . . ."
     The Pardoner started up, and thereupon
65 "Madam," he said, "by God and by St.
     John,
That's noble preaching no one could surpass!
I was about to take a wife; alas!
Am I to buy it on my flesh so dear?
There'll be no marrying for me this year!"
70 "You wait," she said, "my story's not
     begun.
You'll taste another brew before I've done;
You'll find it doesn't taste as good as ale.
And when I've finished telling you my tale
Of tribulation in the married life
75 In which I've been an expert as a wife
That is to say, myself have been the whip.
So please yourself whether you want to sip
At that same cask of marriage I shall broach;
Be cautious before making the approach. . . ."
80   "Madam, I put it to you as a prayer,"
The Pardoner said, "go on as you began!
Tell us your tale, spare not for any man.
Instruct us younger men in your technique."
"Gladly," she answered, "if I am to speak.
85 But still I hope the company won't reprove me
Though I should speak as fantasy may move
     me,
And please don't be offended at my views;
They're really only offered to amuse.
     "Now, gentlemen, I'll on and tell my tale
90 And as I hope to drink good wine and ale
I'll tell the truth. Those husbands that I had,
Three of them were good and two were bad.
The three that I call 'good' were rich and
     old. . . .
I managed them so well by my technique
95 Each was delighted to go out and seek
And buy some pretty things for me to wear,
Happy if I as much as spoke them fair.
God knows how spitefully I used to scold
     them.

"Listen, I'll tell you how I used to hold
     them,
100 You knowing women, who can understand.
First put them in the wrong, and out of
     hand.
No one can be so bold—I mean no man—
At lies and swearing as a woman can.
This is no news, as you'll have realized,
105 To knowing ones, but to the misadvised.
A knowing wife if she is worth her salt
Can always prove her husband is at fault,
And even though the fellow may have heard
Some story told him by a little bird
110 She knows enough to prove the bird is crazy
And get her maid to witness she's a daisy,
With full agreement, scarce solicited.
But listen. Here's the sort of thing I said:
     " 'Now, sir old dotard, what is that you
     say?
115 Why is my neighbor's wife so smart and gay?
She is respected everywhere she goes.
I sit at home and have no decent clothes.
Why haunt her house? What are you doing
     there?
Are you so amorous? Is she so fair?
120 What, whispering secrets to our maid? For
     shame,
Sir ancient lecher! Time you dropped that
     game.
And if I see my gossip or a friend
You scold me like a devil! There's no end
If I as much as stroll towards his house.
125 Then you come home as drunken as a
     mouse,
You mount your throne and preach, chapter
     and verse
—All nonsense—and you tell me it's a curse
To marry a poor woman—she's expensive;
Or if her family's wealthy and extensive
130 You say it's torture to endure her pride
And melancholy airs, and more beside. . . .
     " 'You say that some desire us for our
     wealth,
Some for our shapeliness, our looks, our
     health,
Some for our singing, others for our dancing,

135 Some for our gentleness and dalliant
    glancing,
And some because our hands are soft and
    small;
By your account the devil gets us all. . . .
That's what you say as you stump off to bed,
You brute! You say no man of sense would
    wed,
140 That is, not if he wants to go to Heaven.
Wild thunderbolts and fire from the seven
Planets³ descend and break your withered
    neck!
    " 'You say that buildings falling into
    wreck,
And smoke, and scolding women, are the
    three
145 Things that will drive a man from home.
    Dear me!
What ails the poor old man to grumble so?
    " 'We women hide our faults to let them
    show
Once we are safely married, so you say.
There's a fine proverb for a popinjay!⁴
150   " 'You say that oxen, asses, hounds, and
    horses
Can be tried out on various ploys and
    courses;
And basins too, and dishes when you buy
    them,
Spoons, chairs, and furnishings, a man can
    try them
As he can try a suit of clothes, no doubt,
155 But no one ever tries a woman out
Until he's married her; old dotard crow!
And then you say she lets her vices show.
    " 'You also say we count it for a crime
Unless you praise our beauty all the time,
160 Unless you're always poring on our faces
And call us pretty names in public places;
Or if you fail to treat me to a feast
Upon my birthday—presents at the least—
Or to respect my nurse and her grey hairs,
165 Or be polite to all my maids upstairs
And to my father's cronies and his spies.
That's what you say, old barrelful of lies!
    " 'Then there's our young apprentice,

The Wife of Bath, from the Ellesmere Chaucer.

    handsome Johnny;
Because he has crisp hair that shines as
    bonny
170 As finest gold, and squires me up and down
You show your low suspicions in a frown.
I wouldn't have him, not if you died
    tomorrow!
    " 'And tell me this, God punish you with
    sorrow,
Why do you hide the keys of coffer doors?
175 It's just as much my property as yours.
Do you want to make an idiot of your wife?
Now, by the Lord that gave me soul and life,
    . . .
I think you'd like to lock me in your coffer!
"Go where you please, dear wife," you ought
    to offer,
180 "Amuse yourself! I shan't give ear to malice,

---

3. seven/Planets, the seven "wandering stars" studied by ancient astronomers: the sun, the moon, Mercury, Venus, Mars, Jupiter, and Saturn.
4. popinjay, parrot.

I know you for a virtuous wife, Dame Alice."
We cannot love a husband who takes charge
Of where we go. We like to be at large. . . .
   " 'And when a woman tries a mild display
185 In dress or costly ornament, you say
It is a danger to her chastity,
And then, bad luck to you, start making free
With Bible tags in the Apostle's name;[5]
"And in like manner, chastely and with
    shame,
190 You women should adorn yourselves," said
    he,
"And not with braided hair or jewelry
With pearl or golden ornament." What next!
I'll pay as much attention to your text
And rubric in such things as would a gnat.
195   " 'And once you said that I was like a cat,
For if you singe a cat it will not roam
And that's the way to keep a cat at home.
But when she feels her fur is sleek and gay
She can't be kept indoors for half a day
200 But off she takes herself as dusk is falling
To show her fur and go a-caterwauling.
Which means if I feel gay, as you suppose,
I shall run out to show my poor old clothes.
   " 'Silly old fool! You and your private
    spies!
205 Go on, beg Argus[6] with his hundred eyes
To be my bodyguard, that's better still!
But yet he shan't, I say, against my will.
I'll pull him by the beard, believe you me!
   " 'And once you said that principally three
210 Misfortunes[7] trouble earth, east, west and
    north,
And no man living could endure a fourth.
My dear sir shrew, Jesu cut short your life!
You preach away and say a hateful wife
Is reckoned to be one of these misfortunes.
215 Is there no other trouble that importunes
The world and that your parables could
    condemn?
Must an unhappy wife be one of them?
   " 'Then you compared a woman's love to
    Hell,
To barren land where water will not dwell,
220 And you compared it to a quenchless fire,

The more it burns the more is its desire
To burn up everything that burnt can be.
You say that just as worms destroy a tree
A wife destroys her husband and contrives,
225 As husbands know, the ruin of their lives.'
   "Such was the way, my lords, you
    understand
I kept my older husbands well in hand.
I told them they were drunk and their
    unfitness
To judge my conduct forced me to take
    witness
230 That they were lying. Johnny and my niece
Would back me up. O Lord, I wrecked their
    peace,
Innocent as they were, without remorse!
For I could bite and whinney like a horse
And launch complaints when things were all
    my fault;
235 I'd have been lost if I had called a halt.
First to the mill is first to grind your corn;
I attacked first and they were overborne,
Glad to apologize and even suing
Pardon for what they'd never thought of
    doing.
240   "I'd tackle one for wenching, out of hand,
Although so ill the man could hardly stand,
Yet he felt flattered in his heart because
He thought it showed how fond of him I was.
I swore that all my walking out at night
245 Was just to keep his wenching well in sight.
That was a dodge that made me shake with
    mirth;
But all such wit is given us at birth.
Lies, tears, and spinning are the things God
    gives

---

5. *Apostle's name.* The reference is to 1 Timothy 2:9.
Note that the Wife is accusing her husband of using the
same tactics that she constantly uses herself.
6. *Argus,* in Greek legend, a hundred-eyed giant who
never closed all his eyes in sleep at the same time and
therefore kept constant watch.
7. *three/Misfortunes.* She is alluding to Proverbs
30:21–23: "For three things the earth is disquieted, and
for four which it cannot bear: for a servant when he
reigneth; and a fool when he is filled with meat; for an
odious woman when she is married; and an handmaid
that is heir to her mistress."

alluding
to first
worm?

By nature to a woman, while she lives.
250 So there's one thing at least that I can boast,
That in the end I always ruled the roast;
Cunning or force was sure to make them
    stumble,
And always keeping up a steady
    grumble. . . .
    "I then would say, 'My dear, just take a
    peep!
255 What a meek look on Willikin our sheep!
Come nearer, husband, let me kiss your
    cheek;
You should be just as patient, just as meek;
Sweeten your heart. Your conscience needs
    a probe.
You're fond of preaching patience out of
    Job,[8]
260 And so be patient; practice what you preach,
And if you don't, my dear, we'll have to
    teach
You that it's nice to have a quiet life.
One of us must be master, man or wife,
And since a man's more reasonable, he
265 Should be the patient one, you must
    agree . . .
    "That's how my first three husbands were
    undone.
Now let me tell you of my last but one.
    "He was a reveller, was number four;
That is to say he kept a paramour.
270 Young, strong, and stubborn, I was full of
    rage
And jolly as a magpie in a cage.
Play me the harp and I would dance and sing,
Believe me, like a nightingale in spring,
If I had had a draught of sweetened
    wine. . . .
275   " . . . Whenever it comes back to me,
When I recall my youth and jollity,
It fairly warms the cockles of my heart!
This very day I feel a pleasure start,
Yes, I can feel it tickling at the root.
280 Lord, how it does me good! I've had my
    fruit,
I've had my world and time, I've had my
    fling!

But age that comes to poison everything
Has taken all my beauty and my pith.
Well, let it go, the devil go therewith!
285 The flour is gone, there is no more to say,
And I must sell the bran as best I may;
But still I mean to find my way to fun. . . .
Now let me tell you of my last but one.
    "I told you how it filled my heart with
    spite
290 To see another woman his delight,
By God and all His saints I made it good!
I carved him out a cross of the same wood,
Not with my body in a filthy way,
But certainly by seeming rather gay
295 To others, frying him in his own grease
Of jealousy and rage; he got no peace.
By God on earth I was his purgatory,[9]
For which I hope his soul may be in glory.
God knows he sang a sorry tune, he flinched,
300 And bitterly enough, when the shoe pinched.
And God and he alone can say how grim,
How many were the ways I tortured him.
    "He died when I came back from Jordan
    Stream[10]
And he lies buried under the rood-beam,[11]
305 Albeit that his tomb can scarce supply us
With such a show as that of King Darius
—Apelles[12] sculped it in a sumptuous
    taste—
But costly burial would have been mere
    waste.
Farewell to him, God give his spirit rest!
310 He's in his grave, he's nailed up in his chest.
    "Now of my fifth, last husband let me
    tell.

---

8. Job, Old Testament figure who keeps faith with God despite many sufferings.
9. purgatory, in the belief of some Christians, a place of temporary punishment for sin after death.
10. When I . . . Jordan Stream, when she returned from one of her pilgrimages to the Holy Land.
11. rood-beam, a beam usually between the chancel and the nave of a church, on which was placed a rood or crucifix. Burial within the chancel itself would have been more expensive.
12. Apelles, a famous Greek artist of the fourth century B.C.

God never let his soul be sent to Hell!
And yet he was my worst, and many a blow
He struck me still can ache along my row

315 Of ribs, and will until my dying day. . . .
Though he had beaten me in every bone
He still could wheedle me to love, I own.
I think I loved him best, I'll tell no lie.
He was disdainful in his love, that's why.

320 We women have a curious fantasy
In such affairs, or so it seems to me.
When something's difficult, or can't be had,
We crave and cry for it all day like mad.
Forbid a thing, we pine for it all night,

325 Press fast upon us and we take to flight;
We use disdain in offering our wares.
A throng of buyers sends prices up at fairs,
Cheap goods have little value, they suppose;
And that's a thing that every woman knows.

330 "My fifth and last—God keep his soul in
      health!
The one I took for love and not for wealth,
Had been at Oxford not so long before
But had left school and gone to lodge next
      door,
Yes, it was to my godmother's he'd gone.

335 God bless her soul! *Her* name was Alison.
She knew my heart and more of what I
      thought
Than did the parish priest, and so she
      ought! . . .
   "And so one time it happened that in
      Lent,
As I so often did, I rose and went

340 To see her, ever wanting to be gay
And go a-strolling, March, April, and May,
From house to house for chat and village
      malice.
   "Johnny (the boy from Oxford) and Dame
      Alice
And I myself, into the fields we went.

345 My husband was in London all that Lent;
All the more fun for me—I only mean
The fun of seeing people and being seen
By cocky lads; for how was I to know
Where or what graces Fortune might
      bestow?

350 And so I made a round of visitations,
Went to processions, festivals, orations,
Preachments and pilgrimages, watched the
      carriages
They use for plays and pageants, went to
      marriages,
And always wore my gayest scarlet dress.

355 "These worms, these moths, these mites,
      I must confess,
Got little chance to eat it, by the way.
Why not? Because I wore it every day.
   "Now let me tell you all that came to pass.
We sauntered in the meadows through the
      grass

360 Toying and dallying to such extent,
Johnny and I, that I grew provident
And I suggested, were I ever free
And made a widow, he should marry me.
And certainly—I do not mean to boast—

365 I ever was more provident than most
In marriage matters and in other such.
I never think a mouse is up to much
That only has one hole in all the house;
If that should fail, well, it's goodbye the
      mouse.

370 "I let him think I was as one enchanted
(That was a trick my godmother implanted)
And told him I had dreamt the night away
Thinking of him, and dreamt that as I lay
He tried to kill me. Blood had drenched the
      bed.

375 'But still it was a lucky dream,' I said,
'For blood betokens gold as I recall.'
It was a lie. I hadn't dreamt at all.
'Twas from my godmother I learnt my lore
In matters such as that, and many more.

380 "Well, let me see . . . what had I to
      explain?
Aha! By God, I've got the thread again.
   "When my fourth husband lay upon his
      bier
I wept all day and looked as drear as drear,
As widows must, for it is quite in place,

385 And with a handkerchief I hid my face.
Now that I felt provided with a mate
I wept but little, I need hardly state.

"To church they bore my husband on the
    morrow
With all the neighbors round him venting
    sorrow,
390 And one of them of course was handsome
    Johnny.
So help me God, I thought he looked so
    bonny
Behind the coffin! Heavens, what a pair
Of legs he had! Such feet, so clean and fair!
I gave my whole heart up, for him to hold.
395 He was, I think, some twenty winters old,
And I was forty then, to tell the truth.
But still, I always had a coltish tooth.
Yes, I'm gap-toothed; it suits me well I feel,
It is the print of Venus[13] and her seal.
400 So help me God I was a lusty one,
Fair, young and well-to-do, and full of
      fun! . . .
  "What shall I say? Before the month was
    gone
This gay young student, my delightful John,
Had married me in solemn festival.
405 I handed him the money, lands, and all
That ever had been given me before;
This I repented later, more and more.
None of my pleasures would he let me seek.
By God, he smote me once upon the cheek
410 Because I tore a page out of his book,
And that's the reason why I'm deaf. But
    look,
Stubborn I was, just like a lioness;
As to my tongue, a very wrangleress.
I went off gadding as I had before
415 From house to house, however much he
    swore.
Because of that he used to preach and scold,
Drag Roman history up from days of old,
How one Simplicius Gallus left his wife,
Deserting her completely all his life,
420 Only for poking out her head one day
Without a hat, upon the public way.
  "Some other Roman—I forget his
    name—
Because his wife went to a summer's game
Without his knowledge, left her in the lurch.

425 "And he would take the Bible up and
    search
For proverbs in Ecclesiasticus,[14]
Particularly one that has it thus:
'Suffer no wicked woman to gad about,'
And then would come the saying (need you
    doubt?)
430 *A man who seeks to build his house of sallows,*
A man who spurs a blind horse over fallows,
Or lets his wife make pilgrimage to Hallows,
Is worthy to be hanged upon the gallows.[15]
But all for naught. I didn't give a hen
435 For all his proverbs and his wise old men.
Nor would I take rebuke at any price;
I hate a man who points me out my vice,
And so, God knows, do many more than I.
That drove him raging mad, you may rely.
440 No more would I forbear him, I can promise.
  "Now let me tell you truly by St. Thomas
About that book and why I tore the page
And how he smote me deaf in very rage.
  "He had a book, he kept it on his shelf,
445 And night and day he read it to himself
And laughed aloud, although it was quite
    serious.
He called it *Theophrastus and Valerius*.[16] . . .
  "It was a book that dealt with wicked
    wives;
He knew more legends of them and their
    lives
450 Than there are good ones mentioned in the
    Bible.
For take my word for it, there is no libel
On women that the clergy will not paint,

---

13. gap-toothed . . . Venus. It was believed that people who were gap-toothed (with their front teeth set wide apart) had amorous natures.
14. Ecclesiasticus, one of the books of the Apocrypha, material included in the Vulgate, but not in Jewish or Protestant Bibles. The reference is to Ecclesiasticus 25:25: "Give neither a wicked woman liberty to gad abroad."
15. A man . . . gallows, a proverbial saying that apparently reflects Johnny's opinion of the Wife's pilgrimages. *Sallows* are willow twigs; *fallows* are fields that have been plowed but left unseeded; *hallows* are saints, or (as here) their shrines.
16. Theophrastus and Valerius, a satire on matrimony attributed to Walter Map, a wit and cynic who lived about A.D. 1200.

Except when writing of a woman-saint,
But never good of other women, though.
455 Who called the lion savage?[17] Do you know?
By God, if women had but written stories
Like those the clergy keep in oratories,
More had been written of man's wickedness
Than all the sons of Adam could
        redress. . . .
460   "Now to my purpose as I told you; look,
Here's how I got a beating for a book.
One evening Johnny, glowering with ire,
Sat with his book and read it by the fire.
And first he read of Eve whose wickedness
465 Brought all mankind to sorrow and distress,
Root-cause why Jesus Christ Himself was
        slain
And gave His blood to buy us back again.
Aye, there's the text where you expressly
        find
That woman brought the loss of all mankind.
470   "He read me then how Samson[18] as he
        slept
Was shorn of all his hair by her he kept,
And by that treachery Samson lost his eyes.
And then he read me, if I tell no lies,
All about Hercules and Deianire;[19]
475 She tricked him into setting himself on fire.
    "He left out nothing of the miseries
Occasioned by his wives to Socrates. . . . [20]
    "And then he told how one Latumius
Lamented to his comrade Arrius
480 That in his orchard-plot there grew a tree
On which his wives had hanged themselves,
        all three,
Or so he said, out of some spite or other;
To which this Arrius replied, 'Dear brother,
Give me a cutting from that blessed tree
485 And planted in my garden it shall be!' . . .
    "Who could imagine, who could figure
        out
The torture in my heart? It reached the top
And when I saw that he would never stop
Reading this cursed book, all night no
        doubt,
490 I suddenly grabbed and tore three pages out
Where he was reading, at the very place,

And fisted such a buffet in his face
That backwards down into our fire he fell.
    "Then like a maddened lion, with a yell
495 He started up and smote me on the head,
And down I fell upon the floor for dead.
    "And when he saw how motionless I lay
He was aghast and would have fled away,
But in the end I started to come to.
500 'O have you murdered me, you robber, you,
To get my land?' I said. 'Was that the game?
Before I'm dead I'll kiss you all the same.'
    "He came up close and kneeling gently
        down
He said, 'My love, my dearest Alison,
505 So help me God, I never again will hit
You, love; and if I did, you asked for it.
Forgive me!' But for all he was so meek
I up at once and smote him on the cheek
And said, 'Take that to level up the score!
510 Now let me die. I can't speak any more.'
    "We had a mort of trouble and heavy
        weather
But in the end we made it up together.
He gave the bridle over to my hand,
Gave me the government of house and land,
515 Of tongue and fist, indeed of all he'd got.
I made him burn that book upon the spot.
And when I'd mastered him, and out of
        deadlock
Secured myself the sovereignty in wedlock,
And when he said, 'My own and truest wife,
520 Do as you please for all the rest of life,
But guard your honor and my good estate,'
From that day forward there was no debate.
So help me God I was as kind to him
As any wife from Denmark to the rim

---

17. *Who . . . savage?* In one of Aesop's fables, a lion,
seeing a picture of a lion being killed by a man, points
out that all depends on the point of view; a lion would
paint a man being killed by a lion.
18. *Samson*, Old Testament figure betrayed by a woman.
19. *Hercules and Deianire.* The classical hero Hercules
was unfaithful to his wife, Deianire. She revenged herself
by giving him a poisoned shirt which caused him such
pain that he preferred to build a funeral pyre and die in its
flames.
20. *Socrates.* The Greek philosopher Socrates (469?–399
B.C.) was legendary as a hen-pecked husband.

525 Of India, and as true. And he to me.
And I pray God that sits in majesty
To bless his soul and fill it with his glory.
Now, if you'll listen, I will tell my story."
The Friar laughed when he had heard all this.
530 "Well, Ma'am," he said, "as God may send
me bliss,
This is a long preamble to a tale!"
But when the Summoner heard the Friar
rail,
"Just look!" he cried, "by the two arms of
God!
These meddling friars are always on the
prod!
535 Don't we all know a friar and a fly
Go buzzing into every dish and pie!
What do you mean with your 'preambulation'?
Amble yourself, trot, do a meditation!
You're spoiling all our fun with your
commotion."
540 The Friar smiled and said, "Is that your
motion?

I promise on my word before I go
To find occasion for a tale or so
About a summoner that will make us laugh."
"Well, damn your eyes, and on my own
behalf,"
545 The Summoner answered, "mine be
damned as well
If I can't think of several tales to tell
About the friars that will make you mourn
Before we get as far as Sittingbourne.
Have you no patience? Look, he's in a huff!"
550 Our Host called out, "Be quiet, that's
enough!
Shut up, and let the woman tell her tale.
You must be drunk, you've taken too much
ale.
Now, Ma'am, you go ahead and no demur."
"All right," she said, "it's just as you
prefer,
555 If I have license from this worthy friar."
"Nothing," said he, "that I should more
desire."

The Wife of Bath's Tale

Geoffrey Chaucer

When good King Arthur ruled in ancient
days,
(A king that every Briton loves to praise)
This was a land brimful of fairy folk.
The Elf Queen and her courtiers joined and
broke
5 Their elfin dance on many a green mead,
Or so was the opinion once, I read,
Hundreds of years ago, in days of yore.
But no one now sees fairies any more,
For now the saintly charity and prayer
10 Of holy friars seem to have purged the air;
They search the countryside through field
and stream
As thick as motes that speckle a sunbeam,

Blessing the halls, the chambers, kitchens,
bowers,
Cities and boroughs, castles, courts, and
towers,
15 Thorpes,[1] barns and stables, outhouses and
dairies,
And that's the reason why there are no
fairies. . . .
    Now it so happened, I began to say,
Long, long ago in good King Arthur's day,
There was a knight who was a lusty liver.
20 One day as he came riding from the river
He saw a maiden walking all forlorn

---

1. *Thorpes,* agricultural villages.

Ahead of him, alone as she was born.
And of that maiden, spite of all she said,
By very force he took her maidenhead.
25 This act of violence made such a stir,
So much petitioning of the king for her,
That he condemned the knight to lose his
    head
By course of law. He was as good as dead
(It seems that then the statutes took that
    view)
30 But that the queen, and other ladies too,
Implored the king to exercise his grace
So ceaselessly, he gave the queen the case
And granted her his life, and she could
    choose
Whether to show him mercy or refuse.
35   The queen returned him thanks with all
    her might,
And then she sent a summons to the knight
At her convenience, and expressed her will:
"You stand, for such is the position still,
In no way certain of your life," said she,
40 "Yet you shall live if you can answer me:
What is the thing that women most desire?
Beware the axe and say as I require.
    "If you can't answer on the moment,
    though,
I will concede you this: you are to go
45 A twelvemonth and a day to seek and learn
Sufficient answer, then you shall return.
I shall take gages² from you to extort
Surrender of your body to the court."
    Sad was the knight and sorrowfully sighed,
50 But there! All other choices were denied,
And in the end he chose to go away
And to return after a year and day
Armed with such answer as there might be
    sent
To him by God. He took his leave and went.
55   He knocked at every house, searched
    every place,
Yes, anywhere that offered hope of grace.
What could it be that women wanted most?
But all the same he never touched a coast,
Country, or town in which there seemed to
    be

60 Any two people willing to agree. . . .
    Some say the things we most desire are
    these:
Freedom to do exactly as we please,
With no one to reprove our faults and lies,
Rather to have one call us good and wise.
65 Truly there's not a woman in ten score
Who has a fault, and someone rubs the sore,
But she will kick if what he says is true;
You try it out and you will find so too.
However vicious we may be within
70 We like to be thought wise and void of sin.
Others assert we women find it sweet
When we are thought dependable, discreet
And secret, firm of purpose and controlled,
Never betraying things that we are told.
75 But that's not worth the handle of a rake;
Women conceal a thing? For Heaven's sake!
Remember Midas?³ Will you hear the tale?
    Among some other little things, now stale,
Ovid relates that under his long hair
80 The unhappy Midas grew a splendid pair
Of ass's ears; as subtly as he might,
He kept his foul deformity from sight;
Save for his wife, there was not one that
    knew.
He loved her best, and trusted in her too.
85 He begged her not to tell a living creature
That he possessed so horrible a feature.
And she—she swore, were all the world to
    win,
She would not do such villainy and sin
As saddle her husband with so foul a name;
90 Besides to speak would be to share the
    shame.
Nevertheless she thought she would have
    died
Keeping this secret bottled up inside;
It seemed to swell her heart and she, no
    doubt,
Thought it was on the point of bursting out.

---

2. *gages*, pledges, guarantees.
3. **Midas.** The source is Ovid's *Metamorphoses*, in which,
however, the secret is known by Midas' barber, not his
wife.

The knight and the hag on their wedding night, an illustration by Edward Burne-Jones
(1833–1898) for the Kelmscott Chaucer. 1896.

95   Fearing to speak of it to woman or man
Down to a reedy marsh she quickly ran
And reached the sedge. Her heart was all on
    fire
And, as a bittern bumbles in the mire,
She whispered to the water, near the ground,
100 "Betray me not, O water, with thy sound!
To thee alone I tell it: it appears
My husband has a pair of ass's ears!
Ah! My heart's well again, the secret's out!
I could no longer keep it, not a doubt."
105 And so you see, although we may hold fast
A little while, it must come out at last,
We can't keep secrets; as for Midas, well,
Read Ovid for his story; he will tell.
    This knight that I am telling you about
110 Perceived at last he never would find out
What it could be that women loved the best.
Faint was the soul within his sorrowful

breast
As home he went, he dared no longer stay;
His year was up and now it was the day.
115 As he rode home in a dejected mood,
Suddenly, at the margin of a wood,
He saw a dance upon the leafy floor
Of four and twenty ladies,[4] nay, and more.
Eagerly he approached, in hope to learn
120 Some words of wisdom ere he should return;
But lo! Before he came to where they were,
Dancers and dance all vanished into air!
There wasn't a living creature to be seen
Save one old woman crouched upon the
    green.
125 A fouler-looking creature I suppose
Could scarcely be imagined. She arose

---

4. *dance . . . ladies,* the fairy ring, a familiar element
in Celtic folklore.

And said, "Sir knight, there's no way on from
    here.
Tell me what you are looking for, my dear,
For peradventure that were best for you;
130 We old, old women know a thing or two."
    "Dear Mother," said the knight, "alack
       the day!
I am as good as dead if I can't say
What thing it is that women most desire;
If you could tell me I would pay your hire."
135 "Give me your hand," she said, "and swear
      to do
Whatever I shall next require of you
—If so to do should lie within your might—
And you shall know the answer before night."
"Upon my honor," he answered, "I agree."
140 "Then," said the crone, "I dare to
      guarantee
Your life is safe; I shall make good my claim.
Upon my life the queen will say the same.
Show me the very proudest of them all
In costly coverchief or jewelled caul[5]
145 That dare say no to what I have to teach.
Let us go forward without further speech."
And then she crooned her gospel in his ear
And told him to be glad and not to fear.
    They came to court. This knight, in full
      array,
150 Stood forth and said, "O Queen, I've kept my
      day
And kept my word and have my answer
    ready."
    There sat the noble matrons and the heady
Young girls, and widows too, that have the
    grace
Of wisdom, all assembled in that place,
155 And there the queen herself was throned to
    hear
And judge his answer. Then the knight drew
    near
And silence was commanded through the
    hall.
    The queen then bade the knight to tell
      them all
What thing it was that women wanted most.
160 He stood not silent like a beast or post,

But gave his answer with the ringing word
Of a man's voice and the assembly heard:
    "My liege and lady, in general," said he,
"A woman wants the selfsame sovereignty
165 Over her husband as over her lover,
And master him; he must not be above her.
That is your greatest wish, whether you kill
Or spare me; please yourself. I wait your
    will."
    In all the court not one that shook her head
170 Or contradicted what the knight had said;
Maid, wife, and widow cried, "He's saved his
    life!"
    And on the word up started the old wife,
The one the knight saw sitting on the green,
And cried, "Your mercy, sovereign lady
    queen!
175 Before the court disperses, do me right!
'Twas I who taught this answer to the knight,
For which he swore, and pledged his honor
    to it,
That the first thing I asked of him he'd do
    it.
So far as it should lie within his might.
180 Before this court I ask you then, sir knight,
To keep your word and take me for your
    wife;
For well you know that I have saved your
    life.
If this be false, deny it on your sword!"
    "Alas!" he said, "Old lady, by the Lord
185 I know indeed that such was my behest,
But for God's love think of a new request,
Take all my goods, but leave my body free."
"A curse on us," she said, "if I agree!
I may be foul, I may be poor and old,
190 Yet will not choose to be, for all the gold
That's bedded in the earth or lies above,
Less than your wife, nay, than your very
    love!"
    "My love?" said he. "By heaven, my
    damnation!
Alas that any of my race and station
195 Should ever make so foul a misalliance!"

---

5. *caul,* a netted cap worn by women.

Yet in the end his pleading and defiance
All went for nothing, he was forced to wed.
He takes his ancient wife and goes to bed.
   Now peradventure some may well suspect
200 A lack of care in me since I neglect
To tell of the rejoicings and display
Made at the feast upon their wedding day.
I have but a short answer to let fall;
I say there was no joy or feast at all,
205 Nothing but heaviness of heart and sorrow.
He married her in private on the morrow
And all day long stayed hidden like an owl,
It was such torture that his wife looked foul.
   Great was the anguish churning in his head
210 When he and she were piloted to bed;
He wallowed back and forth in desperate
      style.
His ancient wife lay smiling all the while;
At last she said, "Bless us! Is this, my dear,
How knights and wives get on together here?
215 Are these the laws of good King Arthur's
      house?
Are knights of his all so contemptuous?
I am your own beloved and your wife,
And I am she, indeed, that saved your life;
And certainly I never did you wrong.
220 Then why, this first of nights, so sad a song?
You're carrying on as if you were half-witted!
Say, for God's love, what sin have I
      committed?
I'll put things right if you will tell me how."
   "Put right?" he cried, "That never can be
      now!
225 Nothing can ever be put right again!
You're old, and so abominably plain,
So poor to start with, so lowbred to follow;
It's little wonder if I twist and wallow!
God, that my heart would burst within my
      breast!"
230   "Is that," said she, "the cause of your
      unrest?"
   "Yes, certainly," he said, "and can you
      wonder?"
   "I could set right what you suppose a
      blunder,
That's if I cared to, in a day or two,

If I were shown more courtesy by you.
235 Just now," she said, "you spoke of gentle
      birth,
Such as descends from ancient wealth and
      worth.
If that's the claim you make for gentlemen
Such arrogance is hardly worth a hen.
Whoever loves to work for virtuous ends,
240 Public and private, and who most intends
To do what deeds of gentleness he can,
Take him to be the greatest gentleman.
Christ wills we take our gentleness from
      Him,
Not from a wealth of ancestry long dim,
245 Though they bequeath their whole
      establishment
By which we claim to be of high descent.
Our fathers cannot make us a bequest
Of all those virtues that became them best
And earned for them the name of gentlemen,
250 But bade us follow them as best we
      can. . . .
For of our parents nothing can we claim
Save temporal things, and these may hurt
      and maim.
   "But everyone knows this as well as I;
For if gentility were implanted by
255 The natural course of lineage down the line,
Public or private, could it cease to shine
In doing the fair work of gentle deed?
No vice or villainy could then bear seed. . . .
   "Gentility is only the renown
260 For bounty that your fathers handed down,
Quite foreign to your person, not your own;
Gentility must come from God alone.
That we are gentle comes to us by grace
And by no means is it bequeathed with
      place. . . .
265 And therefore, my dear husband, I conclude
That even if my ancestors were rude,
Yet God on high—and so I hope He will—
Can grant me grace to live in virtue still,
A gentlewoman only when beginning
270 To live in virtue and to shrink from sinning.
   "As for my poverty which you reprove,
Almighty God Himself in whom we move,

Believe, and have our being, chose a life
Of poverty, and every man or wife,
275 Nay, every child can see our Heavenly King
Would never stoop to choose a shameful
　　thing.
No shame in poverty if the heart is gay,
As Seneca[6] and all the learned say.
He who accepts his poverty unhurt
280 I'd say is rich although he lacked a shirt.
But truly poor are they who whine and fret
And covet what they cannot hope to get.
And he that, having nothing, covets not,
Is rich, though you may think he is a
　　sot. . . .
285 And since it's no offense, let me be plain;
Do not rebuke my poverty again.
　　"Lastly you taxed me, sir, with being old.
Yet even if you never had been told
By ancient books, you gentlemen engage
290 Yourselves in honor to respect old age.
To call an old man 'father' shows good
　　breeding,
And this could be supported from my
　　reading.
　　"You say I'm old and fouler than a fen.
You need not fear to be a cuckold, then.
295 Filth and old age, I'm sure you will agree,
Are powerful wardens upon chastity.
Nevertheless, well knowing your delights,
I shall fulfil your worldly appetites.
　　"You have two choices; which one will
　　you try?
300 To have me old and ugly till I die,
But still a loyal, true, and humble wife
That never will displease you all her life,
Or would you rather I were young and pretty
And take your chance what happens in a city
305 Where friends will visit you because of me,
Yes, and in other places too, maybe.
Which would you have? The choice is all
　　your own."
The knight thought long, and with a piteous
　　groan
At last he said, with all the care in life,
310 "My lady and my love, my dearest wife,
I leave the matter to your wise decision.

You make the choice yourself, for the
　　provision
Of what may be agreeable and rich
In honor to us both, I don't care which;
315 Whatever pleases you suffices me."
　　"And have I won the mastery?" said she,
"Since I'm to choose and rule as I think fit?"
"Certainly, wife," he answered her, "that's
　　it."
"Kiss me," she cried. "No quarrels! On my
　　oath
320 And word of honor, you shall find me both,
That is, both fair and faithful as a wife;
May I go howling mad and take my life
Unless I prove to be as good and true
As ever wife was since the world was new!
325 And if tomorrow when the sun's above
I seem less fair than any lady-love,
Than any queen or empress east or west,
Do with my life and death as you think best.
Cast up the curtain, husband. Look at me!"
330 　　And when indeed the knight had looked
　　to see,
Lo, she was young and lovely, rich in
　　charms.
In ecstasy he caught her in his arms,
His heart went bathing in a bath of blisses
And melted in a hundred thousand kisses,
335 And she responded in the fullest measure
With all that could delight or give him
　　pleasure.
　　So they lived ever after to the end
In perfect bliss; and may Christ Jesus send
Us husbands meek and young and fresh in
　　bed,
340 And grace to overbid them when we wed.
And—Jesu hear my prayer!—cut short the
　　lives
Of those who won't be governed by their
　　wives;
And all old, angry niggards of their pence,
God send them soon a very pestilence!
c. 1385–1400

---

6. Seneca (4? B.C.–A.D. 65), Roman Stoic philosopher and
writer.

Comment

A Fifteenth-Century Valentine

The letter below, which is the earliest extant valentine, comes from the Paston Letters, a collection of correspondence written between about 1420 and 1530. The Pastons were a wealthy family living in Norfolk, a county in eastern England. Most of the letters deal with questions of property, which even enter into affairs of the heart, as the letter below, written by Margery Brews to John Paston in February, 1477, poignantly indicates. The question is whether John cares enough to marry her with a rather small dowry. (He did.) The spelling has been modernized.

A knight and lady in a garden. 15th century. *British Library, London*

Right worshipful and well-beloved Valentine, in my most humble wise [way] I recommend me unto you, &c. And heartily I thank you for the letter which that you sent me by John Beckerton, whereby I understand and know that you be purposed to come to Topcroft [Margery's home] in short time, and without any errand or matter but only to have a conclusion of the matter [i.e., her dowry] betwixt my father and you. I would be most glad of any creature alive so that the matter might grow to effect. And there as you say, an [if] you come and find the matter no more toward than you did aforetime you would no more put my father and my lady my mother to no cost nor business for that cause a good while after, which causes my heart to be full heavy; and that if you come and the matter take to none effect, then should I be much more sorry and full of heaviness.

And as for myself, I have done and understand in the matter that [i.e., all that] I can or may, as God knows. And I let you plainly understand that my father will no more money part withal in that behalf but one hundred pounds and fifty marks, which is right far from the accomplishment of your desire. Wherefore, if that you could be content with that good [i.e., that amount of dowry], and my poor person, I would be the merriest maiden on ground. And if you think not yourself so satisfied, or that you might have much more good, as I have understood by you afore, good, true, and loving Valentine, that you take no such labor upon you as to come more for that matter; but let it pass, and never more to be spoken of, as I may be your true lover and bedewoman during my life [i.e., pray for him while she lives].

No more unto you at this time, but Almighty Jesus preserve you both body and soul, &c.

By your Valentine, MARGERY BREWS

THINK AND DISCUSS
Understanding
1. According to the Wife, what makes a good husband? How does she keep him that way?
2. What does the fifth husband's book (see lines 444–485) have to say about women?
3. How does the Wife react to the book?

Analyzing
4. At the beginning of her *Prologue*, the Wife says, "Please don't be offended at my views;/ They're really only offered to amuse" (lines 87–88). Does she mean it?
5. While her fourth husband was away, the Wife "made a round of visitations" (line 350). Why did she go? Why is she currently traveling to Canterbury?
6. In what ways does the story the Wife tells fit her personality and attitudes?

APPLYING: Allusion H₧
See Handbook of Literary Terms, page 894
An **allusion** is a brief reference to a person, place, event, or work of art. An allusion can convey much information concisely. For example, at the beginning of her tale, the Wife alludes to King Arthur, thus providing an immediate setting in time and place and suggesting that her tale will have the same legendary quality.

1. What is the purpose of the allusion to Midas in *The Wife of Bath's Tale* (line 77)?
2. The Wife alludes to St. Paul in line 15 of her *Prologue*, and she has her husband allude to St. Paul in line 188. What different purposes do these two allusions serve?
3. Where might the Wife have learned all these things she alludes to? What might be her purpose for mentioning them at this time?

THINKING SKILLS
Evaluating
To evaluate is to make a judgment based on some sort of standard, as when the Wife judges her husbands to be "All worthy in their way."

1. Are the Wife's arguments about how men and women should treat each other convincing?
2. Is her *Tale* convincing, or does it seem contrived to prove her point?

VOCABULARY
Prefixes and Roots
A prefix is a word part added to the beginning of a root, or base word, to change its meaning. Knowledge of prefixes and roots can sometimes help you understand an unfamiliar word. Answer these questions about words with prefixes.

1. *Precaution* is care taken in advance. Would you expect to find a *preamble* before, in the middle of, or after a work?
2. A *mischance* is an unfortunate happening. Would two people be happy in a *misalliance?*
3. To *exhale* is to breathe out. If your money has been *extorted*, do you have more of it or less?
4. *Disjointed* means "taken apart." If several people *disperse*, where are they?
5. To *project* is to throw or cast forward. Would a *provident* person be prepared for the future?

COMPOSITION ◄▬
Composing a Link
Chaucer often uses brief "links"—short sections of dialogue involving several of the pilgrims—to bridge the large divisions of *The Canterbury Tales*. Prepare a link of your own (it may be in prose) in which several pilgrims react to *The Wife of Bath's Tale*. Your link should be 250–350 words in length, and your audience will be your classmates.

Analyzing the Wife of Bath's Views
Do you feel that the Wife's views on men and women are specifically medieval, or do they have validity today? Write an essay of three to five paragraphs in which you state your opinion of her views. First summarize the Wife's opinion and illustrate it with details from her *Prologue* and *Tale*. Then explain how valid such views are today. Support your statements with details from your personal experiences or reading.

One of the first books from William Caxton's new printing press was a retelling of the adventures of King Arthur and his Knights of the Round Table. The book was distinguished by the lively, cadenced prose style of its author, Sir Thomas Malory. Although today we know the work as *Morte Darthur (The Death of Arthur)*, from one of the adventures it contains, on the title page of Caxton's edition it is called *The Birth, Life and Acts of King Arthur, of his Noble Knights of the Round Table, their marvelous enquests and adventures, the achieving of the San Greal and in the end Le Morte Darthur with the Dolorous Death and Departing out of this World of them All*—surely an all-inclusive title. Only one complete copy of Caxton's first edition, dated 1485, survives today (at the Pierpont Morgan Library in New York).

Scholars have been able to discover only scattered details of Malory's life. In 1433 or 1434, on the death of his father, Malory inherited the family estates in Warwickshire and Leicestershire. Later events indicate that he made the Warwickshire property his home, for in 1436 he served under the Earl of Warwick at the siege of Calais in the Hundred Years' War, and in 1445 he represented Warwickshire in Parliament.

Malory's troubles began in the 1450s when, in a period of less than ten years, he was accused, among other things, of attempting to murder the Duke of Buckingham; of breaking down the doors of the Cistercian Abbey at Coombe with a hundred men; of stealing cattle and sheep; and of assault and kidnaping, extortion, and jailbreaking. The latter charge certainly was true, for in July, 1451, Malory escaped from Coleshill Prison by swimming the moat, and in October, 1454, he broke out of Colchester Castle in the company of a group of armed men. Most of Malory's activities, especially those in which he was accompanied by numbers of other men, sound less like the acts of a felon and more like the armed sorties that took place just before and during the Wars of the Roses.

However, in 1462 Malory was out of jail and with the Earl of Warwick and King Edward IV (of the House of York, who assumed the throne in 1461), fighting against the Scots and French who were supporting the deposed Henry VI (of the House of Lancaster, who had ruled from 1422 to 1461, in a reign broken by periods of madness).

Later, when for political reasons the Earl of Warwick changed sides, shifting his allegiance to the House of Lancaster, Malory followed suit. He was specifically excluded, by name, from the general pardon which Edward extended to the Lancastrians in 1468, and then or shortly thereafter was put into Newgate Prison. Newgate happened to be located just across the road from the Grey Friars monastery, which had a collection of manuscripts, about twenty of them being legends of Arthur, mostly in French. Perhaps this was where Malory obtained the "books of French" that he mentions as his source, for it was in Newgate that he wrote *Morte Darthur*—and it was in Newgate that he died on March 14, 1471.

The Day of Destiny

from **Morte Darthur**
Sir Thomas Malory

Malory's *Morte Darthur* is the most complete single version of the tales of King Arthur and his court that has been written in English. It represents the drawing together of tales from various English and French versions, many of them contradictory. The historical sources of the Arthurian legend remain obscure. Arthur was probably a Celtic chieftain who lived in Britain during the fifth century and fought the invading Anglo-Saxons, Picts, and Scots.

Sometime during the height of the Middle Ages, however, Arthur became associated with the code of chivalry and with medieval French romances about Lancelot and the Holy Grail. Through these diverse sources Arthur ultimately emerged in song and story as the embodiment of the ideal knight.

"The Day of Destiny" describes the end of King Arthur's reign and the dissolution of the order which he, along with his Knights of the Round Table, has established. This end grows out of the corruption within the royal court itself. Arthur's illegitimate son Mordred knows of the secret love between Arthur's wife, Queen Guinevere (gwin′ə vir), and his best friend, Sir Lancelot. One night Mordred leads a band of knights to Guinevere's chamber, where they find the Queen with Lancelot.

Although he is reluctant, Arthur feels obligated to obey the law of the land and to burn his wife at the stake. However, at the last minute Lancelot rescues her, killing the two knights who were guarding her. Lancelot subsequently flees to a castle in France and Arthur forgives Guinevere; but Gawain (gä′wān, gä′win), the brother of the dead knights, demands vengeance on Lancelot. His hatred forces Arthur to lead his men on an attack against Lancelot's French fortress. In the ensuing battles Lancelot seriously wounds Gawain but refuses to kill him.

Meanwhile, Mordred senses his chance. With Arthur away in France, he leads a rebellion in England, claiming the throne and trying to seize Guinevere as his queen. She flees to the Tower of London. Arthur, returning to defend his crown, battles Mordred for the first time at Dover, where Gawain is fatally wounded. Before his death he writes a letter to Lancelot ending their feud and asking Lancelot to return to England to help Arthur. After a second, inconclusive battle with Mordred's forces, Arthur regroups his men and moves westward.

King Arthur, detail from the Nine Heroes Tapestries. French, circa 1385. *Metropolitan Museum of Art, New York*

And quickly King Arthur moved himself with his army along the coastline westward, toward Salisbury. And there was a day assigned betwixt King Arthur and Sir Mordred, that they should meet upon a field beside Salisbury and not far from the coast. And this day was assigned as Monday after Trinity Sunday,[1] whereof King Arthur was passing glad that he might be avenged upon Sir Mordred.

Then Sir Mordred stirred up a crowd of people around London, for those from Kent, Sussex and Surrey, Essex, Suffolk, and Norfolk stayed for the most part with Sir Mordred. And many a full noble knight drew unto him and also to the King; but they that loved Sir Lancelot drew unto Sir Mordred.

So upon Trinity Sunday at night King Arthur dreamed a wonderful dream, and in his dream it seemed that he saw upon a platform a chair, and the chair was fixed to a wheel,[2] and there upon sat King Arthur in richest cloth of gold that might be made. And the King dreamed there was under him, far below him, a hideous deep black water, and therein were all kinds of serpents and dragons and wild beasts foul and horrible. And suddenly the King dreamed that the wheel turned up side down, and he fell among the serpents, and every beast took him by a limb. And then the King cried out as he lay in his bed,

"Help! help!"

And then knights, squires, and yeomen awaked the King, and then he was so amazed that he knew not where he was. And so he remained awake until it was nearly day, and then he fell into a slumber again, neither sleeping nor completely awake.

Then it seemed to the King that there came Sir Gawain unto him with a number of fair ladies with him. So when King Arthur saw him he said,

"Welcome, my sister's son. I thought you had died! And now I see thee alive, great is my debt to Almighty Jesus. Ah, fair nephew, who be these ladies that come hither with you?"

"Sir," said Sir Gawain, "all these be fair ladies for whom I have fought for, when I was a living man. And all these are those that I did battle for

in righteous quarrels, and God hath given them that aid for their earnest prayers; and because I did battle for them for their rights, they brought me hither unto you. Thus hath God given me leave for to warn you of your death: for if ye fight tomorrow with Sir Mordred, as ye both have agreed, doubt ye not ye shall be slain, and the greatest part of your people on both sides. And for the great concern and good that Almighty Jesus has had for you, and for pity of you and many other good men that shall be slain, God hath sent me to you of His special grace to give you warning that in no way ye do battle tomorrow, but instead that ye make a treaty for a month and a day. And request this urgently, so that tomorrow you can delay. For within a month shall come Sir Lancelot with all his noble knights, and rescue you loyally, and slay Sir Mordred and all that ever will stay with him."

Then Sir Gawain and all the ladies vanished, and at once the King called upon his knights, squires, and yeomen, and charged them quickly to fetch his noble lords and wise bishops unto him. And when they were come the King told them of his vision; that Sir Gawain had told him and warned him that if he fought on the morn, he should be slain. Then the King commanded Sir Lucan the Butler and his brother Sir Bedivere the Bold, with two bishops with them, and charged them in any way to make a treaty for a month and a day with Sir Mordred:

"And spare not, offer him lands and goods as much as ye think reasonable."

So then they departed and came to Sir Mordred where he had a grim host of a hundred thousand, and there they entreated Sir Mordred a long time. And at the last Sir Mordred agreed for to take over Cornwall and Kent during King Arthur's lifetime;

---

1. **Trinity Sunday,** the eighth Sunday after Easter.
2. **wheel,** the wheel of fortune, symbolizing the rapid changes of human destiny; it was a favorite medieval image.

From Part IV of *The Most Piteous Tale of the Morte Darthur Saunz Guerdon,* slightly modernized, from the Winchester MS. version in *The Works of Thomas Malory* edited by Eugène Vinaver (Oxford University Press, 1947, 1967).

and after that all England, after the days of King Arthur.

Then were they agreed that King Arthur and Sir Mordred should meet betwixt both their hosts, and each of them should bring fourteen persons. And so they came with this word unto Arthur. Then he said,

"I am glad that this is done"; and so he went into the field.

And when King Arthur departed he warned all his host that if they saw any sword drawn, "look ye come on fiercely and slay that traitor, Sir Mordred, for I in no way trust him." In like manner Sir Mordred warned his host that "and ye see any manner of sword drawn, look that ye come on fiercely and so slay all that before you stand, for in no way will I trust in this treaty." And in the same way said Sir Mordred unto his host: "for I know well my father will be avenged upon me."

And so they met as they had arranged, and were agreed and accorded thoroughly. And wine was fetched, and they drank together. Just then came an adder out of a little heath-bush, and it stung a knight in the foot. And so when the knight felt himself so stung, he looked down and saw the adder; and at once he drew his sword to slay the adder, and thought of no other harm. And when the host on both sides saw that sword drawn, then they blew trumpets and horns, and shouted grimly, and so both hosts attacked each other. And King Arthur mounted his horse and said, "Alas, this unhappy day!" and so rode to his men, and Sir Mordred in like wise.

And never since was there seen a more grievous battle in no Christian land, for there was only slashing and riding, thrusting and striking, and many a grim word was there spoken of one to the other, and many a deadly stroke. But ever King Arthur rode through the battle against Sir Mordred many times and acted full nobly, as a noble king should do, and at all times he never hesitated. And Sir Mordred did his utmost that day and put himself in great peril.

And thus they fought all the day long, and never ceased 'till the noble knights were fallen on the cold earth. And yet they fought still 'till it was near

The combat of Arthur and Mordred at Camlan, from *St. Albans Chronicle*. Circa 1470. *Lambeth Palace Library*

night, and by then was there a hundred thousand lay dead upon the earth. Then was King Arthur wild with wrath beyond measure, when he saw his people so slain because of him.

And so he looked about himself and could see no more of all his host and of good knights left no more alive but two knights: Sir Lucan the Butler and his brother, Sir Bedivere; and yet they were very badly wounded.

"Jesus have mercy!" said the King, "where are all my noble knights gone? Alas, that ever I should see this grievous day! For now," said King Arthur, "I am come to mine end. But would to God," said he, "that I knew now where were that traitor Sir Mordred that hath caused all this mischief."

Then King Arthur looked about and was aware where stood Sir Mordred leaning upon his sword among a great heap of dead men.

"Now give me my spear," said King Arthur unto Sir Lucan, "for yonder I have seen the traitor that all this woe hath wrought."

"Sir, let him be," said Sir Lucan, "for he brings misfortune. And if ye pass this unfortunate day ye shall be right well revenged. And, good lord, remember ye of your night's dream and what the spirit of Sir Gawain told you last night, and God of His great goodness hath preserved you hitherto. And for God's sake, my lord, leave this battle, for, blessed be God, ye have won the field: for yet be here three alive, and with Sir Mordred is not one alive. And therefore if ye leave now, this wicked day of destiny is past!"

"Now come death, come life," said the King, "now I see him yonder alone, he shall never escape my hands! For at a better advantage shall I never have him."

"God speed you well!" said Sir Bedivere.

Then the King took his spear in both his hands, and ran towards Sir Mordred, crying out and saying,

"Traitor, now is thy death-day come!"

And when Sir Mordred saw King Arthur he ran towards him with his sword drawn in his hands, and there King Arthur struck Sir Mordred under the shield, with a thrust of his spear, through and beyond the body more than a foot. And when Sir Mordred felt that he had his death's wound he thrust himself with the might that he had up to the hand guard of King Arthur's spear, and then he smote his father, King Arthur, with his sword holding it in both his hands, upon the side of the head, so that the sword pierced the helmet and the outer membrane of the brain. And with that Sir Mordred dashed down stark dead to the earth.

And noble King Arthur fell in a swoon to the earth, and there he swooned several times, and Sir Lucan and Sir Bedivere several times lifted him up. And so weakly betwixt them they led him to a little chapel not far from the sea, and when the King was there, he thought himself reasonably eased.

Then heard they people cry in the field.

"Now go thou, Sir Lucan," said the King, "and help me to learn what means that noise in the field."

So Sir Lucan departed, though he was grievously wounded in many places; and as he rode he saw and noticed by the moonlight how the plunderers and robbers were come into the field to plunder and to rob many a full noble knight of brooches and bracelets and of many a good ring and many a rich jewel. And those that were not yet dead, there they slew them for their armor and their gold.

When Sir Lucan understood this he came to the King as soon as he might, and told him all which he had heard and seen.

"Therefore by my advice," said Sir Lucan, "it is best that we bring you to some town."

"I would that it were so," said the King, "but I may not stand, my head fails so. . . . Ah, Sir Lancelot!" said King Arthur, "this day have I missed thee! And alas, that ever I was against thee! For now I have my death, whereof Sir Gawain warned me in my dream."

Then Sir Lucan took up the King on one side and Sir Bedivere the other side, and in the lifting up the King swooned, and in the lifting Sir Lucan fell in a swoon, and part of his guts fell out of his body, and with that the noble knight's heart burst. And when the King awoke he beheld Sir Lucan, how he lay foaming at the mouth and part of his guts lay at his feet.

"Alas," said the King, "this is to me a very sad sight, to see this noble duke die so for my sake, for he would have helped me that had more need of help than I! Alas, that he would not complain for himself, for his heart was so set to help me. Now Jesu have mercy upon his soul!"

Then Sir Bedivere wept for the death of his brother.

"Now leave this mourning and this weeping, gentle knight," said the King, "for all this will not help me. For know thou well, if I might live myself, the death of Sir Lucan would grieve me evermore. But my time passeth on fast," said the King. "Therefore," said King Arthur unto Sir Bedivere, "take thou here Excalibur, my good sword, and go with it to the yonder water side; and when thou comest there, I charge thee throw my sword in that water, and come again and tell me what thou seest there."

"My lord," said Sir Bedivere, "your commandment shall be done, and lightly bring you word again."

So Sir Bedivere departed. And on the way he beheld that noble sword, and the pommel and the haft was all precious stones. And then he said to himself, "If I throw this rich sword in the water, of this shall never come good, but harm and loss." And then Sir Bedivere hid Excalibur under a tree, and so as soon as he might he came again unto the King and said he had been at the water and had thrown the sword into the water.

Sir Bedivere returns Excalibur to the Lady of the Lake, from a 14th century French manuscript. *The British Library, London*

"What saw thou there?" said the King.

"Sir," he said, "I saw nothing but waves and wind."

"That is untruly said by thee," said the King. "And therefore go thou lightly again, and do my commandment; as thou art to me beloved and dear, spare not, but throw it in."

Then Sir Bedivere returned again and took the sword in his hand; and yet he thought it a sin and shame to throw away that noble sword. And so again he hid the sword and returned again and told the king that he had been at the water and done his commandment.

"What sawest thou there?" said the King.

"Sir," he said, "I saw nothing but lapping waters and darkening waves."

"Ah, traitor unto me and untrue," said King Arthur, "now hast thou betrayed me twice! Who would believe that thou hast been to me so beloved and dear, and also named so noble a knight, that thou would betray me for the wealth of this sword? But now go again lightly; for thy long tarrying putteth me in great jeopardy of my life, for I am growing cold. And if thou do not now as I bid thee, if ever I may see thee, I shall slay thee by mine own hands, for thou wouldst for my rich sword see me dead."

Then Sir Bedivere departed and went to the sword and lightly took it up, and so he went unto the water side. And there he bound the belt about the hilt, and threw the sword as far into the water as he might. And there came an arm and an hand above the water, and took it and seized it, and shook it thrice and brandished, and then vanished with the sword into the water.

So Sir Bedivere came again to the King and told

him what he saw.

"Alas," said the King, "help me hence, for I dread me I have tarried over long."

Then Sir Bedivere took the King upon his back and so went with him to the water side. And when they were there, even close by the bank floated a little barge with many fair ladies on it, and among them all was a queen, and all of them had black hoods. And all of them wept and shrieked when they saw King Arthur.

"Now put me into that barge," said the King.

And so he did softly, and there received him three ladies with great mourning. And so they set him down, and in one of their laps King Arthur laid his head. And then the queen said,

"Ah, my dear brother! Why have ye tarried so long from me? Alas, this wound on your head hath caught overmuch cold!"

And then they rowed away from the land, and Sir Bedivere beheld all those ladies go away from him. Then Sir Bedivere cried out and said,

"Ah, my lord Arthur, what shall become of me, now ye go from me and leave me here alone among mine enemies?"

"Comfort thyself," said the King, "and do as well as thou mayest, for in me is no trust for to trust in. For I must go into the vale of Avilion[3] to heal me of my grievous wound. And if thou hear never more of me, pray for my soul!"

But ever the queen and ladies wept and shrieked, that it was pitiful to hear. As soon as Sir Bedivere had lost sight of the barge he wept and wailed, and so entered the forest and traveled all night.

And in the morning he was aware, betwixt two wan woods, of a chapel and a hermitage. Then was Sir Bedivere fearful, and thither he went, and when he came into the chapel he saw where lay a hermit groveling on all fours, close there by a tomb was new dug. When the hermit saw Sir Bedivere he knew him well, for he was but little before Bishop of Canterbury that Sir Mordred put to flight.

"Sir," said Sir Bedivere, "what man is there here buried that ye pray so earnestly for?"

"Fair son," said the hermit, "I know not truly but only guess. But this same night, at midnight, there came a number of ladies and brought here a dead corpse and prayed me to bury him. And here they offered a hundred candles, and they gave me a thousand coins."

"Alas!" said Sir Bedivere, "that was my lord King Arthur, which lieth here buried in this chapel."

Then Sir Bedivere swooned, and when he awoke he prayed the hermit that he might stay with him still, there to live with fasting and prayers:

"For from hence will I never go," said Sir Bedivere, "by my will, but all days of my life stay here to pray for my lord Arthur."

"Sir, ye are welcome to me," said the hermit, "for I know you better than you think that I do: for ye are Sir Bedivere the Bold, and the full noble Duke Sir Lucan the Butler was your brother."

Then Sir Bedivere told the hermit all as ye have heard before, and so he remained with the hermit that was before the Bishop of Canterbury. And there Sir Bedivere put upon himself poor clothes, and served the hermit full lowly in fasting and in prayers.

Thus of Arthur I find no more written in books that have been written, nothing more of the very certainty of his brave death I never read . . .

Yet some men say in many parts of England that King Arthur is not dead, but had by the will of Our Lord Jesu gone into another place; and men say that he shall come again, and he shall win the Holy Cross. Yet I will not say that it shall be so, but rather would I say: here in this world he changed his life. And many men say that there is written upon the tomb this:

HIC IACET ARTHURUS,
REX QUONDAM REXQUE FUTURUS.

Here lies Arthur, King Once and King That Will Be.

1468–1470   1485

---

3. *Avilion* (əvil′yən) or Avalan (av′ə lon), "the isle of apples," one of the paradisal islands of Celtic mythology.

THINK AND DISCUSS
Understanding
1. What does Arthur do to try to avoid the battle? Why does he do so?
2. How does the truce between Arthur and Mordred come to be broken?
3. What does Arthur command Bedivere to do? How does Bedivere carry out Arthur's commandment?

Analyzing
4. What is **foreshadowed** by Arthur's dreams on the night before the battle?
5. What **theme** is suggested by the appearance of the adder on the "Day of Destiny"?
6. Arthur insists on fighting Mordred after the battle is over. What does this demonstrate about his character?
7. What remains obscure about Arthur's fate?
8. Discuss the role of magic in this selection.

Extending
9. What do the plunderers Sir Lucan sees on the battlefield suggest about England's future after Arthur's death?
10. Malory mentions that Arthur's *epitaph*—the inscription on his tomb—is "King Once and King That Will Be," and the notion that Arthur did not die but remained alive has persisted for centuries. Why might people be attracted to such a belief?

APPLYING: Protagonist/Antagonist HƷ
See Handbook of Literary Terms, p. 919

In literature, the hero or leading character, with whom the reader identifies, is called the **protagonist**. The person or force opposed to the protagonist is the **antagonist**. For example, in *Beowulf* the protagonist is Beowulf, and one antagonist is Grendel.

1. Who is the protagonist in *Morte Darthur*? How can you tell?
2. Who is the antagonist? How do you know?
3. Beside the antagonist, are there forces that seem to be working against the protagonist?

THINKING SKILLS
Synthesizing
You are synthesizing when you combine parts or elements, sometimes adding your own creative ideas, to reach a new understanding or create a new work.

1. How do King Arthur and Beowulf both contribute to modern concepts of a hero?
2. As a group, create and write an adventure for Arthur that contains all the elements that make up a medieval romance.

COMPOSITION ◆━
Telling Sir Bedivere's Story
Imagine that you are Sir Bedivere and that you wish to write your own first-person account of Arthur's last days. Take notes from "The Day of Destiny" and background articles in this unit. Use them to write an account of the attempted truce, the battle, Arthur's combat with Mordred, your brother's death, and Arthur's departure. If you wish, you may explain your reasons for not immediately throwing Excalibur into the lake.

Interpreting Theme
"The Day of Destiny" presents so much evil and corruption that there is some doubt as to whether, even had Arthur survived, he could do anything about them. Reread this selection and take notes on the evidence that the Kingdom is in trouble. Then write an essay in which you discuss whether the kingdom could survive in the light of these factors.

ENRICHMENT
Researching Arthurian Stories
As a group, prepare a list of Arthurian materials available in your school or community library. Then let each student choose one source to read and report on. Longer works might be shared by several students. Your class report should include a brief plot summary, an explanation of how this story fits into the Arthurian legends, and an analysis of the form and content of the particular work you have read.

The Medieval Romance

In the medieval period the term *romance* meant a long narrative in verse or prose telling of the adventures of a hero. These stories of adventure usually include knights, ladies in distress, kings, and villains. The materials for the medieval romance in English are mainly drawn from the stories of King Arthur and the knights of the Round Table. This subject matter is sometimes called the "Matter of Britain."

Central to the medieval romance is the code of chivalry, the rules and customs connected with knighthood. Originally chivalry (from the French word *chevalier*, which means "knight" or "horseman") referred to the practice of training knights for the purpose of fighting. The concept broadened to include qualitites of the ideal courtly knight in the Middle Ages: bravery, honor, courtesy, protection of the weak, respect for women, generosity, and fairness to enemies. An important element in the code of chivalry is the ideal of courtly love. This concept required a knight to serve a virtuous noblewoman (often married) and to perform brave deeds to prove his devotion while she remained chaste and unattainable.

Chaucer uses Arthur's court as the setting for *The Wife of Bath's Tale* (see page 130), which incidentally furnishes an illustration of how other stories became attached to the original Arthurian legends. *Sir Gawain and the Green Knight* is another story of knights and their deeds in which can be seen various elements of the chivalric code. Malory's *Morte Darthur* (see page 139) is the most complete single version of the tales of King Arthur and his court that has been written in English.

During the Renaissance (see Unit 3) the code of chivalry and the ideal of courtly love are still very much in evidence. Knights and courtiers who write on courtly themes include the Earl of Surrey, Sir Thomas Wyatt, and Sir Walter Raleigh. Edmund Spenser and Sir Philip Sidney write highly formalized portraits of ideal love.

Medieval romance and its attendant codes of chivalry and courtly love faded in the glare of Rationalism during the eighteenth century (see Unit 4), but in the nineteenth century, Romanticism (see Unit 5) helped to revive the ideals of chivalry. Keats's "La Belle Dame Sans Merci" is the story of a knight who has served his ideal love even to his own desolation. In 1869 Alfred, Lord Tennyson related the Arthurian legends in verse form in *The Idylls of the King* (see page 563). Tennyson focuses on the corruption of the chivalric ideal by Lancelot's sinful love for Guinevere, wife of Arthur.

Treatments of the romance themes of chivalry and courtly love continue into our own day. Historical fiction often attempts to recreate the world of the Middle Ages; for example, T. H. White's *The Once and Future King* (1958), or Mary Stewart's triology—*The Crystal Cave* (1970), *The Hollow Hills* (1973), and *The Last Enchantment* (1979)—all based on the Arthurian legends.

One of the most haunting uses of the theme of chivalry in our own century is in the war poetry of Wilfred Owen (see page 769). Young men of Owen's time learned their ideals of courage and heroism from a study of the classical authors of ancient Greece and Rome and from the Medieval romance tradition of chivalry. Owen and Siegfried Sassoon show the collision between the sentiments of courage and honor learned by boys at school with the harsh realities of trench warfare. "Dulce et Decorum Est," a line by the Latin poet Horace that translates as "It is sweet and honorable to die for one's country," is described in Owen's poem as "the old lie." And yet the ideal of chivalry dies hard, as a glance at the comic strip "Prince Valiant," the *Star Wars* movies with their Jedi knights, or the Masters-of-the-Universe characters and cartoons might suggest.

The Norman invasion in 1066 had abrupt and dramatic consequences for the English language. Naturally enough, Norman French was the official language of the governing classes of England; within a short time it was also adopted by the English nobility, as the English and Norman upper classes gradually intermingled. However, English remained the language of the masses, and the social distinction between those who spoke French and those who spoke English persisted until the beginning of the thirteenth century.

The continued use of French by the upper classes was promoted by the close ties between England and France. After the Conquest, the Anglo-Norman kings retained their titles as Dukes of Normandy, and, through contractual marriages between English and Norman nobility, Englishmen began to acquire land and conduct business in Normandy. Had the political ties across the English Channel remained unbroken, it is possible that all of us today might be speaking some form of French. However, shortly after 1200, relations between Normandy and England deteriorated. Families that held land in both countries were forced to surrender their rights in one or the other. In consequence, the nobles of Norman descent who chose to retain their landholdings in England began to think of France as an alien land and of themselves as Englishmen. A growing suspicion of things "foreign" by those descendants of the original Norman invaders who had become firmly invested in England created a growing nationalistic spirit and an increased tolerance of things English, including the language.

The revival of the English language was also aided by the rise of a middle class of tradesmen and craftsmen, together with a slow but general improvement in economic and social conditions for the mass of native Englishmen. As the English-speaking majority gradually became more influential, the use of English in government and trade became both natural and necessary. Early in the fourteenth century writers began turning from Latin and French (which were considered the languages of scholarship and literature, respectively) to English. In 1362 English was declared, by royal decree, the official language of the courts of law.

By 1400 English was totally restored as the language of the realm, but it had been substantially altered and expanded by three and a half centuries of contact with French. For the first two centuries (1066–1250) the incursion of French vocabulary was relatively slight. Words adopted from the French during this period reflect the relationships between the ruling and subordinate classes (*noble, dame, servant, messenger*) or religious concerns (*sermon, communion, confession, clergy, convent*). By 1250, when ties between England and Normandy had loosened and English nationalism was making itself felt, many more French words began to be assimilated into English—particularly words associated with government, law, and business, such as *crown, state, reign, authority, tax, judge, pardon.* Also notable are the number of words from literature (*poet, tragedy, story*), art (*music* and the word *art* itself), medicine (*physician, pain*), fashion (*gown, boot, robe*), and those concerning food (*beef, bacon, olives*) and social life (*dance, recreation*), which were borrowed from French during this period. The dimensions of the change in cultural outlook which accompanied the changes in language can perhaps be inferred from these and the numerous other additions to English vocabulary, concerned as they are, in the main, with beauty, style, comfort, and the good life.

The structure of the language, too, was changing. Between 1066 and 1400 Old English, originally a highly inflected language, became greatly simplified. Inflections were dropped or were merged into the few surviving forms that are familiar today (for instance, *sing, sang, sung*). The Old English verb *help*, for example, had originally four principal parts (*healpan, healp,*

William Caxton presents his *Recuyell of Histories of Troy* to Margaret, Duchess of Burgundy, in the frontispiece of that book. 1475. *The Huntington Library, San Marino, California*

hulpon, holpen) with five or more additional endings to indicate person and number. Today, of course, it has only two principal parts *(help, helped)*, with one additional ending *(-s)* in the present tense. As the Old English inflections and endings gradually disappeared, the grammatical relationships that they expressed were taken over by the pattern and order of words, so that English became an increasingly phrasal language.

During approximately the same period of time, the distinct Anglo-Saxon dialects merged and evolved into four Middle English dialect groups. The most prominent of these was East Midland, the dialect spoken by the people between the Thames and the Humber rivers. This area included the city of London, rapidly developing as a center of government and commerce. Because of London's importance, the East Midland dialect gradually came to be looked on as "the King's English." Around 1370 Geoffrey Chaucer wrote in this dialect, giving it literary status; and when William Caxton introduced printing to England a century later, he used the speech of London as his standard. The speech of the East Midland area thus became a sort of early "standard English" from which both modern English and American English are directly descended.

The changes in the English language that occurred during the three or four centuries following the Norman Conquest were so all-encompassing that few if any of Chaucer's contemporaries would have been able to comprehend the Old English of *Beowulf*. Dramatic as these changes were, they did not take place swiftly; they evolved slowly over the course of generations, and were the result of complex political and social changes in a turbulent age.

THINKING CRITICALLY
ABOUT LITERATURE

UNIT 2   THE MEDIEVAL PERIOD   1066–1500

■ CONCEPT REVIEW

The following excerpt contains many of the important ideas and literary terms found in the period you have just studied. The notes and questions are designed to help you think critically about your reading. Page numbers in the notes refer to an application. A more extensive discussion of these terms is in the Handbook of Literary Terms.

The author of *Sir Gawain and the Green Knight* is unknown. He was probably Chaucer's contemporary, but because he lived in a provincial center far from Chaucer's world of London and the court, the poet worked in an older tradition of **alliteration** that had its roots in Anglo-Saxon verse.

In this scene, King Arthur and his knights of the Round Table are celebrating in Camelot during the Christmas season. Their banquet is interrupted by a giant knight of fierce appearance, on horseback, his body and clothes all "glittering green." The horseman has asked for "good sport," and since he is not wearing armor and carries no weapons except an axe, Arthur assumes that the stranger seeks "unarmored combat." The Green Knight is speaking as the scene opens.

from Sir Gawain and the Green Knight

translated by **Brian Stone**

Stanza 1

"No, it is not combat I crave, for come to that,
On this bench only beardless boys are sitting.
If I were hasped in armor on a high steed,
No man among you could match me, your might being meager.

■ Note the *alliteration* used throughout.

■ **hasped:** fastened.

From *Sir Gawain and the Green Knight*, translated by Brian Stone (Penguin Classics, 1974), pp. 31–37. Copyright © Brian Stone, 1959, 1964, 1974. Reprinted by permission of Penguin Books Ltd.

5 So I crave in this court a Christmas game,
For it is Yuletide and New Year, and young men abound here.
If any in this household is so hardy in spirit,
Of such mettlesome mind and so madly rash
As to strike a strong blow in return for another,
10 I shall offer to him this fine axe freely;
This axe, which is heavy enough, to handle as he please.
And I shall bide the first blow, as bare as I sit here.
If some intrepid man is tempted to try what I suggest,
Let him leap towards me and lay hold of this weapon,
15 Acquiring clear possession of it, no claim from me ensuing.
Then shall I stand up to his stroke, quite still on this floor—
So long as I shall have leave to launch a return blow
Unchecked.
Yet he shall have a year
And a day's reprieve, I direct.
20 Now hasten and let me hear
Who answers, to what effect."

Stanza 2
If he had astonished them at the start, yet stiller now
Were the henchmen in hall, both high and low.
The rider wrenched himself round in his saddle
25 And rolled his red eyes about roughly and strangely,
Bending his brows, bristling and bright, on all,
His beard swaying as he strained to see who would rise.
When none came to accord with him, he coughed aloud,
Then pulled himself up proudly, and spoke as follows:
30 "What, is this Arthur's house, the honor of which
Is bruited abroad so abundantly?
Has your pride disappeared? Your prowess gone?
Your victories, your valor, your vaunts, where are they?
The revel and renown of the Round Table
35 Is now overwhelmed by a word from one man's voice,
For all flinch for fear from a fight not begun!"
Upon this, he laughed so loudly that the lord grieved.
His fair features filled with blood
For a shame.
He raged as roaring gale;
40 His followers felt the same.
The King, not one to quail,
To that cavalier then came.

■ Note that here the Green Knight begins his challenge.

■ **bare:** not wearing armor; unarmed.

■ **Rhythm** (page 94): Note how the rhythm changes here from four strong beats per line, emphasized by the alliteration, to shorter rhyming lines. These last five lines of each stanza are known as the bob and wheel.
■ **year . . . reprieve:** the usual period for a legal contract.
■ **henchmen:** trusted followers.

■ Note how the Green Knight begins to taunt Arthur's knights.

■ **Characterization** (page 113): Arthur's mixed feelings of shame and anger are described. Note in the next stanza how he reacts.

Stanza 3

"By heaven," then said Arthur, "What you ask is foolish,
But as you firmly seek folly, find it you shall.
45 No good man here is aghast at your great words.
Hand me your axe now, for heaven's sake,
And I shall bestow the boon you bid us give."
He sprang towards him swiftly, seized it from his hand,
And fiercely the other fellow footed the floor.
50 Now Arthur had his axe, and holding it by the haft
Swung it about sternly, as if to strike with it.
The strong man stood before him, stretched to his full height,
Higher than any in the hall by a head and more.
Stern of face he stood there, stroking his beard,
55 Turning down his tunic in a tranquil manner,
Less unmanned and dismayed by the mighty strokes
Than if a banqueter at the bench had brought him a drink
    Of wine.
      Then Gawain at Guinevere's side
      Bowed and spoke his design:
60   "Before all, King, confide
      This fight to me. May it be mine."

Stanza 4

"If you would, worthy lord," said Gawain to the king,
"Bid me stir from this seat and stand beside you,
Allowing me without lese-majesty to leave the table,
65 And if my liege lady were not displeased thereby
I should come there to counsel you before this court of nobles.
For it appears unmeet to me, as manners go,
When your hall hears uttered such a haughty request,
Though you gladly agree, for you to grant it yourself,
70 When on the benches about you many such bold men sit,
Under heaven, I hold, the highest-mettled,
There being no braver knights when battle is joined.
I am the weakest, the most wanting in wisdom, I know,
And my life, if lost, would be least missed, truly.
75 Only through your being my uncle, am I to be valued;
No bounty but your blood in my body do I know.
And since this affair is too foolish to fall to you,
And I first asked it of you, make it over to me;
And if I fail to speak fittingly, let this full court judge
    Without blame."
80   Then wisely they whispered of it,
      And after, all said the same:
    That the crowned king should be quit,
      And Gawain given the game.

■ **footed the floor:** jumped off his horse.

■ **banqueter . . . bench:** a man at his seat.

■ **Gawain** gä′wān, gä′win), nephew of Arthur and his noblest knight. **Guinevere** (gwin′ə vir), Arthur's queen.

■ Gawain's characterization begins here.

■ **lese-majesty:** offense against the dignity of a ruler; severe discourtesy.

■ **unmeet:** unsuitable; improper.
■ Note the implied classification of challenges the king should accept and challenges he should let others accept in his place.
■ Gawain was famous for his courtliness and good manners, which he here displays.

■ **No bounty . . . know:** that is, the only good in my body comes from being a blood-relation to you.

■ **quit:** excused from the contest.

Stanza 5

Then the King commanded the courtly knight to rise.
85 He directly uprose, approached courteously,
Knelt low to his liege lord, laid hold of the weapon;
And he graciously let him have it, lifted up his hand
And gave him God's blessing, gladly urging him
To be strong in spirit and stout of sinew.
90 "Cousin, take care," said the King, "To chop once,
And if you strike with success, certainly I think
You will take the return blow without trouble in time."
Gripping the great axe, Gawain goes to the man
Who awaits him unwavering, not quailing at all.
95 Then said to Sir Gawain the stout knight in green,
"Let us affirm our pact freshly, before going farther.
I beg you, bold sir, to be so good
As to tell me your true name, as I trust you to."
"In good faith," said the good knight, "Gawain is my name,
100 And whatever happens after, I offer you this blow,
And in twelve months' time I shall take the return blow
With whatever weapon you wish, and with no one else
      Shall I strive."
          The other with pledge replied,
          "I'm the merriest man alive
105   It's a blow from you I must bide,
          Sir Gawain, so may I thrive."

Stanza 6

"By God," said the Green Knight, "Sir Gawain, I rejoice
That I shall have from your hand what I have asked for here.
And you have gladly gone over, in good discourse,
110 The covenant I requested of the King in full,
Except that you shall assent, swearing in truth,
To seek me yourself, in such place as you think
To find me under the firmament, and fetch your payment
For what you deal me today before this dignified gathering."
115 "How shall I hunt for you? How find your home?"
Said Gawain, "By God that made me, I go in ignorance;
Nor, knight, do I know your name or your court.
But instruct me truly thereof, and tell me your name,
And I shall wear out my wits to find my way there;
120 Here is my oath on it, in absolute honor!"
"That is enough this New Year, no more is needed,"
Said the gallant in green to Gawain the courteous,
"To tell you the truth, when I have taken the blow
After you have duly dealt it, I shall directly inform you
125 About my house and my home and my own name.

■ *Cousin* had a broader meaning in the Middle Ages, and could describe several degrees of relationship. Gawain is Arthur's nephew.
■ **Irony** (page 121): The irony of lines 90–92 and of others—especially the Green Knight's speeches—becomes apparent later.

■ Here Gawain pledges himself to fight no one else until he meets the Green Knight again.

■ Note that the rest of the pledge will send Gawain on a quest to find the Green Knight.
■ **firmament:** heavens; sky.

■ **New Year:** a time associated with friendship and piety.

The Green Knight's decapitated head magically speaks, from a manuscript once belonging to Renaissance antiquarian Sir Robert Cotton (1571–1631). *The British Library*

Then you may keep your covenant, and call on me,
And if I waft you no words, then well may you prosper,
Stay long in your own land and look for no further
      Trial.
     Now grip your weapon grim;
130   Let us see your fighting style."
     "Gladly," said Gawain to him,
     Stroking the steel the while.

Stanza 7

On the ground the Green Knight graciously stood,
With head slightly slanting to expose the flesh.
135 His long and lovely locks he laid over his crown,
Baring the naked neck for the business now due.
Gawain gripped his axe and gathered it on high,
Advanced the left foot before him on the ground,
And slashed swiftly down on the exposed part,
140 So that the sharp blade sheared through, shattering the bones,
Sank deep in the sleek flesh, split it in two,
And the scintillating steel struck the ground.
The fair head fell from the neck, struck the floor,
And people spurned it as it rolled around.
145 Blood spurted from the body, bright against the green.
Yet the fellow did not fall, nor falter one whit,
But stoutly sprang forward on legs still sturdy,
Roughly reached out among the ranks of nobles,
Seized his splendid head and straightway lifted it.

■ Here the Green Knight offers an alternative. If after the blow he says nothing, Gawain is absolved from his pledge.

■ **Protagonist/Antagonist** (page 145): Here, with the physical blow, the earlier verbal conflict is confirmed and a protagonist/antagonist relationship is solidifed.
■ Note the reaction of the people to the Green Knight's severed head.

150 Then he strode to his steed, snatched the bridle,
   Stepped into the stirrup and swung aloft,
   Holding his head in his hand by the hair.
   He settled himself in the saddle as steadily
   As if nothing had happened to him, though he had
         No head.
155   He twisted his trunk about,
       That gruesome body that bled;
       He caused much dread and doubt
       By the time his say was said.

   c. 1380–1400

■ Note that this element of magic is characteristic of the medieval *romance*.

■ In what follows, the Green Knight proceeds to tell Gawain where to find him, so Gawain can keep his pledge after all.

THINK AND DISCUSS
Understanding
1. Where and when does this scene take place?
2. What is the "game" that the Green Knight proposes in stanza 1?
3. How do the knights and ladies react to the Green Knight in stanza 2?
4. In stanza 6, when does the Green Knight promise to reveal his name and home to Gawain?

Analyzing
5. Why does Gawain ask to be allowed to accept the Green Knight's challenge?
6. Describe exactly the "covenant" arrived at between Gawain and the Green Knight. Why do you think so much emphasis is placed upon the exact terms of the agreement?
7. What evidence of magic is there throughout this excerpt?

Extending
8. Do you think the Green Knight's game is a fair one? Explain.
9. Without reading the rest of the poem, would you expect Sir Gawain to keep his part of the covenant? Why or why not?

REVIEWING LITERARY TERMS
Rhythm
1. Analyze the basic rhythmic pattern of the poem. Find one line that you feel best exemplifies that rhythm.
2. Analyze the different rhythmic pattern of the last five lines in each stanza (the "bob and wheel").
3. In a sentence or two, describe the rhythmic structure of the entire excerpt.

Characterization
4. How does Gawain characterize himself in stanza 4?
5. Do his speeches and actions throughout support what he says about himself? Explain.

Irony
6. What is ironic about King Arthur's speech in lines 90–92?
7. Is the phrase "a Christmas game" in line 5 ironic? Explain.
8. How does the Green Knight use verbal irony to force the "good sport" he has come for?

Protagonist/Antagonist
9. How can you tell that the Green Knight is not the protagonist but the antagonist?
10. How can you tell that Gawain and not Arthur is the protagonist of the poem?

■ CONTENT REVIEW

Classifying

1. Classify the characters in this unit according to their occupations. Make up your own categories.
2. Based on what you have read in this unit, devise a system for classifying these or any other selections as medieval romances (see page 146).

Generalizing

3. To what extent do superstition and belief in the supernatural form a part of daily life in medieval England?

Evaluating

4. Which one character from the unit do you consider the most memorable? Why?
5. In this unit you have studied ballads, narrative poetry, and prose fiction. Do you think that any one type is more effective than the others in presenting a picture of medieval England, or do they supplement one another? Explain.

Synthesizing

6. Do you find the people you encounter in medieval literature strikingly different from the people of our own day? Give specific examples to support your conclusions. In particular, you might consider the so-called "battle of the sexes," heroism in the face of danger, and jealousy in love.
7. Which, if any, of the various characters from this unit would make an appropriate role model for today's youth? Explain.

■ COMPOSITION REVIEW

Writing About Knighthood

A number of knights appear in the selections in this unit: Chaucer's Knight and Squire; the Knight in *The Wife of Bath's Tale;* Sir Patrick Spence; Arthur, Mordred, Sir Lucas, and Sir Bedivere from "The Day of Destiny"; Sir Gawain and the Green Knight. Select one or more of these knights and write a paper for your classmates examining how he reflects or departs from the code of knighthood. As part of your explanation of knighthood, you will want to include its professed ideals of courage, loyalty, piety, and respect for women, as well the importance of knighthood as an institution.

Comparing and Contrasting Characters

The Prioress and the Wife of Bath are the preeminent women among the pilgrims, and seem intended as a contrast. In a three-to-five paragraph paper, with your classmates and teacher as audience, compare and contrast the characters of the Prioress and the Wife of Bath as they are described in the *Prologue* to *The Canterbury Tales.* You may also use additional details from *The Wife of Bath's Prologue* and *Tale* for her character.

Writing About a Theme

The theme of death appears in a number of selections in this unit. *The Pardoner's Tale,* "Lord Randal," "Bonny Barbara Allan," "Edward," "Sir Patrick Spence," and "The Day of Destiny" all treat it. Write an essay for a school literary journal analyzing the theme of death in one or more of these selections. Consider its importance, people's attitudes toward it, and what conclusions can be drawn from its treatment.

Writing About the Medieval Period

What do the selections in this unit tell you about life at court or among the middle or lower classes? Write a composition of at least four paragraphs in which you describe what you have learned about life in medieval England. Assume that you are writing for students who are just about to study this unit. See "Writing About a Period or Trend" in the Writer's Handbook.

THE RENAISSANCE 1500–1660

1500	1525	1550	1575

HISTORY AND THE ARTS

- Michelangelo sculpts *David* (Italy)
- da Vinci paints *Mona Lisa* (Italy)
- Balboa (Spain) reaches Pacific Ocean
- Machiavelli: *The Prince* (Italy)
- Luther's Ninety-five Theses (Germany)
- Cortés (Spain) conquers Mexico
- Church of England established
- Cartier (France) explores Canada
- Anne Boleyn executed
- Copernicus's theory of solar system (Poland)
- Ivan crowned czar of Russia
- Drake begins voyage around the world

MONARCHS AND HOUSES

TUDOR

- Henry VII
- Henry VIII
- Edward VI
- Mary I
- Elizabeth I

ENGLISH LITERATURE

- Henry VIII: *Defense of the Seven Sacraments*
- Sonnet form introduced
- More: *Utopia*
- Book of Common Prayer
- Holinshed: *Chronicles*
- Tottel's Miscellany

Mona Lisa by Leonardo da Vinci c. 1503-5. The Louvre, Paris.

A watercolor of the execution of Mary Queen of Scots. 1587.

Miniature portrait of Queen Elizabeth I. Late 16th century.

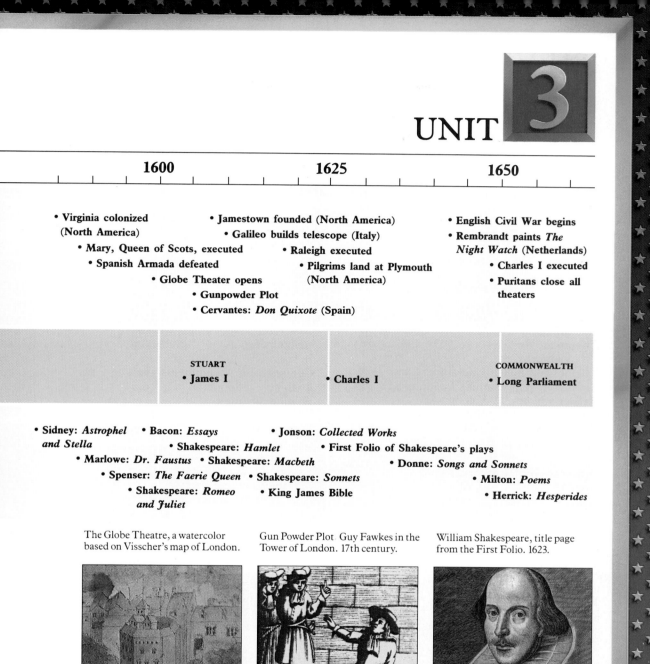

UNIT 3

1600	1625	1650

- Virginia colonized (North America)
  - Jamestown founded (North America)
    - Galileo builds telescope (Italy)
  - Mary, Queen of Scots, executed
    - Spanish Armada defeated
      - Raleigh executed
      - Globe Theater opens
        - Pilgrims land at Plymouth (North America)
        - Gunpowder Plot
        - Cervantes: *Don Quixote* (Spain)
  - English Civil War begins
  - Rembrandt paints *The Night Watch* (Netherlands)
    - Charles I executed
    - Puritans close all theaters

STUART
- James I

- Charles I

COMMONWEALTH
- Long Parliament

- Sidney: *Astrophel and Stella*
  - Bacon: *Essays*
    - Jonson: *Collected Works*
  - Marlowe: *Dr. Faustus*
    - Shakespeare: *Hamlet*
    - Shakespeare: *Macbeth*
      - First Folio of Shakespeare's plays
      - Donne: *Songs and Sonnets*
    - Spenser: *The Faerie Queen*
      - Shakespeare: *Sonnets*
      - Milton: *Poems*
      - Shakespeare: *Romeo and Juliet*
      - King James Bible
        - Herrick: *Hesperides*

The Globe Theatre, a watercolor based on Visscher's map of London.

Gun Powder Plot Guy Fawkes in the Tower of London. 17th century.

William Shakespeare, title page from the First Folio. 1623.

PREVIEW

UNIT 3   THE RENAISSANCE   1500–1660

Authors

Sir Thomas Wyatt
Henry Howard,
    Early of Surrey
Sir Francis Bacon
Queen Elizabeth I
Sir Walter Raleigh

Edmund Spenser
Sir Philip Sidney
William Shakespeare
Christopher Marlowe
Ben Jonson
Richard Lovelace

Robert Herrick
John Donne
George Herbert
Andrew Marvell
John Milton
The King James Bible

Features

Comment: The Death of Raleigh
Reading Shakespearean Drama
Comment: Shakespeare's Theater—
    The Globe
Comment: The Witch-Scenes in *Macbeth*
    (*Macbeth* edition)
Comment: Responses to "The Passionate
    Shepherd"
Themes in English Literature: *Carpe Diem*
Comment: Ben Jonson's Vision of His Son
Reader's Note: "A Valediction"
Reader's Note: "To His Coy Mistress"
Reader's Note: The Twenty-third Psalm
The Changing English Language

Application of Literary Terms

sonnet
analogy
paradox
conceit
apostrophe
connotation/
    denotation

plot
pastoral
symbol
hyperbole
synecdoche
metonymy
blank verse

Review of Literary Terms

metaphor
alliteration
theme

Reading Literature Skillfully

cause/effect

Vocabulary

etymology
archaic meanings
context

Thinking Skills

classifying
generalizing

synthesizing
evaluating

Composition Assignments Include

Analyzing a Sonnet
Writing an Informal Essay
Evaluating Raleigh as a Poet
Writing About Elizabethan Poetic Devices
Creating a Dialogue
Analyzing a *Carpe Diem* Poem
Explaining Symbolism
Writing Concrete Poetry
Analyzing Metaphysical Poetry
Analyzing Symbols of Light and Darkness
Comparing Translations

Enrichment

Interpreting Renaissance Poetry
Researching the Elizabethan Era
Listening to Shakespeare
Blocking a Scene
Holding a Press Conference

Thinking Critically About Literature

Concept Review
Content Review
Composition Review

THE RENAISSANCE   1500–1660

In the opening years of the fourteenth century, there developed in Italy an interest in the manuscripts that had survived from ancient Greece and Rome. As more and more of these were unearthed in libraries and monasteries, Italy fell under the spell of the intellectual movement we have come to call the Renaissance —the rebirth of scholarship based on classical learning and philosophy. As the Renaissance continued to develop and spread from Italy to other European countries, it took on added dimensions. Perhaps stimulated by the discovery that the men and women of ancient Greece and Rome were intelligent, cultured, and creative, the Renaissance gradually became also a rebirth of the human spirit, a realization of the human potential for development. This realization led eventually to many discoveries— including important advances in art, literature, religion, philosophy, science, invention, and geography.

Some of the great Renaissance artists include Michelangelo and Leonardo da Vinci in Italy and Rembrandt van Rijn in the Netherlands. Their works are popular all over the world and are still studied for their beauty, style and artistic innovations. Da Vinci was also an inventor whose notebooks include plans for a flying machine, a parachute, and many types of war machinery.

In religion, the Renaissance spirit brought about the Protestant Reformation, including the founding of the Lutheran Church and the Church of England. Philosophers of the Renaissance include Erasmus in the Netherlands and Niccolò Machiavelli in Italy.

In science, Nikolaus Copernicus, in Poland, asserted that the earth was not the center of the universe, and in Italy, Galileo conducted astronomical investigations with a new invention —the telescope. Their announcements shook the foundations of traditional world views.

The Renaissance was also an age of discovery and colonization of new lands. The Spaniard Vasco de Balboa was the first European to view the Pacific Ocean, and Sir Francis Drake sailed for England around the world, proving once and for all that the earth is round. Hernando Cortés conquered Mexico for Spain, implanting Catholicism but destroying the Indians' civilization, and Jacques Cartier explored Canada for France. Colonies were founded in North America that were to become the United States.

THE RENAISSANCE IN ENGLAND

The Renaissance in England may be divided into three parts: the rise of the Renaissance under the early Tudor monarchs (1500–1558), the height of the Renaissance under Elizabeth I (1558–1603), and the decline of the Renaissance under the Stuart monarchs (1603–1649).

The phenomenon of the Renaissance touched England lightly and fleetingly during Chaucer's time. This early contact was negligible, however, largely because external wars and internal strife ravaged the country for almost a century and a half. In 1485, with the end of the Wars of the Roses and the crowning of Henry VII, domestic unrest ended. Henry immediately set about unifying the country, strengthening the crown, and replenishing the royal treasury.

Under the reign of his son, Henry VIII (1509–1547), England was ripe for the intellectual ferment of the Renaissance. The population had begun to increase rapidly, feudalism was on its deathbed, and there was a steady movement of population to the larger towns and cities, especially London. The population of London, only 93,000 in 1563, had by 1605 more than doubled, to 224,000—a little larger than Grand Rapids, Michigan, today. Part of this growth came about because of the enclosure laws, which meant that large open areas, originally available to everyone, were fenced in, and many agricultural workers, no longer able to pay the higher rents for land, moved to the cities where there was a better chance to find work.

The invention of the printing press, together with improved methods of manufacturing paper, made possible the rapid spread of knowledge. In 1476, during the Wars of the Roses, William Caxton had set up England's first printing press. By 1640, that press and others had printed more than 26,000 different works and editions. It is estimated that by 1530 more than half the population of England was literate.

Renaissance learning made its tardy entry into England near the end of the fifteenth century, carried home by scholars who had traveled in Italy. Earliest among these was the Oxford Group, which introduced what became known as the "New Learning" (or *humanism*—studies concerned with human interest and values) to Oxford University in the 1490s and 1500s. A decade later, the great Dutch humanist, Desiderius Erasmus, was teaching Greek at Cambridge University.

Learning flourished not only at Oxford and Cambridge, but at the lower educational levels too. In 1510 John Colet, one of the original Oxford Group, now Dean of St. Paul's Cathedral, used his inheritance to establish the cathedral school of St. Paul's, the first preparatory school to be devoted to teaching the new learning. Other private schools followed rapidly.

As the Renaissance established itself in England, new types of literature were imported from the European continent. Chief among these were the sonnet, imported by Wyatt and Surrey from Italy, where it had been perfected by Francis Petrarch; and the essay, imported by Bacon from France, where it had been originated by Michel Montaigne. Other verse forms were also borrowed from the Italian and the French, though with lesser impact. Elaborate Renaissance conventions of love poetry found their outlet chiefly in sonnets and sonnet sequences.

Though the non-native influence was strong insofar as poetry was concerned, the native drama continued to develop and gain popularity. Miracle and morality plays remained a favorite form of entertainment, while a new dramatic form, the *interlude*, developed. One of the important ancestors of Elizabethan drama, the interlude was a short play designed to be presented between the courses of a banquet.

While the Renaissance was gathering strength in England, two events occurred that diminished

Detail of Visscher's Map of London. Visible are St. Paul's Cathedral, London Bridge, and the Tower of London. 1616. *British Library*

the influence of the Church. The first was Martin Luther's posting of his Ninety-five Theses on a church door in Wittenberg, Germany, in 1517, an act that heralded the Reformation. The second event was brought about by the desire of Henry VIII for a male heir and his wish to divorce Catherine of Aragon, who had borne only one child, Mary. When the Pope refused to end the marriage, Henry, with an eye also to seizing the vast holdings of the Church, overthrew papal jurisdiction, married Anne Boleyn, and in 1534 was declared, with Parliament's help, head of the Church of England, sometimes called the Anglican Church. Thus England became a Protestant nation.

The Oath of Supremacy, affirming the King as head of both Church and State, was required of those in the service of the Church or the King, as well as those in the learned professions and those attending Oxford or Cambridge Universities. The oath led to ruined careers or martyrdom for many Catholics, who regarded the Pope as the head of the Church.

The problem of succession to the throne continued to trouble Henry. Anne Boleyn gave him one child, Elizabeth, before she was convicted and executed for adultery. Her successor, Jane Seymour, died in childbirth, leaving a sickly son, Edward. Henry's next three marriages—to Anne of Cleves, Catherine Howard, and Catherine Parr—were childless. Eventually three of his children, by three different queens, ruled England.

During the reign of Henry's successor, the child king Edward VI, the movement toward Protestantism continued. However, Queen Mary, the next monarch, was a devout Catholic. Her attempts to restore Catholicism to the country resulted in internal turmoil and much bloodshed.

THE HEIGHT OF THE RENAISSANCE

Under the reign of Elizabeth I (1558–1603), order was restored, and England entered upon her most glorious age. Only twenty-five when she assumed the throne, Elizabeth, who never married, was to rule wisely and well for forty-five years.

That England welcomed its new queen is apparent in a contemporary document. Holins-

Henry VIII, by Hans Holbein the Younger. This is the only surviving painting of Henry definitely attributable to Holbein, the court painter. Circa 1536. *Thyssen-Bornemisza Collection*

hed's *Chronicles* has this to say about Elizabeth's coronation in 1558:

> On her entering the city of London, she was received of the people with prayers, wishes, welcomings, cries, and tender words, all which argued a wonderful earnest love of most obedient subjects towards their sovereign. And on the other side, her grace, by holding up her hands, and merry countenance to such as stood far off, and most

tender and gentle language to those that stood nigh unto her grace, did declare herself no less thankfully to receive her people's good will, than they lovingly offered it to her. And it was not only to those her subjects who were of noble birth that she showed herself thus very gracious, but also to the poorest sort. . . .

Through her policy of middle-of-the-road Protestantism, Elizabeth held in check throughout her reign the proponents of Catholicism on one hand and the growing numbers of Puritan extremists on the other. A master politician, wise in the choice of her counselors, Elizabeth established a strong central government that received the loyal support of her subjects. In 1570, when the Pope excommunicated Elizabeth, his act had the unexpected result of uniting England still more strongly behind its queen. Mary Queen of Scots was a Catholic and heir to the throne after Elizabeth. As such, she represented an invitation to rebellion from within and aggression from without on the part of persons interested in toppling England's Protestant monarchy. Persuaded by her advisors that her cousin's death was a political necessity, Elizabeth set in motion a chain of events that led to Mary's beheading in 1587.

Interested in education, Queen Elizabeth established one hundred free grammar schools in all parts of the country. These schools were open to both sexes of all ranks. Eager to educate their children, many people took advantage of the free schools; this may well have been one of the reasons for England's advancement.

In 1579, Gresham College was founded in London to cater to the needs of the middle class. Unlike the classical curriculum offered by Oxford and Cambridge, its curriculum included law, medicine, and other practical courses suited to the bustling world of London. As the children of the middle class grew better educated, the middle class itself grew in power, its influence showing proportionately in the House of Commons.

During Elizabeth's reign, England began to gain supremacy on the seas. Riches came from ventures like those of the pirate-patriot Sir Francis Drake, whom Elizabeth commissioned to intercept Spanish trading ships on the high seas. Drake's voyage around the world (1577–1580) resulted in his returning to England with a treasure taken from the Spanish—much of which went to swell Elizabeth's treasury. On Drake's return the Queen herself went aboard his ship, the *Golden Hind*, and knighted him then and there.

King Philip II of Spain was, naturally, displeased and, determined to retaliate, sent an invasion fleet called the Armada. Elizabeth's words upon that occasion are noteworthy: "I know I have the body of a weak feeble woman, but I have the heart and stomach of a king—and a king of England, too, and think foul scorn that. . . Spain or any Prince of Europe should dare to invade the borders of my realm." In turn she dispatched the English navy, whose defeat of the Armada in 1588 meant that England would remain Protestant and that it that it would emerge as a dominant sea power.

Elizabeth's reign was an age of courtiers, and many of the men of her court—such as Sir Walter Raleigh and Sir Philip Sidney—lived up to the Renaissance ideal of solider, scholar, and poet. Educated in both classical and modern languages, Elizabeth was herself a poet (see page 173). The queen loved music and dancing, and her court entertainments were notable.

One form of entertainment was the *masque*, a courtly theatrical spectacle. Written for specific occasions and seldom repeated, the masque featured, in addition to song and dance, elegant costumes, elaborate sets, and plots based on mythology or allegory. In an *allegory*, characters are often personifications of abstract ideas such as charity, hope, greed, or envy, and their actions have moral, social, religious, or political significance.

The bustling activity of the court with its swarms of royal agents, foreign ambassadors, churchmen, scholars, poets, actors, musicians, cooks, porters, chambermaids, and other attendants, was reflected in the city of London as a whole. Here carts and coaches, laughing and quarreling throngs of men, women, and children jostled up and down the streets to such an extent that posts had to be set up to keep houses from falling down.

Elizabeth's tastes as well as those of her subjects ran the gamut from public hangings, witch

The Spanish Armada (detail), by Nicholas Hilliard. *The Worshipful Society of Apothecaries of London*

burnings, bearbaitings, and bawdy jokes on up into the rarer atmosphere of exquisite jewels, silks, and brocades, stately dances, and elevated discussions of Christian theology, Greek philosophy, and Italian poetry. Just as Elizabeth could slap and spit at her associates one moment and discuss the elegancies of Italian poetry the next, so her subjects could stop in at the Paris Garden where mastiffs tore at Harry Hunks, the bear, and then pass on to the Globe Theater next door, where Romeo's words dropped gently into Juliet's ears.

Beyond question the Elizabethan period was the golden age of English drama, including among its dramatists Christopher Marlowe, William Shakespeare, and Ben Jonson, along with more than a dozen other first-rate playwrights. Under the skillful handling of these dramatists, blank verse, introduced into the language by Surrey, became the main vehicle for tragedy and comedy. *Hamlet, Macbeth*, and Shakespeare's other tragedies were cast in blank verse (unrhymed iambic pentameter), as were his comedies. The plays of the great dramatists contained something for everyone: low comedy for the uneducated, elevated philosophical concepts for the educated, and strong story lines to engage the attention of everyone.

Because the public theaters attracted large audiences from all levels of society, pickpockets and other criminals were drawn there. As Puritan influence grew in England, more and more complaints were made about the ungodliness of the theaters, and they were occasionally closed. In time of plague, too, their operations were suspended, and the acting companies went on tour.

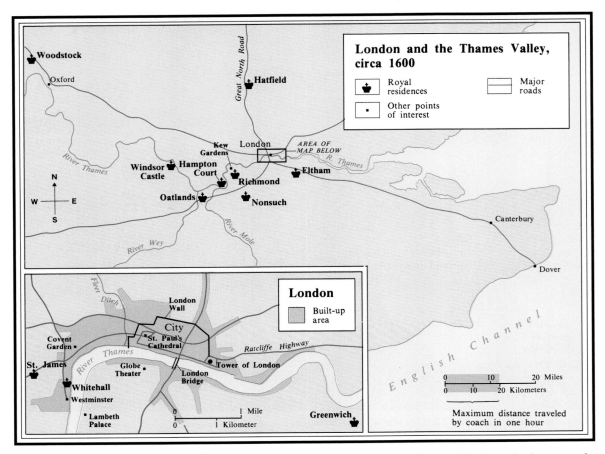

London and the Thames Valley, circa 1600

Royal residences

Other points of interest

Major roads

Woodstock
Oxford
Hatfield
Great North Road
River Thames
Kew Gardens
London
AREA OF MAP BELOW
R. Thames
Windsor Castle
Hampton Court
Richmond
Eltham
Oatlands
Nonsuch
River Wey
River Mole
Canterbury
Dover

N W E S

English Channel

London

Built-up area

Fleet Ditch
London Wall
City
St. Paul's Cathedral
Covent Garden
River Thames
Ratcliffe Highway
St. James
Globe Theater
Tower of London
London Bridge
Whitehall
Westminster
Lambeth Palace
Greenwich

0   1 Mile
0   1 Kilometer

0   10   20 Miles
0   10   20 Kilometers

Maximum distance traveled by coach in one hour

The Puritan influence that forced the occasional closing of the theaters was symptomatic of what was to come. Renaissance exuberance was the exuberance of youth, and as Elizabethan poets warned, youth cannot last forever. Queen Elizabeth's moderate Protestantism and personal presence had maintained England's domestic stability. In 1600, however, when the new century began, Elizabeth was an aging queen not in the best of health. Despite the urging of her counselors, not until she was dying in 1603 did the childless Elizabeth name her successor, King James of Scotland, the son of Mary Queen of Scots.

THE DECLINE OF THE RENAISSANCE

James I, the first Stuart king, had little firsthand knowledge of England, nor was he the kind of leader to rouse patriotic fervor and loyalty in his new subjects. Elizabeth had managed to maintain religious balance between Protestants and Catholics, but under the Stuarts, James and his son Charles I, who succeeded him, that balance was lost. Both monarchs were firm Anglicans (members of the Church of England), opposed to Puritanism. James's active persecution of the Puritans, in fact, led to the founding of the colony of Plymouth in North America in 1620.

There was growing religious and political unrest under James. In 1604 a group of Catholics conceived the idea of blowing up the Parliament building while both Houses were assembled for the opening of Parliament, and King James and his family were in attendance. By November, 1605, the Gunpowder Plot, as it has come to be called, had resulted in the concealment of vast quantities of explosives in the cellar of the Parliament building. At almost the last moment, however, the plot was discovered, and government agents seized one of the leaders, Guy Fawkes, in the cellar. The other conspirators were pursued, and those who were not killed were tried, found guilty, and executed. Today in England, November 5 is celebrated as Guy Fawkes Day with fireworks and bonfires.

Both James and Charles also engaged in struggles with Parliament over finances and what they believed to be their divine right to rule absolutely. The increasing strength of the predominantly Puritan middle class in the House of Commons made confrontation inevitable. This did not occur until the reign of Charles, who settled his disputes with his Parliaments by highhandedly dismissing them. In 1642, civil war erupted, with the king and his supporters, called Royalists or Cavaliers, ranged against the Parliamentary forces, called Puritans or Roundheads, led by Oliver Cromwell. The king was defeated, tried, found guilty of treason, and beheaded in 1649. England was declared to be no longer a monarchy, but a commonwealth under the jurisdiction of Parliament.

At the beginning of the Stuart period, poetry was only a little less exuberant, a little more cynical and introspective than it had been earlier under Elizabeth. A major development was the growth of a group of *metaphysical* poets, led by John Donne. For emphasis, they used "strong" or harsh lines, overriding regular meter; they employed strained metaphors (or *conceits*); and they were intellectual rather than romantic, even in their love poetry.

A number of young Cavaliers, loyal to the king, wrote lyrics about love and loyalty, but even in the love poems it is evident that the freshness of the Elizabethan era had passed. Among the best of these poets were Richard Lovelace and Robert Herrick.

Drama continued to flourish in England under the Stuarts. Shakespeare's great tragedies were written during the reign of King James, and Shakespeare's acting company, taken under the patronage of the king, became known as the King's Men. The theater did in fact remain a popular form of entertainment until the Puritan government closed all playhouses in 1649.

The greatest of the Puritan poets, and one of the greatest English poets, was John Milton, Latin Secretary to the Puritan Commonwealth. While in this position his sight began to fail; eventually he became blind. Sightless, he composed *Paradise Lost*, his greatest work and the most successful English epic.

In 1660, the monarchy was restored, with Charles II (the son of the executed Charles I) on the throne. Theaters were reopened, and—at least for a while—a mood of gaiety reigned.

THINKING ABOUT GRAPHIC AIDS
Using the Time Line

Use the time line on pages 156–157 to answer these questions.

1. What evidence does the time line present as to why the Renaissance period is often called the Elizabethan Age?
2. List the items that deal with world exploration and colonization.
3. Could Shakespeare and his contemporaries have known about the New World?
4. About how long after *Romeo and Juliet* was first presented was it finally printed in book form?
5. Compare this time line with the Unit 2 time line on pages 76–77. For how many years did the House of Tudor hold the English throne?

Using the Map

Use the map on page 164 to answer these questions.

1. About how many square miles did London cover during Elizabeth's reign?
2. How many royal residences are shown in London and the surrounding area?
3. About how long would it have taken Elizabeth to travel by carriage from Hampton Court to Parliament in Westminster?

Thomas Wyatt was born in Kent, and spent most of his adult life at court and abroad in the service of King Henry VIII. Educated at Cambridge, Wyatt went on to a career as courtier and diplomat, serving as ambassador to Spain, to Emperor Charles V, and as a member of a number of diplomatic missions to France and Italy.

Twice imprisoned by Henry, he was twice pardoned and restored to royal favor. Apparently Wyatt had been in love with his first cousin, Anne Boleyn, who later became the second wife of Henry VIII and the mother of the future Queen Elizabeth I. In 1536 Anne Boleyn was charged with adultery and executed. Although Wyatt was imprisoned in the Tower of London for a time, he was exonerated and freed. Continuing in Henry's service, he survived a second imprisonment in 1541, this time on charges of treason, and died of a fever contracted while he was en route to yet another diplomatic mission.

One of the first writers to bring to England from Italy and France the themes and forms of Renaissance poetry, Wyatt is known for introducing the Italian sonnet form into English. Few of Wyatt's poems were published in his lifetime, typical of an age when courtiers privately circulated their poems in manuscript. In 1557, however, after Wyatt's death, *Tottel's Miscellany*, an important collection of early English Renaissance poetry, was published; 97 of its 276 poems are by Wyatt.

H𝕫 **Review METAPHOR in the Handbook of Literary Terms, page 906.**

Whoso List to Hunt   Sir Thomas Wyatt

Whoso list[1] to hunt, I know where is an hind,[2]
But as for me, alas, I may no more.
The vain travail hath wearied me so sore,
I am of them that farthest come behind.
5 Yet may I, by no means, my wearied mind
Draw from the deer; but as she fleeth afore,
Fainting I follow. I leave off therefore,
Since in a net I seek to hold the wind.
Whoso list her hunt, I put him out of doubt,
10 As well as I, may spend his time in vain.
And graven with diamonds in letters plain
There is written, her fair neck round about,
"*Noli me tangere,* [3]for Caesar's I am,
And wild for to hold, though I seem tame."

1557

---

1. *list,* likes.
2. *hind,* female deer.
3. *Noli me tangere,* Do not touch me. [Latin] Tradition has it that the subject of this sonnet was Anne Boleyn, Wyatt's first cousin, with whom he was reputed to be in love. Anne was the wife of Henry VIII and Queen of England.

Henry Howard, Earl of Surrey
1517–1547

Of noble lineage (his father was the Duke of Norfolk and a close adviser to Henry VIII), Surrey received a private education at home. When Surrey was only fifteen, he traveled to France and remained for several months at the French court.

Surrey's first military service occurred in 1536, when he accompanied his father to the north of England to suppress a revolt against Henry VIII. In 1537 he was imprisoned for striking at court a man who accused him of having been sympathetic to the rebels.

Released from prison, he showed his family pride and high spirits to such an extent that in 1539 he was referred to as "the most foolish proud boy in England." In the same year he commanded Henry's forces in Norfolk, and in 1541 he was honored by being made a Knight of the Garter. The strange alliances and misfortunes of Henry's court first touched Surrey personally in 1542 when he was present at the execution of his cousin Catherine Howard, Henry VIII's fifth wife. That same year his quick temper involved him in trouble again and he was briefly imprisoned for challenging another courtier to a duel.

He served in the military in France, where he distinguished himself for bravery and was wounded on the battlefield. In 1546 he and his father were arrested on several charges of treason, and in January, 1547, he was beheaded—just a little more than one week before Henry died.

Although it may seem difficult for one man to have experienced so much in a short life, Surrey was also an accomplished poet. He is represented in *Tottel's Miscellany* (1557) by forty poems. It was he who introduced the English or Shakespearean sonnet form, more natural to the English language than the Italian form. Surrey's poetry is more polished than Wyatt's, but it is generally thought to be less forceful and original in content.

Henry Howard, Earl of Surrey

H

See SONNET in the Handbook of Literary Terms, page 925.

A Lover's Vow

Set me whereas the sun doth parch the green,
Or where his beams may not dissolve the ice,
In temperate heat, where he is felt and seen;
With proud people, in presence sad and wise,
5 Set me in base, or yet in high degree;
In the long night, or in the shortest day;
In clear weather, or where mists thickest be;
In lusty youth, or when my hairs be gray;
Set me in earth, in heaven, or yet in hell;
10 In hill, in dale, or in the foaming flood;
Thrall,[1] or at large—alive whereso I dwell;
Sick or in health, in ill fame or in good;
Yours will I be, and with that only thought
Comfort myself when that my hap[2] is naught.

1557

---

1. *Thrall*, enslaved.
2. *hap*, good fortune.

A young man among roses, miniature by Nicholas
Hilliard. c. 1588. *Victoria and Albert Museum*

Alas, So All Things Now Do Hold Their Peace

Alas! so all things now do hold their peace,[1]
Heaven and earth disturbèd in no thing;
The beasts, the air, the birds their song do cease,
The nightès chare[2] the stars about doth bring.
5 Calm is the sea, the waves work less and less;
So am not I, whom love, alas, doth wring,
Bringing before my face the great increase
Of my desires, whereat I weep and sing,
In joy and woe, as in a doubtful ease.
10 For my sweet thoughts sometime do pleasure
    bring,

But by and by the cause of my disease[3]
Gives me a pang that inwardly doth sting,
When that I think what grief it is again
To live and lack the thing should rid my pain.

1557

---

1. A version of a sonnet by Petrarch, an Italian poet who
lived 1304–1374.
2. *chare*, chariot.
3. *disease*, uneasiness, discomfort.

THINK AND DISCUSS
WHOSO LIST TO HUNT
Understanding
1. According to the speaker, why has he given up hunting the hind?
2. What does he tell others who might want to hunt the hind?

Analyzing
3. What is the significance of the first part of the warning the hind wears around her neck (line 13)?
4. What does the second part of the warning (line 14) imply?

Extending
5. What in Anne Boleyn's life history shows that King Henry VIII enforced the figurative warning written on the hind's collar? (See page 160 of the Background article.)

REVIEWING: Metaphor H𝓩
See Handbook of Literary Terms, p. 906

A **metaphor** is a figure of speech that makes a comparison between two basically unlike things that have something in common. This comparison may be started or implied.

1. What two basically unlike things are compared in this poem?
2. What do they have in common?
3. What different metaphor is contained in line 8?

THINK AND DISCUSS
A LOVER'S VOW
Understanding
1. To whom is this sonnet addressed?
2. What is the "vow" that the lover makes?

Analyzing
3. The last two lines appear to explain the somewhat frenzied tone of the preceding ones. What is the explanation, and how persuasive is it?

Extending
4. How might a modern young woman react to receiving a poem like this?

ALAS, SO ALL THINGS . . .
1. "Alas," the word that opens this sonnet, is an exclamation of sorrow. Where does the first thought of actual sorrow appear?

Analyzing
2. Explain the contrast between the mood of the speaker and that of all the other things.
3. What is the cause of the speaker's uneasiness?

APPLYING: Sonnet H𝓩
See Handbook of Literary Terms, p. 925

A **sonnet** is a lyric poem consisting of fourteen lines of iambic pentameter. The English sonnet expresses its proposition or problem in the first three *quatrains* (four-line stanzas) and resolves it in the concluding *couplet* (pair of lines).

1. What statement does the speaker make in the first twelve lines of "A Lover's Vow"?
2. How is that statement resolved in the last two lines of the poem?
3. Explain the development of thought in "Alas, So All Things . . . ."

COMPOSITION
Writing a Letter to Wyatt
Assume that you are Anne Boleyn and have just seen Wyatt's sonnet. Write him a letter in which you comment on it, either favorably or unfavorably, and explain why you feel as you do. (If you wish, assume instead that you are King Henry VIII and write from his point of view.)

Analyzing a Sonnet
Choose any one of the three sonnets you have read and write a paper in which you explain the sonnet form and analyze how your chosen sonnet fits that form. (Keep in mind that the Wyatt poem is an Italian sonnet, and the two Surrey poems are English sonnets.) Discuss especially the division of thought into proposition and resolution, and mention any poetic devices—such as figurative language—that seem appropriate. See "Writing About Poetry and Poetic Devices" in the Writer's Handbook.

A brilliant child, Bacon entered Trinity College, Cambridge, in 1573, when he was only twelve. Leaving there in 1575, he was admitted to Gray's Inn to study law in 1576. When he was sixteen, he traveled to Paris in the entourage of the British Ambassador, going on to other parts of France, Italy, and Spain, in what had become the typical European tour for promising young men of good family.

In 1579 the death of his father, who was Lord Keeper of the Great Seal to Queen Elizabeth, recalled Bacon to England. He began his political career in 1584 by being elected to Parliament; he was re-elected a number of times. Bypassed during the reign of Elizabeth, Bacon rose rapidly under James; he was knighted in 1603, became Solicitor General in 1607, Attorney General in 1613, a member of the Privy council in 1616, Lord Keeper of the Great Seal (his father's position) in 1617, and Lord Chancellor in 1618, at which time he was created Baron Verulam, and in 1621 Viscount St. Albans.

Bacon's political career ended that same year, when he was charged with misconduct in office, admitted his guilt, and was fined, stripped of his office, and barred from sitting in Parliament. Retiring to the family estate, Bacon continued the writing and scientific experiments he had begun much earlier in life. In 1626, while he was conducting an experiment to determine whether stuffing a chicken with snow would prevent it from spoiling, he contracted a chill that developed into bronchitis, from which he died.

Although Bacon won fame in his day as a philosopher and scientist, he receives most attention today as an author, particularly an essayist. From 1597 to 1625 he published, in three collections, a total of fifty-eight essays and was responsible for introducing the essay form into England. His essays were short, treated a variety of subjects of universal interest, and contained sentences so memorable that many are still quoted today, centuries after they were written.

Bacon is known also for other works, among them *The New Atlantis* (1626), which might be considered an early example of science fiction, in which he describes an ideal state. Of particular interest is the portion dealing with Solomon's House, dedicated to the study of science, which is said to have led to the founding of the Royal Society (for the study of science) some years later. In 1620 *Novum Organum* (*The New Instrument*) was published; written in Latin, the language of learning, it influenced future scientific research through its advocacy of the inductive method of inquiry. The essay you are about to read is frequently quoted and is an example of how much thought Bacon can include in a short piece of writing.

H T See ANALOGY in the Handbook of Literary Terms, page 895.

Of Studies

Sir Francis Bacon

tudies serve for delight, for ornament, and for ability. Their chief use for delight is in privateness and retiring; for ornament, is in discourse; and for ability, is in the judgment and disposition of business; for expert[1] men can execute, and perhaps judge of particulars, one by one; but the general counsels, and the plots and marshaling of affairs come best from those that are learned. To spend too much time in studies is sloth; to use them too much for ornament is affectation; to make judgment wholly by their rules is the humor[2] of a scholar. They perfect nature, and are perfected by experience; for natural abilities are like natural plants, that need pruning by study; and studies themselves do give forth directions too much at large, except they be bounded in by experience. Crafty[3] men contemn studies, simple men admire them, and wise men use them; for they teach not their own use; but that is a wisdom without them and above them, won by observation.

Read not to contradict and confute, nor to believe and take for granted, nor to find talk and discourse, but to weigh and consider. Some books are to be tasted, others to be swallowed, and some few to be chewed and digested; that is, some books are to be read only in parts; others to be read but not curiously,[4] and some few to be read wholly, and with diligence and attention. Some books also may be read by deputy, and extracts made of them by others; but that would be only in the less important arguments and the meaner sort of books; else distilled books are, like common distilled waters, flashy[5] things.

Reading maketh a full man; conference[6] a ready man; and writing an exact man. And, therefore, if a man write little, he had need have a great memory; if he confer little, he had need have a present wit;[7] and if he read little, he had need have much cunning, to seem to know what he doth not. Histories make men wise; poets, witty; the mathematics, subtile; natural philosophy, deep; moral, grave; logic and rhetoric, able to contend: *Abeunt studia in mores!*[8] Nay, there is no stand or impediment in the wit but may be wrought out by fit studies; like as diseases of the body may have appropriate exercises. Bowling is good for the stone and reins,[9] shooting for the lungs and breast, gentle walking for the stomach, riding for the head, and the like. So if a man's wit be wandering, let him study mathematics; for in demonstrations, if his wit be called away never so little, he must begin again. If his wit be not apt to distinguish or find differences, let him study the schoolmen,[10] for they are *cymini sectores!*[11] If he be not apt to beat over matters, and to call up one thing to prove and illustrate another, let him study the lawyers' cases. So every defect of the mind may have a special receipt.

1625

---

1. expert, experienced; practical.
2. humor, whim, disposition.
3. Crafty, skilled in crafts; practical.
4. curiously, thoroughly.
5. flashy, tasteless, flat.
6. conference, conversation.
7. present wit, quick intelligence. The word *wit* is used throughout the essay in this sense.
8. Abeunt . . . mores! Studies develop into habits. [Latin]
9. stone and reins, kidney stone. Reins are kidneys.
10. schoolmen, medieval scholars.
11. cymini sectores, hairsplitters (literally, splitters of cuminseeds). [Latin]

THINK AND DISCUSS
Understanding
1. According to Bacon, what sort of books "may be read by deputy, and extracts made of them by others"? What does he mean by this?

Analyzing
2. This essay is so closely written that to understand and appreciate it fully you must stop and consider the meaning of almost every sentence. Explain in your own words the following: "Studies serve for delight, for ornament, and for ability."
3. Explain: "To spend too much time in studies is sloth; to use them too much for ornament is affectation; to make judgment wholly by their rules is the humor of a scholar."
4. Explain: "Reading maketh a full man; conference a ready man; and writing an exact man."

Extending
5. For what audience does Bacon appear to be writing?

APPLYING: Analogy H?
See Handbook of Literary Terms, p. 895

An **analogy** is a comparison made between two items, situations, or ideas that are somewhat alike but unlike in most respects. Often an unfamiliar or complex object or idea will be explained through comparison to a familiar or simpler one.

1. Explain in your own words what Bacon means in the following analogy: ". . . natural abilities are like natural plants, they need pruning by study."
2. What analogy does Bacon use in the second paragraph, beginning, "Read not to contradict and to confute . . ."?

THINKING SKILLS
Classifying
To classify things is to arrange them into categories or groups according to some system.

Much of "Of Studies" is composed of Bacon's classifications of people and books.

1. Consider the criteria inherent in "Histories make men . . . *mores!*" (page 171, column b, lines 6–9). What is Bacon's system for determining what sort of books should be read to achieve certain ends?
2. As a class, define these categories and then discuss books you have read that you would put into them: "Some books are to be tasted, others to be swallowed, and some few to be chewed and digested."

COMPOSITION ⟨—◆
Writing About Your Reading
Bacon uses the words *reading* and *studies* almost interchangeably. Think back over your experiences with books—in and out of school—and write a short autobiographical sketch about them. Were they pleasant or unpleasant? Did you have any problems? Have you learned anything from books you've read for pleasure? What type of reading do you enjoy most? Title your sketch "Reading Maketh a Full Man (or Woman)," or pick up another quote from Bacon. Share your reading experiences with your classmates.

Writing an Informal Essay
Write an informal essay in which you discuss some personal observations about people or the world around you. Here are some possible titles: "On Waiting in Line," "On Riding in an Elevator," "On Riding a Bicycle (or Motorcycle)," "On Going Shopping," "On Dressing for a Date," "On Filling Out Application Forms." Write informally (use the first person) but thoughtfully, and try to show some of your own personality in what you write. See "Developing Your Style" in the Writer's Handbook.

The woman who gave her name to one of the greatest periods in England's history—the Elizabethan Age—was in every respect a remarkable human being. Too often she is viewed from the regal or historical perspective, without consideration of the personality behind all the pomp and ceremony. Wit, song, and dance made Elizabeth's court a lively place. Not only did she herself enjoy writing poetry, but she enjoyed being honored in the poems of her courtiers. In fact, it was said that one route to advancement at court was to write good verse. For some this was so; for others it was not. Elizabeth at times exhibited a degree of fickleness in her personal relationships, as is hinted in the following poem. (For more biographical data, see the Background article, pages 161–164.)

When I Was Fair and Young

Queen Elizabeth I

When I was fair and young, and favor
  gracèd me,
  Of many was I sought, their mistress for
    to be;
But I did scorn them all, and answered them
  therefore,
    "Go, go, go, seek some otherwhere,
    Impórtune me no more!"

5 How many weeping eyes I made to pine
  with woe,
  How many sighing hearts, I have no skill
    to show;
Yet I the prouder grew, and answered them
  therefore,
    "Go, go, go, seek some otherwhere,
    Impórtune me no more!"

Then spake fair Venus' son, that proud
  victorious boy,[1]

10 And said, "Fine dame, since that you be
  so coy,
  I will so pluck your plumes that you shall
    say no more,
    'Go, go, go, seek some otherwhere,
    Impórtune me no more!' "

When he had spake these words, such
  change grew in my breast,
  That neither night nor day since that, I
    could take any rest,
15 Then lo! I did repent that I had said before,
    "Go, go, go, seek some otherwhere,
    Impórtune me no more!"

1579?   1590

---

1. Venus' son . . . boy. Cupid and his mother Venus were the patrons of lovers in Classical mythology.

THINK AND DISCUSS

WHEN I WAS FAIR AND YOUNG

Understanding

1. Why does Cupid decide to pluck the speaker's plumes?

Analyzing

2. What does the last stanza suggest has happened in the speaker's life?

3. How sincerely repentant does the speaker seem to be?

4. This poem has an unusual **rhythmic** structure, but it is basically in iambic meter, with the number of feet varying from line to line. Line 1 is an *alexandrine*—a line that contains six iambic feet (twelve syllables, with every second syllable stressed; *gracèd* is pronounced in two syllables). What other lines in the first stanza are alexandrines? Is this pattern followed throughout?

Extending

5. Do you think Queen Elizabeth intended this poem to be autobiographical? Explain.

BIOGRAPHY

Sir Walter Raleigh
1552?–1618

Sir Walter Raleigh lived to the fullest the Renaissance ideal of the complete courtier—soldier, statesman, and poet—and was in addition philosopher, historian, explorer, and colonizer. His life ended in a way that was all too common in his times—on the headsman's block on trumped-up charges of treason.

Born in Devonshire about 1552, Raleigh enrolled in Oriel College, Oxford, about 1568, leaving a year later to become a soldier with the Huguenot (French Protestant) army in France. In 1575 he was a member of the Middle Temple of the Inns of Court, apparently on the way to a career in law. However, by 1578 he was fighting with the Dutch against Spain, and then in the Irish campaigns. In the early 1580s he came to Queen Elizabeth's attention and rose rapidly in her favor, becoming her adviser in 1583. He was elevated to knighthood in 1584. In that year, too, with Elizabeth's help he sponsored the first attempt to colonize Virginia, named for Elizabeth, the Virgin Queen.

In 1585 he was in charge of preparations to repel the expected Spanish invasion—indeed, throughout his life he was violently opposed to Spain, especially to Spanish colonization in the New World. Raleigh became Captain of Elizabeth's Guardsmen in 1588, an appointment that made him responsible for her physical safety, an extremely important post in those troubled, often violent times.

By the late 1580s the Earl of Essex had begun to supplant Raleigh as the Queen's favorite, and in 1592 Raleigh incurred royal disfavor by secretly marrying Elizabeth Throckmorton, one of the Queen's maids of honor. When the marriage was discovered, the erring couple were imprisoned in the Tower of London but were released near the end of the year. Although Raleigh never fully regained Elizabeth's favor, he continued to lead an adventurous life in her service. In 1595 he participated in an exploratory voyage to Guyana; in 1596 he was wounded fighting the Spanish in Cadiz, and in the same year he testified against the Earl of Essex at the latter's trial for treason.

Elizabeth was aging, and Raleigh opposed the naming of James as her successor. From the time that James I became king of England in 1603, Raleigh, who was considered dangerous, was in trouble. Almost immediately he was accused of conspiracy against the king, convicted on charges of treason, and sentenced to death. He was pardoned three days before his execution, but kept in prison in the Tower of London, where his wife and son were permitted to join him. There he spent his time writing his *History of the World*, and conducting scientific experiments. In 1616 James I, still holding the sentence of death over Raleigh, permitted him to head a treasure-hunting expedition to Guyana, held by the Spaniards, on condition that he not fight them. But a battle did erupt (though Raleigh was on shipboard at the time); the English were defeated and Raleigh's son killed. The ill-fated expedition returned to England with its leader suffering from malaria.

Upon his return to England, Raleigh was arrested and, on October 29, 1618, beheaded on the old charges of treason. It is said that he asked for the beheading to be done quickly because he felt malarial chills coming on and did not want his enemies to think that he was trembling with fear.

To Queen Elizabeth

Our passions are most like to floods and streams,
The shallow murmur, but the deep are dumb;
So, when affections yield discourse, it seems
The bottom is but shallow whence they come.
5   They that are rich in words must needs
      discover
   That they are poor in that which makes a
      lover.

Wrong not, dear empress of my heart,
   The merit of true passion
With thinking that he feels no smart
10   That sues for no compassion;
Since, if my plaints serve not to prove
   The conquest of your beauty,

They come not from defect of love
   But from excess of duty.

15 For knowing that I sue to serve
   A saint of such perfection
As all desire, yet none deserve,
   A place in her affection,
I rather choose to want[1] relief
20   Than venture the revealing;
When glory recommends the grief,
   Despair distrusts the healing.

---

1. *want*, lack.

Thus those desires that aim too high
    For any mortal lover,
25 When reason cannot make them die
    Discretion doth them cover.
Yet, when discretion doth bereave
    The plaints that they should utter,
Then your discretion may perceive
30   That silence is a suitor.

Silence in love bewrays[2] more woe
    Than words, though ne'er so witty;
A beggar that is dumb, you know,
    Deserveth double pity.
35 Then misconceive not, dearest heart,
    My true though secret passion;
He smarteth[3] most that hides his smart
    And sues for no compassion.
1592?   1655

2. **bewrays**, betrays, reveals.
3. **smarteth**, hurts.

Detail from "A Procession of Queen Elizabeth I,"
attributed to Robert Peake the Elder. c. 1600. *Private Collection*

HZ   **Review ALLITERATION in the Handbook of Literary Terms, page 926.**

Sir Walter Raleigh to His Son

Three things there be that prosper up apace
And flourish, whilst they grow asunder far,
But on a day, they meet all in one place,
And when they meet, they one another mar;
5 And they be these: the wood, the weed, the
    wag.[1]
The wood is that which makes the gallow tree;
The weed is that which strings the hangman's
    bag;
The wag, my pretty knave, betokeneth thee.
Mark well, dear boy, whilst these assemble not,

10 Green springs the tree, hemp grows, the wag is
    wild;
But when they meet, it makes the timber rot,
It frets the halter, and it chokes the child.
Then bless thee, and beware, and let us pray
We part not with thee at this meeting day.
circa 1600

1. **wag**, a mischievous boy, probably a shortening of *waghalter*, one who is likely to swing in the hangman's halter (or noose).

What Is Our Life?

What is our life? a play of passion;
Our mirth, the music of division,[1]
Our mothers' wombs the tiring-houses[2] be
Where we are dressed for this short comedy.
5 Heaven the judicious sharp spectator is,
That sits and marks still[3] who doth act amiss;
Our graves that hide us from the searching sun
Are like drawn curtains when the play is done.
Thus march we playing to our latest rest;
10 Only we die in earnest—that's no jest.

1612

1. *music of division,* music played between acts or other
divisions of a play.
2. *tiring-houses,* dressing rooms.
3. *still,* continuously.

Even Such Is Time

Even such is time, which takes in trust
Our youth, our joys, and all we have,
And pays us but with age and dust,
Who in the dark and silent grave
5 When we have wandered all our ways
Shuts up the story of our days,
And from which earth, and grave, and dust
The Lord shall raise me up, I trust.

1628

Comment

The Death of Raleigh

A scaffold was erected in the old palace yard, upon which after fourteen years reprievement, [Sir Walter Raleigh's] head was cut off; at which time, such abundance of blood issued from his veins, that showed he had stock of nature enough left to have continued him many years in life, though now above three score years old, if it had not been taken away by the hand of violence. And this was the end of the great Sir Walter Raleigh: great sometimes in the favor of Queen Elizabeth, and next to Sir Frances Drake, the great scourge and hate of the Spaniard. . . .

From *Aubrey's Brief Lives,* edited by Oliver Lawson Dick. Copyright 1949 by Oliver Lawson Dick. Reprinted by permission of the publishers, Martin Secker & Warburg Limited and the University of Michigan Press. [First published in 1690.]

THINK AND DISCUSS
TO QUEEN ELIZABETH
Understanding
1. Summarize in one sentence what the speaker is saying to Queen Elizabeth.

Analyzing
2. What is the **analogy** in lines 1–4?
3. Apply the logic of this analogy to the poem itself. Is the poem consistent with, or counter to, the analogy? Explain.

4. According to tradition, Raleigh once spread out his cloak for Queen Elizabeth to walk on. Is this poem reminiscent of the same Raleigh? Explain.

SIR WALTER RALEIGH TO HIS SON

Understanding

1. What does Raleigh mean by "the wood, the weed, the wag" in line 5?

Analyzing

2. What is Raleigh warning his son against? How seriously is this warning to be taken?

3. What does the poem reveal about Raleigh's feelings for his son?

Extending

4. How would you react to a poem like this if you were Raleigh's child?

REVIEWING: Alliteration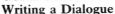

See Handbook of Literary Terms, p. 926

The repetition of sounds, usually consonants, at the beginning of words or accented syllables is called **alliteration.**

1. There are several sets of alliterating words in the poem. What are they?

2. What effect does the alliteration of "the wood, the weed, the wag" have upon the reader? upon the seriousness of the poem's message?

THINK AND DISCUSS

WHAT IS OUR LIFE?

Understanding

1. What images in this poem are drawn from the theater?

2. Who or what judges the actors' performance?

Analyzing

3. What is different about the last line? Relate this line to the rest of the poem.

Extending

4. In what respects may this poem reflect Raleigh's life as a courtier and adventurer?

EVEN SUCH IS TIME

Understanding

1. According to the speaker, what does time pay in exchange for youth and joys?

Analyzing

2. Is this poem a complaint, a philosophical poem, a religious poem, or something else? Explain.

THINKING SKILLS

Synthesizing

One way of synthesizing is to apply personal experience and imagination to a situation, so as to develop new understandings and insights.

1. In his biography, Raleigh is described as fulfilling the Renaissance ideal. Consider the various activities he engaged in during his life. Which of these activities it is still possible for a person to pursue? Is it possible today for one person to do *all* these things?

2. Name one modern person (public figure or not) who in your mind comes closest to being a "Renaissance" person in today's terms.

COMPOSITION

Writing a Dialogue

Based on what you have learned about Queen Elizabeth and Sir Walter Raleigh, write a dialogue between them. The meaning of love would be an appropriate topic, but you may write on any topic you wish. Remember, however, that although they may play with words and banter about serious topics, Elizabeth was nevertheless a powerful queen and Raleigh a gracious courtier.

Evaluating Raleigh as a Poet

Reread the four Raleigh poems (if you wish, add "The Nymph's Reply" on page 266), noting their cleverness and versatility with regard to subjects and poetic forms. Then write an evaluation of Raleigh as a poet, supporting your contentions by references to the poems.

ENRICHMENT

Interpreting Renaissance Poetry

Queen Elizabeth's poem and the Raleigh selections lend themselves well to being read aloud. Plan a class program of readings, including these and any other poems from the period (you might also wish to include some of the Raleigh-Elizabeth dialogue compositions). If possible, play some recordings of Renaissance music as background during your reading.

Unlike the courtier poets, who were satisfied to have their verses circulated in manuscript form, Edmund Spenser wrote for publication—and for the royal favor he hoped would be his through publication.

Coming from an impoverished background (his father was a journeyman clothmaker), Spenser was a "poor boy"—a scholarship student at the Merchant Tailors' School, then under the direction of Richard Mulcaster, one of the great educators of the age. Spenser went on to Pembroke Hall, Cambridge, as a "sizar," a scholarship student who had servant duties to perform; poverty continued to dog his footsteps throughout his life.

After taking his B.A. and M.A., Spenser served as secretary to the Bishop of Rochester, then in 1579 entered the service of the Earl of Leicester. His appointment there was short-lived, for in 1580 he was sent to Ireland as secretary to its new governor, Lord Grey of Wilton. Except for several visits to England, Spenser remained in Ireland for the rest of his life.

In 1579, before he left England, Spenser had published *The Shepheardes Calender*, rich in classical allusions and written in deliberately archaic language. He had also begun his masterpiece, *The Faerie Queene*, a long allegorical poem dedicated to Queen Elizabeth. Not until 1590, and then with the help of Sir Walter Raleigh, was any part of this poem published. Raleigh had visited Spenser at his home, Kilcolman Castle, and the two returned to England together. When the first three books were published, Queen Elizabeth awarded him a pension.

Returning to Ireland, Spenser fell in love with Elizabeth Boyle, to whom he dedicated his sonnet cycle, *Amoretti* (1594)—the title means "little love poems"—which tells the story of their romance. To celebrate their marriage, he composed a beautiful marriage hymn, *Epithalamion* (1594). In 1595 three more books of *The Faerie Queene* were published. These were followed in the same year by another marriage hymn, *Prothalamion*, commissioned by the Earl of Worcester in honor of the double marriage of his two eldest daughters.

Meantime, conditions in Ireland were deteriorating rapidly, and in October, 1598, Spenser's home was burned by the rebels; Spenser and his wife barely escaped with their lives. Sent to London in December, 1598, to plead for reinforcements for the English garrison in Ireland, Spenser became ill. He died in London on January 13, 1599, under conditions suggesting dire poverty. The Earl of Essex paid for his funeral, and he was laid to rest near Chaucer, whom he had long admired, in the Poets' Corner in Westminster Abbey.

HT See PARADOX in the Handbook of Literary Terms, page 915.

from Amoretti

Edmund Spenser

Sonnet 30

My love is like to ice, and I to fire:
How comes it then that this her cold so great
Is not dissolved through my so hot desire,
But harder grows the more I her entreat?
5 Or how comes it that my exceeding heat
Is not allayed by her heart-frozen cold,
But that I burn much more in boiling sweat,
And feel my flames augmented manifold?
What more miraculous thing may be told,
10 That fire, which all things melts, should
    harden ice,
And ice, which is congealed with senseless
    cold,
Should kindle fire by wonderful device?
Such is the power of love in gentle mind,
That it can alter all the course of kind.[1]

                                   1595

Portrait of unidentified young man against a background of flames by Nicholas Hilliard. *Victoria and Albert Museum*

---

1. *kind*, nature.

Sonnet 75

One day I wrote her name upon the strand,
But came the waves and washèd it away:
Again I wrote it with a second hand,
But came the tide and made my pains his
    prey.
5 "Vain man," said she, "that dost in vain
    assay
A mortal thing so to immortalize,
For I myself shall like to this decay,
And eke[1] my name be wipèd out likewise."
"Not so," quoth I, "let baser things devise
10 To die in dust, but you shall live in fame;
My verse your virtues rare shall eternize,
And in the heavens write your glorious
    name.
Where, whenas death shall all the world
    subdue,
Our love shall live, and later life renew."

                               1595

---

1. *eke*, also.

Sir Philip Sidney may be said to epitomize the ideal Renaissance courtier. Of high birth, he received an education that accorded with his background: Shrewsbury School, followed in 1568 by Christ Church College, Oxford, which he left in 1571 without taking his degree, probably because of an outbreak of plague.

Sidney traveled on the European continent, including in his itinerary Paris, where he served for several months as a personal attendant to King Charles IX of France, in which position of honor he undoubtedly learned much about French politics and statesmanship.

Following the Massacre of St. Bartholomew (on August 23, 1572, the eve of the saint's feast), when thousands of French Protestants were killed, Sidney left Paris. For the next several years he traveled in Germany, Hungary, Italy, and the Netherlands, managing to study music and astronomy along the way, and to have his portrait (apparently lost) painted in Venice by Veronese. He did all this before he was twenty-one.

In 1575 Sidney returned to England and to Elizabeth's court. He accompanied Elizabeth on a visit to the estate of the Earl of Essex, where he met the Earl's thirteen-year-old daughter, Penelope. He later immortalized her as the Stella of his sonnet sequence, *Astrophel and Stella*, usually regarded as his greatest literary achievement. This sequence was published posthumously in 1591 and led to a vogue for sonnet sequences.

After a brief assignment as ambassador to Germany, Sidney returned to court in 1580 and possibly incurred Elizabeth's displeasure by writing her a letter opposing her proposed marriage to the Duke of Anjou. Temporarily unwelcome at court, Sidney spent some time with his sister, the Countess of Pembroke, completing for her a prose romance, the *Arcadia*, that he had begun about 1577. Regarded as the second of Sidney's major literary achievements, this book was published in 1590, in revised form, as *The Countess of Pembroke's Arcadia*. Though written chiefly in prose, it did contain some poems. Lost for more than three hundred years, two manuscript copies of Sidney's original *Arcadia* were finally found in 1907.

Sidney's third major literary achievement was a pamphlet titled *An Apology for Poetry*, published in 1595. It is usually considered the single most outstanding work of Elizabethan literary theory and criticism.

In 1583 Sidney was knighted and married Frances Walsingham, the daughter of Sir Francis Walsingham, Elizabeth's Secretary of State. In 1585 Sidney was making plans to sail with Sir Francis Drake on a voyage of discovery to the New World when Queen Elizabeth intervened, sending him to the Netherlands to join the Protestant forces there.

In September, 1586, in a minor skirmish, Sidney received a bullet wound in the left thigh. Tradition has it that after he was wounded Sidney gave the last of his water to a dying foot soldier, saying that the soldier had greater need of it than he. Medical care was still primitive, and Sidney died of his wound twenty-six days later.

Sir Philip Sidney

H𝒯 See CONCEIT in the Handbook of Literary Terms, page 900.

from Arcadia

My true love hath my heart, and I have his,
By just exchange one for the other given:
I hold his dear, and mine he cannot miss;
There never was a bargain better driven.
5 His heart in me keeps me and him in one;
My heart in him his thoughts and senses guides:
He loves my heart, for once it was his own;
I cherish his, because in me it bides.
His heart his wound received from my sight;
10 My heart was wounded with his wounded heart;
For, as from me on him his hurt did light,
So still me-thought in me his hurt did smart:
Both equal hurt, in this change sought our bliss:
My true love hath my heart and I have his.
1580   1590

from Astrophel and Stella

Sonnet 31

With how sad steps, Oh Moon, thou climb'st
   the skies!
How silently, and with how wan a face!
What, may it be that even in heavenly place
That busy archer[1] his sharp arrows tries?
5 Sure, if that long-with-love-acquainted eyes
Can judge of love, thou feel'st a lover's case,
I read it in thy looks—thy languished grace
To me, that feel the like, thy state descries.[2]
Then, even of fellowship, Oh Moon, tell me,
10 Is constant love deemed there but want of
      wit?
Are beauties there as proud as here they be?
Do they above love to be loved, and yet

April in the fields, a detail from a miniature by Simon Beninck. 16th cent. *Victoria and Albert Museum·*

Those lovers scorn whom that love doth
   possess?
Do they call virtue there ungratefulness?[3]
1591

---

1. *archer*, Cupid.
2. *descries*, reveals.
3. *Do . . . ungratefulness?* Do they call ungratefulness a virtue there?

HT See APOSTROPHE in the Handbook of Literary Terms, page 897.

Thou Blind Man's Mark

Thou blind man's mark,[1] thou fool's
    self-chosen snare,
Fond fancy's scum, and dregs of scattered
    thought;
Band[2] of all evils, cradle of causeless care;
Thou web of will, whose end is never wrought;
5 Desire! Desire! I have too dearly bought,
With price of mangled mind, thy worthless ware;
Too long, too long, asleep thou hast me brought,
Who should my mind to higher things prepare.
But yet in vain thou hast my ruin sought;

10 In vain thou mad'st me to vain things aspire;
In vain thou kindlest all thy smoky fire;
For Virtue hath this better lesson taught—
Within myself to seek my only hire,
Desiring naught but how to kill Desire.
1581   **1598**

1. *mark*, target.
2. *Band*, cloth used for swaddling, or wrapping, an infant.

THINK AND DISCUSS
from AMORETTI, SONNET 30
Understanding
1. The speaker demonstrates his perplexity by asking three questions. Summarize each in your own words.

Analyzing
2. How does the final couplet provide an answer to the questions the speaker has asked?

APPLYING: Paradox **HT**
See Handbook of Literary Terms, p. 915
   A **paradox** is a statement, often metaphorical, that seems to be self-contradictory but that has valid meaning. For example, the phrase "freedom in captivity" is paradoxical.

1. What is paradoxical about the central metaphor of Sonnet 30?
2. Is the speaker aware of the paradox? Explain.

THINK AND DISCUSS
SONNET 75
Understanding
1. There are two speakers in this sonnet. Who are they, and which lines are spoken by each?

Analyzing
2. The words *wipèd out* in line 8 are important in tying together the actual and metaphorical worlds of the sonnet. What do they describe in the actual world? in the metaphorical world?

Extending
3. Is the couplet that concludes this sonnet simply a lover's exaggeration, or is there some truth to it? Explain.

from ARCADIA
Understanding
1. In three places the speaker uses terms that deal with barter, or trade. What are they?

Analyzing

2. How do these terms help to express the meaning of the sonnet?

3. Explain: "His heart in me keeps me and him in one" (line 5).

Extending

4. Do you think the poet is more concerned with love or with poetic dexterity? Explain.

APPLYING: Conceit H⊅

See Handbook of Literary terms, p. 900

A **conceit** is a fanciful and sometimes far-fetched metaphor. It has been described as stretching a metaphor to the breaking point.

1. Sidney plays much on the word *heart*. What does the conceit involve?

2. In carrying out the conceit, the speaker mentions that both hearts are wounded. Explain in your own words what she means.

from ASTROPHEL AND STELLA, SONNET 31

Understanding

1. According to the speaker, what do he and the moon have in common?

Analyzing

2. What do the questions the speaker asks the moon (lines 10–14) imply about his own situation on earth?

THOU BLIND MAN'S MARK

Understanding

1. Who or what has taught the speaker to conquer Desire? How is it done?

2. What price has the speaker had to pay for Desire's "worthless ware"?

Analyzing

3. Explain the speaker's current feeling about Desire. Why does he feel this way?

APPLYING: Apostrophe

See Handbook of Literary Terms, p. 897

An **apostrophe** is a figure of speech in which an absent person, an abstract concept such as Truth, or an inanimate object such as Autumn is directly addressed.

1. To whom or what is the apostrophe in this sonnet addressed? How do you know?

2. Which other sonnet by Sidney makes use of an apostrophe? To whom or what is that apostrophe addressed?

VOCABULARY H⊅

Etymology

English has changed enormously over the years, as words were added from various languages, but a good number of the words we still use are from Old or Middle English. Look up the following words in your Glossary; then answer the questions about their etymologies.

bereave   dregs   fond   fret   wan

1. Which word comes from Old English words meaning "to rob away"?

2. Which word has undergone a reversal of meaning from its original meaning of "dark"?

3. Which word comes from a Middle English word meaning "fool"?

4. Which word derives metaphorically from an Old English word meaning "eat"?

5. Which word was singular in its original form but plural in its modern form?

COMPOSITION ◄═▸

Writing a Letter to Elizabeth Boyle

Spenser dedicated his sonnet cycle, *Amoretti*—"little love poems"—to Elizabeth Boyle, whom he later married. Assume that Elizabeth has just shown you Sonnets 30 and 75, sent to her by Spenser, and has asked for your opinion of them and of Spenser as a suitor. How will you answer her? Write Elizabeth Boyle a friendly letter in which you tell what you think of the poetry and of Spenser, although you've never met him. Remember that you yourself are living in the Elizabethan age, when certain manners and kinds of poetry are fashionable.

Writing About Elizabethan Poetic Devices

Reread the poems so far in this unit to find examples of figurative language—particularly **paradox, conceit,** and **apostrophe.** Write a paper of at least five paragraphs explaining how Elizabethan poetry is characterized by the use of certain kinds of poetic devices. Use quotes from the poems to illustrate your points.

BIOGRAPHY

William Shakespeare
1564–1616

More than two hundred contemporary references to Shakespeare have been located among church and legal records, documents in the Public Record Office, and miscellaneous sources. These provide at least an outline of his life, beginning with his baptism on April 26, 1564, in Trinity Church, Stratford-on-Avon, and ending with his burial there on April 25, 1616.

Shakespeare's father, John, was a prosperous glove maker of Stratford who, after holding minor municipal offices, was elected high bailiff (the equivalent of mayor) of Stratford. Shakespeare's mother, Mary Arden, came from an affluent family of landowners.

Shakespeare probably received his early education at the excellent Stratford Grammar School, where he would have learned Latin and a smattering of Greek. In 1582 Shakespeare married Anne Hathaway, who lived in a neighboring hamlet. Susanna, their first child, was born in 1583, followed in 1585 by twins, a boy and a girl, named Hamnet and Judith.

From 1585 to 1592 there is no record of Shakespeare's life, but at some point in this period, Shakespeare must have moved to London and begun a theatrical career. The next reference to him, an unfavorable one, comes from a pamphlet called *A Groatsworth of Wit* (1592), written by Robert Greene. Addressed by Greene to his fellow University Wits who, like him, had been struggling to earn livings as journalists and playwrights, the pamphlet refers to Shakespeare unflatteringly, calling him "an upstart crow, beautified with our feathers, that with his tiger's heart wrapped in a player's hide supposes he is as well able to bombast out a blank verse as the rest of you; and being an absolute *Johannes fac totum*, is in his own conceit the only Shake-scene in a country."

Apparently Shakespeare, whose background was not that of a University Wit but of a "player" (actor), had been taking some playwriting business away from Greene and his friends, possibly updating plays they had once worked on. The "tiger's heart" phrase is an oblique reference to a line in Shakespeare's *Henry VI, Part 3;* "O tiger's heart wrapped in a woman's hide"; "*Johannes fac totum*" means "jack-of-all-trades," probably because Shakespeare was acting and writing; "Shake-scene" is an obvious play on the poet's name. From 1592 to the end of Shakespeare's life, there are many references to him and to his literary output.

Shakespeare's major activity lay in the field of drama. He became a full shareholder in his acting company (the Lord Chamberlain's Men, later the King's Men); he was part-owner of the Globe Theater and later of Blackfriars Theater; and in 1597 he purchased property in Stratford, including New Place, one of the largest houses in the town. He probably retired there about 1610, traveling to London when necessary to take care of his theatrical business. Although some of Shakespeare's plays were published during his lifetime, not until after his death was any attempt made to collect them in a single volume. The First Folio, the first edition of Shakespeare's collected plays, appeared in 1623.

William Shakespeare

HT Review THEME in the Handbook of Literary Terms, page 931.

Shakespeare's Sonnets

In all, 154 sonnets belong to Shakespeare's sonnet sequence. The sonnets were probably written in the 1590s but were first published in 1609. They tell a fragmentary story involving a young man, a "dark lady," and the poet himself, together with a "rival poet." In sonnets 1–126, the young man has the principal role, while in the remainder, the dark lady becomes prominent. Scholars and critics have made many attempts to untangle all the mysteries of Shakespeare's sonnets, as they may shed light on his life, but generally to no avail. It is important to remember that Shakespeare's sonnets were written at a time when such sequences were fashionable, and thus the sonnets may be more an exercise in literary convention than in autobiography.

Sonnet 18

Shall I compare thee to a summer's day?
Thou art more lovely and more temperate:
Rough winds do shake the darling buds of May,
And summer's lease hath all too short a date:
Sometime too hot the eye of heaven shines,
And often is his gold complexion dimmed,
And every fair from fair sometimes declines,
By chance of nature's changing course
    untrimmed,[1]
But thy eternal summer shall not fade
Nor lose possession of that fair thou owest,[2]
Nor shall Death brag thou wander'st in his
    shade,
When in eternal lines to time thou growest.
    So long as men can breathe, or eyes can see,
    So long lives this, and this gives life to thee.

1609

1. *untrimmed*, reduced; shorn of beauty.
2. *fair thou owest*, beauty you possess.

Sonnet 29

When in disgrace with fortune and men's eyes,
I all alone beweep my outcast state,
And trouble deaf heaven with my bootless[1] cries,
And look upon myself and curse my fate,
Wishing me like to one more rich in hope,
Featured like him, like him with friends
    possessed,
Desiring this man's art and that man's scope,
With what I most enjoy contented least—
Yet in these thoughts myself almost
    despising,
Haply I think on thee, and then my state,
Like to the lark at break of day arising
From sullen earth, sings hymns at heaven's gate.
    For thy sweet love remembered such
        wealth brings
    That then I scorn to change my state with
        kings.

1609

1. *bootless*, useless.

Sonnet 30

[handwritten: alliteration of s.]

When to the sessions[1] of sweet silent thought *[handwritten: thinking of the past]*
I summon up remembrance of things past,
I sigh the lack of many a thing I sought,
And with old woes new wail my dear time's
    waste: *[handwritten: depression]*
5 Then can I drown an eye, unused to flow, *[handwritten: friends that R dead]*
For precious friends hid in death's dateless[2]
    night,
And weep afresh love's long since canceled woe,
And moan the expense[3] of many a vanished
    sight:
Then can I grieve at grievances foregone,[4]
10 And heavily from woe to woe tell o'er
The sad account of forebemoanèd moan,
Which I new pay as if not paid before.
    But if the while I think on thee, dear friend,
    All losses are restored and sorrows end.

                             1609

1. *sessions,* literally, the sittings of a law court.
2. *dateless,* endless.
3. *expense,* loss.
4. *foregone,* past.

Sonnet 71

No longer mourn for me when I am dead *[handwritten: ole's dying]*
Than you shall hear the surly sullen bell[1]
Give warning to the world that I am fled
From this vile world, with vilest worms to dwell:
5 Nay, if you read this line, remember not
The hand that writ it; for I love you so,
That I in your sweet thoughts would be forgot,
If thinking on me then should make you woe.
Oh, if, I say, you look upon this verse
10 When I perhaps compounded am with clay,
Do not so much as my poor name rehearse,
But let your love even with my life decay;
    Lest the wise world should look into your moan,
    And mock you with me after I am gone.

[handwritten: don't mourn be happy.]   **1609**

1. *bell,* the bell tolled as someone was dying, in order that
those who heard it might pray for the departing soul.

[handwritten: Italian sonnet 8-6 ABBA/]

Sonnet 116

Let me not to the marriage of true minds
Admit impediments. Love is not love
Which alters when it alteration finds,
Or bends with the remover to remove.[1]
5 Oh no! It is an ever-fixèd mark,
That looks on tempests and is never shaken;
It is the star to every wandering bark, *[handwritten: a ship]*
Whose worth's unknown, although his height
    be taken.
Love's not Time's fool, though rosy lips and
    cheeks
10 Within his bending sickle's compass come;
Love alters not with his brief hours and weeks,
But bears it out even to the edge of doom.
    If this be error and upon me proved,
    I never writ, nor no man ever loved.

                             1609

1. *Or bends . . . remove,* or changes when the loved one
is inconstant.

Detail from *Abbey in an Oak Forest* by Caspar David
Friedrich. 1809–1910. *Staatliche Museen, West Berlin*

[handwritten: Shake 4-8-2]

H/T See CONNOTATION/DENOTATION in the Handbook of Literary Terms, page 901.

Sonnet 130

A My mistress' eyes are nothing like the sun;
B Coral is far more red than her lips' red;
A If snow be white, why then her breasts are dun;
B If hairs be wires, black wires grow on her head;
C I have seen roses damasked,[1] red and white,
D But no such roses see I in her cheeks;
C And in some perfumes is there more delight
D Than in the breath that from my mistress reeks;
E I love to hear her speak, yet well I know
F That music hath a far more pleasing sound;

E I grant I never saw a goddess go;[2]
F My mistress, when she walks, treads on the
  ground.
G And yet, by heaven, I think my love as rare
G As any she[3] belied with false compare.

1609

---

1. *damasked*, mingled.
2. *go*, walk.
3. *any she*, any woman.

THINK AND DISCUSS
SONNET 18
Understanding
1. Which aspects of a summer day are used in this comparison with the beloved? Are any of them favorable?

Analyzing
2. Although this is an English sonnet, its thought can be divided into eight and six lines, like an Italian sonnet. Explain.
3. According to the speaker, what will keep his beloved's "eternal summer" from fading?

Extending
4. Some readers feel that Shakespeare, in this sonnet, was paying greater tribute to his poetry than to his love. What do you think?

REVIEWING: Theme H/T
See Handbook of Literary Terms, p. 931
  Theme is the underlying meaning of a literary work. A theme may be directly stated, but more often it is implied.

1. The theme of Sonnet 18 is not a summer's day, nor even the comparison of the beloved to a summer's day. Reread the couplet and think about its connection to the rest of the sonnet; then explain what the theme is.
2. What other poem that you have read in this unit shares the same theme?

THINK AND DISCUSS
SONNET 29
Understanding
1. What is the speaker's state of mind in lines 1–9?

Analyzing
2. What is striking about the comparison in lines 10–12?

Extending
3. How much of the content of this sonnet is limited to Shakespeare's era, and how much is still appropriate today? Explain.

SONNET 30
Understanding
1. What do lines 1–12 of this sonnet deal with?

Analyzing
2. In lines 1–12, what mood is the speaker in?
3. How does the concluding couplet change everything that preceded it?

Extending

4. Sonnets 29 and 30 are sequential. How does the situation of the speaker differ in the two poems?
5. Despite the different situations, how are the two poems similar?

SONNET 71
Understanding

1. How long does the speaker ask to be mourned after his death?

Analyzing

2. What appears to be the speaker's state of mind?
3. Which words and phrases suggest the unpleasantness of death?
4. Which lines do you think best convey the depth of the speaker's love?
5. How sincere is the advice given by the speaker? Explain.

Extending

6. Shakespeare's sonnets were not published until 1609, when he was forty-five years old. When do you think he may have written this sonnet—when he was very young, not long before its publication, or at another time? Explain.

SONNET 116
Understanding

1. Put the first sentence into your own words. Does the word *admit* mean "acknowledge" or "let in"?
2. How does the speaker regard love that does "admit impediments"?
3. According to the speaker, how long should love last?

Analyzing

4. What **metaphor** is used to show that love should be firm and steady?
5. Comment on the effectiveness of the concluding couplet.

Extending

6. Shakespeare mentions his writing and the effects of time in this sonnet and in Sonnet 18. Compare the two. Which seems to be more mature? Explain.

SONNET 130
Understanding

1. Does the speaker ever say directly that anything is wrong with his mistress? Explain.

Analyzing

2. This is, in a way, an "anti-sonnet". What does it do to each of the following conventions of the sonnet: the beauty of the beloved; her hair, eyes, cheeks, lips, and breath; her voice and walk?
3. What then does the concluding couplet do to the meaning of the entire sonnet? to the conventions of the sonnet?

APPLYING: Connotation/Denotation HP
See Handbook of Literary Terms, p. 901

Connotation refers to the associations and added meanings surrounding a word that are not part of its literal dictionary meaning, or **denotation**. To understand Sonnet 130, you must extend connotation beyond individual words to encompass entire lines of poetry.

1. Line 1 makes a simple statement—its denotation. But what does the line connote about the mistress's eyes?
2. What other lines in the sonnet make simple denotative statements that, however, have unfavorable connotations? Explain each of these.
3. Shakespeare completely changes the connotations of these lines by two devices. One is the use of *if* to indicate conditions contrary to fact. What is the other?

THINKING SKILLS
Generalizing

An author or a reader is generalizing when he or she draws a general conclusion from specific examples.

1. In Sonnet 130, what does Shakespeare imply about sonnets and sonneteers in general?
2. Does he seem to include himself in this generalization? Explain.
3. From the sonnets you have read so far, do you think that Shakespeare's implication is valid? Cite specific poems to support your opinion.

Since the time of Shakespeare, our language and ways of speaking have changed greatly. An awareness of some of Shakespeare's writing techniques and expressions will help you to overcome problems of language and style and enable you to read with increased pleasure and ease. Here are some guidelines for reading *Macbeth*.

Read holistically. To treat something *holistically* is to treat the whole of it, rather than its isolated parts. As you read *Macbeth*, rather than struggling with a difficult passage word by word, read straight through until you come to an end punctuation mark. Aim first to get the sense of the entire passage. Some of the speeches are very long, with involved interruptions, and make their point only in the last two or three lines. Once you comprehend the thought-unit, you can then go back to concentrate on the details.

Use the notes. The notes help you define unfamiliar words as well as understand allusions and particularly difficult lines. A second kind of note, identified by boxed numbers, suggests possible stagings and asks questions designed to help you think about your reading.

Complete contractions. To achieve a regular rhythm in his verse, Shakespeare often subtracts syllables by making contractions. When you come across such words with apostrophes, mentally supply the letters and syllables needed to complete them; for example:

i' = *in*	*'t* = *it*	*ne'er* = *never*
o' = *of*	*o'er* = *over*	*thou'rt* = *thou art*

Find the simple sentence. Many sentences are long and loaded with modifiers and other interrupters. For example, In Act I, Scene 2, the bleeding Captain says, "The merciless Macdonwald—/Worthy to be a rebel, for to that/The multiplying villainies of nature/Do swarm upon him—from the western isles/Of kerns and gallowglasses is supplied. . . ." For sentences like this, you will find it helpful to isolate the subject, verb, and complements, as indicated here by underlining. Then analyze the rest of the sentence.

Rearrange inverted sentences. In modern usage speakers usually place the subject before the verb. Many of Shakespeare's sentences, however, are inverted; for example, Lady Macbeth's doctor says, "More needs she the divine than the physician." When you encounter such passages, simply rearrange the word order to place the subject first. Rearranged, this passage would read: "She needs the divine (priest) more than the physician."

Interpret metaphors. Some of the most important ideas in the play are communicated by means of metaphors. Ask yourself what comparison is implied and then how this comparison affects the overall meaning of the passage. For example, when King Duncan greets Macbeth, to whom he has just given an added title, he says, "I have begun to plant thee, and will labor/To make thee full of growing." In this speech he is using *plant* and *growing* metaphorically to tell Macbeth that other honors will be forthcoming.

Follow the causes and effects. Because *Macbeth* is tightly plotted, events do not happen in isolation, but rather lead one to the other. Event 1 (the cause) will lead to event 2 (the effect), which in turn becomes the cause of event 3, and so on. For example, the three witches tell Macbeth he will be king, but that Banquo's descendents will rule, which causes Macbeth to kill the king and after that to kill Banquo and others. Looking for such chains of causes and effects will help you understand what happens as well as why.

Read passages aloud. You are, after all reading a script meant to be performed by actors. Try reading speeches aloud and visualizing the action as it unfolds. Also listen to or watch actors performing scenes from the play.

HT See PLOT in the Handbook of Literary Terms, page 916.

Macbeth

William Shakespeare

CHARACTERS

DUNCAN, *king of Scotland*

MALCOLM
DONALBAIN } *his sons*

MACBETH
BANQUO } *generals of the king's army*

MACDUFF
LENNOX
ROSS
MENTEITH } *noblemen of Scotland*
ANGUS
CAITHNESS

FLEANCE, *son to Banquo*
SIWARD, *Earl of Northumberland, general of the English forces*

YOUNG SIWARD, *his son*
SEYTON, *an officer attending on Macbeth*
BOY, *son to Macduff*
AN ENGLISH DOCTOR
A SCOTTISH DOCTOR
A CAPTAIN
A PORTER
AN OLD MAN
THREE MURDERERS
LADY MACBETH
LADY MACDUFF
GENTLEWOMAN *attending on Lady Macbeth*
HECATE, *goddess of witchcraft*
THREE WITCHES
APPARITIONS
**LORDS, GENTLEMEN, OFFICERS, SOLDIERS,
ATTENDANTS, AND MESSENGERS**

ACT ONE

SCENE 1

A desert place. (Played on the Tarras,° possibly with the use of the Music Gallery above for one of the three witches.) Thunder and lightning. Enter three WITCHES.

FIRST WITCH. When shall we three meet again
In thunder, lightning, or in rain?

Tarras, terrace. See the diagram of Shakespeare's theater on page 251.

Notes from *On Producing Shakespeare* by Ronald Watkins. First published London 1950 by Michael Joseph, Ltd. Second edition Copyright ©1964 by Benjamin Blom, Inc. Distributed by Arno Press Inc. Reprinted by permission.

SECOND WITCH. When the hurlyburly's done,
    When the battle's lost and won.
5 **THIRD WITCH.** That will be ere the set of sun.
FIRST WITCH. Where the place?
SECOND WITCH.   Upon the heath.
THIRD WITCH. There to meet with Macbeth.
FIRST WITCH. I come, Graymalkin!°
SECOND WITCH. Paddock° calls.
10 **THIRD WITCH.** Anon.
ALL. Fair is foul, and foul is fair,
    Hover through the fog and filthy air.   (*Exeunt.*)°

SCENE 2

A camp near Forres.° (*Played on the Platform.*) *Alarum within.*° *Enter* DUNCAN,
MALCOLM, DONALBAIN, LENNOX, *with* ATTENDANTS, *meeting a bleeding*
CAPTAIN.

DUNCAN. What bloody° man is that? He can report,
    As seemeth by his plight, of the revolt
    The newest state.
MALCOLM.   This is the sergeant°
    Who like a good and hardy soldier fought
5   'Gainst my captivity. Hail, brave friend!
    Say to the King the knowledge of the broil
    As thou didst leave it.

[handwritten margin note: tell the king the battle the came from]

Illustration by Charles Ricketts from *The Tragedie of Macbeth*, reproduced in the Players'
Shakespeare, after the Folio of 1623, Ernest Benn, 1923.

Graymalkin, a gray cat.
Paddock, a toad.

[1] What does line 11 mean? Be alert for characters and events that illustrate this apparent contradiction.

[2] What is the purpose of this scene? In some stage presentations it has been omitted. If you were staging *Macbeth,* would you include it? Why or why not?

Exeunt, exit (plural).
Forres, a town north of Edinburgh.
Alarum within, offstage noises indicating that a battle is going on. An alarum usually consisted of confused sounds of trumpets, drums, clash of arms, and men yelling.

[3] In reading the speeches of Duncan, consider whether he has the characteristics of a strong king.

bloody. Blood is one of the significant motifs that recur in the play. Others are sleeplessness, animal and bird imagery, clothing metaphors (usually of borrowed or ill-fitting garments), darkness and light, hell and devils, and reversal of accepted values. Note throughout what purpose these motifs might serve.

sergeant, In Shakespeare's day, military ranks were not distinguished so clearly as they are now; although the officer is "Captain" in the stage directions and speech headings, Malcolm may not be incorrect in addressing him as "sergeant."

[4] About how old do you guess Malcolm is? As the play progresses, keep this age in mind to see if events support or refute it.

CAPTAIN.   Doubtful it stood,
       As two spent swimmers that do cling together
       And choke their art.° The merciless Macdonwald— *the enemy*
10   Worthy to be a rebel, for to that
       The multiplying villainies of nature
       Do swarm upon him—from the western isles°
       Of kerns° and gallowglasses° is supplied;
       And Fortune, on his damnèd quarrel smiling,
15   Showed like a rebel's whore.° But all's too weak;
       For brave Macbeth—well he deserves that name—
       Disdaining Fortune, with his brandished steel,
       Which smoked with bloody execution,
       Like valor's minion° carvèd out his passage
20   Till he faced the slave;°
       Which ne'er shook hands, nor bade farewell to him,
       Till he unseamed him from the nave to the chaps,°
       And fixed his head upon our battlements.
       DUNCAN. O valiant cousin! Worthy gentleman!
25   CAPTAIN. As whence the sun 'gins his reflection
       Shipwrecking storms and direful thunders break,
       So from that spring whence comfort seemed to come
       Discomfort swells. Mark, King of Scotland, mark:
       No sooner justice had, with valor armed,
30   Compelled these skipping kerns to trust their heels,
       But the Norweyan° lord, surveying vantage,
       With furbished arms and new supplies of men,
       Began a fresh assault.
       DUNCAN.   Dismayed not this *best friends*
       Our captains, Macbeth and Banquo?
       CAPTAIN.   Yes—
35   As sparrows eagles, or the hare the lion.
       If I say sooth, I must report they were
       As cannons overcharged with double cracks,° so they
       Doubly redoubled strokes upon the foe;
       Except they meant to bathe in reeking wounds, *blood of enemy.*
40   Or memorize another Golgotha,°
       I cannot tell.
       But I am faint; my gashes cry for help. → *he's wounded.*
       DUNCAN. So well the words become thee as thy wounds;
       They smack of honor both. Go get him surgeons.
                         (*Exit* CAPTAIN, *attended. Enter* ROSS.)
45   Who comes here?
       MALCOLM.   The worthy thane° of Ross.
       LENNOX. What a haste looks through his eyes! So should he look
       That seems to speak things strange.
       ROSS.   God save the King!

choke their art, hinder their ability to swim.
the western isles, Ireland and the Hebrides.
kerns, lightly-armed Irish foot soldiers.
gallowglasses, Irish foot soldiers armed with axes.
Fortune . . . whore. Fortune falsely seemed to favor Macdonwald. (Fortune was often described as a harlot who was fickle and granted her favors to anyone, regardless of worth.)
minion, darling or favorite.
slave, Macdonwald.

unseamed him . . . chaps, split him from navel to jaws.

Norweyan, Norwegian.

double cracks, doubly charged with powder.

memorize . . . Golgotha (gol′gə thə), make the area as memorable for bloodshed as the place where Christ was crucified.

5   What do the Captain's comments in lines 7–42 indicate about Macbeth as soldier and leader?

thane, a Scottish title, just below an earl.

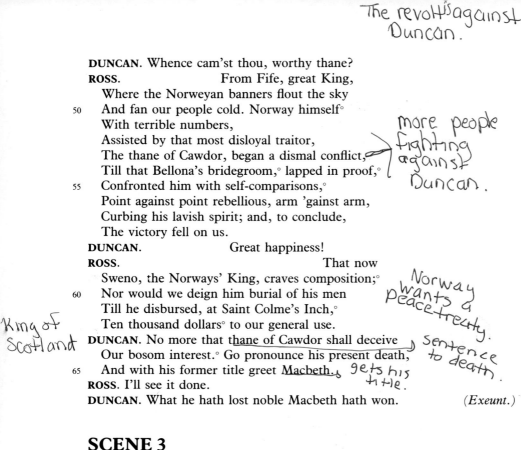

The revolt against Duncan. (handwritten)

DUNCAN. Whence cam'st thou, worthy thane?

ROSS.   From Fife, great King,
Where the Norweyan banners flout the sky

50   And fan our people cold. Norway himself°
With terrible numbers,
Assisted by that most disloyal traitor,
The thane of Cawdor, began a dismal conflict,

more people fighting against Duncan. (handwritten)

Till that Bellona's bridegroom,° lapped in proof,°

55   Confronted him with self-comparisons,°
Point against point rebellious, arm 'gainst arm,
Curbing his lavish spirit; and, to conclude,
The victory fell on us.

DUNCAN.   Great happiness!

ROSS.   That now
Sweno, the Norways' King, craves composition;°

Norway wants a peace treaty. (handwritten)

60   Nor would we deign him burial of his men
Till he disbursed, at Saint Colme's Inch,°
Ten thousand dollars° to our general use.

King of Scotland (handwritten)

DUNCAN. No more that thane of Cawdor shall deceive
Our bosom interest.° Go pronounce his present death,

Sentence to death (handwritten)

65   And with his former title greet Macbeth.

gets his title. (handwritten)

ROSS. I'll see it done.

DUNCAN. What he hath lost noble Macbeth hath won.   *(Exeunt.)*

SCENE 3

*A heath near Forres. (Played on the Platform and in the Study.) Thunder. Enter
the three* WITCHES.

animal images (handwritten)

FIRST WITCH. Where hast thou been, sister?

SECOND WITCH. Killing swine.

THIRD WITCH. Sister, where thou?

FIRST WITCH. A sailor's wife had chestnuts in her lap,

5   And munched, and munched, and munched—"Give me,"
     quoth I.
"Aroint thee,° witch!" the rump-fed ronyon° cries.

will seduce women's husband (handwritten)

Her husband's to Aleppo° gone, master o' the *Tiger,*
But in a sieve I'll thither sail,
And, like a rat without a tail,°

10   I'll do, I'll do, and I'll do.

SECOND WITCH. I'll give thee a wind.

FIRST WITCH. Thou'rt kind.

THIRD WITCH. And I another.

FIRST WITCH. I myself have all the other,

15   And the very ports they blow,
All the quarters that they know

I' the shipman's card.°
I will drain him dry as hay;
Sleep shall neither night nor day
20 Hang upon his penthouse lid;°
He shall live a man forbid;°
Weary sev'nights° nine times nine
Shall he dwindle, peak, and pine;
Though his bark cannot be lost,
25 Yet it shall be tempest-tossed.
Look what I have.
SECOND WITCH. Show me, show me.
FIRST WITCH. Here I have a pilot's thumb,
Wrecked as homeward he did come.   (*Drum within.*)
30 THIRD WITCH. A drum, a drum!
Macbeth doth come!
ALL. The weird sisters, hand in hand
Posters of° the sea and land,
Thus do go about, about;
35 Thrice to thine, and thrice to mine,
And thrice again to make up nine.
Peace! the charm's wound up.   (*Enter* MACBETH *and* BANQUO.)
MACBETH. So foul and fair a day I have not seen.
BANQUO. How far is 't called to Forres? What are these
40 So withered, and so wild in their attire,
That look not like the inhabitants o' the earth,
And yet are on 't? Live you? Or are you aught
That man may question? You seem to understand me,
By each at once her choppy finger laying
45 Upon her skinny lips. You should be women,
And yet your beards forbid me to interpret
That you are so.
MACBETH.   Speak, if you can; what are you?
FIRST WITCH. All hail, Macbeth! hail to thee, thane of Glamis!°
SECOND WITCH. All hail, Macbeth! hail to thee, thane of Cawdor!
50 THIRD WITCH. All hail, Macbeth, that shalt be king hereafter!
BANQUO. Good sir, why do you start, and seem to fear
Things that do sound so fair? I' the name of truth,
Are ye fantastical, or that indeed
Which outwardly ye show? My noble partner
55 You greet with present grace and great prediction
Of noble having and of royal hope,
That he seems rapt withal;° to me you speak not.
If you can look into the seeds of time,
And say which grain will grow and which will not,
60 Speak then to me, who neither beg nor fear
Your favors nor your hate.

---

shipman's card, compass card or chart.
penthouse lid, eyelid.
forbid, accursed.
sev'nights, weeks.

> **7** What do lines 24–25 indicate about the extent of the witches' power?

Posters of, travelers over.

> **8** This incantation might accompany a ritual dance with which the witches mark out in the center of the Platform a charmed circle for Macbeth to step into.

> **9** In line 38, what earlier lines is Macbeth echoing? What does he mean? Why might Shakespeare have given him this line?

> **10** "How . . . Forres?" might be shouted through fog to the distant figures.

> **11** "Live you?" might be spoken at close range.

> **12** In lines 44–45, the witches gesture "silence" in response to Banquo's question, yet they answer Macbeth at once. What does this show about the nature of their spell?

> **13** As he enters, Macbeth might move into the charmed circle the witches have made, reacting from the spell with a shudder. Banquo's course would be in front of the circle. Macbeth would then speak from the circle.

Glamis, (glämz).

> **14** Why *does* Macbeth start (line 51)? As you read on, compare his reaction to the witches' prophecies with Banquo's reaction. What do the reactions of the two men reveal? What might this suggest about the future action of the play?

rapt withal, completely lost in thought.

FIRST WITCH. Hail!

SECOND WITCH. Hail!

THIRD WITCH. Hail!

65 **FIRST WITCH.** Lesser than Macbeth, and greater.

SECOND WITCH. Not so happy, yet much happier.

THIRD WITCH. Thou shalt get° kings, though thou be none. — *will be father of kings.*

    So all hail, Macbeth and Banquo!

FIRST WITCH. Banquo and Macbeth, all hail!

get, beget.

70 **MACBETH.** Stay, you imperfect speakers, tell me more.

    By Sinel's° death I know I am thane of Glamis;

    But how of Cawdor? The thane of Cawdor lives,

    A prosperous gentleman. And to be king

    Stands not within the prospect of belief,

Sinel, Macbeth's father. Macbeth had inherited the title.

75   No more than to be Cawdor. Say from whence

    You owe this strange intelligence? Or why

    Upon this blasted heath you stop our way

    With such prophetic greeting? Speak, I charge you.   *(WITCHES vanish.)*

BANQUO. The earth hath bubbles, as the water has,

80   And these are of them. Whither are they vanished?

15   The witches might vanish through the grave-trap in the Study.

MACBETH. Into the air, and what seemed corporal melted

    As breath into the wind. Would they had stayed!

BANQUO. Were such things here as we do speak about?

    Or have we eaten on the insane root°

85   That takes the reason prisoner?

insane root, a root that causes hallucinations or insanity.

MACBETH. Your children shall be kings.

BANQUO.   You shall be king.

MACBETH. And thane of Cawdor, too; went it not so?

BANQUO. To the selfsame tune and words. Who's here?

                    (Enter ROSS *and* ANGUS.)

ROSS. The King hath happily received, Macbeth,

90   The news of thy success; and when he reads

    Thy personal venture in the rebels' fight,

    His wonders and his praises do contend

    Which should be thine or his. Silenced° with that,

    In viewing o'er the rest o' the selfsame day,

messenger of the king.

Silenced, speechless with admiration.

95   He finds thee in the stout Norweyan ranks,

    Nothing afeared of what thyself didst make,

    Strange images of death.° As thick as hail

    Came post with post,° and everyone did bear

    Thy praises in his kingdom's great defense,

like witches

Nothing . . . death. Macbeth killed, but did not fear death for himself.
post with post, one news-bearer after another.

100   And poured them down before him.

ANGUS.   We are sent

    To give thee from our royal master thanks;

    Only to herald thee into his sight,

    Not pay thee.

ROSS.   And, for an earnest° of a greater honor,

earnest, pledge; promise.

He bade me, from him, call thee thane of Cawdor; — *comes true.*
105 In which addition, hail, most worthy thane!
For it is thine.

BANQUO.   What, can the devil speak true?

MACBETH. The thane of Cawdor lives; why do you dress me — *why do u give me a title not mine.*
In borrowed robes?

ANGUS.   Who was the thane lives yet;
But under heavy judgment bears that life
110 Which he deserves to lose. Whether he was combined
With those of Norway, or did line° the rebel   *line, support.*
With hidden help and vantage, or that with both
He labored in his country's wreck, I know not;
But treasons capital, confessed and proved,
115 Have overthrown him.

MACBETH (aside). *to come* Glamis, and thane of Cawdor!
The greatest is behind.° (*To* ROSS *and* ANGUS) Thanks for your pains.   *behind, to come.*
(*To* BANQUO) Do you not hope your children shall be kings,
When those that gave the thane of Cawdor to me
Promised no less to them?

BANQUO.   That, trusted home,
120 Might yet enkindle you unto the crown,°
Besides the thane of Cawdor. But 'tis strange;
And oftentimes, to win us to our harm,
The instruments of darkness tell us truths,
Win us with honest trifles, to betray's
125 In deepest consequence.
Cousins, a word, I pray you.

MACBETH (aside).   Two truths are told,
As happy prologues to the swelling act
Of the imperial theme.—I thank you, gentlemen.
(*Aside*) This supernatural soliciting
130 Cannot be ill, cannot be good; if ill,
Why hath it given me earnest of success,
Commencing in a truth? I am thane of Cawdor;
If good, why do I yield to that suggestion
Whose horrid image doth unfix my hair
135 And make my seated heart knock at my ribs,
Against the use of nature? Present fears
Are less than horrible imaginings;
My thought, whose murder yet is but fantastical,
Shakes so my single state of man that function
140 Is smothered in surmise, and nothing is
But what is not.°

BANQUO.   Look, how our partner's rapt.

MACBETH (aside). If chance will have me king, why, chance
may crown me,

16 What has Ross said earlier that would allow Macbeth to say, "The greatest is behind"—even if he had not had the confrontation with the witches? Contrast Macbeth's reactions with Banquo's. **That . . . crown.** Complete belief in the witches may arouse in you the ambition to become king. (Note the word *enkindle*.)

17 Note the ambivalent feelings Macbeth expresses in this aside. Which side of his nature seems to predominate here?

My thought . . . is not. My thought, in which the murder is still only a fantasy, so disturbs me that all power of action is smothered by imagination, and only unreal imaginings seem real to me.

Without my stir.

BANQUO.   New honors come upon him,
Like our strange garments,° cleave not to their mold
145   But with the aid of use.

MACBETH (aside).   Come what come may,
Time and the hour runs through the roughest day.

BANQUO. Worthy Macbeth, we stay upon your leisure.°

MACBETH. Give me your favor; my dull brain was wrought
With things forgotten. Kind gentlemen, your pains
150   Are registered where every day I turn
The leaf to read them.° Let us toward the King.
Think upon what hath chanced, and, at more time,
The interim having weighed it, let us speak
Our free hearts each to other.

BANQUO.   Very gladly.
155   MACBETH. Till then, enough. Come, friends.   (Exeunt.)

strange garments, new clothes.

18 In his asides, Macbeth tells the audience, but not the other characters, his secret thoughts. What are they? Read the asides without the intervening comments to get their full impact.

we stay . . . leisure, we await your convenience.

where . . . read them, in my mind and heart.

19 To whom is Macbeth addressing lines 152–154?

SCENE 4

Forres. The palace. (Played on the Platform.) Flourish.° Enter DUNCAN,
MALCOLM, DONALBAIN, LENNOX, *and* ATTENDANTS.

DUNCAN. Is execution done on Cawdor? Are not
Those in commission yet returned?

MALCOLM.   My liege,
They are not yet come back. But I have spoke
With one that saw him die; who did report
5   That very frankly he confessed his treasons,
Implored your Highness' pardon, and set forth
A deep repentance. Nothing in his life
Became him like the leaving it; he died
As one that had been studied in his death
10   To throw away the dearest thing he owed,
As 'twere a careless trifle.

DUNCAN.   There's no art
To find the mind's construction in the face.°
He was a gentleman on whom I built
An absolute trust.

(*Enter* MACBETH, BANQUO, ROSS, *and* ANGUS.)
O worthiest cousin!
15   The sin of my ingratitude even now
Was heavy on me; thou art so far before
The swiftest wing of recompense is slow
To overtake thee. Would thou hadst less deserved,
That the proportion both of thanks and payment
20   Might have been mine! Only I have left to say,

Flourish, a blast of trumpets used to announce the entry of a royal personage.

There's no art . . . face. There is no way of judging a man's thoughts from his appearance.

20 About whom is Duncan speaking? What possible dramatic irony might there be in Macbeth's entrance immediately after this speech? Be alert for other examples of Shakespeare's use of this technique.

21 Considering Duncan's previous message to Macbeth, what might Macbeth expect from Duncan with respect to the succession to the crown?

More is thy due than more than all can pay.

MACBETH. The service and the loyalty I owe,
In doing it, pays itself. Your Highness' part
Is to receive our duties; and our duties

25 Are to your throne and state, children and servants,
Which do but what they should, by doing every thing
Safe toward your love and honor.

DUNCAN.   Welcome hither;
I have begun to plant thee, and will labor
To make thee full of growing. Noble Banquo,

30 That hast no less deserved, nor must be known
No less to have done so, let me enfold thee
And hold thee to my heart.

BANQUO.   There if I grow,
The harvest is your own.

DUNCAN.   My plenteous joys,
Wanton in fullness, seek to hide themselves

35 In drops of sorrow. Son, kinsmen, thanes,
And you whose places are the nearest, know
We will establish our estate upon°
Our eldest, Malcolm, whom we name hereafter
The Prince of Cumberland; which honor must

40 Not unaccompanied invest him only,
But signs of nobleness, like stars, shall shine
On all deservers. From hence to Inverness,°
And bind us further to you.

MACBETH. The rest is labor which is not used for you.°

45 I'll be myself the harbinger, and make joyful
The hearing of my wife with your approach;
So humbly take my leave.

DUNCAN.   My worthy Cawdor!

MACBETH (*aside*). The Prince of Cumberland! that is a step
On which I must fall down, or else o'erleap,

50 For in my way it lies. Stars, hide your fires;
Let not light see my black and deep desires;
The eye wink at the hand; yet let that be
Which the eye fears, when it is done, to see.   (*Exit.*)

DUNCAN. True, worthy Banquo; he is full so valiant,

55 And in his commendations I am fed;
It is a banquet to me. Let's after him,
Whose care is gone before to bid us welcome.
It is a peerless kinsman.   (*Flourish. Exeunt.*)

---

22 | Lines 22–27 make explicit the proper relationship between king and thane. Why do you think Shakespeare gave Macbeth this speech?

23 | What does Duncan mean by lines 28–29?

24 | How does Duncan explain his tears?
establish . . . upon, name as heir to the throne.

25 | How should the actor playing Macbeth react to Duncan's announcement? Why might Duncan pick this moment and this company to name Malcolm his successor?

Inverness, Macbeth's castle.

The rest . . . you. Resting is work for me, when I am doing nothing to help you.

26 | Is Macbeth's reaction in lines 48–53 at all surprising? Is it justified? What does his speech suggest may be his "black and deep desires"?

27 | To whom is Duncan referring in line 54? What do you think Banquo has just been saying to Duncan?

SCENE 5

Inverness. MACBETH's *castle. (Played in the Chamber.) Enter* LADY MACBETH, *reading a letter.*

LADY MACBETH. "They met me in the day of success; and I have learned
by the perfectest report they have more in them than mortal knowledge.
When I burned in desire to question them further, they made themselves
air, into which they vanished. Whiles I stood rapt in the wonder of it, came
5   missives° from the King, who all-hailed me 'Thane of Cawdor'; by which
title, before, these weird sisters saluted me, and referred me to the coming-
on of time, with 'Hail, king that shalt be!' This have I thought good to
deliver thee, my dearest partner of greatness, that thou mightst not lose
the dues of rejoicing, by being ignorant of what greatness is promised thee.
10 Lay it to thy heart, and farewell."
     Glamis thou art, and Cawdor; and shalt be
     What thou art promised. Yet do I fear thy nature;
     It is too full o' the milk of human kindness
     To catch the nearest way. Thou wouldst be great;
15 Art not without ambition, but without
     The illness° should attend it. What thou wouldst highly,
     That wouldst thou holily; wouldst not play false,
     And yet wouldst wrongly win. Thou 'ldst have, great Glamis,
     That which cries, "Thus thou must do, if thou have it";
20 And that which rather thou dost fear to do
     Than wishest should be undone. Hie thee hither,
     That I may pour my spirits in thine ear,
     And chastise with the valor of my tongue
     All that impedes thee from the golden round,°
25 Which fate and metaphysical aid doth seem
     To have thee crowned withal.   *(Enter a* MESSENGER.*)*
                          What is your tidings?
MESSENGER. The King comes here tonight.
LADY MACBETH.   Thou'rt mad to say it!
     Is not thy master with him? Who, were't so,
     Would have informed for preparation.
30 **MESSENGER.** So please you, it is true; our thane is coming;
     One of my fellows had the speed of him,°
     Who, almost dead for breath, had scarcely more
     Than would make up his message.
LADY MACBETH.   Give him tending;
     He brings great news.   *(Exit* MESSENGER.*)*
                     The raven° himself is hoarse
35   That croaks the fatal entrance of Duncan
     Under my battlements. Come, you spirits
     That tend on mortal thoughts,° unsex me here,
     And fill me from the crown to the toe top-full

28 | What does the letter reveal about their relationship? Which phrases in the letter are especially significant?
missives, messages.

29 | How does Lady Macbeth's first reaction to the witches' prophecies differ from Macbeth's?

illness, unscrupulousness.

30 | In what ways does Lady Macbeth's description of her husband reinforce your impression of the ambivalence of his character?

golden round, the crown.

31 | In what tone of voice would she say, "Thou'rt mad. . . . "? What would be her tone in the next sentence? Why?
had the speed of him, outdistanced him.

32 | In line 34a, what thought has just occurred to Lady Macbeth?
raven. Long believed to be a bird of ill omen, the raven was said to foretell death by its croaking.
mortal thoughts, murderous thoughts.

Ellen Terry as Lady Macbeth, by John Singer Sargent. Ellen Terry (1847–1928) played in a wide range of Shakespearean and other classic plays; Lady Macbeth was one of her most celebrated roles. 1889. *National Portrait Gallery, London (on loan from the Tate Gallery)*

Of direst cruelty! make thick my blood;
40   Stop up the access and passage to remorse,
That no compunctious visitings of nature°
Shake my fell purpose, nor keep peace between
The effect and it!° Come to my woman's breasts,
And take my milk for gall, you murdering ministers,
45   Wherever in your sightless substances
You wait on nature's mischief! Come, thick night,
And pall° thee in the dunnest° smoke of hell,
That my keen knife see not the wound it makes,
Nor heaven peep through the blanket of the dark,
50   To cry, "Hold, hold!"   (*Enter* MACBETH.)
                    Great Glamis! Worthy Cawdor!
Greater than both, by the all-hail hereafter!
Thy letters have transported me beyond
This ignorant present, and I feel now
The future in the instant.

MACBETH.   My dearest love,
55   Duncan comes here tonight.

LADY MACBETH.   And when goes hence?

MACBETH. Tomorrow, as he purposes.

LADY MACBETH.   O never
Shall sun that morrow see!
Your face, my thane, is as a book where men
May read strange matters. To beguile the time,
60   Look like the time;° bear welcome in your eye,
Your hand, your tongue. Look like the innocent flower,
But be the serpent under 't. He that's coming
Must be provided for; and you shall put
This night's great business into my dispatch,°
65   Which shall to all our nights and days to come
Give solely sovereign sway and masterdom.

MACBETH. We will speak further.

LADY MACBETH.   Only look up clear;
To alter favor ever is to fear°—
Leave all the rest to me.   (*Exeunt.*)

SCENE 6

Before MACBETH's *castle.* (*Played on the Platform.*) *Hautboys*° *and torches.*
Enter DUNCAN, MALCOLM, DONALBAIN, BANQUO, LENNOX, MACDUFF, ROSS,
ANGUS, *and* ATTENDANTS.

DUNCAN. This castle hath a pleasant seat; the air
Nimbly and sweetly recommends itself
Unto our gentle senses.

---

compunctious . . . nature, natural feelings of compassion.

33 The word *fell* (line 42) has many meanings. Which apply here?

keep peace . . . and it, come between my intention and my carrying out of it.

pall, wrap.

dunnest, darkest; murkiest.

34 At this point, who does Lady Macbeth think will commit the murder?

35 What is Lady Macbeth trying to do in lines 34–50? What character trait is revealed by the conflict between her expressed desires and the nurturing metaphor she uses?

36 How does Macbeth say line 56a—firmly? tentatively?

To beguile . . . time, to deceive the world, appear as it demands or expects.

37 In what senses does Lady Macbeth use the phrase "provided for" in line 63?

38 Is Macbeth completely convinced in line 67a?

To alter . . . fear, to change facial expression shows fear.

Hautboys, a band of oboe-like instruments, generally used by Shakespeare in connection with a procession or a banquet.

39 Note that almost all Duncan's lines may be read in an ominous, ironic sense.

BANQUO.   This guest of summer,
The temple-haunting martlet,° does approve,°
5   By his loved mansionry, that the heaven's breath
Smells wooingly here. No jutty, frieze,
Buttress, nor coign of vantage but this bird
Hath made his pendent bed and procreant cradle;
Where they most breed and haunt, I have observed,
10   The air is delicate.   (*Enter* LADY MACBETH.)
DUNCAN.   See, see, our honored hostess!
The love that follows us sometime is our trouble,
Which still we thank as love. Herein I teach you
How you shall bid God 'ild° us for your pains,
And thank us for your trouble.°
LADY MACBETH.   All our service
15   In every point twice done and then done double
Were poor and single business to contend
Against those honors deep and broad wherewith
Your Majesty loads our house; for those of old,
And the late dignities heaped up to them,
20   We rest your hermits.°
DUNCAN.   Where's the thane of Cawdor?
We coursed him at the heels, and had a purpose
To be his purveyor;° but he rides well,
And his great love, sharp as his spur, hath holp him
To his home before us. Fair and noble hostess,
25   We are your guests tonight.
LADY MACBETH.   Your servants ever
Have theirs, themselves, and what is theirs, in compt,
To make their audit at your Highness' pleasure,
Still to return your own.°⸺⸺⸺→ *trust Macbeth*
DUNCAN.   Give me your hand;
Conduct me to mine host. We love him highly,
30   And shall continue our graces toward him.
By your leave, hostess.   (*Exeunt.*)

SCENE 7

Outside a banqueting hall in MACBETH's *castle. (Played on the Platform.)*
Hautboys and torches. Enter a SEWER,° *and divers* SERVANTS *with dishes and*
service, and pass over the stage. Then enter MACBETH.

MACBETH. If it were done when 'tis done, then 'twere well
It were done quickly; if the assassination
Could trammel up the consequence, and catch
With his surcease° success; that but this blow
5   Might be the be-all and the end-all here,

martlet, martin, a bird of the swallow family.
approve, demonstrate.

[40] Contrast Lines 1–10 with Lady Mabeth's reference to the raven in Act One, Scene 5, lines 34b–36.

God 'ild, literally "God yield," used in returning thanks.
The love . . . your trouble. Duncan means that, since he is there because he loves them, they should thank him even for the trouble he causes them.
[41] What might be ironic in lines 14b–15?
We rest your hermits. Like hermits, we will pray for you.

purveyor, forerunner.

Your servants . . . own. Since we are your servants, all that we have is subject to account and ready to be delivered to you.

Sewer, servant who arranges the dining table.
[42] The servants might "form up for inspection by the Sewer, before marching into the banquet-hall [the Chamber]: noises of merriment from inside will become suddenly louder and more hilarious as they disappear, and will be hushed all at once as an unseen door bangs shut. Macbeth comes swiftly onto the empty Platform in the sudden silence."—Watkins
surcease, death.

Someone will want to murder him.

consequences (?)

But here, upon this bank and shoal of time,
We'd jump° the life to come. But in these cases
We still have judgment here; that we but teach
Bloody instructions, which, being taught, return
10　To plague the inventor; this even-handed justice
Commends the ingredients of our poisoned chalice
To our own lips. He's here in double trust;
First, as I am his kinsman and his subject,
Strong both against the deed; then, as his host,
15　Who should against his murderer shut the door,
Not bear the knife myself. Besides, this Duncan
Hath borne his faculties° so meek, hath been
So clear in his great office, that his virtues
Will plead like angels, trumpet-tongued, against
20　The deep damnation of his taking-off,°
And pity, like a naked, new-born babe,
Striding the blast,° or heaven's cherubim, horsed
Upon the sightless couriers of the air,°
Shall blow the horrid deed in every eye,
25　That tears shall drown the wind. I have no spur
To prick the sides of my intent, but only
Vaulting ambition, which o'erleaps itself
And falls on the other.°　　　　　　(_Enter_ LADY MACBETH.)
　　　　　How now! what news?

LADY MACBETH. He has almost supped; why have you left the chamber?
30　MACBETH. Hath he asked for me?

LADY MACBETH.　　　　　Know you not he has?

MACBETH. We will proceed no further in this business.
He hath honored me of late; and I have bought
Golden opinions from all sorts of people
Which would be worn now in their newest gloss,
35　Not cast aside so soon.

LADY MACBETH.　　　　　Was the hope drunk
Wherein you dressed yourself? Hath it slept since?
And wakes it now, to look so green and pale
At what it did so freely? From this time
Such I account thy love. Art thou afeard
40　To be the same in thine own act and valor
As thou art in desire? Wouldst thou have that
Which thou esteem'st the ornament of life,°
And live a coward in thine own esteem,
Letting "I dare not" wait upon "I would,"
45　Like the poor cat i' the adage?°

MACBETH.　　　　　Prithee, peace.
I dare do all that may become a man;
Who dares do more is none.

R U afraid to get what you want?

jump, risk.

43 This soliloquy has
been a rich source
of titles for mystery books,
such as _Bloody Instructions_
(line 9). How many suit-
able titles can you find?

faculties, royal power.

taking-off, murder.

Striding the blast, riding
the wind.
couriers of the air, winds.
I have . . . the other.
I have nothing to stimu-
late me to the execution of
my purpose but ambition,
which is apt to overreach
itself.

44 In what specific ways
does this soliloquy
support Lady Macbeth's
estimate of Macbeth?

45 What reason does
Macbeth give in
lines 31–35a for not pro-
ceeding with the mur-
der? Is this explanation
in accord with what he
said in his soliloquy (lines
1–28)? If not, why does he
offer a different reason to
his wife?

46 Trace through the
arguments by which
Lady Macbeth works to
convince her husband to
go through with the mur-
der. Is this a plausible
scene? Why or why not?
ornament of life, the
crown.
cat . . . adage. The adage
is "The cat would eat fish,
but would not wet her
feet."

47 How does Macbeth
say lines 45b–47a—

LADY MACBETH. [*evil*] What beast was't, then,
That made you break this enterprise to me?
When you durst do it, then you were a man;
50 And, to be more than what you were, you would
Be so much more the man. Nor time nor place
Did then adhere,° and yet you would make both;
They have made themselves, and that their fitness now
Does unmake you. I have given suck, and know
55 How tender 'tis to love the babe that milks me;
I would, while it was smiling in my face,
Have plucked my nipple from his boneless gums,
And dashed the brains out, had I so sworn as you
Have done to this.

MACBETH.   If we should fail?

LADY MACBETH.   We fail!
60 But screw your courage to the sticking-place,°
And we'll not fail. When Duncan is asleep—
Whereto the rather shall this day's hard journey
Soundly invite him—his two chamberlains
Will I with wine and wassail so convince
65 That memory, the warder of the brain,
Shall be a fume, and the receipt of reason
A limbeck only.° When in swinish sleep
Their drenched natures lie as in a death,
What cannot you and I perform upon
70 The unguarded Duncan? What not put upon
His spongy° officers, who shall bear the guilt
Of our great quell?°

MACBETH.   Bring forth men-children only
For thy undaunted mettle should compose
Nothing but males. Will it not be received,
75 When we have marked with blood those sleepy two
Of his own chamber and used their very daggers,
That they have done 't?

LADY MACBETH.   Who dares receive it other,
As we shall make our griefs and clamour roar
Upon his death?

MACBETH.   I am settled, and bend up
80 Each corporal agent to this terrible feat.°
Away, and mock the time with fairest show;
False face must hide what the false heart doth know.   (*Exeunt.*)

[handwritten marginal notes: "Will kill her baby if she had promised & broken it." / "get them drunk + put the blame on them" / "sense of loyalty"]

pleadingly? mildly? defensively? angrily?

48 Did he explicitly "break this enterprise" (line 48) to her, or did he merely suggest it?

Nor time . . . adhere. There was no suitable time or place to commit the murder.

49 To what earlier speech by Lady Macbeth do lines 54–59a bear a resemblance?

50 Editors of *Macbeth* have punctuated line 59c variously as either "We fail!" or "We fail?" How would the punctuation affect the meaning? ***But screw . . . place.*** The image is drawn from the mechanical device used to prepare a crossbow for firing.

51 Lady Macbeth has been angry. How does her tone change in lines 60–61a? Why? ***memory . . . only,*** memory and reason both will dissipate, like the vapor of the alcohol they drink. This complicated image compares the human brain to the apparatus used in distilling alcohol.

52 Who does Lady Macbeth now say will commit the murder (lines 69–70a)? ***spongy,*** drunken. ***quell,*** murder.

bend up . . . feat, direct all my bodily powers to executing the murder.

53 Macbeth has made up his mind to commit the murder. Has he convinced himself that what he is about to do is morally justified?

THINK AND DISCUSS

SCENES 1–2

Understanding

1. Who is fighting whom? List the characters on both sides of the conflict.
2. What is the cause of the battle?

Analyzing

3. How do the witches, even in Scene 1, establish their supernatural powers?
4. Explain the comparison the Captain makes in lines 7–9 of Scene 2.
5. Why does King Duncan pronounce the death sentence on Macdonwald?

SCENE 3

Understanding

1. What "charm" are the witches casting at the beginning of the scene? Why?

Analyzing

2. What about the witches' greeting startles Macbeth?
3. What, exactly, do they prophesy for Macbeth and Banquo?
4. How does their prophecy immediately begin to come true?
5. An *aside* is a dramatic convention in which characters voice their thoughts, but other characters on stage cannot hear them. Why does Macbeth begin to talk about murder in his aside in lines 129–141? whose murder?

SCENES 4–6

Understanding

1. What does Macbeth tell Duncan (in Scene 4, lines 22–27) about the duties of a king and his subjects?
2. Where are the king and his followers headed at the end of Scene 4? Why?

Analyzing

3. What does Macbeth's letter reveal about the relationship between him and his wife?
4. How does Lady Macbeth **characterize** Macbeth while she is reading his letter?

What does she reveal about herself in this scene?

5. During Scene 5, who does Lady Macbeth assume will commit the murder?
6. In Scene 6, how does Lady Macbeth herself follow the advice she gave Macbeth in Scene 5?

Extending

7. Lady Macbeth prays to the spirits to "unsex" her, suggesting that murder is a thing for men, rather than women, to think about. Do you agree?

SCENE 7

Understanding

1. What is going on off-stage during this scene?
2. What, exactly, is the plan that Macbeth and Lady Macbeth make?

Analyzing

3. A *soliloquy* is a dramatic convention in which a character voices thoughts while alone on stage. What does Macbeth's first soliloquy (lines 1–28) reveal about his state of mind?
4. What reasons does Macbeth voice for *not* murdering Duncan?
5. What reasons does Lady Macbeth give him for committing the murder?

ACT ONE IN REVIEW

Understanding

1. What has happened before the play begins?
2. Trace, in the order in which they occur, the events that lead up to Macbeth's decision to murder Duncan.

Analyzing

3. Shakespeare usually begins his characterizations with the first speeches of his major characters. What have Macbeth and Lady Macbeth revealed about themselves so far?
4. Who seems to be the stronger character so far—Macbeth or Lady Macbeth? Explain why you think so.
5. Metaphors both of mother-like nurturing

and of being "unsexed" have been used by Lady Macbeth and by Macbeth about her. Find these and comment on their **paradoxical** nature.

Extending
6. The opening scene in a Shakespeare play is designed to catch the immediate attention of the audience and can usually be eliminated without harming the plot. How does Scene 1 fit this description? If you were directing the play, would you make any changes in this scene? Explain.

COMPOSITION ━◆━
Spying on Scotland
   Assume that you are a spy in the employ of a foreign country (perhaps Denmark or Ireland), sent to Scotland to determine whether an attack on that country would be successful. Based on what you have seen and heard in Act One, write a report to your king advising him of the situation and making a recommendation as to whether an attack is advisable at this time.

Writing a Humorous Soliloquy
   Select an unpleasant task that awaits you, such as studying for an examination or visiting the dentist. Then work out the pros and cons of that task, following the sequence of thought Macbeth goes through in his "If it were done" soliloquy. Using this speech as your guide, write a humorous soliloquy on your chosen subject. If you wish, try writing it in blank verse. With classmates, make a recording of your soliloquies that can be played for other classes.

ENRICHMENT
Researching the Elizabethan Era
   Literature offers a way of exploring the social customs, politics, beliefs, and values of various historical periods. Select one of the following topics on which to do independent research. Then write a report of your findings that could also be presented orally to the class.

Holinshed's *Chronicles*, the source of *Macbeth*
Elizabethan attitudes toward ghosts
Elizabethan attitudes toward witchcraft
Adult and child acting companies
Public and private theaters
Famous Macbeths (or Lady Macbeths) through the centuries
Critical theories on Macbeth's (or Lady Macbeth's) character
The role of women in Shakespeare's day

ACT TWO

SCENE 1
Court of MACBETH's *castle. (Played on the Platform.) Enter* BANQUO, *and* FLEANCE *bearing a torch before him.*

BANQUO. How goes the night, boy?
FLEANCE. The moon is down; I have not heard the clock.
BANQUO. And she goes down at twelve.
FLEANCE.   I take 't, 'tis later, sir.
BANQUO. Hold, take my sword. There's husbandry° in heaven;
5   Their candles are all out. Take thee that, too.
   A heavy summons lies like lead upon me,
   And yet I would not sleep; merciful powers,
   Restrain in me the cursèd thoughts that nature

husbandry, economy.

| 54 | What might "that" (line 5) be? |
| 55 | What is bothering Banquo? What might his "cursèd thoughts" be? |

Gives way to in repose!

(Enter MACBETH, *and a* SERVANT *with a torch.)*

Give me my sword.

10   Who's there?

MACBETH. A friend.

BANQUO. What sir, not yet at rest? The King's abed.
He hath been in unusual pleasure, and
Sent forth great largess to your offices.°

15   This diamond he greets your wife withal,
By the name of most kind hostess; and shut up
In measureless content.°

MACBETH.   Being unprepared,
Our will became the servant to defect,
Which else should free have wrought.°

BANQUO.   All's well.

20   I dreamt last night of the three weird sisters;
To you they have showed some truth.

MACBETH.   I think not of them;
Yet, when we can entreat an hour to serve,
We would spend it in some words upon that business,
If you would grant the time.

BANQUO.   At your kind'st leisure.

25 MACBETH. If you shall cleave to my consent, when 'tis,°
It shall make honor for you.

BANQUO.   So I lose none
In seeking to augment it, but still keep
My bosom franchised and allegiance clear,
I shall be counseled.°

MACBETH.   Good repose the while!

30 BANQUO. Thanks, sir. The like to you!

(Exeunt BANQUO *and* FLEANCE.)*

MACBETH. Go bid thy mistress, when my drink is ready,
She strike upon the bell. Get thee to bed.   *(Exit* SERVANT.)*
Is this a dagger which I see before me,
The handle toward my hand? Come, let me clutch thee.

35   I have thee not, and yet I see thee still.
Art thou not, fatal vision, sensible
To feeling as to sight? Or art thou but
A dagger of the mind, a false creation,
Proceeding from the heat-oppressèd brain?

40   I see thee yet, in form as palpable
As this which now I draw.
Thou marshal'st me° the way that I was going,
And such an instrument I was to use.
Mine eyes are made the fools o' the other senses,

45   Or else worth all the rest; I see thee still,

208   *The Renaissance*

great largess . . . offices,
many gifts of money to
be distributed among your
servants.

56 Why does Shake-
speare have Banquo
instead of Duncan give the
diamond (line 15)?

shut up . . . content, has
ended his day greatly contented.

Being unprepared . . .
wrought. The unexpected-
ness of Duncan's visit has
prevented us from enter-
taining him as we would
have liked.

If you . . . when 'tis. If
you ally yourself with me,
when the time comes.

So I . . . counseled. As
long as I do not lose my
honor in trying to increase
it, and keep myself free
and my loyalty to Duncan
unstained, I will listen to
you.

57 Why might Banquo
be suspicious at this
point? What do these lines
tell you about his character?

58 If you were directing
a stage production
of *Macbeth*, would you
have the dagger physi-
cally appear before Mac-
beth, or would you have
him address the empty air?

59 What does the imag-
inary dagger reveal
about Macbeth's character
in general, and his feelings
about the murder specifi-
cally?

Thou marshal'st me, you
conduct, lead me.

Sleep = to be at peace. [handwritten]

And on thy blade and dudgeon° gouts of blood,
Which was not so before. There's no such thing;
It is the bloody business which informs°
Thus to mine eyes. Now o'er the one half world
50 Nature seems dead, and wicked dreams abuse
The curtained sleep; witchcraft celebrates
Pale Hecate's° offerings, and withered murder,
Alarumed by his sentinel, the wolf,
Whose howl's his watch, thus with his stealthy pace,
55 With Tarquin's° ravishing strides, toward his design
Moves like a ghost. Thou sure and firm-set earth,
Hear not my steps, which way they walk, for fear
Thy very stones prate of my whereabout,
And take the present horror from the time,
60 Which now suits with it. Whiles I threat, he lives;
Words to the heat of deeds too cold breath gives. (*A bell rings.*)
I go, and it is done; the bell invites me.
Hear it not, Duncan; for it is a knell = *calling.* [handwritten]
That summons thee to heaven or to hell. → *going to kill him.* [handwritten]   (*Exit.*)

this when he decides to murder Duncan. [handwritten]

SCENE 2

The same. (Played in the Study and on the Platform.) Enter LADY MACBETH.

LADY MACBETH. That which hath made them drunk hath made me bold;
What hath quenched them hath given me fire. Hark! Peace!
It was the owl that shrieked, the fatal bellman,° → *omen.* [handwritten]
Which gives the stern'st good-night. He is about it.
5 The doors are open; and the surfeited grooms
Do mock their charge with snores. I have drugged their possets,°
That death and nature do contend about them,
Whether they live or die.
MACBETH (*within*). Who's there? What, ho!
10 LADY MACBETH. Alack, I am afraid they have awaked,
And 'tis not done. The attempt and not the deed
Confounds us. Hark! I laid their daggers ready;
He could not miss 'em. Had he not resembled
My father as he slept, I had done 't.
would have killed him if he didn't look like his father [handwritten]
(*Enter* MACBETH.)
My husband!
15 MACBETH. I have done the deed. Didst thou not hear a noise?
LADY MACBETH. I heard the owl scream and the crickets cry.
Did not you speak?
MACBETH.   When?
LADY MACBETH.   Now.
MACBETH.   As I descended?
LADY MACBETH. Aye.

dudgeon, hilt.

informs, appears.

Hecate (hek′ə tē), goddess of witchcraft.

Tarquin, one of the tyrannical kings of early Rome,
who ravished the chaste
Lucrece.

60 | Macbeth exits through
the Study, which
presumably leads to Dun-
can's chamber.

61 | Lady Macbeth enters
in the Study. Through
the center door might be
seen the beginning of a
flight of stairs leading to
Duncan's apartment.
owl . . . bellman. The
screech of an owl was often
interpreted as an omen of
death. In Elizabethan times,
a bell was rung to indi-
cate that someone was dy-
ing (see John Donne,
"Meditation 17," page 283).
possets, drinks made of
hot milk curdled with
wine or ale.

62 | Macbeth may momen-
tarily appear on the
Tarras as he speaks line 9.

63 | Is Lady Macbeth's
weakness here expect-
ed? How do you account
for it? What might be her
tone here—frightened?
irritated? angry? shaken?

64 | Macbeth descends
the stairs into the
Study.

MACBETH. Hark!
20   Who lies i' the second chamber?
LADY MACBETH.   Donalbain. *[son of Duncan]*
MACBETH (*looking on his hands*). This is a sorry sight.
LADY MACBETH. A foolish thought, to say a sorry sight.
MACBETH. There's one did laugh in 's sleep, and one cried, "Murder!"
    That they did wake each other; I stood and heard them;
25   But they did say their prayers, and addressed them
    Again to sleep. *[people waking up having nightmares of murder]*
LADY MACBETH. There are two° lodged together.
MACBETH. One cried, "God bless us!" and "Amen" the other,
    As they had seen me with these hangman's hands.°
    Listening their fear, I could not say, "Amen,"
30   When they did say, "God bless us!"
LADY MACBETH.   Consider it not so deeply.
MACBETH. But wherefore could not I pronounce "Amen"?
    I had most need of blessing, and "Amen"
    Stuck in my throat.
LADY MACBETH.   These deeds must not be thought
    After these ways; so, it will make us mad.
35 **MACBETH.** Methought I heard a voice cry, "Sleep no more!
    Macbeth does murder sleep," the innocent sleep,
    Sleep that knits up the raveled sleave° of care,
    The death of each day's life, sore labor's bath,
    Balm of hurt minds, great nature's second course,
40   Chief nourisher in life's feast—
LADY MACBETH.   What do you mean?
MACBETH. Still it cried, "Sleep no more!" to all the house;
    "Glamis hath murdered sleep, and therefore Cawdor
    Shall sleep no more; Macbeth shall sleep no more."
LADY MACBETH. Who was it that thus cried? Why, worthy thane,
45   You do unbend your noble strength, to think
    So brainsickly of things. Go get some water,
    And wash this filthy witness from your hand. *[blood]*
    Why did you bring these daggers from the place?
    They must lie there. Go carry them, and smear
50   The sleepy grooms with blood.
MACBETH.   I'll go no more;
    I am afraid to think what I have done;
    Look on 't again I dare not.
LADY MACBETH.   Infirm of purpose!
    Give me the daggers. The sleeping and the dead
    Are but as pictures; 'tis the eye of childhood
55   That fears a painted devil. If he do bleed,
    I'll gild the faces of the grooms withal;
    For it must seem their guilt.°   (*Exit. Knocking within.*)

---

65 Is Macbeth responding to Lady Macbeth here? Where should the actor's attention be directed as he speaks? Think about this as the scene continues. *two*, Malcolm and Donalbain.

hangman's hands. In Elizabethan England, the hangman also had to "draw" —remove the entrails from—some of his victims.

raveled sleave, tangled thread.

66 At what point does Macbeth again become aware of Lady Macbeth? *I'll gild . . . guilt*, a pun on the words *gild* and *guilt*. The pun would have been more obvious to an Elizabethan audience, for *gold* was often used synonymously with *red*.

67 What is Macbeth's state of mind after the murder? Lady Macbeth's? What mistake has Macbeth made? What is illogical about Lady Macbeth's proposed method of remedying it? How do you account for her failure to think straight?

Illustration by Charles Ricketts from *The Tragedie of Macbeth* (Ernest Benn, 1923)

MACBETH.   Whence is that knocking?
    How is 't with me, when every noise appals me?
    What hands are here? Ha! they pluck out mine eyes.
60 Will all great Neptune's ocean wash this blood
    Clean from my hand? No, this my hand will rather
    The multitudinous seas incarnadine,°
    Making the green one red.°   *(Re-enter* LADY MACBETH.*)*
LADY MACBETH. My hands are of your color; but I shame
65 To wear a heart so white. *(Knocking within.)* I hear a knocking
    At the south entry; retire we to our chamber;
    A little water clears us of this deed.

killed a father like figure.

not a coward

incarnadine, redden.
Making . . . red, making
the green sea red.

68 Both now have blood
on their hands. Do
you agree that a "little
water" (line 67) can clear
them of the murder? In
what sense might it? In
what sense not? Contrast
Lady Macbeth's words
with Macbeth's in lines
60–63.

How easy is it, then! Your constancy
Hath left you unattended.° *(Knocking within.)* Hark! more knocking.
70 Get on your nightgown,° lest occasion call us,
And show us to be watchers.° Be not lost
So poorly in your thoughts.
MACBETH. To know my deed, 'twere best not know myself.°

(Knocking within.)

Wake Duncan with thy knocking! I would thou couldst!   *(Exeunt.)*

SCENE 3

The same. (Played in the Study and on the Platform.) Knocking within. Enter a
PORTER.

PORTER. Here's a knocking indeed! If a man were porter of hell-gate, he
should have old° turning the key. *(Knocking within.)* Knock, knock, knock!
Who's there, i' the name of Beelzebub?° Here's a farmer, that hanged
himself on the expectation of plenty.° Come in time; have napkins enow°
5   about you; here you'll sweat for 't. *(Knocking within.)* Knock, knock! Who's
there, in the other devil's name? Faith, here's an equivocator that could
swear in both the scales against either scale; who committed treason enough
for God's sake, yet could not equivocate to heaven. O come in, equivocator.
(Knocking within.) Knock, knock, knock! Who's there? Faith, here's an
10   English tailor come hither for stealing out of a French hose.° Come in,
tailor; here you may roast your goose.° *(Knocking within.)* Knock, knock;
never at quiet! What are you? But this place is too cold for hell. I'll devil-
porter it no further. I had thought to have let in some of all professions that
go the primrose way to the everlasting bonfire.° *(Knocking within.)* Anon,
15   anon! I pray you, remember the porter.°

(He opens the gate. Enter MACDUFF *and* LENNOX.*)*

MACDUFF. Was it so late, friend, ere you went to bed,
That you do lie so late?
PORTER. 'Faith, sir, we were carousing till the second cock:° and drink, sir,
is a great provoker of three things.
20 **MACDUFF.** What three things does drink especially provoke?
PORTER. Marry, sir, nose-painting, sleep, and urine. Lechery, sir, it
provokes, and unprovokes; it provokes the desire, but it takes away the
performance: therefore, much drink may be said to be an equivocator with
lechery: it makes him, and it mars him; it sets him on, and it takes him
25   off; it persuades him, and disheartens him; makes him stand to, and not
stand to; in conclusion, equivocates him in a sleep, and, giving him the
lie, leaves him.
MACDUFF. I believe drink gave thee the lie last night.
PORTER. That it did, sir, i' the very throat on me; but I requited him for
30   his lie; and, I think, being too strong for him, though he took up my legs

~~Pote~~ Porter - comic relief .

Sidenotes:

Your constancy . . . unattended. Your composure has left you.
nightgown, dressing gown.
watchers, awake.

69 | In what manner does Lady Macbeth say, "Be not lost . . . "(lines 71b–72)?

To know . . . myself. It is better to be lost in my thoughts than to be aware of what I have done.

70 | At what pace should Scene 2 be played? What clues in the dialogue tell you?

old, dialect for "plenty of."
Beelzebub, the Devil.
expectation of plenty, because he tried illegally to earn an excess profit on his crops.
napkins enow, enough handkerchiefs to wipe off the sweat caused by the heat of Hell.

71 | To *equivocate* is to hedge or speak ambiguously. By the end of the play, the witches' prophecies will be understood as equivocations.

stealing . . . hose. Tailors were often accused of stealing cloth. Since French hose (breeches) at this period were short and tight, it would take a clever tailor to cut them smaller and steal the excess cloth.
goose, a pressing iron used by a tailor. There may also be a play on the expression "cook your goose."
primrose . . .bonfire, path of pleasure leading to everlasting damnation in Hell.
remember the porter. Here he might hold out his hand for a tip.
second cock, about 3:00 in the morning.

Personifing alcohol

sometime, yet I made a shift to cast him.
MACDUFF. Is thy master stirring?   (*Enter* MACBETH.)
    Our knocking has awakened him; here he comes.
LENNOX. Good-morrow, noble sir.
MACBETH.   Good-morrow, both.
35 MACDUFF. Is the King stirring, worthy thane?
MACBETH.   Not yet.
MACDUFF. He did command me to call timely° on him;
    I have almost slipped the hour.
MACBETH.   I'll bring you to him.
MACDUFF. I know this is a joyful trouble to you;
    But yet 'tis one.
40 MACBETH. The labor we delight in physics° pain.
    This is the door.
MACDUFF.   I'll make so bold to call,
    For 'tis my limited° service.   (*Exit.*)
LENNOX. Goes the King hence today?
MACBETH.   He does; he did appoint so.
LENNOX. The night has been unruly; where we lay,
45   Our chimneys were blown down; and, as they say,
    Lamentings heard i' the air; strange screams of death,
    And prophesying with accents terrible
    Of dire combustion and confused events
    New hatched to the woeful time; the obscure bird°
50   Clamored the livelong night. Some say the earth
    Was feverous and did shake.
MACBETH.   'Twas a rough night.
LENNOX. My young remembrance cannot parallel
    A fellow to it.   (*Re-enter* MACDUFF.)
MACDUFF. O horror, horror, horror! Tongue nor heart
55   Cannot conceive nor name thee!
MACBETH and LENNOX.   What's the matter?
MACDUFF. Confusion now hath made his masterpiece!
    Most sacrilegious murder hath broke ope
    The Lord's anointed temple,° and stole thence
    The life o' the building!
MACBETH.   What is 't you say? The life?
60 LENNOX. Mean you his Majesty?
MACDUFF. Approach the chamber, and destroy your sight
    With a new Gorgon.° Do not bid me speak;
    See, and then speak yourselves.
                (*Exeunt* MACBETH *and* LENNOX.)
          Awake, Awake!
  Ring the alarum-bell. Murder and treason!
65   Banquo and Donalbain! Malcolm! awake!
    Shake off this downy sleep, death's counterfeit,

72 Many expressions in this passage refer to wrestling. "Gave thee the lie" (line 28) means "floored you and put you to sleep." "Took up my legs" (line 30) means "got my feet off the ground." "Cast" (line 31) is a pun meaning both "throw down" and "vomit."

73 What is the dramatic effect of having this comical scene follow immediately the encounter between Macbeth and Lady Macbeth after the murder?

timely, early.
physics, cures.
limited, appointed.

obscure bird, the owl.

74 How would Macbeth say line 51b?

75 Is Macduff's response to the murder (lines 54–55a) a plausible one?

Lord's . . . temple, an allusion to the idea that the king is God's representative. The metaphorical temple is the King's body.

76 Is Macbeth's response in line 59b a plausible one?

Gorgon, a horrible monster of Greek legend. Whoever looked at her was turned to stone.

And look on death itself! Up, up, and see
The great doom's image!° Malcolm! Banquo!
As from your graves rise up, and walk like sprites,
To countenance this horror! Ring the bell.

70

great doom's image, a sight as awful as Judgment Day.

(Bell rings. Enter LADY MACBETH.*)*

LADY MACBETH. What's the business,
That such a hideous trumpet calls to parley
The sleepers of the house? Speak, speak!
MACDUFF.   O gentle lady,
'Tis not for you to hear what I can speak;
The repetition, in a woman's ear,
Would murder as it fell.   *(Enter* BANQUO.*)*
                         O Banquo, Banquo,
Our royal master's murdered!
LADY MACBETH.   Woe, alas!
What, in our house?
BANQUO.   Too cruel anywhere.
Dear Duff, I prithee, contradict thyself,
And say it is not so.

75

80

(Re-enter MACBETH *and* LENNOX, *with* ROSS.*)*

MACBETH. Had I but died an hour before this chance,
I had lived a blessed time; for, from this instant,
There's nothing serious in mortality;°
All is but toys; renown and grace is dead;
The wine of life is drawn, and the mere lees
Is left this vault° to brag of.

85

(Enter MALCOLM *and* DONALBAIN.*)*

DONALBAIN. What is amiss?
MACBETH.   You are, and do not know 't.
The spring, the head, the fountain of your blood
Is stopped; the very source of it is stopped.
MACDUFF. Your royal father's murdered.
MALCOLM.   Oh, by whom?
LENNOX. Those of his chamber, as it seemed, had done 't;
Their hands and faces were all badged° with blood;
So were their daggers, which unwiped we found
Upon their pillows.
They stared, and were distracted; no man's life
Was to be trusted with them.
MACBETH. Oh, yet I do repent me of my fury,
That I did kill them.
MACDUFF.   Wherefore did you so?
MACBETH. Who can be wise, amazed, temperate and furious,
Loyal and neutral, in a moment? No man.
The expedition° of my violent love
Outrun the pauser, reason. Here lay Duncan,

90

95

100

77 Is Lady Macbeth's response in lines 77b–78 what you would expect? How do you account for it?

78 Is Banquo surprised at what has happened? What does he think of Lady Macbeth's response?

mortality, human life.

this vault, the universe.

79 How many meanings can you read into Macbeth's speech (lines 81–86)? Consider what it might mean to the assembled lords, to Macbeth himself, and to the reader.

80 How might Malcolm say line 90b?

badged, marked; splotched.

81 How should the actor playing Macduff react to Macbeth's having killed the grooms? the actor playing Banquo? *expedition*, haste.

His silver skin laced with his golden blood;
And his gashed stabs looked like a breach in nature
105 For ruin's wasteful entrance; there, the murderers,
Steeped in the colors of their trade, their daggers
Unmannerly breeched with gore. Who could refrain,
That had a heart to love, and in that heart
Courage to make 's love known?
LADY MACBETH. Help me hence, ho!
110 **MACDUFF.** Look to the lady.
MALCOLM (*aside to* DONALBAIN). Why do we hold our tongues,
That most may claim this argument for ours?°
DONALBAIN (*aside to* MALCOLM). What should be spoken here,
where our fate,
Hid in an auger-hole,° may rush, and seize us?
Let's away;
115 Our tears are not yet brewed.
MALCOLM (*aside to* DONALBAIN). Nor our strong sorrow
Upon the foot of motion
BANQUO. Look to the lady;

(LADY MACBETH *is carried out.*)

And when we have our naked frailties hid,°
That suffer in exposure, let us meet,
And question this most bloody piece of work,
120 To know it further. Fears and scruples° shake us;
In the great hand of God I stand, and thence
Against the undivulged pretense I fight
Of treasonous malice.°
MACDUFF. And so do I.
ALL. So all.
MACBETH. Let's briefly put on manly readiness,°
125 And meet i' the hall together.
ALL. Well contented.

(*Exeunt all but* MALCOLM *and* DONALBAIN.)

MALCOLM. What will you do? Let's not consort with them.
To show an unfelt sorrow is an office
Which the false man does easy. I'll to England.
DONALBAIN. To Ireland, I: our separated fortune
130 Shall keep us both the safer; where we are,
There's daggers in men's smiles; the near in blood,
The nearer bloody.°
MALCOLM. This murderous shaft that's shot
Hath not yet lighted, and our safest way
Is to avoid the aim. Therefore to horse;
135 And let us not be dainty of° leave-taking,
But shift away; there's warrant in that theft
Which steals itself, when there's no mercy left.° (*Exeunt.*)

---

82 This scene follows classical tradition, in which scenes of bloodshed seldom took place onstage, but were reported in detail by a witness.

83 Some commentators maintain that Lady Macbeth really faints; others claim she only pretends to. Which theory seems more likely? Justify your answer in terms of what you know about Macbeth and Lady Macbeth and their preceding scene.
That most . . . ours, who are most concerned.
auger-hole, obscure hiding place.

when . . . hid, gotten dressed.
scruples, doubts.
Against . . . malice. I will fight against the unknown purpose which prompted this act of treason.

84 Why did Shakespeare give lines 117–123a to Banquo rather than to Macduff?
put . . . readiness, get dressed.

85 How does Malcolm's speech (lines 126–128) relate to "Foul is fair"?
the near . . . bloody, the closer the kinship to Duncan, the greater the chance of being murdered.
dainty of, ceremonious about.
there's warrant . . . left, we are justified in stealing away in these merciless times.

86 What initially makes Malcolm and Donalbain suspicious?

SCENE 4

Outside MACBETH'S *castle. (Played on the Platform.) Enter* ROSS *and an* OLD MAN.

OLD MAN. Threescore and ten I can remember well;
Within the volume of which time I have seen
Hours dreadful and things strange; but this sore night
Hath trifled° former knowings.

ROSS.   Ah, good father,
5 Thou seest, the heavens, as troubled with man's act,
Threaten his bloody stage; by the clock, 'tis day,
And yet dark night strangles the traveling lamp.°
Is 't night's predominance, or the day's shame,
That darkness does the face of earth entomb,
10 When living light should kiss it?

OLD MAN.   'Tis unnatural,
Even like the deed that's done. On Tuesday last
A falcon, towering in her pride of place,
Was by a mousing owl hawked at and killed.

ROSS. And Duncan's horses—a thing most strange and certain—
15 Beauteous and swift, the minions° of their race,
Turned wild in nature—broke their stalls, flung out,
Contending 'gainst obedience, as they would make
War with mankind.

OLD MAN.   'Tis said they eat each other.

ROSS. They did so, to the amazement of mine eyes,
20 That looked upon it.   *(Enter* MACDUFF.*)*
                    Here comes the good Macduff.
How goes the world, sir, now?

MACDUFF.   Why, see you not?

ROSS. Is 't known who did this more than bloody deed?

MACDUFF. Those that Macbeth hath slain.

ROSS.   Alas, the day!
What good could they pretend?°

MACDUFF.   They were suborned.°
25 Malcolm and Donalbain, the King's two sons,
Are stol'n away and fled; which puts upon them
Suspicion of the deed.

ROSS.   'Gainst nature still!
Thriftless ambition, that will ravin up°
Thine own life's means!° Then 'tis most like
30 The sovereignty will fall upon Macbeth.

MACDUFF. He is already named, and gone to Scone°
To be invested.

ROSS.   Where is Duncan's body?

MACDUFF. Carried to Colmekill,°

---

trifled, made trivial.

traveling lamp, the sun.

87 The Elizabethans saw nature as existing in a strictly ordered state. Ross and the Old Man describe events which indicate that the order in nature is awry. Be alert for further indications of unnatural workings in the universe. What might they reflect?

88 What is the symbolic meaning of the falcon-owl incident (lines 11–13)? Watch for specific symbolic significance in other unnatural acts mentioned.

minions, darlings.

What . . . pretend. What profit could they have aimed at?

suborned, hired or bribed.

ravin up, devour.

own life's means, parent.

Scone, ancient residence of Scottish kings.

Colmekill (kōm'kil) Iona Island.

The sacred storehouse of his predecessors,
35 And guardian of their bones.
ROSS.   Will you to Scone?
MACDUFF. No cousin, I'll to Fife.
ROSS.   Well, I will thither.
MACDUFF. Well, may you see things well done there; adieu!
      Lest our old robes sit easier than our new!
ROSS. Farewell, father.
40 OLD MAN. God's benison° go with you; and with those
      That would make good of bad, and friends of foes!

                                                    (*Exeunt.*)

89 Why might Macduff suspect that their old robes (of state)—Duncan's reign—might be "easier" than Macbeth's (line 38)?

benison, blessing.
90 What is the dramatic purpose of this scene?

THINK AND DISCUSS

SCENES 1–2
Understanding
1. By what prearranged signal is Macbeth to murder Duncan? What is to be Lady Macbeth's role in the murder?

Analyzing
2. What might be bothering Banquo so that he "would not sleep"? (See Scene 1, lines 6–9.)
3. What does Macbeth hint to Banquo? How does Banquo respond?
4. How are the descriptions of nature Macbeth uses in his soliloquy (lines 33–61) particularly appropriate?
5. In carrying out the murder, what mistake does Macbeth make? How does Lady Macbeth correct it?
6. Scene 2 is played at a fever pitch. What does it imply about Macbeth and Lady Macbeth as far as Duncan's murder is concerned?
7. How does Macbeth show remorse immediately after the murder? How does Lady Macbeth encourage him?

SCENE 3
Understanding
1. Who knocks at the gate? For what reason have they come?

Analyzing
2. The drunken porter's speeches are an example of *comic relief*. What effect do these speeches have, coming immediately after the murder as they do?
3. What does Macduff's reaction to the discovery of Duncan's body reveal about his character?
4. What mistake does Macbeth make after the discovery of Duncan's body? How does he attempt to excuse it?
5. Discuss the different meanings that Macbeth's speech "Had I but died an hour before. . ." holds for the assembled lords, for Macbeth himself, and for you.
6. Where do Malcolm and Donalbain go? Why?

SCENE 4
Understanding
1. About how much time has elapsed between Scene 3 and Scene 4? How can you tell?
2. What has happened in that time?

Analyzing
3. What unusual events in nature are mentioned in this scene and the last? What meaning do the characters see in these events?
4. What suspicions of Macbeth does Macduff voice?
5. What is the dramatic purpose of this scene?

Understanding

1. Trace the events that occur on the night of the murder.

Analyzing

2. Traditionally, in the second act of a Shakespearean play, the **protagonist** takes some action that cannot be undone or reversed and sets the course of the plot. What is that action in *Macbeth*?
3. How much of the witches' prophecy has come true? What prophecy has yet to be tested?
4. Does Lady Macbeth falter in any way? If so, how?
5. Which characters continue to harbor suspicions of other characters?

Extending

6. Based on what you have seen of their characters and actions, will Macbeth and Lady Macbeth make a good king and queen? Explain your answer.
7. Do you think Shakespeare's placement of the drunken porter scene right after the murder of Duncan adds to or detracts from the play? Explain.

VOCABULARY
Archaic Meanings

Our language is constantly changing, and some of the words that Shakespeare used have altogether different meanings today. For each italicized word in the following passages, write the letter of the meaning Shakespeare intended; then write the letter of the meaning the word has today. You may use your Glossary.

1. ". . . that but this blow/Might be the be-all and the end-all here,/. . . We'd *jump* the life to come." (Act One, Scene 7, lines 4–7)
   a. hurry   c. risk
   b. forget   d. leap
2. "He that's coming/Must be provided for; and you shall put/This night's great business into my *dispatch*. . . ." (Act One, Scene 5, lines 62–64)
   a. care   c. pocket
   b. haste   d. message

3. "There's *husbandry* in heaven;/Their candles are all out." (Act Two, Scene 1, lines 4–5)
   a. farming   c. caution
   b. married men   d. economy
4. "There's no such thing;/It is the bloody business which *informs*/Thus to mine eyes." (Act Two, Scene 1, lines 48–49)
   a. appears   c. vanishes
   b. deceives   d. explains
5. "I'll make so bold to call,/For 'tis my *limited* service." (Act Two, Scene 3, lines 41b–42)
   a. appointed   c. curtailed
   b. dangerous   d. energetic
6. "The *expedition* of my violent love/Outran the pauser, reason." (Act Two, Scene 3, lines 101–102)
   a. haste   c. insanity
   b. journey   d. emotion

COMPOSITION
Updating Shakespeare's Humor

The Porter, pretending to be the porter at the doorway to hell, admits three people: the farmer who was ruined by seeking an excessive (and probably illegal) profit; the equivocator, who could make lies seem true and vice versa; and the tailor who was clever enough to steal cloth in an almost impossible situation. Think about three modern people (not names, just occupations) you would name instead if you were the Porter. In an essay of three to five paragraphs, tell what each of these people did to deserve coming to hell-gate and what criteria you use generally to decide whether or not to admit someone. If you wish, write this assignment in the style of the Porter's speech.

Analyzing Suspense

Critics are in agreement that the scene in which Duncan is murdered reaches an almost unbearable degree of suspense. Reread the scene, and write an essay appropriate for your school literary magazine in which you analyze how Shakespeare managed to achieve and maintain that degree of suspense. Do we ever doubt that a murder will be committed? Do the knocking on the gate and the Porter's scene that follows contribute to, or detract from, that suspense? See "Writing About Drama" in the Writer's Handbook.

ACT THREE

SCENE 1

Forres. The palace. (Played on the Platform and in the Study.) Enter BANQUO.

BANQUO. Thou hast it now—King, Cawdor, Glamis, all—
 As the weird women promised; and, I fear,
 Thou play'dst most foully for 't. Yet it was said
 It should not stand in thy posterity,
5 But that myself should be the root and father
 Of many kings. If there come truth from them—
 As upon thee, Macbeth, their speeches shine—
 Why, by the verities on thee made good,
 May they not be my oracles as well,
10 And set me up in hope? But hush! no more.
 (*Sennet° sounded. Enter* MACBETH, *as king,* LADY MACBETH, *as queen,*
 LENNOX, ROSS, LORDS, LADIES, *and* ATTENDANTS.)
MACBETH. Here's our chief guest.
LADY MACBETH.   If he had been forgotten,
 It had been as a gap in our great feast,
 And all-thing unbecoming.
MACBETH. Tonight we hold a solemn supper, sir,
15 And I'll request your presence.
BANQUO.   Let your Highness
 Command upon me; to the which my duties
 Are with a most indissoluble tie
 Forever knit.
MACBETH. Ride you this afternoon?
20 **BANQUO.** Aye, my good lord.
MACBETH. We should have else desired your good advice,
 Which still hath been both grave and prosperous,°
 In this day's council; but we'll take tomorrow.
 Is 't far you ride?
25 **BANQUO.** As far, my lord, as will fill up the time
 'Twixt this and supper. Go not my horse the better,
 I must become a borrower of the night
 For a dark hour or twain.
MACBETH.   Fail not our feast.
BANQUO. My lord, I will not.
30 **MACBETH.** We hear our bloody cousins are bestowed
 In England and in Ireland, not confessing
 Their cruel parricide, filling their hearers
 With strange invention; but of that tomorrow,
 When therewithal we shall have cause of state

91 How much time has passed by now?

92 Banquo alone of the lords knows about the witches' prophecies, but he has said nothing about them. Why hasn't he? Does he have any plans for action?

Sennet, musical piece played by cornets, generally used to grace a formal procession. It indicates here that Macbeth has achieved the object of his ambition.

93 In what tone of voice does Banquo speak in lines 15b–18?

Which . . . prosperous, which always has been thoughtful and fruitful.
94 Why does Macbeth ask the question in line 24 (and later ones) about Banquo's plans?

95 How should the actor playing Banquo react when Macbeth tells him about Malcolm and Donalbain (lines 30-33)?

35   Craving us jointly.° Hie you to horse; adieu,
        Till you return at night. Goes Fleance with you?
        BANQUO. Aye, my good lord; our time does call upon 's.
        MACBETH. I wish your horses swift and sure of foot;
        And so I do commend you to their backs.
40   Farewell.   (*Exit* BANQUO.)
        Let every man be master of his time
        Till seven at night. To make society
        The sweeter welcome, we will keep ourself
        Till supper-time alone; while then, God be with you.
                    (*Exeunt all but* MACBETH *and an* ATTENDANT.)
45   Sirrah, a word with you; attend those men
        Our pleasure?
        ATTENDANT. They are, my lord, without the palace gate.
        MACBETH. Bring them before us.   (*Exit* ATTENDANT.)
                                    To be thus is nothing,
        But to be safely thus.—Our fears in Banquo
50   Stick deep; and in his royalty of nature
        Reigns that which would be feared. 'Tis much he dares;
        And, to that dauntless temper of his mind,
        He hath a wisdom that doth guide his valor
        To act in safety. There is none but he
55   Whose being I do fear; and, under him,
        My Genius is rebuked; as, it is said,
        Mark Antony's was by Caesar.° He chid the sisters
        When first they put the name of king upon me,
        And bade them speak to him; then prophetlike
60   They hailed him father to a line of kings.
        Upon my head they placed a fruitless crown,
        And put a barren scepter in my gripe,
        Thence to be wrenched with an unlineal hand,
        No son of mine succeeding. If 't be so,
65   For Banquo's issue have I filed° my mind;
        For them the gracious Duncan have I murdered;
        Put rancors in the vessel of my peace
        Only for them; and mine eternal jewel
        Given to the common enemy of man,°
70   To make them kings, the seed of Banquo kings!
        Rather than so, come fate into the list,°
        And champion me to the utterance!° Who's there?
                    (*Re-enter* ATTENDANT, *with two* MURDERERS.)
        Now go to the door, and stay there till we call.   (*Exit* ATTENDANT.)
        Was it not yesterday we spoke together?
75 FIRST MURDERER. It was, so please your Highness.
        MACBETH.   Well, then, now
        Have you considered of my speeches? Know

cause . . . jointly, affairs of state demanding the attention of both of us.

96 In what tone of voice does Macbeth ask the question about Fleance (line 36)?

97 "There can be no better background for this soliloquy than the royal 'state' on which Macbeth sits in his King's robes, wearing his fruitless crown, and grasping his barren sceptre. The setting is more properly one of circumstance than of locality."—Watkins

There is none . . . Caesar. Macbeth's insatiable ambition is silently rebuked by Banquo's innate loyalty. Mark Antony feared Octavius Caesar as a political, not personal, enemy, and this is how Macbeth regards Banquo.

98 *Wrenched* (line 63) has connotations of violence. How has Macbeth interpreted Banquo's loyalty and his silence about the witches' prophecies? What does he fear Banquo may do?

filed, defiled.

mine eternal . . . man, given my soul to the Devil.

list, battlefield.

champion . . . utterance, fight me to the death.

99 How does this soliloquy (lines 47–72) compare with the earlier one (Act One, Scene 7, lines 1–28) in which Macbeth contemplated the murder of Duncan?

Illustration by Charles Ricketts from *The Tragedie of Macbeth* (Ernest Benn, 1923).

That it was he in the times past which held you
So under fortune, which you thought had been
Our innocent self; this I made good to you
80 In our last conference, passed in probation° with you,
How you were borne in hand,° how crossed, the instruments,
Who wrought with them, and all things else that might
To half a soul and to a notion crazed°
Say, "Thus did Banquo."
    FIRST MURDERER.   You made it known to us.
85 **MACBETH.** I did so, and went further, which is now
Our point of second meeting. Do you find
Your patience so predominant in your nature
That you can let this go? Are you so gospeled°
To pray for this good man and for his issue,
90 Whose heavy hand hath bowed you to the grave
And beggared yours forever?
    FIRST MURDERER.   We are men, my liege.
    MACBETH. Aye, in the catalogue ye go for men;
As hounds and greyhounds, mongrels, spaniels, curs,
Shoughs, water-rugs, and demi-wolves are clept°
95 All by the name of dogs. The valued file°
Distinguishes the swift, the slow, the subtle,
The housekeeper, the hunter, every one
According to the gift which bounteous nature
Hath in him closed, whereby he does receive
100 Particular addition, from the bill
That writes them all alike;° and so of men.
Now if you have a station in the file,
Not i' the worst rank of manhood, say 't;
And I will put that business in your bosoms
105 Whose execution takes your enemy off,
Grapples you to the heart and love of us,
Who wear our health but sickly in his life,
Which in his death were perfect.
    SECOND MURDERER.   I am one, my liege,
Whom the vile blows and buffets of the world
110 Have so incensed that I am reckless what
I do to spite the world.
    FIRST MURDERER.   And I another
So weary with disasters, tugged with° fortune,
That I would set my life on any chance,
To mend it, or be rid on 't.
    MACBETH.   Both of you
115 Know Banquo was your enemy.
    BOTH MURDERERS.   True, my lord.
    MACBETH. So is he mine; and in such bloody distance°

100 It is sometimes assumed that the First and Second Murderers are former retainers of Banquo's (the "he" in line 77).
passed in probation, gave detailed proof.
borne in hand, deceived.
notion crazed, half-wit.

gospeled, religious.

Shoughs . . . clept, shaggy dogs, water dogs, and half-wolves are called.
valued file, list according to worth.

Particular . . . alike, specific qualifications along with the general attributes.

tugged with, pulled about by.

such bloody distance, with such hostility.

That every minute of his being thrusts
Against my near'st of life;° and though I could
With barefaced power sweep him from my sight
120 And bid my will avouch it,° yet I must not,
For certain friends that are both his and mine,
Whose loves I may not drop, but wail his fall°
Who I myself struck down; and thence it is
That I to your assistance do make love,
125 Masking the business from the common eye
For sundry weighty reasons.
SECOND MURDERER.   We shall, my lord,
Perform what you command us.
FIRST MURDERER.   Though our lives—
MACBETH. Your spirits shine through you. Within this hour at most
I will advise you where to plant yourselves;
130 Acquaint you with the perfect spy o' the time,
The moment on 't; for 't must be done tonight,
And something from the palace; always thought
That I require a clearness.° And with him—
To leave no rubs nor botches in the work—
135 Fleance his son, that keeps him company,
Whose absence is no less material to me
Than is his father's, must embrace the fate
Of that dark hour. Resolve yourselves° apart;
I'll come to you anon.
BOTH MURDERERS.   We are resolved, my lord.
140 **MACBETH.** I'll call upon you straight; abide within. (*Exeunt* MURDERERS.)
It is concluded. Banquo, thy soul's flight,
If it find heaven, must find it out tonight.   (*Exit.*)

SCENE 2

The palace. (Played in the Chamber.) Enter LADY MACBETH *and a* SERVANT.

LADY MACBETH. Is Banquo gone from court?
SERVANT. Aye, madam, but returns again tonight.
LADY MACBETH. Say to the King I would attend his leisure
For a few words.
SERVANT.   Madam, I will.   (*Exit.*)
LADY MACBETH.   Naught's had, all's spent,
5 Where our desire is got without content.
'Tis safer to be that which we destroy
Than by destruction dwell in doubtful joy.   (*Enter* MACBETH.)
How now, my lord! why do you keep alone,
Of sorriest fancies your companions making,
10 Using those thoughts which should indeed have died

[handwritten annotations: got what we wanted but not happy. better to be murdered than murder.]

thrusts . . . life, threatens my very existence.

bid . . . avouch it, justify
it as an act of royal will.

but . . . fall. I must pretend to lament his death.

101 Critics still puzzle
over the exact mean-
ing of line 130. A plausible
interpretation is that Macbeth will give them the
most accurate report available as to the time when
they should begin watch-
ing for Banquo.
clearness, freedom from
suspicion.

Resolve yourselves, make
up your minds.

102 In what way has Lady
Macbeth changed?

With them they think on? Things without all remedy
Should be without regard; what's done is done.
MACBETH. We have scotched° the snake, not killed it;
She'll close and be herself, whilst our poor malice
15 Remains in danger of her former tooth.
But let the frame of things° disjoint, both the worlds suffer,°
Ere we will eat our meal in fear, and sleep
In the affliction of these terrible dreams
That shake us nightly; better be with the dead,
20 Whom we, to gain our peace, have sent to peace,
Than on the torture of the mind to lie
In restless ecstasy.° Duncan is in his grave;
After life's fitful fever he sleeps well.
Treason has done his worst; nor steel, nor poison,
25 Malice domestic,° foreign levy,° nothing,
Can touch him further.
LADY MACBETH.   Come on,
Gentle my lord, sleek o'er your rugged looks;
Be bright and jovial among your guests tonight.
MACBETH. So shall I, love; and so, I pray, be you.
30 Let your remembrance apply to Banquo;
Present him eminence,° both with eye and tongue;
Unsafe the while, that we
Must lave our honors in these flattering streams,
And make our faces vizards° to our hearts,
35 Disguising what they are.°
LADY MACBETH.   You must leave this.
MACBETH. Oh, full of scorpions is my mind, dear wife!
Thou know'st that Banquo, and his Fleance, lives.
LADY MACBETH. But in them nature's copy's not eterne.°
MACBETH. There's comfort yet; they are assailable;
40 Then be thou jocund. Ere the bat hath flown
His cloistered flight, ere to black Hecate's summons
The shard-borne beetle° with his drowsy hums
Hath rung night's yawning peal, there shall be done
A deed of dreadful note.
LADY MACBETH.   What's to be done?
45 MACBETH. Be innocent of the knowledge, dearest chuck,
Till thou applaud the deed. Come, seeling° night,
Scarf up° the tender eye of pitiful day;
And with thy bloody and invisible hand
Cancel and tear to pieces that great bond°
50 Which keeps me pale! Light thickens, and the crow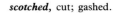
Makes wing to the rooky wood;
Good things of day begin to droop and drowse,
Whiles night's black agents to their preys do rouse.

scotched, cut; gashed.

frame of things, the universe.
both . . . suffer, earth and heaven perish.

restless ecstasy, suffering; torment.
Malice domestic, civil war.
levy, invasion.

103 Considering lines 4–26, how do you judge Macbeth and Lady Macbeth now feel about the murder of Duncan?

Present him eminence, show him special favor.
vizards, masks.
Unsafe . . . are. We are unsafe so long as we must flatter and appear to be what we are not.
But . . . eterne. They will not live forever.
shard-borne beetle, either a dung beetle or a beetle that is borne on (flies with) shards, or horny wing cases.

104 Who is now taking the lead in planning?
seeling, blinding. To *seel* is a technical term used in falconry for sewing up the eyelids of a young hawk to make him used to the hood.
Scarf up, blindfold.
great bond, Banquo's bond of life (?).

105 Compare the planning of Banquo's murder with the planning of Duncan's. What indications are there that the relationship between Macbeth and his wife has changed?

Thou marvel'st at my words; but hold thee still;
Things bad begun make strong themselves by ill.
So, prithee, go with me.   (*Exeunt.*)

SCENE 3

A park near the palace. (Played on the Platform.) Enter three MURDERERS.

FIRST MURDERER. But who did bid thee join with us?
THIRD MURDERER.   Macbeth.
SECOND MURDERER. He needs not our mistrust, since he delivers
    Our offices and what we have to do
    To the direction just.°
FIRST MURDERER.   Then stand with us.
5   The west yet glimmers with some streaks of day;
    Now spurs the lated traveler apace
    To gain the timely inn; and near approaches
    The subject of our watch.
THIRD MURDERER.   Hark! I hear horses.
BANQUO (*within*). Give us a light there, ho!
SECOND MURDERER.   Then 'tis he; the rest
10 That are within the note of expectation°
    Already are i' the court.
FIRST MURDERER.   His horses go about.°
THIRD MURDERER. Almost a mile; but he does usually,
    So all men do, from hence to the palace gate
    Make it their walk.
SECOND MURDERER. A light, a light!
                    (*Enter* BANQUO, *and* FLEANCE *with a torch.*)
THIRD MURDERER.   'Tis he.
15 FIRST MURDERER. Stand to 't.
BANQUO. It will be rain tonight.
FIRST MURDERER.   Let it come down. (*They set upon* BANQUO.)
BANQUO. Oh, treachery! Fly, good Fleance, fly, fly, fly!
    Thou mayest revenge. O slave!   (*Dies.* FLEANCE *escapes.*)
THIRD MURDERER. Who did strike out the light?
FIRST MURDERER.   Was 't not the way?
20 THIRD MURDERER. There's but one down; the son is fled.
SECOND MURDERER. We have lost best half of our affair.
FIRST MURDERER. Well, let's away, and say how much is done. (*Exeunt.*)

SCENE 4

*Hall in the palace. (Played on the Platform and in the Study.) A banquet prepared.
Enter* MACBETH, LADY MACBETH, ROSS, LENNOX, LORDS, *and* ATTENDANTS.

106 Why might Macbeth have involved a third murderer in the plot?

107 The third murderer has been variously identified as: a confidential servant of Macbeth's; the character called Attendant in Scene 1; Ross; Macbeth himself. On the basis of evidence in the play, which seems most likely? (Watkins points out: "There is a purely mechanical reason why a third murderer is necessary: Banquo's body must be carried off, and it takes two to carry him off expeditiously; not only that, but the light struck from the hand of Fleance must also be removed before the change of locality to the ensuing banquet scene. One of the trio must pick up the light.")
He needs not . . . just. We need not distrust him, since he reports accurately what we are to do.

108 The murderers might use the Stage-Posts for their ambush ("Then stand with us," line 4).
note of expectation, list of expected guests.
go about, take the long way to the castle. (Shakespeare had to find some plausible excuse for not bringing the horses onstage.)

109 What are some of the circumstances that contribute to Fleance's escape?

MACBETH. You know your own degrees;° sit down. At first
And last the hearty welcome.

LORDS.   Thanks to your Majesty.

MACBETH. Ourself will mingle with society
And play the humble host.

5   Our hostess keeps her state,° but in best time
We will require her welcome.

LADY MACBETH. Pronounce it for me, sir, to all our friends;
For my heart speaks they are welcome.

                    (FIRST MURDERER *appears at the door.*)

MACBETH. See, they encounter thee with their hearts' thanks.

10   Both sides are even. Here I'll sit i' the midst.
Be large in mirth; anon we'll drink a measure
The table round. (*Moves toward* MURDERER *at door.*) There's blood upon
    thy face.

MURDERER. 'Tis Banquo's then.

MACBETH. 'Tis better thee without than he within.°

15   Is he dispatched?

MURDERER. My lord, his throat is cut; that I did for him.

MACBETH. Thou art the best o' the cutthroats; yet he's good
That did the like for Fleance. If thou didst it,
Thou art the nonpareil.°

MURDERER.   Most royal sir,

20   Fleance is 'scaped.

MACBETH (*aside*). Then comes my fit again; I had else been perfect,
Whole as the marble, founded as the rock,
As broad and general as the casing° air.
But now I am cabined, cribbed, confined, bound in

25   To saucy doubts and fears. But Banquo's safe?

MURDERER. Aye, my good lord; safe in a ditch he bides,
With twenty trenched gashes on his head,
The least a death to nature.

MACBETH.   Thanks for that;
There the grown serpent lies. The worm that's fled

30   Hath nature that in time will venom breed,
No teeth for the present. Get thee gone; tomorrow
We'll hear ourselves° again.   (*Exit* MURDERER.)

LADY MACBETH.   My royal lord,
You do not give the cheer; the feast is sold
That is not often vouched, while 'tis a-making,

35   'Tis given with welcome; to feed were best at home;
From thence the sauce to meat is ceremony;
Meeting were bare without it.°

MACBETH.   Sweet remembrancer!
Now good digestion wait on appetite,
And health on both!

degrees, rank. Guests at state banquets were seated according to rank.

keeps her state, remains seated on her throne (in the Study).

110 Macbeth chooses a place at the table "i' the midst" (in the middle) facing the audience.

111 This whispered conversation between Macbeth and the Murderer could plausibly take place at one side of the Platform, outside one of the Stage-Posts.
'Tis better . . . within. The blood is better on you than in him.

nonpareil, one without equal.

112 Macbeth must react in some way before he speaks line 21. What would be appropriate?
casing, enveloping.

hear ourselves, talk it over.
the feast is . . . it. Unless a host keeps his guests assured of their welcome, the meal is like one bought at an inn, and one might as well dine at home. When one is away from home, ceremony should accompany the meal.
Watch for the point when Macbeth becomes aware of the ghost.

LENNOX.   May't please your Highness sit.

(*The* GHOST OF BANQUO *enters, and sits in* MACBETH's *place.*)

40 **MACBETH.** Here had we now our country's honor roofed,°
Were the graced person of our Banquo present;
Who may I rather challenge for unkindness
Than pity for mischance!°

ROSS.   His absence, sir,
Lays blame upon his promise. Please 't your Highness
45 To grace us with your royal company.

MACBETH. The table's full.

LENNOX.   Here is a place reserved, sir.

MACBETH. Where?

LENNOX. Here, my good lord. What is 't that moves your Highness?

MACBETH. Which of you have done this?

LORDS.   What, my good lord?

50 **MACBETH.** Thou canst not say I did it; never shake
Thy gory locks at me.

ROSS. Gentlemen, rise; his Highness is not well.

LADY MACBETH. Sit, worthy friends. My lord is often thus,
And hath been from his youth. Pray you, keep seat;
55 The fit is momentary; upon a thought°
He will again be well. If much you note him,
You shall offend him and extend his passion;°
Feed, and regard him not. Are you a man?

MACBETH. Aye, and a bold one, that dare look on that
60 Which might appal the devil.

LADY MACBETH.   O proper stuff!
This is the very painting of your fear;
This is the air-drawn dagger which, you said,
Led you to Duncan. Oh, these flaws and starts,
Imposters to° true fear, would well become
65 A woman's story at a winter's fire,
Authorized by her grandam. Shame itself!
Why do you make such faces? When all's done,
You look but on a stool.

MACBETH. Prithee, see there! behold! look! lo! how say you?
70 Why, what care I? If thou canst nod, speak, too.
If charnel houses and our graves must send
Those that we bury back, our monuments
Shall be the maws of kites.°   (GHOST *vanishes.*)

LADY MACBETH.   What, quite unmanned in folly?

MACBETH. If I stand here, I saw him.

LADY MACBETH.   Fie, for shame!

75 **MACBETH.** Blood hath been shed ere now, i' the olden time,
Ere humane statue purged the gentle weal;°
Aye, and since, too, murders have been performed

Too terrible for the ear. The time has been,
That, when the brains were out, the man would die,
80 And there an end; but now they rise again,
With twenty mortal murders on their crowns,°
And push us from our stools; this is more strange
Than such a murder is.

LADY MACBETH.   My worthy lord,
Your noble friends do lack you.

MACBETH.   I do forget.
85 Do not muse at me, my most worthy friends;
I have a strange infirmity, which is nothing
To those that know me. Come, love and health to all;
Then I'll sit down. Give me some wine; fill full.
I drink to the general joy o' the whole table,
90 And to our dear friend Banquo, whom we miss;
Would he were here! To all, and him, we thirst,°
And all to all.

LORDS.   Our duties, and the pledge.

(Re-enter GHOST.*)*

be gone

MACBETH. Avaunt! and quit my sight! Let the earth hide thee!
Thy bones are marrowless, thy blood is cold;
95 Thou has no speculation° in those eyes
Which thou dost glare with!

LADY MACBETH.   Think of this, good peers,
But as a thing of custom; 'tis no other;
Only it spoils the pleasure of the time.

MACBETH. What man dare, I dare.
100 Approach thou like the rugged Russian bear,
The armed rhinoceros, or the Hyrcan tiger;
Take any shape but that, and my firm nerves
Shall never tremble. Or be alive again,
And dare me to the desert with thy sword;
105 If trembling I inhabit then,° protest me
The baby of a girl.° Hence, horrible shadow!
Unreal mockery, hence!

(GHOST vanishes.*)*

                              Why, so; being gone,
I am a man again. Pray you, sit still.

LADY MACBETH. You have displaced the mirth, broke the good meeting,
110 With most admired° disorder.

MACBETH.   Can such things be,
And overcome us like a summer's cloud,
Without our special wonder? You make me strange
Even to the disposition that I owe,°
When now I think you can behold such sights,
115 And keep the natural ruby of your cheeks,
When mine is blanched with fear.

mortal . . . crowns,
deadly wounds on their
heads.

thirst, wish to drink.

speculation, light of living
intelligence.

119 Who hears Macbeth's tirades? How
do Macbeth and Lady
Macbeth explain his
behavior? Do you think
the lords accept the explanation?

If . . . then. If I then still
tremble.
The baby of a girl, puny
infant of an immature mo-
ther. (Some editors interpret it as "a girl's doll.")

120 Who has seen the
ghost? What similar
hallucination occurs ear-
lier in the play, and what
purpose do both incidents
serve?
admired, wondered at.
You make . . . owe. You
make me wonder at my
own disposition.

ROSS.   What sights, my lord?

LADY MACBETH. I pray you, speak not; he grows worse and worse;
    Question enrages him. At once, good night;
    Stand not upon the order of your going,°
120 But go at once.

LENNOX.   Good night; and better health
    Attend his Majesty!

LADY MACBETH.   A kind good-night to all!

             (Exeunt all but MACBETH *and* LADY MACBETH.*)*

MACBETH. It will have blood; they say, blood will have blood.
    Stones have been known to move and trees to speak;
    Augurs and understood relations have
125 By magot-pies and choughs and rooks brought forth
    The secret'st man of blood.° What is the night?

LADY MACBETH. Almost at odds with morning, which is which.

MACBETH. How say'st thou, that Macduff denies his person
    At our great bidding?

LADY MACBETH.   Did you send to him, sir?

130 MACBETH. I hear it by the way; but I will send.
    There's not a one of them but in his house
    I keep a servant feed.° I will tomorrow,
    And betimes I will, to the weird sisters.°
    More shall they speak; for now I am bent to know,
135 By the worst means, the worst. For mine own good,
    All causes shall give way; I am in blood
    Stepped in so far that, should I wade no more,
    Returning were as tedious as go o'er.
    Strange things I have in head, that will to hand;
140 Which must be acted ere they may be scanned.°

LADY MACBETH. You lack the season of all natures, sleep.

MACBETH. Come, we'll to sleep. My strange and self-abuse
    Is the initiate fear that wants hard use;°
    We are yet but young in deed.   *(Exeunt.)*

SCENE 5

A heath. (Perhaps HECATE *on the Tarras, with the three* WITCHES *below.)*
Thunder. Enter the three WITCHES, *meeting* HECATE.

FIRST WITCH. Why, how now, Hecate! you look angerly.

HECATE. Have I not reason, beldams as you are,
    Saucy and overbold? How did you dare
    To trade and traffic with Macbeth
5 In riddles and affairs of death;
    And I, the mistress of your charms,

The close contriver of all harms,
  Was never called to bear my part,
  Or show the glory of our art?
10 And, which is worse, all you have done
  Hath been but for a wayward son,
  Spiteful and wrathful, who, as others do,
  Loves for his own ends, not for you.
  But make amends now. Get you gone,
15 And at the pit of Acheron°
  Meet me i' the morning. Thither he
  Will come to know his destiny.
  Your vessels and your spells provide,
  Your charms and everything beside.
20 I am for the air; this night I'll spend
  Unto a dismal and a fatal end;
  Great business must be wrought ere noon.
  Upon the corner of the moon
  There hangs a vaporous drop profound;
25 I'll catch it ere it come to ground;
  And that, distilled by magic sleights,
  Shall raise such artificial sprites
  As by the strength of their illusion
  Shall draw him on to his confusion.
30 He shall spurn fate, scorn death, and bear
  His hopes 'bove wisdom, grace, and fear;
  And you all know security°
  Is mortals' chiefest enemy.
        (Music and a song within, "Come away, come away," etc.)
  Hark! I am called; my little spirit, see,
35 Sits in a foggy cloud, and stays for me.

                      (Exit.)

FIRST WITCH. Come, let's make haste; she'll soon be back again.

                    (Exeunt.)

Acheron, a river in Hell.

security, overconfidence.

SCENE 6

Forres. The palace. (Played on the Tarras.) Enter LENNOX *and another* LORD.

LENNOX. My former speeches have but hit your thoughts,
  Which can interpret further;° only, I say,
  Things have been strangely borne.° The gracious Duncan
  Was pitied of Macbeth; marry, he was dead.
5 And the right-valiant Banquo walked too late;
  Whom, you may say, if 't please you, Fleance killed,
  For Fleance fled; men must not walk too late.

My former . . . further. My earlier speeches have only given you ideas, from which you can draw your own conclusions.
borne, conducted.

Who cannot want the thought how monstrous
It was for Malcolm and for Donalbain
10   To kill their gracious father? Damnèd fact!
How it did grieve Macbeth! Did he not straight
In pious rage the two delinquents tear,
That were the slaves of drink and thralls of sleep?
Was not that nobly done? Aye, and wisely, too;
15   For 'twould have angered any heart alive
To hear the men deny 't. So that, I say,
He has borne all things well. And I do think
That had he Duncan's sons under his key—
As, an 't please heaven, he shall not—they should find
20   What 'twere to kill a father; so should Fleance.
But, peace! for from broad words° and 'cause he failed
His presence at the tyrant's feast, I hear
Macduff lives in disgrace; sir, can you tell
Where he bestows himself?

LORD.   The son of Duncan,
25   From whom this tyrant holds the due of birth,
Lives in the English court, and is received
Of the most pious Edward° with such grace
That the malevolence of fortune nothing
Takes from his high respect. Thither Macduff
30   Is gone to pray the holy King, upon his aid
To wake Northumberland and warlike Siward;
That by the help of these—with Him above
To ratify the work—we may again
Give to our tables meat, sleep to our nights,
35   Free from our feasts and banquets bloody knives,
Do faithful homage and receive free honors,
All which we pine for now; and this report
Hath so exasperate the King that he
Prepares for some attempt of war.

LENNOX.   Sent he to Macduff?°
40   LORD. He did; and with an absolute "Sir, not I,"
The cloudy° messenger turns me his back,
And hums, as who should say, "You'll rue the time
That clogs° me with this answer."

LENNOX.   And that well might
Advise him° to a caution, to hold what distance
45   His wisdom can provide. Some holy angel
Fly to the court of England and unfold
His message ere he come, that a swift blessing
May soon return to this our suffering country
Under a hand accursed!

LORD.   I'll send my prayers with him.   (*Exeunt.*)

125 Note the indirect suggestions in Lennox's speech. Why is he less than forthright? At what points does his tone of voice change? What is the dramatic effect of these changes?

from broad words, because he spoke frankly.

Edward, Edward the Confessor, King of England 1042–1066.

Sent he . . .? Did he send for Macduff?
cloudy, sullen.
clogs, obstructs.
him, Macduff.

126 What is the dramatic purpose of this scene? What earlier scene does it parallel?
127 Some scholars believe this scene should follow Act Four, Scene 1, where it seems to make better sense. It may have been shifted to its present position when Scene 5 was added, to avoid having two scenes with the witches come together.

Comment

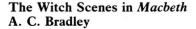

The Witch Scenes in *Macbeth*
A. C. Bradley

On the one hand the Witches are credited by some critics with far too great an influence upon the action; sometimes they are described as goddesses, or even as fates, whom Macbeth is powerless to resist. On the other hand, we are told that, great as is their influence on the action, it is so because they are merely symbolic representations of the unconscious or half-conscious guilt in Macbeth.

As to the former, Shakespeare took as material for his purposes, the ideas about witchcraft that he found existing in people around him and in books like Reginald Scot's *Discovery* (1584). And he used these ideas without changing their substance at all. He selected and improved, avoiding the merely ridiculous, dismissing the sexually loathsome or stimulating, rehandling and heightening whatever could touch the imagination with fear, horror, and mysterious attraction. The Witches, that is to say, are not goddesses, or fates, or, in any way whatever, supernatural beings. They are old women, poor and ragged, skinny and hideous, full of vulgar spite, occupied in killing their neighbors' swine or revenging themselves on sailors' wives who have refused them chestnuts. There is not a syllable in *Macbeth* to imply that they are anything but women. But they have received from evil spirits certain supernatural powers.

Next, while the influence of the Witches' prophecies on Macbeth is very great, it is quite clearly shown to be an influence and nothing more. There is no sign whatever in the play that Shakespeare meant the actions of Macbeth to be forced on him by an external power. The prophecies of the Witches are presented simply as dangerous circumstances with which Macbeth has to deal. Macbeth is, in the ordinary sense, perfectly free in regard to them. That the influence of the first prophecies upon him came as much from himself as from them, is made abundantly clear by the obviously intentional contrast between him and Banquo. Banquo, ambitious but perfectly honest, is scarcely even startled by them, and he remains throughout the scene indifferent to them. But when Macbeth heard them he was not an innocent man. Precisely how far his mind was guilty may be a question; but no innocent man would have started, as he did, with a start of *fear* at the mere prophecy of a crown, or have conceived thereupon *immediately* the thought of murder. Either this thought was not new to him, or he had cherished at least some vaguer dishonorable dream. In either case not only was he free to accept or resist the temptation, but the temptation was already within him. And we are admitting, again, too much when we use the word "temptation" in reference to the first prophecies of the Witches. Speaking strictly we must affirm that he was tempted only by himself. *He* speaks indeed of their "supernatural soliciting"; but in fact they did not solicit. They merely announced events: they hailed him as Thane of Glamis, Thane of Cawdor, and King hereafter. No connection of these announcements with any actions of his was even hinted by them.

When Macbeth sees the Witches again, after the murders of Duncan and Banquo, we observe, however, a striking change. They no longer need to go and meet him; he seeks them out. He has committed himself to his course of evil. Now accordingly they do "solicit." They prophesy, but they also give advice: they bid him be bloody, bold, and secure. We have no hope that he will reject their advice; but so far are they from having, even now, any power to compel him to accept it, that they make careful preparations to deceive him into doing so. And, almost as though to intimate how entirely the responsibility for his deeds still lies with Macbeth, Shakespeare makes his first act after this interview one for which his tempters gave him not a hint—the slaughter of Macduff's wife and children.

To all this we must add that Macbeth himself nowhere betrays a suspicion that his action is, or has been, thrust on him by an external power.

He curses the Witches for deceiving him, but he never attempts to shift to them the burden of his guilt.

We may deal more briefly with the opposite interpretation. According to it the Witches and their prophecies are to be taken merely as symbolical representations of thoughts and desires which have slumbered in Macbeth's breast and now rise into consciousness and confront him. With this idea, which springs from the wish to get rid of a mere external supernaturalism, and to find a psychological and spiritual meaning in that which the groundlings probably received as hard facts, one may feel sympathy. But it is evident that it is rather a "philosophy" of the Witches than an immediate dramatic apprehension of them; and even so it will be found both incomplete and, in other respects, inadequate.

It is incomplete because it cannot possibly be applied to all the facts. Let us grant that it will apply to the most important prophecy, that of the crown; and that the later warning which Macbeth receives, to beware of Macduff, also answers to something in his own breast and "harps his fear aright." But there we have to stop. Macbeth had evidently no suspicion of that treachery in Cawdor through which he himself became Thane; and who will suggest that he had any idea, however subconscious, about Birnam Wood or the man not born of woman?

The theory under consideration is inadequate here chiefly because it is much too narrow. The Witches and their prophecies, if they are to be taken symbolically, must represent not only the evil slumbering in the hero's soul, but all those obscurer influences of the evil around him in the world which aid his own ambition and the incitements of his wife. Such influences, even if we put aside all belief in evil "spirits," are as certain, momentous, and terrifying facts as the presence of inchoate evil in the soul itself; and if we exclude all reference to these facts from our idea of the Witches, it will be greatly impoverished and will certainly fail to correspond with the imaginative effect. The words of the Witches are fatal to the hero only because there is in him something which leaps

Edmund Dulac's poster for *Macbeth*, September 5, 1911. *Victoria and Albert Museum, London*

into light at the sound of them; but they are at the same time the witness of forces which never cease to work in the world around him, and, on the instant of his surrender to them, entangle him inextricably in the web of Fate. If the inward connection is once realized (and Shakespeare has left us no excuse for missing it), we need not fear, and indeed shall scarcely be able, to exaggerate the effect of the Witch scenes in heightening and deepening the sense of fear, horror, and mystery which pervades the atmosphere of tragedy.

From Lecture IX in *Shakespearean Tragedy* by A. C. Bradley. Copyright © by A. C. Bradley. Reprinted by permission of St. Martin's Press, Inc. and Macmillan, London and Basingstoke.

THINK AND DISCUSS

SCENE 1
Understanding
1. About how much time has elapsed since Act Two? How can you tell?
2. What preparations are being made for that night?

Analyzing
3. Why does Macbeth say there is no one he fears but Banquo?
4. Explain in your own words the meaning of Macbeth's "To be thus is nothing" soliloquy.
5. How does Macbeth get the two murderers to undertake Banquo's killing?

Extending
6. Why do you think Macbeth is not satisfied to be king, but wants to be sure that Banquo's descendants will not succeed him?

SCENES 2–3
Understanding
1. What goes wrong with the plot to murder Banquo and Fleance?

Analyzing
2. What is the first indication that Lady Macbeth is ill-at-ease about Duncan's murder? Does Macbeth seem to be feeling the same way? Explain.
3. Does Macbeth take Lady Macbeth into his confidence about the plot to murder Banquo? How do you account for this?

SCENE 4
Understanding
1. According to lines 20–25, what keeps Macbeth from being "perfect"?
2. Explain the meaning of his speech, "blood will have blood" (line 122).

3. Who can see Banquo's ghost at the banquet, and who cannot?

Analyzing
4. According to Macbeth, why does he not sit on his throne as Lady Macbeth does? What dramatic purposes are served by having him sit among the guests?
5. How does Lady Macbeth atempt to cover up for Macbeth at the banquet? Do you think she succeeds, or does she make the situation worse? Explain.
6. What two decisions does Macbeth make after the guests have gone? Has the appearance of Banquo's ghost apparently infuenced him at all in making them?

Extending
7. In some productions of *Macbeth*, Banquo's ghost does not appear physically on stage, so that the apparition is obviously a product of Macbeth's mind. What would be gained by such an approach? What would be lost?

SCENES 5–6
Understanding
1. Who is Hecate? What is she doing here?

Analyzing
2. In Scene 6 Lennox summarizes events. What hints does he give concerning Macbeth?
3. What dramatic purpose is served by Scene 6?

Extending
4. It is often said that Scene 5 was not written by Shakespeare. Does any part of it give you this impression? You might compare the meter and line length in this scene with those of the witches' earlier appearances.

ACT THREE IN REVIEW
Understanding
1. What actions does Macbeth take during this act? What actions does he plan to take at the end of the act?

Analyzing
2. What does Banquo do that enables Macbeth to have him murdered? Is there any connection with a similar act of Duncan's that made his murder possible?
3. What event leaves open the possibility that the witches' prophecy for Banquo can still come true?
4. What indications has Macbeth given so far that his feelings of guilt might yet destroy him?

Extending
5. What do you think is most responsible for the way things have worked out for Macbeth so far—luck, his own actions, or something else?

APPLYING: Plot H🖉
See Handbook of Literary Terms, p. 916

The **plot** of a literary work is a series of happenings organized around a *conflict*. In Elizabethan tragedy, the first act presents background information known as *exposition*. A series of events, the *rising action*, leads to the *climax*, the point at which the fortunes of the *protagonists* are at their highest. In Elizabethan tragedy the structural climax usually occurs in the third act. Then there occurs some action (called the *dramatic reverse*) that triggers a series of events (the *falling action*) that leads to the downfall of the tragic hero. The *resolution* presents the final outcome.

1. What do you regard as the climax of *Macbeth*?
2. Where does the dramatic reverse occur?

COMPOSITION ◁▬
Writing a Diary Entry
Assume that you were one of the invited guests at Macbeth's banquet, and after you were dismissed you decided to record everything you saw in your diary for future reference. Write a diary entry in which you first explain the occasion and describe your host and hostess. Then go on to describe the events of the evening. To make sure you don't forget anything, include also your own thoughts, wonderments, and surmises about what all this means.

Writing About Plot
Conflict is the most essential ingredient of any plot, that which gives it interest and suspense. Looking back on the first three acts of *Macbeth*, list what you believe to be the major conflicts of the play; then arrange them in order of importance. In a four- to six-paragraph essay, identify and describe these conflicts, saving discussion of the most important one for last. See "Writing About Plot" in the Writer's Handbook.

ENRICHMENT
Blocking a Scene
The banquet in Scene 4 requires very careful *blocking* (positioning and movement of characters) because of the many activities going on simultaneously. Macbeth circulates among the guests, speaks to the Murderer at the door, and reacts to Banquo's ghost, who appears and disappears twice. Lady Macbeth tries to cover for her husband, while the guests react in their own ways. Work in small groups to block out this scene on paper, indicating where the various characters should be positioned, where they should move, and how they should react. For example, when the Ghost first appears, should Macbeth move toward it or away, stand or sit? How would you manage the Ghost's entrances and exits, or would you omit him entirely? How should the guests behave while all this is going on? You can use a plan of your school stage or an open platform, such as Shakespeare used (see page 250). Once you have developed your stage directions, assign parts and stage the scene accordingly.

ACT FOUR

SCENE 1

A cavern. In the middle, a boiling caldron. Thunder. Enter the three WITCHES.

FIRST WITCH. Thrice the brinded cat hath mewed.
SECOND WITCH. Thrice and once the hedgepig° whined.
THIRD WITCH. Harpier° cries, " 'Tis time, 'tis time."
FIRST WITCH. Round about the caldron go;
5   In the poisoned entrails throw.
     Toad, that under cold stone
     Days and nights has thirty-one
     Sweltered venom sleeping got,
     Boil thou first i' the charmed pot.
10   **ALL.** Double, double toil and trouble;
     Fire burn and caldron bubble.
     SECOND WITCH. Fillet of a fenny snake,
     In the caldron boil and bake;
     Eye of newt and toe of frog,
15   Wool of bat and tongue of dog,
     Adder's fork and blind-worm's° sting,
     Lizard's leg and howlet's wing,°
     For a charm of powerful trouble,
     Like a hell-broth boil and bubble.
20   **ALL.** Double, double toil and trouble;
     Fire burn and caldron bubble.
     THIRD WITCH. Scale of dragon, tooth of wolf,
     Witches' mummy, maw and gulf°
     Of the ravined° salt-sea shark,
25   Root of hemlock digged i' the dark,
     Liver of blaspheming Jew,
     Gall of goat, and slips of yew°
     Slivered in the moon's eclipse,
     Nose of Turk and Tartar's lips,
30   Finger of birth-strangled babe
     Ditch-delivered by a drab,°
     Make the gruel thick and slab;°
     Add thereto a tiger's chaudron,°
     For the ingredients of our caldron.
35   **ALL.** Double, double toil and trouble;
     Fire burn and caldron bubble.
     SECOND WITCH. Cool it with a baboon's blood,
     Then the charm is firm and good.
                         (*Enter* HECATE *to the other three* WITCHES.)
     HECATE. Oh, well done! I commend your pains;

128 The "cavern" was probably set in the Study.

hedgepig, hedgehog.
Harpier, the Third Witch's familiar spirit.

blind-worm, a small snakelike lizard, thought to be poisonous.
howlet's wing, the wing of a small owl.

maw and gulf, stomach and gullet.
ravined, ravenous.

yew, evergreen tree, thought to be poisonous.

drab, whore.
slab, slimy.
chaudron, entrails.

129 The appearance of Hecate is believed to be a later addition, not

40 And everyone shall share i' the gains.
And now about the caldron sing,
Like elves and fairies in a ring,
Enchanting all that you put in.

(Music and a song, "Black spirits," etc. HECATE *retires.)*

SECOND WITCH. By the pricking of my thumbs,
45 Something wicked this way comes.
Open, locks,
Whoever knocks! *(Enter* MACBETH.*)*

MACBETH. How now, you secret, black, and midnight hags!
What is 't you do?

ALL. A deed without a name.

50 **MACBETH.** I conjure you, by that which you profess,
Howe'er you come to know it, answer me.
Though you untie the winds and let them fight
Against the churches; though the yesty° waves
Confound and swallow navigation up;
55 Though bladed corn be lodged° and trees blown down;
Though castles topple on their warders' heads;
Though palaces and pyramids do slope
Their heads to their foundations; though the treasure
Of nature's germens° tumble all together,
60 Even till destruction sicken;° answer me
To what I ask you.

FIRST WITCH. Speak.

SECOND WITCH. Demand.

THIRD WITCH. We'll answer.

FIRST WITCH. Say, if thou'dst rather hear it from our mouths,
Or from our masters?

MACBETH. Call 'em; let me see 'em.

FIRST WITCH. Pour in sow's blood, that hath eaten
65 Her nine farrow; grease that's sweaten
From the murderer's gibbet throw
Into the flame.

ALL. Come, high or low;
Thyself and office deftly show!

(Thunder. FIRST APPARITION: *an armed Head.)*

MACBETH. Tell me, thou unknown power—

FIRST WITCH. He knows thy thought;
70 Hear his speech, but say thou naught.

FIRST APPARITION. Macbeth! Macbeth! Macbeth! beware Macduff;
Beware the thane of Fife. Dismiss me. Enough.° *(Descends.)*

MACBETH. Whate'er thou art, for thy good caution, thanks;
Thou hast harped° my fear aright; but one word more—

75 **FIRST WITCH.** He will not be commanded; here's another,
More potent than the first.

by Shakespeare—perhaps to provide an excuse for a dance and a song.

130 How has Macbeth's attitude toward the witches changed since his first meeting with them (Act One, Scene 3)? What might this suggest about changes in his character?

yesty, foamy.

Though . . . lodged, though grain, still green, be beaten down.

nature's germens, the seeds or elements through which nature operates.
sicken, is surfeited.

131 In Shakespeare's time, the apparition of a helmeted head came up (presumably from Hell below) through the caldron, which was placed over a trap door. If you were directing a modern production, how would you solve the problems of staging the appearance of the apparitions? What modern equipment might you use?
Dismiss . . . Enough. Note that this is the only apparition that does not equivocate with Macbeth. (Explained in Act Five, Scene 8.)
harped, guessed.

(Thunder. SECOND APPARITION: *a bloody Child.)°*

SECOND APPARITION. Macbeth! Macbeth! Macbeth!

MACBETH. Had I three ears, I 'ld hear thee.

SECOND APPARITION. Be bloody, bold, and resolute; laugh to scorn

80 The power of man, for none of woman born
Shall harm Macbeth.   *(Descends.)*

MACBETH. Then live, Macduff; what need I fear of thee?
But yet I'll make assurance double sure,
And take a bond of fate,° thou shalt not live;

85 That I may tell pale-hearted fear it lies,
And sleep in spite of thunder.

(Thunder. THIRD APPARITION: *a Child crowned,*
with a tree in his hand.)°

What is this,
That rises like the issue of a king,
And wears upon his baby-brow the round
And top of sovereignty?

ALL.   Listen, but speak not to 't.

90 **THIRD APPARITION.** Be lion-mettled, proud, and take no care
Who chafes, who frets, or where conspirers are.
Macbeth shall never vanquished be until
Great Birnam wood to high Dunsinane hill
Shall come against him.   *(Descends.)*

MACBETH.   That will never be;

95 Who can impress° the forest, bid the tree
Unfix his earth-bound root? Sweet bodements!° good!
Rebellion's head, rise never till the wood
Of Birnam rise, and our high-placed Macbeth
Shall live the lease of nature, pay his breath

100 To time and mortal custom.° Yet my heart
Throbs to know one thing; tell me, if your art
Can tell so much—shall Banquo's issue ever
Reign in this kingdom?

ALL.   Seek to know no more.

MACBETH. I will be satisfied; deny me this,

105 And an eternal curse fall on you! Let me know.
Why sinks that caldron? and what noise° is this?   *(Hautboys.)*

FIRST WITCH. Show!

SECOND WITCH. Show!

THIRD WITCH. Show!

110 **ALL.** Show his eyes, and grieve his heart;
Come like shadows, so depart!

(A show of EIGHT KINGS, *the last with a glass° in his hand;*
BANQUO's GHOST *following.)*

MACBETH. Thou art too like the spirit of Banquo; down!
Thy crown does sear mine eyeballs. And thy hair,

bloody Child, Macduff as
a child. (Explained in Act
Five, Scene 8.)

take . . . fate, make
sure that fate's promise is
fulfilled.

Child . . . hand, Malcolm. (Explained in Act
Five, Scene 4.)

impress, conscript; force
to serve as soldiers.
bodements, prophecies.

**pay his breath . . . cus-
tom**, die a natural death.

noise, music.

132 In the "show," the
eight Stuart kings of
Scotland, descending from
Banquo and succeeding
down to James I, the present king, walk in turn
across the back of the
stage.
glass, a magic mirror
showing the future.

Thou other gold-bound brow, is like the first.
115 A third is like the former. Filthy hags!
Why do you show me this? A fourth! Start, eyes!
What, will the line stretch out to the crack of doom?
Another yet! A seventh! I'll see no more;
And yet the eighth appears, who bears a glass
120 Which shows me many more; and some I see
That twofold balls and treble scepters carry.
Horrible sight! Now, I see, 'tis true;
For the blood-boltered° Banquo smiles upon me,
And points at them for his. (APPARITIONS *vanish.*) What, is this so?
125 **FIRST WITCH.** Aye, sir, all this is so; but why
Stands Macbeth thus amazedly?
Come, sisters, cheer we up his sprites,
And show the best of our delights.
I'll charm the air to give a sound,
130 While you perform your antic round;°
That this great King may kindly say
Our duties did his welcome pay.
(*Music. The* WITCHES *dance, and then vanish, with* HECATE.)
MACBETH. Where are they? Gone? Let this pernicious hour
Stand aye accursed in the calendar!
135 Come in, without there!   (*Enter* LENNOX.)
LENNOX.   What's your Grace's will?
MACBETH. Saw you the weird sisters?
LENNOX.   No, my lord.
MACBETH. Came they not by you?
LENNOX.   No, indeed, my lord.
MACBETH. Infected be the air whereon they ride;
And damned all those that trust them! I did hear
140 The galloping of horse; who was 't came by?
LENNOX. 'Tis two or three, my lord, that bring you word
Macduff is fled to England.
MACBETH.   Fled to England!
LENNOX. Aye, my good lord.
MACBETH (*aside*). Time, thou anticipatest my dread exploits;
145 The flighty purpose never is o'ertook
Unless the deed go with it; from this moment
The very firstlings of my heart shall be
The firstlings of my hand.° And even now,
To crown my thoughts with acts, be it thought and done.
150 The castle of Macduff I will surprise;
Seize upon Fife; give to the edge o' the sword
His wife, his babes, and all unfortunate souls
That trace him in his line. No boasting like a fool;
This deed I'll do before this purpose cool.

133 Macbeth speaks "Thou . . . eyeballs" (line 113) as the first king passes. Macbeth continues to comment as each king passes in turn.

134 The balls, or orbs, and scepters (line 121) symbolize the sovereignty of England and Scotland, and the kingdoms of England, Scotland, and Ireland which were united for the first time under James I, eighth of Stuart kings. **blood-boltered,** having hair matted with blood.

antic round, grotesque [or ancient?] round dance.

135 Lines 125–135 are also considered to be a later interpolation, not by Shakespeare.

136 What is the irony of line 139?

The flighty . . . hand. One must act at once if one is to accomplish one's purpose. From now on I shall put my thoughts into immediate action.

155　But no more sights!—Where are these gentlemen?
　　　Come, bring me where they are.　　　　　　　　　　　　*(Exeunt.)*

SCENE 2

Fife. MACDUFF's *castle. (Played in the Chamber.) Enter* LADY MACDUFF, *her*
SON, *and* ROSS.

LADY MACDUFF. What had he done, to make him fly the land?
ROSS. You must have patience, madam.
LADY MACDUFF.　　　　　　　　　　　　He had none;
　　　His flight was madness. When our actions do not,
　　　Our fears do make us traitors.
ROSS.　　　　　　　　　　　You know not
5　Whether it was his wisdom or his fear.
LADY MACDUFF. Wisdom! to leave his wife, to leave his babes,
　　　His mansion and his titles in a place
　　　From whence himself does fly? He loves us not;
　　　He wants the natural touch;° for the poor wren,
10　The most diminutive of birds, will fight,
　　　Her young ones in her nest, against the owl.
　　　All is the fear and nothing is the love;
　　　As little is the wisdom, where the flight
　　　So runs against all reason.
ROSS.　　　　　　　　　My dearest coz,°
15　I pray you, school° yourself; but, for your husband,
　　　He is noble, wise, judicious, and best knows
　　　The fits o' the season.° I dare not speak much further;
　　　But cruel are the times, when we are traitors
　　　And do not know ourselves,° when we hold rumor
20　From what we fear,° yet know not what we fear,
　　　But float upon a wild and violent sea
　　　Each way and move. I take my leave of you;
　　　Shall not be long but I'll be here again;
　　　Things at the worst will cease, or else climb upward
25　To what they were before. My pretty cousin,°
　　　Blessing upon you!
LADY MACDUFF. Fathered he is, and yet he's fatherless.
ROSS. I am so much a fool, should I stay longer,
　　　It would be my disgrace and your discomfort;
30　I take my leave at once.　　　　　　　　　　　　*(Exit* ROSS.*)*
LADY MACDUFF.　　　　　Sirrah,° your father's dead;
　　　And what will you do now? How will you live?
SON. As birds do, mother.
LADY MACDUFF.　　　　　What, with worms and flies?
SON. With what I get, I mean; and so do they.

137 What message has Ross apparently just brought to Lady Macduff?

He wants . . . touch. He lacks natural human affection.

coz, cousin.
school, control.

fits . . . season, violence of the times.

do not . . . ourselves, do not know ourselves (or each other) to be traitors.
hold rumor . . . fear, believe rumors that grow out of fears.

My . . . cousin, Macduff's small son.

138 Ross leaves because he feels like weeping; in Shakespeare's time it was considered disgraceful for a man to weep.
Sirrah, ordinary form of address used in speaking to children and servants.

Illustration by Charles Ricketts from *The Tragedie of Macbeth* (Ernest Benn, 1923).

LADY MACDUFF. Poor bird! thou'ldst never fear the net nor lime,°
35   The pitfall nor the gin.°
   SON. Why should I, mother? Poor birds they are not set for.
      My father is not dead, for all your saying.
   LADY MACDUFF. Yes, he is dead; how wilt thou do for a father?
   SON. Nay, how will you do for a husband?
40 **LADY MACDUFF.** Why, I can buy me twenty at any market.
   SON. Then you'll buy 'em to sell again.
   LADY MACDUFF. Thou speak'st with all thy wit; and yet, i' faith,
      With wit enough for thee.
   SON. Was my father a traitor, mother?
45 **LADY MACDUFF.** Aye, that he was.
   SON. What is a traitor?
   LADY MACDUFF. Why, one that swears and lies.°
   SON. And be all traitors that do so?
   LADY MACDUFF. Every one that does so is a traitor, and must be hanged.
50 **SON.** And must they all be hanged that swear and lie?
   LADY MACDUFF. Every one.
   SON. Who must hang them?
   LADY MACDUFF. Why, the honest men.

lime, birdlime, a sticky substance used to catch birds.
gin, snare.

swears and lies, swears allegiance and then breaks his oath.

SON. Then the liars and swearers are fools, for there are liars and
55   swearers enow to beat the honest men and hang up them.
LADY MACDUFF. Now, God help thee, poor monkey! But how wilt thou
      do for a father?
SON. If he were dead, you'ld weep for him; if you would not, it were a
      good sign that I should quickly have a new father.
60 LADY MACDUFF. Poor prattler, how thou talk'st!

                                                    (*Enter a* MESSENGER.)

MESSENGER. Bless you, fair dame! I am not to you known,
      Though in your state of honor I am perfect.°
      I doubt° some danger does approach you nearly.
      If you will take a homely man's advice,
65   Be not found here; hence, with your little ones.
      To fright you thus, methinks I am too savage;
      To do worse to you were fell cruelty,
      Which is too nigh your person. Heaven preserve you!
      I dare abide no longer.   (*Exit.*)
LADY MACDUFF.   Whither should I fly?
70   I have done no harm. But I remember now
      I am in this earthly world, where to do harm
      Is often laudable, to do good sometime
      Accounted dangerous folly; why, then, alas,
      Do I put up that womanly defense,
75   To say I have done no harm?   (*Enter* MURDERERS.)
                          What are these faces?
FIRST MURDERER. Where is your husband?
LADY MACDUFF. I hope in no place so unsanctified
      Where such as thou mayst find him.
FIRST MURDERER.   He's a traitor.
SON. Thou liest, thou shag-eared° villain!
FIRST MURDERER.   What, you egg!   (*Stabbing him.*)
80   Young fry of treachery!
SON.   He has killed me, mother;
      Run away, I pray you!   (*Dies.*)
(*Exit* LADY MACDUFF, *crying* "*Murder!*" *Exeunt* MURDERERS, *following her.*)

SCENE 3

England. Before the King's palace. (Played on the Platform and in the Study.)
Enter MALCOLM *and* MACDUFF.

MALCOLM. Let us seek out some desolate shade, and there
      Weep our sad bosoms empty.
MACDUFF.   Let us rather
      Hold fast the mortal sword and, like good men,

139 *Macbeth* has only two
humorous scenes:
the broad comedy of the
drunken porter, and the
light comedy of this scene.
What was Shakespeare's
dramatic purpose in plac-
ing Lady Macduff's scene
here?

140 It has been suggested
that the messenger
may have been sent by
Lady Macbeth. Does this
seem possible? Be alert for
possible clues later in the
play.
in your . . . perfect, I
know of your honorable
rank.
doubt, suspect.

shag-eared, often said
to mean *shaggy-haired,*
but Elizabethan criminals
sometimes had their ears
slit, and this could be the
meaning.
141 Trace the murders
committed by Mac-
beth up to this point in
terms of their justifiabili-
ty. What is revealed about
changes in his character?

142 The unusual length
of Scene 3 may be
explained by the fact that
it was customary to give
the chief actor a rest during the fourth act, or
thereabouts, of a tragedy.

Bestride our downfall'n birthdom.° Each new morn
5 New widows howl, new orphans cry, new sorrows
Strike heaven on the face, that it resounds
As if it felt with Scotland and yelled out
Like syllable of dolor.

MALCOLM.   What I believe, I'll wail;
What know, believe; and what I can redress,
10 As I shall find the time to friend,° I will.
What you have spoke, it may be so perchance;
This tyrant, whose sole name blisters our tongues,
Was once thought honest; you have loved him well.
He hath not touched you yet. I am young; but something
15 You may deserve of him through me,° and wisdom
To offer up a weak poor innocent lamb
To appease an angry god.

MACDUFF. I am not treacherous.

MALCOLM.   But Macbeth is.
A good and virtuous nature may recoil
20 In an imperial charge.° But I shall crave your pardon;
That which you are my thoughts cannot transpose;°
Angels are bright still, though the brightest fell;
Though all things foul would wear the brows of grace,
Yet grace must still look so.

MACDUFF.   I have lost my hopes.

25 MALCOLM. Perchance even there where I did find my doubts,
Why in that rawness left you wife and child,
Those precious motives, those strong knots of love,
Without leave-taking? I pray you,
Let not my jealousies be your dishonors,
30 But mine own safeties.° You may be rightly just,
Whatever I shall think.

MACDUFF.   Bleed, bleed, poor country!
Great tyranny! lay thou thy basis sure,
For goodness dare not check thee; wear thou thy wrongs;
The title is affeered!° Fare thee well, lord.
35 I would not be the villain that thou think'st
For the whole space that's in the tyrant's grasp,
And the rich East to boot.

MALCOLM.   Be not offended;
I speak not as in absolute fear of you.
I think our country sinks beneath the yoke;
40 It weeps, it bleeds; and each new day a gash
Is added to her wounds. I think withal
There would be hands uplifted in my right;
And here from gracious England° have I offer
Of goodly thousands; but, for all this,

E.C.
birds - symbols

Bestride . . . birthdom,
defend our fallen father-
land.

143 What is the irony in
Macduff's speech
(lines 2b–8a)?

to friend, suitable.

but something . . . me,
but you may win favor
from Macbeth by betray-
ing me.

recoil . . . charge, reverse
itself through loyalty to
the king.
transpose, change.

Let not . . . safeties. I am
suspicious not to dishonor
you but because I wish to
assure my own safety.

The title . . . affeered.
Your title of tyranny is
confirmed.

England, the king of England.

When I shall tread upon the tyrant's head,
Or wear it on my sword, yet my poor country
Shall have more vices than it had before,
More suffer, and more sundry ways than ever,
By him that shall succeed.

MACDUFF.   What should he be?

50 MALCOLM. It is myself I mean; in whom I know
All the particulars of vice so grafted
That, when they shall be opened, black Macbeth
Will seem as pure as snow, and the poor state
Esteem him as a lamb, being compared
55 With my confineless harms.°

MACDUFF.   Not in the legions
Of horrid hell can come a devil more damned
In evils to top Macbeth.

MALCOLM.   I grant him bloody,
Luxurious,° avaricious, false, deceitful,
Sudden,° malicious, smacking of every sin
60 That has a name; but there's no bottom, none,
In my voluptuousness. Your wives, your daughters,
Your matrons and your maids, could not fill up
The cistern of my lust; and my desire.
All continent impediments would o'erbear
65 That did oppose my will. Better Macbeth
Than such an one to reign.

MACDUFF.   Boundless intemperance
In nature is a tyranny; it hath been
The untimely emptying of the happy throne
And fall of many kings. But fear not yet
70 To take upon you what is yours; you may
Convey° your pleasures in a spacious plenty,
And yet seem cold, the time° you may so hoodwink.
We have willing dames enough; there cannot be
That vulture in you, to devour so many
75 As will to greatness dedicate themselves,
Finding it so inclined.

MALCOLM.   With this there grows
In my most ill-composed affection° such
A stanchless° avarice that, were I king,
I should cut off the nobles for their lands,
80 Desire his jewels and this other's house;
And my more-having would be as a sauce
To make me hunger more; that I should forge
Quarrels unjust against the good and loyal,
Destroying them for wealth.

MACDUFF.   This avarice

confineless harms, unlimited evil.

Luxurious, lustful.
Sudden, violent.

144 What is Malcolm's purpose in making such a confession?

Convey, obtain secretly.
the time, the world.

ill-composed affection, evil disposition.
stanchless, insatiable.

loves women / he won't be king

I would sell all the land / saying how horrible a king he would be

85   Sticks deeper, grows with more pernicious root
       Than summer-seeming° lust, and it hath been
       The sword of our slain kings. Yet do not fear;
       Scotland hath foisons° to fill up your will,
       Of your mere own. All these are portable,
90   With other graces weighed.°
    MALCOLM. But I have none; the king-becoming graces,
       As justice, verity, temperance, stableness,
       Bounty, perseverance, mercy, lowliness,
       Devotion, patience, courage, fortitude,
95   I have no relish of them, but abound
       In the division of each several crime,
       Acting it many ways. Nay, had I power, I should
       Pour the sweet milk of concord into hell,
       Uproar the universal peace, confound
100   All unity on earth.
    MACDUFF.   O Scotland, Scotland!
    MALCOLM. If such a one be fit to govern, speak;
       I am as I have spoken.
    MACDUFF.   Fit to govern!
       No, not to live. O nation miserable,
       With an untitled tyrant bloody-sceptered,
105   When shalt thou see thy wholesome days again,
       Since that the truest issue of thy throne
       By his own interdiction° stands accursed,
       And does blaspheme his breed? Thy royal father
       Was a most sainted king. The queen that bore thee,
110   Oftener upon her knees than on her feet,
       Died every day she lived.° Fare thee well!
       These evils thou repeat'st upon thyself
       Have banished me from Scotland. O my breast,
       Thy hope ends here!
    MALCOLM.   Macduff, this noble passion,
115   Child of integrity, hath from my soul
       Wiped the black scruples, reconciled my thoughts,
       To thy good truth and honor. Devilish Macbeth
       By many of these trains° hath sought to win me
       Into his power, and modest wisdom plucks me
120   From overcredulous haste. But God above
       Deal between thee and me! For even now
       I put myself to thy direction, and
       Unspeak mine own detraction, here abjure
       The taints and blames I laid upon myself,
125   For strangers to my nature. I am yet
       Unknown to woman, never was forsworn,
       Scarcely have coveted what was mine own,

summer-seeming, short-lived.

foisons, plenty.

All these . . . weighed.
These weaknesses are bearable, considering your other virtues.

interdiction, decree.

Died . . . lived, prepared for death by daily prayers and self-sacrifice.

trains, devices.

At no time broke my faith, would not betray
The devil to his fellow, and delight
130 No less in truth than life; my first false speaking
Was this upon myself. What I am truly
Is thine and my poor country's to command;
Whither indeed, before thy here-approach,
Old Siward, with ten thousand warlike men,
135 Already at a point,° was setting forth.
Now we'll together; and the chance of goodness
Be like our warranted quarrel!° Why are you silent?
MACDUFF. Such welcome and unwelcome things at once
'Tis hard to reconcile.   (*Enter a* DOCTOR.)
140 MALCOLM. Well, more anon.—Comes the King forth, I pray you?
DOCTOR. Aye, sir; there are a crew of wretched souls
That stay his cure.° There malady convinces
The great assay of art;° but at his touch—
Such sanctity hath heaven given his hand—
145 They presently amend.
MALCOLM.   I thank you, doctor.   (*Exit* DOCTOR.)
MACDUFF. What's the disease he means?
MALCOLM.   'Tis called the evil:°
A most miraculous work in this good King;
Which often, since my here-remain in England,
I have seen him do. How he solicits heaven,
150 Himself best knows; but strangely-visited people,
All swoln and ulcerous, pitiful to the eye,
The mere despair of surgery, he cures,
Hanging a golden stamp about their necks,
Put on with holy prayers. And 'tis spoken,
155 To the succeeding royalty he leaves
The healing benediction. With this strange virtue,
He hath a heavenly gift of prophecy,
And sundry blessings hang about his throne,
That speak him full of grace.   (*Enter* ROSS.)
MACDUFF.   See, who comes here?
160 MALCOLM. My countryman; but yet I know him not.
MACDUFF. My ever-gentle cousin, welcome hither.
MALCOLM. I know him now. Good God, betimes remove
The means that makes us strangers!
ROSS.   Sir, amen.
MACDUFF. Stands Scotland where it did?
ROSS.   Alas, poor country!
165 Almost afraid to know itself. It cannot
Be called our mother, but our grave; where nothing,
But who knows nothing, is once seen to smile;
Where sighs and groans and shrieks that rend the air

at a point, prepared.

and the chance . . . quarrel, and may our chance of success be as strong as the justness of our cause.

stay his cure, wait for him to cure them.
convinces . . . art, defies cure by any medical skill.

the evil, scrofula, a disease characterized by swelling of the lymphatic glands. It was called "the king's evil" because of a belief that it could be healed by the touch of a king. This curing power was first attributed to Edward the Confessor and later to his successors. This passage was obviously intended to flatter James I, who believed he had this power.

Are made, not marked; where violent sorrow seems
170   A modern ecstasy.° The dead man's knell
      Is there scarce asked for who; and good men's lives
      Expire before the flowers in their caps,
      Dying or ere they sicken.
      MACDUFF.   Oh, relation
      Too nice,° and yet too true!
      MALCOLM.   What's the newest grief?
175 ROSS. That of an hour's age doth hiss the speaker;°
      Each minute teems° a new one.
      MACDUFF.   How does my wife?
      ROSS. Why, well.
      MACDUFF.   And all my children?
      ROSS.   Well, too.
      MACDUFF. The tyrant has not battered at their peace?
      ROSS. No; they were well at peace when I did leave 'em.
180 MACDUFF. Be not a niggard of your speech; how goes 't?
      ROSS. When I came hither to transport the tidings,
      Which I have heavily borne, there ran a rumor
      Of many worthy fellows that were out;°
      Which was to my belief witnessed the rather,
185   For that I saw the tyrant's power afoot.
      Now is the time of help; your eye in Scotland
      Would create soldiers, make our women fight,
      To doff their dire distresses.
      MALCOLM.   Be 't their comfort
      We are coming thither. Gracious England hath
190   Lent us good Siward and ten thousand men;
      An older and a better soldier none
      That Christendom gives out.
      ROSS.   Would I could answer
      This comfort with the like! But I have words
      That would be howled out in the desert air,
195   Where hearing should not latch° them.
      MACDUFF.   What concern they?
      The general cause? Or is it a fee-grief°
      Due to some single breast?
      ROSS.   No mind that's honest
      But in it shares some woe; though the main part
      Pertains to you alone.
      MACDUFF.   If it be mine,
200   Keep it not from me; quickly let me have it.
      ROSS. Let not your ears despise my tongue forever,
      Which shall possess them with the heaviest sound
      That ever yet they heard.
      MACDUFF.   Hum! I guess at it.

A *modern ecstasy*, ordinary feeling.

relation/Too nice, report too exact.

doth hiss the speaker, causes the speaker to be hissed because he is already out of date.
teems, brings forth.
145 | How does Ross reply in line 177a—quickly, or hesitantly?

out, in arms.

latch, catch the sound of.

fee-grief, private grief.

ROSS. Your castle is surprised; your wife and babes
205   Savagely slaughtered. To relate the manner
    Were, on the quarry° of these murdered deer,
    To add the death of you.
MALCOLM.   Merciful heaven!
    What, man! ne'er pull your hat upon your brows;
    Give sorrow words: the grief that does not speak
210   Whispers the o'er-fraught heart, and bids it break.
MACDUFF. My children, too?
ROSS.   Wife, children, servants, all
    That could be found.
MACDUFF.   And I must be from thence!
    My wife killed, too?
ROSS.   I have said.
MALCOLM.   Be comforted;
    Let's make us medicines of our great revenge,
215   To cure his deadly grief.
MACDUFF. He has no children. All my pretty ones?
    Did you say all? O hell-kite! All?
    What, all my pretty chickens and their dam
    At one fell swoop?
220 **MALCOLM.** Dispute it like a man.
MACDUFF.   I shall do so;
    But I must also feel it as a man.
    I cannot but remember such things were,
    That were most precious to me. Did heaven look on
    And would not take their part? Sinful Macduff,
225   They were all struck for thee! Naught, that I am,
    Not for their own demerits, but for mine,
    Fell slaughter on their souls. Heaven rest them now!
MALCOLM. Be this the whetstone of your sword; let grief
    Convert to anger; blunt not the heart, enrage it.
230 **MACDUFF.** Oh, I could play the woman with mine eyes
    And braggart with my tongue! But, gentle heavens,
    Cut short all intermission; front to front
    Bring thou this fiend of Scotland and myself;
    Within my sword's length set him; if he 'scape,
235   Heaven forgive him, too!
MALCOLM.   This tune goes manly.
    Come, go we to the King; our power is ready;
    Our lack is nothing but our leave.° Macbeth
    Is ripe for shaking, and the powers above
    Put on their instruments. Receive what cheer you may;
240   The night is long that never finds the day.   *(Exeunt.)*

---

146 What has happened that might prompt Ross now to tell Macduff the truth about his wife and children?
quarry, heap of dead bodies.

147 To whom is Macduff referring in "He has no children" (line 216)? What does he mean? (Several interpretations are possible.)

148 Why do you think Shakespeare had Macduff learn of Lady Macduff's murder *after* he had convinced Malcolm of his loyalty?

Our lack . . . leave. We only need the King's permission to depart.

THINK AND DISCUSS

SCENE 1
Understanding
1. What three apparitions do the witches show Macbeth? What do they tell him?
2. Of what does the Show of Kings consist?

Analyzing
3. What is Macbeth's reaction to all that the witches show him?
4. What news does Macbeth receive at the end of the scene? What plan does he make because of it?

SCENE 2
Understanding
1. What message has Ross apparently just brought to Lady Macduff?
2. What else does he suggest to her?

Analyzing
3. Describe the circumstances that lead up to the murder of Lady Macduff and her son.
4. What do the visits of Ross and the messenger suggest about the state of affairs in Macbeth's kingdom?
5. What effect is created by the humorous scene between Lady Macduff and her son just before their murders?

Extending
6. As far as the plot of *Macbeth* goes, this scene with Lady Macduff and her son is unnecessary, since the report of their murder is carried to Macduff by Ross. What do you think was Shakespeare's purpose in including it?

SCENE 3
Understanding
1. Where does this scene take place? What are Malcolm and Macduff doing there?

Analyzing
2. Why does Malcolm at first suspect Macduff?
3. Why does Malcolm accuse himself of so many vices?

4. Why does Ross not tell Macduff about his wife and son immediately? What prompts him to tell the truth?
5. With what resolve do Macduff, Malcolm, and Ross end this scene?

Extending
6. How does Shakespeare depict Macduff as bearing his grief? Do you think that this is true to life? Explain.

ACT FOUR IN REVIEW
Understanding
1. What prophecies remain unfulfilled?

Analyzing
2. From Ross's speeches to Malcolm and Macduff, how would you describe the current situation in Scotland?
3. Macbeth has now murdered on four separate occasions: Duncan, Duncan's grooms, Banquo, and Lady Macduff and her son. What reasons had Macbeth for each of these murders?
4. Can you see a pattern in Macbeth's reasons for murder? What does it tell you about Macbeth at this point?

Extending
5. Enumerate the characters who now have motives to retaliate against Macbeth. What do you expect them to do next?

ENRICHMENT
Listening to Shakespeare

Listen to recordings or watch video tapes of several different actors or actresses delivering one of Macbeth's soliloquies or Lady Macbeth's sleepwalking scene in Act Five. Follow the text as you listen and note similarities and differences in their interpretations. In small groups discuss what kind of character you believe each actor is trying to portray—for example, frightened, emotionally unstable, cynical, insane—and determine which reading most closely accords with your image of Macbeth or Lady Macbeth as revealed thus far in the play.

Comment

Shakespeare's Theater—The Globe

There was not one Globe Theater, but two. The first, probably completed in 1599, burned to the ground in 1613. A new Globe, promptly erected on the same spot, stood until 1644, when it was torn down, and houses were erected on its site.

We shall probably never know exactly what the Globe looked like. No contemporary pictures of the theater itself have come down to us, and what evidence there is—in the form of maps, carpenters' contracts, verbal descriptions, and the like—is inconclusive. Still, it is possible to reconstruct a theater that has the same spirit, if not the same appearance, as the original. And so Shakespearean theaters around the world have been designed with permanent open stages, and a full-sized replica is currently under construction in London near the original site south of the Thames River.

The Globe Theater was possibly round but more likely many-sided, with an outside diameter, according to the conjectures of scholars, of about 84 feet. Its three tiers of seats, plus an open area for standees, could accommodate about 2000 spectators.

The main acting area, called the Platform, extended out into the audience. At the back was a curtained recess known as the Study that was usually used for interior scenes. At either side were large permanent doors, similar to the street doors of Elizabethan town houses. These were the main stage entrances. In the floor of the Platform were a number of trap doors leading to the area below stage known as Hell. From these traps arose apparitions, smoke, and fog, and through them actors descended when the action required them to go underground.

On the second level there was another curtained recess called the Chamber, generally used for domestic settings. In front of this was a narrow balcony called the Tarras (terrace) connecting two small bay windows or window stages that flanked it. The Tarras was often used in conjunction with the Platform—for example, to represent a hill, battlements, or a gallery from which observers watched action below.

The third level contained a narrow musicians' gallery that could also be used as an acting area. Above it was a canopied roof supported by two large stage posts that rose from the Platform. Sound effects such as thunder or battle "alarums" were produced in the Huts above the Canopy. The Huts also housed a pulley system used for lowering apparitions or objects supposed to appear from midair.

This entire three-story structure, forming the back of the stage and giving the effect of a large Elizabethan town house, was known as the Tiring House. It was the Globe's permanent set. After 1599 Shakespeare probably wrote most of his plays with this set in mind.

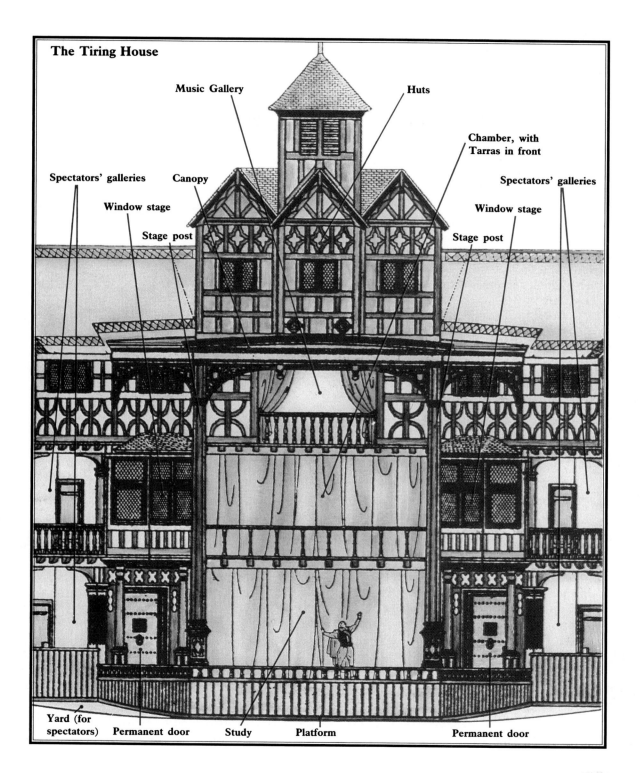

The Tiring House

Music Gallery

Huts

Chamber, with
Tarras in front

Spectators' galleries

Canopy

Spectators' galleries

Window stage

Window stage

Stage post

Stage post

Yard (for
spectators)

Permanent door

Study

Platform

Permanent door

ACT FIVE

SCENE 1

Dunsinane. Anteroom in the castle. (Played in the Chamber.) Enter a DOCTOR
OF PHYSIC° *and a* WAITING-GENTLEWOMAN.

Physic, medicine.

DOCTOR. I have two nights watched with you, but can perceive no truth in
your report. When was it she last walked?

GENTLEWOMAN. Since his Majesty went into the field, I have seen her rise
from her bed, throw her nightgown upon her, unlock her closet, take forth
5 paper, fold it, write upon 't, read it, afterwards seal it, and again return
to bed; yet all this while in a most fast sleep.

DOCTOR. A great perturbation in nature, to receive at once the benefit of
sleep, and do the effects of watching! In this slumbery agitation, besides
her walking and other actual performances, what, at any time, have you
10 heard her say?

GENTLEWOMAN. That, sir, which I will not report after her.

DOCTOR. You may to me; and 'tis most meet you should.

GENTLEWOMAN. Neither to you nor anyone, having no witness to confirm
my speech. (*Enter* LADY MACBETH, *with a taper.*) Lo, you, here she comes!
15 This is her very guise; and, upon my life, fast asleep. Observe her; stand
close.

DOCTOR. How came she by that light?

GENTLEWOMAN. Why, it stood by her; she has light by her continually, 'tis
her command.

20 **DOCTOR.** You see, her eyes are open.

GENTLEWOMAN. Aye, but their sense is shut.

DOCTOR. What is it she does now? Look how she rubs her hands.

GENTLEWOMAN. It is an accustomed action with her, to seem thus washing
her hands. I have known her continue in this a quarter of an hour.

25 **LADY MACBETH.** Yet here's a spot.

DOCTOR. Hark! she speaks. I will set down what comes from her, to satisfy
my remembrance the more strongly.

LADY MACBETH. Out, damned spot! out, I say!—One; two. Why, then 'tis
time to do 't.—Hell is murky! Fie, my lord, fie! a soldier, and afeard? What
30 need we fear who knows it, when none can call our power to account?—Yet
who would have thought the old man to have had so much blood in him?

DOCTOR. Do you mark that?

LADY MACBETH. The thane of Fife had a wife; where is she now?—What,
will these hands ne'er be clean?—No more o' that, my lord, no more o'
35 that; you mar all with this starting.

DOCTOR. Go to, go to; you have known what you should not.

GENTLEWOMAN. She has spoke what she should not, I am sure of that.
Heaven knows what she has known.

LADY MACBETH. Here's the smell of the blood still; all the perfumes of Arabia

149 Note that this scene
is largely in prose—
perhaps because the dis-
jointed remarks of Lady
Macbeth's sleepwalking
do not seem suitable for
poetry; the Doctor and
Gentlewoman, who speak
on a less intense emotional
plane, could not very well
be given poetry to speak
while Lady Macbeth was
present.

150 Note that this act is
made up of a series
of short scenes which take
place alternately at Dun-
sinane Castle and on the
battlefields. On the stage
of the Globe, this could
easily be managed. If you
were making a film of
Macbeth, how would you
handle the frequent shifts?
How might they be dealt
with in a modern stage
production?

40 will not sweeten this little hand. Oh, oh, oh!

DOCTOR. What a sigh is there! The heart is sorely charged.

GENTLEWOMAN. I would not have such a heart in my bosom for the dignity
of the whole body.

DOCTOR. Well, well, well—

45 GENTLEWOMAN. Pray God it be, sir.

DOCTOR. This disease is beyond my practice; yet I have known those which
have walked in their sleep who have died holily in their beds.

LADY MACBETH. Wash your hands, put on your nightgown; look not so
pale.—I tell you yet again, Banquo's buried; he cannot come out on 's

50 grave.

DOCTOR. Even so?

LADY MACBETH. To bed, to bed! There's knocking at the gate. Come, come,
come, come, give me your hand. What's done cannot be undone.—To bed,
to bed, to bed!   (*Exit* LADY MACBETH.)

55 DOCTOR. Will she go now to bed?

GENTLEWOMAN. Directly.

DOCTOR. Foul whisperings are abroad! unnatural deeds
Do breed unnatural troubles; infected minds
To their deaf pillows will discharge their secrets.

60 More needs she the divine than the physician.
God, God forgive us all! Look after her;
Remove from her the means of all annoyance,°
And still keep eyes upon her. So, good night.
My mind she has mated,° and amazed my sight.

65 I think, but dare not speak.

GENTLEWOMAN.   Good night, good doctor.   (*Exeunt.*)

SCENE 2

The country near Dunsinane. (Played on the Platform.) Drum and colors. Enter
MENTEITH, CAITHNESS, ANGUS, LENNOX, *and* SOLDIERS.

MENTEITH. The English power is near, led on by Malcolm,
His uncle Siward, and the good Macduff.
Revenges burn in them; for their dear causes
Would to the bleeding and the grim alarm

5 Excite the mortified man.°

ANGUS.   Near Birnam wood
Shall we well meet them; that way are they coming.

CAITHNESS. Who knows if Donalbain be with his brother?

LENNOX. For certain, sir, he is not. I have a file
Of all the gentry; there is Siward's son,

10 And many unrough° youths that even now
Protest their first of manhood.°

MENTEITH.   What does the tyrant?

---

151 Can you connect each phrase of Lady Macbeth's speeches with some specific aspect of the crimes in which she has been involved?

152 Lady Macbeth is obviously in process of emotional collapse. Have there been signs earlier in the play that this might happen? Note especially her speeches at her last appearance, the end of Act Three, Scene 4.

annoyance, injury to herself.

mated, confounded.

153 How convincingly has Shakespeare portrayed emotional illness?

their dear causes . . . man, their deeply-felt causes would arouse a dead man to bloody battle.

154 Follow young Siward's activities, beginning here with line 9. Why did Shakespeare introduce this episode?

unrough, beardless.

Protest . . . manhood, call themselves men for the first time.

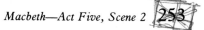

CAITHNESS. Great Dunsinane he strongly fortifies.
Some say he's mad; others that lesser hate him
Do call it valiant fury; but, for certain,
15 He cannot buckle his distempered cause
Within the belt of rule.°

ANGUS.   Now does he feel
His secret murders sticking on his hands;
Now minutely revolts upbraid his faith-breach;°
Those he commands move only in command,
20 Nothing in love; now does he feel his title
Hang loose about him, like a giant's robe
Upon a dwarfish thief.

MENTEITH.   Who then shall blame
His pestered senses to recoil and start,
When all that is within him does condemn
25 Itself for being there?

CAITHNESS.   Well, march we on,
To give obedience where 'tis truly owed.
Meet we the medicine of the sickly weal,
And with him pour we in our country's purge
Each drop of us.°

LENNOX.   Or so much as it needs,
30 To dew the sovereign flower and drown the weeds.
Make we our march towards Birnam.   (*Exeunt, marching.*)

He cannot . . . rule. He cannot control the situation.

Now . . . faith-breach. Every minute, those who revolt against him blame his faithlessness.

Meet we . . . us. We go to meet Malcolm, who will heal the sickness of our country, and to offer our lives in the curing process.

SCENE 3

Dunsinane. A room in the castle. (Played in the Chamber.) Enter MACBETH,
DOCTOR, *and* ATTENDANTS.

MACBETH. Bring me no more reports; let them° fly all.
Till Birnam wood remove to Dunsinane,
I cannot taint° with fear. What's the boy Malcolm?
Was he not born of woman? The spirits that know
5 All mortal consequences have pronounced me thus:
"Fear not, Macbeth; no man that's born of woman
Shall e'er have power upon thee." Then fly, false thanes,
And mingle with the English epicures.°
The mind I sway by° and the heart I bear
10 Shall never sag with doubt nor shake with fear.   (*Enter a* SERVANT.)
The devil damn thee black, thou cream-faced loon!
Where got'st thou that goose look?

SERVANT. There is ten thousand—

MACBETH.   Geese, villain?

SERVANT.   Soldiers, sir.

MACBETH. Go prick thy face, and over-red° thy fear,

them, the thanes.

taint, become infected.

epicures, lovers of luxury.
I sway by, I am directed by.
over-red, redden. The implication is that the servant's blood has gone to his lower body on account of his fear. He is pale, and there is no blood in his liver, where his courage should have resided—hence, *lily-livered.*

Thou lily-livered boy. What soldiers, patch?°
Death of thy soul! those linen cheeks of thine
Are counselors to fear. What soldiers, whey-face?
SERVANT. The English force, so please you.
MACBETH. Take thy face hence.   (*Exit* SERVANT.)
                    Seyton!—I am sick at heart,
20 When I behold—Seyton, I say!—This push°
    Will cheer me ever, or disseat me now.
    I have lived long enough; my way of life
    Is fall'n into the sear, the yellow leaf;
    And that which should accompany old age,
25 As honor, love, obedience, troops of friends,
    I must not look to have; but, in their stead,
    Curses, not loud but deep, mouth-honor, breath,
    Which the poor heart would fain deny, and dare not.
    Seyton!   (*Enter* SEYTON.)
30 SEYTON. What is your gracious pleasure?
    MACBETH.   What news more?
    SEYTON. All is confirmed, my lord, which was reported.
    MACBETH. I'll fight till from my bones my flesh be hacked.
      Give me my armor.
    SEYTON. 'Tis not needed yet.
    MACBETH.   I'll put it on.
35   Send out moe horses, skirr° the country round;
      Hang those that talk of fear. Give me mine armor.
      How does your patient, doctor?
    DOCTOR.   Not so sick, my lord,
      As she is troubled with thick-coming fancies,
      That keeps her from her rest.
    MACBETH.   Cure her of that.
40   Canst thou not minister to a mind diseased,
      Pluck from the memory a rooted sorrow,
      Raze out the written troubles of the brain,
      And with some sweet oblivious antidote
      Cleanse the stuffed bosom of that perilous stuff°
45   Which weighs upon the heart?
    DOCTOR.   Therein the patient
      Must minister to himself.
    MACBETH. Throw physic to the dogs; I'll none of it.
      Come, put mine armor on; give me my staff.
      Seyton, send out.° Doctor, the thanes fly from me.
50   Come sir, dispatch. If thou couldst, doctor, cast
      The water of my land,° find her disease,
      And purge it to a sound and pristine health,
      I would applaud thee to the very echo,
      That should applaud again.—Pull 't off,° I say.—

---

patch, fool.

push, attack.

155 | What *appears* to be Macbeth's emotional state at the beginning of the scene with Seyton (line 29)? How is he actually feeling? What tells you?

skirr, scour.

156 | What do Macbeth's remarks to the doctor about his wife's illness (beginning with line 37) reveal about the state of their relationship at this point?

stuff. Some scholars think this word is a printer's error and should be *grief*.

send out, send out more scouts.

cast . . . land, diagnose my country's illness.

Pull 't off, referring to some part of his armor.

⁵⁵ What rhubarb, senna, or what purgative drug,
Would scour these English hence? Hear'st thou of them?
DOCTOR. Aye, my good lord; your royal preparation
Makes us hear something.
MACBETH.   Bring it° after me.
I will not be afraid of death and bane
⁶⁰ Till Birnam forest come to Dunsinane.
DOCTOR (*aside*). Were I from Dunsinane away and clear,
Profit again should hardly draw me here.   (*Exeunt.*)

it, the armor.

SCENE 4

Country near Birnam wood. (Played on the Platform.) Drum and colors. Enter
MALCOLM, OLD SIWARD *and his* SON, MACDUFF, MENTEITH, CAITHNESS,
ANGUS, LENNOX, ROSS, *and* SOLDIERS, *marching.* English fighters

MALCOLM. Cousins, I hope the days are near at hand
That chambers will be safe.°
MENTEITH.   We doubt it nothing.
SIWARD. What wood is this before us?
MENTEITH.   The wood of Birnam.
MALCOLM. Let every soldier hew him down a bough,
⁵ And bear 't before him; thereby shall we shadow
The numbers of our host, and make discovery°
Err in report of us.
SOLDIERS.   It shall be done.
SIWARD. We learn no other but the confident tyrant
Keeps still in Dunsinane, and will endure
¹⁰ Our setting down before 't.°
MALCOLM.   'Tis his main hope;
For where there is advantage to be given,
Both more and less° have given him the revolt,
And none serve with him but constrainèd things
Whose hearts are absent, too.
MACDUFF.   Let our just censures
¹⁵ Attend the true event,° and put we on
Industrious soldiership.
SIWARD.   The time approaches
That will with due decision make us know
What we shall say we have and what we owe.
Thoughts speculative their unsure hopes relate,
²⁰ But certain issue strokes must arbitrate;°
Toward which advance the war.   (*Exeunt, marching.*)

That chambers . . . safe,
when people can sleep
safely.

157 Note how the equiv-
ocations of the
apparitions begin to be
revealed in lines 3–7.

discovery, Macbeth's scouts.

setting down before 't,
laying siege to it.

Both more and less, both
nobles and common
people.

Let . . . event. Let our
judgment await the actual
outcome of the battle.

Thoughts . . . arbitrate.
We are now speculating
on the basis of our hopes;
only after the battle will
we know the real outcome.

SCENE 5

Dunsinane, Within the castle. (Played on the Tarras and in the Chamber.) Enter
MACBETH, SEYTON, *and* SOLDIERS, *with drum and colors.*

158 The characters enter
on the Tarras.

MACBETH. Hang out our banners on the outward walls;
 The cry is still "They come!" Our castle's strength
 Will laugh a seige to scorn; here let them lie
 Till famine and the ague eat them up.
5 Were they not forced° with those that should be ours,
 We might have met them dareful, beard to beard,
 And beat them backward home.   *(A cry of women within.)*
      What is that noise?
SEYTON. It is the cry of women, my good lord.   *(Exit.)*
MACBETH. I have almost forgot the taste of fears.
10 The time has been my senses would have cooled
 To hear a night-shriek, and my fell of hair°
 Would at a dismal treatise° rouse and stir
 As life were in 't. I have supped full with horrors;
 Direness, familiar to my slaughterous thoughts,
15 Cannot once start me.   *(Re-enter SEYTON.)*
    Wherefore was that cry?
SEYTON. The Queen, my lord, is dead.
MACBETH. She should have died hereafter;
 There would have been a time for such a word.
 Tomorrow, and tomorrow, and tomorrow,
20 Creeps in this petty pace from day to day,
 To the last syllable of recorded time,
 And all our yesterdays have lighted fools
 The way to dusty death. Out, out, brief candle!
 Life's but a walking shadow, a poor player
25 That struts and frets his hour upon the stage
 And then is heard no more; it is a tale
 Told by an idiot, full of sound and fury,
 Signifying nothing.
      (Enter a MESSENGER.)
 Thou comest to use thy tongue; thy story quickly.
30 MESSENGER. Gracious my lord,
 I should report that which I say I saw,
 But know not how to do it.
MACBETH.   Well, say, sir.
MESSENGER. As I did stand my watch upon the hill,
 I looked toward Birnam, and anon, methought,
35 The wood began to move.
MACBETH.   Liar and slave!
MESSENGER. Let me endure your wrath, if 't be not so.
 Within this three mile may you see it coming;
 I say, a moving grove.
MACBETH.   If thou speak'st false,
 Upon the next tree shalt thou hang alive,
40 Till famine cling° thee; if thy speech be sooth,
 I care not if thou dost for me as much.

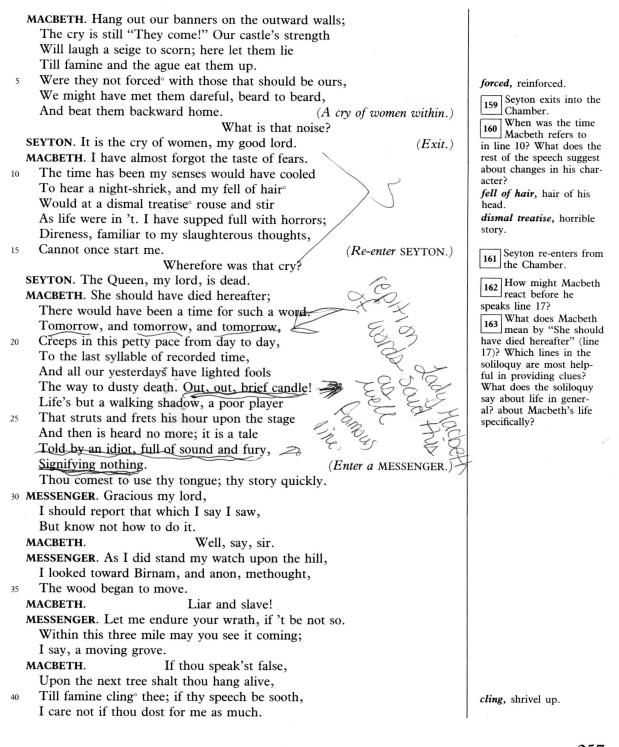

forced, reinforced.

159 Seyton exits into the Chamber.

160 When was the time Macbeth refers to in line 10? What does the rest of the speech suggest about changes in his character?
fell of hair, hair of his head.
dismal treatise, horrible story.

161 Seyton re-enters from the Chamber.

162 How might Macbeth react before he speaks line 17?

163 What does Macbeth mean by "She should have died hereafter" (line 17)? Which lines in the soliloquy are most helpful in providing clues? What does the soliloquy say about life in general? about Macbeth's life specifically?

cling, shrivel up.

I pull in resolution,° and begin
To doubt the equivocation° of the fiend
That lies like truth: "Fear not, till Birnam wood
45 Do come to Dunsinane"; and now a wood
Comes toward Dunsinane. Arm, arm, and out!
If this which he avouches does appear,
There is nor flying hence nor tarrying here.
I 'gin to be aweary of the sun,
50 And wish the estate o' the world were now undone.
Ring the alarum-bell! Blow, wind! come, wrack!°
At least we'll die with harness on our back.   (*Exeunt.*)

I pull in resolution. I weaken in confidence. With these words begins Macbeth's awareness that he has been duped by the witches.
doubt the equivocation, fear the deception.

wrack, ruin; destruction.

SCENE 6

Dunsinane. Before the castle. (Played on the Platform.) Drum and colors. Enter
MALCOLM, OLD SIWARD, MACDUFF, *and their* ARMY, *with boughs.*

MALCOLM. Now near enough; your leavy screens throw down,
And show like those you are. You, worthy uncle,
Shall, with my cousin, your right noble son,
Lead our first battle;° worthy Macduff and we
5 Shall take upon 's what else remains to do,
According to our order.
SIWARD.   Fare you well.
Do we but find the tyrant's power tonight,
Let us be beaten, if we cannot fight.
MACDUFF. Make all our trumpets speak; give them all breath,
10 Those clamorous harbingers of blood and death.   (*Exeunt.*)

battle, division of troops.

they start the war.

SCENE 7

Another part of the field. (Played on the Platform.) Alarums. Enter MACBETH.

MACBETH. They have tied me to a stake; I cannot fly,
But, bearlike, I must fight the course.° What's he
That was not born of woman? Such a one
Am I to fear, or none.   (*Enter* YOUNG SIWARD.)
5 YOUNG SIWARD. What is thy name?
MACBETH.   Thou'lt be afraid to hear it.
YOUNG SIWARD. No; though thou call'st thyself a hotter name
Than any is in hell.
MACBETH.   My name's Macbeth.
YOUNG SIWARD. The devil himself could not pronounce a title
More hateful to mine ear.
MACBETH.   No, nor more fearful.
10 YOUNG SIWARD. Thou liest, abhorrèd tyrant; with my sword
I'll prove the lie thou speak'st.

164 At this point, the Study curtains may have been thrown open to reveal the gate of Macbeth's castle, with perhaps a portcullis hanging under the Tarras. Macbeth stands at bay before the gates.
They have . . . course. In bearbaiting, a popular sport in Shakespeare's time, a bear was tied to a stake and forced to fight rounds with dogs set upon it in relays.

(They fight, and YOUNG SIWARD *is slain.)*

MACBETH. Thou wast born of woman.
    But swords I smile at, weapons laugh to scorn,
    Brandished by man that's of a woman born.   *(Exit.)*
                       (Alarums. Enter MACDUFF.*)*

15 **MACDUFF.** That way the noise is. Tyrant, show thy face!
    If thou be'st slain and with no stroke of mine,
    My wife and children's ghosts will haunt me still.
    I cannot strike at wretched kerns, whose arms
    Are hired to bear their staves; either thou, Macbeth,
20   Or else my sword with an unbattered edge
    I sheathe again undeeded. There thou shouldst be;
    By this great clatter, one of greatest note
    Seems bruited.° Let me find him, fortune!
    And more I beg not.   *(Exit. Alarums.)*
             (Enter MALCOLM *and* OLD SIWARD.*)*

25 **SIWARD.** This way, my lord; the castle's gently rendered,°
    The tyrant's people on both sides do fight;
    The noble thanes do bravely in the war;
    The day almost itself professes yours,
    And little is to do.
MALCOLM.   We have met with foes
30 That strike beside us.
SIWARD.   Enter, sir, the castle.   *(Exeunt. Alarums.)*

SCENE 8

Another part of the field. (Played on the Platform.) Enter MACBETH.

MACBETH. Why should I play the Roman fool and die
    On mine own sword?° Whiles I see lives,° the gashes
    Do better upon them.   *(Enter* MACDUFF.*)*
MACDUFF.   Turn, hell-hound, turn!
MACBETH. Of all men else I have avoided thee.
5 But get thee back; my soul is too much charged
    With blood of thine already.
MACDUFF.   I have no words;
    My voice is in my sword, thou bloodier villain
    Than terms can give thee out!   *(They fight.)*
MACBETH.   Thou losest labor;
    As easy mayst thou the intrenchant° air
10 With thy keen sword impress as make me bleed.
    Let fall thy blade on vulnerable crests;
    I bear a charmèd life, which must not yield
    To one of woman born.
MACDUFF.   Despair thy charm;

bruited, announced by a great noise.

rendered, surrendered.

165 The formal entry into the castle, after surrender, might be made through gates visible in the Study. Victorious soldiers might appear in the window-stages and dip the tyrant's banners, planting those of Malcolm and Siward on the Tarras. Macbeth's next entry and that of Macduff would probably be made through the two stage-doors on the Platform.

Why . . . sword. The Romans considered suicide more honorable than capture.
lives, living persons.

intrenchant, invulnerable.

by born
seasection

And let the angel whom thou still hast served

15 Tell thee Macduff was from his mother's womb
Untimely ripped.

MACBETH. Accursèd be that tongue that tells me so,
For it hath cowed my better part of man!
And be these juggling fiends no more believed

20 That palter with us in a double sense;
That keep the word of promise to our ear,
And break it to our hope. I'll not fight with thee.

MACDUFF. Then yield thee, coward,
And live to be the show and gaze o' the time.

25 We'll have thee, as our rarer monsters are,
Painted upon a pole,° and underwrit,
"Here may you see the tyrant."

MACBETH.   I will not yield,
To kiss the ground before young Malcolm's feet,
And to be baited with the rabble's curse.

30 Though Birnam wood be come to Dunsinane,
And thou opposed, being of no woman born,
Yet I will try the last. Before my body
I throw my warlike shield. Lay on, Macduff,
And damned be him that first cries, "Hold, enough!"

(Exeunt, fighting. Alarums. Retreat. Flourish. Enter, with drum and colors,
MALCOLM, OLD SIWARD, ROSS, *the other* THANES, *and* SOLDIERS.)

35 MALCOLM. I would the friends we miss were safe arrived.

SIWARD. Some must go off;° and yet, by these I see,
So great a day as this is cheaply bought.

MALCOLM. Macduff is missing, and your noble son.

ROSS. Your son, my lord, has paid a soldier's debt;

40 He only lived but till he was a man;
The which no sooner had his prowess confirmed
In the unshrinking station where he fought,
But like a man he died.

SIWARD.   Then he is dead?

ROSS. Aye, and brought off the field; your cause of sorrow

45 Must not be measured by his worth, for then
It hath no end.

SIWARD.   Had he his hurts before?

ROSS. Aye, on the front.

SIWARD.   Why then, God's soldier be he!
Had I as many sons as I have hairs,
I would not wish them to a fairer death;

50 And so, his knell is knolled.

MALCOLM.   He's worth more sorrow,
And that I'll spend for him.

SIWARD.   He's worth no more.

Painted . . . pole, your picture painted on a board which will be suspended on a pole.

166 How do Macbeth's last lines in the play (lines 27–34) relate to his character as described by the Captain in Act One, Scene 2?

go off, die.

167 Compare Siward's reaction to his son's death to the way Macbeth reacted at the news of Duncan's death (Act Two, Scene 3). Compare his reaction to Macduff's reaction when he heard of the murder of his family.

168 Why does Siward say "God's soldier be he!" (line 47b)?

Illustration by Charles Ricketts from *The Tragedie of Macbeth* (Ernest Benn, 1923).

They say he parted well, and paid his score;
And so, God be with him! Here comes newer comfort.

(Re-enter MACDUFF, *with* MACBETH's *head.)*

MACDUFF. Hail, King! for so thou art. Behold, where stands
55 The usurper's cursèd head. The time is free;
I see thee compassed with thy kingdom's pearl,°
That speak my salutation in their minds;
Whose voices I desire aloud with mine—
Hail, King of Scotland!

ALL.   Hail, King of Scotland!

60 MALCOLM. We shall not spend a large expense of time
Before we reckon with your several loves,
And make us even with you. My thanes and kinsmen,
Henceforth be earls, the first that ever Scotland
In such an honor named. What's more to do,
65 Which would be planted newly with the time,
As calling home our exiled friends abroad
That fled the snares of watchful tyranny;
Producing forth the cruel ministers
Of this dead butcher and his fiendlike queen,
70 Who, as 'tis thought, by self and violent hands
Took off her life; this, and what needful else
That calls upon us, by the grace of Grace
We will perform in measure, time, and place;
So, thanks to all at once and to each one,
75 Whom we invite to see us crowned at Scone.

(Flourish. Exeunt.)

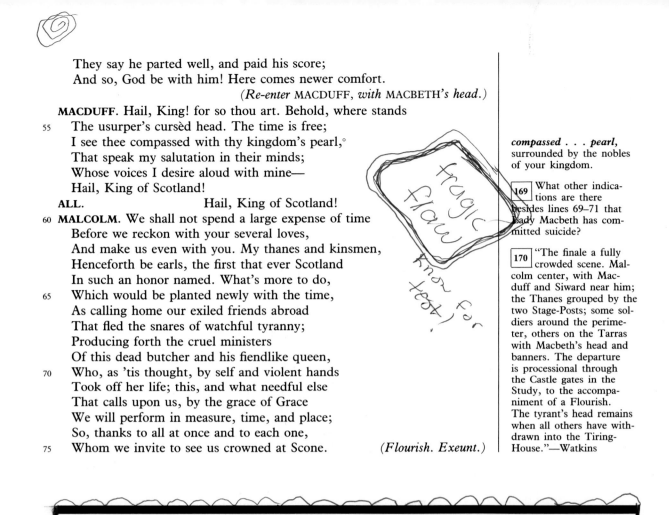

compassed . . . pearl,
surrounded by the nobles
of your kingdom.

169 What other indica-
tions are there
besides lines 69–71 that
Lady Macbeth has com-
mitted suicide?

170 "The finale a fully
crowded scene. Mal-
colm center, with Mac-
duff and Siward near him;
the Thanes grouped by the
two Stage-Posts; some soldiers around the perime-
ter, others on the Tarras
with Macbeth's head and
banners. The departure
is processional through
the Castle gates in the
Study, to the accompa-
niment of a Flourish.
The tyrant's head remains
when all others have withdrawn into the Tiring-
House."—Watkins

THINK AND DISCUSS
SCENE 1
Understanding
1. Explain in your own words what happens in this scene.

Analyzing
2. What subjects does Lady Macbeth talk about in her sleep? What event does she seem to be reliving?
3. What does this indicate about her state of mind?
4. How does the Doctor explain Lady Macbeth's sleepwalking?

SCENES 2–3
Understanding
1. What does Scene 2 reveal about where all the characters are located and what they are doing?

Analyzing
2. Why does Macbeth continue to claim that he is safe?
3. What, actually, is his emotional state? How can you tell?
4. What do Macbeth's remarks about his wife's illness reveal about their relationship at this point?

5. How does the Doctor respond to Macbeth's question about ministering "to a mind diseased"? To whom are they referring?

SCENES 4–5
Understanding

1. What action do the soldiers take in Scene 4 that will make one prophecy come true in an unexpected way?

Analyzing

2. What does Macbeth's soliloquy in Scene 5, lines 17–28, say about life in general? about Macbeth's life in particular?

3. Describe Macbeth's battle plans in lines 1–7. How does he change them in lines 46–52? What causes this change?

SCENES 6–8
Understanding

1. What does Macduff mean when he tells Macbeth that he was "from his mother's womb/Untimely ripped"? (Scene 8, lines 15–16)

2. Who becomes king at Macbeth's death?

Analyzing

3. What is Macbeth's initial attitude toward fighting Macduff? Why does he change?

4. Aside from the revelation about his birth, why is it dramatically appropriate that Macduff is the one finally to kill Macbeth?

5. What assurances does Malcolm give in his final speech that what was wrong in Scotland will now be set right?

6. What indications are there in Act Five that Lady Macbeth commits suicide?

Extending

7. Why does Lady Macbeth fade out of the play almost completely (except for the sleepwalking scene) after Act Three? Would the plot have been weakened if Shakespeare had not done this? Explain.

8. Why might Shakespeare have included the subplot about Young Siward's death?

9. How do Macbeth's last lines in the play relate to his character as described by the Captain in Act One, Scene 2?

READING LITERATURE SKILLFULLY
Cause/Effect

In a tightly-plotted drama such as *Macbeth*, one event causes another, which in turn causes another, and so on. For example, Macbeth believes he is invulnerable because of what he is told by the witches and their apparitions.

1. What actions of Macbeth have caused the situation at the beginning of Act Five?

2. What "impossibility" comes to pass that causes Macbeth to leave his besieged castle?

3. Trace the actions throughout Act Five that are linked by cause and effect to what the apparitions said and that lead Macbeth to his death.

THE PLAY IN REVIEW
Understanding

1. In a sense, the entire tragedy of *Macbeth* is precipitated by three things the witches say to Macbeth in Act One. What are they?

Analyzing

2. Is Duncan **characterized** as an effective king or an ineffective one? Note the situation at the beginning of the play, what Duncan says and does, and how others react to him.

3. How can you tell that Macduff is not the **protagonist** in this play?

4. How sound is Lady Macbeth's judgment of Macbeth's character? How sound is Macbeth's judgment of her?

5. How well do both Macbeth and Lady Macbeth understand themselves and their limitations?

6. According to the classical view, the undoing or downfall of the main character in a tragedy is brought about through a *tragic flaw* in character or through a tragic error. What brings about Macbeth's downfall? Lady Macbeth's?

7. In literature, characters are frequently used as *foils*; that is, the traits of one point up by contrast the traits of another. What traits of Macbeth are thrown into relief by contrast with Duncan? with Young Siward? with Malcolm? How does Lady Macduff serve as a foil for Lady Macbeth?

Extending

8. According the the classical view, tragedy is supposed to arouse feelings of pity and fear in its audience. Is this true of *Macbeth*? Explain.

THINKING SKILLS
Evaluating

To evaluate is to make a judgment based on some sort of standard.

1. Is Macbeth or Lady Macbeth more responsible for the events of the play?
2. Is Macbeth totally evil, or does he have some redeeming qualities? Explain.
3. Is Malcolm likely to become the same sort of ruler his father was? Why or why not?
4. To what extent do the witches control the outcome of the play?

VOCABULARY
Context

Use context clues in the following sentences to write on your paper a definition for each of the italicized words.

1. In his letter to Lady Macbeth, Macbeth says that he has received *missives* from the King telling him he is Thane of Cawdor.
2. Macbeth hurries to Inverness to be the *harbinger* who reports the King's impending visit.
3. Lady Macbeth says she will get the King's chamberlains drunk with wine and *wassail*.
4. After Duncan's murder, his sons Malcolm and Donalbain are accused of *parricide*.
5. To test Macduff's loyalty, Malcolm claims to be so *avaricious* that he would destroy the Scottish nobles for their wealth.
6. When Macbeth learns the circumstances of Macduff's birth, he knows he has been deceived by the *equivocation* of the apparitions.

COMPOSITION
Writing a News Story

Write a front-page story for the *Dunsinane Gazette* on Macbeth's defeat and death. Start by composing a lead sentence that includes the five *W*'s: who, what, when, where, and why. Include the fact that Lady Macbeth has died and the suspicion that she has killed herself. In addition, comment on the suspicious deaths of Duncan and Banquo and on the bloody massacre of Lady Macduff and her son. You may wish to incorporate some quoted remarks to add interest and authority. Before submitting your story, read it aloud to a classmate to test whether your information is clear and understandable.

Analyzing Macbeth's Downfall

Commentators have pointed out that three forces are at work to destroy Macbeth: flaws in his own character, the forces of evil as represented by the witches, and Lady Macbeth. Select the force that you think is most responsible and write a paper analyzing how it contributes to Macbeth's downfall. First go through the play and take notes on evidence to support your view. Construct an outline for the most persuasive case you can make. You will probably want to acknowledge the other forces at work, but show how the one you have chosen is predominant.

ENRICHMENT
Holding a Press Conference

Following the style of your favorite talk show or news program, hold a television press conference to cover Macbeth's defeat and death and Malcolm's becoming king. Have classmates assume the roles of Malcolm, Macduff, Ross, Seyton, the Doctor, Siward, and any bystanders you wish to include. Have commentators report the news and interview the guests about their impressions of what happened. At the end of the program, sum up the significance to the nation of the night's events.

Christopher Marlowe led a short and stormy life, much of which is still shrouded in mystery. The son of a Canterbury shoemaker, he attended King's School, Canterbury, and later Corpus Christi College, Cambridge, holding for six years a scholarship usually awarded to someone intending to enter the ministry.

While still at Cambridge, Marlowe became a government agent (or spy), probably working directly for Sir Francis Walsingham, Queen Elizabeth's Secretary of State. Although he received his B.A. without difficulty, in 1587 the university was about to deny his M.A., possibly because of rumors that he planned to join Catholic emigrés from England at Douay, Belgium, immediately after graduation. However, Elizabeth's Privy Council intervened because of services (unknown to this day) that Marlowe had rendered her, "because it is not Her Majesty's pleasure that anyone employed as he had been in matters touching the benefit of his country should be defamed by those that are ignorant in the affairs he went about." Needless to say, Marlowe received his degree.

In a manner that foreshadowed his own death a few years later, Marlowe became involved in a brawl with William Bradley. Another poet, Thomas Watson, intervened and killed Bradley. Although both men were taken into custody, Watson pleaded self-defense and both were released.

By 1591, Marlowe was established as a playwright and was sharing London lodgings with Thomas Kyd, another playwright. Marlowe's plays cannot be dated with certainty, but it was probably about this time that he wrote *Tamburlaine, Doctor Faustus,* and *The Jew of Malta,* his three greatest tragedies. He had also become friendly with Sir Walter Raleigh and other courtiers.

On May 12, 1593, Kyd was arrested and, under torture, claimed that Marlowe was the author of some atheistical papers found in their lodgings. Called before the Privy Council on May 20, Marlowe was questioned and released, but was required to appear before them daily. On May 30, while the case was still pending, Marlowe was at the inn of the Widow Bull in Deptford with Ingram Frizer, who was in the employ of Thomas Walsingham, and two other men. According to testimony, they quarreled over the bill, and Frizer stabbed Marlowe in self-defense, killing him instantly.

Marlowe's major achievement lay in adapting blank verse to the stage. Ben Jonson expressed his admiration when he referred to"Marlowe's mighty line." Marlowe's ability to compress thought, image, and idea into superb lines of blank verse paved the way for Shakespeare and later practitioners of the art. In addition, Marlowe is known for the towering heroes of his dramas, all of them strong and overpowering until tragedy strikes.

The Passionate Shepherd to His Love

Christopher Marlowe

Come live with me and be my love,
And we will all the pleasures prove
That hills and valleys, dales and fields,
Or woods, or steepy mountain yields.

5 And we will sit upon the rocks,
Seeing the shepherds feed their flocks,
By shallow rivers to whose falls
Melodious birds sing madrigals.[1]

And I will make thee beds of roses
10 And a thousand fragrant posies,
A cap of flowers, and a kirtle[2]
Embroidered all with leaves of myrtle;

A gown made of the finest wool
Which from our pretty lambs we pull;

15 Fair lined slippers for the cold,
With buckles of the purest gold;

A belt of straw and ivy buds,
With coral clasps and amber studs—
And if these pleasures may thee move,
20 Come live with me and be my love.

The shepherd swains shall dance and sing
For thy delight each May morning—
If these delights thy mind may move,
Then live with me and be my love.

1599

---

1. *madrigals*, poems set to music; songs.
2. *kirtle*, a skirt or dress.

Comment

Responses to "The Passionate Shepherd"

Probably one on the most famous poems to emerge from Elizabethan England, "The Passionate Shepherd to His love" has generated many responses—and many parodies. The best and the most famous of these, by Sir Walter Raleigh (see page 174), is "The Nymph's Reply to the Shepherd." In Greek and Roman mythology, a *nymph* was one of the lesser goddesses of nature, who lived in seas, rivers, fountains, springs, hills, woods, or trees. The word came to be applied to any beautiful or graceful young woman. For yet another response to Marlowe's poem, see "The Bait" by John Donne, on page 280.

The Nymph's Reply to the Shepherd

Sir Walter Raleigh

If all the world and love were young,
And truth in every shepherd's tongue,
These pretty pleasures might me move
To live with thee and be thy love.

5 Time drives the flocks from field to fold,

When rivers rage and rocks grow cold;
And Philomel[1] becometh dumb;
The rest complain of cares to come.

The flowers do fade, and wanton fields
10 To wayward winter reckoning yields;
A honey tongue, a heart of gall,
Is fancy's spring, but sorrow's fall.

Thy gowns, thy shoes, thy bed of roses,
Thy cap, thy kirtle, and thy posies,
15 Soon break, soon wither, soon forgotten,
In folly ripe, in reason rotten.

Thy belt of straw and ivy buds,
Thy coral clasps and amber studs,
All these in me no means can move
20 To come to thee and be thy love.

But could youth last and love still breed,
Had joys no date nor age no need,
Then these delights my mind might move
To live with thee and be thy love.

1600

A black-thread embroidery of a shepherd and his gear. 16th cent. *Victoria and Albert Museum*

1. *Philomel*, the nightingale.

THINK AND DISCUSS
THE PASSIONATE SHEPHERD TO HIS LOVE
Understanding
1. What sorts of "delights" does the Shepherd offer the young woman—sophisticated, simple, or something else?

Analyzing
2. How persuasive is the Shepherd? Would his arguments be strong enough to win the young woman away from another suitor? Explain.
3. In "The Nymph's Reply to the Shepherd" (see the Comment article), under what circumstances does she say she would consent to be the Shepherd's love?
4. Do you think she really means this, or is she just being coy?

Extending
5. A reader has commented, "The Passionate Shepherd is a romantic; the Nymph is a realist." Explain whether you agree or disagree.

APPLYING: Pastoral H*T*
See Handbook of Literary Terms, p. 916
   A **pastoral** is a conventional form of lyric poetry presenting an idealized picture of rural life.

1. What aspects of rural life does the Shepherd use to entice the Nymph?
2. Which things that he describes are unlikely to be found in the pastoral life?
3. Does the Nymph seem to have a completely realistic picture of rural life, or does this poem also make use of pastoral conventions? Explain.

Carpe Diem

Among the new types of literature imported into England during the Renaissance was *carpe diem* (kär′pe dē′em) poetry. *Carpe diem* is Latin for "seize (take advantage of) the day," and this poetry dealt with the swift passage of time and the transiency of youth. Usually the speaker was a young man, and usually he was urging a young woman to take advantage of life and love while she was still young and attractive.

The *carpe diem* theme, which goes back to Horace and other Roman poets who wrote verses in Latin, achieved great popularity in Renaissance England. The reasons are easy to understand. Life spans were shorter then: illness, accident, war, and the executioner's axe killed men and women in their prime—if they lived past childhood in the first place. The biographies of the authors in this unit illustrate the point. Wyatt died of fever at 39; Surrey was 30 when he was beheaded; Bacon was 65 when he died of bronchitis; Raleigh was about 66 when he was beheaded; Marlowe was 29 when he was killed; Spenser died at 47; Sidney succumbed to a battle wound at 32; Shakespeare lived only 52 years. Of these eight authors, only Raleigh would have lived long to collect Social Security in modern America. Their average age at death was 45.

Obviously, it was necessary to "seize the day" at an early age, for life was indeed short. Probably the most famous *carpe diem* poem is Marlowe's "The Passionate Shepherd to His Love" (page 266). Here the Shepherd tempts his love with exaggerated and high-flown pictures of the joys of pastoral life. Marlowe's Shepherd was answered by Raleigh in "The Nymph's Rely". Later, Donne parodied Marlowe in "The Bait" (page 280), updating the earlier poem with metaphysical conceits, in one of which the fish are trying to catch the young woman.

Each new movement in poetry altered the basic *carpe diem* theme to suit its own style and philosophy. Herbert, an Anglican priest as well as a poet, uses the *carpe diem* theme in "Virtue" (page 287), but makes major changes as he maintains that the best way to deal with time's rapid passage is to lead a virtuous life. In "To His Coy Mistress" (page 289), Marvell, another metaphysical poet, is at least as concerned with time's swift flight as he is with his mistress.

Among the Cavalier poets, Herrick, also a member of the clergy, produced "To the Virgins, to Make Much of Time" (page 275), a true *carpe diem* poem except that, in keeping with his religious vocation, Herrick does not attempt seduction; instead he advises girls to marry while they are young, or else there may be no takers.

John Milton, a Puritan, also wrote on the *carpe diem* theme, but followed still another approach. In the sonnet "On His Having Arrived at the Age of Twenty-Three" (page 293), he frets over not having accomplished anything important by that point in his life, but he ends by placing his faith in heaven.

The concern with time that is a major aspect of the *carpe diem* theme continues to appear in literature through the years up to the present (though often without the lover/mistress relationship typical of the Renaissance). For instance, it is inherent in Keats's "Ode on a Grecian Urn" (page 514) in the Romantic period; it underlies Arnold's "Dover Beach" (page 613) in the Victorian period; it is the subject of Hopkins's "Spring and Fall: To a Young Child" (page 639) in the New Directions unit; and it is present in Thomas's "Fern Hill" (page 869) in the Twentieth-Century unit. You will probably be able to think of instances of its reappearance in the poetry, song lyrics, movies, and television shows popular among your generation.

Soon after Ben Jonson was born, his father died, and his mother took as her second husband a master bricklayer. With financial help, Ben was able to attend the Westminster School in London, where he studied under William Camden. From that scholar he probably acquired his taste for classical learning.

Too poor to attend either Oxford or Cambridge, Jonson worked for a time with his stepfather as a bricklayer; then he went off to Flanders to fight against the Spanish.

In 1595 or thereabouts, Jonson returned to England. By this time he was married, and he sought employment as an actor and playwright. Induced by Thomas Nashe to collaborate on *The Isle of Dogs* (1597), his first venture into playwriting, Jonson was jailed for a time when the play was judged to have stirred up discontent against the government. His next attempt, *Every Man in His Humor* (1598), in which Shakespeare played a role, was a great success. In this comedy Jonson introduced into the English theater the concept of "humors," the idea that each comic character has a humor, or personality trait, that controls his actions. Shakespeare and other contemporary dramatists were influenced by this idea.

Jonson's quick temper soon got him into further trouble. Before the year was out, he had argued with another actor, Gabriel Spencer, whom he killed in a duel. Imprisoned again, he escaped hanging by reciting his "neck verse"—in an age that valued scholarship, any man who was able to translate a passage of Latin into English could plead benefit of clergy to secure a trial in a church court, where punishments were less harsh than in the secular courts. Jonson's classical knowledge stood him in good stead in this instance, but he was branded on the left thumb to show that he was a convicted felon.

By this time, however, Jonson was on the way to becoming a successful playwright. Among his best comedies are *Volpone* (1606), a further development of his humor theory, and *The Alchemist* (1610). In addition, he ventured into the field of classical tragedy with *Sejanus* (1603), which was not a success, and he wrote many masques, most of them for court performance. Some of his best lyrics were written for the masques.

Jonson was friendly with Shakespeare, Raleigh, and Donne. King James made him poet laureate. A number of young poets, including Herrick and Lovelace (who follow Jonson in this unit), respecting Jonson's talents, called themselves the "Sons of Ben."

Jonson's old age was difficult. After the death of King James, he was no longer called upon to write court masques; in 1628 he suffered a paralyzing stroke, and he may well have been in financial need. When he died in 1637, he was buried in Poets' Corner, Westminster Abbey. Ironically, there is some controversy over whether the first word in the inscription on the slab that marks his grave is in Latin: "Orare (pray for) Ben Jonson"; or in English: "O rare Ben Jonson."

Still to Be Neat

Still[1] to be neat, still to be dressed,
As[2] you were going to a feast;
Still to be powdered, still perfumed:
Lady, it is to be presumed,
5 Though art's hid causes are not found,
All is not sweet, all is not sound.

Give me a look, give me a face,
That makes simplicity a grace;
Robes loosely flowing, hair as free:
10 Such sweet neglect more taketh me
Than all th' adulteries[3] of art;
They strike mine eyes, but not my heart.

1609

---

1. *Still,* always.
2. *As,* as if; as though.
3. *adulteries,* deceits.

Song, to Celia

Drink to me only with thine eyes,
    And I will pledge with mine;
Or leave a kiss but in the cup,
    And I'll not look for wine.
5 The thirst that from the soul doth rise
    Doth ask a drink divine;
But might I of Jove's nectar[1] sup,
    I would not change for thine.

I sent thee late a rosy wreath,
10   Not so much honoring thee
As giving it a hope, that there
    It could not withered be.
But thou thereon didst only breathe,
    And sent'st it back to me;
15 Since when it grows, and smells, I swear,
    Not of itself but thee.

1616

---

1. *nectar,* the drink of the gods.

On My First Son

Farewell, thou child of my right hand,[1] and joy;
    My sin was too much hope of thee, loved boy.
Seven years thou wert lent to me, and I thee pay,
    Exacted by thy fate, on the just day.[2]
5 O, could I lose all father,[3] now! For why
    Will man lament the state he should envy?
To have so soon 'scaped world's and flesh's rage,
    And, if no other misery, yet age!
Rest in soft peace; and, asked, say: Here doth lie
10   Ben Jonson his best piece of poetry[4]—
For whose sake, henceforth, all his vows be such,
As what he loves may never like too much.[5]

1616

---

1. *child of my right hand,* meaning of the Hebrew name Benjamin. Jonson's eldest son, who died of the plague in 1603, was also named Benjamin.
2. *just day,* the boy died on his seventh birthday; may also refer to the Day of Judgment.
3. *lose all father.* abandon the bonds between father and son so he would not feel his grief so keenly.
4. *his best piece of poetry,* his greatest creation, the most nearly perfect thing he made.
5. *As what . . . too much,* that what he loves may never please him too much (and therefore his grief will be less).

Portrait Group, Probably of the Streatfeild Family by William Dobson. The four skulls in the background represent their dead children. Circa 1642. *Yale Center for British Art*

Comment

Ben Jonson's Vision of His Son

At that time [plague] was in London, [Jonson] being in the country at Sir Robert Cotton's house with old Camden, he saw in a vision his eldest son, then a child and at London, appear unto him with the mark of a bloody cross on his forehead, as if it had been cutted with a sword; at which amazed he prayed unto God, and in the morning he came to Mr. Camden's chamber to tell him, who persuaded him it was but an apprehension of his fantasy at which he should not be disjected. In the mean time comes there letters from his wife of the death of that boy in the plague. He appeared to him (he said) of a manly shape, and of that growth that he thinks he shall be at the resurrection.

From *Notes of Ben Jonson's Conversations with William Drummond of Hawthornden*, edited by David Laing, 1842.

Ben Jonson

THINK AND DISCUSS

STILL TO BE NEAT

Understanding

1. Does the speaker prefer artificiality or naturalness in a woman? Explain.

Analyzing

2. What is it that the speaker presumes in lines 4–6?
3. Comment upon the meaning and effectiveness of the last line.

Extending

4. Would the speaker be likely to agree with Sonnet 130 by Shakespeare (page 188)? Explain.

SONG, TO CELIA

Understanding

1. This poem consists of two extended **metaphors,** one in the first stanza and the other in the second. What are they?

Analyzing

2. In the first stanza, what does the soul thirst for?
3. What choice does the speaker indicate he would make in lines 7–8?

Extending

4. Do you consider the first or second metaphor more effective? Why?

ON MY FIRST SON

Understanding

1. How old was Jonson's first son when he died?
2. What "sin" does the speaker confess to?

Analyzing

3. What payment has the speaker made for his sin?
4. How does the speaker attempt to console himself for his son's loss?
5. Comment on the effectiveness of the epitaph, "Here doth lie/Ben Jonson his best piece of poetry."

COMPOSITION ◄━━

Creating a Dialogue

Select either "Still to Be Neat" or "Song, to Celia" and, based on its content, create a dialogue between the speaker and the woman. Try to use some lines from the chosen poem in the speaker's speeches, but you are free to add additional dialogue for him. You will have to invent the woman's responses; she might be skeptical, as is the Nymph in Raleigh's "Reply," or she might be flattered by what he says. Share your dialogue with your classmates and select a number of them to be read aloud for the class.

Analyzing a *Carpe Diem* Poem

Reread "The Passionate Shepherd to His Love" and write a paper of at least five paragraphs in which you discuss the Shepherd's offer in light of your understanding of pastoral and *carpe diem* poetry. Is Marlowe writing a pastoral or is he writing a parody of pastorals? How much of what he describes can actually be found in rural life? What did he expect his readers to think of the poem? What accounts for its popularity and the many answers that have been written to it? What, indeed, accounts for the popularity of *carpe diem* poetry? Organize your thoughts carefully and write for an audience familiar with the materials in this unit.

Possessed of all the attributes needed to be a success at Queen Elizabeth's court, Lovelace was unfortunately born a century too late, into a world in which the courtly characteristics he possessed worked more to his detriment than to his advantage. Born into a wealthy family in Kent and heir to great estates, Lovelace was educated at Charterhouse and at Gloucester Hall, Oxford. Tradition has it that when King Charles and Queen Henrietta Maria visited in Oxford in 1636, they were so taken with Lovelace's handsome face and fine manners that they had arranged to have him get his M.A. on the spot.

After college, Lovelace served at the court of Charles and Henrietta Maria, and he remained steadfastly loyal to his king even when that loyalty cost him his freedom and estates. Without doubt, he is the most romantic—and one of the most unfortunate—of the Cavalier poets.

Cavalier poetry derived its name from the Cavaliers (or Royalists) who supported King Charles I in his war with the Parliamentary forces (the Roundheads). Perhaps because they were aware that an age was ending, the Cavalier poets wrote lyrics, usually light-hearted in tone, in which they celebrated love, loyalty, and bravery. Interested in the arts, Lovelace was an amateur painter and musician as well as poet, but he tended at first to follow the Elizabethan tradition of considering his poetry merely the recreational activity of a highborn gentleman.

After the fall of Charles, Lovelace had the courage to present in 1642 to a very unsympathetic House of Commons a petition in the king's favor. His bravery resulted in his being imprisoned for seven weeks; he used the time to write "To Althea, from Prison," a poem that probably did not endear him to the Puritan cause. Freed, Lovelace left England to fight with the French against the Spaniards. After being wounded at the siege of Dunkirk in 1646, he returned to England, only to be imprisoned again as an enemy of the Puritan Commonwealth. He used his prison time wisely, to prepare his poems for publication; they appeared in 1649 in a volume titled *Lucasta*.

The latter years of Lovelace's life were not happy ones. When he was freed, his estates and their revenues were gone, and he was a poor man. He died of consumption in 1657. In 1659 a posthumous volume of his later poems appeared, titled appropriately enough, *Lucasta: Posthume Poems*.

Richard Lovelace

To Althea, from Prison

When Love with unconfinèd wings
   Hovers within my gates,
And my divine Althea brings
   To whisper at the grates;
5 When I lie tangled in her hair
   And fettered to her eye,
The birds that wanton in the air
   Know no such liberty.

When flowing cups run swiftly round,
10   With no allaying Thames,[1]
Our careless heads with roses bound,
   Our hearts with loyal flames;
When thirsty grief in wine we steep,
   When healths and drafts go free,
15 Fishes that tipple in the deep
   Know no such liberty.

When, like committed linnets, I
   With shriller throat will sing
The sweetness, mercy, majesty,
20   And glories of my King;
When I shall voice aloud how good
   He is, how great should be,
Enlargèd winds, that curl the flood,
   Know no such liberty.

Woodcut from *The life apprehension, arraignement, and execution of Charles Courtney*, 1612. British Library

25 Stone walls do not a prison make,
   Nor iron bars a cage;
Minds innocent and quiet take
   That for an hermitage;
If I have freedom in my love
30   And in my soul am free,
Angels alone, that soar above,
   Enjoy such liberty.

1649

---

1. *no allaying Thames,* no diluting water from the Thames River.

To Lucasta, on Going to the Wars

Tell me not, sweet, I am unkind,
   That from the nunnery
Of thy chaste breast and quiet mind
   To war and arms I fly.

5 True, a new mistress now I chase,
   The first foe in the field;

And with a stronger faith embrace
   A sword, a horse, a shield.

Yet this inconstancy is such
10   As thou too shalt adore;
I could not love thee, dear, so much,
   Loved I not honor more.

1649

Robert Herrick
1591–1674

A Londoner by birth and disposition, Herrick spent nearly thirty years of his life as a country parson in remote Devonshire. As a youth, Herrick was apprenticed to his uncle, Sir William Herrick, a goldsmith and jeweler to the king. It seems that Herrick remained with his uncle until 1613, when he entered Cambridge at the age of twenty-two. He received his B.A. in 1617 and his M.A. in 1620. He was ordained in 1623 and six years later left his beloved London to become a vicar.

At first dissatisfied with the rustic ways of Devonshire, Herrick gradually adjusted and, in many of his lyrics, preserved for future generations the quaint customs of his own corner of southwest England. Herrick, who never married, addressed many of his poems to a series of imaginary mistresses, all of the names taken from classical poetry. A true "Son of Ben," he was at home with the classics, and his poems show an artful simplicity that is the result of constant polishing.

When the Puritans came to power, Herrick lost his parish and in 1647 returned to London—with his poetry. In 1648 his poems were published, in a volume divided into two parts. The first part, *Hesperides*, contained his secular poems, more than eleven hundred of them; the second part, *Noble Numbers*, contained his religious poems, numbering about three hundred. Herrick's work went almost unnoticed; it was not "rediscovered" until the nineteenth century.

In 1662, after the restoration of the monarchy, Herrick again became a vicar. He returned to his parish in Devonshire and lived there for twelve years, until his death in 1674.

Herrick is generally regarded as the best of the Cavalier poets and the "Sons of Ben." All of the Herrick poems that follow were published in *Hesperides* in 1648.

HT   **See SYMBOL in the Handbook of Literary Terms, page 929.**

To the Virgins, to Make Much of Time   *Carpe diem.*
Robert Herrick

Gather ye rosebuds while ye may,
   Old time is still a-flying;
And this same flower that smiles today,
   Tomorrow will be dying.

5 The glorious lamp of heaven, the sun,
   The higher he's a-getting,
The sooner will his race be run,
   And nearer he's to setting.

That age is best which is the first,
10   When youth and blood are warmer;
But being spent, the worse, and worst
    Times still succeed the former.

Then be not coy, but use your time,
    And, while ye may, go marry;
15 For, having lost but once your prime,
    You may forever tarry.

                    1648

Upon Julia's Clothes

Whenas in silks my Julia goes,
Then, then, methinks, how sweetly flows
That liquefaction of her clothes.

Next, when I cast mine eyes, and see
5 That brave[1] vibration, each way free,
O, how that glittering taketh me!

                    1648

---

1. *brave*, bright; splendid.

Delight in Disorder

A sweet disorder in the dress
Kindles in clothes a wantonness.[1]
A lawn[2] about the shoulders thrown
Into a fine distraction;
5 An erring[3] lace, which here and there
Enthralls the crimson stomacher,[4]
A cuff neglectful, and thereby
Ribbons to flow confusèdly;
A winning wave, deserving note,
10 In the tempestuous petticoat;
A careless shoestring, in whose tie
I see a wild civility;
Do more bewitch me than when art
Is too precise in every part.

                  1648

---

1. *wantonness*, gaiety.
2. *lawn*, linen scarf.
3. *erring*, wandering; straying.
4. *stomacher*, cloth laced across the front of a dress.

THINK AND DISCUSS
TO ALTHEA, FROM PRISON
Understanding
1. Each stanza ends with a sort of refrain. What is it, and how does it relate to the title?

Analyzing
2. In lines 5–8 the speaker claims that, although "tangled" and "fettered," he is freer than the birds in the air. Explain this **paradox.**
3. Despite its easy lyricism, this is a poem about three important things: love, imprisonment, and loyalty. What is the speaker's attitude toward each of these?
4. Under what circumstances is it true that "Stone walls do not a prison make,/Nor iron bars a cage" (lines 25–26)?

Extending

5. Which lines in the poem would most antagonize the Puritans?

TO LUCASTA, ON GOING TO THE WARS
Understanding

1. Put into your own words the claim that the speaker makes in lines 11–12.

Analyzing

2. Is this poem concerned more with Lucasta, or more with war? Explain.
3. According to the speaker, why will Lucasta "adore" his "inconstancy"?

TO THE VIRGINS, TO MAKE MUCH OF TIME
Understanding

1. What advice is given to young women in line 14?

Analyzing

2. What elements of the *carpe diem* theme are in this poem?

Extending

3. How does this differ from the other *carpe diem* poems you have read?

APPLYING: Symbol H⫪
See Handbook of Literary Terms, p. 929

A **symbol** is a person, place, event, or object that has meaning in itself but suggests other meanings as well. For example, a flag is a symbol of a country.

1. What do the rosebuds symbolize?
2. In the second stanza, what symbol is used to indicate the swift passage of time?

THINK AND DISCUSS
UPON JULIA'S CLOTHES
Understanding

1. Put into your own words the two sentences that make up this poem.

Analyzing

2. Is this poem more about Julia or her silk dress? Explain.
3. There is a French expression, *mot juste* (mō zhYst'), used in English to signify a word

or phrase that fits a situation perfectly. Is *liquefaction* the *mot juste* to describe Julia's silks? Explain.

DELIGHT IN DISORDER
Understanding

1. What are the subjects of the verb *Do . . . bewitch* in line 13?
2. What comparison is signaled by *more . . . than* in line 13?

Analyzing

3. What **metaphor** does the speaker use in lines 9–10? with what effect?
4. Is the speaker saying that he prefers a careless and untidy woman? Explain.

Extending

5. How does this poem relate to Jonson's "Still to Be Neat" (page 270)?

COMPOSITION ✐
Responding to Lovelace

Assume that you are either Althea or Lucasta, and write a letter to Lovelace in which you respond to the poem he has dedicated to you. Summarize briefly each point he makes in the poem you have chosen; then explain why you agree or disagree with it. Conclude with a general statement in which you either accept or reject his dedication. (If you wish, write a poem entitled "Althea's [or Lucasta's] Reply to Lovelace," and model your writing on Raleigh's "Reply" on page 266.)

Explaining Symbolism

Besides Herrick, many poets in this unit have written about the transiency, or fleeting nature, of youth, and some of them have used their own symbolism. In a paper of at least four paragraphs, explain how Herrick uses rosebuds and the sun as symbols; then discuss how other Renaissance poets have symbolized the same theme. Finally suggest some symbols of your own—such as a burning candle or a rainbow—that would also be appropriate and explain how they might be used. See "Writing About Symbolism" in the Writer's Handbook.

John Donne, one of the great poets and preachers of his age, has left his mark on modern poetry. Born into a Catholic family, Donne was sent to Hart Hall, Oxford, when he was twelve; he also spent some time at Trinity College, Cambridge, and in 1591 was studying law at Lincoln's Inn, in London. In 1596 he participated with Essex and Raleigh in the raid on Cadiz, and in 1597 he voyaged with Essex to the Azores and Spain.

Back in England, attempting to establish himself in a career, Donne became secretary to Sir Thomas Egerton, Lord Keeper of the Great Seal. There he met Egerton's niece, Anne More, fell in love with her, and married her secretly in 1601. When her father learned of the marriage, he was so infuriated that he ruined Donne's career and had him imprisoned. There is a story that from prison Donne wrote the following note to Anne: "John Donne, Anne Donne, Undone."

After his release from prison, Donne lived with Anne in relative poverty. Although he and his father-in-law became reconciled in 1608, not until 1610 did he secure the sort of position for which he was equipped by both intellect and education, becoming secretary to Sir Robert Drury.

As early as 1603, and possibly even earlier, Donne had become an Anglican. After he had written some anti-Catholic pamphlets for Thomas Morton, the Dean of Gloucester, he was asked to take Anglican holy orders to become a priest but refused. In 1615, however, at the urging of King James himself, Donne entered the Anglican priesthood. He became chaplain to the king, then rose rapidly until in 1621 he became Dean of St. Paul's Cathedral, London. A few years earlier, in 1617, Anne had died in childbirth, leaving Donne with seven children (she had borne twelve). Stating that he did not want his children to have a stepmother, Donne did not marry again.

In general, Donne's writing parallels his life. Until he met and fell in love with Anne, he had many love affairs, and his early poetry reflects those affairs and his cynical attitude toward women. After his marriage, he wrote Anne some of the most sincere love poems in the English language. Later, after he became a clergyman, he wrote both religious poetry and religious prose. Some 160 of his sermons have survived, and he was regarded as the foremost preacher of his day.

As he grew older, Donne became concerned with death and the dissolution of the human body. Perhaps the sins of his youth troubled him, perhaps he missed Anne, perhaps his own failing health was a cause of concern. Near the end of his life, he had his portrait painted in his burial shroud, to remind him of his approaching death.

Donne is credited with developing *metaphysical poetry*—poetry that relies for its effects on ingenious and complex **conceits.** Intellectual, strong, often violating traditional rules of scansion, metaphysical poetry requires work on the part of the reader, but the sudden insights it provides justify the effort.

H7 See HYPERBOLE in the Handbook of Literary Terms, page 906.

Song

Go and catch a falling star,
   Get with child a mandrake root,[1]
Tell me where all past years are,
   Or who cleft the devil's foot;
5 Teach me to hear mermaids singing,
   Or to keep off envy's stinging,
      And find
      What wind
Serves to advance an honest mind.

10 If thou be'st born to strange sights,
   Things invisible to see,
Ride ten thousand days and nights,
   Till age snow white hairs on thee,
Thou, when thou return'st, will tell me
15 All strange wonders that befell thee,
      And swear
      Nowhere
Lives a woman true, and fair.

If thou find'st one, let me know;
20   Such a pilgrimage were sweet.
Yet do not; I would not go,
   Though at next door we might meet.
Though she were true when you met her,
And last till you write your letter,
25   Yet she
      Will be
False, ere I come, to two or three.

1633

A mandrake (*Solanaceae mandragora*). The forking root can take odd shapes, and occasionally resembles human arms and legs. Woodcut from *Commentaries on the Six Books of Dioscorides* by Pierandrea Mattioli (Prague, 1563)

---

1. Get . . . mandrake root. Mandrake is a European herb with a forked root, fancied to resemble a human figure. (Recognizing the resemblance as well as the impossibility of a plant's reproducing as humans do, Donne includes this in his catalogue of fantastic achievements.)

The Bait

Come live with me, and be my love,
And we will some new pleasures prove
Of golden sands, and crystal brooks,
With silken lines, and silver hooks.

5 There will the river whispering run
Warmed by thy eyes, more than the sun.
And there th' enamoured fish will stay,
Begging themselves they may betray.

When thou wilt swim in that live bath,
10 Each fish, which every channel hath,
Will amorously to thee swim,
Gladder to catch thee, than thou him.

If thou, to be so seen, be'st loath,
By sun, or moon, thou darkenest both,
15 And if myself have leave to see,
I need not their light, having thee.

Let others freeze with angling reeds,
And cut their legs, with shells and weeds,
Or treacherously poor fish beset,
20 With strangling snare, or windowy net:

Let coarse bold hands, from slimy nest
The bedded fish in banks out-wrest,
Or curious traitors, sleavesilk flies
Bewitch poor fishes' wandering eyes.

25 For thee, thou need'st no such deceit,
For thou thyself art thine own bait;
That fish, that is not catched thereby,
Alas, is wiser far than I.

A Valediction: Forbidding Mourning

As virtuous men pass mildly away,
    And whisper to their souls to go,
Whilst some of their sad friends do say
    The breath goes now, and some say, No;

5 So let us melt, and make no noise,
    No tear-floods, nor sigh-tempests move,
'Twere profanation of our joys
    To tell the laity our love.

Moving of th' earth brings harms and fears,
10   Men reckon what it did and meant,
But trepidation of the spheres,
    Though greater far, is innocent.[1]

Dull sublunary[2] lovers' love
    (Whose soul is sense)[3] cannot admit
15 Absence, because it doth remove
    Those things which elemented[4] it.

But we by a love so much refined
    That our selves know not what it is,
Inter-assurèd of the mind,
20   Care less, eyes, lips, and hands to miss.

Our two souls therefore, which are one,
    Though I must go, endure not yet
A breach, but an expansion,
    Like gold to airy thinness beat.

compass

Valediction, a bidding farewell.
1. *trepidation . . . innocent.* Movements of the heavenly spheres, though greater than those of an earthquake, provoke no fears in (nor danger to) man.
2. *sublunary,* beneath the moon; i.e., earthly and subject to change.
3. *(Whose soul is sense),* whose essence is not mind or spirit.
4. *elemented,* composed.

25 If they be two, they are two so
  As stiff twin compasses[5] are two;
Thy soul, the fixed foot, makes no show
  To move, but doth, if th' other do.

And though it in the center sit,
30   Yet when the other far doth roam,
It leans and hearkens after it,
  And grows erect, as that comes home.

Such wilt thou be to me, who must
  Like th' other foot, obliquely run;
35 Thy firmness makes my circle[6] just,
  And makes me end where I begun.

        1633

---

5. *compasses.* The image is of the instrument used for describing a circle. One branch or leg of the compass is held steady, as a pivot, while the other leg is rotated to draw the circle.
6. *circle.* The circle was a symbol of perfection.

Detail from *Melancholy I* by Albrecht Dürer. The engraving shows the figure of Melancholy holding a compass. *Collection of the Art Institute of Chicago*

Reader's Note

"A Valediction"

Donne wrote this poem to his wife, Anne, just before he left on an extended trip to France. Since Anne was expecting another child, she could not accompany him. According to Donne's biographer, Sir Izaak Walton, Anne had a premonition of impending tragedy. Events later proved her correct, for the child was born dead. Donne, while in France, saw a vision of Anne walking across the bedroom with a dead child in her arms.

"A Valediction" is a farewell message that forbids Anne to mourn Donne's absence. Having established his purpose, Donne needs a reason to support that purpose, and he needs suitable metaphors to express that reason. His reason is simple: he and Anne are insepara-ble because their souls are so intermixed that they have become one (line 21); therefore, even though he must go far away, he and she, being connected by that soul, are not really parted. Here he uses two conceits (ingenious metaphors) to explain why: (1) like gold beaten to airy thinness (line 24), their combined soul will expand, without separation or break, to cover the distance (lines 22–23); or (2) their combined soul is like a pair of compasses, with Anne, the fixed foot, leaning toward Donne, the roaming foot, as he travels, steadying him on his journey and straightening again as he comes home (lines 25–36).

To strengthen his argument, Donne contrasts his and Anne's love (in which they share a single

John Donne

soul) with ordinary love ("dull sublunary lovers' love," line 13,) which cannot admit absence because its "soul" is physical ("sense" or sensation, line 14), and therefore when one of the lovers is gone, he (or she) is physically removed from the other (lines 15–16).

The love of Donne and Anne is also on a higher level, like the concentric spheres of the Ptolemaic system of astronomy (lines 11–12); "tear-floods" and "sigh-tempests" (line 6) would profane it (lines 7–8). Therefore, at parting they should "melt, and make no noise" (line 5), just as "virtuous men pass mildly away, / And whisper to their souls to go" (lines 1–2). Note that Donne does not separate these men from their souls; note also that lines 1–8 are a simile, the first part introduced by "As" (line 1), the second

by "So" (line 5).

Finally, the word "melt" (line 5) may be troublesome. However, an intricate relationship is expressed in lines 4–6, in which "melt" and "tear-floods" (line 6) match, and "breath" (line 4) and "sigh-tempests" (line 6) match; in both pairs the second word represents a superfluity of the first.

Thus, in a series of sometimes outrageous comparisons—conceits, similes, and metaphors drawn from meteorology, theology, geology, Ptolemaic astronomy, metallurgy, and geometry—Donne tells Anne that there is no need to mourn his departure, for their love is so great and their souls so intermingled that they will not really be separated by his journey.

from Holy Sonnets

Sonnet 10

Death, be not proud, though some have called
    thee
Mighty and dreadful, for thou art not so;
For those whom thou think'st thou dost
    overthrow
Die not, poor Death, nor yet canst thou kill me.
5 From rest and sleep, which but thy pictures be,
Much pleasure; then from thee much more must
    flow,
And soonest our best men with thee do go,
Rest of their bones, and soul's delivery.
Thou art slave to fate, chance, kings, and
    desperate men,
10 And dost with poison, war, and sickness dwell,
And poppy[1] or charms can make us sleep
    as well,
And better than thy stroke; why swell'st[2]
    thou then?
One short sleep past, we wake eternally,
And death shall be no more; Death, thou
    shalt die.

1633

Sonnet 14

Batter my heart, three-personed God;[3] for you
As yet but knock, breathe, shine, and seek to
    mend;
That I may rise and stand, o'erthrow me, and
    bend
Your force to break, blow, burn, and make me
    new.
5 I, like an usurped town, to another due,
Labor to admit you, but O, to no end;
Reason, your viceroy in me, me should defend,
But is captived, and proves weak or untrue.
Yet dearly I love you, and would be loved fain,
10 But am betrothed unto your enemy.
Divorce me, untie or break that knot again;
Take me to you, imprison me, for I,
Except you enthral me, never shall be free,
Nor ever chaste, except you ravish me.

1633

---

1. *poppy*, the source of various narcotic drugs.
2. *swell'st*, puff up with pride.
3. *three-personed God*, the Trinity of the Father, the Son, and the Holy Spirit.

See SYNECDOCHE in the Handbook of Literary Terms, page 907.

Meditation 17

Nunc lento sonitu dicunt, Morieris. (Now this bell tolling softly for another, says to me, Thou must die.)

Perchance he for whom this bell tolls may be so ill as that he knows not it tolls for him; and perchance I may think myself so much better than I am, as that they who are about me and see my state, may have caused it to toll for me, and I know not that. The church is catholic, universal, so are all her actions; all that she does belongs to all. When she baptizes a child, that action concerns me; for that child is thereby connected to that head which is my head too, and ingrafted into that body whereof I am a member.[1] And when she buries a man, that action concerns me. All mankind is of one author and is one volume; when one man dies, one chapter is not torn out of the book, but translated into a better language, and every chapter must be so translated. God employs several translators; some pieces are translated by age, some by sickness, some by war, some by justice; but God's hand is in every translation, and his hand shall bind up all our scattered leaves again for that library where every book shall lie open to one another. As therefore the bell that rings to a sermon calls not upon the preacher only, but upon the congregation to come, so this bell calls us all; but how much more me, who am brought so near the door by this sickness.

There was a contention as far as a suit[2] (in which piety and dignity, religion and estimation,[3] were mingled) which of the religious orders should ring to prayers first in the morning; and it was determined that they should ring first that rose earliest. If we understand aright the dignity of this bell that

Statue of John Donne in his burial shroud by Nicholas Stone. 1631. *St. Paul's Cathedral, London*

tolls for our evening prayer, we would be glad to make it ours by rising early, in that application,

---

1. *head . . . member.* That is, the Christian church is the head of all people, as well as a body made up of its members.
2. *contention . . . suit,* a controversy that went as far as a lawsuit.
3. *estimation,* self-esteem.

John Donne

that it might be ours as well as his whose indeed it is. The bell doth toll for him that thinks it doth; and though it intermit again, yet from that minute that that occasion wrought upon him, he is united to God. Who casts not up his eye to the sun when it rises? But who takes off his eye from a comet when that breaks out? Who bends not his ear to any bell which upon any occasion rings? But who can remove it from that bell which is passing a

piece of himself out of this world? No man is an island, entire of itself; every man is a piece of the continent, a part of the main. If a clod be washed away by the sea, Europe is the less, as well as if a promontory were, as well as if a manor of thy friend's or of thine own were. Any man's death diminishes me because I am involved in mankind; and therefore never send to know for whom the bell tolls; it tolls for thee. . . .

1624

THINK AND DISCUSS
SONG
Understanding
1. What seven commands does the speaker issue in stanza 1?

Analyzing
2. What quality do all these commands share?
3. If the reader follows the suggestion in stanza 2, what will happen?
4. Why wouldn't the speaker repeat the reader's "pilgrimage" even if it were successful?
5. What seems to be the speaker's state of mind? What might account for it?

APPLYING: Hyperbole HZ
See Handbook of Literary Terms, p. 906
   A figure of speech involving great exaggeration—such as "I'm freezing to death"—is called **hyperbole.** The effect may be serious or comic.

1. What is exaggereated in the first stanza? What effect does it create?
2. What is exaggerated about the woman in the last stanza? Is the effect the same?

THINK AND DISCUSS
THE BAIT
Understanding
1. List some of the elaborate compliments the speaker pays the woman.

Analyzing
2. What feelings are aroused by such expressions as "live bath" (line 9) and "slimy nest" (line 21)? Why does Donne use such expressions?
3. Explain line 26: "For thou thyself art thine own bait."

Extending
4. This is Donne's updating of Marlowe's "The Passionate Shepherd to His Love" (page 266). Reread the original poem and then discuss the differences introduced in "The Bait."

A VALEDICTION: FORBIDDING MOURNING
Understanding
1. *Valediction* means "a bidding farewell." Who is bidding farewell to whom?
2. What is being described in stanza 1?

Analyzing
3. How does the phrase "pass mildly away" (line 1) interact with the title?
4. Why should the two lovers "make no noise" at their parting? (See lines 5–8.)
5. How do these lovers differ from the "dull, sublunary lovers" of stanza 4?
6. Explain the **conceit** in lines 25–36.

Extending
7. In your opinion, does the cleverness of the poem add to, or detract from, its sincerity?

HOLY SONNET 10

Understanding

1. The entire poem is an **apostrophe.** To whom or what is it addressed?

Analyzing

2. How does the speaker belittle Death's powers?

3. Explain the **paradox** in the last line, "And death shall be no more; Death, thou shalt die."

HOLY SONNET 14

Understanding

1. In line 1 the speaker asks God to *batter* his heart. What synonyms for *batter* occur elsewhere in the poem?

Analyzing

2. For what purpose does the speaker ask God to batter his heart?

3. This sonnet follows both the rhyme scheme and thought division of the Italian sonnet. What is the problem stated in the first eight lines (the *octave*)?

4. In the last six lines (the *sestet*), how does the speaker ask to have his problem resolved?

Extending

5. Compare Holy Sonnets 10 and 14. In which is the speaker suffering more?

MEDITATION 17

Understanding

1. What three reasons are mentioned for tolling a bell? Which reason is most important in this meditation?

Analyzing

2. Discuss the meaning and effectiveness of the two main **analogies:** man as a chapter in a book and man as a piece of the continent.

3. Explain in your own words: ". . . Never send to know for whom the bell tolls; it tolls for thee."

Extending

4. At the time Donne wrote "Meditation 17" he was recovering from a serious illness. How might that fact have influenced his writing?

APPLYING: Synecdoche H/T
See Handbook of Literary Terms, p. 907

A **synecdoche** is a figure of speech in which a part stands for the whole (ten *head* of cattle) or in which the whole stands for a part ("Your *school* called").

1. When Donne writes about the church baptizing a child, who or what does that child represent?

2. Donne writes, "Who can remove it ["his ear"] from that bell which is passing a piece of himself out of this world." What does *ear* stand for? What does "a piece of himself" represent?

COMPOSITION

Responding to Donne's Metaphor

"No man is an island" has often been quoted through the years up until the present day—and was even the title of a modern popular song. What does this metaphor mean to you personally? Write an informal essay of at least four paragraphs in which you first explain your understanding of what Donne meant by his statement; then describe a personal experience of your own or someone else's that illustrates Donne's metaphor in terms of modern life. Examples might include helping a neighbor during a fire, flood, or other emergency, responding to a death or a birth in the family, and so on.

Evaluating Donne's Writings

The samples of Donne's writing you have just read reflect the three phases of his adult life: young man on the loose, loving husband, and devout churchman. Write an essay in which you evaluate his output and show which phase is reflected in each work. Consider especially his versatility, and try to find some common underlying factors in his work. Assume that you will be submitting your essay to a student literary magazine. See "Writing to Analyze an Author's Style" in the Writer's Handbook.

BIOGRAPHY

George Herbert
1593–1633

In his infancy George Herbert, the fifth of seven sons, was dedicated to a life in the church by his mother, a career not uncommon for the younger sons of large, noble families. His father died when Herbert was three. John Donne was a family friend, and certainly Herbert was influenced by that great churchman.

After attending the Westminster School in London, Herbert went on to Trinity College, Cambridge, with the intent of entering the ministry. When he was sixteen he wrote his mother from Cambridge, "My poor abilities in poetry shall be all and ever consecrated to God's glory." After he received his M.A. in 1616, he stayed on at Cambridge, presumably to complete his studies for the ministry.

In 1620, however, Herbert was chosen Orator of Cambridge, a position of honor that normally led to political preferment and high political office. Through this position he became friendly with many powerful nobles and King James himself. At this point, if not sooner, began the struggle between the two facets of his personality, one pulling him toward the church, the other pulling him toward King James's court, where he knew he would be welcomed for his family background (five of his brothers were already in public or diplomatic service), his intellectual achievements, and his attractive personality. In June, 1624, he took a six-month leave of absence from Cambridge to seek preferment at court.

Despite promises, nothing materialized from his time at court. With the death in 1625 of James, he lost his most powerful patron. After a brief period of retirement, in 1626 he took a minor office in the church. In 1627 his mother died, and later that year he resigned as Orator of Cambridge. Herbert had already shown signs of tuberculosis, and he needed to strengthen himself before making any further commitments. In 1629 he was well enough to marry, and in 1630, yielding to his religious vocation, he was ordained and became rector of Bemerton, near Salisbury.

The three years of life that remained to him were probably the happiest he had known, as he took care of his parishioners, completed the religious poems published after his death as *The Temple* (1633), and wrote *A Priest to the Temple, or the Country Parson* (1652), recording in prose his life at Bemerton. Just before his death, Herbert sent the manuscript of *The Temple* to a minister friend with instructions to burn it unless he felt the poems might "turn to the advantage of any dejected poor soul." Fortunately for posterity, the friend recognized the value of the manuscript.

Contained in *The Temple* are more than 160 poems, written in a variety of patterns, but all connected in some way with religion or the religious experience. As the title indicates, the intent of the book is to honor and praise God.

Easter Wings

The shape of this poem is intended to resemble Easter wings—two pairs of them, one for the speaker and one for the Lord. Turn it on its side to see their shape. Originally the lines were printed vertically rather than horizontally.

Lord, who createdst man in wealth and store,[1]
    Though foolishly he lost the same,
        Decaying more and more
           Till he became
5   Most poor:
           With thee
        O let me rise
    As larks, harmoniously,
  And sing this day thy victories:
10 Then shall the fall further the flight in me.

   My tender age in sorrow did begin;
  And still with sicknesses and shame
    Thou didst so punish sin,
      That I became
15   Most thin.
      With thee
    Let me combine,
  And feel this day thy victory;
For, if I imp[2] my wing on thine,
20 Affliction shall advance the flight in me.

                    1633

---

1. *store,* abundance.
2. *imp,* a technical term used in falconry. Additional feathers were grafted (imped) onto a falcon's wings to improve its ability to fly.

Gilded silver angel bearing a reliquary, once part of the royal treasure of France. 15th century. *Louvre, Paris*

Virtue

Sweet day, so cool, so calm, so bright,
    The bridal of the earth and sky:
The dew shall weep thy fall tonight;
    For thou must die.

5 Sweet rose, whose hue, angry and brave,[1]
    Bids the rash gazer wipe his eye:
Thy root is ever in its grave,
    And thou must die.

Sweet spring, full of sweet days and roses,
10   A box where sweets[2] compacted lie;
My music shows ye have your closes,[3]
    And all must die.

Only a sweet and virtuous soul,
    Like seasoned timber, never gives;
15 But though the whole world turn to coal,[4]
    Then chiefly lives.

                    1633

---

1. *angry and brave,* red and splendid.
2. *sweets,* perfumes.
3. *closes,* ending cadences of a song.
4. *coal,* become a cinder at the Last Judgment.

One of the few politically active people to lose nothing during the turbulent years of the Revolution, the Puritan Commonwealth, and the Restoration, Andrew Marvell succeeded in winning the trust of both sides. Born in Winestead-in-Holderness, Yorkshire, he received his early education at Hull Grammar School and called Hull his home for most of his life.

At twelve, Marvell was sent to Cambridge, receiving his B.A. degree from Trinity College in 1639 and staying on there until 1641. By the time he left Cambridge he knew Latin, Greek, Hebrew, Arabic, Syrian, Chaldean, and Persian, a remarkable achievement for one so young.

In 1642 Marvell left England for four years of travel on the European continent, visiting Holland, France, Switzerland, Italy, and Spain, and en route learning Dutch, French, Italian, and Spanish. Returning to England, he found employment in 1650 as tutor to the daughter of Lord Fairfax. For two years he lived at Nun Appleton, Fairfax's country estate in Yorkshire. To these years belong a number of pastoral poems and Marvell's lifelong feeling for the joys of the countryside.

In 1653 Marvell, who had become acquainted with John Milton, was recommended by Milton to become his assistant. A close friendship developed between the two men. In 1659, Marvell became a member of Parliament for Hull, continuing to be re-elected until his death. When the monarchy was restored in 1660, Marvell interceded for Milton and helped to save him from imprisonment or execution.

carpe diem

To His Coy Mistress
Andrew Marvell

1

Had we but world enough, and time,[1]
This coyness, lady, were no crime.
We would sit down, and think which way
To walk, and pass our long love's day.
5 Thou by the Indian Ganges' side
Shouldst rubies find; I by the tide
Of Humber[2] would complain.[3] I would
Love you ten years before the flood,[4]
And you should, if you please, refuse
10 Till the conversion of the Jews.[5]
My vegetable[6] love should grow
Vaster than empires and more slow;
An hundred years should go to praise
Thine eyes, and on thy forehead gaze;
15 Two hundred to adore each breast,

But thirty thousand to the rest;
An age at least to every part,
And the last age should show your heart.
For, lady, you deserve this state;[7]
20 Nor would I love at lower rate.

---

1. *Had . . . time.* Note that the poem opens with a situation contrary to fact.
2. *Humber,* the river that flows through Marvell's home town of Hull.
3. *complain,* i.e., sing plaintive love songs.
4. *flood,* the Biblical flood.
5. *conversion of the Jews.* It was a popular belief that this would occur just before the Last Judgment and the end of the world.
6. *vegetable,* not in the modern sense, but in the sense of living growth.
7. *state,* dignity.

Detail from *Les Bergers (The Shepherds)* by Jean Antoine Watteau, showing elegant people playing "pastorale." Circa 1718. *Staatliche Museen, West Berlin*

2

But[8] at my back I always hear *reality*
Time's wingèd chariot hurrying near;
And yonder all before us lie
Deserts of vast eternity.
25 Thy beauty shall no more be found,
Nor in thy marble vault shall sound
My echoing song; then worms shall try
That long preserved virginity,
And your quaint[9] honor turn to dust.
30 And into ashes all my lust:
The grave's a fine and private place,
But none, I think, do there embrace.

3

Now therefore,[10] while the youthful hue *solution*
Sits on thy skin like morning dew,
35 And while thy willing soul transpires[11]
At every pore with instant fires,
Now let us sport us while we may,

And now, like amorous birds of prey,
Rather at once our time devour
40 Than languish in his slow-chapped[12] power,
Let us roll all our strength and all
Our sweetness up into one ball,
And tear our pleasures with rough strife
Thorough[13] the iron gates of life;
45 Thus, though we cannot make our sun
Stand still, yet we will make him run.[14]

c. 1650   1681

---

8. *But.* This word reverses the situation contrary to fact of stanza 1, and returns to the real world.
9. *quaint,* fastidious; out-of-fashion.
10. *Now therefore.* With these words, the speaker proposes a scheme of action.
11. *transpires,* breathes out.
12. *slow-chapped,* slow-jawed.
13. *Thorough,* through.
14. *Thus, though . . . run.* Since the sun will not stand still for us, let us make him run to keep up with us.

Reader's Note

"To His Coy Mistress"

On the surface a love poem of the *carpe diem* type, urging the speaker's mistress to seize love while she is young enough to enjoy it, this poem is developed in a far more intellectual manner than, for example, Marlowe's "The Passionate Shepherd" (page 266) or Herrick's "To the Virgins" (page 275).

The first line sets up a condition contrary to fact: "*Had* we but world enough and time," meaning that in fact the lovers have neither. The rest of the first stanza provides an elaborate, farfetched, geographical and historical list of the things the lovers would do *if* time and place (eternity and infinity) permitted.

Another three-letter word, "But," matching the "Had" of line 1, opens the second stanza and introduces the world as it really is. Time does not stop, but hurries on, taking youth and life with it. Indisputable is the chilling reality of lines 31 and 32, "The grave's . . . embrace."

Still another three-letter word, "Now," opens the third stanza of the poem. Recognizing the world as it is, the lovers should take advantage of their present moment of youth to defeat their enemy, time. Note the references to time here: like "birds of prey," the lovers should "at once our time devour" (line 39), rather than "languish in his slow-chapped power" (line 40); in other words, they should reverse the normal process. This idea of reversal is amplified in the closing couplet: "though we cannot make our sun [which measures their time] / Stand still, yet we will make him run" (lines 45–46) in order to keep up with them. Taken as an entity, therefore, the poem becomes a challenge to the enemy (time) as well as an invitation to the mistress.

THINK AND DISCUSS
EASTER WINGS
Understanding
1. In lines 1–5 the speaker addresses the Lord. What request does he make of the Lord in lines 6–10?

Analyzing
2. Count the number of poetic feet in each stanza. Technically, how does Herbert achieve the diminishing, then the growing, of his lines?
3. Comment on the appropriateness of "Most poor" (line 5) and "Most thin" (line 15) to their physical position in the poem.
4. In lines 6 and 16, what begins to happen when Herbert combines "With thee" (the Lord)?

Extending
5. Compare Herbert's state of mind in "Easter Wings" with that of Donne in Sonnet 14 ("Batter my heart . . .").

VIRTUE
Understanding
1. In stanzas 1–3, what three different things are **apostrophized**?
2. What **refrain** do stanzas 1–3 share?
3. What happens to this refrain in stanza 4?

Analyzing
4. Discuss the effectiveness of the observation (lines 5–7) that the root of a rose lies in its grave.
5. What relation does the third stanza have to the first two stanzas?
6. How does the fourth stanza relate to the earlier ones?

Extending
7. In what respects is this a *carpe diem* poem like Herrick's "To the Virgins . . ."? In what respects is it different?

TO HIS COY MISTRESS
Understanding
1. The first stanza sounds like a traditional *carpe diem* love poem urging the lady to make the most of time. However, something disturbing happens in the second stanza (lines 21–32). What is it?

Analyzing
2. Relate the last two lines to the rest of the poem.
3. How serious is the speaker when he discusses love? How serious is he when he discusses time? Explain.

Extending
4. In general, is Marvell's poem more like Marlowe's "The Passionate Shepherd to His Love" or Raleigh's "The Nymph's Reply," or is it different from both? Explain.

COMPOSITION
Writing Concrete Poetry
"Easter Wings" is an example of what we now call *concrete poetry*, poems in which words or lines are arranged so that they form the shape of the thing they are describing. Try constructing one of these poems. You do not need rhyming lines. For example, a concrete poem called "Sun" might consist of words or phrases describing how the sun looks or feels. These can be written as rays that emanate from the sun, leaving its circular shape in the middle—or they could be arranged to fill the inside of a circle, their length creating a circular shape. Other possibilities include an egg, a football, a hockey stick, a vase, and so on. Share your creation with your classmates.

Analyzing Metaphysical Poetry
You have been reading metaphysical poetry by Donne, Herbert, and Marvell. Make a list of its characteristics as you see them. Illustrate each characteristic with one or more quotes from the poems (including the titles). Then organize your thoughts and write a paper of four to six paragraphs in which you describe metaphysical poetry for advanced students who are about to study it. See "Writing About a Period or Trend" in the Writer's Handbook.

John Milton was born and brought up in London, the son of a well-to-do scrivener (notary) who also dabbled in real estate. Sent to St. Paul's School, Milton applied himself so energetically to his studies that by 1625 he had mastered Greek, Latin, and Hebrew, as well as a number of modern European languages. He received his B.A. and M.A. from Christ College, Cambridge.

Having decided not to stay at Cambridge to study divinity, Milton spent six years in private study at his father's country house at Horton, Buckinghamshire, reading omnivorously in the varied languages he had mastered. By this time Milton had written several masques and a number of poems in Latin and English, some of which had been published.

Early in 1638 Milton began a tour of Europe that lasted for more than a year. He returned to England in 1639, earlier than he had originally intended, because of the troubled political situation there. Setting up residence in London, he busied himself with his writing and with tutoring his two nephews; later he added several other boys, all of them boarding with him. By this time Milton was seriously considering the epic poem he intended to write, trying to come up with a suitable subject for it.

In 1642 Milton married Mary Powell, who came from a Royalist family. In March, 1649, after he had published a pamphlet justifying the execution of King Charles, Milton was named Latin Secretary in the Council of State of the Puritan government. Warned that he would lose his sight if he continued to do close work, he decided the cause was important enough for him to risk his vision. He became totally blind in 1651, at the age of forty-three. In 1652 Milton's wife died in childbirth, leaving him with three daughters. In 1656 Milton took a second wife, Katherine Woodcock, who died in childbirth in 1658.

With the end of the Puritan regime and the restoration of the Stuart line of kings Milton, who had been a strong supporter of the Puritans and of the execution of Charles I, was regarded as a dangerous enemy. Perhaps because of his age and blindness, perhaps because of the intercession of Andrew Marvell, who had worked as his assistant but was friendly with the Restoration government, Milton escaped execution or lengthy imprisonment, but he was heavily fined and lost most of his property.

No longer active politically, Milton was finally free to write the epic poem he had set aside for so long. He probably began writing *Paradise Lost* about 1660, completing it in 1665. Because he was blind, he dictated the poem to his three daughters, who served as secretaries. In 1663 he married Elizabeth Minshull, who survived him. *Paradise Lost* was published in 1667, followed in 1671 by a shorter sequel, *Paradise Regained,* and a closet drama (not intended for stage production), *Samson Agonistes.* In 1674 Milton died of complications following an attack of gout.

On His Having Arrived at the Age of Twenty-Three

John Milton

How soon hath Time, the subtle thief of youth,
Stolen on his wing my three and twentieth year!
My hasting days fly on with full career,
But my late spring no bud or blossom showeth.[1]
5 Perhaps my semblance[2] might deceive the truth,
That I to manhood am arrived so near;
And inward ripeness doth much less appear,
That some more timely-happy spirits endueth.[3]
Yet be it less or more, or soon or slow,
10 It shall be still in strictest measure even[4]
To that same lot, however mean or high,
Toward which Time leads me, and the will of
　　Heaven;
All is, if I have grace to use it so,
As ever in my great Task-Master's eye.

1631　　　　　　　　　　　　　　　　**1645**

Festina Lente (Latin for "Make haste slowly"). The device of a dolphin curled about an anchor represents the opposites of anchored steadfastness and joyful, bounding motion. From George Wither's A Collection of Emblems (1635).

1. *showeth,* shows.
2. *semblance,* youthful appearance.
3. *endueth,* endows.

4. *even,* adequate; i.e., his "inward ripeness," or inner readiness, will be adequate to whatever destiny Time and Heaven are leading him.

H⌀　**See METONYMY in the Handbook of Literary Terms, page 907.**

On His Blindness　**John Milton**

When I consider how my light is spent,
Ere half my days, in this dark world and wide,
And that one talent[1] which is death to hide
Lodged with me useless, though my soul more
　　bent
5 To serve therewith my Maker, and present
My true account, lest He, returning, chide;
"Doth God exact day-labor, light denied?"
I fondly[2] ask. But Patience, to prevent
That murmur, soon replies: "God doth not need
10 Either man's work or His own gifts; who best

Bear His mild yoke, they serve Him best. His state
Is kingly: thousands at His bidding speed,
And post o'er land and ocean without rest:
They also serve who only stand and wait."

1652　　　　　　　　　　　　　　　　**1673**

1. *talent,* the gift of writing. This refers to Jesus's parable of the "unprofitable servant," condemned for burying his one talent, or coin, instead of spending it. (Matt. 25:15–30)
2. *fondly,* foolishly.

from Paradise Lost BOOK I

John Milton

Like all epic poems, Milton's *Paradise Lost* is a long narrative of events on a grand scale. In the case of *Paradise Lost*, the scale is one of the grandest possible, for the poem has as its setting the entire universe. The main characters are God, His Son, Adam and Eve, and Satan. The theme is the fall of man as embodied in the biblical story of the temptation of Adam and Eve and their expulsion from Paradise.

As if inspired by the earthly event of civil war in his own time and place, Milton envisions a civil war in Heaven, arising over God's appointment of His Son to the seat of honor and power at His right hand. Satan, one of the archangels, desires the exalted position for himself, and with a third of the other angels he wages war against God and His followers. God's forces prove superior; Satan and his rebel host are sent plunging down into Hell, the place that God had prepared for them, as far removed from Heaven as possible.

From this point on Satan vows eternal vengeance. He has heard of God's plan to fashion a new creature called man and to place him in a new region called the world. Why not strike back at God through the corruption of this latest creature of His handiwork?

The story of Satan's meeting with Adam and Eve in the Garden of Eden follows, in the main, the Bible story. Satan tempts Eve, who in turn persuades Adam to eat the forbidden fruit of the Tree of Knowledge. For this disobedience, Adam and Eve are driven from Paradise out into the world. The twelfth and last book of the poem closes with the pair standing hand in hand upon the threshold of the world. Paradise, "so late their happy home," lies behind them. Sadly and penitently they face the future, their punishment softened only by the promise of the ultimate redemption of man by Christ.

Milton began his epic *in medias res*, or "in the middle of the action," waiting until later in the poem to provide a narrative of the earlier events of his story. Thus in Book I the reader is confronted with the terrifying scenes of Satan and his "horrid crew . . . rolling in the fiery gulf" of Hell and of Satan hurling thundering speeches of defiance at the Almighty.

Of man's first disobedience, and the fruit
Of that forbidden tree, whose mortal taste
Brought death into the world, and all our
    woe,
With loss of Eden, till one greater Man[1]
5 Restore us, and regain the blissful seat,
Sing Heávenly Muse,[2] that on the secret top
Of Oreb, or of Sinai,[3] didst inspire
That shepherd,[4] who first taught the chosen
    seed,[5]
In the beginning[6] how the heavens and earth
10 Rose out of Chaos; Or if Sion hill[7]
Delight thee more, and Siloa's brook[8] that
    flowed
Fast by the oracle of God; I thence
Invoke thy aid to my adventurous song,
That with no middle flight intends to soar
15 Above the Aonian mount,[9] while it pursues
Things unattempted yet in prose or rhyme.
And chiefly Thou, O Spirit, that dost prefer
Before all temples the upright heart and pure,
Instruct me, for Thou knowest; Thou from
    the first
20 Wast present, and, with mighty wings
    outspread,
Dovelike sat'st brooding on the vast Abyss
And mad'st it pregnant: What in me is dark
Illumine, what is low raise and support;
That to the height of this great argument
25 I may assert Eternal Providence,
And justify the ways of God to men.[10]
    Say first, [11] for Heaven hides nothing from
    thy view,
Nor the deep tract of Hell, say first what
    cause
Moved our grand Parents in that happy state,
30 Favored of Heaven so highly, to fall off
From their Creator, and transgress His will
For one restraint, lords of the world besides?
Who first seduced them to that foul revolt?[12]
The infernal Serpent; he it was whose guile
35 Stirred up with envy and revenge, deceived
The mother of mankind, what time his
    pride[13]
Had cast him out from Heaven, with all his
    host

Of rebel Angels, by whose aid aspiring
To set himself in glory above his peers,
40 He trusted to have equaled the Most High,
If He opposed; and with ambitious aim
Against the throne and monarchy of God
Raised impious war in Heaven and battle
    proud
With vain attempt. Him the Almighty Power
45 Hurled headlong flaming from the ethereal
    sky
With hideous ruin and combustion down
To bottomless perdition, there to dwell
In adamantine chains and penal fire,
Who durst defy the Omnipotent to arms.
50 Nine times the space that measures day and
    night
To mortal men, he with his horrid crew
Lay vanquished, rolling in the fiery gulf,
Confounded though immortal. But his doom
Reserved him to more wrath; for now the
    thought
55 Both of lost happiness and lasting pain
Torments him; round he throws his baleful
    eyes,
That witnessed[14] huge affliction and dismay
Mixed with obdúrate pride and steadfast hate:
At once as far as angels' ken he views
60 The dismal situation waste and wild;

---

1. **Man,** the Messiah.
2. **Heavenly Muse.** Milton does not name his muse
directly here, but later (Book VII) calls her Urania, meaning "Heavenly," which is the name of the Muse of
Astronomy, though Milton is careful to state there is no
connection between his muse and the pagan Nine Muses.
3. **Oreb . . . Sinai,** twin peaks in Arabia.
4. **shepherd,** Moses, who on Mt. Sinai received the
Word of God.
5. **chosen seed,** the Israelites.
6. **beginning,** a punning reference to the Book of Genesis,
supposedly composed by Moses.
7. **Sion hill,** the height upon which Jerusalem was built.
8. **Siloa's brook,** the stream that flowed near the hill on
which the temple was erected in Jerusalem.
9. **Aonian** (ā ō′nē ən) **mount,** Mount Helicon, representing Greek poetry, which Milton, by writing a Christian
poem, endeavored to surpass.
10. **men.** This concludes the invocation (lines 1–26).
11. **Say first.** Here begins the epic question.
12. **revolt.** The epic question ends here.
13. **pride,** Satan's sin, the most deadly of the Seven
Deadly Sins.
14. **witnessed,** gave evidence of.

A dungeon horrible, on all sides round
As one great furnace flamed, yet from those
    flames
No light, but rather darkness visible[15]
Served only to discover sights of woe,
65 Regions of sorrow, doleful shades, where peace
And rest can never dwell, hope never comes
That comes to all;[16] but torture without end
Still urges, and a fiery deluge, fed
With ever-burning sulphur unconsumed:
70 Such place Eternal Justice had prepared
For those rebellious, here their prison ordained
In utter darkness, and their portion set
As far removed from God and light of Heaven
As from the center thrice to the utmost pole.
75 O how unlike the place from whence they fell!
There the companions of his fall, o'erwhelmed
With floods and whirlwinds of tempestuous fire,
He soon discerns, and weltering[17] by his side
One next himself in power, and next in crime,
80 Long after known in Palestine, and named
Beelzebub.[18] To whom the Arch-Enemy,
And thence in Heaven called Satan,[19] with bold
    words
Breaking the horrid silence thus began:

    Addressing Beelzebub, Satan boldly declares that though he has been thrown into Hell, he will continue to fight God with all his might. Beelzebub is afraid that God is too strong to be overcome. Satan, chiding him for his fears, begins to make plans.

"Seest thou yon dreary plain, forlorn
    and wild,
85 The seat of desolation, void of light,
Save what the glimmering of these livid
    flames
Casts pale and dreadful? Thither let us tend
From off the tossing of these fiery waves,
There rest, if any rest can harbor there,
90 And reassembling our afflicted powers,
Consult how we may henceforth most offend
Our Enemy,[20] our own loss how repair,
How overcome this dire calamity,
What reinforcement we may gain from hope;
95 If not, what resolution from despair."

Thus Satan, talking to his nearest mate,
With head uplift above the wave, and eyes
That sparkling blazed; his other parts
    besides
Prone on the flood, extended long and large,
100 Lay floating many a rood,[21] in bulk as huge
As whom the fables name of monstrous size,
Titanian, or Earth-born,[22] that warred on
    Jove,
Briareos or Typhon,[23] whom the den
By ancient Tarsus held, or that sea-beast
105 Leviathan,[24] which God of all His works
Created hugest that swim the ocean-stream:
Him, haply slumbering on the Norway
    foam,
The pilot of some small night-foundered
    skiff,
Deeming some island, oft, as seamen tell,
110 With fixèd anchor in his scaly rind
Moors by his side under the lee, while night
Invests the sea, and wishèd morn delays:
So stretched out huge in length the Arch-
    Fiend lay
Chained on the burning lake; nor ever
    thence
115 Had risen or heaved his head, but that the
    will
And high permission of all-ruling Heaven
Left him at large to his own dark designs,
That with reiterated crimes he might

---

15. *darkness visible.* It was thought that the flames of hell gave no light.
16. *to all.* The greatest torment of Hell was the total absence of hope of salvation.
17. *weltering,* tossing.
18. *Beelzebub* (bē el′zə bub), from Hebrew meaning "Lord of Flies." In the time of Jesus, Beelzebub was "prince of the demons." (Matthew 12:24; Luke 11:15) In certain medieval literature he was a chief associate of Satan.
19. *Satan,* "the Adversary."
20. *Enemy,* God.
21. *rood,* usually seven or eight yards.
22. *Earth-born.* Both the Titans (giants descended from Heaven) and the earth-born (giants) "warred on Jove."
23. *Briareos* (brē ar′ē əs) *or Typhon* (tī′fən), in Greek mythology, two monsters, the first with a hundred hands, the second with a hundred fire-breathing heads, who attempted to overthrow the dynasty of Jove. Typhon lived in Cilicia (sə lish′ə), of which *Tarsus* (tär′səs) (line 104) was the capital.
24. *Leviathan,* huge sea-monster mentioned in the Bible.

The fallen angels by M. Burgess after John Baptist Medina, from the first illustrated edition of *Paradise Lost* (London, 1688). *British Museum*

Heap on himself damnation, while he sought
120 Evil to others, and enraged might see
How all his malice served but to bring forth
Infinite goodness, grace, and mercy shown
On Man by him seduced, but on himself
Treble confusion, wrath, and vengeance
poured.
125 Forthwith upright he rears from off the pool
His mighty stature; on each hand the flames,
Driven backward, slope their pointing spires,
and rolled
In billows, leave in the midst a horrid vale.
Then with expanded wings he steers his
flight
130 Aloft, incumbent on the dusky air
That felt unusual weight, till on dry land
He lights, if it were land that ever burned
With solid, as the lake with liquid fire;
And such appeared in hue, as when the force
135 Of subterranean wind transports a hill
Torn from Pelorus,[25] or the shattered side
Of thundering Etna, whose combustible
And fueled entrails thence conceiving fire,
Sublimed with mineral fury, aid the winds,
140 And leave a singèd bottom all involved
With stench and smoke: Such resting found
the sole
Of unblest feet. Him followed his next mate,
Both glorying to have scaped the Stygian
flood[26]
As gods, and by their own recovered
strength,
145 Not by the sufferance of Supernal Power.
"Is this the region, this the soil, the clime,"
Said then the lost Archangel, "this the seat
That we must change for Heaven, this
mournful gloom
For that celestial light? Be it so, since He
150 Who now is sovereign can dispose and bid
What shall be right: Farthest from Him is
best,
Whom reason hath equaled, force hath made
supreme
Above His equals.[27] Farewell, happy fields,
Where joy for ever dwells: Hail, horrors!
hail,

155 Infernal world! and thou, profoundest Hell,
Receive thy new possessor: One who brings
A mind not to be changed by place or time.
The mind is its own place, and in itself
Can make a Heaven of Hell, a Hell of
Heaven.
160 What matter where, if I be still the same,
And what I should be, all but less than He
Whom thunder hath made greater? Here at
least
We shall be free; the Almighty hath not built
Here for His envy, will not drive us hence:
165 Here we may reign secure, and in my choice
To reign is worth ambition though in Hell:
Better to reign in Hell, than serve in Heaven.
But wherefore let we then our faithful
friends,
The associates and copartners of our loss,
170 Lie thus astonished on the oblivious pool,
And call them not to share with us their part
In this unhappy mansion, or once more
With rallied arms to try what may be yet
Regained in Heaven, or what more lost in
Hell?"
175   So Satan spake, and him Beelzebub
Thus answered: "Leader of those armies
bright,
Which, but the Omnipotent, none could
have foiled,
If once they hear that voice, their liveliest
pledge
Of hope in fears and dangers, heard so oft
180 In worst extremes, and on the perilous edge
Of battle when it raged, in all assaults
Their surest signal, they will soon resume
New courage and revive, though now they
lie
Groveling and prostrate on yon lake of fire,
185 As we erewhile, astounded and amazed;

---

25. **Pelorus** (pə lôr′ əs), the northeastern promontory of Sicily near the volcano of Mount Etna (line 137).
26. **Stygian** (stij′ē ən) **flood,** the river Styx, one of the four rivers in Hades.
27. **equals.** Note that Satan equates his reason with that of God, and attributes his defeat to the larger number of angels that remained loyal to God.

No wonder, fallen such a pernicious height."
  He scarce had ceased when the superior Fiend
Was moving toward the shore; his ponderous shield,
Ethereal temper, massy, large, and round,
190 Behind him cast; the broad circumference
Hung on his shoulders like the moon, whose orb
Through optic glass the Tuscan artist views
At evening from the top of Fesole,
Or in Valdarno,[28] to descry new lands,
195 Rivers, or mountains in her spotty globe.
His spear, to equal which the tallest pine
Hewn on Norwegian hills, to be the mast
Of some great ammiral,[29] were but a wand,
He walked with to support uneasy steps
200 Over the burning marl, not like those steps
On Heaven's azure; and the torrid clime
Smote on him sore besides, vaulted with fire;
Nathless[30] he so endured, till on the beach
Of that inflamèd sea, he stood and called
205 His legions, Angel forms, who lay entranced
Thick as autumnal leaves that strow the brooks
In Vallombrosa,[31] where the Etrurian shades
High over-arched embower; or scattered sedge
Afloat, when with fierce winds Orion[32] armed
210 Hath vexed the Red Sea coast, whose waves o'erthrew
Busiris and his Memphian chivalry,
While with perfidious hatred they pursued
The sojourners of Goshen,[33] who beheld
From the safe shore their floating carcasses
215 And broken chariot wheels—so thick bestrewn,
Abject and lost, lay these, covering the flood,
Under amazement of their hideous change.
He called so loud that all the hollow deep
Of Hell resounded: "Princes, Potentates,
220 Warriors, the Flower of Heaven, once yours, now lost,
If such astonishment as this can seize
Eternal Spirits; or have ye chosen this place

After the toil of battle to repose
Your wearied virtue, for the ease you find
225 To slumber here, as in the vales of Heaven?
Or in this abject posture have ye sworn
To adore the Conqueror? Who now beholds
Cherub and Seraph rolling in the flood
With scattered arms and ensigns, till anon
230 His swift pursuers from Heaven gates discern
The advantage, and descending, tread us down
Thus drooping, or with linkèd thunderbolts
Transfix us to the bottom of this gulf.
Awake, arise, or be forever fallen!"

> First to rise from the burning lake are the leaders of the fallen angels. Followed by the multitude, they wing their way to the plain and assemble in military formation before their "dread Commander," Satan.

---

235   He, above the rest
In shape and gesture proudly eminent,
Stood like a tower; his form had yet not lost
All her original brightness, nor appeared
Less than Archangel ruined, and the excess
240 Of glory obscured: As when the sun new-risen
Looks through the horizontal misty air
Shorn of his beams, or from behind the moon,

---

28. optic . . . Valdarno. The optic glass is the telescope of Galileo, whom Milton refers to as Tuscan because he lived in Tuscany, a region in central Italy which includes Florence. Fesole (Fiesole, fē ā′zō lā) is a city on a hill near Florence. Valdarno (väl där′nō) is the valley of the River Arno, in which Florence is situated.
29. ammiral, admiral, the flagship bearing the admiral of the fleet.
30. Nathless, nevertheless.
31. Vallombrosa (vä lōm brō′zä), a valley twenty miles east of Florence. Florence and the surrounding country are in ancient Etruria (i trŭr′ē ə) (line 207).
32. Orion, in Greek mythology, a hunter who became a constellation after his death. When the constellation rises late (in November), it is supposed to cause storms.
33. Goshen (gō′shən). Busiris was a mythical king of Egypt (Goshen). Milton considers him the Pharaoh who with his cavalry pursued the children of Israel into the Red Sea (Exodus 14).

In dim eclipse, disastrous twilight sheds
On half the nations, and with fear of change
245 Perplexes monarchs. Darkened so, yet shone
Above them all the Archangel; but his face
Deep scars of thunder had entrenched, and
     care
Sat on his faded cheek, but under brows
Of dauntless courage, and considerate pride
250 Waiting revenge: Cruel his eye, but cast
Signs of remorse and passion, to behold
The fellows of his crime, the followers rather

(Far other once beheld in bliss), condemned
Forever now to have their lot in pain.

In his speech to the army, Satan
announces his intention of seeking
revenge by fraud or guile, not force. Book
I ends with the building of the palace of
Pandemonium (that is, "All Demons"),
and with preparations for a council of war.

1667

THINK AND DISCUSS
ON HIS HAVING ARRIVED . . .
Understanding
1. What does the speaker call Time? What has
Time done?

Analyzing
2. In what respects does the speaker feel he is
less mature than others his age?
3. How does he console himself in the last six
lines?

Extending
4. Is the feeling that time is passing without
a person's having accomplished much also
a feeling common to today's young people?
Explain.

ON HIS BLINDNESS
Understanding
1. Who asks the question in line 7? Who
responds to it?

Analyzing
2. What does the speaker mean by "Doth God
exact day-labor, light denied?"
3. What does he mean by "They also serve who
only stand and wait" (line 14)? How does
that thought comfort him?

Extending
4. Compare this sonnet with the sonnet written
twenty-one years earlier at the age of twenty-
three. How does Milton seem to regard his
accomplishments in each?

APPLYING: Metonymy H▯
See Handbook of Literary Terms, p. 907
   A **metonymy** is a figure of speech in which a
specific term naming an object is substituted for
another word with which it is closely associated; for example, we commonly say "the crown"
when referring to a monarch.

1. In lines 1 and 7, what does *light* represent?
2. In the context of the poem, what does *day-
labor* stand for?
3. To what is the word *yoke* usually applied?
What does it stand for here?

THINK AND DISCUSS
PARADISE LOST
Understanding
1. A classical epic begins with a statement of
the **theme** and an *invocation to the muse*—a
request to a deity for inspiration and help in
writing. Of what does Milton ask his muse
to sing (lines 1–6)?
2. What muse does Milton invoke (lines 6–26)?

3. Lines 27–33 pose the *epic question*, the question that the epic will deal with. Here the epic question has two parts. What are they?

4. Reread the descriptions of Satan in lines 96–101, 126–128, 187–202, and 235–250. Summarize these in a single sentence.

5. Briefly summarize the action in this excerpt. (See especially lines 44–47, 50–53, 59–60, 76–81, 125–126, 129–132, 142, 203–205, 218–225, and 235–237.)

6. A classical epic always includes detailed descriptions of the armor and weapons of the combatants and descriptions of their battles. Find the equivalent in this excerpt.

Analyzing

7. An *epic simile* is an elaborate, extended comparison, introduced by *like* or *as*—or *as whom, as when,* and similar constructions. The first of these, referred to as the Leviathan Simile, begins in line 101. To what beings is Satan compared in this simile?

8. Explain the epic similes in lines 131–141, 205–217, and 237–245.

9. Epic speeches usually begin with the name of the person being addressed and contain elevated language, epithets, and boastfulness. What qualities of epic speech are contained in lines 146–174, 176–187, and 219–234?

10. In the invocation Milton asserts that God ("Eternal Providence") controls everything. How do lines 113–124 support this assertion? Account then for lines 143–145.

11. Satan is not the **protagonist** of *Paradise Lost,* but his **characterization** is so strong that he seems almost an *antihero* (a protagonist with character traits opposed to those of the conventional hero). Discuss this claim.

12. Explain: "The mind is its own place, and in itself/Can make a heaven of Hell, a Hell of Heaven" (lines 158–159) and "Better to reign in Hell than serve in Heaven" (line 167). How do these lines help explain the motivation Milton ascribes to Satan?

Extending

13. Compare Milton's picture of Satan and Hell with other pictures you may be familiar with from literature, movies, and so on.

APPLYING: Blank Verse ✦H
See Handbook of Literary Terms, p. 897

Blank verse is composed of unrhymed iambic pentameter. Of the different poetic meters, iambic is closest to the natural rhythms of spoken English. Nevertheless, poets often introduce variations to avoid monotony.

1. Read aloud lines 1–6 (through *Muse*), emphasizing the syllables you would normally emphasize and pausing where you would normally pause. Which lines follow a perfect iambic pattern?

2. Which lines are run-on? Which are end-stopped?

3. Which lines contain caesuras?

COMPOSITION ✎
Discussing the Sin of Pride

Satan's sin, considered the deadliest of all sins, was pride. Write a composition, with your classmates as audience, in which you discuss this sin as it is presented in *Paradise Lost.* First skim the excerpt to find actions and statements that demonstrate pride. Then write your composition, pointing out evidence of Satan's pride and discussing its effects on him and his followers. You might also discuss why pride was considered the deadliest sin.

Analyzing Symbols of Light and Darkness

Paradise Lost abounds in images of light and darkness, used **symbolically.** Reread the excerpt, listing some of these images. After you have organized them into an outline, write a paper in which you analyze Milton's use of them. Do light and darkness always symbolize the same things? Support your statements by direct quotes from the poem. Consider using this essay as one you submit with your college applications.

Genesis, Chapters 1-3

from **The King James Bible**

No complete translation of the Bible was made into English until the late fourteenth century, when John Wycliffe, a theologian and church reformer who was condemned as a heretic, oversaw a translation. Other "unauthorized" translations appeared in the early sixteenth century, including versions by William Tyndale and Miles Coverdale. Finally, in 1539, the "Great Bible" appeared, under the auspices of the reigning monarch, Henry VIII. This was the first English Bible with official endorsement.

In 1604, James I convened a conference at Hampton Court at which plans were laid for a new version of the Bible by a group of translators. Some fifty or so theologians and scholars began work in various centers of learning (Oxford, Cambridge, Westminster), making extensive use of previous translations, especially those of Tyndale and Wycliffe. The work was issued in 1611 as the "Authorized Version" and has fixed itself so firmly in the imagination of the English-speaking world that no other translation seems able to challenge it.

The King James Bible has been called "the noblest monument of English prose," and deserves the epithet because of the sheer brilliance of its language. The King James version preserves the old language and plain style of the earlier English versions, in contrast to the ornamental style characteristic of some prose in the early seventeenth century. Its extensive use of concrete terms and images, its straightforward phrases and sentences, its balance and parallelism in many passages—all make for a dignified simplicity eminently compatible with religious feeling and ritual. Indeed, the language of the King James Bible has so profoundly affected succeeding generations of writers and has so thoroughly stamped itself in the minds of ordinary people that today it forms a basic part of our everyday speech.

For a comparison of translations of the Bible, see the various versions of the Twenty-third Psalm on page 307.

In the beginning God created the heaven and the earth. And the earth was without form, and void; and darkness was upon the face of the deep. And the Spirit of God moved upon the face of the waters. And God said, "Let there be light": and there was light. And God saw the light, that it was good: and God divided the light from the darkness. And God called the light Day, and the darkness he called Night. And the evening and the morning were the first day.

And God said, "Let there be a firmament in the midst of the waters, and let it divide the waters from the waters." And God made the firmament, and divided the waters which were under the firmament from the waters which were above the firmament: and it was so. And God called the firmament Heaven. And the evening and the morning were the second day.

And God said, "Let the waters under the heaven

be gathered together unto one place, and let the dry land appear": and it was so. And God called the dry land Earth; and the gathering together of the waters called he Seas: and God saw that it was good. And God said, "Let the earth bring forth grass, the herb yielding seed, and the fruit tree yielding fruit after his kind, whose seed is in itself, upon the earth": and it was so. And the earth brought forth grass, and herb yielding seed after his kind, and the tree yielding fruit, whose seed was in itself, after his kind: and God saw that it was good. And the evening and the morning were the third day.

And God said, "Let there be lights in the firmament of the heaven to divide the day from the night; and let them be for signs, and for seasons, and for days, and years: and let them be for lights in the firmament of the heaven to give light upon the earth": and it was so. And God made two great lights; the greater light to rule the day, and the lesser light to rule the night: he made the stars also. And God set them in the firmament of the heaven to give light upon the earth. And to rule over the day and over the night, and to divide the light from the darkness: and God saw that it was good. And the evening and the morning were the fourth day.

And God said, "Let the waters bring forth abundantly the moving creature that hath life, and fowl that may fly above the earth in the open firmament of heaven." And God created great whales, and every living creature that moveth, which the waters brought forth abundantly, after their kind, and every winged fowl after his kind: and God saw that it was good. And God blessed them, saying, "Be fruitful, and multiply, and fill the waters in the seas, and let fowl multiply in the earth." And the evening and the morning were the fifth day.

And God said, "Let the earth bring forth the living creature after his kind, cattle, and creeping thing, and beast of the earth after his kind": and it was so. And God made the beast of the earth after his kind, and cattle after their kind, and every thing that creepeth upon the earth after his kind: and God saw that it was good.

And God said, "Let us make man in our image, after our likeness; and let them have dominion over the fish of the sea, and over the fowl of the air, and over the cattle, and over all the earth, and over every creeping thing that creepeth upon the earth." So God created man in his own image, in the image of God created he him; male and female created he them. And God blessed them, and God said unto them, "Be fruitful, and multiply, and replenish the earth, and subdue it: and have dominion over the fish of the sea, and over the fowl of the air, and over every living thing that moveth upon the earth."

And God said, "Behold, I have given you every herb bearing seed, which is upon the face of all the earth, and every tree, in the which is the fruit of a tree yielding seed; to you it shall be for meat. And to every beast of the earth, and to every fowl of the air, and to every thing that creepeth upon the earth, wherein there is life, I have given every green herb for meat": and it was so.

And God saw every thing that he had made, and behold, it was very good. And the evening and the morning were the sixth day.

Thus the heavens and the earth were finished, and all the host of them. And on the seventh day God ended his work which he had made; and he rested on the seventh day from all his work which he had made. And God blessed the seventh day, and sanctified it: because that in it he had rested from all his work which God created and made.

The Creation of Adam and Eve

These are the generations of the heavens and of the earth when they were created, in the day that the Lord God made the earth and the heavens, and every plant of the field before it was in the earth, and every herb of the field before it grew: for the Lord God had not caused it to rain upon the earth, and there was not a man to till the ground. But there went up a mist from the earth, and watered the whole face of the ground. And the Lord God formed man of the dust of the ground, and breathed into his nostrils the breath of life; and man became a living soul.

And the Lord God planted a garden eastward

in Eden; and there he put the man whom he had formed. And out of the ground made the Lord God to grow every tree that is pleasant to the sight, and good for food; the tree of life also in the midst of the garden, and the tree of knowledge of good and evil. . . .

And the Lord God took the man, and put him into the garden of Eden to dress it and to keep it. And the Lord God commanded the man, saying, "Of every tree of the garden thou mayest freely eat: but of the tree of the knowledge of good and evil, thou shalt not eat of it: for in the day that thou eatest thereof thou shalt surely die."

And the Lord God said, "It is not good that the man should be alone; I will make him an help meet for him." And out of the ground the Lord God formed every beast of the field, and every fowl of the air; and brought them unto Adam to see what he would call them: and whatsoever Adam called every living creature, that was the name thereof. And Adam gave names to all cattle, and to the fowl of the air, and to every beast of the field; but for Adam there was not found an help meet for him.

And the Lord God caused a deep sleep to fall upon Adam, and he slept: and he took one of his ribs, and closed up the flesh instead thereof; and the rib, which the Lord God had taken from man, made he a woman, and brought her unto the man.

And Adam said, "This is now bone of my bones, and flesh of my flesh: she shall be called Woman, because she was taken out of Man."

Therefore shall a man leave his father and his mother, and shall cleave unto his wife: and they shall be one flesh. And they were both naked, the man and his wife, and were not ashamed.

Forbidden Fruit

Now the serpent was more subtil than any beast of the field which the Lord God had made.

And he said unto the woman, "Yea, hath God said, 'Ye shall not eat of every tree of the garden'?"

And the woman said unto the serpent, "We may eat of the fruit of the trees of the garden: but of the fruit of the tree which is in the midst of the garden, God hath said, 'Ye shall not eat of it, neither shall ye touch it, lest ye die.' "

And the serpent said unto the woman, "Ye shall not surely die: for God doth know that in the day ye eat thereof, then your eyes shall be opened, and ye shall be as gods, knowing good and evil."

And when the woman saw that the tree was good for food, and that it was pleasant to the eyes, and a tree to be desired to make one wise, she took of the fruit thereof, and did eat, and gave also unto her husband with her; and he did eat. And the eyes of them both were opened, and they knew that they were naked; and they sewed fig leaves together, and made themselves aprons.

And they heard the voice of the Lord God walking in the garden in the cool of the day: and Adam and his wife hid themselves from the presence of the Lord God amongst the trees of the garden.

And the Lord God called unto Adam, and said unto him, "Where art thou?"

And he said, "I heard thy voice in the garden, and I was afraid, because I was naked; and I hid myself."

And he said, "Who told thee that thou wast naked? Has thou eaten of the tree, whereof I commanded thee that thou shouldest not eat?"

And the man said, "The woman whom thou gavest to be with me, she gave me of the tree, and I did eat."

And the Lord God said unto the woman, "What is this that thou hast done?"

And the woman said, "The serpent beguiled me, and I did eat."

And the Lord God said unto the serpent, "Because thou hast done this, thou art cursed above all cattle, and above every beast of the field; upon thy belly shalt thou go, and dust shalt thou eat all the days of thy life: and I will put enmity between thee and the woman, and between thy seed and her seed; it shall bruise thy head, and thou shalt bruise his heel."

Unto the woman he said, "I will greatly multiply thy sorrow and thy conception; in sorrow thou shalt bring forth children; and thy desire shall be to thy husband, and he shall rule over thee."

And unto Adam he said, "Because thou hast hearkened unto the voice of thy wife, and hast

Adam Naming the Beasts, by William Blake. 1810. *Stirling Maxwell Collection, Pollok House, Glasgow*

eaten of the tree, of which I commanded thee, saying, 'Thou shalt not eat of it': cursed is the ground for thy sake; in sorrow shalt thou eat of it all the days of thy life. Thorns also and thistles shall it bring forth to thee; and thou shalt eat the herb of the field; in the sweat of thy face shalt thou eat bread, till thou return unto the ground; for out of it wast thou taken: for dust thou art, and unto dust shalt thou return."

And Adam called his wife's name Eve; because she was the mother of all living. Unto Adam also and to his wife did the Lord God make coats of skins, and clothed them.

And the Lord God said, "Behold, the man is become as one of us, to know good and evil: and now, lest he put forth his hand, and take also of the tree of life, and eat, and live for ever": therefore the Lord God sent him forth from the garden of Eden, to till the ground from whence he was taken. So he drove out the man; and he placed at the east of the garden of Eden Cherubims, and a flaming sword which turned every way, to keep the way of the tree of life.

1611

THINK AND DISCUSS

Understanding

1. According to Genesis, for what purpose did God create man? woman?
2. From what tree are they not supposed to eat?

Analyzing

3. How does the behavior of Adam and Eve change after they have eaten the forbidden fruit?
4. What punishments are they and the serpent given?
5. Find a passage you consider particularly effective and explore the reasons for its effectiveness. For example, analyze: "In the beginning God created the heaven and the earth."

Extending

6. Imagine that a child, beginning to be conscious of the surrounding world, asks, "Who made the world? Why? How are people made? What about whales? How long did it take?" Show how the opening of Genesis provides possible answers to these questions.

VOCABULARY

Context

Using context as an aid, write on your paper the letter of the most appropriate definition for each italicized word.

1. "Hail Horrors! hail/*infernal* world! and thou profoundest Hell/Receive thy new possessor."
   a. hellish **b.** heavenly **c.** peaceful
2. "And God said unto them, 'Be fruitful, and multiply, and *replenish* the earth.'"
   a. waste **b.** plunder **c.** refill
3. ". . . eyes/That witnessed huge affliction and dismay/Mixed with *obdurate* pride and steadfast hate . . ."
   a. fearful **b.** stubborn **c.** pained
4. "Or in this *abject* posture have ye sworn/To adore the Conqueror?"
   a. visible **b.** proud **c.** wretched
5. "The infernal Serpent; he it was whose *guile*/Stirred up with envy and revenge, deceived/The mother of mankind . . ."
   a. deceit **b.** cleverness **c.** pride

COMPOSITION

Analyzing the Style of Genesis

The repetition of certain words and phrases gives the passages from Genesis a richness and solemnity. Write a composition in which you discuss the effectiveness of this repetition in establishing a style that is rhythmic and flowing, yet appropriate to the serious content of Genesis. First reread the excerpt to find and list repeated words and phrases; then organize your list and use it as the basis for your composition.

Comparing Translations

Read the four different translations of the Twenty-third Psalm in the Reader's Note on page 307. Write a paper comparing the style of these four translations, describing how the style changes over the centuries while the content remains the same. What differences in purpose are suggested? You may find this task easier if you concentrate on one or two lines; for example, lines 2–3 of the King James version. Then note how the other translations differ from it and from one another. Share your paper with your classmates.

Reader's Note

The Twenty-third Psalm

The Bible has been the best seller of all time, and translations of it have been numerous. The achievement of the King James version can best be judged by comparing it with some of the others. Here are four versions of the Twenty-third Psalm: the King James translation, one published before it, and two published later.

from The Great Bible (1539)

The Lord is my shepherd; therefore can I lack nothing. He shall feed me in a green pasture, and lead me forth beside the waters of comfort. He shall convert my soul, and bring me forth in the paths of righteousness for his name's sake. Yea, though I walk through the valley of the shadow of death, I will fear no evil, for thou art with me. Thy rod and thy staff comfort me. Thou shalt prepare a table before me against them that trouble me; thou has anointed my head with oil, and my cup shall be full. But thy loving-kindness and mercy shall follow me all the days of my life and I will dwell in the house of the Lord forever.

from The King James Bible (1611)

The Lord is my shepherd: I shall not want.
He maketh me to lie down in green pastures:
   he leadeth me beside the still waters.
He restoreth my soul: he leadeth me in the
   paths of righteousness for his name's sake.
Yea, thou I walk through the valley of the
   shadow of death, I will fear no evil: for thou
   art with me; thy rod and thy staff they
   comfort me.
Thou preparest a table before me in the
   presence of mine enemies: thou anointest
   my head with oil; my cup runneth over.
Surely goodness and mercy shall follow me all
   the days of my life: and I will dwell in the
   house of the Lord forever.

From *The New English Bible.* Copyright © The Delegates of the Oxford University Press and the Syndics of the Cambridge University Press 1961, 1970. Reprinted by permission.

from The Bay Psalm Book (1640)

The Lord to me a shepherd is,
   want therefore shall not I.
He in the folds of tender grass,
   doth cause me down to lie:
To waters calm me gently leads,
   restore my soul doth he:
He doth in paths of righteousness
   for his name's sake lead me.
Yea though in valley of death's shade
   I walk, none ill I'll fear:
Because thou art with me, thy rod
   and staff my comfort are.
For me a table thou hast spread,
   in presence of my foes:
Thou dost anoint my head with oil,
   my cup it overflows.
Goodness and mercy surely shall
   all my days follow me:
And in the Lord's house I shall dwell
   so long as days shall be.

from The New English Bible (1970)

The Lord is my shepherd; I shall want nothing.
   He makes me lie down in green pastures,
   and leads me beside the waters of peace;
     he renews life within me,
   and for his name's sake guides me in the right path.
   Even thou I walk through a valley dark as death
   I fear no evil, for thou art with me,
thy staff and thy crook are my comfort.
   Thou spreadest a table for me in the sight of my enemies;
   thou hast richly bathed my head with oil,
     and my cup runs over.
   Goodness and love unfailing, these will follow me
     all the days of my life,
   and I shall dwell in the house of the LORD my whole life long.

The Changing English Language

The last years of the fifteenth century mark the end of the Middle English period and the beginning of what is called the early Modern English period. The development of the language during the sixteenth century seems at first both paradoxical and chaotic. On the one hand, there was a movement to make the language more uniform; on the other hand, it continued to be, in both its spoken and written forms, more plastic than it is now.

Some of the confusion during the sixteenth century was due to the persistence of regional dialects. Contributing to the problem of regional variations was the lack of any standard system of spelling and pronunciation. A writer spelled according to his own tastes, and a reader had to have a certain amount of agility and imagination. The word *fellow*, for example, was spelled variously as *fallow*, *felowe*, *felow*, *fallowe*.

During the sixteenth century the first attempts to "improve" and regulate the language were made. Among the forces promoting regulation was the printing press, which eliminated the vagaries and mistakes in handwritten manuscripts and greatly enlarged the number of books and pamphlets available. With the growth of printing came a renewed interest in education (a word, by the way, first used in English in 1531). By Shakespeare's time about half the population of London could at least read, and that number continued to grow.

Among the tens of thousands of items run off the presses during the later part of the century were numerous "how to" books on spelling and usage, and many pamphlets and introductions defending the English vernacular over Latin as the language for all occasions. The preoccupation with a uniform language grew out of the strong sense of national identity; the experimentation with new vocabulary and new means of expression grew out of the adventurous spirit of the Elizabethans and also out of the concern for elegance and style; there was a realization that, in the newly flexible social structure, an elegant style could contribute to upward social mobility.

Of necessity the language had to grow to accommodate the new discoveries being made in scholarship and science. During the later years of the sixteenth century, English vocabulary was tremendously expanded by energetic and sometimes indiscriminate adaptation of words from Latin, Greek, French, Italian, and Spanish to supply terms the native idiom lacked. (Experts estimate that more than ten thousand words were added to English during this period.) So widespread was the importation of foreign terms that the first dictionaries printed in England were listings not of English but of foreign terms.

Latin and Greek contributed thousands of words, among them *antipathy*, *catastrophe*, *external*, *erupt*, *halo*, *anachronism*, *encyclopedia*, *appendix*, *emphasis*, *submerge*, *strenuous*, *inflate*, *infringement*. From French came *bigot*, *alloy*, and *detail*, while *balcony*, *cameo*, *stanza*, and *violin* were borrowed from Italian. Spanish and Portuguese added *alligator*, *negro*, *potato*, *tobacco*, *cannibal*, and many others. Together with, and partially in reaction to, this habit of borrowing and experimenting with foreign terms, there arose a movement to revive and adapt Old English words, adding to the language such forms as *wolfish*, *briny*, *astound*, *doom*, *filch*, and *freak*. It was largely through scholarly writing and literature that most of the new terms gained admittance to the language. The poets of the period—particularly Spenser and Shakespeare—were notorious coiners and borrowers of words.

In contrast to the tremendous embellishment of its vocabulary, the grammatical structure of English underwent relatively few changes in the sixteenth century. Some time in the last part of the century, a shift in the pronunciation of long vowels settled the pronunciation of English close to what it is today.

THINKING CRITICALLY
ABOUT LITERATURE

UNIT 3   THE RENAISSANCE   1500–1660

■ CONCEPT REVIEW

Following is a selection that contains many of the important ideas and literary terms found in Unit 3. It also contains notes and questions designed to help you think critically about your reading. Page numbers in the notes refer to an application or a review. A more extensive discussion of these terms is in the Handbook of Literary Terms.

Sonnet 73

William Shakespeare

That time of year thou mayst in me behold
When yellow leaves, or none, or few, do hang
Upon those boughs which shake against the cold,
Bare ruined choirs where late the sweet birds sang.
5 In me thou see'st the twilight of such day
As after sunset fadeth in the west,
Which by and by black night doth take away,
Death's second self, that seals up all in rest.
In me thou see'st the glowing of such fire,
10 That on the ashes of his youth doth lie
As the deathbed whereon it must expire,
Consumed with that which it was nourished by.
   This thou perceivest, which makes thy love more strong,
   To love that well which thou must leave ere long.

1609

■ **Sonnet** (page 168): Consider what expectations are aroused by a Shakespearean sonnet.
■ **Metaphor** (page 166): Note how each *quatrain* begins with a different metaphor.
■ **Pastoral** (page 267): Watch for pastoral elements.
■ **choirs:** parts of churches used by singers.
■ **Alliteration** (page 176): Note the repeated *b* sounds in line 7.
■ **Symbol** (page 277): Consider how you can tell that "black night" is symbolic.
■ **seals up:** ends; concludes.
■ Note how the fire is *personified* in lines 10–12.
■ **Paradox** (page 180): At first it seems impossible for anything to be consumed by that which nourishes it.
■ The ending *couplet* tells you what kind of sonnet this is.

THINK AND DISCUSS

Understanding

1. What three things does the loved one behold or see in the speaker?
2. To what does *This* in line 13 refer?
3. What is the result of the loved one perceiving *This?*

Analyzing

4. How old does the speaker seem to be? Explain.
5. Why is the loved one's love "more strong"? (See line 14.)
6. What is **personified** in line 8?
7. What elements of *carpe diem* poetry does this sonnet contain?

Extending

8. Is it generally true that people love more strongly that which they are going to lose, or do they love less strongly, for fear of being hurt?

REVIEWING LITERARY TERMS

Sonnet

1. Is this an English or an Italian sonnet? How can you tell?
2. What is its proposition? How many stages does the proposition have?
3. What is its resolution?

Metaphor

4. Lines 1, 5, and 9 introduce three different metaphors. What are they, and what single thing are they all metaphors for?
5. What elements do these metaphors have in common? Which do you think is most effective?

Symbol

6. What does "black night" (line 7) symbolize?

Paradox

7. Consider what becomes of material that feeds a fire; then explain how the fire can be consumed by that which nourished it (line 12).
8. How may this paradox be applied to a human being?

Pastoral

9. What pastoral elements are in this sonnet? What do they contribute to the overall meaning and effect?

Alliteration

10. Which words alliterate in line 8? What is the overall effect on the line of these sounds?

■ CONTENT REVIEW

Classifying

1. Make a chart with the names of the authors from this unit down the side and the following headings across the top: *Courtier, Government Official, Churchman, Playwright, Other.* For each author, place a check under the heading that best describes his or her occupation. If you use *Other,* specify at the bottom of the chart the occupation(s) involved.
2. Which selections from this unit express the *carpe diem* theme—or at least contain aspects of it?

Generalizing

3. From the sonnets you have read in this unit, what were the three most important themes of the sonneteers?
4. The Renaissance has been described as "a rebirth of the human spirit, a realization of the human potential for development." Select one author from this unit and show how that author's works support this generalization.
5. What place did religion have in the literature of this period?

Synthesizing

6. Renaissance poets often used **apostrophe** to address an abstract concept such as Death. What concepts or things in today's world do people tend to apostrophize?
7. If you could travel back to the Renaissance period in a time machine, what person would you most like to meet or what event would you like to witness? Why?

Evaluating

8. It has been claimed that Shakespeare stands at the pinnacle of Renaissance artistry. Support or attack this claim, using as your basis the works included in this unit.

9. Much of the Renaissance output was love poetry of one sort or another. Evaluate it in terms of today's readers. How much of it is still timely?

10. The English Renaissance encompassed the Age of Discovery. To what extent are discovery and exploration inherent in the selections you have read?

■ COMPOSITION REVIEW

Characterizing an Elizabethan

Based on the works you have read in this unit, make a list of the qualities and features that would characterize one of the following members of the court of Queen Elizabeth I: a courtier, a court lady, a sonneteer. Use your imagination to create a name and fill in details. Then write a character sketch about the person you have created. In addition to details of appearance and behavior, you might describe your character in action in a typical court situation. Share your character sketch with your classmates.

Discussing the Theme of Love

Write a paper in which you discuss some of the attitudes toward love displayed by poems in this unit. In addition to the flirtatious, cynical, and serious aspects of love between the sexes, consider also a parent's love for a child (Jonson), a husband's love for his wife (Donne), and a person's love for God (Donne or Herbert). You will probably need to limit your paper to just a few of these attitudes.

Comparing and Contrasting Sonneteers

Among the major practitioners of the sonnet in Renaissance England were Wyatt, Surrey, Spenser, Sidney, Shakespeare, Donne, and Milton. Select any two of these sonneteers and compare and contrast their sonnets with regard to content, structure, and poetic devices.

Evaluating Metaphysical Poetry

"Poetry with ingenious comparisons, far-fetched assertions, and extraordinarily clever phrasing may be interesting but cannot be sincere as genuine love poetry because it does not express deep feeling or profound emotion." In a composition, defend or attack this statement, using examples from the poetry of the Renaissance period to support your position.

Demonstrating Changes in Renaissance Poetry

The Background to this unit mentions that the exuberance of early Renaissance poetry gave way to a more cynical and introspective outlook as the Renaissance waned. Select several poets whose works may be used to demonstrate these changes, and then write a paper in which you demonstrate how at least one poem by each typifies exuberance, cynicism, or introspection.

Analyzing Hamlet as a Protagonist (*Hamlet* edition)

Samuel Taylor Coleridge has said that Hamlet is an intellectual, called upon to act deliberately for human and divine reasons, who keeps resolving to act and yet always delays action. Go back to the play and find evidence to defend or refute this interpretation; then write an essay in which you agree or disagree with Coleridge's analysis, giving reasons to support your answer. See "Writing About Drama" in the Writer's Handbook.

Analyzing Macbeth as a Protagonist (*Macbeth* edition)

Macbeth is, first of all, a play about the murder of a king. This act destroys harmony not only in the character of Macbeth, but also in Scottish society at large. Go back to the play, keeping in mind the relationships among kingship, order, and anarchy. Then write an essay in which you discuss Macbeth's function in the play. Can he be a protagonist and at the same time cause so much disintegration and disorder? Support your case by giving examples from the play.

THE AGE OF REASON

	1660		1680		1700	

HISTORY AND ARTS
- Dryden appointed poet laureate
- Restoration of monarchy
- Theaters reopen
- China open to foreign trade
- Royal Society founded
- Molière: *Tartuffe* (France)
- Plague in London
- London fire
- England and Scotland joined
- Glorious Revolution
- Bank of England founded
- St. Paul's Cathedral rebuilt

MONARCHS AND HOUSES

PROTECTORATE STUART

- Charles II
- James II
- William III and Mary II
- William III
- Anne

HANOVER
- George I

ENGLISH LITERATURE
- Pepys: *Diary* (begun)
- Milton: *Paradise Lost*
- Bunyan: *Pilgrim's Progress*
- Wycherley: *The Country Wife*
- Newton: *Principia*
- Locke: *Essay Concerning Human Understanding*
- Congreve: *The Way of the World*
- Addison & Steele: *The Spectator*
- Pope: *The Rape of the Lock*

She Stoops to Conquer (Act V, Scene 3) by Oliver Goldsmith.

Portrait of Queen Anne, after Kneller, circa 1694.

Robinson Crusoe by Daniel Defoe, first edition, 1719.

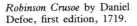

1660–1780

UNIT 4

1740	1760	1780

- **Bach:** *Well-Tempered Clavier* (Germany)
  - **Hogarth:** *A Rake's Progress*
    - **Handel:** *Messiah*
      - **Industrial Revolution begins**
        - **British Museum founded**
          - **Lisbon earthquake (Portugal)**

- **Seven Years' War with France**
  - **Voltaire:** *Candide* (France)
    - **Rousseau:** *The Social Contract* (France)
  - **Encyclopaedia Britannica publ.**
    - **American Revolution begins**
      - **Paine:** *Common Sense* (America)

- **George II**
- **George III**

- **Defoe:** *Robinson Crusoe*
  - **Swift:** *Gulliver's Travels*
    - **Richardson:** *Pamela*

- **Fielding:** *Tom Jones*
  - **Gray:** *Elegy Written in a Country Churchyard*
    - **Johnson:** *Dictionary*
      - **Sterne:** *Tristram Shandy*

- **Goldsmith:** *She Stoops to Conquer*
  - **Smith:** *The Wealth of Nations*
    - **Sheridan:** *The School for Scandal*

Bach and Handel composed for the harpsichord in the 1700s.

Newcomen engine, from a painting of a midlands pithead.

Signing of the Declaration of Independence, by John Trumbull.

PREVIEW

UNIT 4   THE AGE OF REASON   1660–1780

Authors

John Dryden	Joseph Addison	Samuel Johnson
Samuel Pepys	Daniel Defoe	James Boswell
Jonathan Swift	Alexander Pope	Thomas Gray
Sir Richard Steele		

Features
Comment: Size and Scale in *Gulliver's Travels*
Comment: The London Coffeehouses by
    Thomas Babington Macaulay
Themes in English Literature: London
Reader's Note: *The Rape of the Lock* as a Mock
    Epic
Reading a Biography
The Changing English Language

Application of Literary Terms
heroic couplet
satire
point of view
tone
epigram
setting

Review of Literary Terms
irony

Reading Literature Skillfully
fact/opinion

Vocabulary
suffixes
dictionary
pronunciation key

Thinking Skills
classifying
generalizing
evaluating

Composition
Reacting to Satire
Responding to a Quote
Describing the Fire
Characterizing Pepys
Satirizing Your Community
Analyzing Swift's Satire
Analyzing Swift's Use of Irony
Writing a Modern Satire
Writing a Character Sketch
Analyzing a Periodical Essay
Writing a Gentle Satire
Comparing and Contrasting Satires
Writing a Persuasive Essay
Reporting on the Educational System
Summarizing a Plot
Analyzing Pope's Mock Epic
Explaining an Epigram
Analyzing *An Essay on Man*
Describing a Public Figure
Discussing Johnson's Ideas
Writing a Parody
Analyzing Gray's Use of Setting

Enrichment
Readers Theater
Researching *Gulliver's Travels*
Writing Dictionary Definitions

Thinking Critically About Literature
Concept Review
Content Review
Composition Review

THE AGE OF REASON 1660–1780

In Europe in the late seventeenth and eighteenth centuries, there was a general intellectual and literary movement known as the Enlightenment, characterized by *Rationalism*—a philosophy that emphasized the role of reason rather than sensory experience or faith in answering basic questions of human existence. Intellectual freedom and relative freedom from prejudice and superstition in religion and politics were ideals typical of the age. As in all ages, however, behavior often did not match ideals.

In England this movement is more commonly known as the Age of Reason. The English version of this general European movement tended to give an equal place to experience and reason in examining the human condition, and was therefore less strictly "rational" than the French or other continental versions. In England, in fact, many of the most important writers of the period were opposed to the rationalist ideals of social progress and human perfectibility. Because writers based much of their prose and poetry on classical models from ancient Greece and especially Rome, the period is sometimes called the Neoclassical Age.

It was an age, in Europe at least, in which people were concerned with manners and morals, with understanding themselves, their immediate world, and their relations with one another. It was a period influenced by John Locke's *Essay Concerning Human Understanding* (1690), which argued that "our business here is not to know all things, but those which concern our conduct." It was a period stimulated by the discoveries of great scientists like Isaac Newton, whose *Principia* (1687) first set forth the laws of gravitation—a period that advocated the use of scientific method to test old theories and to develop new knowledge.

THE EARLY YEARS, 1660–1700

When in 1660 the Puritan regime was toppled and King Charles II returned triumphantly to the throne, it was to an England generally delighted to have its monarchy restored. Samuel Pepys, who was with the official party that brought the king home, recorded the event in his *Diary*.

The Restoration brought many changes to England. Once again the Anglican Church became the established church, and Puritans were ousted from both government and church positions. Soon after his return, Charles permitted the theaters, closed by the Puritans, to reopen, and he himself sponsored one acting company, the King's Players, while his brother James, the Duke of York, sponsored another.

In 1662 Charles chartered the Royal Society, thus making scientific activities and investigations official. The Society required the use of the scientific method in all of its investigations, and it insisted that reports be written in clear, simple prose.

Not everything ran smoothly, however. Charles had been in exile in France for a number of years, and he brought back some French customs that shocked the more pious people of his realm. Soon a spirit of licentiousness characterized the behavior of the court and the nobility. Additionally, Charles attempted to restore some of the privileges of the Catholics, and himself became a Catholic on his deathbed in 1685. Since Charles left no children, his brother, who was a Catholic, succeeded him as James II. Afraid of the reemergence of Catholicism, the country watched and waited. The Duke of Monmouth, illegitimate son of Charles II, led an uprising against James in 1685. The rebellion failed. When James's second wife gave birth to a son, a Catholic line seemed virtually assured.

By his first marriage, however, James had two daughters, both of whom had been raised as Protestants. The elder, Mary, who was married to the Protestant William of Orange, ruler of the United Provinces of Holland, had been next in line for the English throne until the birth of James's son. Through secret negotiations, William and Mary were offered the throne as joint rulers, and in 1688 William crossed the English Channel with a small army. Immediately the English flocked to his support, and James prudently escaped to France. As a result of this Glorious Revolution (so called because it involved no bloodshed), William and Mary were crowned in 1689. As a condition to their rule, they accepted a Bill of Rights, passed by Parliament, that limited the power of the crown and reaffirmed the supremacy of Parliament. After Mary's death, William was the sole ruler until he died in 1702.

For centuries London had been receiving the bulk of the great population shift from country to town; it was now a thriving city. But quite by coincidence London suffered two major disasters in rapid succession. In 1665 plague ran rampant through the city, killing 70,000 of its inhabitants. Soon after the disease abated, fire broke out in June, 1666, and raged uncontrolled for five days. By the time it was extinguished, 13,000 houses and nearly a hundred churches had been destroyed; two-thirds of the population was homeless. An excerpt from Daniel Defoe's fictional account of the plague begins on page 414. Samuel Pepys's eyewitness account of the fire, taken from the pages of his *Diary*, begins on page 325.

London was rebuilt with wider streets and more solidly constructed buildings. Many of the most beautiful of these, among them St. Paul's Cathedral and the lovely small church of St. Mary-le-Bow, were designed by Sir Christopher Wren, who became England's leading architect.

In 1652, the opening of the first coffeehouse in London had provided a place where men could meet their friends, drink coffee, smoke, and talk. Here the rising middle class rubbed shoulders with writers and members of the upper classes—and sometimes transacted business. In fact, the great insurance firm of Lloyd's of London drew its name, as well as its origin, from Lloyd's Coffeehouse. By the end of the century several thousand coffeehouses were in existence. Macaulay's description of coffeehouse society (see page 361) presents an interesting picture of this facet of English life.

In literature, changes took place that had begun with Ben Jonson's use of classical models early in the seventeenth century. Love sonnets were replaced by satirical verses aimed at correcting individuals and society. Writing in general became less ornate. With the introduction of literary periodicals, the periodical essay, short and intended for consumption by the middle class, became the vogue. Most of the authors in this unit contributed to these periodicals.

With the reopening of the theaters, drama too underwent several changes. The boy actors who had played female roles in Elizabethan drama were replaced by actresses, although some members of the clergy and upper classes considered acting an unsuitable career for a woman. Accompanying this change was the development of the comedy of manners, or Restoration comedy, such as William Wycherley's *The Country Wife* (1675) and William Congreve's *The Way of the World* (1700). This was a sophisticated type of drama that featured multiple plots involving intrigue and infidelity, and deriving much of its humor from characters who tried to adopt manners suitable to a different station in life. Soon these plays became so scandalous that Restoration comedy became synonymous with licentiousness.

THE MIDDLE YEARS, 1700–1744

Queen Anne, the younger sister of Mary II, ruled from 1702–1714. When she died without an heir, the throne went to George I of the German state of Hanover. George, the great-grandson of James I, had Stuart blood, was a Protestant, and was acceptable to the Parliament, even though he spoke German and spent as much time as he could in Hanover. The same was true of his son, George II, who ruled from 1727 to 1760.

Accompanying the changes in monarchs was a growth in the power of the prime minister and his cabinet until, under the first two Hanoverian kings, the country was in effect ruled

Detail of portrait of Sir Christopher Wren holding the plans of St. Paul's Cathedral, apparently begun by Antonio Verrio and completed by Godfrey Kneller and James Thornhill.

by the ministry. England now had two political parties. The Tories favored royal power and the established Church of England and opposed change. The Whigs favored reforms, progress, and parliamentary rather than royal power. During part of Anne's reign and all of the reigns of George I and George II, the Whigs wielded most of the power. They favored the new mercantile middle class living in London and other cities and therefore fostered trade and contributed to the growth of the cities and international commerce.

During the early years of the century the middle class, which had already begun to merge with the landed gentry through intermarriage and common concerns for wealth and property, moved into a position of social dominance.

Meanwhile, the working class was also growing as jobs opened in construction, in mines, and in factories, where they operated the new power-driven machinery that would bring about the Industrial Revolution. Although their voices began to be heard in the eighteenth century, they actually benefited little from England's new riches.

In London, for example, the inequality in the distribution of wealth was appalling. In the streets the silks and brocades and powdered wigs, the gilded coaches and sedan chairs of the rich moved against a background of rags, filth, stench, and crime. Beaux and belles attended plays at Drury Lane Theater, listened to the new art form, Italian opera, or to the chamber music of George Frideric Handel (best known

"The Arrest" from *A Rake's Progress* by William Hogarth. The Rake, a dissolute young man, is arrested for debts. *Sir John Soane's Museum, London*

for his oratorio *The Messiah*), sipped wine and watched fireworks in the arbors of Vauxhall or Ranelagh Gardens, while thousands lived in poverty. Sir Joshua Reynolds and Thomas Gainsborough turned out elegant portraits of prosperous ladies and gentlemen, while William Hogarth savagely satirized the wealthy and protested against the lot of the poor in paintings and graphic works such as *A Rake's Progress*. For most English people, in fact, the uncertainty of life was such that, as Samuel Johnson said, "He that sees before him to his third dinner, has a long prospect."

While the Enlightenment may have swept Europe, it had little effect on the rights of women or on their education. Women were not gen-

erally educated, and they had limited property rights. Daniel Defoe, far ahead of his time, proposed a method of improving the education of women (see page 372).

The middle class exercised a growing influence on literature. Their new wealth afforded them the luxury of reading for pleasure, and they eagerly bought new works as they appeared. Middle-class readers preferred to read about people like themselves, so tragedies gave way to realistic novels such as Samuel Richardson's *Pamela* (1740) or Henry Fielding's *Tom Jones* (1749).

Literary periodicals now came into their own. Aimed at the middle-class coffeehouse audience, such periodicals as *The Spectator* (1711–1712), published by Richard Steele and Joseph Addison, were written to entertain readers and at the same time improve their morals and manners.

After the Glorious Revolution of 1688, there was an adverse reaction to the moral laxity of the Restoration. By 1700 this reaction was felt in the theater and elsewhere. Richard Steele, also a dramatist and a partner in the Drury Lane Theater, popularized a new type of moral comedy that came to be known as sentimental comedy and helped to make the theater respectable again.

Perhaps the greatest moralist of them all, Jonathan Swift, put his satirical pen to use in exposing and ridiculing individual and social evils of his day. His *A Modest Proposal* (see page 337) portrayed in biting satire the plight of the Irish people; in *Gulliver's Travels* (see page 344) his chief targets were governmental and personal hypocrisy and vice. Without doubt, Swift was the greatest prose satirist of the Age of Reason.

THE LATE YEARS, 1744–1780

By 1744 the Hanoverian line of kings had established itself in England. In 1760 George III, the first of this line to be born in England and to speak English as his first language, became king; he ruled for sixty years, until 1820. The first two Georges had supported the Whig party; George III supported the Tories. He also attempted, largely without success, to regain some of the royal powers that through the years had been assumed by Parliament.

The great man of letters of this period was Samuel Johnson. Besides writing periodical essays, poetry, pamphlets, travel journals, criticism, and one heroic tragedy, Johnson successfully completed three major projects, any one of them a lifetime's work for most people. He compiled the first truly comprehensive English dictionary (see page 391); he edited a complete edition of Shakespeare, including both textual and critical notes; and he wrote *Lives of the Poets*, critical biographies of fifty-two of England's poets (see "The Life of Milton," page 396).

Although many of the ideas and literary modes of the Age of Reason lasted through the eighteenth century, by its second half changes had begun to occur. Thomas Gray was a forerunner of the Romantic Age. So too were his air of gentle melancholy and his interest in wild landscapes, older English, Welsh, and Norse poetry, and the common people.

ELSEWHERE IN THE WORLD

The Enlightenment had its rational counterpart in many countries. In France, for example, there was a similar emphasis on satire in works like Molière's *Tartuffe* (1664), which aroused such opposition from the church that it was banned for years, and Voltaire's *Candide* (1759). At the same time there was an emphasis on social and political philosophy that employed Rationalism to build up what satire tore down. In France, Jean Jacques Rousseau wrote *The Social Contract* (1762), while in England Adam Smith wrote *The Wealth of Nations* (1776). These works were typical of a new spirit. At the same time, in the colonies across the Atlantic Ocean Thomas Paine wrote *Common Sense* (1776), and other patriots were constructing their own philosophical document, *The Declaration of Independence* (1776) that announced the American Revolution.

USING GRAPHIC AIDS
Using the Time Line

Use the time line on page 312 to answer these questions.

1. Who was king of England at the time of the American Revolution?
2. Who was the first monarch of a united England and Scotland?
3. About how long did it take to rebuild St. Paul's Cathedral after the London fire?
4. Pepys kept his diary for almost ten years. What events would he have been able to write about?
5. Review the previous time lines on pages 1, 76, and 156. What percent of the monarchs of England have thus far been women?

Dryden left his mark on the literature of his age and succeeding ages in a number of areas: he wrote successful plays, excellent literary criticism, and clever political satire, and he was a talented translator.

After receiving his B. A. from Trinity College, Cambridge, Dryden settled in London and probably held a minor position in the Cromwell government. An early poem, *Heroic Stanzas on the Death of Cromwell* (1659) was followed a year later by *Astraea Redux*, which celebrates the Restoration of the Stuart line to the throne.

The Restoration was kind to Dryden in many ways. With the reopening of the theaters, Dryden turned to playwriting as a source of income; between 1663 and 1681 he averaged a play a year in production. By 1662 he was sufficiently well known to be elected to the Royal Society, a group founded in 1660 and dedicated to promoting scientific inquiry. All his life he retained an interest in science, which appeared in his poems. He also credited the proceedings of the Royal Society for his clear and accurate prose style. In 1663 Dryden married well, taking for his wife Lady Elizabeth Howard, daughter of the Earl of Berkshire and sister of Sir Robert Howard, with whom Dryden collaborated on a play.

In 1667 Dryden published *Annus Mirabilis*, a poem commemorating three events of the previous year: the end of the plague, the Great Fire of London, and the Dutch War. The next year he was made poet laureate, followed two years later by Historiographer Royal. These court appointments brought him added income. His venture into political satire began in 1681, with the publication of *Absalom and Achitophel*, written after an unsuccessful attempt by Charles's illegitimate son, the Duke of Monmouth, to seize the throne. *Mac Flecknoe* (1682) is a further example of literary satire.

Dryden's life reflected the religious turmoil of the age. Born into a Puritan family, he first espoused the Anglican church; then he became a Catholic upon the accession of King James II. With the Glorious Revolution of 1688 and the coming to power of the Protestant monarchs William and Mary in 1689, he kept his Catholic faith but lost his profitable Court appointments as poet laureate and Historiographer Royal.

Dryden began, in his early sixties, a new and successful career as a translator. His translation of Virgil's *Aeneid*, published in 1697, was extremely popular. In his declining years Dryden, respected as the supreme literary figure of his day, spent much of his time at Will's Coffeehouse, to which younger authors and would-be authors came to listen to his conversation and learn from him. Among these was Alexander Pope (see page 376).

See **HEROIC COUPLET** in the Handbook of Literary Terms, page 909.

from Absalom and Achitophel

This satire was written on the eve of the trial of the Duke of Buckingham (the Zimri of the poem), charged with high treason for attempting to prevent the accession to the throne of the Duke of York, later King James II. Buckingham, one of the leaders of the Whig party, tried unsuccessfully to have Parliament declare the Duke of Monmouth—the Absalom (ab′sə ləm) of the poem—next in line for the throne. The Achitophel (ə chit′ə fel) is the Earl of Shaftesbury, who with Buckingham led the Whigs. Dryden drew these names from the Bible—chiefly 2 Samuel —for the parallels which he found with the existing situation in England.

Of these the false *Achitophel* was first:
A name to all succeeding ages cursed.
For close designs, and crooked counsels fit;
Sagacious, bold, and turbulent of wit:
5 Restless, unfixed in principles and place;
In power unpleased, impatient of disgrace.
A fiery soul, which working out its way,
Fretted the pigmy body to decay:
And o'er informed the tenement of clay.
10 A daring pilot in extremity;
Pleased with the danger, when the waves went
    high
He sought the storms; but for a calm unfit,
Would steer too nigh the sands, to boast his Wit.
Great wits are sure to madness near allied;
15 And thin partitions do their bounds divide:
Else, why should he, with wealth and honour
    blessed,
Refuse his age the needful hours of rest?
Punish a body which he coud not please;
Bankrupt of life, yet prodigal of ease?
20 And all to leave, what with his toil he won,
To that unfeathered, two legged thing, a son. . . .

Portrait of the Duke
of Monmouth after
William Wissing(?)
*National Portrait
Gallery, London*

Some of their chiefs were princes of the land:
In the first rank of these did *Zimri* stand:
A man so various,[1] that he seemed to be
25 Not one, but all mankinds epitome.
Stiff in opinions, always in the wrong;
Was everything by starts, and nothing long:
But, in the course of one revolving moon,
Was chemist, fiddler, statesman, and buffoon:
30 Then all for women, painting, rhyming,
    drinking;
Besides ten thousand freaks that died in thinking.

1. *various*, changeable.

John Dryden

Blest madman, who coud every hour employ,
With something new to wish, or to enjoy!
Railing and praising were his usual themes;
35 And both (to show his judgment) in extremes:
So over violent, or over civil,
That every man, with him, was God or Devil.
In squandering wealth was his peculiar art:
Nothing went unrewarded, but desert.[2]

40 Beggered by fools, whom still[3] he found too late:
He had his jest, and they had his estate.
He laught himself from court, then sought relief
By forming parties, but coud ne'er be chief.

1681

---

2. *desert*, what a person deserves.
3. *still*, always.

from Mac Flecknoe

One of Dryden's most effective satires, *Mac Flecknoe* has as its target
Thomas Shadwell, who earned Dryden's ire by praising *The Rehearsal*, a
play in which Dryden was parodied and ridiculed. Flecknoe was an Irish
poet, notorious for his poor poetry, who died in 1678. Calling Shadwell
the son of Flecknoe (in Gaelic *Mac* means "son of"), Dryden proceeds
to use his cutting wit at Shadwell's expense. By an ironic twist of fate,
the royal appointments Dryden lost seven years later with the accession
of William and Mary went to Shadwell, Dryden's "King of Nonsense."

All human things are subject to decay,
And when fate summons, monarchs must obey.
This Flecknoe found, who, like Augustus,[1] young
Was called to empire, and had governed long;
5 In prose and verse was owned, without dispute,
Through all the realms of Nonsense, absolute.
This agèd prince, now flourishing in peace,
And blessed with issue of a large increase;
Worn out with business, did at length debate
10 To settle the succession of the State;
And, pondering which of all his sons was fit
To reign, and wage immortal war with wit,
Cried: " 'Tis resolved; for nature pleads, that he
Should only rule, who most resembles me.
15 Sh——[2] alone my perfect image bears,
Mature in dullness from his tender years:
Sh—— alone, of all my sons, is he
Who stands confirmed in full stupidity.
The rest to some faint meaning make pretense,
20 But Sh—— never deviates into sense.

Some beams of wit on other souls may fall,
Strike through, and make a lucid interval;
But Sh——'s genuine night admits no ray,
His rising fogs prevail upon the day.
25 Besides, his goodly fabric[3] fills the eye,
And seems designed for thoughtless majesty;
Thoughtless as monarch oaks that shade the plain,
And, spread in solemn state, supinely reign.
Heywood and Shirley[4] were but types[5] of thee,
30 Thou last great prophet of tautology."[6]

1682

---

1. *Augustus*, the first emperor of Rome (27 B.C. to A.D. 14); he became emperor at the age of thirty-six.
2. *Sh*——, Shadwell. Satirists commonly used only the initial or the first two letters of the victim's name.
3. *goodly fabric*, bulky body, a reference to Shadwell's obesity.
4. *Heywood and Shirley*, popular playwrights of the early seventeenth century.
5. *types*, prototypes; prefigurings.
6. *tautology*, needless repetition; redundancy.

satire - a technique that employs wit to ridicule an institution or person

THINK AND DISCUSS

ABSALOM AND ACHITOPHEL

Understanding

1. List the words and phrases used to describe Achitophel.
2. What are Zimri's usual themes (line 34)? To what extent did he employ them?

Analyzing

3. What does Dryden mean by calling Zimri "so various, that he seemed to be/Not one, but all mankinds epitome" (lines 24–25)? Is this a negative or positive quality?
4. Explain in your own words the meaning of line 27. Which other lines give you clues?

Extending

5. Explain the meaning of lines 14–15. Do you think this statement is true?

MAC FLECKNOE

Understanding

1. Who does Flecknoe say should rule?
2. What qualities of Shadwell does Flecknoe list?

Analyzing

3. Does Dryden limit his satire to Shadwell's writing, or does he carry it further? Explain.

Extending

4. Suppose you were Shadwell reading this excerpt. How would you feel about it?
5. Whom do you think Dryden satirizes more bitingly, the Duke of Buckingham or Shadwell? Explain.

APPLYING: Heroic Couplet HT
See Handbook of Literary Terms, p. 909

A **heroic couplet** is a pair of poetic lines in rhyming iambic pentameter. The thought ends, or closes, at the end of the second line, and so the heroic couplet can be thought of as a unit. Because it can say so much in so few words, the heroic couplet is especially effective in satire.

> All human things are subject to decay,
> And when fate summons, monarchs must obey.

1. Copy this couplet on separate paper and mark the *scansion* of the lines, using ′ and ‿ for accented and unaccented syllables.
2. Where in line 2 does a *caesura*, or natural pause, occur?
3. In a heroic couplet, the second line may complete the thought of the first, restate it, expand it, or contrast it. What does the second line do in this example?

COMPOSITION

Reacting to Satire

Assume that you are either Shadwell or the Duke of Buckingham, and write Dryden a letter in which you object to his treatment of you in either poem. You might point out the injustice of his attack and ask him what prompted it; you might also tell him what action you plan to take. Make your letter at least three paragraphs long.

Responding to a Quote

In Dryden's *Original and Progress of Satire* (1693), he says about satirical portraits, "There is still a vast difference between the slovenly butchering of a man and the fineness of a stroke that separates the head from the body and leaves it standing in its place." In a composition of three to five paragraphs, first explain the meaning of this claim, and then discuss how well Dryden adheres to it in these two excerpts.

Pepys (pēps) was born in London and lived there most of his life. He was educated at St. Paul's School and Magdalene College, Cambridge. At twenty-two he married Elizabeth St. Michel, the beautiful but poor daughter of a French Huguenot.

What has given Pepys his literary reputation is his private *Diary*, written in a sort of shorthand code (all 3,012 pages of it), covering a period of nearly ten years, from January 1, 1660, to May 31, 1669. Failing vision caused him to give it up. Evidently Pepys did not intend the *Diary* for anyone's eyes but his own, for he includes in it not only the public events at court and in London, but also his own most private thoughts and actions.

In 1660, the year that Pepys began the *Diary*, he became secretary to his distant cousin Edward Montagu, who as Admiral of the Navy was in charge of bringing King Charles II home from France. Pepys, who was with him, recorded the events in his *Diary*. Soon after, Charles awarded Montagu the title of Earl of Sandwich and Pepys's fortunes rose too. He was made Clerk of the Acts in the Navy Office, a position of considerable honor that included a good salary and a fine, rent-free home.

For the next nine years, Pepys faithfully recorded in code in his *Diary* the events, major and minor, of his life. Since he was active in public affairs, these include much of the history of the age: the return and coronation of Charles II; the hanging of Thomas Harrison, one of the Puritans responsible for executing Charles I; the severe outbreak of plague in 1665, during which most Court officials deserted London; the Great Fire of London in 1666; the reopening of the theaters. In addition, Pepys recorded the daily events of his domestic life in great detail, so that we come to know his wife, his servants, his Navy Office associates, his neighbors, and his many friends. Thus, when we read the *Diary* we derive a twofold enjoyment: first, of history in the making, and then of Pepys's reaction to it.

Readers of Pepys's *Diary* tend to remember him for the more gossipy and personal passages that reveal him as a man rather than as a competent administrator and friend of many of the great of his age. For much of his adult life he held a position equivalent to that of a modern Secretary of the Navy; he was on excellent terms with King Charles II, King James II, and other high-ranking courtiers, as well as with Sir Isaac Newton and other scientists; and he had hosts of friends.

When Pepys died in 1703, his will provided that all his books, papers, and collections were to go to Magdalene College; his *Diary*, set aside thirty-four years earlier, was among those papers. In 1818, the diary of John Evelyn, with whom Pepys had been friendly, was published. The references it made to Pepys aroused interest in him. Pepys's *Diary* was located, but deciphering the shorthand code required three years. In 1825 an abridged version was published. An unabridged, annotated edition is now available.

from The Diary

Samuel Pepys

The portion of Pepys's *Diary* included here deals largely with the Great Fire of London, which started on September 2, 1666, and raged out of control for almost a week. Before it was extinguished, it had destroyed two-thirds of London. More than thirteen thousand houses were burned, plus other buildings, including eighty-nine churches. Miraculously, only six people lost their lives, but 250,000 were homeless, camping out in makeshift tents in the fields adjacent to London. It is difficult to comprehend what the burning of London meant in its day. Pepys helps us to realize some of this through his vivid eyewitness descriptions. One thing, however, he does not tell us, for he did not know it: never again was London paralyzed by the plague, for the fire destroyed the rats that carried the plague as well as the old buildings that harbored them. (See map, page 327.)

eptember 2, 1666 (Lord's day). Some of our maids sitting up late last night to get things ready against our feast today, Jane [Pepys's maid] called us up about three in the morning, to tell us of a great fire they saw in the City.[1] So I rose and slipped on my nightgown, and went to her window; and thought it to be on the backside of Mark Lane at the farthest; but, being unused to such fires as followed, I thought it far enough off; and so went to bed again, and to sleep. About seven rose again to dress myself, and there looked out at the window, and saw the fire not so much as it was, and further off. So to my closet[2] to set things to rights, after yesterday's cleaning. By and by Jane comes and tells me that she hears that above 300 houses have been burned down tonight by the fire we saw, and that it is now burning down all Fish Street, by London Bridge. So I made myself ready presently, and walked to the Tower;[3] and there got up upon one of the high places, Sir J. Robinson's little son going up with me; and there I did see the houses at that end of the bridge all on fire, and an infinite great fire on this and the other side the end of the bridge; which, among other people, did trouble me for poor little Michell and our Sarah on the bridge.[4] So down with my heart full of trouble, to the Lieutenant of the Tower, who tells me that it begun this morning in the King's baker's house in Pudding Lane, and that it hath burned St. Magnus's Church and most part of Fish Street already. So I down to the waterside, and there got a boat,[5] and through bridge and there saw a lamentable fire. Poor Michell's house, as far as the Old Swan, already burned that way, and the fire running further, that, in a very little time, it got as far as the Steelyard,[6] while I was there. Everybody endeavoring to remove their goods, and flinging into the river, or bringing them into lighters[7] that

---

1. *the City*, the area within the medieval walls of London; the business district.
2. *closet*, study.
3. *Tower*, the Tower of London, an ancient fort on the Thames.
4. *on the bridge*. In Pepys's time, London Bridge was covered with houses and shops.
5. *boat*. Small boats rowed by "watermen" were a common form of transportation in the city.
6. *the Steelyard*. A German trading area established west of London Bridge on the north side of the Thames.
7. *lighters*, small, flat-bottomed boats.

lay off; poor people staying in their houses as long as till the very fire touched them, and then running into boats, or clambering from one pair of stairs, by the waterside, to another. And, among other things, the poor pigeons, I perceive, were loath to leave their houses, but hovered about the windows and balconies, till some of them burned their wings, and fell down.

Having stayed, and in an hour's time seen the fire rage every way; and nobody, to my sight, endeavoring to quench it, but to remove their goods, and leave all to the fire, and having seen it get as far as the Steelyard, and the wind mighty high, and driving it into the city: and everything, after so long a drought, proving combustible, even the very stones of churches; and, among other things, the poor steeple by which pretty Mrs.——lives, and whereof my old schoolfellow Elborough is parson, taken fire in the very top, and there burned till it fell down; I to Whitehall, with a gentleman with me who desired to go off from the Tower, to see the fire, in my boat; to Whitehall,[8] and there up to the King's closet in the Chapel, where people come about me, and I did give them an account dismayed them all, and word was carried into the King. So I was called for, and did tell the King and Duke of York what I saw; and, that unless his Majesty did command houses to be pulled down, nothing could stop the fire. They seemed much troubled, and the King commanded me to go to my Lord Mayor[9] from him, and command him to spare no houses, but to pull down before the fire every way. The Duke of York bid me tell him, that if he would have any more soldiers, he shall; and so did my Lord Arlington afterwards, as a great secret. Here meeting with Captain Cocke, I in his coach, which he lent me, and Creed with me to Paul's;[10] and there walked along Watling Street, as well as I could, every creature coming away loaden with goods to save, and, here and there, sick people carried away in beds. Extraordinary good goods carried in carts and on backs. At last met my Lord Mayor in Canning Street, like a man spent, with a handkerchief about his neck. To the King's message, he cried like a fainting woman,

"Lord! what can I do? I am spent; people will not obey me. I have been pulling down houses; but the fire overtakes us faster than we can do it." That he needed no more soldiers; and that, for himself, he must go and refresh himself, having been up all night. So he left me, and I him, and walked home, seeing people all almost distracted, and no manner of means used to quench the fire. The houses, too, so very thick thereabouts, and full of matter for burning, as pitch and tar, in Thames Street; and warehouses of oil, and wines, and brandy, and other things. Here I saw Mr. Isaake Houblon, that handsome man, prettily dressed and dirty at his door at Dowgate, receiving some of his brothers' things, whose houses were on fire; and, as he says, have been removed twice already; and he doubts (as it soon proved) that they must be, in a little time, removed from his house also, which was a sad consideration. And to see the churches all filling with goods by people who themselves should have been quietly there at this time.

By this time, it was about twelve o'clock; and so home, and there find my guests, which was Mr. Wood and his wife Barbary Shelden, and also Mr. Moone; she mighty fine, and her husband, for aught I see, a likely man. But Mr. Moone's design and mine, which was to look over my closet, and please him with the sight thereof, which he hath long desired, was wholly disappointed; for we were in great trouble and disturbance at this fire, not knowing what to think of it. However, we had an extraordinary good dinner, and as merry as at this time we could be.

While at dinner, Mrs. Batelier come to enquire after Mr. Woolfe and Stanes (who, it seems, are related to them) whose houses in Fish Street are all burned, and they in a sad condition. She would not stay in the fright.

As soon as dined, I and Moone away, and walked through the City, the streets full of nothing

---

8. **Whitehall,** king's residence and offices in London, upriver from the Tower and the fire.
9. **Lord Mayor,** of London.
10. **Paul's.** Pepys travels back towards the fire, to one of the largest churches in London, which the fire is soon to destroy.

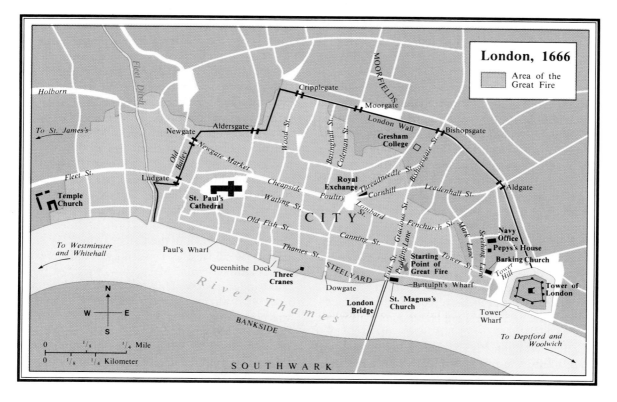

London, 1666

but people and horses and carts loaden with goods, ready to run over one another, and removing goods from one burned house to another. They now removing out of Canning Street, which received goods in the morning, into Lombard Street, and further; and among others, I now saw my little goldsmith Stokes receiving some friend's goods, whose house itself was burned the day after. We parted at Paul's; he home, and I to Paul's Wharf, where I had appointed a boat to attend me, and took in Mr. Carcasse and his brother, whom I met in the street, and carried them below and above bridge too and again to see the fire, which was now got further, both below and above, and no likelihood of stopping it. Met with the King and Duke of York in their barge, and with them to Queenhithe, and there called Sir Richard Browne to them. Their order was only to pull down houses apace, and so below bridge at the waterside; but little was or could be done, the fire coming upon them so fast. Good hopes there was of stopping it at the Three Cranes above, and at Buttulph's Wharf below bridge, if care be used; but the wind carries it into the city, so as we know not, by the waterside, what it do there. River full of lighters and boats taking in goods, and good goods swimming in the water; and only I observed that hardly one lighter or boat in three that had the goods of a house in, but there was a pair of virginals[11] in it. Having seen as much as I could now, I away to Whitehall by appointment, and there walked to St. James's Park; and there met my wife, and Creed, and Wood, and his wife, and walked to my boat; and there upon the water again, and to the fire up and down, it still increasing, and the wind great. So near the fire as we could for smoke; and all over the Thames, with one's face in the wind, you were almost burned with a shower of fire-drops. This is very true; so as houses were burned by these drops and flakes of fire, three or four, nay,

---

11. *virginals,* small legless pianos.

five or six houses, one from another. When we could endure no more upon the water, we to a little ale house on the Bankside, over against the Three Cranes, and there stayed till it was dark almost and saw the fire grow; and, as it grew darker, appeared more and more; and in corners and upon steeples, and between churches and houses, as far as we could see up the hill of the city, in a most horrid, malicious, bloody flame, not like the fine flame of an ordinary fire. Barbary and her husband away before us. We stayed till, it being darkish, we saw the fire as only one entire arch of fire from this to the other side the bridge, and in a bow up the hill for an arch of above a mile long; it made me weep to see it. The churches, houses, and all on fire, and flaming at once; and a horrid noise the flames made, and the cracking of houses at their ruin. So home with a sad heart, and there find everybody discoursing and lamenting the fire; and poor Tom Hater come with some few of his goods saved out of his house, which was burned upon Fish Street Hill. I invited him to lie at my house, and did receive his goods; but was deceived in his lying there, the news coming every moment of the growth of the fire; so as we were forced to begin to pack up our own goods, and prepare for their removal; and did by moonshine, it being brave, dry, and moonshine and warm weather, carry much of my goods into the garden; and Mr. Hater and I did remove my money and iron chests into my cellar, as thinking that the safest place. And got my bags of gold into my office, ready to carry away, and my chief papers of accounts also there, and my tallies into a box by themselves. So great was our fear, as Sir W. Batten hath carts come out of the country to fetch away his goods this night. We did put Mr. Hater, poor man! to bed a little; but he got but very little rest, so much noise being in my house, taking down of goods.

September 3. About four o'clock in the morning, my Lady Batten sent me a cart to carry away all my money and plate and best things to Sir W. Rider's at Bednall Green; which I did, riding myself in my nightgown in the cart; and, Lord! to see how the streets and the highways are crowded with people, running and riding and getting of carts at any rate to fetch away things. I find Sir W. Rider tired with being called up all night and receiving things from several friends. His house full of goods, and much of Sir W. Batten and Sir W. Penn's. I am eased at my heart to have my treasure so well secured. Then home with much ado to find a way. Nor any sleep all this night to me nor my poor wife. But then, and all this day, she and I and all my people[12] laboring to get away the rest of our things, and did get Mr. Tooker to get me a lighter to take them in, and we did carry them (myself some) over Tower Hill, which was by this time full of people's goods, bringing their goods thither. And down to the lighter, which lay at the next quay above the Towerdock. And here was my neighbor's wife, Mrs. ——, with her pretty child and some few of her things, which I did willingly give way to be saved with mine. But there was no passing with anything through the postern, the crowd was so great. At night, lay down a little upon a quilt of W. Hewer in the office (all my own things being packed up or gone); and after me, my poor wife did the like—we having fed upon the remains of yesterday's dinner, having no fire nor dishes, nor any opportunity of dressing anything.

September 4. Up by break of day to get away the remainder of my things, which I did by a lighter at the Iron Gate; and my hands so few, that it was the afternoon before we could get them all away.

Sir W. Penn and I to Tower Street, and there met the fire burning three or four doors beyond Mr. Howells; whose goods, poor man (his trays and dishes, shovels etc., were flung all along Tower Street in the kennels,[13] and people working therewith from one end to the other), the fire coming on in that narrow street, on both sides, with infinite fury. Sir W. Batten, not knowing how to remove his wine, did dig a pit in the garden and laid it in there; and I took the opportunity of laying all the papers of my office that I could not otherwise dispose of. And in the evening Sir W. Penn and I did dig another and put our wine in

---

12. *my people*, Pepys's servants.
13. *kennels*, ditch down the center of the road.

it, and I my Parmesan cheese as well as my wine and some other things.

This night Mrs. Turner, who, poor woman, was removing her goods all this day—good goods, into the garden, and knew not how to dispose of them—and her husband supped with my wife and I at night in the office, upon a shoulder of mutton from the cook's, without any napkin or anything, in a sad manner but were merry. Only, now and then walking into the garden and saw how horridly the sky looks, all on a fire in the night, was enough to put us out of our wits; and indeed it was extremely dreadful, for it looks just as if it was at us, and the whole heaven on fire. I after supper walked in the dark down to Tower Street, and there saw it all on fire at the Trinity house on that side and the Dolphin Tavern on this side, which was very near us—and the fire with extraordinary vehemence. Now begins the practice of blowing up of houses in Tower Street, those next the Tower, which at first did frighten people more than anything; but it stopped the fire where it was done—it bringing down the houses to the ground in the same places they stood, and then it was easy to quench what little fire was in it, though it kindled nothing almost. W. Hewer this day went to see how his mother did, and comes late home, but telling us how he hath been forced to remove her to Islington, her house in Pye Corner being burned. So that it is got so far that way and all the Old Bailey, and was running down to Fleet Street. And Paul's is burned, and all Cheapside. I wrote to my father this night; but the posthouse[14] being burned, the letter could not go.

September 5. I lay down in the office again upon W. Hewer's quilt, being mighty weary, and sore in my feet with going till I was hardly able to stand. About two in the morning my wife calls me up, and tells me of new cries of "Fire!"—it being come to Barking Church, which is the bottom of our land. I up; and finding it so, resolved presently to take her away, and did, and took my gold (which was about £2350). W. Hewer, and Jane down by Proundy's boat to Woolwich; but, Lord! what a sad sight it was by moonlight, to see the whole city almost on fire, that you might see it plain at

John Keeling's fire engine. Fire-fighting equipment lacked efficient pumps and flexible hose.

Woolwich, as if you were by it. There, when I come, I find the gates[15] shut, but no guard kept at all; which troubled me, because of discourse now begun, that there is plot in it,[16] and that the French had done it. I got the gates open, and to Mr. Shelden's, where I locked up my gold, and charged my wife and W. Hewer never to leave the room without one of them in it, night or day. So back again, by the way seeing my goods well in the lighters at Deptford, and watched well by people. Home, and whereas I expected to have seen our house on fire, it being now about seven o'clock, it was not. But to the fire, and there find greater hopes than I expected; for my confidence of finding our office on fire was such, that I durst not ask anybody how it was with us, till I come and saw it not burned. But, going to the fire, I find, by the blowing up of houses, and the great help

14. *posthouse,* post office.
15. *gates,* to the dockyard.
16. *plot in it,* i.e., that the fire has been deliberately set, according to some plot.

given by the workmen out of the King's yards, sent up by Sir W. Penn, there is a good stop given to it, as well as at Mark Lane end as ours; it having only burned the dial of Barking Church, and part of the porch, and was there quenched. I up to the top of Barking steeple, and there saw the saddest sight of desolation that I ever saw; everywhere great fires, oil-cellars, and brimstone, and other things burning. I became afeard to stay there long, and therefore down again as fast as I could, the fire being spread as far as I could see it; and to Sir W. Penn's, and there eat a piece of cold meat, having eaten nothing since Sunday, but the remains of Sunday's dinner. Here I met with Mr. Young and Whistler; and, having removed all my things, and received good hopes that the fire at our end is stopped, they and I walked into the town, and find Fenchurch Street, Gracious Street, and Lombard Street all in dust. The Exchange[17] a sad sight, nothing standing there, of all the statues or pillars, but Sir Thomas Gresham's picture in the corner. Walked into Moorfields, our feet ready to burn, walking through the town among the hot coals, and find that full of people, and poor wretches carrying their goods there, and everybody keeping his goods together by themselves; and a great blessing it is to them that it is fair weather for them to keep abroad night and day; drank there, and paid twopence for a plain penny loaf. Thence homeward, having passed through Cheapside, and Newgate Market, all burned; and seen Anthony Joyce's house in fire; and took up, which I keep by me, a piece of glass of Mercer's Chapel in the street, where much more was, so melted and buckled with the heat of the fire like parchment. I also did see a poor cat taken out of a hole in a chimney, joining to the wall of the Exchange, with the hair all burned off the body, and yet alive. So home at night, and find there good hopes of saving our office; but great endeavors of watching all night, and having men ready; and so we lodged them in the office, and had drink and bread and cheese for them. And I lay down and slept a good night about midnight; though, when I rose, I heard that there had been a great alarm of French and Dutch[18] being risen, which

proved nothing. But it is a strange thing to see how long this time did look since Sunday, having been always full of variety of actions, and little sleep, that it looked like a week or more, and I had forgot almost the day of the week.

September 6. Up about five o'clock, and there met Mr. Gawden at the gate of the office (I intending to go out, as I used every now and then to do, to see how the fire is) to call our men to Bishopsgate, where no fire had yet been near, and there is now one broke out—which did give great grounds to people, and to me too, to think that there is some kind of plot in this (on which many by this time have been taken, and it hath been dangerous for any stranger to walk in the streets); but I went with the men and we did put it out in a little time, so that that was well again. It was pretty to see how hard the women did work in the kennels sweeping of water; but then they would scold for drink and be as drunk as devils. I saw good butts of sugar broke open in the street, and people go and take handfuls out and put into beer and drink it. And now all being pretty well, I took boat and over to Southwark, and took boat on the other side the bridge and so to Westminster, thinking to shift myself,[19] being all in dirt from top to bottom. But could not there find any place to buy a shirt or pair of gloves, Westminster Hall being full of people's goods—those in Westminster having removed all their goods, and the Exchequer money put into vessels to carry to Nonsuch.[20] But to the Swan, and there was trimmed. And then to Whitehall, but saw nobody, and so home. A sad sight to see how the River looks—no houses nor church near it to the Temple—where it stopped. At home did go with Sir W. Batten and our neighbor Knightly (who, with one more, was the only man of any fashion left in all the neighborhood hereabouts, they all removing their goods and leaving their houses to the mercy of the fire) to Sir R. Ford's,

---

17. *the Exchange,* a large building in which merchants met to discuss business; built in 1576 by Sir Thomas Gresham.
18. *French and Dutch,* England's enemies at the time.
19. *shift myself,* change clothes.
20. *Nonsuch,* a royal palace in Surrey.

The flight from the Great Fire in London, by an anonymous Dutch artist. circa 1666.
Museum of London

and there dined, in an earthen platter a fried breast of mutton, a great many of us. But very merry; and indeed as good a meal, though as ugly a one, as ever I had in my life. Thence down to Deptford, and there with great satisfaction landed all my goods at Sir G. Carteret's, safe, and nothing missed I could see, or hurt. This being done to my great content, I home; and to Sir W. Batten's, and there with Sir R. Ford, Mr. Knightly, and one Withers, a professed lying rogue, supped well; and mighty merry and our fears over. From them to the office and there slept, with the office full of laborers, who talked and slept and walked all night long there. But strange it was to see Clothworkers Hall on fire these three days and nights in one body of Flame—it being the cellar, full of Oil.

September 7. Up by five o'clock and, blessed be God, find all well, and by water to Paul's Wharf. Walked thence and saw all the town burned, and a miserable sight of Paul's church, with all the roofs fallen and the body of the choir fallen into St. Faith's[21]—Paul's school also—Ludgate—Fleet Street—my father's house, and the church, and a good part of the Temple the like. So to Creeds lodging near the New Exchange, and there find him laid down upon a bed—the house all

---

21. *St. Faith's*, a chapel under St. Paul's Cathedral.

unfurnished, there being fears of the fire's coming to them. There borrowed a shirt of him—and washed. To Sir W. Coventry at St. James's, who lay without Curtains, having removed all his goods—as the King at Whitehall and everybody had done and was doing. He hopes we shall have no public distractions upon this fire, which is what everybody fears—because of the talk of the French having a hand in it. And it is a proper time for discontents—but all men's minds are full of care to protect themselves and save their goods. The militia is in arms everywhere.

This day our merchants first met at Gresham College, which by proclamation is to be their Exchange. Strange to hear what is bid for houses all up and down here—a friend of Sir W. Riders having £150 for what he used to let for £40/per annum. Much dispute where the Custom House shall be; thereby the growth of the City again to be foreseen. My Lord Treasurer, they say, and others, would have it at the other end of the town. I home late to Sir W. Penn, who did give me a bed—but without curtains or hangings, all being down. So here I went the first time into a naked bed, only my drawers on—and did sleep pretty well; but still, both sleeping and waking, had a fear of fire in my heart, that I took little rest.

1666   1825

THINK AND DISCUSS
Understanding
1. Which episodes about the fire stand out clearest in your mind? Why?
2. Choose one episode and use the map on page 327 to follow Pepy's travels as he reports them.

Analyzing
3. Pepy's *Diary* is important for what it tells of historical events as well as for its **characterization** of Pepys and other historical figures. From this excerpt, what can you tell about Pepys's everyday home life in normal times?
4. During the fire, how does Pepys conduct himself as a public official, husband, and friend?
5. How do the King and the Duke of York seem to feel about Pepys?
6. What do Sir William Penn and Pepys's other friends and neighbors think of him?

Extending
7. Which did you enjoy more, the historical episodes or what Pepys told about himself? Explain.
8. What major differences do you note in comparing the society Pepys describes to society today?

COMPOSITION
Describing the Fire
Write a human-interest story three to five paragraphs long in which you describe the fire as vividly as possible for readers of a newspaper in another city. First look at the picture of the fire on page 331 and review what Pepys says about it. Then use your imagination and place yourself at a vantage point from which you can see the fire. Present your overall impression, and then describe how the fire looks, smells, sounds, and feels, and how it progresses from building to building.

Characterizing Pepys
Write a composition three to five paragraphs long for someone who has not read Pepys's *Diary* in which you characterize Pepys from what he reveals about himself. Is he brave or cowardly, sensitive or insensitive, considerate or inconsiderate? How does he act toward his wife? toward the King and Duke of York? toward friends and servants? Use details and quotes from the *Diary* to support your statements and conclude with your overall impression of him.

BIOGRAPHY

Jonathan Swift
1667–1745

Born into an age that saw satire as one means of improving the human condition, Swift became England's greatest prose satirist. Of his satire Swift wrote to poet Alexander Pope, "the chief end I propose to myself in all my labors is to vex the world rather than divert it."

Although his parents were English, Swift was born in Ireland, and circumstances compelled him to spend most of his life there, though he really wanted to live in or near London. His father died before his birth. Swift's uncle undertook his education, putting him in a boarding school in Kilkenny when he was six; at fifteen he went to Trinity College, Dublin.

Leaving Ireland, Swift went to work as secretary to a distant relative, Sir William Temple, at Moor Park in England. As part of his duties, he tutored Esther Johnson, Temple's ward, then only eight years old. She later became the "Stella" of his letters and poems. Temple died in 1699, leaving one thousand pounds each to Swift and Esther.

Swift had earlier been ordained an Anglican priest, and now he returned again to Ireland as domestic chaplain to Lord Berkeley, Lord Justice of Ireland. Soon Esther and Rebecca Dingley, her companion, followed him. In 1700 he was given the parish of Laracor, near Dublin. For almost ten years, though officially he resided in Ireland, he spent a great deal of time in England, becoming friendly with Addison, Steele, and other authors.

After becoming embroiled in English politics, Swift changed his party from Whig to Tory in 1710, taking over the editorship of the *Examiner*, the official publication of the Tories. From 1710 to 1713, while he was in England, Swift wrote playfully affectionate letters, sometimes two a day, to Stella (Esther) in Dublin. After his death these were published as *Journal to Stella*. In 1713 he was named Dean of St. Patrick's Cathedral, Dublin, a great disappointment to him, for he had been hoping to receive a church in England.

When, in 1714, the Tories lost power, Swift retired to Dublin. Taking an increasing interest in Irish problems, in 1724 he published the *Drapier's Letters*, a series of satirical letters against a projected English scheme to debase the Irish coinage. They so incensed the English government that an award of three hundred pounds was offered for their author; no one revealed Swift's identity.

Gulliver's Travels, Swift's masterpiece on which he had worked for a number of years, was published anonymously in 1726 and immediately became a best seller and the talk of England. Swift's last major publication, probably his bitterest piece of satire, was his *Modest Proposal* (1729).

For most of his adult life, Swift had suffered from an inner ear disorder that caused dizziness and nausea and impaired his hearing. In or before 1727 he was totally deaf. About 1740 his mental faculties began to fail, and in 1742 he was declared of unsound mind. He died in 1745 and was buried in St. Patrick's Cathedral in Dublin.

HT See SATIRE in the Handbook of Literary Terms, page 923.

A Satirical Elegy on the Death of a Late Famous General

Jonathan Swift

At the height of his success as a writer of political pamphlets, Swift had in 1711 attacked the most celebrated and popular general in the British army, the Duke of Marlborough. While granting his great military skill, Swift accused the duke of prolonging the War of the Spanish Succession to make money for himself and several other prominent Whigs. Shortly thereafter Marlborough was dismissed. When he died (June 16, 1722), Swift wrote the following poem. It is perhaps just as well that the poem was not published until 1764, nineteen years after Swift's death.

His Grace! impossible! what, dead!
Of old age, too, and in his bed!
And could that Mighty Warrior fall?
And so inglorious, after all!
5 Well, since he's gone, no matter how,
The last loud trump[1] must wake him now;
And, trust me, as the noise grows stronger,
He'd wish to sleep a little longer.
And could he be indeed so old
10 As by the newspapers we're told?
Threescore, I think, is pretty high;
'Twas time in conscience he should die.
This world he cumbered long enough;
He burnt his candle to the snuff;
15 And that's the reason, some folks think,
He left behind so great a stink.[2]
Behold his funeral appears,
Nor widow's sighs, nor orphan's tears,
Wont[3] at such times each heart to pierce,
20 Attend the progress of his hearse.
But what of that, his friends may say,
He had those honors in his day.
True to his profit and his pride,
He made them weep before he died.

25 Come hither, all ye empty things,
Ye bubbles raised by breath of kings;
Who float upon the tide of state,
Come hither, and behold your fate.
Let Pride be taught by this rebuke,
30 How very mean a thing's a Duke;
From all his ill-got honors flung,
Turned to the dirt from whence he sprung.

1722   **1764**

The Duke of Marlborough marching into Germany. Detail from a Queen Anne playing card by J. Spofforth.

1. *trump*, trumpet signaling the Last Judgment.
2. *stink*. When a candle burned down all the way, its smoldering wick had a foul smell.
3. *wont*, accustomed.

A Description of a City Shower

Jonathan Swift

This poem was published in the *Tatler*, a literary periodical, on October 17, 1710. Swift's description is geographically accurate. The torrents of rainwater flowed from St. Sepulchre's Church in Newgate (St. Pulchre's, line 58) and from Smithfield Market, London's great cattle and beef market where many butchers had their stalls (see line 61), meeting and flowing down Snow Hill and into the Holborn Conduit, then into the Fleet Ditch, an open and smelly sewer, at Holborn Bridge.

Careful observers may foretell the hour
(By sure prognostics) when to dread a shower:
While rain depends,[1] the pensive cat gives o'er
Her frolics, and pursues her tail no more.
5 Returning home at night, you'll find the sink[2]
Strike your offended sense with double stink.
If you be wise, then go not far to dine;
You'll spend in coach hire more than save in
      wine.
A coming shower your shooting corns presage,
10 Old achès throb, your hollow tooth will rage.
Sauntering in coffeehouse is Dulman seen;
He damns the climate and complains of spleen.[3]
    Meanwhile the South, rising with dabbled
      wings,
A sable cloud athwart the welkin[4] flings,
15 That swilled more liquor than it could contain,
And, like a drunkard, gives it up again.
Brisk Susan[5] whips her linen from the rope,
While the first drizzling shower is borne aslope:
Such is that sprinkling which some careless
      quean[6]
20 Flirts on you from her mop, but not so clean:
You fly, invoke the gods; then turning, stop
To rail; she singing, still whirls on her mop.
Not yet the dust had shunned the unequal
      strife,
But, aided by the wind, fought still for life,
25 And wafted with its foe by violent gust,
'Twas doubtful which was rain and which
      was dust.

A cartoon by Isaac Cruikshank. 1797

1. *depends*, literally, hangs overhead; i.e., is imminent.
2. *sink*, sewer.
3. *Dulman . . . spleen.* Dulman (dull man) describes a type. Spleen (melancholy) was commonly attributed to rainy weather.
4. *welkin*, sky.
5. *Susan*, a servant.
6. *quean*, wench.

Ah! where must needy poet seek for aid,
When dust and rain at once his coat invade?
Sole coat, where dust cemented by the rain
30 Erects the nap, and leaves a mingled stain.
    Now in contiguous drops the flood comes
        down,
Threatening with deluge this devoted[7] town.
To shops in crowds the daggled[8] females fly,
Pretend to cheapen[9] goods, but nothing buy.
35 The Templar[10] spruce, while every spout's
        abroach,
Stays till 'tis fair, yet seems to call a coach.
The tucked-up sempstress walks with hasty
        strides,
While streams run down her oiled umbrella's
        sides.
Here various kinds, by various fortunes led,
40 Commence acquaintance underneath a shed.
Triumphant Tories and desponding Whigs[11]
Forget their feuds, and join to save their wigs.
Boxed in a chair[12] the beau impatient sits,
While spouts run clattering o'er the roof by fits,
45 And ever and anon with frightful din
The leather[13] sounds; he trembles from within.
So when Troy chairmen bore the wooden
        steed,[14]
Pregnant with Greeks impatient to be freed
(Those bully Greeks, who, as the moderns do,
50 Instead of paying chairmen, run them
        through),[15]
Laocoön[16] struck the outside with his spear,
And each imprisoned hero quaked for fear.
    Now from all parts the swelling kennels[17]
        flow,

And bear their trophies with them as they go:
55 Filth of all hues and odors seem to tell
What street they sailed from, by their sight
        and smell.
They, as each torrent drives with rapid force,
From Smithfield or St. Pulchre's shape their
        course,
And in huge confluence joined at Snow Hill
        ridge,
60 Fall from the conduit prone to Holborn Bridge.
Sweepings from butchers' stalls, dung, guts,
        and blood,
Drowned puppies, stinking sprats,[18] all
        drenched in mud,
Dead cats, and turnip tops, come tumbling
        down the flood.

1710

---

7. *devoted*, doomed.
8. *daggled*, mud-spattered.
9. *cheapen*, bargain over.
10. *Templar*, law student.
11. *Tories...Whigs*, members of the two leading political parties. (See page 317.) The Tories had just won power.
12. *chair*, sedan chair, an enclosed seat carried on poles by two men. It was a common form of city transportation for the rich.
13. *leather*, roof of the sedan chair.
14. *Troy chairmen . . . steed*, humorous allusion to the Trojan horse, a hollow wooden image that the Greeks used to sneak some hidden warriors into Troy.
15. *run them through*, with swords.
16. *Laocoön* (lā ok′ō on′) Trojan priest who sensed the Greek plot and struck the Trojan horse with his spear. His comrades ignored his warning.
17. *kennels*, street gutters.
18. *sprats*, herrings.

THINK AND DISCUSS
A SATIRICAL ELEGY . . .
Understanding
1. From the exclamations and the questions in the first few lines, what appears to have happened just before the poem begins?

Analyzing
2. What is **ironic** about the General's having died "in his bed"?
3. What is the General accused of in the poem?
4. Why might the General prefer to sleep through the Last Judgment (lines 7–8)?
5. To whom or what is the **apostrophe** in lines

25–33 addressed? What does this suggest about the General?

APPLYING: Satire HT
See Handbook of Literary Terms, p. 923

Satire is the technique that employs wit to ridicule a social institution or human foible, with the intention to inspire reform. The satirist often makes use of **irony** and sarcasm.

1. What is Swift satirizing in lines 1–2?
2. Where in the poem does Swift satirize the General's extending the War of Spanish Succession, with the result that many men were killed unnecessarily?
3. Does Swift make greater use of irony or of sarcasm in this poem? Explain.
4. What elements of an **elegy** does this poem actually contain? What is Swift's purpose in calling it an elegy?
5. Is Swift's intention "to inspire reform"? If so, of whom or what?

THINK AND DISCUSS
A DESCRIPTION OF A CITY SHOWER
Understanding
1. The four verse paragraphs (beginning with lines 1, 13, 31, and 53) describe different phases of the shower. What does each describe?

Analyzing
2. Explain the satire in the following passages: the needy poet (lines 27–30), the daggled females (lines 33–34), the Templar (lines 35–36), and the beau (lines 43–46).

Extending
3. Swift lived in London whenever he could. Does this poem suggest why? Explain.

COMPOSITION
Satirizing Your Community
Choose as your topic some kind of inclement weather: a city shower, an early snowstorm, an extremely windy day, an extended heat wave, and so on. Describe the people you would see and how they react. Try, as Swift did with Dulman, to give them appropriate names. If you wish, try writing in heroic couplets.

Analyzing Swift's Satire
Choose either "A Satirical Elegy . . ." or "A Description of a City Shower" and write a paper for your school literary magazine analyzing Swift's use of satire. Among other things, you might consider the target of his satire, how emotionally involved Swift is, and his use of sarcasm or irony.

HT Review IRONY in the Handbook of Literary Terms, page 912.

A Modest Proposal — Jonathan Swift

verbal irony → the way thing are said & how they should be.

For Preventing the Children of Poor People in Ireland from Being a Burden to Their Parents or Country, and for Making Them Beneficial to the Public

Ireland was ruled by England, and English landlords received all the revenues from the island without any return to the Irish. Apalled by the poverty and deplorable conditions, Swift wrote *A Modest Proposal*, in which he pretends to be a "projector," an expert or social planner, who has a scheme to solve the problem of poverty in Ireland.

Irony → the contrast between what is expected or what appears to be and what actually is

It is a melancholy object to those who walk through this great town,[1] or travel in the country, when they see the streets, the roads, and cabin doors crowded with beggars of the female sex, followed by three, four, or six children, all in rags and importuning every passenger for an alms. These mothers, instead of being able to work for their honest livelihood, are forced to employ all their time in strolling to beg sustenance for their helpless infants; who as they grow up either turn thieves, for want of work, or leave their dear native country to fight for the Pretender[2] in Spain, or sell themselves to the Barbados.[3]

I think it is agreed by all parties that this prodigious number of children in the arms, or on the backs, or at the heels of their mothers, and frequently of their fathers, is, in the present deplorable state of the kingdom, a very great additional grievance; and therefore whoever could find out a fair, cheap, and easy method of making these children sound, useful members of the commonwealth would deserve so well of the public as to have his statue set up for a preserver of the nation.

But my intention is very far from being confined to provide only for the children of professed beggars: it is of a much greater extent and shall take in the whole number of infants at a certain age who are born of parents in effect as little able to support them as those who demand our charity in the streets.

As to my own part, having turned my thoughts for many years upon this important subject and maturely weighed the several schemes of other projectors, I have always found them grossly mistaken in their computation. It is true, a child just dropped from its dam may be supported by her milk for a solar year, with little other nourishment: at most not above the value of two shillings, which the mother may certainly get, or the value in scraps, by her lawful occupation of begging; and it is exactly at one year old that I propose to provide for them in such a manner, as, instead of being a charge upon their parents or the parish, or wanting food and raiment for the rest of their lives, they shall, on the contrary, contribute to the feeding and partly to the clothing of many thousands.

There is likewise another great advantage in my scheme, that it will prevent those voluntary abortions and that horrid practice of women murdering their bastard children, alas! too frequent among us, sacrificing the poor innocent babes, I doubt more to avoid the expense than the shame, which would move tears and pity in the most savage and inhuman breast.

The number of souls in this kingdom being usually reckoned one million and a half, of these I calculate there may be about two hundred thousand couple whose wives are breeders; from which number I subtract thirty thousand couple, who are able to maintain their own children (although I apprehend there cannot be so many, under the present distresses of the kingdom), but this being granted, there will remain an hundred and seventy thousand breeders. I again subtract fifty thousand for those women who miscarry, or whose children die by accident or disease within the year. There only remain one hundred and twenty thousand children of poor parents annually born. The question therefore is, How this number shall be reared and provided for? which, as I have already said, under the present situation of affairs, is utterly impossible by all the methods hitherto proposed. For we can neither employ them in handicraft or agriculture; we neither build houses (I mean in the country) nor cultivate land: they can very seldom pick up a livelihood by stealing till they arrive at six years old, except where they are of towardly[4] parts; although I confess they learn the rudiments much earlier; during which

---

1. *this great town*, Dublin.
2. *the Pretender*, James Stuart (1688–1766), son of King James II, "pretender" or claimant to the throne that his father had lost in the Revolution of 1688. He was Catholic, and Ireland was loyal to him.
3. *sell . . . Barbados*. Because of extreme poverty, many of the Irish bound or "sold" themselves to obtain passage to the West Indies or other British possessions in North America. They agreed to work for their new masters, usually planters, for a specified number of years.
4. *towardly*, dutiful; easily managed.

time they can, however, be properly looked upon only as probationers; as I have been informed by a principal gentleman in the county of Cavan, who protested to me that he never knew above one or two instances under the age of six, even in a part of the kingdom so renowned for the quickest proficiency in that art.

I am assured by our merchants that a boy or a girl before twelve years old is no salable commodity; and even when they come to this age they will not yield above three pounds, or three pounds and half a crown at most, on the exchange; which cannot turn to account either to the parents or kingdom, the change of nutriment and rags having been at least four times that value.

I shall now therefore humbly propose my own thoughts, which I hope will not be liable to the least objection.

I have been assured by a very knowing American of my acquaintance in London that a young healthy child well nursed is at a year old a most delicious, nourishing, and wholesome food, whether stewed, roasted, baked, or boiled; and I make no doubt that it will equally serve in a fricassee or a ragout.[5]

I do therefore humbly offer it to public consideration that of the hundred and twenty thousand children already computed, twenty thousand may be reserved for breed, whereof only one-fourth part to be males; which is more than we allow to sheep, black cattle, or swine; and my reason is that these children are seldom the fruits of marriage, a circumstance not much regarded by our savages; therefore one male will be sufficient to serve four females. That the remaining hundred thousand may, at a year old, be offered in sale to the persons of quality and fortune through the kingdom; always advising the mother to let them suck plentifully in the last month, so as to render them plump and fat for a good table. A child will make two dishes at an entertainment for friends; and when the family dines alone, the fore or hind quarter will make a reasonable dish, and seasoned with a little pepper or salt will be very good boiled on the fourth day, especially in winter.

I have reckoned upon a medium that a child

Engraving, probably 19th century, of an Irish peasant cottage.

just born will weigh twelve pounds, and in a solar year, if tolerably nursed, will increase to twenty-eight pounds.

I grant this food will be somewhat dear, and therefore very proper for landlords, who, as they have already devoured most of the parents, seem to have the best title to the children.

Infant's flesh will be in season throughout the year, but more plentifully in March, and a little before and after: for we are told by a grave author, an eminent French physician,[6] that fish being a prolific diet, there are more children born in Roman Catholic countries about nine months after Lent than at any other season; therefore, reckoning a year after Lent, the markets will be more glutted than usual, because the number of popish infants is at least three to one in this kingdom: and therefore it will have one other collateral advantage, by lessening the number of papists among us.

---

5. *ragout* (ra gü'), a highly seasoned meat stew.
6. *grave author . . . physician,* François Rabelais (c. 1494–1553), who was anything but a "grave author."

I have already computed the charge of nursing a beggar's child (in which list I reckon all cottagers, laborers, and four-fifths of the farmers) to be about two shillings per annum, rags included; and I believe no gentleman would repine to give ten shillings for the carcass of a good fat child, which, as I have said, will make four dishes of excellent nutritive meat, when he has only some particular friend or his own family to dine with him. Thus the squire will learn to be a good landlord and grow popular among his tenants; the mother will have eight shillings net profit and be fit for work till she produces another child.

Those who are more thrifty (as I must confess the times require) may flay the carcass; the skin of which artificially[7] dressed will make admirable gloves for ladies and summer boots for fine gentlemen.

As to our city of Dublin, shambles[8] may be appointed for this purpose in the most convenient parts of it, and butchers we may be assured will not be wanting; although I rather recommend buying the children alive and dressing them hot from the knife as we do roasting pigs.

A very worthy person, a true lover of his country, and whose virtues I highly esteem, was lately pleased, in discoursing on this matter, to offer a refinement upon my scheme. He said that many gentlemen of this kingdom, having of late destroyed their deer, he conceived that the want of venison might be well supplied by the bodies of young lads and maidens, not exceeding fourteen years of age nor under twelve; so great a number of both sexes in every country being now ready to starve for want of work and service; and these to be disposed of by their parents, if alive, or otherwise by their nearest relations. But with due deference to so excellent a friend and so deserving a patriot, I cannot be altogether in his sentiments; for as to the males, my American acquaintance assured me from frequent experience that their flesh was generally tough and lean, like that of our schoolboys, by continual exercise, and their taste disagreeable; and to fatten them would not answer the charge. Then as to the females, it would, I think, with humble submission be a loss to the public, because they soon would become breeders themselves: and besides, it is not improbable that some scrupulous people might be apt to censure such a practice (although indeed very unjustly), as a little bordering upon cruelty; which, I confess, has always been with me the strongest objection against any project, how well soever intended.

But in order to justify my friend, he confessed that this expedient was put into his head by the famous Psalmanazar,[9] a native of the island Formosa, who came from thence to London above twenty years ago: and in conversation told my friend that in his country when any young person happened to be put to death, the executioner sold the carcass to persons of quality as a prime dainty; and that in his time the body of a plump girl of fifteen, who was crucified for an attempt to poison the emperor, was sold to his imperial majesty's prime minister of state, and other great mandarins of the court, in joints from the gibbet, at four hundred crowns. Neither indeed can I deny that if the same use were made of several plump girls in this town, who, without one single groat to their fortunes, cannot stir abroad without a chair, and appear at a playhouse and assemblies in foreign fineries which they never will pay for, the kingdom would not be the worse.

Some persons of a desponding spirit are in great concern about that vast number of poor people who are aged, diseased, or maimed; and I have been desired to employ my thoughts, what course may be taken to ease the nation of so grievous an encumbrance. But I am not in the least pain upon that matter, because it is very well known that they are every day dying and rotting, by cold and famine, and filth and vermin, as fast as can be reasonably expected. And as to the young laborers, they are now in almost as hopeful a condition: they cannot get work, and consequently pine away for want of nourishment to a degree that if at any

---

7. *artificially,* artfully; skillfully.
8. *shambles,* slaughterhouses.
9. *Psalmanazar,* the impostor George Psalmanazar (c. 1679–1763), a Frenchman who passed himself off in England as a Formosan and wrote a totally fictional "true" account of Formosa, in which he described cannibalism.

time they are accidentally hired to common labor, they have not strength to perform it; and thus the country and themselves are happily delivered from the evils to come.

I have too long digressed and therefore shall return to my subject. I think the advantages, by the proposal which I have made, are obvious and many, as well as of the highest importance.

For first, as I have already observed, it would greatly lessen the number of papists, with whom we are yearly overrun, being the principal breeders of the nation, as well as our most dangerous enemies; and who stay at home on purpose to deliver the kingdom to the Pretender, hoping to take their advantage by the absence of so many good Protestants, who have chosen rather to leave their country than stay at home and pay tithes against their conscience to an Episcopal curate.[10]

Secondly, the poorer tenants will have something valuable of their own, which by law may be made liable to distress,[11] and help to pay their landlord's rent; their corn and cattle being already seized, and money a thing unknown.

Thirdly, whereas the maintenance of a hundred thousand children, from two years old and upwards, cannot be computed at less than ten shillings a piece per annum, the nation's stock will be thereby increased fifty thousand pounds per annum, beside the profit of a new dish introduced to the tables of all gentlemen of fortune in the kingdom who have any refinement in taste. And the money will circulate among ourselves, the goods being entirely of our own growth and manufacture.

Fourthly, the constant breeders, besides the gain of eight shillings sterling per annum by the sale of their children, will be rid of the charge of maintaining them after the first year.

Fifthly, this food would likewise bring great custom to taverns: where the vintners will certainly be so prudent as to procure the best receipts[12] for dressing it to perfection, and consequently have their houses frequented by all the fine gentlemen, who justly value themselves upon their knowledge in good eating: and a skillful cook, who understands how to oblige his guests, will contrive to make it as expensive as they please.

Sixthly, this would be a great inducement to marriage, which all wise nations have either encouraged by rewards or enforced by laws and penalties. It would increase the care and tenderness of mothers toward their children, when they were sure of a settlement for life to the poor babes, provided in some sort by the public, to their annual profit instead of expense. We should see an honest emulation among the married women, which of them could bring the fattest child to the market. Men would become as fond of their wives during the time of their pregnancy as they are now of their mares in foal, their cows in calf, or sows when they are ready to farrow; nor offer to beat or kick them (as is too frequent a practice) for fear of a miscarriage.

Many other advantages might be enumerated. For instance, the addition of some thousand carcasses in our exportation of barreled beef, the propagation of swine's flesh, and improvement in the art of making good bacon, so much wanted among us by the great destruction of pigs, too frequent at our tables; which are no way comparable in taste or magnificence to a well-grown, fat, yearling child, which roasted whole will make a considerable figure at a lord mayor's feast, or any other public entertainment. But this and many others I omit, being studious of brevity.

Supposing that one thousand families in this city would be constant customers for infants' flesh, besides others who might have it at merry meetings, particularly weddings and christenings, I compute that Dublin would take off annually about twenty thousand carcasses; and the rest of the kingdom (where probably they will be sold somewhat cheaper) the remaining eighty thousand.

I can think of no one objection that will possibly be raised against this proposal, unless it should be urged that the number of people will be thereby

10. *Protestants . . . curate.* Swift is here attacking the absentee landlords.
11. *distress,* distraint, the legal seizure of property for payment of debts.
12. *receipts,* recipes.

much lessened in the kingdom. This I freely own, and it was indeed one principal design in offering it to the world. I desire the reader will observe that I calculate my remedy for this one individual kingdom of Ireland, and for no other that ever was, is, or, I think, ever can be upon earth. Therefore let no man talk to me of other expedients: of taxing our absentees at five shillings a pound: of using neither clothes nor household furniture, except what is of our own growth and manufacture: of utterly rejecting the materials and instruments that promote foreign luxury: of curing the expensiveness of pride, vanity, idleness, and gaming in our women: of introducing a vein of parsimony, prudence, and temperance: of learning to love our country, in the want of which we differ even from Laplanders and the inhabitants of Topinamboo:[13] of quitting our animosities and factions, nor acting any longer like the Jews, who were murdering one another at the very moment their city was taken:[14] of being a little cautious not to sell our country and conscience for nothing: of teaching landlords to have at least one degree of mercy toward their tenants: lastly, of putting a spirit of honesty, industry, and skill into our shopkeepers; who, if a resolution could now be taken to buy only our native goods, would immediately unite to cheat and exact upon us in the price, the measure, and the goodness, nor could ever yet be brought to make one fair proposal of just dealing, though often and earnestly invited to it.[15]

Therefore, I repeat, let no man talk to me of these and the like expedients, till he has at least some glimpse of hope that there will ever be some hearty and sincere attempt to put them in practice.

But as to myself, having been wearied out for many years with offering vain, idle, visionary thoughts, and at length utterly despairing of success, I fortunately fell upon this proposal; which, as it is wholly new, so it has something solid and real, of no expense and little trouble, full in our own power, and whereby we can incur no danger in disobliging England. For this kind of commodity will not bear exportation, the flesh being of too tender a consistence to admit a long continuance in salt, although perhaps I could name a country which would be glad to eat up our whole nation without it.[16]

After all, I am not so violently bent upon my own opinion as to reject any offer proposed by wise men, which shall be found equally innocent, cheap, easy, and effectual. But before something of that kind shall be advanced in contradiction to my scheme, and offering a better, I desire the author or authors will be pleased maturely to consider two points. First, as things now stand, how they will be able to find food and raiment for an hundred thousand useless mouths and backs. And, secondly, there being a round million of creatures in human figure throughout this kingdom, whose whole subsistence put into a common stock would leave them in debt two millions of pounds sterling, adding those who are beggars by profession to the bulk of farmers, cottagers, and laborers, with their wives and children, who are beggars in effect; I desire those politicians, who dislike my overture, and may perhaps be so bold as to attempt an answer, that they will first ask the parents of these mortals, whether they would not at this day think it a great happiness to have been sold for food at a year old in the manner I prescribe, and thereby have avoided such a perpetual scene of misfortunes as they have since gone through by the oppression of landlords, the impossibility of paying rent without money or trade, the want of common sustenance, with neither house nor clothes to cover them from the inclemencies of the weather, and the most inevitable prospect of entailing the like or greater miseries upon their breed for ever.

I profess, in the sincerity of my heart, that I have not the least personal interest in endeavoring

---

13. *Topinamboo*, a savage area of Brazil.
14. *city was taken*. While the Roman Emperor Titus was besieging Jerusalem, which he took and destroyed in A.D. 70, within the city factions of fanatics were waging bloody warfare.
15. *invited to it*. Swift had already made all these proposals in various pamphlets.
16. *a country . . . without it*. England; this is another way of saying, "The English are devouring the Irish."

to promote this necessary work, having no other motive than the public good of my country, by advancing our trade, providing for infants, relieving the poor, and giving some pleasure to the rich. I have no children by which I can propose to get a single penny; the youngest being nine years old, and my wife past childbearing.

1729

THINK AND DISCUSS
Understanding
1. List some of the shocking details of life in Ireland that the essay casually reveals.
2. In one sentence summarize the "proposal."

Analyzing
3. Who are the major targets of Swift's **satire**?
4. Paragraph 4 refers to "a child just dropped from its dam," and the essay contains other examples of terms usually applied only to animals. Why does Swift use this device?
5. Does Swift suggest that the Irish are in any way responsible for their plight? Explain.
6. Which solution do you think Swift intends his readers to choose: the "modest proposal" or the list of alternatives on page 342, column a, lines 7–32? Explain.

Extending
7. If you did not know this essay is satirical, at what point would you have realized that Swift was "putting you on"?
8. "A Modest Proposal" is classified as nonfiction. How can this be so when Swift makes such outrageous statements?
9. If Swift lived today, what conditions might he be moved to write about?

REVIEWING: Irony HT
See Handbook of Literary Terms, p. 912
Irony is the contrast between what is expected, or what appears to be, and what actually is. In *verbal irony* the intended meaning of a statement is different from, or opposite to, what the statement literally says. "A Modest Proposal" is often referred to as the prime example of sustained verbal irony in English literature.

1. "Whoever could find out a fair, cheap, and easy method of making these children sound, useful members of the commonwealth would deserve so well of the public as to have his statue set up for a preserver of the nation." What is the irony in this statement?
2. List other instances of irony that you find.
3. Explain the effect of *modest* in the title.

COMPOSITION
Analyzing Swift's Use of Irony
The full title of this essay is "A Modest Proposal For Preventing the Children of Poor People in Ireland from Being a Burden to Their Parents or Country, and for Making Them Beneficial to the Public." Write a paper in which you explain why this title is meant to be taken ironically. Suggest some reasons why Swift might have used irony instead of making straightforward statements. See "Writing About Irony and Satire" in the Writer's Handbook.

Writing a Modern Satire
Select a modern abuse and write a satirical essay about it for your school literary magazine. First state the problem; then propose your solution and explain why it would be effective. Your solution need not be as outrageous as Swift's, but try to be controversial.

ENRICHMENT
Readers Theater
Select key sections of "A Modest Proposal" and have one or more students read them aloud while other students, holding pamphlets, pantomime the reactions of an absentee landlord, a native Irishman, a sensitive Londoner, and so on, who are reading the essay for the first time.

H T See POINT OF VIEW in the Handbook of Literary Terms, page 917.

A Voyage to Brobdingnag

from **Gulliver's Travels**

Jonathan Swift

In the first book of *Gulliver's Travels*, Lemuel Gulliver finds himself in the land of the Lilliputians, tiny people only one-tenth his size. Swift uses these tiny people to satirize the pretensions of the English and their customs.

As the second book opens, Gulliver has again gone to sea as a ship's doctor; his ship has just weathered a storm that has blown it so far off course that no one has any idea where the ship is.

n the 16th day of June, 1703, a boy on the topmast discovered land. On the 17th we came in full view of a great island or continent (for we knew not whether) on the south side whereof was a small neck of land jutting out into the sea, and a creek too shallow to hold a ship of above one hundred tons. We cast anchor within a league of this creek, and our Captain sent a dozen of his men well armed in the longboat, with vessels for water if any could be found. I desired his leave to go with them that I might see the country and make what discoveries I could. When we came to land we saw no river or spring, nor any sign of inhabitants. Our men therefore wandered on the shore to find out some fresh water near the sea, and I walked alone about a mile on the other side, where I observed the country all barren and rocky. I now began to be weary, and seeing nothing to entertain my curiosity, I returned gently down towards the creek; and the sea being full in my view, I saw our men already got into the boat, and rowing for life to the ship. I was going to hollow[1] after them, although it had been to little purpose, when I observed a huge creature walking after them in the sea as fast as he could; he waded not much deeper than his knees and took prodigious strides, but our men had the start of him half a league, and the sea thereabouts being full of sharp-pointed rocks, the monster was not able to overtake the boat. This I was afterwards told, for I durst not stay to see the issue of that adventure, but ran as fast as I could the way I first went, and then climbed up a steep hill, which gave me some prospect of the country. I found it fully cultivated; but that which first surprised me was the length of the grass, which, in those grounds that seemed to be kept for hay, was about twenty foot high.

I fell into a highroad, for so I took it to be, although it served to the inhabitants only as a footpath through a field of barley. Here I walked on for some time, but could see little on either side, it being now near harvest, and the corn[2] rising at least forty foot. I was an hour walking to the end of this field, which was fenced in with a hedge of

---

1. *hollow*, call out or exclaim.
2. *corn*, the principal grain of any country; here it means wheat.

at least one hundred and twenty foot high, and the trees so lofty that I could make no computation of their altitude. There was a stile[3] to pass from this field into the next: it had four steps, and a stone to cross over when you came to the utmost. It was impossible for me to climb this stile, because every step was six foot high, and the upper stone above twenty. I was endeavoring to find some gap in the hedge when I discovered one of the inhabitants in the next field advancing towards the stile, of the same size with him whom I saw in the sea pursuing our boat. He appeared as tall as an ordinary spire-steeple, and took about ten yards at every stride, as near as I could guess. I was struck with the utmost fear and astonishment, and ran to hide myself in the corn, from whence I saw him at the top of the stile, looking back into the next field on the right hand; and heard him call in a voice many degrees louder than a speaking trumpet; but the noise was so high in the air that at first I certainly thought it was thunder. Whereupon seven monsters like himself came towards him with reaping hooks in their hands, each hook about the largeness of six scythes. These people were not so well clad as the first, whose servants or laborers they seemed to be. For, upon some words he spoke, they went to reap the corn in the field where I lay. I kept from them at as great a distance as I could, but was forced to move with extreme difficulty, for the stalks of the corn were sometimes not above a foot distant, so that I could hardly squeeze my body betwixt them. However, I made a shift to go forward till I came to a part of the field where the corn had been laid by the rain and wind; here it was impossible for me to advance a step, for the stalks were so interwoven that I could not creep through, and the beards of the fallen ears so strong and pointed that they pierced through my clothes into my flesh. At the same time I heard the reapers not above an hundred yards behind me. Being quite dispirited with toil, and wholly overcome by grief and despair, I lay down between two ridges and heartily wished I might there end my days. I bemoaned my desolate widow and fatherless children; I lamented my own folly and willfulness in attempting a second voyage against the advice of all my friends and relations. In this terrible agitation of mind, I could not forbear thinking of Lilliput,[4] whose inhabitants looked upon me as the greatest prodigy that ever appeared in the world; where I was able to draw an imperial fleet in my hand, and perform those other actions which will be recorded forever in the chronicles of that empire, while posterity shall hardly believe them, although attested by millions. I reflected what a mortification it must prove to me to appear as inconsiderable in this nation as one single Lilliputian would be among us. But this I conceived was to be the least of my misfortunes; for as human creatures are observed to be more savage and cruel in proportion to their bulk, what could I expect but to be a morsel in the mouth of the first among these enormous barbarians who should happen to seize me? Undoubtedly philosophers are in the right when they tell us that nothing is great or little otherwise than by comparison. It might have pleased fortune to let the Lilliputians find some nation where the people were as diminutive with respect to them as they were to me. And who knows but that even this prodigious race of mortals might be equally overmatched in some distant part of the world, whereof we have yet no discovery?

Scared and confounded as I was, I could not forbear going on with these reflections; when one of the reapers approaching within ten yards of the ridge where I lay, made me apprehend that with the next step I should be squashed to death under his foot, or cut in two with his reaping hook. And therefore when he was again about to move, I screamed as loud as fear could make me. Whereupon the huge creature trod short, and looking round about under him for some time, at last espied me as I lay on the ground. He considered a while with the caution of one who endeavors to lay hold on a small dangerous animal in such a manner that it shall not be able either to scratch or to bite him, as I myself have sometimes

---

3. *stile,* a set of steps for ascending and descending.
4. *Lilliput,* the country of the tiny people where Gulliver was shipwrecked on his first voyage.

done with a weasel in England. At length he ventured to take me up behind by the middle between his forefinger and thumb, and brought me within three yards of his eyes, that he might behold my shape more perfectly. I guessed his meaning, and my good fortune gave me so much presence of mind that I resolved not to struggle in the least as he held me in the air about sixty foot from the ground, although he grievously pinched my sides, for fear I should slip through his fingers. All I ventured was to raise mine eyes towards the sun, and place my hands together in a supplicating posture, and to speak some words in an humble melancholy tone, suitable to the condition I then was in. For I apprehended every moment that he would dash me against the ground, as we usually do any little hateful animal which we have a mind to destroy. But my good star would have it that he appeared pleased with my voice and gestures, and began to look upon me as a curiosity, much wondering to hear me pronounce articulate words, although he could not understand them. In the meantime I was not able to forbear groaning and shedding tears and turning my head towards my sides, letting him know, as well as I could, how cruelly I was hurt by the pressure of his thumb and finger. He seemed to apprehend my meaning; for, lifting up the lappet[5] of his coat, he put me gently into it, and immediately ran along with me to his master, who was a substantial farmer, and the same person I had first seen in the field.

The farmer having (as I supposed by their talk) received such an account of me as his servant could give him, took a piece of a small straw about the size of a walking staff, and therewith lifted up the lappets of my coat, which it seems he thought to be some kind of covering that nature had given me. He blew my hairs aside to take a better view of my face. He called his hinds[6] about him, and asked them (as I afterwards learned) whether they had ever seen in the fields any little creature that resembled me. He then placed me softly on the ground upon all four; but I got immediately up, and walked slowly backwards and forwards, to let those people see I had no intent to run away. They all sat down in a circle about me, the better to observe my motions. I pulled off my hat, and made a low bow towards the farmer; I fell on my knees, and lifted up my hands and eyes, and spoke several words as loud as I could; I took a purse of gold out of my pocket, and humbly presented it to him. He received it on the palm of his hand, then applied it close to his eye to see what it was, and afterwards turned it several times with the point of a pin (which he took out of his sleeve), but could make nothing of it. Whereupon I made a sign that he should place his hand on the ground; I then took the purse, and opening it, poured all the gold into his palm. There were six Spanish pieces of four pistoles each, beside twenty or thirty smaller coins. I saw him wet the tip of his little finger upon his tongue, and take up one of my largest pieces, and then another; but he seemed to be wholly ignorant what they were. He made me a sign to put them again into my purse, and the purse again into my pocket, which after offering to him several times, I thought it best to do.

The farmer by this time was convinced I must be a rational creature. He spoke often to me, but the sound of his voice pierced my ears like that of a water mill, yet his words were articulate enough. I answered as loud as I could in several languages, and he often laid his ear within two yards of me, but all in vain, for we were wholly unintelligible to each other. He then sent his servants to their work, and taking his handkerchief out of his pocket, he doubled and spread it on his hand, which he placed flat on the ground with the palm upwards, making me a sign to step into it, as I could easily do, for it was not above a foot in thickness. I thought it my part to obey, and for fear of falling, laid myself at full length upon the handkerchief, with the remainder of which he lapped me up to the head for further security, and in this manner carried me home to his house. There he called his wife, and showed me to her; but she screamed and ran back as women in England do at the sight of a toad or a spider. However, when she had a while seen my behavior, and how well I observed

---

5. *lappet*, flap.
6. *hinds*, servants.

the signs her husband made, she was soon reconciled, and by degrees grew extremely tender of me.

Gulliver is given into the care of the farmer's nine-year-old daughter, Glumdalclitch, who teaches him the language. The farmer decides to make money by displaying Gulliver in the capital. The Queen sends for him, is pleased with Gulliver, and purchases him. At his suggestion, she retains Glumdal-clitch to care for Gulliver. He is presented to the King, who takes an interest in him.

His Majesty sent for three great scholars who were then in their weekly waiting (according to the custom in that country). These gentlemen, after they had a while examined my shape with much nicety, were of different opinions concerning me. They all agreed that I could not be produced according to the regular laws of nature, because I was not framed with a capacity of preserving my life, either by swiftness, or climbing of trees, or digging holes in the earth. They observed by my teeth, which they viewed with great exactness, that I was a carnivorous animal; yet most quadrupeds being an overmatch for me, and field mice, with some others, too nimble, they could not imagine how I should be able to support myself, unless I fed upon snails and other insects; which they offered, by many learned arguments, to evince that I could not possibly do. One of them seemed to think that I might be an embryo, or abortive birth. But this opinion was rejected by the other two, who observed my limbs to be perfect and finished, and that I had lived several years, as it was manifest from my beard, the stumps whereof they plainly discovered through a magnifying glass. They would not allow me to be a dwarf, because my littleness was beyond all degrees of comparison; for the Queen's favorite dwarf, the smallest ever known in that kingdom, was nearly thirty foot high. After much debate, they concluded unanimously that I was only *relplum scalcath*, which is interpreted literally,

Gulliver in the corn, from a French edition of *Gulliver's Travels.* 1795

lusus naturae,[7] a determination exactly agreeable to the modern philosophy of Europe, whose professors, disdaining the old evasion of *occult causes*, whereby the followers of Aristotle[8] endeavor in vain to disguise their ignorance, have invented this wonderful solution of all difficulties, to the unspeakable advancement of human knowledge.

After this decisive conclusion, I entreated to be heard a word or two. I applied myself to the King, and assured his Majesty that I came from a country which abounded with several millions of both sexes, and of my own stature, where the animals, trees, and houses were all in proportion, and where by consequence I might be as able to defend myself, and to find sustenance, as any of his Majesty's subjects could do here; which I took for a full answer to those gentlemen's arguments. To this they only replied with a smile of contempt, saying that the farmer had instructed me very well in my lesson. The King, who had a much better understanding, dismissing his learned men, sent

---

7. **lusus naturae,** a sport, or freak of nature. [Latin]
8. *Aristotle* (ar'ə stot'l), Greek philosopher and scientist (384–322 B.C.).

for the farmer, who by good fortune was not yet gone out of town; having therefore first examined him privately, and then confronted him with me and the young girl, his Majesty began to think that what we told him might possibly be true. He desired the Queen to order that a particular care should be taken of me, and was of opinion that Glumdalclitch should still continue in her office of tending me, because he observed we had a great affection for each other. A convenient apartment was provided for her at Court; she had a sort of governess appointed to take care of her education, a maid to dress her, and two other servants for menial offices; but the care of me was wholly appropriated to herself. The Queen commanded her own cabinetmaker to contrive a box that might serve me for a bedchamber, after the model that Glumdalclitch and I should agree upon. This man was a most ingenious artist, and according to my directions, in three weeks finished for me a wooden chamber of sixteen foot square and twelve high, with sash windows, a door, and two closets, like a London bedchamber. The board that made the ceiling was to be lifted up and down by two hinges, to put in a bed ready furnished by her Majesty's upholsterer, which Glumdalclitch took out every day to air, made it with her own hands, and letting it down at night, locked up the roof over me. A nice[9] workman, who was famous for little curiosities, undertook to make me two chairs, with backs and frames, of a substance not unlike ivory, and two tables, with a cabinet to put my things in. The room was quilted on all sides, as well as the floor and the ceiling, to prevent any accident from the carelessness of those who carried me, and to break the force of a jolt when I went in a coach. I desired a lock for my door to prevent rats and mice from coming in: the smith, after several attempts, made the smallest that ever was seen among them, for I have known a larger at the gate of a gentleman's house in England. I made a shift[10] to keep the key in a pocket of my own, fearing Glumdalclitch might lose it. The Queen likewise ordered the thinnest silks that could be gotten, to make me clothes, not much thicker than an English blanket, very cumbersome till I was accustomed to them. They were after the fashion of the kingdom, partly resembling the Persian, and partly the Chinese, and are a very grave, decent habit.

The Queen became so fond of my company that she could not dine without me. I had a table placed upon the same at which her Majesty ate, just at her left elbow, and a chair to sit on. Glumdalclitch stood upon a stool on the floor, near my table, to assist and take care of me. I had an entire set of silver dishes and plates, and other necessaries, which, in proportion to those of the Queen, were not much bigger than what I have seen of the same kind in a London toyshop, for the furniture of a baby-house: these my little nurse kept in her pocket in a silver box and gave me at meals as I wanted them, always cleaning them herself. No person dined with the Queen but the two Princesses Royal, the elder sixteen years old, and the younger at that time thirteen and a month. Her Majesty used to put a bit of meat upon one of my dishes, out of which I carved for myself; and her diversion was to see me eat in miniature. For the Queen (who had indeed but a weak stomach) took up at one mouthful as much as a dozen English farmers could eat at a meal, which to me was for some time a very nauseous sight. She would craunch[11] the wing of a lark, bones and all, between her teeth, although it were nine times as large as that of a full-grown turkey; and put a bit of bread into her mouth as big as two twelve-penny loaves. She drank out of a golden cup, above a hogshead at a draught. Her knives were twice as long as a scythe set straight upon the handle. The spoons, forks, and other instruments were all in the same proportion. I remember when Glumdalclitch carried me out of curiosity to see some of the tables at Court, where ten or a dozen of these enormous knives and forks were lifted up together, I thought I had never till then beheld so terrible a sight.

It is the custom that every Wednesday (which,

9. *nice,* precise or exact.
10. *made a shift,* arranged or contrived.
11. *craunch,* crunch.

as I have before observed, was their Sabbath) the King and Queen, with the royal issue of both sexes, dine together in the apartment of his Majesty, to whom I was now become a favorite; and at these times my little chair and table were placed at his left hand, before one of the saltcellars. This prince took a pleasure in conversing with me, inquiring into the manners, religion, laws, government, and learning of Europe; wherein I gave him the best account I was able. His apprehension was so clear, and his judgment so exact, that he made very wise reflections and observations upon all I said. But I confess that after I had been a little too copious in talking of my own beloved country, of our trade and wars by sea and land, of our schisms in religion and parties in the state, the prejudices of his education prevailed so far that he could not forbear taking me up in his right hand, and stroking me gently with the other, after an hearty fit of laughing, asked me whether I were a Whig or a Tory. Then turning to his first minister, who waited behind him with a white staff, near as tall as the mainmast of the *Royal Sovereign*,[12] he observed how contemptible a thing was human grandeur, which could ·be mimicked by such diminutive insects as I: "and yet," said he, "I dare engage, these creatures have their titles and distinctions of honor; they contrive little nests and burrows, that they call houses and cities; they make a figure in dress and equipage;[13] they love, they fight, they dispute, they cheat, they betray." And thus he continued on, while my color came and went several times with indignation to hear our noble country, the mistress of arts and arms, the scourge of France, the arbitress of Europe, the seat of virtue, piety, honor, and truth, the pride and envy of the world, so contemptuously treated.

But as I was not in a condition to resent injuries, so, upon mature thoughts, I began to doubt whether I were injured or no. For, after having been accustomed several months to the sight and converse of this people, and observed every object upon which I cast my eyes to be of proportionable magnitude, the horror I had first conceived from their bulk and aspect was so far worn off that if I

had then beheld a company of English lords and ladies in their finery and birthday clothes,[14] acting their several parts in the most courtly manner of strutting and bowing and prating, to say the truth, I should have been strongly tempted to laugh as much at them as this King and his grandees did at me. Neither indeed could I forbear smiling at myself when the Queen used to place me upon her hand towards a looking glass, by which both our persons appeared before me in full view together; and there could be nothing more ridiculous than the comparison; so that I really began to imagine myself dwindled many degrees below my usual size. . . .

I was frequently rallied by the Queen upon account of my fearfulness, and she used to ask me whether the people of my country were as great cowards as myself. The occasion was this. The kingdom is much pestered with flies in summer, and these odious insects, each of them as big as a Dunstable lark, hardly gave me any rest while I sat at dinner, with their continual humming and buzzing about my ears. They would sometimes alight upon my victuals, and leave their loathsome excrement or spawn behind, which to me was very visible, although not to the natives of that country, whose large optics were not so acute as mine in viewing smaller objects. Sometimes they would fix upon my nose or forehead, where they stung me to the quick, smelling very offensively; and I could easily trace that viscous matter, which our naturalists tell us enables those creatures to walk with their feet upwards upon a ceiling. I had much ado to defend myself against these destable animals, and could not forbear starting when they came on my face. It was the common practice of the dwarf to catch a number of these insects in his hand, as schoolboys do among us, and let them out suddenly under my nose, on purpose to frighten me, and divert the Queen. My remedy was to cut

---

12. **Royal Sovereign,** one of the largest ships in the Royal Navy.
13. *equipage,* carriage with its horses, driver, and servants.
14. *birthday clothes,* fashionable London traditionally dressed with splendor for royal birthdays.

them in pieces with my knife as they flew in the air, wherein my dexterity was much admired.

I remember one morning when Glumdalclitch had set me in my box upon a window, as she usually did in fair days to give me air (for I durst not venture to let the box be hung on a nail out of the window, as we do with cages in England), after I had lifted up one of my sashes, and sat down at my table to eat a piece of sweet cake for my breakfast, above twenty wasps, allured by the smell, came flying into the room, humming louder than the drones of as many bagpipes. Some of them seized my cake, and carried it piecemeal away; others flew about my head and face, confounding me with the noise, and putting me in the utmost terror of their stings. However, I had the courage to rise and draw my hanger,[15] and attack them in the air. I dispatched four of them, but the rest got away, and I presently shut my window. These insects were as large as partridges; I took out their stings, found them an inch and a half long, and as sharp as needles. I carefully preserved them all, and having since shown them with some other curiosities in several parts of Europe, upon my return to England I gave three of them to Gresham College,[16] and kept the fourth for myself. . . .

But the greatest danger I ever underwent in that kingdom was from a monkey, who belonged to one of the clerks of the kitchen. Glumdalclitch had locked me up in her closet,[17] while she went somewhere upon business or a visit. The weather being very warm, the closet window was left open, as well as the windows in the door of my bigger box, in which I usually lived, because of its largeness and conveniency. As I sat quietly meditating at my table, I heard something bounce in at the closet window, and skip about from one side to the other, whereat, although I was much alarmed, yet I ventured to look out, but stirred not from my seat; and then I saw this frolicsome animal, frisking and leaping up and down, till at last he came to my box, which he seemed to view with great pleasure and curiosity, peeping in at the door and every window. I retreated to the farther corner of my room, or box, but the monkey looking in at every side, put me into such a fright that I wanted presence of mind to conceal myself under the bed, as I might easily have done. After some time spent in peeping, grinning, and chattering, he at last espied me, and reaching one of his paws in at the door, as a cat does when she plays with a mouse, although I often shifted place to avoid him, he at length seized the lappet of my coat (which, being made of that country cloth, was very thick and strong) and dragged me out. He took me up in his right forefoot, and held me as nurse does a child she is going to suckle, just as I have seen the same sort of creature do with a kitten in Europe: and when I offered to struggle, he squeezed me so hard that I thought it more prudent to submit. I have good reason to believe that he took me for a young one of his own species, by his often stroking my face very gently with his other paw. In these diversions he was interrupted by a noise at the closet door, as if somebody were opening it, whereupon he suddenly leaped up to the window at which he had come in, and thence upon the leads[18] and gutters, walking upon three legs, and holding me in the fourth, till he clambered up to a roof that was next to ours. I heard Glumdalclitch give a shriek at the moment he was carrying me out. The poor girl was almost distracted: that quarter of the palace was all in an uproar; the servants ran for ladders; the monkey was seen by hundreds in the court, sitting upon the ridge of a building, holding me like a baby in one of his forepaws and feeding me with the other, by cramming into my mouth some victuals[19] he had squeezed out of the bag on one side of his chaps, and patting me when I would not eat; whereat many of the rabble below could not forbear laughing; neither do I think they justly ought to be blamed, for without question the sight was ridiculous enough to everybody but myself. Some of the people threw

---

15. *hanger,* sword.
16. *Gresham College,* where the Royal Society, a scientific association, held its meetings.
17. *closet,* a small room used as an office or study.
18. *leads,* roof.
19. *victuals* (vit'ls), food or provisions.

up stones, hoping to drive the monkey down; but this was strictly forbidden, or else very probably my brains had been dashed out.

The ladders were now applied, and mounted by several men; which the monkey observing, and finding himself almost encompassed, not being able to make speed enough with his three legs, let me drop on a ridge tile, and made his escape. Here I sat for some time three hundred yards from the ground, expecting every moment to be blown down by the wind, or to fall by my own giddiness, and come tumbling over and over from the ridge to the eaves. But an honest lad, one of my nurse's footmen, climbed up, and putting me into his breeches pocket, brought me down safe.

I was almost choked with the filthy stuff the monkey had crammed down my throat; but my dear little nurse picked it out of my mouth with a small needle, and then I fell a vomiting, which gave me great relief. Yet I was so weak and bruised in the sides with the squeezes given me by this odious animal that I was forced to keep my bed a fortnight. The King, Queen, and all the Court sent every day to inquire after my health, and her Majesty made me several visits during my sickness. The monkey was killed, and an order made that no such animal should be kept about the palace. . . .

I desired the Queen's woman to save for me the combings of her Majesty's hair, whereof in time I got a good quantity; and consulting with my friend the cabinetmaker, who had received general orders to do little jobs for me, I directed him to make two chair frames, no larger than those I had in my box, and then to bore little holes with a fine awl round those parts where I designed the backs and seats; through these holes I wove the strongest hairs I could pick out, just after the manner of cane chairs in England. When they were finished, I made a present of them to her Majesty, who kept them in her cabinet, and used to show them for curiosities, as indeed they were the wonder of every one that beheld them. The Queen would have made me sit upon one of these chairs, but I absolutely refused to obey her, protesting I would rather die a thousand deaths than place a dishonorable part of my body on those precious hairs that once adorned her Majesty's head. Of these hairs (as I had always a mechanical genius) I likewise made a neat little purse above five foot long, with her Majesty's name deciphered in gold letters, which I gave to Glumdalclitch by the Queen's consent. To say the truth, it was more for show than use, being not of strength to bear the weight of the larger coins; and therefore she kept nothing in it but some little toys that girls are fond of.

The King, who delighted in music, had frequent consorts[20] at court, to which I was sometimes carried, and set in my box on a table to hear them; but the noise was so great that I could hardly distinguish the tunes. I am confident that all the drums and trumpets of a royal army, beating and sounding together just at your ears, could not equal it. My practice was to have my box removed from the places where the performers sat, as far as I could, then to shut the doors and windows of it, and draw the window curtains, after which I found their music not disagreeable.

I had learned in my youth to play a little upon the spinet. Glumdalclitch kept one in her chamber, and a master attended twice a week to teach her: I call it a spinet, because it somewhat resembled that instrument, and was played upon in the same manner. A fancy came into my head that I would entertain the King and Queen with an English tune upon this instrument. But this appeared extremely difficult: for the spinet was near sixty foot long, each key being almost a foot wide; so that, with my arms extended, I could not reach to above five keys, and to press them down required a good smart stroke with my fist, which would be too great a labor and to no purpose. The method I contrived was this: I prepared two round sticks about the bigness of common cudgels; they were thicker at one end than the other, and I covered the thicker ends with a piece of a mouse's skin, that by rapping on them I might neither damage the tops of the keys, nor interrupt the sound. Before the spinet a bench was placed, about

---

20. *consorts,* concerts.

four foot below the keys, and I was put upon the bench. I ran sideling[21] upon it that way and this, as fast as I could, banging the proper keys with my two sticks; and made a shift to play a jig, to the great satisfaction of both their Majesties: but it was the most violent exercise I ever underwent, and yet I could not strike above sixteen keys, nor, consequently, play the bass and treble together, as other artists do; which was a great disadvantage to my performance.

Gulliver spends some time telling the King about the society, economy, and government of England and the wars she has engaged in. As he does so, he unconsciously praises one abuse after another. The King takes careful notes of everything Gulliver says.

His Majesty in other audience was at the pains to recapitulate the sum of all I had spoken; compared the questions he made with the answers I had given; then taking me into his hands, and stroking me gently, delivered himself in these words, which I shall never forget nor the manner he spoke them in. "My little friend Grildrig,[22] you have made a most admirable panegyric[23] upon your country. You have clearly proved that ignorance, idleness, and vice are the proper ingredients for qualifying a legislator. That laws are best explained, interpreted, and applied by those whose interests and abilities lie in perverting, confounding, and eluding them. I observe among you some lines of an institution which in its original might have been tolerable; but these half erased, and the rest wholly blurred and blotted by corruptions. It doth not appear from all you have said how any one virtue is required towards the procurement of any one station among you; much less that men are ennobled on account of their virtue, that priests are advanced for their piety or learning, soldiers for their conduct or valor, judges for their integrity, senators for the love of their country, or counselors for their wisdom. As for yourself," continued the King, "who have spent the greatest part of your life in traveling, I am well disposed to hope you may hitherto have escaped many vices of your country. But by what I have gathered from your own relation, and the answers I have with much pains wringed and extorted from you, I cannot but conclude the bulk of your natives to be the most pernicious race of little odious vermin that nature ever suffered to crawl upon the surface of the earth."

Nothing but an extreme love of truth could have hindered me from concealing this part of my story. It was in vain to discover my resentments, which were always turned into ridicule; and I was forced to rest with patience while my noble and most beloved country was so injuriously treated. I am heartily sorry as any of my readers can possibly be that such an occasion was given, but this prince happened to be so curious and inquisitive upon every particular that it could not consist either with gratitude or good manners to refuse giving him what satisfaction I was able. Yet thus much I may be allowed to say in my own vindication: that I artfully eluded many of his questions, and gave to every point a more favorable turn by many degrees than the strictness of truth would allow. For I have always borne that laudable partiality to my own country, which Dionysius Halicarnassensis[24] with so much justice recommends to an historian. I would hide the frailties and deformities of my political mother, and place her virtues and beauties in the most advantageous light. This was my sincere endeavor in those many discourses I had with that mighty monarch, although it unfortunately failed of success.

But great allowances should be given to a King who lives wholly secluded from the rest of the world, and must therefore be altogether unacquainted with the manners and customs that most prevail in other nations: the want of which knowledge will ever produce many *prejudices*, and

---

21. *sideling*, sideways.
22. *Grildrig*, the name given to Gulliver in Brobdingnag. It means "manikin."
23. *panegyric*, speech or writing in praise of something.
24. *Dionysius Halicarnassensis* (dī′ə nish′ē əs hal′ə kär-nas′sen sis), a Greek writer in the time of Augustus who wrote a history of Rome.

Gulliver and the King, from a 19th century edition of *Gulliver's Travels*.

or iron, according to its bigness, would drive a ball of iron or lead with such violence and speed as nothing was able to sustain its force. That the largest balls thus discharged would not only destroy whole ranks of an army at once, but batter the strongest walls to the ground; sink down ships with a thousand men in each, to the bottom of the sea; and, when linked together by a chain, would cut through masts and rigging; divide hundreds of bodies in the middle, and lay all waste before them. That we often put this powder into large hollow balls of iron, and discharged them by an engine into some city we were besieging; which would rip up the pavements, tear the houses to pieces, burst and throw splinters on every side, dashing out the brains of all who came near. That I knew the ingredients very well, which were cheap and common; I understood the manner of compounding them, and could direct his workmen how to make those tubes of a size proportionable to all other things in his Majesty's kingdom, and the largest need not be above two hundred foot long; twenty or thirty of which tubes, charged with the proper quantity of powder and balls, would batter down the walls of the strongest town in his dominions in a few hours; or destroy the whole metropolis, if ever it should pretend to dispute his absolute commands. This I humbly offered to his Majesty as a small tribute of acknowledgment in return of so many marks that I had received of his royal favor and protection.

The King was struck with horror at the description I had given of those terrible engines and the proposal I had made. He was amazed how so impotent and groveling an insect as I (these were his expressions) could entertain such inhuman ideas, and in so familiar a manner as to appear wholly unmoved at all the scenes of blood and desolation which I had painted as the common effects of those destructive machines; whereof he said some evil genius, enemy to mankind, must have been the first contriver. As for himself, he protested that although few things delighted him so much as new discoveries in art or in nature, yet he would rather lose half his kingdom than be privy to such a secret, which he commanded me,

a certain *narrowness of thinking,* from which we and the politer countries of Europe are wholly exempted. And it would be hard indeed if so remote a prince's notions of virtue and vice were to be offered as a standard for all mankind.

To confirm what I have now said, and further, to show the miserable effects of a *confined education,* I shall here insert a passage which will hardly obtain belief. In hopes to ingratiate myself farther into his Majesty's favor, I told him of an invention discovered between three and four hundred years ago, to make a certain powder, into an heap of which the smallest spark of fire falling would kindle the whole in a moment, although it were as big as a mountain, and make it all fly up in the air together, with a noise and agitation greater than thunder. That a proper quantity of this powder rammed into an hollow tube of brass

as I valued my life, never to mention any more.

A strange effect of *narrow principles* and *short views!* that a prince possessed of every quality which procures veneration, love, and esteem; of strong parts, great wisdom, and profound learning; endued with admirable talents for government, and almost adored by his subjects; should from a *nice, unnecessary scruple,* whereof in Europe we can have no conception, let slip an opportunity put into his hands that would have made him absolute master of the lives, the liberties, and the fortunes of his people. Neither do I say this with the least intention to detract from the many virtues of that excellent King, whose character I am sensible will on this account be very much lessened in the opinion of an English reader: but I take this defect among them to have risen from their ignorance; they not having hitherto reduced politics into a science, as the more acute wits of Europe had done. For I remember very well, in a discourse one day with the King, when I happened to say there were several thousand books among us written upon the art of government, it gave him (directly contrary to my intention) a very mean opinion of our understandings. He professed both to abominate and despise all *mystery, refinement,* and *intrigue,* either in a prince or a minister. He could not tell what I meant by *secrets of state,* where an enemy or some rival nation were not in the case. He confined the knowledge of governing within very *narrow bounds:* to common sense and reason, to justice and lenity,[25] to the speedy determination of civil and criminal causes, with some other obvious topics which are not worth considering. And he gave it for his opinion that whoever could make two ears of corn or two blades of grass to grow upon a spot of ground where only one grew before would deserve better of mankind and do more essential service to his country than the whole race of politicians put together.

Gulliver, having been in Brobdingnag about two years, is taken by the King and Queen on a tour to the south coast of the kingdom. Longing to see the ocean again, Gulliver asks permission to be carried there by a page whom he likes and who earlier had been entrusted with his care.

I shall never forget with what unwillingness Glumdalclitch consented, nor the strict charge she gave the page to be careful of me, bursting at the same time into a flood of tears, as if she had some foreboding of what was to happen. The boy took me out in my box about half an hour's walk from the palace, towards the rocks on the seashore. I ordered him to set me down, and lifting up one of my sashes, cast many a wistful melancholy look towards the sea. I found myself not very well, and told the page that I had a mind to take a nap in my hammock, which I hoped would do me good. I got in, and the boy shut the window close down, to keep out the cold. I soon fell asleep: and all I can conjecture is that while I slept, the page, thinking no danger could happen, went among the rocks to look for birds' eggs; having before observed him from my window searching about, and picking up one or two in the clefts. Be that as it will, I found myself suddenly awaked with a violent pull upon the ring which was fastened at the top of my box for the conveniency of carriage. I felt my box raised very high in the air, and then borne forward with prodigious speed. The first jolt had like to have shaken me out of my hammock, but afterwards the motion was easy enough. I called out several times as loud as I could raise my voice, but all to no purpose. I looked towards my windows, and could see nothing but the clouds and sky. I heard a noise just over my head like the clapping of wings, and then began to perceive the woeful condition I was in; that some eagle had got the ring of my box in his beak, with an intent to let it fall on a rock, like a tortoise in a shell, and then pick out my body and devour it. For the sagacity and smell of this bird enable him to discover his quarry at a great distance, although better concealed than I could be within a two-inch board.

In a little time I observed the noise and flutter of

25. *lenity,* mercy.

wings to increase very fast, and my box was tossed up and down like a signpost in a windy day. I heard several bangs or buffets, as I thought, given to the eagle (for such I am certain it must have been that held the ring of my box in his beak), and then all on a sudden felt myself falling perpendicularly down for above a minute, but with such incredible swiftness that I almost lost my breath. My fall was topped by a terrible squash, that sounded louder to mine ears than the cataract of Niagara; after which I was quite in the dark for another minute, and then my box began to rise so high that I could see light from the tops of my windows. I now perceived that I was fallen into the sea. My box, by the weight of my body, the goods that were in, and the broad plates of iron fixed for strength at the four corners of the top and bottom, floated about five foot deep in water. I did then and do now suppose that the eagle which flew away with my box was pursued by two or three others, and forced to let me drop while he was defending himself against the rest, who hoped to share in the prey. The plates of iron fastened at the bottom of the box (for those were the strongest) preserved the balance while it fell, and hindered it from being broken on the surface of the water. Every joint of it was well grooved, and the door did not move on hinges, but up and down like a sash; which kept my closet so tight that very little water came in. I got with much difficulty out of my hammock, having first ventured to draw back the slip-board on the roof already mentioned, contrived on purpose to let in air, for want of which I found myself almost stifled.

How often did I then wish myself with my dear Glumdalclitch, from whom one single hour had so far divided me! And I may say with truth that in the midst of my own misfortune, I could not forbear lamenting my poor nurse, the grief she would suffer for my loss, the displeasure of the Queen, and the ruin of her fortune. Perhaps many travelers have not been under greater difficulties and distress than I was at this juncture, expecting every moment to see my box dashed in pieces, or at least overset by the first violent blast or a rising wave. A breach in one single pane of glass would have been immediate death, nor could anything have preserved the windows but the strong lattice wires placed on the outside against accidents in traveling. I saw the water ooze in at several crannies, although the leaks were not considerable, and I endeavored to stop them as well as I could. I was not able to lift up the roof of my closet, which otherwise I certainly should have done, and sat on the top of it, where I might at least preserve myself from being shut up, as I may call it, in the hold. Or, if I escaped these dangers for a day or two, what could I expect but a miserable death of cold and hunger! I was four hours under these circumstances, expecting and indeed wishing every moment to be my last.

I have already told the reader that there were two strong staples fixed upon that side of my box which had no window and into which the servant, who used to carry me on horseback, would put a leathern belt, and buckle it about his waist. Being in this disconsolate state, I heard, or at least thought I heard, some kind of grating noise on that side of my box where the staples were fixed; and soon after I began to fancy that the box was pulled or towed along in the sea; for I now and then felt a sort of tugging, which made the waves rise near the tops of my windows, leaving me almost in the dark. This gave me some faint hopes of relief, although I was not able to imagine how it could be brought about. I ventured to unscrew one of my chairs, which were always fastened to the floor; and having made a hard shift to screw it down again directly under the slipping-board that I had lately opened, I mounted on the chair, and putting my mouth as near as I could to the hole, I called for help in a loud voice, and in all the languages I understood. I then fastened my handkerchief to a stick I usually carried, and thrusting it up the hole, waved it several times in the air, that if any boat or ship were near, the seamen might conjecture some unhappy mortal to be shut up in the box.

I found no effect from all I could do, but plainly perceived my closet to be moved along; and in the space of an hour or better, that side of the box where the staples were, and had no window, struck against something that was hard.

I apprehended it to be a rock, and found myself tossed more than ever. I plainly heard a noise upon the cover of my closet, like that of a cable, and the grating of it as it passed through the ring. I then found myself hoisted up by degrees at least three foot higher than I was before. Whereupon I again thrust up my stick and handkerchief, calling for help till I was almost hoarse. In return to which, I heard a great shout repeated three times, giving me such transports of joy as are not to be conceived but by those who feel them. I now heard a trampling over my head, and somebody calling through the hole with a loud voice in the English tongue: "If there be anybody below, let them speak." I answered, I was an Englishman, drawn by ill fortune into the greatest calamity that ever any creature underwent, and begged, by all that was moving, to be delivered out of the dungeon I was in. The voice replied, I was safe, for my box was fastened to their ship; and the carpenter should immediately come and saw an hole in the cover, large enough to pull me out. I answered, that was needless and would take up too much time, for there was no more to be done but let one of the crew put his finger into the ring, and take the box out of the sea into the ship, and so into the captain's cabin. Some of them, upon hearing me talk so wildly, thought I was mad; others laughed; for indeed it never came into my head that I was now got among people of my own stature and strength. The carpenter came, and in a few minutes sawed a passage about four foot square; then let down a small ladder, upon which I mounted, and from thence was taken into the ship in a very weak condition.

1726

Comment

Size and Scale in *Gulliver's Travels*

Samuel Johnson had the following to say of *Gulliver's Travels:* "When once you have thought of big men and little men, it is very easy to do all the rest." Perhaps Johnson was right, but there is more to thinking "of big men and little men" than first meets the eye. Take, for instance, the problem of scale. The Lilliputians were one-tenth Gulliver's size, the Brobdingnagians were twelve times his size.

Consider for a moment what the size of the Brobdingnagians means. Swift's scale of twelve to one corresponds to the number of inches in a foot, and probably this ratio was intentional. To better comprehend the power of Swift's invention, try to picture for yourself the size of a six-foot (by Brobdingnagian standards) Brobdingnagian. To us he would be seventy-two feet tall, the height of a six- or seven-story building.

Or try the concept in reverse: you are $1/12$ the size of Brobdingnagians. Compute $1/12$ of your height; for most of us this is five or six inches. Now measure against your leg how high this would be (just slightly above the ankle bone). Next, picture yourself that height, looking up as far as you can see at the creature towering above you, and picture a world built to his scale. Imagine what an ordinary chair or table would look like, or a television screen. Realize too that with eyes adapted to your "miniature" world, you would see blemishes you never believed possible, that an ordinary eyelash would be frightening because of its length (nearly a foot long by your minuscule standards).

As a further exercise, imagine your everyday world from a different perspective. Try getting down on the floor and examining the room from that perspective—you'll see what the underside of most of your furniture looks like. Now, try to imagine being Gulliver's size in Brobdingnag and seeing those items from his scale. You will perhaps agree with Johnson that, "when once you have thought of big men and little men, it is very easy to do all the rest"—provided you can also think of a world built to that scale.

THINK AND DISCUSS
Understanding
1. How does Gulliver reach Brobdingnag? How does he finally leave?
2. How does Gulliver come to be sold to the Queen?
3. Describe Gulliver's most dangerous adventure at court and how he is saved.
4. In what ways does Swift show how small Gulliver is in comparison with the people of Brobdingnag?

Analyzing
5. Why did Swift think it necessary for Brobdingnag to be in an unknown location?
6. Describe how Gulliver makes gifts for the Queen and plays a jig for the King. Why do you think Swift includes these episodes?
7. What do the three great scholars finally decide Gulliver is? What is **satirized** here?
8. Explain the circumstances that prompt the King to say, "I cannot but conclude the bulk of your natives to be the most pernicious race of little odious vermin that nature ever suffered to crawl upon the surface of the earth." What is the importance of this speech to the meaning of the entire selection?

Extending
9. Some scholars feel that *Gulliver's Travels* is an early example of science fiction or fantasy. Explain why you agree or disagree.

APPLYING: Point of View   H𝓣
See Handbook of Literary Terms, p. 917

The vantage point from which an author presents the actions and characters of a story is called **point of view**. An author selects a particular point of view in order to achieve certain effects. The major points of view are these: *first person* ("I"); *omniscient* or *limited omniscient*; and *third person*, also called *dramatic*.

1. From what point of view is "Gulliver's Travels" told? How do you know?
2. How does this choice of point of view help Swift to satirize English society?

VOCABULARY
Suffixes
A suffix is a word part added to the end of a root to form another word. Suffixes generally change the function of a word in a sentence, but some suffixes carry meaning as well. Many English words are derived from words in which roots and suffixes were already combined in their original languages.

Copy these words on your paper; then look them up in the Glossary. After each word write the suffix, the meaning of the suffix, and the part of speech it forms. For example: *lamentable* -able, "deserving to be _____ ed" (adjective)

disconsolate	prodigious
laudable	supplicate
nicety	veneration

THINKING SKILLS
Classifying
To classify things is to arrange them into categories or groups according to some system.

1. Scan *Gulliver's Travels* to find what kinds of items are used to show his small size according to the Brobdingnagian scale of things. Classify these according to whether they are human, animal (including insects), vegetable, or non-living.
2. Classify the Brobdingnagians mentioned in the selection. Devise your own system.

ENRICHMENT
Researching *Gulliver's Travels*
As a class, divide the entire book of *Gulliver's Travels* into parts of manageable size. Read the part you have chosen and report to the class, summarizing briefly the plot and explaining the satire, so that the entire class understands the nature of Swift's work.

Flamboyant, often in debt, with a temper as quick as his wit, Steele nevertheless was a firm advocate of morality. In combination with Joseph Addison (see page 365), he did much to convert England from Restoration worldliness to a new sense of personal and national decency. Born in Dublin, he attended Charterhouse School in London, where he first met Addison. He went on to Oxford but left Merton College without a degree to accept a commission in the army.

While in the army, Steele wrote *The Christian Hero* (1701), a pamphlet that praised King William III. Following this he wrote three moral comedies, none of them successful; however, these and his later successful comedies did set the vogue for sentimental comedies.

On April 12, 1709, the first issue of *The Tatler* appeared in the London coffee houses. Issued thrice weekly under the motto, "Whatever men do is the subject of this book," it was Steele's attempt to educate the new middle class in manners and morals. On January 2, 1711, after 271 issues, *The Tatler* ceased publication.

A short time later Steele and Addison produced *The Spectator*. The essay that follows is from the second number of *The Spectator* (March 2, 1711) and describes the various individuals who make up The Spectator Club, a coffeehouse group. When *The Spectator* also ceased publication, Steele tried other periodicals: *The Guardian* (1713; 175 issues), *The Englishman* (1713–1714; 57 issues), *The Lover* (1714; 40 issues), and at least five others. It was *The Tatler*, however, that showed the way to its successors.

H℡ **See TONE in the Handbook of Literary Terms, page 932.**

The Spectator Club

Sir Richard Steele

In this essay Steele **characterizes** the members of the Spectator Club. In subsequent essays in *The Spectator*, he and Addison use these characters and the narrator, Mr. Spectator, to satirize some of the minor evils of the age.

---

he first of our society is a gentleman of Worcestershire, of ancient descent, a baronet, his name Sir Roger de Coverley. His great-grandfather was inventor of that famous country-dance[2] which is called after him. All who know that shire are very well acquainted with the parts and merits of Sir Roger. He is a gentleman that is very singular in his behavior, but his singularities proceed from his good sense and are contradictions to the manners of the world only as he thinks the world is in the wrong. However, this humor[3] creates him no enemies, for he does nothing with sourness or obstinacy; and his being unconfined to modes and forms makes him but the readier and more capable to please and oblige all who know him.

When he is in town, he lives in Soho Square. It is said he keeps himself a bachelor by reason he was crossed in love by a perverse, beautiful widow of the next county to him. Before this disappointment Sir Roger was what you call a fine gentleman, had often supped with my Lord Rochester and Sir George Etherege,[4] fought a duel upon his first coming to town, and kicked Bully Dawson[5] in a public coffee house for calling him "youngster." But being ill-used by the above-mentioned widow, he was very serious for a year and a half; and though, his temper being naturally jovial, he at last got over it, he grew careless of himself, and never dressed afterwards.[6] He continues to wear a coat and doublet of the same cut that were in fashion at the time of his repulse, which, in his merry humors, he tells us, has been in and out twelve times since he first wore it.

He is now in his fifty-sixth year, cheerful, gay, and hearty; keeps a good house both in town and country; a great lover of mankind; but there is such a mirthful cast in his behavior that he is rather beloved than esteemed. His tenants grow rich, his servants look satisfied, all the young women profess love to him, and the young men are glad of his company. When he comes into a house, he calls the servants by their names, and talks all the way upstairs to a visit. I must not omit that Sir Roger is a justice of the quorum;[7] that he fills the chair at a quarter-session[8] with great abilities; and three months ago gained universal applause by explaining a passage in the Game Act.[9]

The gentleman next in esteem and authority among us is another bachelor, who is a member of the Inner Temple,[10] a man of great probity, wit, and understanding; but he has chosen his place of residence rather to obey the direction of an old humorsome father than in pursuit of his own inclinations. He was placed there to study the laws of the land, and is the most learned of any of the house in those of the stage.[11] He knows the argument of each of the orations of Demosthenes and Tully,[12] but not one case in the reports of our own courts. No one ever took him for a fool, but none, except his intimate friends, know he has a great deal of wit.[13] This turn makes him at once both disinterested and agreeable. As few of his thoughts are drawn from business, they are most of them fit for conversation. His taste of books is a little too just[14] for the age he lives in; he has read all, but approves of very few. His familiarity

---

1. "*Ast . . . ore.*" But six others and more cry out together with one voice. [Latin]
2. *country-dance,* called the "Roger de Coverley" and similar to the Virginia Reel.
3. *humor,* odd behavior.
4. *Lord Rochester and Sir George Etherege* (eth'ər ij), a poet and a dramatist, respectively, in the reign of Charles II.
5. *Bully Dawson,* notorious London swindler of the seventeenth century.
6. *never dressed afterwards.* He never afterwards dressed in the latest fashion.
7. *justice of the quorum,* justice of the peace.
8. *fills . . . quarter-session,* presides as judge at the quarterly meeting of a local court.
9. *Game Act,* laws controlling the hunting of game, which were evidently as hard to understand as our Income Tax law.
10. *Inner Temple,* one of the four Inns of Court in London, which have the exclusive right of admitting persons to practice at the bar.
11. *those of the stage,* the laws, or rules, that govern the writing of plays.
12. *Demosthenes* (di mos'thə nēz') *and Tully* (tul'i). The former was the most famous orator of ancient Greece. The latter was Marcus Tullius Cicero, a famous Roman orator.
13. *wit,* intellectual ability.
14. *just,* proper; correct.

with the customs, manners, actions, and writings of the ancients makes him a very delicate observer of what occurs to him in the present world. He is an excellent critic, and the time of the play is his hour of business. Exactly at five he passes through New Inn,[15] crosses through Russell Court, and takes a turn at Will's[16] till the play begins. He has his shoes rubbed and his periwig powdered at the barber's as you go into the Rose.[17] It is for the good of the audience when he is at a play, for the actors have an ambition to please him.

The person of next consideration is Sir Andrew Freeport, a merchant of great eminence in the city of London, a person of indefatigable industry, strong reason, and great experience. His notions of trade are noble and generous, and, as every rich man has usually some sly way of jesting which would make no great figure were he not a rich man, he calls the sea the British Common.

He is acquainted with commerce in all its parts and will tell you that it is a stupid and barbarous way to extend dominion by arms; for true power is to be got by arts and industry. He will often argue that if this part of our trade were well cultivated, we should gain from one nation; and if another, from another. I have heard him prove that diligence makes more lasting acquisitions than valor and that sloth has ruined more nations than the sword. He abounds in several frugal maxims, among which the greatest favorite is, "A penny saved is a penny got."

A general trader of good sense is pleasanter company that a general scholar; and Sir Andrew having a natural, unaffected eloquence, the perspicuity of his discourse gives the same pleasure that wit would in another man. He has made his fortunes himself and says that England may be richer than other kingdoms by as plain methods as he himself is richer than other men; though at the same time I can say this of him, that there is not a point in the compass but blows home a ship in which he is an owner.

Next to Sir Andrew in the club room sits Captain Sentry, a gentleman of great courage, good understanding, but invincible modesty. He is one of those that deserve very well, but are very awkward at putting their talents within the observation of such as should take notice of them. He was some years a captain and behaved himself with great gallantry in several engagements and at several sieges; but having a small estate of his own, and being next heir to Sir Roger, he has quitted a way of life in which no man can rise suitably to his merit who is not something of a courtier as well as a soldier.

I have heard him often lament that in a profession where merit is placed in so conspicuous a view, impudence should get the better of modesty. When he has talked to this purpose I never heard him make a sour expression, but frankly confess that he left the world because he was not fit for it. A strict honesty and an even, regular behavior are in themselves obstacles to him that must press through crowds who endeavor at the same end with himself—the favor of a commander. He will, however, in this way of talk, excuse generals for not disposing according to men's desert, or inquiring into it. "For," says he, "that great man who has a mind to help me has as many to break through to come at me as I have to come at him." Therefore he will conclude that the man who would make a figure, especially in a military way, must get over all false modesty and assist his patron against the importunity of other pretenders by a proper assurance in his own vindication. He says it is a civil cowardice to be backward in asserting what you ought to expect, as it is a military fear to be slow in attacking when it is your duty.

With this candor does the gentleman speak of himself and others. The same frankness runs through all his conversation. The military part of his life has furnished him with many adventures, in the relation of which he is very agreeable to the company; for he is never overbearing, though accustomed to command men in the utmost degree

---

15. *New Inn,* part of the Middle Temple, one of the four Inns of Court.
16. *takes a turn at Will's,* plays a game or so of cards at Will's Coffeehouse.
17. *the Rose,* a tavern frequented by authors of plays.

below him; nor ever too obsequious from an habit of obeying men highly above him.

But that our society may not appear a set of humorists,[18] unacquainted with the gallantries and pleasures of the age, we have among us the gallant Will Honeycomb, a gentleman who according to his years should be in the decline of his life, but having ever been very careful of his person and always had a very easy fortune, time has made but very little impression either by wrinkles on his forehead or traces in his brain. His person is well turned, of a good height. He is very ready at that sort of discourse with which men usually entertain women.

He has all his life dressed very well, and remembers habits[19] as others do men. He can smile when one speaks to him, and laughs easily. He knows the history of every mode and can inform you from which of the French king's wenches our wives and daughters had this manner of curling their hair, that way of placing their hoods; whose frailty was covered by such a sort of petticoat, and whose vanity to show her foot made that part of the dress so short in such a year. In a word, all his conversation and knowledge has been in the female world.

This way of talking of his very much enlivens the conversation among us of a more sedate turn; and I find there is not one of the company but myself, who rarely speak at all, but speaks of him as of that sort of man who is usually called a well-bred, fine gentleman. To conclude his character, where women are not concerned, he is an honest, worthy man.

I cannot tell whether I am to account him whom I am next to speak of as one of our company, for he visits us but seldom; but when he does, it adds to every man else a new enjoyment of himself. He is a clergyman, a very philosophic man, of general learning, great sanctity of life, and the most exact good breeding. He has the misfortune to be of a very weak constitution and consequently cannot accept of such cares and business as preferments in his functions would oblige him to. He is therefore among divines what a chamber-counselor[20] is among lawyers. The probity of his mind and the integrity of his life create him followers, as being eloquent or loud advances others. He seldom introduces the subject he speaks upon; but we are so far gone in years that he observes, when he is among us, an earnestness to have him fall on some divine topic, which he always treats with much authority, as one who has no interest in this world, as one who is hastening to the object of all his wishes and conceives hope from his decays and infirmities.

These are my ordinary companions.

---

18. *humorists*, eccentric characters.
19. *habits*, styles.
20. *chamber-counselor*, a lawyer who gives opinions in private, but does not appear in court.

Comment

The London Coffeehouses
by Thomas Babington Macaulay

he coffeehouse must not be dismissed with a cursory mention. It might indeed at that time have been not improperly called a most important political institution. Public meetings, harangues, resolutions, and the rest of the modern machinery of agitation had not yet come into fashion. Nothing resembling the modern newspaper existed. In such circumstances the coffeehouses were the chief organs through which the public opinion of the metropolis vented itself.

The first of these establishments had been set up, in the time of the Commonwealth, by a

Turkey merchant, who had acquired among the Mahometans a taste for their favorite beverage. The convenience of being able to make appointments in any part of the town, and of being able to pass evenings socially at a very small charge, was so great that the fashion spread fast. Every man of the upper or middle class went daily to his coffeehouse to learn the news and to discuss it. Every coffeehouse had one or more orators to whose eloquence the crowd listened with admiration, and who soon became what the journalists of our own time have been called, a fourth Estate of the realm.[1]

The court had long seen with uneasiness the growth of this new power in the state. An attempt had been made to close the coffeehouses. But men of all parties missed their usual places of resort so much that there was an universal outcry. The government did not venture, in opposition to a feeling so strong and general, to enforce a regulation of which the legality might well be questioned. Since that time ten years had elapsed, and during those years the number and influence of the coffeehouses had been constantly increasing. Foreigners remarked that the coffeehouse was that which especially distinguished London from all other cities; that the coffeehouse was the Londoner's home, and that those who wished to find a gentleman commonly asked, not whether he lived in Fleet Street or Chancery Lane, but whether he frequented the Grecian or the Rainbow.

Nobody was excluded from these places who had laid down his penny at the bar. Yet every rank and profession, and every shade of religious and political opinion, had its own headquarters. There were houses near Saint James' Park where fops congregated, their heads and shoulders covered with black or flaxen wigs, not less ample than those which are now worn by the Chancellor and by the Speaker of the House of Commons. The wig came from Paris; and so did the rest of the fine gentleman's ornaments, his embroidered coat, his fringed gloves, and the tassel which upheld his pantaloons. The atmosphere was like that of a perfumer's shop. Tobacco in any other form than that of richly scented snuff was held in abomination. If any clown, ignorant of the usages of the house,

called for a pipe, the sneers of the whole assembly and the short answers of the waiters soon convinced him that he had better go somewhere else. Nor would he have had far to go. For, in general, the coffee rooms reeked with tobacco like a guard room; and strangers sometimes expressed their surprise that so many people should leave their own firesides to sit in the midst of eternal fog and stench.

Nowhere was the smoking more constant than at Will's. That celebrated house, situated between Covent Garden and Bow Street, was sacred to polite letters. There the talk was about poetical justice[2] and the unities of place and time.[3] One group debated whether *Paradise Lost* ought not to have been in rhyme. Under no roof was a greater variety of figures to be seen. There were earls in stars and garters,[4] clergymen in cassocks and bands, pert Templars,[5] sheepish lads from the universities, translators and index makers[6] in ragged coats.

There were coffeehouses where the first medical men might be consulted. There were Puritan coffeehouses where no oath was heard, and where lank-haired men discussed election and reprobation[7] through their noses; and Popish coffee houses where, as good Protestants believed, Jesuits planned over their cups another great fire, and cast silver bullets to shoot the King.

These gregarious habits had no small share in forming the character of the Londoner of that age. He was, indeed, a different being from

---

1. *fourth Estate of the realm.* The original three Estates were: (1) the religious leaders of the House of Lords; (2) the nonreligious leaders of the House of Lords; (3) the common people.
2. *poetical justice,* the ideal justice, in which rewards and punishments are distributed as they should be.
3. *unities of place and time,* a reference to the dramatic unities or rules based on the *Poetics* of Aristotle. The rules decreed that a drama should be confined to one location and should cover not more than twenty-four hours.
4. *stars and garters,* insignia of orders of English knighthood.
5. *Templars,* students or lawyers who lived and worked in one of the Temple buildings belonging to English legal societies.
6. *translators and index makers,* hack writers who translated Latin or Greek poems and prepared indexes for the books of other authors.
7. *election and reprobation,* God's choice of those to be accepted and those to be rejected for salvation.

An early London coffeehouse, signed "AS; 1668." *British Museum*

the rustic Englishman. There was not then the intercourse which now exists between the two classes. Only very great men were in the habit of dividing the year between town and country. Few esquires came to the capital thrice in their lives. Nor was it yet the practice of all citizens in easy circumstances to breathe the fresh air of the fields and woods during some weeks of every summer. A cockney in a rural village was stared at as much as if he had intruded into a kraal of Hottentots.[8]

On the other hand, when the Lord of a Lincolnshire or Shropshire manor appeared in Fleet Street, he was as easily distinguished from the resident population as a Turk or a Lascar.[9]

His dress, his gait, his accent, the manner in which he stared at the shops, stumbled into the gutters, ran against the porters, and stood under the water spouts, marked him out as an excellent subject for the operations of swindlers and banterers. Bullies jostled him into the gutter. Hackney coachmen splashed him from head to foot. Thieves explored with perfect security the huge pockets of his horseman's

---

8. **A cockney . . . kraal of Hottentots.** A native of the poorer section of London, who appeared in a rural village, was stared at as much as if he had intruded into a village of a South African race.

9. **Lascar,** native sailor of the East Indies.

coat, while he stood entranced by the splendor of the Lord Mayor's show. Moneydroppers,[10] sore from the cart's tail,[11] introduced themselves to him, and appeared to him the most honest, friendly gentlemen that he had ever seen. Painted women, the refuse of Lewkner Lane and Whetstone Park, passed themselves on him for countesses and maids of honor. If he asked his way to Saint James', his informants sent him to Mile End.[12] If he went into a shop, he was instantly discerned to be a fit purchaser of everything that nobody else would buy, of secondhand embroidery, copper rings, and watches that would not go. If he rambled into any fashionable coffeehouse, he became a mark for the insolent derision of fops and the grave waggery of Templars.

Enraged and mortified, he soon returned to his mansion, and there, in the homage of his tenants and the conversation of his boon companions, found consolation for the vexations and humiliations which he had undergone. There he was once more a great man and saw nothing above himself except when at the assizes he took his seat on the bench near the Judge, or when at the muster of the militia he saluted the Lord Lieutenant. . . .

---

10. **Moneydroppers,** confidence men who drop money around and pretend to find it for the purposes of fraud.
11. **the cart's tail.** Offenders were tied to the end of a cart and whipped through the streets.
12. **Saint James'** . . . **Mile End,** located at opposite ends of London.

THINK AND DISCUSS
Understanding
1. Besides Mr. Spectator, who are the members of the Spectator Club?

Analyzing
2. Which member do you think will take over the leadership of the Club? Why?
3. What interests do you assume the members have in common?

Extending
4. Could such a group be formed in your community today? Explain.

APPLYING: Tone H╤
See Handbook of Literary Terms, p. 932
The author's attitude, stated or implied, toward a subject or audience determines the **tone** of a literary work. For example, Swift's tone in "A Description of a City Shower" is humorous, but gentle, while in "A Modest Proposal" it is harsh, even vicious.

1. How would you describe Steele's tone in "The Spectator Club"—angry, tragic, melancholy, chatty, hilarious? Explain.

2. Judging from Steele's tone, what sort of people does he expect his readers to be?

COMPOSITION
Writing a Character Sketch
Using the same techniques of **characterization** that Swift uses, write a character sketch about a person you know. You will want to describe your subject's physical appearance, dress, habits, attitudes, and opinions. When you have finished writing, read your sketch aloud to a small group of classmates and discuss what changes might make your sketch more vivid and precise.

Analyzing a Periodical Essay
Reread "The Spectator Club," noting the character traits Mr. Spectator seems to regard as favorable for each of the six members he describes. Then write a composition for your school literary magazine in which you discuss the traits Mr. Spectator admires in a club member. Conclude by generalizing about the kind of traits Steele seems to admire. See "Writing About Nonfiction" in the Writer's Handbook.

BIOGRAPHY

Joseph Addison
1672–1719

Addison was educated at the Charterhouse School, where he met Richard Steele, and the two began a lifelong friendship. After receiving his B.A. and M.A. from Magdalen College, Oxford, Addison spent four years in Europe gaining proficiency in modern languages. Entering government service in 1704, Addison (a Whig) was a Member of Parliament from 1708 to his death, and eventually became Secretary of State.

He first achieved literary notice in 1705 with *The Campaign*, a poem celebrating Marlborough's victory in the Battle of Blenheim, and his classical tragedy *Cato* was a great success. He is best known for his part in the development of the periodical essay, his contributions to *The Tatler* and *The Spectator*.

While Addison was living in Ireland on a government assignment, he saw a copy of *The Tatler*. Suspecting it to be the work of Steele, he sent the paper a contribution and thereafter often wrote for it.

In 1711 he and Steele founded the best and most famous of the periodicals, *The Spectator*, published daily, Monday through Saturday, from March 1, 1711, to December 6, 1712. Continuing in the tradition of *The Tatler*, with its objective of improving manners and morals, *The Spectator* was, however, more Addison's than Steele's. Its anonymous Mr. Spectator reported on people, events, and ideas.

Will Wimble

Joseph Addison

> *Summary*
> - good guy - helps people   - he wanders
> - came from rich family   - not married
> - ~~did handywork around town~~   - can't support her
> Social problem - what his family   - fishes → merchant
> wants him to do.   - hunts

Set at the home of Sir Roger de Coverley, the "country squire" member of the Spectator Club, this essay deals with a problem all too common in eighteenth-century England. The narrator is Mr. Spectator himself.

Gratis anhelans, multa agendo nihil agens.[1]

s I was yesterday morning walking with Sir Roger before his house, a country fellow brought him a huge fish, which, he told him, Mr. William Wimble had caught that very morning; and that he presented it, with his service, to him, and intended to come and dine with him. At the same time he delivered a letter, which my friend read to me as soon as the messenger left him.

---

1. Gratis . . . agens, "Out of breath to no purpose, and very busy about nothing," a quotation from a Roman writer of fables.

SIR ROGER:

I desire you to accept of a jack[2] which is the best I have caught this season. I intend to come and stay with you a week and see how the perch bite in the Black River. I observed, with some concern, the last time I saw you upon the bowling green, that your whip wanted a lash to it. I will bring half a dozen with me that I twisted last week, which I hope will serve you all the time you are in the country. I have not been out of the saddle for six days last past, having been at Eton with Sir John's eldest son. He takes to his learning hugely.

I am, Sir, your humble servant,

WILL WIMBLE

This extraordinary letter and message that accompanied it made me very curious to know the character and quality of the gentleman who sent them, which I found to be as follows:

Will Wimble is younger brother to a baronet and descended of the ancient family of the Wimbles. He is now between forty and fifty; but being bred to no business and born to no estate, he generally lives with his elder brother as superintendent of his game. He hunts a pack of dogs better than any man in the country and is very famous for finding out a hare. He is extremely well versed in all the little handicrafts of an idle man. He makes a May fly[3] to a miracle and furnishes the whole country with angle rods. As he is a good-natured, officious[4] fellow and very much esteemed upon account of his family, he is a welcome guest at every house and keeps up a good correspondence among all the gentlemen about him. He carries a tulip root in his pocket from one to another or exchanges a puppy between a couple of friends that live perhaps in the opposite sides of the county.

Will is a particular favorite of all the young heirs, whom he frequently obliges with a net that he has weaved or a setting dog that he has made himself.[5] He now and then presents a pair of garters of his own knitting to their mothers or sisters and raises a great deal of mirth among them by inquiring, as often as he meets them, *how they wear.* These gentlemenlike manufactures and obliging little humors make Will the darling of the country.

"Angling" from *The Gentleman's Recreation,* by Richard Blome, London, 1686.

Sir Roger was proceeding in the character of him when we saw him make up to us with two or three hazel twigs in his hand that he had cut in Sir Roger's woods as he came through them, in his way to the house. I was very much pleased to observe on one side the hearty and sincere welcome with which Sir Roger received him and on the other the secret joy which his guest discovered at sight of the good old knight.

After the first salutes were over, Will desired Sir Roger to lend him one of his servants to carry a set of shuttlecocks he had with him in a little box to a lady that lived about a mile off, to whom it seems he had promised such a present for above this half year. Sir Roger's back was no

2. *jack,* pike (a kind of fish).
3. *May fly,* a lure used in angling.
4. *officious,* eager to please or help.
5. *made himself,* trained.

sooner turned but honest Will began to tell me of a large cock pheasant that he had sprung in one of the neighboring woods, with two or three other adventures of the same nature. Odd and uncommon characters are the game that I look for and most delight in; for which reason I was as much pleased with the novelty of the person that talked to me as he could be for his life with the springing of a pheasant, and therefore listened to him with more than ordinary attention.

In the midst of his discourse the bell rung to dinner, where the gentleman I have been speaking of had the pleasure of seeing the huge jack he had caught served up for the first dish in a most sumptuous manner. Upon our sitting down to it he gave us a long account how he had hooked it, played with it, foiled it, and at length drew it out upon the bank, with several other particulars that lasted all the first course. A dish of wild fowl that came afterwards furnished conversation for the rest of the dinner, which concluded with a late invention of Will's for improving the quail pipe.[6]

Upon withdrawing into my room after dinner I was secretly touched with compassion toward the honest gentleman that had dined with us and could not but consider with a great deal of concern how so good a heart and such busy hands were wholly employed in trifles, that so much humanity should be so little beneficial to others, and so much industry so little advantageous to himself. The same temper of mind and application to affairs might have recommended him to the public esteem and have raised his fortune to another station of life. What good to his country or himself might not a trader or merchant have done with such useful though ordinary qualifications?

Will Wimble's is the case of many a younger brother of a great family, who had rather see their children starve like gentlemen than thrive in a trade or profession that is beneath their quality. This humor fills several parts of Europe with pride and beggary. It is the happiness of a trading nation like ours that the younger sons, though uncapable of any liberal art or profession, may be placed in such a way of life as may perhaps enable them to vie with the best of their family. Accordingly, we find several citizens that were launched into the world with narrow fortunes rising by an honest industry to greater estates than those of their elder brothers. It is not improbable but Will was formerly tried at divinity, law, or physic;[7] and that, finding his genius did not lie that way, his parents gave him up at length to his own inventions. But certainly, however improper he might have been for studies of a higher nature, he was perfectly well turned for the occupations of trade and commerce.

1711

---

6. *quail pipe*, instrument used for imitating the sound of a quail.
7. *physic*, medicine.

Party Patches

Joseph Addison

In this *Spectator* paper Addison lightly ridicules the ladies, who show their political party preferences by placing "beauty spots," or patches, on one side or the other of their faces.

Qualis ubi audito venantum murmure tigris
Horruit in maculas——[1]

bout the middle of last winter I went to see an opera at the theater in the Haymarket, where I could not but take notice of two parties of very fine women that had placed themselves in the opposite side boxes and seemed drawn up in a kind of battle array one against another.

After a short survey of them, I found they were *patched* differently, the faces on one hand being spotted on the right side of the forehead and those upon the other on the left. I quickly perceived that they cast hostile glances upon one another and that their patches were placed in those different situations as party signals to distinguish friends from foes. In the middle boxes between these two opposite bodies were several ladies who patched indifferently on both sides of their faces and seemed to sit there with no other intention but to see the opera.

Upon inquiry I found that the body of Amazons[2] on my right hand were Whigs, and those on my left, Tories; and that those who had placed themselves in the middle boxes were a neutral party, whose faces had not yet declared themselves. These last, however, as I afterwards found, diminished daily, and took their party with one side or the other; insomuch that I observed in several of them the patches which were before dispersed equally are now all gone over to the Whig or Tory side of the face.

The censorious say that the men whose hearts are aimed at are very often the occasions that one part of the face is thus dishonored and lies under a kind of disgrace, while the other is so much set off and adorned by the owner; and that the patches turn to the right or to the left according to the principles of the man who is most in favor. But whatever may be the motives of a few fantastical coquettes, who do not patch for the public good so much as for their own private advantage, it is certain that there are several women of honor who patch out of principle and with an eye to the interest of their country. Nay, I am informed that some of them adhere so steadfastly to their party and are so far from sacrificing their zeal for the public to their passion for any particular person that in a late draft of marriage articles a lady has stipulated with her husband that, whatever his opinions are, she shall be at liberty to patch on which side she pleases.

I must here take notice that Rosalinda, a famous Whig partisan, has most unfortunately a very beautiful mole on the Tory part of her forehead; which, being very conspicuous, has occasioned many mistakes and given a handle to her enemies to misrepresent her face, as though it had revolted from the Whig interest. But, whatever this natural patch may seem to intimate, it is well known that her notions of government are still the same. This unlucky mole, however, has misled several coxcombs and, like the hanging out of false colors, made some of them converse with Rosalinda in what they thought the spirit of her party, when on a sudden she has given them an unexpected fire that has sunk them all at once.

If Rosalinda is unfortunate in her mole, Nigranilla is as unhappy in a pimple, which forces her, against her inclinations, to patch on the Whig side.

I am told that many virtuous matrons, who formerly have been taught to believe that this artificial spotting of the face was unlawful, are now reconciled by a zeal for their cause to what they could not be prompted by a concern for their beauty. This way of declaring war upon one another puts me in mind of what is reported of the tigress, that several spots rise in her skin when she is angry; or, as Mr. Cowley has imitated the verses that stand as the motto of this paper,

——She swells with angry pride,
And calls forth all her spots on ev'ry side.[3]

When I was in the theater the time abovementioned, I had the curiosity to count the patches

---

1. **"Qualis . . . maculas."** Like the tigress when, at the sound of the hunters, spots appear upon her skin. [Latin]
2. **Amazons,** an ancient race of female warriors.
3. **"She swells . . . side,"** from the *Davideis,* an epic poem by the seventeenth-century poet Abraham Cowley (1618–1667).

on both sides, and found the Tory patches to be about twenty stronger than the Whig; but to make amends for this small inequality, I the next morning found the whole puppet show filled with faces spotted after the Whiggish manner. Whether or no the ladies had retreated hither in order to rally their forces I cannot tell; but the next night they came in so great a body to the opera that they outnumbered the enemy.

This account of party patches will, I am afraid, appear improbable to those who live at a distance from the fashionable world; but as it is a distinction of a very singular nature, and what perhaps may never meet with a parallel, I think I should not have discharged the office of a faithful Spectator had I not recorded it.

I have, in former papers, endeavored to expose this party-rage in women, as it only serves to aggravate the hatreds and animosities that reign among men, and in a great measure deprives the fair sex of those peculiar charms with which nature has endowed them.

When the Romans and Sabines[4] were at war and just upon the point of giving battle, the women who were allied to both of them interposed with so many tears and entreaties that they prevented the mutual slaughter which threatened both parties and united them together in a firm and lasting peace.

I would recommend this noble example to our British ladies at a time when their country is torn with so many unnatural divisions that if they continue it will be a misfortune to be born in it. The Greeks thought it so improper for women to interest themselves in competitions and contentions that for this reason, among others, they forbade them, under pain of death, to be present at the Olympic games,[5] notwithstanding these were the public diversions of all Greece.

As our English women excel those of all nations in beauty, they should endeavor to outshine them in all other accomplishments proper to the sex and to distinguish themselves as tender mothers and faithful wives rather than as furious partisans. Female virtues are of a domestic turn. The family is the proper province for private women to

Detail from *The Laughing Audience,* an etching by William Hogarth. 1733. *British Museum*

shine in. If they must be showing their zeal for the public, let it not be against those who are perhaps of the same family, or at least of the same religion or nation, but against those who are the open, professed, undoubted enemies of their faith, liberty, and country.

When the Romans were pressed with a foreign enemy, the ladies voluntarily contributed all their rings and jewels to assist the government under a public exigence, which appeared so laudable an action in the eyes of their countrymen that from thenceforth it was permitted by a law to pronounce public orations at the funeral of a woman in praise of the deceased person, which till that time was peculiar to men. Would our English ladies, instead of sticking on a patch against those of their own country, show themselves so truly public-spirited as to sacrifice every one her necklace against the common enemy, what decrees ought not to be made in favor of them?

Since I am recollecting upon this subject such passages as occur to my memory out of ancient authors, I cannot omit a sentence in the celebrated funeral oration of Pericles,[6] which he made in honor of those brave Athenians[7] that were slain

4. Romans and Sabines. The Sabines were an ancient people living in central Italy, who were conquered by the Romans.

5. Olympic games, contests in athletics, poetry, and music held every four years by the ancient Greeks in honor of Zeus.

6. Pericles (per'ə klēz'), 490?-429 B.C., Athenian statesman, orator, and military commander.

7. Athenians (ə thē'nē ənz), citizens of Athens, Greece, famous in ancient times for its art and literature.

in a fight with the Lacedaemonians.[8] After having addressed himself to the several ranks and orders of his countrymen, and shown them how they should behave themselves in the public cause, he turns to the female part of his audience: "And as for you (says he) I shall advise you in very few words: Aspire only to those virtues that are peculiar to your sex; follow your natural modesty, and think it your greatest commendation not to be talked of one way or other."

---

8. *Lacedaemonians* (las′ə di mō′nē ənz), citizens of Sparta in ancient Greece. Sparta and Athens were great rivals.

THINK AND DISCUSS
WILL WIMBLE
Understanding
1. Why is Will Wimble an idle gentleman?
2. What does Will do that makes him popular in the neighborhood?

Analyzing
3. How does Mr. Spectator feel about Will's activities?
4. Explain the appropriateness of the Latin *epigraph*, the quotation at the beginning, to the meaning of the whole essay.
5. Mr. Spectator says, "Odd and uncommon characters are the game that I look for and most delight in." What does he mean, and how does he apply it in this essay?

Extending
6. Sir Roger de Coverly was first described in "The Spectator Club" (see page 358). Explain how the details in this essay enhance his character as presented there.
7. What sort of reform does the **satire** in "Will Wimble" attempt to inspire?

PARTY PATCHES
Understanding
1. Explain what patches are and how women used them.
2. What does the placement of the patches signify?

Analyzing
3. In most cases, whom are the women trying to impress by the placement of their patches?

4. Why does Addison make an **allusion** to the Greek Olympic games?
5. Why does he allude to Roman ladies? to Pericles' funeral oration?
6. *Caricature* is the exaggeration of prominent features of appearance or character. Whom does Addison caricature in "Party Patches"? Why?

Extending
7. What seems to you to be the real purpose of Addison's **satire** here? Do you agree with him? Explain.

COMPOSITION
Writing a Gentle Satire
The satire in *The Spectator* is usually gentle, aimed at correcting with a tap rather than with a hard blow, so that Mr. Spectator can remain on good terms with those he satirizes. Write an essay of at least three paragraphs in which you gently satirize a public figure or a group of public figures—singers, sports personalities, politicians, and so on. Share your essay with your classmates.

Comparing and Contrasting Satires
Compare and contrast the satire of "Will Wimble" with that of "Party Patches." You might consider what is being satirized in each, which essay appears more realistic, and which essay shows some degree of sympathy. Write three to four paragraphs with your classmates as your audience.

London

"London, thou art the flower of cities all."
—William Dunbar, c. 1465–c. 1530

London is the capital city of England and the heart of what was once the greatest empire in the world. To English people over the centuries, London has represented all that was both desirable and detestable about English life. In the late Middle Ages, when feudalism was on the wane, London was the magnet that drew former serfs from the land to what was becoming a city. To them London stood for opportunity, a chance to find an occupation that would enable them to rise financially and socially.

Fourteenth-century London produced Geoffrey Chaucer, one of England's greatest authors. The fact that he begins his *Canterbury Tales* in London, at the Tabard Inn in Southwark, indicates the drawing power of the city for those going on pilgrimages or other trips through the countryside. The East Midland dialect of London, which Chaucer used in his works, became the standard language of the country and an ancestor of the English we speak in America today.

In the Renaissance, London, which to an earlier generation had meant the opportunity to leave feudal drudgery behind, now became the major focus of exciting new experiments in life and literature. It was to Queen Elizabeth in London that the English sea captains reported on their successful return from the voyages of discovery. It was in London that the golden age of Elizabethan drama developed. William Shakespeare, attracted by the opportunities there, left Stratford-on-Avon to become England's greatest dramatist and poet.

London also had a seamier side, for if it was the center of culture and ideas, it was also marked by poverty and crime. There was a flourishing underworld, and writers such as Thomas Nashe and Robert Greene wrote about its methods, its thieves' language, and its practitioners.

Beggars, thieves, and highwaymen were the main characters in John Gay's *The Beggar's Opera* (1728), which was adapted by Bertolt Brecht and Kurt Weill into *The Threepenny Opera* in 1928.

London was also the center of the plague in England. Plague had been sporadic since the 1300s, and there was an especially violent outbreak in 1665. Daniel Defoe has given us an extremely thorough fictional account of the plague in *A Journal of the Plague Year* (see page 414).

In the eighteenth century, London reached its peak as the seat of fashion, literature, manners, and gentility. Coffeehouses proliferated, and conversation was a well-developed art. Many would have agreed with Samuel Johnson, who said, "When a man is tired of London, he is tired of life; for there is in London all that life can afford."

By the end of the eighteenth century, the Romantic movement (see Unit 5) advocated life in the country as superior to urban life. London was viewed as the center of vice. The Romantics tended to believe that virtue and inspiration resided in the country, the uncorrupted world of nature.

During the nineteenth century the ambivalence with which London was viewed seemed to increase. London was the capital of an expanding empire, and as such it was a seat of power, wealth, and culture. It was the city of thieves, rogues, prisoners, and the poor portrayed by Dickens. It was also the city of Sherlock Holmes as described by Sir Arthur Conan Doyle. In *A Study in Scarlet* (1887), Dr. Watson, friend of Holmes, describes London as "that great cesspool into which all the loungers and idlers of the Empire are irresistably drained."

Today London remains a magnet for people from other parts of the world, especially from the countries that made up the old empire, and a major world capital of the arts, finance, and trade.

The son of a butcher named Foe, Daniel Defoe was a man who seized, without undue scruples, whatever opportunities presented themselves. As a young man he set up business as a merchant but soon found himself bankrupt. He then turned to writing political verses and pamphlets; eventually he was pilloried, fined, and jailed for a stinging satire on the Church of England's methods of treating religious nonconformists. The people of London supported him to such an extent that on his third and last day in the pillory, flower girls covered it with wreaths, a huge crowd sang the "Hymn to the Pillory" that he had composed while in prison, and somehow the crowd received money to purchase liquor to drink his health.

In Defoe's middle years he was a politician, an adventurer, a spy, and an informer. A Whig by conviction, Defoe had few misgivings about switching parties when the Tories came into power in 1710. When the Tories fell from power in 1714, Defoe switched back to the Whig side with equal ease.

From a total of 250 works, Defoe is best-known for those he wrote in later life, among them *Robinson Crusoe* (1719), *Moll Flanders* (1722), and *A Journal of the Plague Year* (1722). Purporting to be not fiction but true accounts, they have a realistic bite that makes them read like fact. Defoe achieved this by employing *verisimilitude*, a piling up of realistic detail so that what was imaginary appeared to have actually happened. Because of this verisimilitude, he is considered one of the fathers of the modern novel.

The Education of Women

Daniel Defoe

I have often thought of it as one of the most barbarous customs in the world, considering us as a civilized and a Christian country, that we deny the advantages of learning to women. We reproach the sex every day with folly and impertinence, while I am confident, had they the advantages of education equal to us, they would be guilty of less than ourselves.

One would wonder, indeed, how it should happen that women are conversable[1] at all, since they are only beholding to natural parts[2] for all their knowledge. Their youth is spent to teach them to stitch and sew or make baubles. They are taught to read, indeed, and perhaps to write their names or so, and that is the height of a woman's

---

1. *that women are conversable*, that women can converse.
2. *beholding . . . parts*, dependent upon natural abilities.

education. And I would but ask any who slight the sex for their understanding, what is a man (a gentleman, I mean) good for that is taught no more?

I need not give instances or examine the character of a gentleman with a good estate and of a good family and with tolerable parts, and examine what figure he makes for want of education.

The soul is placed in the body like a rough diamond and must be polished, or the luster of it will never appear; and 'tis manifest that as the rational soul distinguishes us from brutes, so education carries on the distinction and makes some less brutish than others. This is too evident to need any demonstration. But why then should women be denied the benefit of instruction? If knowledge and understanding had been useless additions to the sex, God Almighty would never have given them capacities, for He made nothing needless. Besides, I would ask such what they can see in ignorance that they should think it a necessary ornament to a woman? or how much worse is a wise woman than a fool? or what has the woman done to forfeit the privilege of being taught? Does she plague us with her pride and impertinence? Why did we not let her learn, that she might have had more wit? Shall we upbraid women with folly, when 'tis only the error of this inhuman custom that hindered them being made wiser?

The capacities of women are supposed to be greater and their senses quicker than those of the men; and what they might be capable of being bred to is plain from some instances of female wit, which this age is not without; which upbraids us with injustice, and looks as if we denied women the advantages of education for fear they should vie with the men in their improvements.

To remove this objection, and that women might have at least a needful opportunity of education in all sorts of useful learning, I propose the draft of an academy for that purpose. . . .

The academy I propose would differ but little from public schools,[3] wherein such ladies as were willing to study should have all the advantages of learning suitable to their genius.[4] But since some severities of discipline more than ordinary would be absolutely necessary to preserve the reputation of the house, that persons of quality and fortune might not be afraid to venture their children thither, I shall venture to make a small scheme by way of essay.[5]

The house I would have built in a form by itself, as well as in a place by itself. The building should be of three plain fronts, without any jettings or bearing-work,[6] that the eye might at a glance see from one coign to the other; the gardens walled in the same triangular figure, with a large moat, and but one entrance. When thus every part of the situation was contrived as well as might be for discovery, and to render intriguing dangerous, I would have no guards, no eyes, no spies set over the ladies, but shall expect them to be tried by the principles of honor and strict virtue. . . .

In this house, the persons who enter should be taught all sorts of breeding suitable both to their genius and quality, and in particular, music and dancing, which it would be cruelty to bar the sex of, because they are their darlings; but besides this, they should be taught languages, as particularly French and Italian; and I would venture the injury of giving a woman more tongues than one. They should, as a particular study, be taught all the graces of speech and all the necessary air of conversation, which our common education is so defective in that I need not expose it. They should be brought to read books, and especially history; and so to read as to make them understand the world and be able to know and judge of things when they hear of them.

To such whose genius would lead them to it, I would deny no sort of learning; but the chief thing, in general, is to cultivate the understandings of the sex, that they may be capable of all sorts of conversation; that, their parts and judgments

---

3. *public schools.* These were classical schools, such as Rugby and Eton, which prepared students for the universities.
4. *their genius,* their special abilities.
5. *essay,* trial.
6. *without any jettings or bearing-work.* Jettings were parts jutting out from the perpendicular wall; bearing-works were the supports for these parts.

being improved, they may be as profitable in their conversation as they are pleasant.

Women, in my observation, have little or no difference in them, but as they are or are not distinguished by education. Tempers, indeed, may in some degree influence them, but the main distinguishing part is their breeding.

The whole sex are generally quick and sharp. I believe I may be allowed to say generally so, for you rarely see them lumpish and heavy when they are children, as boys will often be. If a woman be well-bred, and taught the proper management of her natural wit, she proves generally very sensible and retentive; and without partiality, a woman of sense and manners is the finest and most delicate part of God's creation, the glory of her Maker, and the great instance of His singular regard to man, His darling creature, to whom He gave the best gift either God could bestow or man receive. And 'tis the sordidest piece of folly and ingratitude in the world to withhold from the sex the due luster which the advantage of education gives to the natural beauty of their minds.

A woman well-bred and well taught, furnished with the additional accomplishments of knowledge and behavior, is a creature without comparison; her society is the emblem of sublimer enjoyments; her person is angelic and her conversation heavenly; she is all softness and sweetness, peace, love, wit, and delight. She is every way suitable to the sublimest wish, and the man that has such a one to his portion has nothing to do but rejoice in her and be thankful.

On the other hand, suppose her to be the very same woman, and rob her of the benefit of education, and it follows thus:

If her temper be good, want of education makes her soft and easy. Her wit, for want of teaching, makes her impertinent and talkative. Her knowledge, for want of judgment and experience, makes her fanciful and whimsical. If her temper be bad, want of breeding makes her worse, and she grows haughty, insolent, and loud. If she be passionate, want of manners makes her termagant and a scold, which is much at one with

Lady Leaving a Circulating Library, a colored mezzotint by J. R. Smith. 1781. *British Museum*

lunatic. If she be proud, want of discretion (which still is breeding) makes her conceited, fantastic, and ridiculous. And from these she degenerates to be turbulent, clangorous, noisy, nasty, and the devil.

Methinks mankind for their own sakes—since, say what we will of the women, we all think fit at one time or other to be concerned with them—should take some care to breed them up to be suitable and serviceable, if they expected no such thing as delight from them. Bless us! what care do we take to breed up a good horse and to break him well! and what a value do we put upon him when it is done, and all because he should be fit for our use! and why not a woman? Since all her ornaments and beauty without suitable behavior is a cheat in nature, like the false tradesman who puts the best of his goods uppermost, that the buyer may think the rest are of the same goodness. . . .

The great distinguishing difference which is seen in the world between men and women is in their education, and this is manifested by comparing it with the difference between one man or woman and another.

And herein it is that I take upon me to make such a bold assertion that all the world are mistaken in their practice about women; for I cannot think that God Almighty ever made them so delicate, so glorious creatures, and furnished them with such charms, so agreeable and so delightful to mankind, with souls capable of the same accomplishments with men, and all to be only stewards of our houses, cooks, and slaves.

Not that I am for exalting the female government in the least; but, in short, I would have men take women for companions, and educate them to be fit for it. A woman of sense and breeding will scorn as much to encroach upon the prerogative of the man as a man of sense will scorn to oppress the weakness of the woman. But if the women's souls were refined and improved by teaching, that word would be lost; to say the *weakness of the sex* as to judgment would be nonsense, for ignorance and folly would be no more found among women than men. I remember a passage which I heard from a very fine woman. She had wit and capacity enough, an extraordinary shape and face, and a great fortune, but had been cloistered up all her time, and, for fear of being stolen, had not had the liberty of being taught the common necessary knowledge of women's affairs. And when she came to converse in the world, her natural wit made her so sensible of the want of education that she gave this short reflection on herself: "I am ashamed to talk with my very maids," says she, "for I don't know when they do right or wrong. I had more need go to school than be married."

I need not enlarge on the loss the defect of education is to the sex, nor argue the benefit of the contrary practice; 'tis a thing will be more easily granted than remedied. This chapter is but an essay at the thing, and I refer the practice to those happy days, if ever they shall be, when men shall be wise enough to mend it.

THINK AND DISCUSS
Understanding
1. According to Defoe, what are women taught in their youth?
2. What subjects are to be taught at the proposed academy? For what purpose?

Analyzing
3. What design does Defoe suggest for the building itself? Why?
4. What advantages would men derive from providing an education for women?
5. *Rationalism* is a philosophy that accepts reason as authority in matters of opinion, belief, or conduct. Defoe says, ". . . 'tis manifest that as the rational soul distinguishes us from brutes, so education carries on the distinction and makes some less brutish than others." How does the rational soul do this? How does education help?

Extending
6. Have all the educational faults that Defoe criticizes been eliminated today? Explain.

COMPOSITION
Writing a Persuasive Essay
Put yourself in the place of an eighteenth-century man or woman reading Defoe's essay. With which parts of it would you agree? With which would you disagree? Organize your thoughts and write a letter to *The Spectator* in which you express them. Support your points with examples and write to convince readers to share your opinions. See "Writing to Persuade an Audience" in the Writer's Handbook.

Reporting on the Educational System
Defoe aims at educational reform for the women of his day. Suggestions and complaints are still made about education today. Think about the current strengths and weaknesses of the educational system in the United States and write a report in which you suggest improvements. Address the report to a concerned citizens' group that has asked for your evaluation.

Despite personal handicaps that would have caused a man of lesser determination to give up, Pope rose to be the leading literary figure of his day. He was a Roman Catholic in an age when adherence to the "Old Faith" prevented him from receiving a university education, voting, or holding public office, and when the tax burden on Catholics was sufficiently high to drive many families into bankruptcy.

In addition, at the age of twelve Pope was stricken with tuberculosis of the spine, a disease that left him dwarfed, crippled, and in almost constant pain. By sheer force of will he managed to educate himself and to become admired as a poet and feared as a satirist, claiming in a late poem, "Yes, I am proud; I must be proud to see/Men not afraid of God, afraid of me."

Pope was born in London, but soon after his illness his father, a retired merchant, moved the family to Binfield, in Windsor Forest, where the rural surroundings were healthier. In 1718 Pope moved to Twickenham, near London, where he spent the rest of his life; he later became known as the "wasp of Twickenham" because of the stinging quality of his satire.

Beginning to write poetry when he was very young, Pope saw his *Pastorals* in print in 1709, when he was only twenty-one. When his *Essay on Criticism* (see page 387) was published two years later, he became famous. In 1712 his mock epic, *The Rape of the Lock,* appeared.

About 1713 Pope was instrumental in forming the Scriblerus Club, a group of writers (including Swift) who met on occasion to satirize the pretensions of learned men. Shortly thereafter Pope announced a subscription for a verse translation of Homer's *Iliad.* Almost at once criticism began, led by the Whigs. Probably most of this adverse comment stemmed from Pope's friendship with Swift, at whom the Whigs were angry because of his recent defection from their party to the Tories. In any event, Pope's Catholicism was attacked, as was his competency in Greek. The stir did not interfere with subscription sales.

For two years Pope labored over his translation, the first volume of which was published in 1715. Two days later a rival translation of the *Iliad* appeared, done by Thomas Tickell, probably with the assistance of Joseph Addison. Though this translation was a failure, Pope was upset by it, for Addison had been his longtime friend. Turning to his pen, Pope wrote a scathing satirical portrait of Addison. So successful was Pope's translation of the *Iliad* that he followed it with a translation of the *Odyssey.*

Pope earned a large income through his poetry, editorial work, and translations. In an age of satire, he was often subjected to vituperative literary attacks, but he gave better than he got, cutting down his enemies with sharply honed heroic couplets. Among his later works are *The Dunciad, An Essay on Man* (see page 387), and *Moral Essays,* all written in heroic couplets.

from The Rape of the Lock

An Heroi-Comical Poem

Alexander Pope

In writing *The Rape of the Lock*, Pope attempted to placate both sides in a real-life quarrel that had arisen when Lord Petre (the Baron in the poem) snipped off a lock of hair from the head of Arabella Fermor (Belinda in the poem). To show how trivial was the basis of the quarrel, Pope exaggerated it still further, puffing it up to epic importance.

Pope apparently succeeded in healing the breach between the families involved. Arabella was pleased with the attention given her. While it would have made the story complete if the real-life hero and heroine had married and lived happily ever after, this was not to be. Lord Petre married a younger and richer heiress and died of smallpox within a year. Arabella married another gentleman and became the mother of six children.

CANTO I

What dire offense from amorous causes
    springs,
What mighty contests rise from trivial things,
I sing—This verse to Caryll,[1] Muse! is due;
This, even Belinda may vouchsafe to view:
5 Slight is the subject, but not so the praise,
If she inspire, and he approve my lays.
    Say what strange motive, Goddess! could
      compel
A well-bred lord to assault a gentle belle?
O say what stranger cause, yet unexplored,
10 Could make a gentle belle reject a lord?
In tasks so bold, can little men engage,
And in soft bosoms dwells such mighty rage?
    Sol through white curtains shot a timorous
      ray,
And oped those eyes that must eclipse the day;
15 Now lap dogs give themselves the rousing
    shake.
And sleepless lovers, just at twelve, awake:
Thrice rung the bell, the slipper knocked the
    ground,
And the pressed watch returned a silver
    sound.[2]

As Belinda dreams, Ariel, her guardian sylph (a kind of spirit), delivers a long speech explaining the life of the sylphs, and concludes with a grave warning.

Belinda still her downy pillow pressed,
20 Her guardian Sylph prolonged the balmy
    rest.
'Twas he had summoned to her silent bed
The morning dream that hovered o'er her
    head.
A youth more glittering than a Birth-night
    beau,[3]
(That even in slumber caused her cheek to
    glow)
25 Seemed to her ear his winning lips to lay,
And thus in whispers said, or seemed to
    say . . . .

1. *Caryll,* John Caryll, who suggested that Pope write the poem to heal the breach between the two families.
2. *pressed . . . sound,* a type of watch in which a pressure on the stem would cause the last hour to strike again.
3. *Birth-night beau,* a gentleman dressed in fine clothes for the sovereign's birthday ball.

"Of these am I, who thy protection claim,
A watchful sprite, and Ariel is my name.
Late, as I ranged the crystal wilds of air,
30 In the clear mirror of thy ruling star
I saw, alas! some dread event impend,
Ere to the main this morning sun descend,
But heaven reveals not what, or how, or
    where:
Warned by the Sylph, oh pious maid,
    beware!
35 This to disclose is all thy guardian can:
Beware of all, but most beware of man!"
    He said; when Shock,[4] who thought she
        slept too long,
Leaped up, and waked his mistress with his
    tongue.
'Twas then, Belinda, if report say true,
40 Thy eyes first opened on a billet-doux;[5]
Wounds, charms, and ardors were no sooner
    read,
But all the vision vanished from thy head.
    And now, unveiled, the toilet[6] stands
        displayed,
Each silver vase in mystic order laid.
45 First, robed in white, the nymph intent
        adores,
With head uncovered, the cosmetic powers.
A heavenly image in the glass appears,
To that she bends, to that her eyes she rears;
The inferior priestess,[7] at her altar's side,
50 Trembling, begins the sacred rites of pride.
Unnumbered treasures ope at once, and here
The various offerings of the world appear;
From each she nicely culls with curious toil,
And decks the goddess with the glittering
    spoil.
55 This casket India's glowing gems unlocks,
And all Arabia[8] breathes from yonder box.
The tortoise here and elephant unite,
Transformed to combs, the speckled and the
    white.
Here files of pins extend their shining rows,
60 Puffs, powders, patches, Bibles, billet-
    doux.
Now awful[9] Beauty puts on all its arms;
The fair each moment rises in her charms,

"The Toilet" by Aubrey Beardsley. The Beardsley illustrations in this poem were done for an edition of *The Rape
of the Lock* published in 1896.

Repairs her smiles, awakens every grace,
And calls forth all the wonders of her face;
65 Sees by degrees a purer blush arise,
And keener lightnings quicken in her eyes.
The busy Sylphs surround their darling care;
These set the head, and those divide the hair,
Some fold the sleeve, while others plait the
    gown;
70 And Betty's[10] praised for labors not her own.

---

4. *Shock*, Belinda's dog.
5. *billet-doux* (bil'ā dū'), love letter. [French]
6. *toilet*, dressing table.
7. *inferior priestess*, Belinda's maid, Betty.
8. *Arabia*, source of perfumes.
9. *awful*, awesome or awe-inspiring.
10. *Betty*, Belinda's maid.

CANTO II

After her elaborate preparations at the dressing table, Belinda sets out, "launched on the bosom of the silver Thames," on her way to Hampton Court, one of the royal palaces near London, and the center of her delightful, sophisticated, and trivial social life.

This nymph, to the destruction of
    mankind,
Nourished two locks, which graceful
    hung behind
In equal curls, and well conspired to deck
With shining ringlets the smooth ivory neck.
75 Love in these labyrinths his slaves detains,
And mighty hearts are held in slender
    chains.
With hairy springes[11] we the birds betray,
Slight lines of hair surprise the finny prey,
Fair tresses man's imperial race ensnare,
80 And beauty draws us with a single hair.
    The adventurous Baron the bright locks
        admired;
He saw, he wished, and to the prize aspired.
Resolved to win, he meditates the way,
By force to ravish, or by fraud betray;
85 For when success a lover's toils attends,
Few ask, if fraud or force attained his ends.

The sylph Ariel, aware of the threat to Belinda, summons his fellow sylphs and sends them to their various stations about Belinda to guard her every precious possession.

"This day, black omens threat the
    brightest Fair
That ever deserved a watchful spirit's
    care;
Some dire disaster, or by force, or slight;
90 But what, or where, the Fates have wrapped
    in night.

Whether the nymph shall break Diana's
    law,[12]
Or some frail china jar receive a flaw;
Or stain her honor, or her new brocade;
Forget her prayers, or miss a masquerade;
95 Or lose her heart, or necklace, at a ball;
Or whether Heaven has doomed that Shock
    must fall.
Haste, then, ye spirits! to your charge repair:
The fluttering fan be Zephyretta's care;
The drops[13] to thee, Brillante, we consign;
100 And, Momentilla, let the watch be thine:
Do thou, Crispissa, tend her favorite lock;
Ariel himself shall be the guard of Shock.
    "To fifty chosen Sylphs, of special note,
We trust the important charge, the petticoat:
105 Oft have we known that sevenfold fence to
    fail,
Though stiff with hoops, and armed with ribs
    of whale;
Form a strong line about the silver bound,
And guard the wide circumference around.
    "Whatever spirit, careless of his charge,
110 His post neglects, or leaves the fair at large,
Shall feel sharp vengeance soon o'ertake his
    sins,
Be stopped in vials, or transfixed with pins;
Or plunged in lakes of bitter washes lie,
Or wedged whole ages in a bodkin's[14] eye:
115 Gums and pomatums[15] shall his flight
    restrain,
While clogged he beats his silken wings in
    vain;
Or alum styptics[16] with contracting power
Shrink his thin essence like a rivelled
    flower:
Or, as Ixion[17] fixed, the wretch shall feel

---

11. *springes*, nooses to catch birds.
12. *Diana's law*, chastity. Diana was the goddess of maidenhood.
13. *drops*, pendant earrings.
14. *bodkin*, a large blunt needle with an eye.
15. *pomatums*, perfumed ointments to keep the hair in place.
16. *alum styptics*, astringents.
17. *Ixion*, in Greek myth, fastened to an endlessly revolving wheel in Hades as punishment for making love to Juno, queen of the gods.

120 The giddy motion of the whirling mill,
In fumes of burning chocolate shall glow,
And tremble at the sea that froths below!"
    He spoke; the spirits from the sails
        descend;
Some, orb in orb, around the nymph extend,
125 Some thrid[18] the mazy ringlets of her hair,
Some hang upon the pendants of her ear;
With beating hearts the dire event they wait,
Anxious, and trembling for the birth of Fate.

CANTO III

Close by those meads, for ever crowned with
    flowers,
130 Where Thames with pride surveys his rising
        towers,
There stands a structure of majestic frame,
Which from the neighboring Hampton takes
    its name.[19]
Here Britain's statesmen oft the fall
    foredoom
135 Here thou, great Anna![20] whom three realms
        obey,
Dost sometimes counsel take—and sometimes
    tea.
    Hither the heroes and the nymphs resort,
To taste awhile the pleasures of a court;
In various talk the instructive hours they
        passed,
140 Who gave the ball, or paid the visit last;
One speaks the glory of the British Queen,
And one describes a charming Indian screen;
A third interprets motions, looks, and eyes;
At every word a reputation dies.
145 Snuff, or the fan, supply each pause of chat,
With singing, laughing, ogling, and all that.
    Meanwhile, declining from the noon of
        day,
The sun obliquely shoots his burning ray;
The hungry judges soon the sentence sign,
150 And wretches hang that jurymen may dine;
    . . .

Belinda joins the pleasure-seekers at
Hampton Court, and wins at a card game,
ombre, over the Baron who covets her
locks. But as the game ends, and they all
partake of refreshments, the Baron seizes
his opportunity.

But when to mischief mortals bend
    their will,
How soon they find fit instruments of ill!
Just then, Clarissa drew with tempting
    grace
A two-edged weapon[21] from her shining
    case;
155 So ladies in romance assist their knight,
Present the spear, and arm him for the
    fight.
He takes the gift with reverence, and
    extends
The little engine on his fingers' ends;
This just behind Belinda's neck he
    spread,
160 As o'er the fragrant steams she bends her
    head:
Swift to the lock a thousand sprites repair,
A thousand wings, by turns, blow back the
    hair;
And thrice they twitched the diamond in her
    ear;
Thrice she looked back, and thrice the foe
    drew near.
165 Just in that instant, anxious Ariel sought
The close recesses of the virgin's thought;
As on the nosegay in her breast reclined,
He watched the ideas rising in her mind,
Sudden he viewed, in spite of all her art,
170 An earthly lover lurking at her heart.
Amazed, confused, he found his power
    expired,
Resigned to fate, and with a sigh retired.

18. *thrid*, thread; pass through.
19. *name*, Hampton Court, a royal palace near London.
20. *Anna*, Queen Anne (1702–1714).
21. *two-edged weapon*, scissors.

"The Rape of the Lock" by Aubrey Beardsley.

The peer now spreads the glittering forfex[22] wide,
To inclose the lock; now joins it, to divide.
175 Even then, before the fatal engine closed,
A wretched Sylph too fondly interposed;
Fate urged the shears, and cut the Sylph in twain
(But airy substance soon unites again).
The meeting points the sacred hair dissever
180 From the fair head, for ever, and for ever!
Then flashed the living lightning from her eyes,
And screams of horror rend the affrighted skies.
Not louder shrieks to pitying Heaven are cast,
When husbands or when lap dogs breathe their last;
185 Or when rich China vessels fallen from high,
In glittering dust and painted fragments lie!
"Let wreaths of triumph now my temples twine,"
(The victor cried) "the glorious prize is mine!
While fish in streams, or birds delight in air,
190 Or in a coach and six the British fair,
As long as Atalantis[23] shall be read,
Or the small pillow grace a lady's bed,
While visits shall be paid on solemn days,
When numerous wax-lights in bright order blaze,
195 While nymphs take treats, or assignations give,
So long my honor, name, and praise shall live!
What time would spare, from steel receives its date,
And monuments, like men, submit to fate!
Steel could the labor of the gods destroy,
200 And strike to dust the imperial towers of Troy;
Steel could the works of mortal pride confound,
And hew triumphal arches to the ground.
What wonder then, fair nymph! thy hairs should feel
The conquering force of unresisted steel?"

CANTO IV

Confusion and hysteria result from the Baron's dastardly deed of cutting off Belinda's lock of hair, and Belinda delivers to the Baron a speech of elevated indignation.

205 "For ever cursed be this detested day,
Which snatched my best, my favorite curl away!
Happy! ah ten times happy had I been,
If Hampton Court these eyes had never seen!
Yet am not I the first mistaken maid,
210 By love of courts to numerous ills betrayed.
Oh had I rather unadmired remained
In some lone isle, or distant northern land;
Where the gilt chariot never marks the way,
Where none learn ombre, none e'er taste bohea![24]
215 There kept my charms concealed from mortal eye,
Like roses that in deserts bloom and die.
What moved my mind with youthful lords to roam?
Oh had I stayed, and said my prayers at home!
'Twas this, the morning omens seemed to tell:
220 Thrice from my trembling hand the patchbox fell;
The tottering china shook without a wind,
Nay, Poll sat mute, and Shock was most unkind!
A Sylph too warned me of the threats of fate,
In mystic visions, now believed too late!
225 See the poor remnants of these slighted hairs!
My hands shall rend what ev'n thy rapine spares:
These, in two sable ringlets taught to break,
Once gave new beauties to the snowy neck;

---

22. *forfex*, scissors.
23. *Atalantis*, a popular book of court scandal and gossip.
24. *bohea*, an expensive tea.

The sister lock now sits uncouth, alone,
230 And in its fellow's fate foresees its own;
Uncurled it hangs, the fatal shears demands;
And tempts once more thy sacrilegious
    hands.
Oh hadst thou, cruel! been content to seize
Hairs less in sight, or any hairs but these!"

CANTO V

235 She said: the pitying audience melt in tears,
But fate and Jove had stopped the Baron's
    ears.
In vain Thalestris with reproach assails,
For who can move when fair Belinda fails?
Not half so fixed the Trojan could remain,
240 While Anna begged and Dido raged in vain.
Then grave Clarissa graceful waved her fan;
Silence ensued, and thus the nymph began.
    "Say why are beauties praised and
        honoured most,
The wise man's passion, and the vain man's
    toast?
245 Why decked with all that land and sea afford,
Why angels called, and angel-like adored?
Why round our coaches crowd the white-
    gloved beaux,
Why bows the side-box from its inmost
    rows?
How vain are all these glories, all our pains,
250 Unless good sense preserve what beauty
    gains:
That men may say, when we the front-box
    grace,
'Behold the first in virtue, as in face!'
Oh! if to dance all night, and dress all day,
Charmed the smallpox, or chased old age
    away,
255 Who would not scorn what housewife's cares
    produce,
Or who would learn one earthly thing of use?
To patch, nay ogle, might become a saint,
Nor could it sure be such a sin to paint.
But since, alas! frail beauty must decay,
260 Curled or uncurled, since locks will turn to
    grey;

Since painted or not painted, all shall fade,
And she who scorns a man, must die a maid;
What then remains, but well our power to
    use,
And keep good humour still whate'er we
    lose?
265 And trust me, dear! good humour can
    prevail,
When airs, and flights, and screams, and
    scolding fail.
Beauties in vain their pretty eyes may roll;
Charms strike the sight, but merit wins the
    soul."
    So spoke the dame, but no applause
    ensued;
270 Belinda frowned, Thalestris called her
    prude.
"To arms, to arms!" the fierce virago[25] cries,
And swift as lightning to the combat flies.
All side in parties, and begin the attack;
Fans clap, silks rustle, and tough
    whalebones crack;
275 Heroes' and heroines' shouts confusedly
    rise,
And bass, and treble voices strike the skies.
No common weapons in their hands are
    found,
Like gods they fight, nor dread a mortal
    wound.

    Belinda attacks the Baron, but to no avail.
They are both deprived of the precious
lock as it rises into the skies immortalized
and transfigured into a heavenly body.

    See fierce Belinda on the Baron flies,
280 With more than usual lightning in her eyes;
Nor feared the chief the unequal fight to try,
Who sought no more than on his foe to die.
But this bold lord, with manly strength
    endued,
She with one finger and a thumb subdued:

---

25. *virago*, a strong, vigorous woman; amazon.

285 Just where the breath of life his nostrils
      drew,
    A charge of snuff the wily virgin threw;
    The Gnomes direct, to every atom just,
    The pungent grains of titillating dust.
    Sudden, with starting tears each eye
      o'erflows,
290 And the high dome re-echoes to his nose.
      "Now meet thy fate," incensed Belinda
        cried,
    And drew a deadly bodkin[26] from her side.
    (The same, his ancient personage to deck,
    Her great-great-grandsire wore about his
      neck
295 In three seal rings; which after, melted down,
    Formed a vast buckle for his widow's gown:
    Her infant grandame's whistle next it grew,
    The bells she jingled, and the whistle blew;
    Then in a bodkin graced her mother's hairs,
300 Which long she wore, and now Belinda
      wears.)
      "Boast not my fall" (he cried) "insulting
        foe!
    Thou by some other shalt be laid as low.
    Nor think, to die dejects my lofty mind;
    All that I dread is leaving you behind!
305 Rather than so, ah let me still survive,
    And burn in Cupid's flames—but burn
      alive."
      "Restore the lock!" she cries; and all
        around
    "Restore the lock!" the vaulted roofs
      rebound.
    Not fierce Othello in so loud a strain
310 Roared for the handkerchief that caused his
      pain.[27]
    But see how oft ambitious aims are crossed,
    And chiefs contend till all the prize is lost!
    The lock, obtained with guilt, and kept with
      pain,
    In every place is sought, but sought in vain:
315 With such a prize no mortal must be blest,
    So Heaven decrees! with Heaven who can
      contest?
      Some thought it mounted to the lunar
        sphere,

Since all things lost on earth, are treasured
      there.
    There heroes' wits are kept in ponderous
      vases,
320 And beaux' in snuffboxes and tweezer-cases.
    There broken vows, and deathbed alms are
      found,
    And lovers' hearts with ends of riband
      bound;
    The courtier's promises and sick man's
      prayers,
    The smiles of harlots, and the tears of heirs.
325 Cages for gnats, and chains to yoke a flea,
    Dried butterflies, and tomes of casuistry.[28]
      But trust the Muse—she saw it upward
        rise,
    Though marked by none but quick poetic
      eyes:
    (So Rome's great founder to the heavens
      withdrew,
330 To Proculus alone confessed in view.)[29]
    A sudden star, it shot through liquid air,
    And drew behind a radiant trail of hair.
    Not Berenice's lock[30] first rose so bright,
    The heavens bespangling with disheveled
      light.
335 The Sylphs behold it kindling as it flies,
    And pleased pursue its progress through the
      skies.
      This the beau monde[31] shall from the Mall[32]
        survey,
    And hail with music its propitious ray.

---

26. *bodkin*, ornamental hairpin shaped like a stiletto.
27. *Othello . . . pain*, In Shakespeare's play, Othello becomes enraged when his wife Desdemona fails to produce a highly prized handkerchief and is convinced she has given it to her supposed lover.
28. *tomes of casuistry*, books of oversubtle reasoning about conscience and conduct.
29. *So Rome's . . . view*. Proculus, a Roman senator, saw Romulus, the founder of Rome, taken to heaven.
30. *Berenice's lock*. The Egyptian queen Berenice dedicated a lock of her beautiful hair to Venus for the safe return of her husband from war; the hair was turned into a comet. There is a constellation known as *Coma Berenicis*, Berenice's hair.
31. *beau monde*, fashionable society.
32. *Mall*, a promenade in St. James's Park in London.

This, the blest lover shall for Venus take,
340 And send up vows from Rosamonda's lake.[33]
This Partridge soon shall view in cloudless
    skies,
When next he looks through Galileo's eyes;
And hence the egregious wizard shall
    foredoom
The fate of Louis, and the fall of Rome.[34]
345   Then cease, bright nymph! to mourn thy
    ravished hair
Which adds new glory to the shining sphere!
Not all the tresses that fair head can boast
Shall draw such envy as the lock you lost.
For, after all the murders of your eye,

350 When, after millions slain, your self shall
    die;
When those fair suns shall set, as set they
    must,
And all those tresses shall be laid in dust;
This lock, the Muse shall consecrate to fame,
And 'midst the stars inscribe Belinda's
    name.
1712   1714

---

33. Rosamonda's lake, in St. James's Park.
34. Partridge . . . Rome. John Partridge (1644-1715)
was an astrologer and almanac-maker who annually
predicted the downfall of the King of France and of the
Pope.

Reader's Note

The Rape of the Lock as a Mock Epic

    A mock epic uses the form and style of an epic poem to satirize a trivial subject by making it appear ridiculous. In *The Rape of the Lock* Pope uses exaggeration as his major tool to show how trivial was the basis for the quarrel between the families of Arabella Fermor and Lord Petre.

    The traditional epic opens with a statement of its theme. Pope states his in the first few lines: "What dire offense from amorous causes springs, / What mighty contests rise from trivial things, / I sing." True to the epic tradition, Pope invokes a Muse, a spirit that inspires the poet. Next, he poses the important epic question, which the rest of the poem will seek to answer: "In tasks so bold [snipping the lock of hair] can little men engage, / And in soft bosoms dwells such mighty rage?"

    Also in the epic tradition are formal speeches, often boastful, delivered in elevated language. Pope provides these in the Baron's triumphal speech (lines 187–204), and in Belinda's reply (lines 205–234).

    The war of the classical epic is here fought by the lords and ladies led respectively by the Baron and Belinda. To Belinda's weapon—a bodkin, or needle—is given the complete genealogy accorded to the hero's armor and weapons in a traditional epic (lines 293–300). The supernatural elements that intervene in the affairs of humans in traditional epics are in Pope's poem the Sylphs and Gnomes.

    Finally, Pope's own device of juxtaposing in a single couplet the great with the trivial occurs throughout the poem. For example:

Here thou, great Anna, whom three realms
    obey,
Dost sometimes counsel take—and some-
    times tea. (lines 135–136)

Not louder shrieks to pitying Heaven are
    cast,
When husbands or when lap dogs breathe
    their last. (lines 183–184)

Pope's purpose in joining these disparate elements is to weld the trivial to the elevated, and to extend both beyond Belinda and the Baron to the follies of the whole human race, from queens to lapdog-loving wives.

THINK AND DISCUSS

Understanding

1. How does the Baron manage to cut off Belinda's lock despite her supernatural protectors?
2. How does Belinda respond? What "chemical warfare" does she use against the Baron?
3. What finally becomes of the lock of hair?

Analyzing

4. The Baron's feelings about Belinda are clear. What are hers about him?
5. How is Belinda made to seem now like a goddess, now like a warrior from classical mythology?
6. Why are these references to classical mythology particularly appropriate to this mock epic?
7. How important are the Sylphs (the spirits) to the **plot**? to the **tone**?
8. What rational element does Clarissa try to introduce? How is her speech received?
9. Pope often juxtaposes the great with the trivial (see the Reader's Note on page 385). Explain the juxtapositions in lines 87–96 and the effect they create.
10. Humor is also created by **irony**. What is the irony in lines 139–140? in lines 149–150?

Extending

11. In what respects has the "war between the sexes" changed from Pope's time to the present day? In what respects has it remained unchanged?
12. Explain how this poem could be popular with the real-life people involved at the same time that it pointed out the absurdity of their quarrel.

THINKING SKILLS

Evaluating

To evaluate is to make a judgment based on some sort of standard.

1. Based on other materials you have read in this unit, how accurate is Pope's evaluation of his own society?
2. How effective is *The Rape of the Lock* as a piece of satire?
3. What interest does this poem—which is several hundred years old and deals with a trivial topic—hold for today's readers?

COMPOSITION

Summarizing a Plot

Skim through "The Rape of the Lock" and make notes on the main actions. Then write a brief plot summary of the excerpt printed here. Revise to combine sentences and to eliminate unnecessary details. Try to condense your summary into no more than ten sentences (two per canto, or section). See "Writing Notes and Summaries" in the Writer's Handbook.

Analyzing Pope's Mock Epic

In an essay of at least five paragraphs, discuss how Pope adapts some of the following epic devices for his mock epic: invocation to the muse, statement of theme, statement of the epic question, elevated language, intervention of supernatural beings, a hero who seems larger than life, boastful speeches by great warriors, descriptions of armor, detailed history of heroes' weapons, great battles, personal combat.

Next to Shakespeare, Pope is probably the most frequently quoted of English poets. The following excerpts are from his *An Essay on Man* and *An Essay on Criticism*, both long poems in polished heroic couplets.

from An Essay on Man   Alexander Pope

Iambic pentameter   couplets are heroic

Know then thyself, presume not God to scan;
The proper study of mankind is Man.
Placed on this isthmus of a middle state,
A being darkly wise, and rudely great:
5 With too much knowledge for the Skeptic[1] side,
With too much weakness for the Stoic's[2] pride,
He hangs between: in doubt to act, or rest;
In doubt to deem himself a god, or beast;
In doubt his mind or body to prefer;
10 Born but to die, and reasoning but to err;
Alike in ignorance, his reason such,
Whether he thinks too little, or too much:

Chaos of thought and passion, all confused;
Still by himself abused, or disabused;
15 Created half to rise, and half to fall;
Great lord of all things, yet a prey to all;
Sole judge of truth, in endless error hurled:
The glory, jest, and riddle of the world!

1733

1. *Skeptic,* a person who questions the possibility or certainty of our knowledge of anything; a doubter.
2. *Stoic,* member of a school of philosophy founded in Athens which taught that one should be free from passion and unmoved by life's happenings.

from An Essay on Criticism   Alexander Pope

1. 'Tis with our judgments as our watches; none
   Go just alike, yet each believes his own.
2. Let such teach others who themselves excel,
   And censure freely who have written well.
3. Music resembles poetry; in each
   Are nameless graces which no methods
     teach.
4. Of all the causes which conspire to blind
   Man's erring judgment, and misguide the
     mind,
   What the weak head with strongest bias rules,
   Is pride, the never-failing vice of fools.
5. Trust not yourself: but your defects to know,

   Make use of every friend—and every foe.
6. A little learning is a dangerous thing;
   Drink deep, or taste not the Pierian spring.[1]
   There shallow draughts intoxicate the brain,
   And drinking largely sobers us again.
7. 'Tis not a lip, or eye, we beauty call,
   But the joint force and full result of all.
8. True wit is Nature to advantage dressed,
   What oft was thought, but ne'er so well
     expressed.

journal entry!

1. *Pierian* (pī ir′ ē ən) *spring,* i.e., inspiration; from Pieria, where the Muses were born.

9. As shades more sweetly recommend the light,
   So modest plainness sets off sprightly wit.
10. Words are like leaves; and where they most abound,
    Much fruit of sense beneath is rarely found.
11. True ease in writing comes from art, not chance,
    As those move easiest who have learned to dance.
12. Those heads, as stomachs, are not sure the best

Which nauseate all, and nothing can digest.
13. Be not the first by whom the new are tried,
    Nor yet the last to lay the old aside.
14. Some praise at morning what they blame at night,
    But always think the last opinion right.
15. We think our fathers fools, so wise we grow;
    Our wiser sons, no doubt, will think us so.
16. Good nature and good sense must ever join;
    To err is human, to forgive divine.

THINK AND DISCUSS
from AN ESSAY ON MAN
Understanding
1. What does Pope say is the proper study of mankind?
2. According to this poem, what are some of the doubts and conflicts that beset people?

Analyzing
3. An *aphorism* is a brief saying embodying a moral. Which **heroic couplet** is also an aphorism?
4. Explain the relationship of the last line to the rest of the poem.

Extending
5. Do you agree or disagree with Pope's evaluation of humanity in this excerpt? Explain.

from AN ESSAY ON CRITICISM
Understanding
1. Select any five of these couplets and rewrite them in your own words.

Analyzing
2. Many of these couplets can be read in two senses: as advice to writers or critics, and as general *maxims*, or guides, for living. Select three different couplets and explain their use in both senses.

APPLYING: Epigram HT
See Handbook of Literary Terms, p. 905

An **epigram** is any short, witty verse or saying, often ending with a wry twist. For example, Dryden's "Great wits are sure to madness near allied;/And thin partitions do their bounds divide. . ." is epigrammatic.

1. What wry twist is contained in epigram 5?
2. Which of the other epigrams also end with wry twists?
3. Which of these epigrams do you consider to have the most application today?

COMPOSITION
Explaining an Epigram

Select any one of the epigrams from *An Essay on Criticism* and use it as the basis for a composition in which you draw on your reading and experience to explain the epigram and demonstrate its applicability to today's world.

Analyzing *An Essay on Man*

In a composition, discuss the thoughts that Pope expresses in this excerpt from *An Essay on Man*. Begin by summarizing his meaning; then show how Pope's ideas reflect his life and other writings as well as the age in which he lived. Go on to illustrate his ideas with examples from our modern world and to discuss what applicability this essay might have today.

One of the most remarkable men of his age, Johnson won renown as a scholar, poet, essayist, conversationalist, literary critic, compiler of the first comprehensive English dictionary—and as the subject of one of the greatest biographies ever written, Boswell's *Life of Johnson* (see page 401).

Born in Lichfield in Staffordshire, the son of a provincial bookseller who was rarely more than a step or two ahead of poverty, Johnson as an infant contracted scrofula (tuberculosis of the lymph glands) from his nurse. The disease marred his face and left him blind in one eye; in addition, it was probably responsible for the occasional nervous twitches that he could not suppress. Johnson attended Pembroke College, Oxford until lack of funds compelled him to leave. From 1729 to 1737 Johnson worked as a bookseller and schoolmaster. In 1735 he married a widow considerably older than he.

In 1737, having completed a tragic drama, *Irene*, Johnson went to London, accompanied by David Garrick, who had been one of his pupils and was to go on to become the most famous actor of his day. From 1737 to 1746 Johnson earned his living by writing for *The Gentleman's Magazine*.

In 1747 Johnson announced the plan for his *Dictionary of the English Language*. He completed this monumental work eight years later. In 1765 he completed his second major project: a new and complete edition of Shakespeare. Johnson's third and last major project, his *Lives of the English Poets*, he completed in 1781 (see page 396).

While the *Dictionary* was underway, Johnson wrote to support himself. From 1750 to 1752 he edited his own periodical, *The Rambler*, which ran for 208 issues; he also wrote essays, book reviews, and articles for other publications. Garrick was successful in having *Irene*, Johnson's tragedy, produced in 1749 at the Drury Lane Theater. When the *Dictionary* was finally published in 1755, Johnson's fame was assured.

During the time that Johnson was editing Shakespeare, he continued to do other literary work. From 1758 to 1760 he wrote *The Idler*, a series of essays, nearly 100 in all. In January, 1759, his *Rasselas* was published, a rare blend of Oriental novel and philosophical tale. Although King George III awarded him a pension in 1762, Johnson continued writing.

On May 16, 1763, Johnson met the young Scotsman, James Boswell, who was to become his biographer. As their friendship ripened, Boswell spent some time almost every year with Johnson. In 1764 Johnson founded the Literary Club, a group of distinguished men who met once a week at the Turk's Head Coffee House in Soho. Among its members were Sir Joshua Reynolds, the great portrait painter; Oliver Goldsmith, physician and author; Edmund Burke, orator and statesman; Garrick; and Boswell.

In 1775 Oxford University awarded the aging Johnson an honorary doctorate. In June, 1783, Johnson suffered a stroke that temporarily left him unable to speak. He died eighteen months later, on December 13, 1784, and was buried in Westminster Abbey.

from **London**

Samuel Johnson

The year after he came to the city, Johnson published, anonymously,
a long satirical poem which he labeled "A poem in imitation of the third
satire of Juvenal." Juvenal was a Roman (A.D. 60?-130?) who wrote bitter
denunciations of the society, culture, and politics of his day.

By numbers, here, from shame or censure
    free,[1]
All crimes are safe, but hated poverty.
This, only this, the rigid law pursues,
This, only this, provokes the snarling Muse;
5 The sober trader, at a tattered cloak,
Wakes from his dream and labors for a joke;
With brisker air the silken courtiers gaze,
And turn the varied taunt a thousand ways.
Of all the griefs that harass the distressed
10 Sure the most bitter is a scornful jest;
Fate never wounds more deep the generous
        heart
Than when a blockhead's insult point the
        dart. . . .
    Prepare for death, if here at night you
        roam,
And sign your will before you sup from
        home.
15 Some fiery fop, with new commission vain,
Who sleeps on brambles till he kills his man;[2]
Some frolic drunkard, reeling from a feast,
Provokes a broil and stabs you for a jest.
Yet ev'n these heroes, mischievously gay,
20 Lords of the street and terrors of the way,
Flushed as they are with folly, youth and
        wine,
Their prudent insults to the poor confine:
Afar they mark the flambeau's bright
        approach,
And shun the shining train and golden
        coach.
25   In vain, these dangers past, your doors
        you close,

Detail from an engraved broadside on the murder of Sir
Edmund Berry Godfrey. 1678. *Pepys Library, Cambridge*

And hope the balmy blessings of repose:
Cruel with guilt, and daring with despair,
The midnight murd'rer bursts the faithless
        bar,
Invades the sacred hour of silent rest,
30 And plants, unseen, a dagger in your breast.
    Scarce can our fields—such crowds at
        Tyburn[3] die—
With hemp the gallows and the fleet supply.
Propose your schemes, ye senatorian band,
Whose "Ways and Means"[4] support the
        sinking land,
35 Lest ropes be wanting, in the tempting
        Spring,
To rig another convoy for the King.

1738

---

1. *By numbers . . . free,* free from shame or censure
because they (crimes) are so frequent.
2. *Who sleeps . . . man,* who cannot rest until he kills his
man.
3. *Tyburn,* place where criminals were executed.
4. *Ways and Means,* term used in the House of Commons
for methods of raising money.

from the Dictionary of the English Language

Samuel Johnson

Johnson's reputation as a scholar and writer was established in 1755 with the publication of his *Dictionary*. Selling for ninety shillings and filling two large volumes, the *Dictionary* was the most comprehensive English lexicon ever published. In Italy and France similar dictionaries, prepared under the direction of national academies, represented the work of forty or more men. Johnson prepared his single-handedly, with the help of six clerks to copy out the quotations which illustrated the proper use of words.

In all, the *Dictionary* consisted of four parts: a comprehensive preface, explaining Johnson's objectives and methods and giving some background on earlier dictionaries; a history of the development of the English language; a grammar; and finally, the body of the dictionary itself, composed of an extensive, carefully selected list of words, some aids to pronunciation, some etymologies, definitions that were divided and numbered when the word had more than one, and the illustrative quotations.

The following entries are selected either for their comprehensiveness or the personal touches they show.

---

alliga′tor. The crocodile. This name is chiefly used for the crocodile of America, between which, and that of Africa, naturalists have laid down this difference, that one moves the upper, and the other the lower jaw; but this is now known to be chimerical, the lower jaw being equally moved by both.

bu′lly. (Skinner derives this word from *burly*, as a corruption in the pronunciation; which is very probably right; or from *bulky*, or *bulleyed*; which are less probable. May it not come from *bull*, the pope's letter, implying the insolence of those who came invested with authority from the papal court?) A noisy, blustering, quarrelling fellow: it is generally taken for a man that has only the appearance of courage.

bu′tterfly. A beautiful insect, so named because it first appears at the beginning of the season for butter.

chi′cken. (3) A term for a young girl.

chiru′rgeon. One that cures ailments, not by internal medicines, but outward applications. It is now generally pronounced, and by many written, *surgeon*.

cough. A convulsion of the lungs, vellicated by some sharp serosity. It is pronounced *coff*.

to cu′rtail. (*curto*, Latin. It was anciently written *curtal*, which perhaps is more proper; but dogs that had their tails cut, being called *curtal* dogs, the word was vulgarly conceived to mean originally *to cut the tail*, and was in time written according to that notion.) (1) To cut off; to cut short; to shorten.

dedica′tion. (2) A servile address to a patron.

den. (1) A cavern or hollow running horizontally, or with a small obliquity, under ground; distinct from a hole, which runs down perpendicularly.

dull. (8) Not exhilarating; not delightful; as, *to*

make dictionaries is dull *work.*

e′ssay. (2) A loose sally of the mind; an irregular indigested piece; not a regular and orderly composition.

exci′se.[1] A hateful tax levied upon commodities, and adjudged not by the common judges of property, but wretches hired by those to whom excise is paid.

fa′vorite. (2) One chosen as a companion by his superior; a mean wretch whose whole business is by any means to please.

fun. (A low cant word.) Sport; high merriment; frolicksome delight.

ga′mbler. (A cant word, I suppose, for *game*, or *gamester*.) A knave whose practice it is to invite the unwary to game and cheat them.

to gi′ggle. To laugh idly; to titter; to grin with merry levity. It is retained in Scotland.

goat. A ruminant animal that seems a middle species between deer and sheep.

gra′vy. The serous juice that runs from flesh not much dried by the fire.

to hiss. To utter a noise like that of a serpent and some other animals. It is remarkable, that this word cannot be pronounced without making the noise which it signifies.

itch. (1) A cutaneous disease extremely contagious, which overspreads the body with small pustules filled with a thin serum, and raised as microscopes have discovered by a small animal. It is cured by sulphur.

lexico′grapher. A writer of dictionaries; a harmless drudge, that busies himself in tracing the original, and detailing the signification of words.

lunch, lu′ncheon. As much food as one's hand can hold.

ne′twork. Any thing reticulated or decussated, at equal distances, with interstices between the intersections.

oats. A grain, which in England is generally given to horses, but in Scotland supports the people.

pa′rasite. One that frequents rich tables, and earns his welcome by flattery.

pa′stern. (1) The knee[2] of an horse.

pa′tron. (1) One who countenances, supports, or protects. Commonly a wretch who supports with insolence, and is paid with flattery.

pe′nsion. An allowance made to any one without an equivalent. In England it is generally understood to mean pay given to a state hireling for treason to his country.

pe′nsioner. (2) A slave of state hired by a stipend to obey his master.

sa′tire. A poem in which wickedness or folly is censured. Proper *satire* is distinguished, by the generality of the reflections, from a *lampoon* which is aimed against a particular person; but they are too frequently confounded.

shre′wmouse. A mouse of which the bite is generally supposed venomous, and to which vulgar tradition assigns such malignity, that she is said to lame the foot over which she runs. I am informed that all these reports are calumnious, and that her feet and teeth are equally harmless with those of any other little mouse. Our ancestors however looked on her with such terror, that they are supposed to have given her name to a scolding woman, whom for her venom they call a *shrew*.

so′nnet. (1) A short poem consisting of fourteen lines, of which the rhymes are adjusted by a particular rule. It is not very suitable to the English language, and has not been used by any man of eminence since Milton.

To′ry. (A cant term, derived, I suppose, from an Irish word signifying a savage.) One who adheres to the ancient constitution of the state, and the apostolical hierarchy of the Church of England, opposed to a Whig.[3]

Whig. (2) The name of a faction.

wi′tticism. A mean attempt at wit.

to worm. (2) To deprive a dog of something, nobody knows what, under his tongue, which is said to prevent him, nobody knows why, from running mad.

1755

---

1. *excise.* Johnson's father had had trouble with the commissioners of excise, in the conduct of his business as a bookseller and maker of parchment.

2. *knee.* In fact, a pastern is part of the foot of a horse. When a lady asked Johnson how he came to define the word in this way, he answered, "Ignorance, Madam, pure ignorance." But he didn't bother to correct his definition until eighteen years later.

3. *opposed to a Whig,* Johnson himself was a Tory.

Letter to Chesterfield

Samuel Johnson

When Johnson, in 1746, first proposed the idea of compiling a dictionary, he discussed the project with Lord Chesterfield, one of the most cultivated noblemen of the age and a man with some scholarly knowledge of language and literature. Chesterfield expressed interest, and in accordance with the custom of literary patronage, gave Johnson a gift of £10. Johnson then addressed to him a detailed *Plan of a Dictionary*, in which Chesterfield is referred to as the patron of the project. Chesterfield read and approved the document before it was published, and apparently promised Johnson his continued assistance and financial support. This, however, never materialized. When the *Dictionary* finally appeared in 1755, Chesterfield expressed the desire to be regarded as its patron. This is the letter Johnson wrote him.

To the Right Honorable
  the Earl of Chesterfield

February 7, 1755.

My Lord,

I have lately been informed by the proprietor of *The World*,[1] that two papers, in which my *Dictionary* is recommended to the public, were written by your Lordship. To be so distinguished is an honor which, being very little accustomed to favors from the great, I know not well how to receive, or in what terms to acknowledge.

When, upon some slight encouragement, I first visited your Lordship, I was overpowered, like the rest of mankind, by the enchantment of your address; and could not forbear to wish that I might boast myself *"Le vainqueur du vainqueur de la terre,"* [2] that I might obtain that regard for which I saw the world contending; but I found my attendance so little encouraged, that neither pride nor modesty would suffer me to continue it. When I had once addressed your Lordship in public, I had exhausted all the art of pleasing which a retired and uncourtly scholar can possess. I had done all that I could; and no man is well pleased to have his all neglected, be it ever so little.

Seven years, my Lord, have now passed, since I waited in your outward rooms, or was repulsed

Portrait of the 4th Earl of Chesterfield, by Allan Ramsay. 1765. *National Portrait Gallery, London*

from your door; during which time I have been pushing on my work through difficulties, of which it is useless to complain, and have brought it, at last, to the verge of publication, without one act of assistance, one word of encouragement, or one smile of favor. Such treatment I did not expect, for I never had a patron before.

1. **The World,** a newspaper run by a friend of Johnson's.
2. **"Le vainqueur . . . de la terre,"** "the conqueror of the conqueror of the world." [French]

The shepherd in Virgil grew at last acquainted with Love, and found him a native of the rocks.[3]

Is not a patron, my Lord, one who looks with unconcern on a man struggling for life in the water, and, when he has reached ground, encumbers him with help? The notice which you have been pleased to take of my labors, had it been early, had been kind; but it has been delayed till I am indifferent, and cannot enjoy it; till I am solitary, and cannot impart it; till I am known, and do not want it. I hope it is no very cynical asperity not to confess obligations where no benefit has been received, or to be unwilling that the public should consider me as owing that to a patron, which Providence has enabled me to do for myself.

Having carried on my work thus far with so little obligation to any favorer of learning, I shall not be disappointed though I should conclude it, if less be possible, with less; for I have been long wakened from that dream of hope, in which I once boasted myself with so much exultation.

My Lord,
  Your Lordship's most humble,
  Most obedient servant,

  Sam. Johnson

---

3. *The shepherd . . . rocks.* Johnson is referring to a passage in the *Eclogues*, a collection of pastorals by the Latin poet Virgil (70–19 B.C.), that speaks of the cruelty of love.

THINK AND DISCUSS
from LONDON
Understanding
1. List some of the evils Johnson describes.

Analyzing
2. What are some of the difficulties the poor face? What does Johnson's **tone** tell you about his attitude toward them?

Extending
3. Do any of these evils or difficulties still exist today? Explain.

from the DICTIONARY
Understanding
1. Find examples that indicate the timelessness of some words and expressions.
2. Find examples that have undergone great change in meaning and acceptability since Johnson's day.

Analyzing
3. In addition to providing definitions, Johnson's *Dictionary* provides insights into his personality. Find examples that reveal Johnson's prejudices or the beliefs of the age.
4. Find examples that show Johnson's ability to enjoy a joke at his own expense.

LETTER TO CHESTERFIELD
Understanding
1. Explain the circumstances under which Johnson wrote this letter.

Analyzing
2. Which statements do you think are most effective in conveying Johnson's pain and anger at Chesterfield's behavior?
3. Which expressions demonstrate his adherence—even if ironical—to polite forms?
4. One critic has referred to Johnson's letter as "impertinent." Explain why you agree or disagree.

Extending
5. How do you suppose Lord Chesterfield reacted to Johnson's letter?

ENRICHMENT
Writing Dictionary Definitions
Select several modern slang or colloquial expressions and prepare personalized definitions for them in the manner of Johnson's *Dictionary*. Do not refer to a dictionary yourself, and assume that your readers have never seen these words in a dictionary. Share your definitions with your classmates; you might even prepare a class *Dictionary of Students' Language*.

Simply put, a **biography** is an account of a person's life, and an **autobiography** is an account of a person's life written (or told) by that person. But biography has not meant the same thing in all periods in history. Although the lives of important people have been recorded for thousands of years, modern biography in a literary sense developed during the Age of Reason. To Johnson goes much of the credit for raising biography to the level of literature, partly due to his style and to his insistence that truth was more important than respect for a subject—or a subject's relatives. Here are some guidelines for reading biography in general and eighteenth-century biography in particular.

Appreciate the form and style. Not all biographies are meant to present a subject's life history from birth to death. Some biographies focus instead on selected periods or aspects of a subject's life. Nor are all biographies written to present a totally objective picture; Johnson, for example, includes his own opinions and prejudices in his *Life of Milton*, and Boswell draws on personal experience for much of his *Life of Johnson*. In reading, try to determine the biographer's purpose.

Understand the chronology. Naturally you would expect to find such vital facts as date and place of birth, family background, education, marriage, and accomplishments. This information might not always be presented in order, however. Noting the important dates mentioned will help you to understand the chronology of the subject's life as well as to see that life in its historical context.

Separate facts from opinions. A *statement of fact* is one that can be proved true or false. If the subject died well before a biography is written, the biographer must research records and gather second-hand accounts. As a reader you have every right to expect that all facts are accurate. Often, however, statements of fact are mixed with *statements of opinion* that include personal opinions, beliefs, or attitudes. You need not automatically reject any such statements, but you should be aware of their nature. Then you can make up your own mind.

Look for devices of characterization. Events and significant actions are a matter of history, but it is in presenting personality that a biographer can make a subject come alive. The same methods of characterization used in fiction can be used in biography. A biographer describes physical traits and personality, speech and behavior, and how other characters reacted to the subject. Obviously, except for autobiography or a case in which the subject has told his or her life to the writer, such things as thoughts and feelings must remain conjectural. Many biographers include letters and journal entries to let subjects speak in their own words.

Enjoy anecdotes and digressions. In an attempt to make a subject come alive, a biographer may include anecdotes—short, interesting, often amusing incidents. Digressions may be used to fill in details or to depart for a while from the chronology. Often you can learn as much about a person from small details as from the main events of his or her life.

Assess honesty and comprehensiveness. In his *Life of Samuel Johnson, LL.D.*, considered by many to be the greatest biography of all time, Boswell tried to present Johnson "unbuttoned," showing the unpleasant as well as the pleasant, the ugly as well as the beautiful. Later, in the 19th century, biographers tended to be discreet; today, biographers tend to "tell all." As you read, judge whether the biography seems honest in not bypassing incidents that might reflect unfavorably on the subject, and whether it seems complete, including all the important aspects of the subject's life.

from The Life of Milton

Samuel Johnson

This excerpt from "The Life of Milton" (one of fifty-two critical biographies included in Johnson's *Lives of the Poets*) concentrates on Milton the man rather than on his poetry. Milton's appearance, habits, learning, religion, politics, and character are thoroughly described by Johnson; although he did not care for Milton's religion or politics, he admired his poetry.

ilton has the reputation of having been in his youth eminently beautiful, so as to have been called the Lady of his college. His hair, which was of a light brown, parted at the foretop, and hung down upon his shoulders, according to the picture which he has given of Adam. He was, however, not of the heroic stature, but rather below the middle size, according to Mr. Richardson, who mentions him as having narrowly escaped from being "short and thick." He was vigorous and active, and delighted in the exercise of the sword, in which he is related to have been eminently skillful. His weapon was, I believe, not the rapier, but the backsword, of which he recommends the use in his book on education.

His eyes are said never to have been bright; but, if he was a dexterous fencer, they must have been once quick.

His domestic habits, so far as they are known, were those of a severe student. He drank little strong drink of any kind, and fed without excess in quantity, and in his earlier years without delicacy of choice. In his youth he studied late at night; but afterwards changed his hours, and rested in bed from nine to four in the summer, and five in winter. The course of his day was best known after he was blind. When he first rose he heard a chapter in the Hebrew Bible, and then studied till twelve; then took some exercise for an hour; then dined; then played on the organ, and sung, or heard another sing; then studied to six; then entertained his visitors till eight; then supped, and, after a pipe of tobacco and a glass of water, went to bed.

So is his life described; but this even tenor appears attainable only in colleges. He that lives in the world will sometimes have the succession of his practice broken and confused. Visitors, of whom Milton is represented to have had great numbers, will come and stay unseasonably; business, of which every man has some, must be done when others will do it.

When he did not care to rise early he had something read to him by his bedside; perhaps at this time his daughters were employed. He composed much in the morning and dictated in the day, sitting obliquely in an elbowchair, with his leg thrown over the arm.

Fortune appears not to have had much of his care. In the civil wars he lent his personal estate to the Parliament, but when, after the contest was decided, he solicited repayment, he met not only with neglect, but "sharp rebuke"; and, having tired both himself and his friends, was given up to poverty and hopeless indignation, till he shewed how able he was to do greater service. He was then made Latin secretary, with two hundred pounds a year, and had a thousand pounds for his *Defence of the People*. His widow, who after his death retired to Namtwich in Cheshire, and died about 1729, is said to have reported that he lost two thousand pounds by entrusting it to a scrivener;[1] and that, in the general depredation upon the Church, he had grasped an estate of about sixty pounds a

Blind Milton Dictating to His Daughters, by Henry Fuseli. *Collection of the Art Institute of Chicago*

year belonging to Westminster Abbey, which, like other sharers of the plunder of rebellion, he was afterwards obliged to return. Two thousand pounds, which he had placed in the Excise Office, were also lost. There is yet no reason to believe that he was ever reduced to indigence: his wants being few were competently supplied. He sold his library before his death, and left his family fifteen hundred pounds; on which his widow laid hold, and only gave one hundred to each of his daughters.

His literature was unquestionably great. He read all the languages which are considered either as learned or polite: Hebrew, with its two dialects, Greek, Latin, Italian, French, and Spanish. In Latin his skill was such as places him in the first rank of writers and critics; and he appears to have cultivated Italian with uncommon diligence. The books in which his daughter, who used to read to him, represented him as most delighting, after Homer, which he could almost repeat, were Ovid's *Metamorphoses* and Euripides. His Euripides is, by Mr. Cradock's kindness, now in my hands: the margin is sometimes noted; but I have found nothing remarkable.

Of the English poets he set most value upon Spenser, Shakespeare, and Cowley. Spenser was apparently his favorite; Shakespeare he may easily be supposed to like, with every other

---

1. *scrivener,* here probably a notary.

skillful reader, but I should not have expected that Cowley, whose ideas of excellence were different from his own, would have had much of his approbation. His character of Dryden, who sometimes visited him, was that he was a good rhymist, but no poet.

His theological opinions are said to have been first Calvinistical, and afterwards, perhaps when he began to hate the Presbyterians, to have extended towards Arminianism.[2] In the mixed questions of theology and government he never thinks that he can recede far enough from popery or prelacy; but what Baudius says of Erasmus seems applicable to him: "magis habuit quod fugeret, quam quod sequeretur."[3] He had determined rather what to condemn than what to approve. He has not associated himself with any denomination of Protestants: we know rather what he was not, than what he was. He was not of the Church of Rome; he was not of the Church of England.

To be of no church is dangerous. Religion, of which the rewards are distant and which is animated only by Faith and Hope, will glide by degrees out of the mind unless it be invigorated and reimpressed by external ordinances, by stated calls to worship, and the salutary influence of example. Milton, who appears to have had full conviction of the truth of Christianity, and to have regarded the Holy Scriptures with the profoundest veneration, to have been untainted by any heretical peculiarity of opinion, and to have lived in a confirmed belief of the immediate and occasional agency of Providence, yet grew old without any visible worship. In the distribution of his hours, there was no hour of prayer, either solitary or with his household; omitting public prayers, he omitted all.

Of this omission the reason has been sought, upon a supposition which ought never to be made, that men live with their own approbation, and justify their conduct to themselves. Prayer certainly was not thought superfluous by him, who represents our first parents as praying acceptably in the state of innocence, and efficaciously after their fall. That he lived without prayer can hardly be affirmed; his studies and meditations were an habitual prayer. The neglect of it in his family was probably a fault for which he condemned himself, and which he intended to correct, but that death, as too often happens, intercepted his reformation.

His political notions were those of an acrimonious and surly republican, for which it is not known that he gave any better reason than that "a popular government was the most frugal; for the trappings of a monarchy would set up an ordinary commonwealth." It is surely very shallow policy, that supposes money to be the chief good; and even this without considering that the support and expense of a Court is for the most part only a particular kind of traffic, by which money is circulated without any national impoverishment.

Milton's republicanism was, I am afraid, founded in an envious hatred of greatness, and a sullen desire of independence; in petulance impatient of control, and pride disdainful of superiority. He hated monarchs in the state and prelates in the church; for he hated all whom he was required to obey. It is to be suspected that his predominant desire was to destroy rather than establish, and that he felt not so much the love of liberty as repugnance to authority.

It has been observed that they who most loudly clamor for liberty do not most liberally grant it. What we know of Milton's character in domestic relations is, that he was severe and arbitrary. His family consisted of women; and there appears in his books something like a Turkish contempt of females, as subordinate and inferior beings. That his own daughters might not break the ranks, he suffered them to be depressed by a mean and penurious education. He thought woman made only for obedience, and man only for rebellion.

1779

2. *Calvinistical, Presbyterians, Arminianism,* complex theological positions. Simply put, Johnson alludes to Milton's early belief in predestination, shared by Calvin and a sect of his followers, the Presbyterians, and to Milton's later doubts about the same subject, shared by the followers of Jacobus Arminius.
3. *"magis habuit . . . sequeretur."* "He was possessed more by what he fled than by what he followed." [Latin] Erasmus (1466?–1536) expressed his humanistic outlook in frequent attacks on the medieval pieties of his time.

THINK AND DISCUSS
Understanding
1. What details of Milton's appearance does Johnson describe in the first two paragraphs? What do they suggest about Milton as a person?
2. What does Johnson criticize about Milton's religion? about his politics?

Analyzing
3. Where in the first two paragraphs does Johnson give his own insights rather than descriptive details?
4. How does Johnson react to the traditional description of the way Milton spent his day? What does this reaction reveal about Johnson's own life?
5. How does Johnson reach the conclusion that Milton did not lead a life "without prayers"? Why would Johnson want to arrive at such a conclusion?

Extending
6. Explain why you are or are not bothered by Johnson's stating his own ideas and prejudices in writing of Milton's life.

READING LITERATURE SKILLFULLY
Fact/Opinion
A statement of fact is one that can be proved true or false, and a statement of opinion is one that includes personal opinions, beliefs, or attitudes. Often the two are mixed.

1. How does Johnson let us know in the first paragraph that he is not reporting facts but second-hand information about Milton?
2. From the information given in the first paragraph construct three statements of fact.
3. After describing Milton's daily habits in paragraph 3, Johnson questions his information in paragraph 4. What is his reason for doing this?
4. What information in paragraph 6 is factual?
5. What information in paragraph 10 is definitely Johnson's opinion?

VOCABULARY
Dictionary
Some words from the selections by Steele, Addison, Defoe, Pope, and Johnson are italicized in the following questions. Answer the questions, giving reasons for your answers. You may use the Glossary if you need to.

1. Would a person who displays *probity* be most likely to be honest, inquisitive, or skeptical?
2. If someone introduced you to a *baronet*, would you be meeting a person in the beef business, a person with a title, or a person who works in a tavern?
3. Would you be most likely to meet a *coxcomb* at a dance, in a barn, or in a butcher shop?
4. If a woman is called a *termagant*, is she redheaded, beautiful, or bad-tempered?
5. If a man displays *asperity*, is he more likely to be smiling, frowning, or nodding?
6. If you knew that a report about someone was *calumnious*, would you think more of that person, or less?
7. Are the brave or the cowardly more likely to behave in a *timorous* way?
8. Is an act of *depredation*, if discovered, more likely to be punished or rewarded?
9. Is a *penurious* person more likely to be a miser, a gambler, or a spendthrift?
10. If someone gave you a *flambeau*, would you put it in a vase, eat it, or use it to guide yourself?

THINKING SKILLS
Generalizing
To generalize is to draw a general conclusion from particular information.

1. What picture of Milton's politics emerges from this selection?
2. Review the selections by Milton and his biography, beginning on page 292. What picture of Milton's religion do you get from combining that information with Johnson's biography of him?

When Boswell and Johnson first met, on May 16, 1763, Boswell, though only twenty-three, was already an accepted member of Edinburgh's literary circles. The eldest son of Alexander Boswell, Lord of Auchinleck, he had studied law in Edinburgh and Glasgow, and had already begun keeping his detailed journal, which was to become the source for several books besides his biography of Johnson.

In December, 1763, Boswell traveled to Europe to complete his education. He studied law for a time at Utrecht, in the Netherlands, then met and became friendly with both Voltaire and Rousseau, French writers and thinkers, and with General Paoli, the Corsican patriot. More than a celebrity-seeker, Boswell was convivial, witty, and intelligent.

When Boswell returned from his travels in February, 1766, he saw Johnson almost immediately, and their friendship grew rapidly. In the twenty-one years they knew each other, however, they did not spend all that much time together, for Boswell was pursuing a separate career in Scotland. He was admitted to the bar, married, and lived in Edinburgh, visiting London about once a year to see Johnson.

In the summer of 1773 Johnson and Boswell undertook an extended tour of the remote and primitive Hebrides, about which both wrote books. Johnson's account, *A Journey to the Western Islands of Scotland*, appeared soon after the tour; Boswell's, titled *The Journal of a Tour to the Hebrides with Samuel Johnson, LL.D.*, was published in 1785, after Johnson's death. Because it recorded Johnson's conversations with and about others without their permission, it caused an immediate stir and evoked some criticism, for people were not accustomed to such candid biography. This criticism was to recur when Boswell's *The Life of Samuel Johnson, LL.D.* was published in 1791.

In later life Boswell made an unsuccessful attempt at entering Scottish politics. To facilitate publishing his biography of Johnson, he moved himself and his family to London in 1786. Three years later his wife died. Boswell spent his remaining years in poor health. When he died in 1795, he was buried at Auchinleck, the family estate in Scotland.

With the discovery of more of Boswell's papers, his writing technique has been closely studied in recent years. Either late at night or early in the morning, he made notes of his activities. Later, when he had time, he converted these into full journal entries; these entries constituted his major source for the *Life*. He painstakingly verified every date and piece of information he gleaned, sending out questionnaires and letters, interviewing people, and reading correspondence. In selecting and presenting details, he worked with a keen dramatic sense, often building to a climax in which Johnson wittily capped whatever conversation was under way. Today we recognize Boswell for the creative artist he was; modern biography owes much to him.

from The Life of Samuel Johnson, LL.D.

James Boswell

Probably the best introduction to Boswell's technique and Johnson's wit is the record in the *Life* of the first meeting of the two:

"At last on Monday the 16th of May, when I was sitting in Mr. Davies's back-parlor, after having drunk tea with him and Mrs. Davies, Johnson unexpectedly came into the shop; and Mr. Davies having perceived him through the glass door in the room in which we were sitting, advancing toward us, he announced his awful approach to me. . . .

"Mr. Davies mentioned my name, and respectfully introduced me to him. I was much agitated, and recollecting his prejudices against the Scotch, of which I had heard much, I said to Davies, 'Don't tell where I come from.'

" 'From Scotland,' cried Davies roguishly. 'Mr. Johnson, (said I) I do indeed come from Scotland, but I cannot help it.' . . . This speech was somewhat unlucky, for with that quickness of wit for which he was so remarkable, he . . . retorted, 'That, Sir, I find is what a very great many of your countrymen cannot help.'

"This stroke stunned me a good deal; and when we had sat down, I felt myself not a little embarrassed, and apprehensive of what might come next. . . .

"I was highly pleased with the extraordinary vigor of his conversation, and regretted that I was drawn away from it by an engagement at another place."

Thus Boswell describes their first meeting. The technique here is similar to that of the rest of the *Life*—dramatic, carefully setting the scene for Johnson's utterances and wit.

On London

alking of a London life, he said, "The happiness of London is not to be conceived but by those who have been in it. I will venture to say, there is more learning and science within the circumference of ten miles from where we now sit, than in all the rest of the kingdom."

BOSWELL. "The only disadvantage is the great distance at which people live from one another."

JOHNSON. "Yes, Sir; but that is occasioned by the largeness of it, which is the cause of all the other advantages."

BOSWELL. "Sometimes I have been in the humor of wishing to retire to a desert."

JOHNSON. "Sir, you have desert enough in Scotland."

I suggested a doubt, that if I were to reside in London, the exquisite zest with which I relished it in occasional visits might go off, and I might grow tired of it.

JOHNSON. "Why, Sir, you find no man, at all intellectual, who is willing to leave London. No, Sir, when a man is tired of London, he is tired of life; for there is in London all that life can afford."

On Eating

At supper this night he talked of good eating with uncommon satisfaction. "Some people (said he) have a foolish way of not minding, or pretending not to mind, what they eat. For my part, I mind my belly very studiously, and very carefully; for I look upon it that he who does not mind his belly will hardly mind anything else."

He now appeared to me *Jean Bull philosophe*,[1] and he was, for the moment, not only serious but vehement. Yet I have heard him, upon other occasions, talk with great contempt of people who were anxious to gratify their palates; and the 206th number of his *Rambler* is a masterly essay against gulosity.[2] His practice, indeed, I must acknowledge, may be considered as casting the balance of his different opinions upon this subject, for I never knew any man who relished good eating more than he did. When at table, he was totally absorbed in the business of the moment; his looks seemed riveted to his plate; nor would he, unless when in very high company, say one word, or even pay the least attention to what was said by others, till he had satisfied his appetite, which was so fierce, and indulged with such intenseness, that while in the act of eating, the veins of his forehead swelled, and generally a strong perspiration was visible. To those whose sensations were delicate, this could not but be disgusting; and it was doubtless not very suitable to the character of a philosopher, who should be distinguished by self-command. But it must be owned that Johnson, though he could be rigidly *abstemious*, was not a *temperate* man either in eating or drinking. He could refrain, but he could not use moderately. He told me that he had fasted two days without inconvenience, and that he had never been hungry but once. They who beheld with wonder how much he ate upon all occasions when his dinner was to his taste could not easily conceive what he must have meant by hunger, and not only was he remarkable for the extraordinary quantity which he ate, but he was, or affected to be, a man of very nice discernment in the science of cookery. He used to descant critically on the dishes which had been at table where he had dined or supped, and to recollect minutely what he had liked.

He about the same time was so much displeased with the performances of a nobleman's French cook, that he exclaimed with vehemence, "I'd throw such a rascal into the river"; and he then proceeded to alarm a lady at whose house he was to sup, by the following manifesto of his skill: "I, Madam, who live at a variety of good tables, am a much better judge of cookery, than any person who has a very tolerable cook, but lives much at home; for his palate is gradually adapted to the taste of his cook; whereas, Madam, in trying by a wider range, I can more exquisitely judge."

When invited to dine, even with an intimate friend, he was not pleased if something better than a plain dinner was not prepared for him. I have heard him say on such an occasion, "This was a good dinner enough, to be sure: but it was not a dinner to *ask* a man to."

On the other hand, he was wont to express, with great glee, his satisfaction when he had been entertained quite to his mind. One day when he had dined with his neighbor and landlord, in Boltcourt, Mr. Allen, the printer, whose old housekeeper had studied his taste in everything, he pronounced this eulogy: "Sir, we could not have had a better dinner, had there been a *Synod*[3] *of Cooks*."

On the Dictionary

That he was fully aware of the arduous nature of the undertaking, he acknowledges; and shows himself perfectly sensible of it in the conclusion

---

1. **Jean Bull philosophe,** John Bull the philosopher [French]. John Bull is the personification of the British nation, the typical Englishman.
2. *gulosity,* excessive appetite; greediness.
3. **Synod,** council; assembly; convention.

Oliver Goldsmith, James Boswell, and Samuel Johnson at the Mitre Tavern, London.
Colored engraving, nineteenth century.

of this "Plan"; but he had a noble consciousness of his own abilities, which enabled him to go on with undaunted spirit.

Dr. Adams found him one day busy at his Dictionary, when the following dialogue ensued.

ADAMS. "This is a great work, Sir. How are you to get all the etymologies?"

JOHNSON. "Why, Sir, here is a shelf with Junius, and Skinner,[4] and others; and there is a Welsh gentleman who has published a collection of Welsh proverbs, who will help me with the Welsh."

ADAMS. "But, Sir, how can you do this in three years?"

JOHNSON. "Sir, I have no doubt that I can do it in three years."

ADAMS. "But the French Academy,[5] which

---

4. *Junius and Skinner.* The sources of many of Johnson's etymologies for the Germanic languages. Franciscus Junius (1589–1677) was a German-born philologist who lived in England and studied Teutonic languages. Stephen Skinner (1623–1667) was a physician and philologist.

5. *French Academy,* a society composed of forty men and women of letters; the chief purpose of the Academy is upholding correct usage of the French language.

consists of forty members, took forty years to compile their Dictionary."

JOHNSON. "Sir, thus it is. This is the proportion. Let me see; forty times forty is sixteen hundred. As three to sixteen hundred, so is the proportion of an Englishman to a Frenchman."

With so much ease and pleasantry could he talk of that prodigious labor which he had undertaken to execute.

On Books and Reading

JOHNSON. "Sir, I love the acquaintance of young people; because, in the first place, I don't like to think myself growing old. In the next place, young acquaintances must last longest, if they do last; and then, Sir, young men have more virtue than old men; they have more generous sentiments in every respect. I love the young dogs of this age: they have more wit and humor and knowledge of life than we had; but then the dogs are not so good scholars. Sir, in my early years I read very hard. It is a sad reflection, but a true one, that I knew almost as much at eighteen as I do now. My judgment, to be sure, was not so good; but I had all the facts. I remember very well, when I was at Oxford, an old gentleman said to me, 'Young man, ply your book diligently now, and acquire a stock of knowledge; for when years come upon you, you will find that poring upon books will be but an irksome task.'"

JOHNSON. "Idleness is a disease which must be combated; but I would not advise a rigid adherence to a particular plan of study. I myself have never persisted in any plan for two days together. A man ought to read just as inclination leads him: for what he reads as a task will do him little good. A young man should read five hours in a day, and so may acquire a great deal of knowledge."

On Pity

JOHNSON. "Pity is not natural to man. Children are always cruel. Savages are always cruel. Pity is acquired and improved by the cultivation of reason. We may have uneasy sensations for seeing a creature in distress, without pity; for we have not pity unless we wish to relieve them. When I am on my way to dine with a friend, and finding it late, have bid the coachman make haste, if I happen to attend when he whips his horses, I may feel unpleasantly that the animals are put to pain, but I do not wish him to desist. No, sir, I wish him to drive on."

Talking of our feeling for the distresses of others:

JOHNSON. "Why, Sir, there is much noise made about it, but it is greatly exaggerated. No, Sir, we have a certain degree of feeling to prompt us to do good; more than that, Providence does not intend. It would be misery to no purpose."

BOSWELL. "But suppose now, Sir, that one of your intimate friends were apprehended for an offense for which he might be hanged."

JOHNSON. "I should do what I could to bail him, and give him any other assistance; but if he were once fairly hanged, I should not suffer."

BOSWELL. "Would you eat your dinner that day, Sir?"

JOHNSON. "Yes, Sir; and eat it as if he were eating it with me. Why, there's Baretti[6] who is to be tried for his life tomorrow, friends have risen up for him on every side; yet if he should be hanged, none of them will eat a slice of plum pudding the less. Sir, that sympathetic feeling goes a very little way in depressing the mind."

The Social Order

I described to him an impudent fellow from Scotland, who affected to be a savage, and railed at all established systems.

JOHNSON. "There is nothing surprising in this, Sir. He wants to make himself conspicuous. He would tumble in a hogsty, as long as you looked at him and called to him to come out. But let him alone, never mind him, and he'll soon give it over."

I added that the same person maintained that

---

6. **Baretti,** a teacher of Italian and friend of Johnson's, who was tried and acquitted for murder.

there was no distinction between virtue and vice.

JOHNSON. "Why, Sir, if the fellow does not think as he speaks, he is lying; and I see not what honor he can propose to himself from having the character of a liar. But if he does really think that there is no distinction between virtue and vice, why, Sir, when he leaves our houses let us count our spoons."

He again insisted on the duty of maintaining subordination of rank.

JOHNSON. "Sir, I would no more deprive a nobleman of his respect, than of his money. I consider myself as acting a part in the great system of society, and I do to others as I would have them to do to me. I would behave to a nobleman as I should expect he would behave to me, were I a nobleman and he Sam Johnson. Sir, there is one Mrs. Macaulay in this town, a great republican. One day when I was at her house, I put on a very grave countenance, and said to her, 'Madam, I am now become a convert to your way of thinking. I am convinced that all mankind are upon an equal footing; and to give you an unquestionable proof, Madam, that I am in earnest, here is a very sensible, civil, well-behaved fellow-citizen, your footman; I desire that he may be allowed to sit down and dine with us.' I thus, Sir, showed her the absurdity of the leveling doctrine. She has never liked me since. Sir, your levelers wish to level *down* as far as themselves; but they cannot bear leveling *up* to themselves. They would all have some people under them; why not then have some people above them?"

On Slavery

After supper I accompanied him to his apartment, and at my request he dictated to me an argument in favor of the negro who was then claiming his liberty, in an action in the Court of Session in Scotland. He had always been very zealous against slavery in every form, in which I with all deference thought that he discovered "a zeal without knowledge." Upon one occasion, when in company with some very grave men at Oxford, his toast was, "Here's to the next insurrection of the negroes in the West Indies."

His violent prejudice against our West Indian and American settlers appeared whenever there was an opportunity. Towards the conclusion of his "Taxation no Tyranny," he says "how is it that we hear the loudest yelps for liberty among the drivers of negroes?"

On Johnson's Character

His figure was large and well-formed, and his countenance of the cast of an ancient statue; yet his appearance was rendered strange and somewhat uncouth, by convulsive cramps, by the scars of that distemper which it was once imagined the royal touch could cure,[7] and by a slovenly mode of dress. He had the use only of one eye; yet so much does mind govern, and even supply the deficiency of organs, that his visual perceptions, as far as they extended, were uncommonly quick and accurate. So morbid was his temperament, that he never knew the natural joy of a free and vigorous use of his limbs; when he walked, it was like the struggling gait of one in fetters; when he rode, he had no command or direction of his horse, but was carried as if in a balloon. That with his constitution and habits of life he should have lived seventy-five years, is a proof that an inherent *vivida vis*,[8] is a powerful preservative of the human frame.

He was prone to superstition, but not to credulity. Though his imagination might incline him to a belief of the marvelous and the mysterious, his vigorous reason examined the evidence with jealousy. He was a sincere and zealous Christian, of high Church-of-England and monarchical principles, which he would not tamely suffer to be questioned; and had, perhaps, at an early period, narrowed his mind somewhat too much, both as to religion and politics. His being impressed with the danger of extreme latitude in either, though

---

7. distemper . . . cure. Scrofula was called the "King's Evil" because of the belief that it could be cured by the monarch's touch. Johnson's mother took him to London when he was two-and-a-half to be touched by Queen Anne, of course to no avail.
8. vivida vis, life force. [Latin]

he was of a very independent spirit, occasioned his appearing somewhat unfavorable to the prevalence of that noble freedom of sentiment which is the best possession of man. Nor can it be denied, that he had many prejudices; which, however, frequently suggested many of his pointed sayings, that rather show a playfulness of fancy than any settled malignity. He was steady and inflexible in maintaining the obligations of religion and morality; both from a regard for the order of society, and from a veneration for the Great Source of all order: correct, nay stern in his taste; hard to please, and easily offended; impetuous and irritable in his temper, but of a most humane and benevolent heart, which showed itself not only in a most liberal charity, as far as his circumstances would allow, but in a thousand instances of active benevolence.

He was afflicted with a bodily disease, which made him often restless and fretful; and with a constitutional melancholy, the clouds of which darkened the brightness of his fancy, and gave a gloomy cast to his whole course of thinking: we, therefore, ought not to wonder at his sallies of impatience and passion at any time; especially when provoked by obtrusive ignorance, or presuming petulance; and allowance must be made for his uttering hasty and satirical sallies even against his best friends. And, surely, when it is considered, that, "amidst sickness and sorrow," he exerted his faculties in so many works for the benefit of mankind and particularly that he achieved the great and admirable Dictionary of our language, we must be astonished at his resolution.

The solemn text, "of him to whom much is given, much will be required," seems to have been ever present to his mind, in a rigorous sense, and to have made him dissatisfied with his labors and acts of goodness, however comparatively great; so that the unavoidable consciousness of his superiority was, in that respect, a cause of disquiet. He suffered so much from this, and from the gloom which perpetually haunted him, and made solitude frightful, that it may be said of him, "If in this life only he had hope, he was of all men most miserable."

He loved praise, when it was brought to him; but was too proud to seek for it. He was somewhat susceptible of flattery. As he was general and unconfined in his studies, he cannot be considered as master of any one particular science; but he had accumulated a vast and various collection of learning and knowledge, which was so arranged in his mind, as to be ever in readiness to be brought forth. But his superiority over other learned men consisted chiefly in what may be called the art of thinking, the art of using his mind; a certain continual power of seizing the useful substance of all that he knew, and exhibiting it in a clear and forcible manner; so that knowledge, which we often see to be no better than lumber in men of dull understanding, was, in him true, evident, and actual wisdom.

His moral precepts are practical; for they are drawn from an intimate acquaintance with human nature. His maxims carry conviction; for they are founded on the basis of common sense, and a very attentive and minute survey of real life. His mind was so full of imagery, that he might have been perpetually a poet; yet it is remarkable, that, however rich his prose is in this respect, his poetical pieces, in general, have not much of that splendor, but are rather distinguished by strong sentiment, and acute observation, conveyed in harmonious and energetic verse, particularly in heroic couplets. Though usually grave, and even awful in his deportment, he possessed uncommon and peculiar powers of wit and humor; he frequently indulged himself in colloquial pleasantry; and the heartiest merriment was often enjoyed in his company; with this great advantage, that, as it was entirely free from any poisonous tincture of vice or impiety, it was salutary to those who shared in it.

He had accustomed himself to such accuracy in his common conversation, that he at all times expressed his thoughts with great force, and an elegant choice of language, the effect of which was aided by his having a loud voice, and a slow deliberate utterance. In him were united a most logical head with a most fertile imagination, which gave him an extraordinary advantage in arguing:

for he could reason close or wide, as he saw best for the moment. Exulting in his intellectual strength and dexterity, he could, when he pleased, be the greatest sophist that ever contended in the lists of declamation; and, from a spirit of contradiction, and a delight in showing his powers, he would often maintain the wrong side with equal warmth and ingenuity: so that, when there was an audience, his real opinions could seldom be gathered from his talk; though, when he was in company with a single friend, he would discuss a subject with genuine fairness; but he was too conscientious to make error permanent and pernicious, by deliberately writing it; and, in all his numerous works, he earnestly inculcated what appeared to him to be the truth; his piety being constant, and the ruling principle of all his conduct.

Such was Samuel Johnson, a man whose talents, acquirements, and virtues were so extraordinary, that the more his character is considered the more he will be regarded by the present age, and by posterity, with admiration and reverence.

THINK AND DISCUSS
Understanding
1. Put into your own words this statement: "In him were united a most logical head with a most fertile imagination."

Analyzing
2. Boswell wanted to write about Johnson so that "he will be seen as he really was," to "delineate him without reserve." What negative characteristics do you find in Boswell's Johnson? What positive characteristics do you find?
3. What role does Boswell play in these scenes? Why does he act this way?
4. Why does Boswell sometimes report Johnson's conversations as if they were part of a play?
5. Why does Boswell call Johnson *Jean Bull philosophe* (402a, 3)?
6. What seems to be Boswell's attitude toward Johnson?

Extending
7. Why do you think people desired Johnson's company?
8. How do you think Johnson felt about Boswell?

COMPOSITION
Describing a Public Figure
Play the part of a modern Boswell and write a description of an imaginary meeting between you and some modern figure you admire. You might base your description on information you have gathered from magazines, television interviews, autobiographies, and so on. Include some dialogue based on your knowledge of your subject's personality and interests. Assume that your description will be published in a national magazine.

Discussing Johnson's Ideas
Some of the ideas Johnson expressed to Boswell are still topics of conversation today; for example, the importance of reading, feelings for the distress of others, class structure, hypocrisy. Select one of these and write an essay in which you quote Johnson's idea, explain it if necessary, and discuss the extent to which it is similar to or different from ideas being expressed today.

After studying at Eton, where he formed close friendships with Horace Walpole, son of the prime minister, and Richard West, Gray went on to Cambridge in 1734, leaving in 1738 without his degree to accompany Walpole on a tour of France and Italy. In 1741, after a disagreement, Gray returned to England alone. Later he and Walpole patched up their quarrel.

Returning to Cambridge in 1742, Gray completed his studies and then made the University his home for the rest of his life, devoting himself to scholarly pursuits. He became expert in the arts, especially literature, and in history; he was, in fact, appointed Professor of Modern History in 1768. Having mastered many regular academic fields, he turned his attention to more unusual ones: pre-Elizabethan poetry and Old Welsh and Norse literature, doing some translations into English. In his interest in these older literatures and in his enjoyment of unspoiled, natural landscapes, he was a forerunner of the Romantic Age.

Shortly after his break with Walpole, Gray in 1742 lost his other close friend, Richard West. Shocked and depressed by West's untimely death, Gray developed a strong streak of melancholy that stayed with him for the rest of his life.

In his later years, Gray lived almost as a recluse, leaving Cambridge only occasionally to vacation in the Lake District or in Scotland, where he could admire the rugged scenery, or to read and do research in the library of the newly opened British Museum in London. Because he kept reworking his poems in an attempt to perfect them, his poetic output was small. Only in his letters, now considered among the best in an age when letter-writing was an art, does Gray show his shy, affectionate nature and gentle humor. When he died in 1771, the churchyard of Stoke Poges, a village in Buckinghamshire, said to be the setting of the "Elegy Written in a Country Churchyard," became his own final resting place.

The "Elegy" presents in carefully selected language a scene of rural serenity; introduces a note of melancholy; goes on to reflect on death, the common man, and the ironies of human destiny; and concludes with the speaker's epitaph for himself.

Elegy Written in a Country Churchyard

Thomas Gray

The curfew tolls the knell of parting day,
  The lowing herd wind slowly o'er the lea,
The plowman homeward plods his weary way,
  And leaves the world to darkness and to
    me.

5 Now fades the glimmering landscape on the
    sight,
  And all the air a solemn stillness holds,
Save where the beetle wheels his droning
    flight,
  And drowsy tinklings lull the distant folds;

Save that from yonder ivy-mantled tower
10   The moping owl does to the moon
    complain
Of such as, wandering near her secret bower,
  Molest her ancient solitary reign.

Beneath those rugged elms, that yew-tree's
    shade,
  Where heaves the turf in many a
    moldering heap,
15 Each in his narrow cell forever laid,
  The rude forefathers of the hamlet sleep.

The breezy call of incense-breathing morn,
  The swallow twittering from the straw-
    built shed,
The cock's shrill clarion, or the echoing
    horn,[1]
20   No more shall rouse them from their lowly
    bed.

For them no more the blazing hearth shall
    burn,
  Or busy housewife ply her evening care;
No children run to lisp their sire's return,
  Or climb his knees the envied kiss to share.

25 Oft did the harvest to their sickle yield;
  Their furrow oft the stubborn glebe has
    broke;
How jocund did they drive their team afield!
  How bowed the woods beneath their
    sturdy stroke!

Let not Ambition mock their useful toil,
30   Their homely joys, and destiny obscure;
Nor Grandeur hear with a disdainful smile
  The short and simple annals of the poor.

The boast of heraldry, the pomp of power,
  And all that beauty, all that wealth e'er
    gave,
35 Awaits alike the inevitable hour:
  The paths of glory lead but to the grave.

Nor you, ye proud, impute to these the fault,
  If Memory o'er their tomb no trophies
    raise,
Where through the long-drawn aisle and
    fretted vault
40   The pealing anthem swells the note of
    praise.

---

1. *horn*, the huntsman's horn.

Can storied urn[2] or animated[3] bust
  Back to its mansion call the fleeting breath?
Can Honor's voice provoke the silent dust,
  Or Flattery soothe the dull cold ear of
    Death?

45 Perhaps in this neglected spot is laid
  Some heart once pregnant with celestial
    fire;
Hands that the rod of empire might have
    swayed,
  Or waked to ecstasy the living lyre.

But Knowledge to their eyes her ample page,
50 Rich with the spoils of time, did ne'er
    unroll;
Chill Penury repressed their noble rage,
  And froze the genial current of the soul.

Full many a gem of purest ray serene,
  The dark unfathomed caves of ocean bear;
55 Full many a flower is born to blush unseen,
  And waste its sweetness on the desert air.

Some village Hampden,[4] that with dauntless
    breast
  The little tyrant of his fields withstood;
Some mute inglorious Milton here may rest,
60 Some Cromwell,[5] guiltless of his country's
    blood.

The applause of listening senates to
    command,
  The threats of pain and ruin to despise,
To scatter plenty o'er a smiling land,
  And read their history in a nation's eyes,

65 Their lot forbade; nor circumscribed alone
  Their growing virtues, but their crimes
    confined;
Forbade to wade through slaughter to a
    throne,
  And shut the gates of mercy on mankind;

The struggling pangs of conscious truth to
    hide,

70 To quench the blushes of ingenuous shame,
  Or heap the shrine of Luxury and Pride
    With incense kindled at the Muse's flame.

Far from the madding crowd's ignoble strife,
  Their sober wishes never learned to stray;
75 Along the cool sequestered vale of life
  They kept the noiseless tenor of their way.

Yet even these bones from insult to protect,
  Some frail memorial still erected nigh,
With uncouth[6] rhymes and shapeless
    sculpture decked,
80 Implores the passing tribute of a sigh.

Their name, their years, spelt by the
    unlettered Muse,
  The place of fame and elegy supply;
And many a holy text around she strews,
  That teach the rustic moralist to die.

85 For who, to dumb forgetfulness a prey,
  This pleasing anxious being e'er resigned,
Left the warm precincts of the cheerful day,
  Nor cast one longing lingering look
    behind?

On some fond breast the parting soul relies,
90 Some pious drops the closing eye requires;
Even from the tomb the voice of Nature
    cries,
  Even in our ashes live their wonted fires.

For thee,[7] who mindful of the unhonored
    dead
  Dost in these lines their artless tale relate;

---

2. *storied urn,* an urn decorated with pictures that tell a story.
3. *animated,* lifelike.
4. *Hampden,* John Hampden (1594–1643), member of the Puritan or Roundhead party who spoke out against royal taxes.
5. *Cromwell,* Oliver Cromwell (1599–1658) was a Puritan military leader who became Lord Protector of the Commonwealth after the execution of Charles I.
6. *uncouth,* strange; odd.
7. *thee,* Gray himself.

Illustration for Gray's "Elegy" by R. Bentley, 1753.

That wreathes its old fantastic roots so
    high,
His listless length at noontide would he
    stretch,
    And pore upon the brook that babbles by.

105 "Hard by yon wood, now smiling as in
      scorn,
    Muttering his wayward fancies he would
      rove;
Now drooping, woeful-wan, like one forlorn,
    Or crazed with care, or crossed in hopeless
      love.

"One morn I missed him on the customed
    hill,
110   Along the heath, and near his favorite tree;
Another came; nor yet beside the rill,
    Nor up the lawn, nor at the wood was he;

"The next, with dirges due, in sad array,
    Slow through the church-way path we saw
      him borne.
115 Approach and read (for thou canst read) the
      lay,
    Graved on the stone beneath yon aged
      thorn."

The Epitaph

Here rests his head upon the lap of earth,
    A youth to Fortune and to Fame unknown;
Fair Science frowned not on his humble birth,
120   *And Melancholy marked him for her own.*

Large was his bounty, and his soul sincere;
    Heaven did a recompense as largely send;
He gave to Misery all he had, a tear;
    He gained from Heaven ('twas all he wished)
    a friend.

125 *No farther seek his merits to disclose,*
    Or draw his frailties from their dread abode,
    (There they alike in trembling hope repose),
    The bosom of his Father and his God.
1742–50   1751

95 If chance, by lonely contemplation led,
    Some kindred spirit shall inquire thy fate,

Haply some hoary-headed swain may say,
    "Oft have we seen him at the peep of
      dawn
Brushing with hasty steps the dews away
100   To meet the sun upon the upland lawn,

"There at the foot of yonder nodding beech

THINK AND DISCUSS

Understanding

1. Identify the subjects of the poem (introduced in stanza 4).
2. Put "The applause . . . forbade" (lines 61–65) into your own words.
3. Who is the person quoted in lines 98–116? To whom is he referring?

Analyzing

4. Which words and phrases in the first three stanzas contribute to the air of melancholy that pervades the poem?
5. What is the speaker's attitude toward "the rude forefathers of the hamlet" as contrasted with his attitude toward the world?
6. To what extent were their poverty and lack of education a handicap? To what extent were they a blessing?
7. According to the epitaph that ends the poem, how satisfactory a life did the speaker live?
8. Note the many instances of **personification** throughout. How does this personification contribute to the thoughts expressed?

APPLYING: Setting H⅄

See Handbook of Literary Terms, p. 924

Setting is the time and place in which the events of a narrative occur. In some works it must be inferred, but in other works it is important enough to influence the action.

1. What time of day is it? How do you know?
2. How does the place where the poem is set influence the content of the poem?
3. Setting also involves the period in history during which events occur. What details in the poem suggest its historical setting?

VOCABULARY

Pronunciation Key

Following each numbered sentence are the pronunciations of two different words. One of these pronunciations is for the word that belongs in the blank. Use the pronunciation key in the Glossary to choose the correct word to complete each sentence. Write the words on separate paper, spelling them correctly.

1. "That he was fully aware of the _____ nature of the undertaking, he acknowledges. . . ."
   a. ə sep′tik   **b.** är′jü əs
2. "To quench the blushes of _____ shame. . . ."
   a. in jē′nyəs   **b.** in jen′yü əs
3. ". . . but he was too conscientious to make error permanent and _____ , by deliberately writing it. . ."
   a. pər nish′əs   **b.** per snik′ə tē
4. "But it must be owned that Johnson, though he could be rigidly _____ , was not a temperate man either in eating or drinking."
   a. ab stē′mē əs   **b.** ab′stə nəns
5. "Heaven did a _____ as largely send."
   a. rek′əm pens   **b.** rek′ən dīt
6. "Some heart once pregnant with _____ fire."
   a. sə les′chəl   **b.** sel′ə brāt

COMPOSITION ✒

Writing a Parody

A *parody* is a humorous imitation of a piece of writing, following the form of the original. Try your hand at writing a brief parody of Gray's *Elegy* to submit to your school literary magazine. Your parody might begin, "The hall-bell clangs the end of history. . ." or "The alarm whines the start of blue Monday. . ." Or, choose your own subject. Follow Gray's verse pattern, including his rhyme scheme, and include personification. Close your elegy with an appropriate epitaph.

Analyzing Gray's Use of Setting

Reread the poem, noting Gray's details of setting. Then write an essay, suitable for your school literary magazine, in which you examine how he uses these details to establish setting and how that setting influences the speaker's train of thought and ultimately the **theme** of the poem.

The desire for order and certainty that emerged amidst the turmoil of the seventeenth century was reflected in the development of the language. Particularly in the latter half of the century, the English people, reacting against the novelties and unregulated spontaneity which characterized Elizabethan expression, began to call for an ordered, rational language.

The Royal Society, founded in 1660 by a group of learned men and scientists, objected to the Elizabethan love of verbal gymnastics on the ground that it was unscientific, and demanded of its members instead "a close, naked, natural way of speaking; positive expressions, clear senses, a native easiness, bringing as near the mathematical plainness as they can."

Those caught in the surge toward greater simplicity and precision—among them Swift, Steele, Addison, Johnson, and Lord Chesterfield—tended to disparage what they called "cant" or "low speech." These arbiters of language realized, as did many of their time, that the English language was in a muddle that the disputes over grammar of the previous centuries had failed to solve: words still had widely variant meanings, spellings, and pronunciations, and the general instability of the language was a barrier to clear communication. In the mishandling of the language the educated and well-to-do seem to have been as guilty as any.

The urge to introduce order into the language is evident in hundreds of projects undertaken during the course of the century. Johnson's ponderous two-volume *Dictionary*, great achievement though it was, offered only a partial solution to the problems of standardizing the language, and before the century ended there were many other attempts. The efforts at standardization spilled over into literary texts. One mid-eighteenth-century editor announced that Shakespeare's works were an "unweeded Garden grown to Seed," and confidently set about the cultivation and pruning he thought necessary. Another overearnest

"On the Publishing Day of *The Dunciad*," attributed to George Dalziel, 1853. Writers hostile to Alexander Pope cannot prevent his latest satire from appearing.

reformer named Bentley tackled Milton's poetry, and got for his pains Pope's ridicule for being a scribbler "whose unwearied pains/ Made Horace dull, and humbled Milton's strains." If there was widespread agreement that the English language needed polishing, there was little agreement about how it should be done, and the controversy continued throughout the century.

While neoclassicism did much to tone down the bizarre and freakish aspects of seventeenth-century speech, it did not, in spite of its insistence on rules and rigidity, stamp out the rich variety which makes English a vital instrument of communication. Although both Johnson and Swift objected to the use of such words as *humbug, prig, doodle, bamboozle, fib, bully, fop, banter, stingy, fun, prude*, they continued in use then as they do today, evidence of the fact that people, not grammar books or dictionaries, make and perpetuate language.

THINKING CRITICALLY
ABOUT LITERATURE

UNIT 4   THE AGE OF REASON   1660–1780

■ CONCEPT REVIEW

The following selection contains many of the important ideas and literary terms found in the period you have just studied. It also contains notes and questions designed to help you think critically about your reading. Page numbers in the notes refer to an application. A more extensive discussion of these terms is in the Handbook of Literary Terms.

A Journal of the Plague Year was written in 1722 in response to the widespread alarm over a new outbreak of the plague in Europe the previous year. Daniel Defoe was only a child during the great plague in 1665 and had no detailed recollection of the events he describes, but he did a great deal of research to make his account convincing.

from A Journal of the Plague Year

Daniel Defoe

Part 1

It pleased God that I was still spared, and very hearty and sound in health, but very impatient of being pent up within doors without air, as I had been for fourteen days or thereabouts, and I could not restrain myself, but I would go to carry a letter for my brother to the post-house. Then it was indeed that I observed a profound silence in the streets. When I came to the post-house, as I went to put in my letter, I saw a man stand in one corner of the yard and talking to another at a window, and a third had opened a door belonging to the office. In the middle of the yard lay a small leather purse with two keys hanging at it, with money in it, but nobody would meddle with it. I asked how long it had lain there; the man at the window said it had lain almost an hour, but that they had not meddled with it, because they did not know but

■ **Point of View** (page 357): Note Defoe's use of the first-person point of view.

■ As you read, notice how observant the narrator is.

■ **Irony** (page 343): This statement is ironic because

the person who dropped it might come back to look for it. I had no such need of money, nor was the sum so big that I had any inclination to meddle with it, or to get the money at the hazard it might be attended with; so I seemed to go away, when the man who had opened the door said he would take it up, but so that if the right owner came for it he should be sure to have it. So he went in and fetched a pail of water, and set it down hard by the purse, then went again and fetched some gunpowder, and cast a good deal of powder upon the purse, and then made a train from that which he had thrown loose upon the purse. The train reached about two yards. After this he goes in a third time and fetches out a pair of tongs red hot, and which he had prepared, I suppose, on purpose, and first setting fire to the train of powder, that singed the purse, and also smoked the air sufficiently. But he was not content with that, but he then takes up the purse with the tongs, holding it so long till the tongs burnt through the purse, and then he shook the money out into the pail of water, so he carried it in. The money, as I remember, was about thirteen shillings and some smooth groats and brass farthings. . . .

of the reason the man at the window gives for not touching the purse.

■ Note the extent to which the man goes to purify the money.

Part 2

Passing through Tokenhouse Yard, in Lothbury, of a sudden a casement violently opened just over my head, and a woman gave three frightful screeches, and then cried, "Oh! death, death, death!" in a most inimitable tone, and which struck me with horror and a chillness in my very blood. There was nobody to be seen in the whole street, neither did any other window open, for people had no curiosity now in any case, nor could anybody help one another, so I went on to pass into Bell Alley.

Just in Bell Alley, on the right hand of the passage, there was a more terrible cry than that, though it was not so directed out at the window; but the whole family was in terrible fright, and I could hear women and children run screaming about the rooms like distracted, when a garret-window opened, and somebody from a window on the other side of the alley called and asked, "What is the matter?" upon which, from the first window it was answered, "O Lord, my old master has hanged himself!" The other asked again, "Is he quite dead?" and the first answered, "Ay, ay, quite dead; quite dead and cold!" This person was a merchant and a deputy alderman, and very rich. I care not to mention the name, though I knew his name too, but that would be an hardship to the family, which is now flourishing again.

But this is but one; it is scarce credible what dreadful cases happened in particular families every day. People in the rage of the distemper, or in the torment of their swellings, which was indeed intolerable, running out of their own government, raving and distracted, and often-times laying violent hands upon themselves, throwing themselves out at their windows, shooting themselves, &c.; mothers murdering their own children in their lunacy, some dying of mere grief as a passion, some of mere fright and surprise without any infection at all, others frighted into idiotism and foolish distractions, some into despair and lunacy, others into melancholy madness. . . .

■ groats. . . farthings: coins worth a small sum.

■ casement: window that opens on hinges.
■ inimitable: impossible to imitate.
■ Tone (page 364): Note the change of tone in this section, which portrays graphically the horrors of the plague.
■ Setting (page 412): The setting is specific, as Defoe gives the names of various thoroughfares in London.

■ Note the cumulative effect of all this detail.

■ government: control.

Part 3

. . . here I must observe also that the plague, as I suppose all distempers do, operated in a different manner on differing constitutions; some were immediately overwhelmed with it, and it came to violent fevers, vomitings, insufferable headaches, pains in the back, and so up to ravings and ragings with those pains; others with swellings and tumors in the neck and groin, or armpits, which till they could be broke put them into insufferable agonies and torment; while others, as I have observed, were silently infected, the fever preying upon their spirits insensibly, and they seeing little of it till they fell into swooning, and faintings, and death without pain.

I am not physician enough to enter into the particular reasons and manner of these differing effects of one and the same distemper. . . . I am only relating what I know, or have heard, or believe of the particular cases, and what fell within the compass of my view; . . . but this may be added too, that though the former sort of those cases, namely, those openly visited, were the worst for themselves as to pain . . . yet the latter had the worst state of the disease; for in the former they frequently recovered, especially if the swellings broke, but the latter was inevitable death; no cure, no help could be possible, nothing could follow but death. . . .

■ Notice the logical yet inquisitive approach typical of the Age of Reason.
■ **constitutions:** physical makeups; natures.
■ Defoe describes the three strains of the plague: pneumonic, bubonic, and septicemic, the last being 100% fatal.

Part 4

. . . the shutting up of houses, so as to confine those that were well with those that were sick, had very great inconveniences in it, and some that were very tragical. . . . But it was authorized by a law, it had the public good in view as the end chiefly aimed at, and all the private injuries that were done by the putting it in execution must be put to the account of the public benefit.

It is doubtful to this day whether, in the whole, it contributed anything to the stop of the infection. . . . Certain it is that if all the infected persons were effectually shut in, no sound person could have been infected by them, because they could not have come near them. But the case was this, and I shall only touch it here, namely, that the infection was propagated insensibly, and by such persons as were not visibly infected, who neither knew whom they infected or who they were infected by. . . .

■ Notice that the public good is placed ahead of individual convenience.

■ **propagated insensibly:** passed on unknowingly.

Part 5

. . . the common people, who, ignorant and stupid in their reflections, as they were brutishly wicked and thoughtless before, were now led by their fright to extremes of folly; and, as I have said before that they ran to conjurers and witches, and all sorts of deceivers, to know what should become of them (who fed their fears, and kept them always alarmed and awake on purpose to delude them and pick their pockets), so they were as mad upon their running after quacks and mountebanks, and every practising old woman, for medicines and remedies; storing themselves with such multitudes of pills, potions, and preservatives, as they were called, that they not only spent their money, but even poisoned themselves beforehand, for fear of the poison of the infection, and prepared their bodies for the plague, instead of preserving them

■ **conjurers:** tricksters; magicians.

■ **mountebanks:** persons who sell useless medicines in public.

Fleeing from the Plague, 1665. *Society of Antiquaries, London*

against it. On the other hand, it is incredible, and scarce to be imagined, how the posts of houses and corners of streets were plastered over with doctors' bills and papers of ignorant fellows, quacking and tampering in physic, and inviting the people to come to them for remedies, which was generally set off with such flourishes as these, viz.: "Infallible preventive pills against the plague." "Never-failing preservatives against the infection." "Sovereign cordials against the corruption of the air." "Exact regulations for the conduct of the body in case of an infection." "Anti-pestilential pills." "Incomparable drink against the plague, never found out before." "An universal remedy for the plague." "The only true plague-water." "The royal antidote against all kinds of infection"; and such a number more that I cannot reckon up; and if I could, would fill a book of themselves to set them down. . . .

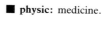 **physic:** medicine.

■ **viz.:** namely.

■ Satire (page 337): In Section 5 Defoe is satirizing the people who prey upon the public's fears and the people who purchase quack remedies.

Part 6

It is here . . . to be observed that after the funerals became so many that people could not toll the bell, mourn or weep, or wear black for one another, as they did before; no, nor so much as make coffins for those that died; so after a while the fury of the infection appeared to be so increased that, in short, they shut up no houses at all. It seemed enough that all the remedies of that kind had been used till they were found fruitless, and that the plague spread itself with an irresistible fury; so that as the fire the succeeding year spread itself, and burned with such violence that the citizens, in despair, gave over their endeavors to extinguish it, so in the plague it came at last to such violence that people sat still looking at one another, and seemed quite abandoned to despair.

■ Note that Defoe inadvertently gives the reason why there were no longer serious visitations of the plague.

Part 7

In the middle of their distress, when the condition of the city of London was so truly calamitous, just then it pleased God, as it were, by His immediate hand to disarm this enemy; the poison was taken out of the sting. It was

■ Note the change in tone as the plague abates.
■ **calamitous:** disastrous.

Thinking Critically About Literature **417**

wonderful; even the physicians themselves were surprised at it. Wherever they visited they found their patients better; either they had sweated kindly, or the tumors were broke, or the carbuncles went down, and the inflammations round them changed color, or the fever was gone, or the violent headache was assuaged, or some good symptom was in the case; so that in a few days everybody was recovering, whole families that were infected and down, that had ministers praying with them, and expected death every hour, were revived and healed, and none died at all out of them.

Nor was this by any new medicine found out, or new method of cure discovered, or by any experience in the operation which the physicians or surgeons attained to; but it was evidently from the secret invisible hand of Him that had at first sent this disease as a judgment upon us; and let the atheistic part of mankind call my saying what they please, it is no enthusiasm; it was acknowledged at that time by all mankind.

■ Note the religious close.

1722

THINK AND DISCUSS
Understanding
1. What is the narrator's errand after fourteen days of being "pent up within doors"?
2. How much good did it do, according to the narrator, to shut up houses? Why was it done?
3. What effect does the narrator say that taking "pills, potions, and preservatives" has on people's health?

Analyzing
4. Why might the three men at the post-house be standing so far apart?
5. Why does the man in the doorway go to such lengths to get at the money in the purse?
6. Defoe is regarded as a master of *verisimilitude*—the art of piling detail upon detail so that his fictional accounts have the authenticity of real life. Find several examples of verisimilitude in this selection.
7. Does Defoe seem more concerned with the physical horrors of the plague, or with the psychological? Explain.

Extending
8. Do you think that Defoe's *Journal* rings more true than an account in a history book would?

9. If you were a Londoner reading this book in 1722, would it increase or diminish your concern about a new outbreak of plague?

REVIEWING LITERARY TERMS
Point of View
1. What does Defoe achieve by using the first-person point of view rather than the third person?

Irony
2. The man at the window says they did not meddle with the purse because they thought the owner might return for it. What is their real reason for not meddling with it?

Tone
3. The tone in Part 1 is matter-of-fact as Defoe reports on what he sees. How does it change in Part 2?

Setting
4. Why might Defoe include such specific locations as Tokenhouse Yard, Lothbury, and Bell Alley?

Satire
5. What does Defoe satirize about the common people?

6. What is Defoe satirizing about the signs plastered on houses and street corners?

■ CONTENT REVIEW

Classifying

1. The writers of the Age of Reason frequently wrote about public issues. Scan the unit to find a number of these issues; then classify chosen selections according to which public issues they address.

2. Two main kinds of satire are often identified: *Horatian* (after the Roman poet Horace), which tends to be gentle and humorous, and *Juvenalian* (after the Roman poet Juvenal), which tends to be harsh and biting. Classify the satire in this unit according to these types.

Generalizing

3. What is meant by *reason* as it is used in "The Age of Reason"?

4. The Age of Reason stressed social relationships and particularly manners—the way people should behave toward one another. What, generally, do the authors in this unit consider to be good manners?

5. The love poetry that characterized the Renaissance is almost totally missing from the Age of Reason. What themes do these writers treat instead? What might explain this change?

Synthesizing

6. The Anglo-Saxons feared "The Violent Face of Nature" (see page 58). Compare and contrast their attitude with that of the writers in this unit, particularly Gray. How do you account for this change?

7. Name some examples of modern biography that you are familiar with and explain what they owe to the models of biography written by Johnson and Boswell.

Evaluating

8. Many of the selections in this unit are bitingly satirical. Do you think any of them are unjustifiably so? Explain.

9. Which of the selections you have read in this unit would you recommend as the one work from this period that every twentieth-century student should read? Why?

■ COMPOSITION REVIEW

Writing About Literary Trends

Literature underwent changes in form, content, and purpose from the beginning of the Age of Reason to its end. Consider Dryden, who comes first in the unit, and Gray, who comes last. Write an essay comparing their works in terms of style and content and suggesting reasons for the differences you describe. See "Writing About a Period or Trend" in the Writer's Handbook.

Comparing and Contrasting Techniques

In a paper of four or more paragraphs, compare and contrast Defoe's description of the plague in *A Journal of the Plague Year* with Pepys's description of the fire in his *Diary*. Consider the immediacy of the accounts, the emphasis on the psychological, the use of physical detail or fact, the audience addressed, and the formality of the writing style.

Evaluating Literary Objectives

According to Addison and Steele, the objectives of their literary periodicals were to enliven morality with wit, and to temper wit with morality. Choose any two or three selections from this unit (including, if you wish, those by Addison and Steele) and discuss how well the selections carry out these objectives.

Analyzing Attitudes Toward Women

Both Addison in "Party Patches" and Defoe in "On the Education of Women" write about how women respond to society's expectations of them and about what the authors think those expectations *ought* to be. Write a paper in which you compare and contrast how women behave, according to these authors, and how they ought to behave. What, according to these authors, causes this behavior? What would need to be changed to cause the kind of behavior the authors would prefer?

Researching Modern Satirists

Is anyone writing satire today? If so, who? Do some research on two or three modern satirists and write a paper describing their subject matter and techniques. Ask your teacher or librarian to help you choose authors to research.

THE ROMANTICS 1780–1830

1785	1790	1795	1800	1805

HISTORY AND ARTS

- Treaty of Paris
- French Revolution begins
- Washington becomes president of the U.S.
  - Mozart: *The Magic Flute* (Austria)
    - Louis XVI of France executed
    - Reign of Terror in France
    - Napoleonic Wars begin
- Act of Union of Great Britain and Ireland
  - Turner paints *Calais Pier*
    - Napoleon crowned Emperor of France

Nelson wins naval Battle of Trafalgar •

MONARCHS AND HOUSES

HANOVER
- George III

ENGLISH LITERATURE

- Burns: *Poems*
  - Blake: *Songs of Experience*
  - Radcliffe: *The Mysteries of Udolpho*
    - Edgeworth: *Castle Rackrent*   • Wordsworth and Coleridge: *Lyrical Ballads*
    - Boswell: *Life of Samuel Johnson, LL.D.*
- Blake: *Songs* • Wollstonecraft: *A Vindication of Innocence   of the Rights of Woman*
    - Godwin: *Political Justice*

The execution of Louis XVI, detail of engraving, 1793.

Detail of frontispiece to 1795 edition of *The Castle of Otranto*.

George III, portrait by the studio of Allen Ramsay.

1810	1815	1820	1825	1830

• Battle of Waterloo

• First railroad built in England

• England abolishes the slave trade

• Congress of Vienna

• Labor unions become legal

• Goethe: *Faust* (Germany)

• Peterloo Massacre

• Beethoven: *Symphony No. 5* (Germany)

Cooper: *The Last of the Mohicans* (U.S.) •

• Prince of Wales becomes Prince Regent

Poe: *Tamerlane and* • *Other Poems* (U.S.)

• War of 1812 begins (U.S.)

Webster's *American* • *Dictionary* published

• Napoleon invades Russia

• George IV

• C. and M. Lamb: *Tales from Shakespeare*

• Hazlitt: *Characters of Shakespeare's Plays*

• Wordsworth: *Poems in Two Volumes*

• Coleridge: *Biographia Literaria*

• Moore: *Irish Melodies*

• Keats: *Endymion*   • De Quincey: *Confessions of an English Opium-Eater*

• Scott: *The Lady of the Lake*

• Byron: *Don Juan*

• Byron: *Childe Harold's Pilgrimage*

• M. Shelley: *Frankenstein*   • C. Lamb: *Essays of Elia*

• Austen: *Pride and Prejudice*

• Scott: *Ivanhoe*

• P. Shelley: *Prometheus Unbound*

• Keats: *The Eve of St. Agnes*

Napoleon at the Battle of Arcole, 1796, by Antoine-Jean Gros.

Detail of *The Death of Nelson* by William Drummond.

The Phoenix, built by George Stephenson.

PREVIEW

UNIT 5 THE ROMANTICS 1780–1830

Authors
William Blake
Robert Burns
Mary Wollstonecraft
William Wordsworth
Samuel Taylor Coleridge

Thomas De Quincey
George Gordon, Lord Byron
Percy Bysshe Shelley
John Keats
Mary Shelley

Features
Comment: Blake's Obscurities
Reading Romantic Poetry
Themes in English Literature:
    The Countryside
Comment: Coleridge's Remarks About
    "Kubla Khan"
Comment: Did Keats Make a Blunder?
Reader's Note: "Ode on a Grecian Urn"
Comment: The Gothic Novel
The Changing English Language

Application of Literary Terms
repetition
dialect
style
simile
mood
rhyme
onomatopoeia
imagery

Review of Literary Terms
rhythm
metaphor
blank verse
sonnet
tone
symbol

Reading Literature Skillfully
author's purpose

Vocabulary
etymology
word analogies
synonyms

Thinking Skills
classifying
generalizing
synthesizing
evaluating

Composition Assignments Include
Writing an Inductive Essay
Writing About a Symbol
Writing a Story
Describing a Walk
Writing to Persuade
Writing a Ballad
Analyzing the Mood of a Poem
Analyzing Byron's Satire
Writing a Persuasive Speech
Writing a Poem
Analyzing Your Writing Process
Writing About a Personal Discovery
Analyzing Imagery
Writing About Characters
Writing About Theme

Enrichment
Presenting a "Romantic" Performance

Thinking Critically About Literature
Concept Review
Content Review
Composition Review

THE ROMANTICS 1780–1830

As its name suggests, the Romantic Age brought a more daring, individual, and imaginative approach to both literature and life. In the late eighteenth and early nineteenth centuries, many of the most important English writers turned away from the values and ideas characteristic of the Age of Reason. The individual, rather than society, was at the center of the Romantic vision. The Romantic writers tended to be optimists who believed in the possibility of progress and social and human reform. As champions of democratic ideals, they sharply attacked all forms of tyranny and the spreading evils of industrialism, such as urban blight, a polluted environment, and the alienation of people from nature and one another.

AN AGE OF REVOLUTION

The impact of the French Revolution in 1789 upon the writers of the age cannot be overemphasized. While impressed by the efforts of the American colonists to wrest power from their British rulers, the English felt personally removed from such events as Valley Forge. France, however, was only a brief passage across the English Channel. For a time, almost every important British writer responded warmly to the cry of the French for "Liberty, Equality, Fraternity." For example, government restrictions that barred his return to France in 1793 were all that kept William Wordsworth from taking up residence in that country and siding with the revolutionaries.

Whereas the writers of the Age of Reason tended to regard evil as a basic part of human nature, the Romantic writers generally saw humanity as naturally good, but corrupted by society and its institutions of religion, education, and government. Thus, the French Revolution gave life and breath to the dreams of some Romantic writers for a society in which there would be liberty and equality for all. It also contributed later to a sense of disillusionment following the Reign of Terror in France, during which the oppressed classes became as violent and corrupt as their former rulers, thereby paving the way for Napoleon's rise to power.

One of the most significant aspects of nineteenth-century English life was the slow but steady application of the principles of democracy. England emerged from the eighteenth century a parliamentary state in which the monarchy was largely a figurehead. The English Parliament was far from a truly representative body, however, until, after years of popular agitation, Parliament finally passed the First Reform Bill of 1832, which liberalized representation in Parliament.

The Industrial Revolution took place in England from 1750–1850. During this period England changed from an agricultural to an industrial society and from home manufacturing to factory production. As the Industrial Revolution gathered force, towns became cities; more and more villagers, forced by economic necessity to seek work in the growing factories, huddled together in filthy slums. Workers—men, women, and children—labored from sunrise to sunset for meager wages. A child able to pull a cart in the suffocating coal mines or to sweep a floor in the textile factories was considered old enough to work by many employers and some parents. For the children of the poor, religious training, medical care, and education were practically nonexistent.

Gradually English society began to awaken to its obligations to the miserable and helpless. Through the efforts of reformers, the church and government assumed their responsibilities. Sunday schools were organized; hospitals were built; movements were begun to reform the prisons and regulate the conditions of child labor.

The effects of revolution abroad, the demand for a more democratic government, and a growing awareness of social injustice at home are all reflected in a new spirit that over a period of years affected practically every aspect of English life.

The Romantic Age in England was part of a movement that affected all the countries of Western Europe. The forms of romanticism were so many and varied, in some instances embracing contradictory values, that it is difficult to speak of the movement as a whole. It tended to align itself with the humanitarian spirit of the democratic revolutionaries; but romantics were not always democrats, and democrats were not always revolutionaries. Perhaps the safest thing to say is that romanticism represented an attempt to rediscover the mystery and wonder of the world, an attempt to go beyond ordinary reality into the deeper, less obvious, and more elusive levels of individual human existence.

The emergence and spread of the romantic spirit in England gradually became apparent in all aspects of life—fashions, manners, and morals. Simplicity and naturalness rather than artificiality and excess characterized this new spirit and lifestyle.

ELSEWHERE IN THE WORLD

The age of revolution also affected Latin America. In the 1780s, colonists revolted against 300 years of foreign rule in Peru, Colombia, Ecuador, and Venezuela. At first, only one uprising was successful, however. In 1794, Pierre Dominique Toussaint l'Overture, a freed black slave in Hispaniola, led a rebellion against the French. He was captured, but his successor led the Haitians to independence in 1803. He became the subject of a poem by Wordsworth.

Simon Bolivar, born in 1783, fought for more than twenty years to win independence for what became Venezuela, Colombia, Panama, Bolivia, and Ecuador. Bolivar dreamed of a kind of united states for all Spanish America, but his dreams were never realized.

In the United States, the population was moving inexorably westward. Settlers from the myriad ethnic groups that had settled the eastern seaboard streamed into Ohio, Kentucky, Indiana, Michigan, and Illinois in search of land and prosperity, and many more immigrants arrived from Europe. The land area of the United States doubled in 1803 with the purchase from France of the Louisiana territory.

The increase in wealth was spectacular for many because of the rapid expansion of shipping, trade, manufacturing, and agriculture. Thousands of acres in the South were planted in cotton after Eli Whitney's invention of the cotton gin, and every pound of cotton was sold as soon as it was grown.

A NEW SPIRIT IN LIFE AND THE ARTS

In literature, the emergence of the Romantic spirit was particularly evident in the writers' choice of subject matter.

For most of the Romantic poets, nature was the principal source of inspiration, spiritual truth, and enlightenment. Nature, according to Samuel Taylor Coleridge in "Frost at Midnight," should be seen as embodying the "eternal language" whereby God teaches and molds the human spirit.

Poets of the Romantic Age focused on the ordinary person and common life in order to affirm the worth and dignity of all human beings, and to repudiate the evils of a class system that artificially designated a few select people as more important than others because of wealth, position, or name.

In 1765 Bishop Thomas Percy published *Reliques of Ancient English Poetry,* a collection of ballads dating back to late medieval times. Several authors, including Thomas Gray, made translations of old Celtic and Scandinavian legends. Other writers produced Gothic novels or romances—that is, stories laid in medieval times and filled with ruined castles, mysterious doors, and supernaturalism of all kinds.

Nineteenth-century plays, especially those by German playwrights Goethe and Schiller, were characterized by emotionalism.

American writers James Fenimore Cooper, William Cullen Bryant, and Edgar Allan Poe were all influenced to some extent by the Ro-

Detail of *A Morning View of Coalbrookdale* by William Williams. Painted in 1777. *Clive House Museum, Shrewsbury*

mantic Age in that their emphasis was on the past, nature, and the Gothic tale of horror, respectively.

English readers turned eagerly to all these writings about medieval times, especially to the old ballads. People longed for literature that dealt with the elemental themes of courage and valor, hatred and revenge, love and death.

Writers of the Age of Reason exposed the follies of society with satire, a sophisticated form of attack; the youthful Romantics spoke out in a voice of anger and outrage. In "London, 1802," Wordsworth calls England "a fen/of stagnant waters" that has lost "manners, virtue, freedom, power." Percy Shelley, in "England in 1819," characterizes the rulers as leeches "who neither see, nor feel, nor know," but who drink the life's blood of a poor and starving populace. Shelley, like many of the other Romantics, was strongly influenced by William Godwin's *Political Justice* (1793), a work that criticized the existing society and outlined a new ethic and Utopian ideal. Mary Shelley's mother, Mary Wollstonecraft, produced an outspoken feminist manifesto, *A Vindication of the Rights of Woman* (1792), and spent her short, intense life living by the ideals she advocated.

Painting, architecture, and music also reflected Romantic ideas. The works of English painters John Constable and J.M.W. Turner focused on dramatic landscapes often peopled by ordinary men and women going about their duties in dignity and peace. In architecture there was a return to the Gothic style of the Middle Ages, which was regarded as an ideal period. Changes in music also occurred. The German composer Ludwig van Beethoven composed symphonies of power and grandeur, often reflecting violent emotions. Other composers frequently made use of motifs from folk music and themes from folk tales in songs and operas.

TWO GENERATIONS OF POETS

In the period from 1786 to 1830, seven major poets emerged who permanently affected the nature of English language and literature. Blake, Burns, Wordsworth, and Coleridge may be regarded as the first generation of Romantic poets, writing most of their major works from 1786 to 1805. Byron, Shelley, and Keats are the second generation, producing their major works between 1810 to 1824.

Though commonly grouped with writers of the eighteenth century because of the time in which they lived and wrote, William Blake and Robert Burns were clearly forerunners of the Romantic movement in subject matter, themes, and style. Both were gifted poets, unaffiliated with any literary group, who poured out their lyrics while living lives of hard labor and obscurity.

As an old man, William Blake, one of the most original minds of his time, had a circle of young admirers; but during most of his life, he lived in relative obscurity in a working-class neighborhood of London. Central to Blake's vision is the concept of "contraries," the necessity of experiencing opposites, such as pain and joy, success and failure, prudence and excess, in order to understand life. Consequently, Blake produced *Songs of Innocence* and *Songs of Experience*, contrasting poems that need to be paired to yield their deepest meaning. Though Blake's talent and achievement were not widely recognized in his time, today his reputation is firmly established.

The publication of *Poems, Chiefly in the Scottish Dialect* (1786) by Robert Burns is a landmark in English literature. Published when he was only twenty-seven, the book made Burns famous and gave the world a memorable collection of poems. His lyrics on love, nature, patriotism, the nobility of the common man, and the spontaneous emotions of the heart, are expressed in native dialect; his treatment of these themes has made him one of the best-loved poets.

In 1798, with the publication of *Lyrical Ballads*, William Wordsworth and Samuel Taylor Coleridge gave official birth to the Romantic Age in literature, setting forth a formula for a new kind of poetry and presenting twenty-three poems that demonstrated the formula in use. The second edition of *Lyrical Ballads*, published in 1800, contained a preface in which Wordsworth stated the poetic principles that he and Coleridge believed in: first, that ordinary life is the best subject for poetry because the feelings of simple people are sincere and natural; second, that the everyday language of these people best conveys their feelings and is therefore best suited to poetry; third, that the expression of feeling is more important in poetry than the development of an action, or story; and finally, that "poetry is the spontaneous overflow of powerful feelings," and "takes its origin from emotion recollected in tranquility." While these principles were often challenged by other writers of Wordsworth's day, they served as a formal declaration of a new spirit in English literature and became a turning point in the history of English poetry.

The important figures of the second generation of Romantic poets were Lord Byron, Percy Bysshe Shelley, and John Keats. Though highly different in personality and artistic temperament, they were similarly intense, precocious, and tragically short-lived. Though a generation older, Wordsworth and Coleridge outlived all three poets. While initially a major source of inspiration for their poetic theory and practice, Wordsworth and Coleridge turned politically conservative as they grew older, leading the young poets, especially Byron and Shelley, to denounce their onetime idols as traitors to their former principles.

During his brief lifetime, George Gordon, Lord Byron, was the most popular poet abroad as well as at home and also the most scandalous. Reckless, bitter, and in constant revolt against society, he succeeded in producing his best work, including his masterpiece *Don Juan*, a satirical narrative that sums up his reflections on life and human nature. Though Byron always declared himself a disciple of Pope and is today regarded as the greatest satirical poet since Pope, he (more than any other poet of the age) epitomized Romanticism by his unswerving dedication to the cause of freedom and liberty and by the Romantic image he imprinted on the public imagination.

Like Byron, Shelley was rebellious, scandalous, and charismatic. The keynote of Shelley's character was his revolt against tyrannical influences, his belief that the church, state, and commerce, as organized and conducted in his time, led to superstition, selfishness, and corruption. As expressed in the preface to one of his longer poems, *Prometheus Unbound*, Shelley always had "a passion for reforming the world." But it is as a lyric poet that he is remembered.

Possibly the most famous line John Keats ever wrote was, "Beauty is truth, truth beauty," in his poem "Ode on a Grecian Urn"; this work explores the relationship between art and life and expresses the gospel of beauty that guided Keats's brilliant but brief artistic career. In spite of illness, family hardship, and a strained love affair, Keats succeeded, during a nine-month period in 1819, in writing his greatest poems.

Overall, the literature of the Romantic Age has about it a sense of the uniqueness of the individual, a deep personal earnestness, a sensuous delight in both the common and exotic things of this world, a blend of intensely felt joy and dejection, a yearning for ideal states of being, and a probing interest in mysterious and mystical experience. If the Romantic vision of the world was occasionally tinged with bitterness or outrage, it was because the Romantics confronted an increasingly mechanical and materialistic society.

THINKING ABOUT GRAPHIC AIDS
Using the Time Line

The time line on pages 420–421 shows the chronological sequence of historic and literary events from 1780–1830. Use the time line to answer these questions.

1. Before he became President, could George Washington have heard *The Magic Flute*, an opera composed by Wolfgang Amadeus Mozart?
2. What British monarch was king at the start of the French Revolution?
3. Could George IV have ridden on a railroad?
4. Napoleon became emperor of what country?
5. Could Goethe (gĕr'tə) have known Beethoven?

BIOGRAPHY

William Blake

1757–1827

During his lifetime and for half a century afterwards, William Blake's poetry and art were largely ignored, even derided as the work of a madman. When he died in 1827, reportedly while improvising hymns of praise on his deathbed, he was buried in an unmarked grave. Today he is recognized as a poet, painter, engraver, and spiritual visionary of extraordinary originality and genius.

William Blake was born in London in 1757 and lived all but three of his seventy years in a working-class section of the city. Blake was educated through the efforts of his father and his own avid reading in the Bible, philosophy, and poetry. At age ten, Blake expressed an interest in becoming a painter and was enrolled in a drawing school and later apprenticed to an engraver. By 1779 he had begun to accept commissions to illustrate and engrave the works of other writers and was launched on his lifetime career as a respected craftsman. His marriage in 1782 to Catherine Boucher, whom he taught to read, write, and assist him in his engraving work, was happy.

As a child Blake was deeply religious and reported having had an experience of mystic revelation when he was only four. On one occasion he informed his parents that he had seen the prophet Ezekiel in a tree and, on another occasion, said that he had seen a tree filled with angels. By the time of his marriage, Blake had become so consumed in mystical beliefs that his wife is said to have remarked: "I have very little of Mr. Blake's company. He is always in Paradise."

While his development as a painter was fairly gradual, as a poet he was precocious; already in his early teens Blake had begun writing verse that displayed a mastery of the lyric form. Between 1783 and 1793 he wrote, illustrated, and printed his most famous lyrics, *Songs of Innocence* and *Songs of Experience*. He prepared his own illustrative engravings for these poems by a process he himself developed, and either he or his wife tinted each illustration.

Absent from Blake's best-known poems are the classical allusions and formal language that characterized the work of his contemporaries; in their place are a childlike simplicity, lyricism, and visual immediacy that link him to other writers of the Romantic movement. Shortly before his death, Blake reaffirmed the artistic creed to which he was faithful all his life: "I have been very near the gates of death, and have returned very weak and an old man, feeble and tottering, but not in spirit and life, not in the real man, the imagination, which liveth forever."

Songs of Innocence appeared in 1789. Five years later Blake published a second volume, which he titled *Songs of Innocence and Experience: Shewing the Two Contrary States of the Human Soul*. Although not all the *Songs of Innocence* have counterparts in the *Songs of Experience*, the subtitle, and the fact that he never published the *Songs of Experience* as a separate volume, suggest that he intended the poems to be matched.

Introduction

from **Songs of Innocence**

Piping down the valleys wild
Piping songs of pleasant glee
On a cloud I saw a child,
And he laughing said to me:

5 "Pipe a song about a Lamb!"
So I piped with merry cheer.
"Piper pipe that song again"—
So I piped, he wept to hear.

"Drop thy pipe thy happy pipe
10 Sing thy songs of happy cheer."
So I sung the same again
While he wept with joy to hear.

"Piper sit thee down and write
In a book that all may read"—
15 So he vanished from my sight,
And I plucked a hollow reed,

And I made a rural pen,
And I stained the water clear,
And I wrote my happy songs,
20 Every child may joy to hear.

1789

Introduction

from **Songs of Experience**

Hear the voice of the Bard!
Who Present, Past, and Future sees;
Whose ears have heard
The Holy Word,
5 That walked among the ancient trees;

The title page to *Songs of Innocence,* by
William Blake. 1789. *British Museum*

Calling the lapsèd Soul[1]
And weeping in the evening dew;
That might control
The starry pole,
10 And fallen, fallen light renew!

"O Earth, O Earth return!
Arise from out the dewy grass;
Night is worn,
And the morn
15 Rises from the slumberous mass.

"Turn away no more:
Why wilt thou turn away
The starry floor
The wat'ry shore
20 Is given thee till the break of day."

1794

---

1. lapsèd Soul, soul fallen from grace after the fall of
Adam and Eve.

Comment

Blake's Obscurities

Few people of his own day understood or appreciated Blake's writings or his drawings. In a letter to a Dr. Trusler whose writings he was asked to illustrate and who objected to the obscurity of his designs, he wrote: "You say that I [need] somebody to Elucidate my Ideas. What is Grand is necessarily obscure to Weak men. That which can be made Explicit to the Idiot is not worthy my care. The wisest of the Ancients considered what is not too Explicit as the fittest for Instruction, because it rouses the faculties to act. I name Moses, Solomon, Aesop, Homer, Plato."

But in the same letter he also says: "But I am happy to find a Great Majority of Fellow Mortals who can Elucidate My Visions, and Particularly they have been elucidated by Children, who have taken a greater delight in contemplating my Pictures than I even hoped. Neither Youth nor Childhood is Folly or Incapacity."

HT See REPETITION in the Handbook of Literary Terms, page 926.

The Lamb

from **Songs of Innocence**

Little Lamb, who made thee?
Dost thou know who made thee?
Gave thee life, and bid thee feed
By the stream and o'er the mead;
5 Gave thee clothing of delight,
Softest clothing, woolly, bright;
Gave thee such a tender voice,
Making all the vales rejoice?
Little Lamb, who made thee?
10 Dost thou know who made thee?

Little Lamb, I'll tell thee,
Little Lamb, I'll tell thee:
He is callèd by thy name,
For he calls himself a Lamb.[1]
15 He is meek, and he is mild;
He became a little child.
I a child, and thou a lamb,
We are callèd by his name.
Little Lamb, God bless thee!
20 Little Lamb, God bless thee!

1789

The Tyger

from **Songs of Experience**

Tyger! Tyger! burning bright
In the forests of the night,
What immortal hand or eye
Could frame thy fearful symmetry?

5 In what distant deeps or skies
Burnt the fire of thine eyes?
On what wings dare he aspire?
What the hand dare seize the fire?

And what shoulder, and what art,
10 Could twist the sinews of thy heart?
And when thy heart began to beat,
What dread hand? and what dread feet?

What the hammer? what the chain?
In what furnace was thy brain?
15 What the anvil? what dread grasp
Dare its deadly terrors clasp?

---

1. Lamb, symbol of Jesus Christ as Redeemer: "Behold the Lamb of God, which taketh away the sin of the world" (John 1:29).

When the stars threw down their spears,
And watered heaven with their tears,
Did he smile his work to see?
20 Did he who made the Lamb make thee?

Tyger! Tyger! burning bright
In the forests of the night,
What immortal hand or eye
Dare frame thy fearful symmetry?

1794

Detail of "The Tyger" by William Blake, from *Songs of Experience.* 1789–94. *Library of Congress*

HT Review RHYTHM in the Handbook of Literary Terms, page 921.

Holy Thursday

from **Songs of Innocence**

'Twas on a Holy Thursday,[1] their innocent
    faces clean,
The children walking two and two, in red
    and blue and green,
Grey-headed beadles walked before, with
    wands[2] as white as snow,
Till into the high dome of Paul's they like
    Thames' waters flow.

5 O what a multitude they seemed, these
    flowers of London town!
Seated in companies they sit with radiance
    all their own.
The hum of multitudes was there, but
    multitudes of lambs,
Thousands of little boys and girls raising
    their innocent hands.

Now like a mighty wind they raise to heaven
    the voice of song,
10 Or like harmonious thunderings the seats of
    Heaven among.
Beneath them sit the agèd men, wise
    guardians of the poor;
Then cherish pity, lest you drive an angel
    from your door.

1789

Holy Thursday

from **Songs of Experience**

Is this a holy thing to see
In a rich and fruitful land,
Babes reduced to misery,
Fed with cold and usurous hand?

5 Is that trembling cry a song?
Can it be a song of joy?
And so many children poor?
It is a land of poverty!

And their sun does never shine,
10 And their fields are bleak and bare,
And their ways are filled with thorns:
It is eternal winter there.

For where-e'er the sun does shine,
And where-e'er the rain does fall,
15 Babe can never hunger there,
Nor poverty the mind appall.

1794

---

1. *Holy Thursday,* Ascension Day, the fortieth day after Easter, when children in orphanages were brought to St. Paul's Cathedral to give thanks for the charity of God, of which human charity is supposedly a reflection.
2. *wands,* rods.

William Blake

THINK AND DISCUSS
INTRODUCTION from *Songs of Innocence;*
INTRODUCTION from *Songs of Experience*

Understanding
1. Who is the speaker of the first poem? Can the speaker of the second poem be identified?
2. What is suggested in the first poem by the image of a child on a cloud?
3. What is the "fallen light" to which the second poem refers?

Analyzing
4. What qualifies the Bard to assume the role of a prophet of redemption?
5. How are both the piper and the Bard appropriate figures for the group of poems each introduces?
6. The setting of the "Introduction" to *Innocence* is probably daytime; the setting of the "Introduction" to *Experience* ranges from evening to daybreak. What do these settings suggest?

THE LAMB and THE TYGER
Understanding
1. What three things that the Lamb has been given by its creator are mentioned in stanza 1?
2. What does stanza 4 suggest has shaped the Tyger's "fearful symmetry"?
3. What two questions are posed in stanza 5 of "The Tyger"?

Analyzing
4. What explanation can be found in the second stanza of "The Lamb" for the capitalization of the word *Lamb?*
5. "The Lamb" and "The Tyger" are matched poems. How is each connected with the Introduction to its category?
6. The contrast between the Lamb and the Tyger is striking. What qualities of each are emphasized by the images of the poems?
7. The last stanza of "The Tyger" is identical to the first except for a single change in wording. How does this change alter the mood of the poem?

Extending
8. What do you think the Lamb and Tyger symbolize in human life?

APPLYING: Repetition
See Handbook of Literary Terms, p. 926
Repetition is a literary technique in which words, lines, phrases, and sounds are repeated for emphasis and unity. Common forms of repetition include **alliteration, assonance, consonance,** parallelism, refrain, and **rhyme.**

1. Point out several examples of the use of repetition in "The Lamb."
2. What is the effect of the conspicuous use of repetition and parallel phrasing in "The Lamb"?

THINK AND DISCUSS
HOLY THURSDAY poems
Understanding
1. Who are the "Grey-headed beadles"?
2. What is meant by a "usurous hand" in line 4 of the second poem?
3. According to the second poem, what season is permanently associated with the "land of poverty"?

Analyzing
4. What effect does Blake gain through the contrasting views of the children in these matched poems?
5. How do these two poems differ in tone?

REVIEWING: Rhythm HT
See Handbook of Literary Terms, p. 921
Rhythm is the arrangement of stressed and unstressed sounds in speech or writing into regular or varied patterns.

1. How does the rhythm of "Holy Thursday" from *Songs of Innocence* reinforce the mood and tone of the poem?
2. Contrast the rhythm of the second poem with that of the first. What effect does this rhythm create?

The Divine Image

from **Songs of Innocence**

To Mercy, Pity, Peace, and Love
All pray in their distress:
And to these virtues of delight
Return their thankfulness.

5 For Mercy, Pity, Peace, and Love
Is God, our father dear,
And Mercy, Pity, Peace, and Love
Is Man, his child and care.

For Mercy has a human heart,
10 Pity a human face:

And Love, the human form divine,
And Peace, the human dress.

Then every man, of every clime,
That prays in his distress,
15 Prays to the human form divine,
Love, Mercy, Pity, Peace.

And all must love the human form,
In heathen, Turk, or Jew.
Where Mercy, Love, and Pity dwell
20 There God is dwelling too.

1789

The Human Abstract

from **Songs of Experience**

Pity would be no more,
If we did not make somebody Poor;
And Mercy no more could be,
If all were as happy as we;

5 And mutual fear brings peace,
Till the selfish loves increase;
Then Cruelty knits a snare,
And spreads his baits with care.

He sits down with holy fears,
10 And waters the ground with tears;
Then Humility takes its root
Underneath his foot.

Soon spreads the dismal shade
Of Mystery over his head;
15 And the Caterpillar and fly
Feed on the Mystery.

And it bears the fruit of Deceit,
Ruddy and sweet to eat;
And the Raven his nest has made
20 In its thickest shade.

The Gods of the earth and sea,
Sought thro' Nature to find this Tree;
But their search was all in vain:
There grows one in the Human Brain.

1794

William Blake

Proverbs of Hell

from **The Marriage of Heaven and Hell**

Between 1783 and 1793, the years he was working on the *Songs of Innocence and Experience,* Blake also completed one major prose work, *The Marriage of Heaven and Hell,* which includes "Proverbs of Hell," a series of aphorisms containing simple and memorable images that further develop a central theme of his works: "Without contraries is no progression." What Blake means is that the interplay between opposites is a necessary condition of learning; that is, an emotion like joy cannot be fully understood without the experience of its opposite, sorrow. Similarly, the innocence of childhood needs to be balanced by the wisdom gained through experience, however painful and disenchanting.

In seed time learn, in harvest teach, in winter enjoy.
Drive your cart and your plow over the bones of the dead.
The road of excess leads to the palace of wisdom.
Prudence is a rich, ugly old maid courted by Incapacity.
5 The cut worm forgives the plow.
A fool sees not the same tree that a wise man sees.
He whose face gives no light, shall never become a star.
Eternity is in love with the productions of time.
All wholesome food is caught without a net or a trap.
10 No bird soars too high, if he soars with his own wings.
If the fool would persist in his folly he would become wise.
Shame is pride's cloak.
Excess of sorrow laughs. Excess of joy weeps.
The roaring of lions, the howling of wolves, the raging of the stormy sea, and the destructive sword,
      are portions of eternity, too great for the eye of man.
15 Let man wear the fell of the lion, woman the fleece of the sheep.
The bird a nest, the spider a web, man friendship.
What is now proved was once only imagined.
Every thing possible to be believed is an image of truth.
The fox provides for himself, but God provides for the lion.
20 Think in the morning. Act in the noon. Eat in the evening. Sleep in the night.
The tygers of wrath are wiser than the horses of instruction.
Expect poison from the standing water.
You never know what is enough unless you know what is more than enough.
The weak in courage is strong in cunning.

25 Damn braces. Bless relaxes.

The crow wished every thing was black, the owl that every thing was white.

Improvement makes strait roads; but the crooked roads without improvements are roads of Genius.

Truth can never be told so as to be understood, and not be believed.

1790-1793   **1793**

Detail, *Nebuchadnezzar* by William Blake. 1795. *Tate Gallery, London*

HT Review **METAPHOR** in the Handbook of Literary Terms, page 906.

A New Jerusalem

from **Milton**

The following poem has long been used as the hymn of the British Labour Party, which represents the working class. Blake's confidence in the goodness of God and the redeemable nature of man are clearly evident in the poem. Many readers have interpreted the "dark Satanic Mills" (line 8) as a reference to the factories springing up in England during Blake's time in which workers slaved long hours for small pay. Other readers insist the mills are not the real ones of industrial England, but are rather the figurative mills of the mind.

William Blake

And did those feet in ancient time[1]
Walk upon England's mountains green?
And was the holy Lamb of God,
On England's pleasant pastures seen?

5 And did the Countenance Divine,
Shine forth upon our clouded hills?
And was Jerusalem builded here,
Among these dark Satanic Mills?

Bring me my Bow of burning gold:
10 Bring me my Arrows of desire:

Bring me my Spear: O clouds unfold!
Bring me my Chariot of fire!

I will not cease from Mental Fight,
Nor shall my Sword sleep in my hand:
15 Till we have built Jerusalem,
In England's green and pleasant Land.

1800-1809?   **1809-1810**

1. *feet . . . time,* an allusion to the legend that during the
part of Jesus' life not covered in the Bible, he traveled to
many lands, including the British Isles.

Woodcut by William Blake
to illustrate R. J. Thorn-
ton's *Pastorals of Virgil,*
1821. *British Museum*

THINK AND DISCUSS
THE DIVINE IMAGE and THE HUMAN ABSTRACT

Understanding

1. How are the virtues of "Mercy, Pity, Peace, and Love" defined in the second stanza of "The Divine Image"?
2. With what four physical features of humans are the virtues of "Mercy, Pity, Peace, and Love" linked (stanza 3)?
3. According to stanza 1 of "The Human Abstract," what two things would have to happen in order for "Pity" and "Mercy" to be eliminated?

4. In "The Human Abstract" why was the search for the Tree "in vain"?

Analyzing

5. Explain the meaning of the terms "The Divine Image" and "The Human Abstract" as defined by each poem.
6. What noble human ideal is expressed in the last stanza of "The Divine Image"?
7. Explain how "The Human Abstract" provides a cynical repudiation of the noble qualities attributed to humanity in "The Divine Image." Draw on specific statements in the poem that support this view.

Extending

8. How are "The Human Abstract" and "Holy Thursday" from *Songs of Experience* similar in subject matter and tone?

PROVERBS OF HELL

Understanding

1. What is the underlying metaphor of the first proverb?
2. What is "the fell of the lion" (line 15)?
3. According to the proverb "The bird a nest, the spider a web, man friendship," what does friendship provide (line 16)?

Analyzing

4. What is meant by "The cut worm forgives the plow"?
5. In general, how are human beings advised by the "Proverbs of Hell" to conduct their lives?
6. What kinds of attitudes and behavior are specifically condemned in the "Proverbs"?
7. How does the proverb that begins with "The roaring of lions, the howling of wolves" (line 14) help explain Blake's attitude toward the creature in "The Tyger"?

Extending

8. Are these proverbs, written so long ago, still applicable to modern people?

THINKING SKILLS

Classifying

To classify things is to arrange them into categories or groups according to some system.

1. Classify the "Proverbs of Hell" according to similarity of idea. Then name three or four ideas that recur with greatest frequency.
2. Explain the classification system inherent in the first proverb (line 1).

THINK AND DISCUSS

A NEW JERUSALEM

Understanding

1. Basically, one question is asked three times in the first six lines. What is that question?
2. What is the "Jerusalem" twice referred to in this poem?

Analyzing

3. What does the poet suggest has driven the Lamb of God away from England?
4. Explain why members of the British Labour Party, who have long used this poem as their hymn, might find the last stanza especially inspiring?

Extending

5. What is the poet suggesting, in the last two stanzas, to be the rightful role of the poet?

REVIEWING: Metaphor H▨

See Handbook of Literary Terms, p. 906

A **metaphor** is a figure of speech involving an implied comparison.

1. The speaker requests a bow, arrows, spear, and a chariot. What kind of person would be likely to use this type of equipment?
2. The equipment described here is not ordinary. It is transformed by metaphor into something else—a bow of burning gold, for example. What does the speaker hope to accomplish with these metaphorical weapons?

COMPOSITION ◄━━

Writing an Inductive Essay

In a paper of at least three paragraphs, describe an incident from your life that illustrates the truth of one of Blake's "Proverbs of Hell." Organize your essay inductively, starting with an extended description of the incident and waiting until the end to use the proverb to state the "lesson in life" the experience has taught you. Strive for heightened suspense through the use of vivid details and dramatic narration.

Writing about a Symbol

Choose a symbol from Blake's poems, such as the Tyger or the tree in "The Human Abstract." Write an essay in which you first explain the meaning of the symbol as used in the poem. Then explain how the symbol has been presented in the poem, citing details from the poem to support your discussion. Conclude by explaining the significance of the symbol to the poem as a whole and to its theme. See "Writing About Symbolism" in The Writer's Handbook.

Robert Burns, the eldest of seven children, was born in a humble two-room cottage in Ayrshire, Scotland, which his father had built from native stone and clay. The history of the family was one of incessant poverty—poor land, high rents, and back-breaking physical labor. Burns worked as a plowboy on the family farm. He described his life during these early years as "the cheerless gloom of a hermit and the unceasing toil of a galley slave."

Though his formal education was limited, his father inspired in him a love of learning that led him to the works of such writers as Shakespeare, Milton, Dryden, and Pope. He also had a firm grounding in English grammar, a reading knowledge of French, and some background in mathematics and surveying. While plowing in the field, often with a book of ballads in his hands, or going about his other labors, he would recollect the Scottish songs and legends his mother had taught him and mentally compose poems and songs in his native dialect that he would write down in the evening. That his early life was not altogether cheerless can be seen in his lilting poems on love and nature.

After the death of his father in 1784, Burns and his brother took over another farm and continued the struggle with poverty. By this time, Burns had been in and out of several love affairs (he admitted that his "sweetest hours" were "spent among the lasses"), and had also fallen into habits of drinking and dissipation that were to plague him the rest of his life. At age twenty-six, discouraged by his poverty and a frustrating love affair, he determined to embark for Jamaica, but first he gathered together a few of his poems which he published under the title *Poems, Chiefly in the Scottish Dialect* (1786).

Much to his surprise, the book was an overnight success, and instead of going to Jamaica, Burns left for Edinburgh to arrange for a second edition and to find himself swept up in the fashionable literary salons of the city. Edinburgh society, however, regarded Burns as primarily a rustic novelty, and he only made matters worse by acting the part of the arrogant, overly eager literary celebrity.

In 1788 Burns married Jean Armour. Disillusioned with city life, they settled on a farm in Dumfries; the next year he was made an excise officer (collector of taxes), a position that required frequent trips of two hundred miles on horseback. His last years were miserable and depressing, marred by recurrent bouts of ill health, but he nevertheless took on the task of helping to create and preserve the songs of his nation. Before his early death at thirty-seven, he had succeeded in contributing three hundred songs to James Johnson's *The Scots Musical Museum* (1787–1803) and George Thomson's *A Select Collection of Original Scottish Airs for the Voice* (1793–1805). Burns's greatest poetic gift was his ability to express the feelings and concerns of ordinary people in a natural, flowing idiom, thus making him a poet for everyone.

HT See DIALECT in the Handbook of Literary Terms, page 902.

To a Mouse

on turning her up in her nest
with the plow, November, 1785

Wee, sleekit,° cow'rin', tim'rous beastie,
O, what a panic's in thy breastie!
Thou need na start awa sae hasty,
      Wi' bickering brattle!°
5 I wad be laith to rin an' chase thee,
      Wi' murd'ring pattle!°

I'm truly sorry man's dominion
Has broken Nature's social union,
An' justifies that ill opinion
10   Which makes thee startle
At me, thy poor earth-born companion,
      An' fellow-mortal!

I doubt na, whiles,° but thou may thieve;·
What then? poor beastie, thou maun live!
15 A daimen-icker in a thrave°
      'S a sma' request;
I'll get a blessin' wi' the lave,°
      And never miss 't!

Thy wee bit housie, too, in ruin!
20 Its silly wa's° the win's are strewin'!
An' naething, now, to big° a new ane,
      O' foggage° green!
An' bleak December's win's ensuin',
      Baith snell° an' keen!

25 Thou saw the fields laid bare and waste,
An' weary winter comin' fast,
An' cozie here, beneath the blast,
      Thou thought to dwell,
Till crash! the cruel coulter° past
30   Out-thro' thy cell.

sleekit, sleek.

brattle, short race.

pattle, plow, spade.

whiles, sometimes.

A daimen-icker in a thrave, an occasional ear or head of grain in a shock.
the lave, the rest.

silly wa's, simple walls.
big, build.
foggage, coarse grass.

snell, biting.

coulter, plowshare.

That wee bit heap o' leaves an' stibble
Has cost thee mony a weary nibble!
Now thou's turn'd out, for a' thy trouble,
　　　　But house or hald,°
35 To thole° the winter's sleety dribble,
　　　　An' cranreuch° cauld!

　　hald, abode.
　　thole, endure.
　　cranreuch, hoarfrost.

But, Mousie, thou art no thy lane,°
In proving foresight may be vain:
The best laid schemes o' mice an' men
　　　　Gang aft a-gley,°
40 An' lea'e us nought but grief an' pain
　　　　For promised joy.

　　lane, alone.

　　gang . . . a-gley, go awry.

Still thou art blest compared wi' me!
The present only toucheth thee:
45 But oh! I backward cast my e'e
　　　　On prospects drear!
An' forward, tho' I canna see,
　　　　I guess an' fear!

1785　　　　　　　　　　　　　　**1786**

John Anderson, My Jo

John Anderson my jo,° John,
　　When we were first acquent,
Your locks were like the raven,
　　Your bonnie brow was brent;°
5 But now your brow is beld,° John,
　　Your locks are like the snaw,°
But blessings on your frosty pow,°
　　John Anderson my jo!

　　jo, sweetheart.

　　brent, smooth.
　　beld, bald.
　　snaw, snow.
　　pow, pate, head.

John Anderson my jo, John,
10　　We clamb the hill thegither,°
And monie a cantie° day, John,
　　We've had wi' ane anither;
Now we maun totter down, John,
　　And hand in hand we'll go,
15 And sleep thegither at the foot,
　　John Anderson my jo!

　　thegither, together.
　　cantie, happy.

1790

A Red, Red Rose

O my luve is like a red, red rose,
  That's newly sprung in June;
O my luve is like the melodie
  That's sweetly played in tune.

5 As fair art thou, my bonnie lass,
  So deep in luve am I;
And I will luve thee still, my dear,
  Till a' the seas gang dry.

Till a' the seas gang dry, my dear,
10 And the rocks melt wi' the sun;
And I will luve thee still, my dear,
  While the sands o' life shall run.

And fare thee weel, my only luve,
  And fare thee weel a while!
15 And I will come again, my luve,
  Tho' it were ten thousand mile!

1794   1796

Auld Lang Syne

Should auld acquaintance be forgot,
  And never brought to min'?
Should auld acquaintance be forgot,
  And auld lang syne?°
CHORUS
5 For auld lang syne, my dear,
  For auld lang syne,
We'll tak a cup o' kindness yet
  For auld lang syne.

And surely ye'll be your pint-stowp,°
10 And surely I'll be mine!
And we'll tak a cup o' kindness yet
  For auld lang syne.

We twa hae run about the braes,°
  And pu'd the gowans° fine;
15 But we've wandered monie a weary fit°
  Sin' auld lang syne.

We twa hae paidled i' burn.°
  From mornin' sun till dine;°
But seas between us braid° hae roared
20 Sin' auld lang syne.

And there's a hand, my trusty fiere,°
  And gie's a hand o' thine;
And we'll tak a right guid-willie waught[3]
  For auld lang syne.

1788   1796

auld lang syne, literally, old long since; that is, old times; the good old days.

ye'll . . . pint-stowp, you will pay for your pint of drink.

braes, hillsides.
gowans, daisies.
fit, foot, step.

paidled i'burn, paddled in brook.
dine, dinner time.
braid, broad.

fiere, friend.

right . . . waught, hearty goodwill draft, or drink.

Robert Burns

THINK AND DISCUSS

TO A MOUSE

Understanding

1. According to stanza 1, what would the speaker be reluctant to do to the mouse?
2. What reason does the speaker give to justify the mouse's occasional theft of an ear of corn?
3. According to stanza 4, what prevents the mouse from building a new nest?

Analyzing

4. Why does the speaker regard the mouse's situation as truly pitiable?
5. Acccording to the second stanza, why is the mouse justified in running away in panic from a "fellow mortal"?
6. What philosophical idea is expressed in the last two stanzas?
7. Why is the speaker's plight—and that of other human beings—always likely to be worse than that of non-human creatures?

Extending

8. What is gained by using the problems of a mouse to make a comment on the human condition?
9. What does Burns reveal about his own personality and attitudes towards nature through his depiction of the mouse's plight?

JOHN ANDERSON, MY JO

Understanding

1. According to stanza 1, in what two ways does the John Anderson of the past differ from the John Anderson of the present?

Analyzing

2. What is the meaning of the climb up and down "the hill the gither"?
3. What are the speaker's feelings about her life with John Anderson?

A RED, RED ROSE

Understanding

1. To what two things does the speaker compare his "luve" in the first stanza?
2. According to stanzas 2 and 3, how long will the speaker love his "bonnie lass"?

Analyzing

3. What situation probably motivated the writing of "A Red, Red Rose"?
4. How old do the lovers appear to be?

Extending

5. In your opinion, can these declarations be taken seriously?

AULD LANG SYNE

Understanding

1. What question is twice raised in the first stanza?
2. In the last stanza what two actions does the speaker propose?

Analyzing

3. According to stanzas 4 and 5, what experiences did the "old acquaintances" enjoy in their youth?
4. What brought about the separation of the old friends?

Extending

5. Why do you think "Auld Lang Syne" is traditionally sung on New Year's Eve?

APPLYING: Dialect HアＴ
See Handbook of Literary Terms, p. 902

Dialect is a regional variety of language, distinguished from other varieties by pronunciation, grammer, and especially vocabulary. Writers occasionally employ dialect to portray characters or establish a particular setting.

1. What do you think was Burns's purpose in using Scottish dialect in these poems?
2. Why do you think people who sing "Auld Lang Syne" make no attempt to translate the unfamiliar dialect?

The second of five children and the oldest daughter of a submissive mother and abusive father, Mary Wollstonecraft had many harsh experiences as she was growing up and during her early adult life that led her to voice objections to what she considered to be the oppression of women. Her father was an alcoholic and a brute, who would explode in violent rages that Mary endeavored to prevent by sleeping outside her parents' bedroom door. As a child, she moved often and had to depend on her own resources for most of her schooling. As a young adult, she helped her sister rid herself of an unhappy marriage and had a close friend die in childbirth. These experiences, along with others, caused her to be critical of the traditional relationships between men and women.

Attempting occupations that were considered appropriate for females, she met with little success. Giving up these "acceptable" occupations, she journeyed to London to begin her writing career. Her writings include essays, reviews, novels, letters, and educational and political books, including an eyewitness account of the French Revolution. Her most famous book, *A Vindication of the Rights of Woman,* was an appeal for women's independence and an attack on the educational restrictions and "mistaken notions of female excellence" that keep women in a state of "ignorance and slavish dependence." The work caused great furor, arousing attacks on the socially unacceptable life of the author and on the straightforward style of the book since, when this work was published, people were not accustomed to this kind of outspokenness, especially from a woman.

While in Paris in 1792 to observe the French Revolution, she fell deeply in love with Gilbert Imlay, an American writer and adventurer, by whom she had a daughter in 1794. Following two suicide attempts as a result of Imlay's neglect and later abandonment, she published in 1796 a travel book, *Letters Written During a Short Residence in Sweden, Norway, and Denmark,* which, besides portraying the austere landscape, contains astute observations on the lot of women in northern countries. The same year she renewed her acquaintance with the social philosopher William Godwin, a friendship that quickly ripened into love and resulted in their marriage in 1797. These were possibly the happiest, most fulfilled years of Mary Wollstonecraft's life as, secure in her husband's love and teeming with ideas and projects for the future, she awaited the birth of their child. On August 30, 1797, Mary Godwin was born, the future author of *Frankenstein*. While the birth was not difficult, Mary Wollstonecraft developed blood poisoning and died ten days later. In her dying words she extolled her husband as "the kindest, best man in the world."

from A Vindication of the Rights of Woman

Mary Wollstonecraft

CHAPTER 2

To account for, and excuse the tyranny of man, many ingenious arguments have been brought forward to prove, that the two sexes, in the acquirement of virtue, ought to aim at attaining a very different character: or, to speak explicitly, women are not allowed to have sufficient strength of mind to acquire what really deserves the name of virtue. Yet it should seem, allowing them to have souls, that there is but one way appointed by providence to lead *mankind* to either virtue or happiness.

If then women are not a swarm of ephemeron[1] triflers, why should they be kept in ignorance under the specious name of innocence? Men complain, and with reason, of the follies and caprices of our sex, when they do not keenly satirize our headstrong passions and grovelling vices. Behold, I should answer, the natural effect of ignorance! The mind will ever be unstable that has only prejudices to rest on, and the current will run with destructive fury when there are no barriers to break its force. Women are told from their infancy, and taught by the example of their mothers, that a little knowledge of human weakness, justly termed cunning, softness of temper, *outward* obedience, and a scrupulous attention to a puerile kind of propriety, will obtain for them the protection of man; and should they be beautiful, every thing else is needless, for at least twenty years of their lives. . . .

The most perfect education, in my opinion is, such an exercise of the understanding as is best calculated to strengthen the body and form the heart. Or, in other words, to enable the individual to attain such habits of virtue as will render it independent. In fact, it is a farce to call any being virtuous whose virtues do not result from the exercise of its own reason. This was Rousseau's opinion respecting men.[2] I extend it to women, and confidently assert, that they have been drawn out of their sphere by false refinement, and not by an endeavour to acquire masculine qualities. Still the regal homage which they receive is so intoxicating, that till the manners of the times are changed, and formed on more reasonable principles, it may be impossible to convince them, that the illegitimate power, which they obtain by degrading themselves, is a curse, and that they must return to nature and equality, if they wish to secure the placid satisfaction that unsophisticated affections impart. But for this epoch we must wait—wait, perhaps, till kings and nobles, enlightened by reason, and, preferring the real dignity of man to childish state, throw off their gaudy hereditary trappings; and if then women do not resign the arbitrary power of beauty, they will prove that they have *less* mind than man. . . .

Many are the causes that, in the present corrupt state of society, contribute to enslave women by cramping their understandings and sharpening

---

1. *ephemeron*, short-lived.
2. *Rousseau's opinion . . . men.* Jean Jacques Rousseau (1712-1778) argued that the individual's natural goodness is distorted by the false values of civilization.

The Poor Teacher by Richard Redgrave. 1844. *Victoria and Albert Museum, London*

their senses. One, perhaps, that silently does more mischief than all the rest, is their disregard of order.

To do every thing in an orderly manner, is a most important precept, which women, who, generally speaking, receive only a disorderly kind of education, seldom attend to with that degree of exactness that men, who from their infancy are broken into method, observe. This negligent kind of guesswork, for what other epithet can be used to point out the random exertions of a sort of instinctive common sense, never brought to the test of reason? prevents their generalizing matters of fact, so they do to-day what they did yesterday, merely because they did it yesterday. . . .

Women are, therefore, to be considered either as moral beings, or so weak that they must be entirely subjected to the superior faculties of men.

Let us examine this question. Rousseau declares, that a woman should never, for a moment feel herself independent, that she should be governed by fear to exercise her *natural* cunning, and made a coquettish slave in order to render her a more alluring object of desire, a *sweeter* companion to man, whenever he chooses to relax himself. He carries the arguments, which he pretends to draw from the indications of nature, still further, and insinuates that truth and fortitude, the corner stones of all human virtue, shall be cultivated with certain restrictions, because with respect to the female character, obedience is the grand lesson which ought to be impressed with unrelenting rigour.

What nonsense! when will a great man arise with sufficient strength of mind to puff away the fumes which pride and sensuality have thus spread over the subject! If women are by nature inferior to men, their virtues must be the same in quality, if not in degree, or virtue is a relative idea; consequently, their conduct should be founded on the same principles and have the same aim.

Connected with man as daughters, wives, and mothers, their moral character may be estimated by their manner of fulfilling those simple duties; but the end, the grand end of their exertions should be to unfold their own faculties, and acquire the dignity of conscious virtue. They may try to render their road pleasant; but ought never to forget, in common with man, that life yields not the felicity which can satisfy an immortal soul. I do not mean to insinuate, that either sex should be so lost, in abstract reflections or distant views, as to forget the affections and duties that lie before them, and are in truth, the means appointed to produce the fruit of life; on the contrary, I would warmly recommend them, even while I assert, that they afford most satisfaction when they are considered in their true subordinate light.

CHAPTER 9

. . . But what have women to do in society? I may be asked, but to loiter with easy grace; surely you would not condemn them all to suckle fools and chronicle small beer![3] No. Women might certainly study the art of healing, and be physicians as well as nurses.

How much more respectable is the woman who earns her own bread by fulfilling any duty, than the most accomplished beauty!—beauty did I say?—so sensible am I of the beauty of moral loveliness, or the harmonious propriety that attunes the passions of a well-regulated mind, that I blush at making the comparison; yet I sigh to think how few women aim at attaining this respectability by withdrawing from the giddy whirl of pleasure, or the indolent calm that stupifies the good sort of women it sucks in.

Proud of their weakness, however, they must always be protected, guarded from care, and all the rough toils that dignify the mind.—If this be the fiat[4] of fate, if they will make themselves insignificant and contemptible, sweetly to waste "life away," let them not expect to be valued when their beauty fades, for it is the fate of the fairest flowers to be admired and pulled to pieces by the careless hand that plucked them. In how many ways do I wish, from the purest benevolence, to impress this truth on my sex; yet I fear that they will not listen to a truth that dear bought experience has brought home to many an agitated bosom, nor willingly resign the privileges of rank and sex for the privileges of humanity, to which those have no claim who do not discharge its duties.

Those writers are particularly useful, in my opinion, who make man feel for man, independent of the station he fills, or the drapery of factitious sentiments. I then would fain convince reasonable men of the importance of some of my remarks, and prevail on them to weigh dispassionately the whole tenor of my observations.—I appeal to their understandings; and, as a fellow-creature, claim, in the name of my sex, some interest in their hearts. I entreat them to assist to emancipate their companion, to make her a *help meet* for them!

Would men but generously snap our chains, and be content with rational fellowship instead of slavish obedience, they would find us more observant daughters, more affectionate sisters, more faithful wives, more reasonable mothers—in a word, better citizens. We should then love them with true affection, because we should learn to respect ourselves; and the peace of mind of a worthy man would not be interrupted by the idle vanity of his wife, nor the babes sent to nestle in a strange bosom, having never found a home in their mother's.[5]

---

3. *to suckle . . . beer*, Shakespeare, *Othello*, Act Two, Scene 1, line 161.
4. *fiat*, dictate, command.
5. *nestle . . . mother's*, given to a nurse to be cared for.

THINK AND DISCUSS
Understanding
1. What reason does the writer give for women's "headstrong passions and groveling vices" (paragraph 2)?
2. What is a reason cited for the enslavement of women (paragraphs 4 and 5)?
3. What does the writer suggest should be the "grand end" of women's "exertions"?
4. What profession, restricted in her time to men only, does the writer state women might take up?

Analyzing
5. What type of teaching and role expectations for women are attacked in the second paragraph?
6. What does the author consider to be a perfect education?
7. What ideas of Rousseau does Wollstonecraft repudiate as "nonsense"?
8. Which writers does Wollstonecraft consider to be particularly useful (next to last paragraph)? Does she include herself in this group?
9. What is Wollstonecraft's message to women who rely solely on their physical beauty to gain the protection of men?

Extending
10. In your opinion, have women attained the level of emancipation Wollstonecraft appeals for in this essay?

APPLYING: Style HT
See Handbook of Literary Terms, p. 928

Style is the distinctive handling of language by an author; it refers not to what is said, but to *how* it is said and can be variously described as *wordy*, *poetic*, *formal*, and so forth.

1. How would you describe the style of "A Vindication of the Rights of Woman"?

2. Compare Wollstonecraft's style with that of some modern nonfiction writers. How do you account for the differences?

THINKING SKILLS
Generalizing
To generalize is to draw a general conclusion from particular information.

1. According to the arguments presented in "A Vindication of the Rights of Woman," what social reforms is Mary Wollstonecraft advocating to enable women to enjoy their natural rights and freedom?
2. Who must take the initiative to bring about these reforms?

COMPOSITION
Writing a Letter
Imagine that Mary Wollstonecraft returned today to discover whether the rights she advocated for women have been realized. In a personal letter, inform her of developments in the women's movement that have instituted the reforms she advocated. Then point up areas still in need of reform. Conclude by commenting on her contribution to the battle for equal rights for women.

Writing a Story
Write a brief story that develops a major theme Wollstonecraft stresses in her essay: "Looks are only skin deep." Create a character totally convinced that physical beauty will unlock the riches of the world, then portray the disillusionment that comes with the failure of the dream. Make sure to illustrate the fate of an individual whose entire existence is devoted solely to sensual rather than intellectual and spiritual development.

In ancient Greece, a *lyric* was a song rendered to the accompaniment of a lyre, a stringed musical instrument. Today the term is used to describe a short poem that expresses intense thought and feeling. It also refers to poetic expressions of considerable complexity, such as the elegy and ode. The poems of the Romantic Age are predominately lyrics, works whose appeal is to the reader's emotions and whose form is whatever the poet felt to be most natural and proper for his or her particular insight.

Here are some guidelines for reading lyric poetry of the Romantic period.

Read the poem aloud. "Lyric" means "song," and lyrical poetry is best read aloud so that the musical qualities of the verse can be enjoyed. Listen for the ways in which the poet has incorporated rhythm and sound devices, such as assonance, consonance, alliteration, and rhyme, to create a musical effect for the ear as well as the eye.

Read imaginatively. Lyric poetry invites readers to open themselves to new experiences through their imaginations and senses. For example, in his sonnet "On First Looking into Chapman's Homer," Keats asks readers to imaginatively project themselves into the mind and emotions of an explorer beholding a new world for the first time in order to experience what the poet felt upon discovering the true grandeur of Homer's writings.

Identify and characterize the speaker of the poem. The speaker in a lyric poem reveals a great deal about his or her character through the expression of personal thoughts and feelings. Ask yourself: How old is the speaker? What personality traits are revealed by the speaker's words and actions as described in the poem? For example, in Keats's sonnet "When I Have Fears," the speaker is clearly a young person fearful of dying before achieving love and

fame, yet sufficiently mature to comprehend the insignificance of human achievement in the context of eternity.

Sense the tone of the poem. Since lyric poetry is an expression of personal feeling, determining the **tone**—the author's attitude toward his or her subject and audience—is essential. Ask yourself: Is the tone of the poem bitter, humorous, objective, casual, or ironic, among many possibilities? For example, the tone of Wordsworth's "My Heart Leaps Up" is one of joy and optimism.

Determine the author's purpose. Look for both direct and indirect clues to help you understand why the poem was written in the first place and what effect was intended. To determine the author's purpose, pay particular attention to the title, to what is stated in the opening paragraph or stanza, to major ideas introduced in each paragraph or stanza, to the overall tone of the work, and to what is stated in the conclusion. Understanding the author's purpose and how he or she managed to achieve it will guide you in your analysis of the style and merits of a particular work.

Remember that *how* a poem is expressed is as important as *what* it means. Shelley declared that "Poets are the unacknowledged legislators of the world," by which he meant that poetry has the power to inspire people to work towards improving the lot of their fellow humans. Lyric poetry is rich in thought-provoking themes, particularly those affecting man's relationship with nature, God, and other humans. Its essential purpose is not to preach or convey practical information but to engage readers in an exploration of new realms of feeling and thought. Like a vase, a musical composition, or an architectural masterpiece, lyric poetry is a crafted art form intended to yield aesthetic satisfaction and enrich the imagination.

Wordsworth was born on April 7, 1770, in Cockermouth, a village on the edge of the Lake District, a scenic mountain region in northwest England. "Fair seed-time had my soul," said Wordsworth of his childhood years spent exploring a landscape of extraordinary beauty and variety. For eight years he attended Hawkshead Grammar School, where his love of reading and poetic inclinations were strongly encouraged. Wordsworth was enrolled at St. John's College, Cambridge, in 1787 as a scholarship student. Uninspired by the classical curriculum, he devoted himself instead to independent reading, long rambles in the countryside, and extended sessions of writing poetry.

During the summer of 1790, instead of studying for his comprehensive examinations, Wordsworth undertook a walking tour of Switzerland and France from which he returned radicalized in his political thinking and fired with enthusiasm for the French Revolution. "Bliss was it in that dawn to be alive,/ But to be young was very Heaven!" is his description of that period in his autobiographical poem, *The Prelude*. After graduation, Wordsworth returned to France in 1792, determined to learn French well enough to qualify as a tutor or gentleman's companion. Here he met and fell in love with Annette Vallon, who bore him a daughter, Caroline. A lack of funds forced Wordsworth's return to England in December of 1792. Cut off from a return to France by the declaration of war between Britain and France in 1793, increasingly disillusioned with the Revolution following the Reign of Terror and the advent of Napoleon, Wordsworth was uncertain about his personal and professional future.

Two critical developments in 1795 marked a major turning point in Wordsworth's life: a bequest of nine hundred pounds from a friend that enabled him to establish a home for his beloved sister Dorothy and himself at Racedown, and the commencement of his friendship and artistic collaboration with Samuel Taylor Coleridge, a creative association that would lead, in 1798, to the publication of a revolutionary volume of poems and ballads. Published anonymously, *Lyrical Ballads* contained twenty-three poems (nineteen by Wordsworth, four by Coleridge) published according to the following scheme: Wordsworth was to "give the charm of novelty to subjects of everyday life"; Coleridge was to let his imagination roam over more unusual and supernatural subject matter. Ironically, though the book included such poems as Coleridge's "Rime of the Ancient Mariner" and Wordsworth's "Tintern Abbey" (now considered among the finest in the English language), it was at first contemptuously received by critics and poets alike. In 1800, an expanded edition was published with a preface written by Wordsworth to explain his theory of poetry, in which he stated that "all good poetry is the spontaneous overflow of powerful feelings." He further asserted that the subject matter of poetry must be taken from "humble and rustic life" and be expressed in the language of "man speaking to man"; that is, in simple, direct speech.

Lines Composed a Few Miles Above Tintern Abbey

William Wordsworth

Wordsworth composed this poem while on a walking tour with his sister Dorothy along the River Wye, which winds back and forth across the border between England and Wales on its way to the Bristol Channel. The beautiful ruin of Tintern Abbey is located in a deep valley at the river's edge. Wordsworth had previously visited the Wye in 1793, five years before this poem was published in *Lyrical Ballads*.

Five years have past; five summers, with the
    length
Of five long winters! and again I hear
These waters, rolling from their mountain
    springs
With a soft inland murmur.—Once again
5 Do I behold these steep and lofty cliffs
That on a wild secluded scene impress
Thoughts of more deep seclusion and
    connect
The landscape with the quiet of the sky.
The day is come when I again repose
10 Here, under this dark sycamore, and view
These plots of cottage ground, these orchard
    tufts,
Which at this season, with their unripe
    fruits,
Are clad in one green hue, and lose
    themselves
Mid groves and copses. Once again I see
15 These hedgerows, hardly hedgerows, little
    lines
Of sportive wood run wild; these pastoral

farms,
Green to the very door; and wreaths of
    smoke
Sent up, in silence, from among the trees,
With some uncertain notice, as might seem
20 Of vagrant dwellers in the houseless woods,
Or of some Hermit's cave, where by his fire
The Hermit sits alone.
                  These beauteous forms,
Through a long absence, have not been to
    me
As is a landscape to a blind man's eye;
25 But oft, in lonely rooms, and 'mid the din
Of towns and cities, I have owed to them,
In hours of weariness, sensations sweet,
Felt in the blood, and felt along the heart;
And passing even into my purer mind,
30 With tranquil restoration:—feelings too
Of unremembered pleasure, such, perhaps,
As have no slight or trivial influence
On that best portion of a good man's life,
His little, nameless, unremembered acts
35 Of kindness and of love. Nor less, I trust,

To them I may have owed another gift,
Of aspect more sublime; that blessèd mood,
In which the burthen of the mystery,
In which the heavy and the weary weight
40 Of all this unintelligible world,
Is lightened—that serene and blessèd mood,
In which the affections gently lead us on—
Until, the breath of this corporeal frame
And even the motion of our human blood
45 Almost suspended, we are laid asleep
In body, and become a living soul;
While with an eye made quiet by the power
Of harmony, and the deep power of joy,
We see into the life of things.

                If this
50 Be but a vain belief, yet, oh! how oft—
In darkness and amid the many shapes
Of joyless daylight; when the fretful stir
Unprofitable, and the fever of the world,
Have hung upon the beatings of my heart—
55 How oft, in spirit, have I turned to thee,
O sylvan Wye![1] thou wanderer through the
    woods,
How often has my spirit turned to thee!
And now, with gleams of half-extinguished
    thought,
With many recognitions dim and faint,
60 And somewhat of a sad perplexity,
The picture of the mind revives again;
While here I stand, not only with the sense
Of present pleasure, but with pleasing
    thoughts
That in this moment there is life and food
65 For future years. And so I dare to hope,
Though changed, no doubt, from what I was
    when first
I came among these hills, when like a roe[2]
I bounded o'er the mountains, by the sides
Of the deep rivers, and the lonely streams,
70 Wherever nature led: more like a man
Flying from something that he dreads than
    one
Who sought the thing he loved. For nature
    then
(The coarser pleasures of my boyish days,
And their glad animal movements all gone by)

Tintern Abbey by Joseph M. W. Turner. Painted about 1794. *British Museum*

75 To me was all in all.—I cannot paint
What then I was. The sounding cataract[3]
Haunted me like a passion: the tall rock,
The mountain, and the deep and gloomy
    wood,
Their colors and their forms, were then to me
80 An appetite; a feeling and a love,
That had no need of a remoter charm,
By thought supplied, nor any interest
Unborrowed from the eye.—That time is past,
And all its aching joys are now no more,
85 And all its dizzy raptures. Not for this
Faint I, nor mourn nor murmur; other gifts
Have followed; for such loss, I would
    believe,

1. **Wye**, a river that runs past Tintern Abbey.
2. **roe**, a small, agile deer.
3. **cataract**, waterfall.

Abundant recompense. For I have learned
To look on nature, not as in the hour
90 Of thoughtless youth, but hearing often
          times
The still, sad music of humanity,
Nor hash nor grating, though of ample
          power
To chasten and subdue. And I have felt
A presence that disturbs me with the joy
95 Of elevated thoughts; a sense sublime
Of something far more deeply interfused,
Whose dwelling is the light of setting suns,
And the round ocean and the living air,
And the blue sky, and in the mind of man;
100 A motion and a spirit, that impels
All thinking things, all objects of all thought,
And rolls through all things. Therefore am
          I still
A lover of the meadows and the woods,
And mountains; and of all that we behold
105 From this green earth; of all the mighty
          world
Of eye, and ear—both what they half create,
And what perceive; well pleased to recognize
In nature and the language of the sense
The anchor of my purest thoughts, the nurse,
110 The guide, the guardian of my heart, and
          soul
Of all my moral being.
                              Nor perchance,
If I were not thus taught, should I the more
Suffer my genial spirits[4] to decay;
For thou art with me here upon the banks
115 Of this fair river; thou my dearest Friend,[5]
My dear, dear Friend; and in thy voice I
          catch
The language of my former heart, and read
My former pleasures in the shooting lights
Of thy wild eyes. Oh! yet a little while
120 May I behold in thee what I was once,
My dear, dear Sister! and this prayer I make,
Knowing that Nature never did betray
The heart that loved her; 'tis her privilege,
Through all the years of this our life, to lead
125 From joy to joy; for she can so inform[6]
The mind that is within us, so impress

With quietness and beauty, and so feed
With lofty thoughts, that neither evil
          tongues,
Rash judgments, nor the sneers of selfish
          men,
130 Nor greetings where no kindness is, nor all
The dreary intercourse of daily life,
Shall e'er prevail against us, or disturb
Our cheerful faith, that all which we behold
Is full of blessings. Therefore let the moon
135 Shine on thee in the solitary walk;
And let the misty mountain winds be free
To blow against thee; and, in after years,
When these wild ecstasies shall be matured
Into a sober pleasure, when thy mind
140 Shall be a mansion for all lovely forms,
Thy memory be as a dwelling place
For all sweet sounds and harmonies; oh!
          then,
If solitude, or fear, or pain, or grief,
Should be thy portion, with what healing
          thoughts
145 Of tender joy wilt thou remember me,
And these my exhortations! Nor,
          perchance—
If I should be where I no more can hear
Thy voice, nor catch from thy wild eyes these
          gleams
Of past existence—wilt thou then forget
150 That on the banks of this delightful stream
We stood together; and that I, so long
A worshiper of Nature, hither came
Unwearied in that service—rather say
With warmer love—oh! with far deeper zeal
155 Of holier love. Nor wilt thou then forget
That after many wanderings, many years
Of absence, these steep woods and lofty
          cliffs,
And this green pastoral landscape, were to me
More dear, both for themselves and for thy
          sake!

                                        1798

---

4. *genial spirits*, native powers.
5. *my dearest Friend*, Wordsworth's sister, Dorothy.
6. *inform*, inspire.

THINK AND DISCUSS

Understanding

1. Where is the speaker situated as he describes the landscape?
2. Where does the speaker say he has spent the past five years (lines 22–29)?
3. In lines 62–65 what are the speaker's "pleasing thoughts" while experiencing "present pleasure"?
4. What is "the cheerful faith" the speaker refers to in lines 125–134?

Analyzing

5. In lines 1–22 the countryside is described. What specific features of the landscape would have to be included in a painting of this scene? Are there any signs of human habitation?
6. Judging from lines 22–65, what three major benefits has Wordsworth derived from having once beheld the beauty of this natural scene? Overall, what "gifts" or sustenance does Wordsworth find in nature?
7. At what times has he felt impelled to recall this particular "picture of the mind"?
8. In lines 65–111 the poet describes two phases of his developing attitude toward nature. How does his present attitude differ from his feelings when he first visited the Wye?
9. At which phase of development in relation to nature does Dorothy now stand? What are her brother's wishes for her?
10. How is Wordsworth's affection for his sister connected with the **themes** of the poem?

Extending

11. Judging from the details provided in the poem, what kind of relationship did Wordsworth appear to enjoy with his sister?
12. Examine the illustration accompanying the poem. Does it convey a "probing interest in mysterious and mystical experience," a "yearning for ideal states of being"?

REVIEWING: Blank Verse H𝟤

See Handbook of Literary Terms, p. 897

Blank verse is unrhymed iambic pentameter. Of all the regular English verse forms it is the most fluid and comes closest to the natural rhythms of English speech, yet it is readily heightened for passages of passion and grandeur.

1. Look at lines 1–24 of "Tintern Abbey." Note that the poet has varied the basic blank verse pattern. The end of line 2 ("and again I hear") should be read as one unit with line 3 and the beginning of line 4. This avoids a sing-song effect that might otherwise have been present. Reread lines 9–14, paying attention to the punctuation and not stopping at the ends of lines.
2. A caesural pause can also affect the blank verse pattern. What line contains such a pause?
3. Read lines 22–23. How is the blank verse pattern altered here?

READING LITERATURE SKILLFULLY

Author's Purpose

Why was this piece written in the first place, and what effect did the author intend? The author's purpose greatly influences the way a particular work is written. In "Tintern Abbey," for example, Wordsworth makes a special point of explaining that this particular setting moved him so deeply that he had to write down his feelings without delay. These feelings then lead naturally to Wordsworth's philosophical speculations.

1. State, in one or two sentences, the author's purpose in "Lines Composed a Few Miles Above Tintern Abbey."
2. How does the **tone** of the poem shift as the poet contrasts his present feelings with those of his youth?
3. How does this shift in tone reinforce the author's purpose?

My Heart Leaps Up   William Wordsworth

My heart leaps up when I behold
  A rainbow in the sky:
So was it when my life began;
So is it now I am a man:
5 So be it when I shall grow old,
  Or let me die!

The Child is father of the Man;
And I could wish my days to be
Bound each to each by natural piety.[1]
1802   1807

___

1. *piety*, reverence, affection.

Composed upon Westminster Bridge, September 3, 1802   William Wordsworth

Earth has not anything to show more fair:
Dull would he be of soul who could pass by
A sight so touching in its majesty;
This City now doth, like a garment, wear
5 The beauty of the morning; silent, bare,
Ships, towers, domes, theaters, and temples
    lie
Open unto the fields, and to the sky;

All bright and glittering in the smokeless air.
Never did sun more beautifully steep
10 In his first splendor, valley, rock, or hill;
Ne'er saw I, never felt, a calm so deep!
The river glideth at his own sweet will:
Dear God! the very houses seem asleep;
And all that mighty heart is lying still!
1802   1807

___

HT   See SIMILE in the Handbook of Literary Terms, page 905.

___

It Is a Beauteous Evening   William Wordsworth

It is a beauteous evening, calm and free,
The holy time is quiet as a Nun
Breathless with adoration; the broad sun
Is sinking down in its tranquillity;
5 The gentleness of heaven broods o'er the
    Sea:

Listen! the mighty Being[1] is awake,
And doth with his eternal motion make
A sound like thunder—everlastingly.

___

1. *Being*, the ocean.

Dear Child!² dear Girl! that walkest with me
    here,
10 If thou appear untouched by solemn
    thought,
Thy nature is not therefore less divine:
Thou liest in Abraham's bosom³ all the year,
And worship'st at the Temple's inner shrine,

God being with thee when we know it not.
1802   1807

---

2. *Dear Child,* Wordsworth's French daughter, Caroline.
3. *in Abraham's bosom,* in the presence of God. See Luke 16:22.

THINK AND DISCUSS
MY HEART LEAPS UP
Understanding
1. What does the "rainbow in the sky" represent?

Analyzing
2. According to the first six lines, what condition of life was essential for Wordsworth, without which he would prefer death?
3. "My Heart Leaps Up" is generally considered a summary of Wordsworth's philosophy. Explain, accounting for the **paradox** expressed in line 7.
4. What does Wordsworth mean by "days. . ./ Bound. . . by natural piety"?

COMPOSED UPON WESTMINSTER BRIDGE, SEPTEMBER 3, 1802
Understanding
1. Is this a Petrarchan or Shakespearean sonnet?
2. Name two qualities of the "City" that Wordsworth found especially awesome.

Analyzing
3. As he stands upon Westminster Bridge in the early morning, what sights and emotions touch the poet's soul?
4. Point out uses of **personification** in the poem. What effect is achieved through ascribing human qualities to the city?

Extending
5. What do you think motivates the exclamation with which the poem ends?

IT IS A BEAUTEOUS EVENING
Understanding
1. What is described in the *octave* of this **sonnet**?
2. What is described in the *sestet*?

Analyzing
3. Describe the **setting**. What state of mind does this setting inspire in the poet?
4. How is Wordsworth's response to the beauty of the evening different from that of his daughter?
5. What explanation does Wordsworth give for the child's attitude being different from his?

Extending
6. Why is the presence of the child essential to the poem and to the poet's perception of this experience?

APPLYING: Simile H⊅
See Handbook of Literary Terms, p. 905
A **simile** is a figure of speech involving a comparison using *like* or *as*. Writers of both prose and poetry use similes to heighten emotional intensity, add vividness of detail, and appeal to the senses.

1. In "It Is a Beauteous Evening," what effect does Wordsworth achieve through comparing the evening to a nun?
2. What is the "sound like thunder"?

The Countryside

For many readers, the Romantic poets are synonymous with "nature poets." Indeed, nature, in particular the English countryside, is a primary poetic subject. But the countryside is far more than just pretty scenery to be described; in the works of the Romantic writers, characteristically the countryside is closely observed, sensuously depicted, lavishly praised, and frequently personified. The centrality of the countryside in the lives and works of these writers is further demonstrated by these recurrent themes.

The countryside is the ideal environment for human happiness and inner harmony. The Romantic poets lived in or explored the most beautiful countrysides of England and Europe and thoroughly relished the rustic scene. Wordsworth lived the greater part of his life in the English Lake District, just south of the Scottish border, and logged miles of walking to store up sensations and "powerful feelings" that could later be recollected and spontaneously "overflow" into his poetry. The years he spent in London only made him all the more conscious of the sights and sensations the stagnant and morally corrupt city denied him.

In Coleridge's "The Rime of the Ancient Mariner," the Mariner's sins are finally forgiven not by a churchman in a cathedral, but by a "hermit good [who] lives in that wood."

The role of the countryside in fostering inner harmony and personal happiness is equally apparent in Mary Shelley's *Frankenstein*. Throughout the novel, the countryside is used to mirror the polarities of Dr. Frankenstein's personality. During his brief periods of "peaceful happiness," of feeling in harmony with himself and the world, Frankenstein dwells amid pleasant landscapes, dotted with inviting human habitations. But during the years he labors to create the monster, seasons come and go without his taking time to "watch the blossom or the expanding leaves." He even confesses that "the fall of a leaf startled me. . . ." And when creating the monster's mate, Frankenstein chooses for his workplace a singularly miserable hovel on one of the most remote, rocky, and barren islands of the Orkneys, alienated from both nature and humanity.

The countryside serves as the fountainhead of poetic imagination. In no writer's work is this more explicitly set forth than in the poems of Wordsworth. In "Tintern Abbey," for example, the poet refers to himself as "A worshiper of Nature" who in his youth found "wild ecstasies" in the countryside. In his mature years, Wordsworth refers to nature as "The anchor of my purest thought, the nurse,/The guide, the guardian of my heart, and soul/Of all my moral being."

In like spirit Keats, in the summer of 1818, undertook a strenuous walking trip expressly, as he wrote in a letter to a friend, to "identify finer scenes, load me with grander Mountains, and strengthen more my reach in Poetry." And in "Ode to the West Wind," Shelley equates the poetic inspiration he seeks to attain with the fierce energy and dynamic force of the West Wind.

The countryside provides a stimulus to apprehension of ideal beauty and spiritual truth. In revolt from the mechanistic conception of the world as composed of physical particles in motion, the Romantics portrayed the landscape as sublime and often invested natural objects with significance beyond themselves. Wordsworth sensed in nature "A motion and a spirit, that impels/All thinking things, all objects of all thought,/And rolls through all things." In "Ode to a Nightingale," Keats represents the song of the nightingale as transcending time and change, as a symbol of immortality and ideal beauty. Thus, as portrayed by the Romantics, the countryside is never simply rural scenery, but a stimulus to thought and visionary power, emblematic also of the divine in man and nature.

H Review SONNET in the Handbook of Literary Terms, page 925.

The World Is Too Much with Us William Wordsworth

The world is too much with us; late and soon,
Getting and spending, we lay waste our
    powers:
Little we see in Nature that is ours;
We have given our hearts away, a sordid
    boon!
5 This Sea that bares her bosom to the moon,
The winds that will be howling at all hours,
And are up-gathered now like sleeping
    flowers;
For this, for everything, we are out of tune;

It moves us not.—Great God! I'd rather be
10 A Pagan suckled in a creed outworn;
So might I, standing on this pleasant lea,
Have glimpses that would make me less
    forlorn;
Have sight of Proteus rising from the sea;
Or hear old Triton[1] blow his wreathèd horn.

1802-1804   **1807**

---

1. *Proteus* (prō'tē əs) . . . *Triton* (trīt'n), sea gods in classical mythology.

London, 1802 William Wordsworth

Milton! thou shouldst be living at this hour:
England hath need of thee: she is a fen
Of stagnant waters: altar, sword, and pen,
Fireside, the heroic wealth of hall and bower,
5 Have forfeited their ancient English dower
Of inward happiness. We are selfish men:
Oh! raise us up, return to us again;
And give us manners, virtue, freedom, power.

Thy soul was like a Star, and dwelt apart;
10 Thou hadst a voice whose sound was like the
    sea:
Pure as the naked heavens, majestic, free;
So didst thou travel on life's common way,
In cheerful godliness; and yet thy heart
The lowliest duties on herself did lay.

1802   **1807**

THINK AND DISCUSS
THE WORLD IS TOO MUCH WITH US
Understanding
1. According to lines 1–4, what activities so consume human energies that people have lost touch with nature?

Analyzing
2. With what aspects of nature does the poet say we are "out of tune"?
3. What is the "creed" that Wordsworth says he would prefer to the materialism of his day?

Extending

4. Do the ideas in the poem apply to contemporary life? Explain.

LONDON, 1802

Understanding

1. What have the people of Wordsworth's age "forfeited"?

2. What four things is Milton asked to restore to English life?

Analyzing

3. Why is England in need of Milton's return?

4. According to the poet, why is Milton the right person to inspire reform?

Extending

5. How much does this sonnet resemble "The World Is Too Much With Us" in theme and tone?

REVIEWING: Sonnet
See Handbook of Literary Terms, p. 925

The **sonnet** is a lyric poem with a traditional form of fourteen iambic pentameter lines. The Italian or Petrarchan sonnet forms basically a two-part poem of eight lines (*octave*) and six lines (*sestet*), with these two parts played off against each other in a great variety of ways. The English or Shakespearean sonnet presents a four-part structure in which an idea or theme is developed in three stages and then brought to a conclusion in the couplet.

1. What kind of sonnets are these?

2. In "The World Is Too Much With Us," how do the point of view and tone change in line 9?

3. In "London, 1802," what change of thought begins the sestet?

Ode: Intimations of Immortality from Recollections of Early Childhood

William Wordsworth

Nature was for Wordsworth a source of spiritual insight. Nowhere does he express this view so clearly as in the "Ode: Intimations of Immortality." As you read the ode, keep these points in mind: (1) In his childhood and youth Wordsworth had a strong intuition that the soul, which is eternal and never dies, comes into a human body at birth from a glorious heavenly home. (2) Gradually, as he grew older, he lost the vision of his childhood belief. (3) In manhood, experiences with nature have brought him comfort and renewed his belief in immortality.

The Child is father of the Man;
And I could wish my days to be
Bound each to each by natural piety.

Stanza 1

There was a time when meadow, grove, and
    stream,
The earth, and every common sight,

To me did seem
Appareled in celestial light,
5 The glory and the freshness of a dream.
It is not now as it hath been of yore;—
Turn wheresoe'er I may,
By night or day,
The things which I have seen I now can see
no more.

Stanza 2

10 The Rainbow comes and goes,
And lovely is the Rose,
The Moon doth with delight
Look round her when the heavens are bare;
Waters on a starry night
15 Are beautiful and fair;
The sunshine is a glorious birth;
But yet I know, where'er I go,
That there hath passed away a glory from the
earth.

Stanza 3

Now, while the birds thus sing a joyous song,
20 And while the young lambs bound
As to the tabor's sound,[1]
To me alone there came a thought of grief:
A timely utterance gave that thought relief,
And I again am strong:
25 The cataracts blow their trumpets from the
steep;
No more shall grief of mine the season wrong;
I hear the Echoes through the mountains
throng,
The Winds come to me from the fields of sleep,
And all the earth is gay;
30 Land and sea
Give themselves up to jollity,
And with the heart of May
Doth every Beast keep holiday—
Thou Child of Joy,
35 Shout round me, let me hear thy shouts, thou
happy Shepherd-boy!

Stanza 4

Ye blessèd Creatures, I have heard the call
Ye to each other make; I see

The heavens laugh with you in your jubilee;
My heart is at your festival,
40 My head hath its coronal,[2]
The fullness of your bliss, I feel—I feel it all.
Oh, evil day! if I were sullen
While Earth herself is adorning,
This sweet May-morning,
45 And the Children are culling
On every side,
In a thousand valleys far and wide,
Fresh flowers; while the sun shines warm,
And the Babe leaps up on his Mother's arm:—
50 I hear, I hear, with joy I hear!
—But there's a Tree, of many, one,
A single Field which I have looked upon,
Both of them speak of something that is gone:
The Pansy at my feet
55 Doth the same tale repeat:
Whither is fled the visionary gleam?
Where is it now, the glory and the dream?

Stanza 5

Our birth is but a sleep and a forgetting:
The Soul that rises with us, our life's Star,[3]
60 Hath had elsewhere its setting,
And cometh from afar:
Not in entire forgetfulness,
And not in utter nakedness,
But trailing clouds of glory do we come
65 From God, who is our home:
Heaven lies about us in our infancy!
Shades of the prison-house begin to close
Upon the growing Boy,
But he beholds the light, and whence it flows
70 He sees it in his joy;
The Youth, who daily farther from the east
Must travel, still is Nature's priest,
And by the vision splendid
Is on his way attended;
75 At length the Man perceives it die away,
And fade into the light of common day.

---

1. *tabor's sound*, drum beat.
2. *coronal*, crown of flowers.
3. *Star*, the sun.

Stanza 6

Earth fills her lap with pleasures of her own;
Yearnings she hath in her own natural kind,
And even with something of a Mother's mind,
80   And no unworthy aim,
    The homely[4] Nurse doth all she can
To make her Foster-child, her Inmate Man,
    Forget the glories he hath known,
And that imperial palace whence he came.

Stanza 7

85 Behold the Child among his new-born blisses,
A six years' Darling of a pigmy size!
See, where 'mid work of his own hand he lies,
Fretted[5] by sallies of his mother's kisses,
With light upon him from his father's eyes!
90 See, at his feet, some little plan or chart,
Some fragment from his dream of human life,
Shaped by himself with newly-learnèd art;
    A wedding or a festival
    A mourning or a funeral,
95   And this hath now his heart,
    And unto this he frames his song:
    Then will he fit his tongue
To dialogues of business, love, or strife;
    But it will not be long
100   Ere this be thrown aside,
    And with new joy and pride
The little Actor cons[6] another part;
Filling from time to time his "humorous
    stage"[7]
With all the Persons, down to palsied Age,
105 That Life brings with her in her equipage;
    As if his whole vocation
    Were endless imitation.

Stanza 8

Thou, whose exterior semblance doth belie
    Thy Soul's immensity;
110 Thou best Philosopher, who yet dost keep
Thy heritage, thou Eye among the blind,
That, deaf and silent, read'st the eternal
    deep,[8]
Haunted forever by the eternal mind—
    Mighty Prophet! Seer blest!
115   On whom those truths do rest,

Which we are toiling all our lives to find,
In darkness lost, the darkness of the grave;
Thou, over whom thy Immortality
Broods like the Day, a Master o'er a Slave,
120 A Presence which is not to be put by;
Thou little Child, yet glorious in the might
Of heaven-born freedom on thy being's
    height,
Why with such earnest pains dost thou
    provoke
The years to bring the inevitable yoke,
125 Thus blindly with thy blessedness at strife?
Full soon thy Soul shall have her earthly
    freight,
And custom lie upon thee with a weight,
Heavy as frost, and deep almost as life!

Stanza 9

    Oh, joy! that in our embers
130   Is something that doth live,
    That nature yet remembers
    What was so fugitive!
The thought of our past years in me doth breed
Perpetual benediction: not indeed
135 For that which is most worthy to be blest;
Delight and liberty, the simple creed
Of Childhood, whether busy or at rest,
With new-fledged hope still fluttering in his
    breast:—
    Not for these I raise
140   The song of thanks and praise;
    But for those obstinate questionings
    Of sense and outward things,
    Fallings from us, vanishings;
    Blank misgivings of a Creature
145 Moving about in worlds not realized,[9]
High instincts before which our mortal Nature
Did tremble like a guilty Thing surprised:

---

4. *homely*, familiar; friendly; simple.
5. *Fretted*, bothered.
6. *cons*, learns.
7. *"humorous stage,"* from a sonnet by Samuel Daniel (1562–1619). *Humorous* means "changeable" or "moody" here.
8. *eternal deep*, mysteries of eternity.
9. *not realized*, not yet truly understood.

But for those first affections,
Those shadowy recollections,
150 Which, be they what they may,
Are yet the fountain light of all our day,
Are yet a master light of all our seeing;
Uphold us, cherish, and have power to
make
Our noisy years seem moments in the being
155 Of the eternal Silence: truths that wake,
To perish never;
Which neither listlessness, nor mad endeavor,
Nor Man nor Boy,
Nor all this is at enmity with joy,
160 Can utterly abolish or destroy!
Hence in a season of calm weather
Though inland far we be,
Our Souls have sight of that immortal sea
Which brought us hither,
165 Can in a moment travel thither,
And see the Children sport upon the shore,
And hear the mighty waters rolling evermore.

Stanza 10

Then sing, ye Birds, sing, sing, a joyous song!
And let the young Lambs bound
170 As to the tabor's sound!
We in thought will join your throng,
Ye that pipe and ye that play,
Ye that through your hearts today
Feel the gladness of the May!
175 What though the radiance which was once so
bright
Be now forever taken from my sight,
Though nothing can bring back the hour
Of splendor in the grass, of glory in the flower;
We will grieve not, rather find
180 Strength in what remains behind;
In the primal sympathy
Which having been must ever be;
In the soothing thoughts that spring
Out of human suffering;
185 In the faith that looks through death,
In years that bring the philosophic mind.

Stanza 11

And O, ye Fountains, Meadows, Hills, and
Groves,

The Cornfield by John Constable. 1826. *National Gallery,
London*

Forebode not any severing of our loves!
Yet in my heart of hearts I feel your might;
190 I only have relinquished one delight
To live beneath your more habitual sway.
I love the Brooks which down their channels
fret,
Even more than when I tripped lightly as
they;
The innocent brightness of a new-born Day
195 Is lovely yet;
The Clouds that gather round the setting sun
Do take a sober coloring from an eye
That hath kept watch o'er man's mortality;
Another race hath been, and other palms are
won.
200 Thanks to the human heart by which we live,
Thanks to its tenderness, its joys, and fears,
To me the meanest flower that blows can give
Thoughts that do often lie too deep for tears.
1802–1804   **1807**

THINK AND DISCUSS

Understanding

1. To what time of life is the speaker referring in stanza 1?
2. What is the "prison house" in line 67?
3. According to lines 129–134, what is it that nature still remembers?
4. In line 151, what is the "fountain light of all our day"?

Analyzing

5. The first four stanzas express a sense of loss. How have the speaker's feelings changed since the days when "every common sight" seemed "appareled in celestial light"?
6. In stanzas 3 and 4, what incidents temporarily restore the speaker's sense of joy? What is meant by "A timely utterance gave that thought relief"?
7. Despite this brief resurgence of joy, what causes the speaker to conclude that "the visionary gleam. . .the glory and the dream" are permanently gone?
8. Stanzas 5 through 8 offer an explanation for the sense of loss the speaker is experiencing. Identify the stages in the journey from birth to manhood described in stanza 5.
9. Why, in stanza 6, does the speaker speak of the earth as a "homely Nurse" and of man as "her Foster-child"? What is the "imperial palace" which is man's true home?
10. In stanzas 7 and 8, the speaker talks of the Child's immensity of soul and addresses him as a "best Philosopher" and "Mighty Prophet! Seer blest!" What is his justification for such extravagant praise?
11. According to lines 121–125, how is the child "at strife" with his own "blessedness"?
12. Stanzas 9–13 offer a consolation to the speaker for his sense of loss and provide reasons for exultation. Why, in stanza 9, does he feel moved to "raise/The song of praise"?
13. What is the "splendor in the grass" (stanza 10) that can never be recaptured? Yet, "what remains behind" as a source of strength and sustenance?
14. What "one delight" has been "relinquished" with the passage of childhood? Is this loss offset by any gains from maturity?

Extending

15. The last three lines of "My Heart Leaps Up" appear as an epigraph, or preface, to this poem. What relation is there between the short poem and the "Intimations Ode"?

COMPOSITION

Describing a Walk

Many of Wordsworth's poems were composed mentally while he was walking. Take an extended walk—through the heart of your city, a particular neighborhood, a park, or uninhabited area. Mentally file observations you can use. Later, write a descriptive paper in which you present a verbal mural of what you have seen and experienced. Use details that appeal to the senses and recreate the scene. Conclude with a discussion of what your walk taught you about yourself or life in general.

Writing to Persuade

Is "The world . . . too much with us," as Wordsworth suggests in his sonnet of that title? Are people today so preoccupied with materialistic goals that they have lost their capacity to be moved by the awesomeness and beauty of nature? In a paper, discuss what aspects of contemporary life inhibit humans from enjoying the beauty and pleasure that nature affords. Consider such factors as the decay of urban centers, the inflationary cost of living, and the impact of the "Electronic Age" on industrial America. In your conclusion suggest what might be done to bring mankind more "in tune" with the natural world. See "Writing to Persuade an Audience" in the Writer's Handbook.

Coleridge was very possibly the most versatile and stimulating mind of his generation—a poet, critic, philosopher, theologian, lecturer, journalist, and charismatic personality. He was simultaneously self-destructive, impetuous, and contradictory. Constantly self-deprecating, Coleridge helped perpetuate the widespread legend of himself as a genius incapable of finishing anything he started, irresponsible, wasteful of his talents, and in the reproachful words of Thomas Carlyle, "sunk inextricably in the depths of putrescent idleness." This is the same man, however, whom Wordsworth termed, "the most wonderful man that I have ever known," and of whom the essayist Charles Lamb stated, "never saw I his likeness, nor probably the world can again."

The youngest of twelve children of a Devonshire vicar, Coleridge was spoiled, precocious, and restless, continually lost in his dream world. After his father died when he was ten years old, Coleridge was sent to school in London, a time of loneliness and intense intellectual growth that he recalled later in his poetry. At age nineteen he went up to Cambridge. Here he spent a studious year before falling into bad habits and sinking deeply into debt.

A decisive meeting with the poet Robert Southey during the summer of 1793 resulted in a scheme for an ideal community to be established on the banks of the Susquehanna River in Pennsylvania. To further the cause, Coleridge became engaged to Sara Fricker, the sister of Southey's fiancée. Following the inevitable collapse of their Utopian dream, Coleridge went through with the marriage to Sara, though inwardly "wretched."

In one extraordinary year, 1798–1799, Coleridge began his stimulating association with Wordsworth and his sister Dorothy, wrote three of his best poems ("The Rime of the Ancient Mariner," "Kubla Khan," and the first part of "Christabel"), and was given 150 pounds a year for life, relieving him of oppressive financial burdens. The relationship between the two poets led to the refining of their poetic gifts and the publication in 1798 of *Lyrical Ballads*. By 1801, Coleridge had become a confirmed opium addict. Suffering from neuralgia and other ailments, a marriage gone sour, and the ebbing of his creative powers, he continued to deteriorate physically and emotionally, a state of mind described in "Dejection: an Ode." At thirty-five he separated from his wife; in 1810 a quarrel with Wordsworth caused a breach in their friendship until a reconciliation in 1828.

Despite his lifelong struggle against the addictive powers of opium, Coleridge's accomplishments were prodigious. His major critical effort, the *Biographia Literaria*, published in 1817, provides an account of the purpose and origin of the *Lyrical Ballads* and an analysis of the excellence and defects of Wordsworth's poetry. From 1819 until his death in 1834, Coleridge lived in London in the house of James Gillman, a surgeon, receiving many distinguished visitors from England and America and acquiring his legendary reputation as a brilliant conversationalist.

Kubla Khan

Samuel Taylor Coleridge

In Xanadu did Kubla Khan[1]
A stately pleasure-dome decree:
Where Alph, the sacred river, ran
Through caverns measureless to man
5   Down to a sunless sea.
So twice five miles of fertile ground
With walls and towers were girdled round:
And there were gardens bright with sinuous rills,
Where blossomed many an incense-bearing tree;
10 And here were forests ancient as the hills,
Enfolding sunny spots of greenery.

But oh! that deep romantic chasm which slanted
Down the green hill athwart a cedarn cover!
A savage place! as holy and enchanted
15 As e'er beneath a waning moon was haunted
By woman wailing for her demon-lover!
And from this chasm, with ceaseless turmoil
   seething,
As if this earth in fast thick pants were
   breathing,
A mighty fountain momently[2] was forced:
20 Amid whose swift half-intermitted burst
Huge fragments vaulted like rebounding hail,
Or chaffy grain beneath the thresher's flail:
And 'mid these dancing rocks at once and ever
It flung up momently the sacred river.
25 Five miles meandering with a mazy motion
Through wood and dale the sacred river ran,
Then reached the caverns measureless to man,
And sank in tumult to a lifeless ocean:
And 'mid this tumult Kubla heard from far
30 Ancestral voices prophesying war!
   The shadow of the dome of pleasure
   Floated midway on the waves;
   Where was heard the mingled measure
   From the fountain and the caves.

A Sea Spell
by Dante Gabriel
Rossetti. 1877.
*Fogg Art Museum,
Harvard University*

35 It was a miracle of rare device,
A sunny pleasure-dome with caves of ice!

   A damsel with a dulcimer
   In a vision once I saw:
   It was an Abyssinian maid,
40   And on her dulcimer she played,
   Singing of Mount Abora.
Could I revive within me
Her symphony and song,
To such a deep delight 'twould win me,
45 That with music loud and long,
I would build that dome in air,
That sunny dome! those caves of ice,
And all who heard should see them there,
And all should cry, Beware! Beware!
50 His flashing eyes, his floating hair!
Weave a circle round him thrice,
And close your eyes with holy dread,
For he on honey-dew hath fed,
And drunk the milk of Paradise.
1797   **1816**

---

1. *Kubla Khan,* founder of the Mongol dynasty in China in the thirteenth century.
2. *momently,* intermittently; at every moment.

Comment

Coleridge's Remarks About "Kubla Khan"

These remarks by Coleridge were prefixed to "Kubla Khan" when it was first published in *Christabel; Kubla Khan, a Vison; The Pains of Sleep* (1816). Coleridge refers to himself in the third person in these remarks.

"The following fragment is here published at the request of a poet of great and deserved celebrity, [Byron] and, as far as the author's own opinions are concerned, rather as a psychological curiosity, than on the ground of any supposed *poetic* merits.

"In the summer of the year 1797, the author, then in ill health, had retired to a lonely farmhouse between Porlock and Linton, on the Exmoor confines of Somerset and Devonshire. In consequence of a slight indisposition, an anodyne had been prescribed, from the effects of which he fell asleep in his chair at the moment that he was reading the following sentence, or words of the same substance, in *Purchas's Pilgrimage:* "Here the Khan Kubla commanded a palace to be built, and a stately garden thereunto. And thus ten miles of fertile ground were inclosed with a wall." The author continued for about three hours in a profound sleep, at least of the external senses, during which time he has the most vivid confidence that he could not have composed less than from two to three hundred lines; if that indeed can be called composition in which all the images rose up before him as *things*, with a parallel production of the correspondent expressions, without any sensation or consciousness of effort. On awaking he appeared to himself to have a distinct recollection of the whole, and taking his pen, ink, and paper, instantly and eagerly wrote down the lines that are here preserved. At this moment he was unfortunately called out by a person on business from Porlock, and detained by him above an hour, and on his return to his room, found, to his no small surprise and mortification, that though he still retained some vague and dim recollection of the general purport of the vision, yet, with the exception of some eight or ten scattered lines and images, all the rest had passed away like the images on the surface of a stream into which a stone has been cast. . . ."

THINK AND DISCUSS

Understanding
1. Name several extraordinary features of the "pleasure-dome," as described in lines 1–24.
2. What vision is described in lines 37–41?

Analyzing
3. In what ways is the "pleasure-dome" shown to be a place of stunning opposites?
4. Readers have often commented that "Kubla Khan" has sinister undertones. Do you find any? What lines or phrases suggest them to you?

5. What, according to lines 42–47, does the poet seek to do? What must first happen?
6. What might "the sacred river" **symbolize** in the poem? Consider its origin, the course it follows, and its final destination.
7. In lines 48–54 what reaction from others does the poet anticipate? Explain.

Extending
8. How is the role of the poet, as portrayed in this poem, similar to that chosen by Coleridge for himself in *Lyrical Ballads?* (You may wish to review the biography of Wordsworth on page 449 that explains the plan for this book.)

APPLYING: Mood
See Handbook of Literary Terms, p. 914

Mood is the overall atmosphere or prevailing emotional aura of a work. For example, a mood can be passionate, serious, reflective, or melancholy, among many possibilities.

1. How would you describe the mood in stanza 1 of "Kubla Khan"?
2. How is the mood sharply altered in the second stanza with the introduction of the words "But oh!"?

VOCABULARY
Etymology

Use your Glossary to answer the following questions about the etymology or history of the words given below. Read each clue and then write on your paper the matching word from the list.

> bard   beadle
> genial   sinuous

1. Which word comes from Old French and means a kind of official person?
2. Which comes from a word in Latin that originally meant "curve"?
3. Which refers to singers of a sort who entertained from before recorded history to the Middle Ages?
4. Which comes from a Latin word, the original form of which we use to mean someone brilliant?

H See RHYME in the Handbook of Literary Terms, page 919.

The Rime of the Ancient Mariner   Samuel Taylor Coleridge

ARGUMENT°

HOW A SHIP, HAVING PASSED THE LINE,° WAS DRIVEN BY STORMS TO THE COLD COUNTRY TOWARD THE SOUTH POLE; AND HOW FROM THENCE SHE MADE HER COURSE TO THE TROPICAL LATITUDE OF THE GREAT PACIFIC OCEAN; AND OF THE STRANGE THINGS THAT BEFELL; AND IN WHAT MANNER THE ANCIENT MARINER CAME BACK TO HIS OWN COUNTRY.

Argument, meaning here "a summary." In 1798, when "The Rime of the Ancient Mariner" was first published in *Lyrical Ballads,* by Samuel Taylor Coleridge and William Wordsworth, the reader was given no reading helps except the Argument. In later editions, Coleridge added the "Gloss," or prose summary, which is printed alongside the poem.

the Line, the Equator.

AN ANCIENT MARINER MEETETH THREE GALLANTS BIDDEN TO A WEDDING FEAST, AND DETAINETH ONE.

PART THE FIRST

It is an ancient Mariner,
    And he stoppeth one of three.
"By thy long gray beard and glittering eye,
    Now wherefore stopp'st thou me?

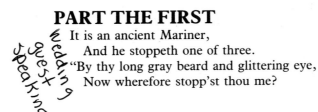

THE WEDDING
GUEST IS
SPELLBOUND BY
THE EYE OF THE
OLD SEAFARING
MAN, AND
CONSTRAINED TO
HEAR HIS TALE.

5 "The Bridegroom's doors are opened wide,
    And I am next of kin;
The guests are met, the feast is set—
    May'st hear the merry din."

He° holds him with his skinny hand;
10   "There was a ship," quoth he.
"Hold off! unhand me, graybeard loon!"
    Eftsoons° his hand dropt he.

He holds him with his glittering eye;
    The Wedding Guest stood still,
15 And listens like a three years' child—
    The Mariner hath his will.

The Wedding Guest sat on a stone—
    He cannot choose but hear;
And thus spake on that ancient man,
20   The bright-eyed Mariner.

"The ship was cheered, the harbor cleared;
    Merrily did we drop
Below the kirk,° below the hill,
    Below the lighthouse top.

THE MARINER
TELLS HOW THE
SHIP SAILED
SOUTHWARD WITH
A GOOD WIND
AND FAIR
WEATHER TILL IT
REACHED THE
LINE.

25 "The Sun came up upon the left;
    Out of the sea came he!
And he shone bright, and on the right
    Went down into the sea.

"Higher and higher every day,
30   Till over the mast at noon—"
The Wedding Guest here beat his breast,
    For he heard the loud bassoon. → *music*

THE WEDDING
GUEST HEARETH
THE BRIDAL
MUSIC; BUT THE
MARINER CON-
TINUETH HIS TALE.

The Bride hath paced into the hall;
    Red as a rose is she;
35 Nodding their heads before her goes
    The merry minstrelsy.°

The Wedding Guest he beat his breast,
    Yet he cannot choose but hear;
And thus spake on that ancient man,
40   The bright-eyed Mariner.

THE SHIP DRAWN
BY STORM
TOWARD THE
SOUTH POLE.

"And now the Storm Blast came, and he
    Was tyrannous and strong;
He struck with his o'ertaking wings,
    And chased us south along.

45 "With sloping masts and dipping prow,

He, the Mariner.

Eftsoons (eft sünz'),
immediately. (Archaic)

kirk, church. (Scottish
and North English)

minstrelsy, group of
singers or musicians.

As who pursued with yell and blow
Still treads the shadow of his foe,
  And forward bends his head,°
The ship drove fast, loud roared the blast,
50 And southward aye we fled.

"And now there came both mist and snow,
  And it grew wondrous cold;
And ice, mast-high, came floating by
  As green as emerald.

55 "And through the drifts the snowy clifts°
  Did send a dismal sheen;
Nor shapes of men nor beasts we ken° —
  The ice was all between.

"The ice was here, the ice was there,
60 The ice was all around;
It cracked and growled, and roared and howled,
  Like noises in a swound!°

"At length did cross an Albatross;
  Thorough° the fog it came;
65 As if it had been a Christian soul,
  We hailed it in God's name.

"It ate the food it ne'er had eat,
  And round and round it flew.
The ice did split with a thunder-fit;
70 The helmsman steered us through!

"And a good south wind sprung up behind;
  The Albatross did follow,
And every day, for food or play,
  Came to the mariners' hollo!

75 "In mist or cloud, on mast or shroud,°
  It perched for vespers nine;°
Whiles all the night, through fog-smoke white,
  Glimmered the white moonshine."

"God save thee, ancient Mariner,
80 From the fiends that plague thee thus!—
'Why look'st thou so?"—"With my crossbow
  I shot the Albatross."

PART THE SECOND

"The Sun now rose upon the right;
  Out of the sea came he,

THE LAND OF ICE,
AND OF FEARFUL
SOUNDS, WHERE
NO LIVING THING
WAS TO BE SEEN;

TILL A GREAT SEA
BIRD CALLED THE
ALBATROSS CAME
THROUGH THE
SNOW-FOG, AND
WAS RECEIVED
WITH GREAT JOY
AND HOSPITALITY.

AND LO! THE
ALBATROSS
PROVETH A BIRD
OF GOOD OMEN,
AND FOLLOWETH
THE SHIP AS IT
RETURNED
NORTHWARD,
THROUGH FOG
AND FLOATING
ICE.

THE ANCIENT
MARINER
INHOSPITABLY
KILLETH
THE PIOUS BIRD OF
GOOD OMEN.

As who . . . head, as a
person who, pursued so
closely that he is running
in his enemy's shadow,
bends forward in an effort
to attain greater speed.

snowy clifts, towering icebergs.

ken, saw. (Archaic)

Like noises in a swound,
like the roaring that a
fainting person hears in his
ears.
Thorough, through.

shroud, rope running
from a mast to the side of
the ship.
for vespers nine, for nine
evenings.

The illustrations are by Gustave Doré (1832–1883), a French illustrator and graphic artist.

₈₅ Still hid in mist, and on the left
    Went down into the sea.

"And the good south wind still blew behind,
    But no sweet bird did follow,
Nor any day, for food or play,
₉₀   Came to the mariners' hollo!

HIS SHIPMATES
CRY OUT AGAINST
THE ANCIENT
MARINER FOR
KILLING THE BIRD
OF GOOD LUCK.

"And I had done a hellish thing,
    And it would work 'em woe;
For all averred I had killed the bird
    That made the breeze to blow.
₉₅ 'Ah, wretch!' said they, 'the bird to slay,
    That made the breeze to blow!'

BUT WHEN THE
FOG CLEARS OFF,
THEY JUSTIFY THE
SAME, AND THUS
MAKE THEMSELVES
ACCOMPLICES IN
THE CRIME.

"Nor dim nor red, like God's own head,
    The glorious Sun uprist;°
Then all averred I had killed the bird
₁₀₀   That brought the fog and mist.
'Twas right,' said they, 'such birds to slay,
    That bring the fog and mist.'

uprist, uprose.

THE FAIR BREEZE
CONTINUES; THE
SHIP ENTERS THE
PACIFIC OCEAN AND
SAILS NORTHWARD,
EVEN TILL IT
REACHES THE LINE.

"The fair breeze blew, the white foam flew,
    The furrow followed free;
₁₀₅ We were the first that ever burst
    Into that silent sea.

THE SHIP HATH
BEEN SUDDENLY
BECALMED.

"Down dropt the breeze, the sails dropt down;
    'Twas sad as sad could be;
And we did speak only to break
₁₁₀   The silence of the sea!

"All in a hot and copper sky,
    The bloody Sun, at noon,
Right up above the mast did stand,
    No bigger than the Moon.

₁₁₅ "Day after day, day after day,
    We stuck, nor breath nor motion;
As idle as a painted ship
    Upon a painted ocean.

AND THE
ALBATROSS
BEGINS TO BE
AVENGED.

"Water, water, everywhere,
₁₂₀   And all the boards did shrink;
Water, water, everywhere,
    Nor any drop to drink.

"The very deep did rot—O Christ!
    That ever this should be!
₁₂₅ Yea, slimy things did crawl with legs

Upon the slimy sea.

"About, about, in reel and rout
    The death fires° danced at night;
The water, like a witch's oils,
130   Burnt green, and blue, and white.

"And some in dreams assurèd were
    Of the spirit that plagued us so;
Nine fathom deep he had followed us
    From the land of mist and snow.

135 "And every tongue, through utter drought,
    Was withered at the root;
We could not speak, no more than if
    We had been choked with soot.

"Ah! well-a-day!—what evil looks
140   Had I from old and young!
Instead of the cross, the Albatross
    About my neck was hung."

PART THE THIRD
"There passed a weary time. Each throat
    Was parched, and glazed each eye.
145 A weary time! a weary time!
    How glazed each weary eye!
When, looking westward, I beheld
    A something in the sky.

"At first it seemed a little speck,
150   And then it seemed a mist;
It moved, and moved, and took at last
    A certain shape, I wist.°

"A speck, a mist, a shape, I wist!
    And still it neared and neared;
155 As if it dodged a water sprite,
    It plunged and tacked and veered.

"With throats unslaked, with black lips baked,
    We could nor laugh nor wail;
Through utter drought all dumb we stood!
160 I bit my arm, I sucked the blood,
    And cried, 'A sail! a sail!'

"With throats unslaked, with black lips baked,
    Agape they heard me call;
Gramercy!° they for joy did grin,

A SPIRIT HAD FOLLOWED THEM; ONE OF THE INVISIBLE INHABITANTS OF THIS PLANET, NEITHER DEPARTED SOULS NOR ANGELS; CONCERNING WHOM THE LEARNED JEW JOSEPHUS AND THE PLATONIC CONSTANTINOPOLITAN, MICHAEL PSELLUS,° MAY BE CONSULTED. THEY ARE VERY NUMEROUS, AND THERE IS NO CLIMATE OR ELEMENT WITHOUT ONE OR MORE.

THE SHIPMATES IN THEIR SORE DISTRESS WOULD FAIN THROW THE WHOLE GUILT ON THE ANCIENT MARINER; IN SIGN WHEREOF THEY HANG THE DEAD SEA BIRD ROUND HIS NECK.

THE ANCIENT MARINER BEHOLDETH A SIGN IN THE ELEMENT AFAR OFF.

AT ITS NEARER APPROACH, IT SEEMETH HIM TO BE A SHIP; AND AT A DEAR RANSOM HE FREETH HIS SPEECH FROM THE BONDS OF THIRST.

A FLASH OF JOY;

---

death fires, luminous glow caused by discharges of atmospheric electricity and often seen on masts of sailing ships in stormy weather.

the learned Jew Josephus (jō sē′fəs) . . . **Michael Psellus** (sel′es). Josephus (37–95) was a historian. Psellus (1018–1079) was a theologian, born in Constantinople, who admired Plato, the famous ancient Greek philosopher.

wist, knew or discovered. (Archaic)

Gramercy (grə mėr′sē), many thanks. (Archaic)

165 And all at once their breath drew in,
    As they were drinking all.

AND HORROR FOLLOWS. FOR CAN IT BE A SHIP THAT COMES ONWARD WITHOUT WIND OR TIDE?

" 'See! see!' I cried, 'she tacks no more!
    Hither to work us weal;°
Without a breeze, without a tide,
170   She steadies with upright keel!'

to work us weal (wēl), to bring us good.

"The western wave was all aflame,
    The day was well-nigh done!
Almost upon the western wave
    Rested the broad bright Sun;
175 When that strange shape drove suddenly
    Betwixt us and the Sun.

IT SEEMETH HIM BUT THE SKELETON OF A SHIP.

"And straight the Sun was flecked with bars
    (Heaven's Mother send us grace!),
As if through a dungeon grate he peered,
180   With broad and burning face.

" 'Alas!' thought I, and my heart beat loud,
    'How fast she nears and nears!
Are those *her* sails that glance in the Sun,
    Like restless gossameres?

AND ITS RIBS ARE SEEN AS BARS ON THE FACE OF THE SETTING SUN. THE SPECTER WOMAN AND HER DEATH MATE, AND NO OTHER ON BOARD THE SKELETON SHIP.

185 " 'Are those *her* ribs through which the Sun
    Did peer, as through a grate?
And is that Woman all her crew?
Is that a Death?° and are there two?
    Is Death that Woman's mate?'

a Death, a skeleton.

LIKE VESSEL, LIKE CREW!

190 "Her lips were red, her looks were free,°
    Her locks were yellow as gold;
Her skin was as white as leprosy;
The Nightmare Life-in-Death was she,
    Who thicks man's blood with cold.

her looks were free. The Specter Woman's manner is bold and brazen.

DEATH AND LIFE-IN-DEATH HAVE DICED FOR THE SHIP'S CREW, AND SHE (THE LATTER) WINNETH THE ANCIENT MARINER.

195 "The naked hulk alongside came,
    And the twain were casting dice;
'The game is done! I've won! I've won!'
    Quoth she, and whistles thrice.

NO TWILIGHT WITHIN THE COURTS OF THE SUN.°

"The Sun's rim dips; the stars rush out;
200   At one stride comes the dark;
With far-heard whisper, o'er the sea,
    Off shot the specter bark.

the courts of the sun, those far northern lands where the sun shines most of the day and night.

AT THE RISING OF THE MOON,

"We listened and looked sideways up!
Fear at my heart, as at a cup,
205   My lifeblood seemed to sip!

472 *The Romantics*

The stars were dim, and thick the night;
The steersman's face by his lamp gleamed
　　　white;
　From the sails the dew did drip—
Till clomb above the eastern bar
210 The hornèd Moon,° with one bright star
　　Within the nether tip.

"One after one, by the star-dogged Moon,
　Too quick for groan or sigh,
Each turned his face with a ghastly pang,
215　And cursed me with his eye.

"Four times fifty living men
　(And I heard nor sigh nor groan),
With heavy thump, a lifeless lump,
　They dropped down one by one.

220 "The souls did from their bodies fly—
　They fled to bliss or woe!
And every soul, it passed me by,
　Like the whizz of my crossbow!"

PART THE FOURTH

"I fear thee, ancient Mariner!
225　I fear thy skinny hand!
And thou art long, and lank, and brown,
　As is the ribbed sea sand.

"I fear thee and thy glittering eye
　And thy skinny hand, so brown."
230 "Fear not, fear not, thou Wedding Guest!
　This body dropt not down.

"Alone, alone, all, all alone,
　Alone on a wide, wide sea!
And never a saint took pity on
235　My soul in agony.

"The many men, so beautiful!
　And they all dead did lie;
And a thousand thousand slimy things
　Lived on; and so did I.

240 "I looked upon the rotting sea,
　And drew my eyes away;
I looked upon the rotting deck,
　And there the dead men lay.

ONE AFTER
ANOTHER

HIS SHIPMATES
DROP DOWN
DEAD,

BUT LIFE-IN-DEATH
BEGINS HER WORK
ON THE ANCIENT
MARINER.

THE WEDDING
GUEST FEARETH
THAT A SPIRIT IS
TALKING TO HIM;

BUT THE ANCIENT
MARINER ASSURETH
HIM OF HIS BODILY
LIFE, AND PROCEED-
ETH TO RELATE HIS
HORRIBLE PENANCE.

HE DESPISETH THE
CREATURES OF
THE CALM,

AND ENVIETH
THAT THEY
SHOULD LIVE, AND
SO MANY LIE
DEAD,

Till clomb . . . Moon,
until the crescent moon
climbed (clomb) high
above the eastern horizon
(bar).

"I looked to Heaven, and tried to pray;
245 But or ever a prayer had gusht,
A wicked whisper came, and made
My heart as dry as dust.

"I closed my lids, and kept them close,
And the balls like pulses beat;
250 For the sky and the sea, and the sea and
the sky
Lay like a load on my weary eye,
And the dead were at my feet.

BUT THE CURSE
LIVETH FOR HIM
IN THE EYE OF THE
DEAD MEN.

"The cold sweat melted from their limbs;
Nor rot nor reek did they;
255 The look with which they looked on me
Had never passed away.

IN HIS LONELINESS
AND FIXEDNESS HE
YEARNETH TOWARD
THE JOURNEYING
MOON, AND THE
STARS THAT STILL
SOJOURN, YET STILL
MOVE ONWARD; AND
EVERYWHERE THE
BLUE SKY BELONGS
TO THEM, AND IS
THEIR APPOINTED
REST AND THEIR
NATIVE COUNTRY
AND THEIR OWN
NATURAL HOMES,
WHICH THEY ENTER
UNANNOUNCED, AS
LORDS THAT ARE
CERTAINLY EXPECTED
AND YET THERE IS A
SILENT JOY AT THEIR
ARRIVAL.

"An orphan's curse would drag to Hell
A spirit from on high;
But oh! more horrible than that
260 Is a curse in a dead man's eye!
Seven days, seven nights, I saw that curse,
And yet I could not die.

"The moving Moon went up the sky,
And nowhere did abide;
265 Softly she was going up,
And a star or two beside—

"Her beams bemocked the sultry main,°
Like April hoarfrost spread;
But where the ship's huge shadow lay,
270 The charmèd water burnt alway
A still and awful red.

BY THE LIGHT OF
THE MOON HE
BEHOLDETH GOD'S
CREATURES OF
THE GREAT CALM,

"Beyond the shadow of the ship,
I watched the water snakes;
They moved in tracks of shining white,
275 And when they reared, the elfish light
Fell off in hoary flakes.

"Within the shadow of the ship
I watched their rich attire;
Blue, glossy green, and velvet black,
280 They coiled and swam; and every track
Was a flash of golden fire.

THEIR BEAUTY
AND THEIR
HAPPINESS.

"O happy living things! no tongue
Their beauty might declare;
A spring of love gushed from my heart;

Her beams . . . main.
The moonbeams looked
cool in contrast to the fiery
sea.

285 And I blessed them unaware!
  Sure my kind saint took pity on me,
    And I blessed them unaware.

"The selfsame moment I could pray;
    And from my neck so free
290 The Albatross fell off, and sank
    Like lead into the sea."

PART THE FIFTH

"Oh, sleep! it is a gentle thing,
    Beloved from pole to pole!
To Mary Queen the praise be given!
295 She sent the gentle sleep from Heaven,
    That slid into my soul.

BY THE GRACE OF
THE HOLY
MOTHER, THE
ANCIENT MARINER
IS REFRESHED
WITH RAIN.

"The silly° buckets on the deck,
    That had so long remained,
I dreamt that they were filled with dew;
300 And when I awoke, it rained.

silly, simple.

"My lips were wet, my throat was cold,
    My garments all were dank,
Sure I had drunken in my dreams,
    And still my body drank.

305 "I moved, and could not feel my limbs;
    I was so light—almost
I thought that I had died in sleep,
    And was a blessed ghost.

HE HEARETH
SOUNDS AND
SEETH STRANGE
SIGHTS AND
COMMOTIONS IN
THE SKY AND THE
ELEMENT.

"And soon I heard a roaring wind;
310   It did not come anear;
But with its sound it shook the sails
    That were so thin and sere.

"The upper air burst into life!
    And a hundred fire-flags sheen;°
315 To and fro they were hurried about;
And to and fro, and in and out,
    The wan stars danced between.

fire-flags sheen, flashes of
lightning shone bright.

"And the coming wind did roar more loud,
    And the sails did sigh like sedge;°
320 And the rain poured down from one black
        cloud;
    The Moon was at its edge.

sedge, coarse grass that
grows in wet ground.

"The thick, black cloud was cleft, and still

The Moon was at its side;
Like waters shot from some high crag,
325 The lightning fell with never a jag,
A river steep and wide.

THE BODIES OF
THE SHIP'S CREW
ARE INSPIRED,
AND THE SHIP
MOVES ON;

"The loud wind never reached the ship,
Yet now the ship moved on!
Beneath the lightning and the Moon
330 The dead men gave a groan.

"They groaned, they stirred, they all uprose;
Nor spake, nor moved their eyes;
It had been strange, even in a dream,
To have seen those dead men rise.

335 "The helmsman steered, the ship moved on;
Yet never a breeze up-blew.
The mariners all 'gan work the ropes,
Where they were wont to do;
They raised their limbs like lifeless tools—
340 We were a ghastly crew.

"The body of my brother's son
Stood by me, knee to knee;
The body and I pulled at one rope,
But he said naught to me."

BUT NOT BY THE
SOULS OF THE
MEN, NOR BY
DEMONS OF
EARTH OR MIDDLE
AIR, BUT BY A
BLESSED TROOP OF
ANGELIC SPIRITS
SENT DOWN BY THE
INVOCATION
OF THE GUARDIAN
SAINT.

345 "I fear thee, ancient Mariner!"
"Be calm, thou Wedding Guest!
'Twas not those souls that fled in pain,
Which to their corses° came again,   *corses*, corpses.
But a troop of spirits blest;

350 "For when it dawned—they dropped their arms
And clustered round the mast;
Sweet sounds rose slowly through their mouths;
And from their bodies passed.

"Around, around, flew each sweet sound,
355 They darted to the Sun;
Slowly the sounds came back again,
Now mixed, now one by one.

"Sometimes a-dropping from the sky
I heard the skylark sing;
360 Sometimes all little birds that are,
How they seemed to fill the sea and air
With their sweet jargoning!

"And now 'twas like all instruments,

Now like a lonely flute;
365 And now it is an angel's song,
That makes the heavens be mute.

"It ceased; yet still the sails made on
A pleasant noise till noon,
A noise like of a hidden brook
370 In the leafy month of June,
That to the sleeping woods all night
Singeth a quiet tune.

"Till noon we quietly sailed on.
Yet never a breeze did breathe;
375 Slowly and smoothly went the ship,
Moved onward from beneath.

THE LONESOME
SPIRIT FROM THE
SOUTH POLE
CARRIES ON THE
SHIP AS FAR AS
THE LINE, IN
OBEDIENCE TO
THE ANGELIC
TROOP, BUT STILL
REQUIRETH
VENGEANCE.

"Under the keel nine fathom deep,
From the land of mist and snow,
The spirit slid and it was he
380 That made the ship to go.
The sails at noon left off their tune,
And the ship stood still also.

"The Sun, right up above the mast,
Had fixed her to the ocean,
385 But in a minute she 'gan stir,
With a short, uneasy motion—
Backwards and forwards half her length
With a short, uneasy motion.

"Then like a pawing horse let go,
390 She made a sudden bound;
It flung the blood into my head,
And I fell down in a swound.

THE POLAR SPIRIT'S
FELLOW DEMONS, THE
INVISIBLE INHABITANTS
OF THE ELEMENT,
TAKE PART IN HIS
WRONG; AND TWO
OF THEM RELATE,
ONE TO THE OTHER,
THAT PENANCE LONG
AND HEAVY FOR THE
ANCIENT MARINER
HATH BEEN ACCORDED
TO THE POLAR SPIRIT,
WHO RETURNETH
SOUTHWARD.

"How long in that same fit I lay,
I have not to declare;
395 But ere my living life returned
I heard and in my soul discerned
Two voices in the air.

" 'Is it he?' quoth one, 'Is this the man?
By Him who died on cross,
400 With his cruel bow he laid full low
The harmless Albatross.

" 'The spirit who bideth by himself
In the land of mist and snow,
He loved the bird that loved the man
405 Who shot him with his bow.'

"The other was a softer voice,
    As soft as honeydew;
Quoth he, 'The man hath penance done
    And penance more will do.' "

PART THE SIXTH

First Voice

410 " 'But tell me, tell me! speak again,
    Thy soft response renewing—
What makes that ship drive on so fast?
    What is the Ocean doing?'

Second Voice

" 'Still as a slave before his lord,
415   The Ocean hath no blast;
His great bright eye most silently
    Up to the Moon is cast—

" 'If he may know which way to go;
    For she guides him smooth or grim.
420 See, brother, see! how graciously
    She looketh down on him.'

First Voice

" 'But why drives on that ship so fast,
    Without or° wave or wind?'

Second Voice

" 'The air is cut away before,
425   And closes from behind.

" 'Fly, brother, fly! more high, more high,
    Or we shall be belated;
For slow and slow that ship will go,
    When the Mariner's trance is abated.'

430 "I woke, and we were sailing on
    As in a gentle weather.
'Twas night, calm night, the Moon was high;
    The dead men stood together.

"All stood together on the deck,
435   For a charnel dungeon° fitter;
All fixed on me their stony eyes
    That in the Moon did glitter.

"The pang, the curse, with which they died,
    Had never passed away;
440 I could not draw my eyes from theirs,

THE MARINER
HATH BEEN CAST
INTO A TRANCE;
FOR THE ANGELIC
POWER CAUSETH
THE VESSEL TO
DRIVE NORTH-
WARD FASTER
THAN HUMAN LIFE
COULD ENDURE.

THE
SUPERNATURAL
MOTION IS
RETARDED; THE
MARINER AWAKES,
AND HIS PENANCE
BEGINS ANEW.

or, either.

charnel (chär'nl) **dungeon**, burial vault.

Nor turn them up to pray.

THE CURSE IS
FINALLY EXPIATED.

"And now this spell was snapt; once more
   I viewed the ocean green,
And looked far forth, yet little saw
445   Of what had else been seen—

"Like one that on a lonesome road
   Doth walk in fear and dread,
And having once turned round, walks on,
   And turns no more his head,
450 Because he knows a frightful fiend
   Doth close behind him tread.

"But soon there breathed a wind on me,
   Nor sound nor motion made;
Its path was not upon the sea,
455   In ripple or in shade.

"It raised my hair, it fanned my cheek
   Like a meadow gale of spring—
It mingled strangely with my fears,
   Yet it felt like a welcoming.

460 "Swiftly, swiftly flew the ship,
   Yet she sailed softly, too;
Sweetly, sweetly blew the breeze—
   On me alone it blew.

AND THE ANCIENT
MARINER BEHOLD-
ETH HIS NATIVE
COUNTRY.

"Oh! dream of joy! is this indeed
465   The lighthouse top I see?
Is this the hill? Is this the kirk?
   Is this mine own countree?

"We drifted o'er the harbor bar,
   And I with sobs did pray—
470 'O let me be awake, my God!
   Or let me sleep alway.'

"The harbor bay was clear as glass,
   So smoothly it was strewn!
And on the bay the moonlight lay,
475   And the shadow of the Moon.

"The rock shone bright, the kirk no less,
   That stands above the rock;
The moonlight steeped in silentness
   The steady weathercock.

THE ANGELIC
SPIRITS LEAVE THE
DEAD BODIES,

480 "And the bay was white with silent light,
   Till rising from the same,

Full many shapes, that shadows were,
    In crimson colors came.

AND APPEAR IN
THEIR OWN FORMS
OF LIGHT.

485 "A little distance from the prow
    Those crimson shadows were;
I turned my eyes upon the deck—
    Oh, Christ! what I saw there!

"Each corse lay flat, lifeless and flat,
    And, by the holy rood!°
490 A man all light, a seraph° man,
    On every corse there stood.

the holy rood (rŭd), the cross of Christ.

seraph (ser′əf), one of the highest order of angels.

"This seraph band, each waved his hand—
    It was a heavenly sight!
They stood as signals to the land,
495   Each one a lovely light;

"This seraph band, each waved his hand;
    No voice did they impart—
No voice; but oh! the silence sank
    Like music on my heart.

500 "But soon I heard the dash of oars,
    I heard the Pilot's cheer;
My head was turned perforce away,
    And I saw a boat appear.

"The Pilot, and the Pilot's boy,
505   I heard them coming fast;
Dear Lord in Heaven! it was a joy
    The dead men could not blast.

"I saw a third—I heard his voice;
    It is the Hermit good!
510 He singeth loud his godly hymns
    That he makes in the wood.
He'll shrieve my soul,° he'll wash away
    The Albatross's blood."

PART THE SEVENTH

THE HERMIT OF
THE WOOD

"This hermit good lives in that wood
515   Which slopes down to the sea;
How loudly his sweet voice he rears!
He loves to talk with marineres
    That come from a far countree.

"He kneels at morn, and noon, and eve—
520   He hath a cushion plump;

He'll shrieve (shrīv) *my soul*. The Hermit of the wood will hear the Ancient Mariner's confession and, after listening to the tale of his wrongdoings, will impose a penance upon him. When this penance is carried out, the Mariner will secure peace and forgiveness for his sins.

It is the moss that wholly hides
   The rotted old oak stump.

"The skiff boat neared; I heard them talk:
   'Why, this is strange, I trow!°
525 Where are those lights so many and fair
   That signal made but now?'

I trow (trō, trou), I think.

APPROACHETH
THE SHIP WITH
WONDER.

" 'Strange, by my faith!' the Hermit said—
   'And they answered not our cheer!
The planks look warped! and see those sails
530   How thin they are and sere!
I never saw aught like to them,
   Unless perchance it were

" 'Brown skeletons of leaves that lag
   My forest brook along;
535 When the ivy tod° is heavy with snow;
And the owlet whoops to the wolf below
   That eats the she-wolf's young.'

the ivy tod, a clump of ivy.

" 'Dear Lord! it hath a fiendish look'—
   (The Pilot made reply)
540 'I am a-feared'—'Push on, push on!'
   Said the Hermit cheerily.

"The boat came closer to the ship,
   But I nor spake nor stirred;

The boat came close beneath the ship,
545 And straight a sound was heard.

"Under the water it rumbled on,
  Still louder and more dread;
It reached the ship, it split the bay;
  The ship went down like lead.

550 "Stunned by that loud and dreadful sound,
  Which sky and ocean smote,
Like one that hath been seven days drowned
  My body lay afloat;
But swift as dreams, myself I found
555 Within the Pilot's boat.

"Upon the whirl, where sank the ship,
  The boat spun round and round;
And all was still, save that the hill
  Was telling of the sound.

560 "I moved my lips—the Pilot shrieked
  And fell down in a fit;
The holy Hermit raised his eyes
  And prayed where he did sit.

"I took the oars; the Pilot's boy,
565 Who now doth crazy go,
Laughed loud and long, and all the while
  His eyes went to and fro.
'Ha! ha!' quoth he, 'full plain I see,
  The Devil knows how to row.'

570 "And now, all in my own countree,
  I stood on the firm land!
The Hermit stepped forth from the boat,
  And scarcely he could stand.

" 'O shrieve me, shrieve me, holy man!'
575 The Hermit crossed his brow.
'Say quick,' quoth he, 'I bid thee say—
  What manner of man art thou?'

"Forthwith this frame of mine was wrenched
  With a woeful agony,
580 Which forced me to begin my tale;
  And then it left me free.

"Since then, at an uncertain hour,
  That agony returns;
And till my ghastly tale is told,

585   This heart within me burns.

"I pass, like night, from land to land;
   I have strange power of speech;
That moment that his face I see,
I know the man that must hear me—
590   To him my tale I teach.

"What loud uproar bursts from that door!
   The wedding guests are there;
But in the garden bower the bride
   And bridemaids singing are;
595 And hark the little vesper bell,
   Which biddeth me to prayer!

"O Wedding Guest! this soul hath been
   Alone on a wide, wide sea;
So lonely 'twas that God himself
600   Scarce seemèd there to be.

"O sweeter than the marriage feast,
   'Tis sweeter far to me,
To walk together to the kirk
   With a goodly company!—

605 "To walk together to the kirk,
   And all together pray,
While each to his great Father bends,
Old men, and babes, and loving friends,
   And youths, and maidens gay!

AND TO TEACH, BY
HIS OWN
EXAMPLE, LOVE
AND REVERENCE
TO ALL THINGS
THAT GOD MADE
AND LOVETH.

610 "Farewell, farewell! but this I tell
   To thee, thou Wedding Guest!
He prayeth well who loveth well
   Both man and bird and beast.

"He prayeth best who loveth best
615   All things both great and small;
For the dear God who loveth us,
   He made and loveth all."

The Mariner, whose eye is bright,
   Whose beard with age is hoar,°
620 Is gone; and now the Wedding Guest
   Turned from the Bridegroom's door.

He went like one that hath been stunned,
   And is of sense forlorn;
A sadder and a wiser man,
625   He rose the morrow morn.   **1798**

hoar, gray or white.

THINK AND DISCUSS
Understanding
1. A *frame* is a narrative device for presenting a story within another story. Explain in your own words how the Mariner starts telling his story to the Wedding Guest.
2. What forces the ship toward the South Pole? What enables it to sail northward again?
3. What forms of suffering must the Mariner endure as payment for having killed the albatross? How do his shipmates suffer?
4. How long is the Mariner forced to suffer "all, all alone" (line 232)?
5. After the Mariner has dropped the guilty weight of the Albaross, what do the "Two voices in the air" (lines 386–409) suggest will happen to the Mariner?
6. What service does the Hermit provide for the Mariner?

Analyzing
7. Describe the sailors' changing reactions to the albatross. (See lines 65, 93, 101, and 139.)
8. The Mariner is given no particular motivation for shooting the albatross. Why might this be so?
9. Why does the Mariner bless the water snakes? What happens as a result?
10. In Part the Fifth how is the ship manned now that the crew is dead? What spiritual forces are involved?
11. In Part the Sixth how is the dying curse of the Mariner's shipmates finally dispelled? What are the Mariner's immediate feelings?
12. In Part the Seventh how do the Hermit, Pilot, and the Pilot's boy react to the Mariner and the sight of his ship?
13. What is the Mariner's final doom or sentence? With what strange powers is he endowed?

Extending
14. The critic Oliver Elton said of this poem, "Coleridge is not . . . concerned with the prevention of cruelty to albatrosses." What do you think *is* Coleridge's concern in this poem? What does he wish to communicate about human experience?

APPLYING: Rhyme HT
See Handbook of Literary Terms, p. 919
Rhyme is the exact repetition of sounds in at least the final accented syllables of two or more words. If the rhyme occurs at the ends of lines, it is called end rhyme. If the rhyme occurs within the line it is called internal rhyme. In the ballad stanza, which Coleridge mainly uses in "Rime of the Ancient Mariner," the second and fourth lines are end-rhymed.

Give examples of end rhyme and internal rhyme in lines 67–74 of "The Rime of the Ancient Mariner."

1. What is the rhyme scheme of lines 62–82?
2. Which of these lines have internal rhymes?
3. What examples of slant rhymes occur in these lines?

COMPOSITION
Writing a Ballad
Write a ballad about the adventures and exploits of a public figure who has received fame or notoriety. Once you have picked your subject, determine the **tone** you wish to adopt; for example, laudatory, satirical, or humorous. Also pinpoint the overall impression you wish to convey about this person and what incidents you intend to incorporate in your narration. One way to begin might be to model your opening lines after the first stanza of "The Rime of the Ancient Mariner": "There was an . . . ."

Analyzing the Mood of a Poem
Write a paper of at least four paragraphs in which you analyze the mood or moods in the poem and discuss how mood helps to contribute to the overall effect of the poem. Go on to discuss what devices Coleridge uses to achieve a certain mood. See "Writing About Mood or Tone" in the Writer's Handbook.

BIOGRAPHY

Thomas De Quincey
1785–1859

The son of a wealthy Manchester merchant, Thomas De Quincey was extraordinarily gifted and sensitive, an individual of vast knowledge. By the age of fifteen he could read, write, and speak Greek "as though it were his native tongue." At the age of seventeen, unhappy with himself and his life at school, he ran away to London, living in poverty while continuing his close reading of the English poets and keeping a diary, which he later drew on for his autobiographical writings. Following a reconciliation with his family, he attended Oxford, where he studied German literature and philosophy as well as English literature. A brilliant but erratic student, he left Oxford in 1808 without a degree because he could not face the emotional ordeal of the oral examination.

An ardent admirer of both Wordsworth and Coleridge, whom he had met in 1807, De Quincey moved to the Lake District, took a home near Wordsworth, and began a close relationship with those Romantic poets living in the area. De Quincey was among the first to recognize the importance of Wordsworth's and Coleridge's *Lyrical Ballads*, and he became an enthusiastic advocate of Romantic literature. After having been warmly accepted by Coleridge, De Quincey anonymously arranged for him to receive a gift of money. By this time De Quincey, like Coleridge, had become addicted to opium to relieve the pains of neuralgia and other ailments, some acquired during his earlier period of hardship in London.

In 1821, part of the *Confessions of an English Opium-Eater* was published in periodical form and, in the following year, in its entirety. Considered De Quincey's masterpiece, the book sold extremely well and was praised for its authentic detail and imaginative prose style. For the remainder of his life De Quincey was a prolific contributor of essays on personal, political, social, critical, historical, and even philosophical subjects to various periodicals.

De Quincey moved to Edinburgh in middle age and remained there until his death on December 8, 1859. In his commentary on the poetry of Pope, De Quincey drew a distinction between "the literature of knowledge" and "the literature of power": "The function of the first is to teach; the function of the second is to move; the first is a rudder; the second, an oar or sail." De Quincey's best work belongs to the literature of power.

The following essay by De Quincey, originally written as a magazine article, considers the scene in Shakespeare's play in which Macbeth and Lady Macbeth are startled by a loud knocking just after they have murdered King Duncan. This occurs in Act Two, at the end of scene 2 and the beginning of scene 3. The essay is a famous example of critical impressionism, in which the emphasis is on the writer's impressions and emotional responses to the subject under discussion, rather than on a rigorously developed logical argument.

On the Knocking at the Gate in *Macbeth*

Thomas De Quincey

From my boyish days I had always felt a great perplexity on one point in *Macbeth*. It was this: the knocking at the gate which succeeds to the murder of Duncan produced to my feelings an effect for which I never could account. The effect was that it reflected back upon the murderer a peculiar awfulness and a depth of solemnity; yet, however obstinately I endeavored with my understanding to comprehend this, for many years I never could see *why* it should produce such an effect.

Here I pause for one moment, to exhort the reader never to pay any attention to his understanding[1] when it stands in opposition to any other faculty of his mind. The mere understanding, however useful and indispensable, is the meanest faculty in the human mind, and the most to be distrusted; and yet the great majority of people trust to nothing else—which may do for ordinary life, but not for philosophical purposes. Of this out of ten thousand instances that I might produce I will cite one. Ask of any person whatsoever who is not previously prepared for the demand by a knowledge of perspective to draw in the rudest way the commonest appearance which depends upon the laws of that science—as, for instance, to represent the effect of two walls standing at right angles to each other, or the appearance of the houses on each side of a street as seen by a person looking down the street from one extremity. Now, in all cases, unless the person has happened to observe in pictures how it is that artists produce these effects, he will be utterly unable to make the smallest approximation to it. Yet why? For he has actually seen the effect every day of his life. The reason is that he allows his understanding to overrule his eyes. His understanding, which includes no intuitive knowledge of the laws of vision, can furnish him with no reason why a line which is known and can be proved to be a horizontal line should not *appear* a horizontal line: a line that made any angle with the perpendicular less than a right angle would seem to him to indicate that his houses were all tumbling down together. Accordingly, he makes the line of his houses a horizontal line, and fails of course to produce the effect demanded. Here, then, is one instance out of many in which not only the understanding is allowed to overrule the eyes, but where the understanding is positively allowed to obliterate the eyes, as it were; for not only does the man believe the evidence of his understanding in opposition to that of his eyes, but (which is monstrous) the idiot is not aware that his eyes ever gave such evidence. He does not know that he has seen (and therefore *quoad*[2] his consciousness has *not* seen) that which he *has* seen every day of his life.

But to return from this digression. My understanding could furnish no reason why the knocking at the gate in *Macbeth* should produce any effect, direct or reflected. In fact, my understanding said positively that it could *not* produce any effect. But I knew better; I felt that it did; and I waited and clung to the problem until further knowledge should enable me to solve it. At length, in 1812, Mr. Williams made his *début* on the stage of Ratcliffe Highway, and executed

---

1. *understanding*, intellect; the reasoning faculty.
2. *quoad* (kwō'ad), relative to. [Latin]

The body of John Williams, about to be buried, from Fairburn's *Authentic and Particular Account of the Horrid Murders in Ratcliffe Highway and New Gravel Lane.* 1811.

those unparalleled murders which have procured for him such a brilliant and undying reputation.[3] On which murders, by the way, I must observe that in one respect they have had an ill effect, by making the connoisseur in murder very fastidious in his taste, and dissatisfied with anything that has been since done in that line. All other murders look pale by the deep crimson of his; and, as an amateur once said to me in a querulous tone, "There has been absolutely nothing *doing* since his time, or nothing that's worth speaking of." But this is wrong; for it is unreasonable to expect all men to be great artists, and born with the genius of Mr. Williams. Now, it will be remembered that in the first of these murders (that of the Marrs) the same incident (of a knocking at the door soon after the work of extermination was complete) did actually occur which the genius of Shakespeare has invented; and all good judges, and the most eminent dilettanti,[4] acknowledged the felicity of Shakespeare's suggestion as soon as it was actually realized. Here, then, was a fresh proof that I had been right in relying on my own feeling, in opposition to my understanding; and again I set myself to study the problem. At length I solved it to my own satisfaction; and

my solution is this: murder, in ordinary cases, where the sympathy is wholly directed to the case of the murdered person, is an incident of coarse and vulgar horror; and for this reason—that it flings the interest exclusively upon the natural but ignoble instinct by which we cleave to life: an instinct which, as being indispensable to the primal law of self-preservation, is the same in kind (though different in degree) amongst all living creatures. This instinct, therefore, because it annihilates all distinctions, and degrades the greatest of men to the level of "the poor beetle that we tread on,"[5] exhibits human nature in its most abject and humiliating attitude. Such an attitude would little suit the purposes of the poet. What then must he do? He must throw the interest on the murderer. Our sympathy must be with *him* (of course I mean a sympathy of comprehension, a

---

3. *Mr. Williams . . . reputation.* In fact, it was in December, 1811, that John Williams, a seaman, murdered two families in the Ratcliffe Highway, a street in the slums of the East End of London.
4. *dilettanti*, literally, lovers of art; here, lovers of the art of murder.
5. *"the poor beetle . . . on,"* Shakespeare, *Measure for Measure,* Act Three, Scene 1, line 78.

sympathy by which we enter into his feelings, and are made to understand them—not a sympathy of pity or approbation). In the murdered person, all strife of thought, all flux and reflux of passion and of purpose, are crushed by one overwhelming panic; the fear of instant death smites him "with its petrific mace."[6] But in the murderer, such a murderer as a poet will condescend to, there must be raging some great storm of passion—jealousy, ambition, vengeance, hatred—which will create a hell within him; and into this hell we are to look.

In *Macbeth*, for the sake of gratifying his own enormous and teeming faculty of creation, Shakespeare has introduced two murderers: and, as usual in his hands, they are remarkably discriminated; but—though in Macbeth the strife of mind is greater than in his wife, the tiger spirit not so awake, and his feelings caught chiefly by contagion from her—yet, as both were finally involved in the guilt of murder, the murderous mind of necessity is finally to be presumed in both. This was to be expressed; and, on its own account, as well as to make it a more proportionable antagonist to the unoffending nature of their victim, "the gracious Duncan,"[7] and adequately to expound "the deep damnation of his taking off,"[8] this was to be expressed with peculiar energy. We were to be made to feel that the human nature—i.e., the divine nature of love and mercy, spread through the hearts of all creatures, and seldom utterly withdrawn from man—was gone, vanished, extinct, and that the fiendish nature had taken its place. And, as this effect is marvellously accomplished in the *dialogues* and *soliloquies* themselves, so it is finally consummated by the expedient under consideration; and it is to this that I now solicit the reader's attention. If the reader has ever witnessed a wife, daughter, or sister in a fainting fit, he may chance to have observed that the most affecting moment in such a spectacle is *that* in which a sigh and a stirring announce the recommencement of suspended life. Or, if the reader has ever been present in a vast metropolis on the day when some great national idol was carried in funeral pomp to his grave, and, chancing to walk near the course

through which it passed, has felt powerfully, in the silence and desertion of the streets, and in the stagnation of ordinary business, the deep interest which at that moment was possessing the heart of man—if all at once he should hear the death-like stillness broken up by the sound of wheels rattling away from the scene, and making known that the transitory vision was dissolved, he will be aware that at no moment was his sense of the complete suspension and pause in ordinary human concerns so full and affecting as at that moment when the suspension ceases, and the goings-on of human life are suddenly resumed. All action in any direction is best expounded, measured, and made apprehensible, by reaction. Now, apply this to the case in *Macbeth*. Here, as I have said, the retiring of the human heart and the entrance of the fiendish heart was to be expressed and made sensible. Another world has stepped in; and the murderers are taken out of the region of human things, human purposes, human desires. They are transfigured: Lady Macbeth is "unsexed";[9] Macbeth has forgot that he was born of woman; both are conformed to the image of devils; and the world of devils is suddenly revealed. But how shall this be conveyed and made palpable? In order that a new world may step in, this world must for a time disappear. The murderers and the murder must be insulated—cut off by an immeasurable gulf from the ordinary tide and succession of human affairs—locked up and sequestered in some deep recess; we must be made sensible that the world of ordinary life is suddenly arrested, laid asleep, tranced, racked into a dread armistice; time must be annihilated, relation to things without abolished; and all must pass self-withdrawn into a deep syncope and suspension of earthly passion. Hence it is that, when the deed is done, when the work of darkness

---

6. *"with its petrific mace,"* Milton, *Paradise Lost*, Book Ten, line 293. *Petrific* means "petrifying."
7. *"the gracious Duncan,"* Shakespeare, *Macbeth*, Act Three, Scene 1, line 66.
8. *"the deep . . . taking off,"* Shakespeare, *Macbeth*, Act One, Scene 7, line 20. "Taking off" means murder.
9. *"unsexed,"* a reference to *Macbeth*, Act One, Scene 5, line 38.

is perfect, then the world of darkness passes away like a pageantry in the clouds: the knocking at the gate is heard, and it makes known audibly that the reaction has commenced; the human has made its reflux upon the fiendish; the pulses of life are beginning to beat again; and the reestablishment of the goings-on of the world in which we live first makes us profoundly sensible of the awful parenthesis that had suspended them.

O mighty poet! Thy works are not as those of other men, simply and merely great works of art, but are also like the phenomena of nature, like the sun and the sea, the stars and the flowers, like frost and snow, rain and dew, hailstorm and thunder, which are to be studied with entire submission of our own faculties, and in the perfect faith that in them there can be no too much or too little, nothing useless or inert, but that, the farther we press in our discoveries, the more we shall see proofs of design and self-supporting arrangement where the careless eye had seen nothing but accident!

1823

THINK AND DISCUSS
Understanding
1. What "one point" in *Macbeth* was a source of perplexity for De Quincey?
2. In what two ways does De Quincey say the character of Macbeth in the scene of Duncan's murder has been differentiated from that of his wife?
3. What does he believe to be "the most affecting moment" of a fainting fit?

Analyzing
4. Which does De Quincey trust more, intellect or feeling? What reason does he give for his perference?
5. What happened that caused De Quincey to understand the effect that the knocking had on him?
6. What is his explanation for the emotional impact of the knocking at the gate?
7. The last paragraph is lavish in its praise of Shakespeare. What are De Quincey's reasons for stating that Shakespeare's works "are not as those of other men"?

Extending
8. What incidents can you recall, either from plays or films, that have impressed on you by means of visual or sound effects the "peculiar awfulness" or "depth of solemnity" of an event?

VOCABULARY
Word Analogies
An analogy is a similarity. On some standardized tests a colon is used to mean "is related to." For example, *hot : cold :: day : night* means "*hot* is related to *cold* in the same way that *day* is related to *night*." In the example, the relationship is that of opposites; other relationships to watch for are *greater* or *less than, the same as, causes* or *is the result of, is a part of,* and so on.

Determine the relationship between the two italicized words in each question. Then select, from the pairs of words that follow, the words that are related in the same way as the words in the first pair. You may use your Glossary if you need to.

1. *primal : modern ::* **a.** advise : encourage; **b.** happy : sad; **c.** age : time.
2. *swarm : teem ::* **a.** free : captive; **b.** lifeless : inactive; **c.** tragedy : farce.
3. *obstinate : flexible ::* **a.** careful : sloppy; **b.** appeal : attract; **c.** principle : rule.
4. *peaceful : querulous ::* **a.** fitness : appropriateness; **b.** childish : juvenile; **c.** hidden : obvious.
5. *confusion : perplexity ::* **a.** rest : exercise; **b.** hint : suggestion; **c.** seriousness : foolishness.

Strikingly handsome, with a reputation for wickedness and free thought, George Gordon, Lord Byron embodied in his life and in his writings the figure subsequently known as the "Byronic hero": a moody individualist, self-exiled from society after exhausting all possibilities of excitement, and tormented by remorse over sins committed in the past.

Byron was descended from two high-strung families with reputations for reckless living and violence. Byron's father, a spendthrift army captain and playboy known as "Mad Jack," dissipated the fortunes of the two heiresses he married and left his widow to rear their three-year-old child in poverty. Byron's mother was tempestuous, proud, and slightly mad, a person who alternately showered her child with love, then taunted him as a "lame brat" because of the deformed right foot with which he was born.

At the age of ten, George Gordon became the sixth Lord Byron upon the death of his great-uncle, inheriting a fortune and the estate of Newstead Abbey. He was later enrolled at Harrow, where he proved to be an indifferent student, but a fine athlete and leader. When Byron entered Cambridge, he was well read in both Latin and Greek, excelled in swimming and boxing, and had already fallen in love twice. After graduation, Byron took the customary Grand Tour of Europe. Returning to London, he published the first two cantos of *Childe Harold*, which were so popular that, as he put it, "I awoke one morning and found myself famous." He took his seat in the House of Lords and made a brilliant speech defending workers who had wrecked machinery that threatened their jobs.

Enjoying his role as the favorite of London society, Byron gained the reputation of being one who was "mad, bad, and dangerous to know." He dressed as he felt a poet should and cultivated a deliberately mysterious air. After several love affairs, he married the nobly born, very proper Annabella Milbanke in an attempt to gain some stability and respectability in his life. After one year of marriage that caused her to question her husband's sanity, his wife returned to her parents with their newborn daughter. The circumstances of the separation scandalized English society and led to Byron's decision, in 1816, to leave England for good.

"Making a public show of a very genuine misery, he swept across Europe the pageant of his bleeding heart." Thus Matthew Arnold described Byron's conduct following his moral banishment from England as he wandered across the Continent. Despite being "half mad during the time . . . between metaphysics, mountains, lakes, love unextinguishable, thoughts unutterable, and the nightmare of my own delinquencies," Byron poured out some of his greatest work.

Even today Byron remains a legend and a paradox—a fiery rebel and a conventional aristocrat, an idealist and a cynic, a scandalous playboy to his countrymen and a hero to the Greeks, to whose war of liberation from Turkish rule his money and energies were committed during the months before his death at Missolonghi on April 19, 1824, at the age of thirty-six.

She Walks in Beauty

George Gordon, Lord Byron

She[1] walks in beauty, like the night
  Of cloudless climes and starry skies;
And all that's best of dark and bright
  Meet in her aspect and her eyes:
5 Thus mellowed to that tender light
  Which heaven to gaudy day denies.

One shade the more, one ray the less,
  Had half impaired the nameless grace
Which waves in every raven tress,
10   Or softly lightens o'er her face;
Where thoughts serenely sweet express
  How pure, how dear their dwelling-place.

And on that cheek, and o'er that brow,
  So soft, so calm, yet eloquent,
15 The smiles that win, the tints that glow,
  But tell of days in goodness spent,
A mind at peace with all below,
  A heart whose love is innocent!

1814   **1815**

---

1. **She,** Lady Wilmot Horton, Byron's beautiful young cousin by marriage, who had appeared in an evening dress of black mourning brightened with spangles.

When We Two Parted

George Gordon, Lord Byron

When we two parted
  In silence and tears,
Half broken-hearted
  To sever for years,
5 Pale grew thy cheek and cold,
  Colder thy kiss;
Truly that hour foretold
  Sorrow to this.

Detail of *Broken Vows* by Philip Hermogenes Calderon. 1856. *Tate Gallery, London*

The dew of the morning
10 Sunk chill on my brow—
It felt like the warning
    Of what I feel now.
Thy vows are all broken,
    And light is thy fame;
15 I hear thy name spoken,
    And share in its shame.

They name thee before me,
    A knell to mine ear;
A shudder comes o'er me—
20 Why wert thou so dear?

They know not I knew thee,
    Who knew thee too well—
Long, long shall I rue thee,
    Too deeply to tell.

25 In secret we met—
    In silence I grieve,
That thy heart could forget,
    Thy spirit deceive.
If I should meet thee
30 After long years,
How should I greet thee?—
    With silence and tears.

1808   1816

THINK AND DISCUSS
SHE WALKS IN BEAUTY
Understanding
1. What does the first stanza of the poem say that "heaven" denies to "gaudy day"?
2. What would "impair" the ideal beauty of the woman described?

Analyzing
3. The poem expresses both physical and spiritual ideals. Keeping in mind that standards of beauty vary from age to age, identify what the speaker considers a physical ideal.
4. What spiritual ideal does the woman described embody?
5. Which aspects of beauty—the physical or the spiritual—does the poem more strongly emphasize?

Extending
6. In your opinion, to what extent does Byron's depiction of ideal physical and spiritual beauty correspond with modern definitions of "ideal beauty"?

WHEN WE TWO PARTED
Understanding
1. What kind of reputation does the woman beloved by the speaker presently enjoy?
2. How did the speaker arrange his earlier meetings with his beloved?

Analyzing
3. As he reflects on the parting from his beloved, what does the speaker recognize as a presentiment of future sorrow?
4. The speaker declares: "Long, long shall I rue thee." What circumstances have made the experience especially unhappy?

from Don Juan *from* Canto I

George Gordon, Lord Byron

The Don Juan legend of the great lover had been popular in Europe for centuries before Byron's version. It first appeared in literary form in a play by the Spanish dramatist Tirso de Molina (1570?–1648). In addition to Byron's *Don Juan* (pronounced jü′ən, not hwän), a play by Molière and Mozart's opera *Don Giovanni* are other famous treatments of the theme.

Byron confided in a letter to Thomas Moore that his poem was probably "too free for these very modest days," and indeed the first five cantos (sections) were published anonymously by Byron, who had already outraged the English public. "Confess, confess, you dog," wrote Byron in a letter, ". . . it may be bawdy but is it not good English? It may be profligate but is it not *life,* is it not *the thing?*"

To his publisher, who had asked for the plan of the poem, Byron wrote: "I had not quite fixed whether to make him end in Hell, or in an unhappy marriage, not knowing which would be the severest. The Spanish tradition says Hell: but it is probably only an Allegory of the other state." By the time of his death, Byron had written sixteen cantos, but *Don Juan* was not in sight of completion.

Stanza 1

I want a hero: an uncommon want,
  When every year and month sends forth
    a new one,
Till, after cloying the gazettes with cant,
  The age discovers he is not the true one;
5 Of such as these I should not care to vaunt,
  I'll therefore take our ancient friend Don
    Juan—
We all have seen him, in the pantomime,
Sent to the devil somewhat ere his time.

10 (Horace makes this the heroic turnpike
    road),
And then your hero tells, whene'er you
    please,
  What went before—by way of episode,
While seated after dinner at his ease,
  Beside his mistress in some soft abode,
15 Palace, or garden, paradise, or cavern,
  Which serves the happy couple for a tavern.

Stanza 6

Most epic poets plunge "in medias res"[1]

---

1. *"in medias res"* (in mā′dē äs räs′), "in the middle of things," from the Latin poet Horace.

Stanza 7

That is the usual method, but not mine—
  My way is to begin with the beginning;
The regularity of my design
20   Forbids all wandering as the worst of
      sinning,
And therefore I shall open with a line
  (Although it cost me half an hour in
      spinning)
Narrating somewhat of Don Juan's father,
And also of his mother, if you'd rather.

Stanza 8

25 In Seville was he born, a pleasant city,
  Famous for oranges and women—he
Who has not seen it will be much to pity,
  So says the proverb—and I quite agree;
Of all the Spanish towns is none more pretty.
30   Cadiz, perhaps—but that you soon may
     see—
Don Juan's parents lived beside the river,
A noble stream, and called the Guadalquivir.

Stanza 9

His father's name was Jóse—*Don*, of course,
  A true Hidalgo,[2] free from every stain
35 Of Moor or Hebrew blood, he traced his
     source
  Through the most Gothic gentlemen of
     Spain;
A better cavalier ne'er mounted horse,
  Or, being mounted, e'er got down again,
Than Jóse, who begot our hero, who
40 Begot—but that's to come—Well, to renew:

Stanza 10

His mother was a learnèd lady, famed
  For every branch of every science
     known—
In every Christian language ever named,
  With virtues equalled by her wit alone:
45 She made the cleverest people quite
     ashamed,
  And even the good with inward envy
     groan,
Finding themselves so very much exceeded

In their own way by all the things that she
  did.

Stanza 13

She knew the Latin—that is, "the Lord's
  prayer,"
50   And Greek—the alphabet—I'm nearly
     sure;
She read some French romances here and
  there,
  Although her mode of speaking was not
     pure;
For native Spanish she had no great care,
  At least her conversation was obscure;
55 Her thoughts were theorems, her words a
  problem,
  As if she deemed that mystery would
     ennoble 'em.

Stanza 15

Some women use their tongues—she *looked*
  a lecture,
  Each eye a sermon, and her brow a
     homily,
An all-in-all sufficient self-director,
60   Like the lamented late Sir Samuel
     Romilly,[3]
The Law's expounder, and the State's
  corrector,
  Whose suicide was almost an anomaly—
One sad example more, that "All is vanity,"—
(The jury brought their verdict in
     "Insanity.")

Stanza 17

65 Oh! she was perfect past all parallel—
  Of any modern female saint's comparison;
So far above the cunning powers of hell,
  Her guardian angel had given up his
     garrison;

---

2. *Hidalgo*, a member of the lower Spanish nobility.
3. *Sir Samuel Romilly*, an English lawyer who
represented Byron's wife in her suit for divorce; he
committed suicide in 1818.

Even her minutest motions went as well
70 As those of the best time-piece made by
       Harrison:[4]
In virtues nothing earthly could surpass her,
Save thine "incomparable oil," Macassar![5]

Stanza 18
Perfect she was, but as perfection is
    Insipid in this naughty world of ours,
75 Where our first parents never learned to kiss
      Till they were exiled from their earlier
         bowers,
    Where all was peace, and innocence, and bliss
      (I wonder how they got through the twelve
         hours),
    Don Jóse, like a lineal son of Eve,
80 Went plucking various fruit without her
       leave.

Stanza 19
He was a mortal of the careless kind,
    With no great love for learning, or the
       learned,
Who chose to go where'er he had a mind,
    And never dreamed his lady was
       concerned;
85 The world, as usual, wickedly inclined
    To see a kingdom or a house o'erturned,
Whispered he had a mistress, some said *two*,
But for domestic quarrels *one* will do.

Stanza 20
Now Donna Inez had, with all her merit,
90   A great opinion of her own good qualities;
Neglect, indeed, requires a saint to bear it,
    And such, indeed, she was in her moralities;
But then she had a devil of a spirit,
    And sometimes mixed up fancies with
       realities,
95 And let few opportunities escape
    Of getting her liege lord into a scrape.

Stanza 23
Don Jóse and his lady quarrelled—*why*,
    Not any of the many could divine,
Though several thousand people chose to try,

100   'Twas surely no concern of theirs nor
         mine;
    I loathe that low vice—curiosity;
       But if there's anything in which I shine,
    'Tis in arranging all my friends' affairs,
    Not having, of my own, domestic cares.

Stanza 24
105 And so I interfered, and with the best
       Intentions, but their treatment was not
          kind;
    I think the foolish people were possessed,
       For neither of them could I ever find,
    Although their porter afterwards confessed—
110   But that's no matter, and the worst's
          behind,
    For little Juan o'er me threw, downstairs,
    A pail of housemaid's water unawares.

Stanza 25
A little curly-headed, good-for-nothing,
    And mischief-making monkey from his
       birth;
115 His parents ne'er agreed except in doting
    Upon the most unquiet imp on earth;
Instead of quarreling, had they been but
       both in
    Their senses, they'd have sent young
       master forth
To school, or had him soundly whipped at
       home.
120 To teach him manners for the time to come.

Stanza 26
Don Jóse and the Donna Inez led
    For some time an unhappy sort of life,
Wishing each other, not divorced, but dead;
    They lived respectably as man and wife,
125 Their conduct was exceedingly well-bred,
    And gave no outward signs of inward
       strife,

---

4. *Harrison*, John Harrison (1693–1776), English
watchmaker who invented the first practical marine
chronometer, enabling sailors to compute accurately their
longitude at sea.
5. *Macassar*, a fragrant oil used as a hair dressing.

Until at length the smothered fire broke out,
And put the business past all kind of doubt.

Stanza 27

For Inez called some druggists and
    physicians,
130   And tried to prove her loving lord was
    mad,
But as he had some lucid intermissions,
    She next decided he was only *bad*;
Yet when they asked her for her depositions,
    No sort of explanation could be had,
135 Save that her duty both to man and God
    Required this conduct—which seemed very
    odd.

Stanza 32

Their friends had tried at reconciliation,
    Then their relations, who made matters
    worse
('Twere hard to tell upon a like occasion
140   To whom it may be best to have
    recourse—
I can't say much for friend or yet relation);
    The lawyers did their utmost for divorce,
But scarce a fee was paid on either side
Before, unluckily, Don Jóse died.

Stanza 33

145 He died: and most unluckily, because,
    According to all hints I could collect
From counsel learned in those kinds of laws
    (Although their talk's obscure and
    circumspect),
His death contrived to spoil a charming
    cause;
150   A thousand pities also with respect
To public feeling, which on this occasion
Was manifested in a great sensation.

Stanza 37

Dying intestate, Juan was sole heir
    To a chancery[6] suit, and messuages,[7] and
    lands,
155 Which, with a long minority and care,
    Promised to turn out well in proper hands:

Inez became sole guardian, which was fair,
    And answered but to nature's just
    demands;
An only son left with an only mother
160 Is brought up much more wisely than another.

Stanza 38

Sagest of women, even of widows, she
    Resolved that Juan should be quite a
    paragon,
And worthy of the noblest pedigree
    (His sire was of Castile, his dam from
    Aragon).
165 Then for accomplishments of chivalry,
    In case our lord the king should go to war
    again,
He learned the arts of riding, fencing,
    gunnery,
And how to scale a fortress—or a nunnery.

Stanza 39

But that which Donna Inez most desired,
170   And saw into herself each day before all
The learnèd tutors whom for him she hired,
    Was that his breeding should be strictly
    moral:
Much into all his studies she inquired,
    And so they were submitted first to her, all,
175 Arts, sciences, no branch was made a
    mystery
To Juan's eyes, excepting natural history.

Stanza 40

The languages, especially the dead,
    The sciences, and most of all the abstruse,
The arts, at least all such as could be said
180   To be the most remote from common use,
In all these he was much and deeply read;
    But not a page of anything that's loose,
Or hints continuation of the species,
Was ever suffered, lest he should grow
    vicious.

---

6. *chancery*, high court in England famous for its delays.
7. *messuages* (mes′wij əz), houses together with adjacent buildings.

Stanza 41

185 His classic studies made a little puzzle,
   Because of filthy loves of gods and
      goddesses,
   Who in the earlier ages raised a bustle,
      But never put on pantaloons or bodices;
   His reverend tutors had at times a tussle,
190   And for their Aeneids, Iliads, and
      Odysseys,
   Were forced to make an odd sort of apology,
   For Donna Inez dreaded the Mythology.

Stanza 44

Juan was taught from out the best edition,
   Expurgated by learnèd men, who place,
195 Judiciously, from out the schoolboy's vision,
   The grosser parts; but, fearful to deface
Too much their modest bard by this
   omission,
   And pitying sore this mutilated case,
They only add them all in an appendix,
200 Which saves, in fact, the trouble of an index.

Stanza 45

For there we have them all "at one fell
   swoop,"
   Instead of being scattered through the
      pages;
They stand forth marshalled in a handsome
   troop,
   To meet the ingenuous youth of future ages,
205 Till some less rigid editor shall stoop
   To call them back into their separate cages,
Instead of standing staring all together,
Like garden gods—and not so decent either.

Stanza 47

Sermons he read, and lectures he endured,
210   And homilies, and lives of all the saints;
To Jerome and to Chrysostom[8] inured,
      He did not take such studies for restraints;
But how faith is acquired, and then ensured,
   So well not one of the aforesaid paints
215 As Saint Augustine in his fine Confessions,[9]
   Which make the reader envy his
      transgressions.

Stanza 48

This, too was a sealed book to little Juan—
   I can't but say that his mamma was right,
If such an education was the true one.
220   She scarcely trusted him from out her
      sight;
   Her maids were old, and if she took a new
      one,
      You might be sure she was a perfect fright;
She did this during even her husband's life—
I recommend as much to every wife.

Stanza 49

225 Young Juan waxed in godliness and grace;
   At six a charming child, and at eleven
With all the promise of as fine a face
   As e'er to man's maturer growth was
      given—.
He studied steadily and grew apace,
230   And seemed, at least, in the right road to
      heaven,
For half his days were passed at church, the
   other
Between his tutors, confessor, and mother.

Stanza 50

At six, I said, he was a charming child,
   At twelve he was a fine, but quiet boy;
235 Although in infancy a little wild,
   They tamed him down amongst them: to
      destroy
His natural spirit not in vain they toiled.
   At least it seemed so; and his mother's joy
Was to declare how sage, and still, and
   steady,
240 Her young philosopher was grown already.

Stanza 54

Young Juan now was sixteen years of age,
   Tall, handsome, slender, but well knit: he
      seemed

---

8. *Jerome . . . Chrysostom,* early Christian writers.
9. *Saint Augustine . . . Confessions.* In his *Confessions*
Saint Augustine (354–430) describes a variety of his
youthful sins.

Active, though not so sprightly, as a page;
  And everybody but his mother deemed
245 Him almost man; but she flew in a rage
  And bit her lips (for else she might have
      screamed)
If any said so, for to be precocious
Was in her eyes a thing the most atrocious.

Stanza 55
Amongst her numerous acquaintance, all
250   Selected for discretion and devotion,
There was the Donna Julia, whom to call
  Pretty were but to give a feeble notion
Of many charms in her as natural
  As sweetness to the flower, or salt to
      ocean,
255 Her zone to Venus, or his bow to Cupid,
(But this last simile is trite and stupid).

Stanza 60
Her eye (I'm very fond of handsome eyes)
  Was large and dark, suppressing half its
      fire
Until she spoke, then through its soft disguise
260   Flashed an expression more of pride than
      ire,
And love than either; and there would arise
  A something in them which was not desire,
But would have been, perhaps, but for the
      soul
Which struggled through and chastened
      down the whole.

Stanza 61
265 Her glossy hair was clustered o'er a brow
  Bright with intelligence, and fair, and
      smooth;
Her eyebrow's shape was like the aërial bow,
  Her cheek all purple with the beam of
      youth,
Mounting, at times, to a transparent glow,
270   As if her veins ran lightning; she, in sooth,
Possessed an air and grace by no means
      common;
Her stature tall—I hate a dumpy woman.

Stanza 62
Wedded she was some years, and to a man
  Of fifty, and such husbands are in plenty;
275 And yet, I think, instead of such a ONE
  'Twere better to have TWO of five-and-
      twenty,
Especially in countries near the sun:
  And now I think on't, "mi vien in mente,"[10]
Ladies even of the most uneasy virtue
280 Prefer a spouse whose age is short of thirty.

Stanza 69
Juan she saw, and, as a pretty child,
  Caressed him often—such a thing might
      be
Quite innocently done, and harmless styled,
  When she had twenty years, and thirteen
      he;
285 But I am not so sure I should have smiled
  When he was sixteen, Julia twenty-three;
These few short years make wondrous
      alterations,
Particularly amongst sunburnt nations.

Stanza 70
Whate'er the cause might be, they had
      become
290   Changed; for the dame grew distant, the
      youth shy,
Their looks cast down, their greetings almost
      dumb,
  And much embarrassment in either eye;
There surely will be little doubt with some
  That Donna Julia knew the reason why,
295 But as for Juan, he had no more notion
Than he who never saw the sea, of ocean.

Stanza 71
Yet Julia's very coldness still was kind,
  And tremulously gentle her small hand
Withdrew itself from his, but left behind
300   A little pressure, thrilling, and so bland

---

10. *"mi vien in mente"* (mē vē en' in men'tā), "it comes
to mind." [Italian]

Detail of *Woman with Guitar* by John Phillip. *Nottingham Castle Museum and Art Gallery, England*

And slight, so very slight, that to the mind
　　'Twas but a doubt; but ne'er magician's wand
Wrought change with all Armida's[11] fairy art
　　Like what this light touch left on Juan's heart.

Stanza 72

305 And if she met him, though she smiled no more,
　　She looked a sadness sweeter than her smile,
As if her heart had deeper thoughts in store
　　She must not own, but cherished more the while

For that compression in its burning core;
310 　Even innocence itself has many a wile,
And will not dare to trust itself with truth,
And love is taught hypocrisy from youth.

Stanza 75

Poor Julia's heart was in an awkward state;
　　She felt it going, and resolved to make
315 The noblest efforts for herself and mate,
　　For honor's, pride's, religion's, virtue's sake.
Her resolutions were most truly great,
　　And almost might have made a Tarquin[12] quake:
She prayed the Virgin Mary for her grace,
320 As being the best judge of a lady's case.

Stanza 76

She vowed she never would see Juan more,
　　And next day paid a visit to his mother,
And looked extremely at the opening door,
　　Which, by the Virgin's grace, let in another;
325 Grateful she was, and yet a little sore—
　　Again it opens, it can be no other,
'Tis surely Juan now—No! I'm afraid
That night the Virgin was no further prayed.

Stanza 77

She now determined that a virtuous woman
330 　Should rather face and overcome temptation,
That flight was base and dastardly, and no man
　　Should ever give her heart the least sensation;
That is to say, a thought beyond the common
　　Preference, that we must feel upon occasion,
335 For people who are pleasanter than others,
But then they only seem so many brothers.

---

11. **Armida,** a sorceress mentioned in *Jerusalem Delivered,* an epic poem by the Italian Renaissance poet Torquato Tasso (1544–1595).
12. *a Tarquin,* one of the legendary kings of ancient Rome, noted for their lustiness.

Stanza 78

And even if by chance—and who can tell?
   The devil's so very sly—she should
     discover
That all within was not so very well,
340   And, if still free, that such a lover
Might please perhaps, a virtuous wife can
     quell
   Such thoughts, and be the better when
     they're over;
And if the man should ask, 'tis but denial:
I recommend young ladies to make trial.

Stanza 79

345 And then there are such things as love divine,
   Bright and immaculate, unmixed and pure,
Such as the angels think so very fine,
   And matrons, who would be no less
     secure,
Platonic, perfect, "just such love as mine":
350   Thus Julia said—and thought so, to be
     sure,
And so I'd have her think, were I the man
On whom her reveries celestial ran.

Stanza 86

So much for Julia. Now we'll turn to Juan.
   Poor little fellow! he had no idea
355 Of his own case, and never hit the true one;
   In feelings quick as Ovid's Miss Medea,[13]
He puzzled over what he found a new one,
   But not as yet imagined it could be a
Thing quite in course, and not at all
     alarming,
360 Which, with a little patience, might grow
     charming.

Stanza 87

Silent and pensive, idle, restless, slow,
   His home deserted for the lonely wood,
Tormented with a wound he could not know,
   His, like all deep grief, plunged in
     solitude:
365 I'm fond myself of solitude or so,
   But then, I beg it may be understood,
By solitude I mean a Sultan's, not

A hermit's, with a harem for a grot.

Stanza 90

Young Juan wandered by the glassy brooks,
370   Thinking unutterable things; he threw
Himself at length within the leafy nooks
   Where the wild branch of the cork forest
     grew;
There poets find materials for their books,
   And every now and then we read them
     through,
375 So that their plan and prosody are eligible,
Unless, like Wordsworth, they prove
     unintelligible.

Stanza 91

He, Juan (and not Wordsworth), so pursued
   His self-communion with his own high
     soul,
Until his mighty heart, in its great mood,
380   Had mitigated part, though not the whole
Of its disease; he did the best he could
   With things not very subject to control,
And turned, without perceiving his
     condition,
Like Coleridge, into a metaphysician.

Stanza 92

385 He thought about himself, and the whole
     earth,
   Of man the wonderful, and of the stars,
And how the deuce they ever could have
     birth;
   And then he thought of earthquakes, and
     of wars,
How many miles the moon might have in
     girth,
390   Of air-balloons, and of the many bars
To perfect knowledge of the boundless
     skies—
And then he thought of Donna Julia's eyes.

1818   1819

---

13. *Ovid's Miss Medea.* In the *Metamorphoses*, Ovid presents Medea as a quick-tempered woman who took dreadful revenge on Jason for deserting her.

THINK AND DISCUSS
Understanding
1. How did Don Jóse and Donna Inez raise Juan? According to the speaker in stanza 25, how *should* they have treated him instead?
2. What happened to Don Jóse's estate following his sudden death?
3. Describe the teachers and servants Juan was surrounded with during his youth.

Analyzing
4. In stanza 6, the speaker refers to one of the **epic** conventions. What is the convention? What use does he intend to make of it in his own epic, as he tells us in stanza 7?
5. In stanza 7, the speaker states that his plan for the poem "Forbids all wandering as the worst of sinning," and then he proceeds immediately to digress. Point out examples of "wandering" in other stanzas.
6. In stanzas 10–18 Donna Inez is described. The speaker says, "Oh! she was perfect past all parallel." What examples of her character and behavior reveal that this statement is **ironic?**
7. What view of marriage is conveyed through the description of Don Jóse and Donna Inez's relationship?
8. What plans does Donna Inez have for her son? What is the speaker's attitude toward these plans?
9. Which aspects of Don Juan's education are most sharply satirized? What comment is the speaker making about the society of his time?
10. The encounter between Donna Julia and Don Juan exploits the stock comedy situation of the beautiful young woman, married to an old husband, who gets involved with a younger man. How sincere are Donna Julia's efforts to resist temptation?

Extending
11. What similarities do you find between *Don Juan* and the poetry of Alexander Pope?

REVIEWING: Tone H2
See Handbook of Literary Terms, p. 932
Tone is the author's attitude toward his or her subject matter and toward the audience. The tone of a poem or a story can be said to be serious, bitter, casual, humorous, or satirical, among many possibilities.

1. How would you describe the tone of *Don Juan?*
2. Find some typical statements that contribute to this tone.

COMPOSITION
Analyzing Byron's Satire
Byron himself described *Don Juan* as "a satire on the abuses of the present state of society." In a paper of six to eight paragraphs, identify and discuss the "abuses" exposed in this excerpt. Start by listing the targets of satire you intend to discuss; then write your analysis, taking up each point in its order of importance. Consider, for example, what the poem has to say about love, marriage, parenting, and education. What human vices, such as hypocrisy, social pretension, and complacency, are specifically attacked? Be sure to incorporate citations from the text to illustrate and enrich your discussion. In your conclusion, you may wish to suggest what positive ideals are being emphasized through the satiric exposure of wrongs.

Writing a Persuasive Speech
Select an aspect of the educational program of your high school that you believe needs improving. In a persuasive paper of five to six paragraphs that could be read to your local school board, start by defining the problem and stating its urgency. After making any necessary concessions, using examples from your own experience and that of your classmates, explain what you perceive as currently harmful to a young person's education. In your conclusion, recommend specific actions you wish the school board to take. Your overall tone should be forceful, but still courteous and respectful.

Like Byron, Shelley was a controversial personality whose reputation was marred by scandal. He was known for his personal charm, unwavering opposition to tyranny, and great gifts. Unlike Byron, whose literary reputation was legendary during his lifetime, Shelley achieved recognition only after death. By the end of the nineteenth century, however, he had become a primary force in English poetry, influencing the work of such later writers as Browning, Swinburne, Hardy, and Yeats.

Shelley was the eldest son of a well-to-do country squire who never understood nor was able to control his maverick child. During his unhappy school years, Shelley was bullied by the older boys because of his slight build and moody shyness; he became known at Eton as "mad Shelley" because of his eccentric ways. Although a brilliant student, he was always resentful of authority. At Oxford his rebelliousness and nonconformist behavior caused him severe problems, especially since he had become a convert to the radical philosophy of William Godwin. His collaboration on a pamphlet entitled *The Necessity of Atheism* resulted in his abrupt expulsion from Oxford and a further strain in his relationship with his parents.

Soon after leaving for London, Shelley eloped with sixteen-year-old Harriet Westbrooke, with whom he had two children. Three years later he fell in love with William Godwin's daughter, Mary, and eloped with her to Switzerland, ringing the final knell on his public reputation. In 1816 Harriet committed suicide and, shortly thereafter, Shelley married Mary Godwin.

In 1818 Shelley and Mary moved to Italy. Shelley's last four years were a time of close friendships, most notably with Byron, and highly productive work, including the writing of a tragedy, *The Cenci;* his masterpiece, *Prometheus Unbound;* and numerous lyrics, such as "Ode to the West Wind," "Ozymandias," "Ode to a Skylark," and "The Cloud." During the year 1821 he published his magnificent elegy for Keats, "Adonais," and *A Defense of Poetry.*

In 1822, when Shelley was approaching his thirtieth birthday, he was drowned while sailing off the Italian coast. His body washed ashore ten days later. A volume of Keats was found in one pocket and a volume of Sophocles in the other. He was cremated by friends on a funeral pyre on the beach. Byron was present and swam out to watch the flames that devoured his friend and fellow exile. Shelley's ashes were buried near Keats's grave in the Protestant Cemetery in Rome. Describing his valued friend, Byron called Shelley, "the best and least selfish man I ever knew. I never knew one who was not a beast in comparison."

Shelley had worshipped Wordsworth when Wordsworth was a liberal activist and a courageous spokesman for "truth and liberty" in literature and politics. In later life, however, Wordsworth grew very conservative, turning his back on causes he earlier espoused. In "To Wordsworth" Shelley laments the change in his former hero.

To Wordsworth

Percy Bysshe Shelley

Poet of Nature, thou has wept to know
That things depart which never may return:
Childhood and youth, friendship and love's
    first glow,
Have fled like sweet dreams, leaving thee to
    mourn.
5 These common woes I feel. One loss is mine
Which thou too feel'st, yet I alone deplore.
Thou wert as a lone star, whose light did shine
On some frail bark in winter's midnight roar:
Thou hast like to a rock-built refuge stood
10 Above the blind and battling multitude:
In honored poverty thy voice did weave
Songs consecrate to truth and liberty,—
Deserting these, thou leavest me to grieve,
Thus having been, that thou shouldst cease to
    be.

1815   1816

England in 1819

An old, mad, blind, despised, and dying king[1]—
Princes, the dregs of their dull race, who flow
Through public scorn—mud from a muddy
    spring;
Rulers who neither see, nor feel, nor know,
5 But leechlike to their fainting country cling,
Till they drop, blind in blood, without a blow;
A people starved and stabbed in the untilled
    field—
An army, which liberticide and prey
Makes as a two-edged sword to all who wield;
10 Golden and sanguine laws which tempt and slay;
Religion Christless, Godless—a book sealed;
A Senate—Time's worst statute[2] unrepealed—
Are graves, from which a glorious Phantom[3]
    may
Burst, to illumine your tempestuous day.

1819   1839

THINK AND DISCUSS

TO WORDSWORTH

Understanding

1. What four "common woes" that Wordsworth experienced and wrote about has Shelley also known?
2. In lines 7–10, to what two things does the poet compare the Wordsworth of the past?

Analyzing

3. Explain the double meaning of the last line, especially of the words "been" and "be."

ENGLAND IN 1819

Understanding

1. To what are England's rulers compared in line 5?
2. What does the poet say is missing from the religion of his day?

Analyzing

3. What is the condition of England as Shelley views it?
4. What specific faults of the country's rulers does the sonnet identify?
5. In the last two lines of the poem, what is predicted?
6. To what does the word "graves" (line 13) refer?
7. What is the tone of the poem?

Extending

8. How does this sonnet compare with Wordsworth's "London, 1802"?

---

1. *An old . . . king,* George III, who died in 1820, blind and insane.
2. *Time's worst statute,* the law restricting the civil liberties of Roman Catholics, which was not repealed until 1829.
3. *Phantom,* revolution.

Ozymandias

Percy Bysshe Shelley

According to an early Greek historian, Ozymandias (oz′i man′dē əs), more commonly known as Ramses II, was an Egyptian pharaoh whose huge statue bore the following inscription: "I am Ozymandias, King of Kings; if anyone wishes to know what I am and where I lie, let him surpass me in some of my exploits."

I met a traveler from an antique land
Who said: Two vast and trunkless legs of stone
Stand in the desert . . . Near them, on the sand,
Half sunk, a shattered visage lies, whose frown,
5 And wrinkled lip, and sneer of cold command,
Tell that its sculptor well those passions read
Which yet survive, stamped on these lifeless
    things,
The hand that mocked them, and the heart
    that fed:[1]
And on the pedestal these words appear:

10 "My name is Ozymandias, king of kings:
Look on my works, ye Mighty, and despair!"
Nothing beside remains. Round the decay
Of that colossal wreck, boundless and bare
The lone and level sands stretch far away.

1817   **1818**

---

1. *The hand . . . fed,* that is, the passions carved in the stone have outlived the hand that sculpted ("mocked" or imitated) them and the pharaoh's heart that nurtured them.

Funerary Temple of Ramses II at Thebes, sketched by David Roberts in 1838.

Ode to the West Wind

Percy Bysshe Shelley

Of the inspiration for "Ode to the West Wind," Shelley wrote: "This poem was conceived and chiefly written in a wood that skirts the Arno, near Florence, and on a day when that tempestuous wind, whose temperature is at once mild and animating, was collecting the vapors which pour down the autumnal rains. They began, as I foresaw, at sunset with a violent tempest of hail and rain, attended by that magnificent thunder and lightning peculiar to the . . . regions."

1

O wild West Wind, thou breath of Autumn's
    being,
Thou, from whose unseen presence the
    leaves dead
Are driven, like ghosts from an enchanter
    fleeing,

Yellow, and black, and pale, and hectic red,
5 Pestilence-stricken multitudes: O thou,
Who chariotest to their dark wintry bed

The wingèd seeds, where they lie cold and
    low,
Each like a corpse within its grave, until
Thine azure sister of the Spring shall blow

10 Her clarion o'er the dreaming earth, and fill
(Driving sweet buds like flocks to feed in air)
With living hues and odors plain and hill:

Wild Spirit, which art moving everywhere;
Destroyer and preserver; hear, oh, hear!

2

15 Thou on whose stream, mid the steep sky's
    commotion,
Loose clouds like earth's decaying leaves are
    shed,

Shook from the tangled boughs of Heaven
    and Ocean,

Angels of rain and lightning: there are spread
On the blue surface of thine aëry surge,
20 Like the bright hair uplifted from the head

Of some fierce Maenad,[1] even from the dim
    verge
Of the horizon to the zenith's height,
The locks of the approaching storm. Thou dirge

Of the dying year, to which this closing night
25 Will be the dome of a vast sepulcher,
Vaulted with all thy congregated might

Of vapors, from whose solid atmosphere
Black rain, and fire, and hail will burst: oh hear!

3

Thou who didst waken from his summer
    dreams
30 The blue Mediterranean, where he lay,
Lulled by the coil of his crystàlline streams,

---

1. **Maenad** (mē′nad), a priestess of Dionysus, Greek god of wine, who was worshiped with savage, orgiastic rites.

Beside a pumice isle in Baiae's bay,[2]
And saw in sleep old palaces and towers
Quivering within the wave's intenser day,

35 All overgrown with azure moss and flowers
So sweet, the sense faints picturing them!
    Thou
For whose path the Atlantic's level powers[3]

Cleave themselves into chasms, while far below
The sea-blooms and the oozy woods which
    wear
40 The sapless foliage of the ocean, know

Thy voice, and suddenly grow gray with fear,
And tremble and despoil themselves: oh, hear!

4

If I were a dead leaf thou mightest bear;
If I were a swift cloud to fly with thee;
45 A wave to pant beneath thy power, and share

The impulse of thy strength, only less free
Than thou, O uncontrollable! If even
I were as in my boyhood, and could be

The comrade of thy wanderings over
    Heaven,
50 As then, when to outstrip the skyey speed
Scarce seemed a vision; I would ne'er have
    striven

As thus with thee in prayer in my sore need.
Oh, lift me as a wave, a leaf, a cloud!
I fall upon the thorns of life! I bleed!

55 A heavy weight of hours has chained and bowed
One too like thee: tameless, and swift, and
    proud.

5

Make me thy lyre, even as the forest is:
What if my leaves are falling like its own!
The tumult of thy mighty harmonies

60 Will take from both a deep, autumnal tone,
Sweet though in sadness. Be thou, Spirit fierce,
My spirit! Be thou me, impetuous one!

Drive my dead thoughts over the universe
Like withered leaves to quicken a new birth!
65 And, by the incantation of this verse,

Scatter, as from an unextinguished hearth
Ashes and sparks, my words among mankind!
Be through my lips to unawakened earth

The trumpet of a prophecy! O Wind,
70 If Winter comes, can Spring be far behind?
1819   1820

---

2. **Baiae's** (bä′yäz) **bay.** The modern village of Baia is a seaport about ten miles from Naples in Italy.
3. **the Atlantic's level powers,** the surface of the ocean.

THINK AND DISCUSS
OZYMANDIAS
Understanding
1. According to lines 1–4, what has happened to the statue?
2. What facial expressions did the sculptor stamp on the "shattered visage"?
3. Besides the statue, what remains of Ozymandias's mighty works?

Analyzing
4. Given the description of the present condition of the statue and landscape, what **irony** is there in the inscription on the pedestal?
5. What does the line "The hand that mocked them, and the heart that fed" ironically explain about both the sculptor and the tyrant Ozymandias?

Extending

6. What comment, if any, is Shelley making on tyranny?

ODE TO THE WEST WIND
Understanding

1. What is the "azure sister of the Spring" (line 9)? What are the "Angels of rain and lightning" (line 18)?
2. According to the third stanza, what has been the effect of the West Wind on "The blue Mediterranean"? On the "Atlantic's level powers"?
3. In stanza 5, what does the speaker ask the West Wind to do with his thoughts and words?

Analyzing

4. "Ode to the West Wind" is divided into five sections. What is the topic of each section?
5. What two contradictory forces does the West Wind represent? What echoes of this **para-dox** do you find throughout the poem? In what sense is the West Wind a spirit "moving everywhere"?
6. In the fourth stanza the poet draws a comparison between himself and the West Wind. How are they alike? In what ways are they different?
7. The fifth stanza begins with the request, "Make me thy lyre," and concludes with the command, "Be through my lips. . ./The trumpet of a prophecy!" What change in the poet's attitude toward himself and in the **tone** of the poem is marked by the movement from "lyre" to "trumpet"?
8. What does Shelley see in the West Wind that he envies and desires for himself as a poet?
9. In what sense would Shelley as poet, like the West Wind, function as both "destroyer" and "preserver"?

Extending

10. How do lines 47–52 echo Wordsworth's conceptions of childhood, as expressed in such poems as "Tintern Abbey" and the "Intimations Ode"?

VOCABULARY
Synonyms

A synonym is a word that means the same as another word. Copy each of the following quotations on separate paper, substituting for the italicized word another word or phrase that is synonymous.

1. "Princes, the *dregs* of their dull race. . . ."
2. ". . .Near them, on the sand,/Half sunk, a shattered *visage* lies. . . ."
3. "Thou dirge/Of the dying year, to which this closing night/Will be the dome of a vast *sepulcher*. . . ."
4. "Be thou me, *impetuous* one!"
5. "Scatter, as from an *unextinguished* hearth/Ashes and sparks, my words among mankind!"

COMPOSITION
Writing a Poem

Shelley's "England in 1819" catalogues social ills in the hope of igniting revolutionary reforms. Using Shelley's sonnet as your model, select some aspect of contemporary life that you feel deserves similar criticism. List the aspects you intend to criticize in your poem; then arrange details to build emotional intensity. You need not use the sonnet form, though it well lends itself to this kind of topic. In the concluding lines of your poem, be sure to make your reader aware whether you hold out any hope for the future.

Analyzing Your Writing Process

In "Ode to the West Wind," Shelley expresses concern about the writer's sources of inspiration and impact on the world. In a paper of six to eight paragraphs, explain the uses of writing in your life and describe your personal "writing process." Consider such questions as these: Why is writing important in your life? How do you go about writing a paper? Is writing relatively easy or hard for you? At what times of the day do you work best and under what conditions? Do you have any special habits or tools that make the writing task easier? Which phases of the process do you find easiest, which most difficult? Overall, portray your actions from the time a paper is first assigned and describe your feelings about what you finally achieve.

John Keats
1795–1821

John Keats was born in London, the eldest of four children. His father, a cockney stable keeper, was killed in a riding accident when John was nine; six years later his mother died of tuberculosis. From the age of eight to fifteen, Keats attended a small school at Enfield, where he distinguished himself as a brilliant student and acquired his love of English poetry. At the age of fifteen, soon after his mother's death, his guardians apprenticed him to an apothecary (druggist) and surgeon. Although he spent some time working in London hospitals and qualified to practice as an apothecary, he abandoned this profession to devote his time to literature.

With support from the critic Leigh Hunt, the poet William Wordsworth, and the essayist Charles Lamb, Keats at age twenty-one began his literary career in earnest. According to a school friend, for Keats "the greatest men in the world were the Poets, and to rank among them was the chief object of his ambition." In 1818 Keats returned home to nurse his younger brother Tom until the latter's death from tuberculosis. Soon after, the publication of *Endymion*, his first sustained poetic effort, received unduly harsh criticism. Critics, mocking his cockney heritage and his medical training, advised him to go back to his "plaster, pills, and ointment boxes" and leave the writing of poetry to the educated and cultured. This adverse publicity kept his poetry from selling and left him almost destitute. Meanwhile, Keats fell in love with the beautiful and lively Fanny Brawne. Their intense and hopeless love affair was an added source of anguish for the passionate young man who desired marriage but found himself thwarted by financial difficulties and worsening health.

Despite sorrow and adversities, the year 1819 was for Keats one of profound growth as a poet. Uplifted by an unusually beautiful and early spring, he produced such exalted works as "The Eve of St. Agnes," "La Belle Dame Sans Merci," and his great odes. The following spring his last book was published—*Lamia, Isabella, The Eve of St. Agnes, and Other Poems* (the book found in Shelley's pocket after his drowning)—a work that one critic has called "the greatest single volume of English poetry of the nineteenth century."

Though deeply influenced by his reading of Spenser, Shakespeare, and Milton, Keats took Wordsworth as his chief poetic guide, believing with him that poetry should be the creation of concrete sensual images in the service of profound creative thought. In contrast to most of his contemporaries, he strove to subordinate his own personality in order to concentrate exclusively on the subject itself, an artistic capacity to which he gave the term, "Negative Capability."

After a desperate flight to Italy to find a warmer climate in which to regain his health, Keats died of tuberculosis on February 23, 1821, at the age of twenty-five. He lies buried in the Protestant Cemetery in Rome under the epitaph he wrote for himself, "Here lies one whose name was writ in water."

When I Have Fears

John Keats

When I have fears that I may cease to be
Before my pen has gleaned my teeming brain,
Before high-pilèd books, in charact'ry,[1]
Hold like rich garners the full-ripened grain;
5 When I behold, upon the night's starred face,
Huge cloudy symbols of a high romance,
And think that I may never live to trace
Their shadows, with the magic hand of chance;
And when I feel, fair creature of an hour,
10 That I shall never look upon thee more,
Never have relish in the faery power
Of unreflecting love!—then on the shore
Of the wide world I stand alone, and think
Till Love and Fame to nothingness do sink.

1818   1848

---

1. *charact'ry*, characters or letters; that is, writing.

On First Looking into Chapman's Homer

John Keats

Charles Cowden Clarke, an old friend and former teacher, stimulated Keats's interest in Greek literature when he presented him with George Chapman's spirited translation of Homer's *Iliad*. To Keats, who knew no Greek, it was a revelation and a delight; he spent the whole night reading it. About ten o'clock the next morning, Keats sent Clarke a communication. It was the following sonnet.

Much have I traveled in the realms of gold,
    And many goodly states and kingdoms seen;
    Round many western islands have I been
Which bards in fealty to Apollo[1] hold.
5 Oft of one wide expanse had I been told
    That deep-browed Homer ruled as his
        demesne;[2]
    Yet did I never breathe its pure serene
Till I heard Chapman speak out loud and bold:
Then felt I like some watcher of the skies
10   When a new planet swims into his ken;
Or like stout Cortez[3] when with eagle eyes
    He stared at the Pacific—and all his men
Looked at each other with a wild surmise—
    Silent, upon a peak in Darien.[4]

1816

---

1. *Apollo*, god of poetry and music.
2. *demesne* (di mēn'), domain.
3. *Cortez*. Balboa, not Cortez, discovered the Pacific Ocean.
4. *Darien*, in Panama.

Did Keats Make a Blunder?

The fact that Balboa, not Cortez, first discovered the Pacific has disturbed commentators on Keats's sonnet "On First Looking into Chapman's Homer" for many years. Why does Keats, who was a voracious reader from boyhood and acquainted with most of the available literature on historic voyages, use Cortez as his symbol of discovery? Perhaps he deliberately chose Cortez to imply that one need not be "the first" to make a discovery for that discovery to have profound personal significance. After all, Keats was not the first to read Chapman's famous translation of Homer (which had been in print for two centuries), nor was his discovery of Chapman's version his first contact with Homer (he had read Pope's translation). He was talking about the satisfactions of an inner voyage, where "first" no longer counts.

La Belle Dame Sans Merci

John Keats

Translated from the French, the title means "the beautiful lady without pity." The poem is probably based on the centuries-old ballad "True Thomas," which tells how a man was enchanted by the Queen of Elfland and lured to her home, where he had to serve her for seven years. Keats takes up that story after the seven years are over and the spell has been broken. The situation is considered to be symbolic of hopeless love.

1

O what can ail thee, Knight-at-arms,
  Alone and palely loitering?
The sedge has withered from the lake
  And no birds sing!

2

5 O what can ail thee, Knight-at-arms,
  So haggard, and so woebegone?
The squirrel's granary is full
  And the harvest's done.

3

I see a lily on thy brow
10 With anguish moist and fever dew,
And on thy cheeks a fading rose
  Fast withereth too.

4

I met a Lady in the Meads,
  Full beautiful, a faery's child,
15 Her hair was long, her foot was light,
  And her eyes were wild.

5

I made a Garland for her head,
  And bracelets too, and fragrant zone;[1]
She looked at me as she did love
20 And made sweet moan.

6

I set her on my pacing steed
  And nothing else saw all day long,
For sidelong would she bend and sing
  A faery's song.

1. *zone*, girdle.

7

25 She found me roots of relish sweet,
And honey wild, and manna dew,
And sure in language strange she said
"I love thee true."

8

She took me to her elfin grot
30 And there she wept and sighed full sore,
And there I shut her wild wild eyes
With kisses four.

9

And there she lullèd me asleep,
And there I dreamed—Ah, woe betide!—
35 The latest dream I ever dreamt
On the cold hill side.

10

I saw pale Kings, and Princes too,
Pale warriors, death-pale were they all;
They cried, "La Belle Dame sans Merci
40 Hath thee in thrall!"

11

I saw their starved lips in the gloam
With horrid warning gapèd wide,
And I awoke, and found me here
On the cold hill's side.

Detail of *La Belle Dame Sans Merci* by John William Waterhouse. 1893. *Hessisches Landesmuseum, Darmstadt*

12

45 And this is why I sojourn here,
Alone and palely loitering;
Though the sedge is withered from the lake
And no birds sing.

1819   **1820**

HT See ONOMATOPOEIA in the Handbook of Literary Terms, page 927.

Ode to a Nightingale

John Keats

After the death of his brother Tom, Keats spent nearly a year with a friend, Charles Armitage Brown, who described the circumstances surrounding the writing of the "Ode to a Nightingale" as follows:

"In the spring a nightingale had built her nest near my house. Keats felt a tranquil and continual joy in her song; one morning he took his chair from the breakfast table to the grass plot under a plum tree, where he sat for two or three hours. When he came into the house, I perceived he had some scraps of paper in his hand, and these he was quietly thrusting behind the books. On inquiry, I found those scraps, four or five in number; the writing was not well legible, and it was difficult to arrange the stanzas. With his assistance I succeeded, and this was his 'Ode to a Nightingale.' ''

The poem is a reverie—a succession of dreamlike thoughts—inspired by the bird's song. In the first stanza the poet is just sinking into the reverie; in the last stanza he comes out of it and back to consciousness of the real world. The first and last stanzas constitute a frame for the reverie proper.

My heart aches, and a drowsy numbness pains
  My sense, as though of hemlock[1] I had drunk,
Or emptied some dull opiate to the drains
  One minute past, and Lethe-wards[2] had sunk:
5 'Tis not through envy of thy happy lot,
  But being too happy in thine happiness—
    That thou, light-wingèd Dryad[3] of the trees,
      In some melodious plot
Of beechen green, and shadows numberless,
10   Singest of summer in full-throated ease.

O for a draft of vintage! that hath been
  Cooled a long age in the deep-delvèd earth,
Tasting of Flora[4] and the country green,
  Dance, and Provençal song,[5] and sunburnt mirth!
15 O for a beaker full of the warm South,
  Full of the true, the blushful Hippocrene,[6]
    With beaded bubbles winking at the brim,
      And purple-stainèd mouth;
That I might drink, and leave the world unseen,
20   And with thee fade away into the forest dim:

Fade far away, dissolve, and quite forget
  What thou among the leaves hast never known,
The weariness, the fever, and the fret
  Here, where men sit and hear each other groan;
25 Where palsy shakes a few, sad, last gray hairs,
  Where youth grows pale, and specter-thin, and dies;
    Where but to think is to be full of sorrow
      And leaden-eyed despairs,
Where Beauty cannot keep her lustrous eyes,

30 Or new love pine at them beyond tomorrow.

Away! away! for I will fly to thee,
  Not charioted by Bacchus[7] and his pards,
But on the viewless[8] wings of Poesy,
  Though the dull brain perplexes and retards:
35 Already with thee! tender is the night,
  And haply the Queen-Moon is on her throne,
    Clustered around by all her starry Fays;
      But here there is no light,
Save what from heaven is with the breezes blown
40   Through verdurous glooms and winding mossy ways.

I cannot see what flowers are at my feet,
  Nor what soft incense hangs upon the boughs,
But, in embalmèd darkness, guess each sweet
  Wherewith the seasonable month endows
45 The grass, the thicket, and the fruit tree wild;
  White hawthorn, and the pastoral eglantine;
    Fast fading violets covered up in leaves;
      And mid-May's eldest child,

---

1. *hemlock,* a poison.
2. *Lethe-wards,* towards Lethe, the river of forgetfulness in Hades.
3. *Dryad,* a tree nymph.
4. *Flora,* goddess of the flowers and the spring.
5. *Provençal song.* Provence in southern France was famous in the Middle Ages for the songs of its troubadours.
6. *Hippocrene,* a fountain on Mt. Helicon in Greece, sacred to the Muses.
7. *Bacchus,* god of wine, who was often represented as riding in a carriage drawn by leopards (pards).
8. *viewless,* invisible.

The Enchanted Castle by Claude Lorrain, a seventeenth-century French painting supposedly remembered by Keats when he wrote the "Ode to a Nightingale." *National Gallery, London*

The coming musk-rose, full of dewy wine,
50   The murmurous haunt of flies on summer eves.

Darkling I listen; and, for many a time,
  I have been half in love with easeful Death,
Called him soft names in many a musèd rhyme,
  To take into the air my quiet breath;
55 Now more than ever seems it rich to die,
  To cease upon the midnight with no pain,
    While thou art pouring forth thy soul abroad
      In such an ecstasy!
Still wouldst thou sing, and I have ears in vain—
60   To thy high requiem become a sod.
Thou wast not born for death, immortal Bird!
  No hungry generations tread thee down;
The voice I hear this passing night was heard
  In ancient days by emperor and clown:[9]
65 Perhaps the selfsame song that found a path
  Through the sad heart of Ruth, when sick for home,

She stood in tears amid the alien corn;[10]
  The same that oft-times hath
Charmed magic casements, opening on the foam
70   Of perilous seas, in faery lands forlorn.

Forlorn! the very word is like a bell
  To toll me back from thee to my sole self!
Adieu! the fancy cannot cheat so well
  As she is famed to do, deceiving elf.
75 Adieu! Adieu! thy plaintive anthem fades
  Past the near meadows, over the still stream,
    Up the hillside; and now 'tis buried deep
      In the next valley glades:
Was it a vision, or a waking dream?
80   Fled is that music—Do I wake or sleep?
1819   **1820**

---

9. *clown,* peasant.
10. *Ruth . . . corn.* According to the Bible story, Ruth left her homeland to go with Naomi, her mother-in-law, to Judah, a foreign country to her, where she worked in the corn (wheat) fields (Ruth 2:1–23).

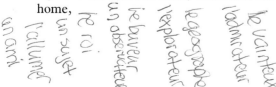

Keats 513

Ode on a Grecian Urn

John Keats

Thou still unravished bride of quietness,
    Thou foster child of Silence and slow Time,
Sylvan historian, who canst thus express
    A flowery tale more sweetly than our rhyme—
5 What leaf-fringed legend haunts about thy
        shape
    Of deities or mortals, or of both,
        In Tempe[1] or the dales of Arcady?[2]
    What men or gods are these? What maidens
        loath?
What mad pursuit? What struggle to escape?
10   What pipes and timbrels? What wild
        ecstasy?

Heard melodies are sweet, but those unheard
    Are sweeter; therefore, ye soft pipes, play
        on;
Not to the sensual ear, but, more endeared,
    Pipe to the spirit ditties of no tone:
15 Fair youth, beneath the trees, thou canst not
        leave
Thy song, nor ever can those trees be bare;
    Bold lover, never, never canst thou kiss,
Though winning near the goal—yet, do not
        grieve;
She cannot fade, though thou hast not thy
        bliss,
20   Forever will thou love, and she be fair!

Ah, happy, happy boughs! that cannot shed
    Your leaves, nor ever bid the spring adieu;
And, happy melodist, unwearièd,
    Forever piping songs forever new;
25 More happy love! more happy, happy love!
    Forever warm and still to be enjoyed,
        Forever panting, and forever young;
All breathing human passion far above,

That leaves a heart high-sorrowful and cloyed,
30   A burning forehead, and a parching
        tongue.

Who are these coming to the sacrifice?
    To what green altar, O mysterious priest,
Lead'st thou that heifer lowing at the skies,
    And all her silken flanks with garlands
        dressed?
35 What little town by river or seashore,
    Or mountain-built with peaceful citadel,
        Is emptied of this folk, this pious morn?
    And, little town, thy streets forevermore
Will silent be; and not a soul to tell
40   Why thou art desolate, can e'er return.

O Attic shape![3] Fair attitude! with brede[4]
    Of marble men and maidens overwrought,
With forest branches and the trodden weed;
    Thou, silent form! dost tease us out of
        thought
45 As doth eternity: Cold Pastoral!
    When old age shall this generation waste,
        Thou shalt remain, in midst of other woe
    Than ours, a friend to man, to whom thou
        say'st,
"Beauty is truth, truth beauty—that is all
50   Ye know on earth, and all ye need to
        know."

1819   1820

---

1. *Tempe* (tem'pē), a beautiful valley in Thessaly in Greece.
2. *Arcady*, Arcadia, a part of ancient Greece, celebrated in pastoral poetry as the home of an ideal shepherd life.
3. *Attic shape*, a shape representing the simple, elegant taste of Athens.
4. *brede*, embroidery.

"Ode on a Grecian Urn"

In "Ode on a Grecian Urn" Keats uses **apostrophe,** addressing the urn directly as a "still unravished bride of quietness," a "foster child of Silence and slow Time," and a "Sylvan historian." Though ancient, the urn has remained fresh and unblemished and is awesomely silent. Since it has remained "young" through many centuries, it can only be a "foster child" of Time, who ages and destroys her natural children. The scenes portrayed are "sylvan," that is, set in a rural, forested region, and depict rustic life. According to Keats, through touch and sight the urn soundlessly communicates its "flowery tale more sweetly" than the poet's "rhyme."

The poem can be seen as developing a series of **paradoxes:** the young lovers, though destined never to touch, enjoy a love "Forever warm . . . Forever panting"; static carvings describe a scene of dynamic action; even in its most ideal moments, art is a reminder of death and decay. The last stanza strikes a positive note. The urn is called a "friend of man," of this and succeeding generations, that can "tease us out of thought / As doth eternity." Great art enables humanity temporarily to transcend mortal limitations; to contemplate the good, the true, and the beautiful, and to perceive life in the context of eternity.

HT **See IMAGERY in the Handbook of Literary Terms, page 910.**

To Autumn

John Keats

1

Season of mists and mellow fruitfulness,
   Close bosom-friend of the maturing sun;
Conspiring with him how to load and bless
   With fruit the vines that round the
       thatch-eaves run;
5 To bend with apples the mossed cottage-trees,
   And fill all fruit with ripeness to the core;
     To swell the gourd, and plump the hazel
       shells
With a sweet kernel; to set budding more,
   And still more, later flowers for the bees,
10   Until they think warm days will never cease,
     For Summer has o'er-brimmed their
       clammy cells.

Detail of *The Cyder Feast,* a wood engraving by Edward Calvert. 1828. *British Museum*

2

Who hath not seen thee oft amid thy store?
  Sometimes whoever seeks abroad may find
Thee sitting careless on a granary floor,
15 Thy hair soft-lifted by the winnowing wind;
Or on a half-reaped furrow sound asleep,
  Drowsed with the fume of poppies, while thy
    hook
    Spares the next swath and all its twinèd
      flowers:
And sometimes like a gleaner thou dost keep
20 Steady thy laden head across a brook;
Or by a cider-press, with patient look,
  Thou watchest the last oozing hours by
    hours.

1819

3

Where are the songs of Spring? Aye, where are
    they?
  Think not of them, thou hast thy music too—
25 While barred clouds bloom the soft-dying day,
  And touch the stubble-plains with rosy hue;
Then in a wailful choir the small gnats mourn
  Among the river sallows,[1] borne aloft
    Or sinking as the light wind lives or dies;
30 And full-grown lambs loud bleat from hilly
    bourn,
  Hedge crickets sing; and now with treble soft
The redbreast whistles from a garden croft,
  And gathering swallows twitter in the skies.

1820

---

1. *sallows*, willows.

THINK AND DISCUSS
WHEN I HAVE FEARS
Understanding
1. What, in lines 1–4, does the speaker fear to lose?
2. What is the fear expressed in lines 5–8?
3. What is the fear expressed in lines 9–11?

Analyzing
4. What possible reason might Keats have had for mentioning his fears in the order in which they are presented?
5. Judging by lines 12–14, what is the emotional effect of these "fears" on the speaker? How does he finally deal with them?

Extending
6. What does the capitalization of "Love" and "Fame" suggest about the young poet's aspirations at this stage of his life?

ON FIRST LOOKING INTO CHAPMAN'S HOMER
Understanding
1. According to lines 1–4, what are the "realms of gold" where the speaker has traveled?
2. What "one wide expanse" had the speaker only heard about until his discovery of Chapman's book?
3. Chapman's book made the speaker feel like what two people?

Analyzing
4. What do lines 7–8 suggest about the poet's earlier experiences in reading Homer?
5. What do **similes** in lines 9–14 express about Keats's feelings after reading Chapman?

Extending
6. Do you think it really matters that Keats mistook Cortez for Balboa as the person who first sighted the Pacific Ocean? (See the "Comment" article on page 510.)

LA BELLE DAME SANS MERCI
Understanding
1. In your own words describe what has happened to the Knight.

Analyzing
2. What aspects of the Knight's behavior and appearance cause the passerby to inquire repeatedly, "O what can ail thee"?
3. Describe the **setting**—both time and place. How does the setting contribute to the **mood** of melancholy and loss?
4. What elements in the poem suggest a medieval romance?
5. What were the effects of his "enthrallment" on the Knight? What are the overtones of the last two lines of the poem in respect to his condition?

ODE TO A NIGHTINGALE
Understanding
1. In lines 1–4, to what is the "drowsy numbness" the speaker experiences compared?
2. According to lines 51–55, with what has the speaker been "half in love"?
3. According to lines 63–70, who has heard the same song of the nightingale in the past?
4. What word returns the speaker from his reverie to reality?

Analyzing
5. Describe the speaker's mental and emotional state when he first hears the nightingale's song. What emotions does the nightingale's song arouse in him?
6. The poem is essentially a reverie on ways of escaping the afflictions of the world. What possible means of escape are contemplated?
7. One of Keats's basic ideas—the permanence and changelessness of beauty—is developed in stanza 7. What does he mean by "Thou wast not born for death, immortal Bird!" (line 61)?
8. Explain how Keats's **allusion** to the Bible story of Ruth confirms both the immortality of the bird's song and his own "forlorn" state in the real world.
9. What does Keats mean by lines 73–74: "the fancy cannot cheat so well/As she is famed to do"?

Extending
10. How does this poem typify the style and subject matter of an ode?

APPLYING: Onomatopoeia   H⅂⊺
See Handbook of Literary Terms, p. 927
Onomatopoeia refers to the use of words, like **buzz,** whose sound imitates the sound of the thing spoken of. It also refers to the use of melodious words to echo the meaning of an extended passage or phrase.

1. In lines 41–50, where has onomatopoeia been used to echo meaning?
2. In what way is the word *forlorn* "like a bell" tolling (lines 71–72)?
3. Find other examples of words or phrases you consider onomatopoetic.

THINK AND DISCUSS
ODE ON A GRECIAN URN
Understanding
1. According to lines 6–10, what figures are pictured on the urn? What are they doing?
2. According to lines 11–14, to what "ear" should the "soft pipes, play on"?
3. What figures and actions, according to lines 31–40, are pictured on the other side of the urn?

Analyzing
4. What examples of **apostrophe** are in lines 1–3? Why does the speaker address the urn in this way?
5. Lines 11–12 state, "Heard melodies are sweet, but those unheard/Are sweeter." Explain in your own words what this might mean.
6. What other **paradoxes** are to be found in the first four stanzas?
7. What autobiographical note seems to be introduced in the third stanza? What is the effect of this?
8. In what other sense, besides its being made of marble, is the urn a "Cold pastoral"?
9. What truth about the human condition does the urn convey? What seems to be Keats's concept of "beauty"?
10. According to some readers, one **theme** of the Ode is the relationship between art and

life. How would you explain this theme?

Extending
11. With what similar theme are both "Ode to a Nightingale" and "Ode on a Grecian Urn" concerned? How do they differ in subject matter and tone?

REVIEWING: Symbol
See Handbook of Literary Terms, p. 929
A **symbol** is something relatively concrete, such as an object, action, character, or scene, that signifies something relatively abstract, such as a concept or idea.

1. In what ways might the youth on the urn symbolize both the artist that never runs out of inspiration and the lover that never ceases to love?
2. What does the urn itself come to symbolize through the poem?

THINK AND DISCUSS
TO AUTUMN
Understanding
1. Who or what is the "Close bosom-friend of the maturing sun"?
2. According to stanza 2, where might someone seeking "abroad" find Autumn? doing what?
3. What five kinds of music, according to the third stanza, does Autumn perform to rival "the songs of Spring"?

Analyzing
4. In this poem the season is **personified.** What kind of person does the speaker suggest Autumn is?
5. Consider "To Autumn" in the context of Keats's life. What hints of melancholy, of things coming to their end, can be found in stanza 3?

Extending
6. How does "To Autumn" demonstrate Keats's theory of "Negative Capability"? (See Keats's biography on page 508.)

APPLYING: Imagery
See Handbook of Literary Terms, p. 910
Imagery is the use of sensory details to pro-

vide vividness in a literary work and arouse emotions or feelings in a reader.

1. To what senses does the imagery of stanza 1 mainly appeal? Find words and phrases that exemplify this imagery.
2. To what senses does the imagery of stanza 2 mainly appeal? stanza 3?

COMPOSITION
Writing About a Personal Discovery
The word "eureka" is commonly used to express the triumph of discovery, such as Keats experienced on discovering Chapman's translation of Homer. In a paper of four to six paragraphs, describe a personal experience in which you made a discovery that similarly altered your thinking, behavior—possibly the course of your life. In your first paragraph, use Keats's poem as a lead-in to your topic. Then go on to describe the event in detail, sharing the thoughts and feelings you experienced at the time. Conclude by identifying the discovery this experience enabled you to make and explain its lasting impact on your life.

Analyzing Imagery
In a paper of five to seven paragraphs, analyze Keats's use of imagery in "Ode to a Nightingale" to portray the reverie induced by the song of the nightingale. Start by providing a rapid overview of the poem and stating the purpose of the paper. Then analyze the images stanza by stanza. To what senses does the poet appeal? What word-pictures and sound effects does he use? In your conclusion explain why a sensual apprehension of the poem is essential to comprehension of its overall meaning. See "Writing about Poetry and Poetic Devices" in the Writer's Handbook.

ENRICHMENT
Preparing a "Romantic" Performance
As a group, prepare a performance for your fellow students or a civic group by reading several short poems from this unit, accompanied by suitable background music by a composer of the Romantic period. Research recordings of Franz Liszt or Frédéric Chopin to find suitable pieces. Practice reading aloud before your presentation.

Mary Shelley
1797–1851

Mary Shelley seemed destined for greatness. Her mother was Mary Wollstonecraft, a liberal thinker and radical feminist who wrote *A Vindication of the Rights of Woman*. Her father, William Godwin, was the author of *Political Justice*, a work that contributed to the political radicalization of the young writers of the era.

Mary Shelley was born on August 30, 1797. Ten days later her mother died, leaving Mary and a half sister in the care of the bereaved and impractical William Godwin. The father quickly remarried a next-door neighbor, Mrs. Mary Jane Clairmont, a widow with two children. Mary Shelley disliked her stepmother intensely but idolized her father and the mother she never knew, for whose death she blamed herself.

Mary Shelley began writing when she was a small child. By the age of nine, she could boast of having heard Coleridge recite "The Rime of the Ancient Mariner" and of hearing Thomas De Quincey relate his theories on the occult. Starting in 1812, she stayed for two years with a family in Scotland, coming home occasionally on visits. On one such visit in 1812 she met the poet Percy Shelley, who had come to serve as a disciple of William Godwin. In May of 1814 they met again and, at the end of July, eloped to the Continent, leaving behind his wife Harriet and two children. The marriage was legalized two years later following Harriet's suicide. By age twenty-four, Mary Shelley was a widow who had lost three of her four children and who faced a hard struggle to support herself and her remaining child. Other than *Frankenstein*, Mary Shelley wrote travel books, four additional novels, biographical sketches, and notes on her husband's poems that scholars have found invaluable.

In her preface to *Frankenstein*, Mary Shelley recounts the fascinating circumstances that inspired the book's creation. On a holiday to Switzerland in the summer of 1816, the Shelleys met Lord Byron, with whom they shared hours of conversation. Since the summer proved "wet and uncongenial," they were confined to the house for days on end, during which they read German ghost stories. One night Byron proposed that each of them try writing a ghost story for their mutual entertainment; Mary Shelley was the only one to complete the task.

For several days she had sought in vain for a story idea, then it came to her in a vivid dream following an evening of discussion of the experiments of Erasmus Darwin to animate lifeless matter. In her own words: "Night waned upon this talk; and even the witching hour had gone by before we retired to rest. When I placed my head on my pillow I did not sleep, nor could I be said to think. My imagination, unbidden, possessed and guided me, gifting the successive images that arose in my mind with a vividness far beyond the normal bounds of reverie. I saw—with shut eyes but acute mental vision—I saw the pale student of unhallowed arts kneeling beside the thing he had put together." The next day the actual writing of *Frankenstein* began.

from Frankenstein

Mary Shelley

In his early adolescence, Victor Frankenstein, the precocious eldest son of a distinguished family in Geneva, pours over the works of Paracelsus and Albertus Magnus, medieval alchemists, and becomes imbued with "a fervent longing to penetrate the secrets of nature" and pursue a career in natural science. During two years of intensive study at the University of Ingolstadt, Frankenstein astounds his professors by his mastery of chemistry and research procedures and his passion to probe "the deepest mysteries of creation." Having exhausted the resources at Ingolstadt, Frankenstein thinks of returning home to his family and fiancée, Elizabeth, but finds his stay protracted by the following incident which he relates to his benefactor, Robert Walton. Victor Frankenstein is speaking:

Part 1

ne of the phenomena which had peculiarly attracted my attention was the structure of the human frame, and, indeed, any animal endued with life. Whence, I often asked myself, did the principle of life proceed? It was a bold question, and one which has ever been considered as a mystery; yet with how many things are we upon the brink of becoming acquainted, if cowardice or carelessness did not restrain our inquiries. I revolved these circumstances in my mind, and determined thenceforth to apply myself more particularly to those branches of natural philosophy which relate to physiology. Unless I had been animated by an almost supernatural enthusiasm, my application to this study would have been irksome, and almost intolerable. To examine the causes of life, we must first have recourse to death. I became acquainted with the science of anatomy: but this was not sufficient; I must also observe the natural decay and corruption of the human body. In my education my father had taken the greatest precautions that my mind should be impressed with no supernatural horrors. I do not ever remember to have trembled at a tale of superstition, or to have feared the apparition of a spirit. Darkness had no effect upon my fancy; and a churchyard was to me merely the receptacle of bodies deprived of life, which, from being the seat of beauty and strength, had become food for the worm. Now I was led to examine the cause and progress of this decay, and forced to spend days and nights in vaults and charnel houses.[1] My attention was fixed upon every object the most insupportable to the delicacy of the human feelings. I saw how the fine form of man was degraded and wasted; I beheld the corruption of death succeed to the blooming cheek of life; I saw how the worm inherited the wonders of the eye and brain. I paused, examining and analyzing all the minutiae of causation, as exemplified in the change from life to death, and death to life, until from the midst of this darkness a sudden light broke in upon me—a light so brilliant and wondrous, yet so simple, that while I became dizzy with the

---

1. *charnel houses,* places where dead bodies or bones are laid.

immensity of the prospect which it illustrated, I was surprised that among so many men of genius who had directed their inquiries towards the same science, that I alone should be reserved to discover so astonishing a secret.

Remember, I am not recording the vision of a madman. The sun does not more certainly shine in the heavens, than that which I now affirm is true. Some miracle might have produced it, yet the stages of the discovery were distinct and probable. After days and nights of incredible labor and fatigue, I succeeded in discovering the cause of generation and life; nay, more, I became myself capable of bestowing animation upon lifeless matter.

The astonishment which I had at first experienced on this discovery soon gave place to delight and rapture. After so much time spent in painful labor, to arrive at once at the summit of my desires was the most gratifying consummation of my toils. But this discovery was so great and overwhelming that all the steps by which I had been progressively led to it were obliterated, and I beheld only the result. What had been the study and desire of the wisest men since the creation of the world was now within my grasp. Not that, like a magic scene, it all opened upon me at once: the information I had obtained was of a nature rather to direct my endeavors so soon as I should point them towards the object already accomplished. . . .

I see by your eagerness, and the wonder and hope which your eyes express, my friend, that you expect to be informed of the secret with which I am acquainted; that cannot be: listen patiently until the end of my story, and you will easily perceive why I am reserved upon that subject. I will not lead you on, unguarded and ardent as I then was, to your destruction and infallible misery. Learn from me, if not by my precepts, at least by my example, how dangerous is the acquirement of knowledge, and how much happier that man is who believes his native town to be the world, than he who aspires to become greater than his nature will allow.

When I found so astonishing a power placed within my hands, I hesitated a long time concerning the manner in which I should employ it. Although I possessed the capacity of bestowing animation, yet to prepare a frame for the reception of it, with all its intricacies of fibers, muscles, and veins, still remained a work of inconceivable difficulty and labor. I doubted at first whether I should attempt the creation of a being like myself, or one of simpler organization; but my imagination was too much exalted by my first success to permit me to doubt of my ability to give life to an animal as complex and wonderful as man. The materials at present within my command hardly appeared adequate to so arduous an undertaking; but I doubted not that I should ultimately succeed. I prepared myself for a multitude of reverses; my operations might be incessantly baffled, and at last my work be imperfect: yet, when I considered the improvement which every day takes place in science and mechanics, I was encouraged to hope my present attempts would at least lay the foundations of future success. Nor could I consider the magnitude and complexity of my plan as any argument of its impracticability. It was with these feelings that I began the creation of a human being. As the minuteness of the parts formed a great hinderance to my speed, I resolved, contrary to my first intention, to make the being of a gigantic stature; that is to say, about eight feet in height, and proportionably large. After having formed this determination, and having spent some months in successfully collecting and arranging my materials, I began.

No one can conceive the variety of feelings which bore me onwards, like a hurricane, in the first enthusiasm of success. Life and death appeared to me ideal bounds, which I should first break through, and pour a torrent of light into our dark world. A new species would bless me as its creator and source; many happy and excellent natures would owe their being to me. No father could claim the gratitude of his child so completely as I should deserve theirs. Pursuing these reflections, I thought that if I could bestow animation upon lifeless matter, I might in process of time (although I now found it impossible) renew life where death had apparently devoted the body to corruption.

These thoughts supported my spirits, while I pursued my undertaking with unremitting ardor. My cheek had grown pale with study, and my person had become emaciated with confinement. Sometimes, on the very brink of certainty, I failed; yet still I clung to the hope which the next day or the next hour might realize. One secret which I alone possessed was the hope to which I had dedicated myself; and the moon gazed on my midnight labors, while, with unrelaxed and breathless eagerness, I pursued nature to her hidden places. Who shall conceive the horrors of my secret toil, as I dabbled among the unhallowed damps of the grave, or tortured the living animal to animate the lifeless clay? My limbs now tremble and my eyes swim with the remembrance; but then a resistless, and almost frantic, impulse urged me forward; I seemed to have lost all soul or sensation but for this one pursuit. It was indeed but a passing trance that only made me feel with renewed acuteness so soon as, the unnatural stimulus ceasing to operate, I had returned to my old habits. I collected bones from charnel houses; and disturbed, with profane fingers, the tremendous secrets of the human frame. In a solitary chamber, or rather cell, at the top of the house, and separated from all the other apartments by a gallery and staircase, I kept my workshop of filthy creation: my eyeballs were starting from their sockets in attending to the details of my employment. The dissecting room and the slaughter-house furnished many of my materials; and often did my human nature turn with loathing from my occupation, whilst, still urged on by an eagerness which perpetually increased, I brought my work near to a conclusion.

The summer months passed while I was thus engaged, heart and soul, in one pursuit. It was a most beautiful season; never did the fields bestow a more plentiful harvest, or the vines yield a more luxuriant vintage: but my eyes were insensible to the charms of nature. And the same feelings which made me neglect the scenes around me caused me also to forget those friends who were so many miles absent, and whom I had not seen for so long a time. I knew my silence disquieted them; and I well remembered the words of my father: "I know that while you are pleased with yourself, you will think of us with affection, and we shall hear regularly from you. You must pardon me if I regard any interruption in your correspondence as a proof that your other duties are equally neglected."

I knew well, therefore, what would be my father's feelings; but I could not tear my thoughts from my employment, loathsome in itself, but which had taken an irresistible hold of my imagination. I wished, as it were, to procrastinate all that related to my feelings of affection until the great object, which swallowed up every habit of my nature, should be completed.

I then thought that my father would be unjust if he ascribed my neglect to vice, or faultiness on my part; but I am now convinced that he was justified in conceiving that I should not be altogether free from blame. A human being in perfection ought always to preserve a calm and peaceful mind, and never to allow passion or a transitory desire to disturb his tranquillity. I do not think that the pursuit of knowledge is an exception to this rule. If the study to which you apply yourself has a tendency to weaken your affections, and to destroy your taste for those simple pleasures in which no alloy can possibly mix, then that study is certainly unlawful, that is to say, not befitting the human mind. If this rule were always observed; if no man allowed any pursuit whatsoever to interfere with the tranquillity of his domestic affections, Greece had not been enslaved; Caesar would have spared his country; America would have been discovered more gradually; and the empires of Mexico and Peru had not been destroyed.

But I forget that I am moralizing in the most interesting part of my tale; and your looks remind me to proceed.

My father made no reproach in his letters, and only took notice of my silence by inquiring into my occupations more particularly than before. Winter, spring, and summer passed away during my labors; but I did not watch the blossom or the expanding leaves—sights which before always yielded me supreme delight—so deeply was I engrossed in my occupation. The leaves of that year had withered before my work drew near to a close; and now every day showed me more plainly how well I had succeeded. But my enthusiasm was checked by my anxiety, and I appeared rather like one doomed by slavery to toil in the mines, or any other unwholesome trade, than an artist occupied by his favorite employment. Every night I was oppressed by a slow fever, and I became nervous to a most painful degree; the fall of a leaf startled me, and I shunned my fellow creatures as if I had been guilty of a crime. Sometimes I grew alarmed at the wreck I perceived that I had become; the energy of my purpose alone sustained me: my labors would soon end, and I believed that exercise and amusement would then drive away incipient disease; and I promised myself both of these when my creation should be complete.

It was on a dreary night of November that I beheld the accomplishment of my toils. With an anxiety that almost amounted to agony, I collected the instruments of life around me, that I might infuse a spark of being into the lifeless thing that lay at my feet. It was already one in the morning; the rain pattered dismally against the panes, and my candle was nearly burnt out, when, by the glimmer of the half-extinguished light, I saw the dull yellow eye of the creature open; it breathed hard, and a convulsive motion agitated its limbs.

How can I describe my emotions at this catastrophe, or how delineate the wretch whom with such infinite pains and care I had endeavored to form? His limbs were in proportion, and I had selected his features as beautiful. Beautiful!—Great God! His yellow skin scarcely covered the work of muscles and arteries beneath; his hair was of a lustrous black, and flowing; his teeth of a pearly whiteness; but these luxuriances only formed a more horrid contrast with his watery eyes, that seemed almost of the same color as the dun white sockets in which they were set, his shriveled complexion and straight black lips.

The different accidents of life are not so changeable as the feelings of human nature. I had worked hard for nearly two years, for the sole purpose of infusing life into an inanimate body. For this I had deprived myself of rest and health. I had desired it with an ardor that far exceeded moderation; but now that I had finished, the beauty of the dream vanished, and breathless horror and disgust filled my heart. Unable to endure the aspect of the being I had created, I rushed out of the room, and continued a long time traversing my bedchamber, unable to compose my mind to sleep. At length lassitude succeeded to the tumult I had before endured; and I threw myself on the bed in my clothes, endeavoring to seek a few moments of forgetfulness. But it was in vain: I slept, indeed, but I was disturbed by the wildest dreams. I thought I saw Elizabeth, in the bloom of health, walking in the streets of Ingolstadt. Delighted and surprised, I embraced her; but as I imprinted the first kiss on her lips, they became livid with the hue of death; her features appeared to change, and I thought that I held the corpse of my dead mother in my arms; a shroud enveloped her form, and I saw the grave-worms crawling in the folds of the flannel. I started from my sleep with horror; a cold dew covered my forehead, my teeth chattered, and every limb became convulsed: when, by the dim and yellow light of the moon, as it forced its way through the window shutters, I beheld the wretch—the miserable monster whom I had created. He held up the curtain of the bed; and his eyes, if eyes they may be called, were fixed on me. His jaws opened, and he muttered some inarticulate sounds, while a grin wrinkled his cheeks. He might have spoken, but I did not hear; one hand was stretched out, seemingly to detain me, but I escaped, and rushed down stairs. I took refuge in the courtyard belonging to the house which I inhabited; where I remained during the rest of the night, walking up and down in the greatest agitation, listening attentively, catching and fearing each sound as if it were to announce the approach of the demoniacal corpse to which I had so miserably given life.

Oh! no mortal could support the horror of that countenance. A mummy again endued with animation could not be so hideous as that wretch.

I had gazed on him while unfinished; he was ugly then; but when those muscles and joints were rendered capable of motion, it became a thing such as even Dante[2] could not have conceived.

I passed the night wretchedly. Sometimes my pulse beat so quickly and hardly that I felt the palpitation of every artery; at others, I nearly sank to the ground through languor and extreme weakness. Mingled with this horror, I felt the bitterness of disappointment; dreams that had been my food and pleasant rest for so long a space were now become a hell to me; and the change was so rapid, the overthrow so complete!

Morning, dismal and wet, at length dawned, and discovered to my sleepless and aching eyes the church of Ingolstadt, its white steeple and clock, which indicated the sixth hour. The porter opened the gates of the court, which had that night been my asylum, and I issued into the streets, pacing them with quick steps, as if I sought to avoid the wretch whom I feared every turning of the street would present to my view. I did not dare return to the apartment which I inhabited, but felt impelled to hurry on, although drenched by the rain which poured from a black and comfortless sky.

I continued walking in this manner for some time, endeavoring, by bodily exercise, to ease the load that weighed upon my mind. I traversed the streets, without any clear conception of where I was, or what I was doing. My heart palpitated in the sickness of fear; and I hurried on with irregular steps, not daring to look about me:—

"Like one who, on a lonely road,
    Doth walk in fear and dread,
And, having once turned round, walks on,
    And turns no more his head;
Because he knows a frightful fiend
    Doth close behind him tread."[3]

Continuing thus, I came at length opposite to the inn at which the various diligences and carriages usually stopped. Here I paused, I knew not why; but I remained some minutes with my eyes fixed on a coach that was coming towards me from the other end of the street. As it drew nearer, I observed that it was the Swiss diligence: it stopped just where I was standing, and, on the door being opened, I perceived Henry Clerval, who, on seeing me, instantly sprung out. "My dear Frankenstein," exclaimed he, "how glad I am to see you! how fortunate that you should be here at the very moment of my alighting!"

Nothing could equal my delight on seeing Clerval; his presence brought back to my thoughts my father, Elizabeth, and all those scenes of home so dear to my recollection. I grasped his hand, and in a moment forgot my horror and misfortune; I felt suddenly, and for the first time during many months, calm and serene joy. I welcomed my friend, therefore, in the most cordial manner, and we walked towards my college. Clerval continued talking for some time about our mutual friends, and his own good fortune in being permitted to come to Ingolstadt. "You may easily believe," said he, "how great was the difficulty to persuade my father that all necessary knowledge was not comprised in the noble art of bookkeeping; and, indeed, I believe I left him incredulous to the last, for his constant answer to my unwearied entreaties was the same as that of the Dutch schoolmaster in the *Vicar of Wakefield:*[4]—'I have ten thousand florins a year without Greek, I eat heartily without Greek.' But his affection for me at length overcame his dislike of learning, and he has permitted me to undertake a voyage of discovery to the land of knowledge."

"It gives me the greatest delight to see you; but tell me how you left my father, brothers, and Elizabeth."

"Very well, and very happy, only a little uneasy that they hear from you so seldom. By the by, I mean to lecture you a little upon their account myself.—But, my dear Frankenstein," continued he, stopping short, and gazing full in my face, "I did not before remark how very ill you appear; so thin and pale; you look as if you had been watching

---

2. Dante (1265–1321), Italian poet, author of the *Inferno.*
3. a stanza from Coleridge's "The Rime of the Ancient Mariner."
4. *Vicar of Wakefield,* a novel by Oliver Goldsmith, published in 1766.

for several nights."

"You have guessed right; I have lately been so deeply engaged in one occupation that I have not allowed myself sufficient rest, as you see: but I hope, I sincerely hope, that all these employments are now at an end, and that I am at length free."

I trembled excessively; I could not endure to think of, and far less to allude to, the occurrences of the preceding night. I walked with a quick pace, and we soon arrived at my college. I then reflected, and the thought made me shiver, that the creature whom I had left in my apartment might still be there, alive, and walking about. I dreaded to behold this monster; but I feared still more that Henry should see him. Entreating him, therefore, to remain a few minutes at the bottom of the stairs, I darted up towards my own room. My hand was already on the lock of the door before I recollected myself. I then paused; and a cold shivering came over me. I threw the door forcibly open, as children are accustomed to do when they expect a specter to stand in waiting for them on the other side; but nothing appeared. I stepped fearfully in: the apartment was empty; and my bedroom was also freed from its hideous guest. I could hardly believe that so great a good fortune could have befallen me; but when I became assured that my enemy had indeed fled, I clapped my hands for joy, and ran down to Clerval.

We ascended into my room, and the servant presently brought breakfast; but I was unable to contain myself. It was not joy only that possessed me; I felt my flesh tingle with excess of sensitiveness, and my pulse beat rapidly. I was unable to remain for a single instant in the same place; I jumped over the chairs, clapped my hands, and laughed aloud. Clerval at first attributed my unusual spirits to joy on his arrival; but when he observed me more attentively he saw a wildness in my eyes for which he could not account; and my loud, unrestrained, heartless laughter, frightened and astonished him.

"My dear Victor," cried he, "what, for God's sake, is the matter? Do not laugh in that manner. How ill you are! What is the cause of all this?"

"Do not ask me," cried I, putting my hands before my eyes, for I thought I saw the dreaded specter glide into the room; "*he* can tell.—Oh, save me! save me!" I imagined that the monster seized me; I struggled furiously, and fell down in a fit.

Poor Clerval! what must have been his feelings? A meeting, which he anticipated with such joy, so strangely turned to bitterness. But I was not the witness of his grief; for I was lifeless, and did not recover my senses for a long, long time.

Part 2

After being away six years, Frankenstein finds his long-delayed homecoming marred by the tragic news of the murder of his youngest brother, William, by an unknown strangler whom Frankenstein, in a moment of intuition, realizes is the monster he created. In a terrible breach of justice, "poor, good" Justine Moritz, a former servant and companion, is executed for the crime, thereby deepening Frankenstein's feelings of personal guilt and despair. Crushed by sorrow and remorse, Frankenstein suffers a nervous collapse like that which followed the creation of the monster and impulsively departs to wander alone in the Alps and, finally, to ascend the summit of Montanvert Mountain. Victor Frankenstein is speaking:

It was nearly noon when I arrived at the top of the ascent. For some time I sat upon the rock that overlooks the sea of ice. A mist covered both that and the surrounding mountains. Presently a breeze dissipated the cloud, and I descended upon the glacier. The surface is very uneven, rising like the waves of a troubled sea, descending low, and interspersed by rifts that sink deep. The field of ice is almost a league in width, but I spent nearly two hours in crossing it. The opposite mountain is a bare perpendicular rock. From the side where I now stood Montanvert was exactly opposite, at the distance of a league; and above it rose Mont Blanc, in awful majesty. I remained in a recess of the rock, gazing on this wonderful and stupendous scene. The sea, or rather the vast river of ice, wound among its dependent mountains, whose aerial summits hung over its recesses. Their icy and glittering peaks shone in the sunlight over the clouds. My heart, which was before sorrowful, now swelled with something like joy; I exclaimed—"Wandering spirits, if indeed ye wander, and do not rest in your narrow beds, allow me this faint happiness, or take me, as your companion, away from the joys of life."

As I said this, I suddenly beheld the figure of a man, at some distance, advancing towards me with superhuman speed. He bounded over the crevices in the ice, among which I had walked with caution; his stature, also, as he approached, seemed to exceed that of man. I was troubled: a mist came over my eyes, and I felt a faintness seize me; but I was quickly restored by the cold gale of the mountains. I perceived, as the shape came nearer (sight tremendous and abhorred!) that it was the wretch whom I had created. I trembled with rage and horror, resolving to wait his approach, and then close with him in mortal combat. He approached; his countenance bespoke bitter anguish, combined with disdain and malignity, while its unearthly ugliness rendered it almost too horrible for human eyes. But I scarcely observed this; rage and hatred had at first deprived me of utterance, and I recovered only to overwhelm him with words expressive of furious detestation and contempt.

"Devil," I exclaimed, "do you dare approach me? and do not you fear the fierce vengeance of my arm wreaked on your miserable head? Begone, vile insect! or rather, stay, that I may trample you to dust! and, oh! that I could, with the extinction of your miserable existence, restore those victims whom you have so diabolically murdered!"

"I expected this reception," said the demon. "All men hate the wretched; how, then, must I be hated, who am miserable beyond all living things! Yet you, my creator, detest and spurn me, thy creature, to whom thou art bound by ties only dissoluble by the annihilation of one of us. You purpose to kill me. How dare you sport thus with life? Do your duty towards me, and I will do mine towards you and the rest of mankind. If you will comply with my conditions, I will leave them and you at peace; but if you refuse, I will glut the maw of death, until it be satiated with the blood of your remaining friends."

"Abhorred monster! fiend that thou art! the tortures of hell are too mild a vengeance for thy crimes. Wretched devil! you reproach me with your creation; come on, then, that I may extinguish the spark which I so negligently bestowed."

My rage was without bounds; I sprang on him, impelled by all the feelings which can arm one being against the existence of another.

He easily eluded me, and said—

"Be calm! I entreat you to hear me, before you give vent to your hatred on my devoted head. Have I not suffered enough that you seek to increase my misery? Life, although it may only be an accumulation of anguish, is dear to me, and I will defend it. Remember, thou hast made me more powerful than thyself; my height is superior to thine; my joints more supple. But I will not be tempted to set myself in opposition to thee. I am thy creature, and I will be even mild and docile to my natural lord and king, if thou wilt also perform thy part, the which thou owest me. Oh, Frankenstein, be not equitable to every other, and trample upon me alone, to whom thy justice, and even thy clemency and affection, is most due. Remember, that I am thy creature; I ought to be thy Adam; but I am rather the fallen angel, whom thou drivest from joy for no misdeed. Everywhere I see bliss, from which I alone am irrevocably excluded. I was benevolent and good; misery made me a fiend. Make me happy, and I shall again be virtuous."

"Begone! I will not hear you. There can be no community between you and me; we are enemies. Begone, or let us try our strength in a fight, in which one must fall."

"How can I move thee? Will no entreaties cause thee to turn a favorable eye upon thy creature, who implores thy goodness and compassion? Believe me, Frankenstein: I was benevolent; my soul glowed with love and humanity: but am I not

Illustration from the 1832 edition of *Frankenstein*.

alone, miserably alone? You, my creator, abhor me; what hope can I gather from your fellow-creatures, who owe me nothing? they spurn and hate me. The desert mountains and dreary glaciers are my refuge. I have wandered here many days; the caves of ice, which I only do not fear, are a dwelling to me, and the only one which man does not grudge. These bleak skies I hail, for they are kinder to me than your fellow-beings. If the multitude of mankind knew of my existence, they would do as you do, and arm themselves for my destruction. Shall I not then hate them who abhor me? I will keep no terms with my enemies. I am miserable, and they shall share my wretchedness. Yet it is in your power to recompense me, and deliver them from an evil which it only remains for you to make so great that not only you and your family, but thousands of others, shall be swallowed up in the whirlwinds of its rage. Let your compassion be moved, and do not disdain me. Listen to my tale: when you have heard that, abandon or commiserate me, as you shall

judge that I deserve. But hear me. The guilty are allowed, by human laws, bloody as they are, to speak in their own defense before they are condemned. Listen to me, Frankenstein. You accuse me of murder; and yet you would, with a satisfied conscience, destroy your own creature. Oh, praise the eternal justice of man! Yet I ask you not to spare me: listen to me; and then, if you can, and if you will, destroy the work of your hands."

"Why do you call to my remembrance," I rejoined, "circumstances, of which I shudder to reflect, that I have been the miserable origin and author? Cursed be the day, abhorred devil, in which you first saw light! Cursed (although I curse myself) be the hands that formed you! You have made me wretched beyond expression. You have left me no power to consider whether I am just to you or not. Begone! relieve me from the sight of your detested form."

"Thus I relieve thee, my creator," he said, and placed his hated hands before my eyes, which I flung from me with violence; "thus I take from thee a sight which you abhor. Still thou canst listen to me, and grant me thy compassion. By the virtues that I once possessed, I demand this from you. Hear my tale; it is long and strange, and the temperature of this place is not fitting to your fine sensations; come to the hut upon the mountain. The sun is yet high in the heavens; before it descends to hide itself behind yon snowy precipices, and illuminate another world, you will have heard my story, and can decide. On you it rests whether I quit for ever the neighborhood of man, and lead a harmless life, or become the scourge of your fellow-creatures, and the author of your own speedy ruin."

As he said this, he led the way across the ice: I followed. My heart was full, and I did not answer him; but, as I proceeded, I weighed the various arguments that he had used, and determined at least to listen to his tale. I was partly urged by curiosity, and compassion confirmed my resolution. I had hitherto supposed him to be the murderer of my brother, and I eagerly sought a confirmation or denial of this opinion.

For the first time, also, I felt what the duties of a creator towards his creature were, and that I ought to render him happy before I complained of his wickedness. These motives urged me to comply with his demand. We crossed the ice, therefore, and ascended the opposite rock. The air was cold, and the rain again began to descend: we entered the hut, the fiend with an air of exultation, I with a heavy heart and depressed spirits. But I consented to listen; and, seating myself by the fire which my odious companion had lighted, he thus began his tale.

Victor Frankenstein listens intently as the monster describes his attempts to become part of the human family, studying in secret the ways of family life, communication, and affectionate relations. The monster further informs Frankenstein that the discovery of books gave him the means to develop his feelings and intellect. As a result, the monster came to realize his similarity to humanity and yet his complete alienation and loneliness, awakening in him the stirrings of envy, resentment, and rebellion. The monster concludes his narrative by demanding that Frankenstein create a female for him as a companion. After some delay, Frankenstein seeks out a lonely cottage in one of the Orkney Islands to accomplish his loathsome task.

But though he begins his labors, he can scarcely bear to enter his laboratory for days at a time. Upon reflecting that the female he has promised to create may be even more "malignant" than her mate, he destroys the creature. The monster sees the act and confronts Frankenstein, vowing angrily, ". . .I go; but remember, I shall be with you on your wedding-night."

The monster keeps his deadly promise: Elizabeth, Frankenstein's bride, is slain on her wedding night; Frankenstein's father perishes in grief; and Frankenstein is doomed to spend his final years in pursuit of his grisly creation—a quest that takes him, finally, to the Arctic wastes and into the protection of Robert Walton, a sensitive explorer who cherishes Frankenstein's friendship and transmits his story. Weakened by his exhausting and perilous journeying, Frankenstein dies on Walton's ship. Late that same night, Walton goes to investigate the source of unearthly sounds emerging from the cabin where the corpse of Frankenstein rests. Robert Walton is speaking:

Part 3

I entered the cabin where lay the remains of my ill-fated and admirable friend. Over him hung a form which I cannot find words to describe; gigantic in stature, yet uncouth and distorted in its proportions. As he hung over the coffin his face was concealed by long locks of ragged hair; but one vast hand was extended, in color and apparent texture like that of a mummy. When he heard the sound of my approach he ceased to utter exclamations of grief and horror and sprung towards the window. Never did I behold a vision so horrible as his face, of such loathsome yet appalling hideousness. I shut my eyes involuntarily and endeavored to recollect what were my duties with regard to this destroyer. I called on him to stay.

He paused, looking on me with wonder; and, again turning towards the lifeless form of his creator, he seemed to forget my presence, and every feature and gesture seemed instigated by the wildest rage of some uncontrollable passion.

"That is also my victim!" he exclaimed: "in his murder my crimes are consummated; the miserable series of my being is wound to its close! Oh, Frankenstein! generous and self-devoted being! what does it avail that I now ask thee to pardon me? I, who irretrievably destroyed thee by destroying all thou lovedst. Alas! he is cold, he cannot answer me."

His voice seemed suffocated; and my first impulses, which had suggested to me the duty of obeying the dying request of my friend, in destroying his enemy, were now suspended by a mixture of curiosity and compassion. I approached this tremendous being; I dared not again raise my eyes to his face, there was something so scaring and unearthly in his ugliness. I attempted to speak, but the words died away on my lips. The monster continued to utter wild and incoherent self-reproaches. At length I gathered resolution to address him in a pause of the tempest of his passion: "Your repentance," I said, "is now superfluous. If you had listened to the voice of conscience, and heeded the stings of remorse, before you had urged your diabolical venegeance to this extremity, Frankenstein would yet have lived."

"And do you dream?" said the demon; "do you think that I was then dead to agony and remorse? . . . But when I discovered that he, the author at once of my existence and of its unspeakable torments, dared to hope for happiness; that while he accumulated wretchedness and despair upon me he sought his own enjoyment in feelings and passions from the indulgence of which I was for ever barred, then impotent envy and bitter indignation filled me with an insatiable thirst for vengeance. I recollected my threat and resolved that it should be accomplished. . . . And now it is ended; there is my last victim!"

I was at first touched by the expressions of his misery; yet, when I called to mind what Frankenstein had said of his powers of eloquence and persuasion, and when I again cast my eyes on the lifeless form of my friend, indignation was rekindled within me. "Wretch!" I said, "it is well that you come here to whine over the desolation that you have made. You throw a torch into a pile of buildings; and when they are consumed you sit among the ruins and lament the fall. Hypocritical fiend! if he whom you mourn still lived, still would he be the object, again would he become the prey, of your accursed vengeance. It is not pity that you feel; you lament only because the victim of your malignity is withdrawn from your power."

"Oh, it is not thus—not thus," interrupted the being; "yet such must be the impression conveyed to you by what appears to be the purport of my actions. Yet I seek not a fellow-feeling in my misery. No sympathy may I ever find. When I first sought it, it was the love of virtue, the feelings of happiness and affection with which my whole being overflowed, that I wished to be participated. . . . But now crime has degraded me beneath the meanest animal. No guilt, no mischief, no malignity, no misery, can be found comparable to mine. When I run over the frightful catalogue of my sins, I cannot believe that I am the same creature whose thoughts were once filled with sublime and transcendent visions of the beauty and the majesty of goodness. But it is even so; the fallen angel becomes a malignant devil. Yet even that enemy of God and man had friends and associates in his desolation; I am alone.

"You, who call Frankenstein your friend, seem to have a knowledge of my crimes and his misfortunes. But in the detail which he gave you of them he could not sum up the hours and months of misery which I endured, wasting in impotent passions. For while I destroyed his hopes, I did not satisfy my own desires. They were for ever ardent and craving; still I desired love and fellowship, and I was still spurned. Was there no injustice in this? Am I to be thought the only criminal when all human kind sinned against me? . . . I, the miserable and the abandoned, am an abortion, to be spurned at, and kicked, and trampled on. Even now my blood boils at the recollection of this injustice.

"But it is true I am a wretch. I have murdered the lovely and the helpless; I have strangled the innocent as they slept, and grasped to death his throat who never injured me or any other living thing. I have devoted my creator, the select specimen of all that is worthy of love and admiration among men, to misery; I have pursued him even to that irremediable ruin. There he lies, white and cold in death. You hate me; but your abhorrence cannot equal that with which I regard myself. I look on the hands which executed the deed; I think on the heart in which the imagination of it was conceived, and long for the moment when these hands will meet my eyes, when that imagination will haunt my thoughts no more.

"Fear not that I shall be the instrument of future mischief. My work is nearly complete. . . . I shall quit your vessel on the ice-raft which brought me thither, and shall seek the most northern extremity of the globe; I shall collect my funeral pile and consume to ashes this miserable frame, that its remains may afford no light to any curious and unhallowed wretch who would create such another as I have been. I shall die. I shall no longer feel the agonies which now consume me, or be the prey of feelings unsatisfied, yet unquenched. He is dead who called me into being; and when I shall be no more the very remembrance of us both will speedily vanish. I shall no longer see the sun or stars, or feel the winds play on my cheeks. Light, feeling, and sense will pass away; and in this condition must I find my happiness. Some years ago, when the images which this world affords first opened upon me, when I felt the cheering warmth of summer, and heard the rustling of the leaves and the warbling of the birds, and these were all to me, I should have wept to die; now it is my only consolation. Polluted by crimes, and torn by the bitterest remorse, where can I find rest but in death?

"Farewell! I leave you, and in you the last of human kind whom these eyes will ever behold. Farewell, Frankenstein! If thou wert yet alive, and yet cherished a desire of revenge against me, it would be better satiated in my life than in my destruction. . . .

"But soon," he cried, with sad and solemn enthusiasm, "I shall die, and what I now feel be no longer felt. Soon these burning miseries will be extinct. I shall ascend my funeral pile triumphantly, and exult in the agony of the torturing flames. The light of that conflagration will fade away; my ashes will be swept into the sea by the winds. My spirit will sleep in peace; or if it thinks, it will not surely think thus. Farewell."

He sprung from the cabin-window, as he said this, upon the ice-raft which lay close to the vessel. He was soon borne away by the waves and lost in darkness and distance.

1817

The Gothic Novel

The Renaissance and the Age of Reason looked on the Middle Ages as a barbarous and superstitious period. The word *Gothic*, meaning "medieval," was used figuratively by the writers of the seventeeth and eighteenth centuries to describe what was considered uncouth or in bad taste. The boorish Squire Western in *Tom Jones* (1749), for example, is "of more than Gothic ignorance." A change in attitude toward the Gothic is indicated by the popularity of Horace Walpole's novel *The Castle of Otranto, a Gothic Story* (1765). Walpole (1717–1797) was an aristocrat with an enthusiasm for Gothic architecture and his novel began the fashion for a pseudo-medieval paraphernalia of weird landscapes, haunted castles, and secret societies.

Some of the most famous Gothic novels, or novels of terror, were written by women. The "Shakespeare of romance," Mrs. Ann Radcliffe (1764–1823) was the author of *The Mysteries of Udolpho* (1794), which Sir Walter Scott called "the most interesting novel in the English language." Mrs. Radcliffe enjoyed foreign travel, and the "awful" setting of her novel, the Castle of Udolpho, was inspired by her memories of a medieval fortress on the Rhine: "Toward the close of day the road wound into a deep valley . . . The sun had just sunk below the top of the mountains . . . whose long shadow stretched athwart the valley; but his sloping rays . . . streamed in full splendor upon the towers and battlements of a castle that spread its extensive ramparts along the brow of the precipice above . . . The whole edifice was invested with the solemn duskiness of evening. Silent, lonely, and sublime, it seemed to stand the sovereign of the scene. . . . ''

The attraction of Mrs. Radcliffe's novel, which was as popular as Walpole's had been, was partly its romantic, dream-like atmosphere, and partly its unmistakable moral message: in the words of one literary historian, "Virtue triumphs; every problem is solved; every occurrence that has inspired the heroine with feelings of supernatural dread receives a natural explanation.''

Mrs. Radcliffe and her many enthusiastic readers were satirized by Jane Austen (1775–1817) in her novel *Northanger Abbey* (begun 1798). In one memorable bit of dialogue, the heroine and her girl friend discuss their favorite reading:

"And when you have finished *Udolpho*, . . . I have made out a list of ten or twelve more of the same kind for you.''

"Have you, indeed! How glad I am—What are they all?''

"I will read you their names directly; here they are, in my pocket-book. *Castle of Wolfenbach, Clermont, Mysterious Warnings, Necromancer of the Black Forest, Midnight Bell, Orphan of the Rhine,* and *Horrid Mysteries.* Those will last us some time.''

"Yes, pretty well; but are they all horrid? Are you sure they are all horrid?''

THINK AND DISCUSS
SECTION 1
Understanding

1. "After days and nights of incredible labor and fatigue," what capability did Frankenstein acquire? How did this make him feel?
2. Where was Frankenstein's laboratory located?
3. What type of "study" does Frankenstein say is "unlawful . . . not befitting the human mind"?
4. What happens to Elizabeth in Frankenstein's nightmare?

Analyzing

5. What qualities of mind make Dr. Frankenstein's search for "the principle of life," which entails days and nights in vaults and graveyards, less horrifying to him than to the average person?
6. Frankenstein reads in Robert Walton's expression an eagerness to know his "secret" —and how to animate lifeless matter. What does he tell Walton he should learn from him instead?
7. Frankenstein states he hesitated a long time before deciding how to employ his newfound power. Why does he finally decide to create a being like himself? How are these plans later modified?
8. Describe the scope of Frankenstein's ambition, at this stage of his labor, for himself and for the world.
9. According to Frankenstein, what are the effects of his hard labor on his body, mind, and emotions?
10. In retrospect, does Frankenstein approve of his creation of the monster? Explain.
11. Describe the events on the "dreary night of November" when Frankenstein beholds the results of his two years of labor.
12. What is the effect on Frankenstein of Clerval's arrival?

SECTIONS 2 AND 3
Understanding

1. Once he recognizes the figure approaching through the mist on the mountains, how does Frankenstein feel, and what does he decide to do?
2. During their meeting, what does the monster threaten to do if Frankenstein refuses to do his "duty" towards him?
3. What reason does the monster give for "hailing" the "bleak skies" and icy mountain caves in which he has been forced to dwell?

4. What reasons does the monster give for urging Frankenstein to come with him to "the hut upon the mountain"?
5. In his conversation with Walton, what does the monster say filled him with "an insatiable thirst for vengence"?
6. What ending has the monster planned for himself?

Analyzing

7. In describing the encounter between Frankenstein and the monster on the mountaintop, what use does Mary Shelley make of the biblical story of the fall of man?
8. Judging from the monster's remarks, what does Mary Shelley believe to be the origin of evil in human life?
9. The monster forcefully rebukes Frankenstein, declaring, "Do your duty towards me. . . ." What duty does Frankenstein neglect to perform? Is the monster justified in feeling he has been wronged?
10. Why does Frankenstein agree to go with the monster to the hut on the mountain to hear his tale? Is he touched by anything the monster says to him?
11. The monster tells Walton: "the fallen angel becomes a malignant devil." What does this statement mean, and how does it summarize the monster's moral history?
12. The monster also declares that "all human kind sinned against me." What specific examples of the injustice he has suffered does the monster cite?
13. Is the monster's remorse over the death of Frankenstein genuine?

OVERVIEW
Analyzing

1. To what extent can it be said that Frankenstein and the monster symbolize the best and worst in each other as well as the essential duality of human nature? Can you think of other works of literature that portray the double nature of humanity, a mixture of both good and evil?
2. At times the monster's words become almost laughable in their sophistication. In your opinion, what aspects of the story are most convincing? Which are least so?

3. The novel has a pronounced didactic component, representing Mary Shelley's attempt to interpret and moralize on her imaginative vision. What do you regard as the moral "lessons" of the story?
4. What is Robert Walton's function in the novel?

Extending

5. How does the portrayal of the monster in the novel differ from the common public conception of the monster fostered by the mass media, especially film versions of the story?
6. What might explain the wide-spread public confusion of Frankenstein with his creation? Why do so many people believe that Frankenstein is actually the monster's name?

COMPOSITION
Writing about Characters

In a paper of five to eight paragraphs, contrast the public conception of the monster with the creature portrayed in Mary Shelley's *Frankenstein*. Start with movie portrayals of the monster, then go on to describe the monster as actually portrayed in the novel. Describe his appearance, behavior, desires, and feelings. In your conclusion, sum up what the monster is intended to represent in the novel, keeping in mind Mary Shelley's allusions to Adam and to Satan, "the fallen angel." See "Writing about Characters" in the Writer's Handbook.

Writing about Theme

Frankenstein is not only a compelling horror story, but also a work of immense relevance to modern life. In a paper of five to six paragraphs, present what you perceive as themes of particular relevance for our times. Consider, for example, what the novel is saying about the human preoccupation with appearances, the moral implications of scientific experimentation, "man's inhumanity to man," and conditions necessary for a balanced life. In your conclusion, you might wish to remind your readers that *Frankenstein* goes far beyond being the simple "ghost story" that Byron asked each of his guests to write. See "Writing about Theme" in the Writer's Handbook.

The Changing English Language

The years prior to and including those of the Romantic Movement are notable for the beginnings of really serious attempts to improve and correct the spoken language—in other words, to set up a standard of pronunciation. In 1773 William Kendrick published the first dictionary that indicated vowel sounds, and he was quickly copied by both English and American lexicographers. Because many of these men felt that words should be pronounced as they are spelled, there was a tendency to reestablish older pronunciations, especially in respect to unaccented syllables. This was especially true in America, which was establishing an English of its own. Americans rebelled against the pronunciations of Samuel Johnson, long the accepted English authority. Although Johnson's *Dictionary* (see page 391) had indicated no pronunciations, his poetry through its meter made clear which pronunciations he regarded as standard. Thus in his poem *The Vanity of Human Wishes* the following words obviously are to be pronounced with only two syllables: *venturous, treacherous, powerful, general, history, quivering, flattering,* and *slippery.* Yet, with the possible exception of *general,* they were three-syllable words in America.

It was not until the Romantic Age that Greek began to affect the English language directly. Many new philosophic and scientific names were being added to the language. Combining two or more words or roots from Latin or Greek gave the language such words as *barometer* and *thermometer.* Another method of creating new words was adding Greek combining forms, prefixes, and suffixes such as *micro-* ("small"), *macro-* ("large"), *tele-* ("far"), *per-* ("maximum"), *-oid* ("like"), *-ic* ("smaller"), and *-ous* ("larger") to words already in use. In this manner words like *microscope, macrocosm, telepathy, peroxide, parotoid, sulphuric,* and *sulphurous* were produced.

Partly as a result of the interest of the romanticists in the Middle Ages, words belonging to

Detail of "The Divine Image" by William Blake, from *Songs of Innocence.* 1789.

the past were reintroduced into the language. The imitation of older ballads revived some archaic words found in such poems. Coleridge uses *eftsoons* for *again, I wis* (from the Middle English *iwis*) for *certainly,* and *een* for *eye.* Keats uses *faeries,* the archaic spelling of *fairies, fay* in place of *faith,* and *sooth* to mean *smooth.* These words, not only old but odd, were scarcely likely to be adopted in conversation, but they served to acquaint readers with the language of England's past. In their search for color the romanticists also included slang and dialect terms, and although these forms are sparsely used in comparison with their use in literature today, they began to find acceptance in writing. Many of the romanticists like to coin their own words; sometimes, as with *fuzzgig* and *critick-asting,* these bordered on the ridiculous.

As you know, the romantic writers were concerned with bringing naturalness and simplicity back into the language. Consequently some of them felt that borrowed or foreign words should be eliminated from the language because they corrupted the mother tongue. This discrimination against foreign words was not widespread, for English had become quite stabilized.

THINKING CRITICALLY
ABOUT LITERATURE

UNIT 5   THE ROMANTICS   1780–1830

■ CONCEPT REVIEW

The following selection contains many of the important ideas and literary terms found in the period you have just studied. It also contains notes and questions designed to help you think critically about your reading. Page numbers in the notes refer to an application. A more extensive discussion of these terms is in the Handbook of Literary Terms.

Wordworth had originally intended to trace his development as a poet in a long philosophical poem. "The Prelude" was meant as a "preparatory poem" to the larger work, which Wordsworth never finished. Since its publication in 1850, "The Prelude" has come to be known as Wordsworth's most famous long poem.

from The Prelude, Book 1

William Wordsworth

Stanza 1

    Fair seed-time had my soul, and I grew up
Fostered alike by beauty and by fear:
Much favored in my birthplace, and no less
In that belovèd Vale to which erelong
5 We were transplanted—there were we let loose
For sports of wider range. Ere I had told
Ten birthdays, when among the mountain slopes
Frost, and the breath of frosty wind, had snapped
The last autumnal crocus, 'twas my joy
10 With store of springes o'er my shoulder hung
To range the open heights where woodcocks run
Along the smooth green turf. Through half the night,
Scudding away from snare to snare, I plied
That anxious visitation—moon and stars

■ Consider what is meant by the *metaphor* in line 1.
■ In line 2 Wordsworth first mentions the two opposing forces in nature that combine to discipline his character and form his conscience.
■ **Vale:** Esthwaite Vale in Lancashire, near Wordsworth's boyhood home.
■ **Ere I . . . birthdays.** Wordsworth was not quite ten years old.
■ **springes:** snares for catching birds.
■ **Scudding:** moving swiftly.

15 Were shining o'er my head. I was alone,
And seemed to be a trouble to the peace
That dwelt among them. Sometimes it befell
In these night wanderings, that a strong desire
O'erpowered my better reason, and the bird
20 Which was the captive of another's toil
Became my prey; and when the deed was done
I heard among the solitary hills
Low breathings coming after me, and sounds
Of undistinguishable motion, steps
25 Almost as silent as the turf they trod.

Stanza 2

Nor less, when spring had warmed the cultured Vale,
Moved we as plunderers where the mother bird
Had in high places built her lodge; though mean
Our object and inglorious, yet the end
30 Was not ignoble. Oh! when I have hung
Above the raven's nest, by knots of grass
And half-inch fissures in the slippery rock
But ill sustained, and almost (so it seemed)
Suspended by the blast that blew amain,
35 Shouldering the naked crag, oh, at that time
While on the perilous ridge I hung alone,
With what strange utterance did the loud dry wind
Blow through my ear! the sky seemed not a sky
Of earth—and with what motion moved the clouds!

Stanza 3

40 Dust as we are, the immortal spirit grows
Like harmony in music; there is a dark
Inscrutable workmanship that reconciles
Discordant elements, makes them cling together
In one society. How strange that all
45 The terrors, pains, and early miseries,
Regrets, vexations, lassitudes interfused
Within my mind, should e'er have borne a part,
And that a needful part, in making up
The calm existence that is mine when I
50 Am worthy of myself! Praise to the end!
Thanks to the means which Nature deigned to employ;
Whether her fearless visitings, or those
That came with soft alarm, like hurtless light
Opening the peaceful clouds; or she may use
55 Severer interventions, ministry
More palpable, as best might suit her aim.

■ Notice how Wordsworth has managed to vary the *rhythm* of his *blank verse* through *run-on lines* and *caesuras*.

■ Lines 21–25 describe fears analogous to those of the Ancient Mariner and Frankenstein after they have violated the sanctity of nature.

■ Consider whether Wordsworth's *tone* in this section is appropriate to his description of a boy exploring nature.

■ **amain:** with full force; violently.

■ This is one of several statements explaining the process by which the poet's mind and soul were shaped.

■ Note the *personification* of Nature as royalty, "deigning" to confer her favors.

Stanza 4

One summer evening (led by her) I found
A little boat tied to a willow tree
Within a rocky cove, its usual home.
60 Straight I unloosed her chain, and stepping in
Pushed from the shore. It was an act of stealth
And troubled pleasure, nor without the voice
Of mountain echoes did my boat move on;
Leaving behind her still, on either side,
65 Small circles glittering idly in the moon,
Until they melted all into one track
Of sparkling light. But now, like one who rows,
Proud of his skill, to reach a chosen point
With an unswerving line, I fixed my view
70 Upon the summit of a craggy ridge,
The horizon's utmost boundary; far above
Was nothing but the stars and the gray sky.
She was an elfin pinnace; lustily
I dipped my oars into the silent lake,
75 And, as I rose upon the stroke, my boat
Went heaving through the water like a swan;
When, from behind that craggy steep till then
The horizon's bound, a huge peak, black and huge,
As if with voluntary power instinct,
80 Upreared its head. I struck and struck again,
And growing still in stature the grim shape
Towered up between me and the stars, and still,
For so it seemed, with purpose of its own
And measured motion like a living thing,
85 Strode after me. With trembling oars I turned,
And through the silent water stole my way
Back to the covert of the willow tree;
There in her mooring place I left my bark,
And through the meadows homeward went, in grave
90 And serious mood; but after I had seen
That spectacle, for many days, my brain
Worked with a dim and undetermined sense
Of unknown modes of being; o'er my thoughts
There hung a darkness, call it solitude
95 Or blank desertion. No familiar shapes
Remained, no pleasant images of trees,
Of sea or sky, no colors of green fields;
But huge and mighty forms, that do not live
Like living men, moved slowly through the mind
100 By day, and were a trouble to my dreams.

■ The "mountain echoes" are the voice of the poet's conscience, activated by the theft of the boat and the sense of having violated the natural harmony of the environment.

■ **Imagery** (page 518): Note the accumulation of visual images developed in lines 69–72.

■ **pinnace:** a light boat or vessel.

■ **instinct:** endowed.

■ **Mood** (page 466): Imagery and personification here combine to create a fearful mood.

■ **bark:** boat.

■ Here the operation of fear on the development of the poet's character is most pronounced.

Stanza 5

Wisdom and Spirit of the universe!
Thou Soul that art the eternity of thought
That givest to forms and images a breath
And everlasting motion, not in vain
105 By day or starlight thus from my first dawn
Of childhood didst thou intertwine for me
The passions that build up our human soul;
Not with the mean and vulgar works of man,
But with high objects, with enduring things—
110 With life and nature—purifying thus
The elements of feeling and of thought,
And sanctifying, by such discipline,
Both pain and fear, until we recognize
A grandeur in the beatings of the heart.
115 Nor was this fellowship vouchsafed to me
With stinted kindness. In November days,
When vapors rolling down the valley made
A lonely scene more lonesome, among woods,
At noon and 'mid the calm of summer nights,
120 When, by the margin of the trembling lake,
Beneath the gloomy hills homeward I went
In solitude, such intercourse was mine;
Mine was it in the fields both day and night,
And by the waters, all the summer long.

Stanza 6

125 And in the frosty season, when the sun
Was set, and visible for many a mile
The cottage windows blazed through twilight gloom,
I heeded not their summons: happy time
It was indeed for all of us—for me
130 It was a time of rapture! Clear and loud
The village clock tolled six—I wheeled about,
Proud and exulting like an untired horse
That cares not for his home. All shod with steel,
We hissed along the polished ice in games
135 Confederate, imitative of the chase
And woodland pleasures—the resounding horn,
The pack loud chiming, and the hunted hare.
So through the darkness and the cold we flew,
And not a voice was idle; with the din
140 Smitten, the precipices rang aloud;
The leafless trees and every icy crag
Tinkled like iron; while far distant hills
Into the tumult sent an alien sound

■ **Style** (page 447): The *apostrophes* in line 101 and elsewhere are typical of Wordsworth's Romantic lyrical style.

■ Lines 104–114 state the *theme* of the poem—the process by which nature builds up "our human soul."

■ Note Wordsworth's contention that the works of man are "mean and vulgar." Note also what he considers to be enduring.

■ **vouchsafed:** granted or given.
■ **With stinted kindness:** stingily.

■ **Simile** (page 455): Here the speaker compares himself to a horse.
■ Here Wordsworth portrays the joys of childhood as rapturously as in "My Heart Leaps Up" and the "Intimations Ode."
■ **Confederate:** joined or allied.

■ **Onomatopoeia** (page 517): *Tinkled* is an example of a word created to imitate a sound.

Of melancholy not unnoticed, while the stars
145 Eastward were sparkling clear, and in the west
The orange sky of evening died away.
Not seldom from the uproar I retired
Into a silent bay, or sportively
Glanced sideway, leaving the tumultuous throng,
150 To cut across the reflex of a star

reflex: reflection.

That fled, and, flying still before me, gleamed
Upon the glassy plain; and oftentimes,
When we had given our bodies to the wind,
And all the shadowy banks on either side
155 Came sweeping through the darkness, spinning still
The rapid line of motion, then at once
Have I, reclining back upon my heels,
Stopped short; yet still the solitary cliffs
Wheeled by me—even as if the earth had rolled
160 With visible motion her diurnal round!

diurnal round: daily turning (on its axis).

Behind me did they stretch in solemn train,
Feebler and feebler, and I stood and watched
Till all was tranquil as a dreamless sleep.
1805   1850

THINK AND DISCUSS
Understanding
1. According to lines 1–2, what two things "fostered" the speaker's character?
2. Describe the speaker's customary outdoor activities.
3. What sort of existence does the speaker say all the troubles listed in lines 45–47 have resulted in?
4. What seasons are described in this excerpt?

Analyzing:
5. How do lines 3–25 illustrate both the beauty and the fear mentioned in line 2?
6. Lines 51–56 refer to three "means" that Nature may employ: "fearless visitings," visitings that came "with soft alarm," and "Severer interventions." Which one of these is exemplified in the narrative in section 4?
7. Describe in your own words the apparition that disturbs the speaker in lines 77–85. What immediate and lasting effect did it have on him?
8. According to section 5, by what process is the "human soul" shaped and developed? What is the role of "pain and fear" in this process?
9. What "happy time" does Wordsworth describe in section 6? What "solitary" experience also proves pleasurable and memorable?

Extending
10. What similarities with poems such as "Tintern Abbey," "My Heart Leaps Up," and the "Intimations Ode" mark this as a poem by Wordsworth?

REVIEWING LITERARY TERMS
Simile
1. In lines 40–41, what simile does the speaker use to describe the growth of the spirit? What is suggested about the development of the spirit through this comparison?
2. What simile is used to describe the motion of the boat in lines 75–76? Explain whether you think the simile is or is not effective in this context.

Imagery
3. To what senses do the images in lines 30–38 appeal? in lines 138–152?

Onomatopoeia
4. Point out uses of onomatopoeia in lines 133–142, both in words and phrases.

Mood
5. Contrast the mood established in lines 21–25 with that established in lines 133–139.
6. The *little boat* that the speaker finds in line 58 he later calls an *elfin pinnace* (line 73) and a *bark* (line 88). How does each word fit the particular mood he is trying to create?

Style
7. Do you think Wordsworth's style is appropriate to his subject matter and theme? Consider such things as his tone, sentence structure, and use of poetic diction and various kinds of figurative language.

■ CONTENT REVIEW
THINKING SKILLS
Classifying
1. List the various kinds of suffering the Mariner is compelled to undergo after slaying the albatross. Classify the items on your list according to *physical, psychological,* and *spiritual suffering* (agonies of conscience and soul).
2. Draw up a list of character traits for either Donna Inez in *Don Juan* or Dr. Frankenstein in Mary Shelley's *Frankenstein.* Classify these items under such headings as *personality, temperament, ambitions, values, beliefs, personal strengths and weaknesses,* or any other categories of your own devising.

Generalizing
3. Looking back over Shelley's poems, what do you find to be his political philosophy?
4. In the poems of Keats, how do the poet's fears of death influence his writing about such lofty themes as art and immortal beauty?

Synthesizing
5. Explain why the term "The Age of Revolt" is an appropriate label for the Romantic period.

Mention specific writers and their works.
6. Explain what you consider to be the finest ideals of the Romantic Age, specific ways of viewing life we should hold on to today.

Evaluating
7. Compare the education of a youth that Byron describes in *Don Juan* with that which Wordsworth describes in "The Prelude" (Concept Review). What do you regard as the strengths of these educational programs? the deficiencies? Which program would more likely develop the "paragon" of moral virtue Donna Inez wished her son to become?
8. As the selections of this unit illustrate, the Romantic writers (particularly Wordsworth) glorified childhood, describing it as a time of idyllic enjoyment of nature and a state of innocence. What strikes you as convincing or unconvincing about this viewpoint? Explain.
9. Is "A Vindication of the Rights of Woman" effective as a piece of persuasion? Explain.

■ COMPOSITION REVIEW
Developing the Creative Imagination
Many of the poems in this unit deal with the evolution of the poet's creative imagination throughout each of the formative stages of life. In an essay of six to eight paragraphs, analyze this theme as developed in such poems as "Tintern Abbey," the "Intimations Ode," Coleridge's "Kubla Khan," and Shelley's "Ode to the West Wind." What is the role of the countryside in the molding of the poetic imagination? What is the source of poetic inspiration? In your conclusion identify what enables the poet to commence writing and produce literary work.

Discussing Nature as a Teacher
The Romantic poets regarded nature as a teacher and source of ultimate wisdom and enlightenment. Looking back on the poems of this unit, discuss some of the "lessons" Nature was able to teach in her role as Teacher. Start by making a list of these lessons, then classifying them according to headings of your own devising. In a paper of five or six paragraphs, present some of the more important lessons these poems portray.

THE VICTORIANS 1830–1880

1840	1850

HISTORY AND ARTS

- Hugo: *The Hunchback of Notre Dame* (France)
- Reform Bill gives vote to middle-class men
- Slavery abolished in British Empire
- Oxford Movement begins
- Factory Act regulates child labor
- Emerson: *Essays* (U.S.)
- Irish Potato Famine begins
- Repeal of Corn Laws
- Melville: *Moby Dick* (U.S.) •
- Marx and Engels: *The Communist Manifesto*
- Pre-Raphaelite Brotherhood founded
- California Gold Rush (U.S.)
- Hawthorne: *The Scarlet Letter* (U.S.)
- Great Exhibition opens
- Crimean War begins
- Thoreau: *Walden* (U.S.)

MONARCHS AND HOUSES

HANOVER

- William IV
- Victoria

ENGLISH LITERATURE

- Tennyson: *Poems, Chiefly Lyrical*
- Dickens: *Pickwick Papers*
- Dickens: *David Copperfield* •
- Macaulay: *History of England* •
- E. Bronte: *Wuthering Heights*
- C. Bronte: *Jane Eyre*   • Arnold: *Poems*
- Thackeray: *Vanity Fair*
- E. Browning: *Sonnets from the Portuguese*
- Tennyson named poet laureate

Child labor, from a 1840 novel by Frances Trollope.

A ceremony marks beginning of construction of Suez Canal.

Queen Victoria, Empress of India, on ivory throne, 1876.

UNIT

1860　　　　　　1870　　　　　　1880

- Indian Army mutinies against British
- Work on Suez Canal begins
- U.S. Civil War begins
- Death of Prince Albert
- President Lincoln assassinated (U.S.)
- Marx: *Das Kapital*

- Tolstoy: *War and Peace* (Russia)
- Unification of Italy
- Irish Land Act
- Wilhelm I proclaimed Emperor of Germany
- Irish Home Rule movement starts
- Verdi: *Aida* (Italy)
- France defeated in Franco-Prussian War

- Wagner: *The Ring of the Neibelung* (Germany)
- Gilbert and Sullivan: *H.M.S. Pinafore*
- Queen Victoria Empress of India

- Mill: *On Liberty*
- Tennyson: *Idylls of the King*
- Darwin: *On the Origin of Species*
- Fitzgerald: *The Rubaiyat of Omar Khayyam*
- Eliot: *The Mill on the Floss*

- Carroll: *Alice in Wonderland*
- R. Browning: *The Ring and The Book*

- Hardy: *The Return of the Native*

U.S. soldiers charge Fort Wagner, South Carolina, in 1863.

Illustration by John Tenniel for *Alice's Adventures in Wonderland*.

Karl Marx, socialist author of *Das Kapital*.

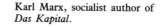

PREVIEW

UNIT 6   THE VICTORIANS   1830–1880

Authors
Elizabeth Barrett Browning
Alfred, Lord Tennyson
Charles Dickens
Robert Browning
George Eliot
Matthew Arnold
John Stuart Mill

Features
Reader's Note: "The Lady of Shalott"
Reader's Note: "The Passing of Arthur"
Reading Victorian Fiction
Comment: G. K. Chesterton on
    David Copperfield
Comment: George Eliot on Realism
Themes in English Literature: The
    Discovery of Childhood
Reader's Note: "Dover Beach"
The Changing English Language

Application of Literary Terms
lyric   dramatic monologue
assonance   inference

Review of Literary Terms
rhyme   point of view
metaphor   imagery

Reading Literature Skillfully
predicting outcomes

Vocabulary
archaic meanings
antonyms

Thinking Skills
classifying
synthesizing
evaluating

Composition
Summarizing Browning's Life in Love
Analyzing Browning's Sonnet Form
Describing a Modern Shalott
Responding to Ulysses' Decision
Writing a Lyric Poem
Explaining the Theme of Lyric 106
Explaining the Symbolism of Excalibur
Analyzing Tennyson's Style
Writing a Lyric Poem
Exploring Tennyson's Figurative Language
Describing a Modern "Duke of Ferrara"
Analyzing Browning's Dramatic Monologue
Explaining Maggie's Character
Analyzing Point of View
Symbolizing the Modern World
Analyzing Imagery and Mood in "Dover Beach"

Enrichment
Exploring the Sonnet Tradition
Researching Tennyson's Sources
Comparing Oral Histories
Researching Portraiture

Thinking Critically About Literature
Concept Review
Content Review
Composition Review

BACKGROUND

THE VICTORIANS 1830–1880

On June 20, 1837, the eighteen-year-old Victoria woke to learn that her uncle King William IV was dead, and that she was Queen. That night she wrote in her diary, "I am very young and perhaps in many, though not in all things, inexperienced, but I am sure, that very few have more real good will and more real desire to do what is fit and right than I have." Victoria proved herself worthy. Her sixty-three-year reign, the longest in English history, became a symbol of stability and propriety.

The Victorian era marks the climax of England's rise to economic and military supremacy. Nineteenth-century England became the first modern, industrialized nation. It ruled the most widespread empire in world history, embracing all of Canada, Australia, New Zealand, India, Pakistan, and many smaller countries in Asia, Africa, and the Caribbean. England's undisputed economic power further extended the nation's dominance—many independent countries were virtual fiefdoms, trading primarily with England and using the English pound sterling as international currency.

Although a great power in the world, internally England was anything but stable, and for some decades its very survival seemed doubtful. The years of war with France had permitted a small group of wealthy, land-owning aristocrats who controlled the government to halt politi-

Queen Victoria and the Prince Consort and their Eldest Children in 1846, by Franz Xavier Winterhalter. *The Royal Collection*

cal reform, stifling dissent by claiming that any change might imperil the war effort. "There was not a city, no, not a town," wrote Coleridge in 1809, "in which a man suspected of holding democratic principles could move abroad without receiving some unpleasant proof of the hatred in which his supposed opinions were held by the great majority of the people." With France defeated, this ruling minority strove to maintain the status quo. When thousands of workers gathered outside Manchester in August of 1819 to hear speeches on "cleanliness, sobriety, order, and peace," the local militia fired into the crowd, killing eleven and wounding four hundred. An English version of the French Revolution seemed perilously close. Middle-class young men of the era, according to the novelist Charles Kingsley, thought "that the masses were their natural enemies and that they might have to fight . . . for the safety of their property and the honor of their sisters."

THE INDUSTRIAL REVOLUTION

Such anger and fear grew out of the profound economic and social changes that swept over England between 1815 and 1850. The Industrial Revolution had started slowly in the eighteenth century, with the invention of the steam engine and machines for spinning and weaving. After the war with France, this revolution began in earnest. In the north of England the newly mechanized textile industry expanded rapidly. One district in Yorkshire increased its textile production from 2.4 million yards in 1839 to 42 million yards in 1849. In 1848 English production of iron equaled that of the rest of the world combined. Much of this iron went into the spreading system of railroads. England opened the first stretch of commercial track in 1830. By 1839 there were 1,200 miles, and by 1850, 7,000 miles.

Increased agricultural production and improved medical techniques contributed to a rapidly expanding population. Despite emigration, the number of people in England doubled between 1801 and 1850. At the same time, there was a massive population shift from rural areas to the newly industrialized cities: Bradford, for example, went from a population of 13,000 in 1801 to 104,000 in 1861. To those in power,

these immense changes sometimes seemed proof of an almost divine blessing on the nation. "The spinning jenny and the railroad, Cunard's liners and the electric telegraph, are to me," says a rather typical optimist in Kingsley's novel *Yeast* (1848), "signs that we are, on some points at least, in harmony with the universe; that there is a mighty spirit working among us, who . . . may be the Ordering and Creating God." The historian T. B. Macaulay asserted in 1835 that the English had become, quite simply, "the greatest and the most highly civilized people that ever the world saw. . . ."

However, in 1845 the writer and politician Benjamin Disraeli pointed out the existence in England of "two nations . . . who are as ignorant of each other's habits, thoughts, and feelings, as if they were . . . of different planets; who are formed by a different breeding, are fed by a different food, are ordered by different manners, and are not governed by the same laws." These "two nations" were the rich and the poor.

In describing the London of 1837 in *Nicholas Nickleby*, Dickens stressed this dramatic and perilous dichotomy. "The rags of the squalid ballad-singer fluttered in the rich light that showed the goldsmith's treasures, pale and pinched-up faces hovered about the windows where was tempting food, hungry eyes wandered over the profusion guarded by one thin sheet of brittle glass—an iron wall to them . . . . Life and death went hand in hand; wealth and poverty stood side by side; repletion and starvation laid them down together."

Rapid industrialization destroyed old jobs as it provided new ones. Population shifts left thousands housed in urban slums with bad water, no sanitation, and little food. Periodic depressions in markets for goods left whole factories unemployed. The government was unequipped to handle such new and large-scale problems. Furthermore, many thoughtful people believed that widespread suffering and even death were inevitable. Malthus had argued in 1798 that the only way to control population growth was starvation or self-control, while Ricardo in 1817 claimed that wages must be just high enough to permit a worker to survive. Anything more, he wrote, would wreck the system. Thus, a man

The Great Exhibition. Moving machinery. 1851. Lithograph by Joseph Nash (1809–78) for Dickinson Bros. *Guildhall Library, City of London*

as influential and powerful as Matthew Arnold's patron, Lord Lansdowne, could quite calmly predict that, in the Irish potato famine of 1845, "one million of persons would die before it was over," and then persuade the government to cut back on its famine relief program. And in the next two years, a million people did die.

Even for those who had a job, life in the new industrial working class was difficult at best. Men, women, and children, accustomed to the varied and independent work habits of farms and small towns, found themselves laboring up to sixteen hours a day, six days a week, in factories without any governmental safety regulations. The work was monotonous. It turned people into "hands," as the factory owners called the anonymous workers, with no control over their lives, hired and fired at the whim of the owner at the fluctuation of the market. Looking at the disparity between classes in 1853, John Ruskin argued that workers feel "that the kind of labor

to which they are condemned is verily a degrading one, and makes them less than men."

The Victorian years did bring increasing efforts to achieve political, social, and economic reforms to meet the changes created by industrialization. In 1832 Parliament passed a Reform Bill that increased the electorate by fifty percent—now one Englishman in five could vote, though the bill carefully excluded workers and women. This same period witnessed the final abolition of slavery throughout the British Empire (1833), and the first legislation regulating child labor (1833). The 1840s, the worst years of the century for unemployment, hunger, and disease, brought radical working-class agitation for the People's Charter, which demanded universal male suffrage and a Parliament in which any man could serve. The government never responded directly to these demands, but Parliament did repeal some of its more unjust laws (such as the Corn Laws, which kept the price of bread unnaturally high), and began to legislate shorter working hours, industrial safety, urban sanitary reform, and so on. Ultimately, mounting economic prosperity reduced radical agitation, and England felt sufficiently secure by 1851 to host "The Great Exhibition," the first World's Fair. By 1867, in a second Reform Bill, most working men gained the vote.

ELSEWHERE IN THE WORLD

Although the English genius for compromise smoothed over much class conflict, the problems created by capitalism did not disappear. And so there were also efforts to change the shape of society itself. In 1848 Engels and Marx published their pamphlet "The Communist Manifesto," and for years Marx worked quietly in the British Museum Library preparing *Das Kapital* (1867), a central document for twentieth-century communism.

There were short-lived flare-ups of radical activity in Europe during the middle of the nineteenth century, but this was more a period of national consolidation. Italy united in a single government in 1870, and, in the same year, the Germans achieved unification under the rule of the Prussian Emperor Wilhelm I.

After the destructive worldwide conflicts of the Napoleonic era, nations in the middle of the nineteenth century restricted themselves to small wars: France and England joined Turkey against Russia in the Crimean War (1853–1856); the young United States of America went through a bloody civil war (1861–1865), marked at its close by the assassination of President Lincoln (1865); and France lost to Germany in the Franco-Prussian War of 1870–1871, a defeat that laid the groundwork for World War I some years later.

The western nations continued to expand their power and influence. United States development accelerated with the California Gold Rush of 1848. The American Commodore Perry "opened" Japan in 1854, forcing the Japanese to trade with foreign countries. In 1859 a British company began construction of the Suez Canal.

It is a period especially rich in literary achievement. In France the Romantic movement culminated in the work of the poet and novelist Victor Hugo, whose *The Hunchback of Notre Dame* (1831) and *Les Miserables* (1860) expressed sympathy with the outcasts of respectable society. Contemporaneously, the United States was enjoying its first cultural flowering, in the essays of Ralph Waldo Emerson (1841), in the appearance of the first great American novels, Nathaniel Hawthorne's *The Scarlet Letter* (1850) and Herman Melville's *Moby Dick* (1851), and in the bracing experiments with prose and poetry by Henry David Thoreau (*Walden*, 1854), Walt Whitman (*Leaves of Grass*, 1855), and Emily Dickinson (writing her lyrics privately in the 1860s and 1870s). After centuries as a backwater nation, Russia suddenly became a political and cultural rival to the western nations. During the middle of the century the Russian novel moved to the forefront of artistic development with Ivan Turgenev's *Fathers and Sons* (1862), Fyodor Dostoyevsky's *Crime and Punishment* (1866), and Leo Tolstoy's *War and Peace* (1868).

The greatest theatrical achievements of the century took place in the opera house. In 1874 the German Richard Wagner completed his masterpiece, *The Ring of the Neibelung*, a cycle of four music dramas based upon Germanic hero tales and myths. The Italian Giuseppe Verdi, in works such as *Aida* (1871), transformed Italian opera into a deeply expressive medium.

LITERARY DEVELOPMENTS IN ENGLAND

During Victoria's reign it became clear that all things were subject to change—that change itself had become a permanent phenomenon. One way to deal with this was to trust in what was happening, and thus developed the Victorian belief in progress.

But serious difficulties arose when one applied such thinking to religion—something that most people thought a fixed aspect of their lives. The very developments in science that were creating the marvels of modern technology now raised questions about the Bible. Lyell's *Principles of Geology* (1830) and Chamber's *Vestiges of Creation* (1844) seemed to prove the earth far older than the Bible said it was, while radical German theologians questioned the divinity of Jesus. The climax to these developments came with the appearance of Charles Darwin's *On the Origin of Species* (1859), suggesting that the processes of biological evolution, rather than specific acts of divine creation, were responsible for the characteristics of living creatures. Such challenges deeply troubled thoughtful people, who felt the need for conclusive answers.

In an era of change, confusion, and alarm, English writers felt compelled to accept social responsibilities. For a nation raised on the warnings of the Sunday sermon, serious writing now frequently took up the burden and the authority of the preacher, both to enlighten, by suggesting new solutions to current problems, and also to inspirit, by moving the heart to new hope.

Victorians were avid readers. With little theater or music, not only the educated elite, but many ordinary people found reading their principal source of entertainment and information. There was in the era not only an esteem, but a passion for verse. At Cambridge and Oxford promising undergraduates neglected their studies to write, read, and argue about poetry. All sorts of poems appeared: lyrics, narratives, verse dramas, epics, a bewildering variety of invention and experiment.

But the dominant form of the era was the novel, in masterworks such as Charlotte Brontë's *Jane Eyre* (1847), her sister Emily Brontë's *Wuthering Heights* (1847), Thackeray's *Vanity Fair* (1849), and Dickens's *Great Expectations* (1860). Victorians bought them in hardbound volumes or paperbound serials that appeared each month, or they borrowed them from privately owned lending libraries. They liked long novels that told stories about their own world: the middle-class struggle for financial security, social acceptance, and love in marriage.

Finally, there were the Victorian writers of nonfiction prose, thinkers trying to refashion how people look at themselves and their world. The Victorians discarded the informal essay of the eighteenth century for the long article on a matter of substance. These frequently appeared first in thick quarterly reviews or in monthly and weekly magazines. Later, the author would gather together such articles into a collection or interweave them into a book. Exposition in such works was frequently not merely to explain; it was to move. In Victorian prose one finds not only the art of the orator, but that of the poet as well.

Probably never in the history of England were the rewards for authorship so great, at least for successful writers. Not only did some, like Tennyson and Dickens, make fortunes by their pens, but readers treated writers as sages or prophets, turning to them to learn ways of thinking and modes of feeling. Browning's every utterance was carefully considered by members of the Browning Society. More significantly, interlocking friendships joined most of the eminent writers of the day. They read aloud to each other from their latest works and shared criticism and ideas. "It was," as the modern historian G. M. Young writes, "a part of the felicity of the [1850s] to possess a literature which was at once topical, contemporary, and classic; to meet the Immortals on the streets, and to read them with added zest for the encounter."

Victoria outlived this generation of writers whose first works appeared when she was a young queen. Another very different group of authors appeared, and the next unit explores the new directions they took.

THINKING ABOUT GRAPHIC AIDS
Using the Time Line

Use the time line on pages 540–541 to answer these questions.

1. Why is this called the Victorian age?
2. Under what monarch was child labor regulated?
3. What accounts for the great wave of Irish emigration beginning in the 1840s?
4. President Lincoln abolished slavery in the U.S. two years before his assassination. For how many years had slavery already been abolished in England?
5. Did the mutiny of the Indian Army against the British result in an independent India? How can you tell?

BIOGRAPHY

Elizabeth Barrett Browning
1806–1861

Elizabeth Barrett Browning became, despite formidable obstacles, one of the most widely read and admired poets of her day. From her earliest years she demonstrated keen independence of spirit. The studies for young ladies of her era did not interest her. Not content with the meager education given Victorian girls, she insisted on learning Greek, Latin, French, Italian, German, and Spanish from tutors, while studying history and philosophy on her own.

What interested her most was literature. She began writing poetry at the age of eight, and in her twentieth year she published her first collection of verse.

Already, though, her health was declining. In her fifteenth year she had started taking opium at a doctor's direction to relieve what was called a "nervous disorder." Unhappily, the drug became not a cure but another problem. In 1838 she suffered a serious breakdown.

When she settled at the family home in London in 1841 it was as a permanent invalid. Elizabeth devoted what energy she had to writing, and in 1844 a two-volume collection of poems won high praise, in part for lyrics such as "The Cry of the Children" that indignantly protested the suffering of children forced to work in factories and mines. It was Robert Browning's letter praising this collection that initiated their celebrated correspondence. In *Sonnets from the Portuguese*, written during 1846, Elizabeth chronicles her growing love for him. Elizabeth's father was violently opposed to even the idea of marriage, and so finally the lovers eloped, fleeing to Italy in September of 1846. Mr. Barrett refused to see them, or their son (born in 1849), ever again. Only in 1849, after several years of marriage, did she finally show *Sonnets from the Portuguese* to Robert. He prevailed upon her to publish them in 1850.

Liberated from her sickroom and stimulated by married life in Florence, Elizabeth continued to write poetry not only about love, but also about political change and social justice. Robert Browning never envied his wife's success. Her development as an artist was, however, tragically cut short by her unexpected death in 1861.

from Sonnets from the Portuguese

Elizabeth Barrett Browning

Sonnet 1

I thought once how Theocritus had sung
Of the sweet years, the dear and wished-for
    years,
Who each one in a gracious hand appears
To bear a gift for mortals, old or young;
5 And, as I mused it in his antique tongue,
I saw in gradual vision, through my tears,
The sweet, sad years, the melancholy years,
Those of my own life, who by turns had flung
A shadow across me. Straightway I was 'ware,
10 So weeping, how a mystic shape did move
Behind me, and drew me backward by the hair;
And a voice said in mastery, while I strove,
"Guess now who holds thee?"—"Death," I
    said. But there
The silver answer rang, "Not Death, but Love."

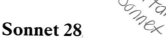

Sonnet 28

My letters! all dead paper, mute and white!
And yet they seem alive and quivering
Against my tremulous hands which loose the
    string
And let them drop down on my knee to-night.
5 This said—he wished to have me in his sight
Once, as a friend: this fixed a day in spring
To come and touch my hand . . . a simple
    thing,
Yet I wept for it!—this, . . . the paper's
    light . . .
Said, *Dear I love thee;* and I sank and quailed
As if God's future thundered on my past.
This said, *I am thine*—and so its ink has paled
With lying at my heart that beat too fast.
And this . . . O Love, thy words have ill
    availed
If, what this said, I dared repeat at last!

Sonnet 43

How do I love thee? Let me count the ways.
I love thee to the depth and breadth and height
My soul can reach, when feeling out of sight
For the ends of Being and ideal Grace.
5 I love thee to the level of everyday's
Most quiet need, by sun and candlelight.
I love thee freely, as men strive for Right;
I love thee purely, as they turn from Praise.
I love thee with the passion put to use
10 In my old griefs, and with my childhood's faith,
I love thee with a love I seemed to lose
With my lost saints—I love thee with the
    breadth,
Smiles, tears, of all my life!—and, if God
    choose,
I shall but love thee better after death.

1845–1846   **1850**

April Love (Detail) by Arthur Hughes. 1855–56. *Tate Gallery, London*

THINK AND DISCUSS
SONNET 1
Understanding
1. Theocritus was a Greek writer of the third century B.C. One of his poems personified the hours. What did past years mean to Theocritus?
2. What do past years mean to the speaker?
3. How does the speaker describe the other character in the poem?
4. What does this other character turn out to be a **personification** of?

Analyzing
5. What does the speaker assume that the "mystic shape" must be? Why do you suppose she makes this assumption?
6. What is surprising about the identity of the "shape"?
7. What does the **allusion** to Theocritus have to do with the conclusion of the sonnet?

Extending
8. What kind of love relationship might the speaker expect, after this introduction?

SONNET 28
Understanding
1. Describe the **setting**. What is the speaker doing?

Analyzing
2. Explain her reaction to the letter saying "Dear I love thee" (line 9).
3. Why do you suppose she refuses to repeat the words of the last letter?

SONNET 43
Understanding
1. What does the speaker try to list in this poem?

Analyzing
2. How is the spatial **metaphor** of line 2 developed?

3. Why does the speaker switch from space to daily life?
4. How do metaphors of time enter in?
5. Explain what you think the speaker means by her "lost saints" in line 12.

Extending
6. In your opinion, is the kind of love described here too extreme an abandonment of individuality? Explain.

COMPOSITION
Summarizing Browning's Life in Love
Although these are but three of the forty-four poems in *Sonnets from the Portuguese*, a reader can still get a sense of the author's life. Write a summary of the story of Elizabeth Barrett Browning's love, to make its progress clear for the ordinary reader. First review the poems and note all the references to phases of her life. Then outline them in chronological order. As you write, use brief quotations from the poems to illustrate your summary.

Analyzing Browning's Sonnet Form
Sonnets traditionally make a shift in thought or feeling after the eighth or the twelfth line. Analyze how Browning works within the tradition, and write an essay explaining your findings to your teacher. Begin with a close examination of the poems to determine if and where a shift occurs in each. Use your introductory paragraph to describe the standard sonnet form and subsequent paragraphs to explain how these three sonnets shift in thought or feeling. See "Writing About Poetry and Poetic Devices" in the Writer's Handbook.

ENRICHMENT
Exploring the Sonnet Tradition
The tradition of the sonnet is a rich one in English literature. Review the sonnets in Units 3 and 5 to select one that strikes you as similar to Browning's poetry. In class read aloud the poem you chose, and then explain the connections you see with these Victorian examples.

Alfred, Lord Tennyson
1809–1892

When Alfred Tennyson arrived at Cambridge University in November of 1827, he was a lanky, remote eighteen-year-old who found it difficult to make friends. Though raised in a crowded country parsonage as one of eleven children, Tennyson as a boy had been given to solitude and depression. This gloom came partly from fears that the epilepsy which had driven his father to alcoholism, violence, and madness would prove hereditary. For the young Tennyson, relief came in writing.

Gradually, a group of Cambridge undergraduates recognized that here was a major new poet. They encouraged Tennyson in his writing and became for him a second, more supportive, family. Tennyson's closest friend from this period was Arthur Henry Hallam, the son of a wealthy historian. It was he who urged Tennyson to publish *Poems, Chiefly Lyrical* (1830). There, for the first time, appeared lyrics such as "The Kraken" that struck a distinctive new note in English literature—combining the rich language of Keats with strangely evocative symbols that resist simple explanation. These poems mark the beginning of Victorian poetry.

Soon Hallam was engaged to marry Tennyson's younger sister, Emily. Together, Tennyson and Hallam traveled to the Pyrenees in the summer of 1830 and to the Rhine two years later. Their close friendship became what R. B. Martin calls "the most emotionally intense period" Tennyson ever knew. Then, while on a trip to Vienna with his father, Hallam suddenly died of a ruptured blood vessel in the brain.

At this critical turning point in his life, Tennyson rejected the depression and madness of his family background and resolutely turned toward achievement through his art. In the two months following the news of his friend's death (October–November, 1833), he drafted "Ulysses," with its defiant cry for action, the first version of "The Passing of Arthur," whose legendary hero bears the same name as Tennyson's friend, and some of the lyrical poems that were to become *In Memoriam, A. H. H.* In these works Tennyson fuses private emotional crises; public, moral conclusions; and symbols drawn from a wide literary heritage, both classical and native. His ability to write of both the private and the public, the present problem described in terms of materials drawn from the past, gave Tennyson the chance to powerfully integrate thought and feeling in his poetry.

The ensuing years were difficult. Tennyson lived on slender grants of money from his family, moving restlessly from one lodging to another, trying to write. His *Poems* (two volumes, 1842) and *The Princess* (1847) started to build a public reputation, but his first great success came in 1850 when, yielding to a friend's insistence, he finally published *In Memoriam*, a cycle of lyrics that laments Hallam's death and chronicles Tennyson's own struggle to regain an appetite for life.

In Memoriam enjoyed enormous public and critical success. It brought profits that enabled Tennyson to marry and live a settled life, and won him the title poet laureate, which he was to hold for nearly half a century.

The Lady of Shalott

Alfred, Lord Tennyson

PART 1

On either side the river lie
Long fields of barley and of rye,
That clothe the wold and meet the sky;
And through the field the road runs by
5   To many-towered Camelot;
And up and down the people go,
Gazing where the lilies blow
Round an island there below,
    The island of Shalott.

10 Willows whiten, aspens quiver,
Little breezes dusk and shiver
Through the wave that runs for ever
By the island in the river
    Flowing down to Camelot.
15 Four gray walls, and four gray towers,
Overlook a space of flowers,
And the silent isle embowers
    The Lady of Shalott.

By the margin, willow-veiled,
20 Slide the heavy barges trailed
By slow horses; and unhailed
The shallop flitteth silken-sailed
    Skimming down to Camelot:
But who hath seen her wave her hand?
25 Or at the casement seen her stand?
Or is she known in all the land,
    The Lady of Shalott?

Only reapers, reaping early
In among the bearded barley,
30 Hear a song that echoes cheerly

From the river winding clearly,
    Down to towered Camelot:
And by the moon the reaper weary,
Piling sheaves in uplands airy,
35 Listening, whispers " 'Tis the fairy
    Lady of Shalott."

PART 2

There she weaves by night and day
A magic web with colors gay.
She has heard a whisper say,
40 A curse is on her if she stay
    To look down to Camelot.
She knows not what the curse may be,
And so she weaveth steadily,
And little other care hath she,
45   The Lady of Shalott.

And moving through a mirror clear
That hangs before her all the year,
Shadows of the world appear.
There she sees the highway near
50   Winding down to Camelot:
There the river eddy whirls,
And there the surly village churls,
And the red cloaks of market girls,
    Pass onward from Shalott.

55 Sometimes a troop of damsels glad,
An abbot on an ambling pad,
Sometimes a curly shepherd lad,
Or long-haired page in crimson clad,
    Goes by to towered Camelot;
60 And sometimes through the mirror blue

The knights come riding two and two:
She hath no loyal knight and true,
    The Lady of Shalott.

But in her web she still delights
65 To weave the mirror's magic sights,
For often through the silent nights
    A funeral, with plumes and lights
    And music, went to Camelot:
Or when the moon was overhead,
70 Came two young lovers lately wed;
"I am half sick of shadows," said
    The Lady of Shalott.

life on the outside.

PART 3

A bow-shot from her bower eaves,
He rode between the barley sheaves,
75 The sun came dazzling through the leaves,
And flamed upon the brazen greaves
    Of bold Sir Lancelot.
A red-cross knight for ever kneeled
To a lady in his shield,
80 That sparkled on the yellow field,
    Beside remote Shalott.

The gemmy bridle glittered free,
Like to some branch of stars we see
Hung in the golden Galaxy.
85 The bridle bells rang merrily
    As he rode down to Camelot:
And from his blazoned baldric slung
A mighty silver bugle hung,
And as he rode his armor rung,
90   Beside remote Shalott.

All in the blue unclouded weather
Thick-jewelled shone the saddle leather,
The helmet and the helmet feather
Burned like one burning flame together,
95   As he rode down to Camelot.
As often through the purple night,
Below the starry clusters bright,
Some bearded meteor, trailing light,
    Moves over still Shalott.

100 His broad clear brow in sunlight glowed;

The Lady of Shalott (Detail) by John William Waterhouse.
1888. *Tate Gallery, London*

On burnished hooves his war horse trode;
From underneath his helmet flowed
His coal black curls as on he rode,
    As he rode down to Camelot.
105 From the bank and from the river
He flashed into the crystal mirror,
"Tirra lirra," by the river
    Sang Sir Lancelot.

She left the web, she left the loom,
110 She made three paces through the room,
She saw the water lily bloom,
She saw the helmet and the plume,
    She looked down to Camelot.
Out flew the web and floated wide;
115 The mirror cracked from side to side;
"The curse is come upon me," cried
    The Lady of Shalott.

Reader's Note

"The Lady of Shalott"

Tennyson first published "The Lady of Shalott" in 1832, but he revised the poem extensively before reprinting it in 1842. Looking back at the passages he later rewrote or dropped altogether, it becomes clear that in its first version the poem pictured the Lady as a fairy-tale princess, giving added emphasis to the unreality of her appearance and her world.

For example, in the first version lines 19–21 read as follows:

The little isle is all inrailed
With a rose-fence, and overtrailed
With roses: by the marge unhailed . . . .

A more luxurious Lady once appeared in lines 24–26 of the first version:

A pearl-garland winds her head:
She leaneth on a velvet bed,
Full royally apparellèd . . . .

And between lines 126–127 stood this stanza in the first version:

A cloudwhite crown of pearl she dight.
All raimented in snowy white
That loosely flew, (her zone in sight,
Clasped with one blinding diamond bright,)
    Her wide eyes fixed on Camelot,
Though the squally eastwind keenly
Blew, with folded arms serenely
By the water stood the queenly
    Lady of Shalott.

PART 4

In the stormy east wind straining,
The pale yellow woods were waning,
120 The broad stream in his banks complaining.
Heavily the low sky raining
        Over towered Camelot;
Down she came and found a boat
Beneath a willow left afloat,
125 And round about the prow she wrote
        The Lady of Shalott.

And down the river's dim expanse
Like some bold seer in a trance,
Seeing all his own mischance—
130 With a glassy countenance
        Did she look to Camelot.
And at the closing of the day
She loosed the chain, and down she lay;
The broad stream bore her far away,
135   The Lady of Shalott.

Lying, robed in snowy white
That loosely flew to left and right—
The leaves upon her falling light—
Through the noises of the night
140   She floated down to Camelot:

And as the boat head wound along
The willowy hills and fields among,
They heard her singing her last song,
        The Lady of Shalott.

145 Heard a carol, mournful, holy,
Chanted loudly, chanted lowly,
Till her blood was frozen slowly,
And her eyes were darkened wholly,
        Turned to towered Camelot.
150 For ere she reached upon the tide
The first house by the water-side,
Singing in her song she died,
        The Lady of Shalott.

Under tower and balcony,
155 By garden wall and gallery,
A gleaming shape she floated by,
Dead-pale between the houses high,
        Silent into Camelot.
Out upon the wharfs they came,
160 Knight and burgher, lord and dame,
And round the prow they read her name,
        The Lady of Shalott.

Who is this? and what is here?

And in the lighted palace near
165 Died the sound of royal cheer;
And they crossed themselves for fear,
All the knights at Camelot:

But Lancelot mused a little space;
He said, "She has a lovely face;
170 God in his mercy lend her grace,
The Lady of Shalott."

1842

H T Review METAPHOR in the Handbook of Literary Terms, page 906.

Ulysses

Alfred, Lord Tennyson

In the legendary Trojan War, the Greeks besieged Troy for ten years to win back the beautiful queen Helen. After their victory the warrior king Ulysses, a victim of hostile gods, wandered for ten more years, sailing unknown seas, battling with monsters, and even journeying to the land of the dead, before he reached his island home of Ithaca. There, he had to kill a band of rivals who wished to seize his wife and lands. With his victory the traditional story, told in Homer's *Odyssey*, comes to an end. Many have speculated on what Ulysses did in later life. Tennyson, following the guess of the medieval poet Dante, concludes that after such adventures Ulysses could not rest content at home.

It little profits that an idle king,
By this still hearth, among these barren crags,
Matched with an agèd wife, I mete and dole
Unequal laws unto a savage race,
5 That hoard, and sleep, and feed, and know not
    me.
I cannot rest from travel: I will drink
Life to the lees: all times I have enjoyed
Greatly, have suffered greatly, both with those
That loved me, and alone; on shore, and when
10 Through scudding drifts the rainy Hyades[1]
Vexed the dim sea: I am become a name;
For always roaming with a hungry heart
Much have I seen and known; cities of men
And manners, climates, councils, governments,
15 Myself not least, but honored of them all;

And drunk delight of battle with my peers,
Far on the ringing plains of windy Troy.
I am part of all that I have met;
Yet all experience is an arch wherethrough
20 Gleams that untraveled world whose margin
    fades
Forever and forever when I move.
How dull it is to pause, to make an end,
To rust unburnished, not to shine in use!
As though to breathe were life! Life piled on life
25 Were all too little, and of one to me
Little remains: but every hour is saved
From the eternal silence, something more,

---

1. *rainy Hyades* (hī′ə dēz′), constellation of stars whose appearance brought rainy weather.

A bringer of new things; and vile it were
For some three suns to store and hoard myself,
30 And this gray spirit yearning in desire
To follow knowledge like a sinking star,
Beyond the utmost bound of human thought.
  This is my son, mine own Telemachus,
To whom I leave the scepter and the isle—
35 Well-loved of me, discerning to fulfill
This labor, by slow prudence to make mild
A rugged people, and through soft degrees
Subdue them to the useful and the good.
Most blameless is he, centered in the sphere
40 Of common duties, decent not to fail
In offices of tenderness, and pay
Meet adoration to my household gods,
When I am gone. He works his work, I mine.
  There lies the port; the vessel puffs her sail:
45 There gloom the dark, broad seas. My mariners,
Souls that have toiled, and wrought, and
   thought with me—
That ever with a frolic welcome took
The thunder and the sunshine, and opposed
Free hearts, free foreheads—you and I are old;
50 Old age hath yet his honor and his toil;
Death closes all: but something ere the end,
Some work of noble note, may yet be done,
Not unbecoming men that strove with gods.
The lights begin to twinkle from the rocks:
55 The long day wanes: the slow moon climbs: the
  deep
Moans round with many voices. Come, my
  friends,
'Tis not too late to seek a newer world.
Push off, and sitting well in order smite
The sounding furrows; for my purpose holds
60 To sail beyond the sunset, and the baths
Of all the western stars, until I die.
It may be that the gulfs will wash us down:
It may be we shall touch the Happy Isles,[2]
And see the great Achilles, whom we knew.
65 Though much is taken, much abides; and
  though
We are not now that strength which in old days
Moved earth and heaven; that which we are,
  we are;
One equal temper of heroic hearts,

Made weak by time and fate, but strong in will
70 To strive, to seek, to find, and not to yield.
1833   1842

---

2. *To sail . . . Happy Isles.* Ulysses conceives of the
world in terms of ancient geography. The stars literally
plunge into the sea (lines 60–61), boats can fall off the
edge of the earth into an abyss (line 62), and somewhere
in the West are the Happy Islands, a paradise for heroes
now dead, like Achilles who fought beside Ulysses at Troy
(lines 63–64).

THINK AND DISCUSS
THE LADY OF SHALOTT
Understanding
1. Describe the **setting**, including the island
of Shalott and the surrounding countryside—and the time in which the poem
is set.
2. Summarize the action in the poem, using no
more than two sentences for each part.

Analyzing
3. Contrast the life of the Lady of Shalott with
that of people in the outside world.
4. Why is the mirror so important to her?
5. Explain how the **imagery** and **figurative language** used to describe Lancelot suggest his
character.
6. According to lines 40–41, what action will
bring a curse upon the Lady? What does she
do in lines 109–113 to activate the curse?
7. Why does the Lady leave her tower?
8. How does she act like a "seer in a trance"
(line 128)?
9. Discuss the **symbolism** of geography and
weather (including the season of the year).
10. How appropriate is Lancelot's reaction to
the Lady's death? Is he true to the image
on his shield?

Extending
11. Connect this fairy-tale story with what you
know about the gap between rich and poor

in Victorian England: to what extent might the Lady represent those who enjoy security and wealth in a world full of starving people? Where does this interpretation break down?

REVIEWING: Rhyme HT
See Handbook of Literary Terms, p. 919

Rhyme is the repetition of sounds in the accented syllables of two or more words. Patterns of rhyming words help create the rhythms and the music of poetry in English.

1. Chart the rhyme scheme in the first stanza of "The Lady of Shalott." Is this rhyme scheme consistent throughout?
2. Identify the slant rhymes in stanza 4 (lines 28–36). What other instances of slant rhyme are in the poem?
3. What kind of rhyme appears in line 60?

VOCABULARY
Archaic Meanings

To fit the language of "The Lady of Shalott" to its setting, Tennyson uses a number of words that were already archaic in his day. Use your Glossary to look up the definitions and etymologies of the following words. Then, for each word, write a sentence that illustrates the meaning that Tennyson intended.

wold (line 3)   shallop (line 22)
blow (line 7)   churls (line 52)
bower (*embower*, line 17)   pad (line 56)

THINK AND DISCUSS
ULYSSES
Understanding

1. How does Ulysses describe his current activities in lines 1–5?
2. Does he decide to leave again? How can you tell?
3. What does he expect Telemachus to do?

Analyzing

4. How does Ulysses **characterize** his wife and his people?
5. Explain why Ulysses has a "hungry heart" (line 12). What is he hungry for?
6. How does he plan to spend the rest of his life?

7. Ulysses seeks "knowledge" (lines 30–32); but what kind of knowledge is this, and what will it gain for him?
8. How do Ulysses' word choices illustrate his attitude towards his son?
9. Discuss how the **setting** (lines 54–56) fits the tone of Ulysses' speech.

Extending

10. Evaluate the contrasting attitudes towards personal responsibility posed by Ulysses' decision. Is he justified in what he does?

REVIEWING: Metaphor HT
See Handbook of Literary Terms, p. 906

A **metaphor** is a figure of speech, stated or implied, comparing two different things that have some shared characteristic. A metaphor does not use a connective such as *like* or *as*.

1. To what is life compared in lines 6–7? What are the shared characteristics?
2. What is the metaphor in lines 22–23?
3. How does this metaphor illustrate Ulysses' attitude towards growing old?

THINKING SKILLS
Classifying

To classify things is to arrange them into categories or groups according to some system.

1. "There are two kinds of people in the world. . ." is the start of many a classification, with conclusions such as "the haves and the have-nots" or "romantics and realists." In contrasting himself and his mariners with his wife, son, and the rest of his people, what two categories is Ulysses implying?
2. As a class, discuss the different groups of "two kinds of people in the world" that you have heard of. Are these groups valid; that is, can everyone actually be put into one or the other?

COMPOSITION
Describing a Modern Shalott

Tennyson sets his story of solitude, frustration, rebellion, and death in a remote, medieval past. Translate the stages of his story into a two-page narrative written for your classmates, describing the life and death of a modern man or woman who lives in a modern Shalott. In what sort of place can your character live so as to be able to see the outside world and yet not be able to communicate with it? Who will be your modern equivalent of Lancelot? What happens to your character after leaving Shalott?

Responding to Ulysses' Decision

Decide whether Ulysses is right in leaving Ithaca: is one's personal fulfillment more important than one's responsibilities to family and society? Then write a paper in which you persuade your classmates of your opinion. First go back through the poem, isolating Ulysses' reasons for leaving, and assessing their relative merits. Outline your essay by listing these arguments from the weakest to the strongest, and plan to devote a paragraph to explaining and evaluating each of them. Support your points with brief quotations of Ulysses' own words.

ENRICHMENT
Researching Tennyson's Sources

Many of Tennyson's poems spring from his imaginative response to books he was reading. He based "Ulysses" on passages from Dante's medieval poem *The Divine Comedy*. Obtain a copy and read the passage from "The Inferno" (Canto 26, lines 86–131) in which Ulysses describes his last voyage. Look for ideas and images that influenced Tennyson, and prepare an informal presentation for your classmates on how Tennyson adapted Dante.

HT See LYRIC in the Handbook of Literary Terms, page 913.

---

from In Memoriam

Alfred, Lord Tennyson

Like the sonnet sequences of the Elizabethan poets, *In Memoriam* is a book-length work built of separate but related poems. However, it is something new in English poetry because, rather than simply expressing conventional love sentiments, *In Memoriam* chronicles the emotional, psychological, and intellectual growth of an individual. In 131 lyrics the poet moved from initial grief, through mounting depression, to virtual despair; and then, thanks to the help of others and the spiritual nourishment of nature, he turns toward a personal recovery based on a new vision of life.

In the few examples that follow, the speaker first recounts his loneliness as he returns to the home of his dead friend and spends the first Christmas without him. Then, with the passage of time and the ebbing of grief, the speaker begins to long for the return of his own inner vitality, symbolized by the coming of a new spring. The sorrowful first Christmas gives way to a more hopeful New Year's Eve, and with the speaker and his world renewed, the lost friend seems somehow close to him once more.

Lyric 7

[handwritten: At friends house In city]

Dark house, by which once more I stand
    Here in the long unlovely street,
    Doors, where my heart was used to beat
So quickly, waiting for a hand,

[handwritten: friends]

5 A hand that can be clasped no more—
    Behold me, for I cannot sleep,
    And like a guilty thing I creep
At earliest morning to the door.

He is not here; but far away *[handwritten: upset]*
10 The noise of life begins again,
    And ghastly thro' the drizzling rain
On the bald street breaks the blank day.

Lyric 27 *[handwritten: captive/linnet]*

I envy not in any moods *[handwritten: no nothing but their cage]*
    The captive void of noble rage,
    The linnet born within the cage, *[handwritten: animal]*
That never knew the summer woods:

5 I envy not the beast that takes
    His license in the field of time, *[handwritten: death]*
    Unfettered by the sense of crime,
To whom a conscience never wakes;

Nor, what may count itself as blest,
10 The heart that never plighted troth
    But stagnates in the weeds of sloth;
Nor any want-begotten rest.

[handwritten: addressing issue of death]

I hold it true, whate'er befall;
    I feel it, when I sorrow most;
15 'Tis better to have loved and lost
Than never to have loved at all.

Lyric 28 *[handwritten: Christmas time]*

The time draws near the birth of Christ:
    The moon is hid; the night is still;
    The Christmas bells from hill to hill
Answer each other in the mist.

5 Four voices of four hamlets round,
    From far and near, on mead and moor,
    Swell out and fail, as if a door

The Doubt: "Can These Dry Bones Live?" (Detail) by Henry Alexander Bowler; this painting was intended to illustrate *In Memoriam*. Exhibited 1855. *Tate Gallery, London*

Were shut between me and the sound:

Each voice four changes on the wind,
10   That now dilate, and now decrease,
   Peace and goodwill, goodwill and peace,
Peace and goodwill, to all mankind.

This year I slept and woke with pain,
   I almost wished no more to wake,
15   And that my hold on life would break
Before I heard those bells again:

But they my troubled spirit rule,
   For they controlled me when a boy;
   They bring me sorrow touched with joy,
20 The merry merry bells of Yule.

Lyric 83 *New Year / Spring*

Dip down upon the northern shore,
   O sweet new-year delaying long;
   Thou doest expectant nature wrong;
Delaying long, delay no more.

5 What stays thee from the clouded noons,
   Thy sweetness from its proper place?
   Can trouble live with April days,
Or sadness in the summer moons?

Bring orchis, bring the foxglove spire,
10   The little speedwell's darling blue,
   Deep tulips dashed with fiery dew,
Laburnums, dropping-wells of fire.

O thou, new-year, delaying long,
   Delayest the sorrow in my blood,
15   That longs to burst a frozen bud
And flood a fresher throat with song.

Lyric 106 *Winter*

Ring out, wild bells, to the wild sky,
   The flying cloud, the frosty light:
   The year is dying in the night;
Ring out, wild bells, and let him die.

5 Ring out the old, ring in the new,
   Ring, happy bells, across the snow:

The year is going, let him go;
Ring out the false, ring in the true.

Ring out the grief that saps the mind,
10   For those that here we see no more;
   Ring out the feud of rich and poor,
Ring in redress to all mankind.

Ring out a slowly dying cause,
   And ancient forms of party strife;
15   Ring in the nobler modes of life,
With sweeter manners, purer laws.

Ring out the want, the care, the sin,
   The faithless coldness of the times;
   Ring out, ring out my mournful rhymes,
20 But ring the fuller minstrel in.

Ring out false pride in place and blood,
   The civic slander and the spite;
   Ring in the love of truth and right,
Ring in the common love of good.

25 Ring out old shapes of foul disease;
   Ring out the narrowing lust of gold;
   Ring out the thousand wars of old,
Ring in the thousand years of peace.

Ring in the valiant man and free,
30   The larger heart, the kindlier hand;
   Ring out the darkness of the land,
Ring in the Christ that is to be.

Lyric 115

Now fades the last long streak of snow,
   Now burgeons every maze of quick
   About the flowering squares, and thick
By ashen roots the violets blow.

5 Now rings the woodland loud and long,
   The distance takes a lovelier hue,
   And drowned in yonder living blue
The lark becomes a sightless song.

Now dance the lights on lawn and lea,
10   The flocks are whiter down the vale,

And milkier every milky sail
On winding stream or distant sea;

Where now the seamew pipes, or dives
  In yonder greening gleam, and fly
15 The happy birds, that change their sky
To build and brood; that live their lives

From land to land; and in my breast
  Spring wakens too; and my regret
  Becomes an April violet,
20 And buds and blossoms like the rest.

Lyric 119
Doors, where my heart was used to beat

So quickly, not as one that weeps
  I come once more; the city sleeps; *night*
I smell the meadow in the street;

5 I hear a chirp of birds; I see
  Betwixt the black fronts long-withdrawn
  A light-blue lane of early dawn,
And think of early days and thee,

And bless thee, for thy lips are bland,
10 And bright the friendship of thine eye;
  And in my thoughts with scarce a sigh
I take the pressure of thine hand. *handshake*

                  1850

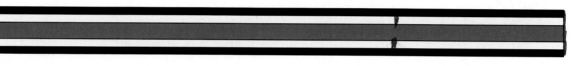

THINK AND DISCUSS
LYRIC 7
Understanding
1. Whose house is this?

Analyzing
2. Why do the closed doors trouble the speaker?
3. Explain how the poem uses **alliteration** to suggest the speaker's feelings.

Extending
4. Why do people grieving for the dead sometimes feel "guilty," as this speaker does (line 7)?

LYRIC 27
Understanding
1. State in your own words what the speaker means in the last stanza.

Analyzing
2. What characteristic is shared by the various creatures he lists?

Extending
3. Would the Lady of Shalott agree that " 'Tis better to have loved and lost/Than never to have loved at all?" Do you agree?

LYRIC 28
Understanding
1. What kind of weather dominates this Christmas season?

Analyzing
2. Explain how **repetition** suggests the sounds of ringing bells.
3. What does the speaker mean by the **metaphor** of sleeping and waking in the fourth stanza?
4. Characterize the **tone** of the phrase "The merry merry bells of Yule" (line 20).

Extending
5. Discuss the particular strains that people grieving for someone feel at holiday times.

LYRIC 83
Understanding
1. To whom or what is the poem **apostrophized**?

Analyzing
2. How do the glimpses of nature—especially

in the last two lines—serve as **metaphors** describing the speaker's hope for a happier life?

Extending

3. Discuss how Tennyson here adapts ideas about the revitalizing power of nature found in the poetry of Wordsworth.

LYRIC 106
Understanding

1. What are the bells ringing for?
2. What sorts of things does the speaker tell the bells to "Ring out"? What does he tell the bells to "Ring in"?

Analyzing

3. In general, what expectations does the speaker have on this New Year's Eve?
4. At what points does he explicitly try to turn away from his past grief?
5. What effects are created by **repetition**?

Extending

6. In your list of hopes for the future, what items differ from those in this list?

LYRIC 115
Understanding

1. What season of the year is described?

Analyzing

2. How can line 4 function as a **metaphor** for the speaker himself?
3. Compare the last stanza of this poem with the last stanza of Lyric 83, and explain what has happened to the speaker.

Extending

4. If someone's "regret/Becomes an April violet. . ." (lines 18–19), does that person betray those once grieved for?

LYRIC 119
Understanding

1. Whose hand does the speaker take?

Analyzing

2. In what ways has this place, first seen in Lyric 7, been transformed?
3. Explain the kind of connection the speaker now has with his lost friend.

APPLYING: Lyric H7
See Handbook of Literary Terms, p. 913

A **lyric** is a relatively short, highly personal poem expressing an emotion or state of mind and usually creating a single impression. Lyric poems frequently suggest musical effects through words.

1. Describe the dominant emotion in Lyric 7.
2. What is the state of mind in Lyric 106?
3. Analyze the structure, meter, and rhyme scheme of these lyrics. What differences do you find?
4. How does Lyric 83 allude to the musical effects in lyric poetry?

THINKING SKILLS
Evaluating

To evaluate is to make a judgment based on some sort of standard.

1. How convincing to you are the expressions of grief in *In Memoriam*?
2. Do you find the affirmation in Lyric 119 convincing, or does it seem merely an act of self-delusion?
3. Evaluate the standards you used to answer questions 1 and 2. How do they differ from the standards of the Victorians?

COMPOSITION
Writing a Lyric Poem

Write a lyric poem, to be shared with your classmates, in which you describe a place you know well that seems transformed by some strong feeling so that the scene itself reflects the emotion. The emotion needn't be sorrow—it might be love, fear, or any other. Choose your own meter and rhyme and try to stick to them.

Explaining the Theme of Lyric 106

Tennyson's Lyric 106 is a classic statement of mid-Victorian hopes and dreams. Write a five-paragraph essay for your teacher in which you explain the speaker's goals. In preparation, review the poem to find the political, social, artistic, and personal hopes expressed there. Devote a paragraph to explaining each of them in your essay. In your introduction, describe the emotional context in which the poem presents its vision of the future.

The Passing of Arthur *from* Idylls of the King

Alfred, Lord Tennyson

While still a schoolboy Tennyson became interested in the ancient tale of King Arthur and his Knights of the Round Table. In 1833 Tennyson wrote the poem "Morte d'Arthur," about the medieval king's death. Between 1857 and 1873 Tennyson wrote eleven other poems about Arthurian legend, with the collective title *Idylls of the King*, an *idyll* being a short narrative poem with modest goals.

"The Passing of Arthur," which includes the 1833 "Morte d'Arthur," describes the end of King Arthur's reign. His queen Guinevere and his best friend Lancelot have betrayed him in an adulterous love affair. While Arthur attacks Lancelot, Guinevere flees to a convent at Almesbury, where Arthur later finds her "lying in the dust," repentant. Arthur's nephew Modred, using this current confusion, has raised a rebellion against the king and is ready to attack Arthur's men. Tennyson's poem begins the night before the battle, as Arthur finds himself tormented by a dream in which Gawain, a former knight, warns vaguely of disaster the next day. Tennyson presents the poem as an old story told by the faithful knight Bedivere many years later.

That story which the bold Sir Bedivere,
First made and latest left of all the knights,
Told, when the man was no more than a
    voice
In the white winter of his age, to those
5 With whom he dwelt, new faces, other minds.

    For on their march to westward, Bedivere,
Who slowly paced among the slumbering host,
Heard in his tent the moanings of the King:
"I found Him in the shining of the stars,
10 I marked Him in the flowering of His fields,
But in His ways with men I find Him not.
I waged His wars, and now I pass and die.
O me! for why is all around us here
As if some lesser god had made the world,
15 But had not force to shape it as he would,

Till the High God behold it from beyond,
And enter it, and make it beautiful?
Or else as if the world were wholly fair,
But that these eyes of men are dense and dim,
20 And have not power to see it as it is.
Perchance, because we see not to the close—
For I, being simple, thought to work His will,
And have but stricken with the sword in vain;
And all whereon I leaned in wife and friend
25 Is traitor to my peace, and all my realm
Reels back into the beast, and is no more.
My God, thou hast forgotten me in my death;
Nay—God my Christ—I pass but shall not
    die."
Then, ere that last weird battle in the West,
30 There came on Arthur sleeping, Gawain
    killed

In Lancelot's war,[1] the ghost of Gawain blown
Along a wandering wind, and past his ear
Went shrilling, "Hollow, hollow all delight!
Hail, King! to-morrow thou shalt pass away.
35 Farewell! there is an isle of rest for thee.
And I am blown along a wandering wind,
And hollow, hollow, hollow all delight."
And fainter onward, like wild birds that
    change
Their season[2] in the night and wail their way
40 From cloud to cloud, down the long wind
    the dream
Shrilled; but in going mingled with dim cries
Far in the moonlit haze among the hills,
As of some lonely city sacked by night,
When all is lost, and wife and child with wail
45 Pass to new lords; and Arthur woke and
    called,
"Who spake? A dream. O light upon the
    wind,
Thine, Gawain, was the voice—are these
    dim cries
Thine? or doth all that haunts the waste and
    wild
Mourn, knowing it will go along with me?"
50 This heard the bold Sir Bedivere and spake:
"O me, my King, let pass whatever will,
Elves,[3] and the harmless glamor of the field;
But in their stead thy name and glory cling
To all high places like a golden cloud
55 For ever; but as yet thou shalt not pass.
Light was Gawain in life, and light in death
Is Gawain, for the ghost is as the man;
And care not thou for dreams from him, but
    rise—
I hear the steps of Modred in the West,
60 And with him many of thy people, and
    knights
Once thine, whom thou hast loved, but
    grosser grown
Than heathen, spitting at their vows and thee.
Right well in heart they know thee for the
    King.
Arise, go forth and conquer as of old."
65 Then spake King Arthur to Sir Bedivere:
"Far other is this battle in the West

Whereto we move, than when we strove in
    youth,
And brake the petty kings, and fought with
    Rome,
Or thrust the heathen from the Roman wall,
70 And shook him thro' the North. Ill doom is
    mine
To war against my people and my knights.
The king who fights his people fights himself.
And they my knights, who loved me once, the
    stroke
That strikes them dead is as my death to me.
75 Yet let us hence, and find or feel a way
Thro' this blind haze, which ever since I saw
One lying in the dust at Almesbury,[4]
Hath folded in the passes of the world."

Then rose the King and moved his host by
    night,
80 And ever pushed Sir Modred, league by league,
Back to the sunset bound of Lyonesse[5]—
A land of old upheaven from the abyss
By fire, to sink into the abyss again;
Where fragments of forgotten peoples dwelt,
85 And the long mountains ended in a coast
Of ever-shifting sand, and far away
The phantom circle of a moaning sea.
There the pursuer could pursue no more,
And he that fled no further fly the King;
90 And there, that day when the great light of
    heaven
Burned at his lowest[6] in the rolling year,
On the waste sand by the waste sea they closed.

---

1. *Lancelot's war.* Arthur's recent attack on Lancelot.
See the headnote on page 563.
2. *wild birds . . . season,* migrating birds flying north
or south according to the season of the year.
3. *Elves,* elemental spirits of the wild, according to
medieval folk belief; one of the peoples of Fairyland.
4. *One . . . Almesbury* (ămz'bĕr ē). According to
Tennyson, Queen Guinevere fled to the nunnery at
Almesbury. Arthur pursued her there. When she heard
his steps approaching the door of her nun's cell, she fell
from her chair "And grovelled with her face against the
5. *Lyonesse* (lī'ō nes'), a legendary country supposed
to have once been attached to the peninsula of Cornwall,
but long since sunk under the sea. Lyonesse is sometimes
identified with Cornwall itself.
6. *Burned at his lowest,* the time of the winter solstice.

Nor ever yet had Arthur fought a fight
Like this last, dim, weird battle of the West.
95 A deathwhite mist slept over sand and sea;
Whereof the chill, to him who breathed it, drew
Down with his blood, till all his heart was cold
With formless fear. And ev'n on Arthur fell
Confusion, since he saw not whom he fought.
100 For friend and foe were shadows in the mist,
And friend slew friend not knowing whom he
    slew;
And some had visions out of golden youth,
And some beheld the faces of old ghosts
Look in upon the battle. And in the mist
105 Was many a noble deed, many a base,
And chance and craft and strength in single
    fights,
And ever and anon with host to host
Shocks, and the splintering spear, the hard
    mail hewn,
Shield-breakings, and the clash of brands,[7] the
    crash
110 Of battleaxes on shattered helms, and shrieks
After the Christ, of those who falling down
Looked up for heaven, and only saw the mist;
And shouts of heathen and the traitor knights,
Oaths, insult, filth, and monstrous blasphemies,
115 Sweat, writhings, anguish, laboring of the lungs
In that close mist, and cryings of the light,
Moans of the dying, and voices of the dead.
Last, as by some one deathbed after wail
Of suffering, silence follows, or thro' death
120 Or deathlike swoon, thus over all that shore,
Save for some whisper of the seething seas,
A dead hush fell; but when the dolorous day
Grew drearier toward twilight falling, came
A bitter wind, clear from the North, and blew
125 The mist aside, and with that wind the tide
Rose, and the pale King glanced across the field
Of battle; but no man was moving there;
Nor any cry of Christian heard thereon,
Nor yet of heathen; only the wan wave
130 Brake in among dead faces, to and fro
Swaying the helpless hands, and up and down
Tumbling the hollow helmets of the fallen,
And shivered brands that once had fought with
    Rome,

And rolling far along the gloomy shores
135 The voice of days of old and days to be.
Then spake King Arthur to Sir Bedivere,
And whiter than the mist that all day long
Had held the field of battle was the King:
"Hearest thou this great voice that shakes the
    world,
140 And wastes the narrow realm whereon we move,
And beats upon the faces of the dead,
My dead, as tho' they had not died for me?—
O Bedivere, for on my heart hath fall'n
Confusion, till I know not what I am,
145 Nor whence I am, nor whether I be King,
Behold, I seem but King among the dead."
    Then spake the bold Sir Bedivere: "My King,
King everywhere! and so the dead have kings,
There also will I worship thee as King.
150 Yet still thy life is whole, and still I live
Who love thee; but who hates thee, he that
    brought
The heathen back among us, yonder stands,
Modred unharmed, the traitor of thine house."
Then spake the King: "My house hath been
    my doom.
155 But call not thou this traitor of my house
Who hath but dwelt beneath one roof with me.
My house are rather they who sware my vows,
Yea, even while they brake them, owned me
    King.
And well for thee, saying in my dark hour,
160 When all the purport of my throne hath failed,
That quick or dead thou holdest me for King.
King am I, whatsoever be their cry;
And one last act of knighthood shalt thou see
Yet, ere I pass." And uttering this the King
165 Made at the man: then Modred smote his liege
Hard on that helm which many a heathen sword
Had beaten thin; while Arthur at one blow,
Striking the last stroke with Excalibur,
Slew him, and all but slain himself, he fell.
170 So all day long the noise of battle rolled
Among the mountains by the winter sea;
Until King Arthur's Table, man by man,

---

7. *brands*, swords.

Had fall'n in Lyonesse about their lord,
King Arthur. Then, because his wound was
　　deep,
175　The bold Sir Bedivere uplifted him,
And bore him to a chapel nigh the field,
A broken chancel[8] with a broken cross,
That stood on a dark strait of barren land:
On one side lay the Ocean, and on one
180　Lay a great water, and the moon was full.
Then spake King Arthur to Sir Bedivere:
"The sequel of to-day unsolders all
The goodliest fellowship of famous knights
Whereof this world holds record. Such a sleep
185　They sleep—the men I loved. I think that we
Shall never more, at any future time,
Delight our souls with talk of knightly deeds,
Walking about the gardens and the halls
Of Camelot, as in the days that were.
190　I perish by this people which I made,—
Tho' Merlin[9] sware that I should come again
To rule once more; but, let what will be, be,
I am so deeply smitten thro' the helm
That without help I cannot last till morn.
195　Thou therefore take my brand Excalibur,
Which was my pride: for thou rememberest
　　how
In those old days, one summer noon, an arm
Rose up from out the bosom of the lake,
Clothed in white samite,[10] mystic, wonderful,
200　Holding the sword—and how I rowed across
And took it, and have worn it, like a king;
And, wheresoever I am sung or told
In aftertime, this also shall be known;
But now delay not: take Excalibur,
205　And fling him far into the middle mere:
Watch what thou seest, and lightly bring me
　　word."
To him replied the bold Sir Bedivere:
"It is not meet, Sir King, to leave thee thus,
Aidless, alone, and smitten thro' the helm—
210　A little thing may harm a wounded man;
Yet I thy hest will all perform at full,
Watch what I see, and lightly bring thee word."
So saying, from the ruined shrine he stept,
And in the moon athwart the place of tombs,
215　Where lay the mighty bones of ancient men,

Old knights, and over them the sea wind sang
Shrill, chill, with flakes of foam. He, stepping
　　down
By zigzag paths, and juts of pointed rock,
Came on the shining levels of the lake.
220　There drew he forth the brand Excalibur,
And o'er him, drawing it, the winter moon,
Brightening the skirts of a·long cloud, ran forth
And sparkled keen with frost against the hilt;
For all the haft twinkled with diamond sparks,
225　Myriads of topaz lights, and jacinth work
Of subtlest jewellery. He gazed so long
That both his eyes were dazzled as he stood,
This way and that dividing the swift mind,
In act to throw: but at the last it seemed
230　Better to leave Excalibur concealed
There in the many-knotted waterflags,
That whistled stiff and dry about the marge.
So strode he back slow to the wounded King.
Then spake King Arthur to Sir Bedivere:
235　"Hast thou performed my mission which I
　　gave?
What is it thou hast seen? or what hast heard?"
And answer made the bold Sir Bedivere:
"I heard the ripple washing in the reeds,
And the wild water lapping on the crag."
240　To whom replied King Arthur, faint and pale:
"Thou has betrayed thy nature and thy name,
Not rendering true answer, as beseemed
Thy fealty, nor like a noble knight:
For surer sign had followed, either hand,
245　Or voice, or else a motion of the mere.
This is a shameful thing for men to lie.
Yet now, I charge thee, quickly go again,
As thou art lief[11] and dear, and do the thing
I bade thee, watch, and lightly bring me word."
250　Then went Sir Bedivere the second time
Across the ridge, and paced beside the mere,
Counting the dewy pebbles, fixed in thought;

---

8. *chancel* (chan′səl), the space around the altar of a church.
9. *Merlin* (mėr′lən), a magician and prophet who was Arthur's chief adviser. At the beginning of the king's reign, Merlin had prophesied that Arthur would not die, but return to rule.
10. *samite* (sam′ ĭt), a rich, heavy silk fabric.
11. *lief* (lēf), beloved.

The Last Sleep of Arthur in Avalon (Detail) by Sir Edward Burne-Jones. 1881–98. *Museo de Arte, Ponce, Puerto Rico*

But when he saw the wonder of the hilt,
How curiously and strangely chased,[12] he smote
255 His palms together, and he cried aloud:
"And if indeed I cast the brand away,
Surely a precious thing, one worthy note,
Should thus be lost for ever from the earth,
Which might have pleased the eyes of many
    men.
260 What good should follow this, if this were done?
What harm, undone? Deep harm to disobey,
Seeing obedience is the bond of rule.

Were it well to obey then, if a king demand
An act unprofitable, against himself?
265 The King is sick, and knows not what he does.
What record, or what relic of my lord
Should be to aftertime, but empty breath
And rumors of a doubt? But were this kept,
Stored in some treasure-house of mighty kings,
270 Some one might show it at a joust of arms,
Saying, 'King Arthur's sword, Excalibur,
Wrought by the lonely maiden of the Lake.
Nine years she wrought it, sitting in the deeps
Upon the hidden bases of the hills.'
275 So might some old man speak in the aftertime
To all the people, winning reverence.
But now much honor and much fame were lost."
So spake he, clouded with his own conceit,[13]
And hid Excalibur the second time,
280 And so strode back slow to the wounded King.
Then spoke King Arthur, breathing heavily:
"What is it thou hast seen? or what has heard?"
And answer made the bold Sir Bedivere:
"I heard the water lapping on the crag,
285 And the long ripple washing in the reeds."
To whom replied King Arthur, much in wrath:
"Ah, miserable and unkind, untrue,
Unknightly, traitor-hearted! Woe is me!
Authority forgets a dying king,
290 Laid widowed of the power in his eye
That bowed the will. I see thee what thou art,
For thou, the latest-left of all my knights,
In whom should meet the offices of all,
Thou wouldst betray me for the precious hilt;
295 Either from lust of gold, or like a girl
Valuing the giddy pleasure of the eyes.
Yet, for a man may fail in duty twice,
And the third time may prosper, get thee hence.
But, if thou spare to fling Excalibur,
300 I will arise and slay thee with my hands."
Then quickly rose Sir Bedivere, and ran,
And, leaping down the ridges lightly, plunged
Among the bulrush beds, and clutched the sword,
And strongly wheeled and threw it. The great
    brand

---

12. *chased* (chās'd), carved or engraved.
13. *conceit*, an idea or notion, often a farfetched one.

305 Made lightnings in the splendor of the moon,
And flashing round and round, and whirled in
an arch,
Shot like a streamer of the northern morn,
Seen where the moving isles of winter shock
By night, with noises of the Northern Sea.[14]
310 So flashed and fell the brand Excalibur.
But ere he dipt the surface, rose an arm
Clothed in white samite, mystic, wonderful,
And caught him by the hilt, and brandished him
Three times, and drew him under in the mere.
315 And lightly went the other to the King.
Then spoke King Arthur, drawing thicker
breath:
"Now see I by thine eyes that this is done.
Speak out: what is it thou hast heard, or seen?"
And answer made the bold Sir Bedivere:
320 "Sir King, I closed mine eyelids, lest the gems
Should blind my purpose, for I never saw,
Nor shall see, here or elsewhere, till I die,
Not tho' I live three lives of mortal men,
So great a miracle as yonder hilt.
325 Then with both hands I flung him, wheeling
him;
But when I looked again, behold an arm,
Clothed in white samite, mystic, wonderful,
That caught him by the hilt, and brandished
him
Three times, and drew him under in the mere."
330 And answer made King Arthur, breathing hard:
"My end draws nigh; 'tis time that I were gone.
Make broad thy shoulders to receive my weight,
And bear me to the margin; yet I fear
My wound hath taken cold, and I shall die."
335 So saying, from the pavement he half rose,
Slowly, with pain, reclining on his arm,
And looking wistfully with wide blue eyes
As in a picture. Him Sir Bedivere
Remorsefully regarded thro' his tears,
340 And would have spoken, but he found not
words;
Then took with care, and kneeling on one knee,
O'er both his shoulders drew the languid hands,
And rising bore him thro' the place of tombs.
But, as he walked, King Arthur panted hard,
345 Like one that feels a nightmare on his bed

When all the house is mute. So sighed the
King,
Muttering and murmuring at his ear, "Quick,
quick!
I fear it is too late, and I shall die."
But the other swiftly strode from ridge to ridge,
350 Clothed with his breath, and looking, as he
walked,
Larger than human on the frozen hills.
He heard the deep behind him, and a cry
Before. His own thought drove him like a goad.
Dry clashed his harness in the icy caves
355 And barren chasms, and all to left and right
The bare black cliff clanged round him, as he
based
His feet on juts of slippery crag that rang
Sharp-smitten with the dint of armed heels—
And on a sudden, lo! the level lake,
360 And the long glories of the winter moon.
Then saw they how there hove a dusky barge,
Dark as a funeral scarf from stem to stern,
Beneath them; and descending they were ware[15]
That all the decks were dense with stately
forms,
365 Black-stoled, black-hooded, like a dream—by
these
Three Queens with crowns of gold. And from
them rose
A cry that shivered to the tingling stars,
And, as it were one voice, an agony
Of lamentation, like a wind that shrills
370 All night in a waste land, where no one comes,
Or hath come, since the making of the world.
Then murmured Arthur, "Place me in the
barge."
So to the barge they came. There those three
Queens
Put forth their hand, and took the King, and
wept.
375 But she, that rose the tallest of them all

---

14. *Shot like a streamer . . . the Northern Sea.* The
comparison here is between the flight of the sword and
the aurora borealis, the "northern light," bands of light
appearing in the sky around the polar regions. The
"moving isles of winter" are icebergs.
15. *ware*, aware.

And fairest, laid his head upon her lap,
And loosed the shattered casque, and chafed
    his hands,
And called him by his name, complaining loud,
And dropping bitter tears against a brow
380 Striped with dark blood: for all his face was
    white
And colorless, and like the withered moon
Smote by the fresh beam of the springing east;
And all his greaves and cuisses dashed with
    drops
Of onset;[16] and the light and lustrous curls—
385 That made his forehead like a rising sun
High from the dais-throne—were parched with
    dust;
Or clotted into points and hanging loose,
Mixed with the knightly growth that fringed his
    lips.
So like a shattered column lay the King;
390 Not like that Arthur who, with lance in rest,
From spur to plume a star of tournament,
Shot thro' the lists at Camelot, and charged
Before the eyes of ladies and of kings.
Then loudly cried the bold Sir Bedivere:
395 "Ah! my Lord Arthur, whither shall I go?
Where shall I hide my forehead and my eyes?
For now I see the true old times are dead,
When every morning brought a noble chance,
And every chance brought out a noble knight.
400 Such times have been not since the light that led
The holy Elders with the gift of myrrh.[17]
But now the whole Round Table is dissolved
Which was an image of the mighty world,
And I, the last, go forth companionless,
405 And the days darken round me, and the years,
Among new men, strange faces, other minds."
And slowly answered Arthur from the barge:
"The old order changeth, yielding place to new,
And God fulfils himself in many ways,
410 Lest one good custom should corrupt the world.
Comfort thyself; what comfort is in me?
I have lived my life, and that which I have done
May He within himself make pure! but thou,
If thou shouldst never see my face again,
415 Pray for my soul. More things are wrought by
    prayer

Than this world dreams of. Wherefore, let thy
    voice
Rise like a fountain for me night and day.
For what are men better than sheep or goats
That nourish a blind life within the brain,
420 If, knowing God, they lift not hands of prayer
Both for themselves and those who call them
    friend?
For so the whole round earth is every way
Bound by gold chains about the feet of God.
But now farewell. I am going a long way
425 With these thou seest—if indeed I go
(For all my mind is clouded with a doubt)—
To the island-valley of Avilion;[18]
Where falls not hail, or rain, or any snow.
Nor ever wind blows loudly; but it lies
430 Deep-meadowed, happy, fair with orchard lawns
And bowery hollows crowned with summer sea,
Where I will heal me of my grievous wound."
So said he, and the barge with oar and sail
Moved from the brink, like some full-breasted
    swan
435 That, fluting a wild carol ere her death,
Ruffles her pure cold plume, and takes the flood
With swarthy webs. Long stood Sir Bedivere
Revolving many memories, till the hull
Looked one black dot against the verge of dawn,
440 And on the mere the wailing died away.
But when that moan had past for ever more,
The stillness of the dead world's winter dawn
Amazed him, and he groaned, "The King is
    gone."
And therewithal came on him the weird rhyme,
445 "From the great deep to the great deep he
    goes."
Whereat he slowly turned and slowly clomb
The last hard footstep of that iron crag;
Thence marked the black hull moving yet, and
    cried,
"He passes to be King among the dead,

---

16. **onset,** combat; "drops/Of onset" are of blood.
17. **holy Elders . . . myrrh.** The three Magi, or priestly
kings, were led by a star to the birthplace of Jesus, each
carrying a gift. One of the gifts was *myrrh* (mėr), a fragrant
resin.
18. **Avilion** (ə vilʹē ən), or *Avalon,* one of the paradisal
isles of Celtic legend, located in the West.

450 And after healing of his grievous wound
He comes again; but—if he come no more—
O me, be yon dark Queens in yon black boat,
Who shrieked and wailed, the three whereat we
gazed
On that high day, when, clothed with living
light,
455 They stood before his throne in silence, friends
Of Arthur, who should help him at his need?"
Then from the dawn it seemed there came, but
faint
As from beyond the limit of the world,

Like the last echo born of a great cry,
460 Sounds, as if some fair city were one voice
Around a king returning from his wars.
Thereat once more he moved about, and clomb
Ev'n to the highest he could climb, and saw,
Straining his eyes beneath an arch of hand,
465 Or thought he saw, the speck that bare the
King,
Down that long water opening on the deep
Somewhere far off, pass on and on, and go
From less to less and vanish into light.
And the new sun rose bringing the new year.

1833, 1869   **1869**

Reader's Note

"The Passing of Arthur"

By the end of the medieval period Arthur's story had gone through many transformations, but its great climax remained his final battle and death, modified by the note of hope in his return. Like many of his contemporaries, Tennyson believed the early 1830s were the end of an era in English history; a traditional, agrarian, aristocratic world was being replaced by a new world of innovation, industrialization, and democracy. Bedivere's lament—"I, the last, go forth companionless,/And the days darken round me, and the years,/Among new men, strange faces, other minds"—articulated something many people felt. Tennyson's poem became an effort to resolve this sense of crisis by strengthening the faint hope with which Malory's account of Arthur concludes into a belief in the future.

Tennyson was, even in the 1830s, already well-read in mythology and theories of myth, and he added to Malory's account a more explicitly optimistic, mythic dimension. Many cultures tell the story of the hero who fails, dies, and then returns. Such stories echo the cycles of the day and the seasons, and reassure the listener that dawn and spring will come again. While Malory is vague about the time of year in which Arthur dies, Tennyson is very explicit:

Arthur fights on New Year's Eve, and dies on New Year's Day. The funeral barge carrying Arthur sails into the sun in "the stillness of the dead world's winter dawn" (line 442). This parallel between Arthur's life and the yearly cycle joins a similar parallel between Arthur and the sun's daily cycle. In the account of his youthful successes, Arthur is described as having a "forehead like a rising sun" (line 385); now, at his dying hour his face looks like "the withered moon/Smote by the fresh beam of the springing east" (lines 381–382). Arthur's resemblance to the cyclic gods of earlier myths promises a more certain return.

Tennyson then adds another dimension with more than one allusion to Jesus. Of course for most Victorian readers, to see in Arthur a resemblance to Jesus was to evoke that trust in his return to life which their religion so consistently taught. Further, it suggested that Arthur might serve as a model for a life of public service and self-sacrifice.

Tennyson gave to his tale the typically Victorian trust in progress. In his last moments Arthur concludes, "The old order changeth, yielding place to new." To his contemporaries, fearful of the changing character of England, Tennyson's conclusions were heartening.

THINK AND DISCUSS
Understanding
1. What message does the dream of Gawain bring?
2. Describe how Arthur receives his fatal wound.
3. What happens to Excalibur?

Analyzing
4. Describe the spiritual crisis that besets Arthur on the night before the battle.
5. In what ways does the setting of the last battle suggest its significance?
6. Why does Arthur wish to throw away Excalibur?
7. Debate the merit of Bedivere's two reasons for keeping Excalibur.
8. How does the end of the poem justify Tennyson's term "Passing"?

Extending
9. What does Arthur imply about the nature of any social order when he says of the rebel knights, "the stroke/That strikes them dead is as my death to me" (lines 73–74)?
10. Does Arthur mean by this the same thing that Donne means in "the bell . . . tolls for thee" ("Meditation 17," page 283)?
11. Explain how Arthur's suggestion that the old order must change lest "one good custom should corrupt the world" (line 410) might apply to issues of your own day.

APPLYING: Assonance
See Handbook of Literary Terms, p. 926
The same vowel sound, appearing in two or more words, constitutes **assonance**. While rhyme is the repetition of the sound of entire syllables, both consonants and vowels, assonance is simply the repetition of vowel sounds.

1. Locate all the long *o* sounds (as in *open*) in lines 30–37.
2. Locate all the short *i* sounds (as in *it*) in lines 366–371.
3. Locate other instances of assonance in this selection. What effects do they create?

COMPOSITION
Explaining the Symbolism of Excalibur
"The Passing of Arthur" is full of symbols of various kinds. Some, like Arthur's crown, are symbols of kingship; some, like the time of the year, are symbols of the end of an age. Write an essay, to be read by your teacher, in which you consider the symbolism of the sword Excalibur. Begin by going back through the poem, noting where Arthur got the sword and how he refers to it throughout. Consider these questions: How is Arthur able to give up Excalibur so easily? Why is Bedivere so hesitant to throw it away? What does the way it disappears suggest about its power? Outline your thoughts before you begin to write.

Analyzing Tennyson's Style
Tennyson wrote "The Passing of Arthur" in a style deliberately different from ordinary speech. Write a paper analyzing for your classmates the style of Tennyson's poetry and discussing how it affects the story he tells. Start by going back through the poem and noting stylistic traits that strike you as unusual. Look especially at Tennyson's use of archaic words, his repetition of certain phrases, and his efforts to make his descriptions sound like the things they describe. Then cluster your observations under three or four headings that can serve as the main paragraphs of your paper. See "Writing to Analyze an Author's Style" in the Writer's Handbook.

ENRICHMENT
Researching Tennyson's Source
Tennyson based "The Passing of Arthur" on a passage from Sir Thomas Malory's *Morte Darthur* (see page 139). Assign study groups to examine sections of Malory's version, such as Bedivere and Excalibur, the arrival of the mysterious queens, Arthur's final words, and the way Arthur departs. Each team should look for words, thoughts, and descriptions that Tennyson adapted from Malory. Then have a research conference, in which each team reports on how the Victorian poet adapted his source.

The Kraken

Alfred, Lord Tennyson

Below the thunders of the upper deep;
Far, far beneath in the abysmal sea,
His ancient, dreamless, uninvaded sleep
The Kraken[1] sleepeth: faintest sunlights flee
5 About his shadowy sides: above him swell
Huge sponges of millennial growth and height;
And far away into the sickly light,
From many a wondrous grot and secret cell
Unnumbered and enormous polypi[2]
10 Winnow with giant arms the slumbering green.

There hath he lain for ages and will lie
Battening upon huge seaworms in his sleep,
Until the latter fire[3] shall heat the deep;
Then once by man and angels to be seen,
15 In roaring he shall rise and on the surface die.

1830

---

1. *Kraken*, mythical sea monster.
2. *polypi* (pol′ip ī′), octopuses, or sea serpents.
3. *latter fire*, the destruction of the earth at the Last Judgment.

Tears, Idle Tears

Alfred, Lord Tennyson

Tears, idle tears, I know not what they mean,
Tears from the depth of some divine despair
Rise in the heart, and gather to the eyes,
In looking on the happy Autumn fields,
5 And thinking of the days that are no more.

Fresh as the first beam glittering on a sail,
That brings our friends up from the underworld,
Sad as the last which reddens over one
That sinks with all we love below the verge;
10 So sad, so fresh, the days that are no more.

Ah, sad and strange as in dark summer dawns
The earliest pipe of half-awakened birds
To dying ears, when unto dying eyes
The casement slowly grows a glimmering square;
15 So sad, so strange, the days that are no more.

Dear as remembered kisses after death,
And sweet as those by hopeless fancy feigned
On lips that are for others; deep as love,
Deep as first love, and wild with all regret;
20 O Death in Life, the days that are no more.

1834   **1847**

Crossing the Bar

Alfred, Lord Tennyson

Tennyson composed this lyric in 1889 after recovering from a serious illness. The "bar" is an underwater ridge of sand across the mouth of a harbor. Once over it, a boat is in open water. Tennyson explained the last lines by saying, "The pilot has been on board all the while, but in the dark I have not seen him." He later requested that this poem appear "at the end of all editions of my poems."

Sunset and evening star,
  And one clear call for me!
And may there be no moaning of the bar,
  When I put out to sea,

5 But such a tide as moving seems asleep,
  Too full for sound and foam,
When that which drew from out the boundless
    deep
  Turns again home.

Twilight and evening bell,
10 And after that the dark!

And may there be no sadness of farewell,
  When I embark;

For though from out our bourne[1] of Time and
    Place
  The flood may bear me far,
15 I hope to see my Pilot face to face
  When I have crossed the bar.

1889   1889

---

1. *bourne*, boundary; limit.

THINK AND DISCUSS

THE KRAKEN

Understanding

1. When will the Kraken finally awake? What will happen to it then?

Analyzing

2. Tennyson uses the art of indirection here—he says virtually nothing about the appearance of the Kraken itself. How does its **setting** help instead to give a sense of what the Kraken is like?

Extending

3. How do creatures such as the Kraken inspire questions about the nature of creation itself?

TEARS, IDLE TEARS

Analyzing

1. Explain the cause of these tears.
2. How does this lyric use **images** of light? (See especially lines 6, 8, 11, and 14.)

Extending

3. Explain how the days of the past constitute a sort of death in anybody's life.

CROSSING THE BAR

Understanding

1. The poem's sustained **metaphor** compares embarking on an ocean voyage to what universal human experience?
2. Who or what is the Pilot?

Analyzing

3. What is "that which drew from out the boundless deep" that now "Turns again home"?
4. Why does the speaker ask for a tide that "seems asleep,/Too full for sound and foam"?

Extending

5. Is this a poem of confidence or fear?

COMPOSITION

Writing a Lyric Poem

Write a lyric poem of at least twenty lines, in which you use setting and mood to suggest, rather than specifically describe, something ominous, like the Kraken. Try to achieve a regular rhythm and, if you wish, use rhyme—establishing in your first stanza a rhyme scheme that you follow throughout.

Exploring Tennyson's Figurative Language

"Tears, Idle Tears" employs a series of **similes**, signaled by the word *as*, to suggest experiences that are beyond words. Write an essay addressed to a friend in which you explore the power of some of these similes to suggest experiences and feelings. Select two or three of Tennyson's similes and devote a paragraph to each. Start with the most specific meaning you can see in each comparison, but then free your associations to make more personal connections. That is the kind of reading Tennyson sought to evoke.

Tennyson 573

Reading VICTORIAN FICTION

From its eighteenth-century beginnings, the English novel has functioned both as entertainment and as a moral analysis of life. Here are some guidelines for reading the Victorian novel excerpts that follow.

Determine the narrative point of view. In *David Copperfield*, the title character tells in the first-person about events that he recalls from his personal angle of vision—a highly subjective one, as he hates some people and admires others. As you read, be aware of his youth and of the limited understanding Dickens has given him.

In George Eliot's *The Mill on the Floss*, an omniscient narrator reports the thoughts and feelings of a variety of characters, as if she knows everything about everyone she describes. But Eliot's omniscient narrator is also a specific personality, who clearly favors some characters and ironically undercuts others because she finds them amusing and flawed. At times she shares with the reader her own philosophical musings.

Watch for class relationships. Victorian novels describe a world governed by a powerful class system that dictated relationships. Characters defer to those of a higher social class but treat with remove—or with disdain—those of a lower class. When, however, we see the servant Peggotty sitting in the parlor arguing with her mistress, the scene suggests that the mistress is incapable of ruling her own home.

Keep in mind unstated cultural values. The Victorian ideal of happiness included a stable family life, financial security, and social respectability, and the plots of their novels usually show central characters striving to achieve those goals. Pay attention to what characters say they want, what they really seem to want, and how they try to get what they want.

Anticipate plot developments. To a large extent, Victorian novels follow certain traditions. Knowing this, you can predict outcomes. For example, when *David Copperfield* begins, Clara Copperfield is a young, pretty widow, clearly dependent upon Peggotty to run the household. In this plot situation readers can expect that she will seek a second marriage. Generally, comic novels end with marriage and financial reward—the traditional "happy ending"—while tragic novels end with death and the perpetuation of injustice. In both cases they don't just stop, they come to conclusions. You can look forward to an end to the story in which, somehow, the conflicts of the plot will be resolved and the problems that it presented will be fixed.

Be aware of the limits imposed on Victorian novelists. There was a fairly wide range of subjects, such as human sexual relationships, that Victorian writers could not describe directly. There was a practical reason for this prohibition. It was common practice to read novels aloud after dinner to the whole family, as the evening's entertainment. Writers addressed this audience and were careful not to offend sensitive family members. But this does not mean that Victorian novels skirt difficult subjects altogether. Rather, they deal with them indirectly.

Look for a social message. There is a message in any "happy ending" in which vice is punished and virtue rewarded. Victorian novelists sought further to respond in their fiction to the perceived needs of the era, diagnosing economic, social, and political injustices, and suggesting remedies. For example, in *David Copperfield*, Dickens attacks misguided educational practices and demonstrates serious concern about emotional cruelty in Victorian family life.

Charles Dickens
1812–1870

After Shakespeare, Charles Dickens is the most popular English writer. During his lifetime Dickens completed fourteen novels, two travel books, and four Christmas novellas. He left, as well, a novel unfinished at his death, and several volumes of essays and sketches associated with the three literary magazines he edited during his career.

Dickens achieved his successes on his own. His boyhood was a struggle for survival. His father, John Dickens, was charming but irresponsible. Though he sired a family of eight children, he was chronically careless about money matters. By the time young Dickens was ten, the family was penniless and living in a slum. He received a sketchy education at best. Then, in his twelfth year, his parents decided he should go to work.

They found him a job in a warehouse pasting labels on bottles of shoe polish. It was an experience he called "the secret agony of my soul." Later in life he kept the secret from all but one of his friends. Dickens never minded hard work, but already, at this young age, he felt intimations of his real abilities, and to work as a drudge six days a week seemed to stifle any chance he had for success in life. He never forgave his parents.

After about half a year, sympathetic relatives rescued the Dickens family, and Charles went back to school filled with hope. At fifteen he began a career as a law clerk, and learned stenography. Soon he was using this skill to record speeches in Parliament, and by the age of twenty he had become a successful newspaper reporter.

Dickens began submitting short fictional sketches to London magazines, and one caught the eye of the publishers Chapman and Hall. They were planning to try a new form of fiction; a series of illustrated comical sketches that would appear serially each month for better than a year. They hired the young Dickens and at the end of March, 1836, the first issue of *The Pickwick Papers* appeared. By November forty thousand readers a month were buying copies, and Dickens found himself a celebrity.

Dickens wrote all his novels for serial publication. His early novels were informal in design—Dickens felt free to introduce characters and incidents at whim, or at the bidding of the public. But at least from the time of *Dombey and Son* (1846–1848) he abandoned this informality for strictly organized novels. With few exceptions, each succeeding novel gained him a wider readership.

Dickens's work always combines the comic and the tragic. His is a comprehensive view of human life and his novels make a vigorous response to the injustice and the suffering of his era. His plots are rich with incident, complex, and full of suspense. They keep the reader turning the page. Finally, and here again the parallel with Shakespeare is compelling, his characters live. While some readers may forget details of plot and scene, the gallery of characters Dickens created remains in the memory and the imagination. His is a densely peopled world, and ultimately this is why so many readers enjoy his novels.

from David Copperfield

Charles Dickens

hether I shall turn out to be the hero of my own life, or whether that station will be held by anybody else, these pages must show. To begin my life with the beginning of my life, I record that I was born (as I have been informed and believe) on a Friday, at twelve o'clock at night. It was remarked that the clock began to strike, and I began to cry, simultaneously. . . .

I was born at Blunderstone, in Suffolk, or "thereby," as they say in Scotland. I was a posthumous child. My father's eyes had closed upon the light of this world six months, when mine opened on it. There is something strange to me, even now, in the reflection that he never saw me; and something stranger yet in the shadowy remembrance that I have of my first childish associations with his white gravestone in the churchyard, and of the indefinable compassion I used to feel for it lying out alone there in the dark night, when our little parlor was warm and bright with fire and candle, and the doors of our house were—almost cruelly, it seemed to me sometimes—bolted and locked against it. . . .

The first objects that assume a distinct presence before me, as I look far back, into the blank of my infancy, are my mother with her pretty hair and youthful shape, and Peggotty with no shape at all, and eyes so dark that they seemed to darken their whole neighborhood in her face, and cheeks and arms so hard and red that I wondered the birds didn't peck her in preference to apples.

I believe I can remember these two at a little distance apart, dwarfed to my sight by stooping down or kneeling on the floor, and I going unsteadily from the one to the other. I have an impression on my mind which I cannot distinguish from actual remembrance, of the touch of Peggotty's forefinger as she used to hold it out to me, and of its being roughened by needlework, like a pocket nutmeg grater.

This may be fancy, though I think the memory of most of us can go farther back into such times than many of us suppose; just as I believe the power of observation in numbers of very young children to be quite wonderful for its closeness and accuracy. Indeed, I think that most grown men who are remarkable in this respect, may with greater propriety be said not to have lost the faculty, than to have acquired it; the rather, as I generally observe such men to retain a certain freshness, and gentleness, and capacity of being pleased, which are also an inheritance they have preserved from their childhood. . . .

What else do I remember? Let me see. There comes out of the cloud, our house—not new to me, but quite familiar, in its earliest remembrance. On the ground floor is Peggotty's kitchen, opening into a back yard; with a pigeon-house on a pole, in the center, without any pigeons in it; a great dog kennel in a corner, without any dog; and a quantity of fowls that look terribly tall to me, walking about, in a menacing and ferocious manner. There is one cock who gets upon a post to crow, and seems to take particular notice of me as I look at him through the kitchen window, who makes me shiver, he is so fierce. Of the geese outside the side gate who come waddling after me with their long necks stretched out when I go that way, I dream at night: as a man environed by wild beasts might dream of lions.

Here is a long passage—what an enormous perspective I make of it!—leading from Peggotty's kitchen to the front door. A dark store room opens out of it, and that is a place to be run past at night; for I don't know what may be among those tubs and jars and old tea chests, when there is nobody in there with a dimly burning light, letting a moldy air come out at the door, in which there is the smell of soap, pickles, pepper, candles, and coffee, all at one whiff. Then there are the two parlors: the parlor in which we sit of an evening, my mother and I and Peggotty—for Peggotty is quite our companion, when her work is done and we are alone—and the best parlor where we sit on a Sunday; grandly, but not so comfortably. There is something of a doleful air about that room to me, for Peggotty has told me—I don't know when, but apparently ages ago—about my father's funeral, and the company having their black cloaks put on. One Sunday night my mother reads to Peggotty and me in there, how Lazarus was raised up from the dead. And I am so frightened that they are afterwards obliged to take me out of bed, and show me the quiet churchyard out of the bedroom window, with the dead all lying in their graves at rest, below the solemn moon.

There is nothing half so green that I know anywhere, as the grass of that churchyard; nothing half so shady as its trees; nothing half so quiet as its tombstones. The sheep are feeding there, when I kneel up, early in the morning, in my little bed in a closet[1] within my mother's room, to look out at it; and I see the red light shining on the sundial, and think within myself, "Is the sundial glad, I wonder, that it can tell the time again?"

Here is our pew in the church. What a highbacked pew! With a window near it, out of which our house can be seen, and *is* seen many times during the morning service, by Peggotty, who likes to make herself as sure as she can that it's not being robbed, or is not in flames. But though Peggotty's eye wanders, she is much offended if mine does, and frowns to me, as I stand upon the seat, that I am to look at the clergyman. But I can't always look at him—I know him without that white thing on, and I am afraid of his wondering why I stare so, and perhaps stopping the service to inquire—and what am I to do? It's a dreadful thing to gape, but I must do something. I look at my mother, but *she* pretends not to see me. I look at a boy in the aisle, and *he* makes faces at me. I look at the sunlight coming in at the open door

Our Pew at Church, by "Phiz" (Hablot Knight Browne).

through the porch, and there I see a stray sheep—I don't mean a sinner, but mutton—half making up his mind to come into the church. I feel that if I looked at him any longer, I might be tempted to say something out loud; and what would become of me then! . . . I look . . . to the pulpit; and think what a good place it would be to play in, and what a castle it would make, with another boy coming up the stairs to attack it, and having the velvet cushion with the tassels thrown down on his head. In time my eyes gradually shut up; and, from seeming to hear the clergyman singing a drowsy song in the heat, I hear nothing, until I fall off the seat with a crash, and am taken out, more dead than alive, by Peggotty.

And now I see the outside of our house, with the latticed bedroom windows standing open to let in the sweet-smelling air, and the ragged old

---

1. *closet,* enclosure.

rooks' nests still dangling in the elm trees at the bottom of the front garden. Now I am in the garden at the back, beyond the yard where the empty pigeon house and dog kennel are—a very preserve of butterflies, as I remember it, with a high fence, and a gate and padlock; where the fruit clusters on the trees, riper and richer than fruit has ever been since, in any other garden, and where my mother gathers some in a basket, while I stand by, bolting furtive gooseberries, and trying to look unmoved. A great wind rises, and the summer is gone in a moment. We are playing in the winter twilight, dancing about the parlor. When my mother is out of breath and rests herself in an elbow chair, I watch her winding her bright curls round her fingers, and straightening her waist, and nobody knows better than I do that she likes to look so well, and is proud of being so pretty.

That is among my very earliest impressions. That, and a sense that we were both a little afraid of Peggotty, and submitted ourselves in most things to her direction, were among the first opinions—if they may be so called—that I ever derived from what I saw.

Peggotty and I were sitting one night by the parlor fire, alone. I had been reading to Peggotty about crocodiles. I must have read very perspicuously, or the good soul must have been deeply interested, for I remember she had a cloudy impression, after I had done, that they were a sort of vegetable. I was tired of reading, and dead sleepy; but having leave, as a high treat, to sit up until my mother came home from spending the evening at a neighbor's, I would rather had died upon my post (of course) than have gone to bed. I had reached that stage of sleepiness when Peggotty seemed to swell and grow immensely large. I propped my eyelids open with my two forefingers, and looked perseveringly at her as she sat at work; at the little bit of wax candle she kept for her thread—how old it looked, being so wrinkled in all directions!—at the little house with a thatched roof, where the yard-measure lived; at her work box with a sliding lid, with a view of Saint Paul's Cathedral (with a pink dome) painted on the top; at the brass thimble on her finger; at herself, whom I thought lovely. I felt so sleepy, that I knew if I lost sight of anything, for a moment, I was gone.

"Peggotty," says I, suddenly, "were you ever married?"

"Lord, Master Davy," replied Peggotty, "What's put marriage in your head!"

She answered with such a start, that it quite awoke me. And then she stopped in her work, and looked at me, with her needle drawn out to its thread's length.

"But *were* you ever married, Peggotty?" says I. "You are a very handsome woman, an't you?"

I thought her in a different style from my mother, certainly; but of another school of beauty, I considered her a perfect example. . . .

"*Me* handsome, Davy!" said Peggotty. "Lawk, no, my dear! But what put marriage in your head?"

"I don't know!—You mustn't marry more than one person at a time, may you, Peggotty?"

"Certainly not," says Peggotty, with the promptest decision.

"But if you marry a person, and the person dies, why then you may marry another person, mayn't you, Peggotty?"

"You MAY," says Peggotty, "if you choose, my dear. That's a matter of opinion."

"But what is your opinion, Peggotty?" said I.

I asked her, and looked curiously at her, because she looked so curiously at me.

"My opinion is," said Peggotty, taking her eyes from me, after a little indecision and going on with her work, "that I never was married myself, Master Davy, and that I don't expect to be. That's all I know about the subject."

"You an't cross, I suppose, Peggotty, are you?" said I, after sitting quiet for a minute.

I really thought she was, she had been so short with me; but I was quite mistaken: for she laid aside her work (which was a stocking of her own), and opening her arms wide, took my curly head within them, and gave it a good squeeze. I know it was a good squeeze, because, being very plump, whenever she made any little exertion after she was dressed, some of the buttons on the back of her gown flew off. And I recollect two bursting to the opposite side of the parlor, while she was hugging me.

"Now let me hear some more about the Crorkindills," said Peggotty, who was not quite right in the name yet, "for I an't heard half enough."

I couldn't quite understand why Peggotty looked so queer, or why she was so ready to go back to the crocodiles. However, we returned to those monsters, with fresh wakefulness on my part, and we left their eggs in the sand for the sun to hatch; and we ran away from them, and baffled them by constantly turning, which they were unable to do quickly, on account of their unwieldy make; and we went into the water after them, as natives, and put sharp pieces of timber down their throats; and in short we ran the whole crocodile gauntlet. *I* did at least; but I had my doubts of Peggotty, who was thoughtfully sticking her needle into various parts of her face and arms, all the time.

We had exhausted the crocodiles, and begun with the alligators, when the garden bell rang. We went out to the door; and there was my mother, looking even unusually pretty, I thought, and with her a gentleman with beautiful black hair and whiskers, who had walked home with us from church last Sunday.

As my mother stooped down on the threshhold to take me in her arms and kiss me, the gentleman said I was a more highly privileged little fellow than a monarch—or something like that; for my later understanding comes, I am sensible, to my aid here.

"What does that mean?" I asked him, over her shoulder.

He patted me on the head; but somehow, I didn't like him or his deep voice, and I was jealous that his hand should touch my mother's in touching me—which it did. I put it away, as roughly as I could.

"Oh Davy!" remonstrated my mother.

"Dear boy!" said the gentleman. "I cannot wonder at his devotion!"

I never saw such a beautiful color on my mother's face before. She gently chid me for being rude; and, keeping me close to her shawl, turned to thank the gentleman for taking so much trouble as to bring her home. She put out her hand to him as she spoke, and, as he met it with his own, she glanced, I thought, at me.

"Let us say 'good night,' my fine boy," said the gentleman, when he had bent his head—*I* saw him!—over my mother's little glove.

"Good night!" said I.

"Come! Let us be the best friends in the world!" said the gentleman, laughing. "Shake hands!"

My right hand was in my mother's left, so I gave him the other.

"Why that's the wrong hand, Davy!" laughed the gentleman.

My mother drew my right hand forward, but I was resolved, for my former reason, not to give it him, and I did not. I gave him the other, and he shook it heartily, and said I was a brave fellow, and went away.

At this minute I see him turn round in the garden, and give us a last look with his ill-omened black eyes, before the door was shut.

Peggotty, who had not said a word or moved a finger, secured the fastenings instantly, and we all went into the parlor. My mother, contrary to her usual habit, instead of coming to the elbow chair by the fire, remained at the other end of the room, and sat singing to herself.

"—Hope you have had a pleasant evening, ma'am," said Peggotty, standing as stiff as a barrel in the center of the room, with a candlestick in her hand.

"Much obliged to you, Peggotty," returned my mother, in a cheerful voice, "I have had a *very* pleasant evening."

"A stranger or so makes an agreeable change," suggested Peggotty.

"A very agreeable change indeed," returned my mother.

Peggotty continuing to stand motionless in the middle of the room, and my mother resuming her singing, I fell asleep, though I was not so sound asleep but that I could hear voices, without hearing what they said. When I half awoke from this uncomfortable doze, I found Peggotty and my mother both in tears, and both talking.

"Not such a one as this, Mr. Copperfield wouldn't have liked," said Peggotty. "That I say, and that I swear!"

"Good Heavens!" cried my mother. "You'll drive me mad! Was ever any poor girl so ill-used by her servants as I am! Why do I do myself the injustice of calling myself a girl? Have I never been married, Peggotty?"

"God knows you have, ma'am," returned Peggotty.

"Then how can you dare," said my mother—"you know I don't mean how can you dare, Peggotty, but how can you have the heart—to make me so uncomfortable and say such bitter things to me, when you are well aware that I haven't, out of this place, a single friend to turn to!"

"The more's the reason," returned Peggotty, "for saying that it won't do. No! That it won't do. No! No price could make it do. No!"—I thought Peggotty would have thrown the candlestick away, she was so emphatic with it.

"How can you be so aggravating," cried my mother, shedding more tears than before, "as to talk in such an unjust manner! How can you go on as if it was all settled and arranged, Peggotty, when I tell you over and over again, you cruel thing, that beyond the commonest civilities nothing whatever has passed! You talk of admiration. What am I to do? If people are so silly as to indulge the sentiment, is it *my* fault? What am I to do, I ask you? Would you wish me to shave my head and black my face, or disfigure myself with a burn, or a scald, or something of that sort? I dare say you would, Peggotty. I dare say you'd quite enjoy it."

Peggotty seemed to take this aspersion very much to heart, I thought.

"And my dear boy," cried my mother, coming to the elbow chair in which I was, and caressing me, "my own little Davy! Is it to be hinted to me that I am wanting in affection for my precious treasure, the dearest little fellow that ever was!"

"Nobody never went and hinted no such a thing," said Peggotty.

"You did, Peggotty!" returned my mother.

"You know you did. What else was it possible to infer from what you said, you unkind creature, when you know as well as I do, that on his account only last quarter I wouldn't buy myself a new parasol, though that old green one is frayed the whole way up, and the fringe is perfectly mangy. You know it is, Peggotty. You can't deny it." Then, turning affectionately to me, with her cheek against mine, "Am I a naughty mama to you, Davy? Am I a nasty, cruel, selfish, bad mama? Say I am, my child; say 'yes,' my dear boy, and Peggotty will love you, and Peggotty's love is a great deal better than mine, Davy. *I* don't love you at all, do I?"

At this, we all fell a-crying together. I think I was the loudest of the party, but I am sure we were all sincere about it. I was quite heartbroken myself, and am afraid that in the first transports of wounded tenderness I called Peggotty a "Beast." That honest creature was in deep affliction, I remember, and must have become quite buttonless on the occasion; for a little volley of those explosives went off, when, after having made it up with my mother, she kneeled down by the elbow chair, and made it up with me.

We went to bed greatly dejected. My sobs kept waking me, for a long time; and when one very strong sob quite hoisted me up in bed, I found my mother sitting on the coverlet, and leaning over me. I fell asleep in her arms, after that, and slept soundly.

Whether it was the following Sunday when I saw the gentleman again, or whether there was any greater lapse of time before he reappeared, I cannot recall. I don't profess to be clear about dates. But there he was, in church, and he walked home with us afterwards. He came in, too, to look at a famous geranium we had, in the parlor window. It did not appear to me that he took much notice of it, but before he went he asked my mother to give him a bit of the blossom. She begged him to choose it for himself, but he refused to do that—I could not understand why—so she plucked it for him, and gave it into his hand. He said he would never, never, part with it any more;

and I thought he must be quite a fool not to know that it would fall to pieces in a day or two.

Peggotty began to be less with us, of an evening, than she had always been. My mother deferred to her very much—more than usual, it occurred to me—and we were all three excellent friends; still we were different from what we used to be, and were not so comfortable among ourselves. Sometimes I fancied that Peggotty perhaps objected to my mother's wearing all the pretty dresses she had in her drawers, or to her going so often to visit at that neighbor's; but I couldn't, to my satisfaction, make out how it was.

Gradually, I became used to seeing the gentleman with the black whiskers. I liked him no better than at first, and had the same uneasy jealousy of him; but if I had any reason for it beyond a child's instinctive dislike, and a general idea that Peggotty and I could make much of my mother without any help, it certainly was not *the* reason that I might have found if I had been older. No such thing came into my mind, or near it. I could observe, in little pieces, as it were; but as to making a net of a number of these pieces, and catching anybody in it, that was, as yet, beyond me.

One autumn morning I was with my mother in the front garden, when Mr. Murdstone—I knew him by that name now—came by, on horseback. He reined up his horse to salute my mother, and said he was going to Lowestoft to see some friends who were there with a yacht, and merrily proposed to take me on the saddle before him if I would like the ride.

The air was so clear and pleasant, and the horse seemed to like the idea of the ride so much himself, as he stood snorting and pawing at the garden gate, that I had a great desire to go. . . .

Mr. Murdstone and I were soon off, and trotting along on the green turf by the side of the road. He held me quite easily with one arm, and I don't think I was restless usually; but I could not make up my mind to sit in front of him without turning my head sometimes, and looking up in his face. He had that kind of shallow black eye—I want a better word to express an eye that has no depth in it to be

looked into—which, when it is abstracted, seems from some peculiarity of light to be disfigured, for a moment at a time, by a cast. Several times when I glanced at him, I observed that appearance with a sort of awe, and wondered what he was thinking about so closely. His hair and whiskers were blacker and thicker, looked at so near, than even I had given them credit for being. A squareness about the lower part of his face, and the dotted indication of the strong black beard he shaved close every day, reminded me of the waxwork that had travelled into our neighborhood some half-a-year before. This, his regular eyebrows, and the rich white, and black, and brown, of his complexion—confound his complexion, and his memory!—made me think him, in spite of my misgivings, a very handsome man. I have no doubt that my poor dear mother thought him so too.

We went to an hotel by the sea, where two gentlemen were smoking cigars in a room by themselves. Each of them was lying on at least four chairs, and had a large rough jacket on. In a corner was a heap of coats and boat-cloaks, and a flag, all bundled up together.

They both rolled on to their feet in an untidy sort of manner when we came in, and said "Halloa, Murdstone! We thought you were dead!"

"Not yet," said Mr. Murdstone.

"And who's this shaver?" said one of the gentlemen, taking hold of me.

"That's Davy," returned Mr. Murdstone.

"Davy who?" said the gentleman. "Jones?"

"Copperfield," said Mr. Murdstone.

"What! Bewitching Mrs. Copperfield's encumbrance?" cried the gentleman. "The pretty little widow?"

"Quinion," said Mr. Murdstone, "take care, if you please. Somebody's sharp."

"Who is?" asked the gentleman, laughing.

I looked up, quickly; being curious to know.

"Only Brooks of Sheffield,"[2] said Mr. Murdstone.

I was quite relieved to find it was only Brooks

---

2. Brooks of Sheffield, famous English makers of knives and other cutting instruments.

of Sheffield; for, at first, I really thought it was I.

There seemed to be something comical in the reputation of Mr. Brooks of Sheffield, for both the gentlemen laughed heartily when he was mentioned, and Mr. Murdstone was a good deal amused also. After some laughing, the gentleman whom he had called Quinion, said:

"And what is the opinion of Brooks of Sheffield, in reference to the projected business?"

"Why, I don't know that Brooks understands much about it at present," replied Mr. Murdstone; "but he is not generally favorable, I believe."

There was more laughter at this, and Mr. Quinion said he would ring the bell for some sherry in which to drink to Brooks. This he did; and when the wine came, he made me have a little, with a biscuit, and, before I drank it, stand up and say "Confusion to Brooks of Sheffield!" The toast was received with great applause, and such hearty laughter that it made me laugh too; at which they laughed the more. In short, we quite enjoyed ourselves. . . .

I observed all day that Mr. Murdstone was graver and steadier than the two gentlemen. They were very gay and careless. They joked freely with one another, but seldom with him. It appeared to me that he was more clever and cold than they were, and that they regarded him with something of my own feeling. I remarked that once or twice when Mr. Quinion was talking, he looked at Mr. Murdstone sideways, as if to make sure of his not being displeased; and that once when Mr. Passnidge (the other gentleman) was in high spirits, he trod upon his foot, and gave him a secret caution with his eyes, to observe Mr. Murdstone, who was sitting stern and silent. Nor do I recollect that Mr. Murdstone laughed at all that day, except at the Sheffield joke—and that, by-the-by, was his own.

We went home early in the evening. . . . When he was gone, my mother asked me all about the day I had had, and what they had said and done. I mentioned what they had said about her, and she laughed, and told me they were impudent fellows who talked nonsense—but I knew it pleased her. I knew it quite as well as I know it now. I took the opportunity of asking if she were at all acquainted with Mr. Brooks of Sheffield, but she answered No, only she supposed he must be a manufacturer in the knife and fork way.

Can I say of her face—altered as I have reason to remember it, perished as I know it is—that it is gone, when here it comes before me at this instant, as distinct as any face that I may choose to look on in a crowded street? Can I say of her innocent and girlish beauty, that it faded, and was no more, when its breath falls on my cheek now, as it fell that night? Can I say she ever changed, when my remembrance brings her back to life, thus only; and, truer to its loving youth than I have been, or man ever is, still holds fast what it cherished then?

I write of her just as she was when I had gone to bed after this talk, and she came to bid me good night. She kneeled down playfully by the side of the bed, and laying her chin upon her hands, and laughing, said:

"What was it they said, Davy? Tell me again. I can't believe it."

" 'Bewitching——' " I began.

My mother put her hand upon my lips to stop me.

"It was never bewitching," she said, laughing. "It never could have been bewitching, Davy. Now I know it wasn't!"

"Yes it was. 'Bewitching Mrs. Copperfield,' " I repeated stoutly. "And 'pretty.' "

"No no, it was never pretty. Not pretty," interposed my mother, laying her fingers on my lips again.

"Yes it was, 'Pretty little widow.' "

"What foolish, impudent creatures!" cried my mother, laughing and covering her face. "What ridiculous men! An't they? Davy dear—"

"Well, Ma."

"Don't tell Peggotty; she might be angry with them. I am dreadfully angry with them myself; but I would rather Peggotty didn't know."

I promised, of course; and we kissed one another over and over again, and I soon fell fast asleep.

It seems to me, at this distance of time, as if

it were the next day when Peggotty broached the striking and adventurous proposition I am about to mention; but it was probably about two months afterwards.

We were sitting as before, one evening (when my mother was out as before), in company with the stocking and the yard-measure, and the bit of wax, and the box with Saint Paul's on the lid, and the Crocodile Book, when Peggotty, after looking at me several times, and opening her mouth as if she were going to speak, without doing it—which I thought was merely gaping, or I should have been rather alarmed—said coaxingly:

"Master Davy, how should you like to go along with me and spend a fortnight at my brother's at Yarmouth? Wouldn't *that* be a treat?"

"Is your brother an agreeable man, Peggotty?" I inquired, provisionally.

"Oh what an agreeable man he is!" cried Peggotty, holding up her hands. "Then there's the sea; and the boats and ships; and the fishermen; and the beach. . . ."

I was flushed by her summary of delights, and replied that it would indeed be a treat, but what would my mother say?

"Why then I'll as good as bet a guinea," said Peggotty, intent upon my face, "that she'll let us go. I'll ask her, if you like, as soon as ever she comes home. There now!"

"But what's she to do while we're away?" said I, putting my small elbows on the table to argue the point. "She can't live by herself."

If Peggotty were looking for a hole, all of a sudden, in the heel of that stocking, it must have been a very little one indeed, and not worth darning.

"I say! Peggotty? She can't live by herself, you know."

"Oh bless you!" said Peggotty, looking at me again at last. "Don't you know? She's going to stay for a fortnight with Mrs. Grayper. Mrs. Grayper's going to have a lot of company."

Oh! If that was it, I was quite ready to go. I waited, in the utmost impatience, until my mother came home from Mrs. Grayper's (for it was that identical neighbor), to ascertain if we could get leave to carry out this great idea. Without being nearly so much surprised as I had expected, my mother entered into it readily; and it was all arranged that night, and my board and lodging during the visit were to be paid for.

The day soon came for our going. It was such an early day that it came soon, even to me, who was in a fever of expectation, and half afraid that an earthquake or a fiery mountain, or some other great convulsion of nature, might interpose to stop the expedition. We were to go in a carrier's cart, which departed in the morning after breakfast. I would have given any money to have been allowed to wrap myself up overnight, and sleep in my hat and boots.

It touches me nearly now, although I tell it lightly, to recollect how eager I was to leave my happy home; to think how little I suspected what I did leave for ever.

I am glad to recollect that when the carrier's cart was at the gate, and my mother stood there kissing me, a grateful fondness for her and for the old place I had never turned my back upon before, made me cry. I am glad to know that my mother cried too, and that I felt her heart beat against mine.

I am glad to recollect that when the carrier began to move, my mother ran out at the gate, and called to him to stop, that she might kiss me once more. I am glad to dwell upon the earnestness and love with which she lifted up her face to mine, and did so.

As we left her standing in the road, Mr. Murdstone came up to where she was, and seemed to expostulate with her for being so moved. I was looking back round the awning of the cart, and wondered what business it was of his. Peggotty, who was also looking back on the other side, seemed anything but satisfied; as the face she brought into the cart denoted.

I sat looking at Peggotty for some time, in a reverie on this supposititious case: whether, if she were employed to lose me like the boy in the fairy tale, I should be able to track my way home again by the buttons she would shed. . . .

Young David, in his innocence, enjoys his holiday with Peggotty's family. Time passes swiftly, and soon he must return home.

Now, all the time I had been on my visit, I had been ungrateful to my home again, and had thought little or nothing about it. But I was no sooner turned towards it, than my reproachful young conscience seemed to point that way with a steady finger; and I felt, all the more for the sinking of my spirits, that it was my nest, and that my mother was my comforter and friend.

This gained upon me as we went along; so that the nearer we drew, and the more familiar the objects became that we passed, the more excited I was to get there, and to run into her arms. But Peggotty, instead of sharing in these transports, tried to check them (though very kindly), and looked confused and out of sorts.

Blunderstone Rookery would come, however, in spite of her, when the carrier's horse pleased—and did. How well I recollect it, on a cold grey afternoon, with a dull sky, threatening rain!

The door opened, and I looked, half laughing and half crying in my pleasant agitation, for my mother. It was not she, but a strange servant.

"Why, Peggotty!" I said ruefully, "isn't she come home!"

"Yes, yes, Master Davy," said Peggotty. "She's come home. Wait a little bit, Master Davy, and I'll—I'll tell you something."

Between her agitation, and her natural awkwardness in getting out of the cart, Peggotty was making a most extraordinary festoon of herself, but I felt too blank and strange to tell her so. When she had got down, she took me by the hand; led me, wondering, into the kitchen; and shut the door.

"Peggotty!" said I, quite frightened. "What's the matter?"

"Nothing's the matter, bless you, Master Davy dear!" she answered, assuming an air of sprightliness.

"Something's the matter, I'm sure. Where's mama?"

"Where's mama, Master Davy?" repeated Peggotty.

"Yes. Why hasn't she come out to the gate, and what have we come in here for? Oh, Peggotty!" My eyes were full, and I felt as if I were going to tumble down.

"Bless the precious boy!" cried Peggotty, taking hold of me. "What is it? Speak, my pet!"

"Not dead, too! Oh, she's not dead, Peggotty?"

Peggotty cried out No! with an astonishing volume of voice; and then sat down, and began to pant, and said I had given her a turn.

I gave her a hug to take away the turn, or to give her another turn in the right direction, and then stood before her, looking at her in anxious inquiry.

"You see, dear, I should have told you before now," said Peggotty, "but I hadn't an opportunity. I ought to have made it, perhaps, but I couldn't azackly"—that was always the substitute for exactly, in Peggotty's militia of words—"bring my mind to it."

"Go on, Peggotty," said I, more frightened than before.

"Master Davy," said Peggotty, untying her bonnet with a shaking hand, and speaking in a breathless sort of way. "What do you think? You have got a Pa!"

I trembled, and turned white. Something—I don't know what, or how—connected with the grave in the churchyard, and the raising of the dead, seemed to strike me like an unwholesome wind.

"A new one," said Peggotty.

"A new one?" I repeated.

Peggotty gave a gasp, as if she were swallowing something that was very hard, and, putting out her hand, said:

"Come and see him."

"I don't want to see him."

—"And your mama," said Peggotty.

I ceased to draw back, and we went straight to the best parlor, where she left me. On one side of the fire, sat my mother; on the other, Mr. Murdstone. My mother dropped her work, and arose hurriedly, but timidly I thought.

"Now, Clara, my dear," said Mr. Murdstone. "Recollect! control yourself, always control yourself! Davy boy, how do you do?"

I gave him my hand. After a moment of suspense, I went and kissed my mother: she kissed me, patted me gently on the shoulder, and sat down again to her work. I could not look at her, I could not look at him. I knew quite well that he was looking at us both; and I turned to the window and looked out there, at some shrubs that were dropping their heads in the cold.

As soon as I could creep away, I crept upstairs. My old dear bedroom was changed, and I was to lie a long way off. I rambled downstairs to find anything that was like itself, so altered it all seemed; and roamed into the yard. I very soon started back from there, for the empty dog kennel was filled up with a great dog—deep-mouthed and black-haired like Him—and he was very angry at the sight of me, and sprung out to get at me.

If the room to which my bed was removed, were a sentient thing that could give evidence, I might appeal to it at this day—who sleeps there now, I wonder!—to bear witness for me what a heavy heart I carried to it. I went up there, hearing the dog in the yard bark after me all the way while I climbed the stairs; and, looking as blank and strange upon the room as the room looked upon me, sat down with my small hands crossed, and thought.

I thought of the oddest things. Of the shape of the room, of the cracks in the ceiling, of the paper on the wall, of the flaws in the window glass making ripples and dimples on the prospect, of the washing stand being rickety on its three legs, and having a discontented something about it. . . . I rolled myself up in a corner of the counterpane, and cried myself to sleep.

I was awakened by somebody saying "Here he is!" and uncovering my hot head. My mother and Peggotty had come to look for me, and it was one of them who had done it.

"Davy," said my mother. "What's the matter?"

I thought it very strange that she should ask me, and answered, "Nothing." I turned over on my face, I recollect, to hide my trembling lip, which answered her with greater truth.

"Davy," said my mother. "Davy, my child!"

I dare say no words she could have uttered, would have affected me so much, then, as her calling me her child. I hid my tears in the bedclothes, and pressed her from me with my hand, when she would have raised me up.

"This is your doing, Peggotty, you cruel thing!" said my mother. "I have no doubt at all about it. How can you reconcile it to your conscience, I wonder, to prejudice my own boy against me, or against anybody who is dear to me? What do you mean by it, Peggotty?"

Poor Peggotty lifted up her hands and eyes, and only answered, in a sort of paraphrase of the grace I usually repeated after dinner, "Lord forgive you, Mrs. Copperfield, and for what you have said this minute, may you never be truly sorry!"

"It's enough to distract me," cried my mother. "In my honeymoon, too, when my most inveterate enemy might relent, one would think, and not envy me a little peace of mind and happiness, Davy, you naughty boy! Peggotty, you savage creature! Oh, dear me!" cried my mother, turning from one of us to the other, in her pettish wilful manner, "what a troublesome world this is, when one has the most right to expect it to be as agreeable as possible!"

I felt the touch of a hand that I knew was neither hers nor Peggotty's, and slipped to my feet at the bedside. It was Mr. Murdstone's hand, and he kept it on my arm as he said:

"What's this? Clara, my love, have you forgotten?—Firmness, my dear!"

"I am very sorry, Edward," said my mother. "I meant to be very good, but I am so uncomfortable."

"Indeed!" he answered. "That's a bad hearing, so soon, Clara."

"I say it's very hard I should be made so now," returned my mother, pouting; "and it is—very hard—isn't it?"

He drew her to him, whispered in her ear, and kissed her. I knew as well, when I saw my mother's head lean down upon his shoulder, and her arm touch his neck—I knew as well that he could mold her pliant nature into any form he chose, as I know, now, that he did it.

"Go you below, my love," said Mr. Murdstone. "David and I will come down, together. My friend," turning a darkening face on Peggotty, when he had watched my mother out, and dismissed her with a nod and a smile: "do you know your mistress's name?"

"She has been my mistress a long time, sir," answered Peggotty. "I ought to know it."

"That's true," he answered. "But I thought I heard you, as I came upstairs, address her by a name that is not hers. She has taken mine, you know. Will you remember that?"

Peggotty, with some uneasy glances at me, curtseyed herself out of the room without replying; seeing, I suppose, that she was expected to go, and had no excuse for remaining. When we two were left alone, he shut the door, and sitting on a chair, and holding me standing before him, looked steadily into my eyes. I felt my own attracted, no less steadily, to his. As I recall our being opposed thus, face to face, I seem again to hear my heart beat fast and high.

"David," he said, making his lips thin, by pressing them together, "if I have an obstinate horse or dog to deal with, what do you think I do?"

"I don't know."

"I beat him."

I had answered in a kind of breathless whisper, but I felt, in my silence, that my breath was shorter now.

"I make him wince, and smart. I say to myself, 'I'll conquer that fellow'; and if it were to cost him all the blood he had, I should do it. What is that upon your face?"

"Dirt," I said.

He knew it was the mark of tears as well as I. But if he had asked the question twenty times, each time with twenty blows, I believe my baby heart would have burst before I would have told him so.

"You have a good deal of intelligence for a little fellow," he said, with a grave smile that belonged to him, "and you understand me very well, I

see. Wash that face, sir, and come down with me. . . ."

Soon Mr. Murdstone's sister Jane joins the unhappy family, and brother and sister begin to separate David from his mother.

There had been some talk on occasions of my going to boarding school. Mr. and Miss Murdstone had originated it, and my mother had of course agreed with them. Nothing, however, was concluded on the subject yet. In the meantime, I learnt lessons at home.

Shall I ever forget those lessons! They were presided over nominally by my mother, but really by Mr. Murdstone and his sister, who were always present, and found them a favorable occasion for giving my mother lessons in that miscalled firmness, which was the bane of both our lives. I believe I was kept at home, for that purpose. I had been apt enough to learn, and willing enough, when my mother and I had lived alone together. I can faintly remember learning the alphabet at her knee. To this day, when I look upon the fat black letters in the primer, the puzzling novelty of their shapes, and the easy good nature of O and Q and S, always seem to present themselves again before me as they used to do. But they recall no feeling of disgust or reluctance. On the contrary, I seem to have walked along a path of flowers as far as the Crocodile Book, and to have been cheered by the gentleness of my mother's voice and manner all the way. But these solemn lessons which succeeded those, I remember as the deathblow at my peace, and a grievous daily drudgery and misery. They were very long, very numerous, very hard—perfectly unintelligible, some of them, to me—and I was generally as much bewildered by them as I believe my poor mother was herself.

Let me remember how it used to be, and bring one morning back again.

I come into the second-best parlor after breakfast, with my books, and an exercise book, and a slate. My mother is ready for me at her writing desk, but not half so ready as Mr. Murdstone in his easy chair by the window (though he pretends to be reading a book), or as Miss Murdstone, sitting near my mother stringing steel beads. The very sight of these two has such an influence over me, that I begin to feel the words I have been at infinite pains to get into my head, all sliding away, and going I don't know where. I wonder where they *do* go, by-the-by?

I hand the first book to my mother. Perhaps it is a grammar, perhaps a history, or geography. I take a last drowning look at the page as I give it into her hand, and start off aloud at a racing pace while I have got it fresh. I trip over a word. Mr. Murdstone looks up. I trip over another word. Miss Murdstone looks up. I redden, tumble over half-a-dozen words, and stop. I think my mother would show me the book if she dared, but she does not dare, and she says softly:

"Oh, Davy, Davy!"

"Now, Clara," says Mr. Murdstone, "be firm with the boy. Don't say 'Oh, Davy, Davy!' That's childish. He knows his lesson, or he does not know it."

"He does *not* know it," Miss Murdstone interposes awfully.

"I am really afraid he does not," says my mother.

"Then you see, Clara," returns Miss Murdstone, "you should just give him the book back, and make him know it."

"Yes, certainly," says my mother; "that is what I intend to do, my dear Jane. Now, Davy, try once more, and don't be stupid."

I obey the first clause of the injunction by trying once more, but am not so successful with the second, for I am very stupid. I tumble down before I get to the old place, at a point where I was all right before, and stop to think. But I don't think about the lesson. I can't. I think of the number of yards of net in Miss Murdstone's cap, or of the price of Mr. Murdstone's dressing gown, or any such ridiculous problem that I have no business with, and don't want to have anything at all to do with. Mr. Murdstone makes a movement of impatience which I have been expecting for a long time. Miss Murdstone does the same. My mother glances submissively at them, shuts the book, and

lays it by as an arrear to be worked out when my other tasks are done.

There is a pile of these arrears very soon, and it swells like a rolling snowball. The bigger it gets, the more stupid *I* get. The case is so hopeless, and I feel that I am wallowing in such a bog of nonsense, that I give up all idea of getting out, and abandon myself to my fate. The despairing way in which my mother and I look at each other, as I blunder on, is truly melancholy. But the greatest effect in these miserable lessons is when my mother (thinking nobody is observing her) tries to give me the clue by the motion of her lips. At that instant, Miss Murdstone, who has been lying in wait for nothing else all along, says in a deep warning voice:

"Clara!"

My mother starts, colors, and smiles faintly. Mr. Murdstone comes out of his chair, takes the book, throws it at me or boxes my ears with it, and turns me out of the room by the shoulders.

Even when the lessons are done, the worst is yet to happen, in the shape of an appalling sum. This is invented for me, and delivered to me orally by Mr. Murdstone, and begins, "If I go into a cheesemonger's shop, and buy five thousand double-Gloucester cheeses at fourpence-halfpenny each, present payment"—at which I see Miss Murdstone secretly overjoyed. I pore over these cheeses without any result or enlightenment until dinner time; when . . . I have a slice of bread to help me out with the cheeses, and am considered in disgrace for the rest of the evening. . . .

The natural result of this treatment, continued, I suppose, for some six months or more, was to make me sullen, dull, and dogged. I was not made the less so, by my sense of being daily more and more shut out and alienated from my mother. I believe I should have been almost stupefied but for one circumstance.

It was this. My father had left in a little room upstairs, to which I had access (for it adjoined my own) a small collection of books which nobody else in our house ever troubled. From that blessed little room *Roderick Random, Peregrine Pickle, Humphrey Clinker, Tom Jones, The Vicar of Wakefield, Don Quixote, Gil Blas,* and *Robinson*

Crusoe, came out, a glorious host, to keep me company.[3] They kept alive my fancy, and my hope of something beyond that place and time. . . . It is astonishing to me now, how I found time, in the midst of my porings and blunderings over heavier themes, to read those books as I did. It is curious to me how I could ever have consoled myself under my small troubles (which were great troubles to me), by impersonating my favorite characters in them—as I did—and by putting Mr. and Miss Murdstone into all the bad ones—which I did too. . . . I had a greedy relish for a few volumes of Voyages and Travels—I forget what, now—that were on those shelves; and for days and days I can remember to have gone about my region of our house, armed with the center-piece out of an old set of boot-trees—the perfect realization of Captain Somebody, of the Royal British Navy, in danger of being beset by savages, and resolved to sell his life at a great price. The Captain never lost dignity, from having his ears boxed with the Latin Grammar. I did; but the Captain was a Captain and a hero, in despite of all the grammars of all the languages in the world, dead or alive.

This was my only and my constant comfort. When I think of it, the picture always rises in my mind, of a summer evening, the boys at play in the churchyard, and I sitting on my bed, reading as if for life. Every barn in the neighborhood, every stone in the church, and every foot of the churchyard, had some association of its own, in my mind, connected with these books, and stood for some locality made famous in them. . . .

The reader now understands as well as I do, what I was when I came to that point of my youthful history to which I am now coming again.

One morning when I went into the parlor with my books, I found my mother looking anxious, Miss Murdstone looking firm, and Mr. Murdstone binding something round the bottom of a cane—a lithe and limber cane, which he left off binding when I came in, and poised and switched in the air.

"I tell you, Clara," said Mr. Murdstone, "I have been often flogged myself."

"To be sure; of course," said Miss Murdstone.

"Certainly, my dear Jane," faltered my mother, meekly. "But—but do you think it did Edward good?"

"Do you think it did Edward harm, Clara?" asked Mr. Murdstone, gravely.

"That's the point!" said his sister.

To this my mother returned, "Certainly, my dear Jane," and said no more.

I felt an apprehension that I was personally interested in this dialogue, and sought Mr. Murdstone's eye as it lighted on mine.

"Now, David," he said—and I saw that cast again, as he said it—"you must be far more careful today than usual." He gave the cane another poise, and another switch; and having finished his preparation of it, laid it down beside him, with an expressive look, and took up his book.

This was a good freshener to my presence of mind, as a beginning. I felt the words of my lessons slipping off, not one by one, or line by line, but by the entire page. I tried to lay hold of them; but they seemed, if I may so express it, to have put skates on, and to skim away from me with a smoothness there was no checking.

We began badly, and went on worse. I had come in, with an idea of distinguishing myself rather, conceiving that I was very well prepared; but it turned out to be quite a mistake. Book after book was added to the heap of failures, Miss Murdstone being firmly watchful of us all the time. And when we came at last to the five thousand cheeses (canes he made it that day, I remember), my mother burst out crying.

"Clara!" said Miss Murdstone, in her warning voice.

"I am not quite well, my dear Jane, I think," said my mother.

I saw him wink, solemnly, at his sister, as he rose and said, taking up the cane:

---

3. *Roderick Random* (1748), *Peregrine Pickle* (1751), and *Humphrey Clinker* (1771) are novels by Tobias Smollett. *Tom Jones* (1749) is a novel by Henry Fielding. *The Vicar of Wakefield* (1766) is a novel by Oliver Goldsmith. *Don Quixote* (1605) is a Spanish novel by Miguel de Cervantes. *Gil Blas* (1715) is a French novel by Le Sage. *Robinson Crusoe* (1719) is a novel by Daniel Defoe.

"Why, Jane, we can hardly expect Clara to bear, with perfect firmness, the worry and torment that David has occasioned her today. That would be stoical. Clara is greatly strengthened and improved, but we can hardly expect so much from her. David, you and I will go upstairs, boy."

As he took me out at the door, my mother ran towards us. Miss Murdstone said, "Clara! are you a perfect fool?" and interfered. I saw my mother stop her ears then, and I heard her crying.

He walked me up to my room slowly and gravely—I am certain he had a delight in that formal parade of executing justice—and when we got there, suddenly twisted my head under his arm.

"Mr. Murdstone! Sir!" I cried to him. "Don't! Pray don't beat me! I have tried to learn, sir, but I can't learn when you and Miss Murdstone are by. I can't indeed!"

"Can't you, indeed, David?" he said. "We'll try that."

He had my head as in a vice, but I twined round him somehow, and stopped him for a moment, entreating him not to beat me. It was only for a moment that I stopped him, for he cut me heavily an instant afterwards, and in the same instant I caught the hand with which he held me in my mouth, between my teeth, and bit it through. It sets my teeth on edge to think of it.

He beat me then, as if he would have beaten me to death. Above all the noise we made, I heard them running up the stairs, and crying out—I heard my mother crying out—and Peggotty. Then he was gone; and the door was locked outside; and I was lying, fevered and hot, and torn, and sore, and raging in my puny way, upon the floor.

How well I recollect, when I became quiet, what an unnatural stillness seemed to reign through the whole house! How well I remember, when my smart and passion began to cool, how wicked I began to feel!

I sat listening for a long while, but there was not a sound. I crawled up from the floor, and saw my face in the glass, so swollen, red, and ugly, that it almost frightened me. My stripes were sore and stiff, and made me cry afresh, when I moved; but they were nothing to the guilt I felt. It lay heavier on my breast than if I had been a most atrocious criminal, I dare say.

It had begun to grow dark, and I had shut the window (I had been lying, for the most part, with my head upon the sill, by turns crying, dozing, and looking listlessly out), when the key was turned, and Miss Murdstone came in with some bread and meat, and milk. These she put down upon the table without a word, glaring at me the while with exemplary firmness, and then retired, locking the door after her.

Long after it was dark I sat there, wondering whether anybody else would come. When this appeared improbable for that night, I undressed, and went to bed; and, there, I began to wonder fearfully what would be done to me. Whether it was a criminal act that I had committed? Whether I should be taken into custody, and sent to prison? Whether I was at all in danger of being hanged?

I never shall forget the waking, next morning; the being cheerful and fresh for the first moment, and then the being weighed down by the stale and dismal oppression of remembrance. Miss Murdstone reappeared before I was out of bed; told me, in so many words, that I was free to walk in the garden for half an hour and no longer; and retired, leaving the door open, that I might avail myself of that permission.

I did so, and did so every morning of my imprisonment, which lasted five days. If I could have seen my mother alone, I should have gone down on my knees to her and besought her forgiveness; but I saw no one, Miss Murdstone excepted, during the whole time—except at evening prayers in the parlor; to which I was escorted by Miss Murdstone after everybody else was placed; where I was stationed, a young outlaw, all alone by myself near the door; and whence I was solemnly conducted by my jailer, before anyone arose from the devotional posture. I only observed that my mother was as far off from me as she could be, and kept her face another way so that I never saw it; and that Mr. Murdstone's hand was bound up in a large linen wrapper.

The length of those five days I can convey

no idea of to anyone. They occupy the place of years in my remembrance. The way in which I listened to all the incidents of the house that made themselves audible to me; the ringing of bells, the opening and shutting of doors, the murmuring of voices, the footsteps on the stairs; to any laughing, whistling, or singing, outside, which seemed more dismal than anything else to me in my solitude and disgrace—the uncertain pace of the hours, especially at night, when I would wake thinking it was morning, and find that the family were not yet gone to bed, and that all the length of night had yet to come—the depressed dreams and nightmares I had—the return of day, noon, afternoon, evening, when the boys played in the churchyard, and I watched them from a distance within the room, being ashamed to show myself at the window lest they should know I was a prisoner—the strange sensation of never hearing myself speak—the fleeting intervals of something like cheerfulness, which came with eating and drinking, and went away with it—the setting in of rain one evening, with a fresh smell, and its coming down faster and faster between me and the church, until it and gathering night seemed to quench me in gloom, and fear, and remorse—all this appears to have gone round and round for years instead of days, it is so vividly and strongly stamped on my remembrance.

On the last night of my restraint, I was awakened by hearing my own name spoken in a whisper. I started up in bed, and putting out my arms in the dark, said:

"Is that you, Peggotty?"

There was no immediate answer, but presently I heard my name again, in a tone so very mysterious and awful, that I think I should have gone into a fit, if it hadn't occurred to me that it must have come through the keyhole.

I groped my way to the door, and putting my own lips to the keyhole, whispered:

"Is that you, Peggotty, dear?"

"Yes, my own precious Davy," she replied. "Be as soft as a mouse, or the Cat'll hear us."

I understood this to mean Miss Murdstone, and was sensible of the urgency of the case; her room being close by.

"How's mama, dear Peggotty? Is she very angry with me?"

I could hear Peggotty crying softly on her side of the keyhole, as I was doing on mine, before she answered. "No. Not very."

"What is going to be done with me, Peggotty dear? Do you know?"

"School. Near London," was Peggotty's answer. I was obliged to get her to repeat it, for she spoke it the first time quite down my throat, in the consequence of my having forgotten to take my mouth away from the keyhole and put my ear there; and though her words tickled me a good deal, I didn't hear them.

"When, Peggotty?"

"Tomorrow."

"Is that the reason why Miss Murdstone took the clothes out of my drawers?" which she had done, though I have forgotten to mention it.

"Yes," said Peggotty. "Box."

"Shan't I see mama?"

"Yes," said Peggotty. "Morning."

Then Peggotty fitted her mouth close to the keyhole, and delivered these words through it with as much feeling and earnestness as a keyhole has ever been the medium of communicating, I will venture to assert: shooting in each broken little sentence in a convulsive little burst of its own.

"Davy, dear. If I ain't ben azackly as intimate with you. Lately, as I used to be. It ain't because I don't love you. Just as well and more, my pretty poppet. It's because I thought it better for you. And for someone else besides. Davy, my darling, are you listening? Can you hear me?"

"Ye—ye—ye—yes, Peggotty!" I sobbed.

"My own!" said Peggotty, with infinite compassion. "What I want to say, is. That you must never forget me. For I'll never forget you. And I'll take as much care of your mama, Davy. As ever I took of you. And I won't leave her. The day may come when she'll be glad to lay her poor head. On her stupid, cross old Peggotty's arm again. And I'll write to you, my dear. Though I ain't no scholar. And I'll—I'll—" Peggotty fell to kissing the keyhole, as she couldn't kiss me . . . and we both of us kissed the keyhole with the greatest affection—I patted it with my hand, I recollect, as if it had been her honest face—and parted. From that night there grew up in my breast, a feeling for Peggotty, which I cannot very well define. She did not replace my mother; no one could do that; but she came into a vacancy in my heart, which closed upon her, and I felt towards her something I have never felt for any other other human being. It was a sort of comical affection too; and yet if she had died, I cannot think what I should have done, or how I should have acted out the tragedy it would have been to me.

In the morning Miss Murdstone appeared as usual, and told me I was going to school; which was not altogether such news to me as she supposed. She also informed me that when I was dressed, I was to come downstairs into the parlor, and have my breakfast. There, I found my mother, very pale and with red eyes: into whose arms I ran, and begged her pardon from my suffering soul.

"Oh, Davy!" she said. "That you could hurt any one I love! Try to be better, pray to be better! I forgive you; but I am so grieved, Davy, that you should have such bad passions in your heart."

They had persuaded her that I was a wicked fellow, and she was more sorry for that, than for my going away. I felt it sorely. I tried to eat my parting breakfast, but my tears dropped upon my bread-and-butter, and trickled into my tea, and choked me. I saw my mother look at me sometimes, and then glance at the watchful Miss Murdstone, and then look down, or look away.

"Master Copperfield's box there!" said Miss Murdstone, when wheels were heard at the gate.

I looked for Peggotty, but it was not she; neither she nor Mr. Murdstone appeared. My former acquaintance, the carrier, was at the door; the box was taken out to his cart, and lifted in.

"Clara!" said Miss Murdstone, in her warning note.

"Ready, my dear Jane," returned my mother. "Good bye, Davy. You are going for your own good. Good bye, my child. You will come home in the holidays, and be a better boy."

"Clara!" Miss Murdstone repeated.

"Certainly, my dear Jane," replied my mother, who was holding me. "I forgive you, my dear boy. God bless you!"

"Clara!" Miss Murdstone repeated.

Miss Murdstone was good enough to take me out to the cart, and to say on the way that she hoped I would repent, before I came to a bad end; and then I got into the cart, and the lazy horse walked off with it.

1849

Comment

G. K. Chesterton on *David Copperfield*

For though there are many other aspects of *David Copperfield*, this autobiographical aspect is, after all, the greatest. It is not only both realistic and romantic; it is realistic because it is romantic. It is human nature described with the human exaggeration. We all know the stiff-necked and humorous old-fashioned nurse, so conventional and yet so original, so dependent and yet so independent. We all know the intrusive stepfather, the abstract strange male, coarse, handsome, sulky, successful, a breaker-up of homes. We know David's poor and aristocratic mother, so proud, so gratified,

so desolate. But while these are real characters they are real characters lit up with the colors of youth and passion. They are real people romantically felt.

When we say the book is true to life we must stipulate that it is especially true to youth: even to boyhood. All the characters seem a little larger than they really were, for David is looking up at them. And the early pages of the book are in particular astonishingly vivid. Parts of it seem like fragments of our forgotten infancy. The dark house of childhood, the loneliness, the things half understood, the nurse with her inscrutable sulks and her more inscrutable tenderness, the sudden deportations to distant places, the seaside and its childish friendships, all this stirs in us when we read it, like something out of a previous existence. Above all, Dickens has excellently depicted the child enthroned in that humble circle which only in after years he perceives to have been humble.

G. K. Chesterton, *Charles Dickens*, New York: Dodd, Mead & Co., 1906.

THINK AND DISCUSS
Understanding
1. Describe the situation that David, Clara Copperfield, and Peggotty are in at the beginning.

Analyzing
2. How do Peggotty and Clara divide the traditional functions of a mother?
3. How is Clara **characterized**?
4. How does David's description of Murdstone's appearance **foreshadow** the sort of person Murdstone is later revealed to be?
5. Why does Peggotty take David to visit her family?
6. What does education become under the direction of the Murdstones?
7. What does fiction mean to David?
8. How does David fight back against his stepfather? What is the ultimate result of his doing so?
9. The novel is told from David's **point of view**. Give examples of the child's visual perspective and limited, or selective, understanding of events.

Extending
10. At the start of his narrative, David raises and leaves open the question of heroism. Do you find a hero in the excerpt you have read? Explain.

READING LITERATURE SKILLFULLY
Predicting Outcomes
You can make use of specific hints—given through characters' thoughts, speeches, and reactions to other characters and events—to predict outcomes in many kinds of fiction.

1. When Murdstone escorts Clara home, David mentions his "ill-omened black eyes." What does he mean?
2. When David returns from his visit with Peggotty's family, how does the weather hint at the emotional situation to come?
3. What hints have been given that Clara will marry Murdstone?

VOCABULARY
Antonyms
Match each word in the left column with its antonym, or opposite, in the right column.

1. aspersion   a. forthright
2. doleful   b. hysterical
3. encumbrance   c. unaccustomed
4. furtive   d. advantage
5. inveterate   e. cheerful
6. perspicuous   f. insensate
7. sentient   g. praise
8. stoical   h. incoherent

ENRICHMENT
Comparing Oral Histories
Retelling childhood memories is a favorite human activity. Explore for yourself the rich variety of such recollections. First, during informal small group discussions, recall for each other the funniest and the strangest of your own childhood memories. Listen carefully to what each person has to say, and when all the stories have been told, decide among yourselves what they had in common. Such repeated elements might be considered typical of childhood. When you rejoin the rest of the class, have a reporter from each discussion group tell everyone what you concluded about childhood memories.

592   *The Victorians*

In contrast to many other successful writers of his era, Robert Browning enjoyed a happy boyhood. He was educated largely at home and spent much of his free time reading some of the six thousand books in his father's library.

At the age of twelve he sent a collection of poems off to a magazine editor (they were rejected), and by late adolescence he had decided to become a poet. His indulgent parents raised no objections, and prepared to go on supporting him indefinitely. This may have hurt Browning's early development as a writer. He was under no constraints to modify what he did to please editors or readers. He wrote just as he wished, and what he wrote struck most people as very odd. His first serious effort (a long, confessional poem) seemed to John Stuart Mill to manifest "a more intense and morbid self-consciousness than I ever knew in any sane being."

Browning responded to that just criticism; he sought to replace his youthful, subjective work with objective, dramatic poetry. He took as his subjects not his own feelings, but the diverse people and places he had read about in his father's library. Yet in his use of geographically and historically distant material, Browning was always conscious of, and speaking to, his contemporaries. His poetry is never just an escape to some lost time.

Browning's poetry remained difficult for many people to read. Rather than the smooth, harmonious verse of Tennyson, Browning favored a rugged, irregular music not very different from the sound of the speaking voice. Some wondered if this was poetry at all. Then, too, Browning typically felt free to make allusions to obscure facts; such references made his poems difficult to grasp, and unnerved some readers. Browning's father continued to pay to have his son's poems published. The public remained indifferent.

But another poet, far more celebrated, did take note of Browning's efforts, and when he sent Elizabeth Barrett a letter (June 10, 1845) praising her latest book, she replied with unexpected praise for his poetry. So began a famous courtship and marriage.

The Brownings settled in Florence, Italy. Both worked hard at their poetry. In 1855 Robert published what modern readers consider one of his greatest achievements, a collection of fifty dramatic monologues titled *Men and Women*. It received mixed reviews. In June of 1861 Elizabeth died. Making a complete break from the happy past, Robert returned to London and to his writing.

And now the public reception of his poetry began to improve. His *Dramatis Personae* collection of 1864 won positive reviews. Then, between 1868 and 1869 he published his most ambitious work, *The Ring and the Book*, a 21,000-line poem in which nine different people consider an obscure Roman murder. The critics placed him in the first rank of English poets.

Robert Browning

 See **DRAMATIC MONOLOGUE** in the Handbook of Literary Terms, page 903.

Porphyria's Lover

The rain set early in tonight,
   The sullen wind was soon awake,
It tore the elm-tops down for spite,
   And did its worst to vex the lake:
5   I listened with heart fit to break.
When glided in Porphyria; straight
   She shut the cold out and the storm,
And kneeled and made the cheerless grate
   Blaze up, and all the cottage warm;
10   Which done, she rose, and from her form
Withdrew the dripping cloak and shawl,
   And laid her soiled gloves by, untied
Her hat and let the damp hair fall,
   And, last, she sat down by my side
15   And called me. When no voice replied,
She put my arm about her waist,
   And made her smooth white shoulder bare,
And all her yellow hair displaced,
   And, stooping, made my cheek lie there,
20   And spread, o'er all, her yellow hair,
Murmuring how she loved me—she
   Too weak, for all her heart's endeavor,
To set its struggling passion free
   From pride, and vainer ties dissever,
25   And give herself to me forever.
But passion sometimes would prevail,
   Nor could tonight's gay feast restrain
A sudden thought of one so pale
   For love of her, and all in vain:
30   So, she was come through wind and rain.
Be sure I looked up at her eyes
   Happy and proud; at last I knew
Porphyria worshiped me: surprise
   Made my heart swell, and still it grew
35   While I debated what to do.
That moment she was mine, mine, fair,

The Bridesmaid by Sir John Everett Millais. 1851. *Fitzwilliam Museum, Cambridge*

   Perfectly pure and good: I found
A thing to do, and all her hair
   In one long yellow string I wound
40   Three times her little throat around,
And strangled her. No pain felt she;
   I am quite sure she felt no pain.
As a shut bud that holds a bee,
   I warily oped her lids: again
45   Laughed the blue eyes without a stain.
And I untightened next the tress
   About her neck; her cheek once more

Blushed bright beneath my burning kiss:
   I propped her head up as before,
50   Only, this time my shoulder bore
Her head, which droops upon it still:
   The smiling rosy little head,
So glad it has its utmost will,
   That all it scorned at once is fled,

55   And I, its love, am gained instead!
Porphyria's love: she guessed not how
   Her darling one wish would be heard.
And thus we sit together now,
   And all night long we have not stirred,
60   And yet God has not said a word!

1836

HT   **See INFERENCE in the Handbook of Literary Terms, page 911.**

My Last Duchess

[handwritten: Talking to ambassador + we never hear what he says.]

The time is the sixteenth century, the scene is the city of Ferrara in northern Italy. The speaker is the Duke of Ferrara.

That's my last duchess painted on the wall,
Looking as if she were alive. I call
That piece a wonder, now: Frà Pandolf's hands
Worked busily a day, and there she stands.
5 Will 't please you sit and look at her? I said
"Frà Pandolf" by design, for never read
Strangers like you that pictured countenance,
The depth and passion of its earnest glance,
But to myself they turned (since none puts by
10 The curtain I have drawn for you, but I)
And seemed as they would ask me, if they durst,
How such a glance came there; so, not the first
Are you to turn and ask thus. Sir, 'twas not
Her husband's presence only, called that spot
15 Of joy into the Duchess' cheek: perhaps
Frà Pandolf chanced to say "Her mantle laps
Over my lady's wrist too much," or "Paint
Must never hope to reproduce the faint
Half-flush that dies along her throat": such stuff
20 Was courtesy, she thought, and cause enough
For calling up that spot of joy. She had

A heart—how shall I say?—too soon made glad,
Too easily impressed; she liked whate'er
She looked on, and her looks went everywhere.
25 Sir, 'twas all one! My favor at her breast,
The dropping of the daylight in the West,
The bough of cherries some officious fool
Broke in the orchard for her, the white mule
She rode with round the terrace—all and each
30 Would draw from her alike the approving
   speech,
Or blush, at least. She thanked men—good!
   but thanked
Somehow—I know not how—as if she ranked
My gift of a nine-hundred-years-old name
With anybody's gift. Who'd stoop to blame
35 This sort of trifling? Even had you skill
In speech—which I have not—to make your will
Quite clear to such an one, and say, "Just this
Or that in you disgusts me; here you miss,
Or there exceed the mark"—and if she let
40 Herself be lessoned so, nor plainly set

Robert Browning

Her wits to yours, forsooth, and made excuse—
E'en then would be some stooping; and I choose
Never to stoop. Oh sir, she smiled, no doubt,
Whene'er I passed her; but who passed without
45 Much the same smile? This grew; I gave
    commands;
Then all smiles stopped together. There she
    stands
As if alive. Will 't please you rise? We'll meet

The company below, then. I repeat,
The Count your master's known munificence
50 Is ample warrant that no just pretense
Of mine for dowry will be disallowed;
Though his fair daughter's self, as I avowed
At starting, is my object. Nay, we'll go
Together down, sir. Notice Neptune, though,
55 Taming a sea-horse, thought a rarity,
Which Claus of Innsbruck cast in bronze for me!

1842

Alphonso d'Este, Second Duke of Ferrara, painted by Girolamo da Carpi. *Museo del Prado, Madrid*

Lucretia de Medici, painted by the school of Angelo Bronzino. *Museo Mediceo, Florence*

Prospice

The Latin word *Prospice* (pros′pi chē) means "Look Forward!" and suggests Browning's unflinching attitude toward death. The last three lines of the poem refer to Elizabeth Barrett Browning, who had died shortly before the poem was written.

Fear death?—to feel the fog in my throat,
  The mist in my face,
When the snows begin, and the blasts denote
     I am nearing the place,
5 The power of the night, the press of the storm,
  The post of the foe;

Where he stands, the Arch Fear in a visible
    form,
    Yet the strong man must go:
For the journey is done and the summit
    attained,
10   And the barriers fall,
Though a battle's to fight ere the guerdon be
    gained,
    The reward of it all.
I was ever a fighter, so — one fight more,
    The best and the last!
15 I would hate that death bandaged my eyes, and
    forebore,
    And bade me creep past.
No! let me taste the whole of it, fare like my
    peers

    The heroes of old,
Bear the brunt, in a minute pay glad life's
    arrears
20   Of pain, darkness and cold.
For sudden the worst turns the best to the brave,
    The black minute's at end,
And the elements' rage, the fiend-voices that rave,
    Shall dwindle, shall blend,
25 Shall change, shall become first a peace out of
    pain,
    Then a light, then thy breast,
O thou soul of my soul! I shall clasp thee again,
    And with God be the rest!

                 1864

THINK AND DISCUSS
PORPHYRIA'S LOVER
Understanding
1. Describe the condition of the room and the speaker before Porphyria's arrival.
2. Where has she come from?
3. Why, according to the speaker, does Porphyria refuse to marry him? (See lines 21–25.)
4. What "thing to do" does the speaker find? What does he do afterward?

Analyzing
5. How does the speaker's **personification** of the storm (lines 1–5) suggest his state of mind?
6. Why does he respond so coldly (in line 15) to Porphyria's tenderness?
7. In lines 15–21 the speaker describes Porphyria caring for him; then in lines 43–55 he depicts his own treatment of her. How has the situation reversed?
8. What does the speaker imply in the last line?

Extending
9. Should literature focus on the kind of mental states found in "Porphyria's Lover"?

APPLYING: Dramatic Monologue HT
See Handbook of Literary Terms, p. 903
    In a **dramatic monologue** a fictional character, speaking in the first person, reveals details of **setting**, dramatic situation, and **characterization**. The audience is usually present, although silent. Since the speaker's thoughts and feelings are subjective, readers must watch for hints as to whether or not they are true.

1. Who are the two characters depicted in "Porphyria's Lover"?
2. Describe the setting.
3. How does the speaker try to justify his murder to himself and his audience?
4. How does the speaker continue to impart qualities of life to Porphyria after she is dead?

THINK AND DISCUSS
MY LAST DUCHESS
Understanding
1. Whom is the Duke talking to?
2. Describe what they look at while the Duke talks.
3. What is the Duke's stated purpose in this conversation?

Analyzing

4. Was the marriage of the Duke and the Duchess one based on love? Explain.
5. How do the Duke's words suggest his feelings about Frà Pandolf?
6. List the things that gave the Duchess pleasure and explain what they reveal about her personality.
7. Why didn't the Duke tell the Duchess how he expected her to behave?
8. Why does he mention the bronze statue by Claus of Innsbruck?

Extending

9. What sort of report do you think the listener is expected to deliver to the Count?
10. What do you, as a modern reader, consider the Duke's main fault?

APPLYING: Inference H
See Handbook of Literary Terms, p. 911

When an author does not say something specifically, but leaves the reader with hints and clues, then the reader makes an **inference**, a reasonable conclusion based on the information the author provides.

1. The Duke presumes that "the depth and passion" of the Duchess's expression in the picture springs from Frà Pandolf's complimenting her on her beauty. Given the little we know about this woman, what do you think might have provoked her "earnest glance" (line 8)?
2. What sort of "commands" (line 45) do you infer he gave?
3. When the Duke insists that he is primarily interested in the Count's "fair daughter's self" (line 52), what inference do you draw?

THINK AND DISCUSS
PROSPICE
Understanding

1. Name the "Arch Fear" of line 7.
2. What do the "barriers" of line 10 divide?
3. What sudden turn occurs in line 21?

Analyzing

4. What **metaphor** dominates this poem?
5. How do its characteristic qualities suggest the speaker's attitude toward life and death?
6. What does the speaker mean by paying "glad life's arrears" in line 19?
7. Explain how two different meanings of "rest" make the last line ambiguous.

Extending

8. Why do you think most of the poem describes the struggle, while only four lines picture the reward?

COMPOSITION
Describing a Modern "Duke of Ferrara"

In Browning's poem, the Duke of Ferrara is a powerful man, and he seems to enjoy using his power over others—including his wife. Write an essay for your classmates in which you describe a modern person in a position of great power. The person you choose may be fictional—from a book, movie, or TV show—or real. Describe how powerful your chosen person is and be sure to include at least one example of that power in use. Does the social and financial position of modern women make it impossible for a modern "Duke of Ferrara" to "give commands" to put an end to someone who annoys him?

Analyzing Browning's Dramatic Monologue

Write a five-paragraph essay for your teacher in which you analyze how Browning employs dramatic monologue in "My Last Duchess." First define the term. Then describe how the words of the Duke create a sense of place and time, a specific listener, and a dramatic situation. Last, analyze the discrepancy between what the Duke says and what you infer actually happened.

ENRICHMENT
Researching Portraiture

Bring to class a number of library books that have color reproductions of portrait paintings from the past. Divide into groups and examine some of these pictures together. What can you tell about the subjects of the portraits from their facial expressions, physical posture, dress, and pictured possessions? What can you tell about the painter's era from the subject, style of painting, degree of formality, and so on?

George Eliot
1819–1880

When Mary Ann Evans began to publish fiction in 1858, she took the pen name George Eliot; this change was an emblem of the seriousness with which she addressed her new career. There were many successful women novelists in mid-Victorian England who wrote under their own names, but there existed a general assumption that they wrote "women's novels." When Evans began to publish her novels under an assumed name she was implicitly asserting her intention to rival the greatest novelists of her day.

Mary Ann Evans's father dominated her childhood. A powerful man, both physically and intellectually, Robert Evans was self-educated. He rose to serve as chief agricultural agent for a wealthy landowner. His daughter Mary Ann showed early intellectual promise and from the ages of five to sixteen she attended a series of schools for girls, in which she acquired a fervent belief in Christianity. On the death of her mother in 1836, Evans came home to keep house for her father—a task that proved increasingly restrictive, but to which she devoted herself.

The death of her father in 1849 freed Evans from domestic responsibilities but posed serious problems. Where and how was she to live? She settled in London, joining a group of free-thinking writers who respected her now formidable abilities. By 1851 she was editing *The Westminster Review*, translating German philosophy, and publishing her own essays on the intellectual questions of the day.

In 1853, in the midst of this stimulating environment, she met G. E. Lewes, another writer and thinker. Soon they fell in love. Lewes was already married, but his wife had deserted him. Divorce proved impossible. Evans decided to defy convention and live with him, calling herself Mrs. Lewes and insisting that in all but law they were husband and wife. In mid-Victorian Britain they had to lead a retired life.

It was Lewes who persuaded Mary Ann Evans to write fiction. Her first novel, *Adam Bede* (1859) enjoyed immediate success. In her second novel, *The Mill on the Floss* (1860) Evans used a setting from England's past to study some of its current problems. The novel's evocative pictures of farms, grain mills, and small towns mirror the places and people Evans knew as a girl and read about in the poetry of Wordsworth. Yet in this world that she depicts she sees some of the critical problems of her era, especially the question of sexual equality.

The Mill on the Floss (1860) describes a rural England that was disappearing even as George Eliot wrote. At the center of the novel is the Tulliver family. Mr. Tulliver owns a flour mill on the Floss River and has two hired men, Luke and Harry, to help him run it. He has been successful in business, even though he has never been formally educated, and despite the fact that he is always embroiled in law suits about property rights. Mr. Tulliver's son Tom is beginning to grow up and his father, in trying to decide what to do with the boy, consults his friend Mr. Riley. Although Mr. Tulliver doesn't know it, his daughter Maggie is listening.

from The Mill on the Floss

George Eliot

 he gentleman in the ample white cravat and shirt-frill, taking his brandy-and-water so pleasantly with his good friend Tulliver, is Mr. Riley, a gentleman with a waxen complexion and fat hands, rather highly educated for an auctioneer and appraiser, but large-hearted enough to show a great deal of *bonhommie*[1] towards simple country acquaintances of hospitable habits. Mr. Riley spoke of such acquaintances kindly as "people of the old school."

The conversation had come to a pause. . . .

"There's a thing I've got i' my head," said Mr. Tulliver at last, in rather a lower tone than usual, as he turned his head and looked steadfastly at his companion.

"Ah!" said Mr. Riley, in a tone of mild interest. He was a man with heavy waxen eyelids and high-arched eyebrows, looking exactly the same under all circumstances. This immovability of face, and the habit of taking a pinch of snuff before he gave an answer, made him trebly oracular to Mr. Tulliver.

"It's a very particular thing," he went on; "it's about my boy Tom."

At the sound of this name, Maggie, who was seated on a low stool close by the fire, with a large book open on her lap, shook her heavy hair back and looked up eagerly. There were few sounds that roused Maggie when she was dreaming over her book, but Tom's name served as well as the shrillest whistle: in an instant she was on the watch, with gleaming eyes, like a Skye terrier suspecting mischief, or at all events determined to fly at any one who threatened it towards Tom.

"You see, I want to put him to a new school at Midsummer," said Mr. Tulliver; "he's comin' away from the 'cademy at Ladyday,[2] an' I shall let him run loose for a quarter; but after that I want to send him to a downright good school, where they'll make a scholard of him."

"Well," said Mr. Riley, "there's no greater advantage you can give him than a good education. Not," he added, with polite significance—"not that a man can't be an excellent miller and farmer, and a shrewd sensible fellow into the bargain, without much help from the schoolmaster."

"I believe you," said Mr. Tulliver, winking, and turning his head on one side, "but that's where it is. I don't *mean* Tom to be a miller and farmer. I see no fun i' that: why, if I made him a miller an' farmer, he'd be expectin' to take to the Mill an' the land, an' a-hinting at me as it was time for me to lay by[3] an' think o' my latter end. Nay, nay, I've seen enough o' that wi' sons. I'll never pull my coat off before I go to bed. I shall give Tom an eddication an' put him to a business, as he may make a nest for himself, an' not want to push me out o' mine. Pretty well if he gets it when I'm dead an' gone. I shan't be put off wi' spoonmeat afore I've lost my teeth."

This was evidently a point on which Mr. Tulliver felt strongly, and the impetus which had given unusual rapidity and emphasis to his speech, showed itself still unexhausted for some minutes afterwards, in a defiant motion of the head from side to side, and an occasional "Nay, nay," like

---

1. *bonhommie,* good-natured friendship.
2. *Ladyday,* March 25th, a legal holiday in England.
3. *lay by,* retire.

a subsiding growl.

These angry symptoms were keenly observed by Maggie, and cut her to the quick. Tom, it appeared, was supposed capable of turning his father out of doors, and of making the future in some way tragic by his wickedness. This was not to be borne; and Maggie jumped up from her stool, forgetting all about her heavy book, which fell with a bang within the fender; and going up between her father's knees, said, in a half-crying, half-indignant voice—

"Father, Tom wouldn't be naughty to you ever; I know he wouldn't."

Mrs. Tulliver was out of the room superintending a choice supper dish, and Mr. Tulliver's heart was touched; so Maggie was not scolded about the book. Mr. Riley quietly picked it up and looked at it, while the father laughed with a certain tenderness in his hard-lined face, and patted his little girl on the back, and then held her hands and kept her between his knees.

"What! they mustn't say any harm o' Tom, eh?" said Mr. Tulliver, looking at Maggie with a twinkling eye. Then, in a lower voice, turning to Mr. Riley, as though Maggie couldn't hear, "She understands what one's talking about so as never was. And you should hear her read—straight off, as if she knowed it all beforehand. And allays at her book! But it's bad—it's bad," Mr. Tulliver added, sadly, checking this blamable exultation; "a woman's no business wi' being so clever; it'll turn to trouble, I doubt. But, bless you!"—here the exultation was clearly recovering the mastery—"she'll read the books and understand 'em better nor half the folks as are growed up."

Maggie's cheeks began to flush with triumphant excitement: she thought Mr. Riley would have a respect for her now; it had been evident that he thought nothing of her before.

Mr. Riley was turning over the leaves of the book, and she could make nothing of his face, with its high-arched eyebrows; but he presently looked at her and said,

"Come, come and tell me something about this book; here are some pictures—I want to know what they mean."

Maggie with deepening color went without hesitation to Mr. Riley's elbow and looked over the book, eagerly seizing one corner, and tossing back her mane, while she said,

"O, I'll tell you what that means. It's a dreadful picture, isn't it? But I can't help looking at it. That old woman in the water's a witch—they've put her in to find out whether she's a witch or no, and if she swims she's a witch, and if she's drowned—and killed, you know—she's innocent, and not a witch, but only a poor silly old woman. But what good would it do her then, you know, when she was drowned? Only, I suppose, she'd go to heaven, and God would make it up to her. And this dreadful blacksmith with his arms akimbo, laughing—oh, isn't he ugly?—I'll tell you what he is. He's the devil *really*" (here Maggie's voice became louder and more emphatic), "and not a right blacksmith; for the devil takes the shape of wicked men, and walks about and sets people doing wicked things, and he's oftener in the shape of a bad man than any other, because, you know, if people saw he was the devil, and he roared at 'em, they'd run away, and he couldn't make 'em do what he pleased."

Mr. Tulliver had listened to this exposition of Maggie's with petrifying wonder. . . .

"Go, go!" said Mr. Tulliver, peremptorily, beginning to feel rather uncomfortable at these free remarks on the personal appearance of a being powerful enough to create lawyers: "shut up the book, and let's hear no more o' such talk. It is as I thought—the child 'ull learn more mischief nor good wi' the books. Go, go and see after your mother."

Maggie shut up the book at once, with a sense of disgrace, but not being inclined to see after her mother, she compromised the matter by going into a dark corner behind her father's chair, and nursing her doll, towards which she had an occasional fit of fondness in Tom's absence, neglecting its toilette, but lavishing so many warm kisses on it that the waxen cheeks had a wasted unhealthy appearance.

"Did you ever hear the like on't?" said Mr.

Tulliver, as Maggie retired. "It's a pity but what she'd been the lad—she'd ha' been a match for the lawyers, *she* would. It's the wonderful'st thing"—here he lowered his voice—"as I picked the mother because she wasn't o'er 'cute[4]—bein' a good-looking woman too, an' come of a rare family for managing; but I picked her from her sisters o' purpose, 'cause she was a bit weak, like; for I wasn't agoin' to be told the rights o' things by my own fireside. But you see when a man's got brains himself, there's no knowing where they'll run to; an' a pleasant sort o' soft woman may go on breeding you stupid lads and 'cute wenches, till it's like as if the world was turned topsy-turvy. It's an uncommon puzzlin' thing."

It was a heavy disappointment to Maggie that she was not allowed to go with her father in the gig when he went to fetch Tom home from the academy; but the morning was too wet, Mrs. Tulliver said, for a little girl to go out in her best bonnet. Maggie took the opposite view very strongly, and it was a direct consequence of this difference of opinion that when her mother was in the act of brushing out the reluctant black crop, Maggie suddenly rushed from under her hands and dipped her head in a basin of water standing near—in the vindictive determination that there should be no more chance of curls that day.

"Maggie, Maggie," exclaimed Mrs. Tulliver, sitting stout and helpless with the brushes on her lap, "what is to become of you if you're so naughty? I'll tell your Aunt Glegg and your Aunt Pullet when they come next week, and they'll never love you any more. O dear, O dear! look at your clean pinafore, wet from top to bottom. Folks 'ull think it's a judgment on me as I've got such a child—they'll think I've done summat wicked."

Before this remonstrance was finished, Maggie was already out of hearing, making her way towards the great attic that ran under the old high-pitched roof, shaking the water from her black locks as she ran, like a Skye terrier escaped from his bath. This attic was Maggie's favorite retreat on a wet day, when the weather was not too cold; here she fretted out all her ill-humors, and talked aloud to the worm-eaten floors and the worm-eaten shelves, and the dark rafters festooned with cobwebs; and here she kept a Fetish[5] which she punished for all her misfortunes. This was the trunk of a large wooden doll, which once stared with the roundest of eyes above the reddest of cheeks; but was now entirely defaced by a long career of vicarious suffering. Three nails driven into the head commemorated as many crises in Maggie's nine years of earthly struggle; that luxury of vengeance having been suggested to her by the picture of Jael destroying Sisera in the old Bible. The last nail had been driven in with a fiercer stroke than usual, for the Fetish on that occasion represented Aunt Glegg. But immediately afterwards Maggie had reflected that if she drove many nails in, she would not be so well able to fancy that the head was hurt when she knocked it against the wall, nor to comfort it, and make believe to poultice it, when her fury was abated; for even Aunt Glegg would be pitiable when she had been hurt very much, and thoroughly humiliated, so as to beg her niece's pardon. Since then she had driven no more nails in, but had soothed herself by alternately grinding and beating the wooden head against the rough brick of the great chimneys that made two square pillars supporting the roof. That was what she did this morning on reaching the attic, sobbing all the while with a passion that expelled every other form of consciousness—even the memory of the grievance that had caused it. As at last the sobs were getting quieter, and the grinding less fierce, a sudden beam of sunshine, falling through the wire lattice across the worm-eaten shelves, made her throw away the Fetish and run to the window. The sun was really breaking out; the sound of the mill seemed cheerful again; the granary doors were open; and there was Yap, the queer white-and-brown terrier, with one ear turned back, trotting about and sniffing vaguely, as if he were in search of a companion. It was

---

4. *'cute*, acute; that is, intelligent.
5. *Fetish*, in primitive cultures, an object believed to possess magical powers; Maggie's fetish, much like a voodoo doll, receives the punishments she cannot inflict on other people.

irresistible. Maggie tossed her hair back and ran downstairs, seized her bonnet without putting it on, peeped, and then dashed along the passage lest she should encounter her mother, and was quickly out in the yard, whirling round like a Pythoness,[6] and singing as she whirled, "Yap, Yap, Tom's coming home!" while Yap danced and barked round her, as much as to say, if there was any noise wanted he was the dog for it.

"Hegh, hegh, Miss, you'll make yourself giddy, an' tumble down i' the dirt," said Luke, the head miller, a tall broad-shouldered man of forty, black-eyed and black-haired, subdued by a general mealiness. . . .

Maggie paused in her whirling and said, staggering a little, "O no, it doesn't make me giddy, Luke; may I go into the mill with you?"

Maggie loved to linger in the great spaces of the mill, and often came out with her black hair powdered to a soft whiteness that made her dark eyes flash out with new fire. The resolute din, the unresting motion of the great stones, giving her a dim delicious awe as at the presence of an uncontrollable force—the meal for ever pouring, pouring—the fine white powder softening all surfaces, and making the very spider-nets look like a fairy lace work—the sweet pure scent of the meal—all helped to make Maggie feel that the mill was a little world apart from her outside everyday life. . . . But the part of the mill she liked best was the topmost story—the cornhutch, where there were the great heaps of grain, which she could sit on and slide down continually. She was in the habit of taking this recreation as she conversed with Luke, to whom she was very communicative, wishing him to think well of her understanding, as her father did.

Perhaps she felt it necessary to recover her position with him on the present occasion, for, as she sat sliding on the heap of grain near which he was busying himself, she said, at that shrill pitch which was requisite in mill-society—

"I think you never read any book but the Bible—did you, Luke?"

"Nay, Miss—an' not much o' that," said Luke, with great frankness. "I'm no reader, I

aren't. . . ."

"Why, you're like my brother Tom, Luke," said Maggie, wishing to turn the conversation agreeably; "Tom's not fond of reading. I love Tom so dearly, Luke—better than anybody else in the world. When he grows up, I shall keep his house, and we shall always live together. I can tell him everything he doesn't know. But I think Tom's clever, for all he doesn't like books: he makes beautiful whipcord and rabbit pens."

"Ah," said Luke, "but he'll be fine an' vexed, as the rabbits are all dead."

"Dead!" screamed Maggie, jumping up from her sliding seat on the corn. "O dear, Luke! What! the lop-eared one, and the spotted doe that Tom spent all his money to buy?"

"As dead as moles," said Luke, fetching his comparison from the unmistakable corpses[7] nailed to the stable-wall.

"O dear, Luke," said Maggie, in a piteous tone, while the big tears rolled down her cheek; "Tom told me to take care of 'em, and I forgot. What *shall* I do?"

"Well, you see, Miss, they were in that far tool house, an' it was nobody's business to see to 'em. I reckon Master Tom told Harry to feed 'em, but there's no countin' on Harry—*he's* an offal creatur as iver come about the primises, he is. He remembers nothing but his own inside—an' I wish it 'ud gripe him."

"O, Luke, Tom told me to be sure and remember the rabbits every day; but how could I, when they didn't come into my head, you know? O, he will be so angry with me, I know he will, and so sorry about his rabbits—and so am I sorry. O, what *shall* I do?"

"Don't you fret, Miss," said Luke, soothingly, "they're nash things, them lop-eared rabbits—they'd happen ha' died, if they'd been fed. Things out o' natur niver thrive: God A'mighty doesn't like 'em. He made the rabbits'

---

6. *Pythoness,* a priestess to the god Apollo, so named because Apollo once slew a monstrous serpent named Python. Such priestesses expressed their devotion in whirling dances.
7. *corpses,* moles killed because they are farm pests.

ears to lie back, an' it's nothin' but contrairiness to make 'em hing down like a mastiff dog's. Master Tom 'ull know better nor buy such things another time. Don't you fret, Miss. Will you come along home wi' me, and see my wife? I'm a-goin' this minute." The invitation offered an agreeable distraction to Maggie's grief, and her tears gradually subsided as she trotted along by Luke's side to his pleasant cottage, which stood with its apple and pear trees, and with the added dignity of a lean-to pig-sty, at the other end of the Mill fields. . . .

Tom was to arrive early in the afternoon, and there was another fluttering heart besides Maggie's when it was late enough for the sound of the gig-wheels to be expected; for if Mrs. Tulliver had a strong feeling, it was fondness for her boy. At last the sound came—that quick light bowling of the gig-wheels—and in spite of the wind, which was blowing the clouds about, and was not likely to respect Mrs. Tulliver's curls and capstrings, she came outside the door, and even held her hand on Maggie's offending head, forgetting all the griefs of the morning.

"There he is, my sweet lad! But, Lord ha' mercy! he's got never a collar on; it's been lost on the road, I'll be bound, and spoilt the set."

Mrs. Tulliver stood with her arms open; Maggie jumped first on one leg and then on the other; while Tom descended from the gig, and said, with masculine reticence as to the tender emotions, "Hallo! Yap—what! are you there?"

Nevertheless he submitted to be kissed willingly enough, though Maggie hung on his neck in rather a strangling fashion, while his blue-grey eyes wandered towards the croft and the lambs and the river, where he promised himself that he would begin to fish the first thing tomorrow morning. He was one of those lads that grow everywhere in England, and, at twelve or thirteen years of age, look as much alike as goslings:—a lad with light-brown hair, cheeks of cream and roses, full lips, indeterminate nose and eyebrows—a physiognomy in which it seems impossible to discern anything but the generic character of boyhood; as different as possible from poor Maggie's phiz, which Nature seemed to have molded and colored with the most decided intention. But that same Nature has the deep cunning which hides itself under the appearance of openness, so that simple people think they can see through her quite well, and all the while she is secretly preparing a refutation of their confident prophecies. Under these average boyish physiognomies that she seems to turn off by the gross, she conceals some of her most rigid, inflexible purposes, some of her most unmodifiable characters; and the dark-eyed, demonstrative, rebellious girl may after all turn out to be a passive being compared with this pink-and-white bit of masculinity with the indeterminate features.

"Maggie," said Tom, confidentially, taking her into a corner, as soon as his mother was gone out to examine his box, and the warm parlor had taken off the chill he had felt from the long drive, "you don't know what I've got in *my* pockets," nodding his head up and down as a means of rousing her sense of mystery. . . .

"What is it?" said Maggie, in a whisper. "I can see nothing but a bit of yellow."

"Why it's . . . a . . . new . . . guess, Maggie!"

"O, I *can't* guess, Tom," said Maggie, impatiently.

"Don't be a spitfire, else I won't tell you," said Tom, thrusting his hand back into his pocket, and looking determined.

"No, Tom," said Maggie, imploringly, laying hold of the arm that was held stiffly in the pocket. "I'm not cross, Tom; it was only because I can't bear guessing. *Please* be good to me."

Tom's arm slowly relaxed, and he said, "Well, then it's a new fishline—two new uns—one for you, Maggie, all to yourself. I wouldn't go halves in the toffee and gingerbread on purpose to save the money; and Gibson and Spouncer fought with me because I wouldn't.[8] And here's hooks; see here! . . . . I say, *won't* we go and fish tomorrow down by the Round Pool? And you shall catch

---

8. **Gibson . . . I wouldn't,** school chums who wanted Tom to spend his pocket money on treats.

Detail of *Spring* by Frederick Walker. 1864.

your own fish, Maggie, and put the worms on, and everything—won't it be fun?"

Maggie's answer was to throw her arms round Tom's neck and hug him, and hold her cheek against his without speaking, while he slowly unwound some of the line, saying, after a pause,

"Wasn't I a good brother, now, to buy you a line all to yourself? You know, I needn't have bought it, if I hadn't liked."

"Yes, very, very good. . . . I *do* love you, Tom."

Tom had put the line back in his pocket, and was looking at the hooks one by one, before he spoke again.

"And the fellows fought me, because I wouldn't give in about the toffee."

"O dear! I wish they wouldn't fight at your school, Tom. Didn't it hurt you?"

"Hurt me? no," said Tom, putting up the hooks again, taking out a large pocketknife, and slowly opening the largest blade, which he looked at meditatively as he rubbed his finger along it. Then he added—

"I gave Spouncer a black eye, I know—that's what he got by wanting to leather *me;* I wasn't going to go halves because anybody leathered me."

"O how brave you are, Tom! I think you're like Samson. If there came a lion roaring at me, I think you'd fight him—wouldn't you, Tom?"

"How can a lion come roaring at you, you silly thing? There's no lions, only in the shows."

"No; but if we were in the lion countries—I mean in Africa, where it's very hot—the lions eat people there. I can show it you in the book where I read it."

"Well, I should get a gun and shoot him."

"But if you hadn't got a gun—we might have gone out, you know, not thinking—just as we go fishing; and then a great lion might run towards us roaring, and we couldn't get away from him. What should you do, Tom?"

Tom paused, and at last turned away contemptuously, saying, "But the lion *isn't* coming. What's the use of talking?"

"But I like to fancy how it would be," said Maggie, following him. "Just think what you would do, Tom."

"O don't bother, Maggie! you're such a silly—I shall go and see my rabbits."

Maggie's heart began to flutter with fear. She dared not tell the sad truth at once, but she walked after Tom in trembling silence as he went out, thinking how she could tell him the news so as to soften at once his sorrow and his anger; for Maggie dreaded Tom's anger of all things—it was quite a different anger from her own.

"Tom," she said, timidly, when they were out of doors, "how much money did you give for your rabbits?"

"Two half-crowns and a sixpence," said Tom, promptly.

"I think I've got a great deal more than that in my steel purse upstairs. I'll ask mother to give it you."

"What for?" said Tom. "I don't want *your* money, you silly thing. I've got a great deal more money than you, because I'm a boy. I always have half-sovereigns and sovereigns for my Christmas boxes, because I shall be a man, and you only have five-shilling pieces, because you're only a girl."

"Well, but, Tom—if mother would let me give you two half-crowns and a sixpence out of my purse to put into your pocket and spend, you know; and buy some more rabbits with it?"

"More rabbits? I don't want any more."

"O, but Tom, they're all dead."

Tom stopped immediately in his walk and turned round towards Maggie. "You forgot to feed 'em, then, and Harry forgot?" he said, his color heightening for a moment, but soon subsiding. "I'll pitch into Harry—I'll have him turned away. And I don't love you, Maggie. You shan't go fishing with me tomorrow. I told you to go and see the rabbits every day." He walked on again.

"Yes, but I forgot—and I couldn't help it, indeed, Tom. I'm so very sorry," said Maggie, while the tears rushed fast.

"You're a naughty girl," said Tom severely, "and I'm sorry I bought you the fishline. I don't love you."

"O, Tom, it's very cruel," sobbed Maggie. "I'd forgive you, if *you* forgot anything—I wouldn't mind what you did—I'd forgive you and love you."

"Yes, you're a silly—but I never *do* forget things—*I* don't."

"O, please forgive me, Tom; my heart will break," said Maggie, shaking with sobs, clinging to Tom's arm, and laying her wet cheek on his shoulder.

Tom shook her off, and stopped again, saying in a peremptory tone, "Now, Maggie, you just listen. Aren't I a good brother to you?"

"Ye-ye-es," sobbed Maggie, her chin rising and falling convulsedly.

"Didn't I think about your fishline all this quarter, and mean to buy it, and saved my money o' purpose, and wouldn't go halves in the toffee, and Spouncer fought me because I wouldn't?"

"Ye-ye-es . . . and I . . . lo-lo-love you so, Tom."

"But you're a naughty girl. Last holidays you licked the paint off my lozenge box, and the holidays before that you let the boat drag my fishline down when I'd set you to watch it, and you pushed your head through my kite, all for nothing."

"But I didn't mean," said Maggie; "I couldn't help it."

"Yes, you could," said Tom, "if you'd minded what you were doing. And you're a naughty girl, and you shan't go fishing with me tomorrow."

With this terrible conclusion, Tom ran away from Maggie towards the mill, meaning to greet Luke there, and complain to him of Harry.

Maggie stood motionless, except from her sobs,

for a minute or two; then she turned round and ran into the house, and up to her attic, where she sat on the floor, and laid her head against the worm-eaten shelf, with a crushing sense of misery. Tom was come home, and she had thought how happy she should be—and now he was cruel to her. What use was anything, if Tom didn't love her? O, he was very cruel! Hadn't she wanted to give him the money, and said how very sorry she was? She knew she was naughty to her mother, but she had never been naughty to Tom—had never *meant* to be naughty to him.

"O, he is cruel!" Maggie sobbed aloud, finding a wretched pleasure in the hollow resonance that came through the long empty space of the attic. She never thought of beating or grinding her Fetish; she was too miserable to be angry.

These bitter sorrows of childhood! when sorrow is all new and strange, when hope has not yet got wings to fly beyond the days and weeks, and the space from summer to summer seems measureless.

Maggie soon thought she had been hours in the attic, and it must be teatime, and they were all having their tea, and not thinking of her. Well, then, she would stay up there and starve herself—hide herself behind the tub, and stay there all night; and then they would all be frightened, and Tom would be sorry. Thus Maggie thought in the pride of her heart, as she crept behind the tub; but presently she began to cry again at the idea that they didn't mind her being there. If she went down again to Tom now—would he forgive her?—perhaps her father would be there, and he would take her part. But, then, she wanted Tom to forgive her because he loved her, not because his father told him. No, she would never go down if Tom didn't come to fetch her. This resolution lasted in great intensity for five dark minutes behind the tub; but then the need of being loved, the strongest need in poor Maggie's nature, began to wrestle with her pride, and soon threw it. She crept from behind her tub into the twilight of the long attic, but just then she heard a quick footstep on the stairs. . . .

It was Tom's step . . . that Maggie heard on the stairs, when her need of love had triumphed over her pride, and she was going down with her swollen eyes and dishevelled hair to beg for pity. At least her father would stroke her head and say, "Never mind, my wench." It is a wonderful subduer, this need of love—this hunger of the heart—as peremptory as that other hunger by which Nature forces us to submit to the yoke, and change the face of the world.

But she knew Tom's step, and her heart began to beat violently with the sudden shock of hope. He only stood still at the top of the stairs and said, "Maggie, you're to come down." But she rushed to him and clung round his neck, sobbing, "O Tom, please forgive me—I can't bear it—I will always be good—always remember things—do love me—please, dear Tom!"

We learn to restrain ourselves as we get older. We keep apart when we have quarrelled, express ourselves in well-bred phrases, and in this way preserve a dignified alienation, showing much firmness on one side, and swallowing much grief on the other. We no longer approximate in our behavior to the mere impulsiveness of the lower animals, but conduct ourselves in every respect like members of a highly civilized society. Maggie and Tom were still very much like young animals, and so she could rub her cheek against his, and kiss his ear in a random, sobbing way; and there were tender fibers in the lad that had been used to answer to Maggie's fondling; so that he behaved with a weakness quite inconsistent with his resolution to punish her as much as she deserved: he actually began to kiss her in return, and say—

"Don't cry, then, Magsie—here, eat a bit o' cake."

Maggie's sobs began to subside, and she put out her mouth for the cake and bit a piece: and then Tom bit a piece, just for company, and they ate together and rubbed each other's cheeks and brows and noses together, while they ate, with a humiliating resemblance to two friendly ponies.

"Come along, Magsie, and have tea," said Tom at last, when there was no more cake except what was downstairs.

So ended the sorrows of this day, and the next morning Maggie was trotting with her own fishing rod in one hand and a handle of the basket in the other, stepping always, by a peculiar gift, in the muddiest places, and looking darkly radiant from under her beaver bonnet because Tom was good to her. She had told Tom, however, that she should like him to put the worms on the hook for her, although she accepted his word when he assured her that worms couldn't feel (it was Tom's private opinion that it didn't much matter if they did). He knew all about worms, and fish, and those things; and what birds were mischievous, and how padlocks opened, and which way the handles of the gates were to be lifted. Maggie thought this sort of knowledge was very wonderful—much more difficult than remembering what was in the books; and she was rather in awe of Tom's superiority, for he was the only person who called her knowledge "stuff," and did not feel surprised at her cleverness. Tom, indeed, was of opinion that Maggie was a silly little thing; all girls were silly—they couldn't throw a stone so as to hit anything, couldn't do anything with a pocketknife, and were frightened at frogs. Still he was very fond of his sister, and meant always to take care of her, make her his housekeeper, and punish her when she did wrong. . . .

It was one of their happy mornings. They trotted along and sat down together, with no thought that life would ever change much for them: they would only get bigger and not go to school, and it would always be like the holidays; they would always live together and be fond of each other. And the mill with its booming—the great chestnut tree under which they played at houses—their own little river, the Ripple, where the banks seemed like home, and Tom was always seeing the water rats, while Maggie gathered the purple plumy tops of the reeds, which she forgot and dropped afterwards . . . these things would always be just the same to them.

Life did change for Tom and Maggie; and yet they were not wrong in believing that the thoughts and loves of these first years would always make part of their lives. We could never have loved the earth so well if we had had no childhood in it,—if it were not the earth where the same flowers come up again every spring that we used to gather with our tiny fingers as we sat lisping to ourselves on the grass—the same hips and haws on the autumn hedgerows—the same redbreasts that we used to call "God's birds," because they did no harm to the precious crops. What novelty is worth that sweet monotony where everything is known, and *loved* because it is known?

The wood I walk in on this mild May day, with the young yellow-brown foliage of the oaks between me and the blue sky, the white starflowers and the blue-eyed speedwell and the ground ivy at my feet—what grove of tropic palms, what strange ferns or splendid broad petalled blossoms, could ever thrill such deep and delicate fibers within me as this home scene? These familiar flowers, these well remembered bird notes, this sky, with its fitful brightness, these furrowed and grassy fields, each with a sort of personality given to it by the capricious hedgerows—such things as these are the mother tongue of our imagination, the language that is laden with all the subtle inextricable associations the fleeting hours of our childhood left behind them.. Our delight in the sunshine on the deep bladed grass today, might be no more than the faint perception of wearied souls, if it were not for the sunshine and the grass in the far-off years which still live in us, and transform our perception into love.

1860

George Eliot on Realism

The notion that peasants are joyous, that the typical moment to represent a man in a smock-frock is when he is cracking a joke and showing a row of sound teeth, that cottage matrons are usually buxom, and village children necessarily rosy and merry, are prejudices difficult to dislodge from the artistic mind, which looks for its subjects into literature instead of life. . . . But no one who has seen much of actual ploughmen thinks them jocund; no one who is well acquainted with the English peasantry can pronounce them merry. The slow gaze, in which no sense of beauty beams, no humor twinkles,—the slow utterance, and the heavy slouching walk, remind one rather of that melancholy animal the camel, than of the sturdy countryman, with striped stockings, red waistcoat, and hat aside, who represents the traditional English peasant. . .

The greatest benefit we owe to the artist, whether painter, poet, or novelist, is the extension of our sympathies. . . . Art is the nearest thing to life; it is a mode of amplifying experience and extending our contact with our fellowmen beyond the bounds of our personal lot. All the more sacred is the task of the artist when he undertakes to paint the life of the People. Falsification here is far more pernicious than in the more artificial aspects of life. It is not so very serious that we should have false ideas about evanescent fashions—about the manners and conversation of beaux and duchesses; but it *is* serious that our sympathy with the perennial joys and struggles, the toil, the tragedy, and the humor in the life of our more heavily-laden fellow-men, should be perverted, and turned towards a false object instead of the true one. . . .

The thing for mankind to know is, not what are the motives and influences which the moralist thinks *ought* to act on the laborer or the artisan, but what are the motives and influences which *do* act on him. We want to be taught to feel, not for the heroic artisan or the sentimental peasant, but for the peasant in all his coarse apathy, and the artisan in all his suspicious selfishness.

From "The Natural History of German Life," published July, 1856.

THINK AND DISCUSS

Understanding

1. Describe Mr. Tulliver's assumptions about the proper education for boys and girls.
2. How does Maggie get rid of her anger?
3. Who is responsible for the rabbits dying?
4. How does Tom show Maggie he forgives her?

Analyzing

5. Why doesn't Mr. Tulliver want his son to become a miller?
6. Explain why Maggie wets her hair the day Tom comes home.
7. In what ways does her impulsive affection limit and hurt Maggie?
8. How does the discussion about lions illustrate the differences between Tom and Maggie?

Extending

9. Do the difficulties that Victorian girls encountered in getting an education, suggested by the scene where the men discuss Maggie's reading, still exist today?
10. Does childhood still connect us with the earth, as the narrator says in the conclusion to this excerpt?

REVIEWING: Point of View HT
See Handbook of Literary Terms, p. 917

The relationship between the teller of the story and the characters in it is called **point of view**. In the *first-person* point of view the narrator is a character in the story. In the *third-person* point of view the narrator is not a participant. There are three kinds of third-person narrators:

In the *third-person objective* point of view, the narrator describes external events only and does not say anything about the character's thoughts and feelings. In the *third-person limited* point of view, the narrator reveals the thoughts and feelings of a single character. In the *third-person omniscient* point of view, the narrator can reveal the inner thoughts and feelings of all the characters. Some novelists, like Eliot, create narrators who seem to be emotionally involved in the characters and events.

1. List the characters in *The Mill on the Floss* whose thoughts and feelings are revealed. What point of view is this?
2. When Tom comes with his piece of cake to call Maggie downstairs, whose feelings are revealed? What effect is created?
3. At times, as in the last two paragraphs, the writer seems to speak in her own voice. How does this influence the way you read the story itself?
4. During the first description of Tom Tulliver (page 604), the narrator pauses for a discussion of heredity and development. Do you think the narrator's comments here are fair?

COMPOSITION
Explaining Maggie's Character

Eliot's Maggie Tulliver is a complex character, pulled in different directions by her strong feelings. Write a comparison/contrast essay in which you describe her inner contradictions to someone who knows nothing about her. Begin by listing her opposing characteristics. For example, Maggie wants to have her own way, yet she eagerly submits to Tom's rule. When you have a sufficient list, use the principal contradictions as the topics in your outline.

Analyzing Point of View

Choose a scene from *The Mill on the Floss* and write a paper analyzing the point of view in that scene. Note what kinds of information the reader gets: Which events are reported objectively? Which character's thoughts and feelings are revealed? How do the other characters look from that perspective? As you study the scene, ask yourself how these authorial strategies affect your reactions. In your paper, include your reactions to the characters revealed, the inner views offered and their implications, and the narrator's comments. See "Writing About Point of View" in the Writer's Handbook.

The Discovery of Childhood

Until the last two centuries, children were usually treated as little adults. Once out of baby clothes they dressed just like their fathers and mothers, and as soon as they were able they began to work alongside their parents, preparing to take up much the same kind of life once they were able. Parents may have loved their children just as tenderly then as now; Ben Jonson's epitaph for his dead son (see page 270) illustrates a father's pride and grief. But Sir Walter Raleigh's short poem of paternal advice (see page 176) is typical of parent/child relationships. He speaks to the son as a man in the making, and warns him of the gallows that "chokes the child" who breaks the law.

Glumdalclitch, in *Gulliver's Travels* (see page 344), illustrates how children spent their days. She has a job fitting her age, which is to take care of this tiny man, and because she is still young she forgets her responsibilities from time to time. Maggie Tulliver is quite like her, forgetting to feed Tom's rabbits, with predictable results. Both *The Mill on the Floss* and *David Copperfield* illustrate how British culture, even in the early nineteenth century, still offered no separate cultural identity for children. The books they read are adult books, like Maggie's tract on witches, or are relentlessly practical, like the crocodile book David reads.

But a revolutionary change was already beginning to take place in British culture, ushered in by the Romantics: the "discovery" of childhood. Blake's *Songs of Innocence* (see page 429) literally give a voice to the child, since those poems look at the world from a child's perspective, which Blake depicts as sweet, but limited. He knew that the naive trust of "The Lamb" must give way to the indignant rage of "The Tyger."

Coleridge and Wordsworth, fascinated with the subject of personal development, came to look upon childhood as a crucial stage in life, a time for the mind and the feelings to discover their full range, under the benevolent teaching power of nature. Wordsworth, in the "Ode: Intimations of Immortality from Recollections of Early Childhood" (see page 458) remembers a time when "The earth, and every common sight,/To me did seem/Appareled in celestial light,/The glory and the freshness of a dream. . . ." Here Wordsworth endows the perceptions of children with a visionary power far superior to that of adults, which leads to the paradox that "The child is father to the Man. . ."

The memories of earliest childhood in Dickens's *David Copperfield* are more domestic: David feels a childhood wonder at the rooster in the back yard and the shadows in the pantry. But to this Dickens adds a characteristic indignation at the injustices which children frequently suffer. Mr. Murdstone, acting on the assumptions of previous centuries, thinks it is a good thing to whip a boy who cannot remember his lessons. Dickens's novel, illustrating a new attitude, attacks that assumption by making Murdstone a villain.

Eliot's *The Mill on the Floss* takes this indignation a step further. She shows how a whole society systematically denies a bright and energetic child the chance to grow and develop, simply because of her gender. Maggie Tulliver is a victim twice over, and yet her buoyant spirit keeps rising again. Here too, along with the emotional frustrations of childhood, seen in Maggie's solitary rages in the attic, there are the moments of poetic revelation, when the mill grinds on, and its sifting powder makes "the very spider-nets look like a fairy lace work. . . ." In such works, British culture recovered for itself something which it had long ignored, and succeeded in making readers more fully aware of themselves.

BIOGRAPHY

Matthew Arnold
1822–1888

The most complex problem of Matthew Arnold's youth was living in the shadow of his celebrated father. Thomas Arnold had taken over the direction of Rugby School in 1828 and within a few years transformed it into a model educational institution. From his sixth year Matthew lived with his parents at Rugby, in a home swarming with bright, ambitious boys from the school. No one needed to tell him of the high expectations his parents held for his success. While Arnold was always a loving and respectful son, perhaps unconsciously he felt the need to rebel. His own academic performance was uneven—at times brilliant, at times very bad. Nevertheless, he won a scholarship to Oxford in 1841.

There he found little challenge in his studies and ample time to turn himself into a dandy, playing whist and billiards, choosing outlandish waistcoats, addressing his friends as "my dear." As one contemporary put it, "a very gentlemanly young man with a slight tinge of the fop that does no harm when blended with talents, good nature, and high spirits."

Arnold's father died unexpectedly of a heart attack in 1842. Matthew remained at Oxford, continuing to study philosophy there until 1846. It was a period of indecision. While many of his contemporaries embarked on professional careers, Arnold remained uncommitted. In 1847 he began to serve as private secretary to Lord Lansdowne, President of the Privy Council and head of the Council on Education. Arnold's duties were light and in his free time he wrote poetry. By 1849 he could publish his first volume, *The Strayed Reveller*. The mixed response to the book kept him unsure of his calling.

Arnold felt intensely the confusion of the modern world—"everything is against one," he wrote in 1849—and he dreamed of a poetry that might help, a poetry that would "not only . . . interest, but also . . . inspirit and rejoice the reader." This he strove for in his own work. But in moments of depression he would insist, "my poems are fragments—i.e., . . . I am fragments . . . the whole effect of my poems is vague and indeterminate." Perhaps Arnold set too high a goal for his art.

Practical matters intervened. In 1850 he proposed to Frances Wightman, and to support himself and his wife he obtained, with the help of Lord Lansdowne, a job in the civil service. For the next thirty-five years Arnold worked as an inspector of private schools for poor children. It was an exhausting job, requiring constant travel. But it permitted Arnold direct involvement in some of the social problems of his day.

Writing poetry became more difficult. In 1853 he told a close friend, "I am past thirty, and three parts iced over—and my pen, it seems to me is even stiffer and more cramped than my feeling." More and more, Arnold turned to prose. He began with essays on literature. As time passed, his range expanded into essays and books on education, political issues, and theology. Arnold became one of the leading intellectuals of his day.

Isolation   Matthew Arnold

The woman addressed here in such pessimistic terms may have been a childhood friend of Arnold's named Mary Claude. By 1848 she was a beautiful and brilliant young writer and ethnologist—an anthropologist who deals with the various racial or cultural groups of people. Arnold evidently arranged to meet her in Switzerland, but she left before he arrived. During the next few months he wrote a series of lyrics in which he gave her the fictitious name of Marguerite. In the series the poem below is titled "To Marguerite—Continued."

Yes! in the sea of life enisled,[1]
With echoing straits between us thrown,
Dotting the shoreless watery wild,
We mortal millions live *alone*.
5 The islands feel the enclasping flow,
And then their endless bounds they know.

But when the moon their hollows lights,
And they are swept by balms of spring,
And in their glens, on starry nights,
10 The nightingales divinely sing;
And lovely notes, from shore to shore,
Across the sounds and channels pour—

O! then a longing like despair
Is to their farthest caverns sent;

15 For surely once, they feel, we were
Parts of a single continent!
Now round us spreads the watery plain—
Oh might our marges[2] meet again!

Who ordered, that their longing's fire
20 Should be, as soon as kindled, cooled?
Who renders vain their deep desire?—
A God, a God their severance ruled!
And bade betwixt their shores to be
The unplumbed, salt, estranging sea.

1852

1. *enisled*, placed apart, as on an island.
2. *marges*, borders, edges, margins.

Self-Dependence

Matthew Arnold

Weary of myself, and sick of asking
What I am, and what I ought to be,
At this vessel's prow I stand, which bears me
Forwards, forwards o'er the starlit sea.

5 And a look of passionate desire
O'er the sea and to the stars I send:
"Ye who from my childhood up have calmed me,
Calm me, ah, compose me to the end!

"Ah, once more," I cried, "ye stars, ye waters,
10 On my heart your mighty charm renew;
Still, still let me, as I gaze upon you,
Feel my soul becoming vast like you!"

From the intense, clear, star-sown vault of
        heaven,
Over the lit sea's unquiet way,
15 In the rustling night-air came the answer:
"Wouldst thou *be* as these are? *Live* as they.

"Unaffrighted by the silence round them,
Undistracted by the sights they see,
These demand not that the things without them
20 Yield them love, amusement, sympathy.

"And with joy the stars perform their shining,   *imagery*
And the sea its long moon-silvered roll;
For self-poised they live, nor pine with noting
All the fever of some differing soul.

25 "Bounded by themselves, and unregardful
In what state God's other works may be,
In their own tasks all their powers pouring,
These attain the mighty life you see."

O air-born voice! long since, severely clear,
30 A cry like thine in mine own heart I hear:
"Resolve to be thyself; and know that he
Who finds himself loses his misery!"

                                        1852

Dover Beach

Matthew Arnold

The sea is calm tonight,
The tide is full, the moon lies fair
Upon the straits; on the French coast the light
Gleams and is gone; the cliffs of England stand,
5 Glimmering and vast, out in the tranquil bay,
Come to the window, sweet is the night air!

Only, from the long line of spray
Where the sea meets the moon-blanched land,
Listen! you hear the grating roar
10 Of pebbles which the waves draw back, and fling,
At their return, up the high strand,
Begin, and cease, and then again begin,
With tremulous cadence slow, and bring
The eternal note of sadness in.

15 Sophocles[1] long ago
Heard it on the Aegean, and it brought
Into his mind the turbid ebb and flow
Of human misery; we
Find also in the sound a thought,

20 Hearing it by this distant northern sea.

The Sea of Faith
Was once, too, at the full, and round earth's
        shore
Lay like the folds of a bright girdle[2] furled.
But now I only hear
25 Its melancholy, long, withdrawing roar,
Retreating, to the breath
Of the night wind, down the vast edges drear
And naked shingles[3] of the world.

Ah, love, let us be true
30 To one another! for the world, which seems
To lie before us like a land of dreams,
So various, so beautiful, so new,

---

1. **Sophocles,** Greek dramatist (495-406 B.C.).
2. **girdle,** in the traditional sense, a garment that encircles, or girds, the body; usually a loose belt around the waist.
3. **shingles,** pebble beaches.

Hath really neither joy, nor love, nor light,
Nor certitude, nor peace, nor help for pain;
35 And we are here as on a darkling plain

Swept with confused alarms of struggle and
    flight,
Where ignorant armies clash by night.

1851   1867

Reader's Note

"Dover Beach"

The town of Dover, sheltered by the towering chalk cliffs of the English south coast, lies within sight of France. For centuries it has served as a port for travelers bound for the continent. Dover's proximity to Europe also makes it one of England's most vulnerable points, and a Norman castle built on a hill above the town stands as a reminder of the dangers to peace and security that occasionally threaten from across the narrow span of the English Channel.

Arnold and his wife visited Dover twice in 1851: in June, just after their wedding, and in October, on their way to a continental vacation. He almost certainly wrote "Dover Beach" during this period, and he clearly poured into this relatively short poem, which seems to be addressed to his wife, the ideas and feelings of the moment.

Arnold begins with the image of the ocean, and that image dominates the poem. But the way his speaker sees the ocean shifts as his ideas and his mood evolve, and it is this change in thought and feeling that constitutes the action of the poem.

At first glance, what the speaker sees is a "calm" (line 1) sea; the tide is "full" (line 2); the French coast is visible, yet at a safe distance. The protecting cliffs of England "stand, / Glimmering and vast" (line 5). He calls his listener to the window to enjoy this scene. But then a shift begins—there is the "grating roar" (line 9) of the waves. The very sounds of these words harshly contrast with the agreeable "calm" and "full" of the first lines. And whereas the speaker first looked from a distance, seeing "the long line of spray" (line 7), he is now much closer and more involved with the scene, as he observes pebbles picked up by the waves and hurled up the shore (line 10).

In the sound of the waves the speaker hears the "eternal note of sadness" (line 14). To Arnold, the Greek playwright Sophocles epitomized "the calm, the cheerfulness, the disinterested objectivity" lacking in the modern spirit, and his works achieved a "noble serenity which always accompanies true insight."

The note of sadness makes the poem's speaker recall what Sophocles heard in the ocean's roar: an objective, distanced vision of human suffering. But as a modern man, the speaker has a more specific, a more subjective association.

His phrase, the "Sea of Faith" (line 21), is intentionally ambiguous. It can refer to a faith in God—in Arnold's time many thoughtful people were troubled by religious doubts and at times it seemed as if an era of calm belief had been replaced by one of disturbing uncertainties. But "Faith" here also includes simple trust in other people and in society. As lines 33–34 indicate, the speaker no longer has faith in "certitude . . . peace . . . [or] help for pain" and lines 25–27 describe his sense of vulnerability, terror, and absolute solitude.

The speaker's only solution is a very modern one—a plea for love and fidelity in one other person (lines 29–30). The scene at the beginning of the poem, with its security and tranquility, seems now only a deception, a "land of dreams" (line 31). In the final lines the speaker looks at a very different ocean. The moonlight is gone. The calm of the full tide has dissolved into confusion. The waves look like warriors in a night battle, fighting in ignorance. In the poem's last words we hear the roar of the waves and understand the despair they have inspired.

Pegwell Bay, Kent (Detail) by William Dyce. 1859–60. *Tate Gallery, London*

THINK AND DISCUSS
ISOLATION
Understanding

1. What is the single, dominant **metaphor** in this poem?

Analyzing

2. What causes the "islands" suddenly to recognize that they were once connected?
3. What does the water represent?
4. If their "marges" could meet again, what would be the result in human terms?

Extending

5. Comment on the speaker's conclusion that "a God" is responsible.

SELF-DEPENDENCE
Understanding

1. What two voices speak in this poem?
2. In the midst of dissatisfaction with himself, what does the speaker wish he could be like?

Analyzing

3. How does the "voice" characterize the differences between nature and human existence?
4. What does the speaker's "heart" tell him to do?

Extending

5. In what ways does this poem react to the Romantic notion that people might find their spirits instructed and elevated through contact with nature?

DOVER BEACH
Understanding

1. Having looked at the scene, what does the speaker ask of himself and his love?

Analyzing

2. Compare and contrast the ways in which Sophocles and the modern speaker use the ocean as a **symbol**.
3. Describe the speaker's vision of the human condition.

REVIEWING: Imagery HⲦ
See Handbook of Literary Terms, p. 910

Specific, concrete, details that appeal to the senses constitute **imagery**. Images provide vividness and tend to arouse emotions in a way that abstract language does not.

1. What does the image of "echoing straits . . . Dotting the shoreless watery wild" in "Isolation" (lines 2–3) suggest about human relationships?
2. What images are involved in the wakening of longing?
3. What three images dominate "Self-Dependence"?

4. "Dover Beach" switches in stanza 5 from images of the sea—to what?

THINKING SKILLS
Synthesizing

To synthesize is to combine elements so as to achieve a new pattern not evident before—a new understanding.

1. In the seventeenth century Donne said, "no man is an island" (page 283), but in the nineteenth century Arnold says that people are indeed like islands. Which position do you feel is more appropriate for the twentieth century? Explain.
2. Donne said further that "every man is a piece of the continent." Arnold acknowledges as much, but complains that the "watery plain" now separates people. If this is true, what do you think caused the separation?
3. Are Donne and Arnold really in disagreement? Explain.

COMPOSITION ⬥
Symbolizing the Modern World

Arnold uses images of islands in the sea to symbolize his sense of life. Write a paper in which you name and describe something that symbolizes your own sense of modern life. Use imagery to help your reader feel about it the same way that you do. Then explain why you think that this object—whatever it is—is an appropriate symbol for life today.

Analyzing Imagery and Mood in "Dover Beach"

The speaker of "Dover Beach" devotes much of the poem to describing a scene, and in so doing establishes a mood for the poem as a whole. Write an essay in which you explain how these images affect the reader's feelings. First select several images from the poem—for example, "grating roar/Of pebbles," which suggests an ominous mood. Use the images you choose as the basis for different paragraphs in your analysis. See "Writing About Mood or Tone" in the Writer's Handbook.

Polite English of the Victorian period—especially the early years—was extremely formal. Men addressed their wives as "Mrs." and husbands were treated with equal courtesy. The utmost formality was extended to strangers, thereby implying they were solemn and important people. There were certain classes of people—the ambitious businessman, the newly rich, the aspiring student—who carried this formality to absurd lengths. They spoke an exaggerated English of their own called *genteelism*.

The first and most important rule of genteelism was to avoid the common word and use instead a learned, bookish synonym. The advocates of genteelism did not help themselves to a piece of bread with jam—they assisted themselves to a portion of bread with preserves; they did not begin a meal—they commenced a collation; they did not use a toothpowder—they employed a dentrifice; they did not shut the door to a room—they closed the portal to an accommodation; and they never used *before*, *except*, or *about*—it was *ere*, *save*, and *anent*.

The rapid advance of invention and mechanization all during the Victorian Age created a need for many new words. Grammarians protested the forming of such words as *telegraph* and *typewriter* by scientists, inventors, and manufacturers, and felt that the making of words should be left to the etymologists.

As American English grew in the nineteenth century, it often used different words from British English to denote the same thing. Compare the following words pertaining to the railroad industry—the first of each pair is American, the second is British: *railroad—railway; conductor—guard; fireman—stoker; car—carriage; track—line; freight—goods; trunk—box;* and *check—register.* Britishers were *ill, clever,* and *homely;* Americans were *sick, smart,* and *friendly.*

As the language grew, when words were needed they were used with little regard for "correctness" in spite of the snobbery of genteelism and the protests of grammarians.

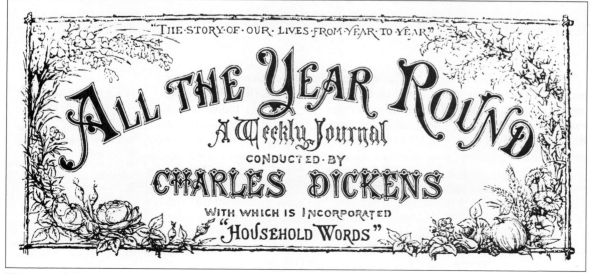

Title page of *All the Year Round*, a periodical founded and edited by Charles Dickens. *The Dickens House, London*

THINKING CRITICALLY
ABOUT LITERATURE

UNIT 6   THE VICTORIANS 1830–1880

■ CONCEPT REVIEW

The following selection contains many of the important ideas and literary terms found in Unit 6. It also contains notes and questions designed to help you think critically about your reading. Page numbers in the notes refer to an application or a review. A more extensive discussion of these terms is in the Handbook of Literary Terms.

John Stuart Mill (1806–1873) was one of the leading writers and thinkers of the Victorian era. His books include *A System of Logic* (1843), *Principles of Political Economy* (1848), *On Liberty* (1859), and *The Subjection of Women* (1869). This passage from Mill's *Autobiography* (1873) describes his quite unusual childhood.

from The Autobiography of John Stuart Mill

John Stuart Mill

I have no remembrance of the time when I began to learn Greek. I have been told that it was when I was three years old. My earliest recollection on the subject, is that of committing to memory what my father termed Vocables, being lists of common Greek words, with their signification in English, which he wrote out for me on cards. Of grammar, until some years later, I learnt no more than the inflections of the nouns and verbs, but, after a course of vocables, proceeded at once to translation; and I faintly remember going through *Aesop's Fables*, the first Greek book which I read. The *Anabasis*, which I remember better, was the second. I learnt no Latin until my eighth year. At that time I had read, under my father's tuition, a number of Greek prose authors. . . . But my father, in all his teaching, demanded of me not only the utmost that I could do, but much that I could by no possibility have done. What he was himself willing to undergo for the sake of my instruction, may be judged from the fact, that I went through the

■ **my father:** James Mill (1773–1836) worked for the East India company and wrote on government and psychology.
■ **Vocables:** words, as heard or seen without consideration of meanings.
■ **Anabasis:** Xenophon's account of the Greek army fighting its way through enemy territory in Asia.
■ This is one of several ambiguous statements in the passage. Consider whether Mill is praising or criticizing his father.

whole process of preparing my Greek lessons in the same room and at the same table at which he was writing: and as in those days Greek and English lexicons were not, and I could make no more use of a Greek and Latin lexicon than could be made without having yet begun to learn Latin, I was forced to have recourse to him for the meaning of every word which I did not know. This incessant interruption, he, one of the most impatient of men, submitted to, and wrote under that interruption several volumes of his History and all else that he had to write during those years.

The only thing besides Greek, that I learnt as a lesson in this part of my childhood, was arithmetic: this also my father taught me: it was the task of the evenings, and I well remember its disagreeableness. But the lessons were only a part of the daily instruction I received. Much of it consisted in the books I read by myself, and my father's discourses to me, chiefly during our walks. From 1810 to the end of 1813 we were living in Newington Green, then an almost rustic neighborhood. My father's health required considerable and constant exercise, and he walked habitually before breakfast, generally in the green lanes towards Hornsey. In these walks I always accompanied him, and with my earliest recollections of green fields and wild flowers, is mingled that of the account I gave him daily of what I had read the day before. To the best of my remembrance, this was a voluntary rather than a prescribed exercise. I made notes on slips of paper while reading, and from these, in the morning walks, I told the story to him; for the books were chiefly histories, of which I read in this manner a great number. . . . Of children's books, any more than of playthings, I had scarcely any, except an occasional gift from a relation or acquaintance: among those I had, *Robinson Crusoe* was preeminent, and continued to delight me through all my boyhood. It was no part however of my father's system to exclude books of amusement, though he allowed them very sparingly. Of such books he possessed at that time next to none, but he borrowed several for me; those which I remember are the *Arabian Nights*, Cazotte's *Arabian Tales*, *Don Quixote*, Miss Edgeworth's *Popular Tales*, and a book of some reputation in its day, Brooke's *Fool of Quality*.

In my eighth year I commenced learning Latin, in conjunction with a younger sister, to whom I taught it as I went on, and who afterwards repeated the lessons to my father: and from this time, other sisters and brothers being successively added as pupils, a considerable part of my day's work consisted of this preparatory teaching. It was a part which I greatly disliked; the more so, as I was held responsible for the lessons of my pupils, in almost as full a sense as for my own: I however derived from this discipline the great advantage of learning more thoroughly and retaining more lastingly the things which I was set to teach: perhaps, too, the practice it afforded in explaining difficulties to others, may even at that age have been useful. . . .

A voluntary exercise, to which throughout my boyhood I was much addicted, was what I called writing histories. I successively composed a Roman history, picked out of Hooke; an abridgement of the *Ancient Universal History*; a History of Holland, from my favorite Watson and from an anonymous compilation; and in my eleventh and twelfth year I occupied myself with

■ Note the special burdens that James Mill undergoes in teaching his son.
■ **lexicons:** dictionaries.

■ **his History:** James Mill was working on *The History of British India*, which he published in 1818.
■ Consider how you would describe the general *tone* of this selection.

■ **Newington Green:** A suburb of London.

■ *Imagery* (page 616): These two images contrast with the setting for the rest of his day's activities.

■ *Robinson Crusoe* was not, however, originally intended as a children's book—nor were most of the other books mentioned later.
■ Mill contrasts these books with what he ordinarily read.

■ Note both the advantages and the disadvantages of his teaching his sisters and brothers.

■ Consider what the *connotation* of words such as "addicted" suggests about Mill's attitude toward such activities.

writing what I flattered myself was something serious. This was no less than a history of the Roman Government, compiled (with the assistance of Hooke) from Livy and Dionysius: of which I wrote as much as would have made an octavo volume. . . .

During this part of my childhood, one of my greatest amusements was experimental science; in the theoretical, however, not the practical sense of the word; not trying experiments—a kind of discipline which I have often regretted not having had—nor even seeing, but merely reading about them. I never remember being so wrapt up in any book, as I was in Joyce's *Scientific Dialogues;* and I was rather recalcitrant to my father's criticisms of the bad reasoning respecting the first principles of physics, which abounds in the early part of that work. I devoured treatises on Chemistry, especially that of my father's early friend and schoolfellow, Dr. Thomson, for years before I attended a lecture or saw an experiment.

From about the age of twelve, I entered into another and more advanced stage in my course of instruction; in which the main object was no longer the aids and appliances of thought, but the thoughts themselves. This commenced with Logic. . . . I know nothing in my education, to which I think myself more indebted for whatever capacity of thinking I have attained. The first intellectual operation in which I arrived at any proficiency, was dissecting a bad argument, and finding in what part the fallacy lay: and though whatever capacity of this sort I attained was due to the fact that it was an intellectual exercise in which I was most perseveringly drilled by my father, yet it is also true that the school logic, and the mental habits acquired in studying it, were among the principal instruments of this drilling. I am persuaded that nothing, in modern education, tends so much, when properly used, to form exact thinkers, who attach a precise meaning to words and propositions, and are not imposed on by vague, loose, or ambiguous terms. . . .

In the course of instruction which I have partially retraced, the point most superficially apparent is the great effort to give, during the years of childhood an amount of knowledge in what are considered the higher branches of education, which is seldom acquired (if acquired at all) until the age of manhood. The result of the experiment shows the ease with which this may be done, and places in a strong light the wretched waste of so many precious years as are spent in acquiring the modicum of Latin and Greek commonly taught to schoolboys; a waste, which has led so many educational reformers to entertain the ill-judged proposal of discarding these languages altogether from general education. If I had been by nature extremely quick of apprehension, or had possessed a very accurate and retentive memory, or were of a remarkably active and energetic character, the trial would not be conclusive; but in all these natural gifts I am rather below than above par; what I could do, could assuredly be done by any boy or girl of average capacity and healthy physical constitution: and if I have accomplished anything, I owe it, among other fortunate circumstances, to the fact that through the early training bestowed on me by my father, I started, I may fairly say, with an advantage of a quarter of a century over my contemporaries.

■ **Inference** (page 598): Note how Mill now seems to regard his Roman history.
■ **Livy and Dionysius:** Historians of ancient Rome.
■ **octavo:** This refers to the size of the pages, about 6 x 9 inches.
■ Note the difference between practical and theoretical science.
■ **recalcitrant:** disobedient; resisting of authority.

■ **Logic:** the principles of reasoning and proof. Here is a classic example of a form of reasoning called a *syllogism:* Major premise: All humans are mortal (must die). Minor premise: Socrates is a human. Conclusion: Socrates is mortal.

■ Consider how Mill's *style* may be influenced by his purpose in writing and his intended audience.

■ Mill's conclusions about his capabilities may not be shared by every reader.

There was one cardinal point in this training, of which I have already given some indication, and which, more than anything else, was the cause of whatever good it effected. Most boys or youths who have had much knowledge drilled into them, have their mental capacities not strengthened, but overlaid by it. They are crammed with mere facts, and with the opinions or phrases of other people, and these are accepted as a substitute for the power to form opinions of their own: and thus the sons of eminent fathers, who have spared no pains in their education, so often grow up mere parroters of what they have learnt, incapable of using their minds except in the furrows traced for them. Mine, however, was not an education of cram. My father never permitted anything which I learnt to degenerate into a mere exercise of memory. He strove to make the understanding not only go along with every step of the teaching, but, if possible, precede it. Anything which could be found out by thinking I never was told, until I had exhausted my efforts to find it out for myself. . . . A pupil from whom nothing is ever demanded which he cannot do, never does all he can.

One of the evils most liable to attend on any sort of early proficiency, and which often fatally blights its promise, my father most anxiously guarded against. This was self-conceit. He kept me, with extreme vigilance, out of the way of hearing myself praised, or of being led to make self-flattering comparisons between myself and others. From his own [dealings] with me I could derive none but a very humble opinion of myself; and the standard of comparison he always held up to me, was not what other people did, but what a man could and ought to do. He completely succeeded in preserving me from the sort of influences he so much dreaded. I was not at all aware that my attainments were anything unusual at my age. If I accidentally had my attention drawn to the fact that some other boy knew less than myself—which happened less often than might be imagined—I concluded, not that I knew much, but that he, for some reason or other, knew little, or that his knowledge was of a different kind from mine. . . .

It is evident that this, among many other of the purposes of my father's scheme of education, could not have been accomplished if he had not carefully kept me from having any great amount of [contact] with other boys. He was earnestly bent upon my escaping not only the ordinary corrupting influence which boys exercise over boys, but the contagion of vulgar modes of thought and feeling; and for this he was willing that I should pay the price of inferiority in the accomplishments which schoolboys in all countries chiefly cultivate. The deficiencies in my education were principally in the things which boys learn from being turned out to shift for themselves, and from being brought together in large numbers. From temperance and much walking, I grew up healthy and hardy, though not muscular; but I could do no feats of skill or physical strength, and knew none of the ordinary bodily exercises. It was not that play, or time for it, was refused me. Though no holidays were allowed, lest the habit of work should be broken, and a taste for idleness acquired, I had ample leisure in every day to amuse myself; but as I had no boy companions, and the animal need of physical activity was satisfied by

■ **Metaphor** (page 557): The metaphorical picture suggested here provokes sympathy for the ordinary student.

■ **Point of view** (page 609): Another kind of personality might complain here that after expecting so much, the elder Mill was far too stingy with his praise.

■ Note the special conditions necessary for such an education.

■ Consider what Mill means by "deficiencies in my education."

walking, my amusements, which were mostly solitary, were in general of a quiet, if not a bookish turn, and gave little stimulus to any other kind even of mental activity than that which was already called forth by the studies: I consequently remained long, and in a less degree have always remained, inexpert in anything requiring manual dexterity; my mind as well as my hands, did its work very lamely when it was applied, or ought to have been applied, to the practical details which, as they are the chief interest of life to the majority of men, are also the things in which whatever mental capacity they have, chiefly shows itself: I was constantly meriting reproof by inattention, inobservance, and general slackness of mind in matters of daily life. My father was the extreme opposite in these particulars: his senses and mental faculties were always on the alert; he carried decision and energy of character in his whole manner and into every action of life: and this, as much as his talents, contributed to the strong impression which he always made upon those with whom he came into personal contact. But the children of energetic parents, frequently grow up unenergetic, because they lean on their parents, and the parents are energetic for them. The education which my father gave me, was in itself much more fitted for training me to *know* than to *do*.

■ Note how Mill *characterizes* both himself and his father throughout.

■ Note the generalization about his education with which Mill concludes.

1873

THINK AND DISCUSS
Understanding
1. List the subjects young Mill studied under his father.
2. Why couldn't he use a dictionary to help him with his Greek vocabulary?
3. What kinds of training did he gain from teaching his younger brothers and sisters?
4. Why did he never get a holiday?

Analyzing
5. How does Mill **characterize** his father? Does he intend this to be a negative or positive characterization? Explain.
6. Find examples of the way Mill uses the **connotations** of words to suggest his evaluations of particular activities.
7. Explain the results of Mill's having been trained "to know" rather than "to do." Does he seem to mind?
8. How would you describe the **tone** of this selection?
9. Discuss how Mill's **style** is a reflection of his education and a further reflection of his intended audience and his purpose for writing.

Extending
10. Compare Mill's childhood reading with that

of David Copperfield and Maggie Tulliver. How do these **allusions** to books define a recurring value in Victorian literature?
11. Do Mill's reasons for valuing the study of logic convince you that it should be a part of everyone's education?
12. When Mill describes the "deficiencies in [his] education," what other aspects of personal development does he neglect to mention?

REVIEWING LITERARY TERMS
Imagery
1. Explain how the image of Mill and his father walking "in the green lanes. . ." affects the reader's feelings for this kind of education.

Inference
2. Given what Mill describes about his childhood, would you accept his inference that in "natural gifts" of memory and quickness of apprehension he was "rather below than above par" compared with other children?
3. At what points do you infer a degree of resentment on Mill's part against his father?

Metaphor
4. When Mill speaks of people "incapable of using their minds except in the furrows

traced for them," what two different things does he compare?

5. To what is self-conceit metaphorically compared? Why is this metaphor particularly appropriate?

Point of view

6. When Mill discusses "the ordinary corrupting influence which boys exercise over boys. . ." what is he talking about? How does his choice of words spring from the peculiarities of his individual perspective on this subject?

7. Compare the point of view here with that of other autobiographies you have read. How does Mill's first-person account differ from the first-person accounts of other writers?

■ CONTENT REVIEW

Classifying

1. Many of the selections in this unit are about love. Classify them according to the kind of love they present or the kinds of conflicts generated by love.

2. Which characters in this unit exercise power over others, and which submit to power? When you have listed the characters, classify them further according to the kinds of power they exercise and the reasons for submission.

Generalizing

3. Mill talks about his father's "system" and his "scheme of education." Describe it.

4. Which selections demonstrate—to one degree or another—that money and wealth can have a destructive influence?

5. As a class, write a brief statement generalizing your understanding of the rights and duties of women in Victorian England.

Synthesizing

6. Faced with inevitable death, do modern people adopt the solutions of Tennyson's Ulysses or of the speaker in Browning's "Prospice"?

7. To what extent do the "two nations" described in the Background—the rich and the poor—still exist today?

Evaluating

8. How accurately—according to your own memories—do Dickens and Eliot picture the way children's minds work?

9. Discuss the extent to which "Sonnets from the Portuguese," *In Memoriam*, and "My Last Duchess" manage to convey a sense of natural speech in spite of the fact that they are in rhyme.

■ COMPOSITION REVIEW

Explaining Character Development

The Victorian fascination with inner change and growth appears both in Tennyson's *In Memoriam* and in Dickens's *David Copperfield*. Write an essay explaining to someone who has not read these works how they illustrate personal progress. For each work, explain the initial state of the protagonist, the processes which help him to change, and his final state.

Analyzing Victorian Quests

Tennyson's "Ulysses," Browning's "Prospice," and Arnold's "Self-Dependence" all feature speakers bound on a quest—a journey in search of something. Write an essay comparing and contrasting these poems. First note the differences you find among the speakers, including their motives and actions. Begin your paper with a description of how the quest appears time and again in Victorian poetry. Then in subsequent paragraphs compare the kinds of journeys taken by these three speakers, their attitudes, and the goals they seek.

Evaluating Visions of the Future

Victorian writers frequently speculated about future developments. Tennyson, in Lyric 106 from *In Memoriam*, envisions future improvements, while Arnold, in "Dover Beach," denies any such hopes. Write an essay to persuade your reader that history has proven one right, one wrong. First do some thinking about the present state of the world, and decide which poem seems to you to make a more accurate prediction. In your essay, first present the problem; then show how incorrect one of these poems is; then show how the other one is correct. Quote as necessary to support your points.

NEW DIRECTIONS 1880–1915

1885	1890	1895	1900

HISTORY AND ARTS

- Verdi: *Otello* (Italy)
- Rodin sculpts *The Thinker* (France)
- James: *Portrait of a Lady* (U.S.)
- Van Gogh paints at Arles, France
- Commercial electricity (U.S.)
- Bismarck resigns as chancellor of Germany
- Puccini: *La Boheme* (Italy)
- Boxer Rebellion in China
- Boer War starts
- Queen Victoria's Diamond Jubilee
- Ibsen: *An Enemy of the People* (Norway)
- Automobile production (France)
- Twain: *Huckleberry Finn* (U.S.)
- Spanish-American War starts
- Fabian Society founded

MONARCHS AND HOUSES

HANOVER • Victoria

ENGLISH LITERATURE

- Hardy: *Jude the Obscure*
- Stevenson: *Treasure Island*
- Yeats: *The Countess Cathleen*
- Wilde: *The Importance of Being Earnest*
- Oxford English Dictionary, Volume 1
- Wells: *The Time Machine*
- Doyle: *A Study in Scarlet*
- Kipling: *The Jungle Book*
- Frazer: *The Golden Bough*
- Housman: *A Shropshire Lad*
- Stoker: *Dracula*

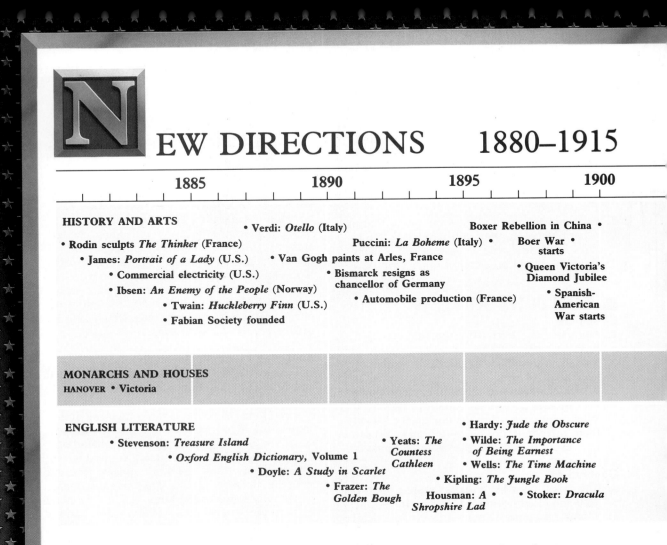

The Thinker, bronze scupture by Auguste Rodin. 1879–1889

Sherlock Holmes, a twentieth-century illustration.

Still Life . . . Sunflowers, by Vincent Van Gogh. 1888

1905   **1910**   **1915**

- **London:** *The Call of the Wild* (U.S.)
- **Wright Brothers' first flight** (U.S.)
- **Russo-Japanese War begins**
- **Abbey Theater founded in Dublin**
- **Chekhov:** *The Cherry Orchard* (Russia)

- **Old-Age Pension Law passed**
- **Strauss:** *Elektra* (Germany)
- **South Africa becomes British dominion**
- **Chinese Republic established**

- **Panama Canal opens**
- **Stravinsky:** *The Rite of Spring* (Russia)
- **Suffragettes demonstrate in London**
- **World War I begins**

SAXE-COBURG
- **Edward VII**

WINDSOR
- **George V**

- **Barrie:** *Peter Pan*
- **Synge:** *The Playboy of the Western World*

- **Conrad:** *The Secret Sharer*
- **Forster:** *Howard's End*
- **Shaw:** *Pygmalion*
- **Lawrence:** *Sons and Lovers*

- **Saki:** *Beasts and Super-Beasts*

Boer War: Crossing the Tuela under heavy fire.

The Wright Brothers' first powered flight, 1903.

King Edward VII, portrait by Sir Luke Fildes. 1912

PREVIEW

UNIT 7   NEW DIRECTIONS   1880–1915

Authors

Thomas Hardy	Joseph Conrad	William Butler Yeats
Gerard Manley Hopkins	A. E. Housman	Saki (H. H. Munro)
Bernard Shaw	Rudyard Kipling	Oscar Wilde

Features
Reader's Note: Imagery in "God's Grandeur"
Reading a Comedy of Ideas
Comment: Shaw and Smollett
Themes in English Literature: Social Class
Comment: Housman on Writing His Poetry
Comment: Yeats and Ronsard
Comment: Yeats on the Source of "Innisfree"
Reader's Note: "Sailing to Byzantium"
Reader's Note: "The Second Coming"
The Changing English Language

Application of Literary Terms
anastrophe
stereotype

Review of Literary Terms
alliteration
dialect
characterization
plot
inference
style

Reading Literature Skillfully
main idea and details

Vocabulary Skills
roots
dictionary
synonyms and antonyms

Thinking Skills
generalizing
synthesizing
evaluating

Composition Assignments
Explaining Multiple Meanings of Words
Analyzing Hopkins's Sound Devices
Explaining Speech Clues to Performance
Analyzing Social Relationships
Analyzing Liza's Characterization
Evaluating Doolittle's Philosophy
Explaining What the Characters Want
Analyzing Dramatic Ironies
Explaining the Point of View
Analyzing Conrad's Symbolism
Imagining Alternative Choices
Persuading to Stay in Competition
Explaining the Themes in "Recessional"
Evaluating the Virtues in "If ____"
Describing a Composite Beast
Analyzing Yeats's Use of Imagery
Writing Tobermory's Last Letter
Analyzing the Irony in "Tobermory"

Enrichment
Creating a Collage of Contrasts
Designing Costumes for *Pygmalion*
Comparing *Pygmalion* and *My Fair Lady*
Debating Leggatt's Crime

Thinking Critically About Literature
Concept Review
Content Review
Composition Review

NEW DIRECTIONS 1880–1915

By 1880 England had become the first modern industrial empire. Its large, urban manufacturing centers, with a highly disciplined work force using advanced machine methods, produced goods that went by rail and then by steamship to consumers all over the world, protected en route by the world's largest navy. British financial power and administrative leadership dominated not only the island nation and its colonial territories, but many other countries as well, so that the English could be found in positions of authority and influence in places as distant as China, Borneo, Morocco, and Argentina. Nevertheless, England's commercial success and position of world leadership were not unaccompanied with problems.

The most persistent and visible of these problems remained the condition of the English working class. As the poet Gerard Manley Hopkins wrote, "It is a dreadful thing for the greatest and most necessary part of a very rich nation to live a hard life without dignity, knowledge, comforts, delight, or hopes in the midst of plenty—which plenty they make." Most industrial laborers still worked a six-day week, dressed poorly, and lived in substandard housing. Few had any education; fewer still went to church, since they were disillusioned with organized religion. In the 1880s and 1890s some middle-class intellectuals became convinced that only radical solutions would remedy these problems, and important writers like William Morris and Bernard Shaw committed themselves to socialism.

Such efforts to effect radical change were hampered in part by steadily improving economic conditions during this period. Thanks to falling prices, real wages rose as much as forty percent. At the same time the government was making efforts at moderate change. In 1884 a series of voting reforms opened the franchise to virtually every adult male, thus effectively creating popular democracy in England. The Education Act of 1891 established free schools for everyone up to the age of twelve.

These crucial developments in social justice at home came at a time of new challenge from abroad. Germany, fresh from its victory in the Franco-Prussian War (1870), and the United States, recovered from its own civil war (1861–1865), now became serious threats to English predominance. The Royal Commission on Trade and Industry (1885–1886) noted, "We are beginning to feel the effects of foreign competition in quarters where our trade formerly enjoyed a virtual monopoly." A central problem was that the machinery of England's industrial base was aging, but no one seemed to want to go to the expense of having it modernized.

BRITISH IMPERIALISM

British investment and energy were going elsewhere, into the expansion and defense of the Empire. Even into the 1870s most people had considered British colonies like India merely as economic burdens. But with the appearance of new commercial rivals, the notion of a worldwide confederation of nations under British control, and hence ready markets for British goods, now became popular. Sometimes through gunboat diplomacy (the policy of using military coercion on weaker nations), sometimes through negotiation and formal treaty, England expanded its empire, gaining control over territories that are now Egypt (1882), Nigeria (1885), Kenya and Uganda (1888), Zimbabwe (1889), and Sudan (1891–1899).

Some of those promoting expansion perceived in the British Empire a strain of high idealism.

Lord Salisbury, a prime minister in the 1880s and 1890s, argued that colonialism could be, for the newly adopted peoples, "a great civilizing, Christianizing force." In a celebrated poem Rudyard Kipling proclaimed, "Take up the White Man's burden—/the savage wars of peace—/Fill full the mouth of Famine/and bid the sickness cease. . ." But in the same year (1899), Joseph Conrad described imperialist adventurers far differently in his novella *Heart of Darkness:* "To tear treasure out of the bowels of the land was their desire, with no more moral purpose at the back of it than there is in burglars breaking into a safe." The debate over imperialism reached a crisis in England's war with the Dutch Boer settlers over South Africa (1899–1902), a war England won, but at the expense of bitter criticism at home and abroad.

Even more divisive was the problem of English control over Ireland. Legally, Ireland was a part of England and its representatives sat in Parliament. But the Roman Catholic Irish resented their Protestant English landlords and demanded home rule. This problem was not effectively solved until 1921, with the establishment of the Irish Free State, and throughout the period before World War I Ireland experienced recurrent political turmoil. This turmoil was accompanied by a remarkable cultural awakening in Ireland. As part of an effort to recover the native culture, there was an attempt to revive the Irish language. Folklorists collected poems and tales of Irish myth and legend that survived in medieval manuscripts or in oral form in remote peasant villages. Most importantly, a series of gifted writers endeavored to create a valid Irish literature, rooted in its people, their language and traditions, and separate from the English. The most important figure in this movement, the poet William Butler Yeats, helped found the Abbey Theatre in Dublin (1904), encouraging a new native drama on Irish themes and in Irish idiom, such as John Millington Synge's *The Playboy of the Western World* (1907).

An important characteristic of this revival, in its efforts to regain a specifically Irish spirit, was its rejection both of Protestant and Catholic Christianity, and its celebration of the pagan mythology of early Ireland. This effort to reach back to the cultural roots of a people and their primitive connection to the land was going on in England as well, most notably in the fiction of Thomas Hardy. His efforts to discover a more elemental human experience in the lives of rural people met frequent criticism. Hardy's disregard for middle-class moral values and what detractors called his "pessimism" offended many readers. Hardy's defiant response was to assert that "the soul has her eternal rights . . . she will not be darkened by statutes, not lullabied by the music of bells." He insisted that his so-called "pessimism" was actually only a part of "the exploration of reality" and a "first step towards the soul's betterment."

A NEW WORLD VIEW

Explorations such as Hardy's were in part the consequence of the ongoing problems posed by modern science. The ideas of Charles Darwin, championed by biologists like Thomas Henry Huxley (who coined the word *agnostic),* seemed to cut through old assumptions about human nature and destiny, leaving people uncertain about themselves and their future. H. G. Wells described this new dismay: "Science is a match that man has just got alight. He thought he was in a room—in moments of devotion, a temple—and that his light would be reflected from and display walls inscribed with wonderful secrets . . . It is a curious sensation, now that the preliminary splutter is over and the flame burns up clear, to see . . . in place of all that human comfort and beauty he anticipated— darkness still" (1891). This sense of darkness and loneliness, of a mysterious universe that seems without order or purpose, pervades the literature of the period.

This new world view had an immediate effect on how people viewed social and moral questions. The confusion in a character from Conrad's novel *The Secret Agent* (1907) is typical: "He was incapable by now of judging what could be true, possible, or even probable in this astounding universe. He was terrified out of all capacity for belief or disbelief. . . ." This grim vision reached a sort of climax in Shaw's play *Heartbreak House,* written just before the outbreak of war in 1914:

HECTOR. And this ship that we are all in?

Piccadilly Circus (detail), by Charles Ginner. 1912. *Tate Gallery, London*

This soul's prison we call England?

CAPTAIN SHOTOVER. The captain is in his bunk, drinking bottled ditch-water; and the crew is gambling in the forecastle. She will strike and sink and split. Do you think the laws of God will be suspended in England's favor because you were born in it?

The literature from this era of challenge, anxiety, and doubt is singularly different from that of the high Victorian period. Though many members of the generation of Tennyson and Browning were still alive, younger writers largely rejected not only their affirmations, but also the way they wrote, seeking instead new forms for new perceptions.

One striking evidence of this is the sudden re-emergence of the theater into English literature.

Since the days of the Puritans there had been strong opposition to any theatrical performances in English society, and this was abetted by the Licensing Act of 1737 that permitted only three London theaters to present serious drama. Although the Act was revoked in 1843, and the numbers of theaters grew, serious plays in English do not reappear until the 1880s and 1890s. When they do, it is partly under the influence of the controversial Norwegian playwright Henrik Ibsen. Ibsen's disciple Bernard Shaw revolutionized British theater in the 1890s with a series of what he called "Plays Unpleasant," because in them "dramatic power is used to force the spectator to face unpleasant fact." Even the fairly lighthearted *Pygmalion* (1913) is also a serious exploration of the English class system.

Much of the important writing of this period

Suffragette Grace Chappelaw selling "Votes for Women" posters, October, 1911.

first appeared in weekly magazines, and these periodicals had an important influence on the character of fiction at the end of the century. Novels in the mid-Victorian period had been long—traditionally 900 pages. This was too long for a magazine, and the novels of this period began to shrink in length. Magazines encouraged the development of the short story (a form the Americans had perfected in the 1840s but which the British had largely ignored until the 1880s) and also of the "tale" or novella, such as Conrad's "The Secret Sharer"—far too long to be a short story, yet still too brief to be a novel. Magazines were aimed at a family readership, and editors tried to maintain strict control over the content of the stories published, though writers like Hardy constantly fought against such restraints. Mid-Victorian fiction typically dealt with middle-class England, but the fiction at the century's close is more varied in its subjects. Hardy's peasant tragedies, Kipling's tales of India, Conrad's sea stories, and the scientific romances of H. G. Wells expanded fiction's reach.

Victorian writers generally, and the poets in particular, accepted the serious responsibility to speak out on the issues of the day, and endeavored to find solutions to the dilemmas of the era. This frequently led to long, complex poems in a wide variety of forms, like Tennyson's *In Memoriam.* Toward the end of the century most poets abandoned this responsibility. Hardy is typical in denying any philosophical importance for his poems. They are, he wrote, "merely what I have often explained to be only a confused heap of impressions. . . ." Consequently, it is the brief, emotionally charged lyric that dominates poetry before the First World War.

ELSEWHERE IN THE WORLD

All over the world revolutionary things were happening in science and technology, and in the arts. In 1905 Albert Einstein published his *Theory of Relativity* in Germany, laying a new foundation for twentieth-century physics. This period saw the introduction of many inventions that have shaped our modern world. Automobiles, developed over decades, began to be produced on a large scale in France in 1891. In the U.S. Thomas Edison, who earlier had developed the phonograph (1877) and the electric light (1879), now opened the first commercial electricity station in New York City (1882). A few years later, the U.S. also saw the first successful airplane flight by the Wright Brothers in 1903.

In France the artistic movement known as Impressionism, begun by a group of painters in 1874, began to flower. Some of the best-known Impressionist artists are Auguste Renoir, Edgar Degas, and Vincent Van Gogh. In music, Richard Strauss in Germany and Igor Stravinsky in Russia were exposing a wary world to new sounds.

EDWARDIAN ENGLAND

Queen Victoria lived until January, 1901, in a realm radically different from the one she first knew and increasingly alien to what she most valued. Her son, nearly sixty years old when he was crowned Edward VII, reigned only nine years. Despite the brevity of the Edwardian period, it saw the development of a national conscience that expressed itself in important social legislation (including the first old-age pensions) that laid the groundwork for the English welfare state. The foremost architect of reform was the brilliant Welsh politican David Lloyd George. In a speech to the House of Commons in 1909 in defense of his budget funding these radical social programs, Lloyd George stated, "This is a war budget. It is for raising money to wage war against poverty and squalidness. I cannot help believing that before this generation has passed away, we shall have advanced a great step toward that good time when poverty, wretchedness, and the human degradation which always followed in its camp will be as remote to the people of this country as the wolves which once infested its forests."

It was also during this period that the woman's suffrage movement entered a more radical phase, its supporters courting arrest and imprisonment in their struggle to win the right to vote. Militant suffragettes like Emmeline Pankhurst and her daughters Christabel and Sylvia represented a dramatic change in the public conception of a woman's role. It was a long way from the Victorian heroine who crocheted, played the piano, and swooned at the slightest provocation, to women like Lady Constance Lytton, who endured forcible feeding in prison, or Emily Wilding Davison, who was killed when she threw herself under the hooves of a horse owned by Edward's son and successor, George V, at the running of the Derby (England's most famous horse race) on June 4, 1913.

George had succeeded his father in May of 1910. Four years later, England became involved in World War I, in the words of historian Paul Johnson, "the greatest moral, spiritual, and physical catastrophe in the entire history of the English people—a catastrophe whose consequences, all wholly evil, are still with us." On the eve of the war, despite the buoyant confidence of many in England that the fighting would be over by Christmas, the British Foreign Secretary Sir Edward Grey observed with a grim foreboding, "The lamps are going out all over Europe; we shall not see them lit again in our lifetime."

THINKING ABOUT GRAPHIC AIDS
Using the Time Line

Use the time line on pages 624–625 to answer these questions.

1. Could Queen Victoria have known about the automobile? the airplane?
2. Name two important social movements during the period.
3. Compare this time line with the Unit 6 time line on pages 540–541. What authors were popular when Queen Victoria ascended to the throne? What authors were popular at the time of her death?
4. How long did the Edwardian period last?
5. Who was the monarch at the outbreak of World War I?

Hardy was born in a thatched cottage in southern Dorsetshire, near the edge of the area he called "Egdon Heath." His father, a skilled stonemason, taught his son to play the violin and sent him to country day schools. At age fifteen Hardy began to study architecture, and in 1861 he went to London to begin a career. In an age of intellectual ferment, Hardy found himself progressively more unsure about his own goals. He tried poetry, considered a career as an actor, and finally decided to write fiction.

In part, this was a practical decision. From the first Hardy aimed his fiction at serial publication in magazines, where it would most quickly pay the bills. However, at the same time, not forgetting an earlier dream, he resolved to keep his tales "as near to poetry in their subject as the conditions would allow." The emotional power of Hardy's fiction disturbed readers from the start, but he persevered, deciding "he was committed to novel-writing as a regular trade, as much as he had formerly been to architecture. . . ." After his first success, *Far from the Madding Crowd* (1874), came *The Return of the Native* (1878), *The Mayor of Casterbridge* (1885), and *Tess of the D'Urbervilles* (1891). Hardy wrote about the Dorset countryside he knew intimately, calling it *Wessex* (the name of the Anglo-Saxon kingdom once located there). He wrote about agrarian working-class people, milkmaids, stonecutters, and shepherds, as George Eliot had done, but not, as in her novels, from the distant perspective of the London intellectual. Hardy's rejection of middle-class moral values disturbed and finally shocked some readers, but as time passed his novels gained in popularity and prestige.

In 1874 he married and in 1885 built a remote country home in Dorset. From 1877 on he spent three to four months a year in fashionable society, while the rest of the time he lived in the country.

In 1895 *Jude the Obscure* elicited such bitter critical attacks that Hardy decided to stop writing novels altogether. He had made enough money anyhow, and could afford to return to an earlier dream. In 1898 he published his first volume of poetry. Over the next twenty-nine years Hardy completed over 900 lyrics. His verse was utterly independent of the taste of his day. "My poetry was revolutionary," he said, "in the sense that I meant to avoid the jewelled line. . . ." Instead, he strove for a rough, natural voice, with rustic diction and irregular meters expressing concrete, particularized impressions of life.

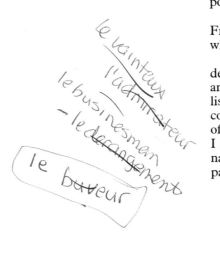

The Darkling Thrush ✓

•hope in dying

I leant upon a coppice gate[1]
  When Frost was spectre-grey,
And winter's dregs made desolate
  The weakening eye of day.
5 The tangled bine-stems scored the sky
  Like strings of broken lyres,
And all mankind that haunted nigh
  Had sought their household fires.

The land's sharp features seemed to be
10 The Century's corpse outleant,
His crypt the cloudy canopy,
  The wind his death-lament.
The ancient pulse of germ and birth
  Was shrunken hard and dry,
15 And every spirit upon earth
  Seemed fervourless as I.

At once a voice arose among
  The bleak twigs overhead

In a full-hearted evensong
20 , Of joy illimited;
  An agèd thrush, frail, gaunt, and small,
  In blast-beruffled plume,
Had chosen thus to fling his soul
  Upon the growing gloom.

25 So little cause for carolings
  Of such ecstatic sound
Was written on terrestrial things
  Afar or nigh around,
That I could think there trembled through
30 His happy good-night air
Some blessèd Hope, whereof he knew
  And I was unaware.

1900   1902

Darkling, in the dark.
1. *coppice gate,* gate to a copse, or wooded grove.

The Man He Killed ✓

•mocking war

"Had he and I but met
  By some old ancient inn,
We should have sat us down to wet
  Right many a nipperkin![1]

5 "But ranged as infantry,
  And staring face to face,
I shot at him as he at me,
  And killed him in his place.

  "I shot him dead because—
10 Because he was my foe,
Just so: my foe of course he was;
  That's clear enough; although

"He thought he'd 'list,[2] perhaps,
  Off-hand like—just as I—
15 Was out of work—had sold his traps[3]—
  No other reason why.

"Yes; quaint and curious war is!
  You shoot a fellow down
You'd treat if met where any bar is,
20 Or help to half-a-crown."[4]

1902

1. *nipperkin,* a half-pint of ale.
2. *'list,* enlist.
3. *traps,* simple personal belongings.
4. *half-a-crown,* an English coin worth about sixty cents at the time of the poem, though far larger in purchasing power.

Thomas Hardy

"Ah, Are You Digging on My Grave?" ✓

[handwritten: husband]

"Ah, are you digging on my grave
    My loved one?—planting rue?"
—"No: yesterday he went to wed
One of the brightest wealth has bred.
5 'It cannot hurt her now,' he said,
    'That I should not be true.'"

"Then who is digging on my grave?
    My nearest dearest kin?"
—"Ah, no: they sit and think, 'What use!

[handwritten: child?]

10 What good will planting flowers produce?
No tendance of her mound can loose
    Her spirit from Death's gin.'"[1]

"But some one digs upon my grave?
    My enemy?—prodding sly?"
15 —"Nay: when she heard you had passed the
        Gate
That shuts on all flesh soon or late,
She thought you no more worth her hate,

[handwritten: enemy]

    And cares not where you lie."

"Then, who is digging on my grave?

20   Say—since I have not guessed!"
—"O it is I, my mistress dear,
Your little dog, who still lives near,
And much I hope my movements here
    Have not disturbed your rest?"

25 "Ah, yes! *You* dig upon my grave . . .
    Why flashed it not on me
That one true heart was left behind!
What feeling do we ever find
To equal among human kind
30   A dog's fidelity!"

"Mistress, I dug upon your grave
    To bury a bone, in case
I should be hungry near this spot
When passing on my daily trot.
35 I am sorry, but I quite forgot
    It was your resting-place."

1914

1. *gin*, a snare or trap for game.

In Time of "The Breaking of Nations"

I
Only a man harrowing clods
    In a slow silent walk
With an old horse that stumbles and nods
    Half asleep as they stalk.

II
5 Only thin smoke without flame
    From the heaps of couch-grass;
Yet this will go onward the same
    Though Dynasties pass.

III
Yonder a maid and her wight[1]
10   Come whispering by:
War's annals will fade into night
    Ere their story die.

1916

"The Breaking of Nations," an allusion to Jeremiah
51:20.
1. *wight*, an archaic word meaning "a human being."

THINK AND DISCUSS
THE DARKLING THRUSH
Understanding
1. Describe the **setting**—both time and place.
2. How does the speaker describe himself and "every spirit upon earth"?
3. What does the speaker think the thrush knows that he doesn't?

Analyzing
4. Explain why the **simile** of "broken lyres" (line 6) fits the speaker's mood.
5. What **metaphor** dominates the second stanza?
6. How does the thrush contrast with his song?
7. To what extent does the speaker learn something from the thrush?

Extending
8. Compare the use of setting and **theme** in Hardy's poems with that of the nature poems of Coleridge and Wordsworth.

THE MAN HE KILLED
Understanding
1. In line 1, *Had* signals a condition contrary to fact. What would have happened if that condition had been met? What happened instead?

Analyzing
2. What details of the poem suggest the speaker's social class?
3. Why does Hardy use words like *nipperkin* and other suggestions of **dialect?**
4. What does the punctuation of stanzas 3 and 4 suggest about the speaker's thoughts?
5. Why did he go to war?

Extending
6. Do you share the speaker's feelings about war?

"AH, ARE YOU DIGGING ON MY GRAVE?"
Understanding
1. Who are the two speakers? Describe their situation.

Analyzing
2. The first speaker keeps trying to figure out who is digging. Is there an order to her questions? Explain.
3. What does Hardy mean to imply through the answers the first speaker gets?
4. What is particularly **ironic** about stanza 6?

Extending
5. To what extent does this poem suggest pessimism about human nature?

IN TIME OF "THE BREAKING OF NATIONS"
Understanding
1. Describe the picture that the **images** of this poem, taken together, create.
2. To whom does the word *their* of line 12 refer?

Analyzing
3. What **connotation** does the word *Only*, which begins the first two stanzas, have in this context?
4. How does this pastoral scene **symbolize** a response to "Dynasties" and "War's annals"?

Extending
5. Hardy's poem insists on quite specific qualities in the things it describes: the man is "slow," the horse "old," the smoke "thin," and the couple "whisper." What effect do these qualities have on your reaction to the scene pictured?

THINKING SKILLS
Synthesizing
To synthesize is to put together parts and elements so as to form a whole. Consider how Hardy's poetry not only is appropriate to, but also helps to define the late nineteenth century.

1. Explain how the problem of death appears in each of these selections.
2. What is Hardy's consistent attitude toward the fact of death?
3. Using what you have learned from the Background to this unit, explain how this aspect of Hardy's work is a reaction to the scientific discoveries of his era.

BIOGRAPHY

Gerard Manley Hopkins
1844–1889

Hopkins was the eldest son of an exceptional family. His father published books of mathematics and poetry, while his mother read German philosophy. Several of their children were artists or musicians, and all took seriously their devotion to the Church of England.

Hopkins's superior work at Highgate School won him admission to Oxford in 1863, where he studied classics. Already he felt a strong inclination to write poetry. But more profound issues intervened. Like many of his contemporaries, Hopkins questioned the religion of his family, and in 1866 he broke with them to join the Roman Catholic Church. After completing his Oxford studies, Hopkins joined the Jesuit order in 1868. In beginning a long period of training for the priesthood, he dramatically burned all his youthful poems.

During the next few years Hopkins felt it wrong to write verse, but in 1875 he wrote a long (280-line) poem commemorating the wreck of the sailing vessel *Deutschland*. Later he told a friend, "I had long had haunting my ear the echo of a new rhythm . . ." and here it burst forth. During the next few years Hopkins studied theology in Wales and in a series of lyrics such as "Pied Beauty" and "God's Grandeur" he celebrated his ecstatic sense of the divine in nature. From the first Hopkins's poetry was unusual. He admired many of the classic poets, but his reaction to their work was, he said, "to make me admire and do otherwise." Judging his own work he confessed, "No doubt my poetry errs on the side of oddness . . . ." But he recognized this was the consequence of his search for the particular, the distinctive in things. Hopkins shared his poems with but a very few friends, and though he dreamed of a wider audience he made little effort to have his works published.

After his ordination in 1877 Hopkins served as a parish priest in industrial towns such as Manchester and Liverpool. From 1881 on he taught classical languages, first at the Jesuit seminary in Stonyhurst, then, from 1884, at the Catholic University College in Dublin. He disliked his teaching responsibilities but scrupulously fulfilled them.

His emotional life grew more troubled. His God, "the only person that I am in love with seldom, especially now, stirs my heart . . ." he told a friend, and he became haunted by the suicides of several Oxford friends. By 1885 he felt overwhelmed by a "constant, crippling" melancholy which, he confessed, "is much like madness." From this dark period come some of Hopkins's greatest poems, sonnets such as "Thou Art Indeed Just, Lord" in which he struggles with the encroaching tragedy of his life. These were a last, splendid gesture. Hopkins had never been very healthy, and in an outbreak of typhoid fever he died in 1889.

A friend and fellow writer, Robert Bridges, saved Hopkins's poems and 29 years later, in 1918, published them to an astonished and, by then, appreciative world. (For more information on Hopkins's poetic theory see the entry *sprung rhythm* in the Glossary of Literary Terms.)

Pied Beauty   Gerard Manley Hopkins ✓

·beauty is all over

Glory be to God for dappled things—
  For skies of couple-color as a brinded[1]
    cow;
    For rose-moles all in stipple[2] upon trout
      that swim;
Fresh-firecoal chestnut-falls;[3] finches' wings;
5 Landscape plotted and pieced—fold,
    fallow, and plow;[4]
    And all trades, their gear and tackle and
    trim.

All things counter,[5] original, spare, strange;
  Whatever is fickle, freckled (who knows
    how?)
    With swift, slow; sweet, sour; adazzle,
    dim;

10 He fathers-forth whose beauty is past
    change:
        Praise him.

1877   1918

---

1. brinded, streaked with different colors. An early form of *brindled*.
2. stipple. In graphic arts, areas of color or shade are sometimes rendered by masses of tiny dots, called *stipples*.
3. Fresh-firecoal chestnut-falls. Newly fallen nuts stripped of their husks look like glowing coals.
4. Landscape . . . plow. Seen from a distance, a landscape can look as if an architect laid it out in square sections—"plotted" it out; or a tailor sewed it together out of square bits of cloth—"pieced" it together. Different sections can be set aside to be used as pastures—"folds"; to sit idly regaining fertility—"fallow"; or be placed under cultivation—"plow."
5. counter, contrary to expectation.

Welsh Mountain Landscape, by James Innes. 1912. *Manchester City Art Gallery*

God's Grandeur

Gerard Manley Hopkins

The world is charged with the grandeur of
  God.
  It will flame out, like shining from shook
  foil;
  It gathers to a greatness, like the ooze of
  oil
Crushed. Why do men then now not reck
  his rod?
5 Generations have trod, have trod, have trod;
  And all is seared with trade; bleared,
  smeared with toil;
  And wears man's smudge and shares
  man's smell: the soil
Is bare now, nor can foot feel, being shod.

And for[1] all this, nature is never spent;
10 There lives the dearest freshness deep
  down things;
And though the last lights off the black West
  went
  Oh, morning, at the brown brink
  eastward, springs—
Because the Holy Ghost over the bent
  World broods with warm breast and with
  ah! bright wings.

1877   1918

---

1. *for,* despite.

Reader's Note

Imagery in "God's Grandeur"

In an early essay Hopkins wrote, "All things
. . . are charged with God, and if we know
how to touch them, give off sparks and take fire
. . . " The **imagery** here is electrical, and refers
to a battery, or to the static electricity which
can build up in cloth or hair. Touching such
objects strikes sparks—shocks and surprises you.
The first line of this poem expresses this idea in
its image of a "charged" world. The second is
related to it. Here we have an image of flaming light rays which Hopkins himself explained
in a letter to a friend. "I mean foil in its sense
of leaf or tinsel . . . Shaken gold foil gives off
broad glares like sheet lightning and also, and
this is true of nothing else, owing to its zigzag
dints and creasings and network of small many
cornered facets, a sort of forked lightning too."

In lines three and four the initial images of

electrical sparks and lightning are replaced by
their opposites. If you put a puddle of heavy oil,
like olive oil, between two surfaces and squeeze
them together, the oil will be crushed into a thin
ooze. But if you then separate the surfaces the
tension within the oil itself will pull oil droplets
back together. It is this kind of internal force
drawing things back together which Hopkins
here contrasts with the radiating energy of the
first lines. He sees both as typical of God's power, reflected in His creation.

In line four the poet wonders why people
no longer fear God's authority—fear the birch
rod which God, like an angry father beating his
children, could use to punish evil. This "rod"
also suggests the lightning rod which carries the
electrical energy of the divine storm to earth and
links the first lines of the poem with this pas-

sage, as the "smear" of line six and "smudge" of line seven link with the oil of line three—though in lines six and seven the oil is the defiling oil of industrial society.

The imagery of the first eight lines, then, describes a god of power and wrath, and an earth sullied by a senseless civilization. The last six lines of the sonnet turn to very different images—a spring of fresh water (line 10), sunset and sunrise (lines 11–12), with a double use of the verb "spring" in line 12, and finally, a multiple image in which God the Holy Ghost, the spiritual dimension of the Christian God, is seen as the dawn of both a new day and a new, regenerated life, and also a dove, a benevolent bird of peace hovering over the world.

Spring and Fall: ✓
To a Young Child
Gerard Manley Hopkins

Márgarét, are you gríeving
Over Goldengrove unleaving?
Leáves, líke the things of man, you
With your fresh thoughts care for, can you?
5 Áh! ás the heart grows older
It will come to such sights colder
By and by, nor spare a sigh
Though worlds of wanwood leafmeal[1] lie;
And yet you wíll weep and know why.
10 Now no matter, child, the name:
Sórrow's spríngs áre the same.
Nor mouth had, no nor mind, expressed
What heart heard of, ghost guessed:
It ís the blight man was born for,
15 It is Margaret you mourn for.
1880   1918

---

1. **wanwood leafmeal,** palely colored autumn leaves ("wan") have fallen to the ground where they lie matted and already disintegrating ("leafmeal").

Autumn Leaves (detail), by Sir John Everett Millais. An example of the Pre-Raphaelite style of painting. 1856. *Manchester City Art Gallery*

Thou Art Indeed Just, Lord ✓

Gerard Manley Hopkins

> *Righteous art thou, O Lord,*
> *when I plead with thee; yet let me talk*
> *with thee of thy judgments: Wherefore*
> *doth the way of the wicked prosper?*
> (Jeremiah 12:1)

Thou art indeed just, Lord, if I contend
With thee; but, sir, so what I plead is just.
Why do sinners' ways prosper? and why
    must
Disappointment all I endeavor end?
5   Wert thou my enemy, O thou my friend,
How wouldst thou worse, I wonder, than
    thou dost
Defeat, thwart me? Oh, the sots and thralls
    of lust
Do in spare hours more thrive than I that
    spend,

Sir, life upon thy cause. See, banks and
    brakes[1]
10 Now, leavèd how thick! lacèd they are again
With fretty chervil,[2] look, and fresh wind
    shakes
Them; birds build—but not I build; no, but
    strain,
Time's eunuch, and not breed one work that
    wakes.
Mine, O thou lord of life, send my roots rain.
1889   **1918**

---

1. **brakes,** thickets.
2. **fretty chervil.** Chervil is an aromatic herb of the parsley family. *Fretty,* meaning "patterned like fretwork," describes its leaves.

THINK AND DISCUSS
PIED BEAUTY
Understanding
1. What does the title mean?

Analyzing
2. Explain how the poem's first and last lines summarize its main idea.
3. Hopkins's verse combines oddly different **images.** Explain the combinations of images in lines 2 and 3. What effect do these combinations have on the reader?
4. How do "all trades" fit the imagery here?
5. Stanza 2 uses no images at all. Explain how adjectives serve the same function.
6. How does God differ from creation?

Extending
7. How does "Pied Beauty" use the tradition of Romantic nature poetry?

GOD'S GRANDEUR
Understanding
1. How have *trade* and *toil* (line 6) obscured the sense of God's presence in creation?
2. What kind of hope does the speaker still retain?

Analyzing
3. How does Hopkins use the octave and sestet of this Petrarchan **sonnet** to divide the ideas in this poem?
4. What characteristics of divine power do the first two sentences describe?
5. Contrast the way power emerges in the last six lines.

REVIEWING: Alliteration

See Handbook of Literary Terms, p. 926

Repeating sounds, especially consonant sounds, at the beginnings of words or in stressed syllables, is called **alliteration.**

1. What sounds alliterate in lines 2–4?
2. Examine the pairs of words that alliterate throughout. How do the words relate? What effect, then, is created by having them alliterate?
3. Why do you suppose Hopkins uses this device in addition to rhyme?

THINK AND DISCUSS

SPRING AND FALL: TO A YOUNG CHILD

Understanding

1. How has Margaret reacted to the falling of the leaves ("unleaving") in the autumn woods ("Goldengrove")?

Analyzing

2. Why does the speaker express surprise in the first four lines?
3. Does the speaker think that maturing will help heal this sorrow?
4. Explain the use of **hyperbole** in line 8.
5. How does the **metaphor** in line 11 provide an explanation of Margaret's feelings now and in the future?

Extending

6. Why is the speaker vague (in line 10) about the source of Margaret's grief?
7. Does this poem offer effective consolation? Does it attempt to?

THOU ART INDEED JUST, LORD

Undersanding

1. What has caused the speaker's spiritual crisis? (See lines 3–4.)
2. *Wert thou* means "if you were." What question does the speaker ask the Lord in lines 5–7? Is it a serious question?

Analyzing

3. Explain how the unusual sentence structure in the first four lines permits Hopkins to end his statements with words especially important to his argument.
4. Explain the multiple meanings of the word *spend* in line 8.

5. How does nature **imagery** emphasize the speaker's despair?

Extending

6. How could the very existence of this poem provide an answer to his prayer?

COMPOSITION

Explaining Multiple Meanings of Words

Hopkins frequently uses words in contexts where they can mean several things simultaneously. He does this for dramatic effect, and to suggest that human experiences are complex and ambiguous. Using an unabridged dictionary, look up all the meanings for these words; *spend, dear, spring, bent, brood.* Find them in "God's Grandeur," and see how many meanings can work within the context of the poem. Organize what you have learned and write a paper, to be read by your teacher, in which you devote a paragraph each to at least three different words. Explain how many meanings the word has in context, and what Hopkins wishes to suggest by using it.

Analyzing Hopkins's Sound Devices

Hopkins employs unusual **rhythms,** along with end **rhyme,** internal rhyme, **alliteration, assonance,** and **onomatopoeia** to give his poems an unusually vigorous and rough sound, to weave together his images and ideas, and, at times, to make a poem sound like the things it describes. Write an essay in which you explain to your teacher where at least three of these sound devices can be found, and the effects each has on the poem. See "Writing About Poetry and Poetic Devices" in the Writer's Handbook.

ENRICHMENT

Creating a Collage of Contrasts

Hopkins's poetry frequently juxtaposes contrasting images, such as "shook foil" and "gathering ooze." Suggest a comparable visual contrast by creating a collage of pictures. First, browse through a variety of old magazines to find images that might creatively interact or conflict with each other. Cut them freely to enhance their dominant effects, and then glue them to a large sheet of poster board in a way that will most effectively present their contrasts.

Theater-goers have certain traditional expectations when they see a comedy. They look forward to some amusing jokes and to a story with a happy ending. Comedy plots hinge on something being wrong that stands in the way of social harmony. The happy endings in traditional comedies, then, witness the correction of foolish excesses in individuals, the replacement of unjust standards with fair ones, and, quite frequently, the getting-together of one or more couples, symbolizing the reconciliation of contrasting forces within society. Shaw, however, was a revolutionary, and his comedies of ideas turn this tradition upside down. Keep the following guidelines in mind as you read *Pygmalion*.

Expect a reversal of the traditional plot. The Pygmalion story illustrates the traditional comedy plot: exposition—Pygmalion doesn't like women; complication—he is pressured to marry, but instead he creates a statue and falls in love with it; resolution—the goddess Venus gives life to the statue, and Pygmalion marries his creation. Thus, the fault that caused the complication is corrected. Shaw's play also pictures the correction of faults and a turn towards new possibilities, but it diverges from what audiences would ordinarily expect.

Watch for the ways the plot is reversed. Who is the discontented Pygmalion here? What form does the complication take? What does Pygmalion expect of his creation, and—even more important—what does his creation expect of Pygmalion? You will also find a striking difference in structure, in that the play appears to lack a traditional ending. Instead of the "resolution" usually found in comedies, we have what Shaw called "the discussion."

Find the humor in the unexpected. Shaw's plays can be very funny, but they are not so because of jokes. Instead, characters acting contrary to expectations create the humor. Watch, for example, for Doolittle's reasons for refusing more money than he has asked for.

Analyze the main ideas. Traditional comic characters represent common human faults: the braggart, the hypochondriac, the foolish lover. Shaw's characters also represent ideas. His people debate with each other because they care intensely about the intellectual positions they take. In "the discussion" that ends *Pygmalion*, winning the argument means not only showing that one is right, but also surviving emotionally as a human being. Be prepared for Shaw's "both/and," his tendency to present the contradictory sides of an argument without seeming to favor one or the other. Because of this, you will find not just one main idea, but several—each represented by one or more characters. The supporting details that prove their arguments lie not only in the words they express, but also in the ways they act.

Discriminate major and minor characters. While Shaw's major characters articulate particular ideas, the minor characters tend to be one-dimensional stereotypes. The major characters struggle with the life energies that surge within them, while the minor characters remain the victims of their condition. An important example of this distinction appears in the way the play depicts love. Shaw once said, "I am a moral revolutionary, interested, not in the class war, but in the struggle between human vitality and the artificial system of morality. . . ."

Note the characters' development. Look for change within a character. The real Shavian hero or heroine grows through recognizing the shams of a false society and the illusions of its conventional ways of thinking. In brushing them aside, the character moves closer to reality. On the other hand, you will find people who lose insight and independence through a disillusionment that leads to failure. There are also characters who do not change at all, but whose presence, like the catalyst in a chemical process, permits change in others.

England's most significant dramatist since the Renaissance was an Irishman, born into an unhappy Dublin family in 1856. His father drank, and the little money he made kept the family in genteel poverty. Shaw's mother and older sister, seeking some sort of a profession, took vocal lessons from a local musician named George Vandaleur Lee, and he moved in with the family in 1865, much to the scandal of the neighbors.

In 1872 Vandaleur Lee went to London and soon after Mrs. Shaw and her daughter followed him. Shaw joined them in 1876. He had no clear sense of his goals in life. He wrote music criticism under Lee's name (1876–1878), sold telephones for the Edison Company (1879), and tried to write fiction, producing five novels no one would publish.

By his own account, Shaw's life changed dramatically in 1882 when he heard a lecture by the American political theorist Henry George. It set Shaw to reading Karl Marx's *Das Kapital* and thinking about the problems of capitalist societies. In 1884, along with a cluster of friends, Shaw helped found the Fabian Society, and for the rest of his life he remained deeply involved in efforts to alter British society through the peaceful redistribution of wealth.

In time, Shaw came to think he might make the theater serve as a vehicle for his ideas, and his first play, *Widowers' Houses*, about slum landlords, premiered in 1892. An early review called it "The most daring play submitted of late years. . ." In 1893 he pushed further, in *Mrs. Warren's Profession*, a serious discussion of prostitution. The official censor refused it a performance license.

But Shaw was convinced now of his calling, despite the reproach of some critics and the erratic enthusiasms of London audiences. In 1898 he began a lifelong practice of publishing his play texts, then a very uncommon practice. To the book editions he added lengthy stage directions, as well as prefaces and epilogues that further elaborated his ideas, thus creating in the print version what he called a "theatre of the mind."

During the first years of this century Shaw produced a sequence of masterpieces such as *Major Barbara* (1905) and *Pygmalion* (1912). After World War I, he became even more theatrically daring with plays such as *Heartbreak House* (1919) and *Back to Methuselah* (1920), a five-play cycle on human development beginning with Adam and, in the last segment, projecting "As Far as Thought Can Reach" to the year A.D. 31920. He received the Nobel prize in 1925.

Shaw bristled with ideas. He was convinced that modern plays should contain, along with the traditional plot conflict and its resolution, what he called "the discussion," a consideration of important problems and suggestions for their resolution. The discussion, he insisted, "is the test of the playwright. . [and] also the real center of his play's interest." The continuing worldwide popularity of Shaw's plays indicates that his ideas still matter.

Pygmalion

Bernard Shaw

CAST OF CHARACTERS

THE DAUGHTER—Miss Eynsford Hill (Clara)
THE MOTHER—Mrs. Eynsford Hill
FREDDY—Mr. Eynsford Hill, *her son*
THE FLOWER GIRL—Eliza (Liza) Doolittle
THE GENTLEMAN—Colonel Pickering
THE NOTE TAKER—Henry Higgins, *a professor of phonetics*

A BYSTANDER
A SARCASTIC BYSTANDER
GENERAL BYSTANDERS
MRS. PEARCE, *Henry Higgins's housekeeper*
ALFRED DOOLITTLE, *Eliza's father*
MRS. HIGGINS, *Henry Higgins's mother*
THE PARLOR-MAID

ACT ONE

London at 11:15 P.M. Torrents of heavy summer rain. Cab whistles blowing frantically in all directions. Pedestrians running for shelter into the portico of St. Paul's Church (not Wren's cathedral but Inigo Jones's church in Covent Garden[1] vegetable market), among them a lady and her daughter in evening dress. They are all peering out gloomily at the rain, except one man with his back turned to the rest, who seems wholly preoccupied with a notebook in which he is writing busily.

The church clock strikes the first quarter.

THE DAUGHTER (*in the space between the central pillars, close to the one on her left*). I'm getting chilled to the bone. What can Freddy be doing all this time? He's been gone twenty minutes.

THE MOTHER (*on her daughter's right*). Not so long. But he ought to have got us a cab by this.

A BYSTANDER (*on the lady's right*). He wont[2] get no cab not until half-past eleven, missus, when they come back after dropping their theater fares.

THE MOTHER. But we must have a cab. We cant stand here until half-past eleven. It's too bad.

THE BYSTANDER. Well, it aint my fault, missus.

THE DAUGHTER. If Freddy had a bit of gumption, he would have got one at the theater door.

---

1. **Covent Garden,** chief fruit, vegetable and flower-market district of London. It originally was a "convent garden" attached to Westminster Abbey. The area also includes St. Paul's Church, designed by the English architect Inigo Jones (1573–1652), and the Covent Garden Opera House.

2. **wont.** One of the spelling reforms advocated by Shaw was the omission of apostrophes in contractions. He retained the punctuation when omission would be confusing (*I'll* rather than *Ill*), or if omission would change pronunciation (*he's* rather than *hes*).

THE MOTHER. What could he have done, poor boy?

THE DAUGHTER. Other people got cabs. Why couldnt he?

FREDDY *rushes in out of the rain from the Southampton Street side, and comes between them closing a dripping umbrella. He is a young man of twenty, in evening dress, very wet round the ankles.*

THE DAUGHTER. Well, havnt you got a cab?

FREDDY. Theres not one to be had for love or money.

THE MOTHER. Oh, Freddy, there must be one. You cant have tried.

THE DAUGHTER. It's too tiresome. Do you expect us to go and get one ourselves?

FREDDY. I tell you theyre all engaged. The rain was so sudden: nobody was prepared; and everybody had to take a cab. Ive been to Charing Cross one way and nearly to Ludgate Circus the other; and they were all engaged.

THE MOTHER. Did you try Trafalgar Square?

FREDDY. There wasn't one at Trafalgar Square.

THE DAUGHTER. Did you try?

FREDDY. I tried as far as Charing Cross Station. Did you expect me to walk to Hammersmith?

THE DAUGHTER. You havnt tried at all.

THE MOTHER. You really are very helpless, Freddy. Go again; and dont come back until you have found a cab.

FREDDY. I shall simply get soaked for nothing.

THE DAUGHTER. And what about us? Are we to stay here all night in this draft, with next to nothing on? You selfish pig—

FREDDY. Oh, very well: I'll go; I'll go. (*He opens his umbrella and dashes off Strandwards,[3] but comes into collision with a flower girl, who is hurrying in for shelter, knocking her basket out of her hands. A blinding flash of lightning, followed instantly by a rattling peal of thunder, orchestrates the incident.*)

THE FLOWER GIRL. Nah then, Freddy: look wh' y' gowin, deah.

FREDDY. Sorry. (*He rushes off.*)

THE FLOWER GIRL (*picking up her scattered flowers and replacing them in the basket*). Theres menners f' yer! Te-oo banches o voylets trod into the mad. (*She sits down on the plinth[4] of the column, sorting her flowers, on the lady's right. She is not at all a romantic figure. She is perhaps eighteen, perhaps twenty, hardly older. She wears a little sailor hat of black straw that has long been exposed to the dust and soot of London and has seldom if ever been brushed. Her hair needs washing rather badly: its mousy color can hardly be natural. She wears a shoddy black coat that reaches nearly to her knees and is shaped to her waist. She has a brown skirt with a coarse apron. Her boots are much the worse for wear. She is no doubt as clean as she can afford to be; but compared to the ladies she is very dirty. Her features are no worse than theirs; but their condition leaves something to be desired; and she needs the services of a dentist.*)

THE MOTHER. How do you know that my son's name is Freddy, pray?

THE FLOWER GIRL. Ow, eez ye-ooa san, is e? Wal, fewd dan y' de-ooty bawmz a mather should, eed now bettern to spawl a pore gel's flahrzn than ran awy athaht pyin. Will ye-oo py me f' them? (*Here, with apologies, this desperate attempt to represent her dialect without a phonetic alphabet must be abandoned as unintelligible outside London.*)

THE DAUGHTER. Do nothing of the sort, mother. The idea!

THE MOTHER. Please allow me, Clara. Have you any pennies?

THE DAUGHTER. No, Ive nothing smaller than sixpence.

THE FLOWER GIRL (*hopefully*). I can give you change for a tanner,[5] kind lady.

THE MOTHER (*to* CLARA). Give it to me. (CLARA *parts reluctantly.*) Now (*To the girl*) this is for your flowers.

THE FLOWER GIRL. Thank you kindly, lady.

THE DAUGHTER. Make her give you the change. These things are only a penny a bunch.

---

3. *Strandwards.* The Strand is the main thoroughfare between the West End, the fashionable residential area, and the business and commercial center of London.
4. *plinth,* the lower, square part of the base of a column.
5. *tanner,* sixpence. [Slang]

THE MOTHER. Do hold your tongue, Clara. (*To the girl*) You can keep the change.

THE FLOWER GIRL. Oh, thank you, lady.

THE MOTHER. Now tell me how you know that young gentleman's name.

THE FLOWER GIRL. I didnt.

THE MOTHER. I heard you call him by it. Dont try to deceive me.

THE FLOWER GIRL (*protesting*). Who's trying to deceive you? I called him Freddy or Charlie same as you might yourself if you was talking to a stranger and wished to be pleasant.

THE DAUGHTER. Sixpence thrown away! Really, mamma, you might have spared Freddy that. (*She retreats in disgust behind the pillar.*)

An elderly gentleman of the amiable military type rushes into the shelter, and closes a dripping umbrella. He is in the same plight as FREDDY, *very wet about the ankles. He is in evening dress, with a light overcoat. He takes the place left vacant by the daughter's retirement.*

THE GENTLEMAN. Phew!

THE MOTHER (*to* THE GENTLEMAN). Oh, sir, is there any sign of its stopping?

THE GENTLEMAN. I'm afraid not. It started worse than ever about two minutes ago. (*He goes to the plinth beside* THE FLOWER GIRL; *puts up his foot on it; and stoops to turn down his trouser ends.*)

THE MOTHER. Oh dear! (*She retires sadly and joins her daughter.*)

THE FLOWER GIRL (*taking advantage of the military gentleman's proximity to establish friendly relations with him*). If it's worse, it's a sign it's nearly over. So cheer up, Captain; and buy a flower off a poor girl.

THE GENTLEMAN. I'm sorry. I havnt any change.

THE FLOWER GIRL. I can give you change, Captain.

THE GENTLEMAN. For a sovereign? Ive nothing less.

THE FLOWER GIRL. Garn! Oh do buy a flower off me, Captain. I can change half-a-crown. Take this for tuppence.

THE GENTLEMAN. Now dont be troublesome: theres a good girl. (*Trying his pockets*) I really havnt any change—Stop: heres three hapence, if thats any use to you. (*He retreats to the other pillar.*)

THE FLOWER GIRL (*disappointed, but thinking three half-pence better than nothing*). Thank you, sir.

THE BYSTANDER (*to the girl*). You be careful: give him a flower for it. Theres a bloke here behind taking down every blessed word youre saying. (*All turn to the man who is taking notes.*)

THE FLOWER GIRL (*springing up terrified*). I aint done nothing wrong by speaking to the gentleman. Ive a right to sell flowers if I keep off the kerb. (*Hysterically*) I'm a respectable girl: so help me, I never spoke to him except to ask him to buy a flower off me. (*General hubbub, mostly sympathetic to* THE FLOWER GIRL, *but deprecating her excessive sensibility. Cries of* Dont start hollerin. Who's hurting you? Nobody's going to touch you. Whats the good of fussing? Steady on. Easy easy, etc., *come from the elderly staid spectators, who pat her comfortingly. Less patient ones bid her shut her head, or ask her roughly what is wrong with her. A remoter group, not knowing what the matter is, crowd in and increase the noise with question and answer:* Whats the row? What she do? Where is he? A tec[6] taking her down. What! him? Yes: him over there: Took money off the gentleman, etc.)

THE FLOWER GIRL (*breaking through them to the gentleman, crying wildly*). Oh, sir, dont let him charge me.[7] You dunno what it means to me. Theyll take away my character and drive me on the streets for speaking to gentlemen. They—

THE NOTE TAKER (*coming forward on her right, the rest crowding after him*). There, there, there, there! who's hurting you, you silly girl? What do you take me for?

THE BYSTANDER. It's all right: he's a gentleman: look at his boots. (*Explaining to* THE NOTE TAKER) She thought you was a copper's nark, sir.

THE NOTE TAKER (*with quick interest*). Whats a copper's nark?

---

6. *tec*, detective. [Slang]

7. *charge me*, bring an accusation against me.

THE BYSTANDER (*inapt at definition*). It's a—well, it's a copper's nark, as you might say. What else would you call it? A sort of informer.

THE FLOWER GIRL (*still hysterical*). I take my Bible oath I never said a word—

THE NOTE TAKER (*overbearing but good-humored*). Oh, shut up, shut up. Do I look like a policeman?

THE FLOWER GIRL (*far from reassured*). Then what did you take down my words for? How do I know whether you took me down right? You just show me what youve wrote about me. (THE NOTE TAKER *opens his book and holds it steadily under her nose, though the pressure of the mob trying to read it over his shoulders would upset a weaker man.*) Whats that? That aint proper writing. I cant read that.

THE NOTE TAKER. I can. (*Reads, reproducing her pronunciation exactly*) "Cheer ap, Keptin; n' baw ya flahr orf a pore gel."

THE FLOWER GIRL (*much distressed*). It's because I called him Captain. I meant no harm. (*To* THE GENTLEMAN) Oh, sir, dont let him lay a charge agen me for a word like that. You—

THE GENTLEMAN. Charge! I make no charge. (*To* THE NOTE TAKER) Really, sir, if you are a detective, you need not begin protecting me against molestation by young women until I ask you. Anybody could see that the girl meant no harm.

THE BYSTANDERS GENERALLY (*demonstrating against police espionage*). Course they could. What business is it of yours? You mind your own affairs. He wants promotion, he does. Taking down people's words! Girl never said a word to him. What harm if she did? Nice thing a girl cant shelter from the rain without being insulted, etc., etc., etc. (*She is conducted by the more sympathetic demonstrators back to her plinth, where she resumes her seat and struggles with her emotion.*)

THE BYSTANDER. He aint a tec. He's a blooming busybody: thats what he is. I tell you, look at his boots.

THE NOTE TAKER (*turning on him genially*). And how are all your people down at Selsey?

THE BYSTANDER (*suspiciously*). Who told you my people come from Selsey?

Lilli Marberd as Liza in the first production of *Pygmalion*, Vienna, 1913.

THE NOTE TAKER. Never you mind. They did. (*To the girl*) How do you come to be up so far east? You were born in Lisson Grove.

THE FLOWER GIRL (*appalled*). Oh, what harm is there in my leaving Lisson Grove? It wasnt fit for a pig to live in; and I had to pay four-and-six a week. (*In tears*) Oh, boo—hoo—oo—

THE NOTE TAKER. Live where you like; but stop that noise.

THE GENTLEMAN (*to the girl*). Come, come! he

cant touch you: you have a right to live where you please.

A SARCASTIC BYSTANDER (*thrusting himself between* THE NOTE TAKER *and* THE GENTLE-MAN). Park Lane, for instance. I'd like to go into the Housing Question with you, I would.

THE FLOWER GIRL (*subsiding into a brooding melancholy over her basket, and talking very low-spiritedly to herself*). I'm a good girl, I am.

THE SARCASTIC BYSTANDER (*not attending to her*). Do you know where I come from?

THE NOTE TAKER (*promptly*). Hoxton.

Titterings. Popular interest in THE NOTE TAKER'*s performance increases.*

THE SARCASTIC ONE (*amazed*). Well, who said I didnt? Bly me! You know everything, you do.

THE FLOWER GIRL (*still nursing her sense of injury*). Aint no call to meddle with me, he aint.

THE BYSTANDER (*to her*). Of course he aint. Dont you stand it from him. (*To* THE NOTE TAKER) See here: what call have you to know about people what never offered to meddle with you?

THE FLOWER GIRL. Let him say what he likes. I dont want to have no truck with him.

THE BYSTANDER. You take us for dirt under your feet, dont you? Catch you taking liberties with a gentleman!

THE SARCASTIC BYSTANDER. Yes: tell him where he come from if you want to go fortune-telling.

THE NOTE TAKER. Cheltenham, Harrow,[8] Cambridge, and India.

THE GENTLEMAN. Quite right. (*Great laughter. Reaction in* THE NOTE TAKER'*s favor. Exclamations of* He knows all about it. Told him proper. Hear him tell the toff[9] where he come from? *etc.*)

THE GENTLEMAN. May I ask, sir, do you do this for your living at a music-hall?

THE NOTE TAKER. Ive thought of that. Perhaps I shall some day.

The rain has stopped; and the persons on the outside of the crowd begin to drop off.

THE FLOWER GIRL (*resenting the reaction*). He's no gentleman, he aint, to intefere with a poor girl.

THE DAUGHTER (*out of patience, pushing her way rudely to the front and displacing* THE GENTLE-MAN, *who politely retires to the other side of the pillar*). What on earth is Freddy doing? I shall get pneumownia if I stay in this draft any longer.

THE NOTE TAKER (*to himself, hastily making a note of her pronunciation of "monia"*). Earlscourt.

THE DAUGHTER (*violently*). Will you please keep your impertinent remarks to yourself.

THE NOTE TAKER. Did I say that out loud? I didnt mean to. I beg your pardon. Your mother's Epsom, unmistakably.

THE MOTHER (*advancing between her daughter and* THE NOTE TAKER). How very curious! I was brought up in Largelady Park, near Epsom.

THE NOTE TAKER (*uproariously amused*). Ha! Ha! What a devil of a name! Excuse me. (*To* THE DAUGHTER) You want a cab, do you?

THE DAUGHTER. Dont dare speak to me.

THE MOTHER. Oh please, please, Clara. (*Her daughter repudiates her with an angry shrug and retires haughtily.*) We should be so grateful to you, sir, if you found us a cab. (THE NOTE TAKER *produces a whistle.*) Oh, thank you. (*She joins her daughter.*)

THE NOTE TAKER *blows a piercing blast.*

THE SARCASTIC BYSTANDER. There! I knowed he was a plain-clothes copper.

THE BYSTANDER. That aint a police whistle: thats a sporting whistle.

THE FLOWER GIRL (*still preoccupied with her wounded feelings*). He's no right to take away my character. My character is the same to me as any lady's.

THE NOTE TAKER. I dont know whether youve noticed it; but the rain stopped about two minutes ago.

THE BYSTANDER. So it has. Why didnt you say so before? and us losing our time listening to your silliness! (*He walks off towards the Strand.*)

THE SARCASTIC BYSTANDER. I can tell where you come from. You come from Anwell.[10] Go back there.

---

8. *Cheltenham, Harrow.* Cheltenham and Harrow are exclusive preparatory schools.
9. *toff,* dandy. [Slang]
10. *Anwell,* Hanwell, an insane asylum.

This and all subsequent illustrations for *Pygmalion* are photographs of the 1974 London production starring Alec McCowen as Higgins, Diana Rigg as Liza Doolittle, Jack May as Colonel Pickering, and Bob Hoskins as Alfred Doolittle.

THE NOTE TAKER (*helpfully*). *H*anwell.

THE SARCASTIC BYSTANDER (*affecting great distinction of speech*). Thenk you, teacher. Haw haw! So long. (*He touches his hat with mock respect and strolls off.*)

THE FLOWER GIRL. Frightening people like that! How would he like it himself?

THE MOTHER. It's quite fine now, Clara. We can walk to a motor bus. Come. (*She gathers her skirts above her ankles and hurries off towards the Strand.*)

THE DAUGHTER. But the cab—(*her mother is out of hearing*). Oh, how tiresome! (*She follows angrily.*)

All the rest have gone except THE NOTE TAKER, THE GENTLEMAN, *and* THE FLOWER GIRL, *who sits arranging her basket and still pitying herself in murmurs.*

THE FLOWER GIRL. Poor girl! Hard enough for her to live without being worried and chivied.

THE GENTLEMAN (*returning to his former place on* THE NOTE TAKER'*s left*). How do you do it, if I may ask?

THE NOTE TAKER. Simply phonetics. The science of speech. Thats my profession: also my hobby. Happy is the man who can make a living by his hobby! You can spot an Irishman or a Yorkshireman by his brogue. *I* can place any man within six miles. I can place him within two miles in London. Sometimes within two streets.

THE FLOWER GIRL. Ought to be ashamed of himself, unmanly coward!

THE GENTLEMAN. But is there a living in that?

THE NOTE TAKER. Oh yes. Quite a fat one. This is an age of upstarts. Men begin in Kentish Town with £80 a year, and end in Park Lane with a hundred thousand. They want to drop Kentish Town; but they give themselves away every time they open their mouths. Now I can teach them—

THE FLOWER GIRL. Let him mind his own business and leave a poor girl—

THE NOTE TAKER (*explosively*). Woman: cease this detestable boohooing instantly; or else seek the shelter of some other place of worship.

THE FLOWER GIRL (*with feeble defiance*). Ive a right to be here if I like, same as you.

THE NOTE TAKER. A woman who utters such depressing and disgusting sounds has no right to be anywhere—no right to live. Remember that you are a human being with a soul and the divine gift of articulate speech: that your native language is the language of Shakespear and Milton and The Bible: and dont sit there crooning like a bilious pigeon.

THE FLOWER GIRL (*quite overwhelmed, looking up at him in mingled wonder and deprecation without daring to raise her head*). Ah-ah-ah-ow-ow-ow-oo!

THE NOTE TAKER (*whipping out his book*). Heavens! what a sound! (*He writes; then holds out the book and reads, reproducing her vowels exactly.*) Ah-ah-ah-ow-ow-ow-oo!

THE FLOWER GIRL (*tickled by the performance, and laughing in spite of herself*). Garn!

THE NOTE TAKER. You see this creature with her kerbstone English: the English that will keep her in the gutter to the end of her days. Well, sir, in three months I could pass that girl off as a duchess at an ambassador's garden party. I could even get her a place as lady's maid or shop assistant, which requires better English.

THE FLOWER GIRL. Whats that you say?

THE NOTE TAKER. Yes, you squashed cabbage leaf, you disgrace to the noble architecture of these columns, you incarnate insult to the English language: I could pass you off as the Queen of Sheba. (*To* THE GENTLEMAN) Can you believe that?

THE GENTLEMAN. Of course I can. I am myself a student of Indian dialects; and—

THE NOTE TAKER (*eagerly*). Are you? Do you know Colonel Pickering, the author of Spoken Sanscrit?

THE GENTLEMAN. I am Colonel Pickering. Who are you?

THE NOTE TAKER. Henry Higgins, author of Higgins's Universal Alphabet.

PICKERING (*with enthusiasm*). I came from India to meet you.

HIGGINS. I was going to India to meet you.

PICKERING. Where do you live?

HIGGINS. 27A Wimpole Street. Come and see me tomorrow.

PICKERING. I'm at the Carlton. Come with me now and lets have a jaw over some supper.

HIGGINS. Right you are.

THE FLOWER GIRL (*to* PICKERING, *as he passes her*). Buy a flower, kind gentleman. I'm short for my lodging.

PICKERING. I really havnt any change. I'm sorry (*he goes away*).

HIGGINS (*shocked at the girl's mendacity*). Liar. You said you could change half-a-crown.

THE FLOWER GIRL (*rising in desperation*). You ought to be stuffed with nails, you ought. (*Flinging the basket at his feet*) Take the whole blooming basket for sixpence.

The church clock strikes the second quarter.

HIGGINS (*hearing in it the voice of God, rebuking him for his Pharisaic*[11] *want of charity to the poor girl*). A reminder. (*He raises his hat solemnly; then throws a handful of money into the basket and follows* PICKERING.)

THE FLOWER GIRL (*picking up a half-crown*). Ah-ow-ooh! (*Picking up a couple of florins*) Aaah-ow-ooh! (*Picking up several coins*) Aaaaaah-ow-ooh! (*Picking up a half-sovereign*) Aaaaaaaaaaaah-ow-ooh!!!

FREDDY (*springing out of a taxicab*). Got one at last. Hallo! (*To the girl*) Where are the two ladies that were here?

THE FLOWER GIRL. They walked to the bus when the rain stopped.

FREDDY. And left me with a cab on my hands! Damnation!

THE FLOWER GIRL (*with grandeur*). Never mind, young man. *I'm going home in a taxi.* (*She sails off to the cab. The driver puts his hand behind him and holds the door firmly shut against her. Quite understanding his mistrust, she shews him her handful of money.*) Eightpence aint no object to me, Charlie. (*He grins and opens the door.*) Angel Court, Drury Lane, round the corner of Mickle-John's oil shop. Lets see how fast you can make her hop it. (*She gets in and pulls the door to with a slam as the taxicab starts.*)

FREDDY. Well, I'm dashed.

---

11. *Pharisaic*, self-righteous. The Pharisees were a strict Jewish sect at the time of Jesus.

THINK AND DISCUSS
ACT ONE
Understanding
1. What is the note-taker Higgins doing on this evening?
2. Describe how he uses his knowledge in dealing with other people.

Analyzing
3. Explain how **setting** permits Shaw to keep an unlikely collection of characters together for some time.
4. What tensions existing between different social classes are depicted?
5. How does language define and fix class status?
6. Why does Higgins throw the Flower Girl (Liza) a handful of coins?
7. How is Liza **characterized** so far? Consider her posture, her persistence in not moving on after the rain ends, and her reaction to Higgins's coins.
8. Has any **plot** complication gotten under way by the end of Act One?

Extending
9. Could such a varied gathering take place in your community? Where would it be?
10. How do you react to the chance meeting between Higgins and Pickering? Do you think Shaw intended the playgoer to believe in the literal possibility of this coincidental meeting?

REVIEWING: Dialect H乙
See Handbook of Literary Terms, p. 902
A **dialect** is a form of speech characteristic of a particular region or class, differing from the standard language used by those in positions of social power.

1. How many different dialects are identified in Act One?
2. Explain the significance of Liza's speaking a dialect so strong that Shaw "abandons" his attempt to represent it.

3. How does Higgins describe "proper" English?

COMPOSITION
Explaining Speech Clues to Performance
In the speeches of their characters, actors and actresses find hints for developing their performances. Choose three speeches by different characters and write an essay explaining how those speeches suggest staging. For example, when Higgins calls Liza a "squashed cabbage leaf" (page 650), his words demonstrate that he feels free to speak abusively to other people. Now, imagine how an actor might portray Higgins on stage. Should he speak loudly and abruptly and stride about with exaggerated self-confidence? See "Writing About Drama" in the Writer's Handbook.

Analyzing Social Relationships
In this act, people ask for money, make threats, and give orders; they meet, separate, even desert one another. First, rank the characters according to how they treat each other, from kind to rude. Then note each character's social class. (You may decide to treat the crowd as one character.) Write an essay analyzing the public manners of different social classes as depicted in this act. Conclude by explaining what you think Shaw wants his audience to infer from the way these people act.

ENRICHMENT
Designing Costumes for *Pygmalion*
Not only speech, but clothing helps to define one's social class and personality. Shaw's characters are very aware of this; for example, Higgins's boots proclaim his status as a "gentleman." Think about Act One from the point of view of a costume designer, and in a class discussion describe, as specifically as possible, how the various characters should dress. Use clues from the text; but when Shaw says nothing, rely on your imagination. If possible, consult some library books on period costume.

ACT TWO

Next day at 11 A.M. HIGGINS's *laboratory in Wimpole Street. It is a room on the first floor, looking on the street, and was meant for the drawing room. The double doors are in the middle of the back wall; and persons entering find in the corner to their right two tall file cabinets at right angles to one another against the walls. In this corner stands a flat writing table, on which are a phonograph, a laryngoscope, a row of tiny organ pipes with bellows, a set of lamp chimneys for singing flames with burners attached to a gas plug in the wall by an indiarubber tube, several tuning-forks of different sizes, a life-size image of half a human head, shewing in section the vocal organs, and a box containing a supply of wax cylinders for the phonograph.*

Further down the room, on the same side, is a fireplace, with a comfortable leather-covered easy-chair at the side of the hearth nearest the door, and a coal-scuttle. There is a clock on the mantelpiece. Between the fireplace and the phonograph table is a stand for newspapers.

On the other side of the central door, to the left of the visitor, is a cabinet of shallow drawers. On it is a telephone and the telephone directory. The corner beyond, and most of the side wall, is occupied by a grand piano, with the keyboard at the end furthest from the door, and a bench for the player extending the full length of the keyboard. On the piano is a dessert dish heaped with fruit and sweets, mostly chocolates.

The middle of the room is clear. Besides the easy-chair, the piano bench, and two chairs at the phonograph table, there is one stray chair. It stands near the fireplace. On the walls, engravings: mostly Piranesi and mezzotint portraits.[1] No paintings.

PICKERING *is seated at the table, putting down some cards and a tuning-fork which he has been using.* HIGGINS *is standing up near him, closing two or three file drawers which are hanging out. He appears in the morning light as a robust, vital, appetizing sort of man of forty or thereabouts, dressed in a professional-looking black frockcoat with a white linen collar and black silk tie. He is of the energetic, scientific type, heartily, even violently interested in everything that can be studied as a scientific subject, and careless about himself and other people, including their feelings. He is, in fact, but for his years and size, rather like a very impetuous baby "taking notice" eagerly and loudly, and requiring almost as much watching to keep him out of unintended mischief. His manner varies from genial bullying when he is in a good humor to stormy petulance when anything goes wrong; but he is so entirely frank and void of malice that he remains likeable even in his least reasonable moments.*

HIGGINS (*as he shuts the last drawer*). Well, I think thats the whole show.

PICKERING. It's really amazing. I havnt taken half of it in, you know.

HIGGINS. Would you like to go over any of it again?

PICKERING (*rising and coming to the fireplace, where he plants himself with his back to the fire*). No, thank you; not now. I'm quite done up for this morning.

HIGGINS (*following him, and standing beside him on his left*). Tired of listening to sounds?

PICKERING. Yes. It's a fearful strain. I rather fancied myself because I can pronounce twenty-four distinct vowel sounds; but your hundred and thirty beat me. I cant hear a bit of difference between most of them.

HIGGINS (*chuckling, and going over to the piano to eat sweets*). Oh, that comes with practice. You hear no difference at first; but you keep on listening, and presently you find theyre all as different as A from B. (MRS. PEARCE *looks in: she is* HIGGINS's *housekeeper.*) Whats the matter?

MRS. PEARCE (*hesitating, evidently perplexed*). A young woman wants to see you, sir.

HIGGINS. A young woman! What does she want?

MRS. PEARCE. Well, sir, she says youll be glad to see her when you know what she's come about. She's quite a common girl, sir. Very common indeed. I should have sent her away, only I thought perhaps you wanted her to talk into

---

1. *Piranesi and mezzotint portraits.* Giovanni Battista Piranesi (1720–1778) was an Italian graphic artist noted for his large prints of buildings of classical and post-classical Rome. A mezzotint is a picture engraved on a roughened copper or steel plate.

your machines. I hope Ive not done wrong; but really you see such queer people sometimes—youll excuse me, I'm sure, sir—

HIGGINS. Oh, thats all right, Mrs. Pearce. Has she an interesting accent?

MRS. PEARCE. Oh, something dreadful, sir, really. I dont know how you can take an interest in it.

HIGGINS (to PICKERING). Lets have her up. Shew her up, Mrs. Pearce. (He rushes across to his working table and picks out a cylinder to use on the phonograph).

MRS. PEARCE (only half resigned to it). Very well, sir. It's for you to say. (She goes downstairs.)

HIGGINS. This is rather a bit of luck. I'll shew you how I make records. We'll set her talking; and I'll take it down first in Bell's Visible Speech; then in broad Romic; and then we'll get her on the phonograph so that you can turn her on as often as you like with the written transcript before you.

MRS. PEARCE (returning). This is the young woman, sir.

THE FLOWER GIRL enters in state. She has a hat with three ostrich feathers, orange, sky-blue, and red. She has a nearly clean apron, and the shoddy coat has been tidied a little. The pathos of this deplorable figure, with its innocent vanity and consequential air, touches PICKERING, who has already straightened himself in the presence of MRS. PEARCE. But as to HIGGINS, the only distinction he makes between men and women is that when he is neither bullying nor exclaiming to the heavens against some feather-weight cross, he coaxes women as a child coaxes its nurse when it wants to get anything out of her.

HIGGINS (brusquely, recognizing her with unconcealed disappointment, and at once, babylike, making an intolerable grievance of it). Why, this is the girl I jotted down last night. She's no use; Ive got all the records I want of the Lisson Grove lingo; and I'm not going to waste another cylinder on it. (To the girl) Be off with you: I dont want you.

THE FLOWER GIRL. Dont you be so saucy. You aint heard what I come for yet. (To MRS. PEARCE, who is waiting at the door for further instructions) Did you tell him I come in a taxi?

MRS. PEARCE. Nonsense, girl! what do you think a gentleman like Mr. Higgins cares what you came in?

THE FLOWER GIRL. Oh, we are proud! He aint above giving lessons, not him: I heard him say so. Well, I aint come here to ask for any compliment; and if my money's not good enough I can go elsewhere.

HIGGINS. Good enough for what?

THE FLOWER GIRL. Good enough for ye-oo. Now you know, dont you? I'm come to have lessons, I am. And to pay for em too: make no mistake.

HIGGINS (stupent[2]). Well!!! (Recovering his breath with a gasp) What do you expect me to say to you?

THE FLOWER GIRL. Well, if you was a gentleman, you might ask me to sit down, I think. Dont I tell you I'm bringing you business?

HIGGINS. Pickering: shall we ask this baggage to sit down, or shall we throw her out of the window?

THE FLOWER GIRL (running away in terror to the piano, where she turns at bay). Ah-ah-oh-ow-ow-ow-oo! (Wounded and whimpering) I wont be called a baggage when Ive offered to pay like any lady.

Motionless, the two men stare at her from the other side of the room, amazed.

PICKERING (gently). What is it you want, my girl?

THE FLOWER GIRL. I want to be a lady in a flower shop stead of selling at the corner of Tottenham Court Road. But they wont take me unless I can talk more genteel. He said he could teach me. Well, here I am ready to pay him—not asking any favor—and he treats me as if I was dirt.

MRS. PEARCE. How can you be such a foolish ignorant girl as to think you could afford to pay Mr. Higgins?

THE FLOWER GIRL. Why shouldnt I? I know what lessons cost as well as you do; and I'm ready to pay.

HIGGINS. How much?

THE FLOWER GIRL (coming back to him, trium-

2. *stupent*, dumfounded.

phant). Now youre talking! I thought youd come off it when you saw a chance of getting back a bit of what you chucked at me last night. *(Confidentially)* Youd had a drop in,[3] hadnt you?

HIGGINS *(peremptorily).* Sit down.

THE FLOWER GIRL. Oh, if youre going to make a compliment of it—

HIGGINS *(thundering at her).* Sit down.

MRS. PEARCE *(severely).* Sit down, girl. Do as youre told.

THE FLOWER GIRL. Ah-ah-ah-ow-ow-oo! *(She stands, half rebellious, half bewildered.)*

PICKERING *(very courteous).* Wont you sit down? *(He places the stray chair near the hearthrug between himself and HIGGINS.)*

THE FLOWER GIRL *(coyly).* Dont mind if I do. *(She sits down.* PICKERING *returns to the hearthrug.)*

HIGGINS. Whats your name?

THE FLOWER GIRL. Liza Doolittle.

HIGGINS *(declaiming gravely).*
Eliza, Elizabeth, Betsy and Bess,
They went to the woods to get a bird's nes':

PICKERING. They found a nest with four eggs in it:

HIGGINS. They took one apiece, and left three in it.
They laugh heartily at their own wit.

LIZA. Oh, dont be silly.

MRS. PEARCE *(placing herself behind* ELIZA's *chair).* You musnt speak to the gentleman like that.

LIZA. Well, why wont he speak sensible to me?

HIGGINS. Come back to business. How much do you propose to pay me for the lessons?

LIZA. Oh, I know whats right. A lady friend of mine gets French lessons for eighteenpence an hour from a real French gentleman. Well, you wouldnt have the face to ask me the same for teaching me my own language as you would for French; so I wont give more than a shilling. Take it or leave it.

HIGGINS *(walking up and down the room, rattling his keys and his cash in his pockets).* You know, Pickering, if you consider a shilling, not as a simple shilling, but as a percentage of this girl's income, it works out as fully equivalent to sixty or seventy guineas from a millionaire.

PICKERING. How so?

HIGGINS. Figure it out. A millionaire has about £150 a day. She earns about half-a-crown.

LIZA *(haughtily).* Who told you I only—

HIGGINS *(continuing).* She offers me two-fifths of her day's income for a lesson. Two-fifths of a millionaire's income for a day would be somewhere about £60. It's handsome. By George, it's enormous! it's the biggest offer I ever had.

LIZA *(rising, terrified).* Sixty pounds! What are you talking about? I never offered you sixty pounds. Where would I get—

HIGGINS. Hold your tongue.

LIZA *(weeping).* But I aint got sixty pounds. Oh—

MRS. PEARCE. Dont cry, you silly girl. Sit down. Nobody is going to touch your money.

HIGGINS. Somebody is going to touch you; with a broomstick, if you dont stop snivelling. Sit down.

LIZA *(obeying slowly).* Ah-ah-ah-ow-oo-o! One would think you was my father.

HIGGINS. If I decide to teach you, I'll be worse than two fathers to you. Here! *(He offers her his silk handkerchief.)*

LIZA. Whats this for?

HIGGINS. To wipe your eyes. To wipe any part of your face that feels moist. Remember: thats your handkerchief; and thats your sleeve. Dont mistake the one for the other if you wish to become a lady in a shop.

LIZA , *utterly bewildered, stares helplessly at him.*

MRS. PEARCE. It's no use talking to her like that, Mr. Higgins: she doesn't understand you. Besides, youre quite wrong: she doesnt do it that way at all. *(She takes the handkerchief.)*

LIZA *(snatching it).* Here! You give me that handkerchief. He give it to me, not to you.

PICKERING *(laughing).* He did. I think it must be regarded as her property, Mrs. Pearce.

MRS. PEARCE *(resigning herself).* Serve you right, Mr. Higgins.

PICKERING. Higgins: I'm interested. What about the ambassador's garden party? I'll say youre the greatest teacher alive if you make that good.

---

3. ***had a drop in,*** had been drinking. [Slang]

I'll bet you all the expenses of the experiment you cant do it. And I'll pay for the lessons.

LIZA. Oh, you are real good. Thank you, Captain.

HIGGINS (*tempted, looking at her*). It's almost irresistible. She's so deliciously low—so horribly dirty—

LIZA (*protesting extremely*). Ah-ah-ah-ah-ow-ow-oo-oo!!! I aint dirty: I washed my face and hands afore I come, I did.

PICKERING. Youre certainly not going to turn her head with flattery, Higgins.

MRS. PEARCE (*uneasy*). Oh dont say that, sir: theres more ways than one of turning a girl's head; and nobody can do it better than Mr. Higgins, though he may not always mean it. I do hope, sir, you wont encourage him to do anything foolish.

HIGGINS (*becoming excited as the idea grows on him*). What is life but a series of inspired follies? The difficulty is to find them to do. Never lose a chance: it doesnt come every day. I shall make a duchess of this draggletailed guttersnipe.

LIZA (*strongly deprecating this view of her*). Ah-ah-ah-ow-ow-oo!

HIGGINS (*carried away*). Yes: in six months —in three if she has a good ear and a quick tongue—I'll take her anywhere and pass her off as anything. We'll start today: now! this moment! Take her away and clean her, Mrs. Pearce. Monkey Brand, if it wont come off any other way. Is there a good fire in the kitchen?

MRS. PEARCE (*protesting*). Yes; but—

HIGGINS (*storming on*). Take all her clothes off and burn them. Ring up Whiteley or somebody for new ones. Wrap her up in brown paper til they come.

LIZA. Youre no gentleman, youre not, to talk of such things. I'm a good girl, I am; and I know what the like of you are, I do.

HIGGINS. We want none of your Lisson Grove prudery here, young woman. Youve got to learn to behave like a duchess. Take her away, Mrs. Pearce. If she gives you any trouble, wallop her.

LIZA (*springing up and running between* PICKERING *and* MRS. PEARCE *for protection*). No! I'll call the police, I will.

MRS. PEARCE. But Ive no place to put her.

HIGGINS. Put her in the dustbin.

LIZA. Ah-ah-ah-ow-ow-oo!

PICKERING. Oh come, Higgins! be reasonable.

MRS. PEARCE (*resolutely*). You must be resonable, Mr. Higgins: really you must. You cant walk over everybody like this.

HIGGINS, *thus scolded, subsides. The hurricane is succeeded by a zephyr of amiable surprise.*

HIGGINS (*with professional exquisiteness of modulation*). *I* walk over everybody! My dear Mrs. Pearce, my dear Pickering, I never had the slightest intention of walking over anyone. All I propose is that we should be kind to this poor girl. We must help her to prepare and fit herself for her new station in life. If I did not express myself clearly it was because I did not wish to hurt her delicacy, or yours.

LIZA , *reassured, steals back to her chair.*

MRS. PEARCE (*to* PICKERING). Well, did you ever hear anything like that, sir?

PICKERING (*laughing heartily*). Never, Mrs. Pearce: never.

HIGGINS (*patiently*). Whats the matter?

MRS. PEARCE. Well, the matter is, sir, that you cant take a girl up like that as if you were picking up a pebble on the beach.

HIGGINS. Why not?

MRS. PEARCE. Why not! But you dont know anything about her. What about her parents? She may be married.

LIZA. Garn!

HIGGINS. There! As the girl very properly says, Garn! Married indeed! Dont you know that a woman of that class looks a worn out drudge of fifty a year after she's married?

LIZA. Whood marry me?

HIGGINS (*suddenly resorting to the most thrillingly beautiful low tones in his best elocutionary style*). By George, Eliza, the streets will be strewn with the bodies of men shooting themselves for your sake before Ive done with you.

MRS. PEARCE. Nonsense, sir. You mustnt talk like that to her.

LIZA (*rising and squaring herself determinedly*). I'm going away. He's off his chump, he is. I dont want no balmies teaching me.

HIGGINS (*wounded in his tenderest point by her insensibility to his elocution*). Oh, indeed! I'm mad, am I? Very well, Mrs. Pearce: you neednt order the new clothes for her. Throw her out.

LIZA (*whimpering*). Nah-ow. You got no right to touch me.

MRS. PEARCE. You see now what comes of being saucy. (*Indicating the door*) This way, please.

LIZA (*almost in tears*). I didnt want no clothes. I wouldnt have taken them. (*She throws away the handkerchief.*) I can buy my own clothes.

HIGGINS (*deftly retrieving the handkerchief and intercepting her on her reluctant way to the door*). Youre an ungrateful wicked girl. This is my return for offering to take you out of the gutter and dress you beautifully and make a lady of you.

MRS. PEARCE. Stop, Mr. Higgins. I wont allow it. It's you that are wicked. Go home to your parents, girl; and tell them to take better care of you.

LIZA. I aint got no parents. They told me I was big enough to earn my own living and turned me out.

MRS. PEARCE. Wheres your mother?

LIZA I aint got no mother. Her that turned me out was my sixth stepmother. But I done without them. And I'm a good girl, I am.

HIGGINS. Very well, then, what on earth is all this fuss about? The girl doesnt belong to anybody—is no use to anybody but me. (*He goes to* MRS. PEARCE *and begins coaxing.*) You can adopt her, Mrs. Pearce: I'm sure a daughter would be a great amusement to you. Now dont make any more fuss. Take her downstairs; and—

MRS. PEARCE. But whats to become of her? Is she to be paid anything? Do be sensible, sir.

HIGGINS. Oh, pay her whatever is necessary: put it down in the housekeeping book. (*Impatiently*) What on earth will she want with money? She'll have her food and her clothes. She'll only drink if you give her money.

LIZA (*turning on him*). Oh you are a brute. It's a lie: nobody ever saw the sign of liquor on me. (*To* PICKERING) Oh, sir; youre a gentleman: dont let him speak to me like that.

PICKERING (*in good-humored remonstrance*). Does it occur to you, Higgins, that the girl has some feelings?

HIGGINS (*looking critically at her*). Oh no, I dont think so. Not any feelings that we need bother about. (*Cheerily*) Have you, Eliza?

LIZA. I got my feelings same as anyone else.

HIGGINS (*to* PICKERING, *reflectively*). You see the difficulty?

PICKERING. Eh? What difficulty?

HIGGINS. To get her to talk grammar. The mere pronunciation is easy enough.

LIZA. I dont want to talk grammar. I want to talk like a lady in a flower-shop.

MRS. PEARCE. Will you please keep to the point, Mr. Higgins? I want to know on what terms the girl is to be here. Is she to have any wages? And what is to become of her when youve finished your teaching? You must look ahead a little.

HIGGINS (*impatiently*). Whats to become of her if I leave her in the gutter? Tell me that, Mrs. Pearce.

MRS. PEARCE. Thats her own business, not yours, Mr. Higgins.

HIGGINS. Well, when Ive done with her, we can throw her back into the gutter; and then it will be her own business again; so thats all right.

LIZA. Oh, youve no feeling heart in you: you dont care for nothing but yourself. (*She rises and takes the floor resolutely.*) Here! Ive had enough of this. I'm going. (*Making for the door.*) You ought to be ashamed of yourself, you ought.

HIGGINS (*snatching a chocolate cream from the piano, his eyes suddenly beginning to twinkle with mischief*). Have some chocolates, Eliza.

LIZA (*halting, tempted*). How do I know what might be in them? Ive heard of girls being drugged by the like of you.

HIGGINS *whips out his penknife; cuts a chocolate in two; puts one half into his mouth and bolts it; and offers her the other half.*

HIGGINS. Pledge of good faith, Eliza. I eat one half: you eat the other. (LIZA *opens her mouth to retort: he pops the half chocolate into it.*) You shall have boxes of them, barrels of them, every day. You shall live on them. Eh?

LIZA (*who has disposed of the chocolate after being nearly choked by it*). I wouldnt have ate it, only I'm too ladylike to take it out of my mouth.

HIGGINS. Listen, Eliza. I think you said you came in a taxi.

LIZA. Well, what if I did? Ive as good a right to take a taxi as anyone else.

HIGGINS. You have, Eliza; and in future you shall have as many taxis as you want. You shall go up and down and round the town in a taxi every day. Think of that, Eliza.

MRS. PEARCE. Mr. Higgins: youre tempting the girl. It's not right. She should think of the future.

HIGGINS. At her age! Nonsense! Time enough to think of the future when you havnt any future to think of. No, Eliza: do as this lady does: think of other people's futures; but never think of your own. Think of chocolates, and taxis, and gold, and diamonds.

LIZA. No: I dont want no gold and no diamonds. I'm a good girl, I am. (*She sits down again, with an attempt at dignity.*)

HIGGINS. You shall remain so, Eliza, under the care of Mrs. Pearce. And you shall marry an officer in the Guards, with a beautiful moustache; the son of a marquis, who will disinherit him for marrying you, but will relent when he sees your beauty and goodness—

PICKERING. Excuse me, Higgins; but I really must interfere. Mrs. Pearce is quite right. If this girl is to put herself in your hands for six months for an experiment in teaching, she must understand thoroughly what she's doing.

HIGGINS. How can she? She's incapable of understanding anything. Besides, do any of us understand what we are doing? If we did, would we ever do it?

PICKERING. Very clever, Higgins; but not to the present point. (*To* ELIZA) Miss Doolittle—

LIZA (*overwhelmed*). Ah-ah-ow-oo!

HIGGINS. There! Thats all youll get out of Eliza. Ah-ah-ow-oo! No use explaining. As a military man you ought to know that. Give her her orders: thats what she wants. Eliza: you are to live here for the next six months, learning how to speak beautifully, like a lady in a florist's shop. If youre good and do whatever youre told, you shall sleep in a proper bedroom, and have lots to eat, and money to buy chocolates and take rides in taxis. If youre naughty and idle you will sleep in the back kitchen among the black beetles, and be walloped by Mrs. Pearce with a broomstick. At the end of six months you shall go to Buckingham Palace in a carriage, beautifully dressed. If the King finds out youre not a lady, you will be taken by the police to the Tower of London, where your head will be cut off as a warning to other presumptuous flower girls. If you are not found out, you shall have a present of seven-and-six-pence to start life with as a lady in a shop. If you refuse this offer you will be a most ungrateful and wicked girl; and the angels will weep for you. (*To* PICKERING) Now are you satisfied, Pickering? (*To* MRS. PEARCE) Can I put it more plainly and fairly, Mrs. Pearce?

MRS. PEARCE (*patiently*). I think youd better let me speak to the girl properly in private. I dont know that I can take charge of her or consent to the arrangement at all. Of course I know you dont mean her any harm; but when you get what you call interested in people's accents, you never think or care what may happen to them or you. Come with me, Eliza.

HIGGINS. Thats all right. Thank you, Mrs. Pearce. Bundle her off to the bathroom.

LIZA (*rising reluctantly and suspiciously*). Youre a great bully, you are. I wont stay here if I dont like. I wont let nobody wallop me. I never asked to go to Bucknam Palace, I didnt. I was never in trouble with the police, not me. I'm a good girl—

MRS. PEARCE. Dont answer back, girl. You dont understand the gentleman. Come with me. (*She leads the way to the door, and holds it open for* ELIZA.)

LIZA (*as she goes out*). Well, what I say is right. I wont go near the King, not if I'm going to have my head cut off. If I'd known what I was letting myself in for, I wouldnt have come here. I always been a good girl; and I never offered to say a word to him; and I dont owe him nothing; and I dont care; and I wont be put upon; and I have my feelings the same as anyone else— MRS. PEARCE *shuts the door; and* ELIZA's *plaints are no longer audible.* PICKERING *comes from the hearth to the chair and sits astride it with his arms on the back.*

PICKERING. Excuse the straight question, Higgins. Are you a man of good character where women are concerned?

HIGGINS (*moodily*). Have you ever met a man of good character where women are concerned?

PICKERING. Yes: very frequently.

HIGGINS (*dogmatically, lifting himself on his hands to the level of the piano, and sitting on it with a bounce*). Well, I havnt. I find that the moment I let a woman make friends with me, she becomes jealous, exacting, suspicious, and a damned nuisance. I find that the moment I let myself make friends with a woman, I become selfish and tyrannical. Women upset everything. When you let them into your life, you find that the woman is driving at one thing and youre driving at another.

PICKERING. At what, for example?

HIGGINS (*coming off the piano restlessly*). Oh, Lord knows! I suppose the woman wants to live her own life; and the man wants to live his; and each tries to drag the other on to the wrong track. One wants to go north and the other south; and the result is that both have to go east, though they both hate the east wind. (*He sits down on the bench at the keyboard.*) So here I am, a confirmed old bachelor, and likely to remain so.

PICKERING (*rising and standing over him gravely*). Come, Higgins! You know what I mean. If I'm to be in this business I shall feel responsible for that girl. I hope it's understood that no advantage is to be taken of her position.

HIGGINS. What! That thing! Sacred, I assure you. (*Rising to explain*) You see, she'll be a pupil; and teaching would be impossible unless pupils were sacred. Ive taught scores of American millionairesses how to speak English: the best-looking women in the world. I'm seasoned. They might as well be blocks of wood. *I* might as well be a

block of wood. It's—

MRS. PEARCE *opens the door. She has* ELIZA's *hat in her hand.* PICKERING *retires to the easy-chair at the hearth and sits down.*

HIGGINS (*eagerly*). Well, Mrs. Pearce: is it all right?

MRS. PEARCE (*at the door*). I just wish to trouble you with a word, if I may, Mr. Higgins.

HIGGINS. Yes, certainly. Come in. (*She comes forward.*) Dont burn that, Mrs. Pearce. I'll keep it as a curiosity. (*He takes the hat.*)

MRS. PEARCE. Handle it carefully, sir, please. I had to promise her not to burn it; but I had better put it in the oven for a while.

HIGGINS (*putting it down hastily on the piano*). Oh! thank you. Well, what have you to say to me?

PICKERING. Am I in the way?

MRS. PEARCE. Not at all, sir. Mr. Higgins: will you please be very particular what you say before the girl?

HIGGINS (*sternly*). Of course. I'm always particular about what I say. Why do you say this to me?

MRS. PEARCE (*unmoved*). No, sir: youre not at all particular when youve mislaid anything or when you get a little impatient. Now it doesnt matter before me: I'm used to it. But you really must not swear before the girl.

HIGGINS (*indignantly*). *I* swear! (*Most emphatically.*) I never swear. I detest the habit. What the devil do you mean?

MRS. PEARCE (*stolidly*). Thats what I mean, sir. You swear a great deal too much. I dont mind your damning and blasting, and what the devil and where the devil and who the devil—

HIGGINS. Mrs. Pearce: this language from your lips! Really!

MRS. PEARCE (*not to be put off*).—but there is a certain word I must ask you not to use. The girl has just used it herself because the bath was too hot. It begins with the same letter as bath. She knows no better: she learnt it at her mother's knee. But she must not hear it from your lips.

HIGGINS (*loftily*). I cannot charge myself with having ever uttered it, Mrs. Pearce. (*She looks at him steadfastly. He adds, hiding an uneasy conscience with a judicial air*) Except perhaps in a moment of extreme and justifiable excitement.

MRS. PEARCE. Only this morning, sir, you applied it to your boots, to the butter, and to the brown bread.

HIGGINS. Oh, that! Mere alliteration, Mrs. Pearce, natural to a poet.

MRS. PEARCE. Well, sir, whatever you choose to call it, I beg you not to let the girl hear you repeat it.

HIGGINS. Oh, very well, very well. Is that all?

MRS. PEARCE. No, sir. We shall have to be very particular with this girl as to personal cleanliness.

HIGGINS. Certainly. Quite right. Most important.

MRS. PEARCE. I mean not to be slovenly about her dress or untidy in leaving things about.

HIGGINS (*going to her solemnly*). Just so. I intended to call your attention to that. (*He passes on to* PICKERING, *who is enjoying the conversation immensely.*) It is these little things that matter, Pickering. Take care of the pence and the pounds will take care of themselves is as true of personal habits as of money. (*He comes to anchor on the hearthrug, with the air of a man in an unassailable position.*)

MRS. PEARCE. Yes, sir. Then might I ask you not to come down to breakfast in your dressing-gown, or at any rate not to use it as a napkin to the extent you do, sir. And if you would be so good as not to eat everything off the same plate, and to remember not to put the porridge saucepan out of your hand on the clean table-cloth, it would be a better example to the girl. You know you nearly choked yourself with a fishbone in the jam only last week.

HIGGINS (*routed from the hearthrug and drifting back to the piano*). I may do these things sometimes in absence of mind; but surely I dont do them habitually. (*Angrily*) By the way: my dressing-gown smells most damnably of benzine.

MRS. PEARCE. No doubt it does, Mr. Higgins. But if you will wipe your fingers—

HIGGINS (*yelling*). Oh very well, very well: I'll wipe them in my hair in future.

MRS. PEARCE. I hope youre not offended, Mr. Higgins.

HIGGINS (*shocked at finding himself thought capable of an unamiable sentiment*). Not at all, not at all. Youre quite right, Mrs. Pearce: I shall be particularly careful before the girl. Is that all?

MRS. PEARCE. No sir. Might she use some of those Japanese dresses you brought from abroad? I really cant put her back into her old things.

HIGGINS. Certainly. Anything you like. Is that all?

MRS. PEARCE. Thank you, sir. Thats all. (*She goes out.*)

HIGGINS. You know, Pickering, that woman has the most extraordinary ideas about me. Here I am, a shy, diffident sort of man. Ive never been able to feel really grown-up and tremendous, like other chaps. And yet she's firmly persuaded that I'm an arbitrary overbearing bossing kind of person. I cant account for it.

MRS. PEARCE *returns.*

MRS. PEARCE. If you please, sir, the trouble's beginning already. Theres a dustman[4] downstairs, Alfred Doolittle, wants to see you. He says you have his daughter here.

PICKERING (*rising*). Phew! I say!

HIGGINS (*promptly*). Send the blackguard up.

MRS. PEARCE. Oh, very well, sir. (*She goes out.*)

PICKERING. He may not be a blackguard, Higgins.

HIGGINS. Nonsense. Of course he's a blackguard.

PICKERING. Whether he is or not, I'm afraid we shall have some trouble with him.

HIGGINS (*confidently*). Oh no: I think not. If theres any trouble he shall have it with me, not I with him. And we are sure to get something interesting out of him.

PICKERING. About the girl?

HIGGINS. No, I mean his dialect.

PICKERING. Oh!

MRS. PEARCE (*at the door*). Doolittle, sir. (*She admits* DOOLITTLE *and retires.*)

ALFRED DOOLITTLE *is an elderly but vigorous dustman, clad in the costume of his profession, including a hat with a black brim covering his neck and shoulders. He has well marked and rather interesting features, and seems equally free from fear and*

---

4. *dustman,* a trash or garbage collector.

conscience. He has a remarkably expressive voice, the result of a habit of giving vent to his feelings without reserve. His present pose is that of wounded honor and stern resolution.

DOOLITTLE (*at the door, uncertain which of the two gentlemen is his man*). Professor Iggins?

HIGGINS. Here. Good morning. Sit down.

DOOLITTLE. Morning, Governor. (*He sits down magisterially.*) I come about a very serious matter, Governor.

HIGGINS (*to* PICKERING). Brought up in Hounslow. Mother Welsh, I should think. (DOOLITTLE *opens his mouth, amazed.* HIGGINS *continues.*) What do you want, Doolittle?

DOOLITTLE (*menacingly*). I want my daughter: thats what I want. See?

HIGGINS. Of course you do. Youre her father, arnt you? You dont suppose anyone else wants her, do you? I'm glad to see you have some spark of family feeling left. She's upstairs. Take her away at once.

DOOLITTLE (*rising, fearfully taken aback*). What!

HIGGINS. Take her away. Do you suppose I'm going to keep your daughter for you?

DOOLITTLE (*remonstrating*). Now, now, look here, Governor. Is this reasonable? Is it fairly to take advantage of a man like this? The girl belongs to me. You got her. Where do I come in? (*He sits down again.*)

HIGGINS. Your daughter had the audacity to come to my house and ask me to teach her how to speak properly so that she could get a place in a flower-shop. This gentleman and my housekeeper have been here all the time. (*Bullying him*) How dare you come here and attempt to blackmail me? You sent her here on purpose.

DOOLITTLE (*protesting*). No, Governor.

HIGGINS. You must have. How else could you possibly know that she is here?

DOOLITTLE. Dont take a man up like that, Governor.

HIGGINS. The police shall take you up. This is a plant—a plot to extort money by threats. I shall telephone the police. (*He goes resolutely to the telephone and opens the directory.*)

DOOLITTLE. Have I asked you for a brass far-

thing? I leave it to the gentleman here: have I said a word about money?

HIGGINS (*throwing the book aside and marching down on* DOOLITTLE *with a poser*). What else did you come for?

DOOLITTLE (*sweetly*). Well, what would a man come for? Be human, Governor.

HIGGINS (*disarmed*). Alfred: did you put her up to it?

DOOLITTLE. So help me, Governor, I never did. I take my Bible oath I aint seen the girl these two months past.

HIGGINS. Then how did you know she was here?

DOOLITTLE (*"most musical, most melancholy"*).[5] I'll tell you, Governor, if youll only let me get a word in. I'm willing to tell you. I'm wanting to tell you. I'm waiting to tell you.

HIGGINS. Pickering: this chap has a certain natural gift of rhetoric. Observe the rhythm of his native woodnotes wild. "I'm willing to tell you: I'm wanting to tell you: I'm waiting to tell you." Sentimental rhetoric! thats the Welsh strain in him. It also accounts for his mendacity and dishonesty.

PICKERING. Oh, please, Higgins: I'm west country[6] myself. (*To* DOOLITTLE) How did you know the girl was here if you didnt send her?

DOOLITTLE. It was like this, Governor. The girl took a boy in the taxi to give him a jaunt. Son of her landlady, he is. He hung about on the chance of her giving him another ride home. Well, she sent him back for her luggage when she heard you was willing for her to stop here. I met the boy at the corner of Long Acre and Endell Street.

HIGGINS. Public house. Yes?

DOOLITTLE. The poor man's club, Governor: why shouldnt I?

PICKERING. Do let him tell his story, Higgins.

DOOLITTLE. He told me what was up. And I ask you, what was my feelings and my duty as a

---

5. *"most . . . melancholy,"* a line from Milton's poem "Il Penseroso."
6. *west country,* the counties in the region southwest of London, especially the remoter ones, like Devon and Cornwall.

father? I says to the boy, "You bring me the luggage," I says—

PICKERING. Why didnt you go for it yourself?

DOOLITTLE. Landlady wouldnt have trusted me with it, Governor. She's that kind of woman: you know. I had to give the boy a penny afore he trusted me with it, the little swine. I brought it to her just to oblige you like, and make myself agreeable. Thats all.

HIGGINS. How much luggage?

DOOLITTLE. Musical instrument, Governor. A few pictures, a trifle of jewelry, and a birdcage. She said she didnt want no clothes. What was I to think from that, Governor? I ask you as a parent what was I to think?

HIGGINS. So you came to rescue her from worse than death, eh?

DOOLITTLE (*appreciatively: relieved at being so well understood*). Just so, Governor. Thats right.

PICKERING. But why did you bring her luggage if you intended to take her away?

DOOLITTLE. Have I said a word about taking her away? Have I now?

HIGGINS (*determinedly*). Youre going to take her away, double quick. (*He crosses to the hearth and rings the bell.*)

DOOLITTLE (*rising*). No, Governor. Dont say that. I'm not the man to stand in my girl's light. Heres a career opening for her, as you might say; and—

MRS. PEARCE *opens the door and awaits orders.*

HIGGINS. Mrs. Pearce: this is Eliza's father. He has come to take her away. Give her to him. (*He goes back to the piano, with an air of washing his hands of the whole affair.*)

DOOLITTLE. No. This is a misunderstanding. Listen here—

MRS. PEARCE. He cant take her away, Mr. Higgins: how can he? You told me to burn her clothes.

DOOLITTLE. Thats right. I cant carry the girl through the streets like a blooming monkey, can I? I put it to you.

HIGGINS. You have put it to me that you want your daughter. Take your daughter. If she has no clothes go out and buy her some.

DOOLITTLE (*desperate*). Wheres the clothes she come in? Did I burn them or did your missus here?

MRS. PEARCE. I am the housekeeper, if you please. I have sent for some clothes for your girl. When they come you can take her away. You can wait in the kitchen. This way, please.

DOOLITTLE, *much troubled, accompanies her to the door; then hesitates; finally turns confidently to* HIGGINS.

DOOLITTLE. Listen here, Governor. You and me is men of the world, aint we?

HIGGINS. Oh! Men of the world, are we? Youd better go, Mrs. Pearce.

MRS. PEARCE. I think so, indeed, sir. (*She goes, with dignity.*)

PICKERING. The floor is yours, Mr. Doolittle.

DOOLITTLE (*to* PICKERING). I thank you, Governor. (*To* HIGGINS, *who takes refuge on the piano bench, a little overwhelmed by the proximity of his visitor; for* DOOLITTLE *has a professional flavor of dust about him.*) Well, the truth is, Ive taken a sort of fancy to you, Governor; and if you want the girl, I'm not so set on having her back home again but what I might be open to an arrangement. Regarded in the light of a young woman, she's a fine handsome girl. As a daughter she's not worth her keep; and so I tell you straight. All I ask is my rights as a father; and youre the last man alive to expect me to let her go for nothing; for I can see youre one of the straight sort, Governor. Well, whats a five-pound note to you? And whats Eliza to me? (*He returns to his chair and sits down judicially.*)

PICKERING. I think you ought to know, Doolittle, that Mr. Higgins's intentions are entirely honorable.

DOOLITTLE. Course they are, Governor. If I thought they wasnt, I'd ask fifty.

HIGGINS (*revolted*). Do you mean to say that you would sell your daughter for £50?

DOOLITTLE. Not in a general way I wouldnt; but to oblige a gentleman like you I'd do a good deal, I do assure you.

PICKERING. Have you no morals, man?

DOOLITTLE (*unabashed*). Cant afford them, Governor. Neither could you if you was as poor as me. Not that I mean any harm, you know. But if Liza is going to have a bit out of this, why not me too?

HIGGINS (*troubled*). I dont know what to do, Pickering. There can be no question that as a matter of morals it's a positive crime to give this chap a farthing. And yet I feel a sort of rough justice in his claim.

DOOLITTLE. Thats it, Governor. Thats all I say. A father's heart, as it were.

PICKERING. Well, I know the feeling; but really it seems hardly right—

DOOLITTLE. Dont say that, Governor. Dont look at it that way. What am I, Governors both? I ask you, what am I? I'm one of the undeserving poor: thats what I am. Think of what that means to a man. It means that he's up agen middle-class morality all the time. If theres anything going, and I put in for a bit of it, it's always the same story: "Youre undeserving; so you cant have it." But my needs is as great as the most deserving widow's that ever got money out of six different charities in one week for the death of the same husband. I dont need less than a deserving man: I need more. I dont eat less hearty than him; and I drink a lot more. I want a bit of amusement, cause I'm a thinking man. I want cheerfulness and a song and a band when I feel low. Well, they charge me just the same for everything as they charge the deserving. What is middle-class morality? Just an excuse for never giving me anything. Therefore, I ask you, as two gentlemen, not to play that game on me. I'm playing straight with you. I aint pretending to be deserving. I'm undeserving; and I mean to go on being undeserving. I like it; and thats the truth. Will you take advantage of a man's nature to do him out of the price of his own daughter what he's brought up and fed and clothed by the sweat of his brow until she's growed big enough to be interesting to you two gentlemen? Is five pounds unreasonable? I put it to you; and I leave it to you.

HIGGINS (*rising, and going over to* PICKERING). Pickering: if we were to take this man in hand

for three months, he could choose between a seat in the Cabinet and a popular pulpit in Wales.

PICKERING. What do you say to that, Doolittle?

DOOLITTLE. Not me, Governor, thank you kindly. Ive heard all the preachers and all the prime ministers—for I'm a thinking man and game for politics or religion or social reform same as all the other amusements—and I tell you it's a dog's life any way you look at it. Undeserving poverty is my line. Taking one station in society with another, it's—it's—well, it's the only one that has any ginger in it, to my taste.

HIGGINS. I suppose we must give him a fiver.

PICKERING. He'll make a bad use of it, I'm afraid.

DOOLITTLE. Not me, Governor, so help me I wont. Dont you be afraid that I'll save it and spare it and live idle on it. There wont be a penny of it left by Monday: I'll have to go to work same as if I'd never had it. It wont pauperize me, you bet. Just one good spree for myself and the missus, giving pleasure to ourselves and employment to others, and satisfaction to you to think it's not been throwed away. You couldnt spend it better.

HIGGINS (*taking out his pocket book and coming between* DOOLITTLE *and the piano*). This is irresistible. Lets give him ten. (*He offers two notes to the dustman.*)

DOOLITTLE. No, Governor. She wouldnt have the heart to spend ten; and perhaps I shouldnt neither. Ten pounds is a lot of money: it makes a man feel prudent like; and then goodbye to happiness. You give me what I ask you, Governor: not a penny more, and not a penny less.

PICKERING. Why dont you marry that missus of yours? I rather draw the line at encouraging that sort of immorality.

DOOLITTLE. Tell her so, Governor; tell her so. I'm willing. It's me that suffers by it. Ive no hold on her. I got to be agreeable to her. I got to give her presents. I got to buy her clothes something sinful. I'm a slave to that woman, Governor, just because I'm not her lawful husband. And she knows it too. Catch her marrying me! Take my advice, Governor: marry Eliza while she's young and dont know no better. If you dont youll be sorry for it after. If you do, she'll be sorry for it after; but better her than you, because youre a man, and she's only a woman and dont know how to be happy anyhow.

HIGGINS. Pickering: if we listen to this man another minute, we shall have no convictions left. (To DOOLITTLE) Five pounds I think you said.

DOOLITTLE. Thank you kindly, Governor.

HIGGINS. Youre sure you wont take ten?

DOOLITTLE. Not now. Another time, Governor.

HIGGINS (handing him a five-pound note). Here you are.

DOOLITTLE. Thank you, Governor. Good morning. (He hurries to the door, anxious to get away with his booty. When he opens it he is confronted with a dainty and exquisitely clean young Japanese lady in a simple blue cotton kimono printed cunningly with small white jasmine blossoms. MRS. PEARCE is with her. He gets out of her way deferentially and apologizes.) Beg pardon, miss.

THE JAPANESE LADY. Garn! Dont you know your own daughter?

DOOLITTLE	⎱ exclaiming	⎰ Bly me! it's Eliza!
HIGGINS	⎬ simul-	⎨ Whats that! This!
PICKERING	⎰ taneously	⎱ By Jove!

LIZA. Dont I look silly?

HIGGINS. Silly?

MRS. PEARCE (at the door). Now Mr. Higgins, please dont say anything to make the girl conceited about herself.

HIGGINS (conscientiously). Oh! Quite right, Mrs. Pearce. (To ELIZA) Yes: damned silly.

MRS. PEARCE. Please, sir.

HIGGINS (correcting himself). I mean extremely silly.

LIZA. I should look all right with my hat on. (She takes up her hat; puts it on; and walks across the room to the fireplace with a fashionable air.)

HIGGINS. A new fashion, by George! And it ought to look horrible!

DOOLITTLE (with fatherly pride). Well, I never thought she'd clean up as good looking as that, Governor. She's a credit to me, aint she?

LIZA. I tell you, it's easy to clean up here. Hot and cold water on tap, just as much as you like, there is. Woolly towels, there is; and a towel horse so hot, it burns your fingers. Soft brushes to scrub yourself, and a wooden bowl of soap smelling like primroses. Now I know why ladies is so clean. Washing's a treat for them. Wish they saw what it is for the like of me!

HIGGINS. I'm glad the bathroom met with your approval.

LIZA. It didnt: not all of it; and I dont care who hears me say it. Mrs. Pearce knows.

HIGGINS. What was wrong, Mrs. Pearce?

MRS. PEARCE (blandly). Oh, nothing, sir. It doesnt matter.

LIZA. I had a good mind to break it. I didnt know which way to look. But I hung a towel over it, I did.

HIGGINS. Over what?

MRS. PEARCE. Over the looking glass, sir.

HIGGINS. Doolittle: you have brought your daughter up too strictly.

DOOLITTLE. Me! I never brought her up at all, except to give her a lick of a strap now and again. Dont put it on me, Governor. She aint accustomed to it, you see: thats all. But she'll soon pick up your free-and-easy ways.

LIZA. I'm a good girl, I am; and I wont pick up no free-and-easy ways.

HIGGINS. Eliza: if you say again that youre a good girl, your father shall take you home.

LIZA. Not him. You dont know my father. All he come here for was to touch you for some money to get drunk on.

DOOLITTLE. Well, what else would I want money for? To put into the plate in church, I suppose. (She puts out her tongue at him. He is so incensed by this that PICKERING presently finds it necessary to step between them.) Dont you give me none of your lip; and dont let me hear you giving this gentleman any of it neither, or youll hear from me about it. See?

HIGGINS. Have you any further advice to give her before you go, Doolittle? Your blessing, for instance.

DOOLITTLE. No, Governor, I aint such a mug as to put up my children to all I know myself. Hard enough to hold them in without that. If you want Eliza's mind improved, Governor, you do it yourself with a strap. So long, gentlemen. (*He turns to go.*)

HIGGINS (*impressively*). Stop. Youll come regularly to see your daughter. It's your duty, you know. My brother is a clergyman; and he could help you in your talks with her.

DOOLITTLE (*evasively*). Certainly. I'll come, Governor. Not just this week, because I have a job at a distance. But later on you may depend on me. Afternoon, gentlemen. Afternoon, maam. (*He takes off his hat to* MRS. PEARCE, *who disdains the salutation and goes out. He winks at* HIGGINS, *thinking him probably a fellow-sufferer from* MRS. PEARCE's *difficult disposition, and follows her.*)

LIZA. Dont you believe the old liar. He'd as soon you set a bull-dog on him as a clergyman. You wont see him again in a hurry.

HIGGINS. I dont want to, Eliza. Do you?

LIZA. Not me. I dont want never to see him again, I dont. He's a disgrace to me, he is, collecting dust, instead of working at his trade.

PICKERING. What is his trade, Eliza?

LIZA. Taking money out of other people's pockets into his own. His proper trade's a navvy;[7] and he works at it sometimes too—for exercise—and earns good money at it. Aint you going to call me Miss Doolittle any more?

PICKERING. I beg your pardon, Miss Doolittle. It was a slip of the tongue.

LIZA. Oh, I dont mind; only it sounded so genteel. I should just like to take a taxi to the corner of Tottenham Court Road and get out there and tell it to wait for me, just to put the girls in their place a bit. I wouldnt speak to them, you know.

PICKERING. Better wait til we get you something really fashionable.

HIGGINS. Besides, you shouldnt cut[8] your old friends now that you have risen in the world. Thats what we call snobbery.

LIZA. You dont call the like of them my friends now, I should hope. Theyve took it out of me often enough with their ridicule when they had the chance; and now I mean to get a bit of my own back. But if I'm to have fashionable clothes,

I'll wait. I should like to have some. Mrs. Pearce says youre going to give me some to wear in bed at night different to what I wear in the daytime; but it do seem a waste of money when you could get something to shew. Besides, I never could fancy changing into cold things on a winter night.

MRS. PEARCE (*coming back*). Now, Eliza. The new things have come for you to try on.

LIZA. Ah-ow-oo-ooh! (*She rushes out.*)

MRS. PEARCE (*following her*). Oh, dont rush about like that, girl. (*She shuts the door behind her.*)

HIGGINS. Pickering: we have taken on a stiff job.

PICKERING (*with conviction*). Higgins: we have.

---

7. *navvy,* unskilled laborer, especially one doing excavation or construction work.
8. *cut,* refuse to recognize socially.

THINK AND DISCUSS
ACT TWO
Understanding

1. What does Liza want from Higgins?
2. Explain the agreement that Higgins and Pickering come to.

Analyzing

3. When Liza appears, she is prepared "to pay like any lady." Explain how this illustrates her notion of upper-class life and, further, her own sense of herself.
4. In what ways does Pickering's presence throughout Act Two modify what happens?
5. How does Higgins's use of the chocolates serve as a warning about the future?
6. List some of the assumptions Higgins has about Liza and her father. What do they indicate about class prejudice?
7. Why does Doolittle follow Liza?

8. Explain how Doolittle redefines conventional ideas about a father's "rights," "morals," the life of "the undeserving poor," and a "bad use" of money.
9. Mrs. Pearce indulges in her own, rather strict instructions to Higgins. What do they tell us about the way he lives? What do they tell us about class differences?
10. Why is everyone so surprised when Liza returns from her bath? How does this **foreshadow** what might happen after she receives training?

Extending

11. Liza, a lower-class woman, wants to improve her condition. Higgins and Pickering turn her plans into a bet to entertain themselves. Discuss how their "taking-over" in this way is a privilege of power. Does this same sort of taking-over still go on?

HT Review CHARACTERIZATION in the Handbook of Literary Terms, page 898.

ACT THREE

It is MRS. HIGGINS's at-home[1] day. Nobody has yet arrived. Her drawing room, in a flat on Chelsea Embankment,[2] has three windows looking on the river; and the ceiling is not so lofty as it would be in an older house of the same pretension. The windows are open, giving access to a balcony with flowers in pots. If you stand with your face to the windows, you have the fireplace on your left and the door in the right-hand wall close to the corner nearest the windows.

MRS. HIGGINS was brought up on Morris and Burne-Jones;[3] and her room, which is very unlike her son's room in Wimpole Street, is not crowded with furniture and little tables and nicknacks. In the middle

of the room there is a big ottoman; and this, with the carpet, the Morris wallpapers, and the Morris chintz window curtains and brocade covers of the ottoman and its cushions, supply all the ornament, and are much too handsome to be hidden by odds and ends of useless things. A few good oil paintings from the exhi-

---

1. **at-home day,** the day one receives callers.
2. **Chelsea Embankment.** Chelsea is a pleasant residential district along the bank of the Thames.
3. **Morris and Burne-Jones.** William Morris and Edward Burne-Jones were members of a decorating firm noted for fine carvings, stained glass, metalwork, wallpapers, chintzes, tiles, and carpets. (See pages 132 and 567.)

bitions in the Grosvenor Gallery thirty years ago (the Burne-Jones, not the Whistler side of them) are on the walls. The only landscape is a Cecil Lawson on the scale of a Rubens.[4] There is a portrait of MRS. HIG-GINS *as she was when she defied fashion in her youth in one of the beautiful Rossettian[5] costumes which, when caricatured by people who did not understand, led to the absurdities of popular estheticism in the eighteen-seventies.*

In the corner diagonally opposite the door MRS. HIG-GINS, *now over sixty and long past taking the trouble to dress out of the fashion, sits writing at an elegantly simple writing-table with a bell button within reach of her hand. There is a Chippendale chair further back in the room between her and the window nearest her side. At the other side of the room, further forward, is an Elizabethan chair roughly carved in the taste of Inigo Jones. On the same side a piano in a decorated case. The corner between the fireplace and the window is occupied by a divan cushioned in Morris chintz.*

It is between four and five in the afternoon.

The door is opened violently; and HIGGINS *enters with his hat on.*

MRS. HIGGINS (*dismayed*). Henry (*scolding him*)! What are you doing here to-day? It is my at-home day: you promised not to come. (*As he bends to kiss her, she takes his hat off, and presents it to him.*)

HIGGINS. Oh, bother! (*He throws the hat down on the table.*)

MRS. HIGGINS. Go home at once.

HIGGINS (*kissing her*). I know, mother. I came on purpose.

MRS. HIGGINS. But you mustnt. I'm serious, Henry. You offend all my friends: they stop coming whenever they meet you.

HIGGINS. Nonsense! I know I have no small talk: but people dont mind. (*He sits on the settee.*)

MRS. HIGGINS. Oh! dont they? Small talk indeed! What about your large talk? Really, dear, you mustnt stay.

HIGGINS. I must. Ive a job for you. A phonetic job.

MRS. HIGGINS. No use, dear. I'm sorry; but I cant get round your vowels; and though I like to get pretty postcards in your patent shorthand, I always have to read the copies in ordinary writing you so thoughtfully send me.

HIGGINS. Well, this isnt a phonetic job.

MRS. HIGGINS. You said it was.

HIGGINS. Not your part of it. Ive picked up a girl.

MRS. HIGGINS. Does that mean that some girl has picked you up?

HIGGINS. Not at all. I don't mean a love affair.

MRS. HIGGINS. What a pity!

HIGGINS. Why?

MRS. HIGGINS. Well, you never fall in love with anyone under forty-five. When will you discover that there are some rather nice-looking young women about?

HIGGINS. Oh, I cant be bothered with young women. My idea of a lovable woman is something as like you as possible. I shall never get into the way of seriously liking young women: some habits lie too deep to be changed. (*Rising abruptly and walking about, jingling his money and his keys in his trouser pockets*) Besides, theyre all idiots.

MRS. HIGGINS. Do you know what you would do if you really loved me, Henry?

HIGGINS. Oh bother! What? Marry, I suppose?

MRS. HIGGINS. No. Stop fidgeting and take your hands out of your pockets. (*With a gesture of despair, he obeys and sits down again.*) Thats a good boy. Now tell me about the girl.

HIGGINS. She's coming to see you.

MRS. HIGGINS. I dont remember asking her.

HIGGINS. You didnt. *I* asked her. If youd known her you wouldnt have asked her.

MRS. HIGGINS. Indeed! Why?

HIGGINS. Well, it's like this. She's a common flower girl. I picked her off the kerbstone.

MRS. HIGGINS. And invited her to my at-home!

HIGGINS (*rising and coming to her to coax her*). Oh,

---

4. *Cecil Lawson . . . Rubens.* Cecil Lawson (1851–1882) was an English landscape painter. Peter Paul Rubens (1577–1640) was a Flemish painter known for his large canvases.
5. *Rossettian,* inspired by the paintings of Dante Gabriel Rossetti (1828–1882), whose work often pictures women in flowing robes. (See page 464.)

thatll be all right. Ive taught her to speak properly; and she has strict orders as to her behavior. She's to keep to two subjects: the weather and everybody's health—Fine day and How do you do, you know—and not to let herself go on things in general. That will be safe.

MRS. HIGGINS. Safe! To talk about our health! about our insides! perhaps about our outsides! How could you be so silly, Henry?

HIGGINS (*impatiently*). Well, she must talk about something. (*He controls himself and sits down again.*) Oh, she'll be all right: dont you fuss. Pickering is in it with me. Ive a sort of bet on that I'll pass her off as a duchess in six months. I started on her some months ago; and she's getting on like a house on fire. I shall win my bet. She has a quick ear; and she's been easier to teach than my middle class pupils because she's had to learn a complete new language. She talks English almost as you talk French.

MRS. HIGGINS. Thats satisfactory, at all events.

HIGGINS. Well, it is and it isnt.

MRS. HIGGINS. What does that mean?

HIGGINS. You see, Ive got her pronunciation all right; but you have to consider not only how a girl pronounces, but what she pronounces; and thats where—

They are interrupted by THE PARLOR-MAID, *announcing guests.*

THE PARLOR-MAID. Mrs. and Miss Eynsford Hill. (*She withdraws.*)

HIGGINS. Oh Lord! (*He rises: snatches his hat from the table; and makes for the door; but before he reaches it his mother introduces him.* MRS. *and* MISS EYNSFORD HILL *are the mother and daughter who sheltered from the rain in Covent Garden. The mother is well bred, quiet, and has the habitual anxiety of straitened means. The daughter has acquired a gay air of being very much at home in society: the bravado of genteel poverty.*)

MRS. EYNSFORD HILL (*to* MRS. HIGGINS). How do you do? (*They shake hands.*)

MISS EYNSFORD HILL. How d'you do? (*She shakes.*)

MRS. HIGGINS (*introducing*). My son Henry.

MRS. EYNSFORD HILL. Your celebrated son! I have so longed to meet you, Professor Higgins.

HIGGINS (*glumly, making no movement in her direction*). Delighted. (*He backs against the piano and bows brusquely.*)

MISS EYNSFORD HILL (*going to him with confident familiarity*). How do you do?

HIGGINS (*staring at her*). Ive seen you before somewhere. I havnt the ghost of a notion where; but Ive heard your voice. (*Drearily*) It doesnt matter. Youd better sit down.

MRS. HIGGINS. I'm sorry to say that my celebrated son has no manners. You mustnt mind him.

MISS EYNSFORD HILL (*gaily*). I dont. (*She sits in the Elizabethan chair.*)

MRS. EYNSFORD HILL (*a little bewildered*). Not at all. (*She sits on the ottoman between her daughter and* MRS. HIGGINS, *who has turned her chair away from the writing-table.*)

HIGGINS. Oh, have I been rude? I didnt mean to be.

He goes to the central window, through which, with his back to the company, he contemplates the river and the flowers in Battersea Park on the opposite bank as if they were a frozen desert.

THE PARLOR-MAID *returns, ushering in* PICKERING.

THE PARLOR-MAID. Colonel Pickering. (*She withdraws.*)

PICKERING. How do you do, Mrs. Higgins?

MRS. HIGGINS. So glad youve come. Do you know Mrs. Eynsford Hill—Miss Eynsford Hill? (*Exchange of bows. The Colonel brings the Chippendale chair a little forward between* MRS. HILL *and* MRS. HIGGINS, *and sits down.*)

PICKERING. Has Henry told you what weve come for?

HIGGINS (*over his shoulder*). We were interrupted: damn it!

MRS. HIGGINS. Oh Henry, Henry, really!

MRS. EYNSFORD HILL (*half rising*). Are we in the way?

MRS. HIGGINS (*rising and making her sit down again*). No, no. You couldnt have come more fortunately: we want you to meet a friend of ours.

HIGGINS (*turning hopefully*). Yes, by George! We

want two or three people. Youll do as well as anybody else.

THE PARLOR-MAID *returns, ushering* FREDDY.

THE PARLOR-MAID. Mr. Eynsford Hill.

HIGGINS (*almost audibly, past endurance*). God of Heaven! another of them.

FREDDY (*shaking hands with* MRS. HIGGINS). Ahdedo?

MRS. HIGGINS. Very good of you to come. (*Introducing*) Colonel Pickering.

FREDDY (*bowing*). Ahdedo?

MRS. HIGGINS. I dont think you know my son, Professor Higgins.

FREDDY (*going to* HIGGINS). Ahdedo?

HIGGINS (*looking at him much as if he were a pickpocket*). I'll take my oath Ive met you before somewhere. Where was it?

FREDDY. I dont think so.

HIGGINS (*resignedly*). It dont matter, anyhow. Sit down. (*He shakes* FREDDY's *hand, and almost slings him on to the ottoman with his face to the windows; then comes round to the other side of it.*)

HIGGINS. Well, here we are, anyhow! (*He sits down on the ottoman next* MRS. EYNSFORD HILL, *on her left.*) And now, what the devil are we going to talk about until Eliza comes?

MRS. HIGGINS. Henry: you are the life and soul of the Royal Society's soirees; but really youre rather trying on more commonplace occasions.

HIGGINS. Am I? Very sorry. (*Beaming suddenly*) I suppose I am, you know. (*Uproariously*) Ha, ha!

MISS EYNSFORD HILL (*who considers* HIGGINS *quite eligible matrimonially*). I sympathize. *I* havnt any small talk. If people would only be frank and say what they really think!

HIGGINS (*relapsing into gloom*). Lord forbid!

MRS. EYNSFORD HILL (*taking up her daughter's cue*). But why?

HIGGINS. What they think they ought to think is bad enough, Lord knows; but what they really think would break up the whole show. Do you suppose it would be really agreeable if I were to come out now with what *I* really think?

MISS EYNSFORD HILL (*gaily*). Is it so very cynical?

HIGGINS. Cynical! Who the dickens said it was cynical? I mean it wouldnt be decent.

MRS. EYNSFORD HILL (*seriously*). Oh! I'm sure you

dont mean that, Mr. Higgins.

HIGGINS. You see, we're all savages, more or less. We're supposed to be civilized and cultured—to know all about poetry and philosophy and art and science, and so on; but how many of us know even the meanings of these names? (*To* MISS HILL) What do you know of poetry? (*To* MRS. HILL) What do you know of science? (*Indicating* FREDDY) What does he know of art or science or anything else? What the devil do you imagine I know of philosophy?

MRS. HIGGINS (*warningly*). Or of manners, Henry?

THE PARLOR-MAID (*opening the door*). Miss Doolittle. (*She withdraws.*)

HIGGINS (*rising hastily and running to* MRS. HIGGINS). Here she is, mother. (*He stands on tiptoe and makes signs over his mother's head to* ELIZA *to indicate to her which lady is her hostess.*)

ELIZA, *who is exquisitely dressed, produces an impression of such remarkable distinction and beauty as she enters that they all rise, quite fluttered. Guided by* HIGGINS's *signals, she comes to* MRS. HIGGINS *with studied grace.*

LIZA (*speaking with pedantic correctness of pronunciation and great beauty of tone*). How do you do, Mrs. Higgins? (*She gasps slightly in making sure of the H in* HIGGINS, *but is quite successful.*) Mr. Higgins told me I might come.

MRS. HIGGINS (*cordially*). Quite right: I'm very glad indeed to see you.

PICKERING. How do you do, Miss Doolittle?

LIZA (*shaking hands with him*). Colonel Pickering, is it not?

MRS. EYNSFORD HILL. I feel sure we have met before, Miss Doolittle. I remember your eyes.

LIZA. How do you do? (*She sits down on the ottoman gracefully in the place just left vacant by* HIGGINS.)

MRS. EYNSFORD HILL (*introducing*). My daughter Clara.

LIZA. How do you do?

CLARA (*impulsively*). How do you do? (*She sits down on the ottoman beside* ELIZA, *devouring her with her eyes.*)

FREDDY (*coming to their side of the ottoman*). Ive certainly had the pleasure.

MRS. EYNSFORD HILL (*introducing*). My son Freddy.

LIZA. How do you do?

FREDDY *bows and sits down in the Elizabethan chair, infatuated.*

HIGGINS (*suddenly*). By George, yes: it all comes back to me! (*They stare at him.*) Covent Garden! (*Lamentably*) What a damned thing!

MRS. HIGGINS. Henry, please! (*He is about to sit on the edge of the table.*) Dont sit on my writing-table: youll break it.

HIGGINS (*sulkily*). Sorry.

He goes to the divan, stumbling into the fender and over the fire-irons on his way; extricating himself with muttered imprecations; and finishing his disastrous journey by throwing himself so impatiently on the divan that he almost breaks it. MRS. HIGGINS *looks at him, but controls herself and says nothing. A long and painful pause ensues.*

MRS. HIGGINS (*at last, conversationally*). Will it rain, do you think?

LIZA. The shallow depression in the west of these islands is likely to move slowly in an easterly direction. There are no indications of any great change in the barometrical situation.

FREDDY. Ha! ha! how awfully funny!

LIZA. What is wrong with that, young man? I bet I got it right.

FREDDY. Killing!

MRS. EYNSFORD HILL. I'm sure I hope it wont turn cold. Theres so much influenza about. It runs right through our whole family regularly every spring.

LIZA (*darkly*). My aunt died of influenza: so they said.

MRS. EYNSFORD HILL (*clicks her tongue sympathetically*)!!!

LIZA (*in the same tragic tone*). But it's my belief they done the old woman in.

MRS. HIGGINS (*puzzled*). Done her in?

LIZA. Y-e-e-e-es, Lord love you! Why should she die of influenza? She come through diphtheria right enough the year before. I saw her with my own eyes. Fairly blue with it, she was. They all thought she was dead; but my father he kept ladling gin down her throat til she came to so sudden that she bit the bowl off the spoon.

MRS. EYNSFORD HILL (*startled*). Dear me!

LIZA (*piling up the indictment*). What call would a woman with that strength in her have to die of influenza? What become of her new straw hat that should have come to me? Somebody pinched it; and what I say is, them as pinched it done her in.

MRS. EYNSFORD HILL. What does doing her in mean?

HIGGINS (*hastily*). Oh, thats the new small talk. To do a person in means to kill them.

MRS. EYNSFORD HILL (*to* ELIZA, *horrified*). You surely dont believe that your aunt was killed?

LIZA. Do I not! Them she lived with would have killed her for a hat-pin, let alone a hat.

MRS. EYNSFORD HILL. But it cant have been right for your father to pour spirits down her throat like that. It might have killed her.

LIZA. Not her. Gin was mother's milk to her. Besides, he'd poured so much down his own throat that he knew the good of it.

MRS. EYNSFORD HILL. Do you mean that he drank?

LIZA. Drank! My word! Something chronic.

MRS. EYNSFORD HILL. How dreadful for you!

LIZA. Not a bit. It never did him no harm what I could see. But then he did not keep it up regular. (*Cheerfully*) On the burst, as you might say, from time to time. And always more agreeable when he had a drop in. When he was out of work, my mother used to give him fourpence and tell him to go out and not come back until he'd drunk himself cheerful and lovinglike. Theres lots of women has to make their husbands drunk to make them fit to live with. (*Now quite at her ease*) You see, it's like this. If a man has a bit of a conscience, it always takes him when he's sober; and then it makes him low-spirited. A drop of booze just takes that off and makes him happy. (*To* FREDDY, *who is in convulsions of suppressed laughter*) Here! what are you sniggering at?

FREDDY. The new small talk. You do it so awfully well.

LIZA. If I was doing it proper, what was you laughing at? (*To* HIGGINS) Have I said anything I oughtnt?

MRS. HIGGINS (*interposing*). Not at all, Miss Doolittle.

LIZA. Well, thats a mercy, anyhow. (*Expansively*) What I always say is—

HIGGINS (*rising and looking at his watch*). Ahem!

LIZA (*looking round at him; taking the hint; and rising*). Well: I must go. (*They all rise*, FREDDY *goes to the door.*) So pleased to have met you. Goodbye. (*She shakes hands with* MRS. HIGGINS.)

MRS. HIGGINS. Goodbye.

LIZA. Goodbye, Colonel Pickering.

PICKERING. Goodbye, Miss Doolittle. (*They shake hands.*)

LIZA (*nodding to the others*). Goodbye, all.

FREDDY (*opening the door for her*). Are you walking across the Park, Miss Doolittle? If so—

LIZA. Walk! Not bloody likely. (*Sensation*) I am going in a taxi. (*She goes out.*)

PICKERING *gasps and sits down.* FREDDY *goes out on the balcony to catch another glimpse of* ELIZA.

MRS. EYNSFORD HILL (*suffering from shock*). Well, I really cant get used to the new ways.

CLARA (*throwing herself discontentedly into the Elizabethan chair*). Oh, it's all right, mamma, quite right. People will think we never go anywhere or see anybody if you are so old-fashioned.

MRS. EYNSFORD HILL. I daresay I am very old-fashioned; but I do hope you wont begin using that expression, Clara. I have got accustomed to hear you talking about men as rotters, and calling everything filthy and beastly; though I do think it horrible and unladylike. But this last is really too much. Dont you think so, Colonel Pickering?

PICKERING. Dont ask me. Ive been away in India for several years; and manners have changed so much that I sometimes dont know whether I'm at a respectable dinner-table or in a ship's forecastle.

CLARA. It's all a matter of habit. Theres no right or wrong in it. Nobody means anything by it. And it's so quaint, and gives such a smart emphasis to things that are not in themselves very witty. I find the new small talk delightful and quite innocent.

MRS. EYNSFORD HILL (*rising*). Well, after that, I think it's time for us to go.

PICKERING and HIGGINS *rise*.

CLARA (*rising*). Oh yes: we have three at-homes to go to still. Goodbye, Mrs. Higgins. Goodbye, Colonel Pickering. Goodbye, Professor Higgins.

HIGGINS (*coming grimly at her from the divan, and accompanying her to the door*). Goodbye. Be sure you try on that small talk at the three at-homes. Dont be nervous about it. Pitch it in strong.

CLARA (*all smiles*). I will. Goodbye. Such nonsense, all this early Victorian prudery!

HIGGINS (*tempting her*). Such damned nonsense!

CLARA. Such bloody nonsense!

MRS. EYNSFORD HILL (*convulsively*). Clara!

CLARA. Ha! ha! (*She goes out radiant, conscious of being thoroughly up to date, and is heard descending the stairs in a stream of silvery laughter.*)

FREDDY (*to the heavens at large*). Well, I ask you— (*He gives it up, and comes to* MRS. HIGGINS.) Goodbye.

MRS. HIGGINS (*shaking hands*). Goodbye. Would you like to meet Miss Doolittle again?

FREDDY (*eagerly*). Yes, I should, most awfully.

MRS. HIGGINS. Well, you know my days.

FREDDY. Yes. Thanks awfully. Goodbye. (*He goes out.*)

MRS. EYNSFORD HILL. Goodbye, Mr. Higgins.

HIGGINS. Goodbye. Goodbye.

MRS. EYNSFORD HILL (*to Pickering*). It's no use. I shall never be able to bring myself to use that word.

PICKERING. Dont. It's not compulsory, you know. Youll get on quite well without it.

MRS. EYNSFORD HILL. Only, Clara is so down on me if I am not positively reeking with the latest slang. Goodbye.

PICKERING. Goodbye.

(*They shake hands.*)

MRS. EYNSFORD HILL (*to* MRS. HIGGINS). You mustnt mind Clara. (PICKERING, *catching from her lowered tone that this is not meant for him to hear, discreetly joins* HIGGINS *at the window.*) We're so poor! and she gets so few parties, poor

child! She doesnt quite know. (MRS. HIGGINS, *seeing that her eyes are moist, takes her hand sympathetically and goes with her to the door.*) But the boy is nice. Dont you think so?

MRS. HIGGINS. Oh, quite nice. I shall always be delighted to see him.

MRS. EYNSFORD HILL. Thank you, dear. Goodbye. (*She goes out.*)

HIGGINS (*eagerly*). Well? Is Eliza presentable? (*He swoops on his mother and drags her to the ottoman, where she sits down in* ELIZA's *place with her son on her left.*)

PICKERING *returns to his chair on her right.*

MRS. HIGGINS. You silly boy, of course she's not presentable. She's a triumph of your art and of her dressmaker's; but if you suppose for a moment that she doesnt give herself away in every sentence she utters, you must be perfectly cracked about her.

PICKERING. But dont you think something might be done? I mean something to eliminate the sanguinary[6] element from her conversation.

MRS. HIGGINS. Not as long as she is in Henry's hands.

HIGGINS (*aggrieved*). Do you mean that my language is improper?

MRS. HIGGINS. No, dearest; it would be quite proper—say on a canal barge; but it would not be proper for her at a garden party.

HIGGINS (*deeply injured*). Well I must say—

PICKERING (*interrupting him*). Come, Higgins: you must learn to know yourself. I havnt heard such language as yours since we used to review the volunteers in Hyde Park twenty years ago.

HIGGINS (*sulkily*). Oh, well, if you say so, I suppose I dont always talk like a bishop.

MRS. HIGGINS (*quieting* HENRY *with a touch*). Colonel Pickering: will you tell me what is the exact state of things in Wimpole Street?

PICKERING (*cheerfully: as if this completely changed the subject*). Well, I have come to live there with Henry. We work together at my Indian Dialects; and we think it more convenient—

---

6. **sanguinary,** a reference to Liza's use of the slang word *bloody.*

MRS. HIGGINS. Quite so. I know all about that: it's an excellent arrangement. But where does this girl live?

HIGGINS. With us, of course. Where should she live?

MRS. HIGGINS. But on what terms? Is she a servant? If not, what is she?

PICKERING (slowly). I think I know what you mean, Mrs. Higgins.

HIGGINS. Well, dash me if I do! Ive had to work at the girl every day for months to get her to her present pitch. Besides, she's useful. She knows where my things are, and remembers my appointments and so forth.

MRS. HIGGINS. How does your housekeeper get on with her?

HIGGINS. Mrs. Pearce? Oh, she's jolly glad to get so much taken off her hands; for before Eliza came, she used to have to find things and remind me of my appointments. But she's got some silly bee in her bonnet about Eliza. She keeps saying "You dont think, sir": doesnt she, Pick?

PICKERING. Yes: thats the formula. "You dont think, sir." Thats the end of every conversation about Eliza.

HIGGINS. As if I ever stop thinking about the girl and her confounded vowels and consonants. I'm worn out, thinking about her, and watching her lips and her teeth and her tongue, not to mention her soul, which is the quaintest of the lot.

MRS. HIGGINS. You certainly are a pretty pair of babies, playing with your live doll.

HIGGINS. Playing! The hardest job I ever tackled: make no mistake about that, mother. But you have no idea how frightfully interesting it is to take a human being and change her into a quite different human being by creating a new speech for her. It's filling up the deepest gulf that separates class from class and soul from soul.

PICKERING (drawing his chair closer to MRS. HIGGINS and bending over to her eagerly). Yes: it's enormously interesting. I assure you, Mrs. Higgins, we take Eliza very seriously. Every week—every day almost—there is some new change. (Closer again) We keep records of every stage—dozens of gramophone disks and photographs—

HIGGINS (assailing her at the other ear). Yes, by George: it's the most absorbing experiment I ever tackled. She regularly fills our lives up: doesnt she, Pick?

PICKERING. We're always talking Eliza.

HIGGINS. Teaching Eliza.

PICKERING. Dressing Eliza.

MRS. HIGGINS. What!

HIGGINS. Inventing new Elizas.

HIGGINS (speaking together.)	You know, she has the most extraordinary quickness of ear:
PICKERING	I assure you, my dear Mrs. Higgins, that girl
HIGGINS	just like a parrot. Ive tried her with every
PICKERING	is a genius. She can play the piano quite beautifully.
HIGGINS	possible sort of sound that a human being can make—
PICKERING	We have taken her to classical concerts and to music
HIGGINS	Continental dialects, African dialects, Hottentot
PICKERING	halls; and it's all the same to her: she plays everything
HIGGINS	clicks, things it took me years to get hold of; and
PICKERING	she hears right off when she comes home, whether it's
HIGGINS	she picks them up like a shot, right away, as if she had
PICKERING	Beethoven and Brahms or Lehar and Lionel Monckton;[7]

---

7. *Lehar and Lionel Monckton,* popular composers of light music.

HIGGINS ⎫ been at it all her life.
PICKERING ⎭ though six months ago,
           she'd never as much as
           touched a piano—

MRS. HIGGINS (*putting her fingers in her ears, as they are by this time shouting one another down with an intolerable noise*). Sh-sh-sh-sh! (*They stop.*)

PICKERING. I beg your pardon. (*He draws his chair back apologetically.*)

HIGGINS. Sorry. When Pickering starts shouting nobody can get a word in edgeways.

MRS. HIGGINS. Be quiet, Henry. Colonel Pickering: dont you realize that when Eliza walked into Wimpole Street, something walked in with her?

PICKERING. Her father did. But Henry soon got rid of him.

MRS. HIGGINS. It would have been more to the point if her mother had. But as her mother didnt something else did.

PICKERING. But what?

MRS. HIGGINS (*unconsciously dating herself by the word*). A problem.

PICKERING. Oh, I see. The problem of how to pass her off as a lady.

HIGGINS. I'll solve that problem. Ive half solved it already.

MRS. HIGGINS. No, you two infinitely stupid male creatures; the problem of what is to be done with her afterwards.

HIGGINS. I dont see anything in that. She can go her own way, with all the advantages I have given her.

MRS. HIGGINS. The advantages of that poor woman who was here just now! The manners and habits that disqualify a fine lady from earning her own living without giving her a fine lady's income! Is that what you mean?

PICKERING (*indulgently, being rather bored*). Oh, that will be all right, Mrs. Higgins. (*He rises to go.*)

HIGGINS (*rising also*). We'll find her some light employment.

PICKERING. She's happy enough. Dont you worry about her. Goodbye. (*He shakes hands as if he were consoling a frightened child, and makes for the door.*)

HIGGINS. Anyhow, theres no good bothering now. The thing's done. Goodbye, mother. (*He kisses her, and follows* PICKERING.)

PICKERING (*turning for a final consolation*). There are plenty of openings. We'll do whats right. Goodbye.

HIGGINS (*to* PICKERING *as they go out together*). Let's take her to the Shakespear exhibition at Earls Court.

PICKERING. Yes: lets. Her remarks will be delicious.

HIGGINS. She'll mimic all the people for us when we get home.

PICKERING. Ripping. (*Both are heard laughing as they go downstairs.*)

MRS. HIGGINS (*rises with an impatient bounce, and returns to her work at the writing-table. She sweeps a litter of disarranged papers out of her way; snatches a sheet of paper from her stationery case; and tries resolutely to write. At the third line she gives it up; flings down her pen; grips the table angrily and exclaims*). Oh, men! men!! men!!!

THINK AND DISCUSS
ACT THREE
Understanding
1. What are Higgins's reasons for taking Liza to his mother's "at-home"?
2. Describe Liza's effect on the Eynsford Hill family.

Analyzing
3. Specify the intellectual position Mrs. Higgins represents. What other characters in the play share her convictions?
4. During the tea, who has better manners, Higgins or Liza? What is the point of this contrast?
5. What has Liza's training achieved by the end of Act Three, and where does it still fall short?
6. How do Higgins's own limitations make the task more difficult?
7. Why does Clara choose to say "bloody nonsense!" at the end of her visit?

Extending
8. Mrs. Higgins's closing exclamation is her explanation for "the problem." Is she right?

REVIEWING: Characterization HT
See Handbook of Literary Terms, p. 898

Characterization describes the various strategies writers use to make literary creations seem like people.

1. How does the way Freddy sits down at Mrs. Higgins's "at home" illustrate his strength of will?
2. In what ways do Freddy's speeches illustrate his intelligence?
3. What do you learn about Freddy's emotional maturity from his reaction to Liza?

THINKING SKILLS
Evaluating

Making a judgment on the basis of some sort of standard is **evaluating**. Evaluate the competing moral codes that Shaw has presented by this point in the play: Mrs. Higgins's propriety, Mr. Doolittle's rules for the "undeserving poor," Higgins's "scientific" assumption that only his research matters, and so on.

1. If achieving simple pleasure is your standard, which is the most sensible code to live by?
2. If you seek acceptance by the members of polite society, which is best?
3. If you want to get a job done quickly, whose code works most successfully?
4. Of all the systems of moral value illustrated in the play, which do you think Shaw wants us to live by, and how does he indicate his preference?

COMPOSITION ◄——
Analyzing Liza's Characterization

Liza has said little about herself, and yet she clearly dominates Shaw's play. Write an essay, to be read by your classmates, analyzing Shaw's methods of characterization. First skim the play to find examples of what she says about herself, what others say about her, how she treats other people, and her emotional reactions, as suggested in the stage directions. In your essay, devote one paragraph each to the best example you can find of each of these, going on to explain what kind of person your examples show Liza to be.

Evaluating Doolittle's Philosophy

Doolittle's fluent arguments for his own way of life momentarily charm and persuade Higgins, and they have the same effect on theater audiences. Take a closer look at this character and what he says, and evaluate both in an essay of at least four paragraphs. To do so, first summarize his philosophy about marriage, child rearing, and money; then present your views on how successful this philosophy would be in life.

ACT FOUR

The Wimpole Street laboratory. Midnight. Nobody in the room. The clock on the mantel-piece strikes twelve. The fire is not alight: it is a summer night.

Presently HIGGINS *and* PICKERING *are heard on the stairs.*

HIGGINS *(calling down to* PICKERING). I say, Pick: lock up, will you? I shant be going out again.

PICKERING. Right. Can Mrs. Pearce go to bed? We dont want anything more, do we?

HIGGINS. Lord, no!

ELIZA *opens the door and is seen on the lighted landing in all the finery in which she has just won* HIGGINS's *bet for him. She comes to the hearth, and switches on the electric lights there. She is tired: her pallor contrasts strongly with her dark eyes and hair; and her expression is almost tragic. She takes off her cloak; puts her fan and flowers on the piano; and sits down on the bench, brooding and silent.* HIGGINS, *in evening dress, with overcoat and hat, comes in, carrying a smoking jacket which he has picked up downstairs. He takes off the hat and overcoat; throws them carelessly on the newspaper stand; disposes of his coat in the same way; puts on the smoking jacket; and throws himself wearily into the easy-chair at the hearth.* PICKERING, *similarly attired, comes in. He also takes off his hat and overcoat, and is about to throw them on* HIGGINS's *when he hesitates.*

PICKERING. I say: Mrs. Pearce will row if we leave these things lying about in the drawing room.

HIGGINS. Oh, chuck them over the bannisters into the hall. She'll find them there in the morning and put them away all right. She'll think we were drunk.

PICKERING. We are, slightly. Are there any letters?

HIGGINS. I didnt look. (PICKERING *takes the overcoats and goes downstairs.* HIGGINS *begins half singing half yawning an air from* La Fanciulla del Golden West.[1] *Suddenly he stops and exclaims)* I wonder where the devil my slippers are!

ELIZA *looks at him darkly; then rises suddenly and leaves the room.*

HIGGINS *yawns again, and resumes his song.*

PICKERING *returns, with the contents of the letter-box in his hand.*

PICKERING. Only circulars, and this coroneted billet-doux[2] for you. (*He throws the circulars into the fender, and posts himself on the hearthrug, with his back to the grate.*)

HIGGINS *(glancing at the billet-doux)*. Money-lender. (*He throws the letter after the circulars.*) ELIZA *returns with a pair of large down-at-heel slippers. She places them on the carpet before* HIGGINS, *and sits as before without a word.*

HIGGINS *(yawning again)*. Oh Lord! What an evening! What a crew! What a silly tomfoolery! (*He raises his shoe to unlace it, and catches sight of the slippers. He stops unlacing and looks at them as if they had appeared there of their own accord.*) Oh! Theyre there, are they?

PICKERING *(stretching himself)*. Well, I feel a bit tired. It's been a long day. The garden party, a dinner party, and the opera! Rather too much of a good thing. But youve won your bet, Higgins. Eliza did the trick, and something to spare, eh?

HIGGINS *(fervently)*. Thank God it's over!

ELIZA *flinches violently; but they take no notice of her; and she recovers herself and sits stonily as before.*

PICKERING. Were you nervous at the garden party? *I* was. Eliza didnt seem a bit nervous.

HIGGINS. Oh, she wasnt nervous. I knew she'd be all right. No: it's the strain of putting the job through all these months that has told on me. It was interesting enough at first, while we were at the phonetics; but after that I got deadly sick of it. If I hadnt backed myself to do it I should have chucked the whole thing up two months ago. It was a silly notion: the whole thing has been a bore.

---

1. **La Fanciulla del Golden West,** *The Girl of the Golden West,* an opera by Puccini that opened in New York in 1910.
2. **coroneted billet-doux.** A billet-doux (bil′ā dü′) is a love letter. This one bears a coronet, or crown, indicating that it is from someone of noble birth; but Higgins's response seems to indicate that the writer is an upstart.

PICKERING. Oh come! the garden party was frightfully exciting. My heart began beating like anything.

HIGGINS. Yes, for the first three minutes. But when I saw we were going to win hands down, I felt like a bear in a cage, hanging about doing nothing. The dinner was worse: sitting gorging there for over an hour, with nobody but a damned fool of a fashionable woman to talk to! I tell you, Pickering, never again for me. No more artificial duchesses. The whole thing has been simple purgatory.

PICKERING. Youve never been broken in properly to the social routine. (*Strolling over to the piano*) I rather enjoy dipping into it occasionally myself: it makes me feel young again. Anyhow, it was a great success: an immense success. I was quite frightened once or twice because Eliza was doing it so well. You see, lots of the real people cant do it at all: theyre such fools that they think style comes by nature to people in their position; and so they never learn. Theres always something professional about doing a thing superlatively well.

HIGGINS. Yes: thats what drives me mad: the silly people dont know their own silly business. (*Rising*) However, it's over and done with; and now I can go to bed at last without dreading tomorrow.

ELIZA's *beauty becomes murderous.*

PICKERING. I think I shall turn in too. Still, it's been a great occasion: a triumph for you. Goodnight. (*He goes.*)

HIGGINS (*following him*). Goodnight. (*Over his shoulder, at the door*) Put out the lights, Eliza; and tell Mrs. Pearce not to make coffee for me in the morning: I'll take tea. (*He goes out.*)

ELIZA *tries to control herself and feel indifferent as she rises and walks across to the hearth to switch off the lights. By the time she gets there she is on the point of screaming. She sits down in* HIGGINS's *chair and holds on hard to the arms. Finally she gives way and flings herself furiously on the floor, raging.*

HIGGINS (*in despairing wrath outside*). What the devil have I done with my slippers? (*He appears at the door.*)

LIZA (*snatching up the slippers, and hurling them at him one after the other with all her force*). There are your slippers. And there. Take your slippers; and may you never have a day's luck with them!

HIGGINS (*astounded*). What on earth—! (*He comes to her.*) What's the matter? Get up. (*He pulls her up.*) Anything wrong?

LIZA (*breathless*). Nothing wrong—with you. Ive won your bet for you, havnt I? Thats enough for you. *I* dont matter, I suppose.

HIGGINS. You won my bet! You! Presumptuous insect! *I* won it. What did you throw those slippers at me for?

LIZA. Because I wanted to smash your face. I'd like to kill you, you selfish brute. Why didnt you leave me where you picked me out of—in the gutter? You thank God it's all over, and that now you can throw me back again there, do you? (*She crisps her fingers*[3] *frantically.*)

HIGGINS (*looking at her in cool wonder*). The creature is nervous, after all.

LIZA (*gives a suffocated scream of fury, and instinctively darts her nails at his face*)!!

HIGGINS (*catching her wrists*). Ah! would you? Claws in, you cat. How dare you show your temper to me? Sit down and be quiet. (*He throws her roughly into the easy-chair.*)

LIZA (*crushed by superior strength and weight*). Whats to become of me? Whats to become of me?

HIGGINS. How the devil do I know whats to become of you? What does it matter what becomes of you?

LIZA. You dont care. I know you dont care. You wouldnt care if I was dead. I'm nothing to you—not so much as them slippers.

HIGGINS (*thundering*). Those slippers.

LIZA (*with bitter submission*). Those slippers. I didnt think it made any difference now.

A *pause.* ELIZA *hopeless and crushed.* HIGGINS *a little uneasy.*

---

3. **crisps her fingers**, clenches and relaxes her fists.

HIGGINS (*in his loftiest manner*). Why have you begun going on like this? May I ask whether you complain of your treatment here?

LIZA. No.

HIGGINS. Has anybody behaved badly to you? Colonel Pickering? Mrs. Pearce? Any of the servants?

LIZA. No.

HIGGINS. I presume you dont pretend that *I* have treated you badly?

LIZA. No.

HIGGINS. I am glad to hear it. (*He moderates his tone.*) Perhaps youre tired after the strain of the day. Will you have a glass of champagne? (*He moves toward the door.*)

LIZA. No. (*Recollecting her manners*) Thank you.

HIGGINS (*good-humored again*). This has been coming on you for some days. I suppose it was natural for you to be anxious about the garden party. But thats all over now. (*He pats her kindly on the shoulder. She writhes.*) Theres nothing more to worry about.

LIZA. No. Nothing more for you to worry about. (*She suddenly rises and gets away from him by going to the piano bench, where she sits and hides her face.*) Oh God! I wish I was dead.

HIGGINS (*staring after in sincere surprise*). Why? In heaven's name, why? (*Reasonably, going to her*) Listen to me, Eliza. All this irritation is purely subjective.

LIZA. I dont understand. I'm too ignorant.

HIGGINS. It's only imagination. Low spirits and nothing else. Nobody's hurting you. Nothing's wrong. You go to bed like a good girl and sleep it off. Have a little cry and say your prayers: that will make you comfortable.

LIZA. I heard your prayers. "Thank God it's all over!"

HIGGINS (*impatiently*). Well, dont you thank God it's all over? Now you are free and can do what you like.

LIZA (*pulling herself together in desperation*). What am I fit for? What have you left me fit for? Where am I to go? What am I do to? Whats to become of me?

HIGGINS (*enlightened, but not at all impressed*). Oh thats whats worrying you, is it? (*He thrusts his hands into his pockets, and walks about in his usual manner, rattling the contents of his pockets, as if condescending to a trivial subject out of pure kindness.*) I shouldnt bother about it if I were you. I should imagine you wont have much difficulty in settling yourself somewhere or other, though I hadnt quite realized that you were going away. (*She looks quickly at him: he does not look at her, but examines the dessert stand on the piano and decides that he will eat an apple.*) You might marry, you know. (*He bites a large piece out of the apple and munches it noisily.*) You see, Eliza, all men are not confirmed old bachelors like me and the Colonel. Most men are the marrying sort (poor devils!); and youre not bad-looking: it's quite a pleasure to look at you sometimes—not now, of course, because youre crying and looking as ugly as the very devil; but when youre all right and quite yourself, youre what I should call attractive. That is, to the people in the marrying line, you understand. You go to bed and have a good nice rest; and then get up and look at yourself in the glass; and you wont feel so cheap.

ELIZA *again looks at him, speechless, and does not stir.*

The look is quite lost on him: he eats his apple with a dreamy expression of happiness, as it is quite a good one.

HIGGINS (*a genial afterthought occurring to him*). I daresay my mother could find some chap or other who would do very well.

LIZA. We were above that at the corner of Tottenham Court Road.

HIGGINS (*waking up*). What do you mean?

LIZA. I sold flowers. I didnt sell myself. Now youve made a lady of me I'm not fit to sell anything else. I wish youd left me where you found me.

HIGGINS (*slinging the core of the apple decisively into the grate*). Tosh, Eliza. Dont you insult human relations by dragging all this cant about buying and selling into it. You neednt marry the fellow if you dont like him.

LIZA. What else am I to do?

HIGGINS. Oh, lots of things. What about your old

idea of a florist's shop? Pickering could set you up in one: he's lots of money. (*Chuckling*) He'll have to pay for all those togs you have been wearing to-day; and that, with the hire of the jewellery, will make a big hole in two hundred pounds. Why, six months ago you would have thought it the millennium to have a flower shop of your own. Come! youll be all right. I must clear off to bed: I'm devilish sleepy. By the way, I came down for something: I forget what it was.

LIZA. Your slippers.

HIGGINS. Oh yes, of course. You shied them at me. (*He picks them up, and is going out when she rises and speaks to him.*)

LIZA. Before you go, sir—

HIGGINS (*dropping the slippers in his surprise at her calling him sir*). Eh?

LIZA. Do my clothes belong to me or to Colonel Pickering?

HIGGINS (*coming back into the room as if her question were the very climax of unreason*). What the devil use would they be to Pickering?

LIZA. He might want them for the next girl you pick up to experiment on.

HIGGINS (*shocked and hurt*). Is that the way you feel towards us?

LIZA. I dont want to hear anything more about that. All I want to know is whether anything belongs to me. My own clothes were burnt.

HIGGINS. But what does it matter? Why need you start bothering about that in the middle of the night?

LIZA. I want to know what I may take away with me. I dont want to be accused of stealing.

HIGGINS (*now deeply wounded*). Stealing! You shouldnt have said that, Eliza. That shews a want of feeling.

LIZA. I'm sorry. I'm only a common ignorant girl; and in my station I have to be careful. There cant be any feelings between the like of you and the like of me. Please will you tell me what belongs to me and what doesnt?

HIGGINS (*very sulky*). You may take the whole damned houseful if you like. Except the jewels. Theyre hired. Will that satisfy you? (*He turns on his heel and is about to go in extreme dudgeon.*)

LIZA (*drinking in his emotion like nectar, and nagging him to provoke a further supply*). Stop, please. (*She takes off her jewels.*) Will you take these to your room and keep them safe? I don't want to run the risk of their being missing.

HIGGINS (*furious*). Hand them over. (*She puts them into his hands.*) If these belonged to me instead of to the jeweller, I'd ram them down your ungrateful throat. (*He perfunctorily thrusts them into his pockets, unconsciously decorating himself with the protruding ends of the chains.*)

LIZA (*taking a ring off*). This ring isnt the jeweller's: it's the one you bought me in Brighton. I dont want it now. (HIGGINS *dashes the ring violently into the fireplace, and turns on her so threateningly that she crouches over the piano with her hands over her face, and exclaims*) Dont you hit me.

HIGGINS. Hit you! You infamous creature, how dare you accuse me of such a thing? It is you who have hit me. You have wounded me to the heart.

LIZA (*thrilling with hidden joy*). I'm glad. Ive got a little of my own back, anyhow.

HIGGINS (*with dignity, in his finest professional style*). You have caused me to lose my temper: a thing that has hardly ever happened to me before. I prefer to say nothing more tonight. I am going to bed.

LIZA (*pertly*). Youd better leave a note for Mrs. Pearce about the coffee; for she wont be told by me.

HIGGINS (*formally*). Damn Mrs. Pearce; and damn the coffee; and damn you; and damn my own folly in having lavished hard-earned knowledge and the treasure of my regard and intimacy on a heartless guttersnipe. (*He goes out with impressive decorum, and spoils it by slamming the door savagely.*)

ELIZA *goes down on her knees on the hearthrug to look for the ring.*

Understanding

1. Where have Higgins, Pickering, and Liza been? for what reason?

Analyzing

2. What do Higgins and Pickering congratulate themselves about?

3. Why is Liza upset? Who has predicted at least some of her concerns earlier?

4. The story of Cinderella ends with the Prince finding her because her foot fits a magic slipper. How has Shaw used this notion, but reversed it?

5. When Higgins suggests that his mother could find a husband for Liza, her response is, "We were above that at the corner of Tottenham Court Road." What does she mean?

6. Higgins claimed he could bridge the gap between social classes by teaching Liza to speak properly. Now, however, she insists that "in my station I have to be careful. There can't be any feeling between the like of you and the like of me." Why not? What is wrong?

7. How intense is the pain Higgins feels when he complains Liza has "wounded me to the heart"?

8. What is the **symbolic** force of the ring that Eliza first throws away, and then later tries to retrieve?

Extending

9. What separates people today? Is it still differences in speech, or are there other, more significant factors that divide us now?

HT Review PLOT in the Handbook of Literary Terms, page 916.

ACT FIVE

MRS. HIGGINS's *drawing room. She is at her writing-table as before.* THE PARLOR-MAID *comes in.*

THE PARLOR-MAID (*at the door*). Mr. Henry, maam, is downstairs with Colonel Pickering.

MRS. HIGGINS. Well, show them up.

THE PARLOR-MAID. Theyre using the telephone, maam. Telephoning to the police, I think.

MRS. HIGGINS. What!

THE PARLOR-MAID (*coming further in and lowering her voice*). Mr. Henry is in a state, maam. I thought I'd better tell you.

MRS. HIGGINS. If you had told me that Mr. Henry was not in a state it would have been more surprising. Tell them to come up when theyve finished with the police. I suppose he's lost something.

THE PARLOR-MAID. Yes, maam (*going*).

MRS. HIGGINS. Go upstairs and tell Miss Doolittle that Mr. Henry and the Colonel are here. Ask her not to come down til I send for her.

THE PARLOR-MAID. Yes, maam.

HIGGINS *bursts in. He is, as* THE PARLOR-MAID *has said, in a state.*

HIGGINS. Look here, mother: heres a confounded thing!

MRS. HIGGINS. Yes, dear. Good morning. (*He checks his impatience and kisses her, whilst* THE PARLOR-MAID *goes out.*) What is it?

HIGGINS. Eliza's bolted.

MRS. HIGGINS (*calmly continuing her writing*). You must have frightened her.

HIGGINS. Frightened her! nonsense! She was left last night, as usual, to turn out the lights and all that; and instead of going to bed she changed her clothes and went right off: her bed wasn't slept in. She came in a cab for her things before seven this morning; and that fool Mrs. Pearce let her have them without telling me a word about it. What am I to do?

MRS. HIGGINS. Do without, I'm afraid, Henry. The girl has a perfect right to leave if she chooses.

HIGGINS (*wandering distractedly across the room*). But I cant find anything. I dont know what appointments Ive got. I'm— (PICKERING *comes in.* MRS. HIGGINS *puts down her pen and turns away from the writing-table.*)

PICKERING (*shaking hands*). Good morning, Mrs. Higgins. Has Henry told you? (*He sits down on the ottoman.*)

HIGGINS. What does that ass of an inspector say? Have you offered a reward?

MRS. HIGGINS (*rising in indignant amazement*). You dont mean to say you have set the police after Eliza.

HIGGINS. Of course. What are the police for? What else could we do? (*He sits in the Elizabethan chair.*)

PICKERING. The inspector made a lot of difficulties. I really think he suspected us of some improper purpose.

MRS. HIGGINS. Well, of course he did. What right have you to go to the police and give the girl's name as if she were a thief, or a lost umbrella, or something? Really! (*She sits down again, deeply vexed.*)

HIGGINS. But we want to find her.

PICKERING. We cant let her go like this, you know, Mrs. Higgins. What were we to do?

MRS. HIGGINS. You have no more sense, either of you, than two children. Why—

THE PARLOR-MAID *comes in and breaks off the conversation.*

THE PARLOR-MAID. Mr. Henry: a gentleman wants to see you very particular. He's been sent on from Wimpole Street.

HIGGINS. Oh, bother! I cant see anyone now. Who is it?

THE PARLOR-MAID. A Mr. Doolittle, sir.

PICKERING. Doolittle! Do you mean the dustman?

THE PARLOR-MAID. Dustman! Oh no, sir: a gentleman.

HIGGINS (*springing up excitedly*). By George, Pick, it's some relative of hers that she's gone to. Somebody we know nothing about. (*To* THE PARLOR-MAID) Send him up, quick.

THE PARLOR-MAID. Yes, sir. (*She goes.*)

HIGGINS (*eagerly, going to his mother*). Genteel relatives! now we shall hear something. (*He sits down in the Chippendale chair.*)

MRS. HIGGINS. Do you know any of her people?

PICKERING. Only her father: the fellow we told you about.

THE PARLOR-MAID (*announcing*). Mr. Doolittle. (*She withdraws.*)

DOOLITTLE *enters. He is resplendently dressed as for a fashionable wedding, and might, in fact, be the bridegroom. A flower in his buttonhole, a dazzling silk hat, and patent leather shoes complete the effect. He is too concerned with the business he has come on to notice* MRS. HIGGINS. *He walks straight to* HIGGINS, *and accosts him with vehement reproach.*

DOOLITTLE (*indicating his own person*). See here! Do you see this? You done this.

HIGGINS. Done what, man?

DOOLITTLE. This, I tell you. Look at it. Look at this hat. Look at this coat.

PICKERING. Has Eliza been buying you clothes?

DOOLITTLE. Eliza! not she. Not half. Why would she buy me clothes?

MRS. HIGGINS. Good morning, Mr. Doolittle. Wont you sit down?

DOOLITTLE (*taken aback as he becomes conscious that he has forgotten his hostess*). Asking your pardon, maam. (*He approaches her and shakes her proffered hand.*) Thank you. (*He sits down on the ottoman, on* PICKERING'*s right.*) I am that full of what has happened to me that I cant think of anything else.

HIGGINS. What the dickens has happened to you?

DOOLITTLE. I shouldnt mind if it had only happened to me: anything might happen to anybody and nobody to blame but Providence, as you might say. But this is something that you done to me: yes, you, Enry Iggins.

HIGGINS. Have you found Eliza? Thats the point.

DOOLITTLE. Have you lost her?

HIGGINS. Yes.

DOOLITTLE. You have all the luck, you have. I aint found her; but she'll find me quick enough now after what you done to me.

MRS. HIGGINS. But what has my son done to you, Mr. Doolittle?

DOOLITTLE. Done to me! Ruined me. Destroyed my happiness. Tied me up and delivered me into the hands of middle-class morality.

HIGGINS (rising intolerantly and standing over DOOLITTLE). Youre raving. Youre drunk. Youre mad. I gave you five pounds. After that I had two conversations with you, at half-a-crown an hour. Ive never seen you since.

DOOLITTLE. Oh! Drunk! am I? Mad? am I? Tell me this. Did you or did you not write a letter to an old blighter in America that was giving five millions to found Moral Reform Societies all over the world, and that wanted you to invent a universal language for him?

HIGGINS. What! Ezra D. Wannafeller! He's dead. (He sits down again carelessly.)

DOOLITTLE. Yes: he's dead; and I'm done for. Now did you or did you not write a letter to him to say that the most original moralist at present in England, to the best of your knowledge, was Alfred Doolittle, a common dustman.

HIGGINS. Oh, after your last visit I remember making some silly joke of the kind.

DOOLITTLE. Ah! you may well call it a silly joke. It put the lid on me right enough. Just give him the chance he wanted to show that Americans is not like us: that they recognize and respect merit in every class of life, however humble. Them words is in his blooming will, in which, Henry Higgins, thanks to your silly joking, he leaves me a share in his Pre-digested Cheese Trust worth three thousand a year on condition that I lecture for his Wannafeller Moral Reform and World League as often as they ask me up to six times a year.

HIGGINS. The devil he does! Whew! (Brightening suddenly) What a lark!

PICKERING. A safe thing for you, Doolittle. They won't ask you twice.

DOOLITTLE. It aint the lecturing I mind. I'll lecture them blue in the face, I will, and not turn a hair. It's making a gentleman of me that I object to. Who asked him to make a gentleman of me? I was happy. I was free. I touched pretty nigh everybody for money when I wanted it, same as I touched you, Enry Iggins. Now I am worrited; tied neck and heels; and everybody touches me for money. It's a fine thing for you, says my solicitor. Is it? says I. You mean it's a good thing for you, I says. When I was a poor man and had a solicitor once when they found a pram in the dust cart, he got me off, and got shut of me and got me shut of him as quick as he could. Same with the doctors: used to shove me out of the hospital before I could hardly stand on my legs, and nothing to pay. Now they finds out that I'm not a healthy man and cant live unless they looks after me twice a day. In the house I'm not let do a hand's turn for myself: somebody else must do it and touch me for it. A year ago I hadnt a relative in the world except two or three that wouldnt speak to me. Now Ive fifty, and not a decent week's wages among the lot of them. I have to live for others and not for myself: thats middle-class morality. You talk of losing Eliza. Dont you be anxious: I bet she's on my doorstep by this: she that could support herself easy by selling flowers if I wasnt respectable. And the next one to touch me will be you, Enry Iggins. I'll have to learn to speak middle-class language from you, instead of speaking proper English. Thats where youll come in; and I daresay thats what you done it for.

MRS. HIGGINS. But, my dear Mr. Doolittle, you need not suffer all this if you are really in earnest. Nobody can force you to accept this bequest. You can repudiate it. Isnt that so, Colonel Pickering?

PICKERING. I believe so.

DOOLITTLE (*softening his manner in deference to her sex*). Thats the tragedy of it, maam. It's easy to say chuck it; but I havnt the nerve. Which of us has? We're all intimidated. Intimidated, maam: thats what we are. What is there for me if I chuck it but the workhouse in my old age? I have to dye my hair already to keep my job as a dustman. If I was one of the deserving poor, and had put by a bit, I could chuck it; but then why should I, acause the deserving poor might as well be millionaires for all the happiness they ever has. They dont know what happiness is. But I, as one of the undeserving poor, have nothing between me and the pauper's uniform but this here blasted three thousand a year that shoves me into the middle class. (Excuse the expression, maam: youd use it yourself if you had my provocation.) Theyve got you every way you turn: it's a choice between the Skilly of the workhouse and the Char Bydis of the middle class;[1] and I havnt the nerve for the workhouse. Intimidated: thats what I am. Broke. Brought up. Happier men than me will call for my dust, and touch me for their tip; and I'll look on helpless, and envy them. And thats what your son has brought me to. (*He is overcome by emotion.*)

MRS. HIGGINS. Well, I'm very glad youre not going to do anything foolish, Mr. Doolittle. For this solves the problem of Eliza's future. You can provide for her now.

DOOLITTLE (*with melancholy resignation*). Yes, maam: I'm expected to provide for everyone now, out of three thousand a year.

HIGGINS (*jumping up*). Nonsense! he cant provide for her. He shant provide for her. She doesnt belong to him. I paid him five pounds for her. Doolittle: either youre an honest man or a rogue.

DOOLITTLE (*tolerantly*). A little of both, Henry, like the rest of us: a little of both.

HIGGINS. Well, you took that money for the girl; and you have no right to take her as well.

MRS. HIGGINS. Henry: dont be absurd. If you want to know where Eliza is, she is upstairs.

HIGGINS (*amazed*). Upstairs!!! Then I shall jolly soon fetch her downstairs. (*He makes resolutely for the door.*)

MRS. HIGGINS (*rising and following him*). Be quiet, Henry. Sit down.

HIGGINS. I—

MRS. HIGGINS. Sit down, dear; and listen to me.

HIGGINS. Oh very well, very well, very well. (*He throws himself ungraciously on the ottoman, with his face towards the windows.*) But I think you might have told us this half an hour ago.

MRS. HIGGINS. Eliza came to me this morning. She told me of the brutal way you two treated her.

HIGGINS (*bounding up again*). What!

PICKERING (*rising also*). My dear Mrs. Higgins, she's been telling you stories. We didnt treat her brutally. We hardly said a word to her; and we parted on particularly good terms. (*Turning on* HIGGINS) Higgins: did you bully her after I went to bed?

HIGGINS. Just the other way about. She threw my slippers in my face. She behaved in the most outrageous way. I never gave her the slightest provocation. The slippers came bang into my face the moment I entered the room—before I had uttered a word. And used perfectly awful language.

PICKERING (*astonished*). But why? What did we do to her?

MRS. HIGGINS. I think I know pretty well what you did. The girl is naturally rather affectionate, I think. Isnt she, Mr. Doolittle?

DOOLITTLE. Very tender-hearted, maam. Takes after me.

MRS. HIGGINS. Just so. She had become attached to you both. She worked very hard for you, Henry! I dont think you quite realize what anything in the nature of brain work means to a girl like that. Well, it seems that when the great day of trial came, and she did this wonderful

---

1. *Skilly . . . Char Bydis of the middle class.* Doolittle is referring to Scylla (sil′ə) and Charybdis (kə rib′dis). In the narrow strait that separates Italy and Sicily there is a dangerous rock and a whirlpool, which the ancient Greeks named Scylla and Charybdis. The expression "to be between Scylla and Charybdis" means to be between two evils, either one of which can be safely avoided only by risking the other.

thing for you without making a single mistake, you two sat there and never said a word to her, but talked together of how glad you were that it was all over and how you had been bored with the whole thing. And then you were surprised because she threw your slippers at you! *I* should have thrown the fire-irons at you.

HIGGINS. We said nothing except that we were tired and wanted to go to bed. Did, we, Pick?

PICKERING (*shrugging his shoulders*). That was all.

MRS. HIGGINS (*ironically*). Quite sure?

PICKERING. Absolutely. Really, that was all.

MRS. HIGGINS. You didnt thank her, or pet her, or admire her, or tell her how splendid she'd been.

HIGGINS (*impatiently*). But she knew all about that. We didnt make speeches to her, if thats what you mean.

PICKERING (*conscience stricken*). Perhaps we were a little inconsiderate. Is she very angry?

MRS. HIGGINS (*returning to her place at the writing-table*). Well, I'm afraid she wont go back to Wimpole Street, especially now that Mr. Doolittle is able to keep up the position you have thrust on her; but she says she is quite willing to meet you on friendly terms and to let bygones be bygones.

HIGGINS (*furious*). Is she, by George? Ho!

MRS. HIGGINS. If you promise to behave yourself, Henry, I'll ask her to come down. If not, go home; for you have taken up quite enough of my time.

HIGGINS. Oh, all right. Very well. Pick: you behave yourself. Let us put on our best Sunday manners for this creature that we picked out of the mud. (*He flings himself sulkily into the Elizabethan chair.*)

DOOLITTLE (*remonstrating*). Now, now, Enry Iggins! have some consideration for my feelings as a middle-class man.

MRS. HIGGINS. Remember your promise, Henry. (*She presses the bell-button on the writing-table.*) Mr. Doolittle: will you be so good as to step out on the balcony for a moment. I dont want Eliza to have the shock of your news until she has made it up with these two gentlemen. Would

you mind?

DOOLITTLE. As you wish, lady. Anything to help Henry to keep her off my hands. (*He disappears through the window.*)

THE PARLOR-MAID *answers the bell.* PICKERING *sits down in* DOOLITTLE's *place.*

MRS. HIGGINS. Ask Miss Doolittle to come down, please.

THE PARLOR-MAID. Yes, maam. (*She goes out.*)

MRS. HIGGINS. Now, Henry: be good.

HIGGINS. I am behaving myself perfectly.

PICKERING. He is doing his best, Mrs. Higgins. *A pause.* HIGGINS *throws back his head; stretches out his legs; and begins to whistle.*

MRS. HIGGINS. Henry, dearest, you dont look at all nice in that attitude.

HIGGINS (*pulling himself together*). I was not trying to look nice, mother.

MRS. HIGGINS. It doesnt matter, dear. I only wanted to make you speak.

HIGGINS. Why?

MRS. HIGGINS. Because you cant speak and whistle at the same time.

HIGGINS *groans. Another very trying pause.*

HIGGINS (*springing up, out of patience*). Where the devil is that girl? Are we to wait here all day? ELIZA *enters, sunny, self-possessed, and giving a staggeringly convincing exhibition of ease of manner. She carries a little work-basket, and is very much at home.* PICKERING *is too much taken aback to rise.*

LIZA. How do you do, Professor Higgins? Are you quite well?

HIGGINS (*choking*). Am I—(*He can say no more.*)

LIZA. But of course you are: you are never ill. So glad to see you again, Colonel Pickering. (*He rises hastily; and they shake hands.*) Quite chilly this morning, isn't it? (*She sits down on his left. He sits beside her.*)

HIGGINS. Dont you dare try this game on me. I taught it to you; and it doesnt take me in. Get up and come home; and dont be a fool.

ELIZA *takes a piece of needlework from her basket, and begins to stitch at it, without taking the least notice of this outburst.*

MRS. HIGGINS. Very nicely put, indeed, Henry.

No woman could resist such an invitation.

HIGGINS. You let her alone, mother. Let her speak for herself. You will jolly soon see whether she has an idea that I havnt put into her head or a word that I havnt put into her mouth. I tell you I have created this thing out of the squashed cabbage leaves of Covent Garden; and now she pretends to play the fine lady with me.

MRS. HIGGINS (*placidly*). Yes, dear; but youll sit down, wont you?

HIGGINS *sits down again, savagely.*

LIZA (*to* PICKERING, *taking no apparent notice of* HIGGINS, *and working away deftly*). Will you drop me altogether now that the experiment is over, Colonel Pickering?

PICKERING. Oh dont. You musnt think of it as an experiment. It shocks me, somehow.

LIZA. Oh, I'm only a squashed cabbage leaf—

PICKERING (*impulsively*). No.

LIZA (*continuing quietly*).—but I owe so much to you that I should be very unhappy if you forgot me.

PICKERING. It's very kind of you to say so, Miss Doolittle.

LIZA. It's not because you paid for my dresses. I know you are generous to everybody with money. But it was from you that I learnt really nice manners; and that is what makes one a lady, isnt it? You see it was so difficult for me with the example of Professor Higgins always before me. I was brought up to be just like him, unable to control myself, and using bad language on the slightest provocation. And I should never have known that ladies and gentlemen didnt behave like that if you hadnt been there.

HIGGINS. Well!!

PICKERING. Oh, thats only his way, you know. He doesnt mean it.

LIZA. Oh, *I* didn't mean it either, when I was a flower girl. It was only my way. But you see I did it; and thats what makes the difference after all.

PICKERING. No doubt. Still, he taught you to speak; and I couldn't have done that, you know.

LIZA (*trivially*). Of course: that is his profession.

HIGGINS. Damnation!

LIZA (*continuing*). It was just like learning to dance in the fashionable way: there was nothing more than that in it. But do you know what began my real education?

PICKERING. What?

LIZA (*stopping her work for a moment*). Your calling me Miss Doolittle that day when I first came to Wimpole Street. That was the beginning of self-respect for me. (*She resumes her stitching.*) And there were a hundred little things you never noticed, because they came naturally to you. Things about standing up and taking off your hat and opening doors—

PICKERING. Oh, that was nothing.

LIZA. Yes: things that showed you thought and felt about me as if I were something better than a scullery-maid; though of course I know you would have been just the same to a scullery-maid if she had been let into the drawing room. You never took off your boots in the dining room when I was there.

PICKERING. You mustnt mind that. Higgins takes off his boots all over the place.

LIZA. I know. I am not blaming him. It is his way, isnt it? But it made such a difference to me that you didnt do it. You see, really and truly, apart from the things anyone can pick up (the dressing and the proper way of speaking, and so on), the difference between a lady and a flower girl is not how she behaves, but how she's treated. I shall always be a flower girl to Professor Higgins, because he always treats me as a flower girl, and always will; but I know I can be a lady to you, because you always treat me as a lady, and always will.

MRS. HIGGINS. Please dont grind your teeth, Henry.

PICKERING. Well, this is really very nice of you, Miss Doolittle.

LIZA. I should like you to call me Eliza, now, if you would.

PICKERING. Thank you, Eliza, of course.

LIZA. And I should like Professor Higgins to call me Miss Doolittle.

HIGGINS. I'll see you damned first.

MRS. HIGGINS. Henry! Henry!

PICKERING (*laughing*). Why dont you slang back at him? Dont stand it. It would do him a lot of good.

LIZA. I cant. I could have done it once; but now I cant go back to it. You told me, you know, that when a child is brought to a foreign country, it picks up the language in a few weeks, and forgets its own. Well, I am a child in your country. I have forgotten my own language, and can speak nothing but yours. Thats the real breakoff with the corner of Tottenham Court Road. Leaving Wimpole Street finishes it.

PICKERING (*much alarmed*). Oh! but youre coming back to Wimpole Street, arnt you? Youll forgive Higgins?

HIGGINS (*rising*). Forgive! Will she, by George! Let her go. Let her find out how she can get on without us. She will relapse into the gutter in three weeks without me at her elbow.

DOOLITTLE *appears at the center window. With*

a look of dignified reproach at HIGGINS, *he comes slowly and silently to his daughter, who, with her back to the window, is unconscious of his approach.*

PICKERING. He's incorrigible, Eliza. You wont relapse, will you?

LIZA. No: not now. Never again. I have learnt my lesson. I dont believe I could utter one of the old sounds if I tried. (DOOLITTLE *touches her on her left shoulder. She drops her work, losing her self-possession utterly at the spectacle of her father's splendor.*) A-a-a-a-a-ah-ow-ooh!

HIGGINS (*with a crow of triumph*). Aha! Just so. A-a-a-a-ahowooh! A-a-a-a-ahowooh! A-a-a-a-ahowooh! Victory! Victory! (*He throws himself on the divan, folding his arms, and spraddling arrogantly.*)

DOOLITTLE. Can you blame the girl? Dont look at me like that, Eliza. It aint my fault. Ive come into some money.

LIZA. You must have touched a millionaire this time, dad.

DOOLITTLE. I have. But I'm dressed something special today. I'm going to St. George's, Hanover Square.[2] Your stepmother is going to marry me.

LIZA (*angrily*). Youre going to let yourself down to marry that low common woman!

PICKERING (*quietly*). He ought to, Eliza. (*To* DOOLITTLE) Why has she changed her mind?

DOOLITTLE (*sadly*). Intimidated, Governor. Intimidated. Middle-class morality claims its victim. Wont you put on your hat, Liza, and come and see me turned off?

LIZA. If the Colonel says I must, I—I'll (*almost sobbing*) I'll demean myself. And get insulted for my pains, like enough.

DOOLITTLE. Dont be afraid: she never comes to words with anyone now, poor woman! respectability has broke all the spirit out of her.

PICKERING (*squeezing* ELIZA's *elbow gently*). Be kind to them, Eliza. Make the best of it.

LIZA (*forcing a little smile for him through her vexation*). Oh well, just to shew theres no ill feeling. I'll be back in a moment. (*She goes out.*)

DOOLITTLE (*sitting down beside* PICKERING). I feel uncommon nervous about the ceremony,

Colonel. I wish youd come and see me through it.

PICKERING. But youve been through it before, man. You were married to Eliza's mother.

DOOLITTLE. Who told you that, Colonel?

PICKERING. Well, nobody told me. But I concluded—naturally—

DOOLITTLE. No: that aint the natural way, Colonel: it's only the middle-class way. My way was always the undeserving way. But dont say nothing to Eliza. She dont know: I always had a delicacy about telling her.

PICKERING. Quite right. We'll leave it so, if you dont mind.

DOOLITTLE. And youll come to the church, Colonel, and put me through straight?

PICKERING. With pleasure. As far as a bachelor can.

MRS. HIGGINS. May I come, Mr. Doolittle? I should be very sorry to miss your wedding.

DOOLITTLE. I should indeed be honored by your condescension, maam; and my poor old woman would take it as a tremenjous compliment. She's been very low, thinking of the happy days that are no more.

MRS. HIGGINS (*rising*). I'll order the carriage and get ready. (*The men rise, except* HIGGINS.) I shant be more than fifteen minutes. (*As she goes to the door* ELIZA *comes in, hatted and buttoning her gloves.*) I'm going to the church to see your father married, Eliza. You had better come in the brougham[3] with me. Colonel Pickering can go on with the bridegroom.

MRS. HIGGINS *goes out.* ELIZA *comes to the middle of the room between the center window and the ottoman.* PICKERING *joins her.*

DOOLITTLE. Bridegroom! What a word! It makes a man realize his position, somehow. (*He takes up his hat and goes towards the door.*)

PICKERING. Before I go, Eliza, do forgive him and come back to us.

---

2. St. George's, Hanover Square, a church where many fashionable weddings took place.
3. brougham (brüm, brō′ǝm), a closed carriage or automobile, having an outside seat for the driver.

LIZA. I dont think papa would allow me. Would you, dad?

DOOLITTLE (*sad but magnanimous*). They played you off very cunning, Eliza, them two sportsmen. If it had been only one of them, you could have nailed him. But you see, there was two; and one of them chaperoned the other, as you might say. (*To* PICKERING) It was artful of you, Colonel; but I bear no malice: I should have done the same myself. I been the victim of one woman after another all my life; and I dont grudge you two getting the better of Eliza. I shant interfere. It's time for us to go, Colonel. So long, Henry. See you in St. George's, Eliza. (*He goes out.*)

PICKERING (*coaxing*). Do stay with us, Eliza. (*He follows* DOOLITTLE.)

ELIZA *goes out on the balcony to avoid being alone with* HIGGINS. *He rises and joins her there. She immediately comes back into the room and makes for the door; but he goes along the balcony quickly and gets his back to the door before she reaches it.*

HIGGINS. Well, Eliza, youve had a bit of your own back, as you call it. Have you had enough? and are you going to be reasonable? Or do you want any more?

LIZA. You want me back only to pick up your slippers and put up with your tempers and fetch and carry for you.

HIGGINS. I havnt said I wanted you back at all.

LIZA. Oh, indeed. Then what are we talking about?

HIGGINS. About you, not about me. If you come back I shall treat you just as I have always treated you. I cant change my nature; and I dont intend to change my manners. My manners are exactly the same as Colonel Pickering's.

LIZA. Thats not true. He treats a flower girl as if she was a duchess.

HIGGINS. And I treat a duchess as if she was a flower girl.

LIZA. I see. (*She turns away composedly, and sits on the ottoman, facing the window.*) The same to everybody.

HIGGINS. Just so.

LIZA. Like father.

HIGGINS (*grinning, a little taken down*). Without accepting the comparison at all points, Eliza, it's quite true that your father is not a snob, and that he will be quite at home in any station of life to which his eccentric destiny may call him. (*Seriously*) The great secret, Eliza, is not having bad manners or good manners or any other particular sort of manners, but having the same manner for all human souls: in short, behaving as if you were in Heaven, where there are no third-class carriages, and one soul is as good as another.

LIZA. Amen. You are a born preacher.

HIGGINS (*irritated*). The question is not whether I treat you rudely, but whether you ever heard me treat anyone else better.

LIZA (*with sudden sincerity*). I dont care how you treat me. I don't mind your swearing at me. I don't mind a black eye: Ive had one before this. But (*standing up and facing him*) I wont be passed over.

HIGGINS. Then get out of my way; for I wont stop for you. You talk about me as if I were a motor bus.

LIZA. So you are a motor bus: all bounce and go, and no consideration for anyone. But I can do without you: dont think I cant.

HIGGINS. I know you can. I told you you could.

LIZA (*wounded, getting away from him to the other side of the ottoman with her face to the hearth*). I know you did, you brute. You wanted to get rid of me.

HIGGINS. Liar.

LIZA. Thank you. (*She sits down with dignity.*)

HIGGINS. You never asked yourself, I suppose, whether *I* could do without you.

LIZA (*earnestly*). Dont you try to get round me. Youll have to do without me.

HIGGINS (*arrogant*). I can do without anybody. I have my own soul: my own spark of divine fire. But (*with sudden humility*) I shall miss you, Eliza. (*He sits down near her on the ottoman.*) I have learnt something from your idiotic notions: I confess that humbly and gratefully. And I have grown accustomed to your voice and appearance. I like them, rather.

LIZA. Well, you have both of them on your gramophone and in your book of photographs. When you feel lonely without me, you can turn the machine on. It's got no feelings to hurt.

HIGGINS. I cant turn your soul on. Leave me those feelings; and you can take away the voice and the face. They are not you.

LIZA. Oh, you are a devil. You can twist the heart in a girl as easy as some could twist her arms to hurt her. Mrs. Pearce warned me. Time and again she has wanted to leave you; and you always got round her at the last minute. And you dont care a bit for her. And you dont care a bit for me.

HIGGINS. I care for life, for humanity; and you are a part of it that has come my way and been built into my house. What more can you or anyone ask?

LIZA. I wont care for anybody that doesnt care for me.

HIGGINS. Commercial principles, Eliza. Like (reproducing her Covent Garden pronunciation with professional exactness) s'yollin voylets (selling violets), isn't it?

LIZA. Dont sneer at me. It's mean to sneer at me.

HIGGINS. I have never sneered in my life. Sneering doesnt become either the human face or the human soul. I am expressing my righteous contempt for Commercialism. I dont and wont trade in affection. You call me a brute because you couldnt buy a claim on me by fetching my slippers and finding my spectacles. You were a fool: I think a woman fetching a man's slippers is a disgusting sight: did I ever fetch your slippers? I think a good deal more of you for throwing them in my face. No use slaving for me and then saying you want to be cared for: who cares for a slave? If you come back, come back for the sake of good fellowship; for youll get nothing else. Youve had a thousand times as much out of me as I have out of you; and if you dare to set up your little dog's tricks of fetching and carrying slippers against my creation of a Duchess Eliza, I'll slam the door in your silly face.

LIZA. What did you do it for if you didnt care for me?

HIGGINS (heartily). Why, because it was my job.

LIZA. You never thought of the trouble it would make for me.

HIGGINS. Would the world ever have been made if its maker had been afraid of making trouble? Making life means making trouble. Theres only one way of escaping trouble; and thats killing things. Cowards, you notice, are always shrieking to have troublesome people killed.

LIZA. I'm no preacher: I dont notice things like that. I notice that you dont notice me.

HIGGINS (jumping up and walking about intolerantly). Eliza: youre an idiot. I waste the treasures of my Miltonic mind by spreading them before you. Once for all, understand that I go my way and do my work without caring two-pence what happens to either of us. I am not intimidated, like your father and your stepmother. So you can come back or go to the devil: which you please.

LIZA. What am I to come back for?

HIGGINS (bouncing up on his knees on the ottoman and leaning over it to her). For the fun of it. Thats why I took you on.

LIZA (with averted face). And you may throw me out to-morrow if I dont do everything you want me to?

HIGGINS. Yes; and you may walk out tomorow if I dont do everything you want me to.

LIZA. And live with my stepmother?

HIGGINS. Yes, or sell flowers.

LIZA. Oh! if I only could go back to my flower basket! I should be independent of both you and father and all the world! Why did you take my independence from me? Why did I give it up? I'm a slave now, for all my fine clothes.

HIGGINS. Not a bit. I'll adopt you as my daughter and settle money on you if you like. Or would you rather marry Pickering?

LIZA (looking fiercely round at him). I wouldnt marry you if you asked me; and youre nearer my age than what he is.

HIGGINS (gently). Than he is: not "than what he is."

LIZA (losing her temper and rising). I'll talk as I like.

Youre not my teacher now.

HIGGINS (reflectively). I dont suppose Pickering would, though. He's as confirmed an old bachelor as I am.

LIZA. Thats not what I want; and dont you think it. Ive always had chaps enough wanting me that way. Freddy Hill writes to me twice and three times a day, sheets and sheets.

HIGGINS (disagreeably surprised). Damn his impudence! (He recoils and finds himself sitting on his heels.)

LIZA. He has a right to if he likes, poor lad. And he does love me.

HIGGINS (getting off the ottoman). You have no right to encourage him.

LIZA. Every girl has a right to be loved.

HIGGINS. What! By fools like that?

LIZA. Freddy's not a fool. And if he's weak and poor and wants me, maybe he'd make me happier than my betters that bully me and dont want me.

HIGGINS. Can he make anything of you? Thats the point.

LIZA. Perhaps I could make something of him. But I never thought of us making anything of one another; and you never think of anything else. I only want to be natural.

HIGGINS. In short, you want me to be as infatuated about you as Freddy? Is that it?

LIZA. No I dont. Thats not the sort of feeling I want from you. And dont you be too sure of yourself or of me. I could have been a bad girl if I'd liked. Ive seen more of some things than you, for all your learning. Girls like me can drag gentlemen down to make love to them easy enough. And they wish each other dead the next minute.

HIGGINS. Of course they do. Then what in thunder are we quarrelling about?

LIZA (much troubled). I want a little kindness. I know I'm a common ignorant girl, and you a book-learned gentleman; but I'm not dirt under your feet. What I done (correcting herself) what I did was not for the dresses and the taxis: I did it because we were pleasant together and I come—came—to care for you; not to want you to make love to me, and not forgetting the difference between us, but more friendly like.

HIGGINS. Well, of course. Thats just how I feel. And how Pickering feels. Eliza: youre a fool.

LIZA. Thats not a proper answer to give me. (She sinks on the chair at the writing-table in tears.)

HIGGINS. It's all youll get until you stop being a common idiot. If youre going to be a lady, youll have to give up feeling neglected if the men you know dont spend half their time snivelling over you and the other half giving you black eyes. If you cant stand the coldness of my sort of life, and the strain of it, go back to the gutter. Work til you are more a brute than a human being; and then cuddle and squabble and drink til you fall asleep. Oh, it's a fine life, the life of the gutter. It's real: it's warm: it's violent: you can feel it through the thickest skin: you can taste it and smell it without any training or any work. Not like Science and Literature and Classical Music and Philosophy and Art. You find me cold, unfeeling, selfish, dont you? Very well: be off with you to the sort of people you like. Marry some sentimental hog or other with lots of money, and a thick pair of lips to kiss you with and a thick pair of boots to kick you with. If you cant appreciate what youve got, youd better get what you can appreciate.

LIZA (desperate). Oh, you are a cruel tyrant. I cant talk to you: you turn everything against me: I'm always in the wrong. But you know very well all the time that youre nothing but a bully. You know I cant go back to the gutter, as you call it, and that I have no real friends in the world but you and the Colonel. You know well I couldnt bear to live with a low common man after you two; and it's wicked and cruel of you to insult me by pretending I could. You think I must go back to Wimpole Street because I have nowhere else to go but father's. But dont you be too sure that you have me under your feet to be trampled on and talked down. I'll marry Freddy, I will, as soon as he's able to support me.

HIGGINS (sitting down beside her). Rubbish! you shall marry an ambassador. You shall marry the Governor-General of India or the Lord-Lieutenant of Ireland, or somebody who wants

a deputy-queen. I'm not going to have my masterpiece thrown away on Freddy.

LIZA. You think I like you to say that. But I havent forgot what you said a minute ago; and I wont be coaxed round as if I was a baby or a puppy. If I cant have kindness, I'll have independence.

HIGGINS. Independence? That's middle-class blasphemy. We are all dependent on one another, every soul of us on earth.

LIZA (*rising determinedly*). I'll let you see whether I'm dependent on you. If you can preach, I can teach. I'll go and be a teacher.

HIGGINS. Whatll you teach, in heaven's name?

LIZA. What you taught me. I'll teach phonetics.

HIGGINS. Ha! ha! ha!

LIZA. I'll offer myself as an assistant to Professor Nepean.

HIGGINS (*rising in a fury*). What! That imposter! that humbug! that toadying ignoramus! Teach him my methods! my discoveries! You take one step in his direction and I'll wring your neck.

(*He lays hands on her.*) Do you hear?

LIZA (*defiantly non-resistant*). Wring away. What do I care? I knew youd strike me some day. (*He lets her go, stamping with rage at having forgotten himself, and recoils so hastily that he stumbles back into his seat on the ottoman.*) Aha! Now I know how to deal with you. What a fool I was not to think of it before! You cant take away the knowledge you gave me. You said I had a finer ear than you. And I can be civil and kind to people, which is more than you can. Aha! (*Purposely dropping her aitches to annoy him*) Thats done you, Enry Iggins, it has. Now I dont care that (*snapping her fingers*) for your bullying and your big talk. I'll advertize it in the papers that your duchess is only a flower girl that you taught, and that she'll teach anybody to be a duchess just the same in six months for a thousand guineas. Oh, when I think of myself crawling under your feet and being trampled on and called names, when all the time I had only to lift up my finger to be as good as you, I could just kick myself.

HIGGINS (*wondering at her*). You damned impudent slut, you! But it's better than snivelling; better than fetching slippers and finding spectacles, isnt it? (*Rising*) By George, Eliza, I said I'd make a woman of you; and I have. I like you like this.

LIZA. Yes: you turn round and make up to me now that I'm not afraid of you, and can do without you.

HIGGINS. Of course I do, you little fool. Five minutes ago you were like a millstone round my neck. Now youre a tower of strength: a consort battleship. You and I and Pickering will be three old bachelors together instead of only two men and a silly girl.

MRS. HIGGINS *returns, dressed for the wedding.* ELIZA *instantly becomes cool and elegant.*

MRS. HIGGINS. The carriage is waiting, Eliza. Are you ready?

LIZA. Quite. Is the Professor coming?

MRS. HIGGINS. Certainly not. He cant behave himself in church. He makes remarks out loud all the time on the clergyman's pronunciation.

LIZA. Then I shall not see you again, Professor. Goodbye. (*She goes to the door.*)

MRS. HIGGINS (*coming to* HIGGINS). Goodbye, dear.

HIGGINS. Goodbye, mother. (*He is about to kiss her, when he recollects something.*) Oh, by the way, Eliza, order a ham and a Stilton cheese, will you? And buy me a pair of reindeer gloves, number eights, and a tie to match that new suit of mine. You can choose the color. (*His cheerful, careless, vigorous voice shows that he is incorrigible.*)

LIZA (*disdainfully*). Number eights are too small for you if you want them lined with lamb's wool. You have three new ties that you have forgotten in the drawer of your washstand. Colonel Pickering prefers double Gloucester to Stilton; and you dont notice the difference. I telephoned Mrs. Pearce this morning not to forget the ham. What you are to do without me I cannot imagine. (*She sweeps out.*)

MRS. HIGGINS. I'm afraid youve spoilt that girl, Henry. I should be uneasy about you and her if she were less fond of Colonel Pickering.

HIGGINS. Pickering! Nonsense; she's going to marry Freddy. Ha! ha! Freddy! Freddy!! Ha ha ha ha ha!!!!! (*He roars with laughter as the play ends.*)

Comment

Shaw and Smollett

The legend of the sculptor who falls in love with his own statue has been used in one form or other for centuries; Plautus, Chaucer, Voltaire, W. S. Gilbert all wrote [works] on the theme, but when *Pygmalion* was produced in Berlin, a German critic immediately recognized the plot as having been drawn from an incident in Smollett's novel, *Peregrine Pickle* (1751). When Shaw was questioned about this, he irritably admitted having read the work in his Dublin boyhood but not since. His memory was evidently a good one for the plot [of *Pygmalion*] follows Smollett's little romance very

closely. In Chapter 87, Peregrine meets a sixteen-year-old beggar-girl in the road. She wears rags, her face is dirty, and she talks the language of Billingsgate [the London fish market whose porters and vendors were notorious for their foul speech], but she has agreeable features. He buys her for a small sum from her mother, takes her home, gets his valet to give her a good scrubbing and rinsing, cuts her hair, and gives her some attractive clothes to wear. He then proceeds to cure her of swearing, a most difficult task, and in a few weeks is able to present her at the table of a country squire, where she says very little but behaves well enough to provoke no comment. She goes to London and lives in private lodgings with a female attendant; she is instructed in dancing and French and attends plays and concerts several times a week. One evening while at cards, she detects a certain lady in the act of cheating; she swears violently and soundly cuffs her to the astonishment of all present.

Richard Hugget, *The Truth About Pygmalion*. New York: Random House, 1969, pages 20–21.

THINK AND DISCUSS
ACT FIVE
Understanding

1. Where does Liza go when she leaves the Wimpole street house?
2. Why was Doolittle given a small fortune?

Analyzing

3. What does "middle-class morality" mean in Doolittle's new life?
4. If many comic plots end with a wedding, how has Shaw both followed the tradition and turned its meaning upside down?
5. Compare Liza's entrance in Act Five to her appearance after a bath in Act Two and her introduction to Mrs. Higgins's "at-home." If the first two define moments of progress in Liza's transformation, what new level of development does she reach here?
6. Define what Higgins and Liza struggle over in the final "discussion."
7. Just what is it Higgins offers when he asks Liza to "come back for the sake of good fellowship. . ."?
8. Why does he like her best when she threatens to betray his secrets to a professional rival?
9. What is the meaning in Higgins's final laugh?
10. Is there anything within the play that serves as convincing evidence about what Liza will do next?

Extending

11. Evaluate the contrast Higgins makes between "the coldness of my life" and marriage to "some sentimental hog. . ."
12. In what ways does Liza become one of the "new women" at the start of the twentieth century?

REVIEWING: Plot HヱＴ
See Handbook of Literary Terms, p. 916

The plot of a play is the interconnected series of events that create a story. A plot usually revolves around a **conflict** between people.

1. What is the central conflict in *Pygmalion?*
2. In what way is that conflict partially resolved at the end of Act Three, and again only partially resolved at the end of Act Five?
3. How does the secondary plot involving Alfred Doolittle serve as a comic parallel to the main plot involving Liza?

READING LITERATURE SKILLFULLY
Main Idea and Details

You can further your understanding, analyzing, and evaluating of a piece of literature by looking for the main idea the author is presenting. (Not every piece of literature has a main idea; in lyric poetry and in much fiction such ideas may be difficult to pin down.) In a comedy of ideas, such as *Pygmalion*, you can expect not just one, but several, ideas to be presented and perhaps debated by the characters.

In such works, the details that support the ideas will be found not only in the speeches of the characters, but in their actions and even in developments of plot.

1. How is Higgins's original contention that improving Liza's speech would improve her condition borne out?
2. What details support Liza's claim that "the difference between a lady and a flower girl is not how she behaves, but how she's treated"? (See page 686.)
3. How is Higgins's "righteous contempt for Commercialism" (page 690) proved or disproved by events of the play and by his own actions?
4. What main idea do you suppose Shaw wanted his audiences to carry home from *Pygmalion?*

VOCABULARY
Roots
Look up the listed words in the Glossary. Then answer the following questions about the structure of the words.

deprecate   magnanimous
incense   perfunctory
infatuate

1. Which word has a root that describes an act that is often performed in church?
2. Which has a root that describes how a light might burn?
3. Which is formed from two roots that mean something large but invisible?
4. Which has a root that can mean something done to criminals?
5. Which has a root with a meaning that might describe a dunce?

COMPOSITION
Explaining What the Characters Want
Henry Higgins says he wants Liza Doolittle to come "home," but she resists. During this verbal struggle, both characters reveal certain assumptions about relationships between men and women, and what each one wants from the other. Write a three paragraph essay in which you explain to your fellow students the feelings and needs that lie behind what each of them says. First summarize their positions; then evaluate their claims. Are they telling the truth? Is what they want really the best for each of them? In a concluding paragraph, explain which one of them seems more sensible to you.

Analyzing Dramatic Ironies
Shaw likes to surprise his audience by refusing to fulfill their expectations. Write an essay analyzing how he uses this dramatic irony to suggest new ideas. First consider the reasons why *Pygmalion* contains the following surprises: (1) the audience looks forward to seeing Liza trying to pass at a large party, but Shaw doesn't let us see the test; (2) Higgins and Pickering do not praise Liza for her success and express boredom with the entire project; (3) Higgins succeeds in creating not a "lady," but a strong-minded and independent woman who walks out on him. In your essay, analyze the meaning inherent in these dramatic reversals. See "Writing About Irony and Satire" in the Writer's Handbook.

ENRICHMENT
Comparing *Pygmalion* and *My Fair Lady*
In 1956 a drastically rewritten musical version of Shaw's play, titled *My Fair Lady* premiered on Broadway, enjoying immense popularity. Later it appeared as a Hollywood movie. Obtain copies of the text for *My Fair Lady* and form two research teams. Have the first read through Act One, Scene 7, comparing it with Shaw's Act Three. The second team should compare Act Two, Scenes 6 and 7 with the end of Shaw's Act Five. Look for the ways in which the Broadway version altered Shaw. Then prepare explanations, to be given to the class as a whole, on the effects derived from the alterations and additions.

Social Class

Thinking about society in terms of class groups is a tradition in English literature from the earliest days. It is important to keep in mind that most literary works are written for a privileged class and express how that class looks at the social order.

The *Beowulf* poet praises what he sees as the social interdependence of the Germanic tribe. Wiglaf reminds Beowulf's men, ". . .as we drank in the mead hall . . .we swore to our lord who bestowed these rings/That we would repay. . .if need like this/Should ever befall him." In this social order survival itself depends upon the cooperation of master and men.

Chaucer's *Tales* begin with a vision of the Christian community, a collection of people who travel together because their social and economic differences are, for the moment, bridged by a common religious goal. Along with the aristocratic and the powerful, Chaucer includes the Knight's Yeoman, craftsmen like the Carpenter, a Cook, and even a poor Plowman, who becomes, in Chaucer's hands, a kind of ideal person: "He was an honest worker, good and true,/Living in peace and perfect charity,/Loving God best with all his heart and mind/And then his neighbor as himself. . ."

Shakespearean drama takes a more aristocratic view of the British social order. Working people like the grave diggers in *Hamlet* and the gatekeeper in *Macbeth* are usually comic, indulging in boisterous punning and excessive drinking. Shakespeare does depict devoted servants, like Juliet's nurse, but he has an instinctive distrust for poor people when they act together, as in the unruly mobs of *Julius Caesar*.

Eighteenth-century writers sometimes depicted class differences with a sympathetic but sentimental eye. Thomas Gray's "Elegy in a Country Churchyard" celebrates the simple lives of the poor, but depicts a social gap that makes the feelings of a poet seem inaccessible to an ordinary worker.

It is the Romantic writers who initiate a revolution in English literature by praising and even exalting poor and working class people for virtues and insights springing from their own way of life. Burns, himself a ploughman, writes songs delighting in everyday country life. Coleridge takes as the visionary protagonist of his "Rime" a common sailor. Shelley, a more overtly radical writer politically, indignantly pictures a poverty-stricken "people starved and stabbed in the untilled field" ("England in 1819").

Industrialism sharpened the sense of division between social groups, and during the nineteenth century a specific language of class division clearly emerges, with people grouped into the "upper" or aristocratic, "middle" or mercantile, and "lower" or working classes. Within these divisions there were innumerable subdivisions, but individuals might move from one to the other thanks to education, money, and so on. Class and class movement became a central subject of the Victorian novel, as in Eliot's *The Mill on the Floss*, depicting the forces that keep a lower middle-class miller and his children in their "proper place." Fearful of an outbreak of class warfare, some novelists described the lives of poor workers and urged government and private charity to alleviate their suffering.

Twentieth-century writers became more immediately committed to social change and to depicting conflicts between classes. Shaw, an avowed revolutionary, uses the comedy of Mr. Doolittle to champion a culture that most playgoers would instinctively have condemned. D. H. Lawrence vividly illustrates economic and sexual oppression, and the class hatred which results, in the story "Tickets Please," in which exploited workers finally and triumphantly attack their master, a scene inconceivable in English literature before this time.

While a number of celebrated writers at the beginning of this century lived unusual and romantic lives, Conrad's is the most exotic, the most surprising. He was born Józef Teodor Konrad Korzeniowski. His father and mother were aristocrats of a Polish nation ruled by Russia. His father was an idealistic patriot and a writer. When Conrad was four years old, the police jailed his father for subversive political activities and in May of 1862 exiled the family to a bleak town in northern Russia near the Ural Mountains. There the harsh climate permanently damaged his parents' already weakened health. In 1863 the family moved to a milder climate in a town 125 miles from Kiev, where the five-year-old Joseph learned to read French and Polish from "a good, ugly governess."

Though finally permitted to return home, the family had already suffered irremediable harm. Conrad's mother died in 1865 when he was seven, and his father died four years later.

Conrad's uncle took responsibility for this melancholy but intelligent eleven-year-old boy, who was already reading Cervantes and Dickens. Romantic adventure novels gave him the desire to escape to the sea, and for several years his uncle unsuccessfully tried to dissuade him. Finally, he gave in, and Conrad, now seventeen, joined the French merchant marine at Marseilles, feeling "like a man in a dream."

He served as apprentice and then steward on ships sailing for the West Indies and the coast of South America. Accompanying a fellow sailor, Conrad even smuggled guns to guerrilla bands in Spain in 1876. This reckless adolescence reached a climax when Conrad lost 800 francs gambling and tried to commit suicide. His uncle arrived and paid his debts, and Conrad entered into a more stable young manhood, joining the British merchant navy in June of 1878. During the next sixteen years he worked his way up to the rank of ship's captain, became a naturalized British subject, and saw the world—Australia, Singapore, Java, Siam (now Thailand), Malaysia, and Sumatra. In 1890 he made a trip—later immortalized in his novella *Heart of Darkness*—up the Congo River to Stanley Falls.

Jungle fever, contracted during this adventure, permanently weakened Conrad's health. And at the same time, a very different interest was taking him over. In 1889 he had begun writing a novel. By 1894 it was complete, and when a publisher accepted it, Conrad shifted his energies to literature.

In the next 29 years he wrote 31 volumes of fiction and reminiscence. Many of his stories and novels derive from the adventures of his young manhood, events now examined with the retrospective eye of an older, more thoughtful man. These novels of the sea, such as *Lord Jim* (1900), as well as later studies of politics such as *Nostromo* (1904), *The Secret Agent* (1907), and *Under Western Eyes* (1911), established Conrad as one of the most important English novelists of the first half of the century.

The Secret Sharer

Joseph Conrad

1

On my right hand there were lines of fishing stakes resembling a mysterious system of half-submerged bamboo fences, incomprehensible in its division of the domain of tropical fishes, and crazy of aspect as if abandoned forever by some nomad tribe of fishermen now gone to the other end of the ocean; for there was no sign of human habitation as far as the eye could reach. To the left a group of barren islets, suggesting ruins of stone walls, towers, and blockhouses, had its foundations set in a blue sea that itself looked solid, so still and stable did it lie below my feet; even the track of light from the westering sun shone smoothly, without that animated glitter which tells of an imperceptible ripple. And when I turned my head to take a parting glance at the tug which had just left us anchored outside the bar, I saw the straight line of the flat shore joined to the stable sea, edge to edge, with a perfect and unmarked closeness, in one leveled floor half-brown, half-blue under the enormous dome of the sky. Corresponding in their insignificance to the islets of the sea, two small clumps of trees, one on each side of the only fault in the impeccable joint, marked the mouth of the river Meinam[1] we had just left on the first preparatory stage of our homeward journey; and, far back on the inland level, a larger and loftier mass, the grove surrounding the great Paknam pagoda, was the only thing on which the eye could rest from the vain task of exploring the monotonous sweep of the horizon. Here and there gleams as of a few scattered pieces of silver marked the windings of the great river; and on the nearest of them, just within the bar, the tug steaming right into the land became lost to my sight, hull and funnel and masts, as though the impassive earth had swallowed her up without an effort, without a tremor. My eye followed the light cloud of her smoke, now here, now there, above the plain, according to the devious curves of the stream, but always fainter and farther away, till I lost it at last behind the miter-shaped hill of the great pagoda. And then I was left alone with my ship, anchored at the head of the Gulf of Siam.

She floated at the starting point of a long journey, very still in an immense stillness, the shadows of her spars flung far to the eastward by the setting sun. At that moment I was alone on her decks. There was not a sound in her—and around us nothing moved, nothing lived, not a canoe on the water, not a bird in the air, not a cloud in the sky. In this breathless pause at the threshold of a long passage we seemed to be measuring our fitness for a long and arduous enterprise, the appointed task of both our existences to be carried out, far from all human eyes, with only sky and sea for spectators and for judges.

There must have been some glare in the air to

---

1. *river Meinam* (mä näm′), now Chao Phraya (chou′ prä yä′), a river in central Thailand (formerly called Siam) flowing south into the gulf of Thailand.

interfere with one's sight, because it was only just before the sun left us that my roaming eyes made out beyond the highest ridges of the principal islet of the group something which did away with the solemnity of perfect solitude. The tide of darkness flowed on swiftly; and with tropical suddenness a swarm of stars came out above the shadowy earth, while I lingered yet, my hand resting lightly on my ship's rail as if on the shoulder of a trusted friend. But, with all that multitude of celestial bodies staring down at one, the comfort of quiet communion with her was gone for good. And there were also disturbing sounds by this time—voices, footsteps forward; the steward flitted along the main-deck, a busily ministering spirit; a hand bell tinkled urgently under the poop deck. . . .

I found my two officers waiting for me near the supper table, in the lighted cuddy.[2] We sat down at once, and as I helped the chief mate, I said:

"Are you aware that there is a ship anchored inside the islands? I saw her mastheads above the ridge as the sun went down."

He raised sharply his simple face, overcharged by a terrible growth of whisker, and emitted his usual ejaculations: "Bless my soul, sir! You don't say so!"

My second mate was a round-cheeked, silent young man, grave beyond his years, I thought; but as our eyes happened to meet I detected a slight quiver on his lips. I looked down at once. It was not my part to encourage sneering on board my ship. It must be said, too, that I knew very little of my officers. In consequence of certain events of no particular significance, except to myself, I had been appointed to the command only a fortnight before. Neither did I know much of the hands forward. All these people had been together for eighteen months or so, and my position was that of the only stranger on board. I mention this because it has some bearing on what is to follow. But what I felt most was my being a stranger to the ship; and if all the truth must be told, I was somewhat of a stranger to myself. The youngest man on board (barring the second mate), and untried as yet by a position of the fullest responsibility, I was willing to take the adequacy of the others for granted.

They had simply to be equal to their tasks; but I wondered how far I should turn out faithful to that ideal conception of one's own personality every man sets up for himself secretly.

Meantime the chief mate, with an almost visible effect of collaboration on the part of his round eyes and frightful whiskers, was trying to evolve a theory of the anchored ship. His dominant trait was to take all things into earnest consideration. He was of a painstaking turn of mind. As he used to say, he "liked to account to himself" for practically everything that came in his way, down to a miserable scorpion he had found in his cabin a week before. The why and the wherefore of that scorpion—how it got on board and came to select his room rather than the pantry (which was a dark place and more what a scorpion would be partial to), and how on earth it managed to drown itself in the inkwell of his writing desk—had exercised him infinitely. The ship within the islands was much more easily accounted for; and just as we were about to rise from table he made his pronouncement. She was, he doubted not, a ship from home[3] lately arrived. Probably she drew[4] too much water to cross the bar except at the top of spring tides. Therefore, she went into that natural harbor to wait for a few days in preference to remaining in an open roadstead.

"That's so," confirmed the second mate, suddenly, in his slightly hoarse voice. "She draws over twenty feet. She's the Liverpool ship *Sephora* with a cargo of coal. Hundred and twenty-three days from Cardiff."

We looked at him in surprise.

"The tugboat skipper told me when he came on board for your letters, sir," explained the young man. "He expects to take her up the river the day after tomorrow."

After thus overwhelming us with the extent of his information he slipped out of the cabin. The mate observed regretfully that he "could not

---

2. *cuddy,* small cabin used, in this case, as an officers' dining room.
3. *from home,* from England.
4. *drew,* displaced. A ship draws more water when it is loaded than when it is empty.

account for that young fellow's whims." What prevented him telling us all about it at once he wanted to know.

I detained him as he was making a move. For the last two days the crew had had plenty of hard work, and the night before they had very little sleep. I felt painfully that I—a stranger—was doing something unusual when I directed him to let all hands turn in without setting an anchor watch. I proposed to keep on deck myself till one o'clock or thereabouts. I would get the second mate to relieve me at that hour.

"He will turn out the cook and the steward at four," I concluded, "and then give you a call. Of course at the slightest sign of any sort of wind we'll have the hands up and make a start at once."

He concealed his astonishment. "Very well, sir." Outside the cuddy he put his head in the second mate's door to inform him of my unheard-of caprice to take a five hours' anchor watch on myself. I heard the other raise his voice incredulously—"What? The Captain himself?" Then a few more murmurs, a door closed, then another. A few moments later I went on deck.

My strangeness, which had made me sleepless, had prompted that unconventional arrangement, as if I had expected in those solitary hours of the night to get on terms with the ship of which I knew nothing, manned by men of whom I knew very little more. Fast alongside a wharf, littered like any ship in port with a tangle of unrelated things, invaded by unrelated shore people, I had hardly seen her yet properly. Now, as she lay cleared for sea, the stretch of her main-deck seemed to me very fine under the stars. Very fine, very roomy for her size, and very inviting. I descended the poop and paced the waist, my mind picturing to myself the coming passage through the Malay Archipelago, down the Indian Ocean, and up the Atlantic. All its phases were familiar enough to me, every characteristic, all the alternatives which were likely to face me on the high seas—everything! . . . except the novel responsibility of command. But I took heart from the reasonable thought that the ship was like other ships, the men like other men, and that the sea was not likely to keep any special surprises expressly for my discomfiture.

Arrived at that comforting conclusion, I bethought myself of a cigar and went below to get it. All was still down there. Everybody at the after end of the ship was sleeping profoundly. I came out again on the quarter-deck, agreeably at ease in my sleeping suit on that warm breathless night, barefooted, a glowing cigar in my teeth, and, going forward, I was met by the profound silence of the fore end of the ship. Only as I passed the door of the forecastle I heard a deep, quiet, trustful sigh of some sleeper inside. And suddenly I rejoiced in the great security of the sea as compared with the unrest of the land, in my choice of that untempted life presenting no disquieting problems, invested with an elementary moral beauty by the absolute straightforwardness of its appeal and by the singleness of its purpose.

The riding light in the forerigging burned with a clear, untroubled, as if symbolic, flame, confident and bright in the mysterious shades of the night. Passing on my way aft along the other side of the ship, I observed that the rope side ladder, put over, no doubt, for the master of the tug when he came to fetch away our letters, had not been hauled in as it should have been. I became annoyed at this, for exactitude in some small matters is the very soul of discipline. Then I reflected that I had myself peremptorily dismissed my officers from duty, and by my own act had prevented the anchor watch being formally set and things properly attended to. I asked myself whether it was wise ever to interfere with the established routine of duties even from the kindest of motives. My action might have made me appear eccentric. Goodness only knew how that absurdly whiskered mate would "account" for my conduct, and what the whole ship thought of that informality of their new captain. I was vexed with myself.

Not from compunction certainly, but, as it were, mechanically, I proceeded to get the ladder in myself. Now a side ladder of that sort is a light affair and comes in easily, yet my vigorous tug, which should have brought it flying on board, merely recoiled upon my body in a totally

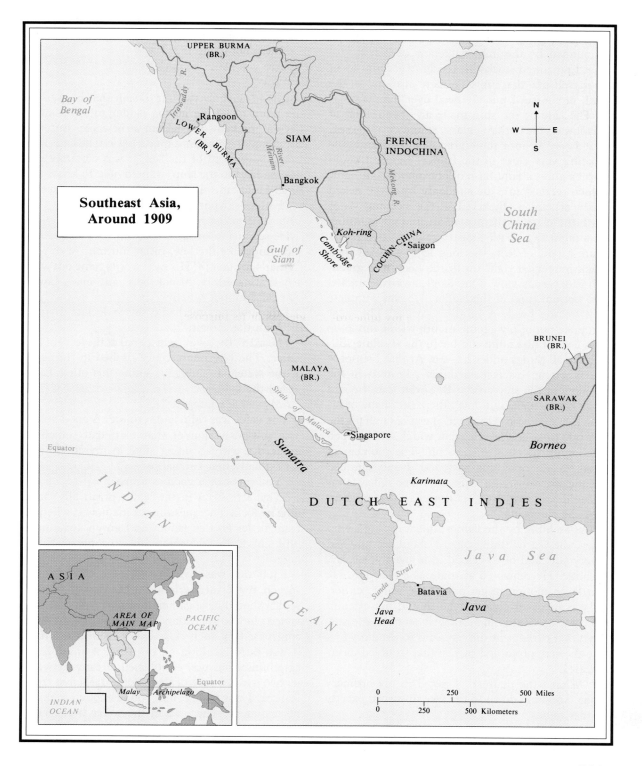

Southeast Asia,
Around 1909

UPPER BURMA
(BR.)

*Bay of
Bengal*

Rangoon

LOWER
BURMA
(BR.)

Irrawaddy R.

SIAM

Bangkok

River Meinam

FRENCH
INDOCHINA

Mekong R.

Koh-ring

*Cambodge
Shore*

COCHIN-CHINA

Saigon

*South
China
Sea*

*Gulf of
Siam*

MALAYA
(BR.)

Strait of Malacca

Singapore

Sumatra

Equator

INDIAN

OCEAN

BRUNEI
(BR.)

SARAWAK
(BR.)

Borneo

D U T C H   E A S T   I N D I E S

Karimata

Java Sea

Sunda Strait

Batavia

*Java
Head*

Java

ASIA

AREA OF
MAIN MAP

*PACIFIC
OCEAN*

Malay Archipelago

Equator

*INDIAN
OCEAN*

N
W   E
S

0		250		500 Miles
0	250	500 Kilometers		

unexpected jerk. What the devil! . . . I was so astounded by the immovableness of that ladder that I remained stockstill, trying to account for it to myself like that imbecile mate of mine. In the end, of course, I put my head over the rail.

The side of the ship made an opaque belt of shadow on the darkling glassy shimmer of the sea. But I saw at once something elongated and pale floating very close to the ladder. Before I could form a guess a faint flash of phosphorescent light, which seemed to issue suddenly from the naked body of a man, flickered in the sleeping water with the elusive, silent play of summer lightning in a night sky. With a gasp I saw revealed to my stare a pair of feet, the long legs, a broad livid back immersed right up to the neck in a greenish cadaverous glow. One hand, awash, clutched the bottom rung of the ladder. He was complete but for the head. A headless corpse! The cigar dropped out of my gaping mouth with a tiny plop and a short hiss quite audible in the absolute stillness of all things under heaven. At that I suppose he raised up his face, a dimly pale oval in the shadow of the ship's side. But even then I could only barely make out down there the shape of his black-haired head. However, it was enough for the horrid, frost-bound sensation which had gripped me about the chest to pass off. The moment of vain exclamations was past, too. I only climbed on the spare spar and leaned over the rail as far as I could, to bring my eyes nearer to that mystery floating alongside.

As he hung by the ladder, like a resting swimmer, the sea lightning played about his limbs at every stir; and he appeared in it ghastly, silvery, fishlike. He remained as mute as a fish, too. He made no motion to get out of the water, either. It was inconceivable that he should not attempt to come on board, and strangely troubling to suspect that perhaps he did not want to. And my first words were prompted by just that troubled incertitude.

"What's the matter?" I asked in my ordinary tone, speaking down to the face upturned exactly under mine.

"Cramp," it answered, no louder. Then slightly anxious, "I say, no need to call anyone."

"I was not going to," I said.

"Are you alone on deck?"

"Yes."

I had somehow the impression that he was on the point of letting go the ladder to swim away beyond my ken—mysterious as he came. But, for the moment, this being appearing as if he had risen from the bottom of the sea (it was certainly the nearest land to the ship) wanted only to know the time. I told him. And he, down there, tentatively:

"I suppose your captain's turned in?"

"I am sure he isn't," I said.

He seemed to struggle with himself, for I heard something like the low, bitter murmur of doubt. "What's the good?" His next words came out with a hesitating effort. "Look here, my man. Could you call him out quietly?"

I thought the time had come to declare myself.

"*I* am the captain."

I heard a "By Jove!" whispered at the level of the water. The phosphorescence flashed in the swirl of the water all about his limbs, his other hand seized the ladder.

"My name's Leggatt."

The voice was calm and resolute. A good voice. The self-possession of that man had somehow induced a corresponding state in myself. It was very quietly that I remarked:

"You must be a good swimmer."

"Yes. I've been in the water practically since nine o'clock. The question for me now is whether I am to let go this ladder and go on swimming till I sink from exhaustion, or—to come on board here."

I felt this was no mere formula of desperate speech, but a real alternative in the view of a strong soul. I should have gathered from this that he was young; indeed, it is only the young who are ever confronted by such clear issues. But at the time it was pure intuition on my part. A mysterious communication was established already between us two—in the face of that silent, darkened tropical sea. I was young, too; young enough to make no comment. The man in the water began suddenly to climb up the ladder, and I hastened away from the rail to fetch some clothes.

Before entering the cabin I stood still, listening in the lobby at the foot of the stairs. A faint snore came through the closed door of the chief mate's room. The second mate's door was on the hook, but the darkness in there was absolutely soundless. He, too, was young and could sleep like a stone. Remained the steward, but he was not likely to wake up before he was called. I got a sleeping suit out of my room and, coming back on deck, saw the naked man from the sea sitting on the main hatch, glimmering white in the darkness, his elbows on his knees and his head in his hands. In a moment he had concealed his damp body in a sleeping suit of the same gray-stripe pattern as the one I was wearing and followed me like my double on the poop. Together we moved right aft, barefooted, silent.

"What is it?" I asked in a deadened voice, taking the lighted lamp out of the binnacle, and raising it to his face.

"An ugly business."

He had rather regular features; a good mouth; light eyes under somewhat heavy, dark eyebrows; a smooth, square forehead; no growth on his cheeks; a small, brown mustache, and a well-shaped, round chin. His expression was concentrated, meditative, under the inspecting light of the lamp I held up to his face; such as a man thinking hard in solitude might wear. My sleeping suit was just right for his size. A well-knit young fellow of twenty-five at most. He caught his lower lip with the edge of white, even teeth.

"Yes," I said, replacing the lamp in the binnacle. The warm, heavy tropical night closed upon his head again.

"There's a ship over there," he murmured.

"Yes, I know. The *Sephora*. Did you know of us?"

"Hadn't the slightest idea. I am the mate of her——" He paused and corrected himself. "I should say I *was*."

"Aha! Something wrong?"

"Yes. Very wrong indeed. I've killed a man."

"What do you mean? Just now?"

"No, on the passage. Weeks ago. Thirty-nine south.[5] When I say a man——"

"Fit of temper," I suggested confidently.

The shadowy, dark head, like mine, seemed to nod imperceptibly above the ghostly gray of my sleeping suit. It was, in the night, as though I had been faced by my own reflection in the depths of a somber and immense mirror.

"A pretty thing to have to own up to for a Conway boy,"[6] murmured my double, distinctly.

"You're a Conway boy?"

"I am," he said, as if startled. Then, slowly . . . "Perhaps you, too——"

It was so; but being a couple of years older I had left before he joined. After a quick interchange of dates a silence fell; and I thought suddenly of my absurd mate with his terrific whiskers and the "Bless my soul—you don't say so" type of intellect. My double gave me an inkling of his thoughts by saying: "My father's a parson in Norfolk. Do you see me before a judge and jury on that charge? For myself I can't see the necessity. There are fellows that an angel from heaven—— And I am not that. He was one of those creatures that are just simmering all the time with a silly sort of wickedness. Miserable devils that have no business to live at all. He wouldn't do his duty and wouldn't let anybody else do theirs. But what's the good of talking! You know well enough the sort of ill-conditioned snarling cur——"

He appealed to me as if our experiences had been as identical as our clothes. And I knew well enough the pestiferous danger of such a character where there are no means of legal repression. And I knew well enough also that my double there was no homicidal ruffian. I did not think of asking him for details, and he told me the story roughly in brusque, disconnected sentences. I needed no more. I saw it all going on as though I were myself inside that other sleeping suit.

"It happened while we were setting a reefed foresail, at dusk. Reefed foresail! You understand

---

5. *thirty-nine south*, degrees of latitude south of the equator.

6. *Conway boy*. The *Conway* was a vessel on which boys learned how to be merchant seamen.

the sort of weather. The only sail we had left to keep the ship running; so you may guess what it had been like for days. Anxious sort of job, that. He gave me some of his cursed insolence at the sheet. I tell you I was overdone with this terrific weather that seemed to have no end to it. Terrific, I tell you—and a deep ship. I believe the fellow himself was half-crazed with funk.[7] It was no time for gentlemanly reproof, so I turned round and felled him like an ox. He up and at me. We closed just as an awful sea made for the ship. All hands saw it coming and took to the rigging, but I had him by the throat, and went on shaking him like a rat, the men above us yelling, 'Look out! look out!' Then a crash as if the sky had fallen on my head. They say that for over ten minutes hardly anything was to be seen of the ship—just the three masts and a bit of the forecastle head and of the poop all awash driving along in a smother of foam. It was a miracle that they found us, jammed together behind the forebitts. It's clear that I meant business, because I was holding him by the throat still when they picked us up. He was black in the face. It was too much for them. It seems they rushed us aft together, gripped as we were, screaming 'Murder!' like a lot of lunatics, and broke into the cuddy. And the ship running for her life, touch and go all the time, any minute her last in a sea fit to turn your hair gray only a-looking at it. I understand that the skipper, too, started raving like the rest of them. The man had been deprived of sleep for more than a week, and to have this sprung on him at the height of a furious gale nearly drove him out of his mind. I wonder they didn't fling me overboard after getting the carcass of their precious shipmate out of my fingers. They had rather a job to separate us, I've been told. A sufficiently fierce story to make an old judge and a respectable jury sit up a bit. The first thing I heard when I came to myself was the maddening howling of that endless gale, and on that the voice of the old man. He was hanging on to my bunk, staring into my face out of his sou'wester.

" 'Mr. Leggatt, you have killed a man. You can act no longer as chief mate of this ship.' "

His care to subdue his voice made it sound monotonous. He rested a hand on the end of the skylight to steady himself with, and all that time did not stir a limb, so far as I could see. "Nice little tale for a quiet tea party," he concluded in the same tone.

One of my hands, too, rested on the end of the skylight; neither did I stir a limb, so far as I knew. We stood less than a foot from each other. It occurred to me that if old "Bless my soul—you don't say so" were to put his head up the companion and catch sight of us, he would think he was seeing double, or imagine himself come upon a scene of weird witchcraft; the strange captain having a quiet confabulation by the wheel with his own gray ghost. I became very much concerned to prevent anything of the sort. I heard the other's soothing undertone.

"My father's a parson in Norfolk," it said. Evidently he had forgotten he had told me this important fact before. Truly a nice little tale.

"You had better slip down into my stateroom now," I said, moving off stealthily. My double followed my movements; our bare feet made no sound; I let him in, closed the door with care, and, after giving a call to the second mate, returned on deck for my relief.

"Not much sign of any wind yet," I remarked when he approached.

"No, sir. Not much," he assented, sleepily, in his hoarse voice, with just enough deference, no more, and barely suppressing a yawn.

"Well, that's all you have to look out for. You have got your orders."

"Yes, sir."

I paced a turn or two on the poop and saw him take up his position face forward with his elbow in the ratlines of the mizzen rigging before I went below. The mate's faint snoring was still going on peacefully. The cuddy lamp was burning over the table on which stood a vase with flowers, a polite attention from the ship's provision merchant—the last flowers we should see for the next three months at the very least. Two bunches of

---

7. *funk*, British slang for panic or cowardly fright.

bananas hung from the beam symmetrically, one on each side of the rudder casing. Everything was as before in the ship—except that two of her captain's sleeping suits were simultaneously in use, one motionless in the cuddy, the other keeping very still in the captain's stateroom.

It must be explained here that my cabin had the form of the capital letter L, the door being within the angle and opening into the short part of the letter. A couch was to the left, the bed place to the right; my writing desk and the chronometers' table faced the door. But anyone opening it, unless he stepped right inside, had no view of what I call the long (or vertical) part of the letter. It contained some lockers surmounted by a bookcase; and a few clothes, a thick jacket or two, caps, oilskin coat, and such like, hung on hooks. There was at the bottom of that part a door opening into my bathroom, which could be entered also directly from the saloon. But that way was never used.

The mysterious arrival had discovered the advantage of this particular shape. Entering my room, lighted strongly by a big bulkhead lamp swung on gimbals above my writing desk, I did not see him anywhere till he stepped out quietly from behind the coats hung in the recessed part.

"I heard somebody moving about, and went in there at once," he whispered.

I, too, spoke under my breath.

"Nobody is likely to come in here without knocking and getting permission."

He nodded. His face was thin and the sunburn faded, as though he had been ill. And no wonder. He had been, I heard presently, kept under arrest in his cabin for nearly seven weeks. But there was nothing sickly in his eyes or in his expression. He was not a bit like me, really; yet, as we stood leaning over my bed place, whispering side by side, with our dark heads together and our backs to the door, anybody bold enough to open it stealthily would have been treated to the uncanny sight of a double captain busy talking in whispers with his other self.

"But all this doesn't tell me how you came to hang on to our side ladder," I inquired, in the hardly audible murmurs we used, after he had told

me something more of the proceedings on board the *Sephora* once the bad weather was over.

"When we sighted Java Head I had had time to think all those matters out several times over. I had six weeks of doing nothing else, and with only an hour or so every evening for a tramp on the quarterdeck."

He whispered, his arms folded on the side of my bed place, staring through the open port. And I could imagine perfectly the manner of this thinking out—a stubborn if not a steadfast operation; something of which I should have been perfectly incapable.

"I reckoned it would be dark before we closed with the land," he continued, so low that I had to strain my hearing near as we were to each other, shoulder touching shoulder almost. "So I asked to speak to the old man. He always seemed very sick when he came to see me—as if he could not look me in the face. You know, that foresail saved the ship. She was too deep to have run long under bare poles. And it was I that managed to set it for him. Anyway, he came. When I had him in my cabin—he stood by the door looking at me as if I had the halter round my neck already—I asked him right away to leave my cabin door unlocked at night while the ship was going through Sunda Straits. There would be the Java coast within two or three miles, off Angier Point. I wanted nothing more. I've had a prize for swimming my second year in the Conway."

"I can believe it," I breathed out.

"God only knows why they locked me in every night. To see some of their faces you'd have thought they were afraid I'd go about at night strangling people. Am I a murdering brute? Do I look it? By Jove! If I had been he wouldn't have trusted himself like that into my room. You'll say I might have chucked him aside and bolted out, there and then—it was dark already. Well, no. And for the same reason I wouldn't think of trying to smash the door. There would have been a rush to stop me at the noise, and I did not mean to get into a confounded scrimmage. Somebody else might have got killed—for I would not have broken out only to get chucked back, and I did not want any more of that work. He refused, looking more sick than ever. He was afraid of the men, and also of that old second mate of his who had been sailing with him for years—a gray-headed old humbug; and his steward, too, had been with him devil knows how long—seventeen years or more—a dogmatic sort of loafer who hated me like poison, just because I was the chief mate. No chief mate ever made more than one voyage in the *Sephora*, you know. Those two old chaps ran the ship. Devil only knows what the skipper wasn't afraid of (all his nerve went to pieces altogether in that hellish spell of bad weather we had)—of what the law would do to him—of his wife, perhaps. Oh, yes! she's on board. Though I don't think she would have meddled. She would have been only too glad to have me out of the ship in any way. The 'brand of Cain'[8] business, don't you see. That's all right. I was ready enough to go off wandering on the face of the earth—and that was price enough to pay for an Abel of that sort. Anyhow, he wouldn't listen to me. 'This thing must take its course. I represent the law here.' He was shaking like a leaf. 'So you won't?' 'No!' 'Then I hope you will be able to sleep on that,' I said, and turned my back on him. 'I wonder that *you* can,' cries he, and locks the door.

"Well, after that, I couldn't. Not very well. That was three weeks ago. We have had a slow passage through the Java Sea; drifted about Carimata for ten days. When we anchored here they thought, I suppose, it was all right. The nearest land (and that's five miles) is the ship's destination; the consul would soon set about catching me; and there would have been no object in bolting to these islets there. I don't suppose there's a drop of water on them. I don't know how it was, but tonight that steward, after bringing me my supper, went out to let me eat it, and left the door unlocked. And I ate it—all there was, too. After I had finished I strolled out on the quarter-deck. I don't know that I meant to do anything. A breath of fresh air was all I wanted, I believe. Then a sudden temptation came over me. I kicked off my slippers and was in the water before I had made up my mind fairly. Somebody heard the splash and they raised an awful hulla-baloo. 'He's gone! Lower the boats! He's committed suicide! No, he's swimming.' Certainly I was swimming. It's not so easy for a swimmer like me to commit suicide by drowning. I landed on the nearest islet before the boat left the ship's side. I heard them pulling about in the dark, hailing, and so on, but after a bit they gave up. Everything quieted down and the anchorage became as still as death. I sat down on a stone and began to think. I felt certain they would start searching for me at daylight. There was no place to hide on those stony things—and if there had been, what would have been the good? But now I was clear of that ship, I was not going back. So after a while I took off all my clothes, tied them up in a bundle with a stone inside, and dropped them in the deep water on the outer side of that islet. That was suicide enough for me. Let them think what they liked, but I didn't mean to drown myself. I meant to swim till I sank—but that's not the same thing. I struck out for another of these little islands, and it was from that one that I first saw your riding light. Something to swim for. I went on easily, and on the way I came upon a flat rock a foot or two above water. In the daytime, I dare say, you might make it out with a glass from your poop. I scrambled up on it and rested myself for a bit. Then I made another start. That last spell must have been over a mile."

His whisper was getting fainter and fainter, and all the time he stared straight out through the porthole, in which there was not even a star to be seen. I had not interrupted him. There was something that made comment impossible in his narrative, or perhaps in himself; a sort of feeling, a quality, which I can't find a name for. And when he ceased, all I found was a futile whisper: "So you swam for our light?"

"Yes—straight for it. It was something to swim for. I couldn't see any stars low down because the coast was in the way, and I couldn't see the land, either. The water was like glass. One might

---

8. **brand of Cain.** In *Genesis* Cain murders his brother Abel, and God drives him out into the wilderness marked on his forehead with a sign of his guilt.

Winter North Atlantic (detail), by Derek George Montague Gardner. This painting shows the *Loch Tay* (built in 1869) running before an Atlantic gale.

have been swimming in a confounded thousand-feet deep cistern with no place for scrambling out anywhere; but what I didn't like was the notion of swimming round and round like a crazed bullock before I gave out; and as I didn't mean to go back . . . No. Do you see me being hauled back, stark naked, off one of these little islands by the scruff of the neck and fighting like a wild beast? Somebody would have got killed for certain, and I did not want any of that. So I went on. Then your ladder——"

"Why didn't you hail the ship?" I asked, a little louder.

He touched my shoulder lightly. Lazy footsteps came right over our heads and stopped. The second mate had crossed from the other side of the poop and might have been hanging over the rail for all we knew.

"He couldn't hear us talking—could he?" My double breathed into my very ear, anxiously.

His anxiety was in answer, a sufficient answer, to the question I had put to him. An answer containing all the difficulty of that situation. I closed the porthole quietly, to make sure. A louder word might have been overheard.

"Who's that?" he whispered then.

"My second mate. But I don't know much more of the fellow than you do."

And I told him a little about myself. I had been appointed to take charge while I least expected anything of the sort, not quite a fortnight ago. I didn't know either the ship or the people. Hadn't had the time in port to look about me or size anybody up. And as to the crew, all they knew was that I was appointed to take the ship home. For the rest, I was almost as much of a stranger on board as himself, I said. And at the moment I felt it most acutely. I felt that it would take very little to make me a suspect person in the eyes of the ship's company.

He had turned about meantime; and we, the two strangers in the ship, faced each other in identical attitudes.

"Your ladder——" he murmured, after a silence. "Who'd have thought of finding a ladder hanging over at night in a ship anchored out here! I felt just then a very unpleasant faintness. After the life I've been leading for nine weeks, anybody would have got out of condition. I wasn't capable of swimming round as far as your rudder chains. And, lo and behold! there was a ladder to get hold of. After I gripped it I said to myself, 'What's the good?' When I saw a man's head looking over I thought I would swim away presently and leave him shouting—in whatever language it was. I didn't mind being looked at. I—I liked it. And then you speaking to me so quietly—as if you had expected me—made me hold on a little longer. It had been a confounded lonely time—I don't mean while swimming. I was glad to talk a little to somebody that didn't belong to the *Sephora*. As to asking for the captain, that was a mere impulse. It could have been no use, with all the ship knowing about me and the other people pretty certain to be round here in the morning. I don't know—I wanted to be seen, to talk with somebody, before I went on. I don't know what I would have said. . . . 'Fine night, isn't it?' or something of the sort."

"Do you think they will be round here presently?" I asked with some incredulity.

"Quite likely," he said faintly.

He looked extremely haggard all of a sudden. His head rolled on his shoulders.

"H'm. We shall see then. Meantime get into that bed," I whispered. "Want help? There."

It was a rather high bed place with a set of drawers underneath. This amazing swimmer really needed the lift I gave him by seizing his leg. He tumbled in, rolled over on his back, and flung one arm across his eyes. And then, with his face nearly hidden, he must have looked exactly as I used to look in that bed. I gazed upon my other self for a while before drawing across carefully the two green serge curtains which ran on a brass rod. I thought for a moment of pinning them together for greater safety, but I sat down on the couch,

and once there I felt unwilling to rise and hunt for a pin. I would do it in a moment. I was extremely tired, in a peculiarly intimate way, by the strain of stealthiness, by the effort of whispering and the general secrecy of this excitement. It was three o'clock by now and I had been on my feet since nine, but I was not sleepy; I could not have gone to sleep. I sat there, fagged out,[9] looking at the curtains, trying to clear my mind of the confused sensation of being in two places at once, and greatly bothered by an exasperating knocking in my head. It was a relief to discover suddenly that it was not in my head at all, but on the outside of the door. Before I could collect myself the words "Come in" were out of my mouth, and the steward entered with a tray, bringing in my morning coffee. I had slept, after all, and I was so frightened that I shouted, "This way! I am here, steward," as though he had been miles away. He put down the tray on the table next the couch and only then said, very quietly, "I can see you are here, sir." I felt him give me a keen look, but I dared not meet his eyes just then. He must have wondered why I had drawn the curtains of my bed before going to sleep on the couch. He went out, hooking the door open as usual.

I heard the crew washing decks above me. I knew I would have been told at once if there had been any wind. Calm, I thought, and I was doubly vexed. Indeed, I felt dual more than ever. The steward reappeared suddenly in the doorway. I jumped up from the couch so quickly that he gave a start.

"What do you want here?"

"Close your port, sir—they are washing decks."

"It is closed," I said, reddening.

"Very well, sir." But he did not move from the doorway and returned my stare in an extraordinary, equivocal manner for a time. Then his eyes wavered, all his expression changed, and in a voice unusually gentle, almost coaxingly:

"May I come in to take the empty cup away, sir?"

---

9. *fagged out*, British slang meaning "exhausted."

"Of course!" I turned my back on him while he popped in and out. Then I unhooked and closed the door and even pushed the bolt. This sort of thing could not go on very long. The cabin was as hot as an oven, too. I took a peep at my double, and discovered that he had not moved, his arm was still over his eyes; but his chest heaved; his hair was wet; his chin glistened with perspiration. I reached over him and opened the port.

"I must show myself on deck," I reflected.

Of course, theoretically, I could do what I liked, with no one to say nay to me within the whole circle of the horizon; but to lock my cabin door and take the key away I did not dare. Directly I put my head out of the companion I saw the group of my two officers, the second mate barefooted, the chief mate in long India-rubber boots, near the break of the poop, and the steward halfway down the poop ladder talking to them eagerly. He happened to catch sight of me and dived, the second ran down on the main-deck shouting some order or other, and the chief mate came to meet me, touching his cap.

There was a sort of curiosity in his eye that I did not like. I don't know whether the steward had told them that I was "queer" only, or downright drunk, but I know the man meant to have a good look at me. I watched him coming with a smile which, as he got into point-blank range, took effect and froze his very whiskers. I did not give him time to open his lips.

"Square the yards by lifts and braces before the hands go to breakfast."

It was the first particular order I had given on board that ship; and I stayed on deck to see it executed, too. I had felt the need of asserting myself without loss of time. That sneering young cub got taken down a peg or two on that occasion, and I also seized the opportunity of having a good look at the face of every foremast man as they filed past me to go to the after braces. At breakfast time, eating nothing myself, I presided with such frigid dignity that the two mates were only too glad to escape from the cabin as soon as decency permitted; and all the time the dual working of my mind distracted me almost to the point of insanity. I was constantly watching myself, my secret self, as dependent on my actions as my own personality, sleeping in that bed, behind that door which faced me as I sat at the head of the table. It was very much like being mad, only it was worse because one was aware of it.

I had to shake him for a solid minute, but when at last he opened his eyes it was in the full possession of his senses, with an inquiring look.

"All's well so far," I whispered. "Now you must vanish into the bathroom."

He did so, as noiseless as a ghost, and then I rang for the steward, and facing him boldly, directed him to tidy up my stateroom while I was having my bath—"and be quick about it." As my tone admitted of no excuses, he said, "Yes, sir," and ran off to fetch his dustpan and brushes. I took a bath and did most of my dressing, splashing, and whistling softly for the steward's edification, while the secret sharer of my life stood drawn up bolt upright in that little space, his face looking very sunken in daylight, his eyelids lowered under the stern, dark line of his eyebrows drawn together by a slight frown.

When I left him there to go back to my room the steward was finishing dusting. I sent for the mate and engaged him in some insignificant conversation. It was, as it were, trifling with the terrific character of his whiskers; but my object was to give him an opportunity for a good look at my cabin. And then I could at last shut, with a clear conscience, the door of my stateroom and get my double back into the recessed part. There was nothing else for it. He had to sit still on a small folding stool, half-smothered by the heavy coats hanging there. We listened to the steward going into the bathroom out of the saloon,[10] filling the water bottles there, scrubbing the bath, setting things to rights, whisk, bang, clatter—out again into the saloon—turn the key—click. Such was my scheme for keeping my second self invisible. Nothing better could be contrived under the circumstances. And there we sat; I at my writing desk ready to appear busy with some papers, he behind me out of sight of the door. It would not

10. *saloon*, large room for general use.

have been prudent to talk in daytime; and I could not have stood the excitement of that queer sense of whispering to myself. Now and then, glancing over my shoulder, I saw him far back there, sitting rigidly on the low stool, his bare feet close together, his arms folded, his head hanging on his breast—and perfectly still. Anybody would have taken him for me.

I was fascinated by it myself. Every moment I had to glance over my shoulder. I was looking at him when a voice outside the door said:

"Beg pardon, sir."

"Well!" . . . I kept my eyes on him, and so when the voice outside the door announced, "There's a ship's boat coming our way, sir," I saw him give a start—the first movement he had made for hours. But he did not raise his bowed head.

"All right. Get the ladder over."

I hesitated. Should I whisper something to him? But what? His immobility seemed to have been never disturbed. What could I tell him he did not know already? Finally I went on deck.

2

The skipper of the *Sephora* had a thin red whisker all round his face, and the sort of complexion that goes with hair of that color; also the particular, rather smeary shade of blue in the eyes. He was not exactly a showy figure; his shoulders were high, his stature but middling—one leg slightly more bandy than the other. He shook hands, looking vaguely around. A spiritless tenacity was his main characteristic, I judged. I behaved with a politeness which seemed to disconcert him. Perhaps he was shy. He mumbled to me as if he were ashamed of what he was saying; gave his name (it was something like Archbold—but at this distance of years I hardly am sure), his ship's name, and a few other particulars of that sort, in the manner of a criminal making a reluctant and doleful confession. He had had terrible weather on the passage out—terrible—terrible—wife aboard, too.

By this time we were seated in the cabin and the steward brought in a tray with a bottle and glasses. "Thanks! No." Never took liquor. Would have some water, though. He drank two tumblerfuls. Terrible thirsty work. Ever since daylight had been exploring the islands round his ship.

"What was that for—fun?" I asked, with an appearance of polite interest.

"No!" He sighed. "Painful duty."

As he persisted in his mumbling and I wanted my double to hear every word, I hit upon the notion of informing him that I regretted to say I was hard of hearing.

"Such a young man, too!" he nodded, keeping his smeary blue, unintelligent eyes fastened upon me. "What was the cause of it—some disease?" he inquired, without the least sympathy and as if he thought that, if so, I'd got no more than I deserved.

"Yes; disease," I admitted in a cheerful tone which seemed to shock him. But my point was gained, because he had to raise his voice to give me his tale. It is not worth while to record that version. It was just over two months since all this had happened, and he had thought so much about it that he seemed completely muddled as to its bearings, but still immensely impressed.

"What would you think of such a thing happening on board your own ship? I've had the *Sephora* for these fifteen years. I am a well-known shipmaster."

He was densely distressed—and perhaps I should have sympathized with him if I had been able to detach my mental vision from the unsuspected sharer of my cabin as though he were my second self. There he was on the other side of the bulkhead, four or five feet from us, no more, as we sat in the saloon. I looked politely at Captain Archbold (if that was his name), but it was the other I saw, in a gray sleeping suit, seated on a low stool, his bare feet close together, his arms folded, and every word said between us falling into the ears of his dark head bowed on his chest.

"I have been at sea now, man and boy, for seven-and-thirty years, and I've never heard of such a thing happening in an English ship. And that it should be my ship. Wife on board, too."

I was hardly listening to him.

"Don't you think," I said, "that the heavy sea

which, you told me, came aboard just then might have killed the man? I have seen the sheer weight of a sea kill a man very neatly, by simply breaking his neck."

"Good God!" he uttered, impressively, fixing his smeary blue eyes on me. "The sea! No man killed by the sea ever looked like that." He seemed positively scandalized at my suggestion. And as I gazed at him, certainly not prepared for anything original on his part, he advanced his head close to mine and thrust his tongue out at me so suddenly that I couldn't help starting back.

After scoring over my calmness in this graphic way he nodded wisely. If I had seen the sight, he assured me, I would never forget it as long as I lived. The weather was too bad to give the corpse a proper sea burial. So next day at dawn they took it up on the poop, covering its face with a bit of bunting; he read a short prayer, and then, just as it was, in its oilskins and long boots, they launched it amongst those mountainous seas that seemed ready every moment to swallow up the ship herself and the terrified lives on board of her.

"That reefed foresail saved you," I threw in.

"Under God—it did," he exclaimed fervently. "It was by a special mercy, I firmly believe, that it stood some of those hurricane squalls."

"It was the setting of that sail which—" I began.

"God's own hand in it," he interrupted me. "Nothing less could have done it. I don't mind telling you that I hardly dared give the order. It seemed impossible that we could touch anything without losing it, and then our last hope would have been gone."

The terror of that gale was on him yet. I let him go on for a bit, then said, casually—as if returning to a minor subject:

"You were very anxious to give up your mate to the shore people, I believe?"

He was. To the law. His obscure tenacity on that point had in it something incomprehensible and a little awful; something, as it were, mystical, quite apart from his anxiety that he should not be suspected of "countenancing any doings of that sort." Seven-and-thirty virtuous years at sea, of which over twenty of immaculate command, and

the last fifteen in the *Sephora*, seemed to have laid him under some pitiless obligation.

"And you know," he went on, groping shame-facedly amongst his feelings, "I did not engage that young fellow. His people had some interest with my owners. I was in a way forced to take him on. He looked very smart, very gentlemanly, and all that. But do you know—I never liked him, somehow. I am a plain man. You see, he wasn't exactly the sort for the chief mate of a ship like the *Sephora*."

I had become so connected in thoughts and impressions with the secret sharer of my cabin that I felt as if I, personally, were being given to understand that I, too, was not the sort that would have done for the chief mate of a ship like the *Sephora*. I had no doubt of it in my mind.

"Not at all the style of man. You understand," he insisted, superfluously, looking hard at me.

I smiled urbanely. He seemed at a loss for a while.

"I suppose I must report a suicide."

"Beg pardon?"

"Sui-cide! That's what I'll have to write to my owners directly I get in."

"Unless you manage to recover him before tomorrow," I assented, dispassionately. . ."I mean, alive."

He mumbled something which I really did not catch, and I turned my ear to him in a puzzled manner. He fairly bawled:

"The land—I say, the mainland is at least seven miles off my anchorage."

"About that."

My lack of excitement, of curiosity, of sur-prise, of any sort of pronounced interest, began to arouse his distrust. But except for the felicitous pretense of deafness I had not tried to pretend anything. I had felt utterly incapable of playing the part of ignorance properly, and therefore was afraid to try. It is also certain that he had brought some ready-made suspicions with him, and that he viewed my politeness as a strange and unnat-ural phenomenon. And yet how else could I have received him? Not heartily! That was impossible for psychological reasons, which I need not state here. My only object was to keep off his inquiries. Surlily? Yes, but surliness might have provoked a point-blank question. From its novelty to him and from its nature, punctilious courtesy was the manner best calculated to restrain the man. But there was the danger of his breaking through my defense bluntly. I could not, I think, have met him by a direct lie, also for psychological (not moral) reasons. If he had only known how afraid I was of his putting my feeling of identity with the other to the test! But, strangely enough—(I thought of it only afterwards)—I believe that he was not a little disconcerted by the reverse side of that weird situation, by something in me that reminded him of the man he was seeking—suggested a mysterious similitude to the young fellow he had distrusted and disliked from the first.

However that might have been, the silence was not very prolonged. He took another oblique step.

"I reckon I had no more than a two-mile pull to your ship. Not a bit more."

"And quite enough, too, in this awful heat," I said.

Another pause full of mistrust followed. Necessity, they say, is mother of invention, but fear, too, is not barren of ingenious suggestions. And I was afraid he would ask me point-blank for news of my other self.

"Nice little saloon, isn't it?" I remarked, as if noticing for the first time the way his eyes roamed from one closed door to the other. "And very well fitted out, too. Here, for instance," I continued, reaching over the back of my seat negligently and flinging the door open, "is my bathroom."

He made an eager movement, but hardly gave it a glance. I got up, shut the door of the bathroom, and invited him to have a look round, as if I were very proud of my accommodation. He had to rise and be shown round, but he went through the business without any raptures whatever.

"And now we'll have a look at my stateroom," I declared, in a voice as loud as I dared to make it, crossing the cabin to the starboard side with purposely heavy steps.

He followed me in and gazed around. My intelligent double had vanished. I played my part.

"Very convenient—isn't it?"

"Very nice. Very comf . . ." He didn't finish and went out brusquely as if to escape from some unrighteous wiles of mine. But it was not to be. I had been too frightened not to feel vengeful; I felt I had him on the run, and I meant to keep him on the run. My polite insistence must have had something menacing in it, because he gave in suddenly. And I did not let him off a single item; mate's room, pantry, storerooms, the very sail locker which was also under the poop—he had to look into them all. When at last I showed him out on the quarter-deck he drew a long, spiritless sigh, and mumbled dismally that he must really be going back to his ship now. I desired my mate, who had joined us, to see to the captain's boat.

The man of whiskers gave a blast on the whistle which he used to wear hanging round his neck, and yelled, "*Sephora's* away!" My double down there in my cabin must have heard, and certainly could not feel more relieved than I. Four fellows came running out from somewhere forward and went over the side, while my own men, appearing on deck, too, lined the rail. I escorted my visitor to the gangway ceremoniously, and nearly overdid it. He was a tenacious beast. On the very ladder he lingered, and in that unique, guiltily conscientious manner of sticking to the point:

"I say . . . you . . . you don't think that ——"

I covered his voice loudly:

"Certainly not. . . . I am delighted. Good-by."

I had an idea of what he meant to say, and just saved myself by the privilege of defective hearing. He was too shaken generally to insist, but my mate, close witness of that parting, looked mystified and his face took on a thoughtful cast. As I did not want to appear as if I wished to avoid all communication with my officers, he had the opportunity to address me.

"Seems a very nice man. His boat's crew told our chaps a very extraordinary story, if what I am told by the steward is true. I suppose you had it from the captain, sir?"

"Yes. I had a story from the captain."

"A very horrible affair—isn't it, sir?"

"It is."

"Beats all these tales we hear about murders in Yankee ships."[11]

"I don't think it beats them. I don't think it resembles them in the least."

"Bless my soul—you don't say so! But of course I've no acquaintance whatever with American ships, not I, so I couldn't go against your knowledge. It's horrible enough for me. . . . But the queerest part is that those fellows seemed to have some idea the man was hidden aboard here. They had really. Did you ever hear of such a thing?"

"Preposterous—isn't it?"

We were walking to and fro athwart the quarterdeck. No one of the crew forward could be seen (the day was Sunday), and the mate pursued:

"There was some little dispute about it. Our chaps took offense. 'As if we would harbor a thing like that,' they said, 'Wouldn't you like to look for him in our coal-hole?' Quite a tiff. But they made it up in the end. I suppose he did drown himself. Don't you, sir?"

"I don't suppose anything."

"You have no doubt in the matter, sir?"

"None whatever."

I left him suddenly. I felt I was producing a bad impression, but with my double down there it was most trying to be on deck. And it was almost as trying to be below. Altogether a nerve-trying situation. But on the whole I felt less torn in two when I was with him. There was no one in the whole ship whom I dared take into my confidence. Since the hands had got to know his story it would have been impossible to pass him off for anyone else, and an accidental discovery was to be dreaded now more than ever. . . .

The steward being engaged in laying the table for dinner, we could talk only with our eyes when I first went down. Later in the afternoon we had a cautious try at whispering. The Sunday quietness of the ship was against us; the stillness of air and water around her was against us; the elements, the men were against us—everything was against us in our secret partnership; time itself—for this could not go on forever. The very trust in Providence was, I suppose, denied to his guilt. Shall I confess

that this thought cast me down very much? And as to the chapter of accidents which counts for so much in the book of success, I could only hope that it was closed. For what favorable accident could be expected?

"Did you hear everything?" were my first words as soon as we took up our position side by side, leaning over my bed place.

He had. And the proof of it was his earnest whisper, "The man told you he hardly dared to give the order."

I understood the reference to be to that saving foresail.

"Yes. He was afraid of it being lost in the setting."

"I assure you he never gave the order. He may think he did, but he never gave it. He stood there with me on the break of the poop after the main topsail blew away, and whimpered about our last hope—positively whimpered about it and nothing else—and the night coming on! To hear one's skipper go on like that in such weather was enough to drive any fellow out of his mind. It worked me up into a sort of desperation. I just took it into my own hands and went away from him, boiling, and—— But what's the use telling you? *You* know! . . . Do you think that if I had not been pretty fierce with them I should have got the men to do anything? Not I! The bo's'n perhaps? Perhaps! It wasn't a heavy sea—it was a sea gone mad! I suppose the end of the world will be something like that; and a man may have the heart to see it coming once and be done with it—but to have to face it day after day——I don't blame anybody. I was precious little better than the rest. Only—I was an officer of that old coal wagon, anyhow——"

"I quite understand," I conveyed that sincere assurance into his ear. He was out of breath with whispering; I could hear him pant slightly. It was all very simple. The same strung-up force which had given twenty-four men a chance, at least, for their lives, had, in a sort of recoil, crushed an unworthy mutinous existence.

---

11. *Yankee ships.* Officers on American ships of that time had a reputation for mistreating their crews.

But I had no leisure to weigh the merits of the matter—footsteps in the saloon, a heavy knock. "There's enough wind to get under way with, sir." Here was the call of a new claim upon my thoughts and even upon my feelings.

"Turn the hands up," I cried through the door. "I'll be on deck directly."

I was going out to make the acquaintance of my ship. Before I left the cabin our eyes met—the eyes of the only two strangers on board. I pointed to the recessed part where the little campstool awaited him and laid my finger on my lips. He made a gesture—somewhat vague—a little mysterious, accompanied by a faint smile, as if of regret.

This is not the place to enlarge upon the sensations of a man who feels for the first time a ship move under his feet to his own independent word. In my case they were not unalloyed. I was not wholly alone with my command; for there was that stranger in my cabin. Or rather, I was not completely and wholly with her. Part of me was absent. That mental feeling of being in two places at once affected me physically as if the mood of secrecy had penetrated my very soul. Before an hour had elapsed since the ship had begun to move, having occasion to ask the mate (he stood by my side) to take a compass bearing of the pagoda, I caught myself reaching up to his ear in whispers. I say I caught myself, but enough had escaped to startle the man. I can't describe it otherwise than by saying that he shied. A grave, preoccupied manner, as though he were in possession of some perplexing intelligence, did not leave him henceforth. A little later I moved away from the rail to look at the compass with such a stealthy gait that the helmsman noticed it—and I could not help noticing the unusual roundness of his eyes. These are trifling instances, though it's to no commander's advantage to be suspected of ludicrous eccentricities. But I was also more seriously affected. There are to a seaman certain words, gestures, that should in given conditions come as naturally, as instinctively as the winking of a menaced eye. A certain order should spring on to his lips without thinking; a certain sign should get itself made, so to speak, without reflection. But all unconscious alertness

had abandoned me. I had to make an effort of will to recall myself back (from the cabin) to the conditions of the moment. I felt that I was appearing an irresolute commander to those people who were watching me more or less critically.

And, besides, there were the scares. On the second day out, for instance, coming off the deck in the afternoon (I had straw slippers on my bare feet) I stopped at the open pantry door and spoke to the steward. He was doing something there with his back to me. At the sound of my voice he nearly jumped out of his skin, as the saying is, and incidentally broke a cup.

"What on earth's the matter with you?" I asked, astonished.

He was extremely confused. "Beg your pardon, sir. I made sure you were in your cabin."

"You see I wasn't."

"No, sir. I could have sworn I had heard you moving in there not a moment ago. It's most extraordinary . . . very sorry, sir."

I passed on with an inward shudder. I was so identified with my secret double that I did not even mention the fact in those scanty, fearful whispers we exchanged. I suppose he had made some slight noise of some kind or other. It would have been miraculous if he hadn't at one time or another. And yet, haggard as he appeared, he looked always perfectly self-controlled, more than calm—almost invulnerable. On my suggestion he remained almost entirely in the bathroom, which, upon the whole, was the safest place. There could be really no shadow of an excuse for anyone ever wanting to go in there, once the steward had done with it. It was a very tiny place. Sometimes he reclined on the floor, his legs bent, his head sustained on one elbow. At others I would find him on the campstool, sitting in his gray sleeping suit and with his cropped dark hair like a patient, unmoved convict. At night I would smuggle him into my bed place, and we would whisper together, with the regular footfalls of the officer of the watch passing and repassing over our heads. It was an infinitely miserable time. It was lucky that some tins of fine preserves were stowed in a locker in my stateroom; hard bread I could always get hold of; and so he lived on stewed chicken, *pâté de foie gras*,[12] asparagus, cooked oysters, sardines—on all sorts of abominable sham delicacies out of tins. My early-morning coffee he always drank; and it was all I dared do for him in that respect.

Every day there was the horrible maneuvering to go through so that my room and then the bathroom should be done in the usual way. I came to hate the sight of the steward, to abhor the voice of that harmless man. I felt that it was he who would bring on the disaster of discovery. It hung like a sword over our heads.

The fourth day out, I think (we were then working down the east side of the Gulf of Siam, tack for tack, in light winds and smooth water)—the fourth day, I say, of this miserable juggling with the unavoidable, as we sat at our evening meal, that man, whose slightest movement I dreaded, after putting down the dishes ran up on deck busily. This could not be dangerous. Presently he came down again; and then it appeared that he had remembered a coat of mine which I had thrown over a rail to dry after having been wetted in a shower which had passed over the ship in the afternoon. Sitting stolidly at the head of the table I became terrified at the sight of the garment on his arm. Of course he made for my door. There was no time to lose.

"Steward," I thundered. My nerves were so shaken that I could not govern my voice and conceal my agitation. This was the sort of thing that made my terrifically whiskered mate tap his forehead with his forefinger. I had detected him using that gesture while talking on deck with a confidential air to the carpenter. It was too far to hear a word, but I had no doubt that this pantomime could only refer to the strange new captain.

"Yes, sir," the pale-faced steward turned resignedly to me. It was this maddening course of being shouted at, checked without rhyme or reason, arbitrarily chased out of my cabin, suddenly called into it, sent flying out of his pantry on incomprehensible errands, that accounted for the growing wretchedness of his expression.

"Where are you going with that coat?"

"To your room, sir."

"Is there another shower coming?"

"I'm sure I don't know, sir. Shall I go up again and see, sir?"

"No! never mind."

My object was attained, as of course my other self in there would have heard everything that passed. During this interlude my two officers never raised their eyes off their respective plates; but the lip of that confounded cub, the second mate, quivered visibly.

I expected the steward to hook my coat on and come out at once. He was very slow about it; but I dominated my nervousness sufficiently not to shout after him. Suddenly I became aware (it could be heard plainly enough) that the fellow for some reason or other was opening the door of the bathroom. It was the end. The place was literally not big enough to swing a cat in. My voice died in my throat and I went stony all over. I expected to hear a yell of surprise and terror, and made a movement, but had not the strength to get on my legs. Everything remained still. Had my second self taken the poor wretch by the throat? I don't know what I could have done next moment if I had not seen the steward come out of my room, close the door, and then stand quietly by the sideboard.

"Saved," I thought. "But, no! Lost! Gone! He was gone!"

I laid my knife and fork down and leaned back in my chair. My head swam. After a while, when sufficiently recovered to speak in a steady voice, I instructed my mate to put the ship round at eight o'clock himself.

"I won't come on deck," I went on. "I think I'll turn in, and unless the wind shifts I don't want to be disturbed before midnight. I feel a bit seedy."

"You did look middling bad a little while ago," the chief mate remarked without showing any great concern.

They both went out, and I stared at the steward clearing the table. There was nothing to be read on that wretched man's face. But why did he avoid

---

12. *pâté de foie gras* (pä tā′ də fwä grä′), paste made of goose liver. [French]

my eyes, I asked myself. Then I thought I should like to hear the sound of his voice.

"Steward!"

"Sir!" Startled as usual.

"Where did you hang up that coat?"

"In the bathroom, sir." The usual anxious tone. "It's not quite dry yet, sir."

For some time longer I sat in the cuddy. Had my double vanished as he had come? But of his coming there was an explanation, whereas his disappearance would be inexplicable. . . . I went slowly into my dark room, shut the door, lighted the lamp, and for a time dared not turn around. When at last I did I saw him standing bolt-upright in the narrow recessed part. It would not be true to say I had a shock, but an irresistible doubt of his bodily existence flitted through my mind. Can it be, I asked myself, that he is not visible to other eyes than mine? It was like being haunted. Motionless, with a grave face, he raised his hands slightly at me in a gesture which meant clearly, "Heavens! what a narrow escape!" Narrow indeed. I think I had come creeping quietly as near insanity as any man who has not actually gone over the border. That gesture restrained me, so to speak.

The mate with the terrific whiskers was now putting the ship on the other tack. In the moment of profound silence which follows upon the hands going to their stations I heard on the poop his raised voice: "Hard alee!" and the distant shout of the order repeated on the main-deck. The sails, in that light breeze, made but a faint fluttering noise. It ceased. The ship was coming round slowly: I held my breath in the renewed stillness of expectation; one wouldn't have thought that there was a single living soul on her decks. A sudden brisk shout, "Mainsail haul!" broke the spell, and in the noisy cries and rush overhead of the men running away with the main brace we two, down in my cabin, came together in our usual position by the bed place.

He did not wait for my question. "I heard him fumbling here and just managed to squat myself down in the bath," he whispered to me. "The fellow only opened the door and put his arm in to hang the coat up. All the same——"

"I never thought of that," I whispered back, even more appalled than before at the closeness of the shave, and marveling at that something unyielding in his character which was carrying him through so finely. There was no agitation in his whisper. Whoever was being driven distracted, it was not he. He was sane. And the proof of his sanity was continued when he took up the whispering again.

"It would never do for me to come to life again."

It was something that a ghost might have said. But what he was alluding to was his old captain's reluctant admission of the theory of suicide. It would obviously serve his turn—if I had understood at all the view which seemed to govern the unalterable purpose of his action.

"You must maroon me as soon as ever you can get amongst these islands off the Cambodge shore," he went on.

"Maroon you! We are not living in a boy's adventure tale," I protested. His scornful whispering took me up.

"We aren't indeed! There's nothing of a boy's tale in this. But there's nothing else for it. I want no more. You don't suppose I am afraid of what can be done to me? Prison or gallows or whatever they may please. But you don't see me coming back to explain such things to an old fellow in a wig[13] and twelve respectable tradesmen, do you? What can they know whether I am guilty or not—or of *what* I am guilty, either? That's my affair. What does the Bible say? 'Driven off the face of the earth.' Very well, I am off the face of the earth now. As I came at night so I shall go."

"Impossible!" I murmured. "You can't."

"Can't?. . . Not naked like a soul on the Day of Judgment. I shall freeze on to this sleeping suit. The Last Day is not yet—and . . . you have understood thoroughly. Didn't you?"

I felt suddenly ashamed of myself. I may say truly that I understood—and my hesitation in letting that man swim away from my ship's side had been a mere sham sentiment, a sort of cowardice.

---

13. *old fellow in a wig.* British judges wear wigs in court.

Bangkok, city of Pagodas, where Conrad took command of the *Otago*. He drew upon experiences of his stay here in writing "The Secret Sharer."

"It can't be done now till next night," I breathed out. "The ship is on the off shore tack and the wind may fail us."

"As long as I know that you understand," he whispered. "But of course you do. It's a great satisfaction to have got somebody to understand. You seem to have been there on purpose." And in the same whisper, as if we two whenever we talked had to say things to each other which were not fit for the world to hear, he added, "It's very wonderful."

We remained side by side talking in our secret way—but sometimes silent or just exchanging a whispered word or two at long intervals. And as usual he stared through the port. A breath of wind came now and again into our faces. The ship might have been moored in dock, so gently and on an even keel she slipped through the water, that did not murmur even at our passage, shadowy and silent like a phantom sea.

At midnight I went on deck, and to my mate's great surprise put the ship round on the other tack. His terrible whiskers flitted round me in silent criticism. I certainly should not have done it if it had been only a question of getting out of that sleepy gulf as quickly as possible. I believe he told the second mate, who relieved him, that it was a great want of judgment. The other only yawned. That intolerable cub shuffled about so sleepily and lolled against the rails in such a slack, improper fashion that I came down on him sharply.

"Aren't you properly awake yet?"

"Yes, sir! I am awake."

"Well, then, be good enough to hold yourself as if you were. And keep a lookout. If there's any current we'll be closing with some islands before daylight."

The east side of the gulf is fringed with islands, some solitary, others in groups. On the blue background of the high coast they seem to float on silvery patches of calm water, arid and gray, or dark green and rounded like clumps of evergreen bushes, with the larger ones, a mile or two long, showing the outlines of ridges, ribs of gray rock under the dank mantle of matted leafage. Unknown to trade, to travel, almost to geography, the manner of life they harbor is an unsolved secret. There must be villages—settlements of fishermen at least—on the largest of them, and some communication with the world is probably kept up by native craft. But all that forenoon, as we headed for them, fanned along by the faintest of breezes,

I saw no sign of man or canoe in the field of the telescope I kept on pointing at the scattered group.

At noon I gave no orders for a change of course, and the mate's whiskers became much concerned and seemed to be offering themselves unduly to my notice. At last I said:

"I am going to stand right in.[14] Quite in—as far as I can take her."

The stare of extreme surprise imparted an air of ferocity also to his eyes, and he looked truly terrific for a moment.

"We're not doing well in the middle of the gulf," I continued, casually. "I am going to look for the land breezes tonight."

"Bless my soul! Do you mean, sir, in the dark amongst the lot of all them islands and reefs and shoals?"

"Well—if there are any regular land breezes at all on this coast one must get close inshore to find them, mustn't one?"

"Bless my soul!" he exclaimed again under his breath. All that afternoon he wore a dreamy, contemplative appearance which in him was a mark of perplexity.

After dinner I went into my stateroom as if I meant to take some rest. There we two bent our dark heads over a half-unrolled chart lying on my bed.

"There," I said, "It's got to be Koh-ring. I've been looking at it ever since sunrise. It has got two hills and a low point. It must be inhabited. And on the coast opposite there is what looks like the mouth of a biggish river—with some towns, no doubt, not far up. It's the best chance for you that I can see."

"Anything. Koh-ring let it be."

He looked thoughtfully at the chart as if surveying chances and distances from a lofty height—and following with his eyes his own figure wandering on the blank land of Cochin-China, and then passing off that piece of paper clean out of sight into uncharted regions. And it was as if the ship had two captains to plan her course for her. I had been so worried and restless running up and down that I had not had the patience to dress that day. I had remained in my sleeping suit, with straw slip-pers and a soft floppy hat. The closeness of the heat in the gulf had been most oppressive, and the crew were used to seeing me wandering in that airy attire.

"She will clear the south point as she heads now," I whispered into his ear. "Goodness only knows when, though, but certainly after dark. I'll edge her in to half a mile, as far as I may be able to judge in the dark——"

"Be careful," he murmured, warningly—and I realized suddenly that all my future, the only future for which I was fit, would perhaps go irretrievably to pieces in any mishap to my first command.

I could not stop a moment longer in the room. I motioned him to get out of sight and made my way on the poop. That unplayful cub had the watch. I walked up and down for a while thinking things out, then beckoned him over.

"Send a couple of hands to open the two quarter-deck ports," I said, mildly.

He actually had the impudence, or else so forgot himself in his wonder at such a incomprehensible order, as to repeat:

"Open the quarter-deck ports! What for, sir?"

"The only reason you need concern yourself about is because I tell you to do so. Have them open wide and fastened properly."

He reddened and went off, but I believe made some jeering remark to the carpenter as to the sensible practice of ventilating a ship's quarter-deck. I know he popped into the mate's cabin to impart the fact to him because the whiskers came on deck, as it were by chance, and stole glances at me from below—for signs of lunacy or drunkenness, I suppose.

A little before supper, feeling more restless than ever, I rejoined for a moment my second self. And to find him sitting so quietly was surprising, like something against nature, inhuman.

I developed my plan in a hurried whisper.

"I shall stand in as close as I dare and then put her round. I will presently find means to smuggle

---

14. *stand in*, sail close to shore.

you out of here into the sail locker, which communicates with the lobby. But there is an opening, a sort of square for hauling the sails out, which gives straight on the quarter-deck and which is never closed in fine weather, so as to give air to the sails. When the ship's way is deadened in stays and all the hands are aft at the main braces you will have a clear road to slip out and get overboard through the open quarter-deck port. I've had them both fastened up. Use a rope's end to lower yourself into the water so as to avoid a splash—you know. It could be heard and cause some beastly complication."

He kept silent for a while, then whispered, "I understand."

"I won't be there to see you go," I began with an effort. "The rest . . . I only hope I have understood, too."

"You have. From first to last"—and for the first time there seemed to be a faltering, something strained in his whisper. He caught hold of my arm, but the ringing of the supper bell made me start. He didn't though; he only released his grip.

After supper I didn't come below again till well past eight o'clock. The faint, steady breeze was loaded with dew; and the wet, darkened sails held all there was of propelling power in it. The night, clear and starry, sparkled darkly, and the opaque, lightless patches shifting slowly against the low stars were the drifting islets. On the port bow there was a big one more distant and shadowily imposing by the great space of sky it eclipsed.

On opening the door I had a back view of my very own self looking at a chart. He had come out of the recess and was standing near the table.

"Quite dark enough," I whispered.

He stepped back and leaned against my bed with a level, quiet glance. I sat on the couch. We had nothing to say to each other. Over our heads the officer of the watch moved here and there. Then I heard him move quickly. I knew what that meant. He was making for the companion; and presently his voice was outside my door.

"We are drawing in pretty fast, sir. Land looks rather close."

"Very well," I answered. "I am coming on deck directly."

I waited till he was gone out of the cuddy, then rose. My double moved, too. The time had come to exchange our last whispers, for neither of us was ever to hear each other's natural voice.

"Look here!" I opened a drawer and took out three sovereigns.[15] "Take this anyhow. I've got six and I'd give you the lot, only I must keep a little money to buy some fruit and vegetables for the crew from native boats as we go through Sunda Straits."

He shook his head.

"Take it," I urged him, whispering desperately. "No one can tell what——"

He smiled and slapped meaningly the only pocket of the sleeping jacket. It was not safe, certainly. But I produced a large old silk handkerchief of mine, and tying the three pieces of gold in a corner, pressed it on him. He was touched, I supposed, because he took it at last and tied it quickly round his waist under the jacket, on his bare skin.

Our eyes met; several seconds elapsed, till, our glances still mingled, I extended my hand and turned the lamp out. Then I passed through the cuddy, leaving the door of my room wide open. . . . "Steward!"

He was still lingering in the pantry in the greatness of his zeal, giving a rub-up to a plated cruet stand the last thing before going to bed. Being careful not to wake up the mate, whose room was opposite, I spoke in an undertone.

He looked round anxiously. "Sir!"

"Can you get me a little hot water from the galley?"

"I am afraid, sir, the galley fire's been out for some time now."

"Go and see."

"Now," I whispered, loudly, into the saloon—too loudly, perhaps, but I was afraid I couldn't make a sound. He was by my side in an instant—the double captain slipped past the stairs—through a tiny dark passage . . . a sliding

---

15. *sovereigns*, British coins, each worth about $5.00 at the time of the story.

door. We were in the sail locker, scrambling on our knees over the sails. A sudden thought struck me. I saw myself wandering barefooted, bareheaded, the sun beating on my dark poll. I snatched off my floppy hat and tried hurriedly in the dark to ram it on my other self. He dodged and fended off silently. I wonder what he thought had come to me before he understood and suddenly desisted. Our hands met gropingly, lingered united in a steady, motionless clasp for a second. . . . No word was breathed by either of us when they separated.

I was standing quietly by the pantry door when the steward returned.

"Sorry, sir. Kettle barely warm. Shall I light the spirit lamp?"

"Never mind."

I came out on deck slowly. It was now a matter of conscience to shave the land as close as possible—for now he must go overboard whenever the ship was put in stays. Must! There could be no going back for him. After a moment I walked over to leeward and my heart flew into my mouth at the nearness of the land on the bow. Under any other circumstances I would not have held on a minute longer. The second mate had followed me anxiously.

I looked on till I felt I could command my voice.

"She will weather," I said then in a quiet tone.

"Are you going to try that, sir?" he stammered out incredulously.

I took no notice of him and raised my tone just enough to be heard by the helmsman.

"Keep her good full."

"Good full, sir."

The wind fanned my cheek, the sails slept, the world was silent. The strain of watching the dark loom of the land grow bigger and denser was too much for me. I had shut my eyes—because the ship must go closer. She must! The stillness was intolerable. Were we standing still?

When I opened my eyes the second view started my heart with a thump. The black southern hill of Koh-ring seemed to hang right over the ship like a towering fragment of the ever-lasting night. On that enormous mass of blackness there was not a gleam to be seen, not a sound to be heard. It

was gliding irresistibly towards us and yet seemed already within reach of the hand. I saw the vague figures of the watch grouped in the waist, gazing in awed silence.

"Are you going on, sir?" inquired an unsteady voice at my elbow.

I ignored it. I had to go on.

"Keep her full. Don't check her way. That won't do now," I said, warningly.

"I can't see the sails very well," the helmsman answered me, in strange, quavering tones.

Was she close enough? Already she was, I won't say in the shadow of the land, but in the very blackness of it, already swallowed up as it were, gone too close to be recalled, gone from me altogether.

"Give the mate a call," I said to the young man who stood at my elbow as still as death. "And turn all hands up."

My tone had a borrowed loudness reverberated from the height of the land. Several voices cried out together: "We are all on deck, sir."

Then stillness again, with the great shadow gliding closer, towering higher, without a light, without a sound. Such a hush had fallen on the ship that she might have been a bark of the dead floating in slowly under the very gate of Erebus.[16]

"My God! Where are we?"

It was the mate moaning at my elbow. He was thunderstruck, and as it were deprived of the moral support of his whiskers. He clapped his hands and absolutely cried out, "Lost!"

"Be quiet," I said, sternly.

He lowered his tone, but I saw the shadowy gesture of his despair. "What are we doing here?"

"Looking for the land wind."

He made as if to tear his hair, and addressed me recklessly.

"She will never get out. You have done it, sir. I knew it'd end in something like this. She will never weather, and you are too close now to stay. She'll drift ashore before she's round. O my God!"

I caught his arm as he was raising it to batter his poor devoted head, and shook it violently.

---

16. gate of Erebus (er′ə bəs), in Greek mythology, the entrance to the land of the dead.

Strong Wind on the Port Quarter, a pastel by John Michael Groves. 1977

"She's ashore already," he wailed, trying to tear himself away.

"Is she? . . . Keep good full there!"

"Good full, sir," cried the helmsman in a frightened, thin, childlike voice.

I hadn't let go the mate's arm and went on shaking it. "Ready about, do you hear? You go forward"—shake—"and stop there"—shake—"and hold your noise"—shake—"and see these headsheets properly overhauled"—shake, shake—shake.

And all the time I dared not look towards the land lest my heart should fail me. I released my grip at last and he ran forward as if fleeing for dear life.

I wondered what my double there in the sail locker thought of this commotion. He was able to hear everything—and perhaps he was able to understand why, on my conscience, it had to be thus close—no less. My first order "Hard alee!" re-echoed ominously under the towering shadow of Koh-ring as if I had shouted in a mountain gorge. And then I watched the land intently. In that smooth water and light wind it was impossible to feel the ship coming-to. No! I could not feel her. And my second self was making now ready to ship out and lower himself overboard. Perhaps he was gone already . . . ?

The great black mass brooding over our very mastheads began to pivot away from the ship's side silently. And now I forgot the secret stranger ready to depart, and remembered only that I was a total stranger to the ship. I did not know her. Would she do it? How was she to be handled?

I swung the mainyard and waited helplessly. She was perhaps stopped, and her very fate hung in the balance, with the black mass of Koh-ring like the gate of the everlasting night towering over her taffrail. What would she do now? Had she way on her yet? I stepped to the side swiftly, and on the shadowy water I could see nothing except a faint phosphorescent flash revealing the glassy smoothness of the sleeping surface. It was impossible to tell—and I had not learned yet the feel of my ship. Was she moving? What I needed was something easily seen, a piece of paper, which I could throw overboard and watch. I had nothing on me. To run down for it I didn't dare. There was no time. All at once my strained, yearning stare distinguished a white object floating within a yard of the ship's side. White on the black water. A phosphorescent flash passed under it. What was that thing? . . . I recognized my own floppy hat. It must have fallen off his head . . . and he didn't bother. Now I had what I wanted—the saving mark for my eyes. But I hardly thought of my other self, now gone from the ship, to be hidden forever from all friendly faces, to be a fugitive and a vagabond on the earth, with no brand of the curse on his sane forehead to stay a slaying hand . . . too proud to explain.

And I watched the hat—the expression of my sudden pity for his mere flesh. It had been meant to save his homeless head from the dangers of the sun. And now—behold—it was saving the ship, by serving me for a mark to help out the ignorance of my strangeness. Ha! It was drifting forward, warning me just in time that the ship had gathered sternway.

"Shift the helm," I said in a low voice to the seaman standing still like a statue.

The man's eyes glistened wildly in the binnacle light as he jumped round to the other side and spun round the wheel.

I walked to the break of the poop. On the over-shadowed deck all hands stood by the forebraces waiting for my order. The stars ahead seemed to be gliding from right to left. And all was so still in the world that I heard the quiet remark, "She's round," passed in a tone of intense relief between two seamen.

"Let go and haul."

The foreyards ran round with a great noise, amidst cheery cries. And now the frightful whiskers made themselves heard giving various orders. Already the ship was drawing ahead. And I was alone with her. Nothing! no one in the world should stand now between us, throwing a shadow on the way of silent knowledge and mute affection, the perfect communion of a seaman with his first command.

Walking to the taffrail, I was in time to make out, on the very edge of a darkness thrown by a towering black mass like the very gateway of Erebus—yes, I was in time to catch an evanescent glimpse of my white hat left behind to mark the spot where the secret sharer of my cabin and of my thoughts, as though he were my second self, had lowered himself into the water to take his punishment: a free man, a proud swimmer striking out for a new destiny.

THINK AND DISCUSS
Understanding
1. Explain the circumstances that make the narrator the only man on deck when Leggatt grips the rope ladder.
2. Describe the risks the narrator takes in getting rid of his secret sharer.

Analyzing
3. Explain why, during their first conversation, Leggatt doesn't ask the narrator for help, and the narrator doesn't explain what he plans to do.
4. How and why does the narrator limit his characterization of the first and second mates?
5. Define the moral ambiguities in Leggatt's killing of the sailor on the *Sephora*.
6. Explain what the narrator means when he says he could not lie "for psychological (not moral) reasons." How, then, does he avoid telling the truth?
7. The narrator repeatedly notes that Leggatt is his double, and that he feels he is two men while Leggatt hides in his cabin. To what extent are these men like each other? How are they different?

8. In what ways might Conrad use Leggatt's name as a meaningful pun? (Look up *legate* in the Glossary before answering this question.)
9. In what ways does the black shadow of Koh-ring represent the gates of Erebus for the narrator?
10. Explain the **symbolic** implications of the narrator's floppy hat.

Extending
11. Leggatt insists that a British judge and jury are not competent to determine "of *what* I am guilty." Discuss the kind of moral position he takes here and whether it has any validity.
12. The narrator ends his story with the judgment that Leggatt swam away to take his punishment as a free man "striking out for a new destiny." Make your own judgment of Leggatt.

REVIEWING: Inference HẬ
See Handbook of Literary Terms, p. 911
   An inference is a reasonable conclusion drawn from fragmentary information or clues.

1. What does the narrator infer about Archbold's character from their encounter?
2. Given the narrator's report of Archbold's visit to his ship, can you infer that Leggatt's account of what happened during the storm is accurate?
3. From the way he now recalls these experiences, what happened subsequently in the narrator's career?

THINKING SKILLS
Generalizing
   General conclusions derived from particular information are **generalizations.**

1. In general, what is the narrator's attitude toward his crew members?
2. How does he usually treat his steward?
3. What attitude do Leggatt and the narrator generally share about the people they left behind in England?

COMPOSITION ◀━▶
Explaining the Point of View
   The first-person narrator of "The Secret Sharer" presents a highly subjective account of what happens. Write an essay of at least four paragraphs to be read by your teacher in which you explain what the narrator is like and how you can tell from his **point of view.** First skim the story to choose passages in which he describes someone's physical appearance, evaluates someone's action, and accounts for his own decision. Devote a paragraph to your best example of each of these. Then, in your final paragraph, describe what kind of captain and what kind of person the narrator is. See "Writing About Point of View" in the Writer's Handbook.

Analyzing Conrad's Symbolism
   Details in "The Secret Sharer" suggest that Conrad might be using the human head as a **symbol,** although readers have never come to an agreement as to what it might symbolize. Write a paper of at least four paragraphs in which you develop your own theory about this symbol. First look through the story to find instances where a head or a hat is mentioned; for example, when the narrator first sees Leggatt, he appears headless. Choose the best instances, and develop them in separate paragraphs. When you have finished writing, compare your theory with those of your classmates. See "Writing About Symbolism" in the Writer's Handbook.

ENRICHMENT
Debating Leggatt's Crime
   Leggatt and the narrator defy the legal and moral conventions of their society, claiming the right to be governed by another code of conduct. Organize and present a debate in class on the topic: Leggatt should be apprehended, tried, and judged according to English maritime law. Assign two teams to argue for and against this assertion. Both teams should review all the evidence given in the story and plan how best to present their side of the issue. During the debate the other members of the class should listen carefully to the arguments of both sides, and when the debate is over they should vote on which side wins.

As the oldest in a family of seven, Housman spent much of his boyhood instructing younger brothers and sisters, anticipating the teaching role he was to take for most of his life. During these years he was very close to his mother, and under her direction he made a close study of the Bible.

Housman entered a private secondary school at age eleven. The next year brought the first major blow in his unhappy life. His mother, exhausted by the strain of childbearing and embittered by her husband's infidelities, died prematurely. Housman brooded over the injustice of her suffering.

At school he was a promising scholar of classical languages and won the prize for poetry two years in a row. In 1877 he entered Oxford on a scholarship. There he found the quality of instruction inadequate, and he soon began skipping lectures and ignoring required reading assignments. With friends he founded and co-edited an under-graduate magazine, *Ye Round Table,* to which he contributed high-spirited parodies of contemporary poetry and fiction. Privately, however, his view of himself and the world grew darker, and by 1880 he was a confirmed atheist.

In 1881 Housman failed the Oxford comprehensive examination in classics. He had clearly overestimated his own studies and foolishly ignored whole areas on which he was to be tested. He returned home, taught in a local school for a few months, and then acquired a civil service job.

Living now in London, Housman resolved to vindicate himself, and in his free time he began on a course of intensive study of the classics. During the next ten years (1882–1892) he wrote over twenty scholarly essays, and when the post of Professor of Latin at the University of London became available in 1893, he applied, informing the College authorities of his failure at Oxford but also enclosing letters of commendation from seventeen authorities in his field. He got the job.

Housman had written poetry, on and off, since his boyhood, but beginning in 1893 a fresh burst of inspiration came to him and by 1895 he had fifty-eight lyrics ready. Published that year at his own expense as *A Shropshire Lad,* the book enjoyed at first a very moderate success, but its reputation grew with time.

Housman's poetry is artfully simple. His subjects are the universal ones, love and death, overshadowed in his treatment by a pervasive pessimism. The "business of poetry," he once said, "is to harmonize the sadness of the universe." While the poems may allude to rural Shropshire, they do not grow out of experience. This is a stylized, literary countryside which owes more to Latin pastoral poetry than to conversations with real shepherds. But the sound of the verse does echo the music of folk ballads and song lyrics, and Housman's language is simple and straightforward.

In his last years Housman enjoyed international acclaim for his scholarly work. But his work as a poet was essentially over. While he tried to present *Last Poems* (1922) as new work, most of its lyrics come from the time of *A Shropshire Lad.* The inspiration of those years never returned to him.

When I Was One-and-Twenty

When I was one-and-twenty
  I heard a wise man say,
"Give crowns and pounds and guineas
  But not your heart away;
5 Give pearls away and rubies
  But keep your fancy free."
But I was one-and-twenty,
  No use to talk to me.

When I was one-and-twenty
10   I heard him say again,
"The heart out of the bosom
  Was never given in vain;
'Tis paid with sighs a plenty
  And sold for endless rue."
15 And I am two-and-twenty,
  And oh, 'tis true, 'tis true.

1896

Comment

Housman on Writing His Poetry

Late in his life A. E. Housman accepted an invitation to lecture on poetry at Cambridge. At the end of his remarks he turned to the definition of the term. "Poetry," he said, ". . . seems to me more physical than intellectual . . ." and he went on to describe the physical "symptoms" which it "provokes": "Experience has taught me, when I am shaving of a morning, to keep watch over my thoughts, because, if a line of poetry strays into my memory, my skin bristles so that the razor ceases to act. This particular symptom is accompanied by a shiver down the spine . . ." Housman's description of how his poems began is equally physical: "Having drunk a pint of beer at luncheon—beer is a sedative to the brain, and my afternoons are the least intellectual portion of my life—I would go out for a walk of two or three hours. As I went along, thinking of nothing in particular, only looking at things around me and following the progress of the seasons, there would flow into my mind, with sudden and unaccountable emotion, sometimes a line or two of verse, sometimes a whole stanza at once, accompanied, not preceded, by a vague notion of the poem which they were destined to form a part of. Then there would usually be a lull of an hour or so, then perhaps the spring would bubble up again . . . When I got home I wrote them down, leaving gaps, and hoping that further inspiration might be forthcoming another day."

Excerpt from "The Name and Nature of Poetry" from *A. E. Housman Selected Prose*, edited by John Carter. Copyright ©1961 by Cambridge University Press. Reprinted by permission.

A. E. Housman

See ANASTROPHE in the Handbook of Literary Terms, page 907.

Loveliest of Trees ✓

Loveliest of trees, the cherry now
Is hung with bloom along the bough,
And stands about the woodland ride,
Wearing white for Eastertide.

5 Now, of my threescore years and ten,
Twenty will not come again,

And take from seventy springs a score,
It only leaves me fifty more.

And since to look at things in bloom
10 Fifty springs are little room,
About the woodlands I will go
To see the cherry hung with snow.

1896

To an Athlete Dying Young ✓

The time you won your town the race
We chaired you through the market place;
Man and boy stood cheering by,
And home we brought you shoulder-high.

5 Today, the road all runners come,
Shoulder-high we bring you home,
And set you at your threshold down,
Townsman of a stiller town.

Smart lad, to slip betimes away
10 From fields where glory does not stay,
And early though the laurel[1] grows
It withers quicker than the rose.

Eyes the shady night has shut
Cannot see the record cut,
15 And silence sounds no worse than cheers
After earth has stopped the ears.

Now you will not swell the rout
Of lads that wore their honors out,

Runners whom renown outran
20 And the name died before the man.

So set, before its echoes fade,
The fleet foot on the sill of shade,
And hold to the low lintel up
The still-defended challenge cup.

25 And round that early-laureled head
Will flock to gaze the strengthless dead,
And find unwithered on its curls
The garland briefer than a girl's.

1896

---

1. laurel. In Greek and Roman times victorious athletes and celebrated poets would be ceremonially crowned with a wreath or garland of laurel leaves.

In a Shoreham Garden, by Samuel Palmer. 1829. *Victoria and Albert Museum*

A. E. Housman

THINK AND DISCUSS

WHEN I WAS ONE-AND-TWENTY

Understanding

1. What wise advice does the speaker ignore?

Analyzing

2. Note, in the advice, the verbs that have to do with trade or commerce. How does the speaker react **ironically** to them?
3. Explain the effect of the long list of things that he *can* give away.

Extending

4. Read the poem aloud, noting its **rhythm** and **rhyme**. How do they affect your reaction to what the speaker is saying?

LOVELIEST OF TREES

Understanding

1. How does the speaker justify taking a day off?

Analyzing

2. What is it about the cherry tree that makes it the "loveliest of trees" for this speaker? Consider, especially, the **connotations** of the poem's final **metaphor**.
3. What is the speaker doing in the second stanza? Why?

Extending

4. Explain the *carpe diem* element in this lyric.

APPLYING: Anastrophe HⱫ
See Handbook of Literary Terms, p. 907

The technique of inverting the normal, customary, or logical sequence of the words in a sentence to achieve greater dramatic emphasis or to create particular rhythms or rhymes is called **anastrophe**. For example, Tennyson's "The Lady of Shalott" begins, "On either side the river lie/Long fields of barley and of rye . . ." in which *fields* and *lie* are inverted from subject-verb order.

1. In ordinary speech, where would "now" appear in the first sentence of "Loveliest of Trees"?

2. Rewrite the last stanza as a conventional sentence and consider why Housman used anastrophe there.

THINK AND DISCUSS

TO AN ATHLETE DYING YOUNG

Understanding

1. What two ceremonies are depicted in this poem?

Analyzing

2. Why does the speaker consider the athlete a "Smart lad" (line 9)?
3. How can the garland (line 27) remain unwithered?
4. Describe in your own words the scene depicted in the last two stanzas.

Extending

5. Explore the ways this poem echoes Thomas Gray's "Elegy Written in a Country Churchyard." (See especially line 36 of that poem.)

COMPOSITION ✎

Imagining Alternative Choices

These Housman lyrics all describe making a decision: to love, to take a day off, to die young. Write a fanciful prose narrative in which a person makes the opposite choice—not to love, to stay at work, or to keep racing. Your narrative should present, in the form of action and description, the consequences of such a decision. Share your narrative with your classmates.

Persuading to Stay in Competition

Housman's "To an Athlete Dying Young" praises the "Smart lad" for slipping away before someone betters his record. Write an essay that persuades a person of your own age to keep competing. Prepare by listing the kinds of arguments Housman and others use to suggest that it is wiser to quit while you are still ahead. Then think of arguments to oppose each of these. Determine what your most convincing ideas are, and organize your paragraphs to move from the weakest to the best.

The world of Kipling's youth has now almost entirely disappeared. He was born in Bombay, into the British Empire at its height, when England ruled the entire subcontinent of India. In his first years a household of native servants cared for him. He spoke their tongue more readily than his own and accompanied them to places Europeans rarely saw.

To guard his health and expand his horizon, Kipling's parents took him to England in 1871. For the next six years he and his sister boarded with an English family and attended local schools. Kipling had been a spoiled and willful child and was unprepared for the tyrannous control exercised by his paid guardians. Though bitterly unhappy he kept his troubles from his parents. In 1878 they enrolled him in the United Services College, a secondary school designed to train the less-than-brilliant sons of not very wealthy families for careers in military service.

At seventeen he returned to India. His father had found him a job as editorial assistant for a newspaper in Lahore. Here Kipling learned the newspaper trade and began to write poems and stories to fill up the occasionally empty column. He entered into the world of colonial administrators and soldiers and began to reproduce it in his writings.

His first book, *Departmental Ditties* (1886), was something new in English literature, describing the personalities and petty aspirations of a colonial society in a strongly cadenced verse derived from ballads and theatrical patter songs. Many of these poems are in dialect. The book sold very well. In the next years Kipling wrote a series of stories first published in newspapers and then collected in book editions sold in Indian railway stations. These were immensely successful, and by 1889 he felt ready to move to England and challenge the literary establishment at its center.

In the 1890s, along with several collections of stories, he published the two volumes of the *Jungle Book* (1894) and the sea tale *Captains Courageous*. In 1901 his finest novel, *Kim*, appeared.

By now Kipling's works had achieved enormous popularity. His poems were recited and sung in music-halls, his stories were a prized feature of the magazines in which they appeared, and his books were best sellers. He became a public figure who frequently contributed topical poems and letters to the newspapers. However, his strong support for the Empire and the military, his enthusiasm for the war in South Africa, and his hatred of Germany made him controversial. When, in October of 1915, he learned that his son was missing in action, he stopped writing fiction.

In the 1920s and 1930s Kipling again began to publish stories and poems, and in fact his latest tales may well be his best. During his lifetime Kipling made a fortune as a writer, was the respected confidant of heads of state and military leaders, and won the Nobel Prize for Literature (1907). After his death a revulsion against his belief in empire and his admiration for force damaged his literary reputation. As time passes, however, the skill and power of his writing are once again drawing serious attention.

Rudyard Kipling

Recessional

A recessional is a hymn sung as the choir leaves the church service. This poem was published in the *London Times* in July, 1897, near the close of the celebration, in London, of the sixtieth anniversary of the accession of Queen Victoria—the Diamond Jubilee. High government officials and troops, as well as kings and representatives of all the important nations of the world, were assembled for the ceremonies. So, too, were soldiers from all the colonies and dominions of the British Empire; and nearly two hundred vessels of the Royal Navy were gathered in English waters. Thus it was a most appropriate time for Kipling to sound a warning, in almost Old Testament manner, to the nation dazzled by the pomp and splendor of the occasion.

God of our fathers, known of old,
Lord of our far-flung battle line,
Beneath whose awful hand we hold
Dominion over palm and pine[1]
5 Lord God of Hosts,[2] be with us yet,
Lest we forget[3]—lest we forget!

The tumult and the shouting dies;[4]
The captains and the kings depart:
Still stands Thine ancient sacrifice,
10 An humble and a contrite heart.[5]
Lord God of Hosts, be with us yet,
Lest we forget—lest we forget!

Far-called, our navies melt away;
On dune and headland sinks the fire:
15 Lo, all our pomp of yesterday
Is one with Nineveh and Tyre![6]
Judge of the Nations, spare us yet,
Lest we forget—lest we forget!

If, drunk with sight of power, we loose
20 Wild tongues that have not Thee in awe,
Such boastings as the Gentiles use,
Or lesser breeds without the Law[7]—
Lord God of Hosts, be with us yet,
Lest we forget—lest we forget!

25 For heathen heart that puts her trust
In reeking tube and iron shard,[8]
All valiant dust that builds on dust,
And guarding, calls not Thee to guard,
For frantic boast and foolish word—
30 Thy Mercy on Thy People, Lord!

1. *palm and pine,* symbolic of the geographical spread of the British Empire from the tropics to the northland.
2. *Lord God of Hosts,* a common Biblical expression.
3. *Lest we forget,* based upon the Biblical passage, "Then beware lest thou forget the Lord." (Deuteronomy 6:12)
4. *The tumult . . . dies,* based upon the Biblical passage, "He smelleth the battle afar off, the thunder of the captains, and the shouting." (Job 39:25)
5. *Thine ancient sacrifice . . . heart,* based upon the Biblical passage, "The sacrifices of God are a broken spirit; a broken and a contrite heart, O God, thou wilt not despise." (Psalms 51:17)
6. *Nineveh* (nĭn′ə və) *and Tyre* (tīr). Nineveh, now buried under the sands, was the capital of ancient Assyria. Tyre, now a seaport on the coast of Palestine, was once a great city of the ancient Phoenicians.
7. *the Gentiles . . . Law,* based upon the Biblical passage, "For when the Gentiles, which have not the law, do by nature the things contained in the law, these, having not the law, are a law unto themselves." (Romans 2:14) In this poem Kipling thinks of the Gentiles as being those who are not English.
8. *reeking tube and iron shard,* gun barrel and fragment of shell.

"Recessional," from *The Five Nations* by Rudyard Kipling. Copyright 1910 by Rudyard Kipling.

If___ ✓

If you can keep your head when all about you
  Are losing theirs and blaming it on you,
If you can trust yourself when all men doubt
  you,
  But make allowance for their doubting too;
5 If you can wait and not be tired by waiting,
  Or being lied about, don't deal in lies,
Or being hated, don't give way to hating,
  And yet don't look too good, nor talk too
  wise:

If you can dream—and not make dreams your
  master;
10 If you can think—and not make thoughts
  your aim;
If you can meet with Triumph and Disaster
  And treat those two impostors just the same;
If you can bear to hear the truth you've spoken
  Twisted by knaves to make a trap for fools,
15 Or watch the things you gave your life to,
  broken,
  And stoop and build 'em up with worn-out
  tools:

If you can make one heap of all your winnings
  And risk it on one turn of pitch-and-toss,
And lose, and start again at your beginnings
20 And never breathe a word about your loss;
If you can force your heart and nerve and sinew
  To serve your turn long after they are gone,
And so hold on when there is nothing in you
  Except the Will which says to them: "Hold
  on!"

25 If you can talk with crowds and keep your virtue,
  Or walk with Kings—nor lose the common
  touch,
If neither foes nor loving friends can hurt you,
  If all men count with you, but none too much;
If you can fill the unforgiving minute
30 With sixty seconds' worth of distance run,
Yours is the Earth and everything that's in it,
  And—which is more—you'll be a Man,
  my son!

Queen Victoria arriving at St. Paul's for the Diamond Jubilee Thanksgiving Service, 1897, by
Andrew C. Gow. 1897. *Guildhall Art Gallery, City of London*

Rudyard Kipling

THINK AND DISCUSS
RECESSIONAL
Understanding
1. This poem is directly addressed to God. To whom is it indirectly addressed?
2. What does the speaker fear his people will forget?

Analyzing
3. How does the poem picture the British Empire?
4. What lesson does the "ancient sacrifice" (line 9) have to teach?
5. Explain the warning implicit in the **allusion** to Nineveh and Tyre.
6. What should the English trust?

Extending
7. To what extent might the warnings in this poem apply to modern-day America?

IF _____
Understanding
1. What are the rewards to be gained by fulfilling all the requirements listed?

Analyzing
2. How does "If _____" picture other people?
3. In adversity, what is the necessary reaction?
4. When all else fails, what human faculty should one rely upon?
5. How can success itself become a danger?
6. Explain the **metaphor** in lines 29–30.
7. What is meant by line 31?

Extending
8. Does the attitude expressed apply equally to women? Do you think Kipling intended it to? Explain.
9. Do you find yourself taking issue with some of the virtues this poem extols?

COMPOSITION
Explaining the Themes in "Recessional"
Kipling's poem describes the British Empire in terms of the lands it embraces and the military power it uses to control those lands, but it also makes use of biblical themes. Write a three-paragraph paper describing to someone who has not read the poem how it alternates between these two very different traditions. In your first paragraph, summarize the poem's themes so that your reader understands Kipling's purpose. In your second paragraph, explain how the poem depicts empire. In your final paragraph, explain how Kipling talks about God and how he connects this with his late-Victorian theme. See "Writing About Theme" in the Writer's Handbook.

Evaluating the Virtues in "If _____"
In the poem Kipling extols certain virtues and conspicuously ignores others: where is knowledge, for example, or love? Write an essay for your classmates in which you evaluate the virtues Kipling praises. To do this, list descriptions of his examples; lines 3–4, for instance, balance self-confidence with openness to criticism. Then classify your descriptions, so that you end up with three or four categories. Devote a paragraph to evaluating each category, including why Kipling praised any virtue and how relevant it is in today's world. In your concluding paragraph, discuss virtues that you think Kipling should also have included.

BIOGRAPHY

William Butler Yeats
1865–1939

As a child Yeats (yāts) divided his time between Dublin and London, where his father worked as a portrait painter, and County Sligo in the West of Ireland, where he lived with his mother's family of sailors and merchants. It was from them that he first became acquainted with the oral literature of the Irish peasantry. He was a mediocre student, uninterested in most of the subjects taught. Finally, he determined to write.

His first books, published before the end of the century, define his lifelong interests. The poems collected in *The Wanderings of Oisin* derive from his intensive study of Irish myth and folklore. For centuries Ireland had been an English colony, its economy exploited and its native culture suppressed. Yeats's early poems and his book on Irish folk tales, *The Celtic Twilight* (1893), were in part political acts. "We had in Ireland," he wrote, "imaginative stories, which the uneducated classes knew and even sang, and might we not make those stories current among the educated classes . . . and at last . . . so deepen the political passion of the nation that all . . . would accept a common design?" Yeat's plays, beginning with *The Countess Cathleen* (1892), had, for some time, this same goal.

It was through his involvement in Irish politics that Yeats first met the revolutionary agitator Maud Gonne. Her beauty and her personality overwhelmed him. Yeats repeatedly proposed marriage but she always refused him, her sole interest fixed on achieving Irish independence.

During the same period Yeats also embarked on a lifelong spiritual quest. Dissatisfied both with his father's atheism and with orthodox religion, he searched for a hidden supernatural dimension in life, joining secret mystical societies, attending séances, and studying alchemy and esoteric philosophy. From this odd lore he acquired not only his belief in a spirit world and reincarnation, but also a body of symbolic images that gave coherence and visual power to his writing. He felt convinced these symbols derived their authority and power from their source in the "Great Memory," the collective unconsciousness of humanity that connects individuals with the *Spiritus Mundi* (Latin for "soul of the world").

In 1905 Yeats and his close friend Lady Augusta Gregory cofounded the Abbey Theatre in Dublin. Here their plays, as well as works by J. M. Synge and Sean O'Casey, created a new, specifically Irish drama that had strong influence both on the modern theater and on Irish politics.

Writing for the stage impressed Yeats with the importance of precise, spare language. As Yeats's poetry dealt with the horror of the Irish fight for independence and looked forward toward an uncertain future world, it acquired the clarity and conciseness that mark twentieth-century style. In his own work Yeats thus began as one of the last romantics but evolved into a leader in modernist, experimental poetry. The evolution of Yeats's art never ceased. The poems written when he was an old man are his most audacious. In 1923 Yeats received the Nobel Prize for Literature.

William Butler Yeats

When You Are Old ✓

When you are old and gray and full of sleep,
And nodding by the fire, take down this
    book,
And slowly read, and dream of the soft look
Your eyes had once, and of their shadows
    deep;

5 How many loved your moments of glad
    grace,
And loved your beauty with love false or
    true,
But one man loved the pilgrim soul in you,
And loved the sorrows of your changing face;

And bending down beside the glowing bars,
10 Murmur, a little sadly, how Love fled
And paced upon the mountains overhead
And hid his face amid a crowd of stars.

                            1892

From *Collected Poems* by William Butler Yeats (New York:
Macmillan, 1956). Reprinted by permission of A. P. Watt Ltd.
on behalf of Michael B. Yeats and Macmillan London Limited.

Portrait of Maud Gonne (detail), by Sara Purser. *The Municipal Gallery of Modern Art, Dublin*

Yeats and Ronsard

"When You Are Old" is, among other things, a rewriting of a sonnet by the French poet Pierre de Ronsard (1524–1585) published in 1552. Yeats's first words simply translate Ronsard's, but their conclusions are very different. When Ronsard looks into the future, he imagines that, "I shall be underground and, a ghost without bones, / By the shadows of myrtle trees I will take my rest. . ." Hoping this pathetic picture might move his beloved to regret her "proud disdain," he suddenly makes this concluding suggestion: "Live now, believe me, don't wait for tomorrow; / Gather today the roses of this life." The effect Ronsard wished his poem to have is clear. But, what does Yeats's poem seek to achieve?

Yeats on the Source of "Innisfree"

. . . Sometimes I told myself very adventurous love-stories with myself for hero, and at other times I planned out a life of lonely austerity, and at other times mixed the ideals and planned a life of lonely austerity mitigated by periodical lapses. I had still the ambition, formed in Sligo in my teens, of living in imitation of Thoreau on Innisfree, a little island in Lough Gill, and when walking through Fleet Street very homesick I heard a little tinkle of water and saw a fountain in a shop-window which balanced a little ball upon its jet, and began to remember lake water. From the sudden remembrance came my poem *Innisfree*, my first lyric with anything in its rhythm of my own music.

From *The Autobiography of William Butler Yeats*, Macmillan, 1965, page 103.

HZ **Review STYLE in the Handbook of Literary Terms, page 928.**

The Lake Isle of Innisfree ✓

I will arise and go now, and go to Innisfree,
And a small cabin build there, of clay and
    wattles made;
Nine bean rows will I have there, a hive for the
    honeybee,
And live alone in the bee-loud glade.

5 And I shall have some peace there, for peace
    comes dropping slow,
Dropping from the veils of the morning to
    where the cricket sings;
There midnight's all a-glimmer, and noon a
    purple glow,
And evening full of the linnet's wings.[1]

I will arise and go now, for always night and
    day
10 I hear lake water lapping with low sounds by
    the shore;
While I stand on the roadway, or on the
    pavements gray,
I hear it in the deep heart's core.

1892

---

1. *Linnet's wings.* The linnet is a small songbird.

From *Collected Poems* by William Butler Yeats (New York: Macmillan, 1956). Reprinted by permission of A. P. Watt Ltd. on behalf of Michael B. Yeats and Macmillan London Limited.

THINK AND DISCUSS
WHEN YOU ARE OLD
Understanding
1. Describe the kind of old age the speaker imagines for the woman he loves.

Analyzing
2. Compare the two kinds of love described in the second stanza. What does the speaker mean by "pilgrim soul"?
3. How do lines 9 and 12 contrast the speaker and his beloved? Which one has the "pilgrim soul"?

Extending
4. Compare the conclusion by Ronsard (in the Comment on page 734) with Yeats's conclusion, and discuss the impact that Romanticism had on "When You Are Old."

THE LAKE ISLE OF INNISFREE
Understanding
1. Where is the speaker living now?
2. What kind of life does he long for?

Analyzing
3. How does his description suggest the spe-cial qualities of life the speaker seeks on this island?
4. What words and phrases are emphasized through **repetition**? Why are they repeated, and how do they link with the poem's **theme**?

Extending
5. Describe your own Innisfree.

REVIEWING: Style H🗹
See Handbook of Literary Terms, p. 928
   Style is the distinctive handling of language found in the work of an author, created through the choice of diction, syntax, figurative language, imagery, and sound devices.

1. How does "arise" typify the kind of diction found in "The Lake Isle of Innisfree"?
2. What effect does **anastrophe** have on the poem's style? Consider especially the syntactic inversion in lines 2, 3, and 11.
3. In what ways does the **figurative language** describing peace (in lines 5–6) evoke a special **mood**?
4. How does the **image** of "linnet's wings" (line 8) characterize the atmospheric quality in the poem?
5. How does the sound of *m* in line 7 help create the poem's world?

The Wild Swans at Coole ✓

The trees are in their autumn beauty,
The woodland paths are dry,
Under the October twilight the water
Mirrors a still sky;
5 Upon the brimming water among the stones
Are nine-and-fifty swans.

Coole (kül). Coole Park was the country estate of Yeats's wealthy friend Lady Augusta Gregory (1852-1932), the Irish playwright and folklorist.

The nineteenth autumn has come upon me
Since I first made my count;
I saw, before I had well finished,
10 All suddenly mount
And scatter wheeling in great broken rings
Upon their clamorous wings.

I have looked upon those brilliant creatures,
And now my heart is sore.
15 All's changed since I, hearing at twilight,
The first time on this shore,
The bell-beat of their wings above my head,
Trod with a lighter tread.

Unwearied still, lover by lover,
20 They paddle in the cold
Companionable streams or climb the air;
Their hearts have not grown old;
Passion or conquest, wander where they will,
Attend upon them still.

25 But now they drift on the still water,
Mysterious, beautiful;
Among what rushes will they build,
By what lake's edge or pool
Delight men's eyes when I awake some day
30 To find they have flown away?

1917

"Swan, Rush, and Iris," a wallpaper design by Walter Crane. 1877. *Victoria and Albert Museum*

William Butler Yeats

Sailing to Byzantium ✓

I

That is no country for old men. The young
In one another's arms, birds in the trees,
—Those dying generations—at their song,
The salmon-falls, the mackerel-crowded
    seas,
5 Fish, flesh, or fowl, commend all summer
    long
Whatever is begotten, born, and dies.
Caught in that sensual music all neglect
Monuments of unaging intellect.

II

An aged man is but a paltry thing,
10 A tattered coat upon a stick, unless
Soul clap its hands and sing, and louder sing
For every tatter in its mortal dress,
Nor is there singing school but studying
Monuments of its own magnificence;
15 And therefore I have sailed the seas and come
To the holy city of Byzantium.

III

O sages standing in God's holy fire
As in the gold mosaic of a wall
Come from the holy fire, perne in a gyre,[1]
20 And be the singing-masters of my soul.
Consume my heart away; sick with desire
And fastened to a dying animal
It knows not what it is; and gather me
Into the artifice of eternity.

IV

25 Once out of nature I shall never take
My bodily form from any natural thing,
But such a form as Grecian goldsmiths make[2]
Of hammered gold and gold enameling
To keep a drowsy Emperor awake;
30 Or set upon a golden bough to sing
To lords and ladies of Byzantium
Of what is past, or passing, or to come.

                       1927

Byzantium, ancient name for the city that became Constantinople and later Istanbul. For Yeats, however, it was not so much a place as an ideal, a symbol for the timeless world of art and intellect as opposed to the natural world of biological change. It was a "holy city": literally, because it was the center of Eastern Christendom; symbolically, because it fostered that development of intellect and imagination that produces artistic perfection. Byzantine art was highly stylized; abandoning all naturalistic representation.
1. *perne in a gyre*. A perne (or *pirn*) is a spool or bobbin; a gyre is a spiraling motion describing a cone. The image seems to be of a long file of sages, spiraling down like the thread flying off a spinning bobbin, forming ever tighter circles that narrow to a single point, the poet who is calling the sages to himself.
2. *such . . . make*. Yeats wrote, "I have read somewhere that in the emperor's palace at Byzantium was a tree made of gold and silver, and artificial birds that sang."

Reprinted with permission of Macmillan Publishing Company and A. P. Watt Ltd. on behalf of Michael B. Yeats and Macmillan London Ltd. from *Collected Poems* by W. B. Yeats. Copyright 1928 by Macmillan Publishing Company, renewed 1956 by Georgie Yeats.

Opposite page: Istanbul and its suburb Galata during the reign of Suleiman (1494?–1566). Note the combination of perspectives. Although the proportions are distorted, many actual landmarks are distinguishable. 16th century. *University Library, Istanbul*

The Man in The Glass

"When you get what you want in your struggle for self
And the world makes you king for a day,
Just go to the mirror and look at yourself
And see what 'the man' has to say.

For it isn't your father or mother or wife
Whose judgement upon you must pass
The fellow whose verdict counts in your life
Is the one staring back from the glass.

You may be like Jack Horner and chisel a plum
And think you're a wonderful guy.
But the 'man in the glass' says you're only a bum,
And you can't look him straight in the eye.

He's the fellow to please never mind all the rest
For he's with you clear to the end.
And you've passed your most dangerous, difficult test
If the 'man in the glass' is your friend.

You may fool the world down the pathway of years
And get pats on the back as you pass.
But your only reward will be heart aches and tears
If you've cheated 'the man in the glass'."

-Author Unkown

"Sailing to Byzantium"

The title suggests this is a poem about a process: the word "Sailing" tells us of something continuously happening—not "I will sail" or "I once sailed," but "I am sailing." (The title for the first draft of the poem suggests this same idea in a different way: "Towards Byzantium.")

The declaration of lines 15–16, "therefore I have sailed the seas and come/To the holy city of Byzantium," might seem to contradict this suggestion, until it becomes clear that the city's name also represents a spiritual state. Though the speaker may already be physically in the city of Byzantium, he is still metaphorically on his journey "out of nature" (line 25) to the ultimate Byzantium of pure spirit, and he isn't there yet.

The fact that the speaker has not reached his goal is important. His poem illustrates how divided his feelings still are about the quest he has undertaken. He has not altogether lost as yet his love for "that sensual music" (line 7) from the land of the young. His is a heart still "sick with desire" (line 21), and at least one reason he now sails away from "the mackerel-crowded seas" (line 4) of youth is that his body ages. It is a "dying animal" (line 22) or "a tattered coat upon a stick" (line 10), and the only escape from the pain and confusion he feels because of his divided self is to cast off that "sick" heart, that "dying" body.

His mind has already perceived a fatal inadequacy in "Those dying generations" (line 3). They are so "Caught in that sensual music" that they "neglect/Monuments of unaging intellect" (lines 7-8). He determines to fix his hope on this form of permanence. These are monuments to that other aspect of self, to the soul's "own magnificence" (line 14); studying them trains the soul (line 13) to sing, and in so doing to rise above the losses of aging, singing "louder . . ./For every tatter in its mortal dress . . ." (lines 11–12). In this "singing school" (line 13) the "singing-masters" (line 20) are those "sages" (line 17) who have achieved spiritual purity. "God's holy fire" (line 17) has burned away every speck of the physical and the imperfect—to these sages the fire is but a golden backdrop, such as one sees behind the saints in Byzantine mosaics. Rather passively the poet calls to these teachers to come and "gather" (line 23) him into their form of eternity—artificial, in the sense that it is entirely the creation of human spirit. There is nothing natural about it.

The strange picture of a golden mechanical bird translates the imagery of stanza 1 into another form of being. The "birds in the trees" (line 2) now become the poet as a fabulous toy; "the young/In one another's arms" (lines 1–2) hearing their own "sensual music" become "a drowsy Emperor" (line 29) and the "lords and ladies of Byzantium" (line 31). There may be a fair bit of irony in this last stanza. Is it better to keep a "drowsy Emperor awake" than to be caught up in "that sensuous music"?

The Second Coming ✓

Turning and turning in the widening gyre[1]
The falcon cannot hear the falconer;
Things fall apart; the center cannot hold;
Mere anarchy is loosed upon the world,
5 The blood-dimmed tide is loosed, and everywhere

The ceremony of innocence is drowned;

The Second Coming. In this poem Yeats borrows a Christian concept—the Second Coming of Christ at the end of the world—in order to develop his own notion of historical change.
1. gyre (jīr), a spiral motion.

The best lack all conviction, while the worst
Are full of passionate intensity.

Surely some revelation is at hand;
10 Surely the Second Coming is at hand.
The Second Coming! Hardly are those words out
When a vast image out of *Spiritus Mundi*[2]
Troubles my sight: somewhere in sands of
    the desert
A shape with lion body and the head of a man,
15 A gaze blank and pitiless as the sun,
Is moving its slow thighs, while all about it
Reel shadows of the indignant desert birds.
The darkness drops again; but now I know

That twenty centuries of stony sleep
20 Were vexed to nightmare by a rocking cradle,
And what rough beast, its hour come round
    at last,
Slouches towards Bethlehem to be born?

1921

2. *Spiritus Mundi,* "soul of the world." [Latin] Yeats believed in the existence of a "Great Memory," a collective unconscious that connected individuals with the *Spiritus Mundi,* and was a reservoir of symbolic images from the past.

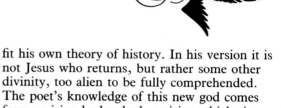

Reader's Note

"The Second Coming"

By the year 1920, Yeats saw the old order of the world flying apart. The horrors of World War I were just past, and now Ireland seemed moving toward anarchy, as squads of assassins from the revolutionary Sinn Fein (shin fān) independence movement and the official Royal Irish Constabulary murdered innocent citizens in opposing terrorist campaigns. "We are," he wrote, "but weasels fighting in a hole." The end of everything he valued seemed at hand, and it made Yeats think of the Second Coming.

In the Gospels, Jesus warns his disciples that he will be crucified, but assures them that he will return again, after an uncertain length of time. Cataclysmic violence will precede this Second Coming, warning everyone that the end of the world is at hand.

Yeats intends his readers to recall this Christian tradition, clearly alluding to the destruction which foreshadows Christ's return in lines 4 to 8 and to his first coming in the reference to Bethlehem (line 22).

But Yeats was no Christian, and he alters the traditional story in a particular way, to make it fit his own theory of history. In his version it is not Jesus who returns, but rather some other divinity, too alien to be fully comprehended. The poet's knowledge of this new god comes from a vision he has had, a vision which rises out of the shared unconscious mind in which all human beings participate and to which Yeats refers by its Latin name, the *Spiritus Mundi,* the "soul of the world." The vision this creates in the poet's mind is vague but menacing—the poet tries to describe it in lines 13–18, but soon loses it, and "darkness drops again" (line 18). He is still so unsure of its meaning that he ends his poem with a question.

What he does understand is that during the past two thousand years (an even number, which seemed to Yeats a complete era in earthly history) this new beast-god has been in stony sleep (line 19), waiting to be born, and angered ("vexed") by the more gentle god of Christianity, symbolized by the "rocking cradle" (line 20) of the infant Jesus. Now this "rough beast" (line 21) is moving toward its own birth, its own, ominous Bethlehem.

THINK AND DISCUSS

THE WILD SWANS AT COOLE

Understanding

1. Describe the **setting**—both time and place.

Analyzing

2. What has changed since the speaker first counted the swans?
3. Why do the hearts of the swans seem not to have grown old?

Extending

4. Does the speaker really want an answer to the question that ends the poem, or does he ask it to conceal a different question?

SAILING TO BYZANTIUM

Understanding

1. What country is described in the first two stanzas? in the last two?
2. What form does the speaker say he will take?
3. What does he seek through this transformation?

Analyzing

4. What kind of images are used in stanza 1 to describe the country the speaker must leave?
5. What is missing from the lives of those who live there?
6. What contrasting qualities do the images have in the last two stanzas?

THE SECOND COMING

Understanding

1. Explain how lines 3–8 characterize modern history, as Yeats perceives it.

Analyzing

2. What happens when the falcon can no longer hear the falconer? How can this **symbolize** what has happened to civilization?
3. Describe the vision from *Spiritus Mundi* that springs to the poet's mind? Why is the beast in the desert?
4. What does its dual nature imply?
5. What lies behind the comparison of its gaze and the light of the sun?

6. Why are the desert birds "indignant" (line 17) at its movement?

Extending

7. Have the sixty-odd years since this poem appeared rendered its fears negligible?

VOCABULARY

Dictionary

Use your Glossary to answer the following questions.

1. What do the Latin roots in *artifice* mean?
2. Write an illustrative sentence that proves your understanding of the word *anarchy*.
3. How does the Latin root of *revelation* influence its religious connotation?
4. Write a word that rhymes with the accented syllable of *clamorous*.
5. How is *mosaic* related to *museum*?

COMPOSITION ◆━━

Describing a Composite Beast

What does the description of the beast "with lion body and the head of a man" suggest about its nature? What qualities would the lion and the man each contribute to this composite? Describe a beast that represents your own vision of today's world. Include parts of as many animals as you wish, but use them for their symbolic, not their literal, attributes. (For example, we usually use an owl to represent wisdom and doves to represent peace or love.) Devote a paragraph to each animal and explain what qualities that animal contributes to your composite.

Analyzing Yeats's Use of Imagery

Yeats's lyrics use the images of a solitary fireplace, an isolated island, and "mysterious, beautiful" swans to express his emotional reactions to his subjects. Write an essay of at least three paragraphs analyzing his technique. Look closely at the connection between these images and the poems in which they appear, to determine how they help express emotion and set a mood.

Born Hector Hugh Munro, "Saki" embodied the cosmopolitan flair, the satiric wit, and the premature end of his generation. Munro's father was the inspector general of the Burmese police, and Munro was born in Burma. When his mother died two years later, he went back to England to be reared by his grandmother and two sternly forbidding aunts. The boy's resentment at their discipline emerged years later in stories which satirize the conventional, the self-righteous, and the cruel.

Munro was a delicate child, given to reading and sketching. He attended local schools and then boarded for two years at Bedford Grammar School. He never went to college. Instead, his father, now retired, returned to Europe to take his children on a tour of Germany, Austria, and Switzerland, after which they settled in the English countryside, where for two years the father directed the final phase of his son's education.

In 1893, aged 22, Munro tried to follow his father's footsteps, enlisting in the Burmese Police. But he could not take the climate, and after one year and seven bouts of fever he returned to England. Now, with his father's financial support, Munro determined to try a different sort of career, and for the next several years he did historical research at the British Museum for a book, finally published in 1900, *The Rise of the Russian Empire*. Critics and readers were not impressed.

So in 1901 he sought yet another role to play, and this time was more successful. In conjunction with a well-known cartoonist, he began writing political satire for the *Westminster Gazette*. To preserve his anonymity Munro took the pen name "Saki" from the cupbearer in the Persian poem *The Rubáiyát of Omar Khayyám*. Munro knew politics and brought to bear on it a mordant wit that delighted readers.

Then in 1902 Munro left England to become a foreign correspondent for the *Morning Post*. During the next six years he reported from the Balkans, Poland, Russia, and, finally, Paris. At the same time he was sending a series of comic short stories back to English newspapers, and published a book of them in 1904.

Munro returned home in 1908, bought a house outside of London, and settled into a relatively quiet life, writing during the day, playing bridge evenings at his club. In his short stories he exhibits a sparkling wit, a careless cruelty, and some deep insights into the malicious side of human nature. In "Tobermory," the marvel of the talking cat is not as important as the threat caused by the cat's knowledge of the hypocrisies and social indiscretions of the members of the house party.

But this tranquil, productive life soon came to an end. In August 1914, on first hearing that England was at war with Germany, Munro enlisted in the army. He was 43 years old. Refusing an officer's commission, Munro faced trench warfare in France at the end of 1915 as a regular infantryman. After a year of brave service he was killed in combat.

Tobermory

Saki

t was a chill, rain-washed afternoon of a late August day, that indefinite season when partridges are still in security or cold storage, and there is nothing to hunt—unless one is bounded on the north by the Bristol Channel, in which case one may lawfully gallop after fat red stags. Lady Blemley's house-party was not bounded on the north by the Bristol Channel, hence there was a full gathering of her guests round the tea table on this particular afternoon. And, in spite of the blankness of the season and the triteness of the occasion, there was no trace in the company of that fatigued restlessness which means a dread of the pianola and a subdued hankering for auction bridge. The undisguised open-mouthed attention of the entire party was fixed on the homely negative personality of Mr. Cornelius Appin. Of all her guests, he was the one who had come to Lady Blemley with the vaguest reputation. Some one had said he was "clever," and he had got his invitation in the moderate expectation, on the part of his hostess, that some portion at least of his cleverness would be contributed to the general entertainment. Until tea-time that day she had been unable to discover in what direction, if any, his cleverness lay. He was neither a wit nor a croquet champion, a hypnotic force nor a begetter of amateur theatricals. Neither did his exterior suggest the sort of man in whom women are willing to pardon a generous measure of mental deficiency. He had subsided into mere Mr. Appin, and the Cornelius seemed a piece of transparent baptismal bluff. And now he was claiming to have launched on the world a discovery beside which the invention of gunpowder, of the printing-press, and of steam locomotion were inconsiderable trifles. Science had made bewildering strides in many directions during recent decades, but this thing seemed to belong to the domain of miracle rather than to scientific achievement.

"And do you really ask us to believe," Sir Wilfrid was saying, "that you have discovered a means for instructing animals in the art of human speech, and that dear old Tobermory has proved your first successful pupil?"

"It is a problem at which I have worked for the last seventeen years," said Mr. Appin, "but only during the last eight or nine months have I been rewarded with glimmerings of success. Of course I have experimented with thousands of animals, but latterly only with cats, those wonderful creatures which have assimilated themselves so marvellously with our civilization while retaining all their highly developed feral instincts. Here and there among cats one comes across an outstanding superior intellect, just as one does among the ruck of human beings, and when I made the acquaintance of Tobermory a week ago I saw at once that I was in contact with a 'Beyond-cat' of extraordinary intelligence. I had gone far along the road to success in recent experiments; with Tobermory, as you call him, I have reached the goal."

Mr. Appin concluded his remarkable statement in a voice which he strove to divest of a triumphant

"Tobermory" from *The Complete Short Stories of Saki* by H. H. Munro. Copyright 1930 by The Viking Press, Inc. Copyright renewed 1958 by The Viking Press, Inc. Reprinted by permission of Viking Penguin Inc.

inflection. No one said "Rats," though Clovis's lips moved in a monosyllabic contortion which probably invoked those rodents of disbelief.

"And do you mean to say," asked Miss Resker, after a slight pause, "that you have taught Tobermory to say and understand easy sentences of one syllable?"

"My dear Miss Resker," said the wonderworker patiently, "one teaches little children and savages and backward adults in that piecemeal fashion; when one has once solved the problem of making a beginning with an animal of highly developed intelligence one has no need for those halting methods. Tobermory can speak our language with perfect correctness."

This time Clovis very distinctly said, "Beyondrats!" Sir Wilfrid was more polite, but equally sceptical.

"Hadn't we better have the cat in and judge for ourselves?" suggested Lady Blemley.

Sir Wilfrid went in search of the animal, and the company settled themselves down to the languid expectation of witnessing some more or less adroit drawing-room ventriloquism.

In a minute Sir Wilfrid was back in the room, his face white beneath its tan and his eyes dilated with excitement.

"By Gad, it's true!"

His agitation was unmistakably genuine, and his hearers started forward in a thrill of awakened interest.

Collapsing into an armchair he continued breathlessly: "I found him dozing in the smoking-room, and called out to him to come for his tea. He blinked at me in his usual way, and I said, 'Come on, Toby; don't keep us waiting'; and, by Gad! he drawled out in a most horribly natural voice that he'd come when he dashed well pleased! I nearly jumped out of my skin!"

Appin had preached to absolutely incredulous hearers; Sir Wilfrid's statement carried instant conviction. A Babel-like chorus of startled exclamation arose, amid which the scientist sat mutely enjoying the first fruit of his stupendous discovery.

In the midst of the clamour Tobermory entered the room and made his way with velvet tread and studied unconcern across to the group seated round the tea table.

A sudden hush of awkwardness and constraint fell on the company. Somehow there seemed an element of embarrassment in addressing on equal terms a domestic cat of acknowledged mental ability.

"Will you have some milk, Tobermory?" asked Lady Blemley in a rather strained voice.

"I don't mind if I do," was the response, couched in a tone of even indifference. A shiver of suppressed excitement went through the listeners, and Lady Blemley might be excused for pouring out the saucerful of milk rather unsteadily.

"I'm afraid I've spilt a good deal of it," she said apologetically.

"After all, it's not my Axminster,"[1] was Tobermory's rejoinder.

Another silence fell on the group, and then Miss Resker, in her best district-visitor manner, asked if the human language had been difficult to learn. Tobermory looked squarely at her for a moment and then fixed his gaze serenely on the middle distance. It was obvious that boring questions lay outside his scheme of life.

"What do you think of human intelligence?" asked Mavis Pellington lamely.

"Of whose intelligence in particular?" asked Tobermory coldly.

"Oh, well, mine for instance," said Mavis, with a feeble laugh.

"You put me in an embarrassing position," said Tobermory, whose tone and attitude certainly did not suggest a shred of embarrassment. "When your inclusion in this house-party was suggested Sir Wilfrid protested that you were the most brainless woman of his acquaintance, and that there was a wide distinction between hospitality and the care of the feeble-minded. Lady Blemley replied that your lack of brain-power was the precise quality which had earned you your invitation, as you were

---

1. **Axminster,** a kind of carpet with a finely tufted, velvetlike pile.

the only person she could think of who might be idiotic enough to buy their old car. You know, the one they call 'The Envy of Sisyphus,'[2] because it goes quite nicely uphill if you push it."

Lady Blemley's protestations would have had greater effect if she had not casually suggested to Mavis only that morning that the car in question would be just the thing for her down at her Devonshire home.

Major Barfield plunged in heavily to effect a diversion.

"How about your carryings-on with the tortoiseshell puss up at the stables, eh?"

The moment he had said it everyone realized the blunder.

"One does not usually discuss these matters in public," said Tobermory frigidly. "From a slight observation of your ways since you've been in this house I should imagine you'd find it inconvenient if I were to shift the conversation on to your own little affairs."

The panic which ensued was not confined to the Major.

"Would you like to go and see if cook has got your dinner ready?" suggested Lady Blemley hurriedly, affecting to ignore the fact that it wanted at least two hours to Tobermory's dinnertime.

"Thanks," said Tobermory, "not quite so soon after my tea. I don't want to die of indigestion."

"Cats have nine lives, you know," said Sir Wilfrid heartily.

"Possibly," answered Tobermory; "but only one liver."

"Adelaide!" said Mrs. Cornett, "do you mean to encourage that cat to go out and gossip about us in the servants' hall?"

The panic had indeed become general. A narrow ornamental balustrade ran in front of most of the bedroom windows at the Towers, and it was recalled with dismay that this had formed a favorite promenade for Tobermory at all hours, whence he could watch the pigeons—and heaven knew what else besides. If he intended to become reminiscent in his present outspoken strain the effect would be something more than disconcerting. Mrs. Cornett, who spent much time at her toilet table, and whose complexion was reputed to be of a nomadic though punctual disposition, looked as ill at ease as the Major. Miss Scrawen, who wrote fiercely sensuous poetry and led a blameless life, merely displayed irritation; if you are methodical and virtuous in private you don't necessarily want everyone to know it. Bertie van Tahn, who was so depraved at seventeen that he had long ago given up trying to be any worse, turned a dull shade of gardenia white, but he did not commit the error of dashing out of the room like Odo Finsberry, a young gentleman who was understood to be reading for the Church and who was possibly disturbed at the thought of scandals he might hear concerning other people. Clovis had the presence of mind to maintain a composed exterior; privately he was calculating how long it would take to procure a box of fancy mice through the agency of the *Exchange and Mart* as a species of hush-money.

Even in a delicate situation like the present, Agnes Resker could not endure to remain too long in the background.

"Why did I ever come down here?" she asked dramatically.

Tobermory immediately accepted the opening.

"Judging by what you said to Mrs. Cornett on the croquet-lawn yesterday, you were out for food. You described the Blemleys as the dullest people to stay with that you knew, but said they were clever enough to employ a first-rate cook; otherwise they'd find it difficult to get anyone to come down a second time."

"There's not a word of truth in it! I appeal to Mrs. Cornett—" exclaimed the discomfited Agnes.

"Mrs. Cornett repeated your remark afterwards to Bertie van Tahn," continued Tobermory, "and said, 'That woman is a regular Hunger Marcher; she'd go anywhere for four square meals a day,' and Bertie van Tahn said—"

---

2. *'The Envy of Sisyphus.'* Sisyphus (sis′ə fəs) is a trickster from Greek mythology. He was finally punished in the Underworld for his crimes, being compelled to roll a great rock up a hill, where, nearing the top, it would break away and roll to the bottom.

Detail of poster, "Tournée du Chat Noir" ("Black Cat Tournament") by Theophile Alexandre Steinlen. *Kunsthalle Bremen, West Germany*

At this point the chronicle mercifully ceased. Tobermory had caught a glimpse of the big yellow Tom from the Rectory working his way through the shrubbery towards the stable wing. In a flash he had vanished through the open French window.

With the disappearance of his too brilliant pupil Cornelius Appin found himself beset by a hurricane of bitter upbraiding, anxious inquiry, and frightened entreaty. The responsibility for the situation lay with him, and he must prevent matters from becoming worse. Could Tobermory impart his dangerous gift to other cats? was the first question he had to answer. It was possible, he replied, that he might have initiated his intimate friend the stable puss into his new accomplishment, but it was unlikely that his teaching could have taken a wider range as yet.

"Then," said Mrs. Cornett, "Tobermory may be a valuable cat and a great pet; but I'm sure you'll agree, Adelaide, that both he and the stable cat must be done away with without delay."

"You don't suppose I've enjoyed the last quarter of an hour, do you?" said Lady Blemley bitterly. "My husband and I are very fond of Tobermory—at least, we were before this horrible accomplishment was infused into him; but now, of course, the only thing is to have him destroyed as soon as possible."

"We can put some strychnine in the scraps he always gets at dinnertime," said Sir Wilfrid, "and I will go and drown the stable cat myself. The coachman will be very sore at losing his pet, but I'll say a very catching form of mange has broken out in both cats and we're afraid of it spreading to the kennels."

"But my great discovery!" expostulated Mr. Appin; "after all my years of research and experiment—"

"You can go and experiment on the shorthorns at the farm, who are under proper control," said

Mrs. Cornett, "or the elephants at the Zoological Gardens. They're said to be highly intelligent, and they have this recommendation, that they don't come creeping about our bedrooms and under chairs, and so forth."

An archangel ecstatically proclaiming the Millennium, and finding that it clashed unpardonably with Henley[3] and would have to be indefinitely postponed, could hardly have felt more crestfallen than Cornelius Appin at the reception of his wonderful achievement. Public opinion, however, was against him—in fact, had the general voice been consulted on the subject it is probable that a strong minority vote would have been in favour of including him in the strychnine diet.

Defective train arrangements and a nervous desire to see matters brought to a finish prevented an immediate dispersal of the party, but dinner that evening was not a social success. Sir Wilfrid had had rather a trying time with the stable cat and subsequently with the coachman. Agnes Resker ostentatiously limited her repast to a morsel of dry toast, which she bit as though it were a personal enemy; while Mavis Pellington maintained a vindictive silence throughout the meal. Lady Blemley kept up a flow of what she hoped was conversation, but her attention was fixed on the doorway. A plateful of carefully dosed fish scraps was in readiness on the sideboard, but sweets and savory and dessert went their way, and no Tobermory appeared either in the dining-room or kitchen.

The sepulchral dinner was cheerful compared with the subsequent vigil in the smoking-room. Eating and drinking had at least supplied a distraction and cloak to the prevailing embarrassment. Bridge was out of the question in the general tension of nerves and tempers, and after Odo Finsberry had given a lugubrious rendering of "Melisande in the Wood," to a frigid audience, music was tacitly avoided. At eleven the servants went to bed, announcing that the small window in the pantry had been left open as usual for Tobermory's private use. The guests read steadily through the current batch of magazines, and fell back gradually on the "Badminton Library" and bound volumes of *Punch*. Lady Blemley made periodic visits to the pantry, returning each time with an expression of listless depression which forestalled questioning.

At two o'clock Clovis broke the dominating silence.

"He won't turn up tonight. He's probably in the local newspaper office at the present moment, dictating the first instalment of his reminiscences. Lady What's-her-name's book won't be in it. It will be the event of the day."

Having made this contribution to the general cheerfulness, Clovis went to bed. At long intervals the various members of the house-party followed his example.

The servants taking round the early tea made a uniform announcement in reply to a uniform question. Tobermory had not returned.

Breakfast was, if anything, a more unpleasant function than dinner had been, but before its conclusion the situation was relieved. Tobermory's corpse was brought in from the shrubbery, where a gardener had just discovered it. From the bites on his throat and the yellow fur which coated his claws it was evident that he had fallen in unequal combat with the big Tom from the Rectory.

By midday most of the guests had quitted the Towers, and after lunch Lady Blemley had sufficiently recovered her spirits to write an extremely nasty letter to the Rectory about the loss of her valuable pet.

Tobermory had been Appin's one successful pupil, and he was destined to have no successor. A few weeks later an elephant in the Dresden Zoological Garden, which had shown no previous signs of irritability, broke loose and killed an Englishman who had apparently been teasing it. The victim's name was variously reported in the papers as Oppin and Eppelin, but his front name was faithfully rendered Cornelius.

"If he was trying German irregular verbs on the poor beast," said Clovis, "he deserved all he got."

1911

---

3. **Henley,** a place on the Thames River in Oxfordshire, the site of an annual regatta since 1839.

THINK AND DISCUSS
Understanding
1. Describe the **setting**.
2. List the human characters. How is each one **characterized** by the narrator?

Analyzing
3. How does the first paragraph of the story **satirize** a particular social world?
4. Explain the **irony** in Lady Blemley's hope that Appin would be "clever."
5. How do the humans alter their treatment of Tobermory when they learn he can talk?
6. What happens to the fabric of this society when the truth is told?
7. How does the reaction to Appin's death complete Saki's satire of these people?

Extending
8. How well, in your opinion, does Tobermory's manner of speaking represent what a cat would say, if it were able?
9. Why does Saki have Tobermory killed?

APPLYING: Stereotype H*
See Handbook of Literary Terms, p. 899

A fixed, generalized idea about a character or situation is a **stereotype;** for example, the sloppy teenager and the boy-gets-girl happy ending are both stereotypical.

1. How do Lord and Lady Blemley fit the stereotype of an English lord and lady?
2. In what ways does Cornelius Appin act like the stereotypical eccentric scientist, and how does the story's plot fit the typical tale of such research gone haywire?
3. How do the guests at this party fulfill the stereotype of proper English people when Tobermory reports negatively about them?

VOCABULARY
Synonyms and Antonyms
Below are three lists. The first column has words from "Tobermory." The second column has synonyms, and the third column has antonyms for these words. On your paper, write the letters of the synonym and antonym for each numbered word.

Words	Synonyms	Antonyms
1. adroit	a. glum	i. domestic
2. assimilate	b. untamed	j. active
3. feral	c. integrate	k. sedentary
4. listless	d. scold	l. secret
5. lugubrious	e. obvious	m. inept
6. nomadic	f. lazy	n. praise
7. ostentatious	g. deft	o. segregate
8. upbraid	h. wandering	p. cheerful

COMPOSITION
Writing Tobermory's Last Letter
Imagine that, just before his untimely death, you met Tobermory and that he dictated a letter to you (because he couldn't hold a pen). First consider to whom he might want to send a letter and what he would say. Write at least three paragraphs, including some comments about honesty, selflessness, and personal initiative in the human beings he has known. In his last paragraph have Tobermory explain what he plans to do next.

Analyzing the Irony in "Tobermory"
In his stories, Saki frequently establishes a dramatic situation and then pulls a switch that is ironic because it reverses what the reader has been led to assume would happen. Write an essay analyzing how this works in "Tobermory." Reread the story to find at least two examples each of verbal and situational irony. As you write, explain in each instance what the reader expects and how Saki surprises with something unexpected. Be sure to discuss the ironic significance of the difference between the two.

The Changing English Language

In 1879 Dr. James Augustus Henry Murray (1837–1915), the President of the Philological Society, began work on the Society's monumental dictionary project. The Philological Society had been organized in 1842. Beginning with some 200 members, the Society's purpose was to investigate the history and structure of language. Up to this time, no English dictionary had included organized and detailed information on the history of words. To correct this deficiency, the Society resolved in January, 1858, to prepare a new dictionary that would display the entire history of every word that was or had been in the English language.

For the next twenty years, first under the editorship of Herbert Coleridge (great-nephew of Samuel Taylor Coleridge), and later of F. J. Furnivall, materials toward the new dictionary were gathered by a large number of volunteer readers, who scoured English literature in search of quotations displaying the meanings of words at different historical periods. (There were a number of American volunteers, and Coleridge at one point suggested that they confine themselves to the literature of the eighteenth century, but his proposal was not closely followed.)

One basic question Murray had to consider during his early years as editor was "What is the English language?" He saw it not as a vocabulary defined by the speech habits of a single class or ethnic group, but rather like a grouping in botany or zoology, its typical species related to other species in which the features characteristic of the group become less and less distinct. The organic grouping that formed the English language he saw as composed of a central core of thousands of words constituting the common vocabulary of the language and linked on every side to more specialized vocabularies. He illustrated this with a diagram:

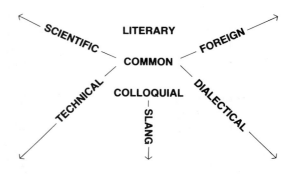

Under Murray, who was the first full-time editor the Society was able to employ, the dictionary project went forward far more swiftly. By April 19, 1882, the first copy was ready for the printer, and by November, 1883, the first volume, *A–B*, was out. Nevertheless, Murray did not live to see the completion of the project. He died in July, 1915 (shortly after completing work on the section *Trink-Turndown*). It was not until June 6, 1928, seventy years since the Philological Society had begun work on its new dictionary "on historical principles," that a banquet was held to celebrate the completion of the project, now known as the *Oxford English Dictionary*.

THINKING CRITICALLY
ABOUT LITERATURE

UNIT 7   NEW DIRECTIONS   1880–1915

■ CONCEPT REVIEW

The following selection contains many of the important ideas and literary terms found in Unit 7. It also contains notes and questions designed to help you think critically about your reading. Page numbers in the notes refer to an application or a review. A more extensive discussion of these terms is in the Handbook of Literary Terms.

When Bernard Shaw's first plays were appearing in London, the most celebrated playwright of the moment was a fellow Irishman, Oscar Wilde. His masterpiece, *The Importance of Being Earnest* (1895), uses highly artificial dialogue to satirize social hypocrisy. In the following scene Jack Worthing, desperately in love with Gwendolen, must face her mother, the indomitable Lady Bracknell, who has just heard of their intention to marry.

from The Importance of Being Earnest

Oscar Wilde

■ Note how Wilde's play exemplifies the *comedy of ideas*.

■ Note how physical position *symbolizes* who dominates in this scene.

■ **Inference** (page 723): Consider what can be inferred from the contrast between "what a really affectionate mother requires" and Lady Bracknell's first question.

LADY BRACKNELL (*sitting down*). You can take a seat, Mr. Worthing. (*Looks in her pocket for notebook and pencil.*)
JACK. Thank you, Lady Bracknell, I prefer standing.
LADY BRACKNELL (*pencil and notebook in hand*). I feel bound to tell you that you are not down on my list of eligible young men, although I have the same list as the dear Duchess of Bolton has. We work together, in fact. However, I am quite ready to enter your name, should your answers be what a really affectionate mother requires. Do you smoke?
JACK. Well, yes, I must admit I smoke.

LADY BRACKNELL. I am glad to hear it. A man should always have an occupation of some kind. There are far too many idle men in London as it is. How old are you?

JACK. Twenty-nine.

LADY BRACKNELL. A very good age to be married at. I have always been of opinion that a man who desires to get married should know either everything or nothing. Which do you know?

JACK (*after some hesitation*). I know nothing, Lady Bracknell.

LADY BRACKNELL. I am pleased to hear it. I do not approve of anything that tampers with natural ignorance. Ignorance is like a delicate exotic fruit; touch it and the bloom is gone. The whole theory of modern education is radically unsound. Fortunately in England, at any rate, education produces no effect whatsoever. If it did, it would prove a serious danger to the upper classes, and probably lead to acts of violence in Grosvenor Square. What is your income?

JACK. Between seven and eight thousand a year.

LADY BRACKNELL (*makes a note in her book*). In land, or in investments?

JACK. In investments, chiefly.

LADY BRACKNELL. That is satisfactory. What between the duties expected of one during one's lifetime, and the duties exacted from one after one's death, land has ceased to be either a profit or a pleasure. It gives one position, and prevents one from keeping it up. That's all that can be said about land.

JACK. I have a country house with some land, of course, attached to it, about fifteen hundred acres, I believe; but I don't depend on that for my real income. In fact, as far as I can make out, the poachers are the only people who make anything out of it.

LADY BRACKNELL. A country house! How many bedrooms? Well, that point can be cleared up afterwards. You have a town house, I hope? A girl with a simple, unspoiled nature, like Gwendolen, could hardly be expected to reside in the country.

JACK. Well, I own a house in Belgrave Square, but it is let by the year to Lady Bloxham. Of course, I can get it back whenever I like, at six months' notice.

LADY BRACKNELL. Lady Bloxham? I don't know her.

JACK. Oh, she goes about very little. She is a lady considerably advanced in years.

LADY BRACKNELL. Ah, nowadays that is no guarantee of respectability of character. What number in Belgrave Square?

JACK. 149.

LADY BRACKNELL (*shaking her head*). The unfashionable side. I thought there was something. However, that could easily be altered.

JACK. Do you mean the fashion, or the side?

LADY BRACKNELL (*sternly*). Both, if necessary, I presume. What are your politics?

JACK. Well, I am afraid I really have none. I am a Liberal Unionist.

■ Watch for lines like this in which expectations are sharply reversed.

■ Consider how this mention of acts of violence parodies real fears born of class differences.

■ **Grosvenor** (grōv′nər) **Square:** an area in the West End, the fashionable residential part of London.

■ **duties:** taxes on inherited wealth were called "death duties." Note the pun on *duties*.

■ **poachers:** people who hunt on private land without permission.

■ **Stereotype** (page 749): Note how Wilde reverses romantic assumptions about innocence and the country.

■ **know:** in the sense of seeing a person socially.

■ **Characterization** (page 675): Observe Lady Bracknell's assumptions about herself.

■ **Liberal Unionist . . . Tories:** The Liberal Party

LADY BRACKNELL. Oh, they count as Tories. They dine with us. Or come in the evening, at any rate. Now to minor matters. Are your parents living?

JACK. I have lost both my parents.

LADY BRACKNELL. Both? . . . That seems like carelessness. Who was your father? He was evidently a man of some wealth. Was he born in what the radical papers call the purple of commerce, or did he rise from the ranks of the aristocracy?

JACK. I am afraid I really don't know. The fact is, Lady Bracknell, I said I had lost my parents. It would be nearer the truth to say that my parents seem to have lost me . . . I don't actually know who I am by birth. I was . . . well, I was found.

LADY BRACKNELL. Found!

JACK. The late Mr. Thomas Cardew, an old gentleman of a very charitable and kindly disposition, found me, and gave me the name of Worthing, because he happened to have a first class ticket for Worthing in his pocket at the time. Worthing is a place in Sussex. It is a seaside resort.

LADY BRACKNELL. Where did the charitable gentleman who had a first class ticket for this seaside resort find you?

JACK (*gravely*). In a handbag.

LADY BRACKNELL. A handbag?

JACK (*very seriously*). Yes, Lady Bracknell. I was in a handbag—a somewhat large, black leather handbag, with handles to it—an ordinary handbag in fact.

LADY BRACKNELL. In what locality did this Mr. James, or Thomas, Cardew come across this ordinary handbag?

JACK. In the cloakroom at Victoria Station. It was given to him in mistake for his own.

LADY BRACKNELL. The cloakroom at Victoria Station?

JACK. Yes. The Brighton line.

LADY BRACKNELL. The line is immaterial. Mr. Worthing, I confess I feel somewhat bewildered by what you have just told me. To be born, or at any rate bred, in a handbag, whether it had handles or not, seems to me to display a contempt for the ordinary decencies of family life that remind one of the worst excesses of the French Revolution. And I presume you know what that unfortunate movement led to? As for the particular locality in which the handbag was found, a cloakroom at a railway station might serve to conceal a social indiscretion—has probably, indeed, been used for that purpose before now—but it could hardly be regarded as an assured basis for a recognized position in good society.

JACK. May I ask you then what you would advise me to do? I need hardly say I would do anything in the world to ensure Gwendolen's happiness.

LADY BRACKNELL. I would strongly advise you, Mr. Worthing, to try and acquire some relations as soon as possible, and to make a definite effort to produce at any rate one parent, of either sex, before the season is quite over.

JACK. Well, I don't see how I could possibly manage to do that. I can produce

split in 1886 over the question of Irish Home Rule, some of the Liberals siding with the Conservatives, or Tories, who supported continued union of Ireland with England.

■ **come in the evening:** Lady Bracknell suggests that the Liberal Unionists (as only partial Tories) are not quite socially acceptable. She may not want them as dinner guests, but is willing to have them visit her during the evening.

■ **Style:** (page 736): In her line, "Was he born . . . " Lady Bracknell parodies the high-flown diction of the newspapers.

■ **Victoria Station:** one of the largest railroad stations in central London.

■ Note the historical *allusion* that comically exaggerates the problem.

the handbag at any moment. It is in my dressing room at home. I really think that should satisfy you, Lady Bracknell.

LADY BRACKNELL. Me, sir! What has it to do with me? You can hardly imagine that I and Lord Bracknell would dream of allowing our only daughter—a girl brought up with the utmost care—to marry into a cloakroom, and form an alliance with a parcel? Good morning, Mr. Worthing!

(LADY BRACKNELL *sweeps out in majestic indignation.*)

1895

■ **Plot** (page 694): Note how a part of the play's comic dramatic tension begins here.

THINK AND DISCUSS

Understanding
1. What does Lady Bracknell discover about Jack during this interview?
2. How, according to her, may he become eligible to marry her daughter?

Analyzing
3. Describe the kind of **setting** in which a scene such as this might take place.
4. Why does Jack insist upon standing up?
5. What does the stage business involving Lady Bracknell's notebook and pencil imply about the way she fulfills the duties of motherhood?
6. How does the line about ignorance as a delicate bloom exemplify the comedy of ideas?
7. How does Wilde **satirize** the rich through Jack's lament about "duties"?
8. Explain how Lady Bracknell's **allusion** to the French Revolution exaggerates the importance of Jack's parentage.

Extending
9. Compare the attitude toward the social establishment expressed here and in *Pygmalion*.

REVIEWING LITERARY TERMS

Inference
1. What can you infer about Lady Bracknell's maternal "affection" from her first question?
2. Using inference, explain what really matters to Lady Bracknell as she seeks a worthy husband for her daughter.

Stereotype
3. Describe the romantic assumption that creates the stereotype of the maiden who lives in the country. How does Lady Bracknell reverse that stereotype?
4. What other stereotypical notions do you find in this selection—either heightened or reversed?

Characterization
5. What do you learn about Lady Bracknell from her hint that she can change either the street number of a London townhouse or what people consider a fashionable place to live?
6. List her other observations that reinforce this sense of her character.

Style
7. Explain how Lady Bracknell parodies the diction of daily newspapers.
8. Characterize the style of Lady Bracknell's own speeches.

Plot
9. What does Lady Bracknell do to precipitate the conflict of the play?
10. How will her insistence on Jack's finding a parent influence the plot?
11. In what way might you expect the handbag to become an important plot device at a later stage of the play?

■ CONTENT REVIEW

Classifying

1. Categorize the various calls to duty in "The Man He Killed," "God's Grandeur," *Pygmalion*, "The Secret Sharer," and "Recessional."

2. Classify the ways that Hopkins, Shaw, Housman, and Yeats see love as a problem.

3. What do people in this period want? Classify the various speakers and protagonists in this unit according to what drives them.

Generalizing

4. How do Conrad and Kipling depict the lives of men who work in the remotest areas of the British empire?

5. Explain in a sentence or two the stereotype of upper-class English society.

6. What has happened to the stereotype of the docile English working man?

Synthesizing

7. Explain how the ironic conclusions to "Ah, Are You Digging On My Grave?", "When I was One-and-Twenty," and "Tobermory" illustrate turn-of-the-century pessimism.

8. What are the shared features of the journeys in "The Secret Sharer" and "Sailing to Byzantium"?

9. As British literature takes its "new directions" into the twentieth century, what features do you find emerging that are most like those of the literature of your own time?

Evaluating

10. How has living in the center of the great British Empire influenced the lives of the characters in this unit—for better or for worse?

11. Which writer most effectively depicts the problems of power: Conrad, Kipling, or Yeats?

12. In this era literature seeks new kinds of heroism. Define the most significant new forms and explain the basis for your judgment.

■ COMPOSITION REVIEW

Describing People of "Good Breeding"

In *Pygmalion*, "Tobermory," and "The Importance of Being Earnest" you read about upper-class society at the turn of the century. Write an essay describing to a reader unfamiliar with this era the dominant characteristics of these people. Begin by listing the most important traits you find in typical characters. Organize your observations into paragraphs on social manners, attitude towards money and power, and priorities and goals, and preface them with an introductory paragraph that establishes the historical context for your reader.

Comparing Approaches to Nature

While the English tradition of nature poetry continued, the poets of this era insisted upon adapting it to their own, personal vision. Select examples from the works of two different authors, and write an essay comparing their poems. Explain how each lyric uses scenes from nature and then compare and contrast the themes that your chosen poets draw from nature.

Analyzing Emotional Commitments

Housman's old man advises, "give not your heart away." Choose examples from two other works in this unit that seem to justify what he says, and use them to illustrate an essay analyzing the retreat from emotional commitment in the literature of this era. First describe the characters you have chosen, considering what they give their hearts to, what happens after they commit themselves, and the implications of what happens. In your concluding paragraph, analyze generally the problems of emotion in an era of social and economic change.

THE TWENTIETH CENTURY

	1925	1935	1945

HISTORY AND ARTS
- Easter Rebellion in Dublin
- Russian Revolution begins
- World War I ends
- Women get the vote
- League of Nations established
- Irish Free State established
- Mussolini comes to power in Italy
- General strike in Britain
- Fitzgerald: *The Great Gatsby* (U.S.)
- Hemingway: *The Sun Also Rises* (U.S.)
- Lindbergh flies solo across Atlantic
- British Broadcasting Corp. organized
- Great Depression starts
- Spanish Civil War begins
- Edward VIII abdicates
- Picasso: *Guernica*
- World War II begins
- Churchill becomes prime minister
- Hitler becomes chancellor of Germany
- United Nations Charter signed
- Williams: *The Glass Menagerie* (U.S.)
- U.S. drops atomic bomb on Japan
- World War II ends
- India gains independence
- State of Israel founded

MONARCHS AND HOUSES

WINDSOR
- George V
- Edward VIII
- George VI

ENGLISH LITERATURE
- Sassoon: *The Old Huntsman*
- Owen: *Poems*
- O'Casey: *The Plough and the Stars*
- Joyce: *Ulysses*
- Waugh: *Decline and Fall*
- Eliot: *The Waste Land*
- O'Connor: *Guests of the Nation*
- Forster: *A Passage to India*
- Brittain: *Testament of Youth*
- Lawrence: *Women in Love*
- Woolf: *Mrs. Dalloway*
- Greene: *Brighton Rock*
- Eliot: *Four Quartets*
- Auden: *The Age of Anxiety*
- Orwell: *Nineteen Eighty-four*

Over the Top by John Nash, a World War I soldier and artist.

Charles Lindbergh in front of his plane, *The Spirit of St. Louis.*

Detail, *Portrait of Marie-Thérèse* by Pablo Picasso, 1937

1915–

1955	1965	1975	1985

- Korean War starts
  - Suez conflict
    - Soviet Union launches *Sputnik*
    - Pasternak: *Dr. Zhivago* (Russia)
      - Britten: *War Requiem*
        - National Theatre founded
          - Beatles gain international popularity
          - U.S. involvement in Vietnam War begins

- Fighting in Northern Ireland
- North Sea oil discovered
  - Britain joins Common Market
    - Silver Jubilee of Queen Elizabeth II
      - Thatcher becomes prime minister
        - Falklands War with Argentina

- Elizabeth II

- Golding: *The Lord of the Flies*
  - Hughes: *The Hawk in the Rain*
  - Bolt: *A Man for All Seasons*
- Thomas: *Under Milk Wood*
  - Pinter: *The Homecoming*
- Tolkien: *The Lord of the Rings*
  - Osborne: *Look Back in Anger*
    - Stoppard: *Jumpers*
    - Greene: *The Honorary Consul*
- Hughes appointed poet laureate

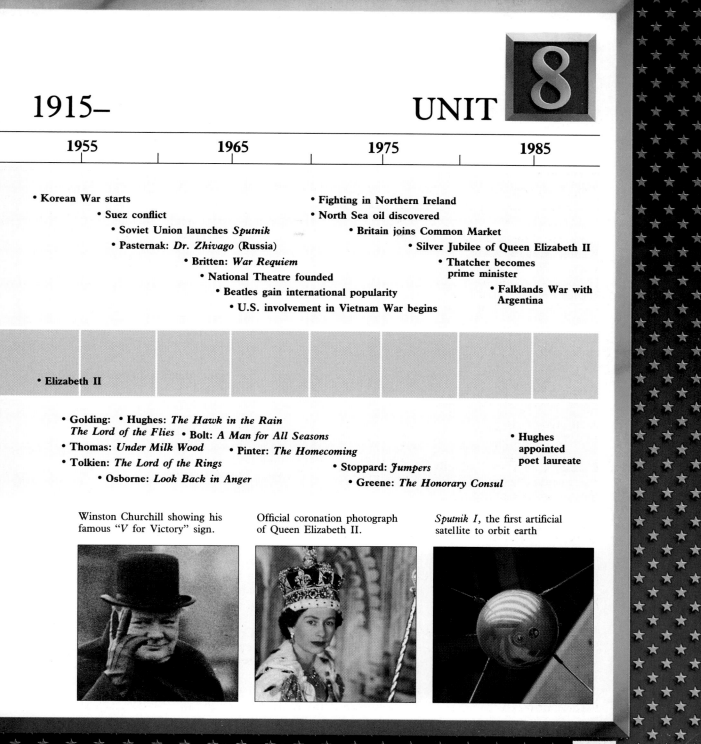

Winston Churchill showing his famous "*V* for Victory" sign.

Official coronation photograph of Queen Elizabeth II.

Sputnik I, the first artificial satellite to orbit earth

PREVIEW

UNIT 8   THE TWENTIETH CENTURY   1915–

Authors

Rupert Brooke
Siegfried Sassoon
Wilfred Owen
Vera Brittain
James Joyce
Katherine Mansfield

Virginia Woolf
George Orwell
D. H. Lawrence
T. S. Eliot
W. H. Auden
Frank O'Connor

Graham Greene
Sylvia Townsend Warner
Dylan Thomas
Stevie Smith
Ted Hughes

Features
Comment: The Language of Heroism
Reading Modern Poetry
Reader's Note: "The Hollow Men"
Themes in English Literature: The Inner Life
Reader's Note: "Fern Hill"
The Changing English Language

Application of Literary Terms
consonance
free verse

Review of Literary Terms
mood
point of view
imagery

Reading Literature Skillfully
propaganda devices
conclusions/generalizations

Vocabulary Skills
word analogies
dictionary
context

Thinking Skills
classifying
generalizing
synthesizing
evaluating

Composition Assignments Include
Writing a War Narration
Writing a Persuasive Essay
Contrasting Views of War
Writing About Irony
Writing an Autobiographical Essay
Contrasting Expectations with Reality
Remembering a Special Gift
Analyzing the Symbolism in
   "The Doll's House"
Writing a Case Study
Writing About First-Hand Experience
Writing a Dialogue
Writing a Character Sketch
Analyzing Eliot's Irony
Writing an Essay of Definition
Writing a Satirical Elegy
Writing a Personal Essay
Analyzing Sibling Rivalry
Writing a Fantasy
Reviewing a Film
Analyzing "Fern Hill"
Writing a Poem

Enrichment
Preparing a Slide Show
Choral Reading
Comparing Versions of the Story

Thinking Critically About Literature
Concept Review
Content Review
Composition Review

THE TWENTIETH CENTURY 1915–

During World War II British civilians heroically endured months of intensive bombing and the threat of invasion; but it is World War I, "the Great War," that must nevertheless be regarded as the cultural watershed for twentieth-century England. Fought mainly in Europe and the Middle East from 1914 to 1918, the war involved on one side the Central Powers—principally Germany, Austria-Hungary, and Turkey—and on the other the Allied Powers—principally Great Britain (and the Commonwealth nations), France, Russia, and (after 1917) the United States. For the British, the chief battlefield was northern France, which became "the Western Front," where vast armies contended in huge, prolonged military actions—called *battles* by the historians, but unlike anything in previous European warfare—resulting in millions of dead and wounded. An ugly and futile bloodbath that decimated a generation, the war precipitated massive social and political changes and shattered romanticized conceptions of war, heroic behavior, and national purpose.

Reflecting on the period from 1901 to 1915, the poet Philip Larkin wrote: "Never such innocence again." Though the quiet surface of Edwardian England was troubled by industrial unrest, the threat of civil war in Ireland, and intensified agitation by the women's suffrage movement, ordinary British people still felt secure in their national identity and their country's position as the most powerful nation in the world. Since England had not been involved in a conflict with a major power since the Crimean War (1854–1856), and had experienced the Boer War (1899–1902) as remote, if unsettling, there was also a universal innocence about the nature of modern warfare.

THE FIRST WORLD WAR

On August 4, 1914, the day war broke out, cheering crowds gathered outside Buckingham Palace, while young men, ardent for what they viewed as the coming test of their manhood in combat, lined up at the recruiting stations to be among the first to enlist. This universal readiness to court death and danger, spawned by the long peace, is everywhere apparent in the letters, poems, and memoirs of the young men of the period. Rupert Brooke, the most popular poet of the prewar era, urged, "Come and die. It'll be great fun!" Among the middle and upper classes, the war was generally regarded as a new kind of "game," to be undertaken in the same spirit of gentlemanly competitiveness as cricket or rugby.

But after only six months of fighting, the war had become a murderous stalemate conducted from trenches. A vast system of underground fortifications stretched from the North Sea to the Alps, and the soldiers of the two sides faced each other across a wilderness of shell craters and barbed wire called "No Man's Land." The trenches were muddy tunnels with only the sight of the sky, in the words of one writer, "to persuade a man that he was not already lost in a common grave." Generals calculated in advance the number of men who would be sacrificed in an attack; then they sent their troops in waves to face enemy machine guns. In 1916, during the eagerly anticipated Battle of the Somme, 60,000 British soldiers were killed or wounded the first day. In the Third Battle of Ypres, 370,000 British soldiers, mired in the mud of No Man's Land created by days of bombardment, were killed, wounded, or frozen to death. (Even during the quietest periods, some 7,000 British soldiers were killed or wounded daily on the Western Front; these losses were referred to as "wastage" by army commanders.) By 1917, the war had come to be, according to one writer, "an enormous carnival of death. Nothing else in the history of Europe, not even the Black Death, had produced such an extravagance of corpses. . . . It was the extinction of the fittest—and for what discernible purpose?"

That a radical transformation in the language, tone, and subject matter of literature was taking place began to be apparent after 1916 in the poetry produced by the young men serving in the front lines. Back in 1914, as illustrated by the opening lines of Rupert Brooke's famous sonnet "The Soldier," the prevailing tone of poetry was still lofty and romantic: "If I should die, think only this of me:/That there's some corner of a foreign field/That is forever England." How different in tone are these lines by a later soldier-poet, Edgell Rickword, describing a dead comrade: "I knew a man, he was my chum,/but he grew darker day by day,/and would not brush the flies away."

Rejecting high-sounding abstractions like "glory," "sacrifice," and "honor" that no longer held any meaning for them, many of the soldier-poets adopted a colloquial, concrete, realistic style, bitter and deeply ironical in tone. Siegfried Sassoon, the most widely-read poet of the war, bitterly satirized generals, politicians, and a civilian population that exhorted the young to fight for their country, while remaining largely ignorant of the slaughter and suffering, those who, in the words of another soldier-poet, Wilfred Owen, "tell with such high zest/To children ardent for some desperate glory,/The old Lie: Dulce et decorum est/Pro patria mori." ("It is sweet and fitting to die for one's country.") Owen was encouraged by Sassoon, whom he idolized, and imbued by him with a compelling sense of mission to tell the truth about modern warfare. Killed one week before the Armistice in 1918, he produced in his last year of life a haunting and accomplished group of savagely ironical poems whose dominant themes are the hideousness and senselessness of the slaughter on the Western Front. Perhaps the most important poet produced by the war, he is also, in the words of Dylan Thomas, "a poet of all times, all places, and all wars."

THE POSTWAR PERIOD

The 1920s were not a tranquil period for Britain. Massive unemployment was created by the return of hundreds of thousands of veterans to civilian life, and bitter labor disputes were the result. Ramsay MacDonald (1866–1937) became the first Labour Party prime minister in January, 1924; but Labour was defeated at the polls later that year, and Stanley Baldwin (1867–1947), a Conservative, became prime minister. Another setback for Labour was the General Strike (May 3–13, 1926), an unsuccessful attempt to support striking coal miners that resulted in retaliatory legislation against trade unions. Baldwin and the Conservatives, who governed England from 1924–1929, were no more successful than their predecessors in dealing with the country's critical economic problems.

Poet, critic, and dramatist, T. S. Eliot, an American expatriate who became a British subject, was the leading spokesman for the modernist poetry that emerged in the 1920s, a poetry characterized by intellectual complexity, allusiveness, precise use of images, and an extreme pessimism. Like the soldier-poets, Eliot turned his back on what he viewed as the inflated rhetoric of the Victorians and insisted on the use of common speech in poetry, as Wordsworth and Coleridge had done earlier. In a famous essay on the metaphysical poets, Eliot argued that, between the time of John Donne and the Victorian period, a "dissociation of sensibility" had occurred, that is, a separation of thought and feeling that modern poetry should seek to bridge through the use of the carefully chosen sensory image—the "objective correlative," in Eliot's phrase. The influence of his poetry—both its technique and its pessimism—was widespread. His most famous work, *The Waste Land* (1922), a highly complex and allusive poem, was seen as a grim metaphor for postwar society.

The revolution in poetry had its counterpart in fiction. The novelists of the eighteenth and nineteenth centuries had written within a defined social context to an audience that shared similar values and beliefs. Modernist writers perceived human beings as living in private worlds and therefore took as their task the illumina-

Enthusiastic crowds at a Southwark recruiting station in December, 1915.

tion of individual experience. Influenced by the work of the noted psychiatrist Sigmund Freud (1856–1939), novelists like James Joyce and Virginia Woolf attempted to reproduce the authentic character of human subjectivity, the so-called *stream of consciousness.* Joyce's *Ulysses* (1922), probably the most influential novel of our time, employs a variety of prose styles and a story line that exactly parallels that of Homer's *Odyssey* to recount the events of a single day (June 16, 1904) in the life of a Dublin man, Leopold Bloom. In *Ulysses* Joyce creates both a microscopically accurate picture of Irish life and a mythical overview of human affairs.

Though a novelist of more narrow limits than Joyce, Virginia Woolf developed a strikingly original and poetic style to convey the inner consciousness of her characters. In novels like *Mrs. Dalloway, To the Lighthouse,* and *The Waves,* she rejected the narrative practice of setting down a series of happenings in chronological sequence as a violation of the truth of human experience: "Life is not a series of gig-lamps symmetrically arranged: life is a luminous halo, a semi-

transparent envelope surrounding us from the beginning of consciousness to the end."

The novels of D. H. Lawrence are more traditional in form than those of Joyce and Woolf, but similarly focused on the inner lives of characters and their felt response to experience. In novels like *Sons and Lovers, The Rainbow,* and *Women in Love,* he explores the frequently ambivalent relationship existing between the sexes, one of intense antagonism, yet mutual dependence and need. Other major themes that dominate his fiction are the conflict between the physical and intellectual sides of human experience and the destruction of the natural world and spontaneous feeling by an encroaching industrial society.

THE 1930s AND 1940s

A worldwide economic depression, the rise of totalitarian powers, the Second World War, and Great Britain's diminished importance in the post-war world darkened the 1930s and 1940s and gave impetus to a literature focused on ideas, social criticism, and ideological debate. It was inevitable that the world depression that began in the late 1920s would have catastrophic effects in highly industrialized and heavily populated Britain. In two years exports and imports declined 35 percent, and three million unemployed roamed the streets of factory towns.

The Spanish Civil War (1936–1939), with Nazi Germany and Fascist Italy assisting one side, and Communist Russia the other, polarized opinion in Britain, with many writers, artists, and intellectuals joining the fight. By the late 1930s there had been some improvement in economic conditions, and Great Britain's foreign policy began to take precedence over its domestic policy. The Second World War, which began in September, 1939, with Hitler's invasion of Poland, was initially a series of disasters for Britain and her allies. During 1939 and 1940 Nazi Germany mastered Europe. Only Britain, now under the able wartime leadership of Winston Churchill (1874–1965) remained to oppose Hitler. But Britons heroically withstood the bombardment of their cities, and with the entry of the United States into the war, and the failure of the German invasion of Russia, the tide began to turn. Although Britain and her allies

Hotel Regina by Neil Davenport. 1978. *Portal Gallery, London*

were eventually victorious, the postwar years were extremely hard. The country was nearly bankrupt, and recovery was slow.

Of the new poets writing during this period, the most important and influential was W. H. Auden. During the 1930s, which he characterized as a "low, dishonest decade," Auden was the acknowledged leader of a circle of writers who aligned themselves with the political left and attempted to expose the social and economic ills of "this country of ours where nobody is well." Although they saw themselves as the creators of a new poetic tradition, the influence of Hopkins, Yeats, and Eliot on these young writers is unmistakable, especially in their use of precise and suggestive images, ironic understatement, and plain speech. Another leftist social critic of the period was George Orwell, who exposed the plight of the English working class in books like *Down and Out in Paris and London* and *The Road to Wigan Pier.*

WORLDWIDE CULTURAL INFLUENCES

The truth of John Donne's "No man is an island" continues to be proved as the world shrinks rapidly, brought about in part through the expansion of the new twentieth-century media, radio, television, and motion pictures. The first commercial radio station in the U.S. opened in 1920 in Pittsburgh, Pennsylvania; England followed soon after with the organization of the British Broadcasting Corporation in 1927. The first public telecasts were seen in the U.S. in 1932, in England, 1936. It was not until after World War II, however, that television became widespread. Today, such celebrated events as the 1981 wedding of Prince Charles, Queen Elizabeth's son and heir, are viewed world-wide.

World travel, forced, at first, by the transportation of troops to different countries during the two World Wars, continues to increase as people eagerly expose themselves to different cultures. Styles in clothing, automobiles, architecture, and so on, are no longer confined within national boundaries.

Music has been called an international language, and the popularity during this century of jazz, swing, and rock in all their various forms has brought about further cultural integration. Motion pictures have exposed all of us to national and ethnic variations in speech, thought, and styles of living.

MODERN ENGLAND

The war years, with the fear of a German invasion and the aerial bombardments of heavily industrialized areas, united the country and forged a spirit of camaraderie among the British that breached (but did not destroy) class barriers and resulted in a landslide victory for the Labour Party in the first postwar election. The new government consolidated the "welfare state," in which the social services were revised and expanded. With bipartisan support the National Health Service Act was passed, providing for the nationalization of hospitals and free medical care for the whole population.

Perhaps England's most notable postwar achievement was the peaceful liquidation of its once vast empire. This imperial loss, coupled with domestic economic problems, caused British statemen to develop a new posture in world affairs. Seeking closer ties with Europe, England accepted an invitation to join the Common Market, a decision taken despite a split in public opinion regarding its future impact on the country's domestic economy.

Some of the poetry of the period, notably the work of Dylan Thomas, was marked by an extravagant, romantic rhetoric. Though simpler in style, the work of Ted Hughes powerfully evokes the world of nature, using a richly textured pattern of metaphor and mythic suggestiveness for its effects.

English drama experienced a renaissance in the 1950s and 1960s, stimulated by the presence of large numbers of first-rate actors and directors and the works of playwrights like John Osborne, John Arden, Harold Pinter, Tom Stoppard, and Edward Bond. Osborne's *Look Back in Anger* (1956) articulated the complaints of the working class against a social system that inhibits upward mobility and personal fulfillment, and launched a movement of socially conscious writers, the "angry young men." In contrast, the work of Harold Pinter, perhaps the most important postwar dramatist in England, is antirealist. Characters move in a nightmarish environment of menace, devoid of communication and love.

Though immensely varied and radically experimental, the literature of the twentieth century is similar to that of previous periods in its overall pattern of continuity and change. While developing new techniques to reflect present realities, modern writers have shown their indebtedness to such past masters as Shakespeare and Donne, Austen and Dickens, Hopkins, Hardy, and Yeats. However, in their rejection of false language and sentiments, in their ironic portrayal of contemporary existence, and in their search for personal identity and meaning in human life, they are the spiritual descendants of the generation whose innocence was lost in the trenches of World War I.

THINKING ABOUT GRAPHIC AIDS
Using the Time Line

Use the time line on pages 756–757 to answer these questions.

1. What major cultural and political changes occurred during the reign of George V?
2. How long after World War I ended did Vera Brittain publish her war memoirs in *Testament of Youth*?
3. Who was the only British monarch to abdicate (resign the throne)?
4. Compare this time line with the Unit 6 time line on pages 540–541. How long after the first suffrage reforms did women finally get the vote in England?
5. Compare the time lines for Units 1–8. For how long has England been one unified country? How many monarchs have ruled in that time?

BIOGRAPHY

Rupert Brooke
1887–1915

An aura of glamor surrounded Rupert Brooke. He was strikingly handsome, personally magnetic, intelligent, and gifted. His death at age twenty-eight during the early months of the Great War made him a legend, the epitome of idealistic young Englishmen ready to perish for their country. "The Soldier," one of five "War Sonnets" published early in 1915, greatly contributed to his immense national popularity, which was enhanced by the posthumous publication of *1914 and Other Poems*. Ironically, Brooke attained his legendary status without ever having engaged in actual combat.

Brooke was educated at Rugby, where his father was a housemaster, and at Kings College, Cambridge, where, for five years, he was the acknowledged leader of the literary community. Before the war the publication of *Poems 1911* and contributions to two volumes of *Georgian Poetry*, edited by his friend Edward Marsh, were well received. Following a nervous collapse in 1913, he traveled extensively in Canada, the United States, and the Pacific, residing for a time in Tahiti, where he did some of his best writing, until drawn home by the outbreak of World War I.

In 1914 Brooke enlisted, receiving a commission in the Royal Naval Division. He participated in the Antwerp Expedition, though seeing no direct action, and was then ordered with his division to the Dardanelles campaign. En route, he contracted blood poisoning and died on a hospital ship anchored off the Greek island of Skyros. His friends buried him in an exquisite olive grove Brooke had admired three days earlier—his "corner of a foreign field/That is for ever England."

Despite his reputation, Brooke is remembered more today for what he represented than for what he wrote. Traditional, patriotic, conventional in subject matter and style, Brooke symbolized the romantic outlook on war that became quickly displaced by the bitterness of soldier-poets directly confronted with the unbelievable horror of life and death in the trenches.

The Soldier

Rupert Brooke

If I should die, think only this of me:
That there's some corner of a foreign field
That is forever England. There shall be
In that rich earth a richer dust concealed;
5 A dust whom England bore, shaped, made
    aware;
Gave, once, her flowers to love, her ways
    to roam,
A body of England's breathing English air,
Washed by the rivers, blest by suns of
    home.

And think, this heart, all evil shed away,
10 A pulse in the eternal mind, no less
Gives somewhere back the thoughts by
    England given;
Her sights and sounds; dreams happy as her
    day;
And laughter, learnt of friends; and
    gentleness,
In hearts at peace, under an English
    heaven.

THINK AND DISCUSS

Understanding

1. If the speaker should die in war, what does he believe his burial place would become?
2. What five things does he say his heart will give back to the world?

Analyzing

3. Is this an Italian or an English sonnet?
4. For what aspects of his English heritage is the speaker especially grateful?
5. What enables the speaker to anticipate and accept the possibility of his death with such a positive and peaceful attitude?

Extending

6. Though written by an Englishman reflecting on his native land, what makes the poem universally applicable?

Siegfried Sassoon's prewar life, richly described in his memoirs, was one of "cultivated idleness," taken up with hunting, book-collecting, and the writing of exquisite verses in the Georgian style (typical of the immediate prewar era) that focused on images of rural England as a source of patriotic ideals. Robert Graves, in his autobiography *Goodbye to All That,* tells of meeting Sassoon in France and showing him the initial drafts of his first book of poems: "He frowned and said that war should not be written about in such a realistic way. In return, he showed me some of his own poems. One of them began: 'Return to greet me, colors that were my joy, / Not in the woeful crimson of men slain . . . ' Sassoon had not yet been in the trenches. I told him, in my old-soldier manner, that he would soon change his style."

The change from conventional idealist to satiric realist, brought about by his personal experiences at the front, is strikingly apparent in Sassoon's two collections of war poems, *The Old Huntsman* (1917) and *Counter-Attack* (1918). Known to his company as "Mad Jack," Sassoon fought with exceptional bravery in France, was awarded two medals, and rose to the rank of captain. By summer of 1917, however, he was convinced that the war was being unjustifiably prolonged and issued a statement reproduced by the press calling for an instant negotiated peace. Instead of being court-martialed as he had hoped, he was judged temporarily insane and hospitalized. During one of his hospital stays he met Wilfred Owen, whom he encouraged in his writing.

Though a poet of more limited range than Owen, Sassoon was the most widely read poet of World War I and a master of satiric verse. His war poems are characterized by a direct, epigrammatic, colloquial style and a tone of intense anger and bitterness toward civilians, journalists, and politicians ignorant of the hell soldiers were going through. After the war, Sassoon produced poetry of inferior quality, but continued to write enlightening autobiographies and memoirs. He was also instrumental in bringing Wilfred Owen to the attention of the reading public.

Base Details

If I were fierce, and bald, and short of breath,
    I'd live with scarlet Majors[1] at the Base,
And speed glum heroes up the line to death.
    You'd see me with my puffy petulant face,
5 Guzzling and gulping in the best hotel,
    Reading the Roll of Honor. "Poor young chap,"
I'd say—"I used to know his father well;
    Yes, we've lost heavily in this last scrap."

And when the war is done and youth stone dead,
10 I'd toddle safely home and die—in bed.

                       1918

1. *scarlet Majors.* The Staff officers serving in safety and relative comfort behind the lines wore cap-bands and lapel-tabs of bright red; line officers serving at the front wore khaki tabs.

Suicide in the Trenches

I knew a simple soldier boy
Who grinned at life in empty joy,
Slept soundly through the lonesome dark,
And whistled early with the lark.

5 In winter trenches, cowed and glum,
With crumps[1] and lice and lack of rum,
He put a bullet through his brain.
No one spoke of him again.

       . . .

You smug-faced crowds with kindling eye
10 Who cheer when soldier lads march by,
Sneak home and pray you'll never know
The hell where youth and laughter go.

                       1918

1. *crumps,* soldiers' slang for exploding shells, from the sound made by them.

"Base Details," "Suicide in the Trenches," and "Does It Matter?" from *Collected Poems* by Siegfried Sassoon. Copyright 1918 by E. P. Dutton. Copyright © 1946 by Siegfried Sassoon. Reprinted by permission of Viking Penguin Inc. and George Sassoon.

Does It Matter?

Does it matter?—losing your legs? . . .
For people will always be kind,
And you need not show that you mind
When the others come in after hunting
5 To gobble their muffins and eggs.

Does it matter?—losing your sight? . . .
There's such splendid work for the blind;
And people will always be kind,
As you sit on the terrace remembering
10 And turning your face to the light.

Do they matter?—those dreams from the
    pit? . . .
You can drink and forget and be glad,
And people won't say that you're mad;
For they'll know you've fought for your
    country
15 And no one will worry a bit.

                       1918

Siegfried Sassoon

THINK AND DISCUSS

BASE DETAILS

Understanding

1. According to the poem, what is the main job of the "scarlet Majors at the Base"?
2. Where do these "scarlet Majors" usually die?

Analyzing

3. What criticism of military leaders does this poem make?
4. Explain the double meaning of the title.
5. What is the **tone** of the poem? Is it appropriate?

Extending

6. What does this poem imply about the attitudes of soldiers in World War I toward their superior officers? What do you think accounts for this attitude?

SUICIDE IN THE TRENCHES

Understanding

1. What was the reaction of the speaker to the suicide of the "soldier boy"?

Analyzing

2. What words in the first stanza show the boy to have been innocent and naive?
3. Judging from the few details we are given, why did he kill himself?
4. Why are the "smug-faced" advised to "Sneak home and pray"?

Extending

5. Are you surprised that the boy described in the first stanza commits suicide? What point about war is the poet making?

DOES IT MATTER?

Understanding

1. What three losses does the poem discuss?
2. Name two ways, according to the poem, that war casualties can escape from their misery.

Analyzing

3. In what tone does the poet answer the repeated question "Does it matter?" What effect does this tone create?
4. What individuals and attitudes does the poem attack?

Extending

5. Are handicapped veterans today treated any better than in Sassoon's day? Consider, for example, the treatment of veterans from the Korean and Vietnam wars.

COMPOSITION

Writing a War Narration

Imagine yourself a casualty of war, reconstructing the awful circumstances that have handicapped you for life. Tell the story of your war experience, narrating events as they happened rather than just summarizing them. Pick a war setting with which you have the most familiarity through your reading or viewing of films. You may wish to use flashbacks to return to the battlefront scene of your calamity. Make sure to tell how you felt before the war and how you feel now about life and your future.

Writing a Persuasive Essay

The media have given a great deal of attention to the treatment of veterans, especially those from the Vietnam War. Write an essay to persuade your classmates that veterans are, or are not, being treated better today than those from previous wars. You may wish to do some research to bolster your argument. State your position in your first paragraph, and in the second paragraph make any necessary concessions to undercut the case for the opposition. Then take up your argument, point by point, in separate paragraphs, providing concrete examples wherever possible. Depending on your viewpoint, conclude either by suggesting needed reforms or applauding the public's treatment of veterans of recent wars. You may wish to read your paper to a friend to test its persuasiveness.

Wilfred Owen
1893–1918

Wilfred Owen went to France in December of 1916, in time to participate in some of the hardest fighting during the cold winter of 1917. In June of 1917, he was hospitalized following a nervous collapse and remained in England until September of 1918, when he volunteered to return to the front, though convinced he was fated to die. This year of reprieve enabled Owen to develop a supportive friendship with his literary idol, Siegfried Sassoon, and gave him the necessary time to carry out his self-assigned mission to tell the truth about modern warfare.

In the famous Preface to the collection of poems he planned, Owen wrote: "Above all I am not concerned with Poetry. . . . My subject is War, and the pity of War. . . . The Poetry is in the pity." The truth is that he was deeply concerned about his craft but had come to reject the romantic poetic tradition he had formerly worked in as false to facts and feelings. His esthetic conversion is evident in a letter home on February 4th, 1917, in which he described "the universal pervasion of Ugliness. Hideous landscapes, vile noises, foul language . . . everything unnatural, broken, blasted; the distortion of the dead, whose unburiable bodies sit outside the dug-outs all day, all night, the most execrable sights on earth. In poetry we call them the most glorious." Owen's poetry, in contrast, is startlingly blunt, ironic, and graphically explicit in its physical description of the daily "crucifixion" of youth on the battlefield. It is also stylistically distinctive in its use of multiple sound effects achieved through the employment of assonance, alliteration, and consonance.

One week before the Armistice of 1918 and two weeks after being decorated for gallantry, Wilfred Owen was killed by machine-gun fire. He had published only four poems during his lifetime and was unknown as a poet, except to a few friends. Through the efforts of his mother and friends, eight of Owen's poems were published in assorted periodicals in 1919, followed, in 1920, by the publication of his collected poems, edited by Siegfried Sassoon. They have come to be praised as the work of the finest poet of World War I and of a major writer of this century.

Dulce et Decorum Est

Bent double, like old beggars under sacks,
Knock-kneed, coughing like hags, we
    cursed through sludge,
Till on the haunting flares we turned our backs
And towards our distant rest began to trudge.
5 Men marched asleep. Many had lost their boots
But limped on, blood-shod. All went lame;
    all blind;
Drunk with fatigue; deaf even to the hoots
Of tired, outstripped Five-Nines[1] that dropped
    behind.

Gas! GAS! Quick, boys!—An ecstasy of
    fumbling,
10 Fitting the clumsy helmets just in time;
But someone still was yelling out and stumbling
And flound'ring like a man in fire or lime . . .
Dim, through the misty panes and thick
    green light,
As under a green sea, I saw him drowning.

15 In all my dreams, before my helpless sight,
He plunges at me, guttering, choking, drowning.

If in some smothering dreams you too could
    pace
Behind the wagon that we flung him in,
And watch the white eyes writhing in his face,
20 His hanging face, like a devil's sick of sin;
If you could hear, at every jolt, the blood
Come gargling from the froth-corrupted lungs,
Obscene as cancer, bitter as the cud
Of vile, incurable sores on innocent tongues,—
25 My friend, you would not tell with such high
    zest
To children ardent for some desperate glory,
The old Lie: Dulce et decorum est
Pro patria mori.[2]
1917   1920

---

1. **Five-Nines,** shells containing poison gas. The subject of this poem is a gas attack. The use of poison gas on the Western Front, first by the Germans and then the Allies, was widely viewed as immoral.
2. **Dulce . . . mori** (dŭl′chā et dǝ côr′ǝm est prō pä′trē-e môr′ē). "It is sweet and honorable to die for one's country," a quotation from one of Horace's *Odes* well known to British schoolboys.

Arms and the Boy

Let the boy try along this bayonet-blade
How cold steel is, and keen with hunger of
    blood;
Blue with all malice, like a madman's flash;
And thinly drawn with famishing for flesh.

5 Lend him to stroke these blind, blunt bullet-
    leads
Which long to nuzzle in the hearts of lads,
Or give him cartridges of fine zinc teeth,
Sharp with the sharpness of grief and death.

For his teeth seem for laughing round an apple.
10 There lurk no claws behind his fingers supple;
And God will grow no talons at his heels,
Nor antlers through the thickness of his curls.
1918   1920

Arms . . . Boy. The title is an ironic play on the opening words of Virgil's *Aeneid*: "Of arms and the man I sing . . ."

H**T** See CONSONANCE in the Handbook of Literary Terms, page 926.

Anthem for Doomed Youth

What passing-bells[1] for these who die as cattle?
  Only the monstrous anger of the guns.
  Only the stuttering rifles' rapid rattle
Can patter out their hasty orisons.[2]
5 No mockeries now for them; no prayers nor bells,
  Nor any voice of mourning save the choirs,—
The shrill, demented choirs of wailing shells;
  And bugles calling for them from sad shires.[3]

What candles may be held to speed them all?
10   Not in the hands of boys, but in their eyes

Shall shine the holy glimmers of good-byes.
  The pallor of girls' brows shall be their pall;
Their flowers the tenderness of patient minds,
And each slow dusk a drawing-down of blinds.
1917   1920

---

1. *passing-bells,* church bells rung for the dying or the dead.
2. *orisons* (ôr′ə zənz), prayers.
3. *bugles . . . shires,* played at funeral services held for them in their home counties (shires).

Over the Top by John Nash. *Imperial War Museum, London*

Comment

The Language of Heroism

In his book *The Great War and Modern Memory*, literary historian Paul Fussell observes that one of the casualties of World War I was the system of "high" diction relating to warfare to which several generations of readers had become accustomed. "The tutors in this special diction had been the boys' books of George Alfred Henty; the male romances of Rider Haggard; the poems of Robert Bridges; and especially the Arthurian poems of Tennyson and the pseudo-medieval romances of William Morris." As examples of this "high" diction, Fussell offers a series of equivalents:

A friend is a . . . . *comrade*
A horse is a . . . . *steed,* or *charger*
The enemy is . . . . *the foe,* or *the host*
Danger is . . . . *peril*
To conquer is to . . . . *vanquish*
To be earnestly brave is to be . . . . *gallant*

To be cheerfully brave is to be . . . . *plucky*
To be stolidly brave is to be . . . .*staunch*
The dead on the battefield are . . . . *the fallen*
The front is . . . . *the field*
Obedient soldiers are . . . . *the brave*
Warfare is . . . . *strife*
To die is to . . . . *perish*
The draft-notice is . . . . *the summons*
To enlist is to . . . . *join the colors*
One's death is one's . . . . *fate*
The sky is . . . . *the heavens*
What is contemptible is . . . . *base*
The legs and arms of young men are . . . . . *limbs*
Dead bodies constitute . . . . *ashes,* or *dust*
The blood of young men is . . . . *"the red / Sweet wine of youth"*—R. Brooke

From *The Great War and Modern Memory* by Paul Fussell. Copyright © 1975 by Oxford University Press, Inc. Reprinted by permission.

Disabled

He sat in a wheeled chair, waiting for dark,
And shivered in his ghastly suit of grey,
Legless, sewn short at elbow. Through the
    park
Voices of boys rang saddening like a hymn,
5 Voices of play and pleasure after day,
Till gathering sleep had mothered them from
    him.

About this time Town used to swing so gay
When glow-lamps budded in the light blue
    trees,
And girls glanced lovelier as the air grew dim,—
10 In the old times, before he threw away his
    knees.
Now he will never feel again how slim
Girls' waists are, or how warm their subtle
    hands;

All of them touch him like some queer disease.

There was an artist silly for his face,
15 For it was younger than his youth, last year.
Now, he is old; his back will never brace;
He's lost his color very far from here,
Poured it down shell-holes till the veins ran
    dry,
And half his lifetime lapsed in the hot race,
20 And leap of purple spurted from his thigh.

One time he liked a blood-smear down his leg,
After the matches, carried shoulder-high.
It was after football, when he'd drunk a peg,
He thought he'd better join.—He wonders
    why.
25 Someone had said he'd look a god in kilts,

That's why; and may be, too, to please his
    Meg;
Aye, that was it, to please the giddy jilts[1]
He asked to join. He didn't have to beg;
Smiling they wrote his lie; aged nineteen years.
30 Germans he scarcely thought of; all their guilt,
And Austria's, did not move him. And no fears
Of Fear came yet. He thought of jewelled hilts
For daggers in plaid socks; of smart salutes;
And care of arms; and leave; and pay arrears;
35 *Esprit de corps;*[2] and hints for young recruits.
And soon, he was drafted out with drums and
    cheers.

Some cheered him home, but not as crowds
    cheer Goal.
Only a solemn man who brought him fruits

Thanked him; and then inquired about his soul.
40 Now, he will spend a few sick years in
    Institutes,
And do what things the rules consider wise,
And take whatever pity they may dole.
Tonight he noticed how the women's eyes
Passed from him to the strong men that were
    whole.
45 How cold and late it is! Why don't they come
And put him into bed? Why don't they come?
1917   **1920**

1. *jilts*, girls.
2. *Esprit de corps* (e sprē′ də kôr′), group spirit, morale.
[*French*]

THINK AND DISCUSS
DULCE ET DECORUM EST
Understanding
1. Are these men returning from or going into battle?
2. To what is death by poisoned gas compared?
3. What is done with the soldier who was gassed?

Analyzing
4. What is the physical and mental condition of the men described in the first stanza?
5. What explicit horrors of life in the front lines does the poem itemize?
6. What is the meaning of the quotation that ends the poem? What is its purpose?

Extending
7. What, in your opinion, marks this as a poem of the twentieth century?

ARMS AND THE BOY
Understanding
1. What two things is the boy in the poem asked to do?

Analyzing
2. According to the last stanza, what would have to happen to the boy for him to use bullets and bayonets as they were intended?
3. How do the **images** of the poem support this idea?

Extending
4. The title is an **allusion** to the opening line ("Of arms and the man I sing. . .") of Virgil's heroic epic *The Aeneid.* Why does Owen want the reader to make a connection between his work and Virgil's?

ANTHEM FOR DOOMED YOUTH
Understanding
1. What replaces church bells, prayers, and choirs for youth killed at the front?
2. What replaces candles and flowers?

Wilfred Owen

Analyzing

3. Why, according to the poem, would the traditional funeral rituals, such as prayers, bells, and choirs, be "mockeries"?
4. What point is the poet trying to make by using the word *anthem*, given the kind of "music" he creates?

Extending

5. What do you think this poem is saying about war and its effect on traditional rituals and values?

APPLYING: Consonance H⚡
See Handbook of Literary Terms, p. 926

   Wilfred Owen's poetry makes rich use of **consonance**—the repetition of consonant sounds followed or preceded by different vowel sounds—as a way of achieving interesting sound effects in his poetry. Consonance is also an effective device for creating mood and unifying meaning in a poem. **Consonantal rhyme** is the rhyming of beginning and ending consonants, such as *grain/groin*, used as a variant to syllabic rhyming.

1. Where has Owen utilized consonance and consonantal rhyme in "Anthem for Doomed Youth"?
2. What **mood** has been created through this use of consonance?
3. Point out instances of consonantal rhyme in "Arms and the Boy."

THINK AND DISCUSS
DISABLED
Understanding

1. How severely disabled is the boy described?
2. What did the boy have to do in order to enlist?
3. Who greeted the boy on his return from the front?

Analyzing

4. What two main contrasts are developed in the poem? for what effect?
5. Contrast the young man's motives for enlisting with the reality he experienced.
6. What accounts for the boy's particularly bitter attitude toward women?

Extending

7. Compare this poem with Sassoon's "Does It Matter?" in **tone, theme,** and **point of view**. Which poem, do you feel, better conveys the plight of disabled veterans?

THINKING SKILLS
Generalizing

   To generalize is to draw a general statement or rule from particular information.

1. What general attitude toward war did Rupert Brooke represent? State this attitude in one sentence.
2. What was the general attitude toward war of Siegfried Sassoon and Wilfred Owen? State it in one sentence.
3. Put into one sentence the attitude you and some of your peers now hold toward war.

COMPOSITION ✏
Contrasting Views of War

   Rupert Brooke's treatment of death in war obviously differs greatly from that of Siegfried Sassoon and Wilfred Owen. In an essay of four to five paragraphs, contrast the idealistic view of war conveyed in Brooke's "The Soldier" with the realistic view presented in Sassoon's "Suicide in the Trenches" and Owen's "Dulce et Decorum Est" and "Anthem for Doomed Youth." Consider differences in tone, word choice, and patriotic feeling. Take up the idealistic viewpoint first, then the realistic. In your conclusion try to account for the differences you have found.

Writing About Irony

   One of the chief literary devices employed by Sassoon and Owen is **irony**. Their subjects, their **imagery**, their diction, even the titles of their poems all contribute to an ironic effect. Select a poem by one author and write an essay in which you examine the use of irony in it. Point out the irony, explain whether it is verbal, situational, or dramatic, and explain why the author used it. What effect upon the reader does it create? See "Writing About Irony" in the Writer's Handbook.

The product of an Edwardian middle-class background, Vera Brittain broke away from her sheltered family life in 1915 to serve four trying years as a Red Cross nurse in army hospitals in London, Malta, and France. After the Armistice she returned to Oxford to complete her studies and eventually launch a career as a writer and social activist.

For almost ten years after the Armistice, Brittain struggled to find the appropriate medium through which to convey the impact of World War I on her own life and on the lives of the men and women of her generation. She first contemplated writing a novel, then reproducing the diary she had kept from 1913 to 1918, using fictitious names for the people mentioned. Finally she resolved that the truth of the experience could only be revealed by setting her personal story against the larger background of war and social change. The subtitle of *Testament of Youth*—"An Autobiographical Study of the Years 1900–1925"—emphasizes her intent to present history through an account of personal life.

A best seller when it was first published in 1933, *Testament of Youth* is especially significant for what it reveals about the upbringing of middle-class women in Edwardian England and about women's participation in and response to the events of 1914–1918. In the Foreward to her book, Brittain declares that what she has written "constitutes, in effect, the indictment of a civilization." She is particularly critical of her age for denying women equal opportunities for education and work, for engaging in an endless and futile war that slaughtered many of England's most promising youth, and for failing to prepare young people to deal with reality and change. As she poignantly recounts, World War I shattered an entire generation so that nothing could ever again be the same.

Part I of *Testament of Youth* covers the years 1900 to Christmas, 1915, and describes Brittain's childhood, her education, and her relationship with Roland Leighton, a brilliant and sensitive school friend of her brother Edward. On the historical level, this opening section describes the impact of the first year of war on English society. The precocious daughter of provincial, middle-class parents, Brittain spent the first eighteen years of her life sheltered, chaperoned, and intellectually thwarted. Like other girls of her class and time, she was admonished to avoid conversation alone with boys, to wear flowing skirts and high-necked blouses, and to aspire to matrimony and motherhood. While being courted by Roland Leighton, she was constantly supervised, her letters opened, her daily actions closely scrutinized. Since her parents believed only boys should seek higher education, Brittain was forced to wage a lengthy campaign to persuade them to allow her to spend a year preparing for the rigorous entrance and scholarship examinations for Oxford. When war broke out, Vera had just received her acceptance to Oxford and was preoccupied by her budding romance with Leighton.

from Testament of Youth

Vera Brittain

When the Great War broke out, it came to me not as a superlative tragedy, but as an interruption of the most exasperating kind to my personal plans. . . .

It would not, I think, be possible for any present-day girl of the same age even to imagine how abysmally ignorant, how romantically idealistic, and how utterly unsophisticated my more sensitive contemporaries and I were at that time. The naiveties of the diary which I began to write consistently soon after leaving school, and kept up until more than half way through the War, must be read in order to be believed. My "Reflective Record, 1913," is endorsed on its title page with the following comprehensive aspirations:

"To extend love, to promote thought, to lighten suffering, to combat indifference, to inspire activity."

"To know everything of something and something of everything."

My diary for August 3rd, 1914, contains a most incongruous mixture of war and tennis.

The day was Bank Holiday,[1] and a tennis tournament had been arranged at the Buxton Club. I had promised to play with my discouraged but still faithful suitor,[2] and did not in the least want to forgo the amusement that I knew this partnership would afford me—particularly as the events reported in the newspapers seemed too incredible to be taken quite seriously.

"I do not know," I wrote in my diary, "how we all managed to play tennis so calmly and take quite an interest in the result. I suppose it is because we all know so little of the real meaning of war that we are so indifferent. B. and I had to owe 30. It was good handicapping as we had a very close game with everybody." . . .

After that[3] events moved, even in Buxton, very quickly. The German cousins of some local acquaintances left the town in a panic. My parents rushed over in the car to familiar shops in Macclesfield and Leek, where they laid in stores of cheese, bacon, and butter under the generally shared impression that by next week we might all be besieged by the Germans. Wild rumors circulated from mouth to mouth; they were more plentiful than the newspapers, over which a free fight broke out on the station platform every time a batch came by train from London or Manchester. Our elderly cook, who had three Reservist sons, dissolved into continuous tears and was too much upset to prepare the meals with her usual competence; her young daughter-in-law, who had had a baby only the previous Friday, became hyster-

---

1. **Bank Holiday,** any day except Saturday or Sunday on which banks are legally closed. August 3, 1914 was a Monday.
2. **suitor,** not Roland Leighton, but an earlier male friend.
3. **that,** August 4, when at midnight, since the Germans had not responded to an English ultimatum that they withdraw from Belgium, the English entered the war.

ical and had to be forcibly restrained from getting up and following her husband to the station. One or two Buxton girls were hurriedly married to officers summoned to unknown destinations. Pandemonium swept over the town. Holiday trippers wrestled with one another for the *Daily Mail;* habitually quiet and respectable citizens struggled like wolves for the provisions in the food-shops, and vented upon the distracted assistants their dismay at learning that all prices had suddenly gone up.

My diary for those few days reflects *The Times*[4] in its most pontifical mood. "Germany has broken treaty after treaty, and disregarded every honorable tie with other nations. . . . Germany has destroyed the tottering hopes of peace. . . . The great fear is that our bungling Government will declare England's neutrality. . . . If we at this critical juncture refuse to help our friend France, we should be guilty of the grossest treachery."

I prefer to think that my real sentiments were more truly represented by an entry written nearly a month later after the fabulously optimistic reports of the Battle of Le Cateau.[5] I had been over to Newcastle-under-Lyme to visit the family dentist, and afterwards sat for an hour in a tree-shadowed walk called The Brampton and meditated on the War. It was one of those shimmering autumn days when every leaf and flower seems to scintillate with light, and I found it "very hard to believe that not far away men were being slain ruthlessly, and their poor disfigured bodies heaped together and crowded in ghastly indiscrimination into quickly provided common graves as though they were nameless vermin. . . . It is impossible," I concluded, "to find any satisfaction in the thought of 25,000 slaughtered Germans, left to mutilation and decay; the destruction of men as though beasts, whether they be English, French, German, or anything else, seems a crime to the whole march of civilization." . . .

My father vehemently forbade Edward, who was still under military age, to join anything whatsoever. Having himself escaped immersion in the public-school tradition, which stood for militaristic heroism unimpaired by the damping exercise

of reason, he withheld his permission for any kind of military training, and ended by taking Edward daily to the mills to divert his mind from the War. Needless to say, these uncongenial expeditions entirely failed of their desired effect, and constant explosions—to which, having inherited so many of my father's characteristics, I seemed only to add by my presence—made our house quite intolerable. A new one boiled up after each of Edward's tentative efforts at defiance, and these were numerous, for his enforced subservience seemed to him synonymous with everlasting disgrace. One vague application for a commission which he sent to a Notts and Derby regiment actually was forwarded to the War Office—"from which," I related with ingenuous optimism, "we are expecting to hear every post."

When my father discovered this exercise of initiative, his wrath and anxiety reached the point of effervescence. Work of any kind was quite impossible in the midst of so much chaos and apprehension, and letters to Edward from Roland, describing his endeavors to get a commission in a Norfolk regiment, did nothing to ease the perpetual tension. Even after the result of my Oxford Senior[6] came through, I abandoned in despair the Greek textbooks that Roland had lent me. I even took to knitting for the soldiers, though only for a very short time; utterly incompetent at all forms of needlework, I found the simplest bed-socks and sleeping-helmets altogether beyond me. "Oh, how I wish I could wake up in the morning," concludes one typical day's entry describing these commotions, "to find this terrible war the dream it seems to me to be!"

At the beginning of 1915 I was more deeply and ardently in love than I have ever been or am ever likely to be, yet at that time Roland and I had hardly been alone together, and never at all without the constant possibility of observation and interruption. In Buxton our occasional walks had

---

4. *The Times*, of London, England's most influential newspaper.
5. *Le Cateau*, August 26, 1914, a costly British victory.
6. *Oxford Senior*, an entrance exam.

always been taken either through the town in full view of my family's inquisitive acquaintances, or as one half of a quartet whose other members kept us continually in sight. At Uppingham[7] every conversation that we had was exposed to inspection and facetious remark by schoolmasters or relatives. In London we could only meet under the benevolent but embarrassingly interested eyes of an aunt. Consequently, by the middle of January, our desire to see one another alone had passed beyond the bounds of toleration.

In my closely supervised life, a secret visit to London was impossible even en route for Oxford; I knew that I should be seen off by a train which had been discussed for days and, as usual, have my ticket taken for me. But Leicester was a conceivable rendezvous, for I had been that way before, even though from Buxton the obvious route was via Birmingham. So for my family's benefit, I invented some objectionable students, likely to travel by Birmingham, whom I wanted to avoid. Roland, in similar mood, wrote that if he could not get leave he would come without it.

When the morning arrived, my mother decided that I seemed what she called "nervy," and insisted upon accompanying me to Miller's Dale, the junction at which travellers from Buxton change to the main line. I began in despair to wonder whether she would elect to come with me all the way to Oxford, but I finally escaped without her suspecting that I had any intention other than that of catching the first available train from Leicester. The usual telegram was demanded, but I protested that at Oxford station there was always such a rush for a cab that I couldn't possibly find time to telegraph until after tea.

At Leicester, Roland, who had started from Peterborough soon after dawn, was waiting for me with another sheaf of pale pink roses. He looked tired, and said he had had a cold; actually, it was incipient influenza and he ought to have been in bed, but I did not discover this till afterwards.

To be alone with one another after so much observation was quite overwhelming, and for a time conversation in the Grand Hotel lounge moved somewhat spasmodically. But constraint disappeared when he told me with obvious pride that he had asked his own colonel for permission to interview the colonel of the 5th Norfolks, who were stationed some distance away and were shortly going to the front, with a view to getting a transfer.

"Next time I see the C.O.," he announced, "I shall tell him the colonel of the 5th was away. I shall say I spent the whole day looking for him—so after lunch I'm coming with you to Oxford."

I tried to subdue my leaping joy by a protest about his cold, but as we both knew this to be insincere it was quite ineffective. I only stipulated that when we arrived he must lose me at the station; "chap. rules," even more Victorian than the social code of Buxton, made it inexpedient for a woman student to be seen in Oxford with a young man who was not her brother.

So we found an empty first-class carriage and travelled together from Leicester to Oxford. It was a queer journey; the memory of its profound unsatisfactoriness remains with me still. I had not realized before that to be alone together would bring, all too quickly, the knowledge that being alone together was not enough. It was an intolerable realization, for I knew too that death might so easily overtake us before there could be anything more. I was dependent, he had only his pay, and we were both so distressingly young.

Thus a new constraint arose between us which again made it difficult to talk. We tried to discuss impersonally the places that we wanted to see when it was possible to travel once more; we'd go to Florence together, he said, directly the War was over.

"But," I objected—my age-perspective being somewhat different from that of to-day—"it wouldn't be proper until I'm at least thirty."

"Don't worry," he replied persuasively. "I'm sure I can arrange for it to be 'proper' before you get to that age!"

And then, somehow, we found ourselves suddenly admitting that each had kept the other's

---

7. **Uppingham,** the private school attended by Edward Brittain and his friends.

letters right from the beginning. We were now only a few miles from Oxford, and it was the first real thing that we had said. As we sat together silently watching the crimson sun set over the flooded land, some quality in his nearness became so unbearable that, all unsophisticated as I was, I felt afraid. I tried to explain it to myself afterwards by a familiar quotation: "There is no beauty that hath not some strangeness in the proportion."[8]

Like so many of the idealistic but naive young men of his generation, Roland Leighton regarded going to war as a duty, a test of heroism, and a potentially glamorous adventure. In a letter to Brittain describing his determination to secure a commission, he wrote: "I feel that I am meant to take an active part in this War. It is to me a very fascinating thing—something, if very horrible, yet very ennobling and very beautiful, something whose elemental reality raises it above the reach of all cold theorizing." On Wednesday, March 31, 1915, Vera saw Roland off to the front and returned home to the dreary realization that the war was beginning to overshadow everything in her life—school, personal relationships, ambitions, and dreams.

The next day I saw him off, although he had said that he would rather I didn't come. In the early morning we walked to the station beneath a dazzling sun, but the platform from which his train went out was dark and very cold. In the railway carriage we sat hand in hand until the whistle blew. We never kissed and never said a word. I got down from the carriage still clasping his hand, and held it until the gathering speed of the train made me let go. He leaned through the window looking at me with sad, heavy eyes, and I watched the train wind out of the station and swing round the curve until there was nothing left but the snowy distance, and the sun shining harshly on the bright, empty rails.

When I got back to the house, where everyone mercifully left me to myself, I realized that my hands were nearly frozen. Vaguely resenting the physical discomfort, I crouched beside the morning-room fire for almost an hour, unable to believe that I could ever again suffer such acute and conscious agony of mind. On every side there seemed to be cause for despair and no way out of it. I tried not to think because thought was intolerable, yet every effort to stop my mind from working only led to a fresh outburst of miserable speculation. I tried to read; I tried to look at the gaunt white hills across the valley, but nothing was any good, so in the end I just stayed huddled by the fire, immersed in a mood of blank hopelessness in which years seemed to have passed since the morning.

At last I fell asleep for some moments, and awoke feeling better; I was, I suppose, too young for hope to be extinguished for very long. Perhaps, I thought, Wordsworth or Browning or Shelley would have some consolation to offer; all through the War poetry was the only form of literature that I could read for comfort, and the only kind that I ever attempted to write. So I turned at once to Shelley's "Adonais,"[9] only to be provoked to new anguish by the words:

O gentle child, beautiful as thou wert,
Why didst thou leave the trodden paths of men
Too soon, and with weak hands though mighty
    heart
Dare the unpastured dragon in his den?

But the lovely cadences stirred me at last to articulateness; there was no one to whom I wanted to talk, but at least I could tell my diary a good deal of the sorrow that seemed so fathomless. . . .

That morning (April 17, 1915) I left the reassuring study of *The Times* to take part in one of the first national "flag-days" organized during the War. As I wandered with my basket of primroses

---

8. *"There . . . proportion."* Brittain is slightly misquoting from Sir Francis Bacon's essay "Of Beauty." Bacon actually wrote, "There is no excellent beauty that hath not some strangeness in the proportion."
9. *Shelley's "Adonais,"* the pastoral elegy composed in 1821 by Percy Shelley in honor of John Keats, who had died that year at the age of 25.

up and down the Buxton streets, blindingly white as they always became in the midday sunshine, my thoughts swung dizzily between the conviction that Roland would return and the certainty that he could never possibly come back. I had little patience to spare for my mother's middle-aged acquaintances, who patronized me as they bought my primroses, and congratulated me on putting aside my "studies" to "do my bit in this terrible War." I took their pennies with scant ceremony, and one by one thrust them with a noisy clatter into my tin.

"Those who are old and think this War so terrible do not know what it means to us who are young," I soliloquized angrily. "When I think how suddenly, instantly, a chance bullet may put an end to that brilliant life, may cut it off in its youth and mighty promise, faith in the 'increasing purpose' of the ages grows dim."

The fight around Hill 60 which was gradually developing, assisted by the unfamiliar horror of gas attacks, into the Second Battle of Ypres,[10] did nothing to restore my faith in the benevolent intentions of Providence. With that Easter vacation began the wearing anxiety of waiting for letters which for me was to last, with only brief intervals, for more than three years, and which, I think, made all non-combatants feel more distracted than anything else in the War. Even when the letters came they were four days old, and the writer since sending them had had time to die over and over again. My diary, with its long-drawn-out record of days upon days of miserable speculation, still gives a melancholy impression of that nerve-racking suspense.

"Morning," it observes, "creeps on into afternoon, and afternoon passes into evening, while I go from one occupation to another, in apparent unconcern—but all the time this gnawing anxiety beneath it all."

Ordinary household sounds became a torment. The clock, marking off each hour of dread, struck into the immobility of tension with the shattering effect of a thunderclap. Every ring at the door suggested a telegram, every telephone call a long-distance message giving bad news. With some of us the effect of this prolonged apprehension still lingers on; even now I cannot work comfortably in a room from which it is possible to hear the front-door bell.

Having successfully completed her first-year exams at Oxford, Vera dropped all studies to commence training as a Red Cross nurse in Devonshire Hospital. In August, Roland returned home on leave, a sadly strained reunion for the young lovers, despite their becoming officially engaged. Frustrated and depressed by lack of privacy and the brevity of their time together, they parted in a mood of despair and foreboding that was to persist in the grim weeks following Roland's return to France.

As September wore on and the Battle of Loos[11] came nearer, an anxious stillness seemed to settle upon the country, making everyone taut and breathless. The Press and personal letters from France were alike full of anticipation and suspense. Roland wrote vaguely but significantly of movements of troops, of great changes impending, and seemed more obsessed with the idea of death than ever before. One letter, describing how he had superintended the reconstruction of some old trenches, was grim with a disgust and bitterness that I had never known him put into words:

"The dugouts have been nearly all blown in, the wire entanglements are a wreck, and in among the chaos of twisted iron and splintered timber and shapeless earth are the fleshless, blackened bones of simple men who poured out their red, sweet wine of youth[12] unknowing, for nothing more tangible than Honor or their Country's Glory or another's Lust of Power. Let him who thinks War is a glorious, golden thing, who loves to

---

10. *Second Battle of Ypres* (ē′prə), beginning April 22, 1915. This was the first action in which poison gas was used.
11. *Battle of Loos*, beginning September 25, 1915.
12. *red, sweet wine of youth.* Here Leighton ironically quotes a famous line from Rupert Brooke's poem "The Dead." See "The Language of Heroism," page 772.

(Left to right) Edward Brittain, Roland Leighton, and Victor Richardson at Uppingham School O.T.C. camp in July, 1915.

roll forth stirring words of exhortation, invoking Honor and Praise and Valor and Love of Country with as thoughtless and fervid a faith as inspired the priests of Baal to call on their own slumbering deity, let him but look at a little pile of sodden grey rags that cover half a skull and a shinbone and what might have been Its ribs, or at this skeleton lying on its side, resting half crouching as it fell, perfect but that it is headless, and with the tattered clothing still draped round it; and let him realize how grand and glorious a thing it is to have distilled all Youth and Joy and Life into a fetid heap of hideous putrescence! Who is there who has known and seen who can say that Victory is worth the death of even one of these?"

Had there really been a time, I wondered, when I believed that it was?

"When I think of these things," I told him in reply, "I feel that that awful Abstraction, the Unknown God, must be some dread and wrathful deity before whom I can only kneel and plead for mercy, perhaps in the words of a quaint hymn of

George Herbert's[13] that we used to sing at Oxford:

Throw away Thy wrath!
Throw away Thy rod!
O my God
Take the gentle path!"

In October, Vera received orders to report to First London General Hospital, Camberwell, an army hospital to which she had applied, lying about her age. Here she experienced miserable living conditions, twelve-hour workdays, and daily exposure to grisly wounds in the surgical wards, in addition to incessant anxiety over Roland's safety and the possible weakening of their love by separation and war. The last week of 1915 she spent in nervous, yet ecstatic anticipation of Roland's leave on December 25, Christmas Day.

Certainly the stage seemed perfectly set for his leave. Now that my parents had at last migrated temporarily to the Grand Hotel at Brighton, our two families were so near; the Matron had promised yet again that my own week's holiday should coincide with his, and even Edward wrote cheerfully for once to say that as soon as the actual date was known, he and Victor[14] would both be able to get leave at the same time.

"Very wet and muddy and many of the communication trenches are quite impassable," ran a letter from Roland written on December 9th. "Three men were killed the other day by a dugout falling in on top of them and one man was drowned in a sump hole. The whole of one's world, at least of one's visible and palpable world, is mud in various stages of solidity or stickiness. . . . I can be perfectly certain about the date of my leave by tomorrow morning and will let you know."

And, when the final information did come, hurriedly written in pencil on a thin slip of paper torn from his Field Service notebook, it brought the enchanted day still nearer than I had dared to hope.

"Shall be home on leave from 24th Dec.–31st. Land Christmas Day. R."

Even to the unusual concession of a leave which began on Christmas morning after night-duty the Matron proved amenable, and in the encouraging quietness of the winter's war, with no Loos in prospect, no great push in the west even possible, I dared to glorify my days—or rather my nights—by looking forward. In the pleasant peace of Ward 25, where all the patients, now well on the road to health, slept soundly, the sympathetic Scottish Sister teased me a little for my irrepressible excitement.

"I suppose you won't be thinking of going off and getting married? A couple of babies like you!"

It was a new and breath-taking thought, a flame to which Roland's mother—who approved of early marriages and believed that ways and means could be left to look after themselves far better than the average materialistic parent supposed—added fuel when she hinted mysteriously, on a day off which I spent in Brighton, that *this* time Roland might not be content to leave things as they were. . . . Suppose, I meditated, kneeling in the darkness beside the comforting glow of the stove in the silent ward, that during this leave we *did* marry as suddenly as, in the last one, we became "officially" engaged? Of course it would be what the world would call—or did call before the War—a "foolish" marriage. But now that the War seemed likely to be endless, and the chance of making a "wise" marriage had become, for most people, so very remote, the world was growing more tolerant. No one—not even my family now, I thought—would hold out against us, even though we hadn't a penny beyond our pay. What if, after all, we did marry thus foolishly? When the War was over we could still go back to Oxford, and learn to be writers—or even lecturers; if we were determined enough about it we could return there, even though—oh, devastating, sweet speculation!—I

---

13. **hymn of George Herbert's,** "Discipline," by the seventeenth-century religious poet George Herbert (see pages 286–287).
14. **Victor,** another school friend of Edward Brittain's.

might have had a baby.

I had never much cared for babies or had anything to do with them; before that time I had always been too ambitious, too much interested in too many projects, to become acutely conscious of a maternal instinct. But on those quiet evenings of night-duty as Christmas approached, I would come, half asleep, as near to praying as I had been at any time, even when Roland first went to France or in the days following Loos.

"Oh, God!" my half-articulate thoughts would run, "do let us get married and let me have a baby—something that is Roland's very own, something of himself to remember him by if he goes. . . . It shan't be a burden to his people or mine for a moment longer that I can help, I promise. I'll go on doing war-work and give it all my pay during the War—and as soon as ever the War's over I'll go back to Oxford and take my Finals so that I can get a job and support it. So *do* let me have a baby, dear God!"

Directly after breakfast, sent on my way by exuberant good wishes from Betty and Marjorie and many of the others, I went down to Brighton. All day I waited there for a telephone message or a telegram, sitting drowsily in the lounge of the Grand Hotel, or walking up and down the promenade, watching the grey sea tossing rough with white surf-crested waves, and wondering still what kind of crossing he had had or was having.

When, by ten o'clock at night, no news had come, I concluded that the complications of telegraph and telephone on a combined Sunday and Christmas Day had made communication impossible. So, unable to fight sleep any longer after a night and a day of wakefulness, I went to bed a little disappointed, but still unperturbed. Roland's family, at their Keymer cottage, kept an even longer vigil; they sat up till nearly midnight over their Christmas dinner in the hope that he would join them, and, in their dramatic, impulsive fashion, they drank a toast to the Dead.

The next morning I had just finished dressing, and was putting the final touches to the pastel-blue crêpe-de-Chine blouse, when the expected message came to say that I was wanted on the telephone. Believing that I was at last to hear the voice for which I had waited for twenty-four hours, I dashed joyously into the corridor. But the message was not from Roland but from Clare;[15] it was not to say that he had arrived home that morning, but to tell me that he had died of wounds at a Casualty Clearing Station on December 23rd.

Section II of *Testament of Youth* depicts Vera's life during the grimmest war years, 1916 to the Armistice of 1918. Plunged into anguish and nightmarish confusion by the death of Roland, Vera suffered through months of loneliness, strained communication with family and friends, and unresolved perplexity about the meaning of Roland's death.

Whenever I think of the weeks that followed the news of Roland's death, a series of pictures, disconnected but crystal clear, unroll themselves like a kaleidoscope through my mind.

A solitary cup of coffee stands before me on a hotel breakfast-table; I try to drink it, but fail ignominiously.

Outside, in front of the promenade, dismal grey waves tumble angrily over one another on the windy Brighton shore, and, like a slaughtered animal that still twists after life has been extinguished, I go on mechanically worrying because his channel-crossing must have been so rough.

It is Sunday, and I am out for a solitary walk through the dreary streets of Camberwell before going to bed after the night's work. In front of me on the frozen pavement a long red worm wriggles slimily. I remember that, after our death, worms destroy this body—however lovely, however beloved—and I run from the obscene thing in horror.

It is Wednesday, and I am walking up the Brixton Road on a mild, fresh morning of early spring. Half-consciously I am repeating a line from Rupert Brooke: "The deep night, and birds singing, and

---

15. *Clare*, Roland Leighton's sister.

Vera Brittain as a V.A.D. nurse

clouds flying . . ." For a moment I have become conscious of the old joy in rainwashed skies and scuttling, fleecy clouds, when suddenly I remember—Roland is dead and I am not keeping faith with him; it is mean and cruel, even for a second, to feel glad to be alive.

In Sussex, by the end of January, the season was already on its upward grade; catkins hung bronze from the bare, black branches, and in the damp lanes between Hassocks and Keymer the birds sang loudly. How I hated them as I walked back to the station one late afternoon, when a red sunset turned the puddles on the road into gleam-ing pools of blood, and a new horror of mud and death darkened my mind with its dreadful obses-sion. Roland, I reflected bitterly, was now part of the corrupt clay into which war had transformed the fertile soil of France; he would never again know the smell of a wet evening in early spring.

I had arrived at the cottage that morning to find his mother and sister standing in helpless distress in the midst of his returned kit, which was lying, just opened, all over the floor. The garments sent back included the outfit that he had been wear-ing when he was hit. I wondered, and I wonder still, why it was thought necessary to return such relics—the tunic torn back and front by the bul-let, a khaki vest dark and stiff with blood, and a pair of blood-stained breeches slit open at the top by someone obviously in a violent hurry. Those gruesome rags made me realize, as I had never realized before, all that France really meant. Eigh-teen months afterwards the smell of Etaples vil-lage, though fainter and more diffused, brought back to me the memory of those poor remnants of patriotism.

"Everything," I wrote later to Edward, "was damp and worn and simply caked with mud. And I was glad that neither you nor Victor nor anyone who may some day go to the front was there to see. If you had been, you would have been over-whelmed by the horror of war without its glory. For though he had only worn the things when living, the smell of those clothes was the smell of graveyards and the Dead. The mud of France which covered them was not ordinary mud; it had not the usual clean pure smell of earth, but it was as though it were saturated with dead bodies—dead that had been dead a long, long time . . . . There was his cap, bent in and shapeless out of recogni-tion—the soft cap he wore rakishly on the back of his head—with the badge thickly coated with mud. He must have fallen on top of it, or perhaps one of the people who fetched him in trampled on it."

What actually happened to the clothes I never knew, but, incongruously enough, it was amid this heap of horror and decay that we found, surrounded by torn bills and letters, the black manuscript notebook containing his poems. On the flyleaf he had copied a few lines written by John Masefield[16] on the subject of patriotism:

"It is not a song in the street and a wreath on a column and a flag flying from a window and a pro-Boer under a pump.[17] It is a thing very holy and very terrible, like life itself. It is a burden to be borne, a thing to labor for and to suffer for and to die for, a thing which gives no happiness and no pleasantness—but a hard life, an unknown grave, and the respect and bowed heads of those who follow."

The months of unrelieved pain and hopelessness following the death of Roland were further darkened by the departure of Vera's brother Edward for the front in February of 1916 and his later wounding in action, for which he earned the Military Cross. In September, Vera was assigned to eight months of duty on the island of Malta, where the remoteness of the war and exposure to daily sunshine effected a resurgence of hopefulness and personal vitality. In April, 1917, news of the blinding of her and Edward's beloved friend Victor by a bullet in the head abruptly ended Vera's "interval of heaven" and sent her swiftly back to England on a quixotic mission to marry and care for her disabled friend in symbolic tribute to Roland. Shortly after her return, Victor died. Another dear friend, Geoffrey, her confidant in the weeks following Roland's death, was killed at the front. Reflecting on these overwhelming losses, Edward wrote: ". . . we have lost almost all there was to lose and what have we gained? Truly as you say has patriotism worn very threadbare. . . ." With Edward at the front, her fiancé and dearest male friends gone, Vera found life at home intolerable and requested assignment to France. In August of 1917 she crossed the channel to begin work at No. 24 General Hospital, Etaples, caring for the wounded on both sides and exposing herself to considerable personal danger.

"Never in my life have I been so absolutely filthy as I get on duty here," I wrote to my mother on December 5th in answer to her request for a description of my work.

"Sister A. has six wards and there is no V.A.D.[18] in the next-door one, only an orderly, so neither she nor he spend very much time in here. Consequently I am Sister, V.A.D. and orderly all in one (somebody said the other day that no one less than God Almighty could give a correct definition of the job of a V.A.D.!) and after, quite apart from the nursing, I have stoked the stove all night, done two or three rounds of bed-pans and kept the kettles going and prepared feeds on exceedingly black Beatrice oil-stoves and refilled them from the steam kettles, literally wallowing in paraffin all the time, I feel as if I had been dragged through the gutter! Possibly acute surgical is the heaviest kind of work there is, but acute medical is, I think, more wearing than anything else on earth. You are kept on the go the whole time and in the end there seems nothing definite to show for it—except that one or two people are still alive who might otherwise have been dead."

The rest of my letter referred to the effect, upon ourselves, of the new offensive at Cambrai.[19]

"The hospital is very heavy now—as heavy as when I came; the fighting is continuing very long this year, and the convoys keep coming down, two or three a night. . . . Sometimes in the middle of the night we have to turn people out of bed and make them sleep on the floor to make room for more seriously ill ones that have come down from the line. We have heaps of gassed cases at present who came in a day or two ago; there are 10 in this ward alone. I wish those people who write so glibly about this being a holy War,

---

16. *John Masefield* (1878–1967), English poet.
17. *a pro-Boer . . . pump.* Public opinion had been strongly divided on the subject of the Boer War (1899–1902), with a number of the British sympathetic to the Boer cause. Here Masefield alludes to the false patriotism of a mob punishing someone opposed to English imperialism by dousing them with water.
18. *V.A.D.,* a nurse of the Voluntary Aid Detachment. "Sister" is the title of a head nurse in a hospital ward.
19. *Cambrai,* beginning November 20, 1917, the first action in which a notable use was made of tanks.

and the orators who talk so much about going on no matter how long the War lasts and what it may mean, could see a case—to say nothing of 10 cases—of mustard gas in its early stages—could see the poor things burnt and blistered all over with great mustard-colored suppurating blisters, with blind eyes—sometimes temporarily, sometimes permanently—all sticky and stuck together, and always fighting for breath, with voices a mere whisper, saying that their throats are closing and they know they will choke. The only thing one can say is that such severe cases don't last long; either they die soon or else improve—usually the former; they certainly never reach England in the state we have them here, and yet people persist in saying that God made the War, when there are such inventions of the Devil about. . . .

While enduring front-line hardship in an understaffed and besieged camp hospital, Vera was simultaneously forced to deal with the complaints and crises of her parents, who were becoming increasingly incapable of coping with wartime stress and her extended absence. Torn between loyalty to her work and to her family, Vera painfully vacillated between intense resentment toward her parents and guilt over her inability to sympathize with anyone living outside the combat zone. In April, 1918, following her mother's collapse, Vera reluctantly returned to England to take charge of her parents' household and settle into weeks of dreary domesticity and heightened anxiety over the safety of Edward, now stationed on the Italian front.

The despondency at home was certainly making many of us in France quite alarmed: because we were women we feared perpetually that, just as our work was reaching its climax, our families would need our youth and vitality for their own support. One of my cousins, the daughter of an aunt, had already been summoned home from her canteen work in Boulogne; she was only one of many, for as the War continued to wear out strength and spirits, the middle-aged generation, having irrevocably yielded up its sons, began to lean with increasing weight upon its daughters. Thus the desperate choice between incompatible claims—by which the women of my generation, with their carefully trained consciences, have always been tormented—showed signs of afflicting us with new pertinacity. . . .

Early in April a letter arrived from my father to say that my mother had "crocked up" and had been obliged, owing to the inefficiency of the domestic help then available, to go into a nursing-home. What exactly was wrong remained unspecified, though phrases referred to "toxic heart" and "complete general breakdown." My father had temporarily closed the flat and moved into an hotel, but he did not, he told me, wish to remain there. "As your mother and I can no longer manage without you," he concluded, "it is now your duty to leave France immediately and return to Kensington."

I read these words with real dismay, for my father's interpretation of my duty was not, I knew only too well, in the least likely to agree with that of the Army, which had always been singularly unmoved by the worries of relatives. What was I to do? I wondered desperately. There was my family, confidently demanding my presence, and here was the offensive,[20] which made every pair of experienced hands worth ten pairs under normal conditions. I remembered how the hastily imported V.A.D.s had gone sick at the 1st London during the rush after the Somme; a great push was no time in which to teach a tyro her job. How much of my mother's breakdown was physical and how much psychological—the cumulative result of pessimism at home? It did not then occur to me that my father's sense of emergency was probably heightened by a subconscious determination to get me back to London before the Germans reached the Channel ports, as everyone in England felt certain they would. I only knew that no one in France would believe a domestic difficulty to be so insol-

---

20. *the offensive*, the last great German offensive of the war, beginning March 21, 1918.

uble; if I were dead, or a male, it would have to be settled without me. I should merely be thought to have "wind-up," to be using my mother's health as an excuse to escape the advancing enemy or the threatening air raids.

Half-frantic with the misery of conflicting obligations, I envied Edward his complete powerlessness to leave the Army whatever happened at home. Today, remembering the violent clash between family and profession, between "duty" and ambition, between conscience and achievement, which has always harassed the women now in their thirties and forties, I find myself still hoping that if the efforts of various interested parties succeed in destroying the fragile international structure built up since the Armistice, and war breaks out on a scale comparable to that of 1914, the organizers of the machine will not hesitate to conscript all women under fifty for service at home or abroad. In the long run, an irrevocable allegiance in a time of emergency makes decision easier for the older as well as for the younger generation. What exhausts women in wartime is not the strenuous and unfamiliar tasks that fall upon them, nor even the hourly dread of death for husbands or lovers or brothers or sons; it is the incessant conflict between personal and national claims which wears out their energy and breaks their spirit. . . .

It seemed to me then, with my crude judgments and black-and-white values, quite inexplicable that the older generation, which had merely looked on at the War, should break under the strain so much more quickly than those of us who had faced death or horror at first hand for months on end. Today, with middle-age just round the corner, and children who tug my anxious thoughts relentlessly back to them whenever I have to leave them for a week, I realize how completely I underestimated the effect upon the civilian population of year upon year of diminishing hope, diminishing food, diminishing light, diminishing heat, of waiting and waiting for news which was nearly always bad when it came. . . .

For some time now, my apprehensions for Edward's safety had been lulled by the long qui-

escence of the Italian front, which had seemed a haven of peace in contrast to our own raging vortex. Repeatedly, during the German offensive, I had thanked God and the Italians who fled at Caporetto[21] that Edward was out of it, and rejoiced that the worst I had to fear from this particular push was the comparatively trivial danger that threatened myself. But now I felt the familiar stirrings of the old tense fear which had been such a persistent companion throughout the War, and my alarm was increased when Edward asked me a week or two later to send him "a funny cat from Liberty's[22] . . . to alleviate tragedy with comedy."

On Sunday morning, June 16th, I opened the *Observer*, which appeared to be chiefly concerned with the new offensive—for the moment at a standstill—in the Noyon-Montdidier sector of the Western Front, and instantly saw at the head of a column the paragraph for which I had looked so long and so fearfully:

> "ITALIAN FRONT ABLAZE
> GUN DUELS FROM MOUNTAIN TO SEA
> BAD OPENING OF AN OFFENSIVE

"The following Italian official *communiqué* was issued yesterday:

"From dawn this morning the fire of the enemy's artillery, strongly countered by our own, was intensified from the Lagerina Valley to the sea. On the Asiago Plateau, to the east of the Brenta and on the middle Piave, the artillery struggle has assumed and maintains a character of extreme violence."

A day or two later, more details were published of the fighting in Italy, and I learnt that the Sherwood Foresters[23] had been involved in the "show" on the Plateau. After that I made no pretense at doing anything but wander restlessly round Kensington or up and down the flat, and,

---

21. *Caporetto,* the rout of the Italian second army by a combined Austro-German attack, October 24, 1917.
22. *Liberty's,* a London department store.
23. *Sherwood Foresters,* Edward Brittain's regiment.

though my father retired glumly to bed every evening at nine o'clock, I gave up writing the semi-fictitious record which I had begun of my life in France. Somehow I couldn't bring myself even to wrap up the *Spectator* and *Saturday Review* that I sent every week to Italy, and they remained in my bedroom, silent yet eloquent witnesses to the dread which my father and I, determinedly conversing on commonplace topics, each refused to put into words.

By the following Saturday we had still heard nothing of Edward. The interval usually allowed for news of casualties after a battle was seldom so long as this, and I began, with an artificial sense of lightness unaccompanied by real conviction, to think that there was perhaps, after all, no news to come. I had just announced to my father, as we sat over tea in the dining-room, that I really must do up Edward's papers and take them to the post office before it closed for the week-end, when there came the sudden loud clattering at the front-door knocker that always meant a telegram.

For a moment I thought that my legs would not carry me, but they behaved quite normally as I got up and went to the door. I knew what was in the telegram—I had known for a week—but because the persistent hopefulness of the human heart refuses to allow intuitive certainty to persuade the reason of that which it knows, I opened and read it in a tearing anguish of suspense.

"Regret to inform you Captain E. H. Brittain M.C. killed in action Italy June 15th."

"No answer," I told the boy mechanically, and handed the telegram to my father, who had followed me into the hall. As we went back into the dining-room I saw, as though I had never seen them before, the bowl of blue delphiniums on the table; their intense color, vivid, ethereal, seemed too radiant for earthly flowers.

Then I remembered that we should have to go down to Purley and tell the news to my mother. . . .

Long after [her father] had gone to bed and the world had grown silent, I crept into the dining-room to be alone with Edward's portrait. Carefully closing the door, I turned on the light and looked at the pale, pictured face, so dignified, so steadfast, so tragically mature. He had been through so much—far, far more than those beloved friends who had died at an earlier stage of the interminable War, leaving him alone to mourn their loss. Fate might have allowed him the little, sorry compensation of survival, the chance to make his lovely music in honor of their memory. It seemed indeed the last irony that he should have been killed by the countrymen of Fritz Kreisler,[24] the violinist whom of all others he had most greatly admired.

And suddenly, as I remembered all the dear afternoons and evenings when I had followed him on the piano as he played his violin, the sad, searching eyes of the portrait were more than I could bear, and falling on my knees before it I began to cry "Edward! Oh, Edward!" in dazed repetition, as though my persistent crying and calling would somehow bring him back. . . .

After a summer of stagnation and grief, Vera signed on for a demeaning month of duty at St. Jude's Hospital, then moved to Queen Alexandra's Hospital, Millbank, where she stayed until April, 1919, functioning like an automaton in the aftermath of Edward's death. Not surprisingly, Vera observed Armistice Day in a spirit of sorrowful reminiscence and realistic assessment of the impact of the tragic war years.

When the sound of victorious guns burst over London at 11 a.m. on November 11th, 1918, the men and women who looked incredulously into each other's faces did not cry jubilantly: "We've won the War!" They only said: "The War is over."

From Millbank I heard the maroons[25] crash with terrifying clearness, and, like a sleeper who is determined to go on dreaming after being told to wake up, I went on automatically washing the dressing bowls in the annex outside my hut. Deeply buried beneath my consciousness there stirred the vague memory of a letter that I had

---

24. *Fritz Kreisler* (1875–1962), Austrian violinist.
25. *maroons,* fireworks that simulate the sound of cannon.

written to Roland in those legendary days when I was still at Oxford, and could spend my Sundays in thinking of him while the organ echoed grandly through New College Chapel. It had been a warm May evening, when all the city was sweet with the scent of wallflowers and lilac, and I had walked back to Micklem Hall after hearing an Occasional Oratorio by Handel,[26] which described the mustering of troops for battle, the lament for the fallen and the triumphant return of the victors.

"As I listened," I told him, "to the organ swelling forth into a final triumphant burst in the song of victory, after the solemn and mournful dirge over the dead, I thought with what mockery and irony the jubilant celebrations which will hail the coming of peace will fall upon the ears of those to whom their best will never return, upon whose sorrow victory is built, who have paid with their mourning for the others' joy. I wonder if I shall be one of those who take a happy part in the triumph—or if I shall listen to the merriment with a heart that breaks and ears that try to keep out the mirthful sounds."

And as I dried the bowls I thought: "It's come too late for me. Somehow I knew, even at Oxford, that it would. Why couldn't it have ended rationally, as it might have ended, in 1916, instead of all that trumpet-blowing against a negotiated peace, and the ferocious talk of secure civilians about marching to Berlin? It's come five months too late—or is it three years? It might have ended last June, and let Edward, at least, be saved! Only five months—it's such a little time, when Roland died nearly three years ago." . . .

Late that evening, when supper was over, a group of elated V.A.D.s who were anxious to walk through Westminster and Whitehall to Buckingham Palace prevailed upon me to join them. Outside the Admiralty a crazy group of convalescent Tommies[27] were collecting specimens of different uniforms and bundling their wearers into flagstrewn taxis; with a shout they seized two of my companions and disappeared into the clamorous crowd, waving flags and shaking rattles. Wherever we went a burst of enthusiastic cheering greeted our Red Cross uniform, and complete strangers adorned with wound stripes rushed up and shook me warmly by the hand. After the long, long blackness, it seemed like a fairy-tale to see the street lamps shining through the chill November gloom.

I detached myself from the others and walked slowly up Whitehall, with my heart sinking in a sudden cold dismay. Already this was a different world from the one that I had known during four life-long years, a world in which people would be light-hearted and forgetful, in which themselves and their careers and their amusements would blot out political ideals and great national issues. And in that brightly lit, alien world I should have no part. All those with whom I had really been intimate were gone; not one remained to share with me the heights and the depths of my memories. As the years went by and youth departed and remembrance grew dim, a deeper and ever deeper darkness would cover the young men who were once my contemporaries.

For the time I realized, with all that full realization meant, how completely everything that had hitherto made up my life had vanished with Edward and Roland, with Victor and Geoffrey. The War was over; a new age was beginning; but the dead were dead and would never return.

1933

---

26. **Handel** (1685–1759), German composer long resident in England.
27. **Tommies,** British soldiers.

THINK AND DISCUSS

AUGUST 1914–CHRISTMAS 1915

Understanding

1. What was Vera Brittain's immediate reaction to the news of the outbreak of World War I?

2. What made life in the Brittain household intolerable during the first weeks of the war?

3. What excuse enabled Brittain to meet Roland and be alone with him?

4. What news did Roland's sister Clare call to communicate on Christmas Eve?

Analyzing

5. How does Brittain **characterize** herself and her entire generation at the outbreak of the war?

6. Describe the behavior of the general public during the first weeks of the war.

7. What does Brittain prefer to think were her "real sentiments" about England's involvement in the war, even before she had been personally affected?

8. Contrast the "rules of courtship" that she and Roland were compelled to observe with those followed in today's society.

9. Already in her diary entry of April 7, 1915, Brittain is beginning to show signs of bitterness and strain. How does her participation in the "flag-day" deepen her sense of disillusionment with the older generation?

10. Why, even years later, did she find it uncomfortable to work in a room where it was "possible to hear the front-door bell"?

11. Having been informed of Roland's Christmas leave, Brittain says, "I dared to glorify my days—or rather my nights—by looking forward." What fantasies helped sustain her during the days of anxious waiting?

Extending

12. Compare Roland's description of the suffering of the men at the front and his attack on idealistic attitudes toward war with Wilfred Owen's "Dulce et Decorum Est." What similarities do you find?

JANUARY 1916–NOVEMBER 11, 1918

Understanding

1. In what condition were the personal effects Roland's family received?

2. In her letter home after the offensive at Cambrai, what awful symptoms of gassing in her patients does Brittain describe?

3. What family situation forced her to leave her nursing position at the front and return to England?

Analyzing

4. What contradictory feelings following Roland's death contributed to Brittain's personal torment?

5. Why did the copied lines of John Masefield found in the kit of Roland's belongings seem "incongruous"?

6. Writing in the early 1930s, Brittain expresses the hope that, in any future war, women will be conscripted as well as men. What caused her to feel this way?

7. What was her reaction to the news of Edward's death on the Italian front?

8. Describe Brittain's reaction on November 11, 1918, to news of the Armistice. What realization about the lasting impact of the war became clear to her that day?

Extending

9. Where, in her memoir, does Brittain show herself in conflict with her parents? Do you think her complaints are justified? How did her views of the "older generation" change when she herself reached middle age?

REVIEWING: Mood HZ
See Handbook of Literary Terms, p. 914

The **mood** of any work is the overall atmosphere or prevailing emotional aura it communicates to the reader. Shifts of mood in literature can occur quite abruptly with a change of events and fortune.

1. Contrast the mood of *Testament of Youth* in the periods immediately before and after Christmas, 1915.
2. What is the mood of Brittain's description of Armistice Day?
3. How would you describe the overall mood of this selection? Is it appropriate for the subject matter and **theme?**

VOCABULARY
Word Analogies
Determine the relationship between the two italicized words in each question. Then select, from the pairs of words that follow, the words that are related in the same way as the words in the first pair. You may use your Glossary.

1. *facetious : serious* :: **a.** mirth : humor; **b.** soothe : upset; **c.** wretched : miserable.
2. *irritable : petulant* :: **a.** coax : persuade; **b.** quiet : noisy; **c.** stern : gentle.
3. *sophisticated : ingenuous* :: **a.** carefree : playful; **b.** smart : intelligent; **c.** proud : humble.
4. *scintillate : glitter* :: **a.** unpleasant : painful; **b.** brave : cowardly; **c.** honest : sinister.
5. *oozing : suppurating* :: **a.** cheap : expensive; **b.** ruin : destroy; **c.** friendly : hostile.

READING LITERATURE SKILLFULLY
Propaganda Devices
Language is a powerful tool for creating opinion. When opinions or beliefs are created and spread systematically, they may be called **propaganda.** Although we often think of it negatively, the word *propaganda* can refer to language that has either a negative or positive effect on people. One of the most effective devices for spreading propaganda is **loaded language**—words and phrases chosen deliberately for their emotional connotations.

1. What is propagandistic about "Dulce et decorum est pro patria mori," as it was originally used by the Latin writer, Horace?
2. Explain how the following entry from Brittain's diary reflects her acceptance of someone else's opinion: "The great fear is that our bungling Government will declare England's neutrality" (see page 777). How does Brittain later react to these words of hers?
3. In what sense is Brooke's poem "The Soldier" propagandistic?
4. Discuss whether there are any social contexts in which the systematic forming of public opinions is desirable.

ENRICHMENT
Preparing a Slide Show
Work in small groups to prepare a slide show on some aspect of World War I, such as the following:

Trench warfare
1914–1918: The Loss of Innocence
The poems of Owen, Brooke, or Sassoon
The Italian or Russian front
A major battle (Marne, Somme, etc.)
Red Cross hospitals
Letters from the front
The Poems of Roland Leighton in *Testament of Youth*

After completing any necessary research, draft a script. Find and photograph pictures that illustrate your narrative. Once your pictures are developed, revise and tape your text, synchronizing pictures and narrative. Include background music where appropriate. Your goal should be to make your presentation both informative and inspirational.

BIOGRAPHY

James Joyce
1882–1941

On the basis of a few poems, a play, and four works of fiction—*Dubliners, A Portrait of the Artist as a Young Man, Ulysses,* and *Finnegans Wake*—James Joyce has come to be regarded as the most original and influential writer of the twentieth century. He was born in Dublin, the eldest of a family of ten children. His father was a civil servant, continually in financial difficulties; his mother was mild-mannered and pious. For several years Joyce attended Clongowes Wood College, a famous Jesuit boarding school, before his family's increasing poverty made this impossible. He later attended University College, Dublin, where he was a brilliant scholar, accomplished in Latin, French, Italian, and Norwegian (the last to enable him to read the plays of the Norwegian dramatist Henrik Ibsen, whom he intensely admired). It was his success in publishing a review of Ibsen's play *When We Dead Awaken* in the London *Fortnightly Review* in 1900 when he was just eighteen that confirmed Joyce in his resolution to become a writer. Disillusionment with Catholicism and the cultural climate of Dublin caused him to leave Ireland for a self-imposed exile in the Italian city of Trieste, and later in Paris and Zurich. Joyce's life during these years was a continual struggle against poverty, eye diseases, and the hostility of censors. During his later years, however, he began to enjoy an international reputation as a modern literary master.

Joyce said that his purpose in writing the short stories collected in *Dubliners* (1914) was to produce "a chapter of the moral history of my country and I chose Dublin for the scene because the city seemed to me the center of paralysis." He wanted to give "the Irish people . . . one good look at themselves in my nicely polished looking glass." The style of *Dubliners* marks a sharp break with the fiction of the nineteenth century. Joyce locates the center of the action in the minds of his characters. Incident and plot are subordinated to psychological revelation. Each word and detail has a calculated purpose, and the meaning of the story is presented as an *epiphany*—a moment of heightened awareness that can occur as a result of a trivial encounter, object, or event. *A Portrait of the Artist as a Young Man* (1916), Joyce's artistic and spiritual autobiography, represents a further working out of this narrative technique. *Ulysses* (1922), perhaps this century's most famous novel, is a dazzlingly original attempt to tell the story of a group of Dubliners on a single day and at the same time present a symbolic view of human history. Portions of Joyce's next novel, *Finnegans Wake* (1939), appeared first in Paris in periodicals under the title *Work in Progress*. This book, which occupied Joyce for fifteen years or more, carried the stylistic experimentation of *Ulysses* even further.

In form and content, most of Joyce's work was controversial. During his lifetime publication was often delayed, and his works were banned, burned, pirated, and confiscated. The ruling of a U.S. federal court judge in 1933 permitting the American publication of *Ulysses* was a landmark in the fight against censorship.

Araby

James Joyce

 orth Richmond Street, being blind, was a quiet street except at the hour when the Christian Brothers' School set the boys free. An uninhabited house of two storeys stood at the blind end, detached from its neighbors in a square ground. The other houses of the street, conscious of decent lives within them, gazed at one another with brown imperturbable faces.

The former tenant of our house, a priest, had died in the back drawing-room. Air, musty from having been long enclosed, hung in all the rooms, and the waste room behind the kitchen was littered with old useless papers. Among these I found a few paper-covered books, the pages of which were curled and damp: *The Abbot*, by Walter Scott, *The Devout Communicant* and *The Memoirs of Vidocq*.[1] I liked the last best because its leaves were yellow. The wild garden behind the house contained a central apple-tree and a few straggling bushes under one of which I found the late tenant's rusty bicycle-pump. He had been a very charitable priest; in his will he had left all his money to institutions and the furniture of his house to his sister.

When the short days of winter came, dusk fell before we had well eaten our dinners. When we met in the street the houses had grown somber. The space of sky above us was the color of ever-changing violet and towards it the lamps of the street lifted their feeble lanterns. The cold air stung us and we played till our bodies glowed. Our shouts echoed in the silent street. The career of our play brought us through the dark muddy lanes behind the houses where we ran the gauntlet of the rough tribes from the cottages, to the back doors of the dark dripping gardens where odors arose from the ashpits, to the dark odorous stables where a coachman smoothed and combed the horse or shook music from the buckled harness. When we returned to the street, light from the kitchen windows had filled the areas. If my uncle was seen turning the corner we hid in the shadow until we had seen him safely housed. Or if Mangan's sister came out on the doorstep to call her brother in to his tea we watched her from our shadow peer up and down the street. We waited to see whether she would remain or go in and, if she remained, we left our shadow and walked up to Mangan's steps resignedly. She was waiting for us, her figure defined by the light from the half-opened door. Her brother always teased her before he obeyed and I stood by the railings looking at her. Her dress swung as she moved her body and the soft rope of her hair tossed from side to side.

Every morning I lay on the floor in the front parlor watching her door. The blind was pulled down to within an inch of the sash so that I could not be seen. When she came out on the doorstep my heart leaped. I ran to the hall, seized my books and followed her. I kept her brown figure always in my eye and, when we came near the point at which our ways diverged, I quickened my pace and passed her. This happened morning after morning. I had never spoken to her, except for a few casual words, and yet her name was like a summons to all my foolish blood.

Her image accompanied me even in places the most hostile to romance. On Saturday evenings when my aunt went marketing I had to go to carry some of the parcels. We walked through the flaring streets, jostled by drunken men and bargaining women, amid the curses of laborers, the shrill litanies of shopboys who stood on guard by the barrels of pigs' cheeks, the nasal chanting of street-singers, who sang a *come-you-all* about O'Donovan Rossa, or a ballad about the troubles in our native land. These noises converged in a single

---

1. *Vidocq.* François-Eugène Vidocq (1775–1857) was an ex-thief who offered his services to Napoleon's government in 1809 and was made head of a special police force composed of former thieves. What was published as his *Memoirs* in 1828 is probably not by him.

sensation of life for me: I imagined that I bore my chalice safely through a throng of foes. Her name sprang to my lips at moments in strange prayers and praises which I myself did not understand. My eyes were often full of tears (I could not tell why) and at times a flood from my heart seemed to pour itself out into my bosom. I thought little of the future. I did not know whether I would ever speak to her or not or, if I spoke to her, how I could tell her of my confused adoration. But my body was like a harp and her words and gestures were like fingers running upon the wires.

One evening I went into the back drawing room in which the priest had died. It was a dark rainy evening and there was no sound in the house. Through one of the broken panes I heard the rain impinge upon the earth, the fine incessant needles of water playing in the sodden beds. Some distant lamp or lighted window gleamed below me. I was thankful that I could see so little. All my senses seemed to desire to veil themselves and, feeling that I was about to slip from them, I pressed the palms of my hands together until they trembled, murmuring: "*O love! O love!*" many times.

At last she spoke to me. When she addressed the first words to me I was so confused that I did not know what to answer. She asked me was I going to *Araby*. I forgot whether I answered yes or no. It would be a splendid bazaar, she said she would love to go.

"And why can't you?" I asked.

While she spoke she turned a silver bracelet round and round her wrist. She could not go, she said, because there would be a retreat that week in her convent. Her brother and two other boys were fighting for their caps and I was alone at the railings. She held one of the spikes, bowing her head towards me. The light from the lamp opposite our door caught the white curve of her neck, lit up her hair that rested there and, falling, lit up the hand upon the railing. It fell over one side of her dress and caught the white border of a petticoat, just visible as she stood at ease.

"It's well for you," she said.

"If I go," I said, "I will bring you something."

What innumerable follies laid waste my waking and sleeping thoughts after that evening! I wished to annihilate the tedious intervening days. I chafed against the work of school. At night in my bedroom and by day in the classroom her image came between me and the page I strove to read. The syllables of the word *Araby* were called to me through the silence in which my soul luxuriated and cast an eastern enchantment over me. I asked for leave to go to the bazaar on Saturday night. My aunt was surprised and hoped it was not some Freemason affair.[2] I answered few questions in class. I watched my master's face pass from amiability to sternness; he hoped I was not beginning to idle. I could not call my wandering thoughts together. I had hardly any patience with the serious work of life which, now that it stood between me and my desire, seemed to me child's play, ugly monotonous child's play.

On Saturday morning I reminded my uncle that I wished to go to the bazaar in the evening. He was fussing at the hallstand, looking for the hatbrush, and answered me curtly:

"Yes, boy, I know."

As he was in the hall I could not go into the front parlor and lie at the window. I left the house in bad humor and walked slowly towards the school. The air was pitilessly raw and already my heart misgave me.

When I came home to dinner my uncle had not yet been home. Still it was early. I sat staring at the clock for some time and, when its ticking began to irritate me, I left the room. I mounted the staircase and gained the upper part of the house. The high, cold, empty, gloomy rooms liberated me and I went from room to room singing. From the front window I saw my companions playing below in the street. Their cries reached me weakened and indistinct and, leaning my forehead against the cool glass, I looked over at the dark house where she lived. I may have stood there for an hour, seeing nothing but the brown-clad figure cast by my imagination, touched discreetly by the lamplight

---

2. *Freemason affair.* The Freemasons are a worldwide secret society whose purpose is mutual aid and fellowship. The Roman Catholic Church has traditionally opposed Freemasonry.

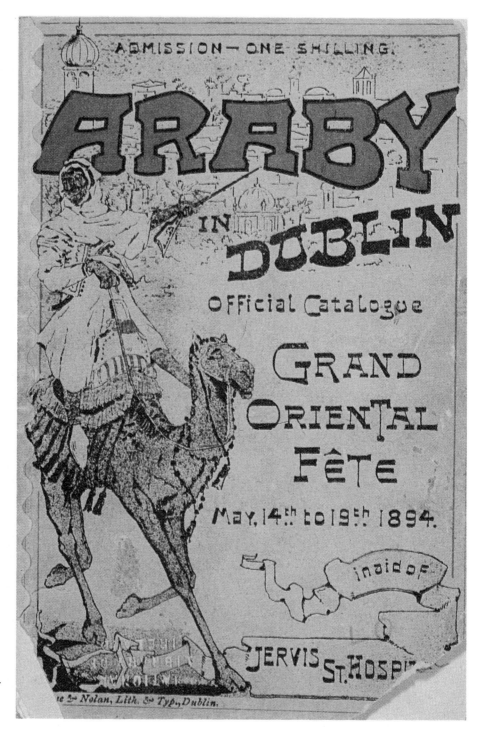

The program of the
bazaar Araby in Dublin.
May 14–19, 1894.
National Library of Ire-
land, Dublin

at the curved neck, at the hand upon the railings, and at the border below the dress.

When I came downstairs again I found Mrs. Mercer sitting at the fire. She was an old garrulous woman, a pawnbroker's widow, who collected used stamps for some pious purpose. I had to endure the gossip of the tea-table. The meal was prolonged beyond an hour and still my uncle did not come. Mrs. Mercer stood up to go; she was sorry she couldn't wait any longer, but it was late, as the night air was bad for her. When she had gone I began to walk up and down the room, clenching my fists. My aunt said:

"I'm afraid you may put off your bazaar for this night of Our Lord."

At nine o'clock I heard my uncle's latchkey in the hall door. I heard him talking to himself and heard the hallstand rocking when it had received the weight of his overcoat. I could interpret these signs. When he was midway through his dinner I asked him to give me the money to go to the bazaar. He had forgotten.

"The people are in bed and after their first sleep now," he said.

I did not smile. My aunt said to him energetically:

"Can't you give him the money and let him go? You've kept him late enough as it is."

My uncle said he was very sorry he had forgotten. He said he believed in the old saying: "All work and no play makes Jack a dull boy." He asked me where I was going and, when I had told him a second time he asked me did I know *The Arab's Farewell to His Steed*.[3] When I left the kitchen he was about to recite the opening lines of the piece to my aunt.

I held a florin[4] tightly in my hand as I strode down Buckingham Street toward the station. The sight of the streets thronged with buyers and glaring with gas recalled to me the purpose of my journey. I took my seat in a third-class carriage of a deserted train. After an intolerable delay the train moved out of the station slowly. It crept onward among ruinous houses and over the twinkling river. At Westland Row Station a crowd of people pressed to the carriage doors; but the porters moved them back, saying that it was a special train for the bazaar. I remained alone in the bare carriage. In a few minutes the train drew up beside an improvised wooden platform. I passed out on to the road and saw by the lighted dial of a clock that it was ten minutes to ten. In front of me was a large building which displayed the magical name.

I could not find any sixpenny entrance and, fearing that the bazaar would be closed, I passed in quickly through a turnstile, handing a shilling to a weary-looking man. I found myself in a big hall girdled at half its height by a gallery. Nearly all the stalls were closed and the greater part of the hall was in darkness. I recognised a silence like that which pervades a church after a service. I walked into the center of the bazaar timidly. A few people were gathered about the stalls which were still open. Before a curtain, over which the words *Café Chantant*[5] were written in colored lamps, two men were counting money on a salver. I listened to the fall of the coins.

Remembering with difficulty why I had come I went over to one of the stalls and examined porcelain vases and flowered tea-sets. At the door of the stall a young lady was talking and laughing with two young gentlemen. I remarked their English accents and listened vaguely to their conversation.

"O, I never said such a thing!"

"O, but you did!"

"O, but I didn't!"

"Didn't she say that?"

"Yes, I heard her."

"O, there's a . . . fib!"

Observing me the young lady came over and asked me did I wish to buy anything. The tone of her voice was not encouraging; she seemed to have spoken to me out of a sense of duty. I looked humbly at the great jars that stood like eastern

---

3. *The Arab's . . . Steed*, a famous Victorian poem by Mrs. Caroline E. S. Norton (1808–1877), "the Byron of her sex."
4. *florin*, a former English coin, worth two shillings.
5. *Café Chantant*, a cafe where singers or musicians entertain.

guards at either side of the dark entrance to the stall and murmured:

"No, thank you."

The young lady changed the position of one of the vases and went back to the two young men. They began to talk of the same subject. Once or twice the young lady glanced at me over her shoulder.

I lingered before her stall, though I knew my stay was useless, to make my interest in her wares seem the more real. Then I turned away slowly and walked down the middle of the bazaar. I allowed the two pennies to fall against the sixpence in my pocket. I heard a voice call from one end of the gallery that the light was out. The upper part of the hall was now completely dark.

Gazing up into the darkness I saw myself as a creature driven and derided by vanity; and my eyes burned with anguish and anger.

1914

THINK AND DISCUSS

Understanding

1. At what times of the day does the narrator manage to catch glimpses of Mangan's sister?
2. Where does the narrator get the idea of going to the bazaar?

Analyzing

3. While we are never told the narrator's age, judging from the description of his thoughts and behavior, how old does he appear to be?
4. How does the narrator reveal his infatuation with the girl and inexperience with women?
5. How does his environment contrast with his fantasy?
6. Why does he offer to bring Mangan's sister a gift from the bazaar?
7. What circumstances make the narrator late to the bazaar?
8. How do his expectations of Araby differ from what he actually experiences?

Extending

9. The story's *epiphany,* or moment of heightened awareness, occurs in the final paragraph. Why do you think the narrator feels as he does? How might such an experience permanently change him and affect his future behavior?

COMPOSITION ◄═══

Writing an Autobiographical Essay

According to common belief, "No one ever forgets the first experience of falling in love." In an essay of five to six paragraphs, recall the first time you fell in love or became infatuated. How old were you? Like Joyce, tell how you found ways to see or encounter the object of your affection. Then describe the course of this relationship. In your conclusion, tell what finally happened and how you felt then compared with now. Be sure to explain what lasting impression this first experience of falling in love had on you. Feel free to inject humor where appropriate.

Contrasting Expectations with Reality

Life is filled with episodes, like the one the narrator experiences in "Araby," in which individuals discover that reality seldom matches expectations. Describe one such episode from your own life—such as a trip, a party, a date, the prom—about which you had expectations that were not realized. In three to five paragraphs, contrast what you had hoped to experience with what actually occurred. In your first paragraph prepare your readers for the contrast to come. Then go on to describe your high hopes, telling why you thought they might come true. Last, explain what actually happened to frustrate your expectations. Describe your reaction to the failure of your dreams and the overall impact of this experience on your life. Ask a friend to evaluate how successfully you have presented the contrast promised in your opening.

BIOGRAPHY

Katherine Mansfield
1888–1923

Born Kathleen Mansfield Beauchamp, she was the daughter of a wealthy New Zealand banker, later knighted, who took her and her sisters to London to be educated at Queen's College. A talented cellist, she studied music at the Royal Academy of Music, but later realized that writing, not music, was her true calling. In 1911, through a chance meeting in Germany, she became friends with the celebrated literary critic and editor John Middleton Murry, with whom she collaborated on a short-lived literary magazine. They were married in 1918. By the end of the war, she had become a virtual invalid, moving from climate to climate for relief from incurable tuberculosis. She died in France on January 9, 1923, at the age of thirty-four.

Mansfield was strongly influenced by the short fiction of the Russian writer Chekhov, and, like him, wrote stories which depend more on atmosphere, character, and the nuances of language than on plot. Like James Joyce and Virginia Woolf in the novel, she developed a poetic and subtly crafted style to convey the inner feelings of her characters and present shifting points of view. Many of her stories center on children and on old people in isolated circumstances and are deeply affecting in their sympathetic portrayal of the lonely, the rejected, and the victimized. It has been suggested that her consciousness of the imminence of death heightened her awareness and helps account for the sensitivity for which her stories are noted.

Like Vera Brittain, Katherine Mansfield suffered the devastating loss of a brother in the war and later stated that this tragedy inspired her to dedicate her life to commemorating the "lovely time when we were both alive." The New Zealand of her childhood that she had so readily abandoned for the cosmopolitan life of England and the Continent increasingly provided the incidents and settings for her stories.

The Doll's House

Katherine Mansfield

hen dear old Mrs. Hay went back to town after staying with the Burnells she sent the children a doll's house. It was so big that the carter and Pat carried it into the courtyard, and there it stayed, propped up on two wooden boxes beside the feed-room door. No harm could come of it; it was summer. And perhaps the smell of paint would have gone off by the time it had to be taken in. For, really, the smell of paint coming from that doll's house ("Sweet of old Mrs. Hay, of course; most sweet and generous!")—but the smell of paint was quite enough to make any one seriously ill, in Aunt Beryl's opinion. Even before the sacking was taken off. And when it was . . .

There stood the doll's house, a dark, oily, spinach green, picked out with bright yellow. Its two solid little chimneys, glued on to the roof, were painted red and white, and the door, gleaming with yellow varnish, was like a little slab of toffee. Four windows, real windows, were divided into panes by a broad streak of green. There was actually a tiny porch, too, painted yellow, with big lumps of congealed paint hanging along the edge.

But perfect, perfect little house! Who could possibly mind the smell? It was part of the joy, part of the newness.

"Open it quickly, some one!"

The hook at the side was stuck fast. Pat pried it open with his pen-knife, and the whole house-front swung back, and—there you were, gazing at one and the same moment into the drawing-room and dining-room, the kitchen and two bedrooms. That is the way for a house to open! Why don't all houses open like that? How much more exciting than peering through the slit of a door into a mean little hall with a hatstand and two umbrellas! That is—isn't it?—what you long to know about a house when you put your hand on the knocker. Perhaps it is the way God opens houses at dead of night when He is taking a quiet turn with an angel. . . .

"O-oh!" The Burnell children sounded as though they were in despair. It was too marvelous; it was too much for them. They had never seen anything like it in their lives. All the rooms were papered. There were pictures on the walls, painted on the paper, with gold frames complete. Red carpet covered all the floors except the kitchen; red plush chairs in the drawing-room, green in the dining-room; tables, beds with real bedclothes, a cradle, a stove, a dresser with tiny plates and one big jug. But what Kezia liked more than anything, what she liked frightfully, was the lamp. It stood in the middle of the dining-room table, an exquisite little amber lamp with a white globe. It was even filled all ready for lighting, though, of course, you couldn't light it. But there was something inside that looked like oil, and that moved when you shook it.

The father and mother dolls, who sprawled very stiff as though they had fainted in the drawing-room, and their two little children asleep upstairs, were really too big for the doll's house. They didn't look as though they belonged. But the lamp was perfect. It seemed to smile at Kezia, to say, "I live here." The lamp was real.

The Burnell children could hardly walk to school fast enough the next morning. They burned to tell everybody, to describe, to—well—to boast about their doll's house before the school-bell rang.

"I'm to tell," said Isabel, "because I'm the eldest. And you two can join in after. But I'm to tell first."

There was nothing to answer. Isabel was bossy, but she was always right, and Lottie and Kezia knew too well the powers that went with being eldest. They brushed through the thick buttercups at the road edge and said nothing.

"And I'm to choose who's to come and see it first. Mother said I might."

For it had been arranged that while the doll's house stood in the courtyard they might ask the girls at school, two at a time, to come and look. Not to stay to tea, of course, or to come traipsing through the house. But just to stand quietly in the courtyard while Isabel pointed out the beauties, and Lottie and Kezia looked pleased. . . .

But hurry as they might, by the time they had reached the tarred palings of the boys' playground the bell had begun to jangle. They only just had time to whip off their hats and fall into line before the roll was called. Never mind, Isabel tried to make up for it by looking very important and mysterious and by whispering behind her hands to the girls near her, "Got something to tell you at playtime."

Playtime came and Isabel was surrounded. The girls of her class nearly fought to put their arms round her, to walk away with her, to beam flatteringly, to be her special friend. She held quite a court under the huge pine trees at the side of the playground. Nudging, giggling together, the little girls pressed up close. And the only two who stayed outside the ring were the two who were always outside, the little Kelveys. They knew better than to come anywhere near the Burnells.

For the fact was, the school the Burnell children went to was not at all the kind of place their parents would have chosen if there had been any choice. But there was none. It was the only school for miles. And the consequence was all the children in the neighborhood, the Judge's little girls, the doctor's daughters, the storekeeper's children, the milkman's, were forced to mix together. Not to speak of there being an equal number of rude, rough little boys as well. But the line had to be drawn somewhere. It was drawn at the Kelveys. Many of the children, including the Burnells, were not allowed even to speak to them. They walked past the Kelveys with their heads in the air, and as they set the fashion in all matters of behavior, the Kelveys were shunned by everybody. Even the teacher had a special voice for them, and a special

smile for the other children when Lil Kelvey came up to her desk with a bunch of dreadfully common-looking flowers.

They were the daughters of a spry, hardworking little washerwoman, who went about from house to house by the day. This was awful enough. But where was Mr. Kelvey? Nobody knew for certain. But everybody said he was in prison. So they were the daughters of a washerwoman and a jail-bird. Very nice company for other people's children! And they looked it. Why Mrs. Kelvey made them so conspicuous was hard to understand. The truth was they were dressed in "bits" given to her by the people for whom she worked. Lil, for instance, who was a stout, plain child, with big freckles, came to school in a dress made from a green art-serge table-cloth of the Burnells', with red plush sleeves from the Logans' curtains. Her hat, perched on top of her high forehead, was a grown-up woman's hat, once the property of Miss Lecky, the postmistress. It was turned up at the back and trimmed with a large scarlet quill. What a little guy she looked! It was impossible not to laugh. And her little sister, our Else, wore a long white dress, rather like a nightgown, and a pair of little boy's boots. But whatever our Else wore she would have looked strange. She was a tiny wishbone of a child, with cropped hair and enormous solemn eyes—a little white owl. Nobody had ever seen her smile; she scarcely ever spoke. She went through life holding on to Lil, with a piece of Lil's skirt screwed up in her hand. Where Lil went our Else followed. In the playground, on the road going to and from school, there was Lil marching in front and our Else holding on behind. Only when she wanted anything, or when she was out of breath, our Else gave Lil a tug, a twitch, and Lil stopped and turned round. The Kelveys never failed to understand each other.

Now they hovered at the edge; you couldn't stop them listening. When the little girls turned round and sneered, Lil, as usual, gave her silly, shamefaced smile, but our Else only looked.

And Isabel's voice, so very proud, went on telling. The carpet made a great sensation, but so did the beds with real bedclothes, and the stove with an oven door.

When she finished Kezia broke in. "You've forgotten the lamp, Isabel."

"Oh, yes," said Isabel, "and there's a teeny little lamp, all made of yellow glass, with a white globe that stands on the dining-room table. You couldn't tell it from a real one."

"The lamp's best of all," cried Kezia. She thought Isabel wasn't making half enough of the little lamp. But nobody paid any attention. Isabel was choosing the two who were to come back with them that afternoon and see it. She chose Emmie Cole and Lena Logan. But when the others knew they were all to have a chance, they couldn't be nice enough to Isabel. One by one they put their arms round Isabel's waist and walked her off. They had something to whisper to her, a secret. "Isabel's *my* friend."

Only the little Kelveys moved away forgotten; there was nothing more for them to hear.

Days passed, and as more children saw the doll's house, the fame of it spread. It became the one subject, the rage. The one question was, "Have you seen Burnells' doll house? Oh, ain't it lovely!" "Haven't you seen it? Oh, I say!"

Even the dinner hour was given up to talking about it. The little girls sat under the pines eating their thick mutton sandwiches and big slabs of johnny cake spread with butter. While always, as near as they could get, sat the Kelveys, our Else holding on to Lil, listening too, while they chewed their jam sandwiches out of a newspaper soaked with large red blobs. . . .

"Mother," said Kezia, "can't I ask the Kelveys just once?"

"Certainly not, Kezia."

"But why not?"

"Run away, Kezia; you know quite well why not."

At last everybody had seen it except them. On that day the subject rather flagged. It was the dinner hour. The children stood together under the pine trees, and suddenly, as they looked at the Kelveys eating out of their paper, always by themselves, always listening, they wanted to be horrid to them. Emmie Cole started the whisper.

Doll house at Wenham built in 1884 by Benjamin Chamberlain for his daughters.

"Lil Kelvey's going to be a servant when she grows up."

"O-oh, how awful!" said Isabel Burnell, and she made eyes at Emmie.

Emmie swallowed in a very meaning way and nodded to Isabel as she'd seen her mother do on those occasions.

"It's true—it's true—it's true," she said.

Then Lena Logan's little eyes snapped. "Shall I ask her?" she whispered.

"Bet you don't," said Jessie May.

"Pooh, I'm not frightened," said Lena. Suddenly she gave a little squeal and danced in front of the other girls. "Watch! Watch me! Watch me now!" said Lena. And sliding, gliding, dragging one foot, giggling behind her hand, Lena went over to the Kelveys.

Lil looked up from her dinner. She wrapped the rest quickly away. Our Else stopped chewing. What was coming now?

"Is it true you're going to be a servant when you grow up, Lil Kelvey?" shrilled Lena.

Dead silence. But instead of answering, Lil only gave her silly, shame-faced smile. She didn't seem to mind the question at all. What a sell[1] for Lena! The girls began to titter.

Lena couldn't stand that. She put her hands on

---

1. *What a sell*, what a come-down, disappointment.

her hips; she shot forward. "Yah, yer father's in prison!" she hissed, spitefully.

This was such a marvellous thing to have said that the little girls rushed away in a body, deeply, deeply excited, wild with joy. Some one found a long rope, and they began skipping. And never did they skip so high, run in and out so fast, or do such daring things as on that morning.

In the afternoon Pat called for the Burnell children with the buggy and they drove home. There were visitors. Isabel and Lottie, who liked visitors, went upstairs to change their pinafores. But Kezia thieved out[2] at the back. Nobody was about; she began to swing on the big white gates of the courtyard. Presently, looking along the road, she saw two little dots. They grew bigger, they were coming towards her. Now she could see that one was in front and one close behind. Now she could see that they were the Kelveys. Kezia stopped swinging. She slipped off the gate as if she was going to run away. Then she hesitated. The Kelveys came nearer, and beside them stalked their shadows, very long, stretching right across the road with their heads in the buttercups. Kezia clambered back on the gate; she had made up her mind; she swung out.

"Hullo," she said to the passing Kelveys.

They were so astonished that they stopped. Lil gave her silly smile. Our Else stared.

"You can come and see our doll's house if you want to," said Kezia, and she dragged one toe on the ground. But at that Lil turned red and shook her head quickly.

"Why not?" asked Kezia.

Lil gasped, then she said, "Your ma told our ma you wasn't to speak to us."

"Oh, well," said Kezia. She didn't know what to reply. "It doesn't matter. You can come and see our doll's house all the same. Come on. Nobody's looking."

But Lil shook her head still harder.

"Don't you want to?" asked Kezia.

Suddenly there was a twitch, a tug at Lil's skirt. She turned round. Our Else was looking at her with big, imploring eyes; she was frowning; she wanted to go. For a moment Lil looked at our Else very doubtfully. But then our Else twitched her skirt again. She started forward. Kezia led the way. Like two little stray cats they followed across the courtyard to where the doll's house stood.

"There it is," said Kezia.

There was a pause. Lil breathed loudly, almost snorted; our Else was still as a stone.

"I'll open it for you," said Kezia kindly. She undid the hook and they looked inside.

"There's the drawing-room and the dining-room, and that's the—"

"Kezia!"

Oh, what a start they gave!

"Kezia!"

It was Aunt Beryl's voice. They turned round. At the back door stood Aunt Beryl, staring as if she couldn't believe what she saw.

"How dare you ask the little Kelveys into the courtyard?" said her cold, furious voice. "You know as well as I do, you're not allowed to talk to them. Run away, children, run away at once. And don't come back again," said Aunt Beryl. And she stepped into the yard and shooed them out as if they were chickens.

"Off you go immediately!" she called, cold and proud.

They did not need telling twice. Burning with shame, shrinking together, Lil huddling along like her mother, our Else dazed, somehow they crossed the big courtyard and squeezed through the white gate.

"Wicked, disobedient little girl!" said Aunt Beryl bitterly to Kezia, and she slammed the doll's house to.

The afternoon had been awful. A letter had come from Willie Brent, a terrifying, threatening letter, saying if she did not meet him that evening in Pulman's Bush, he'd come to the front door and ask the reason why! But now that she had frightened those little rats of Kelveys and given Kezia a good scolding, her heart felt lighter. That ghastly pressure was gone. She went back to the house humming.

---

2. *thieved out,* sneaked away.

When the Kelveys were well out of sight of Burnells', they sat down to rest on a big red drainpipe by the side of the road. Lil's cheeks were still burning; she took off the hat with the quill and held it on her knee. Dreamily they looked over the hay paddocks, past the creek, to the group of wattles where Logan's cows stood waiting to be milked. What were their thoughts?

Presently our Else nudged up close to her sister. But now she had forgotten the cross lady. She put out a finger and stroked her sister's quill; she smiled her rare smile.

"I seen the little lamp," she said, softly.

Then both were silent once more.

1923

THINK AND DISCUSS
Understanding
1. What does Kezia like best about the doll's house?
2. Where did Lil Kelvey get the dress and hat she wears to school?
3. What does Lena say to the Kelveys that makes her schoolmates "wild with joy"?
4. What causes Aunt Beryl to act so venomously toward the Kelvey girls?

Analyzing
5. What is the significance of the doll's house for Isabel? What is it for Kezia?
6. **Characterize** Lil and Else. How do they relate to each other?
7. Why has the line been "drawn" to exclude the Kelveys socially?
8. To what forms of social cruelty are the Kelveys subjected by the other children and by adults?
9. Is the cruelty shown by Aunt Beryl of the same quality as that shown by the little girls, or is it of another type? Explain.
10. Why, when taunted by Lena, does Lil simply respond with her "silly, shamefaced smile?"
11. What special meaning is conveyed by Else's statement, "I seen the little lamp"? How would the effect of that statement differ if spoken by Lil instead of Else?

Extending
12. The girls of the story exhibit a high degree of class consciousness and snobbery. Would this kind of behavior be likely to occur in today's world?

COMPOSITION
Remembering a Special Gift
Over a lifetime, certain gifts stand out as being very special and deeply treasured. In a paper of three to four paragraphs, describe the best gift you ever received. Was it a surprise or something you have yearned for? In your first paragraph tell how you happened to get the gift. Then describe it in detail so that the reader understands the great pleasure it gave you. Were you, like the Burnell children, quick to let others know about your new possession, or did you keep it to yourself? Does the gift continue to have the same meaning for you today? In your conclusion sum up how receiving this gift enhanced your life.

Analyzing the Symbolism in "The Doll's House"
The doll's house represents something to all these characters, and the emphasis on the little lamp suggests that it carries special **symbolic** force. Write an essay of three to five paragraphs analyzing what the doll's house and the lamp mean to Kezia and her friends and to Lil and Else. Consider Mansfield's choice of a doll's house; would another gift have worked as well? You may wish also to incorporate your answer to question 11 in your analysis.

Virginia Woolf was the daughter of Sir Leslie Stephen (1832–1904), the editor of one of the great Victorian scholarly projects, the multivolume *Dictionary of National Biography*. She was educated at home by her father and had the run of his extensive library. After his death she moved to London with her brother and sister. Their homes in the Bloomsbury district, near the British Museum, became the meeting places of a famous group of intellectuals. Among the members of the Bloomsbury Group were the economist John Maynard Keynes, the biographer Lytton Strachey, and the novelist E. M. Forster. Another member of the group was the writer Leonard Woolf, whom she married in 1912. In 1917 they founded the Hogarth Press, which published her books as well as those of a number of other important modern writers, like T. S. Eliot and E. M. Forster.

Woolf began her career as a writer doing book reviews and articles for literary journals and newspapers. At the same time she began her first novel, *The Voyage Out*, which was accepted by a publisher in 1913 but not issued until 1915. The delay was caused by one of the episodes of mental illness that were to trouble her throughout her life.

During the 1920s her work became increasingly experimental. In novels like *Mrs. Dalloway* (1925), *To the Lighthouse* (1927), and *The Waves* (1931), she rebelled against the social fiction of the prewar period with its emphasis on detailed descriptions of character and setting. Instead she attempted to express the timeless inner consciousness of her characters. Influenced by James Joyce's *Ulysses*, she used the techniques of "stream of consciousness" and "interior monologue," moving from one character to another to reveal a variety of mental responses to the same event. Another aspect of her work during this period appeared in *A Room of One's Own* (1929), a long essay in which she forcefully presented the difficulties facing the woman writer.

The outbreak of World War II was a shattering event for Woolf. Nevertheless, she managed to complete a brief, enigmatic final novel, *Between the Acts* (1941). "Written in the gloomiest days of the war," the English critic Cyril Connolly observed, "while the Spitfires and Messerschmitts fell around her Sussex home in the Battle of Britain, and published before the tide of war had turned, her book is about the eternal England, the beautiful threatened civilization which she had always loved . . ." On the morning of March 28, 1941, she walked across the water meadows to the River Ouse and drowned herself, "the one experience," she once confided to a friend, "I shall never describe."

The New Dress   Virginia Woolf

abel had her first serious suspicion that something was wrong as she took her cloak off and Mrs. Barnet, while handing her the mirror and touching the brushes and thus drawing her attention, perhaps rather markedly, to all the appliances for tidying and improving hair, complexion, clothes, which existed on the dressing table, confirmed the suspicion—that it was not right, not quite right, which growing stronger as she went upstairs and springing at her with conviction as she greeted Clarissa Dalloway, she went straight to the far end of the room, to a shaded corner where a looking glass hung and looked. No! It was not *right*. And at once the misery which she always tried to hide, the profound dissatisfaction—the sense she had had, ever since she was a child, of being inferior to other people—set upon her, relentlessly, remorsefully, with an intensity which she could not beat off, as she would when she woke at night at home, by reading Borrow or Scott;[1] for oh these men, oh these women, all were thinking—"What's Mabel wearing? What a fright she looks! What a hideous new dress!"—their eyelids flickering as they came up and then their lids shutting rather tight. It was her own appalling inadequacy; her cowardice; her mean, water-sprinkled blood that depressed her. And at once the whole of the room where, for ever so many hours, she had planned with the little dressmaker how it was to go, seemed sordid, repulsive; and her own drawing room so shabby, and herself, going out, puffed up with vanity as she touched the letters on the hall table and said, "How dull!" to show off—all this now seemed unutterably silly, paltry, and provincial. All this had been absolutely destroyed, shown up, exploded, the moment she came into Mrs. Dalloway's drawing room.

What she had thought that evening when, sitting over the teacups, Mrs. Dalloway's invitation came, was that, of course, she could not be fashionable. It was absurd to pretend it even—fashion meant cut, meant style, meant thirty guineas at least—but why not be original? Why not be herself, anyhow? And, getting up, she had taken that old fashion book of her mother's, a Paris fashion book of the time of the Empire, and had thought how much prettier, more dignified, and more womanly they were then, and so set herself—oh it was foolish—trying to be like them, pluming herself in fact, upon being modest and old-fashioned and very charming, giving herself up, no doubt about it, to an orgy of self-love, which deserved to be chastised, and so rigged herself out like this.

But she dared not look in the glass. She could not face the whole horror—the pale yellow, idiotically old-fashioned silk dress with its long skirt and its high sleeves and its waist and all the things that looked so charming in the fashion book, but not on her, not among all these ordinary people. She felt like a dressmaker's dummy standing there, for young people to stick pins into.

"But, my dear, it's perfectly charming!" Rose Shaw said, looking her up and down with that little satirical pucker of the lips which she expected—Rose herself being dressed in the height of the fashion, precisely like everybody else, always.

We are all like flies trying to crawl over the edge of the saucer, Mabel thought, and repeated the phrase as if she were crossing herself, as if she

---

1. ***Borrow or Scott,*** George Borrow and Walter Scott, popular writers of the 19th century.

"The New Dress" from *A Haunted House and Other Stories* by Virginia Woolf, copyright 1944, 1972 by Harcourt Brace Jovanovich Inc. Reprinted by permission of the publisher, the estate of Virginia Woolf and the Hogarth Press.

were trying to find some spell to annul this pain, to make this agony endurable. Tags of Shakespeare, lines from books she had read ages ago, suddenly came to her when she was in agony, and she repeated them over and over again. "Flies trying to crawl," she repeated. If she could say that over often enough and make herself see the flies, she would become numb, chill, frozen, dumb. Now she could see flies crawling slowly out of a saucer of milk with their wings stuck together; and she strained and strained (standing in front of the looking glass, listening to Rose Shaw) to make herself see Rose Shaw and all the other people there as flies, trying to hoist themselves out of something, or into something, meager, insignificant, toiling flies. But she could not see them like that, not other people. She saw herself like that—she was a fly, but the others were dragonflies, butterflies, beautiful insects, dancing, fluttering, skimming, while she alone dragged herself up out of the saucer. (Envy and spite, the most detestable of the vices, were her chief faults.)

"I feel like some dowdy, decrepit, horribly dingy old fly," she said, making Robert Haydon stop just to hear her say that, just to reassure herself by furbishing up a poor weak-kneed phrase and so showing how detached she was, how witty, that she did not feel in the least out of anything. And, of course, Robert Haydon answered something quite polite, quite insincere, which she saw through instantly, and said to herself, directly he went (again from some book), "Lies, lies, lies!" For a party makes things either much more real, or much less real, she thought; she saw in a flash to the bottom of Robert Haydon's heart; she saw through everything. She saw the truth. *This* was true, this drawing room, this self, and the other false. Miss Milan's little workroom was really terribly hot, stuffy, sordid. It smelled of clothes and cabbage cooking; and yet, when Miss Milan put the glass in her hand, and she looked at herself with the dress on, finished, an extraordinary bliss shot through her heart. Suffused with light, she sprang into existence. Rid of cares and wrinkles, what she had dreamed of herself was there—a beautiful woman. Just for a second (she had not dared look longer, Miss Milan wanted to know about the length of the skirt), there looked at her, framed in the scrolloping[2] mahogany, a gray-white mysteriously smiling, charming girl, the core of herself, the soul of herself; and it was not vanity only, not only self-love that made her think it good, tender, and true. Miss Milan said that the skirt could not well be longer; if anything the skirt, said Miss Milan, puckering her forehead, considering with all her wits about her, must be shorter; and she felt, suddenly, honestly, full of love for Miss Milan, much, much fonder of Miss Milan than of anyone in the whole world, and could have cried for pity that she should be crawling on the floor with her mouth full of pins, and her face red and her eyes bulging—that one human being should be doing this for another, and she saw them all as human beings merely, and herself going off to her party, and Miss Milan pulling the cover over the canary's cage, or letting him pick a hempseed from between her lips, and the thought of it, of this side of human nature and its patience and its endurance and its being content with such miserable, scanty, sordid little pleasures filled her eyes with tears.

And now the whole thing had vanished. The dress, the room, the love, the pity, the scrolloping looking glass, and the canary's cage—all had vanished, and here she was in a corner of Mrs. Dalloway's drawing room, suffering tortures, woken wide awake to reality.

But it was all so paltry, weak-blooded, and petty-minded to care so much at her age with two children, to be still so utterly dependent on people's opinions and not have principles or convictions, not to be able to say as other people did, "There's Shakespeare! There's death! We're all weevils in a captain's biscuit"—or whatever it was that people did say.

She faced herself straight in the glass; she pecked at her left shoulder; she issued out into the room, as if spears were thrown at her yellow dress from all sides. But instead of looking fierce or tragic, as Rose Shaw would have done—Rose would

2. *scrolloping,* possessing heavy, florid ornament.

Kensington Garden dresses for June, 1808, show the Empire waistline. Fashion plate from *Le Beau Monde.*

have looked like Boadicea[3]—she looked foolish and self-conscious, and simpered like a schoolgirl and slouched across the room, positively slinking, as if she were a beaten mongrel, and looked at a picture, an engraving. As if one went to a party to look at a picture! Everybody knew why she did it—it was from shame, from humiliation.

"Now the fly's in the saucer," she said to herself, "right in the middle, and can't get out, and the milk," she thought, rigidly staring at the picture, "is sticking its wings together."

"It's so old-fashioned," she said to Charles Burt, making him stop (which by itself he hated) on his way to talk to someone else.

She meant, or she tried to make herself think that she meant, that it was the picture and not her dress that was old-fashioned. And one word of praise, one word of affection from Charles would have made all the difference to her at the moment. If he had only said, "Mabel, you're looking charming tonight!" it would have changed her life. But then she ought to have been truthful and direct.

Charles said nothing of the kind, of course. He was malice itself. He always saw through one, especially if one were feeling particularly mean, paltry, or feeble-minded.

"Mabel's got a new dress!" he said, and the poor fly was absolutely shoved into the middle of the saucer. Really, he would like her to drown, she believed. He had no heart, no fundamental kindness, only a veneer of friendliness. Miss Milan was much more real, much kinder. If only one could feel that and stick to it always. "Why," she asked herself—replying to Charles much too pertly, letting him see that she was out of temper, or "ruffled" as he called it ("Rather ruffled?" he said and went on to laugh at her with some woman over there)—"Why," she asked herself, "can't I feel one thing always, feel quite sure that Miss Milan is right, and Charles wrong and stick to it, feel sure about the canary and pity and love and not

---

3. **Boadicea** (bō′ə di sē′ə), British queen who led a revolt against the Romans.

be whipped all round in a second by coming into a room full of people?" It was her odious, weak, vacillating character again, always giving at the critical moment and not being seriously interested in conchology, etymology, botany, archaeology, cutting up potatoes and watching them fructify[4] like Mary Dennis, like Violet Searle.

Then Mrs. Holman, seeing her standing there, bore down upon her. Of course a thing like a dress was beneath Mrs. Holman's notice, with her family always tumbling downstairs or having the scarlet fever. Could Mabel tell her if Elmthorpe was ever let for August and September? Oh, it was a conversation that bored her unutterably!—it made her furious to be treated like a house agent or a messenger boy, to be made use of. Not to have value, that was it, she thought, trying to grasp something hard, something real, while she tried to answer sensibly about the bathroom and the south aspect and the hot water to the top of the house; and all the time she could see little bits of her yellow dress in the round looking glass which made them all the size of boot buttons or tadpoles; and it was amazing to think how much humiliation and agony and self-loathing and effort and passionate ups and downs of feeling were contained in a thing the size of a three-penny bit. And what was still odder, this thing, this Mabel Waring, was separate, quite disconnected; and though Mrs. Holman (the black button) was leaning forward and telling her how her eldest boy had strained his heart running, she could see her, too, quite detached in the looking glass, and it was impossible that the black dot, leaning forward, gesticulating, should make the yellow dot, sitting solitary, self-centered, feel what the black dot was feeling, yet they pretended.

"So impossible to keep boys quiet"—that was the kind of thing one said.

And Mrs. Holman, who could never get enough sympathy and snatched what little there was greedily, as if it were her right (but she deserved much more for there was her little girl who had come down this morning with a swollen knee-joint), took this miserable offering and looked at it suspiciously, grudgingly, as if it were a halfpenny when it ought to have been a pound and put it away in her purse, must put up with it, mean and miserly though it was, times being hard, so very hard; and on she went, creaking, injured Mrs. Holman, about the girl with the swollen joints. Ah, it was tragic, this greed, this clamor of human beings, like a row of cormorants,[4] barking and flapping their wings for sympathy—it was tragic, could one have felt it and not merely pretended to feel it!

But in her yellow dress tonight she could not wring out one drop more; she wanted it all, all for herself. She knew (she kept on looking into the glass, dipping into that dreadfully showing up blue pool) that she was condemned, despised, left like this in a backwater, because of her being like this a feeble, vacillating creature; and it seemed to her that the yellow dress was a penance which she had deserved, and if she had been dressed like Rose Shaw, in lovely, clinging green with a ruffle of swansdown, she would have deserved that; and she thought that there was no escape for her—none whatever. But it was not her fault altogether, after all. It was being one of a family of ten; never having money enough, always skimping and paring; and her mother carrying great cans, and the linoleum worn on the stair edges, and one sordid little domestic tragedy after another—nothing catastrophic, the sheep farm failing, but not utterly; her eldest brother marrying beneath him but not very much—there was no romance, nothing extreme about them all. They petered out respectably in seaside resorts; every watering place had one of her aunts even now asleep in some lodging with the front windows not quite facing the sea. That was so like them—they had to squint at things always. And she had done the same—she was just like her aunts. For all her dreams of living in India, married to some hero like Sir Henry Lawrence,[6] some empire builder (still the sight of a native in a turban filled her with romance), she had failed utterly. She had married Hubert, with his safe, permanent underling's job in the Law

---

4. *fructify* (fruc′tə fī), bear fruit.
5. *cormorants,* large, supposedly greedy, sea birds.
6. *Sir Henry Lawrence,* English general in India.

Courts, and they managed tolerably in a smallish house without proper maids and hash when she was alone or just bread and butter, but now and then—Mrs. Holman was off, thinking her the most dried up, unsympathetic twig she had ever met, absurdly dressed, too, and would tell everyone about Mabel's fantastic appearance—now and then, thought Mabel Waring, left alone on the blue sofa, punching the cushion in order to look occupied, for she would not join Charles Burt and Rose Shaw, chattering like magpies and perhaps laughing at her by the fireplace—now and then, there did come to her delicious moments, reading the other night in bed, for instance, or down by the sea on the sand in the sun at Easter—let her recall it—a great tuft of pale sand grass standing all twisted like a shock of spears against the sky, which was blue like a smooth china egg, so firm, so hard, and then the melody of the waves—"Hush, hush," they said, and the children's shouts paddling—yes, it was a divine moment, and there she lay, she felt, in the hand of the Goddess who was the world; rather a hard-hearted, but very beautiful Goddess, a little lamb laid on the altar (one did think these silly things, and it didn't matter so long as one never said them). And also with Hubert sometimes she had quite unexpectedly—carving the mutton for Sunday lunch, for no reason, opening a letter, coming into a room—divine moments, when she said to herself (for she would never say this to anybody else), "This is it. This has happened. This is it!" And the other way about it was equally surprising—that is, when everything was arranged—music, weather, holidays, every reason for happiness was there—then nothing happened at all. One wasn't happy. It was flat, just flat, that was all.

Her wretched self again, no doubt! She had always been a fretful, weak, unsatisfactory mother, a wobbly wife, lolling about in a kind of twilight existence with nothing very clear or very bold, or more one thing than another, like all her brothers and sisters, except perhaps Herbert—they were all the same poor water-veined creatures who did nothing. Then in the midst of this creeping, crawling life, suddenly she was on the crest of a wave.

That wretched fly—where had she read the story that kept coming into her mind about the fly and the saucer?—struggled out. Yes, she had those moments. But now that she was forty, they might come more and more seldom. By degrees she would cease to struggle any more. But that was deplorable! That was not to be endured! That made her feel ashamed of herself!

She would go to the London Library tomorrow. She would find some wonderful, helpful, astonishing book, quite by chance, a book by a clergyman, by an American no one had ever heard of; or she would walk down the Strand and drop, accidentally, into a hall where a miner was telling about the life in the pit, and suddenly she would become a new person. She would be absolutely transformed. She would wear a uniform; she would be called Sister Somebody; she would never give a thought to clothes again. And forever after she would be perfectly clear about Charles Burt and Miss Milan and this room and that room; and it would be always, day after day, as if she were lying in the sun or carving the mutton. It would be it!

So she got up from the blue sofa, and the yellow button in the looking glass got up too, and she waved her hand to Charles and Rose to show them she did not depend on them one scrap, and the yellow button moved out of the looking glass, and all the spears were gathered into her breast as she walked toward Mrs. Dalloway and said, "Good night."

"But it's too early to go," said Mrs. Dalloway, who was always so charming.

"I'm afraid I must," said Mabel Waring. "But," she added in her weak, wobbly voice which only sounded ridiculous when she tried to strengthen it, "I have enjoyed myself enormously."

"I have enjoyed myself," she said to Mr. Dalloway, whom she met on the stairs.

"Lies, lies, lies!" she said to herself, going downstairs, and "Right in the saucer!" she said to herself as she thanked Mrs. Barnet for helping her and wrapped herself round and round and round in the Chinese cloak she had worn these twenty years.

THINK AND DISCUSS
Understanding
1. What about Mabel's new dress makes her feel that it is all wrong for this occasion?
2. What is Mabel's reaction to the polite remarks addressed to her at the party?

Analyzing
3. What do Mabel's repeated references to the fly crawling out of a saucer reveal about her feelings of self-worth and social adequacy?
4. How does her remembrance of the hours spent at the dressmaker's contrast with her feelings at the time?
5. Contrast Mabel's dreams with the circumstances of her life and marriage.
6. What has Mabel found to be **paradoxical** about her experience of happiness?
7. What changes in her personality do Mabel's plans to become a new person call for?

Extending
8. Mabel walks into Mrs. Dalloway's drawing room feeling "as if spears were thrown at her yellow dress from all sides." When she leaves, "all the spears were gathered into her breast. . . ." Is it society or her own sense of inferiority that makes her feel this way? Is she really the target of gossip and social disdain she envisions herself to be?

REVIEWING: Point of View H𝟐
See Handbook of Literary Terms, p. 917
Point of view is the relationship between the teller of the story and the characters in it. The teller may adopt a first-person, a third-person limited, or a third-person omniscient point of view. *Stream of consciousness* is a technique in which a writer moves directly inside characters' minds with complete omniscience. Inner feelings, memories, ideas, and observations are portrayed as occurring simultaneously with external experience. The characters' thoughts come and go in seemingly random, but actually controlled, fashion, much as they do in people's minds.

1. From what point of view is "The New Dress" told?
2. How had Mabel hoped she would appear in her new dress? How does she think she appears when at Mrs. Dalloway's party?
3. Is this how others see her?

THINKING SKILLS
Evaluating
To evaluate is to make a judgment based on some sort of standard.

1. How effectively does Woolf use point of view and the stream-of-consciousness technique to create a fictional world?
2. What are some of the limitations of the stream-of-consciousness technique?

COMPOSITION ◆━
Exploring Other Points of View
In "The New Dress" we perceive events only from Mabel Waring's point of view. Write three brief accounts of the party Mabel attended as they might have been recorded in the journals of Mrs. Dalloway, Robert Haydon, and Mrs. Holman. First reread those sections of the story in which these characters are involved in order to make your writing faithful to the facts of the narrative. Then, in your entries, let the writers describe their encounter with Mabel, evaluate her behavior and her unusual attire, and state how they intend to treat her the next time they meet. See "Writing About Point of View" in the Writer's Handbook.

Writing a Case Study
Assume that you are a social worker whom Mabel has asked for help in overcoming her inferiority complex. Write a case study that provides information such as the client's age, appearance, and profession; significant facts about the client's background and current family situation; a description of the client's problem, with examples of her behavior; and recommendations for overcoming the problem. Be sure to maintain an objective, professional tone to invest your report with a sense of authority.

Born Eric Arthur Blair, Orwell was driven by a lifelong commitment to speak out unpleasant truths, becoming the "wintry conscience of a generation." He was born in Bengal, the son of a minor Indian civil servant. Returning to England, he went to an expensive preparatory school. He won a scholarship to Eton, but instead of continuing on to a university, he joined the Imperial Police in Burma (see "Shooting an Elephant," page 812). In Burma his sense of justice was outraged by the corrupting effects of imperialism both on the colonizers and on the colonized. Resigning from the Imperial Police, he returned to England, determined to become a writer. Troubled by the effects of poverty on the working class, he decided to find out more about their condition, becoming a dishwasher, a farm worker, a tramp, and chronicling his experiences in *Down and Out in Paris and London* (1933).

When the Spanish Civil War broke out in 1936, Orwell, who had become a socialist, went and fought on the side of the Republicans (those loyal to Spain's leftist government) against the military revolt led by General Franco. After being wounded he returned to England, disillusioned by the brutality of communist purges in Spain, which he described in one of his finest books, *Homage to Catalonia* (1938).

Orwell wrote a series of novels in the late 1930s, concluding with *Coming Up for Air* (1939), which reveals Orwell's nostalgia for the life of an earlier England and his fear and hatred of everything that threatened it, from American-style food to the threat of fascist militarism. When the war came, Orwell was rejected for military service, and worked for a time for the BBC. During this period Orwell became an active journalist, writing many newspaper articles and reviews. Many critics locate Orwell's genius in his essays. They cover a broad spectrum of subjects, including politics, both serious and popular literature, language (see The Changing English Language, page 886), and censorship. "Good prose is like a window pane," he once observed, and his own prose style is clear and concise. What made him distinctive as a thinker was his ability to eloquently and provocatively express what many people felt obscurely and inarticulately.

While remaining a socialist, Orwell often chastised the left. The two books that made him famous, *Animal Farm* (1945) and *Nineteen Eighty-four* (1949), were both inspired by his lifelong hatred of totalitarianism. The first is a satire on Stalinist Russia in the form of a beast fable; the second is a "dystopia," a grimly realistic account of a future society in which all freedom has been extinguished. Orwell died at the age of forty-six of tuberculosis.

Shooting an Elephant

George Orwell

In Moulmein, in Lower Burma, I was hated by large numbers of people—the only time in my life that I have been important enough for this to happen to me. I was sub-divisional police officer of the town, and in an aimless, petty kind of way anti-European feeling was very bitter. No one had the guts to raise a riot, but if a European woman went through the bazaars alone somebody would probably spit betel juice over her dress. As a police officer I was an obvious target and was baited whenever it seemed safe to do so. When a nimble Burman tripped me up on the football field and the referee (another Burman) looked the other way, the crowd yelled with hideous laughter. This happened more than once. In the end the sneering yellow faces of young men that met me everywhere, the insults hooted after me when I was at a safe distance, got badly on my nerves. The young Buddhist priests were the worst of all. There were several thousands of them in the town and none of them seemed to have anything to do except stand on street corners and jeer at Europeans.

All this was perplexing and upsetting. For at that time I had already made up my mind that imperialism was an evil thing and the sooner I chucked up my job and got out of it the better. Theoretically—and secretly, of course—I was all for the Burmese and all against their oppressors, the British. As for the job I was doing, I hated it more bitterly than I can perhaps make clear. In a job like that you see the dirty work of Empire at close quarters. The wretched prisoners huddling in the stinking cages of the lock-ups, the grey, cowed faces of the long-term convicts, the scarred buttocks of the men who had been flogged with bamboos—all these oppressed me with an intolerable sense of guilt. But I could get nothing into

perspective. I was young and ill-educated and I had to think out my problems in the utter silence that is imposed on every Englishman in the East. I did not even know that the British Empire is dying, still less did I know that it is a great deal better than the younger empires that are going to supplant it. All I knew was that I was stuck between my hatred of the empire I served and my rage against the evil-spirited little beasts who tried to make my job impossible. With one part of my mind I thought of the British Raj[1] as an unbreakable tyranny, as something clamped down, *in saecula saeculorum*,[2] upon the will of prostrate peoples; with another part I thought that the greatest joy in the world would be to drive a bayonet into a Buddhist priest's guts. Feelings like these are the normal by-products of imperialism; ask any Anglo-Indian official, if you can catch him off duty.

One day something happened which in a round-about way was enlightening. It was a tiny incident in itself, but it gave me a better glimpse than I had had before of the real nature of imperialism—the real motives for which despotic governments act. Early one morning the sub-inspector at a police station the other end of the town rang me up on the phone and said that an elephant was ravaging the bazaar. Would I please come and do something about it? I did not know what I could do, but I wanted to see what was happening and I got on to a pony and started out. I took my rifle, an old

---

1. **British Raj,** the British Empire in the East, including what is now India, Pakistan, Bangladesh, and Burma. *Raj* is a Hindu word meaning "rule."
2. *in saecula saeculorum* (in sā′kü lä sā′kü lôr′əm), forever. [Latin]

.44 Winchester and much too small to kill an elephant, but I thought the noise might be useful *in terrorem*. Various Burmans stopped me on the way and told me about the elephant's doings. It was not, of course, a wild elephant, but a tame one which had gone "must." It had been chained up as tame elephants always are when their attack of "must" is due, but on the previous night it had broken its chain and escaped. Its mahout,[3] the only person who could manage it when it was in that state, had set out in pursuit, but he had taken the wrong direction and was now twelve hours' journey away, and in the morning the elephant had suddenly reappeared in the town. The Burmese population had no weapons and were quite helpless against it. It had already destroyed somebody's bamboo hut, killed a cow and raided some fruit-stalls and devoured the stock; also it had met the municipal rubbish van, and, when the driver jumped out and took to his heels, had turned the van over and inflicted violence upon it.

The Burmese sub-inspector and some Indian constables were waiting for me in the quarter where the elephant had been seen. It was a very poor quarter, a labyrinth of squalid bamboo huts, thatched with palm-leaf, winding all over a steep hillside. I remember that it was a cloudy stuffy morning at the beginning of the rains. We began questioning the people as to where the elephant had gone, and, as usual, failed to get any definite information. That is invariably the case in the East; a story always sounds clear enough at a distance, but the nearer you get to the scene of events the vaguer it becomes. Some of the people said that the elephant had gone in one direction, some said that he had gone in another, some professed not even to have heard of any elephant. I had almost made up my mind that the whole story was a pack of lies, when we heard yells a little distance away. There was a loud, scandalized cry of "Go away, child! Go away this instant!" and an old woman with a switch in her hand came round a corner of a hut, violently shooing away a crowd of naked children. Some more women followed, clicking their tongues and exclaiming; evidently there was something there that the children ought not to have seen. I rounded the hut and saw a man's dead body sprawling in the mud. He was an Indian, a black Dravidian coolie, almost naked, and he could not have been dead many minutes. The people said that the elephant had come suddenly upon him round the corner of the hut, caught him with its trunk, put its foot on his back and ground him into the earth. This was the rainy season and the ground was soft, and his face had scored a trench a foot deep and a couple of yards long. He was lying on his belly with arms crucified and head sharply twisted to one side. His face was coated with mud, the eyes wide open, the teeth bared and grinning with an expression of unendurable agony. (Never tell me, by the way, that the dead look peaceful. Most of the corpses I have seen looked devilish.) The friction of the great beast's foot had stripped the skin from his back as neatly as one skins a rabbit. As soon as I saw the dead man I sent an orderly to a friend's house nearby to borrow an elephant rifle. I had already sent back the pony, not wanting it to go mad with fright and throw me if it smelled the elephant.

The orderly came back in a few minutes with a rifle and five cartridges, and meanwhile some Burmans had arrived and told us that the elephant was in the paddy fields below, only a few hundred yards away. As I started forward practically the whole population of the quarter flocked out of their houses and followed me. They had seen the rifle and were all shouting excitedly that I was going to shoot the elephant. They had not shown much interest in the elephant when he was merely ravaging their homes, but it was different now that he was going to be shot. It was a bit of fun to them, as it would be to an English crowd; besides, they wanted the meat. It made me vaguely uneasy. I had no intention of shooting the elephant—I had merely sent for the rifle to defend myself if necessary—and it is always unnerving to have a crowd following you. I marched down the hill, looking and feeling a fool, with the rifle over my shoulder

---

3. **"must . . . mahout.** *Must* is a frenzied state occurring periodically in male elephants; a mahout (mə hout′) is an elephant-driver.

and an ever-growing army of people jostling at my heels. At the bottom, when you got away from the huts, there was a metalled road and beyond that a miry waste of paddy fields a thousand yards across, not yet ploughed but soggy from the first rains and dotted with coarse grass. The elephant was standing eighty yards from the road, his left side towards us. He took not the slightest notice of the crowd's approach. He was tearing up bunches of grass, beating them against his knees to clean them and stuffing them into his mouth.

I had halted on the road. As soon as I saw the elephant I knew with perfect certainty that I ought not to shoot him. It is a serious matter to shoot a working elephant—it is comparable to destroying a huge and costly piece of machinery—and obviously one ought not to do it if it can possibly be avoided. And at that distance, peacefully eating, the elephant looked no more dangerous than a cow. I thought then and I think now that his attack of "must" was already passing off; in which case he would merely wander harmlessly about until the mahout came back and caught him. Moreover, I did not in the least want to shoot him. I decided that I would watch him for a little while to make sure that he did not turn savage again, and then go home.

But at that moment I glanced round at the crowd that had followed me. It was an immense crowd, two thousand at the least and growing every minute. It blocked the road for a long distance on either side. I looked at the sea of yellow faces above the garish clothes—faces all happy and excited over this bit of fun, all certain that the elephant was going to be shot. They were watching me as they would watch a conjuror about to perform a trick. They did not like me, but with the magical rifle in my hands I was momentarily worth watching. And suddenly I realized that I should have to shoot the elephant after all. The people expected it of me and I had got to do it; I could feel their two thousand wills pressing me forward, irresistibly. And it was at this moment, as I stood there with the rifle in my hands, that I first grasped the hollowness, the futility of the white man's dominion in the East. Here was I, the white man with his gun, standing in front of the unarmed native crowd—seemingly the leading actor of the piece; but in reality I was only an absurd puppet pushed to and fro by the will of those yellow faces behind. I perceived in this moment that when the white man turns tyrant it is his own freedom that he destroys. He becomes a sort of hollow, posing dummy, the conventionalized figure of a sahib.[4] For it is the condition of his rule that he shall spend his life in trying to impress the "natives" and so in every crisis he has got to do what the "natives" expect of him. He wears a mask, and his face grows to fit it. I had got to shoot the elephant. I had committed myself to doing it when I sent for the rifle. A sahib has got to act like a sahib; he has got to appear resolute, to know his own mind and do definite things. To come all that way, rifle in hand, with two thousand people marching at my heels, and then to trail feebly away, having done nothing—no, that was impossible. The crowd would laugh at me. And my whole life, every white man's life in the East, was one long struggle not to be laughed at.

But I did not want to shoot the elephant. I watched him beating his bunch of grass against his knees, with that preoccupied grandmotherly air that elephants have. It seemed to me that it would be murder to shoot him. At that age I was not squeamish about killing animals, but I had never shot an elephant and never wanted to. (Somehow it always seems worse to kill a *large* animal.) Besides, there was the beast's owner to be considered. Alive, the elephant was worth at least a hundred pounds; dead, he would only be worth the value of his tusks—five pounds, possibly. But I had to act quickly. I turned to some experienced-looking Burmans who had been there when we arrived, and asked them how the elephant had been behaving. They all said the same thing: he took no notice of you if you left him alone, but he might charge if you went too close to him.

It was perfectly clear to me what I ought to do. I ought to walk up to within, say, twenty-five yards of the elephant and test his behavior. If he charged

---

4. *sahib* (sä′ib), in British India, a European.

I could shoot, if he took no notice of me it would be safe to leave him until the mahout came back. But also I knew that I was going to do no such thing. I was a poor shot with a rifle and the ground was soft mud into which one would sink at every step. If the elephant charged and I missed him, I should have about as much chance as a toad under a steam-roller. But even then I was not thinking particularly of my own skin, only the watchful yellow faces behind. For at that moment, with the crowd watching me, I was not afraid in the ordinary sense, as I would have been if I had been alone. A white man mustn't be frightened of "natives"; and so, in general, he isn't frightened. The sole thought in my mind was that if anything went wrong those two thousand Burmans would see me pursued, caught, trampled on and reduced to a grinning corpse like that Indian up the hill. And if that happened it was quite probable that some of them would laugh. That would never do. There was only one alternative. I shoved the cartridges into the magazine and lay down on the road to get a better aim.

The crowd grew very still, and a deep, low, happy sigh, as of people who see the theatre curtain go up at last, breathed from innumerable throats. They were going to have their bit of fun after all. The rifle was a beautiful German thing with cross-hair sights. I did not then know that in shooting an elephant one should shoot to cut an imaginary bar running from ear-hole to ear-hole. I ought therefore, as the elephant was sideways on, to have aimed straight at his ear-hole; actually I aimed several inches in front of this, thinking the brain would be further forward.

When I pulled the trigger I did not hear the bang or feel the kick—one never does when a shot goes home—but I heard the devilish roar of glee that went up from the crowd. In that instant, in too short a time, one would have thought, even for the bullet to get there, a mysterious, terrible change had come over the elephant. He neither stirred nor fell, but every line of his body had altered. He looked suddenly stricken, shrunken, immensely old, as though the frightful impact of the bullet had paralyzed him without knocking him down.

At last, after what seemed a long time—it might have been five seconds, I dare say—he sagged flabbily to his knees. His mouth slobbered. An enormous senility seemed to have settled upon him. One could have imagined him thousands of years old. I fired again into the same spot. At the second shot he did not collapse but climbed with desperate slowness to his feet and stood weakly upright, with legs sagging and head dropping. I fired a third time. That was the shot that did for him. You could see the agony of it jolt his whole body and knock the last remnant of strength from his legs. But in falling he seemed for a moment to rise, for as his hind legs collapsed beneath him he seemed to tower upwards like a huge rock toppling, his trunk reaching skyward like a tree. He trumpeted, for the first and only time. And then down he came, his belly towards me, with a crash that seemed to shake the ground even where I lay.

I got up. The Burmans were already racing past me across the mud. It was obvious that the elephant would never rise again, but he was not dead. He was breathing very rhythmically with long rattling gasps, his great mound of a side painfully rising and falling. His mouth was wide open—I could see far down into caverns of pale pink throat. I waited a long time for him to die, but his breathing did not weaken. Finally I fired my two remaining shots into the spot where I thought his heart must be. The thick blood welled out of him like red velvet, but still he did not die. His body did not even jerk when the shots hit him, the tortured breathing continued without a pause. He was dying, very slowly and in great agony, but in some world remote from me where not even a bullet could damage him further. I felt that I had got to put an end to that dreadful noise. It seemed dreadful to see the great beast lying there, powerless to move and yet powerless to die, and not even to be able to finish him. I sent back for my small rifle and poured shot after shot into his heart and down his throat. They seemed to make no impression. The tortured gasps continued as steadily as the ticking of a clock.

In the end I could not stand it any longer and went away. I heard later that it took him half an hour to die. Burmans were arriving with dahs[5] and baskets even before I left, and I was told they had stripped his body almost to the bones by the afternoon.

Afterwards, of course, there were endless discussions about the shooting of the elephant. The owner was furious, but he was only an Indian and could do nothing. Besides, legally I had done the right thing, for a mad elephant has to be killed, like a mad dog, if its owner fails to control it. Among the Europeans opinion was divided. The older men said I was right, the younger men said it was a damn shame to shoot an elephant for killing a coolie, because an elephant was worth more than any damn Coringhee coolie. And afterwards I was very glad that the coolie had been killed; it put me legally in the right and it gave me a sufficient pretext for shooting the elephant. I often wondered whether any of the others grasped that I had done it solely to avoid looking a fool.

1936

---

5. *dah* (dä), a heavy Burmese knife.

THINK AND DISCUSS
Understanding
1. Name some of the abuses to which Europeans in Burma were subjected in Orwell's time.
2. What are the "crimes" the elephant commits that make the natives demand its death?
3. Why does the elephant take so long to die?

Analyzing
4. As a member of the Imperial Police in Burma, Orwell found himself hating both the empire he served and the Burmese. What accounts for the mixed feelings he describes?
5. List Orwell's reasons for not wanting to kill the elephant. Then explain why, against his better judgment, he still goes ahead and kills the elephant.
6. Explain what makes the shooting of the elephant both **ironic** and horrible.
7. What lesson does he feel this episode offers into the "real nature of despotism—the real motives for which despotic governments act"?
8. What reaction of the younger Europeans to the incident supports Orwell's criticism of British imperialism?

Extending
9. Judging from this selection, what abuses of power in the modern world would Orwell be likely to attack if he were living today?

COMPOSITION
Writing a Persuasive Letter
In "Shooting an Elephant," Orwell states that, in a job such as he held in Burma, "you see the dirty work of Empire at close quarters." Write the letter he might have written home to a close friend or relative about the evils of imperialism as he has come to know them first hand. To make your reader more receptive to what you have to say, acknowledge the pride Englishmen take in the British Empire, but suggest that it is unwarranted. Then go on to describe the hatred of the natives toward the British, the wretched condition of the prisons and mistreatment of the prisoners, and the contemptuous attitude of the Europeans toward the native population. To conclude your letter, sum up the negative effects of imperialism on the white man.

Writing About First-hand Experience
The glamor surrounding the British Empire quickly faded for Orwell once he was able to view its operation for himself in Burma. In a paper of four to six paragraphs, tell about a job you have held that proved far different from what you had expected. What things did you not realize about the job until you actually had to do it? Conclude with advice to classmates who might be considering similar employment.

Like the hero of his early novel *Sons and Lovers* (1913), David Herbert Lawrence was born in an English coal-mining town, the son of an uneducated miner and an ambitious mother who was a schoolteacher. During his childhood, the tensions and conflicts between his parents were fierce and disturbing, and, in large measure, responsible for the development of a strong attachment to his mother that later inhibited his relationships with other women. While responsive to his father's working-class values and earthiness, Lawrence was steered by his mother toward a middle-class life and strict moral behavior. Ultimately Lawrence sided with his father, opting for the primitive and instinctual, but first he had to break out of his environment.

After graduating from high school, Lawrence taught for a few years before establishing himself in London literary circles as a writer. In 1912 he declared his emancipation from the past by eloping with an aristocratic German, Frieda von Richthofen. Until his death in 1930, the Lawrences wandered the globe in search of a place undamaged by modern civilization that might also alleviate Lawrence's worsening tuberculosis.

Lawrence's first novel, *The White Peacock*, appeared shortly after his mother's death in 1911 and introduces two types of characters that reappear in his later fiction: the overly intellectual, civilized individual and the more primitive, sensual man who rejects middle-class values and deplores the destruction of natural life caused by industrialization. In 1913 Lawrence's reputation began to spread with the publication of a volume of poems and the novel *Sons and Lovers*, a powerful fictional portrait of Lawrence as the incipient artist struggling to break free from his possessive mother and establish an authentic identity. *The Rainbow* (1915) relates the history of three generations of the Brangwens, a family living in rural England during the last half of the nineteenth century. *Women in Love* (1920) continues the story of the Brangwens but focuses more specifically on the quest for ideal relationships between both men and women and men with other men.

Like Joyce and Woolf, Lawrence sought in his fiction to reveal character from within, to capture the exact feelings produced by immediate experience. Detached from his characters in their conflicts, he could present their arguments without taking sides—a remarkable accomplishment for a writer of strong and passionate opinions. Lawrence's reputation as a poet continues to grow. His keen-sighted observations of nature and animals are conveyed in simple language whose artistic purity attains dignity and grandeur. *Studies in Classical American Literature* (1923) is possibly the most original collection of critical essays published in this century. Since most of his work is an exploration of the primitive and sexual in human nature, Lawrence was constantly in trouble with the censors. It was a price he was willing to pay in his revolt against puritanism, mediocrity, and the dehumanization of an industrial society.

Tickets, Please

D. H. Lawrence

There is in the Midlands a single-line tramway system which boldly leaves the county town and plunges off into the black, industrial countryside, up hill and down dale, through the long ugly villages of workmen's houses, over canals and railways, past churches perched high and nobly over the smoke and shadows, through stark, grimy cold little marketplaces, tilting away in a rush past cinemas and shops down to the hollow where the collieries are, then up again, past a little rural church, under the ash trees, on in a rush to the terminus, the last little ugly place of industry, the cold little town that shivers on the edge of the wild, gloomy country beyond. There the green and creamy colored tramcar seems to pause and purr with curious satisfaction. But in a few minutes—the clock on the turret of the Cooperative Wholesale Society's shops gives the time—away it starts once more on the adventure. Again there are the reckless swoops downhill, bouncing the loops: again the chilly wait in the hilltop marketplace: again the breathless slithering round the precipitous drop under the church: again the patient halts at the loops, waiting for the outcoming car: so on and on, for two long hours, till at last the city looms beyond the fat gasworks, the narrow factories draw near, we are in the sordid streets of the great town, once more we sidle to a standstill at our terminus, abashed by the great crimson and cream-colored city cars, but still perky, jaunty, somewhat dare-devil, green as a jaunty sprig of parsley out of a black colliery garden.

To ride on these cars is always an adventure. Since we are in war-time, the drivers are men unfit for active service: cripples and hunchbacks. So they have the spirit of the devil in them. The ride becomes a steeplechase. Hurray! we have leapt in a clear jump over the canal bridges—now for the four-lane corner. With a shriek and a trail of sparks we are clear again. To be sure, a tram often leaps the rails—but what matter! It sits in a ditch till other trams come to haul it out. It is quite common for a car, packed with one solid mass of living people, to come to a dead halt in the midst of unbroken blackness, the heart of nowhere on a dark night, and for the driver and the girl conductor to call: "All get off—car's on fire!" Instead, however, of rushing out in a panic, the passengers stolidly reply: "Get on—get on! We're not coming out. We're stopping where we are. Push on, George." So till flames actually appear.

The reason for this reluctance to dismount is that the nights are howlingly cold, black, and windswept, and a car is a haven of refuge. From village to village the miners travel, for a change of cinema, of girl, of pub. The trams are desperately packed. Who is going to risk himself in the black gulf outside, to wait perhaps an hour for another tram, then to see the forlorn notice "Depot Only," because there is something wrong! Or to greet a unit of three bright cars all so tight with people that they sail past with a howl of derision. Trams that pass in the night.

This, the most dangerous tram-service in England, as the authorities themselves declare, with pride, is entirely conducted by girls, and driven by rash young men, a little crippled, or by delicate young men, who creep forward in terror. The girls are fearless young hussies. In their ugly blue uniform, skirts up to their knees, shapeless old peaked caps on their heads, they have all the *sang-*

"Tickets, Please" from *The Collected Stories of D. H. Lawrence*, Vol. II. Copyright 1922 by Thomas B. Seltzer. Copyright renewed 1950 by Frieda Lawrence. Reprinted by permission of Viking Penguin Inc., Laurence Pollinger Limited and the Estate of Frieda Lawrence Ravagli.

froid[1] of an old non-commissioned officer. With a tram packed with howling colliers, roaring hymns downstairs and a sort of antiphony of obscenities upstairs, the lasses are perfectly at their ease. They pounce on the youths who try to evade their ticket-machine. They push off the men at the end of their distance. They are not going to be done in the eye—not they. They fear nobody—and everybody fears them.

"Hello, Annie!"

"Hello, Ted!"

"Oh, mind my corn, Miss Stone. It's my belief you've got a heart of stone, for you've trod on it again."

"You should keep it in your pocket," replies Miss Stone, and she goes sturdily upstairs in her high boots.

"Tickets, please."

She is peremptory, suspicious, and ready to hit first. She can hold her own against ten thousand. The step of that tram-car is her Thermopylae.[2]

Therefore, there is a certain wild romance aboard these cars—and in the sturdy bosom of Annie herself. The time for soft romance is in the morning, between ten o'clock and one, when things are rather slack: that is, except marketday and Saturday. Thus Annie has time to look about her. Then she often hops off her car and into a shop where she has spied something, while the driver chats in the main road. There is very good feeling between the girls and the drivers. Are they not companions in peril, shipmates aboard this careering vessel of a tram-car, forever rocking on the waves of a stormy land.

Then, also, during the early hours, the inspectors are most in evidence. For some reason, everybody employed in this tram-service is young: there are no grey heads. It would not do. Therefore the inspectors are of the right age, and one, the chief, is also good-looking. See him stand on a wet, gloomy morning, in his long oilskin, his peaked cap well down over his eyes, waiting to board a car. His face ruddy, his small brown moustache is weathered, he has a faint impudent smile. Fairly tall and agile, even in his waterproof, he springs aboard a car and greets Annie.

"Hello, Annie! Keeping the wet out?"

"Trying to."

There are only two people in the car. Inspecting is soon over. Then for a long and impudent chat on the foot-board, a good, easy, twelve-mile chat.

The inspector's name is John Thomas Raynor—always called John Thomas, except sometimes, in malice, Coddy. His face sets in fury when he is addressed, from a distance, with this abbreviation. There is considerable scandal about John Thomas in half a dozen villages. He flirts with the girl conductors in the morning, and walks out with them in the dark night, when they leave their tram-car at the depot. Of course, the girls quit the service frequently. Then he flirts and walks out with the newcomer: always providing she is sufficiently attractive, and that she will consent to walk. It is remarkable, however, that most of the girls are quite comely, they are all young, and this roving life aboard the car gives them a sailor's dash and recklessness. What matter how they behave when the ship is in port? Tomorrow they will be aboard again.

Annie, however, was something of a Tartar, and her sharp tongue had kept John Thomas at arm's length for many months. Perhaps, therefore, she liked him all the more: for he always came up smiling, with impudence. She watched him vanquish one girl, then another. She could tell by the movement of his mouth and eyes, when he flirted with her in the morning, that he had been walking out with this lass, or the other, the night before. A fine cock-of-the-walk he was. She could sum him up pretty well.

In this subtle antagonism they knew each other like old friends, they were as shrewd with one another almost as man and wife. But Annie had always kept him sufficiently at arm's length. Besides, she had a boy of her own.

The Statutes fair, however, came in November,

---

1. *sang-froid* (säN frwȧ′), calmness, composure; literally, "cold blood." [French]

2. *Thermopylae* (ther mop′ə lē), a narrow mountain pass in Greece where in 480 B.C. a small force (principally Spartans) held off a huge army of Persians.

at Bestwood. It happened that Annie had the Monday night off. It was a drizzling ugly night, yet she dressed herself up and went to the fairground. She was alone, but she expected soon to find a pal of some sort.

The roundabouts were veering round and grinding out their music, the side-shows were making as much commotion as possible. In the coconut shies there were no coconuts, but artificial wartime substitutes, which the lads declared were fastened into the irons. There was a sad decline in brilliance and luxury. None the less, the ground was muddy as ever, there was the same crush, the press of faces lighted up by the flares and the electric lights, the same smell of naphtha and a few fried potatoes, and of electricity.

Who should be the first to greet Miss Annie on the showground but John Thomas. He had a black overcoat buttoned up to his chin, and a tweed cap pulled down over his brows, his face between was ruddy and smiling and handy as ever. She knew so well the way his mouth moved.

She was very glad to have a "boy." To be at the Statutes without a fellow was no fun. Instantly, like the gallant he was, he took her on the Dragons, grim-toothed, roundabout switchbacks. It was not nearly so exciting as a tram-car actually. But, then, to be seated in a shaking, green dragon, uplifted above the sea of bubble faces, careering in a rickety fashion in the lower heavens, whilst John Thomas leaned over her, his cigarette in his mouth, was after all the right style. She was a plump, quick, alive little creature. So she was quite excited and happy.

John Thomas made her stay on for the next round. And therefore she could hardly for shame repulse him when he put his arm round her and drew her a little nearer to him, in a very warm and cuddly manner. Besides, he was fairly discreet, he kept his movement as hidden as possible. She looked down, and saw that his red, clean hand was out of sight of the crowd. And they knew each other so well. So they warmed up to the fair.

After the dragons they went on the horses. John Thomas paid each time, so she could but be complaisant. He, of course, sat astride on the outer horse—named "Black Bess"—and she sat sideways, towards him, on the inner horse—named "Wildfire." But of course John Thomas was not going to sit discreetly on "Black Bess," holding the brass bar. Round they spun and heaved, in the light. And round he swung on his wooden steed, flipping one leg across her mount, and perilously tipping up and down, across the space, half lying back, laughing at her. He was perfectly happy; she was afraid her hat was on one side, but she was excited.

He threw quoits on a table, and won for her two large, pale blue hat-pins. And then, hearing the noise of the cinemas, announcing another performance, they climbed the boards and went in.

Of course, during these performances pitch darkness falls from time to time, when the machine goes wrong. Then there is a wild whooping, and a loud smacking of simulated kisses. In these moments John Thomas drew Annie towards him. After all, he had a wonderfully warm, cozy way of holding a girl with his arm, he seemed to make such a nice fit. And, after all, it was pleasant to be so held: so very comforting and cozy and nice. He leaned over her and she felt his breath on her hair; she knew he wanted to kiss her on the lips. And, after all, he was so warm and she fitted in to him so softly. After all, she wanted him to touch her lips.

But the light sprang up; she also started electrically, and put her hat straight. He left his arm lying nonchalantly behind her. Well, it was fun, it was exciting to be at the Statutes with John Thomas.

When the cinema was over they went for a walk across the dark, damp fields. He had all the arts of love-making. He was especially good at holding a girl, when he sat with her on a stile in the black, drizzling darkness. He seemed to be holding her in space, against his own warmth and gratification. And his kisses were soft and slow and searching.

So Annie walked out with John Thomas, though she kept her own boy dangling in the distance. Some of the tram-girls chose to be huffy. But there, you must take things as you find them in this life.

There was no mistake about it, Annie liked John

Thomas a good deal. She felt so rich and warm in herself whenever he was near. And John Thomas really liked Annie, more than usual. The soft, melting way in which she could flow into a fellow, as if she melted into his very bones, was something rare and good. He fully appreciated this.

But with a developing acquaintance there began a developing intimacy. Annie wanted to consider him a person, a man: she wanted to take an intelligent interest in him, and to have an intelligent response. She did not want a mere nocturnal presence, which was what he was so far. And she prided herself that he could not leave her.

Here she made a mistake. John Thomas intended to remain a nocturnal presence; he had no idea of becoming an all-round individual to her. When she started to take an intelligent interest in him and his life and his character, he sheered off. He hated intelligent interest. And he knew that the only way to stop it was to avoid it. The possessive female was aroused in Annie. So he left her.

It is no use saying she was not surprised. She was at first startled, thrown out of her count. For she had been so *very* sure of holding him. For a while she was staggered, and everything became uncertain to her. Then she wept with fury, indignation, desolation, and misery. Then she had a spasm of despair. And then, when he came, still impudently, on to her car, still familiar, but letting her see by the movement of his head that he had gone away to somebody else for the time being, and was enjoying pastures new, then she determined to have her own back.

She had a very shrewd idea what girls John Thomas had taken out. She went to Nora Purdy. Nora was a tall, rather pale, but well-built girl, with beautiful yellow hair. She was rather secretive.

"Hey!" said Annie, accosting her; then softly: "Who's John Thomas on with now?"

"I don't know," said Nora.

"Why, tha does," said Annie, ironically lapsing into dialect. "Tha knows as well as I do."

"Well, I do, then," said Nora. "It isn't me, so don't bother."

A "clippie," one of the women conductors who replaced men during the First World War, in September, 1917.

"It's Cissy Meakin, isn't it?"

"It is, for all I know."

"Hasn't he got a face on him!" said Annie. "I don't half like his cheek. I could knock him off the foot-board when he comes round at me."

"He'll get dropped on one of these days," said Nora.

"Ay, he will, when somebody makes up their mind to drop it on him. I should like to see him taken down a peg or two, shouldn't you?"

"I shouldn't mind," said Nora.

"You've got quite as much cause to as I have," said Annie. "But we'll drop on him one of these days, my girl. What? Don't you want to?"

"I don't mind," said Nora.

But as a matter of fact, Nora was much more vindictive than Annie.

One by one Annie went the round of the old flames. It so happened that Cissy Meakin left the tramway service in quite a short time. Her mother made her leave. Then John Thomas was on the *qui vive*. He cast his eyes over his old flock. And his eyes lighted on Annie. He thought she would be safe now. Besides, he liked her.

She arranged to walk home with him on Sunday night. It so happened that her car would be in the depot at half-past nine: the last car would come in at 10:15. So John Thomas was to wait for her there.

At the depot the girls had a little waiting-room of their own. It was quite rough, but cozy, with a fire and an oven and a mirror, and table and wooden chairs. The half-dozen girls who knew John Thomas only too well had arranged to take service this Sunday afternoon. So, as the cars began to come in, early, the girls dropped into the waiting-room. And instead of hurrying off home, they sat around the fire and had a cup of tea. Outside was the darkness and lawlessness of wartime.

John Thomas came on the car after Annie, at about a quarter to ten. He poked his head easily into the girls' waiting-room.

"Prayer-meeting?" he asked.

"Ay," said Laura Sharp. "Ladies only."

"That's me!" said John Thomas. It was one of his favorite exclamations.

"Shut the door, boy," said Muriel Baggaley.

"Oh, which side of me?" said John Thomas.

"Which tha likes," said Polly Birkin.

He had come in and closed the door behind him. The girls moved in their circle, to make a place for him near the fire. He took off his greatcoat and pushed back his hat.

"Who handles the teapot?" he said.

Nora Purdy silently poured him out a cup of tea.

"Want a bit o' my bread and drippin'?" said Muriel Baggaley to him.

"Ay, give us a bit."

And he began to eat his piece of bread.

"There's no place like home, girls," he said.

They all looked at him as he uttered this piece of impudence. He seemed to be sunning himself in the presence of so many damsels.

"Especially if you're not afraid to go home in the dark," said Laura Sharp.

"Me! By myself I am."

They sat till they heard the last tram come in.

In a few minutes Emma Houselay entered.

"Come on, my old duck!" cried Polly Birkin.

"It *is* perishing," said Emma, holding her fingers to the fire.

"But—I'm afraid to, go home in, the dark," sang Laura Sharp, the tune having got into her mind.

"Who're you going with to-night, John Thomas?" asked Muriel Baggaley coolly.

"To-night?" said John Thomas. "Oh, I'm going home by myself to-night—all on my lonely-o."

"That's me!" said Nora Purdy, using his own ejaculation.

The girls laughed shrilly.

"Me as well, Nora," said John Thomas.

"Don't know what you mean," said Laura.

"Yes, I'm toddling," said he, rising and reaching for his overcoat.

"Nay," said Polly, "We're all here waiting for you."

"We've got to be up in good time in the morning," he said, in the benevolent official manner.

They all laughed.

"Nay," said Muriel, "Don't leave us all lonely, John Thomas. Take one!"

"I'll take the lot, if you like," he responded gallantly.

"That you won't, either," said Muriel. "Two's company; seven's too much of a good thing."

"Nay—take one," said Laura. "Fair and square, all above board and say which."

"Ay," cried Annie, speaking for the first time. "Pick, John Thomas; let's hear thee."

"Nay," he said. "I'm going home quiet tonight. Feeling good, for once."

"Whereabouts?" said Annie. "Take a good 'un, then. But tha's got to take one of us!"

"Nay, how can I take one," he said, laughing uneasily. "I don't want to make enemies."

"You'd only make *one*," said Annie.

"The chosen *one*," added Laura.

"Oh, my! Who said girls!" exclaimed John Thomas, again turning, as if to escape. "Well—goodnight."

"Nay, you've got to make your pick," said

Muriel. "Turn your face to the wall, and say which one touches you. Go on—we shall only just touch your back—one of us. Go on—turn your face to the wall, and don't look, and say which one touches you."

He was uneasy, mistrusting them. Yet he had not the courage to break away. They pushed him to a wall and stood him there with his face to it. Behind his back they all grimaced, tittering. He looked so comical. He looked around uneasily.

"Go on!" he cried.

"You're looking—you're looking!" they shouted.

He turned his head away. And suddenly, with a movement like a swift cat, Annie went forward and fetched him a box on the side of the head that sent his cap flying and himself staggering. He started round.

But at Annie's signal they all flew at him, slapping him, pinching him, pulling his hair, though more in fun than in spite or anger. He, however, saw red. His blue eyes flamed with strange fear as well as fury, and he butted through the girls to the door. It was locked. He wrenched at it. Roused, alert, the girls stood round and looked at him. He faced them, at bay. At that moment they were rather horrifying to him, as they stood in their short uniforms. He was distinctly afraid.

"Come on, John Thomas! Come on! Choose!" said Annie.

"What are you after? Open the door," he said.

"We shan't—not till you've chosen!" said Muriel.

"Chosen what?" he said.

"Chosen the one you're going to marry," she replied.

He hesitated a moment.

"Open the blasted door," he said, "and get back to your senses." He spoke with official authority.

"You've got to choose!" cried the girls.

"Come on!" cried Annie, looking him in the eye. "Come on! Come on!"

He went forward, rather vaguely. She had taken off her belt, and swinging it, she fetched him a sharp blow over the head with the buckle end. He sprang and seized her. But immediately the other girls rushed upon him, pulling and tearing and beating him. Their blood was now thoroughly up. He was their sport now. They were going to have their own back, out of him. Strange, wild creatures, they hung on him and rushed at him to bear him down. His tunic was torn right up the back. Nora had hold at the back of his collar, and was actually strangling him. Luckily the button burst. He struggled in a wild frenzy of fury and terror, almost mad terror. His tunic was simply torn off his back, his shirtsleeves were torn away, his arms were naked. The girls rushed at him, clenched their hands on him, and pulled at him: or they rushed at him and pushed him, butted him with all their might: or they struck him wild blows. He ducked and cringed and struck sideways. They became more intense.

At last he was down. They rushed on him, kneeling on him. He had neither breath nor strength to move. His face was bleeding with a long scratch, his brow was bruised.

Annie knelt on him, the other girls knelt and hung on to him. Their faces were flushed, their hair wild, their eyes were all glittering strangely. He lay at last quite still, with face averted, as an animal lies when it is defeated and at the mercy of the captor. Sometimes his eye glanced back at the wild faces of the girls. His breast rose heavily, his wrists were torn.

"Now, then, my fellow!" gasped Annie at length. "Now then—now—"

At the sound of her terrifying, cold triumph, he suddenly started to struggle as an animal might, but the girls threw themselves upon him with unnatural strength and power, forcing him down.

"Yes—now, then!" gasped Annie at length.

And there was a dead silence, in which the thud of heart-beating was to be heard. It was a suspense of pure silence in every soul.

"Now you know where you are," said Annie.

The sight of his white, bare arm maddened the girls. He lay in a kind of trance of fear and antagonism. They felt themselves filled with supernatural strength.

Suddenly Polly started to laugh—to giggle wildly—helplessly—and Emma and Muriel joined in. But Annie and Nora and Laura remained the same, tense, watchful, with gleaming eyes. He winced away from these eyes.

"Yes," said Annie, in a curious low tone, secret and deadly. "Yes! You've got it now. You know what you've done, don't you? You know what you've done."

He made no sound nor sign, but lay with bright, averted eyes, and averted, bleeding face.

"You ought to be *killed*, that's what you ought," said Annie, tensely. "You ought to be *killed*." And there was a terrifying lust in her voice.

Polly was ceasing to laugh, and giving long-drawn Oh-h-hs and sighs as she came to herself.

"He's got to choose," she said vaguely.

"Oh, yes, he has," said Laura, with vindictive decision.

"Do you hear—do you hear?" said Annie. And with a sharp movement, that made him wince, she turned his face to her.

"Do you hear?" she repeated, shaking him.

But he was quite dumb. She fetched him a sharp slap on the face. He started, and his eyes widened. Then his face darkened with defiance after all.

"Do you hear?" she repeated.

He only looked at her with hostile eyes.

"Speak!" she said, putting her face devilishly near his.

"What?" he said, almost overcome.

"You've got to *choose!*" she cried, as if it were some terrible menace, and as if it hurt her that she could not exact more.

"What?" he said, in fear.

"Choose your girl, Coddy. You've got to choose her now. And you'll get your neck broken if you play any more of your tricks, my boy. You're settled now."

There was a pause. Again he averted his face. He was cunning in his overthrow. He did not give in to them really—no, not if they tore him to bits.

"All right, then," he said. "I choose Annie." His voice was strange and full of malice. Annie let go of him as if he had been a hot coal.

"He's chosen Annie!" said the girls in chorus.

"Me!" cried Annie. She was still kneeling, but away from him. He was still lying prostrate, with averted face. The girls grouped uneasily around.

"Me!" repeated Annie, with a terrible bitter accent.

Then she got up, drawing away from him with strange disgust and bitterness.

"I wouldn't touch him," she said.

But her face quivered with a kind of agony, she seemed as if she would fall. The other girls turned aside. He remained lying on the floor, with his torn clothes and bleeding, averted face.

"Oh, if he's chosen—" said Polly.

"I don't want him—he can choose again," said Annie, with the same rather bitter hopelessness.

"Get up," said Polly, lifting his shoulder. "Get up."

He rose slowly, a strange, ragged, dazed creature. The girls eyed him from a distance, curiously, furtively, dangerously.

"Who wants him?" cried Laura, roughly.

"Nobody," they answered, with contempt. Yet each one of them waited for him to look at her, hoped he would look at her. All except Annie, and something was broken in her.

He, however, kept his face closed and averted from them all. There was a silence of the end. He picked up the torn pieces of his tunic, without knowing what to do with them. The girls stood about uneasily, flushed, panting, tidying their hair and their dress unconsciously, and watching him. He looked at none of them. He espied his cap in a corner, and went and picked it up. He put it on his head, and one of the girls burst into a shrill, hysterical laugh at the sight he presented. He, however, took no heed, but went straight to where his overcoat hung on a peg. The girls moved away from contact with him as if he had been an electric wire. He put on his coat and buttoned it down. Then he rolled his tunic-rags into a bundle, and stood before the locked door, dumbly.

"Open the door, somebody," said Laura.

"Annie's got the key," said one.

Annie silently offered the key to the girls. Nora unlocked the door.

"Tit for tat, old man," she said. "Show yourself a man, and don't bear a grudge."

But without a word or sign he had opened the door and gone, his face closed, his head dropped.

"That'll learn him," said Laura.

"Coddy!" said Nora.

"Shut up, for God's sake!" cried Annie fiercely, as if in torture.

"Well, I'm about ready to go, Polly. Look sharp!" said Muriel.

The girls were all anxious to be off. They were tidying themselves hurriedly, with mute, stupefied faces.

1922

THINK AND DISCUSS

Understanding

1. During World War I, who were the drivers and conductors on the Midlands system?
2. What "mistake" does Annie make that causes John Thomas to drop her as a girlfriend?
3. What do the girls tell John Thomas he must do before they let him go?

Analyzing

4. Describe the **mood** and **tone** created by the first few paragraphs.
5. What marked change is there in the **style** and tone of the closing episode?
6. What indications are given that, in each other, John Thomas and Annie have found their match?
7. What does the fact that the story is set in wartime and the girls wear uniforms have to do with the events of the story?
8. Does John Thomas deserve the harsh treatment he endures at the hands of his former girlfriends? Is he ever in real danger?
9. At the end of the story, why do the six girls behave so strangely after they have succeeded in humiliating John Thomas?

Extending

10. Why do you think Annie refuses John Thomas after he selects her? What does the narrator mean by "something was broken in her"?
11. How do the characters and events of the story reflect the changing status of women in twentieth-century life? What, in your opinion, do Annie, Nora Purdy, and the other girls have in common with militant feminists today?

COMPOSITION

Writing a Description

In "Tickets, Please," Lawrence uses strong verbs in portraying action, such as the reckless motion of the tram-car and the girls' fight with John Thomas. Write a description of three to four paragraphs in which you portray a scene of intense action, such as a sporting event, a rock concert, a street brawl, a baby-sitting crisis. First describe the setting of the action. Then describe the event itself, using verbs that show the action. Conclude by describing the aftermath of the event. Read your paper aloud to a classmate to detect any descriptions needing more extensive detail.

Writing a Dialogue

Write a scene that might take place between Annie and John Thomas the morning after the girls attack him. While he has promised to marry her, Annie is also the woman responsible for the physical and psychological abuse he has suffered. Before writing, think carefully what mood you wish to establish. Would John Thomas be angry? humbled? revengeful? Would Annie be embarrassed? frightened? ashamed? In your dialogue, have the characters review the events of the previous night and the reasons for the girls' hostility. Then have them discuss their future together. How will the past evening's events affect their relationship? Set up your dialogue as for a play, with stage directions in parentheses.

The Piano

D. H. Lawrence

"The Piano" comes from a notebook containing drafts of early poems.
It is an early version of the poem eventually published as "Piano" in
Lawrence's *New Poems* (1918).

Somewhere beneath that piano's superb
   sleek black
Must hide my mother's piano, little and
   brown, with the back
That stood close to the wall, and the front's
   faded silk both torn,
And the keys with little hollows, that my
   mother's fingers had worn.

5 Softly, in the shadows, a woman is singing
   to me
Quietly, through the years I have crept back
   to see
A child sitting under the piano, in the boom
   of the shaking strings
Pressing the little poised feet of the mother
   who smiles as she sings.

The full throated woman has chosen a
   winning, living song
10 And surely the heart that is in me must belong
To the old Sunday evenings, when darkness
   wandered outside
And hymns gleamed on our warm lips, as we
watched mother's fingers glide.

Or this is my sister at home in the old front
   room
Singing love's first surprised gladness, alone
   in the gloom.
15 She will start when she sees me, and
   blushing, spread out her hands
To cover my mouth's raillery, till I'm bound
   in her shame's heart-spun bands.

A woman is singing me a wild Hungarian air
And her arms, and her bosom, and the
   whole of her soul is bare,
And the great black piano is clamoring as
   my mother's never could clamor
20 And my mother's tunes are devoured of this
   music's ravaging glamor.

"The Piano" and "Piano" from *The Complete Poems of D. H. Lawrence* edited by Vivian de Sola Pinto and Warren Roberts. Copyright © 1964 by Angelo Ravagli and C. M. Weekley, Executors of the Estate of Frieda Lawrence Ravagli. Reprinted by permission of Viking Penguin Inc., Laurence Pollinger Ltd. and the Estate of Mrs. Frieda Lawrence Ravagli.

The Piano Lesson by Malcolm Drummond (1880–1945). *Art Gallery of South Australia, Adelaide*

Piano

D. H. Lawrence

Softly, in the dusk, a woman is singing to me;
Taking me back down the vista of years, till
    I see
A child sitting under the piano, in the boom
    of the tingling strings
And pressing the small, poised feet of a
    mother who smiles as she sings.

5 In spite of myself, the insidious mastery of
    song
Betrays me back, till the heart of me weeps
    to belong
To the old Sunday evenings at home, with
    winter outside
And hymns in the cozy parlor, the tinkling
    piano our guide.

So now it is vain for the singer to burst into
    clamor
10 With the great black piano appassionato.
    The glamor
Of childish days is upon me, my manhood is
    cast
Down in the flood of remembrance, I weep
    like a child for the past.

                                1918

Snake

D. H. Lawrence

A snake came to my water-trough
On a hot, hot day, and I in pajamas for the
    heat,
To drink there.

In the deep, strange-scented shade of the
    great dark carob-tree
5 I came down the steps with my pitcher
And must wait, must stand and wait, for
    there he was at the trough before me.

He reached down from a fissure in the earth-
    wall in the gloom
And trailed his yellow-brown slackness soft-
    bellied down, over the edge of the stone
    trough
And rested his throat upon the stone bottom,
10 And where the water had dripped from the
    tap, in a small clearness,

He sipped with his straight mouth,
Softly drank through his straight gums, into
    his slack long body,
Silently.

Someone was before me at my water-trough,
15 And I, like a second comer, waiting.

He lifted his head from his drinking, as cattle
    do,
And looked at me vaguely, as drinking cattle
    do,
And flickered his two-forked tongue from his
    lips, and mused a moment,

From *The Complete Poems of D. H. Lawrence* edited by Vivian de Sola Pinto and Warren Roberts. Copyright © 1964 by Angelo Ravagli and C. M. Weekley, Executors of the Estate of Frieda Lawrence Ravagli. Reprinted by permission of Viking Penguin Inc., Laurence Pollinger Ltd. and the Estate of Mrs. Freida Lawrence Ravagli.

And stooped and drank a little more,
20 Being earth-brown, earth-golden from the
     burning bowels of the earth
On the day of Sicilian July, with Etna[1]
     smoking.

The voice of my education said to me
He must be killed,
For in Sicily the black, black snakes are
     innocent, the gold are venomous.

25 And voices in me said, If you were a man
You would take a stick and break him now,
     and finish him off.
But must I confess how I liked him,
How glad I was he had come like a guest in
     quiet, to drink at my water-trough
And depart peaceful, pacified, and
     thankless,
30 Into the burning bowels of this earth?

Was it cowardice, that I dared not kill him?
Was it perversity, that I longed to talk to him?
Was it humility, to feel so honored?
I felt so honored.

35 And yet those voices:
If you were not afraid, you would kill him!

And truly I was afraid, I was most afraid,
But even so, honored still more
That he should seek my hospitality
40 From out the dark door of the secret earth.

He drank enough
And lifted his head, dreamily, as one who
     has drunken,
And flickered his tongue like a forked night
     on the air, so black;
Seeming to lick his lips,
45 And looked around like a god, unseeing, into
     the air,
And slowly turned his head,
And slowly, very slowly, as if thrice adream,
Proceeded to draw his slow length curving
     round

And climb again the broken bank of my wall-
     face.

50 And as he put his head into that dreadful
     hole,
And as he slowly drew up, snake-easing his
     shoulders, and entered farther,
A sort of horror, a sort of protest against his
     withdrawing into that horrid black hole,
Deliberately going into the blackness, and
     slowly drawing himself after,
Overcame me now his back was turned.

55 I looked round, I put down my pitcher,
I picked up a clumsy log
And threw it at the water-trough with a
     clatter.

I think it did not hit him.
But suddenly that part of him that was left
     behind convulsed in undignified haste,
60 Writhed like lightning, and was gone
Into the black hole, the earth-lipped fissure
     in the wall-front,
At which, in the intense still noon, I stared
     with fascination.

And immediately I regretted it.
I thought how paltry, how vulgar, what a
     mean act!
65 I despised myself and the voices of my
     accursed human education.

And I thought of the albatross,[2]
And I wished he would come back, my
     snake.

For he seemed to me again like a king,
Like a king in exile, uncrowned in the
     underworld,

---

1. Etna, an active volcano on the Mediterranean island
of Sicily.
2. the albatross, an allusion to Coleridge's *Rime of the
Ancient Mariner*, in which a sailor shoots an albatross, a
large sea bird, and is cursed for it.

₇₀ Now due to be crowned again.

And so, I missed my chance with one of the
    lords
Of life.

And I have something to expiate;
A pettiness.

Taormina.[3]
1923

---

3. *Taormina* (tä ôr mē′nä), an ancient town on the east
coast of Sicily, where Lawrence was living in July, 1912,
when the incident recorded in this poem took place.

Intimates

D. H. Lawrence

Don't you care for my love? she said
    bitterly.

I handed her the mirror, and said:
Please address these questions to the proper
    person!
Please make all requests to head-quarters!
₅ In all matters of emotional importance
please approach the supreme authority
    direct!—
So I handed her the mirror.

And she would have broken it over my
    head,
but she caught sight of her own reflection
₁₀ and that held her spellbound for two seconds
while I fled.

1932

From *The Complete Poems of D. H. Lawrence* edited by Vivian
de Sola Pinto and Warren Roberts. Copyright © 1964 by Angelo
Ravagli and C. M. Weekley, Executors of the Estate of Frieda
Lawrence Ravagli. Reprinted by permission of Viking Penguin
Inc., Laurence Pollinger Ltd. and the Estate of Mrs. Frieda
Lawrence Ravagli.

THINK AND DISCUSS
THE PIANO *and* **PIANO**
Understanding
1. What episode is the basis of both versions of
   this poem?
2. Where did the speaker like to sit when his
   mother played the piano?
3. What character included in "The Piano" has
   been omitted in "Piano"?

Analyzing
4. How does the speaker's representation of his
   feelings differ in these two versions?
5. How do the two poems differ in **mood**?

THE SNAKE
Understanding
1. In Sicily, which snakes are venomous? Which
   are harmless?

2. What is the "mean act" that the speaker immediately regrets?

Analyzing
3. What is the speaker's internal conflict as he watches the snake drinking at the water-trough?
4. Why does the speaker feel more "honored" than "afraid" by the visit of the snake?
5. How do the speaker's feelings change as he observes the snake drink and withdraw into "that horrid black hole"?
6. Explain what the speaker means by the last two lines.
7. What sound devices suggest the movement of the snake?
8. Point out instances where the snake is **personified**. What is the effect of this personification?

Extending
9. The poem dramatizes the conflict between how we are taught to think about certain creatures and how we actually feel in their presence. What does the poem imply about the proper relationship of human beings to the natural world?

INTIMATES
Understanding
1. What prevents the woman from breaking the mirror over the speaker's head?

Analyzing
2. What criticism of the woman is implied by the speaker's words and actions?
3. Does the poem offer any proof that the speaker's criticism of the woman is justified?
4. What is the **tone** of the poem?
5. To what two sets of "intimates" does the title refer?

Extending
6. In your opinion, does this poem describe a lovers' quarrel or the end of a relationship? What would have to happen before intimacy could be re-established?

COMPOSITION ◄━━
Writing a Personal Narrative
Everyone has hidden fears—of snakes, spiders, heights, crowded places, and so on—that create inner terror and need to be confronted and overcome. In a narrative of four to six paragraphs, tell about your most fearful phobia. Provide an account of the events that made you acquire this fear, and then explain what efforts you have taken to overcome it. The use of humor and personal anecdotes will lend interest and appeal to your narrative.

Analyzing the Writer's Craft
"The Piano" is an early version of the poem eventually published as "Piano." In a paper of three to five paragraphs, compare these two poems, pointing out significant revisions Lawrence has made in word choice, **imagery, point of view, rhythm, tone,** and organization. First reread the poems several times and draw up a list of revisions. Your thesis should state that you intend to explain how, through revision, Lawrence has succeeded in producing a better poem than he started with. In this kind of comparative analysis, it is wise to proceed from the general to the specific; that is, first take up such overall matters as organization of ideas, events described, and point of view, and then move on to specific differences in word choice, imagery, rhythm, and tone. See "Writing About Poetry and Poetic Devices" in the Writer's Handbook.

Following World War I, writers such as T. S. Eliot, W. H. Auden, Dylan Thomas, and their followers brought about a revolution in poetic taste and practice. Like the painters influenced by cubism and abstract expressionism or composers influenced by the atonal works of Stravinsky, Schoenberg, and Bartok, "modernist" poets developed new techniques to express their vision of the post-war world. While some of their works are admittedly difficult, modern poetry as a whole employs the language of common speech to provide rich insights into the people and events of modern life. Here are some guidelines to help you as you study the modern poets.

Use the footnotes. Intellectual complexity, allusiveness, and intricacy of form are all characteristics of modern poetry. In your reading you are likely to come across lines from foreign languages or allusions you don't recognize. For example, some of Eliot's poems, such as "The Hollow Men," have epigraphs that need to be interpreted and applied to the poem. W. H. Auden, in his elegy "In Memory of W. B. Yeats," presumes knowledge of the life of Yeats and political events of the 1930s. The footnotes help by providing such information.

Expect innovative use of language. Modern poets have sought to use language that is fresh, exact, and innovative. In "Fern Hill," for example, Dylan Thomas, rejecting cliché, writes "once below a time" instead of "once upon a time" and "All the moon long" instead of "All the night long." He speaks of the "lilting house" and "whinnying green stable," using adjectives that describe the inhabitants instead of the places being named. He also invents new words as they serve his purpose, as in "windfall light," to suggest a waterfall of light carried on the currents of the wind.

Identify the speaker and tone. Remember that the "I" of the poem is not necessarily the poet,

but rather a *persona* through whom the experience of the poem is being conveyed. With any poem that uses the pronoun "I," such as Eliot's "Journey of the Magi," try to establish the age, social status, and character traits of the speaker. Ask yourself: Why has the poet chosen this particular person to narrate the poem? Then pinpoint the tone—the author's attitude toward the subject matter and audience. You can expect that the tone of much of twentieth-century poetry will be ironic, satiric, or pessimistic.

Savor the sounds, images, and surprises. Modern poetry is musical, sensual, and surprising. It is also highly varied in subject matter. Modern poets have exercised the freedom to write about any subject they please, from bullfrogs (Ted Hughes) to drowning (Stevie Smith). To compensate for the limitations of syllabic rhyme, they have resorted to frequent use of consonantal, assonantal, and half-rhymes. Thomas's "Fern Hill," for example, utilizes assonantal rhymes throughout. Modern poets have sought above all to create poetry that will not only "mean," but "be"—that is, be appreciated for its form and music as well as meaning.

Read the poem aloud. Since modern poetry was crafted to be *heard* as well as read, performing the poem is the best way to get at its meaning. Listening to the readings of others can also be helpful. Whenever possible, obtain recordings of the poets reading their own works. You will gain invaluable insights into what interpretations the writers intended.

Draw your own conclusions. Try to read *holistically*, allowing the images of the poem "to fall into the memory successively," as Eliot advised; that is, let the images accumulate to form a total impression. Then you can draw a conclusion about what these images collectively suggest, or else formulate a generalization about the overall idea they lead you to.

On June 21, 1917, the *Times Literary Supplement* reviewed *Prufrock and Other Observations*, a volume of poems by T. S. Eliot, an American who had recently settled in London; the reviewer was unenthusiastic. Thirty-one years later, Eliot was awarded the Nobel Prize. During the intervening years he had emerged as the pivotal figure of modern English literature, the person most directly responsible for changing the course of literary style and taste. He did this through his poetry and plays, works like *The Waste Land* (1922) and *Murder in the Cathedral* (1935), which reflected disillusionment with commercial values and hunger for spiritual revitalization. He did this as well through his work as critic, editor, and publisher. He founded an influential literary journal, *The Criterion*, in 1922, and seven years later became a director of the publishers Faber and Faber, where he introduced the work of W. H. Auden (see pages 840–846).

Eliot famously defined his beliefs as "classicist in literature, royalist in politics, and Anglo-Catholic in religion." In his criticism he discussed his distaste for romanticism and "self-expression," never wavering in his insistence that poetry is "art"—something deliberately crafted and therefore a *patterning* of feeling rather than the feelings themselves. He turned away from the Romantics and Victorians and toward Shakespeare, the metaphysical poets of the seventeenth century, and the nineteenth-century French Symbolists, all of whom he preferred for their use of "common speech," precise sensory images, and ironic wit. While Eliot's poetry is often difficult, at times overly dry, confusingly allusive, and disconnected, every word and phrase has been calculated to directly *reveal*, rather than *explain*, an idea or emotion.

"The Love Song of J. Alfred Prufrock" was written while Eliot was still a student at Harvard. He did graduate work at Harvard, the Sorbonne in Paris, and Oxford, then settled in London, becoming a British subject in 1917. Though his writings attracted attention from the start, because of financial pressures he taught school for a time, later worked in a bank, and in 1925 joined the publishing firm of Faber and Gwyer (later Faber and Faber). During his later years, fame led Eliot into the thick of editing and publishing, though he remained personally shy, aloof, and reclusive.

Eliot's recurrent theme is the sense of loss; in the words of one critic, "the lost vision, the lost purpose, the lost meaning, the lost sense of fellowship, the lost sense of self." In 1927 Eliot became a convert to the Anglican church, and in his later poetry, most impressively in *Ash Wednesday* (1930) and *Four Quartets* (1943), he turned to the theme of spiritual recovery and renewal. His verse dramas, such as *Murder in the Cathedral, The Family Reunion* (1939), and *The Cocktail Party* (1950), contain fine passages but lack characterization and genuine dramatic vitality.

HT See FREE VERSE in the Handbook of Literary Terms, page 908.

The Hollow Men   T. S. Eliot

Mistah Kurtz—he dead.[1]
A penny for the Old Guy[2]

I

We are the hollow men
We are the stuffed men
Leaning together
Headpiece filled with straw. Alas!
5   Our dried voices, when
We whisper together
Are quiet and meaningless
As wind in dry grass
Or rats' feet over broken glass
10   In our dry cellar

Shape without form, shade without color,
Paralyzed force, gesture without motion;

Those who have crossed
With direct eyes,[3] to death's other Kingdom[4]
15   Remember us—if at all—not as lost
Violent souls, but only
As the hollow men
The stuffed men.

II

Eyes[5] I dare not meet in dreams
20   In death's dream kingdom
These do not appear:
There, the eyes are
Sunlight on a broken column
There, is a tree swinging
25   And voices are
In the wind's singing
More distant and more solemn
Than a fading star.

Let me be no nearer
30   In death's dream kingdom
Let me also wear
Such deliberate disguises
Rat's coat, crowskin, crossed staves
In a field[6]
35   Behaving as the wind behaves
No nearer—

Not that final meeting
In the twilight kingdom

---

1. ***Mistah Kurtz—he dead.*** Eliot's first epigraph is a quotation from Joseph Conrad's novella *Heart of Darkness.* Kurtz is a European trader who goes into "the heart of darkness"—the central African jungle—with European standards of life and conduct. Because he has no moral or spiritual strength to sustain him, he soon turns into a barbarian. He differs, however, from Eliot's "hollow men"; he is not paralyzed, as they are, but commits acts of overwhelming evil; and he is not blind as they are, but at his death glimpses the nature of his actions when he exclaims, "The horror! The horror!" Kurtz is thus one of the "lost/Violent souls" mentioned in lines 15-16.
2. ***A penny . . . Guy,*** traditional cry of English children soliciting money for fireworks to celebrate Guy Fawkes Day, November 5, which commemorates the thwarting of the Gunpowder Plot of 1605 in which Guy Fawkes and other conspirators planned to blow up both Houses of Parliament. On this day straw-stuffed images of Fawkes called *guys* are burned.
3. ***Those . . . direct eyes,*** those who have represented something positive (direct), either for good or evil.
4. ***death's other Kingdom,*** the afterlife; eternity.
5. ***Eyes,*** the eyes of those in the afterworld who had confident faith; those who represent positive spiritual force as opposed to the spiritual stagnation or paralysis of the "hollow men."
6. ***Rat's coat . . . in a field,*** a scarecrow decorated with dead rats and crows.

III

This is the dead land
40 This is cactus land
Here the stone images
Are raised, here they receive
The supplication of a dead man's hand
Under the twinkle of a fading star.

45 Is it like this
In death's other kingdom
Waking alone
At the hour when we are
Trembling with tenderness
50 Lips that would kiss
Form prayers to broken stone.

IV

The eyes are not here
There are no eyes here
In this valley of dying stars
55 In this hollow valley
This broken jaw of our lost kingdoms

In this last of meeting places
We grope together
And avoid speech
60 Gathered on this beach of the tumid river

Sightless, unless
The eyes reappear
As the perpetual star
Multifoliate rose[7]
65 Of death's twilight kingdom
The hope only
Of empty men.

V

Here we go round the prickly pear
Prickly pear prickly pear
70 *Here we go round the prickly pear*
At five o'clock in the morning.[8]

Between the idea
And the reality
Between the motion
75 And the act
Falls the Shadow
            For Thine is the Kingdom[9]

Between the conception
And the creation
80 Between the emotion
And the response
Falls the Shadow
            Life is very long

Between the desire
85 And the spasm
Between the potency
And the existence
Between the essence
And the descent
90 Falls the Shadow
            For Thine is the Kingdom

For Thine is
Life is
For Thine is the

95 *This is the way the world ends*
This is the way the world ends
This is the way the world ends
Not with a bang but a whimper.

                                    1925

---

7. Multifoliate rose, in Dante's *Divine Comedy* a symbol
of Paradise, in which the saints are the many petals of
the rose.
8. Here we go . . . morning, a parody of the children's
rhyme "Here we go round the mulberry bush."
9. For Thine . . . Kingdom, a phrase from the Lord's
Prayer.

Reader's Note

"The Hollow Men"

In "The Hollow Men" all the richness and complexity of culture which gives *The Waste Land* such thickness of texture disappears. The poem takes place in a twilight realm of disembodied men and forces. The complexity of relations making up the subjective realm of Eliot's ideal descriptions of it is replaced by the vagueness and impalpability of "Shape without form, shade without color, / Paralyzed force, gesture without motion." The hollow men are walking corpses ("Mistah Kurtz—he dead"), and their emptiness is the vacuity of pure mind detached from any reality. They are cut off from one another. Their voices are whispers, "quiet and meaningless." Groping together, they "avoid speech." They are detached from nature, and live in a place which is devoid of any spiritual presence, a "dead land," a "cactus land," a "valley of dying stars," hollow like the men themselves. The eyes of the hollow men are not only averted from one another, but from those other eyes, the returning look from the divine place which those who cross "with direct eyes" to "death's other Kingdom" will encounter. There are no eyes in the hollow valley, and the empty men are bereft of God. Even within their own hollowness detachment is the law. The "Shadow" which falls between idea and reality, conception and creation, emotion and response, desire and spasm, potency and existence, is the paralysis which seizes men who live in a completely subjective world. Mind had seemed the medium which binds all things together in the unity of an organic culture. Now it is revealed to be the Shadow which isolates things from one another, reduces them to abstraction, and makes movement, feeling, and creativity impossible. "The Hollow Men" is an eloquent analysis of the vacuity of subjective idealism, and the state of the hollow men appears in Eliot's later work as the "distraction, delusion, escape into dream, pretense" of the unenlightened people in his plays, each one of whom is a "fugitive from reality."

From *Poets of Reality* by J. Hillis Miller. Published by the Belknap Press of Harvard University Press. Copyright © 1965 by the President and Fellows of Harvard College. Reprinted by permission of the publisher.

Journey of the Magi T. S. Eliot

"A cold coming we had of it,
Just the worst time of the year
For a journey, and such a long journey:
The ways deep and the weather sharp,
5 The very dead of winter."[1]
And the camels galled, sore-footed,
   refractory,
Lying down in the melting snow.
There were times we regretted
The summer palaces on slopes, the terraces,
10 And the silken girls bringing sherbet.
Then the camel men cursing and grumbling
And running away, and wanting their liquor
   and women,
And the night-fires going out, and the lack
   of shelters,
And the cities hostile and the towns
   unfriendly
15 And the villages dirty and charging high prices:
A hard time we had of it.
At the end we preferred to travel all night,
Sleeping in snatches,
With the voices singing in our ears, saying
20 That this was all folly.

Then at dawn we came down to a temperate
   valley,
Wet, below the snow line, smelling of
   vegetation,
With a running stream and a water-mill beating
   the darkness,
And three trees on the low sky.
25 And an old white horse galloped away in the
   meadow.
Then we came to a tavern with vine-leaves over the
   lintel,
Six hands at an open door dicing for pieces
   of silver,
And feet kicking the empty wine-skins.[2]

But there was no information, and so we
   continued
30 And arrived at evening, not a moment too
   soon
Finding the place; it was (you may say)
   satisfactory.

All this was a long time ago, I remember,
And I would do it again, but set down
This set down
35 This: were we led all that way for
Birth or Death? There was a Birth, certainly,
We had evidence and no doubt. I had seen
   birth and death,
But had thought they were different; this
   Birth was
Hard and bitter agony for us, like Death,
   our death.
40 We returned to our places, these Kingdoms,
But no longer at ease here, in the old
   dispensation,[3]
With an alien people clutching their gods.
I should be glad of another death.

1927

Magi, the "wise men from the east" who journeyed to
Bethlehem to see the infant Jesus. (Matthew 2:1–12)
1. *"A cold . . . winter,"* adapted from a nativity sermon
by the seventeenth-century preacher Lancelot Andrewes
(1555–1626).
2. *Then at dawn . . . wineskins.* Images in this passage
suggest both renewal of life ("vegetation"; "running
stream") and death, foreshadowing events in the life of
Jesus. The "three trees" suggest the Crucifixion; the men
"dicing for pieces of silver" recall both the thirty pieces
of silver received by Judas for betraying Jesus and the
gambling of the soldiers for Jesus' garments at the foot of
the Cross. The white horse is mentioned in Revelation 6:2
and 19:11 in passages alluding to the end of the world.
3. *the old dispensation,* the old pagan religion.

THINK AND DISCUSS
THE HOLLOW MEN
Understanding
1. To what are the hollow men compared in section I?
2. What is the relationship of the speaker to the hollow men?
3. What does the speaker seek to avoid by adopting disguises (in line 32)?
4. How does the world end for the hollow men?

Analyzing
5. According to section I, how do those who have crossed "With direct eyes" to eternity remember the hollow men?
6. What indication is there in section II that the speaker, like the other hollow men, has given up the struggle to revitalize his life?
7. In sections III and IV, what elements of the physical environment reflect the emotional and spiritual emptiness of the hollow men?
8. What is the only hope for their regeneration?
9. What is meant by the "Shadow" to which the poem repeatedly refers? What is the effect of this "Shadow" on such human actions as thinking, creating, and feeling?
10. What do the fragments of the Lord's Prayer and the parody of "Here we go round the mulberry bush" suggest about the spiritual condition of the hollow men?
11. How are the hollow men shown to be unlike Mistah Kurtz and the Old Guy mentioned in the epigraph?

Extending
12. Why do you think Eliot chose to portray people of the post-World War I era as "hollow men"? What criticism of modern life is intended? Do you think that Eliot, if he were writing today, would hold a similar view of society?

READING LITERATURE SKILLFULLY
Conclusions/Generalizations

When you let images accumulate to form a total impression, then you can draw a conclusion about what impression these images collectively suggest or formulate a generalization about the overall idea they lead you to. In "The Hollow Men," for example, appear many images of eyes. The eyes of the narrator and the other hollow men are averted and, later, sightless, as opposed to the "direct eyes" of those of confident faith. A logical conclusion to be drawn from these cumulative images is that the hollow men are spiritually blind.

1. What images of dryness and sterility do you find in "The Hollow Men"?
2. What conclusion can you draw from the many comparisons of the hollow men to scarecrows?
3. What conclusion can you draw from the prevalence of unfinished sentences in section V?

THINK AND DISCUSS
JOURNEY OF THE MAGI
Understanding
1. Who is the speaker? How old does he appear to be?
2. To what kind of life have the travelers been accustomed?
3. After returning from their journey, how do the travelers feel about being back home in their kingdoms?

Analyzing
4. The speaker's account falls into three distinct parts. What are they?
5. What makes the journey so physically arduous and emotionally taxing?
6. What is **symbolically** suggested by the change of **setting** in lines 21–24?

7. Why does the speaker say, "this Birth was/Hard and bitter agony for us, like Death, our death"? But why then does he also say of his journey he "would do it again" (line 33)?
8. Why are the words *Birth* and *Death* capitalized in lines 36 and 38–39, but not elsewhere in the last stanza?
9. What does the speaker mean when he says in the last line that he "should be glad of another death"?

Extending
10. Is this poem simply a retelling of the biblical story of the Three Wise Men? What else might the travelers and their journey represent?

APPLYING: Free Verse H🖋
See Handbook of Literary Terms, p. 908

Free verse is a type of poetry that differs from conventional verse forms in being "free" from a fixed pattern of meter and rhyme. Free verse may employ a wide variety of sound devices, **repetition, imagery,** figures of speech, and **symbolism** to create a poetic effect. Free verse is also highly rhythmic, with lines arranged in tightly organized rhythmic patterns.

1. Point out instances in "Journey of the Magi" where the poetic lines form thoughts.
2. Where has Eliot employed **consonance** and **alliteration** to reinforce the meaning of the lines?
3. Where has repetition been used in the poem, and for what purpose?

COMPOSITION ◄━━▸
Writing a Character Sketch

"The Hollow Men" is a devastating portrayal of human beings devoid of spiritual substance. In a paper of five to seven paragraphs, portray a person you regard as the direct *oppo-site* of "the hollow men"—an individual who is forceful, productive, and admirable in character and achievement. First list traits and accomplishments that make this individual especially admirable. In your thesis statement, mention those outstanding qualities and achievements you intend to portray. Then take up each item in order, illustrating them with appropriate anecdotes. Save discussion of this person's most outstanding trait for your conclusion.

Analyzing Eliot's Irony

"Journey of the Magi" is a highly ironic poem that transforms a celebrated story of wonder and joy into quite a different kind of experience. In three to five paragraphs, write an analysis of the ironic aspects of this poem. Start by describing the events and tone of the biblical story of the "three wise men." (You may wish to research this by reading Matthew 2:1–12.) Then describe Eliot's treatment of the story, stressing in what ways he departs from other versions. In your conclusion, discuss the lasting impact of the experience on the travelers. What special meaning is contained in Eliot's ironic version of the story?

ENRICHMENT
Choral Reading

The poems of T. S. Eliot lend themselves especially well to reading aloud. Eliot himself recorded much of his poetry and was acclaimed for his distinctive readings. As a class, prepare a choral reading of "The Hollow Men." Start by determining which sections of the poem should be read by solo voices and which by combined voices or the entire chorus. Try to capture the multiple rhythms of the poem and vary tempo and vocal tone to match the shifting moods. After careful rehearsal, make a tape recording to play for other classes. If possible, listen to Eliot's reading of the poem to decide whether any changes should be made in your interpretation.

BIOGRAPHY

W. H. Auden
1907–1973

Auden's career as a poet was a complex and influential one. From its confused, precocious beginnings in the 1920s (while he was still an undergraduate), Auden's poetry evolved through political commitment during the 1930s and '40s, to religious reflection in his later years. For more than four decades his poetry succeeded in capturing the horrors, anxieties, and hopes of the times. It was Auden who characterized the 1930s as a "low, dishonest decade" and most memorably crystallized the mood of social dissatisfaction and impending crisis that prevailed during the years leading up to the outbreak of World War II. The postwar period has come to be known as "The Age of Anxiety," from the title of a volume of his poems published in 1948.

He was born in York, the son of a distinguished physician who moved his family to Birmingham when Auden was a year old. He enjoyed a stable and comfortable childhood and acquired an interest in science (at one time intending to be a mining engineer). He was educated at Oxford where he had a great influence on a number of his fellow undergraduates, including Louis MacNeice, Stephen Spender, and C. Day Lewis. This group shared a need to create new poetic techniques to express a heightened social consciousness and a zeal for political reform.

After graduating from Oxford in 1928, Auden spent a year in Berlin, where he was strongly influenced by contemporary German literature, particularly the work of the Marxist poet and playwright Bertolt Brecht. During the early 1930s Auden taught school in England and Scotland. In 1937 he went to Spain, where he drove an ambulance for the Republicans (those loyal to Spain's leftist government). He later recalled this visit as the beginning of his disillusionment with the left and his return to Christianity.

In 1939 Auden settled in the United States, becoming an American citizen in 1946. Beginning in 1948, he divided his time between New York and Europe, summering first on the Italian island of Ischia and later in Austria. During this period Auden spent much of his time editing, translating, and collaborating with his friend the American poet Chester Kallman on a series of opera libretti. He was elected Professor of Poetry at Oxford in 1956. In 1972 he transferred his winter residence from New York to Oxford, where his old college had provided him with a small house. He died in Vienna in 1973.

Auden delighted in playing with words, in employing a variety of rhythms, and in creating striking literary effects. But he was also insistent that "Art is not enough": poetry must also fulfill a moral function, principally that of dispelling hate and promoting love. "Poetry is not concerned with telling people what to do," he once wrote, "but with extending our knowledge of good and evil . . . leading us to the point where it is possible for us to make a rational moral choice."

The Unknown Citizen   W. H. Auden

(To JS/07/M/378
This Marble Monument
Is Erected by the State)

He was found by the Bureau of Statistics to be
One against whom there was no official
    complaint,
And all the reports on his conduct agree
That, in the modern sense of an old-
    fashioned word, he was a saint,
5 For in everything he did he served the
    Greater Community.
Except for the War till the day he retired
He worked in a factory and never got fired,
But satisfied his employers, Fudge Motors Inc.
Yet he wasn't a scab[1] or odd in his views,
10 For his Union reports that he paid his dues,
(Our report on his Union shows it was sound)
And our Social Psychology workers found
That he was popular with his mates and liked
    a drink.
The Press are convinced that he bought a
    paper every day
15 And that his reactions to advertisements
    were normal in every way.
Policies taken out in his name prove that he
    was fully insured,
And his Health-card shows he was once in
    hospital but left it cured.
Both Producers Research and High-Grade
    Living declare
He was fully sensible to the advantages of
    the Instalment Plan
20 And had everything necessary to the Modern
    Man,
A phonograph, a radio, a car and a frigidaire.
Our researchers into Public Opinion are content
That he held the proper opinions for the time
    of year;
When there was peace, he was for peace;
    when there was war, he went.

Drawing by Modell; © 1977, The New Yorker Magazine, Inc.

25 He was married and added five children to
    the population,
Which our Eugenist[2] says was the right
    number for a parent of his generation.
And our teachers report that he never
    interfered with their education.
Was he free? Was he happy? The question
    is absurd:
Had anything been wrong, we should
    certainly have heard.

1940

---

1. *scab,* worker who will not join a labor union or who takes a striker's job.
2. *Eugenist,* an expert in eugenics, the science of improving the human race by a careful selection of parents in order to breed healthier and more intelligent children.

Who's Who   W. H. Auden

A shilling life[1] will give you all the facts:
How Father beat him, how he ran away,
What were the struggles of his youth, what
    acts
Made him the greatest figure of his day:
5 Of how he fought, fished, hunted, worked
    all night,
Though giddy, climbed new mountains; named
    a sea;
Some of the last researchers even write
Love made him weep his pints like you and me.

With all his honors on, he sighed for one

10 Who, say astonished critics, lived at home;
Did little jobs about the house with skill
And nothing else; could whistle; would sit
    still
Or potter round the garden; answered some
Of his long marvellous letters but kept none.

                                    1936

Musée des Beaux Arts   W. H. Auden

About suffering they were never wrong,
The Old Masters; how well they understood
Its human position; how it takes place
While someone else is eating or opening a
    window or just walking dully along;
5 How, when the aged are reverently,
    passionately waiting
For the miraculous birth, there always must
    be
Children who did not specially want it to
    happen, skating
On a pond at the edge of the wood:
They never forgot
10 That even the dreadful martyrdom must run
    its course
Anyhow in a corner, some untidy spot
Where the dogs go on with their doggy life
    and the torturer's horse
Scratches its innocent behind on a tree.

In Brueghel's *Icarus*,[1] for instance: how
    everything turns away
15 Quite leisurely from the disaster; the

    ploughman may
Have heard the splash, the forsaken cry,
But for him it was not an important failure;
    the sun shone
As it had to on the white legs disappearing
    into the green
Water; and the expensive delicate ship that
    must have seen
20 Something amazing, a boy falling out of the sky,
Had somewhere to get to and sailed calmly on.

                                    1940

The Fall of Icarus by Pieter Brueghel the Elder (1525?–1569). *Musée Royaux des Beaux-Arts de Belgique, Brussels*

In Memory of W. B. Yeats (*d. Jan. 1939*) **W. H. Auden**

1

He disappeared in the dead of winter:
The brooks were frozen, the airports almost
  deserted,
And snow disfigured the public statues;
The mercury sank in the mouth of the dying
  day.
5 O all the instruments agree
The day of his death was a dark cold day.

Far from his illness
The wolves ran on through the evergreen
  forests,

The peasant river was untempted by the
  fashionable quays;
10 By mourning tongues
The death of the poet was kept from his
  poems.

But for him it was his last afternoon as
  himself,
An afternoon of nurses and rumors;
The provinces of his body revolted,
15 The squares of his mind were empty,
Silence invaded the suburbs,

The current of his feeling failed: he became
    his admirers.

Now he is scattered among a hundred cities
And wholly given over to unfamiliar affections;
20 To find his happiness in another kind of wood
And be punished under a foreign code of
    conscience.
The words of a dead man
Are modified in the guts of the living.

But in the importance and noise of tomorrow
25 When the brokers are roaring like beasts on
    the floor of the Bourse,[1]
And the poor have the sufferings to which
    they are fairly accustomed,
And each in the cell of himself is almost
    convinced of his freedom;
A few thousand will think of this day
As one thinks of a day when one did
    something slightly unusual.
30 O all the instruments agree
The day of his death was a dark cold day.

2
You were silly like us: your gift survived it all;
The parish of rich women, physical decay,
Yourself; mad Ireland hurt you into poetry.
35 Now Ireland has her madness and her
    weather still,
For poetry makes nothing happen: it survives
In the valley of its saying where executives
Would never want to tamper; it flows south
From ranches of isolation and the busy griefs,
40 Raw towns that we believe and die in; it
    survives,
A way of happening, a mouth.

3
Earth, receive an honored guest;
William Yeats is laid to rest:
Let the Irish vessel lie
45 Emptied of its poetry.

Time that is intolerant

Of the brave and innocent,
And indifferent in a week
To a beautiful physique,

50 Worships language and forgives
Everyone by whom it lives;
Pardons cowardice, conceit,
Lays its honors at their feet.

Time that with this strange excuse
55 Pardoned Kipling and his views,
And will pardon Paul Claudel,[2]
Pardons him for writing well.

In the nightmare of the dark
All the dogs of Europe bark,
60 And the living nations wait,
Each sequestered in its hate;

Intellectual disgrace
Stares from every human face,
And the seas of pity lie
65 Locked and frozen in each eye.

Follow, poet, follow right
To the bottom of the night,
With your unconstraining voice
Still persuade us to rejoice;

70 With the farming of a verse
Make a vineyard of the curse,
Sing of human unsuccess
In a rapture of distress;

In the deserts of the heart
75 Let the healing fountains start,
In the prison of his days
Teach the free man how to praise.

1940

---

1. *Bourse* (bûrs), the stock exchange in Paris.
2. *Kipling . . . Claudel.* Kipling and the French poet
and playwright Paul Claudel (1868-1955) were both criticized for their violently right-wing views.

THINK AND DISCUSS

THE UNKNOWN CITIZEN

Understanding

1. What **setting** is suggested by the epigraph? How is the Unknown Citizen referred to in these lines?
2. For what kinds of conformist behavior is the Unknown Citizen praised?
3. According to the poem, what things are "necessary to the Modern Man"?

Analyzing

4. Why was no official complaint ever brought against the Unknown Citizen?
5. The poem profiles both a person and a society. What kind of world did the Unknown Citizen inhabit?
6. What aspects of this society are most bitingly **satirized**?
7. What literary devices have been used to create the satiric effect?
8. In the next-to-last line the speaker asks, "Was he free? Was he happy?" Judging from the **tone** of the poem, is the answer given by the speaker one that the poet endorses?
9. Explain the double meaning of "Unknown" in the title.

Extending

10. In your opinion, how strong is the pressure for conformity in today's society? In what areas of life is this pressure most noticeable?

WHO'S WHO

Understanding

1. What degree of fame would a reference book like *Who's Who* say the man described in the poem had achieved in his lifetime?

Analyzing

2. Lines 1–8 deal with the public personality of a great man; lines 9–14 deal with someone else. Who is this second person, and what kind of life does this person lead?

3. Why might the great man sigh for this person and write "long marvellous letters" to him or her?
4. What did the other person do with the famous man's letters? Why?
5. What is the **paradox** in this sonnet?
6. Explain the ambiguity and **irony** of the title.

Extending

7. Judging from the clues given in the poem, what do you think made the great man strive so hard for fame? Does achieving it appear to have given him what he sought?

MUSÉE DES BEAUX ARTS

Understanding

1. According to the first stanza, what also takes place while individuals are suffering, as in childbirth or martyrdom?

Analyzing

2. What truth about human suffering does the speaker feel that the Old Masters illustrate in their paintings?
3. How does Brueghel's painting *The Fall of Icarus* illustrate this truth?

Extending

4. Why do you think Auden chose the name of a famous Belgian art museum for his title? Does it seem appropriate for what he has to say?

IN MEMORY OF W. B. YEATS

Understanding

1. What was the public reaction to the death of W. B. Yeats?
2. According to section 3, what generally happens to the reputation of a great writer after death?

Analyzing

3. The traditional **elegy** exalts the memory of the dead person and suggests that even nature is temporarily altered by this person's

death. What details about the day of Yeats's death and the effect on the general public reveal this poem to be an "anti-elegy"?

4. What shift in **point of view** occurs in section 2?
5. What contrast is drawn between the poet's life and his work?
6. What grim political and social conditions of the Europe of 1939 does the poem point out?
7. What role does the speaker suggest the poet should assume in the modern world?

Extending

8. What, in your opinion, is more important: how a person lived or what that person wrote or created? Should the details of a person's life influence our feelings about his or her creative accomplishments?

THINKING SKILLS
Synthesizing

To synthesize is to put together parts and elements so as to form a whole. Synthesis can involve personal experience. For example, it was Auden who synthesized historical events, the work of other authors, and his own experiences to name the period after World War II "the Age of Anxiety."

1. What do you think were some of the elements Auden synthesized in order to come up with that name?
2. What would you name the period you are living in?

COMPOSITION
Writing an Essay of Definition

People sometimes speak of themselves as "just your average citizen," or "an ordinary guy." How do you refer to your peers? How do you label someone who is "out," as opposed to someone who is "in"? Choose a term used in your school, social circle, or community to designate a certain type of person or group of people. In a paper of three to five paragraphs, define it and give illustrations. To develop your ideas, start by offering a general definition of the type of person you have chosen. Then go on to describe the characteristic appearance, dress, personality traits, and behavior. You may find that telling what a person is *not* is a good way of pointing up what that person actually is.

Writing a Satirical Elegy

In "The Unknown Citizen" Auden creates a satirical elegy to criticize certain modern values. Write an elegy of your own, in the style of Auden's, in which you attack some aspect of contemporary life of which you disapprove. Topics such as the national obsession with thinness, the commercialization of holidays, urban blight, violence in the media, or corruption in government would be appropriate targets. When you have decided what you will criticize, create a character to elegize who has done those things. Remember that your task is to condemn through the use of ironic praise. Your readers should be able to recognize from the start that what you say is the opposite of what you mean.

Themes IN ENGLISH LITERATURE

The Inner Life

Writers of earlier times shared with their readers a common value system and sense of what was significant in human life. This helped determine their choice of subjects and themes as well as their methods of expression. In contrast, the modern age has witnessed the disintegration of a public background of belief, and it is their own personal visions of life and reality that modern writers express. When asked, "What is reality?," Virginia Woolf responded, "It would seem to be something very erratic, very undependable—now to be found in a dusty road, now in a scrap of newspaper in the street, now a daffodil in the sun. It lights up a group in a room and stamps some casual saying." (1922) Reality is thus perceived as dependent on an individual's mood or reactions at a given moment. The task of writers, Woolf implies, is to chart the pluralistic universe that lives inside them.

This personalized view of reality has resulted in significant changes in the subject matter and style of modern poetry and fiction. It has led to the creation of works concerned foremost with the exploration of the moods, thoughts, and feelings of individuals—their inner life.

One important consequence of this emphasis has been a departure from formally plotted narratives to stories that are virtually plotless. For example, stories such as Joyce's "Araby" and "Eveline" and Woolf's "The New Dress" contain little action, but build up *epiphanies*, or moments of intense personal revelation. Not *what* happens, but *how* the character feels about an experience is what is regarded as most important.

There has also been a departure from older notions of time. Where time was once seen as moving in a straight line, from one event to another, twentieth-century writers have come to think of it as a continual blend of past with present. Virginia Woolf's novel *Mrs. Dalloway* deals with the events of only a single day, yet reveals all that is relevant about the past of the characters by examining the ways in which present consciousness is colored by retrospective memory.

Efforts to portray the inner life have also contributed to an enhanced awareness of the complexity of the human personality. Beneath the public mask she wears, Mabel Waring, in Woolf's "The New Dress," is portrayed as a seething cauldron of conflicting feelings of love, hate, self-pity, anger, jealousy, hopefulness, and despair.

Both heroes and villains become dwarfed under such intensive scrutiny. As the critic David Daiches remarked, "If we come too close to our hero his heroism dissolves." To lay open a character's inner life is to show this person as fallible, vulnerable, even pitiable. The emergence of the "anti-hero" in modern literature is an inevitable consequence of this kind of revelation of individuals as they really are.

To depict complex psychological experiences, modern writers search for new sources of symbolism, imagery, and modes of expression. Joyce's *Ulysses* and *Finnegan's Wake* exemplify such verbal inventiveness, along with Eliot's "The Waste Land," with its use of mythical, Christian, oriental, and anthropological imagery.

Other important consequences have been the increased importance placed on the search for identity and a heightened sense of the difficulties humans face in the quest for love or permanent relationships. A great many of the interior landscapes of modern literature, not surprisingly, are painted in somber hues, portraying moods of loneliness, inadequacy, emptiness, and loss. As such portrayals of the inner life invariably reveal, the face one puts on or meets is never what it seems.

BIOGRAPHY

Frank O'Connor

1903–1966

In his autobiography, *An Only Child*, Frank O'Connor traces his life from his birth in a slum in Cork to his release in 1923 from imprisonment as a revolutionary during the civil war that followed the establishment of the Irish Free State two years earlier. Born Michael O'Donovan, his early life was hard, unhappy, and poverty-stricken. His father was a laborer, his mother a cleaning woman, and lack of money a perpetual problem. O'Connor states that he received no education worth mentioning. Nevertheless, he was able to look back on his Irish childhood with humor and compassion—qualities that are dominant in most of his stories.

O'Connor learned Gaelic from his grandmother, and his knowledge of this language enabled him to collaborate with William Butler Yeats on translations of Gaelic poems. He began writing as a boy, but was undecided whether to become a painter or a writer. He abandoned painting, he claimed, because it was too expensive. O'Connor toured Ireland on a bicycle, thereby becoming more intimately acquainted with the manners and speech of the Irish people and storing up scenes and subjects that would later appear in his many stories. Of these stories, Yeats once said, "O'Connor was doing for Ireland what Chekhov did for Russia."

O'Connor served for several years as director of the Abbey Theatre, and became a member of the Irish Academy of Letters. In 1952 he moved permanently to the United States, where he published *The Stories of Frank O'Connor* and other collections, wrote for *The New Yorker*, and taught writing courses at Stanford, Harvard, and Northwestern. *The Lonely Voice* (1962) is a lucid and sensitive study of the short story that also reveals his talent as a teacher and critic.

My Oedipus Complex

Frank O'Connor

ather was in the army all through the war—the first war, I mean—so, up to the age of five, I never saw much of him, and what I saw did not worry me. Sometimes I woke and there was a big figure in khaki peering down at me in the candlelight. Sometimes in the early morning I heard the slamming of the front door and the clatter of nailed boots down the cobbles of the lane. These were Father's entrances and exits. Like Santa Claus he came and went mysteriously.

In fact, I rather liked his visits, though it was an uncomfortable squeeze between Mother and him when I got into the big bed in the early morning. He smoked, which gave him a pleasant musty smell, and shaved, an operation of astounding interest. Each time he left a trail of souvenirs—model tanks and Gurkha knives with handles made of bullet cases, and German helmets and cap badges and button-sticks, and all sorts of military equipment—carefully stowed away in a long box on top of the wardrobe, in case they ever came in handy. There was a bit of the magpie about Father; he expected everything to come in handy. When his back was turned, Mother let me get a chair and rummage through his treasures. She didn't seem to think so highly of them as he did.

The war was the most peaceful period of my life. The window of my attic faced southeast. My mother had curtained it, but that had small effect. I always woke with the first light and, with all the responsibilities of the previous day melted, feeling myself rather like the sun, ready to illumine and rejoice. Life never seemed so simple and clear and full of possibilities as then. I put my feet out from under the clothes—I called them Mrs. Left and Mrs. Right—and invented dramatic situations for them in which they discussed the problems of the day. At least Mrs. Right did; she was very demonstrative, but I hadn't the same control of Mrs. Left, so she mostly contented herself with nodding agreement.

They discussed what Mother and I should do during the day, what Santa Claus should give a fellow for Christmas, and what steps should be taken to brighten the home. There was that little matter of the baby, for instance. Mother and I could never agree about that. Ours was the only house in the terrace without a new baby, and Mother said we couldn't afford one till Father came back from the war because they cost seventeen and six. That showed how simple she was. The Geneys up the road had a baby, and everyone knew they couldn't afford seventeen and six. It was probably a cheap baby, and Mother wanted something really good, but I felt she was too exclusive. The Geneys' baby would have done us fine.

Having settled my plans for the day, I got up, put a chair under the attic window, and lifted the frame high enough to stick out my head. The window overlooked the front gardens of the terrace behind ours, and beyond these it looked over a deep valley to the tall, red-brick houses terraced up the opposite hillside, which were all still in shadow, while those at our side of the valley were all lit up, though with long strange shadows that made them seem unfamiliar; rigid and painted.

After that I went into Mother's room and climbed into the big bed. She woke and I began to tell her of my schemes. By this time, though I never seem to have noticed it, I was petrified in my nightshirt, and I thawed as I talked until, the last frost melted, I fell asleep beside her and woke

---

Oedipus (ed′ə pəs, ē′də pəs) ***Complex,*** (in psychoanalysis) a strong childhood attachment for the parent of the opposite sex, often accompanied by a feeling of rivalry, hostility, or fear toward the other parent.

again only when I heard her below in the kitchen, making the breakfast.

After breakfast we went into town; heard Mass at St. Augustine's and said a prayer for Father, and did the shopping. If the afternoon was fine we either went for a walk in the country or a visit to Mother's great friend in the convent, Mother St. Dominic. Mother had them all praying for Father, and every night, going to bed, I asked God to send him back safe from the war to us. Little, indeed, did I know what I was praying for!

One morning, I got into the big bed, and there, sure enough, was Father in his usual Santa Claus manner, but later, instead of uniform, he put on his best blue suit, and Mother was as pleased as anything. I saw nothing to be pleased about, because, out of uniform, Father was altogether less interesting, but she only beamed, and explained that our prayers had been answered, and off we went to Mass to thank God for having brought Father safely home.

The irony of it! That very day when he came in to dinner he took off his boots and put on his slippers, donned the dirty old cap he wore about the house to save him from colds, crossed his legs, and began to talk gravely to Mother, who looked anxious. Naturally, I disliked her looking anxious, because it destroyed her good looks, so I interrupted him.

"Just a moment, Larry!" she said gently.

This was only what she said when we had boring visitors, so I attached no importance to it and went on talking.

"Do be quiet, Larry!" she said impatiently. "Don't you hear me talking to Daddy?"

This was the first time I had heard those ominous words, "talking to Daddy," and I couldn't help feeling that if this was how God answered prayers, he couldn't listen to them very attentively.

"Why are you talking to Daddy?" I asked with as great a show of indifference as I could muster.

"Because Daddy and I have business to discuss. Now, don't interrupt again!"

In the afternoon, at Mother's request, Father took me for a walk. This time we went into town instead of out to the country, and I thought at first, in my usual optimistic way, that it might be an improvement. It was nothing of the sort. Father and I had quite different notions of a walk in town. He had no proper interest in trams, ships, and horses, and the only thing that seemed to divert him was talking to fellows as old as himself. When I wanted to stop he simply went on, dragging me behind him by the hand; when he wanted to stop I had no alternative but to do the same. I noticed that it seemed to be a sign that he wanted to stop for a long time whenever he leaned against a wall. The second time I saw him do it I got wild. He seemed to be settling himself forever. I pulled him by the coat and trousers, but, unlike Mother who, if you were too persistent, got into a wax and said: "Larry, if you don't behave yourself, I'll give you a good slap," Father had an extraordinary capacity for amiable inattention. I sized him up and wondered would I cry, but he seemed to be too remote to be annoyed even by that. Really, it was like going for a walk with a mountain! He either ignored the wrenching and pummeling entirely, or else glanced down with a grin of amusement from his peak. I had never met anyone so absorbed in himself as he seemed.

At teatime, "talking to Daddy" began again, complicated this time by the fact that he had an evening paper, and every few minutes he put it down and told Mother something new out of it. I felt this was foul play. Man for man, I was prepared to compete with him any time for Mother's attention, but when he had it all made up for him by other people it left me no chance. Several times I tried to change the subject without success.

"You must be quiet while Daddy is reading, Larry," Mother said impatiently.

It was clear that she either genuinely liked talking to Father better than talking to me, or else that he had some terrible hold on her which made her afraid to admit the truth.

"Mummy," I said that night when she was tucking me up, "do you think if I prayed hard God would send Daddy back to the war?"

She seemed to think about that for a moment.

"No, dear," she said with a smile. "I don't think

he would."

"Why wouldn't he, Mummy?"

"Because there isn't a war any longer, dear."

"But, Mummy, couldn't God make another war, if he liked?"

"He wouldn't like to, dear. It's not God who makes wars, but bad people."

"Oh!" I said.

I was disappointed about that. I began to think that God wasn't quite what he was cracked up to be.

Next morning I woke at my usual hour, feeling like a bottle of champagne. I put out my feet and invented a long conversation in which Mrs. Right talked of the trouble she had with her own father till she put him in the Home. I didn't quite know what the Home was but it sounded the right place for Father. Then I got my chair and stuck my head out of the attic window. Dawn was just breaking, with a guilty air that made me feel I had caught it in the act. My head bursting with stories and schemes, I stumbled in next door, and in the half-darkness scrambled into the big bed. There was no room at Mother's side so I had to get between her and Father. For the time being I had forgotten about him, and for several minutes I sat bolt upright, racking my brains to know what I could do with him. He was taking up more than his fair share of the bed, and I couldn't get comfortable, so I gave him several kicks that made him grunt and stretch. He made room all right, though. Mother waked and felt for me. I settled back comfortably in the warmth of the bed with my thumb in my mouth.

"Mummy!" I hummed, loudly and contentedly.

"Sssh! dear," she whispered. "Don't wake Daddy!"

This was a new development, which threatened to be even more serious than "talking to Daddy." Life without my early-morning conferences was unthinkable.

"Why?" I asked severely.

"Because poor Daddy is tired."

This seemed to me a quite inadequate reason, and I was sickened by the sentimentality of her "poor Daddy." I never liked that sort of gush; it always struck me as insincere.

"Oh!" I said lightly. Then in my most winning tone: "Do you know where I want to go with you today, Mummy?"

"No, dear," she sighed.

"I want to go down the Glen and fish for thornybacks with my new net, and then I want to go out to the Fox and Hounds, and—"

"Don't-wake-Daddy!" she hissed angrily, clapping her hand across my mouth.

But it was too late. He was awake, or nearly so. He grunted and reached for the matches. Then he stared incredulously at his watch.

"Like a cup of tea, dear?" asked Mother in a meek, hushed voice I had never heard her use before. It sounded almost as though she were afraid.

"Tea?" he exclaimed indignantly. "Do you know what the time is?"

"And after that I want to go up the Rathcooney Road," I said loudly, afraid I'd forget something in all those interruptions.

"Go to sleep at once, Larry!" she said sharply.

I began to snivel. I couldn't concentrate, the way that pair went on, and smothering my early-morning schemes was like burying a family from the cradle.

Father said nothing, but lit his pipe and sucked it, looking out into the shadows without minding Mother or me. I knew he was mad. Every time I made a remark Mother hushed me irritably. I was mortified. I felt it wasn't fair; there was even something sinister in it. Every time I had pointed out to her the waste of making two beds when we could both sleep in one, she had told me it was healthier like that, and now here was this man, this stranger, sleeping with her without the least regard for her health!

He got up early and made tea, but though he brought Mother a cup he brought none for me.

"Mummy," I shouted, "I want a cup of tea, too."

"Yes, dear," she said patiently. "You can drink from Mummy's saucer."

That settled it. Either Father or I would have to leave the house. I didn't want to drink from

Mother's saucer; I wanted to be treated as an equal in my own home, so, just to spite her, I drank it all and left none for her. She took that quietly, too.

But that night when she was putting me to bed she said gently: "Larry, I want you to promise me something."

"What is it?" I asked.

"Not to come in and disturb poor Daddy in the morning. Promise?"

"Poor Daddy" again! I was becoming suspicious of everything involving that quite impossible man.

"Why?" I asked.

"Because poor Daddy is worried and tired and he doesn't sleep well."

"Why doesn't he, Mummy?"

"Well, you know, don't you, that while he was at the war Mummy got the pennies from the Post Office?"

"From Miss MacCarthy?"

"That's right. But now, you see, Miss MacCarthy hasn't any more pennies, so Daddy must go out and find us some. You know what would happen if he couldn't?"

"No," I said, "tell us."

"Well, I think we might have to go out and beg for them like the poor old woman on Fridays. We wouldn't like that, would we?"

"No," I agreed, "We wouldn't."

"So you'll promise not to come in and wake him?"

"Promise."

Mind you, I meant that. I knew pennies were a serious matter, and I was all against having to go out and beg like the old woman on Fridays. Mother laid out all my toys in a complete ring round the bed so that, whatever way I got out, I was bound to fall over one of them.

When I woke I remembered my promise all right. I got up and sat on the floor and played—for hours, it seemed to me. Then I got my chair and looked out the attic window for more hours. I wished it was time for Father to wake; I wished someone would make me a cup of tea. I didn't feel in the least like the sun; instead, I was bored and so very, very cold! I simply longed for the warmth and depth of the big featherbed.

At last I could stand it no longer. I went into the next room. As there was still no room at Mother's side I climbed over her and she woke with a start.

"Larry," she whispered, gripping my arm very tightly, "what did you promise?"

"But I did, Mummy," I wailed, caught in the very act. "I was quiet for ever so long."

"Oh, dear, and you're perished!" she said sadly, feeling me all over. "Now, if I let you stay will you promise not to talk?"

"But I want to talk, Mummy," I wailed.

"That has nothing to do with it," she said with a firmness that was new to me. "Daddy wants to sleep. Now, do you understand that?"

I understood it only too well. I wanted to talk, he wanted to sleep—whose house was it, anyway?

"Mummy," I said with equal firmness, "I think it would be healthier for Daddy to sleep in his own bed."

That seemed to stagger her, because she said nothing for a while.

"Now, once for all," she went on, "you're to be perfectly quiet or go back to your own bed. Which is it to be?"

The injustice of it got me down. I had convicted her out of her own mouth of inconsistency and unreasonableness, and she hadn't even attempted to reply. Full of spite, I gave Father a kick, which she didn't notice but which made him grunt and open his eyes in alarm.

"What time is it?" he asked in a panic-stricken voice, not looking at Mother but the door, as if he saw someone there.

"It's early yet," she replied soothingly. "It's only the child. Go to sleep again. . . . Now, Larry," she added, getting out of bed, "you've wakened Daddy and you must go back."

This time, for all her quiet air, I knew she meant it, and knew that my principal rights and privileges were as good as lost unless I asserted them at once. As she lifted me, I gave a screech, enough to wake the dead, not to mind Father. He groaned.

"That damn child? Doesn't he ever sleep?"

"It's only a habit, dear," she said quietly,

Blarney Lane, Cork, Ireland, where Frank O'Connor lived as a child.

though I could see she was vexed.

"Well, it's time he got out of it," shouted Father, beginning to heave in the bed. He suddenly gathered all the bedclothes about him, turned to the wall, and then looked back over his shoulder with nothing showing only two small, spiteful, dark eyes. The man looked very wicked.

To open the bedroom door, Mother had to let me down, and I broke free and dashed for the farthest corner, screeching. Father sat bolt upright in bed.

"Shut up, you little puppy!" he said in a choking voice.

I was so astonished that I stopped screeching. Never, never had anyone spoken to me in that tone before. I looked at him incredulously and saw his face convulsed with rage. It was only then that I fully realized how God had codded me, listening to my prayers for the safe return of this monster.

"Shut up, you!" I bawled, beside myself.

"What's that you said?" shouted Father, making a wild leap out of bed.

"Mick, Mick!" cried Mother. "Don't you see the child isn't used to you?"

"I see he's better fed than taught," snarled Father, waving his arms wildly. "He wants his bottom smacked."

All his previous shouting was as nothing to these obscene words referring to my person. They really made my blood boil.

"Smack your own!" I screamed hysterically. "Smack your own! Shut up! Shut up!"

At this he lost his patience and let fly at me. He did it with the lack of conviction you'd expect of a man under Mother's horrified eyes, and it ended up as a mere tap, but the sheer indignity of being struck at all by a stranger, a total stranger who had cajoled his way back from the war into our big bed as a result of my innocent intercession, made me completely dotty. I shrieked and shrieked, and danced in my bare feet, and Father, looking awkward and hairy in nothing but a short grey army shirt, glared down at me like a mountain out for murder. I think it must have been then that I realized he was jealous too. And there stood Mother in her nightdress, looking as if her heart was broken between us. I hope she felt as she looked. It seemed to me that she deserved it all.

From that morning out my life was a hell. Father and I were enemies, open and avowed. We conducted a series of skirmishes against one another, he trying to steal my time with Mother and I his. When she was sitting on my bed, telling me a story, he took to looking for some pair of old boots which he alleged he had left behind him at the beginning of the war. While he talked to Mother I played loudly with my toys to show my total lack of concern. He created a terrible scene one evening when he came in from work and found me at his box, playing with his regimental badges, Gurkha knives and buttonsticks. Mother got up and took the box from me.

"You mustn't play with Daddy's toys unless he lets you, Larry," she said severely. "Daddy doesn't play with yours."

For some reason Father looked at her as if she had struck him and then turned away with a scowl.

"Those are not toys," he growled, taking down the box again to see had I lifted anything. "Some of those curios are very rare and valuable."

But as time went on I saw more and more how he managed to alienate Mother and me. What made it worse was that I couldn't grasp his method or see what attraction he had for Mother. In every possible way he was less winning than I. He had a common accent and made noises at his tea. I thought for a while that it might be the newspapers she was interested in, so I made up bits of news of my own to read to her. Then I thought it might be the smoking, which I personally thought attractive, and took his pipes and went round the house dribbling into them till he caught me. I even made noises at my tea, but Mother only told me I was disgusting. It all seemed to hinge round that

unhealthy habit of sleeping together, so I made a point of dropping into their bedroom and nosing round, talking to myself, so that they wouldn't know I was watching them, but they were never up to anything that I could see. In the end it beat me. It seemed to depend on being grownup and giving people rings, and I realized I'd have to wait.

But at the same time I wanted him to see that I was only waiting, not giving up the fight. One evening when he was being particularly obnoxious, chattering away and well above my head, I let him have it.

"Mummy," I said, "do you know what I'm going to do when I grow up?"

"No, dear," she replied. "What?"

"I'm going to marry you," I said quietly.

Father gave a great guffaw out of him, but he didn't take me in. I knew it must only be pretense. And Mother, in spite of everything, was pleased. I felt she was probably relieved to know that one day Father's hold on her would be broken.

"Won't that be nice?" she said with a smile.

"It'll be very nice," I said confidently. "Because we're going to have lots and lots of babies."

"That's right, dear," she said placidly. "I think we'll have one soon, and then you'll have plenty of company."

I was no end pleased about that because it showed that in spite of the way she gave in to Father she still considered my wishes. Besides, it would put the Geneys in their place.

It didn't turn out like that, though. To begin with, she was very preoccupied—I supposed about where she would get the seventeen and six—and though Father took to staying out late in the evenings it did me no particular good. She stopped taking me for walks, became as touchy as blazes, and smacked me for nothing at all. Sometimes I wished I'd never mentioned the confounded baby—I seemed to have a genius for bringing calamity on myself.

And calamity it was! Sonny arrived in the most appalling hullabaloo—even that much he couldn't do without a fuss—and from the first moment I disliked him. He was a difficult child—so far as I was concerned he was always difficult—and demanded far too much attention. Mother was simply silly about him, and couldn't see when he was only showing off. As company he was worse than useless. He slept all day, and I had to go round the house on tiptoe to avoid waking him. It wasn't any longer a question of not waking Father. The slogan now was "Don't-wake-Sonny!" I couldn't understand why the child wouldn't sleep at the proper time, so whenever Mother's back was turned I woke him. Sometimes to keep him awake I pinched him as well. Mother caught me at it one day and gave me a most unmerciful flaking.

One evening, when Father was coming in from work, I was playing trains in the front garden. I let on not to notice him; instead, I pretended to be talking to myself, and said in a loud voice: "If another bloody baby comes into this house, I'm going out."

Father stopped dead and looked at me over his shoulder.

"What's that you said?" he asked sternly.

"I was only talking to myself," I replied, trying to conceal my panic. "It's private."

He turned and went in without a word. Mind you, I intended it as a solemn warning, but its effect was quite different. Father started being quite nice to me. I could understand that, of course. Mother was quite sickening about Sonny. Even at mealtimes she'd get up and gawk at him in the cradle with an idiotic smile, and tell Father to do the same. He was always polite about it, but he looked so puzzled you could see he didn't know what she was talking about. He complained of the way Sonny cried at night, but she only got cross and said that Sonny never cried except when there was something up with him—which was a flaming lie, because Sonny never had anything up with him, and only cried for attention. It was really painful to see how simple-minded she was. Father wasn't attractive, but he had a fine intelligence. He saw through Sonny, and now he knew that I saw through him as well.

One night I woke with a start. There was someone beside me in the bed. For one wild moment I felt sure it must be Mother, having come to her senses and left Father for good, but then I heard Sonny in convulsions in the next room, and Mother saying: "There! There! There!" and I knew it wasn't she. It was Father. He was lying next to me, wide awake, breathing hard and apparently mad as hell.

After a while it came to me what he was mad about. It was his turn now. After turning me out of the big bed, he had been turned out himself. Mother had no consideration now for anyone but that poisonous pup, Sonny. I couldn't help feeling sorry for Father. I had been through it all myself, and even at that age I was magnanimous. I began to stroke him down and say: "There! There!" He wasn't exactly responsive.

"Aren't you asleep either?" he snarled.

"Ah, come on and put your arm around us, can't you?" I said, and he did, in a sort of way. Gingerly, I suppose, is how you'd describe it. He was very bony but better than nothing.

At Christmas he went out of his way to buy me a really nice model railway.

1952

THINK AND DISCUSS

Understanding

1. What is the basic source of conflict between father and son?
2. Why, according to the narrator, was the war "the most peaceful period" of his life?

Analyzing

3. What are some of the narrator's complaints about his father after he returns home?
4. What tactics does the child employ in the battle with his father for the mother's attention? How successful is he in these efforts?
5. What happens when the family triangle is squared by the arrival of Sonny?
6. What, precisely, is the **point of view?** How can you tell that, although the narrator is a child, the author is older?
7. Much of the humor in this story depends on the narrator's innocence and the **irony** that stems from his naivete. Give some key examples of this.

Extending

8. What does the title contribute to the overall effect of the story? Does it influence how you feel about the narrator?

COMPOSITION

Writing a Personal Essay

The relationship with a sibling (brother or sister) can be one of the most significant in a person's life. In a personal essay of five to eight paragraphs, describe the special relationship you share with a sibling. Tell what this person is like, what interests and values you share, and what experiences you regard as most memorable. Conclude by explaining what this relationship has contributed to your life and personal development.

Analyzing Sibling Rivalry

In an essay of four to six paragraphs that could be helpful to parents as well as peers, identify what you regard as major causes of sibling rivalry (aside from the jealousy typically aroused by the addition of a new child to a family). In your opinion, is it just a passing phase of childhood (as in O'Connor's story), or an experience that has lasting consequences in a person's life? What can parents do to prevent jealousy and resentment between siblings? Illustrate your discussion with examples from personal life and observation. Conclude by summing up the harmful effects you believe sibling rivalry can have on a person's emotional and psychological development.

Graham Greene
1904–

A great-nephew of Robert Louis Stevenson, Greene was the son of the headmaster of a school in Hertfordshire. He attended his father's school until, unhappy at the contrast between the comforts of his home life and the cruelties of the classroom, he ran away. He was sent for treatment to a psychoanalyst in whose London home he lived for six months, a period he later described as one of the happiest in his life.

Greene went to Oxford, publishing a book of poetry, *Babbling April* (1925), in the year he graduated. During the next two years he married, became a journalist (eventually joining the staff of the London *Times*), and converted to Roman Catholicism. After the publication of his first novel, *The Man Within* (1929), he left *The Times*, becoming a free-lance writer and reviewer.

Greene is both a prolific writer and an experienced traveler, and over the years his novels have been set in a number of exotic places: *Stamboul Train* (1932) on the Orient Express; *The Power and the Glory* (1940) in Mexico; *The Heart of the Matter* (1948) in Nigeria; *The Quiet American* (1956) in Vietnam; *A Burnt-Out Case* (1961) in Central Africa; *The Comedians* (1966) in Haiti; *The Honorary Consul* (1973) in Argentina.

Two important influences on Greene's writing have been his Catholicism and the cinema. As a Catholic, Greene reflects on his religious convictions and probes the nature of good and evil on both the personal and doctrinal level. Greene has done excellent work both as a film critic and as a screenwriter—*The Third Man* (1949)—and his narrative method and imagery often reveal the influence of the cinema.

Greene has made a classification of his fiction into "entertainments" and "novels." The former are, for the most part, literary thrillers, such as *A Gun for Sale* (1936), *The Ministry of Fear* (1943), and *The Third Man*. His more serious works, including *Brighton Rock* (1938), *The Power and the Glory*, *The Heart of the Matter*, *The End of the Affair* (1948), and *A Burnt-Out Case*, are set, in the words of one recent critic, in "hell . . . a hideously negative and at the same time vividly realized place." In Greene's world, evil is omnipresent, and he makes it felt. Both novels and entertainments are marked by careful plotting and characterization, and an economy and precision of language.

A Shocking Accident   Graham Greene

1

erome was called into his house-master's room in the break between the second and the third class on a Thursday morning. He had no fear of trouble, for he was a warden—the name that the proprietor and headmaster of a rather expensive preparatory school had chosen to give to approved, reliable boys in the lower forms[1] (from a warden one became a guardian and finally before leaving, it was hoped for Marlborough or Rugby,[2] a crusader). The housemaster, Mr. Wordsworth, sat behind his desk with an appearance of perplexity and apprehension. Jerome had the odd impression when he entered that he was a cause of fear.

"Sit down, Jerome," Mr. Wordsworth said. "All going well with the trigonometry?"

"Yes, sir."

"I've had a telephone call, Jerome. From your aunt. I'm afraid I have bad news for you."

"Yes, sir?"

"Your father has had an accident."

"Oh."

Mr. Wordsworth looked at him with some surprise. "A serious accident."

"Yes, sir?"

Jerome worshipped his father: the verb is exact. As man re-creates God, so Jerome re-created his father—from a restless widowed author into a mysterious adventurer who travelled in far places—Nice, Beirut, Majorca, even the Canaries. The time had arrived about his eighth birthday when Jerome believed that his father either "ran guns" or was a member of the British Secret Service. Now it occurred to him that his father might have been wounded in "a hail of machine-gun bullets."

Mr. Wordsworth played with the ruler on his desk. He seemed at a loss how to continue. He said, "You know your father was in Naples?"

"Yes, sir."

"Your aunt heard from the hospital today."

"Oh."

Mr. Wordsworth said with desperation, "It was a street accident."

"Yes sir?" It seemed quite likely to Jerome that they would call it a street accident. The police of course had fired first; his father would not take human life except as a last resort.

"I'm afraid your father was very seriously hurt indeed."

"Oh."

"In fact, Jerome, he died yesterday. Quite without pain."

"Did they shoot him through the heart?"

"I beg your pardon. What did you say, Jerome?"

"Did they shoot him through the heart?"

"Nobody shot him, Jerome. A pig fell on him." An inexplicable convulsion took place in the nerves of Mr. Wordsworth's face; it really looked for a moment as though he were going to laugh. He closed his eyes, composed his features and said rapidly as though it were necessary to expel the story as quickly as possible, "Your father was walking along a street in Naples when a pig fell on him. A shocking accident. Apparently in the poorer quarters of Naples they keep pigs on their balconies. This one was on the fifth floor. It had grown too fat. The balcony broke. The pig fell on your father."

Mr. Wordsworth left his desk rapidly and went

---

1. *lower forms,* lower grades.
2. *Marlborough or Rugby,* two famous public schools. The well-known English public schools—like Marlborough and Rugby—are private boarding schools for the sons of wealthy people.

to the window, turning his back on Jerome. He shook a little with emotion.

Jerome said, "What happened to the pig?"

2

This was not callousness on the part of Jerome, as it was interpreted by Mr. Wordsworth to his colleagues (he even discussed with them whether, perhaps, Jerome was yet fitted to be a warden). Jerome was only attempting to visualize the strange scene to get the details right. Nor was Jerome a boy who cried; he was a boy who brooded, and it never occurred to him at his preparatory school that the circumstances of his father's death were comic—they were still part of the mystery of life. It was later, in his first term at his public school, when he told the story to his best friend, that he began to realize how it affected others. Naturally after that disclosure he was known, rather unreasonably, as Pig.

Unfortunately his aunt had no sense of humor. There was an enlarged snapshot of his father on the piano; a large sad man in an unsuitable dark suit posed in Capri[3] with an umbrella (to guard him against sunstroke), the Faraglione rocks forming the background. By the age of sixteen Jerome was well aware that the portrait looked more like the author of *Sunshine and Shade* and *Rambles in the Balearics* than an agent of the Secret Service. All the same he loved the memory of his father: he still possessed an album filled with picture-postcards (the stamps had been soaked off long ago for his other collection), and it pained him when his aunt embarked with strangers on the story of his father's death.

"A shocking accident," she would begin, and the stranger would compose his or her features into the correct shape for interest and commiseration. Both reactions, of course, were false, but it was terrible for Jerome to see how suddenly, midway in her rambling discourse, the interest would become genuine. "I can't think how such things can be allowed in a civilized country," his aunt

A scene from *A Shocking Accident*, a short film based on Graham Greene's story, which won the 1983 Academy Award as the best live action short film.

---

3. *Capri*, an island in the Bay of Naples.

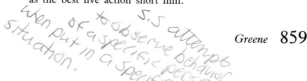

would say. "I suppose one has to regard Italy as civilized. One is prepared for all kinds of things abroad, of course, and my brother was a great traveller. He always carried a water-filter with him. It was far less expensive, you know, than buying all those bottles of mineral water. My brother always said that his filter paid for his dinner wine. You can see from that what a careful man he was, but who could possibly have expected when he was walking along the Via Dottore Manuele Panucci on his way to the Hydrographic Museum that a pig would fall on him?" That was the moment when the interest became genuine.

Jerome's father had not been a very distinguished writer, but the time always seems to come, after an author's death, when somebody thinks it worth his while to write a letter to the *Times Literary Supplement* announcing the preparation of a biography and asking to see any letters or documents or receive any anecdotes from the friends of the dead man. Most of the biographies, of course, never appear—one wonders whether the whole thing may not be an obscure form of blackmail and whether many a potential writer of a biography or thesis finds the means in this way to finish his education at Kansas or Nottingham. Jerome, however, as a chartered accountant, lived far from the literary world. He did not realize how small the menace really was, or that the danger period for someone of his father's obscurity had long passed. Sometimes he rehearsed the method of recounting his father's death so as to reduce the comic element to its smallest dimensions—it would be of no use to refuse information, for in that case the biographer would undoubtedly visit his aunt who was living to a great old age with no sign of flagging.

It seemed to Jerome that there were two possible methods—the first led gently up to the accident, so that by the time it was described the listener was so well prepared that the death came really as an anti-climax. The chief danger of laughter in such a story was always surprise. When he rehearsed this method Jerome began boringly enough.

"You know Naples and those high tenement buildings? Somebody once told me that the Neapolitan always feels at home in New York just as the man from Turin feels at home in London because the river runs in much the same way in both cities. Where was I? Oh, yes. Naples, of course. You'd be surprised in the poorer quarters what things they keep on the balconies of those sky-scraping tenements—not washing, you know, or bedding, but things like livestock, chickens or even pigs. Of course the pigs get no exercise whatever and fatten all the quicker." He could imagine how his hearer's eyes would have glazed by this time. "I've no idea, have you, how heavy a pig can be, but these old buildings are all badly in need of repair. A balcony on the fifth floor gave way under one of those pigs. It struck the third floor balcony on its way down and sort of ricochetted into the street. My father was on the way to the Hydrographic Museum when the pig hit him. Coming from that height and that angle it broke his neck." This was really a masterly attempt to make an intrinsically interesting subject boring.

The other method Jerome rehearsed had the virtue of brevity.

"My father was killed by a pig."

"Really? In India?"

"No, in Italy."

"How interesting. I never realized there was pig-sticking[4] in Italy. Was your father keen on polo?"

In course of time, neither too early nor too late, rather as though, in his capacity as a chartered accountant, Jerome had studied the statistics and taken the average, he became engaged to be married: to a pleasant fresh-faced girl of twenty-five whose father was a doctor in Pinner. Her name was Sally, her favorite author was still Hugh Walpole,[5] and she had adored babies ever since she had been given a doll at the age of five which moved its eyes and made water. Their relationship was contented rather than exciting, as became the love-

---

4. *pig-sticking*, the hunting of wild boars with a spear, especially in India.
5. *Hugh Walpole* (1884-1941), a popular English novelist of the 1920s and 1930s. Greene is suggesting that Sally is a person of conventional tastes.

affair of a chartered accountant; it would never have done if it had interfered with the figures.

One thought worried Jerome, however. Now that within a year he might himself become a father, his love for the dead man increased; he realized what affection had gone into the picture-postcards. He felt a longing to protect his memory, and uncertain whether this quiet love of his would survive if Sally were so insensitive as to laugh when she heard the story of his father's death. Inevitably she would hear it when Jerome brought her to dinner with his aunt. Several times he tried to tell her himself, as she was naturally anxious to know all she could that concerned him.

"You were very small when your father died?"

"Just nine."

"Poor little boy," she said.

"I was at school. They broke the news to me."

"Did you take it very hard?"

"I can't remember."

"You never told me how it happened."

"It was very sudden. A street accident."

"You'll never drive fast, will you, Jemmy?" (She had begun to call him "Jemmy.") It was too late then to try the second method—the one he thought of as the pig-sticking one.

They were going to marry quietly in a registry-office and have their honeymoon at Torquay. He avoided taking her to see his aunt until a week before the wedding, but then the night came, and he could not have told himself whether his apprehension was more for his father's memory or the security of his own love.

The moment came all too soon. "Is that Jemmy's father?" Sally asked, picking up the portrait of the man with the umbrella.

"Yes, dear. How did you guess?"

"He has Jemmy's eyes and brow, hasn't he?"

"Has Jerome lent you his books?"

"No."

"I will give you a set for your wedding. He wrote so tenderly about his travels. My own favorite is *Nooks and Crannies*. He would have had a great future. It made that shocking accident all the worse."

"Yes?"

Jerome longed to leave the room and not see that loved face crinkle with irresistible amusement.

"I had so many letters from his readers after the pig fell on him." She had never been so abrupt before.

And then the miracle happened. Sally did not laugh. Sally sat with open eyes of horror while his aunt told her the story, and at the end, "How horrible," Sally said. "It makes you think, doesn't it? Happening like that. Out of a clear sky."

Jerome's heart sang with joy. It was as though she had appeased his fear for ever. In the taxi going home he kissed her with more passion than he had ever shown and she returned it. There were babies in her pale blue pupils, babies that rolled their eyes and made water.

"A week today," Jerome said, and she squeezed his hand. "Penny for your thoughts, my darling."

"I was wondering," Sally said, "what happened to the poor pig?"

"They almost certainly had it for dinner," Jerome said happily and kissed the dear child again. **1967**

THINK AND DISCUSS

Understanding

1. What are Jerome's fantasies about his father and his profession?
2. What did Jerome's father actually do for a living?
3. What reason does Jerome give for not wanting potential biographers or his fiancée to talk with his aunt about his father's death?

Analyzing

4. Does Jerome's question—"What happened to the pig?"—seem to you a sincere response to the report of his father's death, or an insensitive one?
5. What indications are we given that Jerome's father was not the idealized adventurer his son had made him out to be?
6. Why does Jerome feel the need to devise two different versions of his father's death? Which version, in your opinion, seems more likely to achieve the result Jerome was after?
7. What is amusing about Jerome's decision to marry and his method of choosing a fiancée?
8. How does Sally demonstrate that she is the ideal mate for Jerome?
9. Aren't all accidents "shocking"? Why is Greene's title an apt one for this story?

Extending

10. It has been said that "Everything is funny so long as it is happening to someone else." What incidents reported by the press or depicted in the media can you recall that could be regarded as "shocking" in their consequences, yet laughable because of the circumstances in which they occurred? Have you personally been involved in such an incident?

VOCABULARY

Dictionary

Knowledge of one or two words can frequently unlock the meaning of an entire sentence. Use your Glossary to define any of the italicized words you do not know. Then explain the meaning of the whole sentence.

1. "The housemaster, Mr. Wordsworth, sat behind his desk with an appearance of *perplexity* and *apprehension*."
2. ". . . the stranger would compose his or her features into the correct shape for interest and *commiseration*."
3. "Jerome's heart sang with joy. It was as though she had *appeased* his fear for ever."
4. "It struck the third floor balcony on its way down and sort of *ricochetted* into the street."
5. "This was really a masterly attempt to make an *intrinsically* interesting subject boring."

ENRICHMENT

Comparing Versions of the Story

View the 1983 Academy Award-winning film version of this short story. Compare the film and written versions, paying attention to point of view, characterization, and tone. Which version, in your opinion, most fully conveys the simultaneous sadness and ludicrousness of the situation?

BIOGRAPHY

Sylvia Townsend Warner
1893–1978

"Dry, ironic, compassionate, a joker, a scholar," is the summary of Sylvia Townsend Warner by one recent critic. She was the only child of a housemaster at Harrow, a famous English preparatory school. In one of the autobiographical sketches that Warner occasionally contributed to *The New Yorker*, she recalls that, as an emancipated Victorian, her father "had a fine set of irrefutable doubts." Among other things, the elder Warner, as a schoolmaster, quite naturally "doubted the benefit of learning to read." He felt that the child's native capacities to see, remember, and reflect independently were lost once he or she discovered easy access to information in books: "So long after my contemporaries had become literate, I was left to be observant, retentive, and rational." She was educated at home by her parents, had the run of her father's library, and grew up solitary and precociously learned.

Her first artistic commitment was to music, not to literature. She intended to go to Vienna to study composition with Arnold Schoenberg (1874-1951), one of the leading composers of the twentieth century, but was prevented by the outbreak of World War I. Instead she became a musicologist, remaining until 1928 as one of a group of scholars editing a ten-volume collection of Tudor Church music. A meeting with the writer David Garnett led to the publication of her first book of poetry, *The Espalier* (1925), and her first novel *Lolly Willowes* (1926). *Lolly Willowes* proved popular, especially in the U.S., where it was the first choice of the new Book-of-the-Month Club, creating an American audience for her works and leading eventually to her long association with *The New Yorker* magazine.

In the 1930s Warner became convinced that the only adequate defense against the growing power of fascism was communism. She became a member of the Communist Party of Great Britain in 1935, and made several brief trips to Spain during the Civil War in support of the Loyalist cause. Outside of these trips to Spain, Warner's life was a quiet one. In the early 1930s she moved to the first of a series of cottages she occupied in the Dorset countryside. Warner continued to write fine verse—notably *Opus 7* (1931), a brilliant satirical narrative, and the posthumously published *Twelve Poems* (1980). But her reputation is largely based on her polished, original prose—seven novels, many short stories, and a fine biography of English writer T. H. White.

The Phoenix

Sylvia Townsend Warner

Lord Strawberry, a nobleman, collected birds. He had the finest aviary in Europe, so large that eagles did not find it uncomfortable, so well laid out that both hummingbirds and snowbuntings had a climate that suited them perfectly. But for many years the finest set of apartments remained empty, with just a label saying: "PHOENIX.[1] *Habitat: Arabia.*"

Many authorities on bird life had assured Lord Strawberry that the phoenix is a fabulous bird, or that the breed was long extinct. Lord Strawberry was unconvinced: his family had always believed in phoenixes. At intervals he received from his agents (together with statements of their expenses) birds which they declared were the phoenix but which turned out to be orioles, macaws, turkey buzzards dyed orange, crossbreeds, ingeniously assembled from various plumages. Finally Lord Strawberry went to Arabia, where, after some months, he found a phoenix, won its confidence, caught it, and brought it home in perfect condition.

It was a remarkably fine phoenix, with a charming character—affable to the other birds in the aviary and much attached to Lord Strawberry. On its arrival in England it made a great stir among ornithologists, journalists, poets, and milliners, and was constantly visited. But it was not puffed up by these attentions, and when it was no longer in the news, and the visits fell off, it showed no pique or rancor. It ate well, and seemed perfectly contented.

It costs a great deal of money to keep up an aviary. When Lord Strawberry died he died penniless. The aviary came on the market. In normal times the rarer birds, and certainly the phoenix, would have been bid for by the trustees of Europe's great zoological societies or by private persons in the U.S.A.; but as it happened Lord Strawberry died just after a world war, when both money and bird-seed were hard to come by (indeed the cost of bird-seed was one of the things which had ruined Lord Strawberry). The London *Times* urged in a leader[2] that the phoenix be bought for the London Zoo, saying that a nation of bird-lovers had a moral right to own such a rarity; and a fund, called the Strawberry Phoenix Fund, was opened. Students, naturalists, and school children contributed according to their means; but their means were small, and there were no large donations. So Lord Strawberry's executors (who had the death duties[3] to consider) closed with the higher offer of Mr. Tancred Poldero, owner and proprietor of Poldero's Wizard Wonderworld.

For quite a while Mr. Poldero considered his phoenix a bargain. It was a civil and obliging bird, and adapted itself readily to its new surroundings. It did not cost much to feed, it did not mind children; and though it had no tricks, Mr. Poldero supposed it would soon pick up some. The publicity of the Strawberry Phoenix Fund was now most helpful. Almost every contributor now saved up another half-crown in order to see the phoenix. Others who had not contributed to the fund, even paid double to look at it on the five-shilling days.

But then business slackened. The phoenix was as handsome as ever, and as amiable; but, as Mr. Poldero said, it hadn't got Udge. Even at popular prices the phoenix was not really popular. It was too quiet, too classical. So people went instead to watch the antics of the baboons, or to admire the crocodile who had eaten the woman.

One day Mr. Poldero said to his manager, Mr. Ramkin:

"How long since any fool paid to look at the

---

1. *phoenix* (fē′niks), a legendary bird of Arabia, reputed to live for five hundred years, then to burn itself to ashes in a fire of its own creation and rise again, its youth renewed.
2. *leader*, an editorial.
3. *death duties*, taxes on the estate of a deceased person.

Chinese illustration of a phoenix. 19th century. *Bibliothèque Nationale, Paris*

phoenix?"

"Matter of three weeks," replied Mr. Ramkin.

"Eating his head off," said Mr. Poldero. "Let alone the insurance. Seven shillings a week it costs me to insure that bird, and I might as well insure the Archbishop of Canterbury."

"The public don't like him. He's too quiet for them, that's the trouble. Won't mate nor nothing. And I've tried him with no end of pretty pollies, ospreys, and Cochin-Chinas, and the Lord knows what. But he won't look at them."

"Wonder if we could swap him for a livelier one," said Mr. Poldero.

"Impossible. There's only one of him at a time."

"Go on!"

"I mean it. Haven't you ever read what it says on the label?"

They went to the phoenix's cage. It flapped its wings politely, but they paid no attention. They read:

"PANSY. *Phoenix phoenixissima formosissima arabiana.* This rare and fabulous bird is UNIQUE. The World's Old Bachelor. Has no mate and doesn't want one. When old, sets fire to itself and emerges miraculously reborn. Specially imported from the East."

"I've got an idea," said Mr. Poldero. "How old do you suppose that bird is?"

"Looks in its prime to me," said Mr. Ramkin.

"Suppose," continued Mr. Poldero, "we could somehow get him alight? We'd advertize it beforehand, of course, work up interest. Then we'd have a new bird, and a bird with some romance about it, a bird with a life-story. We could sell a bird like that."

Mr. Ramkin nodded.

"I've read about it in a book," he said. "You've got to give them scented woods and what not, and they build a nest and sit down on it and catch fire spontaneous. But they won't do it till they're old. That's the snag."

"Leave that to me," said Mr. Poldero. "You get those scented woods, and I'll do the ageing."

It was not easy to age the phoenix. Its allowance of food was halved, and halved again, but though it grew thinner its eyes were undimmed and its plumage glossy as ever. The heating was turned off; but it puffed out its feathers against the cold, and seemed none the worse. Other birds were put into its cage, birds of a peevish and quarrelsome nature. They pecked and chivied it; but the phoenix was so civil and amiable that after a day or two they lost their animosity. Then Mr. Poldero tried alley cats. These could not be won by good manners, but the phoenix darted above their heads and flapped its golden wings in their faces, and daunted them.

Mr. Poldero turned to a book on Arabia, and read that the climate was dry. "Aha!" said he. The phoenix was moved to a small cage that had a sprinkler in the ceiling. Every night the sprinkler was turned on. The phoenix began to cough. Mr. Poldero had another good idea. Daily he stationed himself in front of the cage to jeer at the bird and abuse it.

When spring was come, Mr. Poldero felt justified in beginning a publicity campaign about the ageing phoenix. The old public favorite, he said, was nearing its end. Meanwhile he tested the bird's reactions every few days by putting a few tufts of foul-smelling straw and some strands of rusty barbed wire into the cage, to see if it were interested in nesting yet. One day the phoenix began turning over the straw. Mr. Poldero signed a contract for the film rights. At last the hour seemed ripe. It was a fine Saturday evening in May. For some weeks the public interest in the ageing phoenix had been working up, and the admission charge had risen to five shillings. The enclosure was thronged. The lights and the cameras were trained on the cage, and a loud-speaker proclaimed to the audience the rarity of what was about to take place.

"The phoenix," said the loud-speaker, "is the aristocrat of bird-life. Only the rarest and most expensive specimens of oriental wood, drenched in exotic perfumes, will tempt him to construct his strange love-nest."

Now a neat assortment of twigs and shavings, strongly scented, was shoved into the cage.

"The phoenix," the loud-speaker continued, "is as capricious as Cleopatra, as luxurious as la du Barry,[4] as heady as a strain of wild gypsy music. All the fantastic pomp and passion of the ancient East, its languorous magic, its subtle cruelties . . ."

"Lawks!" cried a woman in the crowd. "He's at it!"

A quiver stirred the dulled plumage. The phoenix turned its head from side to side. It descended, staggering, from its perch. Then wearily it began to pull about the twigs and shavings.

The cameras clicked, the lights blazed full on the cage. Rushing to the loud-speaker Mr. Poldero exclaimed:

"Ladies and gentlemen, this is the thrilling moment the world has breathlessly awaited. The legend of centuries is materializing before our modern eyes. The phoenix . . ."

The phoenix settled on its pyre[5] and appeared to fall asleep.

The film director said:

"Well, if it doesn't evaluate more than this, mark it instructional."

At that moment the phoenix and the pyre burst into flames. The flames streamed upwards, leaped out on every side. In a minute or two everything was burned to ashes, and some thousand people, including Mr. Poldero, perished in the blaze.

1940

---

4. *la du Barry*, Countess du Barry (1746-1793), mistress of King Louis XV of France.
5. *pyre* (pīr), a pile of wood for burning a dead body as a funeral rite.

THINK AND DISCUSS

Understanding

1. What is special about the phoenix?
2. Why, after Lord Strawberry's death, is it necessary to sell his aviary?

Analyzing

3. Contrast the two owners of the phoenix and their treatment of the bird.
4. What words are used to **characterize** the phoenix?
5. Why doesn't the phoenix prove to be popular at Poldero's Wizard Wonderworld? What does this suggest about public taste?
6. To what specific forms of abuse does Mr. Poldero subject the bird? Why?
7. What is the major target of **satire** in the story? Are there any other targets? Explain.

Extending

8. It has been said that the public is fickle. What other wonders in the modern world can you think of that the public seems to take for granted?

VOCABULARY

Context

Using clues from context as an aid, write on your paper the most appropriate definition for each of the italicized words in the following passages from "The Phoenix." Be sure you can pronounce all the words.

1. "He had the finest *aviary* in Europe, so large that eagles did not find it uncomfortable, so well laid out that both hummingbirds and snow buntings had a climate that suited them perfectly." **a.** poultry farm; **b.** birdhouse; **c.** museum; **d.** pet shop.
2. "At intervals he received from his agents (together with statements of their expenses) birds which they declared were the phoenix but which turned out to be orioles, macaws, turkey buzzards dyed orange, etc., or stuffed crossbreeds ingeniously assembled from various *plumages*." **a.** countries; **b.** fossils; **c.** collectors; **d.** feathers.

3. "On [the phoenix's] arrival in England it made a great stir among *ornithologists*, journalists, poets, and milliners, and was constantly visited." **a.** poultry farmers; **b.** writers; **c.** scientists who study birds; **d.** cooks.
4. "But [the phoenix] was not puffed up by these attentions, and when it was no longer in the news, and the visits fell off, it showed no pique or *rancor*." **a.** hunger; **b.** resentment; **c.** affection; **d.** interest.
5. "Other birds were put into its cage, birds of a peevish or quarrelsome nature. They pecked and chivied it; but the phoenix was so civil and amiable that after a day or two they lost their *animosity*." **a.** feathers; **b.** ability to fly; **c.** dislike; **d.** friendliness.

COMPOSITION

Writing a Fantasy

Numerous stories and films today involve fantastical creatures that somehow find their way into the modern world. Write a story involving the discovery of a fantastic creature of your own invention. Start by jotting down the qualities of this creature you intend to emphasize: physical appearance, personality and behavior traits, supernatural powers, and so on. Decide how the creature will be discovered, what effect its presence will have on the discoverers, and what eventually will be done with it. Will the appearance of this creature prove a blessing or curse to society?

Reviewing a Film

Like Poldero's Wonder Wizardland, many current films and TV shows cater to the public's desire for violence and sensationalism. Write a review of four to six paragraphs of a film you have seen that you found offensive for these reasons. First state your main objections to the film. Then provide a concise summary of the plot. Go on to discuss the violent and sensationalized aspects of the film, saving the worst for last. Conclude with an overall evaluation of the artistic and humanistic merits of the film. Be ready to read your paper aloud to the class.

BIOGRAPHY

Dylan Thomas
1914–1953

As a result of his exuberant lifestyle, highly popular public readings, and widely publicized death in 1953 at the age of thirty-nine, Dylan Thomas became a celebrity whose public personality temporarily threatened to overshadow his poetry. No modern poet has generated such an outpouring of emotion, gossip, reminiscence, and criticism, nor attained his level as a "cult" figure. One of his biographers explains that Thomas met the need of his society for a romantic rebel: "He was an answer to the machine; his poems contain few images drawn from the twentieth century." Now that time has faded the public legend he can more truly be seen as the greatest lyric poet of his generation and a dramatist and essayist of original humor and charm.

Dylan Thomas was born in Swansea, Wales, a place he periodically fled but which provided the setting and stimulus of his best work. His father was a schoolteacher and poet whose readings of Shakespeare, the Bible, and other poets stimulated Thomas's early fascination with words. When later asked how he had come to write poetry, Thomas would recall his joy in nursery rhymes, stating that "what the words stood for, symbolized, or meant, was of very secondary importance; what mattered was the *sound* of them as I heard them for the first time on the lips of the remote and incomprehensible grown-ups who seemed, for some reason, to be living in my world." Thomas left school at sixteen to work as a newspaper reporter, but poetry writing, which he had been doing since he was a small boy, was more to his taste. He published his first volume of poetry at nineteen and continued to publish well-received books of verse during the 1930s. *Portrait of the Artist as a Young Dog*, a collection of stories about his childhood and youth, appeared in 1940. Another book of boyhood reminiscences, *Quite Early One Morning* (1954), and a verse play, *Under Milk Wood* (1954), were published after his death. During World War II Thomas worked for the BBC as a documentary film editor and also as a radio broadcaster; his magnificent Welsh voice enchanted listeners, as did his generous inclusion of the works of other poets in his readings.

In a letter to a friend, Thomas wrote: "I like things that are difficult to write and difficult to understand . . . I like contradicting my images, saying two things at once in one word, four in two and one in six." Not surprisingly, many of Thomas's poems are frustratingly difficult, especially those in his first two collections, *Eighteen Poems* (1934) and *Twenty-Five Poems* (1936). *Deaths and Entrances* (1946), his most famous collection of poems, reveals a movement away from obscurity to a simpler, more direct, yet ceremonial style. While the young Dylan Thomas was obsessed with mortality, an awareness that "the force" that gives life to plants and people is also the "destroyer," the later Thomas came to the realization that ". . . death shall have no dominion" in a cosmos in which all living things exist in a perpetual cycle of change and rebirth.

Fern Hill

Dylan Thomas

Now as I was young and easy under the apple
    boughs
About the lilting house and happy as the grass
    was green,
    The night above the dingle starry,
      Time let me hail and climb
5   Golden in the heydays of his eyes,
And honored among wagons I was prince of the
    apple towns
And once below a time I lordly had the trees
    and leaves
    Trail with daisies and barley
    Down the rivers of the windfall light.

10 And as I was green and carefree, famous among
    the barns
About the happy yard and singing as the farm
    was home,
    In the sun that is young once only,
      Time let me play and be
    Golden in the mercy of his means,
15 And green and golden I was huntsman and
    herdsman, the calves
Sang to my horn, the foxes on the hills barked
    clear and cold,
    And the sabbath rang slowly
    In the pebbles of the holy streams.

All the sun long it was running, it was lovely,
    the hay
20 Fields high as the house, the tunes from the
    chimneys, it was air
    And playing, lovely and watery
      And fire green as grass.
    And nightly under the simple stars
As I rode to sleep the owls were bearing the
    farm away,
25 All the moon long I heard, blessed among
    stables, the night-jars
    Flying with the ricks, and the horses
    Flashing into the dark.

And then to awake, and the farm, like a
    wanderer white
With the dew, come back, the cock on his
    shoulder: it was all
30   Shining, it was Adam and maiden,
      The sky gathered again
    And the sun grew round that very day.
So it must have been after the birth of the simple
    light
In the first, spinning place, the spellbound
    horses walking warm
35   Out of the whinnying green stable
    On to the fields of praise.

And honored among foxes and pheasants by the
    gay house
Under the new made clouds and happy as the
    heart was long,
    In the sun born over and over,
40   I ran my heedless ways,
    My wishes raced through the house high
    hay
And nothing I cared, at my sky blue trades,
    that time allows

In all his tuneful turning so few and such
      morning songs
Before the children green and golden
45   Follow him out of grace.

Nothing I cared, in the lamb white days, that
      time would take me
Up to the swallow thronged loft by the shadow
      of my hand,

In the moon that is always rising,
      Nor that riding to sleep
50   I should hear him fly with the high fields
And wake to the farm forever fled from the
      childless land.
Oh as I was young and easy in the mercy of his
      means,
    Time held me green and dying
Though I sang in my chains like the sea.

1946

The Cinder Path by Spencer Gore. 1912. *Tate Gallery, London*

Reader's Note

"Fern Hill"

If one sought to describe this poem within the compass of a single phrase, it might be called "an elegy in praise of lost youth." Lament and celebration sound throughout the work: the latter strongly at the beginning, the former gaining tone as the poem progresses.

But, as with all great threnodies (lamentations) in English—with Milton's *Lycidas*, Gray's *Elegy*, Shelley's *Adonais*, and Arnold's *Thyrsis*—the particularity of the cause of grief is lost in a sorrow which speaks for all men. Nostalgic recollection of a child's farm holiday is the leaping-off point for the poem; but—once launched—so intense and poignant a memory overtakes the poet, that his words convey more than a merely topographical homesickness. The farm becomes Eden before the Fall, and time the angel with a flaming sword.

But no such intrusive personification operates within the poem. The farm is invested with a light as radiant as the unforfeited Garden, and time exercises its function as irrevocably as God's excluding angel. So, though at the end we are faced with nothing worse than a farmstead which cannot be revisited, in actual poetic terms we have experienced the states of innocence and eternity, and been subjected to corruption, time, and change.

The poem is constructed from six nine-line stanzas, with only an infrequent rhyme. The absence of rhyme suffices to make the lyrically undulating lines more natural. The artifice and architectonic of the poem consists not in the usual technical devices, but in the repetition, in later stanzas, of *motifs* established in the first. These *motifs* are not worked out with any mechanical regularity; and their place and precedence in the poem are not formally observed. The *motifs* I find to be mainly three: that of the unwitting situation of childhood; that of the delight in this situation; that of time's operation, by which the situation becomes a fate.

Do Not Go Gentle into That Good Night

Do not go gentle into that good night,
Old age should burn and rave at close of day;
Rage, rage against the dying of the light.

Though wise men at their end know dark is right,
5 Because their words had forked no lightning they
Do not go gentle into that good night.

Good men, the last wave by, crying how bright
Their frail deeds might have danced in a green
   bay,
Rage, rage against the dying of the light.

10 Wild men who caught and sang the sun in flight,
And learn, too late, they grieved it on its way,
Do not go gentle into that good night.

Grave men, near death, who see with blinding
   sight
Blind eyes could blaze like meteors and be gay,
15 Rage, rage against the dying of the light.

And you, my father, there on the sad height,
Curse, bless, me now with your fierce tears,
   I pray.
Do not go gentle into that good night.
Rage, rage against the dying of the light.

1951

THINK AND DISCUSS

FERN HILL

Understanding

1. What five adjectives does the speaker use in the first two stanzas to describe himself as a boy at Fern?

2. When he was a child, what did the speaker believe happened to the farm every night when he went to bed? the next morning?

Analyzing

3. What details of his childhood holidays does the poet recall? What do they reveal about the way children characteristically perceive the world?

4. In addition to the "I" of the poem, Time is the dominant presence, **personified** in three distinct forms. What view of Time is developed in the first four stanzas?

5. In what form is Time personified in stanza 5, and what action is Time performing? What period of a person's life does this stanza describe?

6. What final image of Time is presented in the concluding lines of the poem?

7. Why, in lines 30–36, does the speaker **allude** to Adam and the Garden of Eden?

8. **Symbolically,** what happens to the farm in the last stanza? Why is such a happening inevitable?

9. What color scheme is carried out in the poem, and how does it reinforce the change in **mood** in stanza 6?

Extending

10. What is the **theme** of this poem? What similarities and differences can you find in Wordsworth's treatment of the same theme?

DO NOT GO GENTLE INTO THAT GOOD NIGHT

Understanding

1. In the first line, what does the speaker tell his father *not* to do?

2. What does the speaker advise his father to do instead?

Analyzing

3. Who are the "wise," "good," "wild," and "grave" men mentioned in the poem?

4. How do these four kinds of people react to death, and why do they behave as they do?

5. What fact of life do all these reactions serve to illustrate?

6. Why does the son ask his dying father both to "curse" and "bless" him?

7. This poem is a *villanelle* (see Glossary of Literary Terms, page 968). Because of the restrictions imposed by this poetic form, the words of the poem necessarily carry a cargo of multiple meanings. Pick out words and phrases that are clearly ambiguous and explain the possible meanings.

8. How do lines 1 and 3 change in meaning as they are repeated throughout the poem?

9. Identify the pun and explain the **paradox** present in stanza 5.

Extending

10. Do you think Thomas's advice to his father is applicable to everyone? Can you think of situations when death might be welcomed rather than resisted?

HT Review IMAGERY in the Handbook of Literary Terms, p. 910.

A Child's Christmas in Wales

Dylan Thomas

 ne Christmas was so much like another, in those years around the sea-town corner now and out of all sound except the distant speaking of the voices I sometimes hear a moment before sleep, that I can never remember whether it snowed for six days and six nights when I was twelve or whether it snowed for twelve days and twelve nights when I was six. All the Christmases roll down toward the two-tongued sea, like a cold and headlong moon bundling down the sky that was our street; and they stop at the rim of the ice-edged, fish-freezing waves, and I plunge my hands in the snow and bring out whatever I can find. In goes my hand into that wool-white bell-tongued ball of holidays resting at the rim of the carol-singing sea, and out come Mrs. Prothero and the firemen.

It was on the afternoon of the day of Christmas Eve, and I was in Mrs. Prothero's garden, waiting for cats, with her son Jim. It was snowing. It was always snowing at Christmas. December, in my memory, is white as Lapland, though there were no reindeers. But there were cats. Patient, cold and callous, our hands wrapped in socks, we waited to snowball the cats. Sleek and long as jaguars and horrible-whiskered, spitting and snarling, they would slink and sidle over the white back-garden walls, and the lynx-eyed hunters, Jim and I, fur-capped and moccasined trappers from Hudson Bay, off Mumbles Road, would hurl our deadly snowballs at the green of their eyes. The wise cats never appeared. We were so still, Eskimo-footed arctic marksmen in the muffling silence of the eternal snows—eternal, ever since Wednesday—that we never heard Mrs. Prothero's first cry from her igloo at the bottom of the garden. Or, if we heard it at all, it was, to us, like the far-off challenge of our enemy and prey, the neighbour's polar cat. But soon the voice grew louder.

"Fire!" cried Mrs. Prothero, and she beat the dinner-gong.

And we ran down the garden, with the snowballs in our arms, toward the house; and smoke, indeed, was pouring out of the dining-room, and the bong was bombilating,[1] and Mrs. Prothero was announcing ruin like a town crier in Pompeii.[2] This was better than all the cats in Wales standing on the wall in a row. We bounded into the house, laden with snowballs, and stopped at the open door of the smoke-filled room. Something was burning all right; perhaps it was Mr. Prothero, who always slept there after midday dinner with a newspaper over his face. But he was standing in the middle of the room, saying, "A fine Christmas!" and smacking at the smoke with a slipper.

"Call the fire brigade," cried Mrs. Prothero as she beat the gong.

"They won't be there," said Mr. Prothero, "it's Christmas."

There was no fire to be seen, only clouds of smoke and Mr. Prothero standing in the middle of them, waving his slipper as though he were conducting.

"Do something," he said.

And we threw all our snowballs into the

---

1. *bombilating*, humming; booming.
2. *Pompeii* (pom pā'), city in ancient Italy buried by an eruption of Mount Vesuvius in A. D. 79.

smoke—I think we missed Mr. Prothero—and ran out of the house to the telephone box.

"Let's call the police as well," Jim said.

"And the ambulance."

"And Ernie Jenkins, he likes fires."

But we only called the fire brigade, and soon the fire engine came and three tall men in helmets brought a hose into the house and Mr. Prothero got out just in time before they turned it on. Nobody could have had a noisier Christmas Eve. And when the firemen turned off the hose and were standing in the wet, smoky room, Jim's aunt, Miss Prothero, came downstairs and peered in at them. Jim and I waited, very quietly, to hear what she would say to them. She said the right thing, always. She looked at the three tall firemen in their shining helmets, standing among the smoke and cinders and dissolving snowballs, and she said: "Would you like anything to read?"

Years and years and years ago, when I was a boy, when there were wolves in Wales, and birds the color of red-flannel petticoats whisked past the harp-shaped hills, when we sang and wallowed all night and day in caves that smelt like Sunday afternoons in damp front farmhouse parlors, and we chased, with the jawbones of deacons, the English and the bears, before the motor car, before the wheel, before the duchess-faced horse when we rode the daft and happy hills bareback, it snowed and it snowed. But here a small boy says: "It snowed last year, too. I made a snowman and my brother knocked it down and I knocked my brother down and then we had tea."

"But that was not the same snow," I say. "Our snow was not only shaken from whitewash buckets down the sky, it came shawling out of the ground and swam and drifted out of the arms and hands and bodies of the trees; snow grew overnight on the roofs of the houses like a pure and grandfather moss, minutely white-ivied the walls and settled on the postman, opening the gate, like a dumb, numb thunderstorm of white, torn Christmas cards."

"Were there postmen then, too?"

"With sprinkling eyes and wind-cherried noses, on spread, frozen feet they crunched up to the doors and mittened on them manfully. But all that the children could hear was a ringing of bells."

"You mean that the postman went rat-a-tat-tat and the doors rang?"

"I mean that the bells that the children could hear were inside them."

"I only hear thunder sometimes, never bells."

"There were church bells, too."

"Inside them?"

"No, no, no, in the bat-black, snow-white belfries, tugged by bishops and storks. And they rang their tidings over the bandaged town, over the frozen foam of the powder and ice-cream hills, over the crackling sea. It seemed that all the churches boomed for joy under my window; and the weathercocks crew for Christmas, on our fence."

"Get back to the postmen."

"They were just ordinary postmen, fond of walking and dogs and Christmas and the snow. They knocked on the doors with blue knuckles. . . ."

"Ours has got a black knocker. . . ."

"And then they stood on the white Welcome mat in the little, drifted porches and huffed and puffed, making ghosts with their breath, and jogged from foot to foot like small boys wanting to go out."

"And then the Presents?"

"And then the Presents, after the Christmas box.[3] And the cold postman, with a rose on his button-nose, tingled down the tea-tray-slithered run of the chilly glinting hill. He went in his ice-bound boots like a man on fishmonger's slabs. He wagged his bag like a frozen camel's hump, dizzily turned the corner on one foot, and, by God, he was gone."

"Get back to the Presents."

"There were the Useful Presents: engulfing mufflers of the old coach days, and mittens made for giant sloths; zebra scarfs of a substance like silky gum that could be tug-o'-warred down to the galoshes; blinding tam-o'-shanters like patchwork

---

3. **Christmas box**, Christmas gift given to a postman.

Snow Scene by W. Park. 1879.

tea cozies and bunny-suited busbies and balacla-vas[4] for victims of head-shrinking tribes; from aunts who always wore wool next to the skin there were mustached and rasping vests that made you wonder why the aunts had any skin left at all; and once I had a little crocheted nose bag from an aunt now, alas, no longer whinnying with us. And pic-tureless books in which small boys, though warned with quotations not to, *would* skate on Farmer Giles' pond and did and drowned; and books that told me everything about the wasp, except why."

"Go on to the Useless Presents."

"Bags of moist and many-colored jelly babies and a folded flag and a false nose and a tram-conductor's cap and a machine that punched tick-ets and rang a bell; never a catapult; once, by mistake that no one could explain, a little hatch-

et; and a celluloid duck that made, when you pressed it, a most unducklike sound, a mewing moo that an ambitious cat might make who wished to be a cow; and a painting book in which I could make the grass, the trees, the sea and the ani-mals any color I pleased, and still the dazzling sky-blue sheep are grazing in the red field under the rainbow-billed and pea-green birds. Hard-boileds, toffee, fudge and allsorts, crunches, cracknels, humbugs, glaciers, marzipan, and butterwelsh for the Welsh. And troops of bright tin soldiers who, if they could not fight, could always run. And Snakes-and-Families and Happy Ladders. And Easy Hobbi-Games for Little Engineers, complete

---

4. *busbies . . . balaclavas,* two kinds of hats.

with instructions. Oh, easy for Leonardo![5] And a whistle to make the dogs bark to wake up the old man next door to make him beat on the wall with his stick to shake our picture off the wall. And a packet of cigarettes: you put one in your mouth and you stood at the corner of the street and you waited for hours, in vain, for an old lady to scold you for smoking a cigarette, and then with a smirk you ate it. And then it was breakfast under the balloons."

"Were there Uncles, like in our house?"

"There are always Uncles at Christmas. The same Uncles. And on Christmas mornings, with dog-disturbing whistle and sugar fags, I would scour the swatched town for the news of the little world, and find always a dead bird by the white Post Office or by the deserted swings; perhaps a robin, all but one of his fires out. Men and women wading or scooping back from chapel, with taproom noses and wind-bussed cheeks, all albinos, huddled their stiff black jarring feathers against the irreligious snow. Mistletoe hung from the gas brackets in all the front parlors; there was sherry and walnuts and bottled beer and crackers[6] by the dessertspoons; and cats in their fur-abouts watched the fires; and the high-heaped fire spat, all ready for the chestnuts and the mulling pokers. Some few large men sat in the front parlors, without their collars, Uncles almost certainly, trying their new cigars, holding them out judiciously at arms' length, returning them to their mouths, coughing, then holding them out again as though waiting for the explosion; and some few small aunts, not wanted in the kitchen, nor anywhere else for that matter, sat on the very edges of their chairs, poised and brittle, afraid to break, like faded cups and saucers."

Not many those mornings trod the piling streets: an old man always, fawn-bowlered, yellow-gloved and, at this time of year, with spats of snow, would take his constitutional to the white bowling green and back, as he would take it wet or fine on Christmas Day or Doomsday; sometimes two hale young men, with big pipes blazing, no overcoats and wind-blown scarfs, would trudge, unspeaking, down to the forlorn sea, to work up

an appetite, to blow away the fumes, who knows, to walk into the waves until nothing of them was left but the two curling smoke clouds of their inextinguishable briars. Then I would be slapdashing home, the gravy smell of the dinners of others, the bird smell, the brandy, the pudding and mince, coiling up to my nostrils, when out of a snow-clogged side lane would come a boy the spit of myself, with a pink-tipped cigarette and the violet past of a black eye, cocky as a bullfinch, leering all to himself. I hated him on sight and sound, and would be about to put my dog whistle to my lips and blow him off the face of Christmas when suddenly he, with a violet wink, put *his* whistle to *his* lips and blew so stridently, so high, so exquisitely loud, that gobbling faces, their cheeks bulged with goose, would press against their tinseled windows, the whole length of the white echoing street. For dinner we had turkey and blazing pudding, and after dinner the Uncles sat in front of the fire, loosened all buttons, put their large moist hands over their watch chains, groaned a little and slept. Mothers, aunts and sisters scuttled to and fro, bearing tureens. Auntie Bessie, who had already been frightened, twice, by a clock-work mouse, whimpered at the sideboard and had some elderberry wine. The dog was sick. Auntie Dosie had to have three aspirins, but Auntie Hannah, who liked port, stood in the middle of the snow-bound back yard, singing like a big-bosomed thrush. I would blow up balloons to see how big they would blow up to; and, when they burst, which they all did, the Uncles jumped and rumbled. In the rich and heavy afternoon, the Uncles breathing like dolphins and the snow descending, I would sit among festoons and Chinese lanterns and nibble dates and try to make a model man-o'-war, following the Instructions for Little Engineers, and produce what might be mistaken for a sea-going tramcar. Or I would go out, my bright new boots squeaking, into the white world, on to the seaward hill, to call on Jim and Dan and Jack and to pad through

---

5. **Leonardo**, Leonardo da Vinci (1452–1519), Italian painter, architect, engineer, and scientist.
6. *crackers*, party favors containing jokes or gifts, a Christmas tradition in Great Britain.

the still streets, leaving huge deep footprints on the hidden pavements.

"I bet people will think there's been hippos."

"What would you do if you saw a hippo coming down our street?"

"I'd go like this, bang! I'd throw him over the railings and roll him down the hill and then I'd tickle him under the ear and he'd wag his tail."

"What would you do if you saw *two* hippos?"

Iron-flanked and bellowing he-hippos clanked and battered through the scudding snow toward us as we passed Mr. Daniel's house.

"Let's post Mr. Daniel a snowball through his letter box."

"Let's write things in the snow."

"Let's write, 'Mr. Daniel looks like a spaniel' all over his lawn."

Or we walked on the white shore. "Can the fishes see it's snowing?"

The silent one-clouded heavens drifted on to the sea. Now we were snow-blind travelers lost on the north hills, and vast dewlapped dogs, with flasks round their necks, ambled and shambled up to us, baying "Excelsior."[7] We returned home through the poor streets where only a few children fumbled with bare red fingers in the wheel-rutted snow and catcalled after us, their voices fading away, as we trudged uphill, into the cries of the dock birds and the hooting of ships out in the whirling bay. And then, at tea the recovered Uncles would be jolly; and the ice cake loomed in the center of the table like a marble grave. Auntie Hannah laced her tea with rum, because it was only once a year.

Bring out the tall tales now that we told by the fire as the gaslight bubbled like a diver. Ghosts whooed like owls in the long nights when I dared not look over my shoulder; animals lurked in the cubbyhole under the stairs where the gas meter ticked. And I remember that we went singing carols once, when there wasn't the shaving of a moon to light the flying street. At the end of a long road was a drive that led to a large house, and we stumbled up the darkness of the drive that night, each one of us afraid, each one holding a stone in his hand in case, and all of us too brave to say a word. The wind through the trees made noises as of old

and unpleasant and maybe webfooted men wheezing in caves. We reached the black bulk of the house.

"What shall we give them? Hark the Herald?"

"No," Jack said, "Good King Wenceslas. I'll count three."

One, two, three, and we began to sing, our voices high and seemingly distant in the snow-felted darkness round the house that was occupied by nobody we knew. We stood close together, near the dark door.

Good King Wenceslas looked out
On the Feast of Stephen . . .

And then a small, dry voice, like the voice of someone who has not spoken for a long time, joined our singing: a small, dry, eggshell voice from the other side of the door: a small dry voice through the keyhole. And when we stopped running we were outside *our* house; the front room was lovely; balloons floated under the hot-water-bottle-gulping gas; everything was good again and shone over the town.

"Perhaps it was a ghost," Jim said.

"Perhaps it was trolls," Dan said, who was always reading.

"Let's go in and see if there's any jelly left," Jack said. And we did that.

Always on Christmas night there was music. An uncle played the fiddle, a cousin sang "Cherry Ripe," and another uncle sang "Drake's Drum." It was very warm in the little house. Auntie Hannah, who had got on to the parsnip wine, sang about Bleeding Hearts and Death, and then another in which she said her heart was like a Bird's Nest; and then everybody laughed again; and then I went to bed. Looking through my bedroom window, out into the moonlight and the unending smoke-colored snow, I could see the lights in the windows of all the other houses on our hill and hear the music rising from them up the long, steadily falling night. I turned the gas down, I got into bed. I said some words to the close and holy darkness, and then I slept.

1945   1950

---

7. *Excelsior,* a Latin word meaning "ever upward."

THINK AND DISCUSS
A CHILD'S CHRISTMAS IN WALES

Understanding
1. What does the family do for entertainment on Christmas night?
2. How do the children entertain themselves on their own?

Analyzing
3. Explain how Thomas has combined many Christmases into this one essay. How has he signaled the reader what he is doing?
4. For what purpose has Thomas introduced the "small boy" who speaks up in the essay?
5. Thomas makes effective use of compound words like "two-tongued sea"—which are similar to the kennings used in *Beowulf*—to present **metaphors** and **similes** in an original way. Point out several examples of this technique.

Extending
6. In this essay Thomas describes what many would regard as "an old-fashioned Christmas." In what ways are family gatherings and the celebration of holidays different today? What is basically the same?

REVIEWING: Imagery H𝈎
See Handbook of Literary Terms, p. 910

"A Child's Christmas in Wales" is rich in **imagery,** concrete sensory details, such as "birds the color of red-flannel petticoats," that evoke changing moods and feelings by stimulating the senses of the reader. This essay includes appeals to all the five senses—sight, sound, taste, smell, and touch.

1. What images depict the outdoor world of snow and cold?
2. What images depict the indoor world of warmth and cheer?
3. What different images portray postmen?
4. What images portray the "small aunts"? What do these images suggest about the role of these aunts in the family?

THINKING SKILLS
Classifying

To classify things is to arrange them into categories or groups according to some system.

1. How does Thomas classify his presents? What does he include in each category?
2. Name some presents you have received that would fit into either category.
3. What details suggest that Thomas uses the terms *Uncles* and *Aunts* as categories to include relatives of various kinds?

COMPOSITION ✒
Recalling a Special Holiday

Christmas obviously meant a lot to Dylan Thomas. What is your favorite holiday? In a paper of five to seven paragraphs, describe the way in which you and your family typically celebrate this holiday. What people are generally involved? Where do you traditionally gather, and what events highlight the day? Be sure to include sensory details, as Thomas does in "A Child's Christmas in Wales," to make your description more colorful and vivid.

Analyzing "Fern Hill"

Write a five- to seven-paragraph analysis of "Fern Hill" that could be included in a class book on "Insights into Poetry." In your first paragraph state the **theme** and purpose of the poem. Then describe the organization, stanza by stanza. In succeeding paragraphs point out original uses of words, figures of speech, **imagery,** sound devices, visual effects, and **symbolism.** Make sure to identify and **characterize** the speaker and to point out the various **moods** and **tone** of the poem. Cite passages from the poem that illustrate your analysis. In your conclusion describe the emotional effect of the poem on the reader.

When *Novel on Yellow Paper* by "Stevie Smith" appeared in 1936, there was uncertainty for a time as to who this individual was. The poet Robert Nicols wrote Virginia Woolf telling her he was certain that *she* was Stevie Smith, and that the new book was her best novel yet. Eventually the author's identity was established, and this led to the publication of her first book of poetry, *A Good Time Was Had by All* (1937). The literary reputation established with these books has grown slowly but steadily since.

Born in the Yorkshire city of Hull, she lived most of her life in the London suburb of Palmer's Green, sharing a small, unfashionable house with her beloved aunt, whom she dubbed "the Lion of Hull." "Very few in this suburb know me as Stevie Smith, & I should like to keep it that way," she wrote in 1956. Christened "Florence Margaret," she acquired her nickname at the age of about twenty. She was horseback riding with a friend, and some boys called to her, "Come on Steve," (after the famous jockey Steve Donoghue) and the name stuck.

After attending the progressive North London Collegiate School for Girls, she went to work instead of continuing on to a university, becoming a secretary in a magazine publishing company, work she apparently enjoyed and continued until her aunt became bedridden and required her constant care. She published two more novels, *Over the Frontier* (1938) and *The Holiday* (1949); a number of books of poetry, including *Tender Only to One* (1938), *Harold's Leap* (1950), *Not Waving but Drowning* (1957), and *The Frog Prince and Other Poems* (1966); as well as several books of her curious drawings, notably *Some Are More Human Than Others* (1958). *Me Again* (1981) collects some of her short stories, essays, reviews, and letters, as well as previously unpublished poems and drawings.

In her poetry, she made use of nursery rhymes, popular songs, even hymns, employing clever twists and witty verbal maneuvers to create verse that is fresh and immediately engaging. While many of her poems are lightly humorous, even zany, they also reveal an underlying preoccupation with death, and, occasionally, a chilling fascination with the gruesome and macabre. Every collection of her poetry included a sampling of her odd drawings, like the one that accompanies "The Frog Prince," page 880.

The Frog Prince

I am a frog
I live under a spell
I live at the bottom
Of a green well

5 And here I must wait
Until a maiden places me
On her royal pillow
And kisses me
In her father's palace.

10 The story is familiar
Everybody knows it well
But do other enchanted people feel as
 nervous
As I do? The stories do not tell,

Ask if they will be happier
15 When the changes come,
As already they are fairly happy
In a frog's doom?

I have been a frog now
For a hundred years
20 And in all this time
I have not shed many tears.

I am happy, I like the life,
Can swim for many a mile
(When I have hopped to the river)
25 And am for ever agile.

And the quietness,
Yes, I like to be quiet
I am habituated
To a quiet life,

30 But always when I think these thoughts
As I sit in my well
Another thought comes to me and says:
It is part of the spell

Drawing by Stevie Smith.

To be happy
35 To work up contentment
To make much of being a frog
To fear disenchantment

Says, It will be *heavenly*
To be set free
40 Cries, *Heavenly* the girl who disenchants
And the royal times, *heavenly*,
And I think it will be.

Come then, royal girl and royal times,
Come quickly,
45 I can be happy until you come
But I cannot be heavenly,
Only disenchanted people
Can be heavenly.

1937

Not Waving but Drowning

Nobody heard him, the dead man,
But still he lay moaning:
I was much farther out than you thought
And not waving but drowning.

5 Poor chap, he always loved larking
And now he's dead
It must have been too cold for him his heart
    gave way,
They said.

Oh no no no, it was too cold always
10 (Still the dead one lay moaning)
I was much too far out all my life
And not waving but drowning.

1957

Stevie Smith, *The Collected Poems of Stevie Smith*. Copyright © 1972 by the Estate of Stevie Smith. Reprinted by permission of New Directions Publishing Corporation, agents for the Estate of Stevie Smith and James MacGibbon.

THINK AND DISCUSS
THE FROG PRINCE
Understanding
1. Where has the speaker lived while under the spell that changed him into a frog? How long has he lived there?
2. What must happen for him to be "heavenly"?

Analyzing
3. Why does the Frog Prince feel "nervous" (lines 11–12)?
4. What aspects of a frog's life has he come to enjoy?
5. Besides having been turned into a frog, what else does the Frog Prince fear might be part of the spell?
6. How do the last four lines, especially the ambiguous use of *disenchanted*, explain why the Frog Prince is nevertheless eager for the maiden to come quickly and break the spell of enchantment?

Extending
7. The Frog Prince expresses curiosity about what other people feel who have been placed under a spell. What are some of the things folk tales and myths never go into about their worlds?

NOT WAVING BUT DROWNING
Understanding
1. Why doesn't anyone heed the drowning man's cries for help?
2. What reason do people give for the man's death?

Analyzing
3. What two kinds of "drowning" are described in the poem?
4. What social criticism is implied by the **repetition** of the line "not waving but drowning" and the repeated references to the cold?

Extending
5. All his life the man in the poem sent out signals for help that were either misinterpreted or ignored. What other ways can you think of that people use to signal their need for help and personal attention?

BIOGRAPHY

Ted Hughes

1930–

Ted Hughes was born in Yorkshire and grew up in the West Country. He took a degree at Cambridge, where he was primarily interested in folklore and anthropology. In 1956 he married an American poet, the late Sylvia Plath. His first book of poetry, *The Hawk in the Rain*, appeared the following year.

Much of Hughes's poetry deals with the natural world. He frequently writes of the savagery and cunning of animals and of similar qualities in human beings. His viewpoint is always unsentimental, sometimes to the point of harshness. His work shows a variety of influences: folklore, mythology, anthropology, as well as the poetry of Thomas Hardy, D. H. Lawrence, and Robert Graves.

Hughes's second book of poetry, *Lupercal*, won England's prestigious Hawthornden Prize in 1961. *Wodwo* (1967) was a compilation of both poetry and prose, including short stories and a radio play. *Crow* (1970), a cycle of poems in which Hughes attempts to create a fragmentary mythology centered on a trickster figure drawn from primitive mythology, became something of a best-seller (at least for books of verse). In addition to verse, Hughes has written a number of plays, and several books for children.

Some critics have attacked Hughes for the grimness of his poetic subject matter and the violence of his language. His admirers contend, however, that his language is vibrant and passionate, and that his recognition of violence in man and nature is a valid perception.

In 1984 Hughes was appointed poet laureate.

Pike

Ted Hughes

Pike, three inches long, perfect
Pike in all parts, green tigering the gold.
Killers from the egg: the malevolent aged grin.
They dance on the surface among the flies.

5 Or move, stunned by their own grandeur,
Over a bed of emerald, silhouette
Of submarine delicacy and horror.
A hundred feet long in their world.

In ponds, under the heat-struck lily pads—
10 Gloom of their stillness:
Logged on last year's black leaves, watching upwards.
Or hung in an amber cavern of weeds

The jaws' hooked clamp and fangs
Not to be changed at this date;
15 A life subdued to its instrument;
The gills kneading quietly, and the pectorals.

Three we kept behind glass,
Jungled in weed: three inches, four,
And four and a half: fed fry to them—
20 Suddenly there were two. Finally one

With a sag belly and the grin it was born
    with.
And indeed they spare nobody.
Two, six pounds each, over two feet long,
High and dry and dead in the willow-herb—

25 One jammed past its gills down the other's
    gullet:
The outside eye stared: as a vice locks—
The same iron in this eye
Though its film shrank in death.

A pond I fished, fifty yards across,
30 Whose lilies and muscular tench
Had outlasted every visible stone

Of the monastery that planted them—

Stilled legendary depth:
It was as deep as England. It held
35 Pike too immense to stir, so immense and old
That past nightfall I dared not cast

But silently cast and fished
With the hair frozen on my head
For what might move, for what eye might move.
40 The still splashes on the dark pond,

Owls hushing the floating woods
Frail on my ear against the dream
Darkness beneath night's darkness had freed,
That rose slowly towards me, watching.

1959

Bullfrog

Ted Hughes

With their lithe, long, strong legs,
Some frogs are able
To thump upon double-
Bass strings, though pond water deadens and
    clogs.

5 But you, bullfrog, you pump out
Whole fogs full of horn—a threat
As of a liner looming. True
That, first hearing you
Disgorging your gouts of darkness like a
    wounded god,
10 Not utterly fantastically, I expected
(As in some antique tale depicted)
A broken-down bull up to its belly in mud,

Sucking black swamp up, belching out black
    cloud

And a squall of gudgeon and lilies.
                                    A surprise

15 Now, to see you, a boy's prize,
No bigger than a rat, with all dumb silence
In your little old woman hands.

1959

Fern

Ted Hughes

Here is the fern's frond, unfurling a gesture,
Like a conductor whose music will now be
    pause
And the one note of silence
To which the whole earth dances gravely.

5 The mouse's ear unfurls its trust,
The spider takes up her bequest,
And the retina
Reins the creation with a bridle of water.

And, among them, the fern
10 Dances gravely, like the plume
Of a warrior returning, under the low hills,

Into his own kingdom.

1967

Wood engraving of ferns, French, nineteenth century.

THINK AND DISCUSS

PIKE

Understanding

1. What happened to the three pike "kept behind glass"?
2. What happened to the two large pike found "in the willow-herb"?

Analyzing

3. Why, though only "three inches long," are baby pike already "a hundred feet long in their world"?
4. How does the line "A life subdued to its instrument" explain the dread pike inspire?
5. What is significant about the **setting** for the fishing in the last four stanzas?
6. What "dream" has darkness "freed" that leaves the speaker's hair "frozen" on his head (standing on end)?
7. Point out specific **images** and uses of color that make the pike appear **paradoxically** beautiful in spite of their malevolence.

Extending

8. It is characteristic of Hughes's verse to use plants, objects, or animals as **symbols** of some larger general concept. What larger concept might pike represent in this poem?

BULLFROG

Understanding

1. To what is the noise of the bullfrog compared?
2. To what four things is the bullfrog itself compared?

Analyzing

3. Contrast the description of the bullfrog in the first fourteen lines of the poem with that in the last three.
4. What personal experience might the poet be recalling in this poem?

FERN

Understanding

1. Name three things in nature, aside from the fern's frond, whose roundness and intricate perfection the poem celebrates.
2. What two **similes** describe the unfurling and dance-like movement of the frond?

Analyzing

3. Explain lines 6–8. What is the spider's "bequest"? What is the "bridle of water" with which the retina "Reins the creation"?
4. What words suggest the roundness of the cyclic rhythms of nature?

Extending

5. What importance is conferred on the fern through the use of **personification?** Do you feel it is warranted?

COMPOSITION ✎

Describing an Animal

Following the techniques used by Ted Hughes in "Pike" and "Bullfrog," write a five- to seven-paragraph description of an animal you have observed closely. One way to approach the subject might be to trace the events in a typical day in the life of this animal. Use precise sensory details to describe how it moves, responds, feels to the touch, communicates, and so on. What specific incidents reveal the character and temperament of this animal? In your conclusion, explain whether it deserves a nomination to the Hall of Fame or the Rogue's Gallery.

Writing a Poem

Using **imagery** and figures of speech, such as **similes, metaphors,** and **personification,** describe something in the plant or animal kingdom—such as a tree, a lake, a flower, a bird, a horse—that you esthetically appreciate. Pinpoint first what it is that you find most appealing, such as color, movement, size, texture, and so on. Using either free or structured verse, pay tribute to your subject, as Hughes does in "Fern," showing through word pictures why your admiration is warranted.

Scene from 1955 film of *Nineteen Eighty-four*.

In the twentieth century the English language has continued to grow and change. The *Oxford English Dictionary*, published in ten volumes from 1884 to 1928 (see page 750), had swelled to twelve volumes and a supplement by 1933. The word *head* now had more than forty meanings; the word *green* had more than fifty. New words continued to be added to the language. Two world wars provided such terms as *zeppelin, U-boat, blitzkrieg, jeep, concentration camp,* and *A-bomb;* from the sciences came *neurosis, antibiotic, radio, television,* and *transistor;* from the arts came *montage, surrealism,* and *absurdist.*

As the language continued to change, words took on new meanings. *Scan* once meant to study with great care; now it means to glance at hastily. *Sophistication,* once a term of condemnation, now signifies approval. Some words once frowned on in polite society are now acceptable. To have described an act of courage as being *plucky* would have been considered vulgar in Victorian drawing rooms. And to have used the word *gutsy* would have branded the speaker as a social outcast.

The widespread use of manipulative language by propagandists and advertisers disturbed many people. Probably the best-known analyst of the corruption of English by politicians and salesmen in the recent past was George Orwell (see pages 811–816). In essays like "Politics and the English Language" he protested against bad language habits that corrupt thinking: "Modern writing at its worst does not consist in picking out words for the sake of their meaning and inventing images in order to make the meaning clearer. It consists in gumming together long strips of words which have already been set in order by someone else, and making the results presentable by sheer humbug."

Orwell's novel *Nineteen Eighty-four* depicts a slave society ruled by a self-perpetuating elite. The official language is named *Newspeak*. Each year words are eliminated from its vocabulary. The purpose of impoverishing the language is to narrow the range of thought of the citizens, so that it will become increasingly difficult for them to express, or even to form, an unorthodox concept. Ultimately, they will cease to think altogether. In order to create more mental confusion in the citizens, the elite promotes the practice of *doublethink,* the ability to hold two contradictory beliefs simultaneously. Such words as *Newspeak* and *doublethink* have themselves now passed into the language. Perhaps Orwell's bleak fantasy should be seen more as a warning than a prediction. But in a world replete with official euphemism, in which murder is referred to as "termination with extreme prejudice," Orwell's admonition to rid ourselves of bad language habits, like euphemism, as "a necessary first step toward political regeneration," is useful.

THINKING CRITICALLY
ABOUT LITERATURE

UNIT 8   THE TWENTIETH CENTURY   1915–

■ CONCEPT REVIEW

The following selection contains many of the important ideas and literary terms found in Unit 8. It also contains notes and questions designed to help you think critically about your reading. Page numbers in the notes refer to an application or a review. A more extensive discussion of these terms is in the Handbook of Literary Terms.

This story, like "Araby," is from *Dubliners*, a collection of narratives that Joyce wrote to portray what he termed the "spiritual paralysis" of Dublin, the city where he grew up and which he fled as a young man. In this story an opportunity to marry and escape a brutal and stagnating environment leads Eveline to make a decision that will determine the course of the rest of her life.

Eveline

James Joyce

She sat at the window watching the evening invade the avenue. Her head was leaned against the window curtains and in her nostrils was the odor of dusty cretonne. She was tired.

Few people passed. The man out of the last house passed on his way home; she heard his footsteps clacking along the concrete pavement and afterwards crunching on the cinder path before the new red houses. One time there used to be a field there in which they used to play every evening with other people's children. Then a man from Belfast bought the field and built houses in it—not like their little brown houses but bright brick houses with shining roofs. The children of the avenue used to play together in that field—the Devines, the

■ **cretonne:** a strong cotton, linen, or rayon cloth with designs printed in colors.

■ **Imagery** (page 878): Note the images of touch, smell, sound, and sight in these opening sentences that establish the *setting*.

Waters, the Dunns, little Keogh the cripple, she and her brothers and sisters. Ernest, however, never played: he was too grown up. Her father used often to hunt them in out of the field with his blackthorn stick; but usually little Keogh used to keep nix and call out when he saw her father coming. Still they seemed to have been rather happy then. Her father was not so bad then; and besides, her mother was alive. That was a long time ago; she and her brothers and sisters were all grown up; her mother was dead. Tizzie Dunn was dead, too, and the Waters had gone back to England. Everything changes. Now she was going to go away like the others, to leave her home.

Home! She looked round the room, reviewing all its familiar objects which she had dusted once a week for so many years, wondering where on earth all the dust came from. Perhaps she would never see again those familiar objects from which she had never dreamed of being divided. And yet during all those years she had never found out the name of the priest whose yellowing photograph hung on the wall above the broken harmonium beside the colored print of the promises made to Blessed Margaret Mary Alacoque. He had been a school friend of her father. Whenever he showed the photograph to a visitor her father used to pass it with a casual word: "He is in Melbourne now."

She had consented to go away, to leave her home. Was that wise? She tried to weigh each side of the question. In her home anyway she had shelter and food; she had those whom she had known all her life about her. Of course she had to work hard, both in the house and at business. What would they say of her in the Stores when they found out that she had run away with a fellow? Say she was a fool, perhaps; and her place would be filled up by advertisement. Miss Gavan would be glad. She had always had an edge on her, especially whenever there were people listening.

"Miss Hill, don't you see these ladies are waiting?"

"Look lively, Miss Hill, please."

She would not cry many tears at leaving the Stores.

But in her new home, in a distant unknown country, it would not be like that. Then she would be married—she, Eveline. People would treat her with respect then. She would not be treated as her mother had been. Even now, though she was over nineteen, she sometimes felt herself in danger of her father's violence. She knew it was that that had given her the palpitations. When they were growing up he had never gone for her, like he used to go for Harry and Ernest, because she was a girl; but latterly he had begun to threaten her and say what he would do to her only for her dead mother's sake. And now she had nobody to protect her. Ernest was dead and Harry, who was in the church decorating business, was nearly always down somewhere in the country. Besides, the invariable squabble for money on Saturday nights had begun to weary her unspeakably. She always gave her entire wages—seven shillings—and Harry always sent up what he could but the trouble was to get any money from her father. He said she used to squander the money, that she had no head, that he wasn't going to give her his hard-earned money to throw about the streets, and much more, for he was usually fairly bad on

■ **nix:** an old slang word, originally used by thieves to refer to the member of a gang who kept watch.

■ **Point of view** (page 810): Note how the story makes us see Eveline's life and environment through *her* eyes.

■ Note the sensory details used to suggest the shabby condition of the room.

■ **Blessed . . . Alacoque** (1647–1690): a French nun who experienced visions of Jesus Christ. Her visions and teaching have had considerable effect on the devotional life of Roman Catholics.

■ **the Stores:** a department store.

■ **palpitations:** a very rapid beating of the heart.

■ Note the details that *characterize* Eveline's father.

Saturday night. In the end he would give her the money and ask her had she any intention of buying Sunday's dinner. Then she had to rush out as quickly as she could and do her marketing, holding her black leather purse tightly in her hand as she elbowed her way through the crowds and returning home late under her load of provisions. She had hard work to keep the house together and to see that the two young children who had been left to her charge went to school regularly and got their meals regularly. It was hard work—a hard life—but now that she was about to leave it she did not find it a wholly undesirable life.

She was about to explore another life with Frank. Frank was very kind, manly, openhearted. She was to go away with him by the night boat to be his wife and to live with him in Buenos Aires where he had a home waiting for her. How well she remembered the first time she had seen him; he was lodging in a house on the main road where she used to visit. It seemed a few weeks ago. He was standing at the gate, his peaked cap pushed back on his head and his hair tumbled forward over a face of bronze. Then they had come to know each other. He used to meet her outside the Stores every evening and see her home. He took her to see *The Bohemian Girl* and she felt elated as she sat in an unaccustomed part of the theater with him. He was awfully fond of music and sang a little. People knew that they were courting and, when he sang about the lass that loves a sailor, she always felt pleasantly confused. He used to call her Poppens out of fun. First of all it had been an excitement for her to have a fellow and then she had begun to like him. He had tales of distant countries. He had started as a deck boy at a pound a month on a ship of the Allan Line going out to Canada. He told her the names of the ships he had been on and the names of the different services. He had sailed through the Straits of Magellan and he told her stories of the terrible Patagonians. He had fallen on his feet in Buenos Aires, he said, and had come over to the old country just for a holiday. Of course, her father had found out the affair and had forbidden her to have anything to say to him.

"I know these sailor chaps," he said.

One day he had quarreled with Frank and after that she had to meet her lover secretly.

The evening deepened in the avenue. The white of two letters in her lap grew indistinct. One was to Harry; the other was to her father. Ernest had been her favorite but she liked Harry too. Her father was becoming old lately, she noticed; he would miss her. Sometimes he could be very nice. Not long before, when she had been laid up for a day, he had read her out a ghost story and made toast for her at the fire. Another day, when their mother was alive, they had all gone for a picnic to the Hill of Howth. She remembered her father putting on her mother's bonnet to make the children laugh.

Her time was running out but she continued to sit by the window, leaning her head against the window curtain, inhaling the odor of dusty cretonne. Down far in the avenue she could hear a street organ playing. She knew the air. Strange that it should come that very night to remind her of the

■ Note the various clues that indicate Eveline is beginning to waver in her decision to leave home.

■ *The Bohemian Girl:* an opera by the Irish-born composer Michael Balfe (1808–1870).

■ **Patagonians:** primitive people inhabiting the desolate southern part of South America.

■ **Hill of Howth:** a hill on a peninsula that forms the north shore of Dublin Bay.

promise to her mother, her promise to keep the home together as long as she could. She remembered the last night of her mother's illness; she was again in the close dark room at the other side of the hall and outside she heard a melancholy air of Italy. The organ player had been ordered to go away and given sixpence. She remembered her father strutting back into the sickroom saying: "Damned Italians! coming over here!"

As she mused the pitiful vision of her mother's life laid its spell on the very quick of her being—that life of commonplace sacrifices closing in final craziness. She trembled as she heard again her mother's voice saying constantly with foolish insistence: "Derevaun Seraun! Derevaun Seraun!"

She stood up in a sudden impulse of terror. Escape! She must escape! Frank would save her. He would give her life, perhaps love, too. But she wanted to live. Why should she be unhappy? She had a right to happiness. Frank would take her in his arms, fold her in his arms. He would save her.

She stood among the swaying crowd in the station at the North Wall. He held her hand and she knew that he was speaking to her, saying something about the passage over and over again. The station was full of soldiers with brown baggages. Through the wide doors of the sheds she caught a glimpse of the black mass of the boat, lying in beside the quay wall, with illumined portholes. She answered nothing. She felt her cheek pale and cold and, out of a maze of distress, she prayed to God to direct her, to show her what was her duty. The boat blew a long mournful whistle into the mist. If she went, tomorrow she would be on the sea with Frank, steaming toward Buenos Aires. Their passage had been booked. Could she still draw back after all he had done for her? Her distress awoke a nausea in her body and she kept moving her lips in silent fervent prayer.

A bell clanged upon her heart. She felt him seize her hand:

"Come!"

All the seas of the world tumbled about her heart. He was drawing her into them: he would drown her. She gripped with both hands at the iron railing.

"Come!"

No! No! No! It was impossible. Her hands clutched the iron in frenzy. Amid the seas she sent a cry of anguish.

"Eveline! Evvy!"

He rushed beyond the barrier and called to her to follow. He was shouted at to go on but he still called to her. She set her white face to him, passive, like a helpless animal. Her eyes gave him no sign of love or farewell or recognition.

1914

■ **Mood** (page 790): Note how the sound of the organ music and the vision of her mother dramatically alter the mood of the story.

■ **"Deveraun Seraun"**: possibly corrupt Gaelic for "the end of pleasure is pain."

■ Remember that many of Joyce's stories end with an *epiphany*. Watch for one here.

■ Note how the *theme* is expressed indirectly through images as is typical in the work of 20th century writers.

THINK AND DISCUSS
Understanding
1. What is Eveline doing as the story opens?
2. What does she do for a living?
3. What is the cause of Eveline's "palpitations"?
4. Where has Frank offered to take her?

Analyzing
5. Describe the **setting.** How does it influence the course of the story?
6. How is Eveline's father **characterized?** What makes him difficult to live with?
7. What reasons does Eveline have for wanting to leave home? for wanting to stay?
8. What reason does Eveline's father give for forbidding her to see Frank? What other personal reason might he have?
9. Judging from Eveline's description of Frank and their brief courtship, what kind of life might she have enjoyed as Frank's wife?
10. What causes Eveline to send Frank away without a "sign of love or farewell or recognition"?
11. Is there an *epiphany?* If so, what is it and where does it come?
12. What is the **theme** of the story? Is it stated or implied?

Extending
13. Compare "Eveline" with "Araby." What similarities of **plot,** character, setting, and theme stamp them as the work of the same writer?
14. How does the theme of "Eveline" tie in with the larger theme of "the inner life" dealt with extensively in the works of twentieth-century writers?

REVIEWING LITERARY TERMS
Imagery
1. What sensory details enable us to visualize Eveline's home and neighborhood?
2. How does imagery contribute to Eveline's final decision?

Mood
3. What mood is established in the first three paragraphs?
4. How is the mood sharply altered by Eveline's memory of her mother?
5. What mood is captured in the scene at the station, in the paragraph beginning, "She stood among the swaying crowd . . . "?

Point of View
6. From what point of view is "Eveline" told? How does this point of view contribute to the overall effect of the story?

■ CONTENT REVIEW
Classifying
1. The "outsider" is a characteristic figure in twentieth-century literature. Which of the selections in this unit make use of this figure?
2. Which selections in Unit 8 can be classified as **elegies?**
3. List the selections in this unit down one side of a piece of paper. Across the top write these headings: *Childhood, Nature, Inner Life, Social Criticism, War.* Construct a chart of **themes,** placing check marks where appropriate. Which selections contain two or more themes at once?

Generalizing
4. Write your own definition of *modern poetry.* Cite examples of twentieth-century poetry to illustrate various aspects of your definition.
5. Children are pivotal characters in a number of selections in this unit. What joys or sorrows are experienced by the children in these selections?
6. Social criticism is apparent in much of twentieth-century writing. What are some of the aspects of modern life attacked in this unit? What criticism is leveled against them?

Synthesizing

7. Auden called the period following World War II "The Age of Anxiety." Think of an abstract noun that could be applied to each unit in this book, and write an epithet for it, following the pattern of "The Age of _____."

8. When people talk about "the good old days," they are usually thinking of a way of life now lost to us. Are we, in our modern world, missing some important values that people had in earlier times? If so, what are they? How can we regain them?

Evaluating

9. The **sonnet** has been used by poets in almost every period since the Renaissance. Compare "The Soldier," "Anthem for Doomed Youth," and "Who's Who" with sonnets in earlier units. What is there about the sonnet form that makes it so popular?

10. To what extent do twentieth-century writers use humor as a tool for social criticism? How effective is the use of humor in selections in this unit?

■ COMPOSITION REVIEW

Analyzing Twentieth-Century Skepticism

In a paper of five to eight paragraphs, analyze how the works of Sassoon, Owen, and Brittain illustrate the transformation from nineteenth-century idealism and naïveté into twentieth-century skepticism and despair as a result of England's prolonged and tragic involvement in World War I. What illusions about patriotism, military and national leaders, and war itself were shattered in the trenches of World War I? Use quotations from the works of these three writers to illustrate your analysis.

Describing Modern Poetry

Assume that Alfred, Lord Tennyson has returned to earth to investigate the state of poetry in twentieth-century life. Write a letter in which you introduce him to modern poetry, making reference to poems such as "The Hollow Men," "In Memory of W. B. Yeats," "Fern Hill," and "Pike." Acknowledge from the start that Tennyson will very likely be surprised by changes in subject matter and style. Point out some of the techniques and themes that differentiate modern poetry from the Victorian poetry with which Tennyson was familiar and which he personally wrote. Conclude by offering some explanations as to why such radical changes have taken place.

Comparing Twentieth-Century Humorists

The stories of Greene and Warner are humorous, yet in a cynical way. In a paper of six to eight paragraphs compare the use of humor in the stories of these writers, explaining what is cynical, mocking, or scornful in the authors' attitudes toward people and events. What faults of humans and society in general account for the negative outlook in these stories?

Analyzing the Theme of the Inner Life

In the works of many twentieth-century writers, not what happens, but how a character feels about an experience is what is emphasized. In a paper of four to six paragraphs, analyze the treatment of the theme of the inner life in the stories of Joyce, Mansfield, Woolf, and Lawrence, identifying any distinctive techniques used to portray the characters' thoughts, moods, and inner feelings. What do these interior landscapes suggest about the possibility of happiness and meaningful personal relationships in modern society? Which selections portray the moods of loneliness, loss, and alienation so characteristic of twentieth century literature?

HANDBOOK OF LITERARY TERMS

■ ALLUSION

I reached out a hand from under the blankets and
rang the bell for Jeeves.

"Good evening, Jeeves."

"Good morning, sir."

This surprised me.

"Is it morning?"

"Yes, sir."

"Are you sure? It seems very dark outside."

"There is a fog, sir. If you will recollect, we are now
in autumn—season of mists and mellow fruitfulness."

"Oh? Yes. Yes, I see. . . ."

P. G. Wodehouse
from **The Code of the Woosters**

Did you recognize that Jeeves is quoting the
first line of John Keats's poem "To Autumn"
(page 515)? The befuddled narrator, Bertie
Wooster, doesn't—but then, Bertie is the last
person one would expect to appreciate poetry.
In giving this line to Jeeves, the author
underscores the difference between the butler's
knowledge and Bertie's, and in doing so creates
humor. To appreciate the humor, however, the
reader must recognize the allusion.

An **allusion** is a brief reference to a person,
event, place, or work of art. Allusions may refer
to myth, literature, history, religion, or any
aspect of ancient or modern culture. An allusion
can concisely convey much information. See if
you can recognize the allusion in the cartoon in
the next column.

The reference in the caption of the cartoon
is to the first line of Thomas Gray's "Elegy
Written in a Country Churchyard" (page 409),
which reads, "The curfew tolls the knell of parting day. . . ."

©Punch/Rothco

"How does the Knell of Parting Day toll again?"

Sometimes, understanding an allusion is crucial to a reader's understanding of a work; at
other times, allusions serve simply to establish
character, mood, setting, and so on. For example, Chaucer has the Wife of Bath allude to
scripture and the lives of saints in her "Prologue" and "Tale" (page 122). Her use—and
misuse—of these allusions reveals much about
her character. In Wordsworth's "The World Is
Too Much with Us" (page 457), the allusions
to Proteus and Triton serve to underscore the
speaker's desire for a simpler existence, one
more "in tune" with nature.

P. G. Wodehouse, *The Code of the Woosters* (Random House, 1975).

An allusion can be a simple, passing reference to a title, person, or event. Any of several other well-known novels might have been used instead of *Middlemarch* in the following passage:

> She was by way of being terrified of him—he was so fearfully clever, and the first night when she had sat by him, and he talked about George Eliot, she had been really frightened, for she had left the third volume of *Middlemarch* in the train and she never knew what happened in the end. . . .

> *Virginia Woolf*
> *from* **To the Lighthouse**

An allusion can also rely more heavily on the reader's recognition of the specific reference. The following passage is much funnier if you know the old nursery rhyme "Peter Piper picked a peck of pickled peppers":

> . . . to paraphrase the idle legend of Peter Piper, who had never found his way into their nursery, If the greedy little Gradgrinds grasped at more than this, what was it for good gracious goodness' sake that the greedy little Gradgrinds grasped at?

> *Charles Dickens*
> *from* **Hard Times**

■ ALLUSION

A brief reference to a person, event, or place, real or fictitious, or to a work of art. An allusion may or may not be central to the meaning of a literary work.

Virginia Woolf, *To the Lighthouse* (Harcourt, Brace & World, Inc., 1927).

■ Apply to "**The Wife of Bath's Prologue**" and "**Tale**" on pages 122 and 130.

■ ANALOGY

As the painter in his picture, so the artist in his book, aims at the production by honourable artifice of a peculiar atmosphere. "The artist," says Schiller, "may be known rather by what he *omits*"; and in literature, too, the true artist may be best recognised by his tact of omission. For to the grave reader words too are grave; and the ornamental word, the figure, the accessory form or colour or reference, is rarely content to die to thought precisely at the right moment, but will inevitably linger awhile stirring a long "brainwave" behind it of perhaps quite alien associations.

> *Walter Pater*
> *from* "**Style**"

1. To what is a writer compared in the passage above?
2. What, according to Pater, do both books and pictures benefit from?

Pater draws a comparison to lead his readers to see how words, like visual images, should be carefully chosen and manipulated for maximum effectiveness. This type of comparison is called an **analogy**. In literature, an analogy is a comparison made between two objects, situations, or ideas that are basically different but that are alike in some ways. The word *analogy* derives from a term originally used by the Greeks to mean similarity in proportional relationships. A classic example of this is "As A is to B, so C is to D." Often, a writer will compare an unfamiliar or complex object or idea to a simpler one in order to explain the first more clearly.

Analogies can be stated in a particular form. Pater's analogy can be verbalized as "An artist is to a painting as a writer is to a book." Another way to present this analogy is as follows:

artist: painting :: writer: book

Analogies are more than simple comparisons. Usually, the similarities are developed to clarify a point. The point that Pater is making is

that both pictures and words benefit from pruning—a screening out of unnecessary elements.

Read the following poem and answer the questions about the analogy in it.

The Toys

My little Son, who looked from thoughtful eyes
And moved and spoke in quiet grown-up wise,
Having my law the seventh time disobeyed,
I struck him, and dismissed
5 With hard words and unkissed,
—His Mother, who was patient, being dead.
Then, fearing lest his grief should hinder sleep,
I visited his bed,
But found him slumbering deep,

10 With darkened eyelids, and their lashes yet
From his late sobbing wet.
And I, with moan,
Kissing away his tears, left others of my own;
For, on a table drawn beside his head,
15 He had put, within his reach,
A box of counters and a red-veined stone,
A piece of glass abraded by the beach,
And six or seven shells,
A bottle with bluebells,
20 And two French copper coins, ranged there
          with careful art,
To comfort his sad heart.
So when that night I prayed
To God, I wept, and said:
Ah, when at last we lie with trancèd breath,
25 Not vexing Thee in death,
And Thou rememberest of what toys
We made our joys,
How weakly understood
Thy great commanded good,
30 Then, fatherly not less
Than I whom Thou hast moulded from the clay,
Thou'lt leave Thy wrath, and say,
"I will be sorry for their childishness."

Coventry Patmore

1. To what use had the son put his toys?
2. To what is the relationship between father and son compared?
3. To what use are the "toys" put in lines 26–27? What sort of "toys" might the speaker be referring to here?
4. How does the speaker hope that God will react?

■ ANALOGY

A comparison made between two objects, situations, or ideas that are somewhat alike but unlike in most respects. Frequently an unfamiliar or complex object or idea will be compared to a familiar or simpler one.

■ Apply to **"Of Studies"** on page 171.

■ ANASTROPHE

The Cloak, the Boat, and the Shoes

"What do you make so fair and bright?"

"I make the cloak of Sorrow:
O lovely to see in all men's sight
Shall be the cloak of Sorrow,
5 In all men's sight."

"What do you build with sails for flight?"

"I build a boat for Sorrow:
O swift on the seas all day and night
Saileth the rover Sorrow,
10 All day and night."

"What do you weave with wool so white?"

"I weave the shoes of Sorrow:
Soundless shall be the footfall light
In all men's ears of Sorrow,
15 Sudden and light."

William Butler Yeats

Examine the word order in the poem above. How does it differ from that of conventional English? Yeats has used **anastrophe**—the inversion of the usual order of parts of a sentence. For example, in conventional order, lines 3–5 would read: "The cloak of sorrow shall be lovely to see in all men's sight." How would lines 8–10 and 13–15 read?

Writers use anastrophe to emphasize a word or idea or to achieve a certain rhythm or rhyme. Coleridge wrote, poetry is "the best words in their best order" —but that order is not always the conventional one.

■ ANASTROPHE

Inversion of the usual order of the parts of a sentence, primarily for emphasis or to achieve a certain rhythm or rhyme.

From *The Poems of W. B. Yeats: A New Edition*, edited by Richard J. Finneran (New York: Macmillan, 1983). Reprinted by permission of A. P. Watt Ltd. on behalf of Michael B. Yeats and Macmillan London Ltd.

■ Apply to "**Loveliest of Trees**" on page 726.

■ BLANK VERSE

Read the following passage aloud and listen for the rhythm:

Our revels now are ended. These our actors,
As I foretold you, were all spirits, and
Are melted into air, into thin air.
And, like the baseless fabric of this vision,
5 The cloud-capped towers, the gorgeous palaces,
The solemn temples, the great globe itself—
Yea, all which it inherit—shall dissolve
And, like this insubstantial pageant faded,
Leave not a rack behind. We are such stuff
10 As dreams are made on, and our little life
Is rounded with a sleep.

William Shakespeare
from **The Tempest**

Like many of his contemporaries, Shakespeare often wrote in **blank verse**—unrhymed iambic pentameter. A line of iambic pentameter has ten syllables, with accents on the second, fourth, sixth, eighth, and tenth syllables.

First used by the Earl of Surrey in the sixteenth century, blank verse became popular among English poets and playwrights who discovered that its rhythm reflects the natural cadence of English speech. It has been used in poetry more frequently than any other type of rhythm.

For example, read the following aloud:

For on their march to westward, Bedivere, who slowly paced among the slumbering host, heard in his tent the moanings of the King: "I found Him in the shining of the stars. I marked Him in the flowering of His fields. But in His ways with men I find Him not. I waged His wars, and now I pass and die."

The lines on the previous page were altered from Tennyson's "The Passing of Arthur," published in 1869. Compare them with the original on page 563, written in poetic lines. Like most well-written blank verse, these lines, if read properly, sound natural and unforced. To get the best effect from blank verse, read for the sense, as indicated by the punctuation and sentence structure, and ignore the way the poetic lines break.

Although blank verse is written in iambic pentameter, a blank-verse line can, in a play, be split between two speakers. The following dialogue from Shakespeare's *The Tempest* illustrates this point:

1a **ALONSO.** Arise, and say how thou camest here!
1b **MIRANDA.** Oh, wonder!
2 How many goodly creatures are there here!
3 How beauteous mankind is! Oh, brave new world,
4a That has such people in 't!
4b **PROSPERO.** 'Tis new to thee.

A line or lines of a blank-verse passage may, at times, depart from the regular iambic pentameter pattern, as do the two examples here from *The Tempest*. Such shifts in meter provide variety and allow the writer to achieve particular dramatic effects.

■ BLANK VERSE

Unrhymed iambic pentameter, a line of five feet, each with an unstressed syllable followed by a stressed one.

■ Apply to *Paradise Lost* on page 294.

■ CHARACTERIZATION

In the following novel excerpt, Mr. Woodhouse is recovering from the marriage of his daughter's former governess to a neighbor. Read the selection and answer the questions that follow.

The compliments of his neighbours were over; he was no longer teased by being wished joy of so sorrowful an event; and the wedding-cake, which had been a great distress to him, was all eat up. His own stomach could bear nothing rich, and he could never believe other people to be different from himself. What was unwholesome to him, he regarded as unfit for any body; and he had, therefore, earnestly tried to dissuade them from having any wedding-cake at all, and when that proved vain, as earnestly tried to prevent any body's eating it. He had been at the pains of consulting Mr. Perry, the apothecary, on the subject. Mr. Perry was an intelligent, gentlemanlike man, whose frequent visits were one of the comforts of Mr. Woodhouse's life; and, upon being applied to, he could not but acknowledge, (though it seemed rather against the bias of inclination,) that wedding-cake might certainly disagree with many—perhaps with most people, unless taken moderately. With such an opinion, in confirmation of his own, Mr. Woodhouse hoped to influence every visitor of the new-married pair; but still the cake was eaten; and there was no rest for his benevolent nerves till it was all gone.

There was a strange rumour in Highbury of all the little Perrys being seen with a slice of Mrs. Weston's wedding-cake in their hands: but Mr. Woodhouse would never believe it.

Jane Austen
from **Emma**

1. Why does Mr. Woodhouse try to prevent anyone from having wedding-cake?
2. How do other people seem to treat Mr. Woodhouse?
3. What do you learn about the kind of person Mr. Woodhouse is?
4. What do you learn about Mr. Perry?

The methods an author uses to introduce and describe a character are called **characterization**. A character's physical appearance and personality traits may be described. (In the example above, you learn nothing about Mr. Woodhouse's appearance but much about his personality.) The thoughts and feelings of a character may be described. The character's speech and behavior tell you a great deal, as do the reactions of other characters. Any or all of these methods may be used in the same work.

Stereotype

A **stereotype** is a conventional character, based on fixed, generalized ideas about people or groups of people. The character Murdstone in *David Copperfield* (page 576) in many ways fits the stereotype of a villain. Sometimes an author will deliberately use stereotypes as a kind of background or as foils for the main character. A cartoon-like character, centered around one main idea, may be called "flat," or two-dimensional.

"Round" characters are more fully developed, or three-dimensional. They are more believable, both in action and in motivation. Liza Doolittle in *Pygmalion*, for example, is a complex and very believable character. An author creates round characters by giving them individual but real characteristics and then by exploring how a person with those characteristics would react in various circumstances.

Finally, some characters are *dynamic*—they develop and grow in response to events. Other characters, however, are *static*—they are at the end what they were in the beginning, untouched by any event or personality in the narrative.

What techniques of characterization can you find in the following example?

Oh! but he was a tight-fisted hand at the grindstone. Scrooge! a squeezing, wrenching, grasping, scraping, clutching, covetous, old sinner! Hard and sharp as flint, from which no steel had ever struck out generous fire; secret, and self-contained, and solitary as an oyster. The cold within him froze his old features, nipped his pointed nose, shrivelled his cheek, stiffened his gait; made his eyes red, his thin lips blue; and spoke out shrewdly in his grating voice. A frosty rime[1] was on his head, and on his eyebrows, and his wiry chin. He carried his own low temperature always about with him; he iced his office in the dog-days, and didn't thaw it one degree at Christmas. . . .

Nobody ever stopped him in the street to say, with gladsome looks, "My dear Scrooge, how are you? When will you come to see me?" No beggars implored him to bestow a trifle, no children asked him what it was o'clock, no man or woman ever once in all his life inquired the way to such and such a place, of Scrooge. Even the blind men's dogs appeared to know him; and when they saw him coming on, would tug their owners into doorways and up courts; and then would wag their tails as though they said, "No eye at all is better than an evil eye, dark master!"

Charles Dickens
from **A Christmas Carol**

---

1. *rime*, white frost; hoarfrost.

■ CHARACTERIZATION

The methods an author uses to develop the personality of a character in a literary work. An author can describe a character's appearance and personality, speech and behavior, thoughts and feelings, and interactions with other characters. Characters may be "round" or "flat"—as is a *stereotype*—and dynamic or static.

■ Apply to the Prologue to *The Canterbury Tales* on page 97.

■ CONCEIT

As lines, so loves, oblique may well
Themselves in every angle greet;
But ours, so truly parallel,
Though infinite, can never meet.

Andrew Marvell
from "**The Definition of Love**"

1. *Oblique* means either "slanting" or "indirect; not straightforward." Which definition might apply to lines? Which might apply to loves?
2. To what kind of lines does the speaker compare the love between him and his beloved? What qualities of those lines does their love share?

In these lines, Marvell compares love to parallel lines—infinite, but never meeting. Elsewhere in the poem he claims that Fate has placed him and his beloved on opposite poles of the earth, so that they cannot embrace without causing the earth to collapse.

These comparisons are examples of **conceit** —an elaborate and surprising figure of speech comparing two very dissimilar things. Often employing puns and paradoxes, a conceit may develop an analogy or metaphor as far as (or further than) it can logically go.

Conceit is common in the metaphysical poetry of the seventeenth century, poetry that exhibits a highly intellectual style that is witty, subtle, and sometimes fantastic.

In one type of conceit, borrowed from Italian love poetry, a despairing lover describes his idealized mistress—beautiful, but cold and cruel. Teeth are described as pearls, lips as rubies, and so on. In the following example, the poet argues the artificiality of these comparisons, but still compares his love to a star:

Ingrateful Beauty Threatened

Know, Celia, since thou art so proud,
  'Twas I that gave thee thy renown;
Thou hadst in the forgotten crowd
  Of common beauties lived unknown,
5 Had not my verse exhaled thy name,
And with it imped the wings of fame.

That killing power is none of thine,
  I gave it to thy voice and eyes;
Thy sweets, thy graces, all are mine;
10   Thou art my star, shin'st in my skies;
Then dart not from thy borrowed sphere
Lightning on him that fixed thee there.

Tempt me with such affrights no more,
  Lest what I make I uncreate;
15 Let fools thy mystic forms adore,
  I'll know thee in thy mortal state;
Wise poets that wrapped truth in tales
Knew her themselves through all her veils.

Thomas Carew

1. Where did Celia get her power and her fame?
2. The speaker claims to have given Celia the status of a "star." What does he request her not to do?
3. With what does he threaten her?

■ CONCEIT

An elaborate and surprising figure of speech comparing two very dissimilar things. It usually involves intellectual cleverness and ingenuity.

■ Apply to "**Arcadia**" on page 182.

■ CONNOTATION/DENOTATION

Drawing by Modell; ©1983, The New Yorker Magazine, Inc.

"Oh, come, come, Mr. Bryant. It went down a few points, yes, but I wouldn't say it plummeted."

What word has Mr. Bryant apparently used to describe his stock? Why does his stockbroker use different words to describe the same occurrence?

Everyone is aware of the effect that a choice of words can have. (Would you rather drive a "used" car or one that was "previously owned"?) Advertisers make use of this effect, as do most people in their daily lives when they choose one word over another to describe or request something, praise or blame someone.

The emotional associations surrounding a word are known as the word's **connotation.** For example, what do you think of when you hear the word *winter*? Some people associate winter with cars that won't start, icy winds, and layers of uncomfortable clothing. Such associations are not universal, however. Others associate winter

with rain, making snow sculpture, skating, skiing, or the holiday season.

The literal meaning of *winter* does not, of course, include any of these things. The dictionary meaning of a word is its **denotation.** Stripped of positive or negative associations, the denotation remains constant; it is the connotations that can change from individual to individual.

Examine this dictionary definition; then read the verses from a song on the next page.

win ter (win′tər), *n.* **1** the coldest of the four seasons; time of the year between autumn and spring. **2** a year of life; *a man of eighty winters.* **3** the last period of life. **4** period of decline, dreariness, or adversity. —*adj.* **1** of, having to do with, or characteristic of winter; *winter clothes, winter weather.* **2** of the kind that may be kept for use during the winter: *winter apples.* —*v.i.* pass the winter: *Robins winter in the south.* —*v.t.* keep, feed, or manage during winter: *We wintered our cattle in the warm valley.* [Old English]

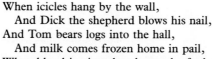

When icicles hang by the wall,
   And Dick the shepherd blows his nail,
And Tom bears logs into the hall,
   And milk comes frozen home in pail,
5 When blood is nipped and ways be foul,
Then nightly sings the staring owl, To-whit!
To-who!—a merry note,
While greasy Joan doth keel the pot.

10 When all aloud the wind doth blow,
   And coughing drowns the parson's saw,
And birds sit brooding in the snow,
   And Marian's nose looks red and raw,
When roasted crabs hiss in the bowl,
15 Then nightly sings the staring owl,
     To-whit!
To-who!—a merry note,
While greasy Joan doth keel the pot.

William Shakespeare
from **Love's Labour's Lost**

1. What words and phrases of negative connotation do you find in Shakespeare's song?
2. What positive connotation is there?
3. Dictionaries reflect usage, and after centuries of use certain metaphorical meanings have taken their place alongside more literal ones. In the entry on page 901, which definitions of winter seem to have metaphorical origins?

■ CONNOTATION

The emotional associations surrounding a word, as opposed to its literal meaning. A connotation may be personal, or it may have universal associations.

■ DENOTATION

The strict, literal meaning of a word.

■ Apply to Sonnet 130 on page 188.

■ DIALECT

"If ye might have had a king's daughter,
   Yersell ye had to blame;
Ye might have taken the king's daughter,
   For ye kend that I was nane."

Anonymous
from **"The Demon Lover"**

How is the English in the ballad stanza above different from the English you speak? What words are different? How is the word order different as well?

A form of speech that is characteristic of a particular region or class, differing from the standard language in pronunciation, vocabulary, and grammatical form, is known as a **dialect.** The dialect in the example reflects the speech of the Scottish border region from which this ballad came.

Dialectal differences may be relatively slight, or they may be so great that mutual comprehension becomes difficult. There are American, Australian, and Scottish dialects of English, for example. And Scottish English contrasts with Scottish Gaelic, which is quite different. The point at which dialects become separate languages is not always clear.

In literature, dialect may serve several purposes. It can characterize those speaking and those spoken about, and it can create mood or atmosphere.

The following passage is from a nineteenth-century novel. What can you infer from the differing dialects of the speakers?

So resolved, I grasped the latch and shook it vehemently. Vinegar-faced Joseph projected his head from a round window of the barn.

"What are ye for?" he shouted. "T' maister's down i' t' fowld. Go round by th' end ot' laith, if ye went to spake to him."

"Is there nobody inside to open the door?" I hallooed, responsively.

"There's nobbut t' missis; and shoo'll not oppen't an ye mak yer flaysome dins till neeght."

"Why? Cannot you tell her who I am, eh, Joseph?"

"Nor-ne me! I'll hae no hend wi't," muttered the head, vanishing.

Emily Brontë
from **Wuthering Heights**

Dialect as a characteristic hasn't disappeared; twentieth-century speakers of English also speak various dialects, whether in cities or in small towns. The following passage presents a twentieth-century example:

"It's your pig this time, then, Tim," I said and the farmer nodded seriously.

"Aye, right as owt yesterday and laid flat like a dead 'un this morning. Never looked up when I filled his trough and by gaw when a pig won't tackle his grub there's summat far wrong." Tim dug his hands inside the broad leather belt which encircled his oversized trousers and which always seemed to be about to nip his narrow frame in two and led the way gloomily into the sty.

James Herriott
from **All Creatures Great and Small**

■ DIALECT

A regional variety of language, with a particular pronunciation, grammar, and vocabulary.

James Herriot, *All Creatures Great and Small* (Bantam, 1972).

■ Apply to **"To a Mouse"** on page 439.

■ DRAMATIC MONOLOGUE

"The Patriot" probably refers to a hero in Italy's struggle to free herself from Austria. Read the poem and answer the questions.

The Patriot
An Old Story

I

It was roses, roses, all the way,
   With myrtle mixed in my path like mad:
The house-roofs seemed to heave and sway,
   The church-spires flamed, such flags they had,
5 A year ago on this very day.

II

The air broke into a mist with bells,
   The old walls rocked with the crowd and cries.
Had I said, "Good folk, mere noise repels—
   But give me your sun from yonder skies!"
10 They had answered, "And afterward, what else?"

III

Alack, it was I who leaped at the sun
   To give it my loving friends to keep!
Naught man could do, have I left undone:
   And you see my harvest, what I reap
15 This very day, now a year is run.

IV

There's nobody on the house-tops now—
   Just a palsied few at the windows set;
For the best of the sight is, all allow,
   At the Shambles' Gate—or, better yet,
20 By the very scaffold's foot, I trow.

V

I go in the rain, and, more than needs,
   A rope cuts both my wrists behind;
And I think, by the feel, my forehead bleeds,
   For they fling, whoever has a mind,
25 Stones at me for my year's misdeeds.

HANDBOOK OF LITERARY TERMS

Dramatic Monologue **903**

HANDBOOK OF LITERARY TERMS

VI

Thus I entered, and thus I go!
  In triumphs, people have dropped down
    dead.
"Paid by the world, what dost thou owe
  Me?"—God might question; now
    instead,
30 'Tis God shall repay: I am safer so.

Robert Browning

1. Who is the speaker in this poem?
2. To whom is he speaking?
3. Why was he acclaimed a year ago?
4. Where is he going now? Why?
5. What can you infer about his attitude toward others and toward himself?

A poem such as this, in which the speaker is a specific character, usually in a specific dramatic situation, addressing a silent audience, is called a **dramatic monologue.** The dramatic monologue reveals aspects of the speaker's personality and also reveals the circumstances that led to his or her discourse. The audience, although silent, is present.

Perfected by Robert Browning in the nineteenth century, dramatic monologue differs from other lyric poetry in that the speaker is a specific character. It also differs from *soliloquy*, a dramatic convention that allows a character alone on stage to speak his or her thoughts aloud, in that the dramatic monologue carries the entire weight of characterization and plot.

■ DRAMATIC MONOLOGUE

A lyric poem in which the speaker is a specific character in a specific dramatic situation, addressing someone whose replies are not recorded.

■ Apply to **"Porphyria's Lover"** on page 594.

■ ELEGY

Break, Break, Break

Break, break, break,
  On thy cold gray stones, O Sea!
And I would that my tongue could utter
  The thoughts that arise in me.

5 O, well for the fisherman's boy,
  That he shouts with his sister at play!
O, well for the sailor lad,
  That he sings in his boat on the bay!

And the stately ships go on
10 To their haven under the hill;
But O for the touch of a vanished hand,
  And the sound of a voice that is still!

Break, break, break,
  At the foot of thy crags, O Sea!
15 But the tender grace of a day that is dead
  Will never come back to me.

Alfred, Lord Tennyson

Tennyson honors his dead friend, Arthur Hallam, in this **elegy**—a lyric of meditation or lament, most often over death.

In its original Greek form the elegy had a definite structure (alternating hexameters and pentameters). It was adapted into English poetry not as a form but as a quality of emotional expression.

In most elegies, there is a formality of language and structure that reflects the solemnity of death and the sense of personal loss. Many elegies, at their conclusion, shift in tone from despair to a joyous recognition of immortality, or to an acceptance of death. Does Tennyson do this in "Break, Break, Break"?

■ ELEGY

A solemn, reflective poem, usually about death, written in a formal style.

■ Apply to **"The Wife's Lament"** on page 51.

■ EPIGRAM

What is an epigram? A dwarfish whole;
Its body brevity and wit its soul.

Samuel Taylor Coleridget

Coleridge wrote these lines to provide an example of the very thing they define. An **epigram** is a short, witty verse or saying, often ending with a wry twist.

What is the "twist" in the following epigram?

Sir, I admit your general Rule
That Every Poet is a Fool:
But you yourself may serve to show it,
That every Fool is not a Poet.

Alexander Pope

Epigrams were originally inscriptions, usually in verse, on a tomb. Today, the form refers to any short poem or saying that expresses a single thought in a concise, witty way. An epigram can be a couplet or quatrain that exists as an independent poem or as a unit in a larger work.

In the late sixteenth and seventeenth centuries, the epigram was a favorite form of such poets as Herrick, Donne, and Jonson. Other well-known epigrammists include Dryden, Pope, Coleridge, and Yeats.

When a brief saying includes a moral, such as Pope's "Know then thyself, presume not God to scan;/The proper study of mankind is Man," it is called instead an *aphorism*.

■ EPIGRAM

Any short, witty verse or saying often ending with a wry twist.

■ Apply to "**An Essay on Criticism**" on page 387.

■ FIGURATIVE LANGUAGE

Where My Books Go

All the words that I utter,
    And all the words that I write,
Must spread out their wings untiring,
    And never rest in their flight,
5 Till they come where your sad, sad heart is,
    And sing to you in the night,
Beyond where the waters are moving,
    Storm-darken'd or starry bright.

William Butler Yeats

Yeats uses the words *wings*, *flight*, and *sing* in his poem, but he is not writing about birds. Rather, he is discussing his poetry.

A writer, through words, can cause a reader to see things in new ways, to venture into a world of imagination. Any language that goes beyond the literal meaning of words is called **figurative language.** The various devices of figurative language are called *figures of speech*.

Writers of English have always used figurative language. The early Anglo-Saxon poems, including *Beowulf* (page 10), relied on a specific figure of speech called a *kenning*. This was a metaphorical compound word such as "ring-giver" for king or "whale-road" for a rough sea.

The most common figures of speech that you will encounter in *England in Literature* are *simile, metaphor, hyperbole, personification, apostrophe, synecdoche*, and *metonymy*.

Simile

As flies to wanton boys are we to the gods,
They kill us for their sport.

A **simile** is a direct comparison between two basically unlike things that have something in common. A simile is usually signaled by the word *as*, as in the quotation from Shakespeare's *King Lear* above, or by the word *like*, as in Raleigh's "To Queen Elizabeth" (page 175): "Our passions are most like to floods and streams."

From *The Poems of W. B. Yeats: A New Edition,* edited by Richard J. Finneran (New York: Macmillan, 1983). Reprinted by permission of A. P. Watt Ltd. on behalf of Michael B. Yeats and Macmillan London Ltd.

A simile may be extended over many lines; when this occurs in an epic poem it is called an *epic simile,* as in Milton's *Paradise Lost* (page 294):

. . . Angel forms, who lay entranced
Thick as autumnal leaves that strow the brooks
In Vallombrosa, where the Etrurian shades
High over-arched embower; or scattered sedge
5 Afloat, when with fierce winds Orion armed
Hath vexed the Red Sea coast. . . .

Metaphor

A **metaphor** also compares two basically unlike things that have something in common, but unlike similes, metaphors use no connective such as *like* or *as.* The comparison in a metaphor may be stated (We are all puppets) or implied (Who is pulling your strings?). In *Rasselas,* for example, Samuel Johnson compares life to a river: "Do not suffer life to stagnate, it will grow muddy for want of motion: commit yourself again to the current of the world."

A metaphor that is developed at great length, often through a whole work or a great part of it, is called an *extended metaphor.* Wyatt's "Whoso List to Hunt" (page 166) contains an extended metaphor, with the hunter representing the love-struck poet and the deer representing the poet's beloved. Extended metaphors are common in poetry but exist in prose as well.

Hyperbole

A great exaggeration (such as "I'm so hungry I could eat a horse") is called **hyperbole.** Its purpose is not to deceive, but to emphasize, for either serious or comic effect. For example, in Burns's "A Red, Red Rose" (page 441), the speaker claims he will love his lady until all the seas go dry. Byron uses hyperbole for comic effect in *Don Juan* (page 493). And Wordsworth, in "Daffodils," describes a field of daffodils in this way:

Continuous as the stars that shine
And twinkle on the Milky Way,
They stretch'd in never-ending line
Along the margin of a bay:
5 Ten thousand saw I at a glance,
Tossing their heads in sprightly dance.

Personification

In **personification,** a writer endows abstractions, ideas, animals, or inanimate objects with human qualities. What is personified in the following passage?

I have been the continual sport of what the world calls fortune; and though I will not wrong her by saying, She has ever made me feel the weight of any great or signal evil; —yet with all the good temper in the world, I affirm it of her, that in every stage of my life, and at every turn and corner where she could get fairly at me, the ungracious Duchess has pelted me with a set of as pitiful misadventures and cross accidents as ever small Hero sustained.

Lawrence Sterne
from **Tristram Shandy**

"Don't let him scare you. He's all hyperbole."

■ INFERENCE

© Punch/Rothco

1. Where are these men?
2. What is strange about their drinks?
3. What is happening?

If you answered that they are on a plane that seems to be heading downward at a rather alarming angle, you have made an **inference**—a reasonable conclusion about the behavior of a character or the meaning of an event, drawn from limited information. In this case the information is the details provided by the cartoonist. Characters in literature are constantly making inferences:

"So far as I can follow you, then, Mr. Holmes," said Sir Henry Baskerville, "someone cut out this message with a scissors—"

"Nail-scissors," said Holmes. "You can see that it was a very short-bladed scissors, since the cutter had to take two snips over 'keep away.' "

Sir Arthur Conan Doyle
from **The Hound of the Baskervilles**

An inference is a guess, but it is an educated one. You must pay careful attention to the text to find the clues that the author has included. Such clues might lie in speech, behavior, description, or narration. Your inference will be valid only when it is based on valid clues.

In the following passage, Jane Eyre has come to serve as governess for Adèle, the young ward of Edward Rochester, a somber, moody man, brusque in his speech, but capable of unexplained changes in his manner. Although Jane is interested in him, she cannot imagine that he might return her feelings. Read the passage and answer the questions.

"How do you do?" he asked.

"I am very well, sir."

"Why did you not come and speak to me in the room?"

I thought I might have retorted the question on him who put it; but I would not take that freedom. I answered:—"I did not wish to disturb you, as you seemed engaged, sir."

"What have you been doing during my absence?"

"Nothing particular; teaching Adèle as usual."

"And getting a good deal paler than you were—as I saw at first sight. What is the matter?" . . .

"I am tired, sir."

He looked at me for a minute.

"And a little depressed," he said. "What about? Tell me."

"Nothing—nothing, sir. I am not depressed."

"But I affirm that you are: so much depressed that a few more words would bring tears to your eyes—indeed, they are there now, shining and swimming. . . . If I had time, and was not in mortal dread of some prating prig of a servant passing, I would know what all this means. Well, to-night I excuse you; but understand that so long as my visitors stay, I expect you to appear in the drawing-room every evening; it is my wish; don't neglect it. Now go, and send Sophie for Adèle. Good-night, my ——" He stopped, bit his lip, and abruptly left me.

Charlotte Brontë
from **Jane Eyre**

1. How do you think Jane and Mr. Rochester have treated each other before this time?
2. What does he infer about Jane's mood? Upon what clues does he base his inference?
3. What do you infer he means to say after *my?*
4. Why does he stop and leave abruptly?

■ INFERENCE

A reasonable conclusion about the behavior of a character or the meaning of an event drawn from the limited information presented by the author. Inferences may or may not be valid.

■ Apply to "**My Last Duchess**" on page 595.

■ IRONY

© Punch/Rothco

"It's ironic really—I started telling jokes at school to stop people bullying me."

1. The character about to be executed is a court jester. Why did he start telling jokes?
2. The king, in the background, is signing "thumbs down" to tell the executioner to go ahead. What do you think the jester has done to warrant this death sentence?
3. In what way did things not work out as the jester had hoped?

A contrast between what is expected or hoped for and what actually happens, or between what appears to be and what actually is, is called **irony.** In the cartoon, the very thing the jester hoped would stop people from bullying him is what has led to his downfall.

There are three kinds of irony. In *verbal irony,* the intended meaning of a statement or work is different from (often the opposite of) what the statement or work literally says. For example, you would be using irony if someone spilled catsup on your favorite sweater, and you said, "That's okay, I look good in red." Jonathan Swift, in "A Modest Proposal" (page 337), makes devastating use of verbal irony. *Understatement,* in which something is expressed less emphatically than it might be, is a form of verbal irony often used for humorous or cutting

effect. Samuel Johnson's remark in his "Letter to Chesterfield" (page 393) is an understatement: "To be so distinguished [by Chesterfield's praise of Johnson's *Dictionary*] is an honor which, being very little accustomed to favors from the great, I know not well how to receive."

Irony of situation refers to a contrast between what is expected or intended and what actually happens. The jester in the cartoon is experiencing such irony. Read the example that follows. From the description of the outside of the houses, how would you expect living conditions to be? How are they actually?

The houses themselves were substantial and very decent. One could walk all round, seeing little front gardens with auriculas and saxifrage in the shadow of the bottom block, sweet-williams and pinks in the sunny top block; seeing neat front windows, little porches, little privet hedges, and dormer windows for the attics. But that was outside; that was the view on to the uninhabited parlors of all the colliers' wives. The dwelling-room, the kitchen, was at the back of the house, facing inward between the blocks, looking at a scrubby back garden, and then at the ash-pits. And between the rows, between the long lines of ash-pits, went the alley, where the children played, and the women gossiped and the men smoked. So, the actual conditions of living in the Bottoms, that was so well built and that looked so nice, were quite unsavoury because people must live in the kitchen, and the kitchens opened on to that nasty alley of ash-pits.

D. H. Lawrence
from Sons and Lovers

Dramatic Irony refers to a situation in which the reader or audience knows facts that one or more characters in the work do not know. Oscar Wilde's *The Importance of Being Earnest* (page 751) relies heavily on dramatic irony for its humor, with two characters claiming to be named Ernest, when, in fact, neither one is.

What kind of irony can you find in the poem on the next page? For what purpose has the author created this irony?

D. H. Lawrence, *Sons and Lovers* (Mitchell Kennerly, 1913).

The Chimney Sweeper

When my mother died I was very young,
And my father sold me while yet my tongue
Could scarcely cry " 'weep! 'weep! 'weep! 'weep!"
So your chimneys I sweep, & in soot I sleep.

5 There's little Tom Dacre, who cried when his head,
That curled like a lamb's back, was shaved;
     so I said
"Hush, Tom! never mind it, for when your
     head's bare
You know that the soot cannot spoil your
     white hair."

And so he was quiet, & that very night,
10 As Tom was a-sleeping, he had such a sight!—
That thousands of sweepers, Dick, Joe, Ned,
     & Jack,
Were all of them locked up in coffins of black.

And by came an Angel who had a bright key,
And he opened the coffins & set them all free;
15 Then down a green plain leaping, laughing,
     they run,
And wash in a river, and shine in the Sun.

Then naked & white, all their bags left behind,
They rise upon clouds and sport in the wind;
And the Angel told Tom, if he'd be a good boy,
20 He'd have God for his father, & never want joy.

And so Tom awoke; and we rose in the dark,
And got with our bags & our brushes to work.
Tho' the morning was cold, Tom was happy
     & warm;
So if all do their duty they need not fear harm.

William Blake

■ IRONY

**A contrast between what appears to be and
what really is. In *verbal irony,* words imply the
opposite of what they literally mean. *Irony of
situation* presents a state of affairs that is the
opposite of what is expected. *Dramatic irony*
occurs in fiction or drama when the reader
knows more than a character or characters do.**

■ Apply to "**The Pardoner's Prologue**" and "**Tale**" on pages
114 and 116.

■ LYRIC

Mother, I Cannot Mind My Wheel

Mother, I cannot mind my wheel:
    My fingers ache, my lips are dry:
Oh! if you felt the pain I feel!
    But oh, who ever felt as I?

5 No longer could I doubt him true;
    All other men may use deceit:
He always said my eyes were blue,
    And often swore my lips were sweet.

Walter Savage Landor

In the poem above, what is the basic emotion?
Is the speaker's tone personal or impersonal?
  This example is a **lyric**—a short poem that
presents an emotion or state of mind rather than

a story. Any emotion, from grief to love to joy, can be featured. Usually a lyric will have a single speaker.

The term *lyric* originally meant poetry intended to be sung to the accompaniment of a lyre, a harplike instrument. Modern lyric poetry still retains some characteristics of music in its treatment of sound and rhythm, ideas and structure.

A lyric may be as formal as a sonnet or as irregular as free verse. Other kinds of lyric poetry include *elegy, dramatic monologue,* and *ode.*

An *ode* is a lyric written to celebrate or commemorate a special occasion. Odes, usually long, complex poems, are marked by dignified language and intellectual tone.

What state of mind is expressed in the following lyric? What idea is expressed?

The Silver Swan

The silver swan, who living had no note,
When death approached, unlocked her silent
    throat;[1]
Leaning her breast against the reedy shore,
Thus sung her first and last, and sung no
    more:
5 "Farewell, all joys; Oh death, come close
    mine eyes;
More geese than swans now live, more fools
    than wise."

              Anonymous

---

1. *who living . . . throat,* a reference to the legend that swans utter no sounds until they are dying. This legend is the origin of the term *swan song.*

■ LYRIC

A poem, usually short, that expresses some basic emotion or state of mind. It usually creates a single impression and is highly personal. It may be rhymed or unrhymed, in any of a number of forms.

■ Apply to **"In Memoriam"** on page 558.

■ MOOD

A Dirge

Rough wind, that moanest loud
    Grief too sad for song;
Wild wind, when sullen cloud
    Knells all the night long;
5 Sad storm, whose tears are vain,
Bare woods, whose branches strain,
Deep caves and dreary main,—
    Wail, for the world's wrong!

        Percy Bysshe Shelley

How does this poem make you feel? What images lead to this feeling?

The overall atmosphere or prevailing emotional aura of a work is called **mood.** Mood may be described as *light, happy, bleak, tragic,* and so on.

An author establishes mood partly through description of setting and partly through the people or objects chosen to be described. In the example, Shelley uses the words *moanest, grief, sullen, knells,* and *dreary* to construct a mood of hopelessness. In contrast, in the first eighteen lines of the Prologue to the *Canterbury Tales* (page 97), Chaucer creates an atmosphere of rebirth and renewal through his description of the "sweet showers" of April.

Read the following passages. What moods do they convey? What techniques does each author use to establish mood?

With blackest moss the flower-plots
   Were thickly crusted, one and all
The rusted nails fell from the knots
   That held the pear to the gable-wall.
5 The unbroken sheds looked sad and strange,
   Unlifted was the clinking latch;
   Weeded and worn the ancient thatch
Upon the lonely moated grange.
     She only said, "My life is dreary,
10   He cometh not," she said;
     She said, "I am aweary, aweary,
      I would that I were dead!"

Alfred, Lord Tennyson
from "Mariana"

Song

The year's at the spring,
And day's at the morn;
Morning's at seven;
The hillside's dew-pearled;
5 The lark's on the wing;
The snail's on the thorn;
God's in his heaven—
All's right with the world!

Robert Browning

It was a bright cold day in April, and the clocks were striking thirteen. Winston Smith, his chin nuzzled into his breast in an effort to escape the vile wind, slipped quickly through the glass doors of Victory Mansions, though not quickly enough to prevent a swirl of gritty dust from entering along with him.

George Orwell
from 1984

■ MOOD

The overall atmosphere or prevailing emotional aura of a work.

■ Apply to **"Kubla Khan"** on page 464.

■ PARADOX

WAR IS PEACE
FREEDOM IS SLAVERY
IGNORANCE IS STRENGTH

George Orwell
from 1984

The above slogans seem impossible, but the world of Orwell's novel *1984* is based on contradictions like this—that within the society are supposed to make sense. Such a statement that seems to be self-contradictory but that has valid meaning is called a **paradox.** Often, you must interpret a paradox metaphorically to get its meaning.

Writers use paradox to emphasize ideas or to create a sense of irony. It is a central device in metaphysical and Elizabethan poetry.

Read the following example and answer the questions.

I grieve and dare not show my discontent,
I love and yet am forced to seem to hate,
I do, yet dare not say I ever meant,
I seem stark mute but inwardly do prate.
5   I am and not, I freeze and yet am burned,
  Since from myself another self I turned.

Queen Elizabeth I
from "On Monsieur's Departure"

1. What four things does the speaker do that are not true to how she feels?
2. What does she mean by "I am and not"?
3. What is the cause of these paradoxical statements?

■ PARADOX

A statement, often metaphorical, that seems to be self-contradictory but that has valid meaning.

George Orwell, *1984*. Orlando: Harcourt Brace Jovanovich, Inc. 1949

■ Apply to **"Amoretti"** on page 180.

■ PASTORAL

Spring, the sweet spring, is the year's
    pleasant king,
Then blooms each thing, then maids dance in
    a ring,
Cold doth not sting, the pretty birds do
    sing:
    Cuckoo, jug-jug, pu-we, to-witta-
      woo! . . .

5 The fields breathe sweet, the daisies kiss
    our feet,
Young lovers meet, old wives a-sunning sit,
In every street these tunes our ears do
    greet:
    Cuckoo, jug-jug, pu-we, to-witta-woo!
    Spring, the sweet spring!

Thomas Nashe
from **"Spring, the Sweet Spring"**

Is this a vision of real country life? The
details in Nashe's poem are characteristic of a
pastoral—a conventional form of lyric poetry
that presents an idealized picture of rural life.
What details from the poem prove that it is idealized and not true to life?

Pastorals, by evoking a simple life in a golden
age that never existed, often comment, through
contrast, on politics, religion, and the corruption of the city or the court.

Pastoral romances and plays were developed
in England in the 16th and 17th centuries,
often translated from Italian and Spanish works.
Milton and Shelley were noted for pastoral
elegies. Certain poets, such as Wordsworth,
have been referred to as pastoral poets because
they use rural settings.

■ PASTORAL

**A conventional form of lyric poetry presenting
an idealized picture of rural life.**

■ Apply to **"The Passionate Shepherd to His Love"** on
page 266.

■ PLOT

The series of related events that make up
a story is its **plot.** Most plots are *chronological*; that is, they proceed in the order in
which events happen, but many variations are
possible. In a carefully constructed plot, events
form a pattern, with each incident linked in a
cause-effect relationship with other incidents.

The first part of a plot is the *exposition*. In
the exposition, the author introduces the main
character or characters, establishes the setting,
and gives whatever background information the
reader needs. Sometimes exposition is achieved
through *flashbacks*, narratives or scenes out of
chronological order, presenting events that happened before the opening of the work.

The *conflict* is the struggle between two
opposing forces. There are four basic kinds of
conflict:

- a person against another person or opponent
- a person against nature
- a person against society
- two elements within a person struggling for
mastery

The *rising action,* or *complication,* is the building of tension or struggle between conflicting
characters or forces. There may be many ups
and downs for the main character, and at times
the struggle may seem to go in one direction,
then in another, before the conflict is resolved.

The *climax* is the decisive or turning point in
a story or play when the action changes course
and begins to resolve itself. In an Elizabethan
tragedy, a structural climax occurs in the third
act. This is the point at which the fortunes
of the protagonists are at their highest. Not
every story or play has this kind of dramatic
climax, and in some works the designation of
a particular action as climax may be open to
interpretation. Sometimes a character may simply resolve a problem in his or her mind. At
times there is no resolution of the plot; the climax then comes when a character realizes that a
resolution is impossible. The term *climax* is also
used to mean the point of greatest interest or

excitement in a work, where the reader or audience has the most intense emotional response.

In the *resolution*, the conflict is finally decided one way or another, and all questions are usually answered. Resolution is also called *denouement*, from a French word meaning, literally, "the untying." In a mystery story the denouement is the explanation or summation of clues, motives, red herrings, and any loose ends not earlier explained. In other kinds of stories, the resolution gives a final accounting of what happens to the main characters.

Events that lead from the climax to the denouement are sometimes called the *falling action*, those events which bring the story to a close. The climax and the denouement may appear very close together, or, in a novel, several chapters apart.

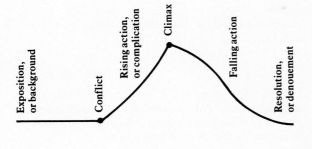

■ PLOT

In the simplest sense, a series of happenings in a literary work; but it is often used to refer to the action as it is organized around a conflict and builds through complication to a climax, followed by a resolution or denouement.

■ Apply to the Shakespeare play on page 191.

■ POINT OF VIEW

1. Why is the man on the right laughing at the man on the left?
2. Why are you able to laugh at the man on the right?

The vantage point from which an author presents the actions and characters of a story is called **point of view.** Most events can be seen from more than one point of view. You are able to laugh at the man in the cartoon because you know something he doesn't—that he is in the same condition as the man he is laughing at.

In literature, a story related by a character is said to be told from the *first-person* point of view. The character uses pronouns such as *I* or *we*, and may participate in the action a great deal or hardly at all. In the first-person point of view, the information presented must be limited to what the character knows, experiences, or infers. The reader, however, may draw inferences from that information.

I have a great deal of difficulty in beginning to write my portion of these pages, for I know I am not clever. I always knew that. I can remember, when I was a very little girl indeed, I used to say to my doll when we were alone together, "Now, Dolly, I am not clever, you know very well, and you must be patient with me, like a dear!" And so she used to sit propped up in a great armchair, with her beautiful complexion and rosy lips, staring at me—or not so much at me, I think, as at nothing—while I busily stitched away, and told her every one of my secrets.

Charles Dickens
from **Bleak House**

1. Is this story being told by a little girl or by an older woman? How can you tell?
2. Would you expect this character to turn out "not clever," as she claims? Why or why not?

A story related by a *narrator* who is not a character in the story is said to be told from the *third-person* point of view. The narrator will use pronouns like *he, she,* and *they.* Further, the third-person narrator may be *omniscient*—able to relate the thoughts, feelings, and perceptions of any or all of the characters as the need arises. Or, the third-person narrator may be *limited*—following the thoughts, feelings, and perceptions of only one character and tending to view events from that character's perspective.

In a related technique called *stream of consciousness,* the flow of thought of one or more characters is created through images, perceptions, and memories that come and go in seemingly random, but actually controlled, fashion, much as they do in people's minds.

A third-person narrator who describes only what can be seen, like a newspaper reporter, is said to use an *objective* or *dramatic* point of view. From which third-person point of view is the following passage related?

Jude had to leave early next morning for his usual week of absence at lodgings; and it was with a sense of futility that he threw into his basket upon his tools and other necessaries the unread book he had brought with him.

He kept his impassioned doings a secret almost from himself. Arabella, on the contrary, made them public among all her friends and acquaintance.

Thomas Hardy
from **Jude the Obscure**

Take care not to assume that any of these points of view is the same as that of the author. Rather, an author creates a mask or voice called a *persona.* In the first-person point of view, the persona is the character telling the story. But even in the third-person point of view, the narrator may be a persona. A narrator's attitude toward his or her subject is capable of much variation; it can range from one of apparent indifference to one of extreme conviction and feeling.

Some writers mix points of view, by placing the narrator seemingly within the story. This "self-conscious" narrator may address the reader directly and even discuss the difficulties involved in writing the story:

Reader take care; I have unadvisedly led thee to the top of as high a hill as Mr. Allworthy's, and how to get thee down without breaking my neck I do not well know. However, let us e'en venture to slide down together, for Miss Bridget rings her bell and Mr. Allworthy is summoned to breakfast, where I must attend, and, if you please, shall be glad of your company. . . .

Henry Fielding
from **Tom Jones**

This point of view was used by novelists of the eighteenth and nineteenth centuries—Eliot uses it in *The Mill on the Floss* (page 600)—but it is rare in the twentieth century.

■ POINT OF VIEW

The vantage point from which an author presents the actions and characters in a story. The story may be related by a character (*first-person* point of view) or by a narrator who does not participate in the action (*third-person* point of view). Further, the third-person narrator may be *omniscient*—able to see into the minds of all characters; *limited*—confined to a single character's perceptions; or *objective*—describing only what can be seen.

■ Apply to "**A Voyage to Brobdingnag**" on page 344.

■ PROTAGONIST/ ANTAGONIST

Most stories present at least one main character, called the **protagonist.** Originally, the protagonist was the actor who played the leading part in a Greek drama. The protagonist may or may not be a hero but is always the character most central to the action.

In a story told from the first-person point of view, the narrator may or may not be the protagonist. In the stories of Arthur Conan Doyle, for example, Dr. Watson, the narrator, tells the exploits of Sherlock Holmes, the protagonist. In *David Copperfield* (page 576), however, David is both narrator and protagonist.

A character who opposes the protagonist is called the **antagonist.** The antagonist is sometimes evil. Often, however, the antagonist is merely a character who causes conflict in the protagonist. Sometimes, an antagonist is a concept, such as Fate or Death.

In *Beowulf* (page 10); the hero Beowulf is the protagonist, and Grendel is the antagonist. In *Paradise Lost* (page 294), Satan is the antagonist.

When a character's traits are the opposite of those of another character, he or she is called a *foil.* The foil points up, through contrast, the strengths or weaknesses of another character. Henry Higgins and Liza Doolittle are foils to one another in *Pygmalion* (page 644). A foil is sometimes a one-dimensional stereotype.

■ PROTAGONIST

The leading character in a literary work.

■ ANTAGONIST

A character who opposes the protagonist. An antagonist whose traits are opposite those of the protagonist is a *foil*.

■ Apply to **"The Day of Destiny"** on page 139.

■ RHYME

"Whenever I think of you,
it makes me want to write something
where the lines end with the same sound."

Rhyme is the exact repetition of sounds in at least the final accented syllables of two or more words. Everyone knows some rhymes; people of all ages are drawn to rhymes in poems, song lyrics, riddles, slogans, and so on. Skillfully used, rhyme complements and reinforces the sense of what is being said. It contributes toward the total communicated effect of a poem.

Rhyme scheme is any pattern of rhyme in a stanza or poem. For purposes of study, the pattern is labeled as shown below, with the first rhyme and all the words rhyming with it labeled *a*; the second rhyme labeled *b*; the third rhyme *c*; and so on:

Requiem

Under the wide and starry sky	*a*
Dig the grave and let me lie:	*a*
Glad did I live and gladly die,	*a*
And I laid me down with a will.	*b*
5 This is the verse you grave for me:	*c*
Here he lies where he longed to be;	*c*
Home is the sailor, home from sea,	*c*
And the hunter home from the hill.	*b*

Robert Louis Stevenson

The most common types of rhymes are end rhymes, internal rhymes, slant rhymes, and feminine rhymes.

End rhyme is the rhyming of words at the ends of lines of poetry. The rhymes in "Requiem" are generally end rhymes.

Internal rhyme is the rhyming of words or accented syllables within a line that may or may not have a rhyme at the end as well. "We three shall flee across the sea to Italy" is an example. Internal rhyme can be used to achieve variety or emphasis within a line. What internal rhymes can you find in this example?

> Thy face is far from this our war,
> Our call and counter-cry,
> I shall not find Thee quick and kind,
> Nor know Thee till I die.
> 5 Enough for me in dreams to see
> And touch Thy garments' hem:
> Thy feet have trod so near to God
> I may not follow them!
>
> *Rudyard Kipling*
> **from "To the True Romance"**

Slant rhyme, sometimes called half rhyme, occurs when the vowel sounds are not quite identical, as in the first and third lines below, from Browning's "Porphyria's Lover" (page 594).

> And I untightened next the tress
> About her neck; her cheek once more
> Blushed bright beneath my burning kiss . . .

Feminine rhyme extends over two or more syllables. These syllables may be one word or several (as in "No matter—no *matter/* If I can get *at her* . . ." from Gilbert and Sullivan's *The Gondoliers*). In feminine rhyme the last syllable or syllables are unaccented, as opposed to *masculine rhyme*, in which the accent falls on the last syllable. What feminine rhymes can you find in the following poem? what masculine rhymes?

Charm

> The owl is abroad, the bat, and the toad,
> And so is the catamountain;
> The ant and the mole sit both in a fold,

> And frog peeps out o' the fountain;
> 5 The dogs they do bay, and the timbrels
> play;
> The spindle is now a-turning;
> The moon it is red, and the stars are fled,
> But all the sky is a-burning.
>
> *Ben Jonson*

Some critics classify any patterns in sound as rhyme. Alliteration and assonance might be considered a form of rhyme under this very broad classification.

Read the following stanzas and chart their rhyme scheme. Then identify all the kinds of rhyme that you can find.

> When I had wings, my brother,
> Such wings were mine as thine:
> Such life my heart remembers
> In all as wild Septembers
>
> 5 As this when life seems other,
> Though sweet, than once was mine;
> When I had wings, my brother,
> Such wings were mine as thine.
>
> Such life as thrills and quickens
> 10 The silence of thy flight,
> Or fills thy note's elation
> With lordlier exultation
> Than man's, whose faint heart sickens
> With hopes and fears that flight
> 15 Such life as thrills and quickens
> The silence of thy flight.
>
> *Algernon Swinburne*
> **from "To a Seamew"**

■ RHYME

Exact repetition of sounds in at least the final accented syllables of two or more words. Common types of rhyme include *end rhyme*, *internal rhyme*, *slant rhyme*, and *feminine rhyme*.

■ Apply to "**The Rime of the Ancient Mariner**" on page 466.

■ RHYTHM

There lived a wife at Usher's Well
  And a wealthy wife was she;
She had three stout and stalwart sons
  And sent them o'er the sea.

    These lines are from the ballad "The Wife of Usher's Well." Because the ballad was meant to be sung, the regular beat is particularly apparent. Like most songs, ballads have a regular beat, or **rhythm.**

    Rhythm refers to the pattern of sounds in speech or writing, created by the arrangement of stressed and unstressed syllables. A poem may have rhymed or unrhymed lines; it may be composed in strict metrical form or in free verse; but it always has rhythm.

    In poetry, the pattern of stressed and unstressed syllables is called *meter.* Meter is measured by feet. A *foot* is a group of syllables usually consisting of one accented syllable and one or more unaccented syllables. The use of the word *foot* originally referred to the movement of the foot in beating time.

    Lines of poetry can be *scanned,* or divided into feet, by indicating the stressed and unstressed syllables. This process is called *scansion.* Stressed syllables are marked with the symbol ′ and unstressed syllables with the symbol ‿ . Then the feet are divided by slashes. The result looks like this:

Come live / with me / and be / my Love,

And we / will all / the pleas- / ures prove.

    The arrangement of accented and unaccented syllables in a foot results in four basic meters: iambic, trochaic, anapestic, and dactyllic.

    An *iamb* consists of an unaccented syllable followed by an accented syllable (‿ ′), as in *until.* The following lines, from Coleridge's "Kubla Khan" (page 464), are basically iambic:

And all / should cry, / Beware! / Beware!

His flash- / ing eyes, / his float- / ing hair!

    A *trochee* consists of an accented syllable followed by an unaccented syllable (′ ‿), as in *answer.* It is the opposite of the iamb. The following lines, from Shakespeare's *Macbeth,* are basically trochaic:

Double, / double / toil and / trouble;

Fire / burn and / caldron / bubble.

    An *anapest* consists of two unaccented syllables followed by an accented syllable (‿ ‿ ′), as in *interfere.* The following line, from Shelley's "Cloud," is anapestic:

Like a child / from the womb, / like a ghost /

    from the tomb . . .

    A *dactyl* consists of one accented syllable followed by two unaccented syllables (′ ‿ ‿), as in *settlement.* It is the opposite of the anapest. The following line, from Charles Kingsley's *Andromeda,* is basically dactylic:

Loosing his / arms from her / waist he flew /

    upward, a- / waiting the / sea beast.

    Few poems are written in metrical feet of a single kind; most poets vary their meters somewhat. A *spondee* consists of two accented syllables (′ ′), as in *sea beast* above. It serves occasionally as a substitute foot to vary the meter, as in the third foot below, from Donne's Holy Sonnet 14 (page 282):

As yet / but knock, / breathe, shine, /

    and seek / to mend . . .

    Poetry varies not only in meter, but in the number of feet in a line. The following terms represent the number of feet in a line of poetry: *monometer* (one foot), *dimeter* (two feet), *trimeter* (three feet), *tetrameter* (four feet), *pentameter* (five feet), *hexameter* (six feet), *heptameter* (seven feet), and *octameter* (eight feet). The most common line lengths are pentameter, tetrameter, and trimeter.

The most common combination of meter and feet in English poetry is iambic pentameter, as are these lines from Marlowe's *Doctor Faustus*:

The mir- / acles / that mag- / ic will / perform

Will make / thee vow / to stud- / y noth- / ing else.

Finally, poetic lines can be *end-stopped* or *run-on*. An end-stopped line is a line of poetry that contains a complete thought, thus necessitating the use of a semicolon, colon, or period at the end. Both of these lines, from Pope's "An Essay on Man" (page 387), are end-stopped:

Know then thyself, presume not God to scan;
The proper study of mankind is Man.

A run-on line is a line in which the thought continues beyond the end of the poetic line. In the first line of the following example, from

Dryden's "To the Memory of Mr. Oldham," there should be no pause after *thine*:

For sure our souls were near allied, and thine
Cast in the same poetic mold with mine.

How many feet are there in each line of "The Wife of Usher's Well," at the beginning of this article? How would you describe the rhythm of that ballad stanza, in terms of feet and meter? Are the lines end-stopped or run-on?

■ RHYTHM

The arrangement of stressed and unstressed sounds in speech or writing. Rhythm, or meter, may be regular or it may vary within a line or work. The four most common metrical feet are *iamb*, *trochee*, *anapest*, and *dactyl*.

■ Apply to the Folk Ballads on page 86.

■ SATIRE

The pigs had set aside the harness-room as a headquarters for themselves. Here, in the evenings, they studied blacksmithing, carpentering, and other necessary arts from books which they had brought out of the farmhouse. Snowball also busied himself with organizing the other animals into what he called Animal Committees. He was indefatigable at this. He formed the Egg Production Committee for the hens, the Clean Tails League for the cows, the Wild Comrades' Re-education Committee (the object of this was to tame the rats and rabbits), the Whiter Wool Movement for the sheep, and various others, besides instituting classes in reading and writing. On the whole, these projects were a failure. The attempt to tame the wild creatures, for instance, broke down almost immediately. They continued to behave very much as before, and when treated with generosity, simply took advantage of it. The cat joined the Re-education Committee and was very active in it for some days. She was seen one day sitting on a roof and talking to some sparrows who were just out of her reach. She was telling them that all animals were now comrades and that any sparrow who chose could come and perch on her paw; but the sparrows kept their distance.

George Orwell
from **Animal Farm**

Animals are not really Orwell's subject. Who or what is? What is Orwell making fun of in the passage above? How do you know?

In *Animal Farm*, Orwell attacks stubborn and greedy rulers in a totalitarian state. *Animal Farm* is a **satire**—a type of literature that ridicules vices and follies, usually for the purpose of producing some change in attitude or action.

Irony and *sarcasm* are often used in satire. Sarcasm is the use of language to hurt or ridicule. It is less subtle in tone than irony. Boswell, in the *Life of Samuel Johnson, LL.D.* (page 401) reports that, during their first meeting, he said, "I do indeed come from Scotland, but I cannot help it." Johnson replied (referring to the immigration of Scots to England), "That, Sir, I find is what a very great many of your countrymen cannot help." Johnson's retort is an example of sarcasm.

Closely related to satire is *parody,* a humorous imitation of the style, subject matter, and so on, of serious writing, usually for the purpose of making the original appear ridiculous. Eliot's "The Hollow Men" (page 834) includes a parody of the children's rhyme "Here we go round the mulberry bush," used for serious effect.

Why is the following passage satiric? What point is Conrad making?

At no time of the world's history have men been at a loss how to inflict mental and bodily anguish upon their fellow-creatures. This aptitude came to them in the growing complexity of their passions and the early refinement of their ingenuity. But it may safely be said that primeval man did not go to the trouble of inventing tortures. He was indolent and pure of heart. He brained his neighbour ferociously with a stone axe from necessity and without malice.

Joseph Conrad
from **Nostromo**

■ SATIRE

The technique that employs wit to ridicule a subject, usually some social institution or human foible, often with the intention to inspire reform.

■ Apply to **"A Satirical Elegy . . ."** on page 334.

■ SETTING

She Dwelt Among the Untrodden Ways

She dwelt among the untrodden ways
　　Beside the springs of Dove,
A Maid whom there were none to praise
　　And very few to love:

5 A violet by a mossy stone
　　Half hidden from the eye!
—Fair as a star, when only one
　　Is shining in the sky.

She lived unknown, and few could know
10　　When Lucy ceased to be;
But she is in her grave, and oh,
　　The difference to me!

William Wordsworth

Where did Lucy dwell? When?
Wordsworth chooses to place this poem in the past and in a natural, rural environment that reflects Lucy's pure, simple character.
Setting is the time and place in which the actions of a narrative occur. It can be general (somewhere in England in the 19th century) or specific (a parlor in New Orleans, June, 1990). The setting may be described by the narrator or one of the characters, or it may be suggested through dialogue, action, or imagery. Setting can contribute strongly to the mood or atmosphere of a work—as well as to its plausibility.
In Shelley's *Frankenstein* (page 520), setting is used to reinforce the mood and the action:

It was on a dreary night of November that I beheld the accomplishment of my toils. With an anxiety that almost amounted to agony, I collected the instruments of life around me, that I might infuse a spark of being into the lifeless thing that lay at my feet. It was already one in the morning; the rain pattered dismally against the panes, and my candle was nearly burnt out, when, by the glimmer of the half- extinguished light, I saw the dull yellow eye of the creature open; it breathed hard, and a convulsive motion agitated its limbs.

What time and place does each of the following settings establish? what mood?

A Saturday afternoon in November was approaching the time of twilight, and the vast tract of unenclosed wild known as Egdon Heath embrowned itself moment by moment. Overhead the hollow stretch of whitish cloud shutting out the sky was as a tent which had the whole heath for its floor.

Thomas Hardy
from **The Return of the Native**

The mansion of the eighteenth century Earl had been changed in the twentieth century into a Club. And it was pleasant, after dining in the great room with the pillars and the chandeliers under a glare of light to go out on to the balcony overlooking the Park. The trees were in full leaf, and had there been a moon, one could have seen the pink and cream coloured cockades on the chestnut trees. But it was a moonless night; very warm, after a fine summer's day.

Virginia Woolf
from "**The Searchlight**"

■ SETTING

The time (both time of day and period in history) and place in which the action of a narrative occurs.

Virginia Woolf, "The Searchlight" from *A Haunted House* (Harcourt, Brace Jovanovich, Inc., 1972).

■ Apply to "**Elegy Written in a Country Churchyard**" on page 409.

■ SONNET

A **sonnet** is a lyric poem consisting of fourteen lines with rhymes arranged according to one or another of certain schemes.

The *Italian*, or *Petrarchan*, sonnet (after the Italian poet Petrarch) is usually rhymed *abbaabba/cdecde* with variations permitted in the *cdecde* rhyme scheme. It forms basically a two-part poem of eight lines (*octave*) and six lines (*sestet*) respectively. These two parts are played off against each other in a great variety of ways. The octave presents a proposition, dilemma, or question, while the sestet provides a comment, application, or solution. The following poem is basically an Italian sonnet in form. How is it different from the traditional Italian sonnet?

The Sonnet

A Sonnet is a moment's monument—
Memorial from the Soul's eternity
To one dead deathless hour. Look that it be,
Whether for lustral rite or dire portent,
5 Of its own arduous fullness reverent:
Carve it in ivory or in ebony,
As Day or Night may rule; and let Time see
Its flowering crest impearled and orient.

A Sonnet is a coin; its face reveals
10 The Soul—its converse, to what Power 'tis
    due:—
Whether for tribute to the august appeals
Of Life, or dower in Love's high retinue,
It serve; or 'mid the dark wharf's cavernous
    breath,
In Charon's palm it pay the toll[1] to Death.

Dante Gabriel Rossetti

---

1. *Charon's palm . . . toll.* In Greek mythology, Charon (ker′ən, kar′ən) was the boatman who ferried the spirits of the dead across the river Styx to Hades. Each spirit was expected to pay him a coin for this service.

Instead of presenting a proposition and solution, Rossetti presents one extended metaphor in the octave and another in the sestet. (Also, the rhyme in the sestet differs from the scheme presented above.)

The *English*, or *Shakespearean*, sonnet is usually rhymed *abab/cdcd/efef/gg*, presenting a four-part structure. The first three parts of four lines each (*quatrains*) may present three statements or examples and the final part of two lines (*couplet*) a conclusion or application. The couplet often provides a comment on the preceding lines or gives them a twist. The following illustrates the English sonnet form:

Sonnet 76

Why is my verse so barren of new pride?
So far from variation or quick change?
Why with the time do I not glance aside
To new-found methods and to compounds
    strange?
5 Why write I still all one, ever the same,
And keep invention in a noted weed,
That every word doth almost tell my name,
Showing their birth and where they did
    proceed?
Oh, know, sweet love, I always write of you,
10 And you and love are still my argument;
So all my best is dressing old words new,
Spending again what is already spent.
    For as the sun is daily new and old,
    So is my love still telling what is told.

William Shakespeare

In the first two quatrains, Shakespeare asks why he writes the same thing over and over instead of something new. In the third quatrain, he answers that his subjects—his love and love itself—remain constant. In the couplet, he strengthens this claim by comparing his love with the natural cycle of the sun.

■ SONNET

A lyric poem with a traditional form of fourteen iambic pentameter lines. Sonnets fall into two groups, according to their rhyme schemes: Italian (Petrarchan) or English (Shakespearean).

■ Apply to **"A Lover's Vow"** on page 168.

HANDBOOK OF LITERARY TERMS

■ SOUND DEVICES

The device of repetition is basic to art as well as writing. The design of this American quilt relies heavily upon repetition of color and form.

'Tis not enough no harshness gives offence,
The sound must seem an echo to the sense.

Pope's lines from *An Essay on Criticism* have universal application, for writers of both poetry and prose use various sound devices to achieve certain effects in their work. These devices can reinforce meaning, unify thought, or create a musical effect. Some of these are repetition, alliteration, assonance, consonance, and onomatopoeia.

Repetition
The most basic sound device is **repetition**—of a sound, word, phrase, or more. Rhyme is repetition, as are some of the other sound devices discussed here. Repetition can serve obvious functions, as in these lines from Browning's "How They Brought the Good News from Ghent to Aix":

I sprang to the stirrup, and Joris, and he;
I galloped, Dirck galloped, we galloped all
    three . . .

Can you hear the horses' hooves in that second line?
More subtly used, repetition can serve to emphasize ideas or to provide unity to a work, whether in prose or poetry.

Alliteration
The repetition of consonant sounds at the beginnings of words or within words, particularly in accented syllables, is called **alliteration**; for example: *P*eter *P*iper *p*icked a *p*eck of *p*ickled *p*eppers. Alliterative words may be found in one line of a poem, or in several, and more than one sound can be alliterated in a given line. What sounds are alliterated in the following lines from Coleridge's "The Rime of the Ancient Mariner" (page 466)?

Swiftly, swiftly flew the ship,
Yet she sailed softly too:
Sweetly, sweetly blew the breeze—
On me alone it blew.

Anglo-Saxon poets used alliteration heavily. Sound devices like alliteration helped people memorize spoken or sung poems, and so were crucial to the survival of oral literature.

Assonance
The repetition of similar vowel sounds followed by different consonant sounds in stressed

syllables or words is called **assonance.** It is often used instead of rhyme. *Hate* and *great* are examples of rhyme; *hate* and *grade* are examples of assonance. In ". . . that hoard, and sleep, and feed, and known not me," from Tennyson's "Ulysses," the words *sleep, feed,* and *me* are assonant.

Consonance

The repetition of consonant sounds that are preceded by different vowel sounds is called **consonance.** Examples are *born* and *burn.* Consonance is sometimes synonymous with *slant rhyme.* What examples of consonance can you find in the following lines from Keats's "Ode to a Nightingale" (page 511)?

Forlorn! the very word is like a bell
To toll me back from thee to my sole self.

Consonance is an effective device for linking sound, mood, and meaning. In the lines above, the *l* sounds reinforce the melancholy mood of the poem.

Onomatopoeia

The use of words whose sounds suggest the natural sounds of an object or activity is called **onomatopoeia.** Some single words in which sound suggests meaning are: *hiss, smack, buzz,* and *hum.* Onomatopoeia can add to a poem's mood. Some sounds seem peaceful, some humorous, and some aggressive. What mood is created by the following lines from Tennyson's *The Princess?*

The moan of doves in immemorial elms,
And murmuring of innumerable bees.

Contrast this with the onomatopoeia found in Owen's "Dulce et Decorum Est" (page 770):

Knock-kneed, coughing like hags, we cursed
    through sludge,
Till on the haunting flares we turned our backs
And towards our distant rest began to trudge.

What sound devices can you find in the poem in the next column? What specific effects do these devices create? What is the overall effect of the sound upon the meaning?

The Three Companions

"O where are you going?" said reader to rider,
"That valley is fatal when furnaces burn,
Yonder's the midden[1] whose odours will madden,
That gap is the grave where the tall return."

5 "O do you imagine," said fearer to farer,
"That dusk will delay on your path to the pass,
Your diligent looking discover the lacking
Your footsteps feel from granite to grass?"

"O what was that bird," said horror to hearer,
10 "Did you see that shape in the twisted trees?
Behind you swiftly the figure comes softly,
The spot on your skin is a shocking disease?"

"Out of this house" —said rider to reader,
"Yours never will" —said farer to fearer,
15 "They're looking for you" —said hearer to horror,
As he left them there, as he left them there.

                                    W. H. Auden

---

1. *midden,* dunghill; refuse heap.

■ SOUND DEVICES

The tools of *repetition, alliteration, assonance, consonance,* and *onomatopoeia.* When used skillfully, they affect the musical quality of a work and contribute to the mood and meaning.

"The Three Companions" by W. H. Auden from *W. H. Auden: Collected Poems.* Edited by Edward Mendelson. Copyright 1934 and renewed 1962 by W. H. Auden. Reprinted by permission of Random House, Inc. and Faber and Faber Limited.

■ Apply repetition to "**The Lamb**" on page 430.
■ Apply alliteration to *Beowulf* on page 10.
■ Apply assonance to "**The Kraken**" on page 572.
■ Apply consonance to "**Anthem for Doomed Youth**" on page 771.
■ Apply onomatopoeia to "**Ode to a Nightingale**" on page 511.

HANDBOOK OF LITERARY TERMS

■ STYLE

Look at these two pictures at the bottom of the page. What is the subject of each? What colors predominate in picture A? in picture B? Are the forms specific or vague? Which picture has more texture? Which picture shows more formal balance?

Although they share a similar subject matter, these two pictures differ greatly in **style,** the distinctive handling of their medium by the artists. In literature, style refers to the way writers use language to suit their ideas. Once authors choose a purpose for writing, they choose words and shape sentences and paragraphs to serve that purpose. Style involves the specific choices made with regard to diction, sentence structure and syntax, and types of figurative language, as well as use of rhythm and rhyme. Some writers have a style that is unique and distinguishable from other writers. Such styles might be labeled *conversational, terse, flamboyant,* and so on. A particular writer can likewise display a variety of styles, depending on the purpose of each work.

Diction is the author's choice of words or phrases. This choice involves both the connotation and denotation of a word as well as levels of usage. Diction can be formal, informal, ornate, simple, pedantic, conversational, and so on. In *Pygmalion* (page 644), Shaw makes use of a wide variety of dictions when he has each character speak in a way that is appropriate to his or her education and background.

A literary form is also part of a writer's style. A poet, for example, can choose to write in sonnet form, free verse, blank verse, or couplets. Within a chosen form, the writer can organize ideas in varying ways as well.

The use of figurative language can be ornamental or essential in establishing meaning. Further, imagery and figures of speech can be used heavily or sparingly, if at all.

Analyze the style of each of the following poems in as many ways as you can. How are they alike? How are they different?

Waiting Both

A star looks down at me,
And says: "Here I and you
Stand, each in our degree.
What do you mean to do,—
5   Mean to do?"

I say: "For all I know,
Wait, and let Time go by,
Till my change come,"— "Just so."
The star says: "So mean I:—
10   So mean I."

Thomas Hardy

"Waiting Both" reprinted with permission of Macmillan Publishing Company from *The Complete Poems of Thomas Hardy*, edited by James Gibson. Copyright 1925 by Macmillan Publishing Company, renewed 1953 by Lloyds Bank Ltd.

Sonnet 64

When I have seen by Time's fell hand defaced
The rich-proud cost of outworn buried age;
When sometime lofty towers I see down-razed
And brass eternal slave to mortal rage;
5   When I have seen the hungry ocean gain
Advantage on the kingdom of the shore,
And the firm soil win of the watery main,
Increasing store with loss, and loss with store;
When I have seen such interchange of state,
10 Or state itself confounded to decay,
Ruin hath taught me thus to ruminate
That Time will come and take my love away.
   This thought is as a death, which cannot choose
   But weep to have that which it fears to lose.

William Shakespeare

1. Both poems discuss a similar subject. What is it?
2. Which poem uses more imagery?
3. How do the sentence structures differ?
4. What is the tone of each poem?

Hardy, writing at the end of the nineteenth century, presents a conversation between his speaker and a star. He unifies his poem with rhyme (*abab*/*cdcd*), repetition (the last line of each stanza) and dialogue. Shakespeare, on the other hand, uses a much more formal structure: the English sonnet. In three quatrains and a couplet, he uses Renaissance conventions to establish the depth of his love, which is sure to be taken away by time. Where Hardy's language is simple and conversational, Shakespeare's is formal. How might the styles of these poems reflect the times in which they were written?

■ STYLE

The distinctive handling of language by an author. Style involves an author's choice and arrangement of words, as well as the tone, mood, imagery, sound effects, and other literary devices that may or may not appear in a work.

■ Apply to **"A Vindication of the Rights of Woman"** on page 444.

■ SYMBOL

If you received a heart on Valentine's Day, what would it mean to you? What would it mean to you to send or receive a rose?

A **symbol** is something relatively concrete, such as an object, action, character, or scene, that signifies something relatively abstract, such as a concept or idea. For centuries, both a heart and a rose have symbolized love.

Different flowers have come to symbolize different things. In Shakespeare's *Hamlet*, Ophelia says, as she distributes flowers and herbs to the other characters:

There's rosemary, that's for remembrance; pray you, love, remember. And there is pansies, that's for thoughts.

The same object can symbolize different things to different people, depending upon different contexts in which it is used.

. . . Just as flowers have flourished in legend it was natural that they should gather symbolic significance to stand for ideas and ideals that mankind has cherished. The ingenuous pansy was called in rural England by such humble names as kiss-me-at-the-garden-gate and three-faces-under-a-hood, but in the Middle Ages it had been symbolic of the Trinity for having three different colors in one blossom. And because pansy comes

Excerpt from *The Lore and Legends of Flowers* by Robert L. Crowell. (Thomas Y. Crowell) Text copyright © 1982 by Robert L. Crowell. Reprinted by permission of Harper & Row, Publishers, Inc.

from the French *pensée,* meaning "thought," the name was considered in the language of love to be an oblique reference to thinking of one's beloved. Some flowers have been used symbolically in different ways in many different religions. The rose was sacred to the Greek god, Dionysus, famous for revelry, and to the Roman goddess, Venus, famous for carnal love. Later it was sacred to the Virgin Mary and was embodied in the rosary.

Robert L. Crowell
from **The Lore and Legends of Flowers**

Originally, the word *symbol* meant a throwing together or fusion. A symbol, unlike a sign, has more than one meaning.

A symbol may form the framework of an entire work. Some symbols are based on traditional associations—a ring for marriage, for example, or a skull for poison. Other symbols are less universal in their connotations. To determine whether a poem or passage is symbolic, consider the following:

- Is a particular idea or image stressed or repeated?
- Does the author emphasize certain words to suggest a symbolic interpretation?
- Does the author equate something concrete with something abstract?
- Do characterization or imagery suggest a symbolic interpretation?

What symbols can you find in the following poem?

Symbols

I watched a rosebud very long
    Brought on by dew and sun and shower,
    Waiting to see the perfect[1] flower:
Then, when I thought it should be strong,
    It opened at the matin hour
        And fell at evensong.[2]

I watched a nest from day to day,
    A green nest full of pleasant shade,
    Wherein three speckled eggs were laid:
But when they should have hatched in May,
    The two old birds had grown afraid
        Or tired, and flew away.

Then in my wrath I broke the bough
    That I had tended so with care,

15 Hoping its scent should fill the air;
I crushed the eggs, not heeding how
    Their ancient promise had been fair:
        I would have vengeance now.

But the dead branch spoke from the sod,[3]
20 And the eggs answered me again:
    Because we failed dost thou complain?
Is thy wrath just? And what if God,
    Who waiteth for thy fruits in vain,
        Should also take the rod?[4]

Christina Rossetti

---

1. *perfect,* finished; full-grown.
2. *matin . . . evensong,* times for church services held in the morning and evening, respectively.
3. *dead branch . . . sod.* In Genesis 4, God says to Cain, who has murdered his brother Abel, "the voice of thy brother's blood crieth unto me from the ground."
4. *rod,* i.e., punishment.

1. Why does the speaker watch the rosebud "very long"? What is her reward for doing so?
2. Why does the speaker watch the nest? What happens to the eggs?
3. Why does the speaker break the bough and the eggs?
4. How do the branch and the eggs answer the speaker?
5. Explain how the rosebud and the eggs might represent human beings, in God's eyes.

For additional examples of literary symbols, examine the city in "Sailing to Byzantium" (page 738) and the road in "To an Athlete Dying Young" (page 726).

■ SYMBOL

Something relatively concrete, such as an object, action, character, or scene, that signifies something relatively abstract, such as a concept or idea.

■ Apply to **"To the Virgins, to Make Much of Time"** on page 275.

■ THEME

Song

When I am dead, my dearest,
  Sing no sad songs for me;
Plant thou no roses at my head,
  Nor shady cypress tree:
5 Be the green grass above me
  With showers and dewdrops wet;
And if thou wilt, remember,
  And if thou wilt, forget.

Christina Rossetti
from "Song"

What is the above stanza about? That's easy—death. But what does the speaker have to *say* about the subject of death?

When she dies, the speaker suggests, she wants no formal remembrances. Even her beloved may remember or forget her, as he chooses. Thus, the poem reflects on the significance of remembrance after death.

The underlying meaning of a literary work is its **theme.** A theme is usually not stated overtly; instead, it is implied through characterization, action, image, and tone. Occasionally, however, an author states the theme:

My theme is memory, that winged host that soared about me one grey morning of war-time.

These memories, which are my life— for we possess nothing certainly except the past—were always with me . . . . These memories are the memorials and pledges of the vital hours of a lifetime.

Evelyn Waugh
from **Brideshead Revisited**

Theme is related to, but not the same, as motif. A *motif* is a character, incident, idea, or object that recurs in various works or in various parts of the same work. In Shakespeare's son-nets (page 186), the nature and effect of time is a recurrent motif. Theme differs, too, from subject. The subject is the topic about which an author is writing.

Not all works have clear themes. Some mystery or science-fiction novels, for example, simply present narratives. Other literary works have more than one theme.

What is the subject of the following poem? What is its theme?

The Walk

You did not walk with me
Of late to the hill-top tree
  By the gated ways,
  As in earlier days;
5 You were weak and lame,
  So you never came,
And I went alone, and I did not mind,
Not thinking of you as left behind.

I walked up there to-day
10 Just in the former way:
  Surveyed around
  The familiar ground
  By myself again:
  What difference, then?
15 Only that underlying sense
Of the look of a room on returning thence.

Thomas Hardy

■ THEME

The main idea or underlying meaning of a literary work. A theme may be directly stated but more often is implied.

■ Apply to **"The Ecclesiastical History of the English People"** on page 60.

HANDBOOK OF LITERARY TERMS

■ TONE

I Travelled Among Unknown Men

I travelled among unknown men,
    In lands beyond the sea;
Nor, England! did I know till then
    What love I bore to thee.

5   'Tis past, that melancholy dream!
    Nor will I quit thy shore
A second time; for still I seem
    To love thee more and more.

Among thy mountains did I feel
10   The joy of my desire;
And she I cherished turned her wheel
    Beside an English fire.

Thy mornings showed, thy nights concealed,
    The bowers where Lucy played;
15 And thine too is the last green field
    That Lucy's eyes surveyed.

William Wordsworth

What adjective would best describe the author's attitude toward his subject? Is Wordsworth sarcastic, flippant, ironic, or serious? How do you know?

An author's attitude toward the subject or audience is the **tone** of a work. By recognizing tone, a reader can determine whether a writer views the subject with sympathy, disdain, humor, or affection. Tone provides the emotional meaning of a work.

Tone in writing is like tone of voice—it can alter the meaning of the words. A person who speaks highly of another while sneering is actually stating dislike. Similarly, in writing, an author can use positive words to condemn a person or event. The tone in which something is said may change or reverse the literal meaning of the words. Any of the following might provide a clue to the tone in a work: word choice, style, choice of images, treatment of characters and events—even sound and rhyme. Further, all of the elements of poetry can help convey tone: connotation, imagery, metaphor, irony, understatement, and so on.

Determine the tone of the following poem. How does it differ from Wordsworth's poem on a related subject?

The English Are So Nice!

The English are so nice
so awfully nice
they are the nicest people in the world.

And what's more, they're very nice about
    being nice
5   about your being nice as well!
if you're not nice they soon make you feel it.

Americans and French and Germans and
    so on
they're all very well
but they're not *really* nice, you know.
10 They're not nice in *our* sense of the word, are they
    now?
That's why one doesn't have to take them
    seriously.
We must be nice to them, of course,
of course, naturally—
But it doesn't really matter what you say to
    them,
15 they don't really understand
you can just say anything to them:
be nice, you know, just nice
but you must never take them seriously, they
    wouldn't understand.
just be nice, you know! oh, fairly nice,
20 not too nice of course, they take advantage
but nice enough, just nice enough
to let them feel they're not quite as nice as
    they might be.

D. H. Lawrence

■ TONE

The author's attitude toward his or her subject matter and toward the audience. Tone can be stated or implied.

■ Apply to **"The Spectator Club"** on page 358.

WRITER'S HANDBOOK

CONTENTS

The Writing Process

Whether you are writing a lengthy research paper or answering an essay test question, the strategy for writing about literature is the same. It is essential that you read the assignment carefully, organize your thoughts, get them down on paper, and revise your writing until it expresses exactly what you want to say. This article will give you specific tips on how to apply three steps of the **writing process**—prewriting, writing, and revising.

PREWRITING

It may seem strange that getting ready to write usually requires more time than the actual writing. Yet going through the preliminary thinking and planning stage thoroughly makes the writing itself both easier and faster, and it also insures that you will achieve a better paper.

Sample Assignment

Analyze the plot structure of Lawrence's "Tickets Please," paying particular attention to the plot elements of exposition, conflict, and climax.

1. Identify the Task

Determine exactly what you are required to do. Read the assignment carefully and note key words that will direct your writing:

analyze: examine various elements to see what they contribute to meaning or effect.

argue: take a stand about some question and supply reasons to support your position.

compare/contrast: point out similarities and differences.

defend: write in favor of an opinion.

describe: give a picture of something.

discuss: consider various possibilities, perhaps more than one interpretation.

explain: make something clear.

illustrate: give examples, quotations, or other textual evidence.

interpret: express your understanding of a work and support your interpretation with references to the text.

persuade; convince: supply reasons why readers should agree with your opinion.

support: prove ideas, claims, or opinions with evidence or argument.

In addition, identify your intended audience. Your audience will determine the amount of background or explanation you need to supply as well as the sophistication of your style and vocabulary.

2. Begin by Reading Carefully

Reading carefully often means reading more than once, perhaps the entire selection or perhaps just parts of it. Check meanings of words and passages you don't at first understand. Acquaint yourself with the literary devices an author uses and pay attention to structure, relationships, and the progression of events or ideas. Careful reading often involves asking yourself questions and making notes as you read.

3. Think It Through

Class discussion may give you ideas to help you get started, but you should do some careful thinking on your own. Ask yourself questions: What is my purpose? What do I know about _____? What inferences can I draw? What would best illustrate _____? What does this word or sentence mean? Why does this idea (theme, image, etc.) recur?

Try *brainstorming* by yourself or with classmates. Jot down your random thoughts and see if some pattern or central idea begins to emerge. Charts and cluster diagrams are often helpful in this preliminary phase.

4. Take Notes

Some note-taking you may do casually as you first read; at other times, you needn't start taking notes until you begin work on a specific assignment. You may even go back to take additional notes when you discover what you need. (See "Writing Notes and Summaries" in the Writer's Handbook, page 942.)

5. Make a Working Plan

Your next task is to limit or focus your ideas and find a way to present them with the supporting evidence you have gathered. To manage your materials, classify and arrange them in a way that is useful to your purpose. The sample assignment asks you specifically to consider the exposition, conflict, and climax of "Tickets Please." This immediately suggests that you should devote at least one paragraph to each of these three elements. You can use one of the following methods, but keep in mind that this is a *working* plan that you can change as needed.

Write a purpose statement. A simple statement of your purpose will help you organize your ideas. You may be able to use this statement as the basis for your thesis statement when you write.

Construct an outline. Make it as simple or complex as necessary for your purpose. Refer to it as you write to make sure you stay on the right track, and after writing use it again to check your work. (See the model outline on page 936.)

Cluster. Group examples, bits of evidence, and so on that strike you as similar in some way. From these clusters, you may be able to form generalizations that will become the main divisions of your paper.

6. Write a Thesis Statement

Assignments that ask for a single-paragraph response can be developed around a topic sentence. Longer papers, however, need a thesis statement, generally placed in the opening paragraph, that explains your subject and the aspects of it that you will cover. Such a statement can provide a structure for organizing your ideas.

Often the wording of the assignment will supply much of the wording of your thesis statement. Note how the model thesis statement at the top of the next column incorporates words and ideas from the sample assignment.

In "Tickets Please" Lawrence establishes background through an unusual exposition and then moves from the establishment of conflict through a suspenseful rising action to a violent, unexpected climax.

WRITING

Write your first, rough draft quickly, getting your thoughts down as rapidly as possible. Keep in mind your overall purpose. Follow your plans and notes, but don't worry if some extra points creep in or if you repeat yourself. You can cut or add material later. If you are uncertain of a fact, mark the spot and return to it later.

Write on one side of the paper and leave plenty of space for additions and changes or for cutting and pasting. At this stage, don't worry about mechanics—spelling, punctuation, and so on. If possible, start early enough so you can put your rough draft away and let it get cold before you come back later for a fresh look.

REVISING

Plan to revise at least once for ideas and content and your expression of them. Then before and after you copy your paper for final submission, edit for errors in spelling, grammar, punctuation, and usage. You can use these questions as a checklist:

Content, Organization, and Style
• Does the paper fulfill the assignment?
• Is there a strong thesis statement to express the main points and to make clear the organization of material?
• Does the paper have a sense of progression toward the most important ideas, which should be saved for the last?
• Does the paper read well aloud? Where could sentences be combined, *and*'s be eliminated, or similar sentence openings be changed to reduce choppiness and monotony?
• What can be cut? (Be ruthless! Don't use a phrase like "at that point in time" when *then*

does the job. Strike out anything that doesn't bear on your subject or that repeats what you have just said.

- Are the paragraphs proportional? Except when used for surprise effect, a paragraph of two sentences next to one of ten or twelve sentences implies a need for more detail or better organization of material.
- Are the opening and closing paragraphs forceful, interesting, and complementary? (The last paragraph should not be simply a restatement of the first but a summation of all that has been discussed.)
- Which sentences in passive voice could be more effectively phrased in active voice?

Grammar, Usage, and Mechanics

- Are all the words spelled correctly?
- Is all of the punctuation logical and helpful in making the meaning clear?
- Are capitals, numerals, and abbreviations used correctly? Are quotation marks and underscoring (italics) used correctly?
- Are quotations exact?
- Are sentences constructed clearly to avoid such common errors as incorrect pronoun form or reference, incorrect form of the verb, or faulty agreement?
- Are there any errors in word choice or usage?

Finally, before handing in your paper, proofread the completed manuscript to catch whatever errors might have slipped in while you were typing or copying.

The model outline and essay shown here and on the next page were written to fulfill the sample assignment on page 934.

You will find this article helpful in completing the assignment on page 25 and most of the other composition assignments in this book.

Outline

I. Introduction (include thesis statement)
II. Section 1 (Exposition in present tense)
  A. Setting
    1. Midlands city
    2. Wartime (W.W. I)
    3. Tramline conductors and ticket-takers
  B. Characters
    1. Annie
    2. John Thomas
III. Section 2 (past tense)
  A. Annie and John Thomas "step out"
  B. Their relationship builds
    1. Suited for each other
    2. But a "subtle antagonism"
  C. John Thomas leaves her
IV. Conflict
  A. Conflict between characters
    1. Annie wants commitment
    2. John Thomas not ready
  B. Old conflict with new twist
    1. Annie not satisfied to be discarded
    2. She plans revenge
V. Section 3—the "paying back"
  A. Annie plans with other girls
    1. Reader suspense—what is she planning?
    2. Will they go along?
  B. Climax—John Thomas must choose among girls
  C. Falling action & denouement
    1. Annie doesn't want what she has got by force
    2. "He can choose again"
VI. Conclusion

A Close Look at Plot in "Tickets, Please"

D. H. Lawrence's story "Tickets, Please" falls into three parts. He establishes background through an unusual exposition and then moves from the establishment of conflict through a suspenseful rising action to a violent, unexpected climax.

The first several paragraphs provide exposition. The setting is a mining community in the Midlands during World War I. Interestingly, this section is in present tense—"There is in the Midlands," "To ride on these cars is always an adventure," and so on, as if the setting still exists. Working girls take tickets on the trams (trolleys), while the drivers are men "unfit for active service." Two characters are singled out: Annie, who is aggressive and flirtatious, and John Thomas, the inspector, who scandalizes the villages by "walking out" with the girls at night.

Section two shifts to past tense as the plot is set in motion. Annie, after treating John Thomas indifferently for some time, "steps out" with him and has fun. From the first they have to overcome a "subtle antagonism," but both need a companion of the opposite sex. They become better acquainted until Annie, not satisfied with a "mere nocturnal presence," starts to take too much of an interest in John's life, and he starts to avoid her.

The plot so far: girl gets boy; girl loses boy. It's an age-old conflict, here given the added complication that the girl is a determined young woman, the wayward boy is her boss, and the setting is wartime, when relationships are tense. Annie moves from weeping, to fury, to despair, and then to a plan. Annie knows that she is not unique, that John Thomas has loved and left many others, but from the first she has been established as a spunky kind who always has a comeback. Determined to regain control, she plots with the other "discards" to get revenge.

The third section is dramatic and fast-paced. The girls begin by luring John Thomas into their waiting-room. At this point, the reader is still in suspense as to what they are going to do. Then, with ever-increasing menace, they begin to badger him to choose among them. Taunting turns to physical violence as they slap, pinch, and pull his hair. Though it is done at first "more in fun than in spite or anger," they lose control and actually bloody him. The climax comes when John Thomas makes his desperate choice—Annie. But she no longer wants what she has won by force. "I wouldn't touch him," she says, ". . . he can choose again." After the violence there is silence; John Thomas is humiliated and the girls embarrassed. They are all anxious to leave. This conclusion is far more realistic than a "girl regains boy" finish would have been.

Looking back over the story, a reader sees that Lawrence has structured his plot skillfully indeed, and that his present-tense exposition, contemporary conflict, and realistic conclusion all lead to the reader's feeling of having witnessed some very real events.

WRITER'S HANDBOOK

Developing Your Style

For any writer, developing an effective style is a lifelong endeavor requiring discipline and constant effort. It involves designing, constructing, recasting, and polishing—sometimes destroying and starting afresh. To determine an appropriate style, a writer must keep in mind the subject, the audience, and the occasion, and arrange words, images, and details toward a definite goal. You can examine the works of famous authors to see what makes their style effective, but it is more important to present your own ideas in your own way and be willing to revise until you are satisfied that you have done your best.

1. Find Your Own Voice

Use words and sentence constructions that are natural to you. Avoid expressions that seem impressive or sophisticated but do not ring true for you. Know your audience and adjust your tone accordingly; obviously you will not use the same tone discussing the poetry of Wordsworth that you would use addressing a pep rally. Remember that simplicity and honesty have always been marks of good style. As the Greek philosopher Aristotle said, "A good style must, first of all, be clear. It must not be mean [poor; common] or above the dignity of the subject. It must be appropriate."

2. Immediately Get Your Reader's Attention

George Orwell's memoir "Shooting an Elephant" begins in this way: "In Moulmein, in Lower Burma, I was hated by large numbers of people—the only time in my life that I have been important enough for this to happen to me." The reader is intrigued—Why was he hated, and why did that signify importance?—and eager to continue. Don't begin, "I am going to write about . . . ." Instead, launch into your subject in a vivid, inviting fashion. If a personal anecdote or something that you have read elsewhere is appropriate, use it.

3. Strive for Clarity

Being clear is a courtesy to your reader, who usually does not have the patience to dig for your meaning—and should not be expected to. Follow the guidelines at the top of the next column for constructing clear, easy-to-read sentences.

- Avoid circumlocutions; get to the point.
- Place modifiers within reach of what they modify.
- Keep pronoun references, verb tenses, and sequence clear.
- Within both sentences and longer units, use transitions that link precisely but unobtrusively.
- Introduce quotations, paraphrases, and examples clearly.

4. Strive for Brevity

Don't waste your reader's time. Say things once clearly. Instead of "at this point in time," say *then* or *now*. Instead of "due to the fact that," say *because*. Choose details wisely and know when enough is enough. Avoid needless repetition of words and ideas.

5. Give Your Writing Energy

Write active, not passive, sentences. Say, "We agreed" rather than "The decision was reached"; "They fought the fire," instead of "The fire was fought." Keep your prose moving with strong and vivid verbs. For example, Virginia Woolf in "Great Men's Houses" paints a picture with active verbs: "Up in the attic under a skylight Carlyle *groaned*, as he *wrestled* with his history. . . ." In "Youth" Joseph Conrad writes, "[Rats] had *destroyed* our sails, *consumed* more stores than the crew, affably *shared* our beds . . ."

6. Choose Fresh Images and Figures of Speech

Eliot uses imagery to describe *The Mill on the Floss:* "the unresting motion of the great stones . . . the fine white powder softening all surfaces . . . the sweet pure scent of the meal. . . ." And Shaw has Higgins speak figuratively in *Pygmalion:* "I suppose the woman wants to live her own life; and the man wants to live his; and each tries to draw the other on to the wrong track. One wants to go north and the other south, and the result is that both have to go east . . . ." Try to avoid inevitable and easy comparisons; if you've heard a comparison before, it's probably a cliché. (But note how startlingly right is Thomas's "Happy as the grass was green.") Aim for comparisons that are unusual, but never contrived.

7. Vary Sentence Patterns

Alternate long sentences with short ones. Sometimes place modifers before the main clause. Try using details cumulatively to build a description or balancing parallel phrases and sentences to give force to ideas. Note the balance and sense of rightness in this sentence from Wilde's *The Importance of Being Earnest:*

> What between the duties expected of one during one's lifetime, and the duties exacted from one after one's death, land has ceased to be either a profit or a pleasure.

8. Strive for Flair

You may not go as far as Oscar Wilde, who reported that he spent the morning putting a comma in and the afternoon taking it out, but searching thoughtfully for the right word, the apt image, and the telling detail is a necessary part of the process of achieving a forceful and interesting style. Allow yourself a sense of experimentation, of exploration; if your result is too bizarre, you can always change it later. If you have fun writing, though, chances are your reader will have fun reading. Sincerity and a general good nature mark the style of a writer who cares about both material and reader.

Finally, keep in mind that even the most experienced writers occasionally develop blocks and experience frustration. If you approach your writing one step at a time, however, you can achieve a composition that is well organized, well written—and worth reading.

No matter what the assignment, keep matters of style in mind as you review and evaluate your writing. Refer to the revision checklist on pages 935–936. In addition, ask yourself the following questions:

- Does the opening sentence attract a reader's attention?
- Is the language strong, direct, and concise?
- Is the tone polite—neither flattering, talking down to the reader, nor dogmatic?
- Are imagery and figurative language carefully chosen to contribute to the overall effect?
- Are sentence patterns varied?
- Are ideas expressed clearly and forcefully?

You will find this article helpful in completing the assignment on page 172 and most of the other composition assignments in this book.

Writing to Persuade an Audience

Good literature presents issues and ideas that are open to various interpretations—many of them defensible. In a sense, all expository writing based on literature is persuasive, for you as a writer are trying to win your reader's confidence in your interpretation, to gain respect for your scholarship and understanding. In addition, writing assignments on literature may offer a statement, judgment, or position with which you are to agree or disagree, providing reasons for your opinion. When you write to persuade readers, you must carefully consider various positions, decide which one makes the best sense to you, and then persuade your readers that your conclusion is a valid one.

PREWRITING

Sample Assignment

In 1912, the time of the action in *Pygmalion,* speech was only one barrier among many contributing to almost insurmountable class distinctions. Using evidence from the play, argue that Liza was right or wrong in declaring that she would never marry Higgins, even if he asked her.

1. Go to the Sources

Don't take a stand or make any decisions about arguing right or wrong until you have carefully reread the selection. As you read, look for evidence—statements, details, actions, and so on that will help you support an interpretation. In the case of this assignment, such evidence would include speeches by characters, notes on the characters' backgrounds, instances of class distinctions in practice, and so on. Take notes on these items.

2. State Your Position

Once you know your material thoroughly, take a stand and stick by it. This may seem obvious, but actually many persuasive papers fail because the writer appears undecided. After careful consideration, suppose that you have decided to support Liza's decision. You might state your position in this way:

Liza is right: she and Higgins might be interesting and amusing foils for each other, but the differences in their backgrounds, positions, and—most important—motivations—would almost certainly spell a disastrous marriage.

This statement may eventually be refined into a thesis statement. For now, it can direct the rest of your prewriting activities. Notice how, even at this stage, the statement suggests three different aspects of the position that might be discussed.

3. Consider Your Audience

Ask yourself what knowledge and what kinds of opinions your intended readers have. Then ask what kind of approach will best convince them. Avoid an approach that might offend or sound insincere—badgering, excessive flattering, talking down, and so on. Be cautious in appeals to emotion, but on the other hand, don't just disregard your audience's emotions and possible biases. For instance, some readers like "happily-ever-after" endings. How will you avoid saying "that's sentimentality" and get them to accept the ending of *Pygmalion?*

4. Adopt a Tone

Decide on a tone before beginning to write. Don't attempt to bludgeon or attack other positions with sarcasm. An open and direct tone, showing respect for other positions but firmly maintaining your own, is always good.

WRITING

Here are some points to consider as you actually begin writing.

5. Order Your Argument

In presenting a logical argument, you have different organizational strategies to choose from. You could begin each paragraph with a general statement and then give evidence to support it (a deductive organization), or you could give your examples first and then draw a conclusion from them (an inductive organization). The position statement on page 940 implies three arguments; you would use the same approach for each of them. Generally, it is most effective to save your strongest argument for last.

6. Differentiate Between Fact and Opinion

The best evidence comes straight from the text. Ask yourself, "Does the text say this, or do I just think it?" Inferences can be used as evidence—particularly in compositions about literature—but be sure that your inferences are valid. Reject unsupported opinions and sweeping generalizations signaled by words like *always* or *no one*.

7. Use Evidence Fairly

Do not try to give yourself an advantage by quoting out of context or twisting statements around to mean what you want them to mean, instead of what the author intended.

8. Refute Opposing Viewpoints

By becoming aware of other viewpoints—and what validity they might have—you are better able to defend your own. Then in your writing, acknowledge those other viewpoints but refute, or disprove, them by showing that yours is more valid. The overall effect will be to strengthen your position. For example, if you undertook to argue that Liza should marry Higgins, you could concede that their marriage might have conflicts, but that their long experience in working (and fighting) together toward a common goal could bring them to triumph over problems.

9. Come to a Conclusion

After presenting your main points, conclude with some kind of summary, in fresh language, of your position. Don't just repeat or echo the first paragraph. Leave your reader with a sense of closure. Notice how, in this model concluding paragraph, the three arguments are smoothly integrated in a restatement of the original position.

Model

Although the original legend of Pygmalion is a story of love triumphing over all, Shaw's play is not a love story in any sense. Higgins has no romantic interest in Liza; she is his creation. If Liza entertains any romantic notions about Higgins, they are effectively squashed by his callous treatment of her. All she wants now is to get on with her life. Thus, while differences in their backgrounds and positions work strongly against the possibility of their marriage, it is the differences in their motivations that make it ultimately impossible.

REVISING

Evaluate your rough draft, using the checklist on pages 935–936. Also consider the following questions:

- Does the paper take a firm and clear stand?
- Are the main points in the argument clearly expressed in main idea statements in each paragraph?
- Do the points seem to flow in a definite direction?
- Is there sufficient and valid support for each argument? Are all conclusions based on evidence?
- Is the tone consistent and convincing?
- Reread the first and last paragraphs. Are the promises made in the first fulfilled? Does the last draw a conclusion?

You will find this article helpful in completing assignments on pages 36, 375, and 462.

Writing Notes and Summaries

Notes and summaries are in a sense part of the preparation for writing about literature. They serve as a kind of shorthand for evaluating and selecting materials, for condensing and storing information and ideas. They are also ways of learning, for with such writing you attempt to get at the essential, to choose the important and give it order for use later, and to dig out ideas and clarify them by paraphrasing—putting them into your own words. While summarizing usually serves as a prewriting skill, an assignment such as a book review may request that you briefly summarize a work before you focus on some specific aspect of it.

PREWRITING

Sample Assignments

Summarize the plot of Mansfield's "The Doll's House" in one paragraph.

Put into your own words the thoughts expressed in Yeats's "When You Are Old."

1. Write a Summary

The following guidelines will help you write your summary.

Be brief. Make every word count. Decide what information is essential to your summary and eliminate all superfluous details. Never include dialogue or quotations, and eliminate most description. If your summary need include only certain aspects of a plot—for example, those that contribute to the irony of a story—choose your material accordingly.

Be complete. An idea summary should include major ideas; a plot summary should include major actions. You might be surprised to discover how few actions can convey the overall sense of a plot, however. While any summary of the plot of "The Doll's House" should undoubtedly include some mention of *why* Aunt Beryl shoos away Lil and Else, details of Beryl's state of mind would be out of place.

Use the present tense. In summarizing literary works, use the present tense: When Kezia *shows* her friends her new doll's house, they *gaze* in rapture. Using the present tense throughout will help you avoid awkward tense shifts.

2. Take Notes

For a plot summary, list the major actions and events in the narrative. If you are summarizing an entire book, try writing a one-sentence summary as you complete each chapter. Combined with transitional words and phrases, these sentences would form a useful first-draft summary of the whole book. For nonfiction selections, list major ideas with subordinating ideas underneath.

A few sheets of paper will provide adequate notes for many assignments. If you plan on taking a lot of notes, however, use notecards. The extra trouble it takes to identify each card will be repaid by the ease with which you can organize them in different ways. Notes can take various forms:

Direct quotation. Copy the author's exact words in the order in which they appear. Use quotation marks and identify the source. Use ellipses (. . .) to show where words have been left out. When you quote poetry, use a slash to indicate the end of a line.

Paraphrase. Put into your own words the sense of a passage. See "Write a Paraphrase" on the next page.

List. Jot down words, details, images, and so on that you find significant.

Chart. Classify your notes under headings that are significant to your plan.

Generalization. Jot down your reactions, questions, and comments as they occur to you.

Whatever form of notes you take, always record your exact source—page, act, poetic line, and so on. Especially for notes from secondary sources (library research), recording complete information now will save you time later.

3. Organize Your Notes

Use the requirements of the assignment as a guide to organizing your notes. You might find grouping or clustering sufficient for your purposes. Otherwise, construct an outline with as much detail as you need.

4. Write a Paraphrase

A paraphrase is a restatement or simplification in your own words, to help your reader (or yourself) understand a passage or selection. A paraphrase is not necessarily longer or shorter than the original; it runs parallel to the original but simplifies it. The difference between a paraphrase and a summary is in the fullness of treatment. The summary may or may not run parallel to the original but in any event condenses it considerably. The paraphrase is useful for working with short units, especially those you want to integrate into your literature paper. Contrast the samples of both in the following section.

WRITING

Study these models of both paraphrase and summary for the poem "When You Are Old" by W. B. Yeats (see page 734). The original poem has 100 words.

Model

Paraphrase: When you are old and you sit sleepily by the fire, pick up my book (my poem) and read it slowly. Dreaming then of how beautiful your eyes were in youth, you may recall that lots of people loved you for your happy young way of moving and your beauty. Some of them loved you truly, and some falsely. You will realize then (when you read my poem) that I loved you for your questing soul (your spirit of always looking for something), and that I appreciated your sadness when you began to change, to grow older. If you bend down looking into the glow of the fire, you may say softly you regret that the love we shared has fled to some high place and hid from us. (129 words)

Model

Summary: When in old age you read my poem, you may realize that although others loved your youth and beauty, I loved your soul. Then you will regret the loss of our love. (32 words)

REVISING

Notes, summaries, and paraphrases written for your own purposes need not, of course, be revised. If you include a summary or paraphrase as part of a composition assignment, however, revise it as you would any other writing. In addition to reviewing the checklist on pages 935–936, ask yourself these questions:

- Have you a good reason for including a summary or paraphrase? Have you made that reason clear?
- Are there any unnecessary words or phrases that can be eliminated?
- In fiction, are the important elements of setting, character identification and relationships, and the main events of the plot made clear?
- In nonfiction, are the main idea and the author's purpose made clear?
- Would the author recognize the plot or ideas?

You will find this article helpful in completing assignments on pages 113 and 386.

Writing About Plot and Plot Devices

The **plot** of a piece of narrative fiction usually contains the following elements: *exposition*, the setting, characters, and any background information necessary to understand the story; *conflict*, an interior or exterior struggle involving the main characters; *rising action*, a series of events leading to the climax; *climax*, the turning point or point of greatest tension; *falling action* and *resolution*, the working out of the conflict. Assignments on writing about plot may ask you to discuss the plot of a work as a whole or may ask you to focus on a single element of plot. In any case, you will have to understand the whole story, novel, or play and its plot components before responding to the assignment.

PREWRITING

Sample Assignment

Discuss the different levels of conflict in Conrad's *The Secret Sharer* and determine which conflict is most essential to driving the plot.

1. Examine the Plot Components

First review the elements of plot to be sure you understand them and how they function together. (See PLOT in the Handbook of Literary Terms, page 916.) As you reread the work to discover the plot elements, ask yourself the following questions:

How is exposition presented? What are you told at the beginning about characters, setting, and what has gone on before? How are you told—directly, by the narrator, or indirectly, through dialogue or other devices? Are there flashbacks to show earlier action? One further question may or may not be significant, depending on the selection: Why has the author chosen this particular point and not another to begin telling the action of the story?

What conflict or conflicts arise? What causes the conflict? Is the conflict between characters, between a character and an outside force, or within a character? In what ways does the conflict create or influence the other events that make up the plot? Often the motivations of several characters will conflict; to the extent that motivation drives the plot you must consider characterization as well.

What is the climax of the action? At what point do events reach a climax and conflicts begin to be resolved? Is there preparation for the resolution, so that the ending seems fitting?

You should be aware that the very concept of plot has undergone changes over the years. Shakespeare and many other early dramatists adhered rather closely to classical models; the climax of a Shakespearean drama is considered to come in the third act, when the fortunes of the protagonist are at the highest. Later writers do not necessarily follow the same models; the climax of a twentieth-century novel, for example, may come at the very end. In some dramas and short stories there may be little conflict and no climax in the traditional sense at all.

2. Look for Chains of Cause and Effect

In a well-plotted narrative, events do not simply occur; they are *caused*. An action by one character will cause another character to act; that character's action will cause further actions, and so on throughout the entire plot. In skillful hands, such plotting can seem entirely natural and inevitable. As you analyze a plot, look for chains of cause and effect. Tracing them will become an important part of your analysis.

3. Consider Possible Subplots

In a long story or novel, there may be more than one plot. If so, how do main plot and subplot(s) relate? How does the author show connections? (In the entire novel *The Mill on the*

Floss, for example, George Eliot skillfully weaves together several plots.)

4. Consider Plot Structure

How does the story or novel develop? How are the events related? Is there a frame story or flashbacks? Many works are not written in chronological order; if so, how does the author make clear the order of events and the relation-ships among them? Even when the assignment focuses on certain elements of plot, you need to understand the entire structure. To do this, you might find it helpful to construct a chronology of some sort, listing the events as they happen. The following chart shows the major events in *The Secret Sharer.* Note how the two chains of events start separately, then converge.

(2 weeks ago) Captain assigned to ship (Now) Captain takes command of ship Captain takes night watch	(3 weeks ago) Leggatt kills *Sephora* sailor Archbold relieves Leggatt of duty & places him under arrest (Now) Leggatt escapes by swimming

Captain discovers Leggatt swimming
Captain hides Leggatt
Archbold visits ship
Captain deceives Archbold
ship leaves Gulf of Siam
Captain & Leggatt plot Leggatt's escape
Captain sails close to land
Leggatt swims to freedom

WRITING

Study the following paragraph, the opening paragraph in an essay fulfilling the sample assignment on *The Secret Sharer:*

Model

There are many levels of conflict operating simultaneously in Conrad's *The Secret Sharer:* Both the Captain and Leggatt experience physical conflict with the sea and societal conflict with maritime laws or traditions. In addition the Captain experiences internal conflict in his decision to hide the escaped man. But it is Leggatt's physical conflict—ac-cidental as it is—with the man he kills that drives the plot of the story.

See also page 937 for a complete model com-position analyzing the plot of Lawrence's "Tickets Please."

REVISING

Evaluate your rough draft, by using the check-list on pages 935–936. In addition, ask yourself these questions:

- Is the connection between story events made clear to the reader?
- Are conflicts sufficiently explained?
- Is the climax identified?
- Have any unusual aspects of plot structure, such as a frame story or flashbacks, been accounted for?
- Is the author's purpose made clear?
- Are sufficient examples from the text given to support any generalizations?

You will find this article helpful in completing assignments on pages 235 (*Macbeth* edition) and 251 (*Hamlet* edition).

Writing About Characters

Writing about fictional characters can involve several different processes. You may be asked to describe a character as a human being, covering physical characteristics, personality, actions, motivations, reactions to other characters, and so on, or to explain how that character changes during the course of the story. Often, you will be asked to compare and contrast one character with another. Or, you may be asked to analyze the techniques of **characterization** a writer uses to create believable characters in a work.

PREWRITING

Sample Assignment

Discuss the methods of characterization Eliot uses in *The Mill on the Floss* to make Maggie a realistic, complex character. Does the narrator contribute anything significant to the characterization during the "self-conscious" passages (in which the narrator addresses the reader directly)?

1. Think It Through

First review the techniques of characterization available to writers. (See CHARACTERIZATION in the Handbook of Literary Terms, page 898.) As you look back through the story, take notes on the different ways you learn about the characters—descriptions, speeches, actions, and so on. Keep in mind that an author may not use all the methods in one work. Ask yourself the following questions.

What details of physical description are given? Appearance may or may not be important to a characterization. In this story Maggie's age is certainly important. In *The Secret Sharer*, Leggatt's appearance takes on a peculiar significance because the narrator sees him as a mirror image.

What personality traits are described? Often, an author tells you directly about a character's personality; for example, "There were few sounds that roused Maggie when she was dreaming over her book . . . ."

What do the character's speech and behavior tell you? These elements are vitally important in understanding characterization. (In a drama, they may be all you have to go on.) Both speech and behavior express the character's thoughts and emotions—unless, of course, the character feels a need to hide his or her real feelings.

Are thoughts and feelings described directly? You may be told what is going on in a character's mind; for example, "Maggie's heart began to flutter with fear. She dared not tell the sad truth at once . . . ." If not, you must infer thoughts and feelings from speech and behavior.

How do the other characters react to the main character? Maggie's father, for example, tells her to talk about her book no more, but soon afterward, he comments to his friends, "It's a pity but what she'd been the lad—she'd ha' been a match for the lawyers, *she* would." Such reactions may provide strong clues to personality traits and motivations. Keep in mind, however, that because other characters have their own motivations, you may or may not be able to take their assessments at face value.

These are the main, traditional methods of characterization that you need to consider. Depending upon the type of selection, you might also consider the following questions.

What is the character's social context? Very significant to Maggie's character is the fact that she is a girl growing up in rural England of the 1860s, when education for women was still considered by many to be a waste of time, if not downright dangerous.

What is the main conflict? How does it affect the character's motivations? This information may be directly revealed, or you may have to infer it from other details.

How does the point of view affect characterization? In a story told from the first-person point of view, for example, you must consider whether the first-person narrator has anything to gain or lose by telling the truth. Often, you must infer what information is valid and what is shaped by the narrator's biases or limited knowledge. *The*

Mill on the Floss contains a further dimension in the form of a "self-conscious" narrator, who talks directly to the reader: "Life did change for Tom and Maggie: and yet they were not wrong in believing that the thoughts and loves of these first years would always make part of their lives."

Are the characters' names significant? Authors sometimes use names to suggest character. Dickens is famous for this with Thomas Grad-grind, Mr. Murdstone, and others, while in Lawrence's "Tickets Please," Annie is Miss Stone.

2. Summarize Your Findings

You may by now have a lot of isolated notes. Take time to organize them carefully. You may find it helpful to construct a chart like this:

Exposition and Description	Character's Speeches	Character's Actions	Other Characters' Reactions
—Attic Maggie's "favorite retreat on a wet day" —Keeps a "fetish" doll that she punishes for all her misfortunes —Maggie and Tom "like young animals"	—Maggie eagerly explains picture of witch and devil (page 601) —"I can tell him everything he doesn't know. But I think Tom's clever, for all he doesn't like books" —"I *do* love you, Tom"	—Pleads for Tom with her father —"Maggie's cheeks began to flush with triumphant excitement" when she thinks Mr. Riley will respect her —Maggie beats the Fetish's head —Forgets to feed Tom's rabbits	—Father: "She understands what one's talking about" —Luke treats her gently and invites her home with him —Tom: "naughty girl" & she can't fish with him. —Tom thinks she's a "silly little thing" (like all girls)

3. Analyze the Characterization

Keep the assignment in mind. Here, you will want to see whether Eliot has used all the methods of characterization available as well as to see what information is presented in the passages that address the reader directly.

4. Develop Your Thesis Statement

Your thesis statement will help you establish the scope of your paper.

George Eliot not only utilizes most of the standard methods of characterization, but also adds another dimension by having the "self-conscious" narrator address the reader directly upon occasion.

WRITING

There are two possible ways to develop this topic. One would be to discuss all the things you discover from exposition, from the characters' speeches and actions, from the reactions of other characters, and so on. This method could lead to some repetition, but on the other hand, it could provide you with a kind of built-in check list of methods. Another way would be to discuss Maggie's physical characteristics, thoughts, feelings, and so on, pointing out how Eliot presents information on each aspect of Maggie's character.

REVISING

In addition to the checklist on pages 935–936, consider these points:

• Does the thesis statement mention the title and author and the points to be considered or the characters to be discussed?
• Are examples from the story included to support the points made?
• Are quotations exact and accurate?

You will find this article helpful in completing assignments on pages 49, 121, and 532.

Writing About Point of View

The author behind every fictional narrative chooses a **point of view,** a perspective from which to tell the story. The author's choice of point of view determines how the actions and characters are presented. Depending upon the point of view, a narrator may be an active participant in the events that make up the plot, or may be distanced from the action.

Poetry is also said to have a point of view; here, the person narrating the story or expressing his or her thoughts or feelings is called the *speaker.* The speaker may be a character, or *persona,* or may be unidentified.

PREWRITING

Writing assignments about point of view may ask you to analyze what that point of view is, or else to show how the author's choice of point of view affects plot, theme, or some other element. Other kinds of assignments may ask you instead to imagine the story told from a different point of view and discuss how it would differ.

Sample Assignment

The story of *Frankenstein* is told from a variety of points of view. The frame story is told from Robert Walton's point of view. Walton relates the story told to him by Victor Frankenstein, who in turn relates the story told to him by the monster. Discuss how the entire story would be changed if it were narrated primarily by the monster.

1. Think It Through

Review what you know about point of view. (See POINT OF VIEW in the Handbook of Literary Terms, page 917.)

The first-person point of view. The narrator will use pronouns such as *I, we,* and *our.* The narrator may take an active part in events or stand aside and report on them.

The third-person omniscient point of view. The narrator will use pronouns such as *he, she, they,* and *them.* At some point during the narrative, the narrator will describe the ideas or feelings of all or most of the main characters. For example, study the quotations at the top of the next column.

" 'Go, go!' said Mr. Tulliver, peremptorily, beginning to feel rather uncomfortable. . . ."

"Maggie shut up the book at once, with a sense of disgrace. . . ."

Tom "promised himself that he would begin to fish the first thing tomorrow morning."

The fact that all these characters' thoughts and emotions are presented in *The Mill on the Floss* identifies the point of view in that work as third-person omniscient.

The third-person limited point of view. Descriptions of thoughts and feelings will be presented for one character only. Also, the action will tend to follow that same character; that is, usually only events that happen in the character's presence are described, with other outside events reported through dialogue.

The third-person objective or dramatic point of view. The narrator reports everything that can be seen or heard but does not describe characters' thoughts or feelings and makes no comment on the action. This point of view appears rather infrequently in narrative prose.

2. Analyze the Point of View

Who is the narrator? Is he or she a major or minor character in the story? If not, into whose thoughts is the reader admitted?

Are there any shifts in point of view? The sample assignment on *Frankenstein* notes that the story is told from various points of view. Be aware of such shifts in narrator and the effect they have on the story. Sometimes the same incident is related from the point of view of more than one character. Then the reader must determine which—if any—of the points of view comes closest to the truth.

Is the theme of the work influenced by point of view? In *Frankenstein*, the theme of scientific curiosity (and responsibility) is developed through Victor Frankenstein as narrator, but when the monster tells his own story, the theme of evils caused by society is brought out.

Is characterization affected? Decide how one character's perceptions filter the information provided about other characters. For example, note how the youth and naiveté of Larry, the narrator in "My Oedipus Complex" (page 849), affect the way the other characters are presented.

Is the plot affected? Note how the first-person narrator in "The Secret Sharer" (page 698) shapes the plot of this story. Note also how involved a reader becomes in the narrator's belief —whether true or not—in the parallels between his life and Leggatt's.

Is the tone affected? The objective tone of the narrator in "A Shocking Accident" (page 858) provides irony and humor in a story that could appear tragic from another point of view. Authors choose a narrator who will convey a tone most appropriate to the story.

3. Imagine an Alternate Point of View

The assignment on *Frankenstein* requires that you do this, but it is a useful approach for other types of assignments as well. For example, how would "The New Dress" (page 805) be changed if Mabel told her own story, rather than the narrator? How would the story be changed if an omniscient narrator told the thoughts and feelings of all the characters, instead of just Mabel's stream of consciousness? Why did Woolf choose the point of view she did?

WRITING

The following paragraphs present a partial analysis of the point of view in *Frankenstein* and begin a transition into a discussion of how the story would be changed if narrated by the monster.

Model

Victor cannot now view his creation (whose features Victor had originally selected as "beautiful") as anything other than a monster. His every reference to the creature conveys the same revulsion; Victor calls him *wretch, monster, demon, devil, vile insect,* and more; he describes his "eyes, if eyes they may be called" and his "shriveled complexion and straight black lips"; he expresses his own feelings of rage and horror and violently repels any physical contact between them; he even attempts to "extinguish the spark which I so negligently bestowed."

The creature, at the same time, is not only acutely aware of how he is reviled by human beings—including his own creator—but of how much he needs Frankenstein's compassion and help. "I was benevolent," he claims; "my soul glowed with love and humanity. . . ." Then he begs the right "by human laws" of speaking in his own defense.

REVISING

Evaluate your first draft, using the checklist on pages 935–936. Also consider these questions:

- Is the point of view specifically—and correctly—identified?
- Is the effect of the point of view shown on appropriate aspects of the story?
- Is the term *narrator* or *speaker* (not *author*) used consistently throughout?
- Do quotations or specific references to the story support the general statements?

You will find this article helpful in completing assignments on pages 609, 723, and 810.

Writing About Theme

Theme is the underlying meaning in a work of literature. Do not confuse theme, which is often a generalization about life, with the subject or a plot summary. Seldom is a theme stated explicitly; instead it may be implied through characterization, action, setting, symbol, image, tone, and so on. You can come to grasp the theme of a work by extracting the central idea of that work.

PREWRITING

Writing assignments about theme may require you to identify the theme of a literary work, or they may state the theme and ask you to explain how the author has reinforced this theme through particular literary devices.

Sample Assignment

State in a sentence or two what you consider to be the theme of Eliot's "The Hollow Men"; then demonstrate how that theme can be inferred from imagery, allusion, mood, characterization, and other literary devices. Consider whether Eliot's theme is meant to apply to all the world, or only to a certain world at a certain time.

1. Review the Work

Be sure you understand how to tell the theme of a work. (See THEME in the Handbook of Literary Terms, page 931.) Then reread the work and examine it closely. Use the footnotes and the Glossary to be sure you understand the vocabulary and—in the case of this poem—the allusions referred to in the assignment. Consider the title, which is often a clue to theme. In Eliot's poem, the title "The Hollow Men" is a strong clue, but it is not enough in itself to be a statement of theme. Consider also the following questions.

How do imagery and figurative language contribute to theme? Note words and phrases such as "Headpiece filled with straw," and "meaningless/As wind in dry grass" that suggest the spiritual emptiness of "The Hollow Men." Note also the recurring motifs, such as eyes and shadows.

Do setting, tone, symbolism, and point of view suggest the theme? Why, for example, is the scarecrow a particularly appropriate symbol? Elements such as these can be clues to theme. Take note of the interplay of these elements, especially in stories and longer works. Remember that writers adopt a tone and point of view that best conveys a theme.

2. State the Theme

Sometimes a theme will be stated by an author; Chaucer's Pardoner, for example, announces that he has a text: "Avarice is the root of all evil" (see page 114). Or, a poet may sum up a theme in a final line or two, as in "I could not love thee, dear, so much,/Loved I not honor more" from Lovelace's "To Lucasta, on Going to the Wars" (see page 274). More often you will need to state the theme yourself. Do not make it too broad ("Men are hollow") or too narrow ("The world ends not with a bang but a whimper"). Do not let it become unfocused ("The hollow men are those who do not have direct eyes and are prevented from meaningful action"). Attempt to distill the essence of the theme so that readers can readily identify it.

Remember that not every work has a theme. Some works are written purely for entertainment; a mystery story, for example, may have no real theme. Such works may offer an experience or leave you with an impression, but offer little by way of underlying meaning. Other works, such as informational articles, are meant to be taken at surface value. Yet, one of the distinguishing characteristics of good literature is that there is some deeper meaning that can teach us more about life and about ourselves.

3. Relate Each Part to the Whole

As you analyze the work, recognize how each element relates to the theme. Look closely, for example, at the image created by the nursery-rhyme parody "Here we go round the prickly pear." At first it may seem out of keeping with the generally somber mood of the poem, but ultimately it fits the theme because the rhyme describes an essentially meaningless activity, and the original mulberry bush has become a prickly pear, befitting the "cactus land" setting.

4. Organize Your Material

If you use a system of questions to analyze a story, your notes will organize themselves naturally as answers and serve as the basis for the body paragraphs of your paper. In dealing with longer works such as a novel or play, you will find it helpful to write summaries of each section of the work and establish the thematic contribution of each part. Long works may deal with several themes that may or may not be connected. In analyzing the theme of a poem such as "The Hollow Men," you might look for subthemes in each of the five sections before relating them all to the overall theme of the poem.

WRITING

The sample assignment asks for a kind of extension, an application of the theme to the world in general. Note how this was addressed in the model paragraph at the top of the next column.

Model

Yet although the speaker seems to be describing the end of the whole world, there may be some slight ray of hope in this otherwise bleak poem. "*We* are the hollow men," says the speaker, aligning himself with those who are spiritually void—and perhaps explaining the lack of a more objective, more hopeful viewpoint. Recognizing a problem, however, can be the first step to its solution. Furthermore there were "Those . . . with direct eyes . . . ." There do exist people who have represented something positive, either for good or evil. "The eyes are not *here*," he continues. Where are they then? In "death's other Kingdom"—eternity—where they are "Sunlight on a broken column" and where "voices are/In the wind's singing." Even if the speaker sees little hope for himself or those of his generation, still it might be possible for some of humankind to avoid the world ending "Not with a bang but a whimper."

REVISING

Use the checklist on pages 935–936 to evaluate your work. In addition, ask yourself the following questions:

- Is the theme stated? If so, has the statement of theme been correctly identified?
- Is the theme implied? If so, does your paper state it clearly?
- Is the thesis statement supported by reference to literary techniques and devices such as imagery, symbolism, setting, tone, characterization, and so on?
- Is each part of the work related to the theme of the whole?
- Is the theme distinguished from mere plot summary or subject?

You will find this article helpful in completing assignments on pages 64, 94, 532, and 732.

Writing to Analyze an Author's Style

Style is the distinct and individual way an author handles language. When you say that you like a particular author, or that you find an author difficult to read, you are probably responding—at least in part—to style. When you are asked to analyze an author's style or to compare the styles of two or more authors, you will need to consider first all the elements that were discussed in Lesson 2, "Developing Your Style." (See also STYLE in the Handbook of Literary Terms, page 928.) In addition, you will need to consider literary devices such as point of view, theme, tone, mood, and symbolism. Most importantly, note the choice of words, the way they are arranged, and the sounds and images they convey.

PREWRITING

Sample Assignment

Analyze Pope's style in "The Rape of the Lock" and show how that style reflects the age in which he lived.

1. Think It Through

In preparing to analyze an author's style, re-read the selection and make notes. As you read, ask yourself the following questions.

What is the author's diction? Is the level of vocabulary plain, difficult, obscure, formal? Does the author use specific, concrete words, or is the language general and abstract? Is the use of words vivid and fresh or dull, even turgid?

What kinds of sentence structure are used? Are sentences long or short, simple or complex? What can you determine about number, kinds, and placement of modifiers? word order for emphasis? use of parallelism to balance thoughts? economy and repetition? In "The Rape of the Lock" the sentence structure is very largely controlled through Pope's use of the heroic couplet, but note what variety he is able to achieve nevertheless.

What imagery predominates? How do sense impressions contribute to description, mood, and so on? Are some images repeated? to what effect? Is there a pattern of images that can be identified?

Does the author use language figuratively? If so, to what purpose? What makes figures of speech

effective or not effective? Note that the style of many prose writers can be described as poetic. For example, Dylan Thomas makes much use of imagery and figurative language in "A Child's Christmas in Wales" (see page 873).

What allusions are there? Allusions appeal to readers whose cultural background is sufficient to understand them. When does an allusive style leave a reader out? When you know the allusion, how does it achieve economy? What are other possible effects?

You would expect to find allusions in an epic —even a mock epic, such as "The Rape of the Lock." Note the number of allusions Pope makes to classical (Greek and Roman) history and mythology. In addition, Pope not only alludes to fairy tales, he has practically invented a whole invisible world populated by the guardian sylphs.

Is there any symbolism? Do some images or figures take on significance as symbols? If so, are these obvious or subtle? Do they occur singly or repeatedly? to what effect?

How does tone affect the style? Is the voice serious, satiric, objective, didactic, reportorial, bitter, happy, sad, and so on? Pope's tone here could be described as mock serious—even pompous—befitting his mock epic.

How much dialogue is there and how often? What makes it seem natural or artificial? Does it further plot and reflect the characters as individuals?

What is the effect of sound and rhythm? Read a passage or two aloud. Identify features of

sound—alliteration, assonance, onomatopoeia—
and words that describe sounds. Determine the
pace and fluency of prose; the rhyme or meter of
poetry.

2. Put the Style in Context

No one writes in a vacuum. Although an author's style may be distinctive and individual, it
nevertheless has a cultural context. An author
may adopt the diction and literary conventions
of his or her period in history or may choose
to rebel against them—or again may choose to
adopt an archaic style (as does Coleridge in "The
Rime of the Ancient Mariner," page 466; Tennyson in "The Passing of Arthur," page 563; and
others). An author's specific audience and purpose also influence style. You may or may not
like certain types of literary styles—in some composition assignments there are opportunities for
you to voice your likes and dislikes—but it is
not fair to judge a selection ineffective because
of a style that is unfamiliar to you.

3. Develop Your Thesis Statement

By now you have some terms you can use to
describe different aspects of style. Now describe
the overall effect. Is it plain or flowery, spare or
poetic, lean or fat? Is it one that you would like
to read more of or imitate—or parody? In the
case of "The Rape of the Lock" you would certainly note that Pope's style operates on two
levels.

> For all the seriousness—even pomposity—
> of Pope's satirical style, the reader can almost
> sense the twinkle in Pope's eye and feel his
> nudge in the ribs, particularly when he has
> brought off an especially clever juxtaposition,
> such as, "Not louder shrieks to pitying Heaven
> are cast,/When husbands or when lap dogs
> breathe their last."

WRITING

The sample assignment asks—in addition to an
analysis of Pope's style—for a demonstration of
how that style reflects the period in which Pope
lived. The model paragraph responds to that part
of the assignment.

Model

The Age of Reason was also an age of satire.
John Dryden had perfected the use of the heroic couplet and had used it extensively in his
many popular political satires. Pope knew and
respected Dryden from an early age. Satire
was rife in London during this period; everyone, it seemed, was writing it. Pope also
helped to form the Scriblerus Club, a group
of satirical writers, and would have known
other writers and their works from his participation in London society. At the time of
writing "The Rape of the Lock," Pope was already famous for *An Essay on Criticism*, written
in heroic couplets, and well-versed in the satirical approach. He was surely familiar with the
epics of classical Greece and Rome; only a few
years later he would publish his own successful translations of the *Iliad* and the *Odyssey*. It
was natural, then, that when Pope turned his
attention to the Lord Petre–Arabella Fermor
quarrel, he should satirize it in the form of a
mock epic written in heroic couplets.

REVISING

In addition to reviewing the revision checklist
on pages 935–936, ask yourself these questions:

- Is the style concisely described in a word or a
  phrase?
- Are the major stylistic elements dealt with
  specifically?
- Are the points in the thesis statement adequately illustrated with quotes or specific references to the text?
- If such things as commentary on plot or characterization appear, are they employed for a purpose?
- Is any analysis of style given some historical
  context?

You will find this article helpful in completing
assignments on pages 285 and 571.

Writing About Poetry and Poetic Devices

Assignments on writing about poetry may ask you to analyze an entire poem and explain what makes it work, or they may focus on one or more specific elements of a poem. Sometimes you may be asked to compare how two or more poets use a certain poetic device. A full analysis of all the elements of a literary work and how they operate together is called an *explication*. To explicate a poem, you must—in effect—pull it completely apart to examine each line and each device and then put it back together again to show the overall effect that is created by all these elements working together.

PREWRITING

Sample Assignment

Analyze Hardy's poem "The Man He Killed" to show how characterization and various poetic devices operate together to make a philosophical statement about war.

Such assignments may or may not include the term *explication*, but when you are asked to consider all the elements of a work and the overall effect they create, use the approach outlined here—or your own variation of it.

1. Read the Work Closely

Begin, as with any paper about literature, with close reading. With poems—especially those that seem difficult at first—this means reading slowly and thoughtfully more than once. Be sure you understand the various poetic devices that you encounter. (See especially FIGURATIVE LANGUAGE, page 905, and SOUND DEVICES, page 926, in the Handbook of Literary Terms.) In addition, ask yourself the following questions.

What is the poem about? Determine the subject and what is being said about the subject.

Who is the speaker? How do you know? The speaker is not the same as the poet. Hardy, for example, creates a persona, an English infantryman. Here, the quotation marks are a clue. Sometimes it can be hard to distinguish between persona and poet, for many poems are quite autobiographical, but to be on the safe side use the term *speaker* unless you are discussing the poet's writing techniques.

What is the overall mood, controlling image, or dramatic situation? Hardy's poem is dramatic—it has plot, something not all poems have. The speaker provides a setting and situation, rather like the exposition in a drama. Because this poem is a narrative, it has an outcome. Consider that outcome. In what way is it ironic?

In a lyric poem, you will need to look instead for imagery and the way that one or more images contribute to the mood or to the ideas being expressed.

What is the poetic form? Notice that Hardy uses the ballad stanza. Consider the conventions of this stanza pattern and of the sorts of poems (folk or literary ballads) it is usually used for. What does the use of this old folk tradition contribute to the meaning of this poem? Why is it appropriate to the persona Hardy chose to tell the story? What does each stanza add as the poem unfolds?

What instances are there of rhyme, rhythm, figurative language, and sound devices? Carefully note each literary technique you find. Its presence is deliberate; your job is to figure out why the poet included it and what it contributes to the effect of the entire poem.

What can you tell from diction and sentence structure? Note the plain language and use of dialect in words like *wet, nipperkin, traps;* the dropped syllable in *list;* and *half-a-crown.* These all reinforce the speaker's identity as an English soldier. Note the punctuation—particularly the dashes—that suggest the speaker's hesitation as he thinks about what he will say. What does that hesitation signify?

What does it all mean? It's a good idea to start and end with this question. You almost always make new discoveries about depth of meaning as you analyze the elements that contribute to the total effect. Is the poem a comment by only one soldier? What is the tone of "quaint and curious war is"? Is the comment ironic? an understatement? How does this phrase fit the character of the speaker? Why, for instance, doesn't he say, "War is hell"?

2. Take Notes

You may not need to take notes on everything you discover. Instead, look for and note details and quotations that will help you fulfill the specific assignment or that will help you support the thesis statement that you may already have in mind.

3. Organize Your Thoughts

Plan your paper to go from the general to the specific, and then back to the general. Deal with overall effects; then go into how they are created. Finally, sum up your findings.

WRITING

The model at the top of the next column shows the first two paragraphs of a paper responding to the sample assignment. Note how the thesis statement (the last sentence in paragraph 1) announces the three main divisions of the paper to follow. Note also the way in which the close analysis is introduced.

Model

"The Man He Killed" by Thomas Hardy is a comment on the irony of war. To make this comment, Hardy chooses the persona of an English infantryman, who speaks about his experience of killing an enemy soldier. The character of the speaker, the dramatic situation, and Hardy's use of the conventions of ballad story-telling all combine to reveal regret over the ways fate twists the lives of men caught in war.

The speaker is an ordinary man who uses plain words, at times revealing his background and simplicity through his dialect. If he had met his enemy at an inn, he says, they might have "wet . . . a nipperkin." He is convivial—he'd have treated the dead man to a drink if they had met at a bar. Instead, he went to war by chance because he was out of work, and he speculates . . . .

REVISING

The most important thing to look for as you reread your paper is whether you have addressed the assignment exactly. If the assignment asks you to focus your discussion on a single element, determining how that element functions within the structure of the poem, don't try to do more. If, however, the assignment asks for a full analysis, be sure you have at least considered all the poetic devices that appear in the particular work you are analyzing. In addition to the checklist on pages 935–936, here are some other points to look for:

- Does the thesis statement mention or at least summarize all the elements that will be considered in the paper?
- Can some points profitably be combined?
- Does the conclusion put back together the elements that have been taken apart for analysis?

You will find this article helpful in completing assignments on pages 169, 518, 550, 641, and 831.

Writing About Drama

Writing about drama shares many characteristics with writing about other narrative fiction. A play, however, presents its own challenges: usually the story is told entirely through dialogue and action, and there is no narrator to provide exposition, description, conflict, characterization, and so on. Writing assignments may ask you to concentrate on any of these elements of narrative fiction, or they may ask you to consider the dramatic conventions of a particular play.

PREWRITING

Assignments on writing about characters in a play may ask you to consider the traditional methods of characterization, but they more likely will ask you to describe the relationships among characters or the ways in which a particular character develops. Assignments on writing about plot may involve the plot as a whole or may concentrate on one or more of the elements of plot.

Sample Assignment

Exposition is not always confined to the first act of a play; in *Pygmalion* there is some exposition in each of the five acts to let the audience know what has happened since the previous act. Analyze Shaw's technique of exposition in Act Four.

1. Think It Through

Who are the major characters? In writing about Shakespearean drama especially, you may refer to the main character as the protagonist and to the opposing character as the antagonist. In *Pygmalion*, Liza and Higgins do not have a protagonist/antagonist relationship; rather they are foils —opposites that emphasize each other's traits by contrast. Other characters may be considered major if they contribute largely to the development of the plot or to whatever changes may occur in the main character.

Who are the minor characters? What function do they serve? In Shakespeare you will find many characters that do not speak. Usually they fill crowd scenes or serve as attendants. Modern drama can also include crowd scenes, as in Act One of *Pygmalion*, but in Act Three, the minor characters of the Eynsford Hill family have a specific function: they provide an appreciative audience for Liza's first tryout in society.

What is the setting? Shakespearean drama was played on a comparatively bare stage, with very little in the way of props. The viewer had to imagine setting from the action and dialogue. Shaw, on the other hand, provides very detailed stage directions about setting; here, the setting contributes largely to the audience's understanding of the social context of the characters.

Does the plot development fit the traditional pattern? Shakespearean drama closely adheres to the traditional pattern of exposition, conflict, rising action, climax, falling action, and resolution. Modern drama may or may not fit this pattern. For example, the conflict may begin before the opening of the play, and exposition may be presented throughout. Many modern plays lack the traditional climax, falling action, and resolution. In *Pygmalion*, the climax might be said to occur off-stage at the parties and opera where Liza's performance wins Higgins's bet. In other plays the climax might come at the very end.

What is the theme? Is the author's purpose to reflect or comment on society and its values? Do any characters or events carry symbolic meaning?

2. Review the Selection

Here are some further questions to ask while considering the sample assignment.

What do you learn from the setting and costumes? Because a play usually does not include an explanation of what is going on, a playwright must choose very carefully which scenes to present and what to include in those scenes. In Act Four the facts that it is midnight and that the characters are all in formal dress suggest that they are returning home from a social engagement.

What do you learn from the action? Everyone seems tired; it has apparently been an exhausting engagement. Higgins and Pickering behave at home as their usual, comfortable selves, but Liza seems withdrawn. Not until she throws Higgins's slippers at him and they begin their argument do we begin to understand what she is upset about.

What do you learn from the dialogue? Not until several minutes into the act does Pickering mention "a garden party, a dinner party, and the opera," and continues, "But you've won your bet, Higgins." At last the audience has confirmation of what it has been guessing: Liza has passed her big test.

3. Organize Your Thoughts

Reread your assignment to be sure your composition does what it is supposed to do. Then plan how you will present your material. The three questions about setting and costumes, action, and dialogue suggest possible divisions for your paper. Or, you might approach it chronologically, presenting information as the audience receives it.

WRITING

As you write, support your points. You might simply mention your evidence, or you might paraphrase lines of dialogue or stage directions. Or, you might run a quotation into your text. To do this, introduce the quote briefly but clearly, interpreting it if necessary or pointing out its relevance to your thesis: "Higgins reveals his confident snobbism when he tells Liza, 'You shall marry the Governor-General of India or the Lord-Lieutenant of Ireland, or somebody who wants a deputy-queen. I'm not going to have my masterpiece thrown away . . . .' "

Note how the model paragraph at the top of the next column takes the chronological approach to presenting exposition.

Model

At the opening of Act Four the clock strikes midnight and Liza, Higgins, and Pickering enter the laboratory wearing evening clothes—apparently they have all been to an important social engagement. Since Act Three ended with Higgins and Pickering laughing over plans to take Liza to the Shakespeare exhibition at Earl's Court, the audience remains unsure as to what has just transpired. Higgins and Pickering proceed to settle into their domestic routine—Higgins putting on his smoking jacket and looking for his slippers and Pickering fetching the mail—without a word of what has just happened. Only Liza seems changed. For all her finery, "She is tired . . . and her expression is almost tragic." Shaw maddeningly prolongs the moment with Higgins's offhand comment, "Oh Lord! What an evening! . . . What a silly tomfoolery!" It is not until Pickering's next line, mentioning the garden party, the dinner party, and the opera, that the audience finally understands what is going on . . . .

REVISING

Use the checklist on pages 935–936 and the following questions to evaluate your first draft:

- Are all the elements of narrative fiction taken into account?
- Are the specific elements of drama dealt with that are called for in the assignment?
- Are quotations exact, word-for-word?
- Are quotations or paraphrases introduced in such a way that the reader understands their relevance?

You will find this article helpful in completing assignments on page 218 (*Macbeth* edition), 311 (*Hamlet* edition), and 651.

Writing About Mood or Tone

Mood and tone are related, but the two are different. **Tone** is the author's attitude as it is reflected in the work; you sense it in the writing "voice." **Mood** is the effect a work has on the reader, the feeling that the reader carries away from a work—rather like a piece of music that puts you in a happy mood or makes you feel sad. This doesn't just happen; an author may use many literary devices to elicit a certain response from a reader. When you write about mood in literature, it is your job not only to identify the mood, but also to analyze how it is created.

PREWRITING

Sample Assignments

Describe the mood in Thomas's "Fern Hill" and how the mood changes in response to the ideas expressed. Demonstrate how Thomas creates this shifting mood through imagery and word choice.

Describe the tone of Johnson's "Letter to Chesterfield." Consider carefully Johnson's adherence to polite social conventions and demonstrate how Johnson's tone nevertheless pierces through those conventions. Is this a letter written by a writer out of control of his tone, or did Johnson deliberately let his tone show through? Why?

1. Think It Through

Be sure you understand the terms. (See MOOD, page 914, or TONE, page 932 in the Handbook of Literary Terms.) Mood can be described by any number of terms that run the spectrum from *light* and *playful* to *somber* or *tragic*. Tone can generally be described by those same words, but also by terms like *objective* or *emotional, optimistic* or *pessimistic, formal* or *informal, ironic, satiric, cynical,* or *bitter*. Probably the best way to get an initial sense of either mood or tone is to read the work holistically—to get a feeling for the whole—before attempting any close analysis. Ask yourself the following questions.

Does any of the above descriptive words come to mind as you read? If so, it is a good candidate for the descriptive word you want. Trust your instincts. Just as you can usually tell when someone in conversation is being sarcastic, dryly

humorous, and so on, you can often sense the same thing in writing.

Does the work maintain the same mood or tone throughout? If not, try to define the shifting moods or tones. See if you can spot at what points these shifts occur. This will help you figure out the reasons for them.

Is there any external evidence (author, title, reading context, and so on) to suggest that a particular work is satirical? Once you know that Jonathan Swift, for example, is renowned as a satirist, you will be ready *not* to accept everything he says at face value. Most of the authors in the Age of Reason, in fact, employed satire to some degree. You will also find much satire in the writings of twentieth-century authors.

Is there any internal evidence (irony, hyperbole, understatement, and so on) to suggest satire? Recognizing that a work has satirical elements may help you understand passages that may otherwise seem puzzling or even outrageous. Satirical approaches may range from the delicate to the very sharp, from comic needling to rapier-like wit, or they can be bitter, even sometimes cruelly destructive. Such elements are not always easy to spot, but they are vital to your understanding of a work.

Is the tone deliberate? You may not always be able to control your tone when you dash off an angry letter to a store that has sent you the wrong merchandise; you can always control your tone when you recopy that letter before sending it or when you revise a piece of writing for publication. If you are in doubt, assume that the tone is deliberate.

What does the tone or mood add to your understanding of the work? Depending upon the type of writing, either tone or mood can be vital to comprehension, or either can be so far in the background as to be practically unnoticeable.

2. Gather Your Evidence

Because both mood and tone are qualities that you sense in reading, pinpointing their causes may be particularly challenging. While all the elements in a work may help produce a certain effect, pay attention to the author's diction—particularly to the use of connotative language or "loaded" words. Vivid imagery and figurative language contribute greatly to mood, as well.

WRITING

Even though mood and tone are general qualities that may permeate a work, there is no need for you to be general in writing about them. When you have done your best job of describing them and of pinpointing the words, phrases, images, figures of speech—even sentence structure—that contribute to them, take a stand. State your opinion firmly and support it. Use direct quotations, pointing out the qualities they possess or the effects they create. Be sure to conclude with a description of the overall effect of the whole work, to which the tone or mood you are analyzing contribute.

The model that follows is a partial response to the first sample assignment on Thomas's "Fern Hill." Notice the use of direct quotations and the emphasis upon specific words and phrases.

Model

While he is at play, the speaker is the center of a little universe consisting of nature, the somehow magical farm, and his own fantasies of himself as a ruler. He was "*honored* among wagons" and "*prince* of the apple towns," who "*lordly* had the trees and leaves . . . ." With all creation at his command, the speaker felt

unthinking (later, "heedless") joy; he was "happy as the grass was green."

Color plays an important role in creating this mood of blissful innocence. *Golden* is used four times, and *green* is used no less than seven times, with almost as many connotations. These colors appear in startlingly original combinations: "happy as the grass was green," "green and carefree," "green and golden," "fire green as grass," "whinnying green stable" —even "green and dying," but that only later, after the speaker has wakened to a "farm forever fled" and realizes that his "green" (happy) days were an illusion of "green" (inexperienced) youth.

REVISING

As you evaluate your first draft, consider whether or not you have managed to be specific about a topic that may in itself be vague. In addition to the checklist on pages 935–936, ask yourself these questions:

- Is the mood or tone described by a carefully-chosen word or phrase?
- Are quotations well chosen to demonstrate specific points?
- Are quotations exact?
- Do any sections tend to ramble or to repeat the same thing in different words?
- Are quotations and other examples explained in terms of significance or application to the thesis?

You will find this article helpful in completing assignments on pages 484 and 616.

WRITER'S HANDBOOK

Writing About Irony and Satire

Irony is not what it appears to be; what is presented literally is not what is meant. It is this contrast that makes irony a useful device in satire. For **satire,** instead of criticizing its subject directly, does so indirectly, through ridicule. Because of this two-faced nature of irony and satire, there are always at least two things to consider in writing about them: the literal meaning and the satirical subtext, or *real* meaning. Satire makes use of more than just irony: hyperbole, understatement, and other literary devices may also serve a satirical function.

PREWRITING

Writing assignments dealing with irony may ask you to identify and explain an ironical statement or situation, to analyze an author's use of irony, or to point out how irony contributes to the overall meaning or theme. Assignments dealing with satire may ask you to point out satirical elements in a work, to identify the subjects of satire, or to explain the purpose of the satire, or they may ask you to analyze the satire by examining the author's technique and use of various literary devices. (See IRONY, page 912, or SATIRE, page 923, in the Handbook of Literary Terms.)

Sample Assignments

Discuss the irony in Smith's "Not Waving but Drowning." Be sure to tell whether the irony is verbal, situational, dramatic, or a combination of these, and to explain what effect irony has on the poem as a whole.

In the first book of *Gulliver's Travels*, Lemuel Gulliver travels to Lilliput, where the people, although only one-tenth Gulliver's size, are fiercely warlike. In the second book, the situation is reversed, and Gulliver himself is tiny by contrast to the people of the country. Consider how this contributes to the effect of the satire in "A Voyage to Brobdingnag." If Swift's English readers managed to feel themselves morally superior to the Lilliputians, how has Swift prevented any chance of that in this selection?

1. Think It Through

Read the work closely. Be aware and wary. As you read, ask yourself the following questions.

What external evidence is there of irony or satire? Consider the title, author, and the general reading context. For example, all the selections by Swift included in *England in Literature* have some elements of satire, and most of the other authors of the Age of Reason wrote in a satirical vein as well. Many twentieth-century authors make use of irony and satire in their writings.

What internal evidence is there? Look especially for statements that don't seem to mean what they say or that suggest a reversal or twist of other statements in the work. Hyperbole, understatement, and paradox are clues, as are seemingly outrageous statements made with a straight face. Humor often indicates the presence of irony or satire. Generally speaking, when the overall effect of a work is different from what might be suggested by a plot summary, suspect a satirical approach by the author.

Is the satire obvious or subtle? Readers have been known to miss the fact that a work is satirical, thereby misunderstanding that work completely. Swift's "A Modest Proposal" has caused much outrage among readers for just that reason. You may not be able to pinpoint just where an author is being satirical, or just what devices that author uses. Your feeling about the overall effect of a work may be all you have to go on.

What is the tone of the work? Satire can range from harsh and biting to light and amusing—even affectionate. Try to find a word or phrase that describes your reaction.

What is the purpose of the satire? Much satire throughout history has been written to correct personal or social evils, but satire may also poke gentle fun at individuals or institutions, with little purpose beyond entertaining.

2. Organize Your Thoughts

Refer to the original assignment, to be sure you are covering all the elements of the work that you are supposed to cover. If the assignment asks for an analysis, be sure to consider the subject of the satire (including, if appropriate, the historical context), the purpose of the satire, and the various literary techniques used by the author. Note especially words, sentences, and paragraphs where you can pinpoint the use of a certain literary device, such as hyperbole.

3. Test Your Thesis

You can use an evaluation by a peer or classmate at any point in the writing process and with any assignment, but such an evaluation might be particularly useful here. Ask your reader—who should be familiar with the selection—how well you have understood the selection and whether you have missed any important points you should include.

WRITING

Notice how the irony and satire are shown to be interrelated in these paragraphs, based on the second sample assignment.

Model

Gulliver is so far dealing with three different races of peoples: the Lilliputians, at one-tenth human scale; the English, at human scale; and the Brobdingnagians, at twelve times human scale. A reader might well expect that the tiniest, most relatively powerless people would be the most peaceful, while the largest, most relatively powerful people would be most given to warfare. But Swift creates a powerful irony here. The tiniest people, the Lilliputians, are the fiercest and most warlike of the three, while the largest people, the Brobdingnagians, are the most peaceful.

The subject of Swift's satire is, of course, neither the Lilliputians nor the Brobdingnagians, for he has created both races. Rather he is satirizing the English by putting them in the middle of these extremes and comparing them both up and down. The result is that any readers who might have felt themselves morally superior to the Lilliputians, tiny yet ridiculously bellicose, find themselves in exactly the same position as the Lilliputians when the King of the Brobdingnagians refers to the English as "the most pernicious race of little odious vermin that nature ever suffered to crawl upon the surface of the earth." For although Gulliver tries to make "allowances" for the King's "*prejudices*, and a certain *narrowness of thinking*, from which we and the politer countries of Europe are wholly exempted," no thinking reader can miss the irony in that last clause.

REVISING

Evaluate your rough draft, using the checklist on pages 935–936. In addition, ask yourself the following questions:

- Have you identified the author's purpose?
- Have you given a context for each example?
- Have you explained the meaning and function of each quotation?
- Have you identified literary devices—hyperbole, paradox, and so on—whenever possible?
- Have you discussed the overall effect of the irony or satire?

You will find this article helpful in completing assignments on pages 343, 695, and 774.

Writing About Symbolism

Interpreting symbolism requires you to look for more than appears on the surface of a work. **Symbolism** begins with a relatively concrete object, action, character, scene, and so on—which then takes on another dimension of meaning. This meaning will be relatively abstract, a concept or idea that goes beyond the literal statement on the page. Arriving at that symbolic meaning depends on your sensitivity as a reader and on your ability to follow the writer's intent in using words and images symbolically.

PREWRITING

Some writing assignments on symbolism may tell you what symbol to look for and ask you to interpret it. Other assignments may ask you to find the symbol or symbols as well. Still other assignments may simply ask you to interpret a work; then it is up to you to spot whether there *is* a symbol, as well as what it means. (See SYMBOL in the Handbook of Literary Terms, page 992.)

Sample Assignment

Analyze the symbolism in Shelley's "Ozymandias." Consider first what symbolic statement King Ozymandias was making. Then show what symbolic statement Shelley makes through his use of Ozymandias. In what way is the setting symbolic as well?

1. Read the Work Closely

As you read and reread the work, look for images or word combinations that are stressed or repeated—or perhaps stand out as being unique or unusual. Consider also whether any character in a work (or the speaker in a poem) seems to feel particular significance in an object, action, and so on. If so, the object may or may not carry the same symbolic meaning for the reader as for the character. As you read, ask youself the following questions.

What is the symbol? Keep in mind that although the symbol itself can be an object, action, character—or something else—it will always be something relatively concrete. Don't confuse the symbol with its abstract meaning.

What does the symbol stand for? A symbol is economical, for a few words can carry a wealth of meaning. If a character seems to place particular significance in an object, that significance may well be the symbolic meaning of the object. Consider then *why* the object might be symbolic to the character. But a symbol can also be ambiguous, meaning different things to different people. (Think of what a flag might mean to an immigrant, to a conscientious objector, to someone held hostage in a foreign country—or to an enemy.) Part of the challenge in writing about symbols is to come up with a sound interpretation and then to support it with evidence from the context of the work. In some cases you may want to offer more than one interpretation, showing the relative strengths and weaknesses of each.

Is the symbol repeated? Often you will find a symbol recurring, its significance gaining new dimensions with every appearance. In some works, a symbol might in the end take on a completely different significance from what it had in the beginning. Be sure you note each recurrence throughout the work.

How does the symbolic meaning extend through the rest of the work? A symbol and its meaning may apply to only a small section of a work, or it may have application to a part of the work far removed. If that is the case, an author will usually—but not always—repeat the symbol in some form or other.

Is a symbolic interpretation justified? Not every work carries symbolic meanings. Many authors prefer plain, straightforward writing. Don't try to assign meaning to a work by hunting for symbols where they are not intended.

Also, don't confuse symbolism with metaphor.

WRITER'S HANDBOOK

A writer uses metaphor to imply a comparison, to equate two things, both of which are usually concrete. In using a symbol, the writer lets an object stand for an abstraction.

Is the symbolic meaning traditional or original? Some literary symbols are almost traditional; for example, life is often thought of as a journey. When you are analyzing a symbol, ask yourself if the meaning seems clear because others have used it, because the meaning is part of a cultural context. Keep in mind that an author may use a traditional symbol, but give it a new twist, one that you should take into account.

2. Organize Your Thoughts

Any or all of the above questions may apply to the work you are analyzing. The most important thing about symbols is the way in which their meanings add depth and complexity to a work. If you can show that this is true, perhaps you need not concern yourself much further with *why* an author chose to use symbolism.

WRITING

In your introduction, establish immediately the identity of the symbol or symbols you will discuss and, if possible, summarize the symbolic meanings very briefly. Then begin your analysis by showing how and in what context each symbol is introduced. The rest of your paper will be devoted to what the symbol means in detail, how that meaning is reflected throughout the work, and possibly to how you arrived at that meaning and why your interpretation is better than any other.

In the model that follows, note how the question about setting in the last part of the sample assignment is introduced.

Model

The setting goes even further to demonstrate the futility of pride and earthly grandeur. The land is *antique,* suggesting that centuries have passed since Ozymandias

erected his statue. The countryside is now a barren desert. The inscription mentions *works* that supposedly were on such a grand scale as to make even the "Mighty" despair upon seeing them, but "Nothing beside remains." The last sentence of the poem, then, presents a panorama—almost as if a movie camera were panning the horizon—of "lone and level sands" that "stretch far away." By this point, the "trunkless legs of stone" that are the sole remains of Ozymandias's statue seem lost, even pathetic, in this arid landscape. Nature is infinitely more vast and more permanent than any of mankind's efforts—and nature, Shelley seems to say, cares not at all.

REVISING

Symbolic meanings can be complex, but that doesn't mean that your analysis should become so complex that it is difficult for a reader to follow. Have a classmate evaluate your first draft for clarity; then go over it yourself, using the checklist on pages 935–936. Also consider these points:

- Is the initial appearance of the symbol described? Is each recurrence discussed?
- Is there consideration of what significance the symbol has to the character(s), and perhaps why?
- Is the straightforward, literal meaning of the symbol presented, as well as the symbolic meaning?
- Is there a demonstration of how the symbolic meaning reflects on the meaning of the work as a whole?

You will find this article helpful in completing assignments on pages 277, 434, and 723.

WRITER'S HANDBOOK

Writing About a Period or Trend

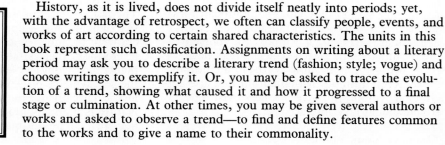

History, as it is lived, does not divide itself neatly into periods; yet, with the advantage of retrospect, we often can classify people, events, and works of art according to certain shared characteristics. The units in this book represent such classification. Assignments on writing about a literary period may ask you to describe a literary trend (fashion; style; vogue) and choose writings to exemplify it. Or, you may be asked to trace the evolution of a trend, showing what caused it and how it progressed to a final stage or culmination. At other times, you may be given several authors or works and asked to observe a trend—to find and define features common to the works and to give a name to their commonality.

PREWRITING

Sample Assignment

What characteristics do the selections in Unit 5 share that earn for them and their authors the description *Romantic?* Does any selection seem out of place in this grouping?

1. Think It Through

Such an assignment implies, first of all, that you have read all of the selections in the unit and understand them reasonably well. You will need to deal with specific selections, of course—but later. First you must deal with the general period. The unit Background, authors' biographies, and Reader's Notes and Comments will be invaluable here. As you review these materials, ask yourself the following questions.

What are the most important characteristics of the literary period? List these characteristics as you encounter them. From the Background and authors' biographies you will note that some of these characteristics are a closeness to nature and love of its beauty; an ascendancy of emotion over reason; an emphasis on a simple life and common people; a belief in making simple language the vehicle for poetry; a stress on the innocence of children; and so on. Any one of these features might serve as the subject for a composition, but here you are striving to understand how they all function together as different aspects of a larger philosophical picture.

Are causes and effects important? Any information you can glean about what prompted an author to write about a certain subject or why that author wrote in a certain form or style might be useful. You may or may not be able to use the information in your paper, but at the least it will contribute to your own general understanding of the period or trend.

Are the lives of the authors significant? Note that Unit 5 is titled *The Romantics,* referring to the authors, not just their works. Wordsworth, for example, was passionately interested in the French Revolution and in so-called liberal causes and ideals. Percy Shelley's "To Wordsworth," in fact, laments Wordsworth's abandonment of those ideals. Again, such information may help your understanding, whether or not you can use it in your paper. The Romantics wrote a lot about nature; consider whether their view of nature was realistic or idealized. Which of them, for example, actually spent time out of doors?

What other cultural elements seem to share similar characteristics? Are they important? For example, there is a Romantic period in music that parallels the Romantic period in literature, and the music shares certain traits, such as emotionalism and an interest in nature, with the literature. Study the fine art that appears as illustrations with various selections. Can you find elements in it that parallel elements in the literature? If you cannot use this information in your writing,

it may nevertheless give you insights into the period to know what the writers were listening to and looking at and what other artists were thinking and doing.

Do any selections not *share the same characteristics? Why?* Note that this question is asked specifically in the assignment; you must at least consider it. If you do find a selection that seems not to fit, perhaps the author was deliberately writing in the style of a different period—or perhaps your list of Romantic characteristics needs revision.

2. Gather Your Evidence

The assignment asks you to consider literary works—not the authors' lives or other cultural influences. Turn now to the selections in Unit 5 and review them, looking for the selections that provide the best examples of the characteristics you have listed earlier. Try to find at least one example for each characteristic.

3. Organize Your Thoughts

Because you are dealing with a generalization (the period or trend) and with many specific examples that support that generalization, it will pay you to plan your paper carefully. The assignment itself may suggest an organizational pattern—here, you may decide to devote a paragraph to each characteristic and its examples. Be sure that your final paragraph comes to some conclusion and does not just summarize what you have written earlier.

WRITING

To avoid a paper with a great number of short paragraphs, try to combine similar traits or characteristics into one paragraph. Use your first paragraph or your thesis statement to define terms and to limit the scope of your paper. Note the way in which the definition is introduced in the model at the top of the next column.

Model

For centuries the word *romance* has meant far more than the modern usage of "love story." To Medieval writers, for example, it referred to a specific literary form that included adventure, elements of the supernatural, and an emphasis on chivalry and courtly romance. By the time of the Romantic period (1780–1830), it implied a belief in progress and social and human reform. But this belief led writers in diverse paths: the natural beauty of the countryside was used to contrast the political and social ills of the city; the common people were raised to the status of role models; a yearning for a former (although nonexistent) "golden age" led to deliberately archaic writing; and an emphasis on emotionalism led not only to philosophical musings about childhood, but to the gothic novel as well.

REVISING

Evaluate your first draft, using the checklist on pages 935–936. Also consider these questions:

- Can certain points be combined?
- Are there any vague statements that can be made more specific?
- Are paragraphs parallel and equal? Do they discuss elements that are of approximately equal weight?
- Are quotation marks used correctly for quoted passages?
- Are titles and authors' names spelled correctly? Are titles indicated by underlining (for complete works) or quotation marks (for individual poems and shorter works)?

You will find this article helpful in completing assignments on pages 155, 291, and 419.

Writing About Nonfiction

Basically, fiction deals with imaginary people and happenings; nonfiction deals with real people and happenings. **Nonfiction** is a very broad term, however, encompassing biography and autobiography; essays; journals, diaries, and letters; history; and various kinds of explanatory texts. Assignments on writing about nonfiction may direct you to any of these genres and ask you to consider content and ideas, form and structure, or style and literary devices.

PREWRITING

Sample Assignment

How does Bacon develop his thoughts in the essay "Of Studies"? Does he use an inductive approach (from the specific to the general), a deductive approach (the reverse), or something else? Analyze his approach and attempt an explanation as to why he chose this approach instead of another.

1. Think It Through

Your preparation should always begin with a close reading of the work. As you read, ask yourself the following questions.

What is the author's purpose? Much fiction is written primarily to entertain, but nonfiction may have a variety of purposes, including information, persuasion, or preservation of thoughts and experience. To identify the author's purpose, it may help to consider the audience the author was writing for.

How is the purpose reflected in the structure and development of the work? Purpose can shape both choice of subject and method of organization. Examples of different methods of organization include the following: (1) an illustration or explanation, followed by supporting details or examples; (2) an analysis of causes and effects, including a discussion of why other causes and effects are not applicable; (3) an account of events in chronological order; (4) a comparison or contrast—as of two books in a review or two types of education in an essay.

Has the author adopted a persona? Why? More often than in other types of writing, the voice in nonfiction may be the author's own. There are

exceptions, as with Swift's persona of a social planner in "A Modest Proposal." Even though the nonfiction writer usually speaks as and for himself or herself, however, be aware that the writer *always* selects, choosing what to put in and what to leave out to give the impression desired. In biography and autobiography, for example, you need to ask if the writer is honest, fully or partially revealing, selective for a purpose, or even biased.

Which elements of style are most apparent? Generally, nonfiction style will be straightforward, but great differences are still possible. Consider, for example, the differences between Boswell's *The Life of Samuel Johnson, LL.D.* and Brittain's *Testament of Youth.* Here, the styles are influenced by the subjects and the historical periods as well as by the authors' personalities.

What ideas are put forth? An assignment may ask you to analyze ideas and the arguments used to support them or to respond to the ideas with your own ideas. In either case, be sure you understand the ideas expressed.

What anecdotal material is included? What is its function? In "Will Wimble," Addison does not lead with his thesis; rather, he begins with an anecdote of having met Wimble. When he does present his thesis at the end, it seems a natural outgrowth of the narrative illustration. Anecdotes may be used in this way, or they may simply provide interest or insight into characters or situations.

2. Form Your Thesis

Review the assignment to make sure you understand exactly what aspect of the literature you are supposed to consider. Now may be a good time to form a thesis statement. You can change it later if you want to, but it will give direction to your next steps.

3. Gather Your Evidence

The type of evidence you need depends to a large extent on your thesis statement. If you are discussing an author's ideas, for example, you will need illustrations of those ideas. Go back through the selection, taking careful notes. Since the sample assignment asks for an analysis of Bacon's development of thought, you would probably find it helpful to outline his essay. Then you would look for examples of conclusions that Bacon states, as well as examples of any materials he uses to support those conclusions. In "Of Studies," you would soon find that Bacon *doesn't* use examples to support his conclusions. That would seem to put his development into the "something else" category mentioned in the assignment. If this is not yet reflected in your thesis statement, change the thesis now.

4. Organize Your Thoughts

The outline form of organization is particularly useful for this type of writing. Your outline should reflect the major divisions in your thesis statement.

WRITING

In responding to the sample assignment, you would certainly need to define that "something else" category—perhaps even give it a name. Note this approach to a definition in the following model.

Model

Certainly Bacon does not develop his thoughts in an inductive way, proceeding from a number of examples to a conclusion that grows out of those examples. But if a deductive approach—going from the general to the specific—necessarily includes examples to support each conclusion, neither does that describe Bacon's development of thought. Instead, he presents each conclusion in a flat, declaratory manner without any examples to illustrate his conclusions and without even explaining to his readers just how he has arrived at those conclusions.

Bacon *does* make use of analogies; for example, he states, "Some books are to be tasted, others to be swallowed, and some few to be chewed and digested . . . ." But these analogies are really just restatements of his conclusions: ". . . that is, some books are to be read only in parts; others to be read but not curiously, and some few to be read wholly, and with diligence and attention." Nowhere does Bacon give any example of what *kind* of books he is referring to, much less any specific titles . . . .

REVISING

In addition to the checklist on pages 935–936, consider these questions:

- Are the author's ideas presented accurately and fairly and not taken out of context?
- If you have included a summary, does it contain unneeded description or elaboration that could be eliminated?
- If you have included a paraphrase, does it accurately reflect the meaning of the original passage?
- If you have included your personal opinion, have you given reasons for it?

You will find this article helpful in completing assignments on pages 364 and 407.

GLOSSARY OF LITERARY TERMS

Words within entries in SMALL CAPITAL LETTERS refer to other entries in the Glossary of Literary Terms. Some entries are followed by a cross-reference to the Handbook of Literary Terms, where a more detailed explanation may be found.

For pronunciation symbols, see the pronunciation key on page 980.

alexandrine (al′ig zan′drən), a line of IAMBIC HEXAMETER:

Most loath- / some, filth- / y, foul, /

and full / of vile / disdain.

Spenser, *The Faerie Queen*

allegory (al′ə gôr′ē), a NARRATIVE either in VERSE or prose, in which characters, action, and sometimes SETTING represent abstract concepts apart from the literal meaning of the story. The underlying meaning may have moral, social, religious, or political significance, and the characters are often PERSONIFICATIONS of abstract ideas such as charity, hope, greed, or envy. Spenser (page 179) used allegory in *The Faerie Queene*.

alliteration (ə lit′ə rā′shən), the repetition of consonant sounds at the beginnings of words or within words, particularly in accented syllables. It can be used to reinforce meaning, to unify thought, or simply to produce a musical effect. "*G*rim and *g*reedy the *g*ruesome monster . . . " (*Beowulf*, page 10) is an example. See also Sound Devices in the Handbook of Literary Terms.

allusion (ə lü′zhən), a brief reference to a person, event, place, work of art, etc. Auden's "Musée des Beaux Arts" (page 842) alludes to *Icarus*, a painting by Brueghel, and to the Greek MYTH that inspired the painting. See also the Handbook of Literary Terms.

analogy (ə nal′ə jē), a comparison made between two objects, situations, or ideas that are somewhat alike but unlike in most respects. Frequently an unfamiliar or complex object or idea will be explained through comparison to a familiar or simpler one. In "Of Studies" (page 171), Bacon makes an analogy between the growth of natural human abilities and that of plants in nature. See also the Handbook of Literary Terms.

anapest (an′ə pest), a three-syllable metrical FOOT consisting of two unaccented syllables followed by an accented syllable, as in *interfere*. The following line is in anapestic TRIMETER:

You can drink / and forget / and be glad . . . .
Sassoon, "Does It Matter?" page 767

See also Rhythm in the Handbook of Literary Terms.

anastrophe (ə nas′trə fē), inversion of the usual order of the parts of the sentence, primarily for emphasis or to achieve a certain RHYTHM or RHYME. In this example both lines contain anastrophe:

The Lord to me a shepherd is,
Want therefore shall not I.
Bay Psalm Book, page 307

See also the Handbook of Literary Terms.

antagonist (an tag′ə nist), a character in a story or play who opposes the chief character or PROTAGONIST. In *Beowulf* (page 10) Grendel is an antagonist, as is Satan in Milton's *Paradise Lost* (page 294). See also Protagonist/Antagonist in the Handbook of Literary Terms.

aphorism (af′ə riz′əm), a brief saying embodying a moral, such as Pope's "Know then thyself, presume not God to scan;/The proper study of mankind is Man," from *An Essay on Man* (page 387).

apostrophe (ə pos′trə fē), a figure of speech in which an absent person, an abstract concept, or an inanimate object is directly addressed. "Milton! thou shouldst be living at this hour . . . " from Wordsworth's "London, 1802" (page 457) is an example of the first; "Death, be not proud . . . " from Donne's Holy Sonnet 10 (page 282) is an example of the second; and "O sylvan Wye! thou wanderer through the woods . . . " from Wordsworth's "Tintern Abbey" (page 450) is an example of the third. See also Figurative Language in the Handbook of Literary Terms.

archetype (är′kə tīp), an image, story pattern, or character type that recurs frequently in literature and evokes strong, often unconscious, associations in the reader. For example, the wicked witch and the enchanted prince are character types widely dispersed throughout folk tales and literature. "Kubla Khan" by Coleridge (page 464) derives much of its power from its use of archetypal images such as the "demon lover." The story of a hero who undertakes a dangerous quest, as in *Beowulf* (page 10) or *Sir Gawain and the Green Knight* (page 149), is a recurrent story pattern.

argument, a prose summary or synopsis of what is in a story or play, both with regard to PLOT and meaning. There is an argument at the beginning of Coleridge's "The Rime of the Ancient Mariner" (page 466).

assonance (as'n əns), the repetition of similar vowel sounds followed by different consonant sounds in stressed syllables or words. It is often used instead of RHYME. *Hate* and *great* are examples of rhyme; *hate* and *grade* are examples of assonance. In ". . . That hoard, and sleep, and feed, and know not me" from Tennyson's "Ulysses" (page 555), the words *sleep*, *feed*, and *me* are assonant. See also Sound Devices in the Handbook of Literary Terms.

autobiography (See BIOGRAPHY.)

ballad, a NARRATIVE song or poem passed on in the oral tradition. It often makes use of REPETITION and DIALOGUE. An example is "Edward" (page 87). If the author of a ballad is unknown, it is called a *folk ballad*; if the author is known, it is called a *literary ballad*.

ballad stanza, a STANZA usually consisting of four alternating lines of IAMBIC TETRAMETER and TRIMETER and rhyming the second and fourth lines:

> The wind sae cauld blew south and north,
>   And blew into the floor;
> Quoth our goodman to our goodwife,
>   "Gae out and bar the door."
>
>   "Get Up and Bar the Door," page 91

biography, any account of a person's life. Examples are Johnson's *Life of Milton* (page 396) and Boswell's *Life of Johnson* (page 401). AUTOBIOGRAPHY is the story of all or part of a person's life written by the person who lived it. Brittain's *Testament of Youth* (page 776) is an autobiography.

blank verse, unrhymed IAMBIC PENTAMETER:

> I may / assert / Eter- / nal Prov- / idence,
>
> And jus- / tify / the ways / of God / to men.
>   Milton, *Paradise Lost*, page 294

The Shakespeare play (page 191) and "Ulysses" (page 555) are also written in blank verse. See also the Handbook of Literary Terms.

cacophony (kə kof'ə nē), a succession of harsh, discordant sounds in either poetry or prose, used to achieve a specific effect. Note the harshness of sound and difficulty of articulation in these lines:

> And all is seared with trade; bleared, smeared
>   with toil;
> And wears man's smudge and shares man's
>   smell: the soil
> Is bare now, nor can foot feel, being shod.
>   Hopkins, "God's Grandeur," page 638

caesura (si zhùr'ə, si zyür'ə), a pause in a line of VERSE, usually near the middle. It most often reflects the sense of the line and is frequently greater than a normal pause. It is used to add variety to regular METER and therefore to add emphasis to certain words. A caesura can be indicated by punctuation, the grammatical construction of a sentence, or the placement of lines on a page. For purposes of study, the mark indicating a caesura is two short, vertical lines:

> Born but to die, ‖ and reasoning but to err;
> Alike in ignorance, ‖ his reason such,
> Whether he thinks too little, ‖ or too much . . .
>
>   Pope, from *An Essay on Man*, page 387

The caesura was a particularly important device in Anglo-Saxon poetry (see the Reader's Note on page 15). However, it is a technique used in many forms of poetry, such as the SONNET, the HEROIC COUPLET, and BLANK VERSE.

canto, one of the main divisions of a long poem. Byron's *Don Juan* (page 493) is divided into cantos.

caricature (kar'ə kə chùr), exaggeration of prominent features of appearance or character. Dickens often used caricature, as, for example, in the characters of the Murdstones in *David Copperfield* (page 576).

carpe diem (kär'pe dē'əm), Latin for "seize the day," the name applied to a THEME frequently found in LYRIC poetry: enjoy life's pleasures while you are able. An example is Herrick's "To the Virgins, To Make Much of Time" (page 275).

Cavalier poetry, a type of LYRIC poetry of the late Renaissance period, influenced by Ben Jonson and the Elizabethan court poets, and consisting mostly of love poems. The Cavalier poets were supporters of Charles I and included Lovelace and Herrick. An example of Cavalier poetry is Lovelace's "To Althea, from Prison" (page 274).

characterization, the methods an author uses to develop the personality of a character in a literary work. A character's physical traits and personality may be described, as are those of John Thomas in Lawrence's "Tickets, Please" (page 818). A character's speech and behavior may be described, as are those of the father in

O'Connor's "My Oedipus Complex" (page 849). The thoughts and feelings of a character or the reactions of other characters to an individual may be shown, as in Greene's "A Shocking Accident" (page 858). Any or all of these methods may be used in the same work. See also the Handbook of Literary Terms.

Classicism, a style of literature characterized by attention to form and influenced by the classical writers of Greece and Rome. Many authors have been influenced by Classicism, and it flourished especially during the Age of Reason. Pope's *An Essay on Man* (page 387) is an example of Classicism.

climax, the decisive or turning point in a story or play when the action changes course and begins to resolve itself. In *Hamlet*, the hesitation and failure of the hero to kill Claudius at prayer in Act Three is often regarded as the climax of the play. In *Macbeth*, the banquet scene in Act Three where the ghost of Banquo appears to Macbeth is often regarded as the climax. Not every story or play has this kind of dramatic climax. Sometimes a character may simply resolve a problem in his or her mind. At times there is no resolution of the PLOT; the climax then comes when a character realizes that a resolution is impossible. Climax is also used to mean the point of greatest interest in a work, where the reader or audience has the most intense emotional response. See also Plot in the Handbook of Literary Terms.

comedy, a play written primarily to amuse the audience. In addition to arousing laughter, comic writing often appeals to the intellect. Thus the comic mode has often been used to "instruct" the audience about the follies of certain social conventions and human foibles. Shaw does this in *Pygmalion* (page 644). When used in this way, the comedy tends toward SATIRE.

comic relief, an amusing episode in a serious or tragic literary work, especially a drama, that is introduced to relieve tension. The gravediggers' scene in *Hamlet*, Act Five, Scene 1, is an example of comic relief, as is the drunken porter at the gate in *Macbeth*, Act Two, Scene 3.

conceit, an elaborate and surprising figure of speech comparing two very dissimilar things. It usually involves intellectual cleverness and ingenuity. In the last three STANZAS of "A Valediction: Forbidding Mourning" (page 280), Donne compares his soul and that of his love to the two legs or branches of a draftsman's compass used to make a circle. The previously unseen likeness as developed by the poet helps us to see and understand the subject described (the relationship of the lovers' souls) more clearly. See also the Handbook of Literary Terms.

conflict, the struggle between two opposing forces. The four basic kinds of conflict are these: a person against another person or ANTAGONIST, as in *Beowulf* (page

10) or O'Connor's "My Oedipus Complex" (page 849); a person against nature, as in "The Seafarer" (page 71); a person against society, as in Shaw's *Pygmalion* (page 644); and two elements within a person struggling for mastery, as in Joyce's "Eveline" (page 887). See also Plot in the Handbook of Literary Terms.

connotation (kon'ə tā'shən), the emotional associations surrounding a word, as opposed to the word's literal meaning or DENOTATION. Some connotations are fairly general, others quite personal. Shakespeare's Sonnet 30 (page 187) uses connotation to create a MOOD of longing. Many of the words used by Shakespeare in this sonnet suggest associations that cluster around a sense of loss. See also the Handbook of Literary Terms.

consonance (kon'sə nəns), the repetition of consonant sounds that are preceded by different vowel sounds:

For*l*orn! the very word is like a be*ll*
To to*ll* me back from thee to my so*l*e se*l*f.
　　　　　Keats, "Ode to a Nightingale," page 511

Consonance is an effective device for linking sound, mood, and meaning. In the lines above, the *l* sounds reinforce the melancholy mood. See also Sound Devices in the Handbook of Literary Terms.

couplet, a pair of rhyming lines with identical METER:

True wit is Nature to advantage dressed,
What oft was thought, but ne'er so well
　　　expressed.
　　　　　Pope, from *An Essay on Criticism*, page 387

dactyl (dak'tl), a three-syllable metrical FOOT consisting of an accented syllable followed by two unaccented syllables, as in *settlement*. The following line is basically in dactylic HEXAMETER:

Loosing his / arms from her / waist he flew /

upward, a- / waiting the / sea beast.
　　　　　Charles Kingsley, *Andromeda*

See also Rhythm in the Handbook of Literary Terms.

denotation (dē'nō tā'shən), the strict, literal meaning of a word. (See also CONNOTATION.)

denouement (dā'nü mäN'), the resolution of the PLOT. The word is derived from a French word meaning "to untie." See also Plot in the Handbook of Literary Terms.

dialect, a form of speech characteristic to a particular region or class, differing from the standard language in pronunciation, vocabulary, and grammatical form.

Burns's poem, "To a Mouse" (page 439) is written in the Scottish dialect. In Shaw's *Pygmalion* (page 644), Liza Doolittle, as a flower girl, speaks in the Cockney dialect characteristic to a certain part of London. See also the Handbook of Literary Terms.

dialogue, conversation between two or more people in a literary work. Dialogue can serve many purposes; among them are these: CHARACTERIZATION of those speaking and those spoken about, as in Greene's "A Shocking Accident" (page 858); the creation of MOOD or atmosphere, as in Mary Shelley's *Frankenstein* (page 520); the advancement of the PLOT, as in Saki's "Tobermory" (page 744); and the development of a THEME, as in Lawrence's "Tickets, Please" (page 818).

diary, a record of daily happenings written by a person for his or her own use. The diarist is moved by a need to record daily routine and confess innermost thoughts. The diary makes up in immediacy and frankness what it lacks in artistic shape and coherence. An example is the *Diary* of Pepys (page 325). (See also JOURNAL.)

diction, the author's choice of words and phrases in a literary work. This choice involves both the CONNOTATION and DENOTATION of a word as well as levels of usage. In *Pygmalion* (page 644), Shaw makes use of a wide variety of dictions when he has each character speak in a way that is appropriate to his or her education and background.

drama, a literary work in verse or prose, written to be acted, that tells a story through the speech and actions of the characters. A drama may be a TRAGEDY, such as *Hamlet* or *Macbeth* (page 191), or a COMEDY, such as *Pygmalion* (page 644).

dramatic convention, any of several devices that the audience accepts as reality in a dramatic work. For instance, the audience accepts that an interval between acts may represent hours, days, weeks, months, or years; that a bare stage may be a meadow or an inner room; that audible dialogue is supposed to represent whispered conversation; or that a blackout signals the end of a scene.

dramatic monologue (mon′l ôg), a LYRIC poem in which the speaker addresses someone whose replies are not recorded. Sometimes the one addressed seems to be present, sometimes not. Examples are "Porphyria's Lover" (page 594) and "My Last Duchess" (page 595). See also the Handbook of Literary Terms.

elegy, a solemn, reflective poem, usually about death, written in a formal style. Examples are Gray's "Elegy Written in a Country Churchyard" (page 409) and Auden's "In Memory of W. B. Yeats" (page 843). See also the Handbook of Literary Terms.

end rhyme, the rhyming of words at the ends of lines of poetry. (See RHYME.) See also Rhyme in the Handbook of Literary Terms.

end-stopped line, a line of poetry that contains a complete thought, thus necessitating the use of a semicolon, colon, or period at the end:

Great lord of all things, yet a prey to all;
Sole judge of truth, in endless error hurled:
The glory, jest, and riddle of the world!

Pope, from *An Essay on Man*, page 387

(See also RUN-ON LINE.)

epic, a long NARRATIVE poem (originally handed down in oral tradition—later a literary form) dealing with great heroes and adventures; having a national, world-wide, or cosmic setting; involving supernatural forces; and written in a deliberately ceremonial STYLE. Examples are *Beowulf* (page 10) and *Paradise Lost* (page 294).

epigram, any short, witty VERSE or saying, often ending with a wry twist:

'Tis with our judgments as our watches; none
Go just alike, yet each believes his own.
Pope, from *An Essay on Criticism*, page 387

See also the Handbook of Literary Terms.

epigraph, a motto or quotation at the beginning of a book, poem, or chapter, often indicating the THEME. An example is found at the beginning of Eliot's "The Hollow Men" (page 834).

epilogue, a concluding section added to a work in order to round it out or interpret it. Shaw wrote an epilogue to *Pygmalion* in which he told what happened to the characters after the play ended.

epiphany (i pif′ə nē), a moment of enlightenment in which the underlying truth, essential nature, or meaning of something is suddenly made clear. Each of Joyce's stories builds up to an epiphany. In "Eveline" (page 887), it is the moment when she realizes she cannot go away with Frank.

epistle, in general, any letter; specifically, a long, formal, and instructional composition in prose or VERSE. Pope's *Essay on Man* (page 387) consists of four verse epistles.

epitaph, a brief statement commemorating a dead person, often inscribed on a tombstone. Gray's "Elegy Written in a Country Churchyard" (page 409) has an epitaph at the end, and Malory's *Morte Darthur* (page 139) concludes with Arthur's epitaph.

epithet, a descriptive expression, usually mentioning a quality or attribute of the person or thing being described. In *Beowulf* (page 10) the epithet *Spear-Danes* is used for the Danes. Often the epithet *Lion-Heart* is applied to King Richard I.

essay, a brief composition that presents a personal viewpoint. An essay may present a viewpoint through formal analysis and argument, as in Bacon's "Of Studies" (page 171), or it may be more informal in style, as in Addison's "Will Wimble" (page 365).

exposition, background information about the SETTING, characters, and other elements of a story. See also Plot in the Handbook of Literary Terms.

extended metaphor, a comparison that is developed at great length, often through a whole work or a great part of it. It is common in poetry but is used in prose as well. Wyatt's "Whoso List to Hunt" (page 166) contains an extended metaphor, with the hunter representing the love-struck poet and the deer representing the poet's beloved. (See METAPHOR.) See also Figurative Language in the Handbook of Literary Terms.

fable, a brief TALE in which the characters are often animals, told to point out a moral truth.

falling action, the resolution of a dramatic PLOT, which takes place after the CLIMAX. See also Plot in the Handbook of Literary Terms.

fantasy, a work that takes place in an unreal world, concerns incredible characters, or employs FICTIONAL scientific principles. There are elements of fantasy in Swift's "A Voyage to Brobdingnag" (page 344) and in Saki's "Tobermory" (page 744). (See also SCIENCE FICTION.)

fiction, a type of literature drawn from the imagination of the author that tells about imaginary people and happenings. NOVELS and SHORT STORIES are fiction. Examples are Eliot's *The Mill on the Floss* (page 600) and Mansfield's "A Doll's House" (page 799).

figurative language, language used in a nonliteral way to express a suitable relationship between essentially unlike things, in order to furnish new effects or fresh insights. The more common figures of speech are SIMILE, METAPHOR, PERSONIFICATION, HYPERBOLE, and SYNECDOCHE. See also the Handbook of Literary Terms.

foil, a character whose traits are the opposite of those of another character, and who thus points up the strengths or weaknesses of the other character. Henry Higgins and Liza Doolittle are foils to one another in *Pygmalion* (page 644).

folk literature, a type of early literature that was passed orally from generation to generation, and only written down after centuries. The authorship of folk literature is unknown. Folk literature includes MYTHS, FABLES, fairy tales, EPICS, and LEGENDS. Examples are *Beowulf* (page 10) and the Folk Ballads (page 84).

foot, a group of syllables in VERSE usually consisting of one accented syllable and one or more unaccented syllables. A foot may occasionally, for variety, have two accented syllables (a SPONDEE) or two unaccented syllables. In the following lines the feet are divided by slashes:

Come líve / with mé / and bé / my Lóve,

And wé / will áll / the plea- / sures próve . . .
Marlowe, "The Passionate Shepherd," page 266

The most common line lengths are five feet (PENTAMETER), four feet (TETRAMETER), and three feet (TRIMETER). The lines quoted above are IAMBIC tetrameter. (See also RHYTHM.) See also Rhythm in the Handbook of Literary Terms.

foreshadowing, a hint given to the reader of what is to come. In "Sir Patrick Spence" (page 89), the reader begins to suspect at least as early as line 16 that disaster awaits the title character. See also the Handbook of Literary Terms.

frame, a NARRATIVE device presenting a story or group of stories within the frame of a larger narrative. In Chaucer's *The Canterbury Tales* (page 96), the pilgrimage is the frame unifying and providing continuity for the stories told by the pilgrims.

free verse, a type of poetry that differs from conventional VERSE forms in being "free" from a fixed pattern of METER and RHYME, but using RHYTHM and other poetic devices. An example is Eliot's "The Hollow Men" (page 834). See also the Handbook of Literary Terms.

gothic novel, a NOVEL written in a STYLE characterized by mystery, horror, and the supernatural, and usually having a medieval or other period SETTING. An example is Mary Shelley's *Frankenstein* (page 520).

hero, the central character in a NOVEL, SHORT STORY, DRAMA, or other work of fiction. David Copperfield is the hero of Dickens's *David Copperfield* (page 576). When the central character is a woman, she is usually called a *heroine*. See also Protagonist in the Handbook of Literary Terms.

heroic couplet, a pair of rhymed VERSE lines in IAMBIC PENTAMETER:

All human things are subject to decay,
And when fate summons, monarchs must obey.
Dryden, from *Mac Flecknoe*, page 322

See also the Handbook of Literary Terms.

hexameter, a metrical line of six FEET:

How man- / y weep- / ing eyes / I made /

to pine / with woe . . .

Elizabeth I, "When I was Fair and Young," page 173

See also Rhythm in the Handbook of Literary Terms.

humor, in literature, writing whose purpose is to amuse or to evoke laughter. Humorous writing can be sympathetic to human nature or satirical. Some forms of humor are IRONY, SATIRE, PARODY, and CARICATURE.

hyperbole (hī pėr′bə lē), a figure of speech involving great exaggeration. The effect may be serious or comic. Byron uses hyperbole for comic effect in *Don Juan*, for example in stanza 17 (page 494). See also Figurative Language in the Handbook of Literary Terms.

iamb (ī′amb), a two-syllable metrical FOOT consisting of an unaccented syllable followed by an accented syllable, as in *until*. The following line is in iambic PENTAMETER:

For God's / sake, hold / your tongue, /

and let / me love . . .

Donne, "The Canonization"

See also Rhythm in the Handbook of Literary Terms.

imagery, the sensory details that provide vividness in a literary work and tend to arouse emotions or feelings in a reader that abstract language does not. Shakespeare's Sonnet 130 (page 188) is rich in specific, concrete details that appeal to the senses. See also the Handbook of Literary Terms.

incremental repetition, a form of REPETITION in which successive STANZAS advance the story or reveal a situation by changes in a single phrase or line. Often a question and answer form is used. An example is the ballad "Edward" (page 87).

inference, a reasonable conclusion about the behavior of a character or the meaning of an event, drawn from the limited information presented by the author. In Browning's "My Last Duchess" (page 595), the Duke is the speaker, and the reader can infer a great deal about his character. See also the Handbook of Literary Terms.

in medias res (in mā′dē äs räs′), Latin for "in the middle of things." In a traditional EPIC the opening scene often begins in the middle of the action. *Paradise Lost* (page 294) opens with Satan and his angels already defeated and in Hell; later in the poem the story of the battle between Satan and the forces of Heaven, which led to this defeat, is told. This device may be used in any NARRATIVE form.

internal rhyme, the rhyming of words or accented syllables within a line that may or may not have a RHYME at the end as well: "We three shall flee across the sea to Italy." See also Rhyme in the Handbook of Literary Terms.

inversion (See ANASTROPHE.)

invocation (in′və kā′shən), the call on a deity or muse (classical goddess who inspired a poet) for help and inspiration. It is found at the beginning of traditional EPIC poems. In *Paradise Lost* (page 294) Milton invokes the "Heavenly Muse" instead of one of the traditional muses of poetry.

irony, the term used to describe a contrast between what appears to be and what really is. In *verbal irony*, the intended meaning of a statement or work is different from (often the opposite of) what the statement or work literally says. An example is Swift's "A Modest Proposal" (page 337). *Understatement*, in which an idea is expressed less emphatically than it might be, is a form of verbal irony often used for humorous or cutting effect. An example is Johnson's remark in his "Letter to Chesterfield" (page 393): "To be so distinguished is an honor which, being very little accustomed to favors from the great, I know not well how to receive." *Irony of situation* refers to an occurrence that is contrary to what is expected or intended, as in Hardy's "Ah, Are You Digging on My Grave?" (page 634). *Dramatic irony* refers to a situation in which events or facts not known to a character on stage or in a fictional work are known to another character and the audience or reader. In Pope's *The Rape of the Lock* (page 377), events known to the sylph Ariel and to the reader are unknown to Belinda. See also the Handbook of Literary Terms.

journal, a formal record of a person's daily experiences. It is less intimate or personal than a DIARY and more chronological than an AUTOBIOGRAPHY. *A Journal of the Plague Year* (page 414) is a fictional attempt by Defoe to create the impression of an actual journal.

kenning, a metaphorical compound word used as a poetic device. In *Beowulf* (page 10) there are many examples of kennings: the king is the "ring-giver," the rough sea is the "whale-road," and the calm sea is the "swan-road."

legend, a story handed down from the past, often associated with some period in the history of a people. A legend differs from a MYTH in having some historical truth and often less of the supernatural. Malory's *Morte Darthur* (page 139) is based on legends of King Arthur and the Knights of the Round Table.

literary ballad (See BALLAD.)

lyric, a poem, usually short, that expresses some basic emotion or state of mind. It usually creates a single impression and is highly personal. It may be rhymed or unrhymed. A SONNET is a lyric poem. Other examples of lyrics are Burns's "A Red, Red Rose" (page 441) and most of the shorter poems of the Romantics. See also the Handbook of Literary Terms.

masque, an amateur dramatic court entertainment with fine costumes and scenery, frequently given in England in the 1500s and 1600s. The term is also used for a PLAY written for such an entertainment. Jonson wrote many masques.

maxim (See APHORISM.)

memoir (mem'wär, mem'wôr), a form of AUTOBIOGRAPHY that is more concerned with personalities, events, and actions of public importance than with the private life of the writer. Orwell's "Shooting an Elephant" (page 812) is an example of memoir.

metaphor, a figure of speech that makes a comparison, without the use of a connective such as *like* or *as*, between two basically unlike things that have something in common. This comparison may be stated (She was a stone) or implied (Her stony silence filled the room). In "Meditation 17" (page 283) Donne compares the individual to a chapter in a book and, later, to a piece of a continent. (See also SIMILE and FIGURATIVE LANGUAGE.) See also Figurative Language in the Handbook of Literary Terms.

metaphysical (met'ə fiz'ə kəl) **poetry,** poetry exhibiting a highly intellectual style that is witty, subtle, and sometimes fantastic, particularly in the use of CONCEITS. See especially the poems of Donne (page 278).

meter, the pattern of stressed and unstressed syllables in POETRY. (See RHYTHM.) See also Rhythm in the Handbook of Literary Terms.

metonymy (mə ton'ə mē), a figure of speech in which a specific word naming an object is substituted for another word with which it is closely associated. An example is in Genesis (page 302): "In the sweat of thy face shalt thou eat bread." Here, *sweat* is used to represent hard physical labor. See also Figurative Language in the Handbook of Literary Terms.

miracle play, a type of PLAY produced during the medieval and early Renaissance periods, based on the life of Christ, stories from the Bible, or LEGENDS of the saints. It is also called a *mystery play.*

mock epic, a SATIRE using the form and style of an EPIC poem to treat a trivial incident. Pope's *The Rape of the Lock* (page 377) is a mock epic.

monologue (See SOLILOQUY and DRAMATIC MONOLOGUE.)

mood, the overall atmosphere or prevailing emotional aura of a work. Coleridge's "Kubla Khan" (page 464) might be described as having a hypnotic, dreamlike mood or atmosphere. (See TONE for a comparison.) See also the Handbook of Literary Terms.

moral, the lesson or inner meaning to be learned from a FABLE, TALE, or other story. The moral of "The Pardoner's Tale" (page 116), as stated by the Pardoner, is "Avarice is the root of all evil."

morality play, a type of PLAY popular in the 1400s and 1500s in which the characters are PERSONIFICATIONS of abstract qualities such as Vice, Virtue, Mercy, Shame, Wealth, Knowledge, Ignorance, Poverty, and Perseverance.

motif (mō tēf'), a character, incident, idea, or object that appears over and over in various works or in various parts of the same work. In Shakespeare's SONNETS (page 186) the effect of time is a recurrent motif.

motivation, the process of presenting a convincing cause for the actions of a character in a dramatic or fictional work in order to justify those actions. Motivation usually involves a combination of external events and the character's psychological traits.

myth, a traditional story connected with the religion of a people, usually attempting to account for something in nature. A myth has less historical background than a LEGEND. Milton's *Paradise Lost* (page 294) has mythic elements in its attempts to interpret aspects of the universe.

narrative, a story or account of an event or a series of events. It may be told either in POETRY or in prose, and it may be either fictional or true. Defoe's *A Journal of the Plague Year* (page 414) and Milton's *Paradise Lost* (page 294) are narratives.

narrative poetry, a poem that tells a story or recounts a series of events. It may be either long or short. EPICS and BALLADS are types of narrative poetry.

narrator, the teller of a story. The teller may be a character in the story, as in O'Connor's "My Oedipus Complex" (page 849); an anonymous voice outside the story, as in Greene's "A Shocking Accident" (page 858); or the author, as in Brittain's *Testament of Youth* (page 776). A narrator's attitude toward his or her subject is capable of much variation; it can range from one of indifference to one of extreme conviction and feeling. (See also PERSONA and POINT OF VIEW.) See also Point of View in the Handbook of Literary Terms.

Naturalism, writing that depicts events as rigidly determined by the forces of heredity and environment. The world described tends to be bleak. There are elements of Naturalism in the work of Thomas Hardy, George Eliot, and D. H. Lawrence.

Neoclassicism, writing of a later period that shows the influence of the Greek and Roman classics. The term is often applied to English literature of the eighteenth century. (See also CLASSICISM and Unit 4.)

nonfiction, any writing that is not FICTION; any type of prose that deals with real people and happenings. BIOGRAPHY and history are types of nonfiction. An example is the excerpt from Boswell's *Life of Johnson* (page 401).

novel, a long work of NARRATIVE prose fiction dealing with characters, situations, and SETTINGS that imitate those of real life. Among the authors in this text who have written novels are Charles Dickens, George Eliot, Thomas Hardy, Joseph Conrad, D. H. Lawrence, James Joyce, Evelyn Waugh, and Graham Greene.

novella (nō vel′ə), a story that is longer than a SHORT STORY usually is, but shorter than a NOVEL. Conrad's "The Secret Sharer" (page 698) might be termed a novella.

ode, a long LYRIC poem, formal in STYLE and complex in form, often written in commemoration or celebration of a special quality, object, or occasion. Examples are Shelley's "Ode to the West Wind" (page 505) and Keats's "Ode to a Nightingale" (page 511).

onomatopoeia (on′ə mat′ə pē′ə), a word or words used in such a way that the sound imitates the sound of the thing spoken of. Some single words in which sound suggests meaning are *hiss, smack, buzz,* and *hum.* An example in which sound echoes sense throughout the whole phrase is "The murmurous haunt of flies on summer eves," from Keats's "Ode to a Nightingale" (page 511). See also Sound Devices in the Handbook of Literary Terms.

ottava rima (ō tä′və rē′mə), a STANZA pattern consisting of eight lines of IAMBIC PENTAMETER with the rhyme scheme *abababcc.* Byron's *Don Juan* (page 493) is written in ottava rima.

parable, a brief fictional work that concretely illustrates an abstract idea or teaches some lesson or truth. It differs from a FABLE in that its characters are generally people rather than animals, and it differs from an ALLEGORY in that its characters do not necessarily represent abstract qualities. Chaucer's *The Wife of Bath's Tale* (page 130) has elements of the parable.

paradox, a statement, often metaphorical, that seems to be self-contradictory but that has valid meaning:

> When I lie tangled in her hair
> And fettered to her eye,
> The birds that wanton in the air
> Know no such liberty.
>> Lovelace, "To Althea, from Prison," page 274

See also the Handbook of Literary Terms.

parallelism, an arrangement of parts of a sentence, paragraph, or other unit of composition in which one element equal in importance to another is similarly developed and phrased. An example is Doolittle's words in *Pygmalion* (page 644): "I'm willing to tell you. I'm wanting to tell you. I'm waiting to tell you." In POETRY, an example is Sassoon's "Does It Matter?" (page 767).

parody, a humorous imitation of serious writing. It follows the form of the original, but often changes the sense to ridicule the writer's STYLE. Eliot's "The Hollow Men" (page 834) has a parody of the children's rhyme "Here we go round the mulberry bush." (See also SATIRE.)

pastoral, a conventional form of LYRIC poetry presenting an idealized picture of rural life. An example is Marlowe's "The Passionate Shepherd to His Love" (page 266). See also the Handbook of Literary Terms.

pentameter (pen tam′ə tər), a metrical line of five FEET:

> When to / the ses- / sions of / sweet si- /
>
> lent thought . . .
>> Shakespeare, Sonnet 30, page 187

See also Rhythm in the Handbook of Literary Terms.

persona (pər sō′nə), the mask or voice of the author or the author's creation in a particular work. Jonathan Swift is the author of *Gulliver's Travels* (page 344), but even though the NARRATIVE is told from the *first-person* POINT OF VIEW, we are not to assume that Swift is expressing his personal opinions. Rather, he has created a persona in the form of the NARRATOR, Lemuel Gulliver. "A Shocking Accident" (page 858) is told from the *omniscient* point of view, but Greene has assumed a voice or persona—detached, witty, ironic—in telling the story. (See also NARRATOR and POINT OF VIEW.)

personification (pər son′ə fə kā′shən), the representation of abstractions, ideas, animals or inanimate objects as human beings by endowing them with human qualities. Death is personified in Donne's Holy Sonnet 10 (page 282). Personification is one kind of FIGURATIVE LANGUAGE. See also Figurative Language in the Handbook of Literary Terms.

play (See DRAMA.)

plot, in the simplest sense, a series of happenings in a literary work. The term is also used to refer to the action as it is organized around a CONFLICT and builds through complication to a CLIMAX followed by a DENOUEMENT or resolution. See the Shakespeare play (page 191). See also the Handbook of Literary Terms.

poetry, a type of literature that creates an emotional response by the imaginative use of words patterned to produce a desired effect through RHYTHM, sound, and meaning. Poetry may be RHYMED or unrhymed. Among the many forms of poetry are the EPIC, ODE, LYRIC, SONNET, BALLAD, ELEGY, BLANK VERSE, and FREE VERSE.

point of view, the vantage point from which an author presents the actions and characters of a story. The story may be related by a character (the *first-person* point of view), as in Dickens's *David Copperfield* (page 576), or the story may be told by a NARRATOR who does not participate in the action (the *third-person* point of view). Further, the third-person narrator may be *omniscient* (om nish′ənt)—able to see into the minds of all characters, as in Lawrence's "Tickets, Please" (page 818). Or the third-person narrator may be *limited*—confined to a single character's perceptions, as in Joyce's "Evaline" (page 887). An author who describes only what can be seen, like a newspaper reporter, is said to use an *objective* or *dramatic* point of view. (See also NARRATOR and PERSONA.) See also the Handbook of Literary Terms.

prologue, a section preceding the main body of a work and serving as an introduction. An example is the *Prologue* to *The Canterbury Tales* (page 97).

protagonist (prō tag′ə nist), the leading character or HERO in a literary work. David Copperfield is the protagonist of Dickens's *David Copperfield* (page 576). (See also ANTAGONIST.) See also the Handbook of Literary Terms.

proverb, a short, wise saying, often handed down from the past, that expresses a truth or shrewd observation about life. "Haste makes waste" is an example. There are many proverbs in the Bible.

psalm (säm, sälm), a song or poem in praise of God. The term is most often applied to the songs or hymns in the Book of Psalms in the Bible. An example is the Twenty-third Psalm, four versions of which are given on page 307.

quatrain (kwot′rān), a verse STANZA of four lines. This stanza may take many forms, according to line lengths and RHYME patterns. Here is one example:

Gather ye rosebuds while ye may,
    Old time is still a-flying;

And this same flower that smiles today,
    Tomorrow will be dying.
Herrick, "To the Virgins," page 275

Rationalism, a philosophy that emphasizes the role of reason rather than of sensory experience and faith in answering basic questions of human existence. It was most influential during the Age of Reason (1660–1780) and influenced such writers of that period as Swift and Pope.

Realism, a way of representing life that emphasizes ordinary people in everyday experiences. O'Connor's story, "My Oedipus Complex" (page 849) is an example of Realism.

refrain, the REPETITION of one or more lines in each STANZA of a poem. The ballad "Edward" (page 87) makes use of refrain.

repetition, a poetic device in which a sound, word, or phrase is repeated for style and emphasis, as in Hopkins's "God's Grandeur" (page 638). See also Sound Devices in the Handbook of Literary Terms.

resolution (See FALLING ACTION.) See also Plot in the Handbook of Literary Terms.

rhyme, the exact repetition of sounds in at least the final accented syllables of two or more words:

Hither the heroes and the nymphs resort,
To taste awhile the pleasures of a court.
Pope, *The Rape of the Lock*, page 377

(See also RHYME SCHEME, INTERNAL RHYME, END RHYME, and SLANT RHYME.) See also the Handbook of Literary Terms.

rhyme scheme, any pattern of rhyme in a STANZA. For purposes of study, the pattern is labeled as shown below, with the first rhyme and all the words rhyming with it labeled *a*, the second rhyme and all the words rhyming with it labeled *b*, and so on:

Queen and huntress, chaste and fair,	*a*
Now the sun is laid to sleep,	*b*
Seated in thy silver chair	*a*
State in wonted manner keep;	*b*
Hesperus entreats thy light,	*c*
Goddess excellently bright.	*c*

Jonson, "To Cynthia"

See also Rhyme in the Handbook of Literary Terms.

rhythm, the arrangement of stressed and unstressed sounds into patterns in speech or writing. Rhythm, or METER, may be regular, or it may vary within a line or work. The four most common meters are IAMB (⌣ ′), TROCHEE (′ ⌣), ANAPEST (⌣⌣′), and DACTYL (′⌣⌣). See also the Handbook of Literary Terms.

rising action, the part of a dramatic PLOT that leads

up to the CLIMAX. In rising action, the complication caused by the CONFLICT of opposing forces is developed. See also Plot in the Handbook of Literary Terms.

romance, a long NARRATIVE in poetry or prose that orginated in the medieval period. Its main elements are adventure, love, and magic. There are elements of the romance in the excerpts from *Morte Darthur* (page 139) and *Sir Gawain and the Green Knight* (page 149).

Romanticism, a type of literature that, unlike REALISM, tends to portray the uncommon. The material selected tends to deal with extraordinary people in unusual settings having unusual experiences. In romantic literature there is often a stress on the past and an emphasis on nature. Examples are Coleridge's "Kubla Khan" (page 464) and Shelley's *Frankenstein* (page 520). There are many other examples in Unit 5.

run-on line, a line in which the thought continues beyond the end of the poetic line. For example, there should be no pause after *thine* in the first line below:

For sure our souls were near allied, and thine
Cast in the same poetic mold with mine.
          Dryden, "To the Memory of Mr. Oldham"

satire, the technique that employs wit to ridicule a subject, usually some social institution or human foible, with the intention of inspiring reform. IRONY and sarcasm are often used in writing satire, and PARODY is closely related. Swift's poetry and prose (page 333), Byron's *Don Juan* (page 493), and Shaw's *Pygmalion* (page 644) all provide examples of satire. See also the Handbook of Literary Terms.

scansion (skan'shən), the result of *scanning*, or marking off lines of POETRY into FEET and indicating the stressed and unstressed syllables. (See RHYTHM and FOOT.) See also Rhythm in the Handbook of Literary Terms.

science fiction, a fictional literary work that uses scientific and technological facts and hypotheses as a basis for stories about such subjects as extraterrestrial beings, adventures in the future or on other planets, and travel through time. Science fiction is a form of FANTASY.

sermon, a written version of a speech on some aspect of religion, morality, conduct, or the like, meant to be delivered in a church. Donne wrote many sermons.

setting, the time (both time of day and period in history) and place in which the action of a NARRATIVE occurs. The setting may be suggested through DIALOGUE and action, or it may be described by the NARRATOR or one of the characters. Setting contributes strongly to the MOOD, atmosphere, and plausibility of a work. The setting is important in Wordsworth's "Lines Composed a Few Miles Above Tintern Abbey" (page 450) and Yeats's "The Wild Swans at Coole" (page 736). See also the Handbook of Literary Terms.

short story, a short prose NARRATIVE that is carefully crafted and usually tightly constructed. The short story form developed in the 1800s. This book includes short stories by Saki, Joyce, Lawrence, Mansfield, Warner, Woolf, O'Connor, and Greene.

simile (sim'ə lē), a figure of speech involving a direct comparison, using *like* or *as*, between two basically unlike things that have something in common:

And now, like amorous birds of prey,
Rather at once our time devour . . .
          Marvell, "To His Coy Mistress," page 289

In this example the similarity between the lovers and the birds of prey is their hungry appetite. (See METAPHOR for comparison.) See also Figurative Language in the Handbook of Literary Terms.

slant rhyme, rhyme in which the vowel sounds are not quite identical, as in the first and third lines below:

And I untightened next the tress
   About her neck; her cheek once more
Blushed bright beneath my burning kiss . . .
          Browning, "Porphyria's Lover," page 594

(See also CONSONANCE.) See also Rhyme in the Handbook of Literary Terms.

soliloquy (sə lil'ə kwē), a DRAMATIC CONVENTION that allows a character alone on stage to speak his or her thoughts aloud. If someone else is on stage but cannot hear the character's words, the soliloquy becomes an *aside*. The Shakespeare play (page 191) has examples of soliloquy. (Compare with DRAMATIC MONOLOGUE.)

sonnet, a LYRIC poem with a traditional form of fourteen IAMBIC PENTAMETER lines. Sonnets fall into two groups, according to their RHYME SCHEMES. The *Italian* or *Petrarchan* sonnet, named after the Italian poet Petrarch, is usually rhymed *abbaabba/cdecde* (with variations permitted in the *cdecde* rhyme scheme). It forms basically a two-part poem of eight lines (*octave*) and six lines (*sestet*) respectively. These two parts are played off against each other in a great variety of ways. An example is Wyatt's "Whoso List to Hunt" (page 166). The *English* or *Shakespearean* sonnet is usually rhymed *abab/cdcd/efef/gg*, presenting a four-part structure in which an idea or theme is developed in three QUATRAINS and then brought to a conclusion in the COUPLET. Shakespeare's sonnets (page 186) are examples of this type. See also the Handbook of Literary Terms.

GLOSSARY OF LITERARY TERMS

speaker, the person who is speaking in a poem, as in Lawrence's "Snake" (page 828). (See also NARRATOR.)

spondee (spon'dē'), a metrical FOOT of two accented syllables, as in *pipe dream.* It serves occasionally as a substitute to vary the meter, as in the third foot below:

As yet / but knock, / breathe, shine, /

and seek / to mend . . .
Donne, Holy Sonnet 14, page 282

See also Rhythm in the Handbook of Literary Terms.

sprung rhythm, a metrical form in which the accented or stressed syllables are *scanned* without regard to the number of unstressed syllables in a FOOT. A foot may have from one to four syllables, with the accent always on the first syllable. The term was invented and the technique developed by Gerard Manley Hopkins. The following line is scanned according to Hopkins's theory:

And for all / this, / nature is / never / spent . . .
Hopkins, "God's Grandeur," page 638

The first foot has three syllables, the second foot one, the third foot three, the fourth foot two, and the fifth foot one, with the accent on the first syllable of each foot.

stage directions, directions given by the author of a PLAY to indicate the action, costumes, SETTING, arrangement of the stage, and so on. For examples of stage directions, see Shaw's *Pygmalion* (page 644), where they are printed in italic type.

stanza, a group of lines that are set off and form a division in a poem, sometimes linked with other stanzas by RHYME. Hopkins's "Pied Beauty" (page 637) has two stanzas.

stereotype (ster'ē ə tīp', stir'ē ə tīp'), a conventional character, PLOT, or SETTING that possesses little or no individuality but that may be used for a purpose. The character of Murdstone in Dickens's *David Copperfield* (page 576) in many ways fits the stereotype of a villain. See also Characterization in the Handbook of Literary Terms.

stream of consciousness, the recording or re-creation of a character's flow of thought. Raw images, perceptions, and memories come and go in seemingly random, but actually controlled, fashion, much as they do in people's minds. James Joyce and Virginia Woolf often used stream of consciousness in their writings.

style, the distinctive handling of language by an author. It involves the specific choices made with regard to DICTION, syntax, FIGURATIVE LANGUAGE, and so on. For a comparison of two very different styles, see Wordsworth's "Ode: Intimations of Immortality" (page 458) and Pope's *The Rape of the Lock* (page 377). See also the Handbook of Literary Terms.

symbol, something relatively concrete, such as an object, action, character, or scene, that signifies something relatively abstract, such as a concept or idea. In Yeats's "Sailing to Byzantium" (page 738), the city of Byzantium is a symbol for the unity of all aspects of life—religious, aesthetic, practical, and intellectual. See also the Handbook of Literary Terms.

synecdoche (si nek'də kē), a figure of speech in which a part stands for the whole, as in "hired *hands.*" *Hands* (the part) stands for the whole (those who do manual labor; those who work with their hands). The term also refers to a figurative expression in which the whole stands for a part, as in "call the *law.*" *Law* (the whole) represents the police (a part of the whole system of law). See also Figurative Language in the Handbook of Literary Terms.

tale, a simple prose or verse NARRATIVE, either true or fictitious. "The Passing of Arthur" (page 563), from Tennyson's *Idylls of the King,* is a tale.

terza rima (ter'tsä rē'mä), a VERSE form with a three-line STANZA rhyming *aba/bcb/cdc,* and so on:

Thou who didst waken from his summer dreams
The blue Mediterranean, where he lay,
Lulled by the coil of his crystalline streams,

Beside a pumice isle in Baiae's bay,
And saw in sleep old palaces and towers
Quivering within the wave's intenser day . . .
Shelley, "Ode to the West Wind," page 505

tetrameter (te tram'ə tər), a metrical line of four FEET:

Had we / but world / enough / and time . . .
Marvell, "To His Coy Mistress," page 289

See also Rhythm in the Handbook of Literary Terms.

theme, the underlying meaning of a literary work. A theme may be directly stated but more often is implied. In Mansfield's "The Doll's House" (page 799), the topic or subject is described, at least in part, in the title, but an important theme is the pain of childhood. See also the Handbook of Literary Terms.

tone, the author's attitude, either stated or implied, toward his or her subject matter and toward the audience. In the *Prologue* to *The Canterbury Tales* (page 97), Chaucer's tone is both sympathetic and IRONIC. He pretends to be an innocent observer, supplying details about each pilgrim in a haphazard manner; yet these details, when carefully weighed, have a telling ironic force. The irony, however, is blended with HUMOR and compassion. See also the Handbook of Literary Terms.

tragedy, dramatic or NARRATIVE writing in which the main character suffers disaster after a serious and significant struggle, but faces his or her downfall in such a way as to attain heroic stature. An example is the Shakespeare play (page 191).

trimeter (trim′ə tər), a metrical line of three FEET:

Down to / a sun- / less sea.
> Coleridge, "Kubla Khan," page 464

See also Rhythm in the Handbook of Literary Terms.

trochee (trō′kē), a metrical FOOT made up of one accented syllable followed by an unaccented syllable, as in *answer*:

Double, / double, / toil and / trouble;

Fire / burn and / caldron / bubble.
> Shakespeare, *Macbeth*, Act Four, Scene 1

See also Rhythm in the Handbook of Literary Terms.

verse, in its most general sense, a synonym for POETRY. Verse may also be used to refer to poetry carefully composed as to RHYTHM and RHYME SCHEME, but of inferior literary value. Sometimes the word *verse* is used to mean a line or STANZA of poetry.

verisimilitude (ver′ə sə mil′ə tüd), the appearance of truth or reality in fiction. For example, Defoe achieves verisimilitude in *A Journal of the Plague Year* (page 414) by piling detail upon detail so that his fictional account has the authenticity of real life.

villanelle (vil′ə nel′), a poetic form normally consisting of five three-line STANZAS and a final QUATRAIN, rhyming *aba/aba/aba/aba/aba/abaa*, and with lines 1 and 3 repeating alternately as REFRAINS throughout. An example is Thomas's "Do Not Go Gentle into That Good Night" (page 871).

GLOSSARY

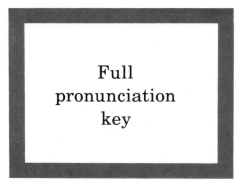

Full
pronunciation
key

The pronunciation of each word is shown just after the word, in this way: **ab bre vi ate** (ə brē′vē āt). The letters and signs used are pronounced as in the words below. The mark ′ is placed after a syllable with primary or heavy accent, as in the example above. The mark ′ after a syllable shows a secondary or lighter accent, as in **ab bre vi a tion** (ə brē′vē ā′shən).

Some words, taken from foreign languages, are spoken with sounds that do not otherwise occur in English. Symbols for these sounds are given in the key as "foreign sounds."

a	hat, cap	j	jam, enjoy	u	cup, butter		**foreign sounds**
ā	age, face	k	kind, seek	u̇	full, put		
ä	father, far	l	land, coal	ü	rule, move		Y as in French *du*.
		m	me, am				Pronounce (ē) with the lips
b	bad, rob	n	no, in	v	very, save		rounded as for (ü).
ch	child, much	ng	long, bring	w	will, woman		
d	did, red			y	young, yet		à as in French *ami*.
		o	hot, rock	z	zero, breeze		Pronounce (ä) with the lips
e	let, best	ō	open, go	zh	measure, seizure		spread and held tense.
ē	equal, be	ô	order, all				
ėr	term, learn	oi	oil, voice	ə	represents:		œ as in French *peu*.
		ou	house, out		a in about		Pronounce (ā) with the lips
f	fat, if				e in taken		rounded as for (ō).
g	go, bag	p	paper, cup		i in pencil		
h	he, how	r	run, try		o in lemon		N as in French *bon*.
		s	say, yes		u in circus		The N is not pronounced,
i	it, pin	sh	she, rush				but shows that the vowel
ī	ice, five	t	tell, it				before it is nasal.
		th	thin, both				
		ŦH	then, smooth				H as in German *ach*.
							Pronounce (k) without
							closing the breath passage.

Grammatical
key

adj.	adjective	*prep.*	preposition
adv.	adverb	*pron.*	pronoun
conj.	conjunction	*v.*	verb
interj.	interjection	*v.i.*	intransitive verb
n.	noun	*v.t.*	transitive verb
sing.	singular	*pl.*	plural
pt.	past tense	*pp.*	past participle

a bash (ə bash′), *v.t.* embarrass and confuse; make uneasy and somewhat ashamed; disconcert. [< Old French *esbaïss-*, a form of *esbaïr* astonish] —**a bash′ment**, *n.*

a bate (ə bāt′), *v.*, **a bat ed, a bat ing.** —*v.t.* **1** lessen in force or intensity; reduce or decrease. **2** put an end to; stop. —*v.i.* become less in force or intensity; diminish.

ab hor (ab hôr′), *v.t.*, **-horred, -hor ring.** regard with horror or disgust; hate completely; detest; loathe.

ab ject (ab′jekt, ab jekt′), *adj.* **1** so low or degraded as to be hopeless; wretched; miserable. **2** deserving contempt; despicable. [< Latin *abjecturm* cast down < *ab-* down + *jacere* to throw]

ab jure (ab jur′), *v.t.*, **-jured, -jur ing.** **1** swear to give up; renounce. **2** retract formally or solemnly; repudiate. **3** refrain from; avoid. [< Latin *abjurare* < *ab-* away + *jurare* swear]

-able, *suffix forming adjectives from verbs and nouns.* **1** that can be ____ed: *Enjoyable = that can be enjoyed.* **2** giving ____; suitable for ____: *Comfortable = giving comfort.* **3** inclined to ____: *Peaceable = inclined to peace.* **4** deserving to be ____ed: *Lovable = deserving to be loved.* **5** liable to be ____: *Breakable = liable to be broken.* [< Old French < Latin *-abilem*]

a bode (ə bōd′), *n.* **1** place of residence; dwelling; house or home. —*v.* a pt. and a pp. of **abide.**

a bom i na ble (ə bom′ə nə bəl), *adj.* **1** arousing disgust and hatred; detestable; loathsome. **2** very unpleasant; disagreeable.

a bom i nate (ə bom′ə nāt), *v.t.*, **-nat ed, -nat ing.** **1** feel extreme disgust for; detest; loathe. **2** dislike. [< Latin *abominatum* deplored as an ill omen < *ab-* off + *ominari* prophesy < *omen* omen]

a bom i na tion (ə bom′ə nā′shən), *n.* **1** something that arouses strong disgust. **2** a feeling of disgust; loathing.

ab ste mi ous (ab stē′mē əs), *adj.* **1** sparing in eating, drinking, etc.; moderate; temperate. **2** very plain; restricted. [< Latin *abstemius*] —**ab ste′mi ous ly**, *adv.* —**ab ste′mi ous ness**, *n.*

ab sti nence (ab′stə nəns), *n.* **1** an abstaining; partly or entirely giving up certain pleasures, food, drink, etc. **2** Also, **total abstinence,** a refraining from drinking any alcoholic liquor.

ab struse (ab strüs′), *adj.* hard to understand; difficult; recondite. [< Latin *abstrusum* concealed < *abs-* away + *trudere* to thrust] —**ab struse′ly**, *adv.* —**abstruse′ness**, *n.*

a bys mal (ə biz′mal), *adj.* **1** too deep or great to be measured; bottomless: *abysmal ignorance.* **2** of the lowest depths of the ocean. **3** INFORMAL. extremely bad; of very low quality. —**a bys′mal ly**, *adv.*

a byss (ə bis′), *n.* **1** a bottomless or very great depth; chasm. **2** anything too deep or great to be measured; lowest depth. **3** the chaos before the Creation. [< Greek *abyssos* < *a-* without + *byssos* bottom]

ac com plice (ə kom′plis), *n.* person who knowingly aids another in committing a crime or other wrong act. [< earlier *a complice* a confederate < Middle French *complice* < Late Latin *complicem* < Latin *complicare* fold together]

ac crue (ə krü′), *v.i.*, **-crued, -cru ing.** **1** come as a natural product or result. **2** grow or arise as the product of money invested. [< Old French *acreüe* an increase < *acreistre* to increase < Latin *accrescere* < *ad-* to + *crescere* grow] —**ac crue′ment**, *n.*

ac qui si tion (ak′wə zish′ən), *n.* **1** act of acquiring. **2** something acquired or gained; addition to an existing group.

ac quit tance (ə kwit′ns), *n.* a written release from a debt or obligation.

ac ri mo ni ous (ak′rə mō′nē əs), *adj.* bitter and irritating in disposition or manner; caustic.

a cute (ə kyüt′), *adj.* **1** acting keenly on the senses; sharp; intense. **2** coming quickly to a crisis; brief and severe. **3** crucial; critical. **4** quick in perceiving and responding to impressions; keen. **5** quick in discernment; sharp-witted; clever. **6** high in pitch; shrill. **7** having or ending in a sharp point. **8** (of a vowel) having an acute accent over it. **9** having one or more acute angles. —*n.* an acute accent. [< Latin *acutum* sharpened < *acuere* sharpen] —**a cute′ly**, *adv.* —**a cute′ness**, *n.*

ad age (ad′ij), *n.* a well-known proverb.

ad a man tine (ad′ə man′tēn′, ad′ə man′tīn), *adj.* unyielding; firm; immovable.

a hat	i it	oi oil	ch child		a in about
ā age	ī ice	ou out	ng long		e in taken
ä far	o hot	u cup	sh she	ə =	i in pencil
e let	ō open	u̇ put	th thin		o in lemon
ē equal	ô order	ü rule	ŦH then		u in circus
ėr term			zh measure		< = derived from

ad dle (ad′l), *v.*, **-dled, -dling,** *adj.* —*v.t.*, *v.i.* **1** make or become muddled. **2** make or become rotten. —*adj.* **1** muddled; confused. **2** rotten. [Old English *adela* muck]

a droit (ə droit′), *adj.* **1** resourceful in reaching one's objective; ingenious; clever. **2** skillful in the use of the hands or body; dexterous. [< French < *à droit* rightly] —**a droit′ly**, *adv.* —**a droit′ness**, *n.*

af fec ta tion (af′ek tā′shən), *n.* **1** behavior that is not natural, but assumed to impress others; pretense. **2** mannerism, choice of language, etc., that indicates a tendency toward this.

af flic tion (ə flik′shən), *n.* **1** condition of continued pain or distress; misery. **2** cause of continued pain or distress; misfortune.

a gue (ā′gyü), *n.* **1** a malarial fever with chills and sweating that alternate at regular intervals. **2** any fit of shaking or shivering; chill.

a kim bo (ə kim′bō), *adj.* with the hands on the hips and the elbows bent outward. [Middle English *in kenebowe,* apparently, in keen bow, at a sharp angle]

al lay (ə lā′), *v.t.*, **-layed, -lay ing.** **1** put at rest; quiet. **2** relieve (pain, trouble, thirst, etc.); alleviate. [Old English *ālecgan* < *ā-away, off* + *lecgan* to lay]

al loy (*n.* al′oi, ə loi′; *v.* ə loi′), *n.* **1** metal made by melting and mixing two or more metals, or a metal and a nonmetal, to secure some desirable quality or qualities, as toughness, resistance to weak, etc. Brass is an alloy of copper and zinc. **2** an inferior metal mixed with a more valuable one. **3** any injurious addition; impurity. —*v.t.* **1** make into an alloy. **2** make less valuable by mixing with a cheaper metal. **3** make worse by mixing with something bad; debase.

al lude (ə lüd′), *v.i.*, **-lud ed, -lud ing.** refer indirectly *(to);* mention slightly in passing. [< Latin *alludere* < *ad-* + *ludere* to play]

al lure (ə lür′), *v.*, **-lured, -lur ing,** *n.* —*v.t.* tempt or attract very strongly; fascinate; charm. —*n.* great charm: fascination. [< Middle French *alurer* < *a-* to + *leurre* lure]

am big u ous (am big′yü əs), *adj.* **1** having or permitting more than one interpretation or explanation; equivocal. **2** of doubtful position or classification. **3** not clearly defined; doubtful; uncertain.

a me na ble (ə mē′nə bəl, ə men′ə bəl), *adj.* **1** open to influence, suggestion, advice, etc.; responsive; submissive. **2** accountable or answerable to some jurisdiction or authority. —**a me′na ble ness**, *n.* —**a me′na bly**, *adv.*

a miss (ə mis′), *adv.* **1** in a wrong way; wrongly. **2 take amiss,** be offended at (something not intended to offend). —*adj.* improper; wrong. [Middle English *a mis* by mistake]

am i ty (am′ə tē), *n.*, *pl.* **-ties.** peace and friendship, especially between nations; friendly relations; friendliness.

an ar chy (an′ər kē), *n.* **1** absence of a system of government and law. **2** disorder and confusion; lawlessness. **3** anarchism. [< Medieval Latin *anarchia* < Greek < *an-* without + *archos* ruler]

an i mos i ty (an′ə mos′ə tē), *n.*, *pl.* **-ties.** keen hostile feelings; active dislike or enmity; ill will.

an nals (an′lz), *n.pl.* **1** historical events; history. **2** a written account of events year by year. [< Latin *annales (libri)* annual (books) < *annus* year]

an ni hi late (ə nī′ə lāt), *v.t.*, **-lat ed, -lat ing.** destroy completely; wipe out of existence. —*v.i.* cease to be; vanish; disappear. [< Late Latin *annihilatum* brought to nothing < Latin *ad-* to + *nihil* nothing] —**an ni′hi la′tive**, *adj.* —**an ni′hi la′tor**, *n.*

an nul (ə nul′), *v.t.,* **-nulled, -nul ling.** **1** destroy the force of; make void; nullify. **2** do away with; cancel. **3** reduce to nothing; annihilate. [< Late Latin *annullare* < Latin *ad-* to + *nullus* none]

a noint (ə noint′), *v.t.* **1** apply an ointment, oil, or similar substance to; cover or smear with oil, etc. **2** consecrate by applying oil. **3** rub or smear with any other substance or liquid. **—a noint′er,** *n.* **—a noint′ment,** *n.*

a nom a ly (ə nom′ə lē), *n., pl.* **-lies.** **1** something anomalous. **2** deviation from the rule; irregularity.

a non (ə non′), *adv.* ARCHAIC. **1** in a little while; soon. **2** at another time; again. **3 ever and anon,** now and then. [Old English *on ān* into one]

an tiph o ny (an tif′ə nē), *n., pl.* **-nies** a responsive alternation between two groups, especially of singers.

a pace (ə pās′), *adv.* very soon; swiftly; quickly; fast.

ap os tol i cal (ap′ə stol′ə kəl), *adj.* **1** of or having to do with an apostle or apostles. **2** of the Apostles, their beliefs, teachings, time, or nature. Also, **apostolic.** [< Greek *apostolos* messenger < *apo-* + *stellein* send]

a poth e car y (ə poth′ə ker′ē), *n., pl.* **-car ies.** druggist; pharmacist. [< Late Latin *apothecarius* shopkeeper < Latin *apotheca* storehouse < Greek *apothēkē* < *apo-* + *tithenai* put]

ap pa ri tion (ap′ə rish′ən), *n.* **1** a supernatural sight or thing; ghost or phantom. **2** the appearance of something strange, remarkable, or unexpected.

ap pas sio na to (ä pä′sya nä′tō), *adj.* (in music) with passion or strong feeling. [< Italian]

ap pease (ə pēz′), *v.t.,* **-peased, -peas ing.** **1** put an end to by satisfying (an appetite or desire). **2** make calm or quiet; pacify.**3** give in to the demands of (especially those of a potential enemy). [< Old French *apaisier* < *a-* to + *pais* peace] **—appeas′er,** *n.* **—ap peas′ing ly,** *adv.*

ap pre hen si ble (ap′ri hen′sə bəl), *adj.* understandable. [< Latin *apprehendere* < *ad-* upon + *prehendere* seize]

ap pre hen sion (ap′ri hen′shən), *n.* **1** expectation of misfortune; dread of impending danger; fear. **2** arrest. **3** understanding.

ap pro ba tion (ap′rə bā′shən), *n.* favorable opinion; approval.

ap pur te nance (ə pėrt′n əns), *n.* addition to something more important; added thing; accessory.

ar bi trar y (är′bə trer′ē), *adj.* **1** based on one's own wishes, notions, or will; not going by rule or law. **2** fixed or determined by chance. **3** using or abusing unlimited power; tyrannical; despotic. **—ar′bi trar′i ly,** *adv.* **—ar′bi trar′i ness,** *n.*

ar chae ol o gy (är′kē ol′ə jē), *n.* the scientific study of the people, customs, and life of ancient times, antedating the keeping of historic records. Through excavation, identification, and study of the remains of ancient cities and of tools, pottery, monuments, or any other remains, archaeology is able to reconstruct a picture of life in the past. Also, **archeology.**

ar chi pel a go (är′kə pel′ə gō, är′chə pel′ə gō), *n., pl.* **-gos** or **-goes.** **1** group of many islands. **2** sea having many islands in it. [< Italian *arcipelago* < *arci-* chief + *pelago* sea]

ar dent (ärd′nt), *adj.* **1** glowing with passion; passionate; impassioned. **2** very enthusiastic; eager. **3** burning; fiery; hot. **4** glowing. **—ar′dent ly,** *adv.* [< Latin *ardentem* burning]

ar du ous (är′jü əs), *adj.* **1** hard to do; requiring much effort; difficult. **2** using up much energy; strenuous. [< Latin *arduus* steep] **—ar′du ous ly,** *adv.* **—ar′du ous ness,** *n.*

ar gu ment (är′gyə mənt), *n.* **1** discussion by persons who disagree. See synonym study below. **2** a giving reasons for or against something. **3** reason or reasons offered for or against something. **4** summary or synopsis of what is in a book, poem, etc. **5** ARCHAIC. plot.

ar raign (ə rān′), *v.t.* **1** bring before a court of law to answer an indictment. **2** call to account; find fault with; accuse. [< Anglo-French *arainer* < Old French *a-* to + *raisnier* speak]

ar rant (ar′ənt), *adj.* thoroughgoing; downright.

ar ras (ar′əs), *n.* curtain, screen, or hangings of tapestry.

ar ray (ə rā′), *n.* **1** proper order; regular arrangement; formation. **2** display of persons or things; imposing group. **3** clothes, especially for some special or festive occasion; dress; attire. **—v.t.** **1** put in order for some purpose; marshal. **2** dress in fine clothes; adorn.

ar rears (ə rirz′), *n.pl.* **1** money due but not paid; unpaid debts. **2** unfinished work; things not done on time. **3 in arrears,** behind in payments, work, etc. [< Old French *arere* < Popular Latin *ad retro* to the rear]

ar ti fice (är′tə fis), *n.* **1** a clever device or trick. **2** trickery; craft. **3** skill or ingenuity. [< Latin *artificium* < *artem* art + *facere* make]

as cend ent (ə sen′dənt), *adj.* **1** moving upward; rising. **2** superior; paramount; controlling. **—n.** position of power; controlling influence. Also, **ascendant.**

a sep tic (ə sep′tik, ā sep′tik), *adj.* free from the living germs causing infection. **—a sep′ti cal ly,** *adv.*

as per i ty (ə sper′ə tē), *n., pl.* **-ties.** harshness or sharpness of temper, especially as shown in tone or manner.

as per sion (ə spėr′zhən), *n.* a damaging or false statement; slander.

as sail (ə sāl′), *v.t.* **1** attack repeatedly with violent blows. **2** attack with hostile words, arguments, or abuse. **3** (of a feeling) come over (a person) strongly; beset; trouble. **—as sail′a ble,** *adj.* [< Old French *asalir* < Latin *ad-* at + *salire* to leap]

as say (ə sā′; *also especially for n.* as′ā), *v.t.* **1** examine by testing or trial; test. **2** ARCHAIC. attempt. **—n.** **1** examination; test. **2** ARCHAIC. attempt; trial.

as sent (ə sent′), *v.i.* express agreement; agree; consent. **—n.** acceptance of a proposal, statement, etc.; agreement. [< Latin *assentire* < *ad-* along with + *sentire* feel, think]

as sig na tion (as′ig nā′shən), *n.* **1** a secret meeting of lovers. **2** the appointment of a time and place for such a meeting. **3** an allotting; apportionment.

as sim i late (ə sim′ə lāt), *v.,* **-lat ed, -lat ing. —v.t.** **1** take in and make part of oneself; absorb; digest. **2** cause to be like the people of a nation in customs, viewpoint, character, etc. **3** make (a speech sound, usually a consonant) more like the sound which follows or precedes. **—v.i.** **1** become absorbed; be digested. **2** become like the people of a nation in customs, viewpoint, character, etc. **3** become like. [< Latin *assimilatum* made similar < *ad-* to + *similis* like] **—as sim′i la′tor,** *n.*

as size (ə sīz′), *n.* **1** session of a court of law. **2 assizes,** *pl.* the periodic sessions of a court of law held in each county of England. [< Old French *assise,* ultimately < Latin *assidere.* sit by]

as suage (ə swāj′), *v.t.,* **-suaged, -suag ing.** **1** make (angry or excited feelings, etc.) less intense; calm or soothe. **2** make (physical or mental pain) easier or milder; relieve or lessen. **3** satisfy or appease (appetites or desires).

a sun der (ə sun′dər), *adv.* in pieces; into separate parts. **—adj.** apart or separate from each other.

-ate[1], *suffix forming adjectives, verbs, and nouns.* **1** of or having to do with ____: *Collegiate = having to do with college.* **2** having or containing ____: *Compassionate = having compassion.* **3** having the form of ____; like ____: *Stellate = having the form of a star.* **4** become ____: *Maturate = become mature.* **5** cause to be ____: *Alienate = cause to be alien.* **6** produce ____: *Ulcerate = produce ulcers.* **7** supply or treat with ____: *Aerate = treat with air.* **8** combine with ____: *Oxygenate = combine with oxygen.* [< Latin *-atus, -atum,* past participle endings]

-ate[2], *suffix forming nouns.* office, rule, or condition of ____: *Caliphate = rule of a caliph.* [< Latin *atus*]

-ate[3], *suffix forming nouns.* salt or ester of ____ic acid: *Sulfate = salt or ester of sulfuric acid.* [special use of *-ate*[1]]

a tro cious (ə trō′shəs), *adj.* **1** monstrously wicked or cruel; very savage or brutal; heinous. **2** INFORMAL. shockingly bad or unpleasant; abominable. **—a tro′cious ly,** *adv.* **—a tro′cious ness,** *n.* [< Latin *atrocitatem* < *atrox* fierce]

aught (ôt), *pron.* ARCHAIC. anything. Also, **ought.**

aug ment (ôg ment′), *v.t., v.i.* make or become greater in size, number, amount, or degree; increase or enlarge.

au gur (ô′gər), *n.* **1** priest in ancient Rome who made predictions and gave advice from signs and omens. **2** soothsayer; fortune-teller. **—v.t.** **1** guess from signs or omens; predict; foretell. **2** be a sign or promise of. —*v.i.* **1 augur ill,** be a bad sign. **2 augur well,** be a good sign. [< Latin]

au gur y (ô′gyər ē), *n., pl.* **-gur ies. 1** prediction; sign; omen. **2** art or practice of foretelling events by interpreting such signs and omens as the flight of birds, thunder and lightning, etc.

au gust (ô gust′), *adj.* inspiring reverence and admiration; majestic; venerable. [< Latin *augustus* < *augere* to increase] —**au gust′ly,** *adv.* —**au gust′ness,** *n.*

aus pi cious (ô spish′əs), *adj.* **1** with signs of success; favorable. **2** prosperous; fortunate. —**aus pi′cious ly,** *adv.*

av ar ice (av′ər is), *n.* too great a desire for money or property; greed for wealth.

av a ri cious (av′ə rish′əs), *adj.* greatly desiring money or property; greedy for wealth. —**av′a ri′cious ly,** *adv.* —**av′a ri′cious ness,** *n.*

a vaunt (ə vônt′, ə vänt′), *interj.* ARCHAIC. begone! get out! go away!

a ver (ə vėr′), *v.t.,* **a verred, a ver ring.** state positively to be true; assert; affirm. [< Old French *averer,* ultimately < Latin *ad-* + *verus* true]

a vi ar y (ā′vē er′ē), *n., pl.* **-ar ies.** house, enclosure, or large cage in which many birds, especially wild birds, are kept; birdhouse. [< Latin *aviarium* < *avis* bird]

a vouch (ə vouch′), *v.t.* **1** declare positively to be true; affirm. **2** vouch for; guarantee. **3** acknowledge; avow. [< Old French *avochier* < *a-* to + *vochier* to call] —**a vouch′ment,** *n.*

awl (ôl), *n.* a sharp-pointed tool used for making small holes in leather or wood. [Old English *æl*]

az ure (azh′ər), *n.* the clear blue color of the unclouded sky; sky blue. —*adj.* sky-blue. [< Old French *l′azur* the azure < Arabic *lāzuward* < Persian *lajward* lapis lazuli]

badge (baj) *v.t.,* **-badged, badging.** mark or distinguish with a badge.

bail iff (bā′lif), *n.* **1** (in England) an overseer or steward of an estate. The bailiff collects rents, directs the work of employees, etc., for the owner. **2** the chief magistrate in certain towns in England.

bait (bāt), *n.* anything, especially food, used to attract fish or other animals so that they may be caught. —*v.t.* **1** put bait on (a hook) or in (a trap). **2** tempt; attract. **3** attack; torment. **4** torment or worry by unkind or annoying remarks. [< Scandinavian (Old Icelandic) *beita* cause to bite]

bal dric (bôl′drik), *n.* belt, usually of leather and richly ornamented, hung from one shoulder to the opposite side of the body to support the wearer's sword, bugle, etc. Also, **baldrick.**

bale (bāl), *n.* ARCHAIC. **1** evil; harm. **2** sorrow; pain. [Old English *bealu*]

bale ful (bāl′fəl), *adj.* **1** full of hurtful or deadly influence; destructive. **2** full of misfortune; disastrous. —**bale′ful ly,** *adv.* —**bale′ful ness,** *n.*

balm (bäm), *n.* **1** a fragrant, oily, sticky substance obtained from certain kinds of trees, used to heal or to relieve pain; balsam. **2** a healing or soothing influence. **3** a fragrant ointment or oil used in anointing. **4** sweet odor; fragrance.

balm y[1] (bä′mē, bäl′mē), *adj.,* **balm i er, balm i est. 1** mild, gentle, and soothing. **2** fragrant. [< *balm*] —**balm′i ly,** *adv.* —**balm′i ness,** *n.*

balm y[2] (bä′mē, bäl′mē), *adj.,* **balm i er, balm i est.** BRITISH SLANG. silly; crazy. [variant of *barmy*]

ban dy (ban′dē), *v.,* **-died, -dy ing,** *adj.* —*v.t.* **1** hit or throw back and forth; toss about. **2** give and take; exchange. **3** pass from one to another in a circle or group. —*adj.* having a bend or curve outward.

bane (bān), *n.* **1** cause of death, ruin, or harm. **2** destruction of any kind; ruin; harm. [Old English *bana* murderer]

bar bar ous (bär′bər əs), *adj.* **1** not civilized; savage. **2** savagely cruel; brutal. **3** rough and rude; coarse; unrefined. **4** (of a word or expression) not in accepted use.

bard (bärd), *n.* **1** a Celtic minstrel and poet who from earliest times to the Middle Ages sang his own poems, usually to harp accompaniment, celebrating marital exploits, etc. **2** any poet. [< Irish and Scottish Gaelic]

a hat	i it	oi oil	ch child		a in about
ā age	ī ice	ou out	ng long		e in taken
ä far	o hot	u cup	sh she	ə =	i in pencil
e let	ō open	u̇ put	th thin		o in lemon
ē equal	ô order	ü rule	ŦH then		u in circus
ėr term			zh measure	**<** = derived from

bark (bärk), *n.* **1** a three-masted ship, square-rigged on the first two masts and fore-and-aft-rigged on the other. **2** ARCHAIC. boat; ship. Also, **barque.**

bar on et (bar′ə nit), *n.* man in Great Britain ranking next below a baron and next above a knight. He has "Sir" before his name and "Bart." after it. EXAMPLE: Sir John Brown, Bart.

bar row (bar′ō), *n.* mount of earth or stones over an ancient grave. [Old English *beorg*]

base (bās), *adj.,* **bas er, bas est. 1** morally low or mean; selfish and cowardly. **2** fit for an inferior person or thing; menial; unworthy. **3** ARCHAIC. of humble birth or origin. [< Old French *bas* < Medieval Latin *bassus* low.]

bea dle (bē′dl), *n.* a minor parish officer in the Church of England whose duties include keeping order and waiting on the clergy. [< Old French *bedel*]

beak er (bē′kər), *n.* **1** a large cup or drinking glass with a wide mouth. **2** contents of a beaker.

be guile (bi gīl′), *v.t.,* **-guiled, -guil ing. 1** trick or mislead (a person); deceive; delude. **2** take away from deceitfully or cunningly. **3** win the attention of; entertain. **4** while away (time) pleasantly.

be hest (bi hest′), *n.* command; order.

bel dam (bel′dəm), *n.* **1** an old woman. **2** an ugly old woman; hag; witch.

be lie (bi lī′), *v.t.,* **-lied, -ly ing. 1** give a false idea of; misrepresent. **2** show to be false; prove to be mistaken. **3** fail to come up to; disappoint.

ben e dic tion (ben′ə dik′shən), *n.* **1** the asking of God's blessing, as at the end of a church service or a marriage ceremony. **2** the form or ritual of this invocation. **3** blessing. [< Latin *benedictionem* < *benedicere* bless < *bene* well + *dicere* say.]

ben e fice (ben′ə fis), *n.* a permanent office or position in the church created by proper ecclesiastical authority and consisting of a sacred duty and the income that goes with it.

be nev o lence (bə nev′ə ləns), *n.* **1** desire to promote the happiness of others; goodwill; kindly feeling. **2** act of kindness; something good that is done; generous gift. **3** (formerly) a forced loan to an English king, now illegal. [< Latin *benevolentia* < *bene* well + *velle* to wish]

be queath (bi kwēŦH′, bi kwēth′), *v.t.* **1** give or leave (especially money or other personal property) by a will. **2** hand down or leave to posterity; pass along. [Old English *becwethan* < *be-* to, for + *cwethan* say] —**be queath′er.** *n.*

be reave (bi rēv′), *v.t.,* **-reaved** or **-reft, -reav ing. 1** leave desolate and alone. **2** deprive ruthlessly; rob. [Old English *berēafian* < *be-* away + *rēafian* rob]

be reft (bi reft′), *adj.* bereaved. —*v.* a pt. and a pp. of **bereave.**

be smirch (bi smėrch′), *v.t.* **1** make dirty. **2** sully. [*be-* thoroughly + *smirch* discolor, Middle English *smorchen*]

be times (bi tīmz′), *adv.* ARCHAIC. **1** early. **2** before it is too late. **3** in a short time; soon.

be trothed (bi trōŦHd′, bi trôtht′), *n.* person engaged to be married. —*adj.* engaged to be married.

bide (bīd), *v.,* **bid ed** or **bode, bid ed, bid ing.** —*v.i.* **1** remain or continue in some state or action; wait. **2** ARCHAIC. dwell; reside. —*v.t.* ARCHAIC. put up with; endure; suffer. [Old English *bīdan*]

bier (bir), *n.* **1** a moveable stand or framework on which a coffin or dead body is placed before burial. **2** such a stand together with the coffin. [Old English *bēr.* Related to *beran* BEAR.]

bil ious (bil′yəs), *adj.* **1** suffering from or caused by some trouble with bile or the liver. **2** having to do with bile. **3** peevish; bad-tempered. **—bil′ious ly,** *adv.* **bil′ious ness,** *n.*

bin na cle (bin′ə kəl), *n.* box or stand that contains a ship's compass, placed hear the helm. [alteration of *bittacle,* ultimately < Latin *habitaculum* dwelling place < *habitare* dwell]

bit tern (bit′ərn), *n.* any of several small herons found chiefly in marshes, characterized by a peculiar booming cry.

black guard (blag′ärd, blag′ərd), *n.* a low, contemptible person; scoundrel. **—v.t.** abuse with vile language; revile. **—v.i.** behave like a blackguard.

blanc mange (blə mänzh′), *n.* a sweet dessert made of milk boiled and thickened with gelatin, cornstarch, etc., flavored and cooled in a mold. [< Old French *blanc-manger* white food]

blas phe my (blas′fə mē), *n., pl.* **-mies.** abuse or contempt for God or sacred things; profanity.

bla zon (blā′zn), *v.t.* **1** make known; proclaim. **2** decorate; adorn. **3** describe or paint (a coat of arms). **4** display; show. **—n. 1** coat of arms, or a shield with a coat of arms on it. **2** description or painting of a coat of arms. **3** display; show. [< Old French *blason* shield] **—bla′zon er,** *n.*

blear (blir), *adj.* **1** (of the eyes) dim from water, tears, etc. **2** indistinct; dim. **—v.t. 1** dim (the eyes) with tears, etc. **2** blur.

blench (blench), *v.i., v.t.* turn white or pale; blanch

blight (blīt), *n.* **1** disease of plants that causes leaves, stems, fruits, and tissues to wither and die. **2** bacterium, fungus, or virus that causes such a disease. **3** anything that withers hope or causes destruction or ruin. **4** decay; deterioration. **—v.t. 1** cause to wither and die. **2** destroy; ruin. **—v.i.** be blighted; suffer from blight [origin uncertain]

blithe (blīтн, blīth), *adj.* **1** happy and cheerful; gay; joyous. **2** heedless. [Old English *blīthe*] **—blithe′ly,** *adv.* **—blithe′- ness,** *n.*

blithe some (blīтн′səm, blīth′səm), *adj.* blithe. **—blithe′- some ly,** *adv.* **blithe′some ness,** *n.*

blow (blō), *n., v.,* **blew, blown, blow ing. —n. 1** a state of blossoming; bloom. **2** display of blossoms. **—v.i.** blossom. [Old English *blōwan*]

bode (bōd), *v.t.,* **bod ed, bod ing. 1** be a sign of; indicate beforehand; portend; foreshadow. **2 bode ill,** be a bad sign. **3 bode well,** be a good sign.

bod kin (bod′kən), *n.* **1** a large, blunt needle with an eye, used for drawing tape or cord through a hem, loops, etc. **2** a small dagger; stiletto. [Middle English *boydekyn* dagger]

bol ster (bōl′stər), *n.* **1** a long, firmly stuffed pillow, placed under the softer pillows on a bed or used as a back on a couch. **2** cushion or pad, often ornamental. **—v.t. 1** support with a bolster. **2** keep from falling; support; prop. [Old English]

boon (bün), *n.* **1** great benefit; blessing. **2** ARCHAIC. something asked for or granted as a favor. [< Scandinavian (Old Icelandic) *bón* petition]

boor ish (bur′ish), *adj.* like a boor; rude or rustic. [< Low German *bur* or Dutch *boer* farmer] **—boor′ish ly,** *adv.* **—boor′- ish ness,** *n.*

boss (bôs, bos), *n.* a raised ornament of silver, ivory, or other material on a flat surface. [< Old French *boce* swelling, hump.]

bot a ny (bot′n ē), *n.* **1** branch of biology that deals with plants and plant life; study of the structure, growth, classification, diseases, etc., of plants. **2** the plant life of a particular area. **3** botanical facts or characteristics concerning a particular plant or group of plants. [< Greek *botanē* plant]

bourn[1] or **bourne**[1] (bôrn, bōrn), *n.* a small stream; brook.

bourn[2] or **bourne**[2] (bôrn, bōrn, burn), *n.* ARCHAIC. **1** boundary; limit. **2** goal; aim. [< Middle French *bourne*]

bow er (bou′ər), *n.* **1** shelter of leafy branches. **2** summerhouse or arbor. [Old English *būr* dwelling]

brace[1] (brās), **braced, brac ing.** *v.t.* **1** give strength of firmness to; support. **2** prepare (oneself). **3** give strength and energy to; refresh.

brace[2] (brās), *n.* OBSOLETE. armor for the arm.

brand (brand), *n.* ARCHAIC. sword.

bran dish (bran′dish), *v.t.* wave or shake threateningly; flourish. **—n.** a threatening shake; flourish. [< Old French *brandiss-,* a form of *brandir* to brand < *brand* sword]

bream (brēm, brim), *n., pl.* **breams** or **bream.** a yellowish freshwater fish related to the carp, common in Europe.

breed (brēd), *v.,* **bred, breed ing,** *n.* **—v.t. 1** produce (young). **2** raise or grow, especially under controlled conditions so as to get new or improved kinds. **3** be the cause of; produce. **4** bring up; train. **5** convert (nonfissionable material) into fissionable material. **—v.i. 1** produce young. **2** be produced or caused. **—n. 1** group within a species, developed by artificial selection and maintained by controlled propagation, having certain distinguishable characteristics, as of color, size, shape, etc. **2** a line of descendants from a particular parentage. **3** kind; sort; type. [Old English *brēdan*] **—breed′a ble,** *adj.*

brin ded (brin′did), *adj.* ARCHAIC. brindled; gray, tan, or tawny with darker streaks and spots.

broad (brôd), *adv.* outspokenly.

brogue (brōg), *n.* **1** an Irish accent or pronunciation of English. **2** a strongly marked accent or pronunciation peculiar to any dialect.

bruit (brüt), *v.t.* spread a report or rumor of; announce; report. **—n.** ARCHAIC. report; rumor.

brusque (brusk), *adj.* abrupt in manner or speech; blunt. [< French < Italian *brusco* coarse] **—brusque′ly,** *adv.*

buck ler (buk′lər), *n.* **1** a small, round shield used to parry blows or thrusts. **2** means of protection; defense.

bull (bùl), *n.* a formal announcement or official decree from the pope. [< Medieval Latin *bulla* < Latin, amulet, bubble]

bul wark (bùl′wərk), *n.* **1** person, thing, or idea that is a defense or protection. **2** wall of earth or other material for defense against an enemy; rampart. **3** breakwater. **4** Usually, **bulwarks,** *pl.* side of a ship extending like a fence above the deck.

bur geon (bėr′jən), *v.i.* **1** grow or shoot forth; bud; sprout. **2** grow or develop rapidly; flourish. **—n.** a bud; sprout. [< Old French *burjon* a bud]

bur gess (bėr′jis), *n.* citizen of an English borough.

burgh er (bėr′gər), *n.* citizen of a burgh or town; citizen.

byr ny (bėr′nē), *n.* a shirt of armor.

ca dav er ous (kə dav′ər əs), *adj.* **1** pale and ghastly. **2** thin and worn. **3** of or like a cadaver. **—ca dav′er ous ly,** *adv.*

ca dence (kād′ns), *n.* **1** the measure or beat of music, dancing, marching, or any movement regularly repeating itself; rhythm: *the cadence of a drum.* **2** fall of the voice. **3** a rising and falling sound; modulation. [< French < Italian *cadenza* < Latin *cadere* to fall.]

ca jole (kə jōl′), *v.t.,* **-joled, -jol ing.** persuade by pleasant words, flattery, or false promises; coax.

ca lum ni ous (kə lum′nē əs), *adj.* slanderous. **—ca lum′ni- ous ly,** *adv.*

cal um ny (kal′əm nē), *n., pl.* **-nies.** a false statement made to injure someone's reputation; slander. [< Latin *calumnia*]

can dor (kan′dər), *n.* **1** a saying openly what one really thinks; honesty in giving one's view or opinion, frankness and sincerity. **2** fairness; impartiality. [< Latin, whiteness < *candere* to shine]

cant (kant), *n.* **1** insincere talk; moral or religious statements that many people make, but few really believe or follow out. **2** the peculiar language of a special group, using many strange words; jargon; argot.

ca price (kə prēs′), *n.* **1** a sudden change of mind without reason; unreasonable notion or desire; whim. **2** tendency to change suddenly and without reason. **3** capriccio. [< French < Italian *capriccio,* literally, a shiver]

ca pri cious (kə prish′əs, kə prē′shəs), *adj.* likely to change suddenly without reason; changeable; fickle; *capricious weather.* **—ca pri′cious ly,** *adv.* **—ca pri′cious ness,** *n.*

car bun cle (kär′bung kəl), *n.* a very painful, inflamed swelling under the skin caused by infection.

car di nal (kärd′n əl), *adj.* **1** of first importance; chief; principal. **2** bright, rich red.

ca reer (kə rir′), *n.* **1** a general course of action or progress through life. **2** way of living; occupation; profession. **3 in full career,** at full speed; going with force.

car nal (kär′nl), *adj.* **1** of or connected with the appetites and passions of the body; sensual. **2** sexual. **3** worldly; not spiritual. **—car′nal ly,** *adv.*

car niv or ous (kär niv′ər əs), *adj.* **1** of or having to do with an order of mammals that feed chiefly on flesh. **2** using other animals as food; flesh-eating. **—car niv′or ous ly,** *adv.* **—car niv′or ous ness,** *n.*

ca rouse (kə rouz′), *v.,* **roused, -rous ing.** *n.* *—v.i.* drink heavily; take part in noisy revels. *—n.* a noisy revel or drinking party. **—ca rous′er,** *n.* **—ca rous′ing ly,** *adv.*

car ri on (kar′ē ən), *n.* **1** dead and decaying flesh. **2** rottenness; filth. *—adj.* **1** dead and decaying. **2** feeding on dead and decaying flesh. **3** rotten; filthy.

case ment (kās′mənt), *n.* **1** window or part of a window which opens on hinges like a door. **2** any window. **3** a casing; covering; frame.

casque (kask), *n.* a piece of armor to cover the head; helmet.

cas ti gate (kas′tə gāt), *v.t.,* **-gat ed, -gat ing. 1** censure, chasten, or punish in order to correct. **2** criticize severely. [< Latin *castigatum* chastened < *castus* pure]

cat a ract (kat′ə rakt′), *n.* **1** a large, steep waterfall. **2** a violent rush or downpour of water; flood.

cat call (kat′kôl′), *n.* a shrill cry or whistle to express disapproval. Actors who perform poorly are sometimes greeted by catcalls from the audience. *—v.i.* make catcalls. *—v.t.* attack with catcalls.

cat er waul (kat′ər wôl), *v.i.* howl like a cat; screech. *—n.* such a howl or screech. [Middle English *caterwrawe* < *cater* cat + *wrawe* wait, howl]

caul (kôl), *n.* ARCHAIC. a close-fitting cap of net, worn by women. [Old English *cawl* basket, net]

cav a lier (kav′ə lir′), *n.* **1** horseman, mounted soldier, or knight. **2** a courteous gentleman. **3** a courteous escort for a lady.

cel e brate (sel′ə brāt), *v.,* **-brat ed, -brat ing.** *—v.t.* **1** observe (a special time or day) with the proper ceremonies or festivities. **2** perform publicly with the proper ceremonies and rites. **3** praise; honor; laud. *—v.i.* observe a festival or event with ceremonies or festivities.

ce les tial (sə les′chəl), *adj.* **1** of the sky; having to do with the heavens. **2** of or belonging to heaven as the place of God and the angels; heavenly; divine. [< Latin *caelestis* < *caelum* heaven] **—ce les′tial ly,** *adv.*

cen so ri ous (sen sôr′ē əs, sen sōr′ē əs), *adj.* too ready to find fault; severely critical.

cen sure (sen′shər), *n., v.,* **-sured, -sur ing.** *—n.* **1** expression of disapproval; unfavorable opinion; criticism. **2** penalty, as a public rebuke or suspension from office. **3** ARCHAIC. opinion. *—v.t.* express disapproval of; find fault with; criticize. See **blame** for synonym study. [< Latin *censura* < *censere* appraise] **—cen′sur er,** *n.*

cere ment (sir′mənt), *n.* Often, **cerements,** *pl.* cloth or garment in which a dead person is wrapped for burial.

cer e mo ni ous (ser′ə mō′nē əs), *adj.* **1** full of ceremony. **2** very formal; extremely polite. **—cer′e mo′ni ous ly,** *adv.*

chal ice (chal′is), *n.* **1** cup or goblet. **2** cup that holds the wine used in the Communion service.

cham ber lain (chām′bər lən), *n.* **1** person who manages the household of a sovereign or great noble. **2** a high official of a royal court. **3** treasurer. [< Old French *chamberlenc*]

cha os (kā′os), *n.* **1** very great confusion; complete disorder. **2** Also, **Chaos.** the infinite space in which formless matter was thought to have existed before the ordered universe came into being. [< Latin < Greek]

charnel house, place where dead bodies or bones are laid.

char y (cher′ē, char′ē), *adj.,* **char i er, char i est. 1** showing caution; careful; wary. **2** shy. **3** sparing; stingy.

chasm (kaz′əm), *n.* **1** a deep opening or crack in the earth; gap. **2** a wide difference of feelings or interests between people or groups. [< Latin *chasma* < Greek]

chaste (chāst), *adj.* **1** pure; virtuous. **2** decent; modest. **3** simple in taste or style; not excessively ornamented. [< Old French < Latin *castus* pure] **—chaste′ly,** *adv.* **—chaste′ness,** *n.*

chas ten (chā′sn), *v.t.* **1** punish to improve; discipline. **2** restrain from excess or crudeness; moderate. **3** make chaste in character or style; purify; refine. **—chas′ten er,** *n.* **—chas′ten-**

ing ly, *adv.* **—chas′ten ment,** *n.*

chas tise (cha stīz′), *v.t.,* **-tised, -tis ing. 1** inflict punishment or suffering on to improve; punish. **2** criticize severely; rebuke. [variant of *chasten*] **—chas tis′a ble,** *adj.* **—chas tis′er,** *n.*

cher ub (cher′əb), *n., pl.* **cher u bim** for 1 and 2, **cher ubs** for 3 and 4. **1** one of the second highest order of angels. **2** picture or statue of a child with wings, or of a child's head with wings but not body. **3** a beautiful innocent, or good child. **4** person with a chubby, innocent face. **—cher′ub like′,** *adj.*

cher u bim (cher′ə bim, cher′yə bim), *n.* **1** a pl. of **cherub** (defs. 1 and 2). **2** (formerly) cherub.

cher u bin (cher′ə bin, cher′yə bin), *n.* cherub.

chid (chid), *v.* pp. of **chide.**

chide (chīd), *v.,* **chid ed, chid, chid ing.** *—v.t.* find fault with; reproach or blame; scold. *—v.i.* find fault; speak in rebuke.

chi mer i cal (kə mer′ə kəl, kī mer′ə kəl), *adj.* **1** being or having to do with a chimera. **2** unreal; imaginary. **3** wildly fanciful; absurd; impossible.

chol er (kol′ər), *n.* an irritable disposition; anger.

chol er ic (kol′ər ik), *adj.* **1** having an irritable disposition; easily made angry. **2** enraged; angry; wrathful.

churl (chérl), *n.* **1** a rude, surly person; boor. **2** person of low birth; peasant. **3** person stingy in money matters; miser. **4** (in Anglo-Saxon and medieval England) a freeman of the lowest rank; ceorl. [Old English *ceorl*]

cic a trice (sik′ə tris), *n.* cicatrix; a scar left by a healed wound.

cir cum scribe (sér′kəm skrīb′, sér′kəm skrīb), *v.t.,* **-scribed, -scrib ing. 1** draw a line around; mark the boundaries of; bound. **2** limit; restrict.

cir cum spect (sér′kəm spekt), *adj.* watchful on all sides; cautious or prudent; careful. [< Latin *circumspectum* < *circum* around + *specere* look] **—cir′cum spect′ly,** *adv.* **—cir′cum spect′ness,** *n.*

cir cum vent (sér′kəm vent′), *v.t.* **1** get the better of or defeat by trickery; outwit. **2** go around. **3** catch in a trap. [< Latin *circumventum* circumvented < *circum* around + *venire* come] **—cir′cum ven′tion,** *n.*

cis tern (sis′tərn), *n.* an artificial reservoir for storing water, especially a tank below ground. [< Latin *cisterna* < *cista* box]

ci vil i ty (sə vil′ə tē), *n., pl.* **-ties. 1** polite behavior; courtesy. **2** act or expression of politeness or courtesy.

clam or ous (klam′ər əs), *adj.* **1** loud and noisy; shouting. **2** making noisy demands or complaints. **—clam′or ous ly,** *adv.*

clan gor ous (klang′ər əs, klang′gər əs), *adj.* clanging.

clar i on (klar′ē ən), *adj.* clear and shrill. *—n.* **1** a trumpet with clear, shrill tones. **2** sound of or like this trumpet. [< Medieval Latin *clarionem* < Latin *clarus* clear]

cleave¹ (klēv), *v.,* **cleft** or **cleaved** or **clove, cleft** or **cleaved** or **clo ven, cleav ing.** *—v.t.* **1** cut, divide, or split open. **2** pass through; pierce; penetrate. **3** make by cutting. *—v.i.* **1** split, especially into layers. **2** pass; penetrate.

cleave² (klēv), *v.i.,* **cleaved** or (ARCHAIC) **clave, cleav ing.** hold fast; cling; adhere. [Old English *cleofian*]

cleft (kleft), *v.* a pt. and a pp. of **cleave¹.** *—adj.* split; divided. *—n.* space or opening made by splitting; crack; fissure. [Old English *(ge) clyft*]

clem en cy (klem′ən sē), *n., pl.* **-cies. 1** gentleness in the use of power or authority; mercy or leniency. **2** mildness.

clepe (klēp), *v.t.,* **cleped** or **clept, clep ing.** ARCHAIC. call, name.

a	hat	i	it	oi	oil	ch	child		a in about
ā	age	ī	ice	ou	out	ng	long		e in taken
ä	far	o	hot	u	cup	sh	she	ə =	i in pencil
e	let	ō	open	ù	put	th	thin		o in lemon
ē	equal	ô	order	ü	rule	ŦH	then		u in circus
ėr	term					zh	measure	<	= derived from

GLOSSARY

clois ter (kloi′stər), *n.* **1** a covered walk, often along the wall of a building, with a row of pillars on the open side or sides. A cloister is sometimes built around the courtyard of a monastery, church, or college building. **2** place of religious retirement; convent or monastery. **3** a quiet place shut away from the world. —*v.t.* shut away in a quiet place. [< Old French *cloistre* < Latin *claustrum* closed place, lock < *claudere* to close]

cloister (def. 1)

clout (klout), *n.* ARCHAIC. **1** cloth or rag. **2** garment. [Old English *clūt* small piece of cloth or metal]

cloy (kloi), *v.t., v.i.* **1** make or become weary by too much, too sweet, or too rich food. **2** make or become weary by too much of anything pleasant. —**cloy′ing ly,** *adv.* —**cloy′ing ness,** *n.*

coign (koin), *n.* a projecting corner. [variant of *coin*]

coign of vantage, a good location for watching or doing something.

coil (koil), *n.* ARCHAIC. trouble; turmoil. [origin uncertain]

coin age (koi′nij), *n.* **1** the making of coins. **2** act or process of making up; inventing. **3** word, phrase, etc., invented.

col lab o ra tion (kə lab′ə rā′shən), *n.* **1** act of working together. **2** an aiding or cooperating traitorously.

col lat er al (kə lat′ər əl), *adj.* **1** related but less important; secondary; indirect. **2** side by side; parallel. **3** additional **4** secured by stocks, bonds, etc. —*n.* stocks, bonds. etc., pledged as security for a loan. —**col lat′er al ly,** *adv.*

col lier y (kol′yər ē), *n., pl.* **-lier ies.** a coal mine and its buildings and equipment.

col lo qui al (kə lō′kwē əl), *adj.* used in everyday, informal talk, but not in formal speech or writing; conversational. —**col lo′qui al ly,** *adv.*

comb er (kō′mər), *n.* **1** breaker. **2** person or thing that combs.

com bus ti ble (kəm bus′tə bəl), *adj.* capable of taking fire and burning; easily burned. —*n.* a combustible substance. —**com bus′ti bly,** *adv.*

come ly (kum′lē), *adj.,* **-li er, -li est. 1** pleasant to look at: attractive. **2** fitting; suitable; proper. [Old English *cȳmlic*]

com men da tion (kom′ən dā′shən), *n.* **1** praise; approval. **2** recommendation. **3** a handing over to another for safekeeping; entrusting.

com mis e rate (kə miz′ə rāt′), *v.t., v.i.,* **-rat ed, -rat ing.** feel or express sorrow for another's suffering or trouble; sympathize with; pity. —**com mis′e ra′tion,** *n.*

com mo tion (kə mō′shən), *n.* **1** violent movement; agitation; turbulence. **2** bustle or stir; confusion.

com pass (kum′pəs), *v.t.* accomplish; obtain.

com pi la tion (kom′pə lā′shən), *n.* **1** act of compiling; collecting and bringing together in one list or account. **2** book, list, etc., that has been compiled.

com plai sant (kəm plā′snt, kəm plā′znt), *adj.* **1** obliging; gracious; courteous. **2** compliant. —**com plai′sant ly,** *adv.*

com pound (*adj.* kom′pound, kom pound′; *n.* kom′pound; *v.* kom pound′, kəm pound′), *adj.* **1** having more than one part. **2** formed of many similar parts combined into a single structure. —*n.* something made by combining parts; mixture. —*v.t.* **1** mix; combine. **2** add to; increase; multiply. [< Old French *compondre* put together < Latin *componere* < *com-* together + *ponere* put]

com prise (kəm prīz′), *v.t.,* **-prised, -pris ing. 1** consist of; include. **2** make up; compose; constitute.

compt (kompt), *n.* ARCHAIC. count.

com punc tion (kəm pungk′shən), *n.* **1** uneasiness of the mind because of wrongdoing; pricking of conscience; remorse. **2** a slight or passing regret. [< Late Latin *compunctionem* < Latin *compungere* to prick, sting < *com-* + *pungere* to prick]

com punc tious (kəm pungk′shəs), *adj.* having or feeling compunction; regret; pricking of conscience.

con-, *prefix.* form of **com-** before *n,* as in *connote,* and before consonants except *b, h, l, m, p, r, w,* as in *concern.*

con., **1** against [for Latin *contra*]. **2** conclusion.

con chol o gy (kong kol′ə jē), *n.* branch of zoology that deals with the shells of mollusks.

con cord (kon′kôrd, kong′kôrd), *n.* **1** agreement; harmony. **2** (in music) a harmonious combination of tones sounded together. **3** treaty. [< Old French *concorde* < Latin *concordia* < *com-* together + *cordis* heart]

con cu bine (kong′kyə bin, kon′kyə bin), *n.* woman who lives with a man without being legally married to him.

con du it (kon′dü it, kon′dit), *n.* **1** channel or pipe for carrying liquids long distances. **2** pipe or underground passage for electric wires or cables.

con fab u late (kən fab′yə lāt), *v.i.* **-lat ed, -lat ing,** talk together informally and intimately; chat. [ultimately < Latin < *com-* together + *fabulari* talk < *fabula* fable]

con fla gra tion (kon′flə grā′shən), *n.* a great and destructive fire.

con flu ence (kon′flü əns), *n.* **1** a flowing together. **2** place where two or more rivers, streams, etc., come together. **3** a coming together of people or things; throng.

con found (kon found′, kən found′ *for 1, 2, 4, 5;* kon′found′ *for 3*), *v.t.* **1** confuse; mix up. **2** surprise and puzzle. **3** damn. **4** ARCHAIC. make uneasy and ashamed. **5** ARCHAIC. defeat; overthrow. [< Old French *confondre* < Latin *confundere* pour together, mix up, confuse] —**con found′er,** *n.*

con fute (kən fyüt′), *v.t.,* **-fut ed, -fut ing. 1** prove (an argument, testimony, etc.) to be false or incorrect. **2** prove (a person) to be wrong; overcome by argument.

con gen ial (kən jē′nyəl), *adj.* **1** having similar tastes and interests; getting on well together. **2** agreeable; suitable. —**con gen′ial ly,** *adv.*

con jec ture (kən jek′chər), *n., v.,* **-tured, -tur ing,** —*n.* **1** formation of an opinion admittedly without sufficient evidence for proof; guessing. **2** a guess. —*v.t., v.i.* guess. [< Latin *conjectura* < *conjicere* discuss, throw together < *com-* together + *jacere* throw] —**con jec′tur a ble,** *adj.* —**con jec′tur er,** *n.*

con ju ra tion (kon′jə rā′shən), *n.* **1** an invoking by a sacred name; conjuring. **2** the practice of magic. **3** a magic form of words used in conjuring; magic spell. **4** ARCHAIC. a solemn appeal.

con jure (kon′jər, kən jur′), *v.t.,* **-jured, -jur ing. 1** compel (a spirit, devil, etc.) to appear or disappear by a set form of words. **2** make a solemn appeal to; request earnestly; entreat.

con sign (kən sin′), *v.t.* **1** hand over; deliver. **2** send; transmit. **3** set apart; assign.

con so la tion (kon′sə lā′shən), *n.* **1** a consoling. **2** a being consoled. **3** a comforting person, thing, or event. —*adj.* between losers in an earlier round of a tournament.

con so nan cy (kon′sə nən sē), *n.* **1** harmony; agreement; accordance. **2** harmony of sounds; simultaneous combination of tones in music that is agreeable to the ear. Also, **consonance.**

con strain (kən strān′), *v.t.* **1** force; compel. **2** confine; imprison. **3** repress; restrain. [< Old French *constreindre* < Latin *constringere* < *com-* together + *stringere* pull tightly]

con sum mate (*v.* kon′sə māt; *adj.* kən sum′it), *v.,* **-mat ed, -mat ing,** *adj.* —*v.t.* bring to completion; realize; fulfill. —*adj.* in the highest degree; complete; perfect. —**con sum′mate ly,** *adv.*

con sum ma tion (kon′sə mā′shən), *n.* completion; fulfillment.

con tempt i ble (kən temp′tə bəl), *adj.* deserving contempt or scorn; held in contempt; mean; low; worthless. —**con tempt′i ble ness,** *n.* —**con tempt′i bly,** *adv.*

con ten tion (kən ten′shən), *n.* **1** statement or point that one has argued for; statement maintained as true. **2** an arguing; disputing; quarreling. **3** argument; dispute; quarrel. **4** struggle; contest; competition. [< Latin *contentionem* < *contendere*]

con tig u ous (kən tig′yü əs), *adj.* **1** in actual contact; touching. **2** adjoining; near. [< Latin *contiguus* < *contingere* touch closely] —**con tig′u ous ly,** *adv.* —**con tig′u ous ness,** *n.*

con ti nence (kon′tə nəns), *n.* **1** control of one's actions and feelings; self-restraint; moderation. **2** chastity.

con ti nent (kon′tə nənt), *adj.* **1** showing restraint with regard to the desires or passions; using self-control; temperate. **2** chaste.

[< Latin *continentem* holding in, refraining < *com-* in + *tenere* to hold] —**con′ti nent ly,** *adv.*

con trite (kən trīt′, kon′trīt), *adj.* **1** broken in spirit by a sense of guilt; penitent. **2** showing deep regret and sorrow. [< Latin *contritus* crushed < *com-* together + *terere* to rub, grind]

con tu me ly (kon tü′mə lē, kon tyü′mə lē; kon′tü mə lē, kon′tyə mə lē), *n., pl.* **-lies. 1** insolent contempt; insulting words or actions; humiliating treatment. **2** a humiliating insult. [< Latin *contumelia,* related to *contumacia* contumacy]

con vey ance (kən vā′əns), *n.* **1** a carrying; transmission; transportation. **2** thing that carries people and goods; vehicle. **3** communications. **4** transfer of ownership. **5** document showing such a transfer; deed.

con vo ca tion (kon′və kā′shən), *n.* **1** a calling together; assembling by a summons. **2** assembly.

con vulse (kən vuls′), *v.t.,* **-vulsed, -vuls ing. 1** shake violently. **2** cause violent disturbance in; disturb violently. **3** throw into convulsions; shake with muscular spasms. **4** throw into fits of laughter; cause to shake with laughter. [< Latin *convulsum* torn away < *com-* + *vellere* to tear]

con vul sion (kən vul′shən), *n.* **1** Often, **convulsions,** *pl.* a violent, involuntary contracting and relaxing of the muscles; spasm; fit. **2** a fit of laughter. **3** a violent disturbance.

con vul sive (kən vul′siv), *adj.* **1** violently disturbing. **2** having convulsions. **3** producing convulsions. —**con vul′sive ly,** *adv.* —**con vul′sive ness,** *n.*

coo lie (kü′lē), *n.* formerly, an unskilled laborer in China, India, etc., hired for very low wages. Also, **cooly.** [< Hindustani *qūlī*]

co quette (kō ket′), *n.* woman who tries to attract men; flirt.

co quet tish (kō ket′ish), *adj.* **1** of a coquette. **2** like a coquette; like a coquette's.

cor dial (kôr′jəl), *adj.* **1** warm and friendly in manner; hearty; sincere. **2** strengthening; stimulating. —*n.* **1** food, drink, or medicine that strengthens or stimulates. **2** liqueur. —**cor′dial ly,** *adv.* —**cor′dial ness,** *n.*

cor mor ant (kôr′mər ənt), *n.* **1** any of a family of large, and supposedly greedy, black sea birds with hooked bills and webbed feet. **2** a greedy person. [< Old French *cormareng* < *corp* raven + *marenc* of the sea]

cor por al (kôr′pər əl), *adj.* of the body: *corporal punishment.* [< Latin *corporalem* < *corpus* body] —**cor′por al ly,** *adv.*

cor po re al (kôr pôr′ē əl, kôr pōr′ē əl), *adj.* **1** of or for the body; **2** material; tangible. —**cor po′re al ly,** *adv.* —**cor po′re al ness,** *n.*

corse let (kôrs′lit), *n.* armor for the upper part of the body. Also, **corslet.**

coun te nance (koun′tə nəns), *n., v.,* **-nanced, -nanc ing.** —*n.* **1** expression of the face. **2** face; features. **3** approval; encouragement. **4** calmness; composure. —*v.t.* approve or encourage; sanction. [< Old French *contenance* < Medieval Latin *continentia* demeanor < Latin, self-control < *continere.*]

course (kôrs, kōrs), *v.,* **coursed, cours ing.** —*v.i.* **1** race; run: *The blood courses through the arteries.* **2** hunt with dogs. —*v.t.* **1** cause (dogs) to hunt for game. **2** run through.

cov ert (kuv′ərt, kō′vərt), *adj.* kept from sight; concealed; secret; hidden. —*n.* **1** a hiding place; shelter. **2** thicket in which animals hide.

cov et (kuv′it), *v.t.* desire eagerly (something that belongs to another).

cov et ous (kuv′ə təs), *adj.* desiring things that belong to others. —**cov′et ous ly,** *adv.* —**cov′et ous ness,** *n.*

cox comb (koks′kōm′), *n.* **1** a vain, empty-headed man; conceited dandy. **2** cockscomb.

coz en (kuz′n), *v.t., v.i.* deceive or trick; cheat; beguile.

cra ven (krā′vən), *adj.* cowardly. —*n.* coward. [< Old French *cravente* overcome < Popular Latin *crepantare* < Latin *crepare* crush; burst] —**cra′ven ly,** *adv.* —**cra′ven ness,** *n.*

cre dent (krēd′nt), *adj.* ARCHAIC. giving credence; believing.

cre du li ty (krə dü′lə tē, krə dyü′lə tē), *n.* a too great readiness to believe.

cre tonne (kri ton′, krē′ton), *n.* a strong cotton, linen, or rayon

corselet

cloth with designs printed in colors on one or both sides.

crib (krib), *v.t.,* **cribbed, crib bing.** shut up in a small space.

croft (krôft, kroft), *n.* BRITISH. **1** a small, enclosed field. **2** a very small rented farm. [Old English]

crone (krōn), *n.* a withered old woman. [< Middle Dutch *croonje* < Old French *carogne* carcass, hag. Doublet of CARRION]

crook (krůk), *n.* **1** hook; bend; curve. **2** a hooked, curved, or bent part. **3** a shepherd's staff, curved on its upper end into a hook.

cru et (krü′it), *n.* a glass bottle to hold vinegar, oil, etc., for the table. [< Old French, diminutive of *cruie* pot]

cuck old (kuk′əld), *n.* husband of an unfaithful wife. —*v.t.* make a cuckold of. [< Old French *cucuault* < *coucou* cuckoo]

cud (kud), *n.* mouthful of food brought back from the first stomach of cattle or other ruminant animals for a slow, second chewing in the mouth. [Old English *cudu, cwidu*]

cud dy (kud′ē), *n., pl.* **-dies.** a small cabin on a boat.

cudg el (kuj′əl), *n., v.,* **-eled, -el ing** or **-elled, -el ling.** —*n.* **1** a short, thick stick used as a weapon; club. **2 take up the cudgels for,** defend strongly. —*v.t.* beat with a cudgel. [Old English *cycgel*]

cuisse (kwis), *n.* piece of armor to protect the thigh.

cull (kul), *v.t.* **1** pick out; select. **2** pick over; make selections from.

cum ber (kum′bər), *v.t.* encumber. —*n.* encumbrance. [< Old French *combrer* impede < *combre* barrier]

cu pid i ty (kyü pid′ə tē), *n.* eager desire to possess something; greed.

cur so ry (kėr′sər ē), *adj.* without attention to details; hasty and superficial. [< Latin *cursorius* of a race < *currere* to run] —**cur′sor i ly,** *adv.* —**cur′sor i ness,** *n.*

cut purse (kut′pėrs′), *n.* pickpocket.

da is (dā′is; British dās), *n.* a raised platform at one end of a hall or large room for a throne, seats of honor, a lectern, etc. [< Old French *deis* < Latin *discus* quoit, dish < Greek *diskos.* Doublet of DESK, DISCUS, DISH, and DISK.]

dal li ance (dal′ē əns), *n.* **1** a dallying; trifling. **2** flirtation.

dal li ant (dal′ē ənt), *adj.* OBSOLETE. tending to dalliance.

dam sel (dam′zəl), *n.* ARCHAIC. a young girl; maiden.

dank (dangk), *adj.* unpleasantly damp or moist. [Middle English *danke*]

das tard ly (das′tərd lē), *adj.* like a dastard; mean and cowardly; sneaking. —**das′tard li ness,** *n.*

daunt less (dônt′lis, dänt′lis), *adj.* not to be frightened or discouraged; brave. —**daunt′less ly,** *adv.*

dearth (dėrth), *n.* **1** too small a supply; great scarcity or lack. **2** scarcity of food; famine. [Middle English *derthe*]

dec la ma tion (dek′lə mā′shən), *n.* **1** act or art of declaiming; making formal speeches. **2** a formal speech or selection of poetry, prose, etc., for reciting. **3** loud and emotional talk.

de co rum (di kôr′əm, di kōr′əm), *n.* proper behavior; good taste in conduct, speech, dress, etc.

de crep it (di krep′it), *adj.* **1** broken down or weakened by old age; old and feeble. **2** worn out or broken down from use. [< Latin *decrepitum* broken down < *de-* + *crepare* to creak]

de cus sate (di kus′āt), *adj., v.,* **-sat ed, -sat ing.** —*adj.* **1** crossed; intersecting. **2** (of leaves, etc.) arranged along the stem in pairs, each pair at right angles to the pair next above or below. —*v.t., v.i.* to cross; intersect.

deem (dēm), *v.t., v.i.* form or have an opinion; think, believe, or consider. [Old English *dēman* < *dōm* judgment]

a hat	i it	oi oil	ch child		a in about
ā age	ī ice	ou out	ng long		e in taken
ä far	o hot	u cup	sh she	ə =	i in pencil
e let	ō open	ů put	th thin		o in lemon
ē equal	ô order	ü rule	⟤H then		u in circus
ėr term			zh measure	< = derived from

de fec tive (di fek′tiv), *adj*. **1** having a defect or defects; not perfect or complete; faulty. **2** lacking one or more of the usual forms of grammatical inflection. **3** below normal in behavior or intelligence. —*n*. person who has some defect.

de fer (di fėr′), *v.i.*, **-ferred, -fer ring.** yield in judgment or opinion.

def er ence (def′ər əns), *n*. **1** respect for the judgment, opinion, wishes, etc., of another. **2** great respect. **3 in deference to,** out of respect for.

def e ren tial (def′ə ren′shəl), *adj*. showing deference; respectful. —**def′e ren′tial ly,** *adv*. [< Middle French *déférer* < Latin *deferre* < *de-* down + *ferre* carry]

de gree (di grē′), *n*. rank: *A noble is a person of high degree.*

de lin e ate (di lin′ē āt), *v.t.*, **-at ed, -at ing. 1** trace the outline of. **2** draw; sketch. **3** describe in words; portray.

de ment ed (di men′tid), *adj*. mentally ill; insane; crazy. [< Latin *dementem* < *de-* out + *mentem* mind] —**de ment′ed ly,** *adv*. —**de ment′ed ness,** *n*.

dep o si tion (dep′ə zish′ən, dē′pə zish′ən), *n*. **1** act of putting out of office or a position of authority; removal from power. **2** the giving of testimony under oath. **3** testimony, especially a sworn statement in writing. **4** a depositing. **5** thing deposited; deposit.

dep re cate (dep′rə kāt), *v.t.*, **-cat ed, -cat ing. 1** express strong disapproval of. **2** depreciate; belittle. [< Latin *deprecatum* pleaded in excuse, averted by prayer < *de-* from, away + *precari* pray] —**dep′re cat′ing ly,** *adv*.

dep re da tion (dep′rə dā′shən), *n*. act of plundering; robbery; ravaging. [< Latin *depraedationem* < *de-* + *praeda* booty]

de ride (di rīd′), *v.t.*, **-rid ed, -rid ing.** make fun of; laugh at in scorn. [< Latin *deridere* < *de-* down + *ridere* to laugh]

de ri sion (di rizh′ən), *n*. **1** scornful laughter; ridicule. **2** object of ridicule. [< Latin *derisionem* < *deridere*. See DERIDE.]

des cant (*v.* des kant′, des kant′; *n.* des′kant), *v.i.* talk at great length; discourse. —*n*. an extended comment; discourse.

de scry (di skrī′), *v.t.*, **-scried, -scry ing. 1** catch sight of; be able to see; make out. **2** discover by observation; detect.

des e crate (des′ə krāt), *v.t.*, **-crat ed, -crat ing.** treat or use without respect; disregard the sacredness of; profane.

des o late (*adj.* des′ə lit; *v.* des′ə lāt), *adj.*, *v.*, **-lat ed, -lat ing.** —*adj*. **1** laid waste; devastated; barren. **2** unhappy; forlorn; wretched. **3** left alone; solitary; lonely. **4** dreary; dismal. —*v.t.* **1** make unfit to live in; lay waste. **2** make unhappy. **3** deprive of inhabitants. [< Latin *desolatum* < *de-* + *solus* alone] —**des′o late ly,** *adv*. —**des′o late ness,** *n*.

des o la tion (des′ə lā′shən), *n*. **1** act of making desolate; devastation. **2** a ruined, lonely, or deserted condition. **3** a desolate place. **4** lonely sorrow; sadness.

de spond en cy (di spon′dən sē), *n*. loss of heart, courage, or hope; discouragement; dejection.

des pot ic (des pot′ik), *adj*. of a despot; having unlimited power; tyrannical. —**des pot′i cal ly,** *adv*. [< Greek *despotēs* master]

deuce (düs, dyüs), *interj*. exclamation of annoyance meaning "bad luck" or "the devil." [apparently < *deuce* two; a die with two spots (thought of as unlucky)]

dew lap (dü′lap′, dyü′lap′), *n*. the loose fold of skin under the throat of cattle and some other animals.

dex ter i ty (dek ster′ə tē), *n*. **1** skill in using the hands or body. **2** skill in using the mind; cleverness.

dex ter ous (dek′stər əs), *adj*. **1** skillful in using the hands or body. **2** having or showing skill in using the mind; clever. Also, **dextrous.** —**dex′ter ous ly,** *adv*. —**dex′ter ous ness,** *n*.

di a dem (dī′ə dem), *n*. **1** a crown. **2** an ornamental band of cloth formerly worn as a crown. **3** royal power or authority.

DEWLAP

dif fi dent (dif′ə dənt), *adj*. lacking in self-confidence; shy. —**dif′fi dent ly,** *adv*.

di gres sion (də gresh′ən, dī gresh′ən), *n*. a digressing; turning aside from the main subject in talking or writing.

di lec tion (də lec′shən), *n*. OBSOLETE. love.

dil i gence[1] (dil′ə jəns), *n*. constant and earnest effort to accomplish what is undertaken; industry.

dil i gence[2] (dil′ə jəns), *n*. a public stagecoach formerly used in France and other parts of Europe. [< French *(carosse de) diligence* fast (coach)]

din gle (ding′gəl), *n*. a small, deep, shady valley.

dire (dīr), *adj.*, **dir er, dir est.** causing great fear or suffering; dreadful. [< Latin *dirus*] —**dire′ly,** *adv*. —**dire′ness,** *n*.

dire ful (dīr′fəl), *adj*. dire; dreadful; terrible. —**dire′ful ly,** *adv*. —**dire′ful ness,** *n*.

dirge (dėrj), *n*. a funeral song or tune. [contraction of Latin *dirige* direct! (first word in office for the dead)] —**dirge′like′,** *adj*.

dirk (dėrk), *n*. dagger. —*v.t.* stab with a dirk. [origin unknown]

dis-, *prefix*. **1** opposite of; lack of; not: *Dishonest = not honest; opposite of honest. Discomfort = lack of comfort.* **2** do the opposite of: *Disentangle = do the opposite of entangle.* **3** apart; away, as in *dispel*. [< Latin]

dis burse (dis bėrs′), *v.t.*, **-bursed, -burs ing.** pay out; expend. [< Old French *desbourser* < *des-* dis-, away + *bourse* purse < Late Latin *bursa*] —**dis burs′er,** *n*.

dis cern (də zėrn′, də sėrn′), *v.t.* see clearly; perceive the difference between (two or more things); distinguish or recognize.

dis cern ment (də zėrn′mənt, də sėrn′mənt), *n*. keenness in seeing and understanding; good judgment; shrewdness.

dis com fi ture (dis kum′fi chŭr, dis kum′fi chər), *n*. **1** defeat of plans or hopes; frustration. **2** confusion. **3** ARCHAIC. a complete defeat; rout.

dis con cert (dis′kən sėrt′), *v.t.* disturb the self-possession of; embarrass greatly; confuse. —**dis′con cert′ing ly,** *adv*.

dis con so late (dis kon′sə lit), *adj*. **1** without hope; forlorn; unhappy. **2** causing discomfort; cheerless. [< Medieval Latin *disconsolatus* < Latin *dis-* + *consolari* to console] —**dis con′so late ly,** *adv*. —**dis con′so late ness,** *n*.

dis count (dis′kount, dis kount′; *n.*, *adj.* dis′kount), *v.t.* **1** deduct (a certain percentage) of the amount or cost. **2** leave out of account; disregard. —*v.i.* sell goods at a discount. —*n*. deduction from the amount or cost. —*adj*. selling goods at prices below those suggested by manufacturers.

dis course (*n.* dis′kôrs, dis′kōrs; *v.* dis kôrs′, dis kōrs′), *n.*, *v.*, **-coursed, -cours ing.** —*n*. **1** a formal or extensive speech or writing. **2** talk; conversation. —*v.i.* **1** speak or write formally or at length on some subject. **2** talk; converse. [< Latin *discursus* a running about < *dis-* + *cursus* a running]

dis gorge (dis gôrj′), *v.*, **-gorged, -gorg ing.** —*v.i.* throw up the contents; empty; discharge. —*v.t.* **1** throw out from the throat; vomit forth. **2** pour forth; discharge. **3** give up unwillingly.

di shev eled or **di shev elled** (də shev′əld), *adj*. not neat; rumpled; mussed; disordered.

dis in ter est ed (dis in′tər ə stid, dis in′tər es′tid), *adj*. **1** free from selfish motives; impartial; fair. **2** uninterested. —**dis in′ter est ed ly,** *adv*. —**dis in′ter est ed ness,** *n*.

dis pas sion ate (dis pash′ə nit), *adj*. free from emotion or prejudice; calm and impartial. —**dis pas′sion ate ly,** *adv*.

dis patch (dis pach′), *v.t.* **1** send off to some place or for some purpose. **2** get done promptly or speedily; settle; conclude. **3** kill. **4** INFORMAL. finish off; eat up. —*n*. **1** a sending off a letter, a messenger, etc., to a particular place or on a specified errand. **2** a written message or communication, such as special news or government business. **3** promptness in doing anything; speed. **4** a putting to death; a killing. **5** ARCHAIC. care. Also, **despatch.** [< Italian *dispacciare* or Spanish *despachar*]

dis perse (dis pėrs′), *v.*, **-persed, -pers ing.** —*v.t.* **1** send or drive off in different directions; scatter. **2** divide (light) into rays of different colors. —*v.i.* spread in different directions; scatter. [< Latin *dispersum* dispersed < *dis-* apart + *spargere* to scatter] —**dis pers′er,** *n*.

dis po si tion (dis′pə zish′ən), *n*. **1** one's habitual ways of acting toward others or of thinking about things; nature.

dis qui et (dis kwī′ət), *v.t.* make uneasy or anxious; disturb. —*n.*

GLOSSARY

uneasy feelings; anxiety. **—dis qui′et ing ly,** *adv.*

dis sev er (di sev′ər), *v.t.* cut into parts; sever; separate. **—***v.i.* separate. **—dis sev′er ment,** *n.*

dis si pate (dis′ə pāt), *v.,* **-pat ed, -pat ing. —***v.t.* **1** spread in different directions; scatter. **2** cause to disappear; dispel. **3** spend foolishly; squander. **—***v.i.* **1** scatter so as to disappear; disperse. **2** indulge excessively in sensual or foolish pleasures.

dis sol u ble (di sol′yə bəl), *adj.* capable of being dissolved.

dis suade (di swād′), *v.t.,* **-suad ed, -suad ing. 1** persuade not to do something. **2** advise against. [< Latin *dissuadere* < *dis-* against + *suadere* to urge]

dis tem per (dis tem′pər), *n.* **1** any sickness of the mind or body; disorder; disease. **2** disturbance. **—***v.t.* make unbalanced; disturb; disorder.

dis till ment or **dis til ment** (dis til′mənt), *n.* ARCHAIC. **1** extract. **2** something distilled.

di verse (də vėrs′, dī vėrs′), *adj.* **1** not alike; different. **2** varied; diversified. **—di verse′ly,** *adv.* **—di verse′ness,** *n.*

di ver sion (də vėr′zhən, dī vėr′zhən), *n.* **1** a turning aside; diverting. **2** distraction from work, care, etc.; amusement; entertainment; pastime. **3** attack or feint intended to distract an opponent's attention from the point of main attack.

doff (dof, dôf), *v.t.* **1** take all; remove: *doff one's hat.* **2** get rid of; throw aside. [contraction of *do off*]

dog mat ic (dôg mat′ik, dog mat′ik), *adj.* **1** of dogma; doctrinal. **2** positive and emphatic in asserting opinions. **3** asserted in a positive and emphatic manner. [< Latin < Greek, opinion < *dokein* think] **—dog mat′i cal ly,** *adv.*

dole (dōl), *n.* ARCHAIC. sorrow; grief.

dole ful (dōl′fəl), *adj.* very sad or dreary; mournful; dismal. **—dole′ful ly,** *adv.* **—dole′ful ness,** *n.*

do lor (dō′lər), *n.* sorrow; grief. [< Latin < *dolere* grieve]

dol or ous (dol′ər əs, dō′lər əs), *adj.* **1** full of or expressing sorrow; mournful. **2** causing or giving rise to sorrow; grievous; painful. **—dol′or ous ly,** *adv.* **—dol′or ous ness,** *n.*

do min ion (də min′yən), *n.* power or right of governing and controlling; rule; control.

dot ard (dō′tərd), *n.* person who is weak-minded and childish because of old age.

dot ing (dō′ting), *adj.* foolishly fond; too fond. **—dot′ing-ly,** *adv.*

dou blet (dub′lit), *n.* **1** a man's close-fitting jacket. Men in Europe wore doublets from the 1400's to the 1600's. **2** pair of two similar or equal things; couple. **3** one of a pair. **4** one of two or more words in a language, derived from the same original source but coming by different routes. EXAMPLE: *fragile* and *frail.*

dow er (dou′ər), *n.* **1** a widow's share for life of her dead husband's property. **2** dowry.

dow ry (dou′rē), *n.,* *pl.* **-ries. 1** money or property that a woman brings to the man she marries. **2** natural gift, talent, or quality; natural endowment. Also, **dower.**

draught (draft), *n.* draft; a single act of drinking or the amount taken in a single drink.

dregs (dregz), *n. pl.* **1** the solid bits of matter that settle to the bottom of a liquid. **2** the least desirable part. [< Scandinavian (Old Icelandic) *dregg,* singular]

dudg eon[1] (duj′ən), *n.* **1** a feeling of anger or resentment. **2 in high dudgeon,** very angry; resentful. [origin unknown]

dudg eon[2] (duj′ən), *n.* OBSOLETE. a wooden handle on a dagger.

dul ci mer (dul′sə mər), *n.* a musical instrument with metal strings, played by striking the strings with two hammers.

dun (dun), *adj.,* **dun ner, dun nest,** *n.* **—***adj.* dull, grayish-brown**—***n.* **1** a dull, grayish brown. **2** horse of a dun color. [Old English *dunn*]

du ress (dů res′, dyů res′; dûr′es, dyûr′es), *n.* **1** use of force; compulsion. The law does not require a person to fulfill a contract signed under duress. **2** imprisonment; confinement.

ec cle si ast (i klē′zē ast), *n.* a member of the clergy.

ec sta sy (ek′stə sē), *n.,* *pl.* **-sies. 1** condition of very great joy; thrilling or overwhelming delight. **2** any strong feeling that completely absorbs the mind; uncontrollable emotion. **3** trance. **4** ARCHAIC. madness. [< Greek *ekstasis* distraction, trance < *existanai* put out of place < *ex-* out + *histanai* to place]

a hat	i it	oi oil	ch child		a in about
ā age	ī ice	ou out	ng long		e in taken
ä far	o hot	u cup	sh she	ə = {	i in pencil
e let	ō open	ů put	th thin		o in lemon
ē equal	ô order	ü rule	ᵾн then		u in circus
ėr term			zh measure	< = derived from

ec stat ic (ek stat′ik), *adj.* **1** full of ecstasy. **2** caused by ecstasy. **—ec stat′i cal ly,** *adv.*

ed dy (ed′ē), *n.,* *pl.* **-dies,** *v.,* **-died, -dy ing. —***n.* water, air, smoke, etc., moving against the main current, especially when having a whirling motion; small whirlpool or whirlwind. **—***v.i., v.t.* **1** move against the main current in a whirling motion; whirl. **2** move in circles.

ed i fi ca tion (ed′ə fə kā′shən), *n.* an edifying; moral improvement; spiritual benefit; instruction.

ef fi ca cious (ef′ə kā′shəs), *adj.* producing the desired results; effective. **—ef′fi ca′cious ly,** *adv.* **—ef′fi ca′cious ness,** *n.*

e gre gious (i grē′jəs), *adj.* **1** remarkably or extraordinarily bad; outrageous; flagrant. **2** remarkable; extraordinary. **—e gre′-gious ly,** *adv.* **—e gre′gious ness,** *n.*

el o cu tion ar y (el′ə kyü′shə ner′ē), *adj.* of or having to do with elocution, the art of speaking or reading clearly and expressively in public. [< Latin *elocutionem* < *eloqui* speak out]

e lude (i lüd′), *v.t.,* **e lud ed, e lud ing. 1** avoid or escape by cleverness, quickness, etc.; slip away from; evade. **2** baffle; mournful; pastime. **3** attack or feint intended to distract an opponent's attention from the point of main attack.

e lu sive (i lü′siv), *adj.* **1** hard to describe or understand; baffling. **2** tending to elude or escape; evasive.

e ma ci ate (i mā′shē āt), *v.t.,* **-at ed, -at ing.** make unnaturally thin; cause to lose flesh or waste away. **—e ma′ci a′tion,** *n.*

em blem (em′bləm), *n.* **1** object or representation that stands for an invisible quality, idea, etc., by some connection of thought; sign of an idea; symbol. **2** a heraldic device. [< Latin *emblema* inlaid work < Greek *emblēma* insertion < *en-* in + *ballein* to throw]

em bow er (em bou′ər), *v.t.* enclose in a shelter of leafy branches.

em i nence (em′ə nəns), *n.* **1** rank or position above all or most others; high standing. **2** a high place; high point of land. **3 Em-inence,** title of honor given to a cardinal in the Catholic Church.

em i nent (em′ə nənt), *adj.* **1** above all or most others; outstanding; distinguished. **2** conspicuous; noteworthy. **3** high; lofty. **4** standing out above other things; prominent. [< Latin *eminentem* standing out, prominent < *ex-* out + *minere* jut] **—em′i nent-ly,** *adv.*

em u late (em′yə lāt), *v.t.,* **-lat ed, -lat ing. 1** copy or imitate in order to equal or excel the achievements or qualities of an admired person. **2** vie with; rival. **—em′u la′tion,** *n.*

en cour age (en kėr′ij), *v.t.,* **-aged, -ag ing. 1** give courage, hope, or confidence to; urge on; hearten. **2** stimulate (persons or personal efforts) by helping or showing approval; support. **3** promote the development of; foster. **—en cour′ag er,** *n.* **—en-cour′ag ing ly,** *adv.* [< *en-* + Old French *corage* < *cuer* heart < Latin *cor*]

en croach (en krōch′), *v.i.* **1** go beyond proper or usual limits; make gradual inroads on: **2** trespass upon the property or rights of another, especially stealthily or by gradual advances; intrude. [< Old French *encrochier* < *en-* in + *croc* hook]

en cum brance (en kum′brəns), *n.* **1** something useless or in the way; hindrance; burden. **2** claim, mortgage, etc., on property. Also, **incumbrance.**

en due (en dü′, en dyü′), *v.t.,* **-dued, -du ing. 1** provide with a quality or power; furnish; supply. **2** clothe. Also, **indue.**

en gen der (en jen′dər), *v.t.* **1** bring into existence; produce; cause. **2** beget. [< Old French *engendrer* < Latin *ingenerare* < *in-* in + *generare* create]

en graft (en graft′), *v.t.* **1** graft (a shoot, etc.) from one tree or plant into another. **2** fix in; implant. Also, **ingraft.**

en kin dle (en kin′dl), *v.t.,* **-dled, -dling.** kindle; set on fire, light, or arouse. **—en kin′dler,** *n.*

en sign (en′sīn, en′sən), *n.* a flag or banner:

en trails (en′trālz, en′trəlz), *n.pl.* **1** the inner parts of the body of a human being or animal. **2** the intestines; bowels.

en treat (en trēt′), *v.t.* ask or keep asking earnestly; beg and pray. [< Old French *entraitier* < *en-* in + *traitier* to treat] —**en treat′ing ly,** *adv.*

en treat y (en trē′tē), *n.,* *pl.* **-treat ies.** an earnest request; prayer or appeal.

en voy (en′voi, än′voi), *n.* **1** messenger or representative. **2** diplomat ranking next below an ambassador and next above a minister. **3** any person sent to represent a government or ruler for diplomatic purposes.

ep i cure (ep′ə kyùr), *n.* person who has a refined taste in eating and drinking and who is very particular in choosing fine foods, wines, etc.

ep i thet (ep′ə thet), *n.* **1** a descriptive expression; word or phrase expressing some quality or attribute. **2** an insulting or contemptuous word or phrase used in place of a person's name. **3** the part of a scientific name of an organism which denotes a species, variety, or other division of a genus.

e pit o me (i pit′ə mē), *n.* **1** a condensed account; summary. An epitome contains only the most important points of a literary work, subject, etc. **2** person or thing that is typical or representative of something. [< Greek *epitomē* < *epitemnein* cut short < *epi-* + *temnein* to cut]

ep och (ep′ək, ē′pok), *n.* **1** period of time; era; age. **2** period of time in which striking things happened. **3** the starting point of such a period. **4** one of the divisions of time into which a geological period is divided. [< Greek *epochē* a stopping, fixed point in time < *epechein* to stop < *epi-* up + *echein* to hold]

eq ui page (ek′wə pij), *n.* **1** carriage. **2** carriage with its horses, driver, and servants. **3** equipment; outfit. **4** articles for personal ornament or use.

e quiv o cal (i kwiv′ə kəl), *adj.* **1** having two or more meanings; intentionally vague or ambiguous. **2** undecided; uncertain. **3** questionable; suspicious. [< Late Latin *aequivocus* ambiguous < Latin *aequus* equal + *vocare* to call]

e quiv o cate (i kwiv′ə kāt), *v.i.,* **-cat ed, -cat ing. 1** use expressions of double meaning in order to mislead. **2** avoid committing oneself on some matter. —**e quiv′o cat′ing ly,** *adv.* —**e quiv′o ca′tor,** *n.*

e quiv o ca tion (i kwiv′ə kā′shən), *n.* **1** the use of expressions with double meaning in order to mislead. **2** an equivocal expression. **3** avoidance of committing oneself on some matter.

es tate (e stāt′), *n.* **1** a large piece of land belonging to a person; landed property. **2** condition or stage in life.

es thet i cism (es thet′ə siz′əm), *n.* appreciation of beauty or the cultivation of the arts.

e ther e al (i thir′ē əl), *adj.* **1** light; airy; delicate. **2** not of the earth; heavenly. **3** of or having to do with the upper regions of space.

et y mol o gy (et′ə mol′ə jē), *n.,* *pl.* **-gies. 1** the derivation of a word. **2** account or explanation of the origin and history of a word. **3** study dealing with linguistic changes, especially with individual word origins. [< Greek *etymologia* < *etymon* the original sense or form of a word (neuter of *etymos* true, real) + *-logos* treating of]

eu ca lyp tus (yü′kə lip′təs), *n.,* *pl.* **-tus es, -ti** (-tī). any of a genus of tall evergreen trees of the myrtle family, found mainly in Australia and neighboring islands; gum tree. It is valued for its timber and for a medicinal oil made from its leaves.

eu nuch (yü′nək), *n.* **1** a castrated man. **2** a castrated man in charge of a harem or the household of an Oriental ruler. [< Greek *eunouchos* < *eunē* bed + *echein* keep, be in charge of]

ev a nes cent (ev′ə nes′nt), *adj.* gradually disappearing; soon passing away; vanishing.

e ven song (ē′vən sông′, ē′vən song′), *n.* vespers.

e vince (i vins′), *v.t.,* **e vinced, e vinc ing. 1** show clearly; manifest. **2** show that one has (a certain quality, trait, etc.)

ex-¹, *prefix.* **1** former; formerly: *Ex-president = former president.* **2** out of; from; out: *Express = press out.* **3** thor-

oughly; utterly: *Exterminate = terminate (finish or destroy) thoroughly.* [< Latin < *ex* out of, without]

ex-², *prefix.* from; out of, as in *exodus.* [< Greek]

ex act i tude (eg zak′tə tüd, eg zak′tə tyüd), *n.* exactness.

ex com mu ni ca tion (ek′skə myü′nə kā′shən), *n.* **1** a formal cutting off from membership in the church; prohibition from participating in any of the rites of the church. **2** an official statement announcing this.

ex er tion (eg zėr′shən), *n.* **1** strenuous action; effort. **2** a putting into action; active use; use.

ex hor ta tion (eg′zôr tā′shən, ek′sôr tā′shən), *n.* **1** strong urging; earnest advice or warning. **2** speech, sermon, etc., that exhorts. [< Latin *exhortari* < *ex-* + *hortari* urge strongly]

ex i gence (ek′sə jəns), *n.* exigency.

ex pe di ent (ek spē′dē ənt), *adj.* **1** helping to bring about a desired result; useful; advantageous. **2** giving or seeking personal advantage; based on self-interest. —*n.* means of bringing about a desired result: *When the truth wouldn't convince them I used the expedient of telling a believable lie.* —**ex pe′di ent ly,** *adv.*

ex pe di tion (ek′spə dish′ən), *n.* **1** journey for some special purpose, such as exploration, scientific study, or for military purposes. **2** the people, ships, etc., making such a journey. **3** efficient and prompt action; speed. **4** ARCHAIC. haste.

ex pi ate (ek′spē āt), *v.t.,* **-at ed, -at ing.** pay the penalty of; make amends for a wrong, sin, etc.; atone for.

ex pos tu late (ek spos′chə lāt), *v.i.,* **-lat ed, -lat ing.** reason earnestly with a person, protesting against something that person means to do or has done; remonstrate in a friendly way.

ex pur gate (ek′spər gāt), *v.t.* **-gat ed, -gat ing.** remove objectionable passages or words from (a book, letter, etc.). [< Latin *expurgatum* purged out < *ex-* out + *purgare* to purge]

ex tant (ek′stənt, ek stant′), *adj.* still existing; not destroyed or lost.

ex tin guish (ek sting′gwish), *v.t.* **1** put out; quench. **2** bring to an end; snuff out; destroy. **3** eclipse or obscure by superior brilliancy; outshine. **4** annual (a right, claim, etc.); nullify. [< Latin *exstinguere* < *ex-* out + *stinguere* quench] —**ex tin′guish a ble,** *adj.* —**ex tin′guish er,** *n.*

ex tort (ek stôrt′), *v.t.* obtain (money, a promise, etc.) by threats, force, fraud, or illegal use of authority. [< Latin *extortum* twisted out < *ex-* out + *torquere* twist] —**ex tort′er,** *n.*

ex ul ta tion (eg′zul tā′shən, ek′sul tā′shən), *n.* an exulting; great rejoicing; triumph.

fa ce tious (fə sē′shəs), *adj.* **1** having the habit of joking; being slyly humorous. **2** said in fun; not to be taken seriously. [< Latin *facetia* jest < *facetus* witty]

fac tion (fak′shən), *n.* **1** group of persons in a political party, church, club, etc., acting together or having a common purpose. **2** strife or quarreling among the members of a political party, church, club, neighborhood, etc.

fac ti tious (fak tish′əs), *adj.* developed by effort; not natural; artificial. [< Latin *factitius* < *facere* do. Doublet of FETISH.]

fag (fag), *v.,* **fagged, fag ging,** *n.* —*v.t.* tire by work; weary. —*v.i.* **1** work hard or until wearied. **2** BRITISH. act as a fag. —*n.* **1** drudgery. **2** drudge. **3** BRITISH. boy who waits on an older boy in certain schools. **4** SLANG. cigarette. [Middle English *fagge* fag end]

fain (fān), ARCHAIC. —*adv.* gladly; willingly. —*adj.* **1** willing, but not eager. **2** obliged. **3** glad. **4** eager. [Old English *fægen*]

fal con (fôl′kən, fal′kən, fô′kən), *n.* any of various hawks trained to hunt and kill other birds and small game. [< Late Latin *falconem* < Latin *falcem* sickle (because of the hooked talons)]

fal con er (fôl′kə nər, fal′kə nər, fô′kə nər), *n.* **1** person who hunts with falcons; hawker. **2** person who breeds and trains falcons for hunting.

fal la cy (fal′ə sē), *n.,* *pl.* **-cies. 1** a false idea; mistaken belief; error. **2** mistake in reasoning; misleading or unsound argument.

far row (far′ō), *n.* litter of pigs. [Old English *fearh*]

far thing (fär′ᵀHing), *n.* a former British coin equal to a fourth of a British penny.

fas tid i ous (fa stid′ē əs), *adj.* hard to please; dainty in taste; easily disgusted. —**fas tid′i ous ly,** *adv.* —**fas tid′i ous ness,** *n.* [< Latin *fastidiosus* < *fastidium* loathing]

fast ness (fast'nis), *n*. **1** a strong, safe place; stronghold. **2** a being fast or firm; firmness. **3** a being quick or rapid; swiftness.

fath om (faᴛʜ'əm), *v.t.* **1** measure the depth of (water); sound. **2** get to the bottom of; understand fully. —**fath'om a ble,** *adj*.

fe al ty (fē'əl tē), *n., pl.* **-ties. 1** loyalty and duty owed by a vassal to his feudal lord. **2** loyalty; faithfulness; allegiance.

feign (fān), *v.t.* **1** put on a false appearance of; make believe; pretend. **2** make up to deceive; invent falsely. —*v.i.* make oneself appear; pretend (to be).

fe lic i tous (fə lis'ə təs), *adj*. **1** well chosen for the occasion; appropriate; well-worded; apt. **2** having a gift for apt speech.

fe lic i ty (fə lis'ə tē), *n., pl.* **-ties. 1** great happiness; bliss. **2** good fortune; blessing.

fen (fen), *n*. low, marshy land covered wholly or partially with shallow, often stagnant water. [Old English *fenn*]

fer al (fir'əl), *adj*. **1** having reverted from domestication back to the original wild or untamed state. **2** wild; untamed. **3** brutal; savage. [< Latin *fera* wild beast < *ferus* wild]

fer vent (fėr'vənt), *adj*. **1** showing great warmth of feeling; very earnest; ardent. **2** hot; glowing; intense. —**fer'vent ly,** *adv*.

fer vid (fėr'vid), *adj*. **1** full of strong feeling; intensely emotional; ardent; spirited. **2** intensely hot. —**fer'vid ly,** *adv*. —**fer'vid ness,** *n*.

fes toon (fe stün'), *n*. a string or chain of flowers, leaves, ribbons, etc., hanging in a curve between two points. —*v.t.* **1** decorate with festoons. **2** hang in curves.

fet id (fet'id, fē'tid), *adj*. smelling very bad; stinking.

fet ter (fet'ər), *n*. **1** chain or shackle for the feet to prevent escape. **2** Usually, **fetters,** *pl*. anything that shackles or binds; restraint. —*v.t.* **1** bind with chains; chain the feet of. **2** bind; restrain: *Fetter your temper.* [Old English *feter.* Related to FOOT.]

fi del i ty (fə del'ə tē, fī del'ə tē), *n., pl.* **-ties. 1** steadfast faithfulness; loyalty. **2** exactness, as in a copy; accuracy. **3** the ability of a radio transmitter or receiver or other device to transmit or reproduce an electric signal or sound accurately. [< Latin *fidelitatem* < *fidelis* faithful [< *fides* faith. Doublet of FEALTY.]

fil i al (fil'ē əl), *adj*. of a son or daughter; due from a son or daughter toward a mother or father: *filial affection.*

fir ma ment (fėr'mə mənt), *n*. arch of the heavens; sky.

fis sure (fish'ər), *n*. **1** a long, narrow opening; split; crack. **2** a splitting apart; division into parts.

flag on (flag'ən), *n*. container for liquids, usually having a handle, a spout, and a cover.

flail (flāl), *n*. instrument for threshing grain by hand, consisting of a wooden handle at the end of which a stouter and shorter pole or club is fastened so as to swing freely. —*v.t.* **1** strike with a flail. **2** beat; thrash. [<Old French *flaiel* < Latin *flagellum* whip]

flam beau (flam'bō), *n., pl.* **-beaux** or **-beaus** (-bōz). **1** a flaming torch. **2** a large, decorated candlestick. [<French]

flo rin (flôr'ən, flor'ən), *n*. a former coin of Great Britain.

fold (fōld), *n*. **1** pen to keep sheep in. **2** sheep kept in a pen. —*v.t.* put or keep (sheep) in a pen.

fond (fond), *adj*. **1 fond of,** having a liking for. **2** loving; affectionate. **3** loving foolishly or too much; doting. **4** cherished. **5** ARCHAIC. foolish. [Middle English *fonned,* past participle of *fonnen* be foolish < *fonne* fool] —**fond'ly,** *adv*. —**fond'ness,** *n*.

for done (fôr dün'), *adj*. ARCHAIC. overcome with fatigue; exhausted.

fore cas tle (fōk'səl, fôr'kas'əl, fōr'kas'əl), *n*. **1** the upper deck in front of the foremast. **2** the sailors' quarters in the forward part of a merchantman. Also, **fo'c'sle.**

for lorn (fôr lôrn'), *adj*. **1** left alone and neglected; deserted; abandoned. **2** wretched in feeling or looks; unhappy. **3** hopelessness; desperate.

for spent (fôr spent'), *adj*. ARCHAIC. worn-out.

found ling (found'ling), *n*. baby or little child found abandoned.

fran chise (fran'chīz), *v.t.* set free.

fret (fret), *v*., **fret ted, fret ting,** *n*. —*v.i.* **1** be peevish, unhappy, discontented, or worried. **2** become gnawed or corroded; waste away. —*v.t.* **1** make peevish, unhappy, discontented, or worried; harass; vex; provoke. **2** eat or wear away. **3** make or form by wearing away. **4** agitate or ruffle. —*n*. condition of worry or discontent; peevish complaining. [Old English *fretan* eat]

---

a hat	i it	oi oil	ch child	a in about
ā age	ī ice	ou out	ng long	e in taken
ä far	o hot	u cup	sh she	ə = { i in pencil
e let	ō open	ủ put	th thin	o in lemon
ē equal	ô order	ü rule	ᴛʜ then	u in circus
ėr term			zh measure	< = derived from

—**fret'ter,** *n*.

frieze (frēz), *n*. **1** a horizontal band of decoration around a room, building, mantel, etc. **2** a horizontal band, often ornamented with sculpture between the cornice and architrave of a building.

fruc ti fy (fruk'tə fī), *v*., **-fied, -fying.** —*v.i.* bear fruit. —*v.t.* make fruitful or productive; cause to bear fruit; fertilize. [<Latin *fructificare* < *fructus* fruit + *facere* make]

fru gal (frü'gəl), *adj*. **1** avoiding waste; tending to avoid unnecessary spending; saving; thrifty. **2** costing little; barely sufficient [<Latin *frugalis* < *frugi* temperate, useful, ultimately < *fructus* fruit, produce. See FRUIT.]

-ful, suffix added to nouns to form adjectives or other nouns. **1** full of ____: *Cheerful = full of cheer.* **2** showing ____: *Careful = showing care.* **3** having a tendency to ____: *Harmful = having a tendency to harm.* **4** enough to fill a ____: *Cupful = enough to fill a cup.* **5** that can be of ____: *Useful = that can be of use.* **6** having the qualities of ____: *Masterful = having the qualities of a master.* [Old English < adjective *full* full]

funk (fungk), INFORMAL. —*n*. **1** condition of panic or fear. **2** a depressed state of mind; bad mood —*v.t.* **1** be afraid of. **2** shrink from; shirk. —*v.i.* flinch or shrink through fear; try to back out of anything. [origin uncertain]

fur bish (fėr'bish), *v.t.* **1** brighten by rubbing or scouring; polish. **2** restore to good condition; make usable again. [< Old French *forbiss-,* a form of *forbir* to polish]

fur tive (fėr'tiv), *adj*. **1** done quickly and with stealth to avoid being noticed; secret. **2** sly; stealthy. —**fur'tive ly,** *adv*.

fus tian (fus'chən), *n*. a coarse, heavy cloth made of cotton and flax, used for clothing in Europe throughout the Middle Ages. —*adj*. made of fustian.

gall (gôl), *v.t.* **1** make sore by rubbing. **2** annoy; irritate. —*v.i.* become sore by rubbing.

gall ing (gô'ling), *adj*. that galls; chafing; irritating.

gam bol (gam'bəl), *n*. a running and jumping about in play; caper; frolic. —*v.i.* run and jump about in play; frolic.

gar ner (gär'nər), *v.t.* **1** gather and store away. **2** collect or deposit. —*n*. **1** storehouse for grain. **2** a store of anything.

gar nish (gär'nish), *n*. **1** something laid on or around food as a decoration. **2** decoration; trimming. —*v.t.* **1** decorate (food). **2** decorate; trim. [<Old French *garniss-,* a form of *garnir* provide, defend < Germanic. Related to WARN.]

gar ru lous (gar'ə ləs, gar'yə ləs), *adj*. **1** talking too much; talkative. **2** using too many words; wordy. [<Latin *garrulus* < *garrire* to chatter] —**gar'ru lous ly,** *adv*. —**gar'ru lousness,** *n*.

gaunt (gônt, gänt), *adj*. **1** very thin and bony; with hollow eyes and a starved look. **2** looking bare and gloomy; desolate. —**gaunt'ly,** *adv*. —**gaunt'ness,** *n*.

gaunt let (gônt'lit, gänt'lit), *n*. **1** a former punishment or torture in which the offender had to run between two rows of people who struck him or her with clubs or other weapons. **2 run the gauntlet, a** pass between two rows of people each of whom strikes the runner as he or she passes. **b** be exposed to unfriendly attacks or severe criticism. Also, **gantlet.** [< Swedish *gatlopp* a running through a lane]

geld ing (gel'ding), *n*. a horse that has been castrated.

gen ial (jē'nyəl), *adj*. **1** smiling and pleasant; cheerful and friendly; kindly. **2** helping growth; pleasantly warming; comforting. [< Latin *genialis,* literally, belonging to the genius < *genius* genius] —**ge ni al i ty** (jē'nē al'ə tē), *n*. —**gen'ial ly,** *adv*. —**gen'ial ness,** *n*.

GLOSSARY

991

gen teel (jen tēl′), *adj.* **1** belonging or suited to polite society, **2** polite; well-bred; fashionable; elegant. **—gen teel′ly,** *adv.*

gib bet (jib′it), *n.* **1** an upright post with a projecting arm at the top, from which the bodies of criminals were hung after execution. **2** gallows. —*v.t.* **1** hang on a gigget.

gibe (jīb), *v.,* **gibed, gib ing,** *n.* —*v.i.* speak in a sneering way; jeer; scoff; sneer. —*n.* a jeer; taunt; sneer. Also, **jibe.**

gim bals (jim′bəlz, gim′bləz), *n. pl.* device consisting of a pair of pivoting rings, one within the other and with axes at right angles to each other, for keeping an object horizontal, as a ship's compass by counteracting the roll and pitch of a ship. [earlier *gimmal* interlocking rings < Old French *gemel* twin < Latin *gemellus*]

glean (glēn), *v.t.* **1** gather (grain) left on a field by reapers. **2** gather little by little. —*v.i.* gather grain left on a field by reapers. **—glean′ er,** *n.*

glebe (glēb), *n.* **1** portion of land assigned to a parish church clergyman. **2** ARCHAIC. earth, soil, or land.

gloam (glōm), *n.* ARCHAIC. twilight.

goad (gōd), *n.* **1** a sharp-pointed stick for driving cattle; gad. **2** anything which drives or urges one on. —*v.t.* drive or urge on.

gos sa mer (gos′ə mər), *n.* **1** film or thread of cobweb spun by small spiders, which is seen floating in the air in calm weather. **2** a very thin, light cloth or coat. **3** anything very light and thin. —*adj.* like gossamer; very light and thin; filmy. [Middle English *gossomer* goose summer, name for "Indian summer," as the season for goose and cobwebs.]

gout (gout), *n.* drop, splash, or clot: *gouts of blood.*

gran dam (gran′dam), *n.* ARCHAIC. **1** grandmother. **2** an old woman. [< Anglo-French *graund dame,* literally, great lady]

gran dee (gran dē′), *n.* **1** a Spanish or Portuguese nobleman of the highest rank. **2** person of high rank or great importance.

greave (grēv), *n.* Often, **greaves,** *pl.* armor for the leg below the knee. [< Old French *greves,* plural]

groat (grōt), *n.* an old English silver coin worth fourpence.

grot (grot), *n.* cave or cavern.

ground (ground), *n.* piece of cloth used as background for embroidery or decoration. [Old English *grund* bottom]

grov el (gruv′əl, grov′əl), *v.,* **-eled, -el ing** or **-elled, -el ling.** **1** lie face downward; crawl at someone's feet; cringe. **2** abase or humble oneself.

gudg eon (guj′ən), *n.* a small Eurasian freshwater fish of the same family as the carp, that is often used for bait.

guer don (gèrd′n), *n., v.t.* reward. [< Old French *guerdoner* to reward < *guerdon* reward < Old High German *widarlōn* repayment]

guile (gīl), *n.* crafty deceit; sly tricks; cunning.

guin ea (gin′ē), *n.* a former British gold coin, not made since 1813, equal to 21 shillings.

gules (gyülz), *n. adj.* (in heraldry) red.

gut ter snipe (gut′ər snīp′), *n.* **1** urchin who lives in the streets. **2** any ill-bred person.

hab er dash er (hab′ər dash′ər), *n.* dealer in the things men wear, such as hats, ties, shirts, socks, etc.

hab i ta tion (hab′ə tā′shən), *n.* **1** place to live in; home; dwelling. **2** an inhabiting.

hag (hag) *n.* **1** a very ugly old woman, especially one who is vicious or malicious. **2** witch. [Middle English *hagge*]

hag gard (hag′ərd), *adj.* looking worn from pain, fatigue, worry, hunger, etc.; careworn; gaunt. [perhaps < Old French *hagard*]

hal low (hal′ō), *v.t.* **1** make holy; make sacred; sanctify. **2** honor as holy or sacred. [Old English *hālgian* < *hālig* holy]

hap ly (hap′lē), *adv.* ARCHAIC. by chance.

ha rangue (hə rang′), *n., v.,* **-rangued, -rangu ing.** —*n.* **1** a noisy, vehement speech. **2** a long, pompous, formal speech. —*v.t.* address (someone) with a harangue. —*v.i.* deliver a harangue.

har ass (har′əs, hə ras′), *v.t.* **1** trouble by repeated attacks; harry. **2** distress with annoying labor, care, misfortune, etc.; disturb; worry; torment. [< French *harasser* < Old French *harer* set

a dog on < *hare* a shout to excite dogs to attack] **—har′ ass ment,** *n.*

har bin ger (här′bən jər), *n.* one that goes ahead to announce another's coming; forerunner: *The robin is a harbinger of spring.* —*v.t.* announce beforehand; foretell. [< Old French *herbergere* provider of shelter (hence, one who goes ahead), ultimately < *herberge* lodging, of Germanic origin. Related to HARBOR.]

har mo ni ous (här mō′nē əs), *adj.* **1** agreeing in feelings, ideas, or actions; getting along well together; amicable. **2** arranged so that the parts are orderly or pleasing; going well together; congruous. **3** sweet-sounding; musical; melodious.

har mo ni um (här mō′nē əm), *n.* a small organ with metal reeds. [< French]

har row (har′ō), *n.* a heavy frame with iron teeth or upright disks, used by farmers to break up ground into fine pieces before planting seeds. —*v.t.* **1** pull a harrow over (land, etc.). **2** hurt; wound. **3** cause pain or torment to; distress.

har ry (har′ē), *v.,* **-ried, -ry ing.** —*v.t.* **1** raid and rob with violence; lay waste; pillage. **2** keep troubling; worry; torment. —*v.i.* make predatory raids. [Old English *hergian* < *here* army]

hart (härt), *n., pl.* **harts** or **hart.** a male deer, especially the male European red deer after its fifth year; stag. [Old English *heorot*]

hasp (hasp), *v.t.* ARCHAIC. enclose in armor; buckle.

hatch ment (hach′mənt), *n.* a square tablet set diagonally, bearing the coat of arms of a dead person.

ha ven (hā′vən), *n.* **1** harbor or port. **2** place of shelter and safety. [Old English *hæfen*]

head stall (hed′stôl′), *n.* the part of a bridle or halter that fits around a horse's head.

heark en (här′kən), *v.i.* pay attention to what is said; listen attentively; listen. Also, **harken.**

heart en (härt′n), *v.t.* cheer up; encourage. **—heart′en er,** *n.*

heath (hēth), *n.* **1** open wasteland with heather or low bushes growing on it, but few or no trees; moor. **2** heather. [Old English *hēth*]

hea then (hē′ᵺən), *n., pl.* **-thens** or **-then,** *adj.* —*n.* person who does not believe in the God of the Bible; person who is not a Christian, Jew, or Moslem; pagan. **—hea′then ness,** *n.*

help meet (help′mēt′), *n.* helpmate.

hem lock (hem′lok), *n.* **1** a poisonous plant of the same family as parsley, with spotted reddish-purple stems, finely divided leaves, and small white flowers. **2** poison made from it.

hent (hent), *n.* OBSOLETE. intent; purpose.

her mit age (hèr′mə tij), *n.* **1** dwelling place of a hermit. **2** a solitary or secluded dwelling place.

hie (hī), *v.,* **hied, hie ing** or **hy ing.** —*v.i.* go quickly; hasten; hurry. —*v.t.* cause to hasten. [Old English *hīgian*]

hi e rar chy (hī′ə rär′kē), *n., pl.,* **-chies.** **1** organization of persons or things arranged one above the other according to rank, class, or grade. **2** group of church officials or different ranks. [< Medieval Latin *hierarchia* < Greek *hieros* sacred + *archos* ruler]

hoar (hôr′ē, hōr), *adj.* hoary.

hoar frost (hôr′frôst′, hôr′frost′; hōr′frôst′, hōr′frost′), *n.* the white, feathery crystals of ice formed when dew freezes; rime.

hoar y (hôr′ē, hōr′ē), *adj.,* **hoar i er, hoar i est.** **1** white or gray. **2** white or gray with age. **3** old; ancient. **—hoar′i ness,** *n.*

holp (hōlp), *v,* ARCHAIC. a pp. of **help.**

hom age (hom′ij, om′ij), *n.* **1** dutiful respect; reverence. **2** (in the Middle Ages) a pledge of loyalty and service by a vassal to a lord. **3** thing done or given to show such acknowledgment. [<Old French < Medieval Latin *hominaticum* < Latin *hominem* human being, man]

hom i ly (hom′ə lē), *n., pl.* **-lies.** **1** sermon, usually on some part of the Bible. **2** serious moral talk or writing that warns, urges, or advises. [<Greek *homilia* < *homilos* a throng, assembly]

hos tel ry (hos′tl rē), *n., pl.* **-ries.** inn or hotel.

hul la ba loo (hul′ə bə lü′), *n., pl* **-loos.** a loud noise or disturbance; uproar.

hur dy-gur dy (hèr′dē gèr′dē), *n. pl.* **-dies.** hand organ.

hur ly-bur ly (hèr′lē bèr′lē), *n. pl.* **-lies.** disorder and noise; commotion; tumult.

hus band ry (huz′bən drē), *n.* **1** farming; *animal husbandry.* **2** careful management of one's affairs or resources; thrift. **3** ARCHAIC. economy.

hus sy (huz′ē, hus′ē), *n.*, *pl.* **-sies.** **1** a bad-mannered or pert girl. **2** an indecent or immoral woman. [Middle English *huswif* housewife]

ig no min i ous (ig′nə min′ē əs), *adj.* **1** shameful; disgraceful; dishonorable. **2** contemptible. **3** lowering one's dignity; humiliating. —**ig′no min′i ous ly,** *adv.*

il lu mine (i lü′mən), *v.t.*, **-mined, -min ing.** make bright; illuminate.

im mi nent (im′ə nənt), *adj.* likely to happen soon; about to occur. —**im′mi nent ly,** *adv.*

im pec ca ble (im pek′ə bəl), *adj.* **1** free from fault; irreproachable. **2** not capable of or liable to sin. [<Latin *impeccabilis* < *in-* not + *peccare* to sin] —**im pec′ca bly,** *adv.*

im ped i ment (im ped′ə mənt), *n.* **1** hindrance; obstruction. **2** some physical defect, especially a defect in speech.

im per cep ti ble (im′pər sep′tə bəl), *adj.* that cannot be perceived or felt; very slight, gradual, subtle, or indistinct. —**im′per cep′ti bly,** *adv.*

im per i ous (im pir′ē əs), *adj.* **1** haughty or arrogant; domineering; overbearing. **2** not to be avoided; necessary; urgent. —**im per′i ous ly,** *adv.* —**im per′i ous ness,** *n.*

im per turb a ble (im′pər tèr′bə bəl), *adj.* not easily excited or disturbed; calm. —**im′per turb′a ble ness,** *n.* —**im′per turb′a bly,** *adv.*

im pet u ous (im pech′ü əs), *adj.* acting or done with sudden or rash energy; hasty. —**im pet′u ously,** *adv.* —**im pet′u ous ness,** *n.*

im pe tus (im′pə təs), *n.* **1** the force with which a moving body tends to maintain its velocity and overcome resistance. **2** a driving force; cause of action or effort; incentive.

im pinge (im pinj′), *v.i.*, **-pinged, -ping ing.** **1** hit; strike. **2** trespass; encroach; infringe.

im pi ous (im′pē əs, im pī′əs), *adj.* not pious; not having or not showing reverence for God; wicked; profane. —**im′pi ous ly,** *adv.* —**im′pi ous ness,** *n.*

im por tune (im′pôr tün′, im′pôr tyün′, im pôr′chən), *v.*, **-tuned, -tun ing,** *adj.* —*v.t.* ask urgently or repeatedly; annoy with pressing demands. —*adj.* importunate.

im por tu ni ty (im′pôr tü′nə tē, im′pôr tyü′nə tē), *n.*, *pl.* **-ties.** persistence in asking; act of demanding again and again.

im pre ca tion (im′prə kā′shən), *n.* **1** an imprecating; cursing. **2** curse.

im preg na ble (im preg′nə bəl), *adj.* able to resist attack; not yielding to force, persuasion, etc. —**im preg′na bly,** *adv.*

im pu dence (im′pyə dəns), *n.* **1** a being impudent; shameless boldness; great rudeness; insolence. **2** impudent conduct or language.

im pu dent (im′pyə dənt), *adj.* shamelessly bold; very rude and insolent. —**im′pu dent ly,** *adv.*

im pute (im pyüt′), *v.t.*, **-put ed, -put ing.** consider as belonging; attribute; charge to a person or a cause; blame.

in-¹, *prefix.* not; the opposite of; the absence of: *Inexpensive = not expensive. Inattention = the absence of attention.* [<Latin]

in-², *prefix.* in; into; on; upon: *Incase = (put) into a case. Intrust = (give) in trust.* [<Latin < *in,* preposition]

in can ta tion (in′kan tā′shən), *n.* **1** set of words spoken as a magic charm or to cast a magic spell. **2** the use of such words.

in car nate (in kär′nit, in kär′nāt), *adj.* embodied in flesh, especially in human form; personified; typified. [< Latin *incarnatum,* < *in-* + *carnem* flesh]

in cense (in sens′), *v.t.*, **-censed, -cens ing.** make very angry; fill with rage. [< Latin *incensum* inflamed, enraged, set on fire < *in-* (intensive) + *candere* glow white]

in cer ti tude (in sèr′tə tüd, in sèr′tə tyüd), *n.* uncertainty; doubt.

in cip i ent (in sip′ē ənt), *adj.* just beginning; in an early stage; commencing. —**in cip′i ent ly,** *adv.*

in co her ent (in′kō hir′ənt), *adj.* **1** having or showing no logical connection of ideas; not coherent; disconnected; confused. **2** not sticking together; loose. —**in′co her′ent ly,** *adv.*

in con gru ous (in kong′grü əs), *adj.* **1** not appropriate; out of place. **2** lacking in agreement or harmony; not consistent. —**in con′gru ous ly,** *adv.* —**in con′gru ous ness,** *n.*

in con ti nen cy (in kon′tə nən sē), *n.* lack of self-control. Also, **incontinence.**

a hat	**i** it	**oi** oil	**ch** child		a in about
ā age	**ī** ice	**ou** out	**ng** long		e in taken
ä far	**o** hot	**u** cup	**sh** she	ə =	i in pencil
e let	**ō** open	**ů** put	**th** thin		o in lemon
ē equal	**ô** order	**ü** rule	**ŦH** then		u in circus
èr term			**zh** measure	**<** = derived from

in cor por al (in kôr′pər al), *adj.* OBSOLETE. incorporeal; not made of any material substance; insubstantial.

in cor ri gi ble (in kôr′ə jə bəl, in kor′ə jə bəl), *adj.* too firmly fixed in bad ways, an annoying habit, etc., to be reformed or changed. —**in cor′ri gi bly,** *adv.*

in cre du li ty (in′krə dü′lə tē, in′krə dyü′lə tē), *n.* lack of belief; doubt.

in cred u lous (in krej′ə ləs), *adj.* **1** not ready to believe; doubting; skeptical. **2** showing a lack of belief. **in cred′u lous ly,** *adv.*

in cul cate (in kul′kāt, in′kul kāt), *v.t.*, **-cat ed, -cat ing.** impress (ideas, opinions, etc.) on the mind of another by frequent repetition; teach persistently. [< Latin *inculcatum* impressed upon, originally, trampled in < *in-* in + *calcem* heel] —**in′cul ca′tion,** *n.* —**in cul′ca tor,** *n.*

in de fat i ga ble (in′di fat′ə gə bəl), *adj.* never getting tired or giving up; tireless. [< Latin *indefatigabilis* < *in-* not + *defatigare* tire out < *de-* completely + *fatigare* to tire]

in di gence (in′də jəns), *n.* extreme need; poverty.

in dis sol u ble (in′di sol′yə bəl), *adj.* that cannot be dissolved, undone, or destroyed; lasting; firm. —**in′dis sol′u bly,** *adv.*

in do lent (in′dl ənt), *adj.* disliking work; lazy; idle; —**in′do lent ly,** *adv.*

in due (in dü′, in dyü′), *v.t.*, **-dued, -du ing.** **1** provide with a quality or power; furnish; supply. **2** clothe. Also, **endue.**

in ert (in ėrt′), *adj.* **1** having no power to move or act; lifeless. **2** inactive; slow; sluggish. **3** with few or no active chemical, physiological, or other properties; rarely combining with other elements. [< Latin *inertem* idle, unskilled < *in-* without + *artem* art, skill] —**in ert′ly,** *adv.*

in ex pe di ent (in′ik spē′dē ənt), *adj.* not expedient; not practicable, suitable, or wise. —**in′ex pe′di ent ly,** *adv.*

in ex plic a ble (in′ik splik′ə bəl, in ek′splə kə bəl), *adj.* that cannot be explained, understood, or accounted for; mysterious.

in ex tri ca ble (in ek′strə kə bəl), *adj.* **1** that one cannot get out of. **2** that cannot be disentangled or solved.

in fal li ble (in fal′ə bəl), *adj.* **1** free from error; that cannot be mistaken. **2** absolutely reliable; sure. **3** (in the Roman Catholic Church) incapable of error in the exposition of doctrine on faith and morals (said of the pope as head of the church) —**in fal′li bly,** *adv.* [< *in-* + Medieval Latin *fallibilis* < Latin *fallere* deceive]

in fat u ate (in fach′ü āt), *v.t.*, **-at ed, -at ing.** **1** inspire with a foolish or extreme passion. **2** make foolish. [< *infatuatum* made foolish < *in-* + *fatuus* foolish]

in fer nal (in fèr′nl), *adj.* **1** of or having to do with hell. **2** of the lower world which the ancient Greeks and Romans thought of as the abode of the dead. **3** fit to have come from hell; hellish; diabolical. [< Late Latin *infernalis* < *infernus* hell < Latin, lower < *inferus* situated below] —**in fer′nal ly,** *adv.*

in firm (in fèrm′), *adj.* **1** lacking strength or health; physically weak or feeble, especially through age. **2** without a firm purpose; not steadfast; faltering. **3** not firm, solid, or strong.

in fir mi ty (in fèr′mə tē), *n.*, *pl.* **-ties.** **1** weakness; feebleness. **2** sickness; illness. **3** weakness, flaw, or defect in a person's character.

in form (in fôrm′), *v.t.* **1** give knowledge, facts, or news to; tell. **2** animate or inspire. **3** ARCHAIC. appear. —*v.i.* **1** make an accusation or complaint; accuse: *The thief who was caught informed against the others.* **2** give information. [< Latin *informare* give form to, instruct < *in-* into + *forma* form]

in fuse (in fyüz′), *v.t.*, **-fused, -fus ing.** **1** introduce as by pouring; put in; instill. **2** inspire.

in gen ious (in jē′nyəs), *adj.* **1** skillful in making; good at inventing. **2** cleverly planned or made. [< Latin *ingeniosus* < *ingenium* natural talent < *in-* in + *gignere* beget, be born] —**in gen′ious ly,** *adv.* **in gen′ious ly,** *adv.* —**in gen′ious ness,** *n.*

in gen u ous (in jen′yü əs), *adj.* **1** free from restraint or reserve; frank and open; sincere. **2** simple and natural; innocent; naïve. [< Latin *ingenuus,* originally, native < *in-* in + *gignere* beget] —**in gen′u ous ly,** *adv.* **in gen′u ous ness,** *n.*

in graft (in gaft′), *v.t.* **1** graft (a shoot, etc.) from one tree or plant into another. **2** fix in; implant. Also, **engraft.**

in gra ti ate (in grā′shē āt), *v.t.,* **-at ed, -at ing.** bring (oneself) into favor; make (oneself) acceptable. **in gra′ti at′ing ly,** *adv.*

in junc tion (in jungk′shən), *n.* **1** a formal order from a court of law ordering a person or group to do, or refrain from doing, something. **2** an authoritative or emphatic order; command.

in sa tia ble (in sā′shə bəl), *adj.* that cannot be satisfied; extremely greedy. —**in sa′tia bly,** *adv.*

in scru ta ble (in skrü′tə bəl), *adj.* that cannot be understood; so mysterious or obscure that one cannot make out its meaning; incomprehensible. —**in scru′ta bly.** *adv.*

in sid i ous (in sid′ē əs), *adj.* **1** seeking to entrap or ensnare; wily or sly; crafty; tricky. **2** working secretly or subtly; developing without attracting attention. —**in sid′i ous ly,** *adv.* —**in sid′i ous ness,** *n.* [< Latin *insidiosus* < *insidiae* ambush < *insidere* sit in < *in-* in + *sedere* sit]

in sin u ate (in sin′yü āt), *v.,* **-at ed, -at ing.** *v.t.* **1** suggest in an indirect way; hint. **2** push in or get in by an indirect, subtle way. —*v.i.* make insinuations. [< Latin *insinuatum* wound or twisted into < *in-* in + *sinus* a curve, winding]

in sip id (in sip′id), *adj.* **1** without any particular flavor; tasteless. **2** lacking interest or spirit; dull, colorless, or weak. —**in sip′id ly,** *adv.* —**in sip′id ness,** *n.* [< Late Latin *insipidus* < Latin *in-* not + *sapidus* tasty]

in so lent (in′sə lənt), *adj.* boldly rude; intentionally disregarding the feelings of others; insulting. [< Latin *insolentem* arrogant, contrary to custom < *in;* not + *solere* be accustomed]

in ter (in tėr′), *v.t.,* **-terred, -ter ring.** put (a dead body) into a grave or tomb; bury.

inter-, *prefix.* **1** one with the other; with or on each other; together. **2** between. **3** between or among a group. [< Latin < *inter* among, between, during, Related to UNDER.]

in ter ces sion (in′tər sesh′ən), *n.* **1** act or fact of interceding. **2** prayer pleading for others.

in ter dic tion (in′tər dik′shən), *n.* prohibition based on authority; formal order forbidding something.

in ter fuse (in′tər fyüz′), *v.t., v.i.,* **-fused, -fus ing. 1** spread through; be diffused through; permeate. **2** fuse together; blend; mix. [< Latin *interfusum* poured between < *inter-* between + *fundere* pour] —**in′ter fu′sion,** *n.*

in ter im (in′tər im), *n.* time between; the meantime. —*adj.* for the meantime; temporary.

in ter lude (in′tər lud), *n.* **1** anything thought of as filling the time between two things; interval. **2** piece of music played between the parts of a song, church service, play, etc. **3** entertainment between the acts of a play. [< Medieval Latin *interludium* < Latin *inter-* between + *ludus* a play]

in ter mit (in′tər mit′), *v.t., v.i.,* **-mit ted, -mit ting.** stop for a time; discontinue; suspend.

in ter stice (in tėr′stis), *n., pl.* **-sti ces** (-stə sēz′). a small or narrow space between things or parts; narrow chink, crack, or opening.

in tes tate (in tes′tāt, in tes′tit), *adj.* having made no will: *die intestate.* —*n.* person who has died without making a will.

in ti mate (in′tə māt), *v.t.,* **-mat ed, -mat ing. 1** suggest indirectly; hint. **2** make known; announce; notify. [< Latin *intimatum* made known, brought in < *intimus* inmost, superlative of *in* in] —**in′ti mat′er,** *n.*

in trep id (in trep′id), *adj.* very brave; fearless; dauntless; courageous. —**in trep′id ly,** *adv.* —**in trep′id ness,** *n.*

in trin sic (in trin′sik), *adj.* **1** belonging to a thing by its very nature; essential; inherent. **2** originating or being inside the part on which it acts. —**in trin′si cal ly,** *adv.*

in vest (in vest′), *v.t.* install in office with a ceremony.

in vet er ate (in vet′ər it), *adj.* **1** confirmed in a habit, practice, feeling, etc.; habitual. **2** long and firmly established; deeply rooted. [< Latin *inveteratum* grown old, long established < *in-* in + *vetus, veteris* old] —**in vet′er ate ly,** *adv.*

in vig o rate (in vig′ə rāt′, *v.t.,* **-rat ed, -rat ing.** give vigor to; fill with life and energy. —**in vig′o ra′tive,** *adj.*

in vin ci ble (in vin′sə bəl), *adj.* unable to be conquered; impossible to overcome; unconquerable. [< Latin *invincibilis* < *in-* not + *vincere* conquer]

in vo ca tion (in′və kā′shən), *n.* **1** a calling upon in prayer; appeal for help or protection. **2** a calling forth of spirits with magic words or charms. **3** set of magic words used to call forth spirits; incantation. [< Latin *invocationem* < *invocare.* See INVOKE.]

in voke (in vōk′), *v.t.,* **-voked, -vok ing. 1** call on in prayer; appeal to for help or protection. **2** appeal to for confirmation or judgment. **3** ask earnestly for; beg for.

ire (īr), *n.* anger; wrath. [< Old French < Latin *ira*]

ir re me di a ble (ir′i mē′dē ə bəl), *adj.* that cannot be corrected or remedied; incurable. —**ir′re me′di a bly,** *adv.*

ir res o lute (i rez′ə lüt), *adj.* not resolute; unable to make up one's mind; hesitating; vacillating.

ir re triev a ble (ir′i trē′və bəl), *adj.* that cannot be retrieved or recovered; impossible to recall or restore to its former condition. —**ir′re triev′a bil′i ty,** *n.* —**ir′re triev′a ble ness,** *n.* —**ir′re triev′a bly,** *adv.*

isth mus (is′məs), *n.* a narrow strip of land with water on both sides, connecting two larger bodies of land. [< Latin < Greek *isthmos*]

isthmus

ja cinth (jā′sinth, jas′inth), *n.* a reddish-orange gem.

joc und (jok′ənd, jō′kənd), *adj.* feeling, expressing, or communicating mirth or cheer; cheerful; merry; gay.

join ture (join′chər), *n.* property given to a woman at the time of her marriage. [< Old French < Latin *junctura* a joining < *jungere* to join. Doublet of JUNCTURE.]

joust (joust, just, jüst), *n.* **1** combat between two knights on horseback, armed with lances, especially as part of a tournament. **2 jousts,** *pl.* a tournament. —*v.i.* fight with lances on horseback.

jo vi al (jō′vē əl), *adj.* good-hearted and full of fun; good-humored and merry. [< Latin *Jovialis* of the planet Jupiter (those born under the planet's sign being supposedly cheerful) < *Jovis* Jove] —**jo′vi al ly,** *adv.* —**jo′vi al ness,** *n.*

ju bi lant (jü′bə lənt), *adj.* expressing or showing joy; rejoicing. [< Latin *jubilantem* < *jubilum* wild shout] —**ju′bi lant ly,** *adv.*

ju di cious (jü dish′əs), *adj.* having, using, or showing good judgment; wise; sensible. —**ju di′cious ly,** *adv.* —**ju di′cious ness,** *n.*

jump (jump), *v.i.* **1** spring from the ground; leap; bound. **2** give a sudden start or jerk. **3** rise suddenly. **4** (in checkers) pass over and capture an opponent's piece. **5** come (to) too quickly; arrive (at) too soon. **6** (in bridge) make a bid higher than necessary to raise a previous bid. **7** continue on another page of a newspaper or magazine. —*v.t.* **1** leap over. **2** cause to jump. **3** pounce upon; attack. **4** SLANG. evade by running away. **5** SLANG. get on by jumping. **6** go around; bypass, as an electric circuit. **7** skip over or pass over. **8** (in checkers) pass over and capture (an opponent's piece). **9** (in bridge) raise a partner's bid by more than one trick. **10** (of a train, subway, etc.) leave (rails or tracks). **11** ARCHAIC. risk.

junc ture (jungk′chər), *n.* **1** point or line where two things join; joint. **2** point of time, especially a critical time or state of affairs. **3** a joining.

ka lei do scope (kə lī′də skōp), *n.* **1** tube containing bits of colored glass and two mirrors. As it is turned, it reflects continually changing patterns. **2** a continually changing pattern or object.

ken (ken), *n.*, *v.*, **kenned** or **kent** (kent), **ken ning.** —*n.* **1** range of sight. **2** range of knowledge. —*v.t.* SCOTTISH. know. —*v.i.* SCOTTISH. have knowledge.

kin dle (kin′dl), *v.*, **-dled, -dling.** —*v.t.* **1** set on fire; light. **2** stir up; arouse. **3** light up; brighten. —*v.i.* **1** catch fire; begin to burn. **2** become stirred up or aroused.

kirk (kėrk), *n.* SCOTLAND AND NORTH ENGLAND. church.

kite (kīt), *n.* any of various falconlike hawks usually having long, pointed wings and a long notched or forked tail.

knave (nāv), *n.* **1** a tricky, dishonest man; rogue; rascal. **2** ARCHAIC. a male servant or any man of humble birth or position.

knav er y (nā′vər ē), *n.*, *pl.* **-er ies.** **1** behavior of a knave or rascal; trickery; dishonesty. **2** a tricky, dishonest act.

knead (nēd), *v.t.* **1** press or mix together (dough or clay) into a soft mass. **2** make or shape by kneading. **3** press and squeeze with the hands; massage.

knell (nel), *n.* **1** sound of a bell rung slowly after a death or at a funeral. **2** a warning sign of death, failure, etc. —*v.i.* **1** (of a bell) ring slowly, especially for a death or at a funeral; toll. **2** give a warning sign of death, failure, etc.

knoll (nōl), *v.i.* ARCHAIC. knell.

la bur num (lə bėr′nəm), *n.* any of a genus of small trees or shrubs of the pea family, having hanging clusters of bright-yellow flowers. [< Latinbc]

lab y rinth (lab′ə rinth′), *n.* **1** number of connecting passages so arranged that it is hard to find one's way from point to point; maze. **2** any confusing, complicated arrangement.

lag gard (lag′ərd), *n.* person who moves too slowly or falls behind; backward person. —*adj.* falling behind; backward. —**lag′gard ly,** *adv.* —**lag′gard ness,** *n.*

la i ty (lā′ə tē), *n.*, *pl.* **-ties.** the people who are not members of the clergy or of a professional class; laymen collectively.

la ment (lə ment′), *v.t.* **1** express grief for; mourn for. **2** regret. —*v.i.* express grief; mourn; weep. —*n.* **1** expression of grief or sorrow; wail. **2** poem, song, or tune that expresses grief.

lam en ta ble (lam′ən tə bəl, lə men′tə bəl), *adj.* **1** to be regreted or pitied; deplorable. **2** inferior; pitiful. —**lam′en ta bly,** *adv.*

lam en ta tion (lam′ən tā′shən), *n.* loud grief; cries of sorrow; mourning: wailing.

lan guish (lang′gwish), *v.i.* **1** become weak or weary; lose energy; droop. **2** suffer under any unfavorable conditions. **3** grow dull, slack, or less intense. **4** long or pine *(for)*. **5** assume a soft, tender look for effect.

lan guor ous (lang′gər əs), *adj.* **1** languid; without energy; weak; weary. **2** quiet; still. —**lan′guor ous ly,** *adv.*

lan yard (lan′yərd), *n.* a loose cord around the neck on which to hang a knife, whistle, etc. Also, **laniard.**

lar gess or **lar gesse** (lär′jis), *n.* **1** a generous giving. **2** a generous gift or gifts. [< Old French *largesse* < *large* generous]

lark (lärk), *n.* a merry adventure; frolic; prank. —*v.i.* have fun; play pranks; frolic. [origin uncertain]

la ryn go scope (lə ring′gə skōp), *n.* instrument with mirrors for examining the larynx.

las si tude (las′ə tüd, las′ə tyüd), *n.* lack of energy; weariness; languor. [< Latin *lassitudo* < *lassus* tired]

lat i tude (lat′ə tüd, lat′ə tyüd), *n.* room to act or think; freedom from narrow rules; scope.

lat tice (lat′is), *n.*, *v.*, **-ticed, -tic ing.** —*n.* **1** structure of crossed wooden or metal strips with open spaces between them. **2** window, gate, etc., having a lattice. —**lat′tice like′,** *adj.*

laud a ble (lô′də bəl), *adj.* worthy of praise; commendable. —**laud′a ble ness,** *n.* —**laud′a bly,** *adv.*

lave (lāv), *v.*, **laved, lav ing.** *v.t.* **1** wash; bathe. **2** wash or flow against; *The stream laves its banks.* —*v.i.* ARCHAIC. bathe.

lay (lā), *n.* **1** a short lyric or narrative poem to be sung. **2** song; tune. [< Old French *lai*]

lea (lē), *n.* a grassy field; meadow; pasture. [Old English *lēah*]

league (lēg), *n.* measure of distance, varying at different periods

a hat	i it	oi oil	ch child		a in about
ā age	ī ice	ou out	ng long		e in taken
ä far	o hot	u cup	sh she	ə =	i in pencil
e let	ō open	ù put	th thin		o in lemon
ē equal	ô order	ü rule	ŦH then		u in circus
ėr term			zh measure	< = derived from	

and in different countries, usually about 3 miles (5 kilometers).

lech er (lech′ər), *n.* person, especially a man, who indulges in lechery, a gross indulgence of lust.

lech er ous (lech′ər əs), *adj.* lewd; lustful. —**lech′er ous ly,** *adv.* —**lech′er ous ness,** *n.*

lee (lē), *n.* **1** shelter; protection. **2** side or part sheltered or away from the wind. —*adj.* sheltered or away from the wind. [Old English *hlēo*]

leech (lēch), *n.* person who tries persistently to get money and favors from others without doing anything to earn them; parasite.

lees (lēz), *n.pl.* **1** the most worthless part of anything; dregs. **2** sediment deposited in the container by wine and some other liquids. [< Old French *lias,* plural of *lie,* probably < Late Latin *lia*]

lee ward (lē′wərd, lü′ərd), *adj.*, *adv.* **1** on the side away from the wind. **2** in the direction toward which the wind is blowing. —*n.* side away from the wind; lee.

leg ate (leg′it), *n.* ambassador representative, especially a representative of the pope. [< Latin *legatus* < *legare* to delegate, originally, provide with a contract < *lex, legis* contract, law]

lep er ous (lep′ər əs), *adj.* OBSOLETE. leprous; of or like leprosy, a chronic, infectious disease that attacks the skin and nerves, causing lumps and spots.

lese maj es ty (lēz maj′ə stē), crime or offense against the sovereign power in a state; treason. [< Middle French *lèse-majesté* < Latin *laesa majestas* insulted sovereignty]

-less, *suffix forming adjectives from verbs and nouns.* **1** without a ____; that has no ____: *Homeless = without a home.* **2** that does not ____: *Ceaseless = that does not cease.* **3** that cannot be ____ed: *Countless = that cannot be counted.* [Old English *-lēas* < *lēas* without]

let (let), *n.*, *v.*, **let ted** or **let, let ting.** —*n.* **1 without let or hindrance,** with nothing to prevent, hinder, or obstruct. **2** interference with the ball in tennis and similar games, especially a serve that hits the net and must be played over. **3** ARCHAIC. prevention; hindrance; obstruction. —*v.t.* ARCHAIC. prevent; hinder; obstruct. [Old English *lettan* hinder < *læt* late]

lev y (lev′ē), *v.*, **lev ied, lev y ing,** *n.*, *pl.* **lev ies.** —*v.t.* **1** order to be paid. **2** draft or enlist (citizens) for an army. —*n.* **1** money collected by authority or force. **2** citizens drafted or enlisted for an army.

lex i con (lek′sə kən, lek′sə kon), *n.* **1** dictionary, especially of Greek, Latin, or Hebrew. **2** the vocabulary of a language or of a certain subject, group, or activity.

li ber ti cide (li bėr′ti sīd), *n.* destruction of liberty.

lib er tine (lib′ər tēn′), *n.* person without moral restraints; immoral or licentious person. —*adj.* without moral restraints.

liege (lēj), *n.*, *v.*, in the Middle Ages: **1** lord having a right to the homage and loyal service of his vassals. **2** vassal obliged to give homage and loyal service to his lord; liegeman. —*adj.* **1** having a right to the homage and loyal service of vassals. **2** obliged to give homage and loyal service to a lord.

liege man (lēj′mən), *n.*, *pl.* **-men.** **1** vassal. **2** a faithful follower.

lim it (lim′it), *n.* **1** farthest edge or boundary; point where something ends or must end. **2 limits,** *pl.* boundary; bounds. **3** (in mathematics) a value toward which terms of a sequence or values of a function approach indefinitely near. **4** an established maximum amount. **5 the limit,** SLANG. as much as, or more than, one can stand. —*v.t.* **1** set a limit to; restrict. **2** ARCHAIC. appoint. [< Latin *limitem* boundary] —**lim′it a ble,** *adj.*

lin e al (lin′ē əl), *adj.* in the direct line of descent. —**lin′e al ly,** *adv.*

GLOSSARY

lin net (lin′it), *n.* a small finch of Europe, Asia, and Africa, having brown or gray plumage, the color changing at different ages and seasons. [< Middle French *linette*]

lin tel (lin′tl), *n.* a horizontal beam or stone over a door, window, etc., to support the structure above it. [< Old French, threshold, ultimately < Latin *limitem* limit]

LINTEL →

← SILL

liq ue fac tion (lik′wə fak′shən), *n.* **1** act or process of liquefying. **2** liquefied condition.

liq uor (lik′ər), *n.* OBSOLETE. fluid.

list less (list′lis), *adj.* seeming too tired to care about anything; not interested in things; not caring to be active; languid. [< *list*⁴] —**list′less ly,** *adv.* —**list′less ness,** *n.*

lists (lists), *n.pl.* **1** place where knights fought in tournaments or tilts. **2** any place or scene of combat. **3 enter the lists,** join in a contest; take part in a fight, argument, etc. [Old English *liste* border]

lit a ny (lit′n ē), *n., pl.* **-nies. 1** prayer consisting of a series of words or requests said by a minister or priest and the congregation's responses. **2** a repeated series.

liv er y (liv′ər ē), *n., pl.* **-er ies. 1** any special uniform provided for the servants of a household, or adopted by any group or profession. **2** any characteristic dress, garb, or outward appearance. **3** the feeding, stabling, and care of horses for pay.

liv id (liv′id), *adj.* **1** having a dull-bluish or grayish color, as from a bruise. **2** very pale. **3** flushed; reddish. **4** very angry.

loath (lōth, lōᴛʜ), *adj.* unwilling or reluctant; averse. Also, **loth.** [Old English *lāth* hostile] —**loath′ness,** *n.*

loi ter (loi′tər), *v.i.* **1** linger idly or aimlessly on one's way; move or go in a slow or lagging manner. **2** waste time in idleness; idle; loaf. —*v.t.* spend (time) idly: *loiter the hours away.* [< Middle Dutch *loteren* be loose]

loll (lol), *v.i.* **1** recline or lean in a lazy manner. **2** hang loosely or droop; dangle. —*v.t.* allow to hang or droop. —*n.* a lolling. [Middle English *lollen*]

low (lō), *v.i., v.t.* make the sound of a cow; moo. —*n.* the sound a cow makes; mooing.

lu cid (lü′sid), *adj.* **1** marked by clearness of reasoning, expression, or arrangement; easy to follow or understand. **2** clear in intellect; rational; sane. **3** translucent; clear. —**lu′cid ly,** *adv.* —**lu′cid ness,** *n.*

lu di crous (lü′də krəs), *adj.* causing derisive laughter; amusingly absurd; ridiculous. [< Latin *ludicrus* < *ludus* sport]

lu gu bri ous (lü gü′brē əs, lü gyü′brē əs), *adj.* too sad; overly mournful. —**lu gu′bri ous ly,** *adv.* —**lu gu′bri ous ness,** *n.*

lu na cy (lü′nə sē), *n., pl.* **-cies. 1** insanity. **2** extreme folly. [< *lunatic*]

-ly¹, *suffix forming adverbs from adjectives.* **1** in a ____ manner: *Cheerfully = in a cheerful manner.* **2** in ____ ways or respects: *Financially = in financial respects.* **3.** to a ____ degree or extent: *Greatly = to a great degree.* **4** in, to, or from a ____ direction: *Northwardly = to or form the north.* **5** in a ____ place: *Thirdly = in the third place.* **6** at a ____ time: *Recently = at a recent time.* [Old English *-līce < -līc* -ly]

-ly², *suffix forming adjectives from nouns.* **1** like a ____: *Ghostly = like a ghost.* **2** like that of a ____; characteristic of a ____: *Sisterly = like that of a sister.* **3** suited to a ____; fit or proper for a ____: *Gentlemanly = suited to a gentleman.* **4** of each or every ____; occurring once per ____: *Daily = of every day.* **5** being a ____; that is a ____: *Heavenly = that is a heaven.* [Old English *-līc < līc* body, form]

mag nan i mous (mag nan′ə məs), *adj.* **1** noble in soul or mind; generous in forgiving; free from mean or petty feelings or acts; unselfish. **2** showing or arising from a generous spirit: *a magnanimous attitude toward a conquered enemy.* [< Latin *magnanimus < magnus* great + *animus* spirit] —**mag nan′i mous ly,** *adv.*

mail (māl), *n.* a flexible armor made of metal rings or small loops of chain linked together, or of overlapping plates, for protecting the body against arrows, spears, etc.

mal e fac tion (mal′ə fak′shən), *n.* an evil deed; crime.

ma lev o lence (mə lev′ə ləns), *n.* the wish that evil may happen to others; ill will; spite.

ma lev o lent (mə lev′ə lənt), *adj.* wishing evil to happen to others; showing ill will; spiteful. —**ma lev′o lent ly,** *adv.*

ma li cious (mə lish′əs), *adj.* **1** showing active ill will; wishing to hurt or make suffer; spiteful. **2** proceeding from malice: *malicious mischief.* —**ma li′cious ly,** *adv.* —**ma li′cious ness,** *n.*

man ci ple (man′sə pəl), *n.* a purchasing agent for a college or other institution; steward.

man date (man′dāt, man′dit), *n.* **1** an order or command: *a royal mandate.* **2** order from a higher court or official to a lower one.

man i fest (man′ə fest), *adj.* apparent to the eye or to the mind; plain; clear. —*v.t.* **1** show plainly; reveal; display. **2** put beyond doubt; prove. —*n.* list of cargo of a ship or aircraft. [< Latin *manifestus* palpable < *manus* hand + *-festus* (able to be) seized]

man i fold (man′ə fōld), *adj.* **1** of many kinds; many and various: *manifold duties.* **2** having many parts or forms. **3** doing many things at the same time. —*adv.* many times.

man na (man′ə), *n.* **1** (in the Bible) the food miraculously supplied to the Israelites in the wilderness. **2** food for the soul or mind. **3** any necessity unexpectedly supplied.

marge (märj), *n.* ARCHAIC. margin.

mark (märk), *n.* a former English coin.

marl (märl), *n.* a loose, crumbly soil containing clay and calcium carbonate, used as a fertilizer. —*v.t.* fertilize with marl.

mar tial (mär′shəl), *adj.* **1** of war; suitable for war. **2** such as war requires; brave; **3** given to fighting; warlike. [< Latin *Martialis* of Mars < *Mars* Mars] —**mar′tial ly,** *adv.*

mart let (märt′lit), *n.* a common European martin.

mat in (mat′n), *n.* the early morning.

mat ins (mat′nz), *n.pl.* **1** first of the seven canonical hours in the breviary of the Roman Catholic Church. **2** service for this hour, often joined to lauds. Also, **mattins** for 2.

mead (mēd), *n.* ARCHAIC. meadow. [Old English *mǣd*]

meal y (mē′lē), *adj.*, **meal i er, meal i est. 1** like meal; dry and powdery. **2** pale. **3** mealy-mouthed. **4** flecked as if with meal; spotty. —**meal′i ness,** *n.*

me an der (mē an′dər), *v.i.* **1** follow a winding course. **2** wander aimlessly. —*n.* **1** a winding course. **2** aimless wandering. **3** a loop in a river or stream.

med i ta tive (med′ə itā′tiv), *adj.* **1** fond of meditating; thoughtful. **2** expressing meditation. —**med′i ta′tive ly,** *adv.*

men dac i ty (men das′ə tē), *n., pl.* **-ties. 1** habit of telling lies; untruthfulness. **2** a lie; falsehood. [< Latin *mendacem* lying]

me ni al (mē′nē əl, mē′nyəl), *adj.* suited to or belonging to a servant; low; mean; servile. —*n.* servant who does the humblest and most unpleasant tasks. —**me′ni al ly,** *adv.*

mer ce nar y (mėr′sə ner′ē), *adj., n., pl.* **-nar ies.** —*adj.* **1** working for money only; acting with money as the motive. **2** done for money or gain. —*n.* **1** soldier serving for pay in a foreign army. **2** person who works merely for pay. [< Latin *mercenarius < merces* wages < *merx, mercis* wares]

mere (mir), *n.* ARCHAIC. lake or pond. [Old English, body of water]

met a phys i cal (met′ə fiz′ə kəl), *adj.* **1** of or having to do with metaphysics. **2** highly abstract; hard to understand; abstruse. **3** ARCHAIC. supernatural. —**met′a phys′i cal ly,** *adv.*

met a phy si cian (met′ə fə zish′ən), *n.* person skilled in or familiar with metaphysics, a branch of philosophy that tries to discover and explain reality and knowledge.

mete (mēt), *v.t.*, **met ed, met ing. 1** give to each person a proper or fair share; distribute; allot. [Old English *metan*]

met tle (met′l), *n.* **1** quality of disposition or temperament. **2** spirit; courage. **3 on one's mettle,** ready to do one's best. [variant of *metal*]

met tle some (met′l səm), *adj.* full of mettle; spirited; courageous.

mew (myü), *n.* **1** sound made by a cat or kitten; meow. **2** a similar sound made by certain birds. —*v.i.* make this sound; meow. [probably imitative]

mid dling (mid′ling), *adj.* medium in size, quality, grade, etc.; ordinary; average. —*adv.* INFORMAL OR DIALECT. moderately; fairly. —*n.* **middlings,** *pl.* **a** products of medium size, quality, grade, or price. **b** coarse particles of ground wheat mixed with bran, used in making a very nutritious flour. [< *mid-* + Old English *-ling* condition] —**mid′dling ly,** *adv.*

mien (mēn), *n.* manner of holding the head and body; way of acting and looking; bearing; demeanor: *the mien of a judge.*

mil len ni al (mə len′ē əl), *adj.* **1** of a thousand years. **2** like that of the millennium; fit for the millennium. —**mil len′ni al ly,** *adv.*

min ion (min′yən), *n.* **1** servant or follower willing to do whatever is ordered; servile or obsequious person. **2** a darling; favorite.

mi nu ti ae (mi nü′shē ē, mi nyü′shē ē), *n.pl.* very small matters; trifling details. [< Latin, trifles, plural of *minutia* smallness < *minutum* made small]

mis-, *prefix.* **1** bad: *Misgovernment = bad government.* **2** badly: *Misbehave = behave badly.* **3** wrong: *Mispronunciation = wrong pronunciation.* **4** wrongly: *Misapply = apply wrongly.* [Old English or < Old French *mes-*]

mis al li ance (mis′ə lī′əns), *n.* an unsuitable alliance or association, especially in marriage.

mis chance (mis chans′), *n.* **1** bad luck; misfortune. **2** piece of bad luck; unlucky accident.

mis cre ant (mis′krē ənt), *n.* a base or wicked person; villain.

mis hap (mis′hap, mis hap′), *n.* an unlucky accident.

mis sive (mis′iv), *n.* a written message; letter.

mit i gate (mit′ə gāt), *v.t., v.i.,* **-gat ed, -gat ing.** make or become mild or milder; make or become less harsh; soften. Anger, grief, pain, punishments, heat, cold, and many other conditions may be mitigated. [< Latin *mitigatum* made gentle < *mitis* gentle]

miz zen or **miz en** (miz′n), *n.* **1** a fore-and-aft sail on the mizzenmast. **2** mizzenmast. —*adj.* of or on the mizzenmast. [< Middle French *misaine* < Italian *mezzana* < Latin *medianus* in the middle < *medius* middle]

mod i cum (mod′ə kəm), *n.* a small or moderate quantity.

mort (môrt), *n.* a great quantity.

mor ti fi ca tion (môr′tə fə kā′shən), *n.* **1** a feeling of shame; humiliation. **2** cause or source of shame or humiliation.

mor ti fy (môr′tə fī), *v.t., v.i.,* **-fied, -fy ing.** **1** wound the feelings of; make feel humbled and ashamed; humiliate. **2** overcome (bodily desires and feelings) by pain and self-denial. [< Old French *mortifier* < Latin *mortificare* to kill < *mortem* death + *facere* to make]

mo sa ic (mō zā′ik), *n.* **1** decoration made of small pieces of stone, glass, wood, etc., of different colors inlaid to form a picture or design. **2** such a picture or design. Mosaics are used in the floors, walls, or ceilings of some fine buildings. **3** art or process of making such a picture or design. **4** anything like a mosaic. **5** mosaic disease. —*adj.* formed by, having to do with, or resembling a mosaic. [< Medieval Latin *mosaicus, musaicus* of the Muses, artistic]

mote (mōt), *n.* **1** speck of dust. **2** any very small thing.

mot ley (mot′lē), *adj.* **1** made up of parts or kinds that are different or varied. **2** of different colors like a clown's suit.

moun te bank (moun′tə bangk), *n.* **1** person who sells quack medicines in public, appealing to the audience by tricks, stories, etc. **2** anybody who tries to deceive people by tricks, stories, etc.; charlatan.

mul ti tude (mul′tə tüd, mul′tə tyüd), *n.* a great many; crowd; host. [< Latin *multitudo* < *multus* much]

mul ti tu di nous (mul′tə tüd′n əs, mul′tə tyüd′n əs), *adj.* **1** forming a multitude; very numerous; existing or occurring in great numbers. **2** including many parts, elements, items, or features. —**mul′ti tu′di nous ness,** *n.*

mu nif i cence (myü nif′ə səns), *n.* very great generosity. [< Latin *munificentia,* ultimately < *munus* gift + *facere* to make]

mu se um (myü zē′əm), *n.* building or rooms where a collection of objects illustrating science, ancient life, art, history, or other subjects is kept and displayed. [< Latin < Greek *mouseion* seat of the Muses < *Mousa* Muse]

must (must), *n.* a state of violent destructiveness, occurring peri-

odically in male elephants. —*adj.* become violently destructive.

mus ter (mus′tər), *v.t.* **1** gather together; assemble; collect. **2** summon. **3** number; comprise. **4 muster in,** enlist. **5 muster out,** discharge. —*v.i.* come together; gather; assemble. —*n.* **1** assembly; collection. **2** a bringing together of troops or others for review, service, roll call, etc. **3** list of those assembled; roll. **4** the number assembled. **5 pass muster,** be inspected and approved; meet the required standards. [< Old French *mostrer* < Latin *monstrare* to show < *monstrum* portent]

mu ti nous (myüt′n əs), *adj.* **1** given to or engaged in mutiny; rebellious. **2** like or involving mutiny; characterized by mutiny. **3** not controllable; unruly. —**mu′ti nous ly,** *adv.* —**mu′ti nous ness,** *n.*

myr tle (mėr′tl), *n.* any of a genus of shrubs of the myrtle family, especially an evergreen shrub of southern Europe with shiny leaves, fragrant white flowers, and black berries.

na ive ty (nä ēv′tē), *n., pl.* **-ties.** naïveté; unspoiled freshness or artlessness.

nec tar (nek′tər), *n.* **1** (in Greek and Roman myths) the drink of the gods. **2** any delicious drink. **3** a sweet liquid found in many flowers. [< Latin < Greek *nektar*] —**nec′tar like′,** *adj.*

neg li gent (neg′lə jənt), *adj.* **1** given to or showing neglect; neglectful. **2** careless; indifferent. —**neg′li gent ly,** *adv.*

-ness, *suffix added to adjectives to form nouns.* **1** quality or condition of being ____: *Preparedness = condition of being prepared.* **2** ____ action; ____ behavior: *Carefulness = careful action; careful behavior.* [Old English *-ness, -niss*]

ni ce ty (nī′sə tē), *n., pl.* **-ties.** **1** carefulness and delicacy in handling; exactness; accuracy. **2 to a nicety,** just right.

nig gard (nig′ərd), *n.* a stingy person; miser. —*adj.* stingy.

nigh (nī), *adv.* **1** near (in position, time, relationship, etc.). **2** nearly; almost. —*adj.* **1** near; close. **2** (of one of a team of horses) left; near. —*prep.* near. —*v.t., v.i.* ARCHAIC. draw near. [Old English *nēah*]

noc tur nal (nok tėr′nl), *adj.* **1** of the night. **2** in the night. —**noc tur′nal ly,** *adv.* [< Latin *nocturnus* of the night < *noctem* night]

no mad (nō′mad, nom′ad), *n.* **1** member of a tribe that moves from place to place to have food or pasture for its cattle. **2** wanderer. —*adj.* **1** wandering from place to place to find pasture. **2** wandering. [< Greek *nomados,* ultimately < *nemein* to pasture]

no mad ic (nō mad′ik), *adj.* of nomads or their life; wandering.

no men cla ture (nō′mən klā′chər, nō men′klə chər), *n.* set or system of names or terms: *the nomenclature of music.* [< Latin *nomenclatura < nomen* name + *calare* to call]

non cha lant (non′shə lənt, non′shə länt′), *adj.* without enthusiasm; coolly unconcerned; indifferent.

nose gay (nōz′gā′), *n.* bunch of flowers; bouquet. [< *nose* + obsolete *gay* something gay or pretty]

nought (nôt), *n.* **1** nothing. **2** zero; 0. Also, naught. [Old English *nāwiht < nā* no + *wiht* thing]

nun ner y (nun′ər ē), *n., pl.* **-ner ies.** building or buildings where nuns live; convent.

nu tri ment (nü′trə mənt, nyü′trə mənt), *n.* that which is required by an organism for life and growth; nourishment; food.

ob dur ate (ob′dər it, ob′dyər it), *adj.* **1** stubborn or unyielding; obstinate. **2** hardened in feelings or heart; not repentant. [< Latin *obduratum* hardened < *ob-* against + *durare* harden] —**ob′dur ate ly,** *adv.* —**ob′dur ate ness,** *n.*

o blique (ə blēk′; *military* ə blīk′), *adj., v.,* **o bliqued,**

o bliquing.—*adj.* **1** neither perpendicular to nor parallel with a given line or surface; not straight up and down or straight across; slanting. **2** not straightforward; indirect. —*v.i., v.t.* have or take an oblique direction; slant. —**o blique′ly,** *adv.*

o bliq ui ty (ə blik′wə tē), *n., pl.* **-ties. 1** indirectness or crookedness of thought, speech, or behavior, especially conduct that is not upright and moral. **2** inclination, or degree of inclination.

o blit e rate (ə blit′ə rāt′), *v.t.,* **-rat ed, -rat ing. 1** remove all traces of; blot out; efface: *The heavy rain obliterated the footprints.* **2** blot out so as to leave no distinct traces; make unrecognizable.

o bliv i on (ə bliv′ē ən), *n.* **1** condition of being entirely forgotten: *Many ancient cities have long since passed into oblivion.* **2** fact of forgetting; forgetfulness. [< Latin *oblivionem* < *oblivisci* forget]

o bliv i ous (ə bliv′ē əs), *adj.* **1** not mindful; forgetful: *The book was so interesting that I was oblivious of my surroundings.* **2** bringing or causing forgetfulness. —**o bliv′i ous ly,** *adv.* —**o bliv′i ous ness,** *n.*

oblivious (def. 1)—The photographer was oblivious of approaching danger.

ob se quies (ob′sə kwēz), *n.pl.* funeral rites or ceremonies; stately funeral.

ob se qui ous (əb sē′kwē əs), *adj.* polite or obedient from hope of gain or from fear; servile; fawning. [< Latin *obsequiosus* < *obsequium* dutiful service < *ob-* after + *sequi* follow]

ob sti na cy (ob′stə nə sē), *n., pl.* **-cies. 1** a being obstinate; stubbornness. **2** an obstinate act.

ob sti nate (ob′stə nit), *adj.* **1** not giving in; stubborn. **2** hard to control, treat, or remove; persistent. [< Latin *obstinatum* determined < *ob-* by + *stare* to stand] —**ob′sti nate ly,** *adv.*

oc cult (ə kult′, ok′ult), *adj.* **1** beyond the bounds of ordinary knowledge; mysterious. **2** outside the laws of the natural world; magical. **3** not disclosed; secret; revealed only to the initiated. —*n.* **the occult,** forces beyond ordinary knowledge supposed to involve the supernatural. —*v.t.* (v.i.) (in astronomy) block or be blocked from sight. [< Latin *occultum* hidden < *ob-* up + *celare* to hide] —**oc cult′ly,** *adv.* —**oc cult′ness,** *n.*

oc ta vo (ok tā′vō, ok tä′vō), *n., pl.* **-vos. 1** the page size of a book in which each leaf is one eighth of a whole sheet of paper. **2** book having pages of this size, usually about 6 by 9 inches (15 by 23 centimeters). [< Medieval Latin *in octavo* in an eighth]

o di ous (ō′dē əs), *adj.* very displeasing; hateful; offensive. [< Latin *odiosus* < *odium* odium] —**o′di ous ly,** *adv.* —**o′di ous ness,** *n.*

of fal (ô′fəl, of′əl), *n.* **1** the waste parts of an animal killed for food. **2** garbage; refuse. [< *off* + *fall*]

of fi cious (ə fish′əs), *adj.* too ready to offer services or advice; minding other people's business; meddlesome. —**of fi′cious ly,** *adv.* —**of fi′cious ness,** *n.*

o men (ō′mən), *n.* **1** sign of what is to happen; object or event that is believed to mean good or bad fortune; augury; presage. **2** prophetic meaning; foreboding. —*v.t.* be a sign of; presage; forebode.

om i nous (om′ə nəs), *adj.* unfavorable; threatening: *ominous clouds.* —**om′i nous ly,** *adv.* —**om′i nous ness,** *n.*

om nip o tent (om nip′ə tənt), *adj.* **1** having all power; almighty. **2** having very great power or influence. —*n.* **the Omnipotent,** God. —**om nip′o tent ly,** *adv.*

o paque (ō pāk′), *adj.* **1** not letting light through; not transparent or translucent. **2** not conducting heat, sound, electricity, etc. **3** not shining; dark; dull. **4** hard to understand; obscure. **5** stupid. —*n.* something opaque. [< Latin *opacus* dark, shady]

o pi ate (ō′pē it, ō′pē āt), *n.* **1** any medical preparation containing opium or a derivative of opium and used especially to dull pain or bring sleep. **2** anything that quiets, soothes, etc.

op u lent (op′yə lənt), *adj.* **1** having wealth; rich. **2** showing wealth; costly and luxurious: *an opulent home.* **3** abundant; plentiful: *opulent hair.* [< Latin *opulentem* < *ops* power, resources] —**op′u lent ly,** *adv.*

o ra cle (ôr′ə kəl, or′ə kəl), *n.* **1** (in ancient Greece and Rome) an answer believed to be given by a god through a priest or priestess to some question. **2** place where the god was believed to give such answers. **3** the priest, priestess, or other means by which the god's answer was believed to be given. **4** a very wise person. **5** a very wise answer. [< Latin *oraculum* < *orare* speak formally]

o rac u lar (ô rak′yə lər, ō rak′yə lər), *adj.* **1** of or like an oracle. **2** with a hidden meaning that is ambiguous or difficult to make out. **3** very wise. —**o rac′u lar ly,** *adv.*

o ra to ry (ôr′ə tôr′ē, ôr′ə tōr′ē; or′ə tôr′ē, or′ə tōr′ē), *n., pl.* **-ries.** a small chapel, room, or other place set apart for private prayer. [< Late Latin *oratorium* < Latin *orare* plead, pray]

or chis (ôr′kis), *n.* orchid, especially any of a genus of terrestrial orchids of temperate regions. A common North American species has a spike of pink-purple flowers with a white lip.

ord nance (ôrd′nəns), *n.* **1** cannon or artillery. **2** military apparatus or supplies of all kinds, such as weapons, vehicles, ammunition, etc. [variant of *ordinance*]

o ri son (ôr′ə zən, or′ə zən; ôr′ə sən, or′ə sən), *n.* prayer.

or ni thol o gist (ôr′nə thol′ə jist), *n.* an expert in ornithology, a branch of zoology dealing with the study of birds.

os ten ta tious (os′ten tā′shəs), *adj.* **1** done for display; intended to attract notice. **2** showing off; liking to attract notice. —**os′ten ta′tious ly,** *adv.* —**os′ten ta′tious ness,** *n.*

ot to man (ot′ə mən), *n.* **1** a low, cushioned seat without back or arms. **2** a cushioned footstool.

-ous, *suffix forming adjectives from nouns.* **1** full of; having much; having: *Joyous* = *full of joy.* **2** characterized by: *Zealous* = *characterized by zeal.* **3** having the nature of: *Idolatrous* = *having the nature of an idolater.* **4** of or having to do with: *Monogamous* = *having to do with monogamy.* **5** like: *Thunderous* = *like thunder.* **6** committing or practicing: *Bigamous* = *practicing bigamy.* **7** inclined to: *Blasphemous* = *inclined to blasphemy.* **8** (in chemistry) indicating the presence in a compound of the designated element in a lower valence than indicated by the suffix *-ic,* as in *stannous, ferrous, sulfurous.* [< Old French *-os, -us* < Latin *-osum*]

o ver ture (ō′vər chər, ō′vər chùr), *n.* **1** proposal or offer. **2** a musical composition played by the orchestra as an introduction to an opera, oratorio, or other long musical composition.

pac tion (pak′shən), *n.* an agreement.

pad (pad), *v.,* **pad ded, pad ding,** *n.* —*v.t.* walk along (a path, road, etc.); tramp; trudge. —*v.i.* **1** go on foot; tramp or trudge along; walk. **2** walk or trot softly. —*n.* **1** a dull sound, as of footsteps on the ground. **2** a slow horse for riding on a road. [probably < earlier Dutch, *path*]

pa go da (pə gō′də), *n.* temple or other sacred building having many stories, with a roof curving upward from each story, found in India, China, Japan, and other Asian countries. [< Portuguese *pagode* < Tamil *pagavadi* < Sanskrit *bhagavatī* goddess]

pal frey (pôl′frē), *n., pl.* **-freys.** ARCHAIC. a gentle riding horse, especially one used by women.

palm er (pä′mər, päl′mər), *n.* **1** pilgrim returning from the Holy Land bringing a palm branch as a token. **2** any pilgrim.

palm y (pä′mē, päl′mē), *adj.,* **palm i er, palm i est. 1** abounding in or shaded by palms. **2** flourishing; prosperous.

pal pa ble (pal′pə bəl), *adj.* **1** readily seen or heard and recognized; obvious. **2** that can be touched or felt; tangible.

pal pi ta tion (pal′pə tā′shən), *n.* **1** a very rapid beating of the heart; throb. **2** a quivering; trembling.

pal sy (pôl′zē), *n., pl.* **-sies,** *v.,* **-sied, -sy ing.** —*n.* paralysis, especially a form of paralysis occurring with Parkinson's disease. —*v.t.* afflict with palsy.

pal ter (pôl′tər), *v.i.* **1** talk or act insincerely; trifle deceitfully. **2** act carelessly; trifle. **3** haggle. [origin unknown] —**pal′ter er,** *n.*

pal try (pôl′trē), *adj.,* **-tri er, -tri est. 1** almost worthless; trifling; petty; mean. **2** of no worth; despicable; contemptible. [probably related to Low German *paltrig* ragged, torn]

pan de mo ni um (pan′də mō′nē əm), *n.* **1** place of wild disorder or lawless confusion. **2** wild uproar or lawlessness. **3 Pandemonium, a** abode of all the demons; hell. **b** hell's capital. In Milton's *Paradise Lost,* it is the palace built by Satan as the central part of hell. [< Greek *pan-* + *daimōn* demon]

par a gon (par′ə gon), *n.* model of excellence or perfection.

par a sol (par′ə sôl, par′ə sol), *n.* a light umbrella used as a protection from the sun.

par ley (pär′lē), *n., pl.* **-leys. 1** conference or informal talk. **2** an informal discussion with an enemy during a truce about terms of surrender, exchange of prisoners, etc. —*v.i.* **1** discuss terms, especially with an enemy. **2** ARCHAIC. speak; talk. [< Old French *parlee,* past participle of *parler* speak < Late Latin *parabolare* < *parabola* speech, story]

par ri cide (par′ə sīd), *n.* **1** act of killing one's parent or parents. **2** person who kills his or her parent or parents.

par si mo ny (pä′sə mō′nē), *n.* extreme economy; stinginess. [< Latin *parsimonia* < *parcere* to spare]

par ti cle (pär′tə kəl), *n.* **1** a very little bit. **2** any of the extremely small units that make up matter, such as a molecule, atom, electron, proton, or neutron. [< Latin *particula,* diminutive of *partem* part]

pate (pāt), *n.* top of the head; head: *a bald pate.* [Middle English]

pa thos (pā′thos), *n.* **1** quality in speech, writing, music, events, or a scene that arouses a feeling of pity or sadness; power of evoking tender or melancholy emotion. **2** a pathetic expression or utterance. [< Greek, suffering, feeling < *path-,* stem of *paschein* suffer]

peer less (pir′lis), *adj.* without an equal; matchless. —**peer′less ly,** *adv.* —**peer′less ness,** *n.*

pelf (pelf), *n.* money or riches, thought of as bad or degrading. [< Old French *pelfre* spoils]

pe nal (pē′nl), *adj.* **1** of, having to do with, or given as punishment. **2** liable to be punished.

pend ent (pen′dənt), *adj.* **1** hanging; suspended. **2** overhanging. **3** pending.

pe nur i ous (pi nùr′ē əs, pi nyùr′ē əs), *adj.* **1** mean about spending or giving money: stingy. **2** in a condition of penury; extremely poor. —**pe nur′i ous ly,** *adv.* —**pe nur′i ous ness,** *n.*

pen ur y (pen′yər ē), *n.* great poverty; extreme want; destitution. [< Latin *penuria* want, need]

per-, *prefix.* throughout; thoroughly; utterly; very: *Perfervid = very fervid. Peruse = use* (i.e., read) *thoroughly.* [< Latin, through, thoroughly, to the end, to destruction]

per chance (pər chans′), *adv.* perhaps. [< Anglo-French *par chance* by chance]

per di tion (pər dish′ən), *n.* **1** loss of one's soul and the joys of heaven; damnation. **2** hell. **3** utter loss or destruction; complete ruin.

pe remp tor y (pə remp′tər ē, per′əmp tôr′ē, per′əmp tōr′ē), *adj.* **1** leaving no choice; decisive; final; absolute. **2** allowing no denial or refusal. **3** imperious; dictatorial. [< Latin *peremptorius* that puts an end to, ultimately < *per-* to the end + *emere* to take] —**pe remp′tor i ly,** *adv.* —**pe remp′tor i ness,** *n.*

per fid i ous (pər fid′ē əs), *adj.* deliberately faithless; treacherous. —**per fid′i ous ly,** *adv.* —**per fid′i ous ness,** *n.*

per force (pər fôrs′, pər fōrs′), *adv.* by necessity; necessarily. [< Old French *par force* by force]

per func tor y (pər fungk′tər ē), *adj.* done merely for the sake of getting rid of the duty; done from force of habit; mechanical; indifferent. [< Late Latin *perfunctorius* < Latin *per-* through + *fungi* execute] —**per func′tor i ly,** *adv.* —**per func′tor i ness,** *n.*

per ni cious (pər nish′əs), *adj.* **1** that will destroy or ruin; causing great harm or damage; very injurious. **2** fatal; deadly. [< Latin *perniciosus,* ultimately < *per-* completely + *necis* death] —**per ni′cious ly,** *adv.* —**per ni′cious ness,** *n.*

per plex i ty (pər plek′sə tē), *n., pl.* **-ties. 1** a perplexed condition; being puzzled; confusion; bewilderment. **2** an entangled or confused state. **3** something that perplexes.

per snick e ty (pər snik′ə tē), *adj.* INFORMAL. **1** overly fastidious; fussy. **2** requiring precise and careful handling. Also, **persnickety.** [origin uncertain]

per spi cu i ty (pér′spə kyü′ə tē), *n.* ease in being understood; clearness in expression; lucidity.

per spic u ous (pər spik′yü əs), *adj.* easily understood; clear; lucid. —**per spic′u ous ly,** *adv.* —**per spic′u ous ness,** *n.*

per ti nac i ty (pèrt′n as′ə tē), *n.* great persistence; holding firmly to a purpose, action, or opinion.

pe rus al (pə rü′zəl), *n.* **1** a careful reading. **2** a detailed examination.

pe ruse (pə rüz′), *v.t.,* **-rused, -rus ing. 1** read, especially thoroughly and carefully. **2** examine in detail, in order to learn; look at with attention.

per verse (pər vèrs′), *adj.* **1** contrary and willful; obstinately opposing what is wanted, reasonable, or required. **2** persistent in wrong. **3** morally bad; perverted; depraved. **4** not correct; wrong: *perverse reasoning.* [< Latin *perversum* turned away, perverted] —**per verse′ly,** *adv.* —**per verse′ness,** *n.*

pes tif er ous (pe stif′ər əs), *adj.* **1** bringing disease or infection; pestilential. **2** bringing moral evil; pernicious. **3** troublesome; annoying. —**pes tif′er ous ly,** *adv.*

pes ti lence (pes′tl əns), *n.* **1** any infectious or contagious epidemic disease that spreads rapidly, often causing many deaths. **2** the bubonic plague.

pes ti lent (pes′tl ənt), *adj.* **1** often causing death. **2** harmful to morals; destroying peace; pernicious. **3** troublesome; annoying. [< Latin *pestilentem* < *pestis* plague]

pet ri fy (pet′rə fī), *v.,* **-fied, -fy ing.** —*v.t.* **1** turn into stone; change (organic matter) into a substance like stone. **2** make hard as stone; stiffen; deaden. **3** paralyze with fear, horror, or surprise: *The bird was petrified as the snake came near.* —*v.i.* **1** become stone or a substance like stone. **2** become rigid like stone; harden. [< French *pétrifier* < Latin *petra* stone + *facere* make]

pet u lance (pech′ə ləns), *n.* a being petulant; peevishness.

pet u lant (pech′ə lənt), *adj.* likely to have little fits of bad temper; irritable over trifles; peevish. [< Latin *petulantem*] —**pet′u lant ly,** *adv.*

phos pho res cence (fos′fə res′ns), *n.* **1** act or process of giving out light without burning or any very slow burning without noticeable heat. **2** light given out in this way. **3** (in physics) light given off by a substance as a result of the absorption of certain rays, as X rays or ultraviolet rays, and continuing for a period of time after the substance has ceased to be exposed to these rays.

phos pho res cent (fos′fə res′nt), *adj.* showing phosphorescence.

phys ic (fiz′ik), *n., v.,* **-icked, -ick ing.** —*n.* medicine, especially one that acts as a laxative. —*v.t.* **1** give a laxative to. **2** give medicine to. **3** act like a medicine on; cure.

phys i og no my (fiz′ē og′nə mē, fiz′ē on′ə mē), *n., pl.* **-mies. 1** kind of features or type of face one has; one's face. **2** art of estimating character from the features of the face or the form of the body. **3** the general aspect or looks of a countryside, a situation, etc. [< Greek *physis* nature + *gnōmon* judge < *gnōnai* recognize]

pique (pēk), *n., v.,* **piqued, pi quing.** —*n.* a feeling of anger at being slighted; wounded pride. —*v.t.* **1** cause a feeling of anger in; wound the pride of.

plac id (plas′id), *adj.* pleasantly calm or peaceful; quiet. [< Latin *placidus* < *placere* to please] —**plac′id ly,** *adv.* —**plac′id ness,** *n.*

plaint (plānt), *n.* **1** complaint. **2** ARCHAIC. lament.

plain tive (plān′tiv), *adj.* expressive of sorrow; mournful; sad. [< Old French *plaintif* < *plaint* plaint] —**plain′tive ly,** *adv.* —**plain′tive ness,** *n.*

a hat	i it	oi oil	ch child	a in about
ā age	ī ice	ou out	ng long	e in taken
ä far	o hot	u cup	sh she	ə = i in pencil
e let	ō open	ù put	th thin	o in lemon
ē equal	ô order	ü rule	ŦH then	u in circus
ėr term			zh measure	< = derived from

plight (plīt), *v.t.* promise solemnly; pledge: *plight one's loyalty.* —*n.* a solemn promise; pledge.

plum age (plü′mij), *n.* feathers of a bird. [< Old French < *plume* plume]

ply (plī), *v.*, **plied, ply ing.** —*v.t.* **1** work with; use. **2** keep up work on; work away at or on. **3** urge again and again. —*v.i.* go back and forth regularly between certain places.

pol i tic (pol′ə tik), *adj.* **1** wise in looking out for one's own interests; prudent; shrewd. **2** showing wisdom or shrewdness. **3** scheming; crafty. **4** political —**pol′i tic ly,** *adv.*

pom mel (pum′əl, pom′əl), *n.*, *v.*, **-meled, -mel ing** or **-melled, -mel ling.** —*n.* **1** part of a saddle that sticks up at the front. **2** a rounded knob on the hilt of a sword, dagger, etc. —*v.t.* pummel; strike or beat.

pon der ous (pon′dər əs), *adj.* **1** very heavy. **2** heavy and clumsy. **3** dull; tiresome. —**pon′der ous ly,** *adv.* —**pon′der ous ness,** *n.*

pon tif i cal (pon tif′ə kəl), *adj.* **1** of or having to do with the pope; papal. **2** of or having to do with a bishop; episcopal. **3** pompous; dogmatic. —**pon tif′i cal ly,** *adv.*

pop in jay (pop′in jā), *n.* a vain, overly talkative person; conceited, silly person.

pop pet (pop′it), *n.* BRITISH DIALECT. a term of affection for a girl or child.

por tent (pôr′tent, pōr′tent), *n.* **1** a warning of coming evil; sign; omen. **2** ominous significance.

por ten tous (pôr ten′təs, pōr ten′təs), *adj.* **1** indicating evil to come; ominous; threatening. **2** amazing; extraordinary. —**por ten′tous ly,** *adv.* —**por ten′tous ness,** *n.*

pos ter i ty (po ster′ə tē), *n.* **1** generations of the future. **2** all of a person's descendants.

pos tern (pō′stərn, pos′tərn), *n.* **1** a small back door or gate. **2** any small or private entrance. —*adj.* rear; lesser.

post hu mous (pos′chə məs), *adj.* **1** happening after death. **2** published after the death of the author. **3** born after the death of the father. —**post′hu mous ly,** *adv.*

poul tice (pōl′tis), *n.*, *v.*, **-ticed, -tic ing.** —*n.* a soft, moist mass of mustard, herbs, etc., applied to the body as a medicine. —*v.t.* put a poultice on. [< Latin *pultes,* plural of *puls* mush]

pox (poks), *n.* **1** any disease characterized by eruption of pustules on the skin, such as chicken pox or smallpox. **2** syphilis.

prate (prāt), *v.*, **prat ed, prat ing.** —*v.i.* talk a great deal in a foolish way. —*v.t.* say in an empty or foolish way. —*n.* a prating; empty or foolish talk. [< Middle Dutch *praeten*]

prat tle (prat′l), *v.*, **-tled, -tling.** —*v.i.* **1** talk or tell freely and carelessly, as some children do. **2** talk or tell in a foolish way. **3** babble. —*v.t.* say in a foolish or childish way. —*n.* **1** childish or foolish talk. **2** babble. [< *prate*] —**prat′tler,** *n.*

pre-, *prefix.* **1** before in time, rank, etc.: *Precambrian = before the Cambrian.* **2** before in position, space, etc.; in front of: *Premolar = in front of the molars.* **3** beforehand; in advance: *Prepay = pay in advance.* [< Latin *prae-, pre-*]

pre am ble (prē′am′bəl), *n.* **1** a preliminary statement; introduction to a speech or a writing. The reasons for a law and its general purpose are often stated in a preamble. **2** a preliminary or introductory fact or circumstance, especially one showing what is to follow. [< Medieval Latin *praeambulum* < Late Latin, walking before < Latin *prae-* pre- + *ambulare* to walk]

pre cept (prē′sept), *n.* rule of action or behavior; guiding principle.

prec i pice (pres′ə pis), *n.* **1** a very steep or almost vertical face of rock; cliff or steep mountainside. **2** situation of great peril; critical position.

pre curse (prē kėrs′), *n.* OBSOLETE. an announcing, sign, or warning of something to come.

pre fer ment (pri fėr′mənt), *n.* **1** advancement; promotion. **2** position or office giving social or financial advancement, especially one in the church. **3** act of preferring.

prel a cy (prel′ə sē), *n.*, *pl.* **-cies. 1** position or rank of a prelate. **2** prelates. **3** church government by prelates.

prel ate (prel′it), *n.* member of the clergy of high rank, such as a bishop.

pre rog a tive (pri rog′ə tiv), *n.* **1** right or privilege that nobody else has. **2** special superiority of right or privilege, such as may derive from an official position, office, etc. [< Latin *praerogativa* allotted to vote first < *praerogare* ask for a vote first < *prae-* pre- + *rogare* ask]

pres age (pres′ij; *also* pri sāj′ *for v.*), *n.*, *v.*, **pre saged, pre sag ing.** —*n.* **1** sign felt as a warning; omen. **2** a feeling that something is about to happen; presentiment; foreboding. —*v.t.* **1** give warning of; predict. **2** have or give a presentiment or prophetic impression of. [< Latin *praesagium* < *prae-* pre- + *sagus* prophetic] —**pre sag′er,** *n.*

pre script (*n.* prē′skript; *adj.* pri skript′, prē′skript), *n.* that which is prescribed; rule; order; direction. —*adj.* prescribed.

pre sump tu ous (pri zump′chü əs), *adj.* acting without permission or right; too bold; forward. —**pre sump′tu ous ly,** *adv.* —**pre sump′tu ous ness,** *n.*

pre tense (prē′tens, pri tens′), *n.* **1** make-believe; pretending. **2** a false appearance. **3** a false claim. **4** claim. **5** a showing off; display; ostentation. **6** anything done to show off. Also, **pretence.**

pri mal (prī′məl), *adj.* **1** of early times; first; primeval. **2** chief; fundamental. —**pri′mal ly,** *adv.*

pri or ess (prī′ər is), *n.* head of a convent or priory for women. Prioresses usually rank below abbesses.

pris tine (pris′tēn′, pris′tən, pris′tīn), *adj.* as it was in its earliest time or state; original; primitive. —**pris′tine ly,** *adv.*

prith ee (priᴛн′ē), *interj.* ARCHAIC. I pray thee; I ask you.

priv y (priv′ē), *adj.* **1** private. **2** ARCHAIC. secret; hidden. **3 privy to,** having secret or private knowledge of.

pro-, *prefix.* **1** forward, as in *project.* **2** forth; out, as in *prolong, prolapse.* **3** on the side of; in favor of, as in *pro-British.* **4** in place of; acting as, as in *pronoun, proconsul.* [< Latin, forward, forth, for]

pro bi ty (prō′bə tē, prob′ə tē), *n.* high principle; uprightness; honesty. [< Latin *probitatem* < *probus* good]

pro cras ti nate (prō kras′tə nāt), *v.i.*, *v.t.*, **-nat ed, -nat ing.** put things off until later; delay, especially repeatedly. —**pro cras′ti na′tion,** *n.* —**pro cras′ti na′tor,** *n.*

pro cre ant (prō′krē ənt), *adj.* generating; having to do with procreation: *a procreant breed of birds.*

prod i gal (prod′ə gəl), *adj.* **1** given to extravagant or reckless spending; wasteful. **2** abundant; lavish. —*n.* person who is wasteful or extravagant; spendthrift.

pro di gious (prə dij′əs), *adj.* **1** very great; huge; vast. **2** wonderful; marvelous. —**pro di′gious ly,** *adv.*

prod i gy (prod′ə jē), *n.*, *pl.* **-gies. 1** person endowed with amazing brilliance, talent, etc., especially a remarkably talented child. **2** a marvelous example.

prof a na tion (prof′ə nā′shən), *n.* act of profaning.

pro fane (prə fān′), *adj.*, *v.*, **-faned, -fan ing.** —*adj.* **1** characterized by contempt or disregard for God or holy things; irreverent. **2** not sacred; worldly; secular. **3** ritually unclean or polluted. —*v.t.* **1** treat (holy things) with contempt or disregard; desecrate. **2** put to wrong or unworthy use. [< Latin *profanus* not sacred < *pro-* in front (outside) of + *fanum* temple, shrine] —**pro fane′ly,** *adv.* —**pro fane′ness,** *n.* —**pro fan′er,** *n.*

prom on to ry (prom′ən tôr′ē, prom′ən tōr′ē), *n.*, *pl.* **-ries.** a high point of land extending from the coast into the water; headland.

prop a gate (prop′ə gāt), *v.*, **-gat ed, -gat ing.** —*v.i.* produce offspring; reproduce. —*v.t.* **1** increase in number or intensity; multiply. **2** cause to increase in number by the production of young **3** spread (news, knowledge, etc.); extend. **4** pass on; send further.

prop a ga tion (prop′ə gā′shən), *n.* **1** the breeding of plants or animals. **2** a spreading; getting more widely believed; making more widely known.

pro pi tious (prə pish′əs), *adj.* **1** holding well; favorable. **2** favorably inclined; gracious. [< Latin *propitius,* originally, falling forward < *pro-* forward + *petere* go toward] —**pro pi′tious ly,** *adv.* —**pro pi′tious ness,** *n.*

pro pri e ty (prə prī′ə tē), *n.*, *pl.* **-ties. 1** quality or condition of being proper; fitness. **2** proper behavior. **3 proprieties,** *pl.*

conventional standards or requirements of proper behavior. [< Latin *proprietatem* appropriateness, property < *proprius* one's own, proper]

pros o dy (pros′ə dē), *n.* **1** the science of poetic meters and versification. **2** any system or style of versification: *Latin prosody.*

prov i dence (prov′ə dəns), *n.* **1** God's care and help. **2 Providence,** God. **3** instance of God's care and help. **4** a being provident; prudence.

prov i dent (prov′ə dənt), *adj.* **1** having or showing foresight; careful in providing for the future; prudent. **2** economical; frugal.

pro vi sion al (prə vizh′ə nəl), *adj.* for the time being; temporary: *a provisional agreement, a provisional governor.*

pro vi sion al ly (prə vizh′ə nə lē), *adv.* **1** for the time being; temporarily. **2** conditionally.

psal ter y (sôl′tər ē), *n., pl.* **-ter ies.** an ancient musical instrument played by plucking the strings. [Old English *saltere*]

pub li can (pub′lə kən), *n.* **1** BRITISH. keeper of a pub. **2** a tax collector of ancient Rome.

pu er ile (pyü′ər əl), *adj.* **1** foolish for a grown person to say or do; childish. **2** youthful; juvenile. [< Latin *puerilis* < *puer* boy, child]

punc til i ous (pungk til′ē əs), *adj.* **1** very careful and exact. **2** paying strict attention to details of conduct and ceremony.

pun gent (pun′jənt), *adj.* **1** sharply affecting the organs of taste and smell. **2** sharp; biting. **3** stimulating to the mind; keen; lively. **—pun′gent ly,** *adv.*

pur ga tion (pėr′gā′shən), *n.* a purging; cleansing.

pur ga tive (pėr′gə tiv), *n.* medicine that causes emptying of the bowels. Castor oil is a purgative. —*adj.* purging, especially causing the bowels to empty.

pur ga to ry (pėr′gə tôr′ē, pėr′gə tōr′ē), *n., pl.* **-ries.** **1** (in Roman Catholic belief) a temporary condition or place in which the souls of those who have died penitent are purified from venial sin or the effects of sin by punishment. **2** any condition or place of temporary suffering or punishment.

pur port (*v.* pər pôrt′, pər pōrt′; *n.* pėr′pôrt, pėr′pōrt), *v.t.* **1** claim or profess. **2** have as its main idea; mean. —*n.* meaning; main idea. **—pur port′ed ly,** *adv.*

pur vey or (pər vā′ər), *n.* **1** person who supplies provisions. **2** person who supplies anything.

pus tule (pus′chul), *n.* a small bump on the skin, filled with pus and inflamed at the base. [< Latin *pustula*]

pu tres cence (pyü tres′ns), *n.* putrescent condition.

pu tres cent (pyü tres′nt), *adj.* **1** becoming putrid; rotting. **2** having to do with putrefaction.

pyre (pīr), *n.* **1** pile of wood for burning a dead body as a funeral rite. **2** any large pile or heap of burnable material. [< Greek *pyra* < *pyr* fire]

quack (kwak), *n.* **1** a dishonest person who pretends to be a doctor. **2** an ignorant pretender to knowledge or skill of any sort; charlatan. —*adj.* not genuine.

quad ru ped (kwod′rə ped), *n.* animal that has four feet. —*adj.* four-footed. [< Latin *quadrupedem* < *quadru-* four + *pedem* foot]

quail (kwāl), *v.i.* be afraid; lose courage; shrink back in fear.

quell (kwel), *v.t.* **1** put down (disorder, rebellion, etc.). **2** put an end to; overcome. [Old English *cwellan* to kill] **—quell′a ble,** *adj.* **—quell′er,** *n.*

quer u lous (kwer′ə ləs, kwer′yə ləs), *adj.* complaining; fretful; peevish. [< Latin *querulus* < *queri* complain] **—quer′u lous ly,** *adv.* **—quer′u lous ness,** *n.*

qui es cence (kwī es′ns), *n.* absence of activity; a quiet state; stillness.

quill (kwil), *n.* a large, stiff feather. **—quill′-like′,** *adj.*

quin tes sence (kwin tes′ns), *n.* **1** the purest form of some quality; pure essence. **2** the most perfect example of something. [< Medieval Latin *qu inta essentia* fifth essence; with reference to a fifth element supposed by medieval philosophers to be more pervasive than the four elements (earth, water, fire, and air)]

qui vive? (kē vēv′), **1** who goes there? **2 on the qui vive,** watchful; alert. [< French, literally, (long) live who?; expecting such a reply as *Vive le roi!* Long live the king!]

a hat	i it	oi oil	ch child		a in about
ā age	ī ice	ou out	ng long		e in taken
ä far	o hot	u cup	sh she	ə =	i in pencil
e let	ō open	ù put	th thin		o in lemon
ē equal	ô order	ü rule	₮H then		u in circus
ėr term			zh measure		< = derived from

quix ot ic (kwik sot′ik), *adj.* **1** resembling Don Quixote; extravagantly chivalrous or romantic. **2** visionary; not practical. **—quix ot′i cal ly,** *adv.*

ra di ance (rā′dē əns), *n.* **1** vivid brightness. **2** radiation.

rail (rāl), *v.i.* complain bitterly; use violent and reproachful language: *rail at one's hard luck.*

rail ler y (rā′lər ē), *n., pl.* **-ler ies.** **1** good-humored ridicule; joking; teasing. **2** a bantering remark.

rai ment (rā′mənt), *n.* ARCHAIC. clothing; garments.

ran cor (rang′kər), *n.* bitter resentment or ill will; extreme hatred or spite. [< Late Latin, rankness < Latin *rancere* be rank]

rapt (rapt), *adj.* **1** lost in delight. **2** so busy thinking of or enjoying one thing that one does not know what else is happening. [< Latin *raptum* seized] **—rapt′ly,** *adv.* **—rapt′ness,** *n.*

rav age (rav′ij), *v.,* **-aged, -ag ing,** *n.* —*v.t.* damage greatly; lay waste; destroy. —*n.* violence; destruction; great damage. **—rav′ag er,** *n.*

rav el (rav′əl), *v.,* **-eled, -el ing** or **-elled, -el ling,** *n.* —*v.i.* **1** fray out; separate into threads. **2** become tangled, involved, or confused. —*v.t.* **1** separate the threads of; fray. **2** make plain or clear; unravel. —*n.* an unraveled thread or fiber.

re buke (ri byük′), *v.,* **-buked, -buk ing,** *n.* —*v.t.* express disapproval of; reprove. —*n.* expression of disapproval; scolding. [< Anglo-French *rebuker* < Old French *rebuchier* < *re-* back + *buchier* to strike]

re cal ci trant (ri kal′sə trənt), *adj.* resisting authority or control; disobedient. —*n.* a recalcitrant person or animal.

re ca pit u late (rē′kə pich′ə lāt), *v.t., v.i.,* **-lat ed, -lat ing.** repeat or recite the main points of; tell briefly; sum up.

re cog ni zance (ri kog′nə zəns, ri kon′ə zəns), *n.* in law: **1** bond binding a person to do some particular act. **2** sum of money to be forfeited if the act is not preformed.

rec om pense (rek′əm pens), *v.,* **-pensed, -pens ing,** *n.* —*v.t.* **1** pay (a person); pay back; reward. **2** make a fair return for (an action, anything lost, damage done, or hurt received). —*n.* **1** payment; reward. **2** return; amends. [< Late Latin *recompensare* < Latin *re-* back + *compensare* compensate]

rec on dite (rek′ən dīt, ri kon′dīt), *adj.* **1** hard to understand; profound. **2** little known; obscure. **3** hidden from view; concealed. [< Latin *reconditum* stored away < *re-* back + *com-* up + *-dere* to put] **—rec′on dite′ly,** *adv.* **—rec′on dite′ness,** *n.*

re course (rē′kôrs, rē′kōrs; ri kôrs′, ri kōrs′), *n.* **1** a turning for help or protection; appealing. **2 have recourse to,** turn to for help; appeal to.

re dress (*v.* ri dres′; *n.* rē′dres, ri dres′), *v.t.* set right; repair; remedy. —*n.* **1** a setting right; reparation; relief. **2** the means of a remedy. [< Middle French *redresser* < *re-* again + *dresser* straighten, arrange]

reeve (rēv), *n.* **1** the chief official of a town or district. **2** bailiff; steward; overseer. [Old English *(ge)rēfa*]

re frac tor y (ri frak′tər ē), *adj.* **1** hard to manage; stubborn; obstinate. **2** not yielding readily to treatment.

re gal (rē′gəl), *adj.* **1** belonging to a king or queen; royal. **2** fit for a king or queen; stately; splendid; magnificent. [< Latin *regalis* < *regem* king. Doublet of ROYAL, REAL[2], RIAL.] **—re′gal ly,** *adv.*

re it e rate (rē it′ə rāt′), *v.t.,* **-rat ed, -rat ing.** say or do several times; repeat (an action, demand, etc.) again and again: *reiterate a command.* **—re it′e ra′tion,** *n.*

re lent less (ri lent′lis), *adj.* without pity; not relenting; unyielding. —**re lent′less ly,** *adv.* —**re lent′less ness,** *n.*

re miss (ri mis′), *adj.* **1** careless or slack in doing what one has to do; neglectful; negligent: *be remiss in one's duty.* **2** characterized by carelessness, negligence, or inattention. [< Latin *remissum* remitted] —**re miss′ly,** *adv.* —**re miss′ness,** *n.*

re mon strance (ri mon′strəns), *n.* act of remonstrating; protest; complaint.

re mon strate (ri mon′strāt), *v.i.,* **-strat ed, -strat ing.** speak, reason, or plead in complaint or protest.

re morse (ri môrs′), *n.* deep, painful regret for having done wrong; compunction; contrition. [< Late Latin *remorsum* tormented, bit again < Latin *re-* back + *mordere* to bite]

re morse less (ri môrs′lis), *adj.* **1** without remorse. **2** pitiless; cruel. —**re morse′less ly,** *adv.* —**re morse′less ness,** *n.*

ren coun ter (ren koun′tər), *n.* a hostile meeting; battle.

rend (rend), *v.t.,* **rent, rend ing. 1** pull apart violently; tear. **2** split. **3** disturb violently. **4** remove with force or violence.

ren dez vous (rän′də vü), *n., pl.* **-vous** (-vüz). **1** an appointment or engagement to meet at a fixed place or time; meeting by agreement. **2** a meeting place; gathering place.

re past (ri past′), *n.* meal; food. [< Old French, ultimately < Latin *re-* again + *pascere* to feed]

re pine (ri pīn′), *v.i.,* **-pined, -pin ing.** be discontented; fret; complain. —**re pin′er,** *n.*

re plen ish (ri plen′ish), *v.t.* fill again; provide a new supply for; renew. [< Old French *repleniss-,* a form of *replenir,* fill again, ultimately < Latin *re-* again + *plenus* full] —**re plen′ish er,** *n.* —**re plen′ish ment,** *n.*

re quite (ri kwīt′), *v.t.,* **-quit ed, -quit ing. 1** pay back; make return for. **2** make return to; reward. **3** make retaliation for; avenge. [< *re-* + *quite,* variant of *quit*] —**re quit′er,** *n.*

req ui em or **Req ui em** (rek′wē əm, rē′kwē əm), *n.* **1** Mass for the dead; musical church service for the dead. **2** music for it. **3** any musical service or hymn for the dead. [< Latin, accusative of *requies* rest; the first word of the Mass for the dead]

re quit al (ri kwī′tl), *n.* **1** repayment; payment; return. **2** act of requiting.

re signed (ri zīnd′), *adj.* submitting to or accepting what comes without complaint. —**re sign′ed ly,** *adv.* —**re sign′ed ness,** *n.*

re splend ent (ri splen′dənt), *adj.* very bright; shinning; splendid: *the resplendent sun, a face resplendent with joy.* [< Latin *resplendentem* < *re-* back + *splendere* to shine] —**re splend′ent ly,** *adv.*

re tain er (ri tā′nər), *n.* **1** person who serves a person of rank; attendant; follower. **2** person who retains.

re ten tive (ri ten′tiv), *adj.* **1** able to hold or keep. **2** able to remember easily. —**re ten′tive ly,** *adv.* —**re ten′tive ness,** *n.*

re tic u late (*adj.* ri tik′yə lit, ri tik′yə lāt; *v.* ri tik′yə lāt), *adj., v.,* **-lat ed, -lat ing.** —*adj.* covered with or resembling a network. Reticulate leaves have the veins arranged like the threads of a net. —*v.t.* cover or mark with a network. —*v.i.* form a network.

rev e la tion (rev′ə lā′shən), *n.* **1** act of making known. **2** the thing made known. **3** disclosure of divine truth and will to humankind. **4 Revelation,** the last book of the New Testament, supposed to have been written by the apostle John. [< Latin *revelationem* < *revelare* reveal]

rev el ry (rev′əl rē), *n., pl.* **-ries.** boisterous reveling or festivity.

re ver be rate (ri vėr′bə rāt′), *v.,* **-rat ed, -rat ing.** —*v.i.* **1** echo back. **2** be cast back; be reflected a number of times, as light or heat. —*v.t.* **1** reecho (a sound or noise). **2** cast back; reflect (light or heat). —**re ver′be ra′tion,** *n.*

ric o chet (rik′ə shā′; *British* rik′ə shet′), *n., v.,* **-cheted** (-shād′). **-chet ing** (-shā′ing) or **-chet ted** (-shet′id), **-chetting** (-shet′ing). —*n.* the skipping or jumping motion of an object after glancing off a flat surface. —*v.i.* move with a skipping or jumping motion. [< French]

rill (ril), *n.* a tiny stream; little brook.

ri val (rī′vəl), *n., adj., v.,* **-valed, -val ing** or **-valled, -val-**

ling. —*n.* **1** person who wants and tries to get the same thing as another or who tries to equal or do better than another; competitor. **2** thing that will bear comparison with something else; equal; match. **3** ARCHAIC. partner. —*adj.* wanting the same thing as another; trying to outdo or equal another; competing. —*v.t.* **1** try to equal or outdo; compete with. **2** equal; match. [< Latin *rivalis* one who uses the same stream as another < *rivus* stream]

riv elled (riv′əld), *adj.* ARCHAIC. full of wrinkles or small folds.

riv en (riv′ən), *adj.* torn apart; split. —*v.* a pp. of *rive.*

road stead (rōd′sted), *n.* place near the shore where ships may anchor; road.

ru di ment (rü′də mənt), *n.* **1** part to be learned first; beginning. **2** something in an early stage; undeveloped or imperfect form.

rue[1] (rü), *v.,* **rued, ru ing,** *n.* —*v.t.* be sorry for; regret. —*n.* sorrow; regret. [Old English *hrēowan*]

rue[2] (rü), *n.* a strong-smelling, woody herb of the same family as the citrus, with yellow flowers, and bitter leaves that were formerly much used in medicine. [< Old French < Latin *ruta*]

rue ful (rü′fəl), *adj.* **1** sorrowful; unhappy; mournful. **2** causing sorrow or pity. —**rue′ful ly,** *adv.*

ruf fi an (ruf′ē ən), *n.* a rough, brutal, or cruel person; bully; hoodlum. —*adj.* rough; brutal; cruel. [< Middle French < Italian *ruffiano* pander]

ru mi nant (rü′mə nənt), *n.* any of a suborder of even-toed, hoofed, herbivorous mammals which chew the cud and have a stomach with four separate cavities, including cattle, deer, sheep, goats, giraffes, and camels. —*adj.* belonging to the group of ruminants. [< Latin *ruminantem* chewing a cud < *rumen* gullet]

sac ri le gious (sak′rə lij′əs, sak′rə lē′jəs), *adj.* injurious or insulting to sacred persons or things. —**sac′ri le′gious ly,** *adv.* —**sac′ri le′gious ness,** *n.*

saf fron (saf′rən), *n.* **1** an autumn crocus with purple flowers having orange-yellow stigmas. **2** an orange yellow. —*adj.* orange-yellow.

sa ga cious (sə gā′shəs), *adj.* **1** wise in a keen, practical way; shrewd. **2** intelligent. [< Latin *sagacem*] —**sa ga′cious ly,** *adv.* —**sa ga′cious ness,** *n.*

sa gac i ty (sə gas′ə tē), *n.* keen, sound judgment; mental acuteness; shrewdness.

sage (sāj), *adj.,* **sag er, sag est,** *n.* —*adj.* **1** showing wisdom or good judgment: *a sage reply.* **2** wise: *a sage adviser.* —*n.* a very wise person. —**sage′ly,** *adv.* —**sage′ness,** *n.*

sal ly (sal′ē), *v.,* **-lied, -ly ing,** *n., pl.* **-lies.** —*v.i.* **1** go suddenly from a defensive position to attack an enemy. **2** rush forth suddenly; go out. **3** set out briskly or boldly. —*n.* **1** a sudden attack on an enemy made from a defensive position; sortie. **2** a sudden rushing forth. **3** a going forth; trip; excursion. **4** a witty remark.

sal u tar y (sal′yə ter′ē), *adj.* **1** beneficial. **2** good for the health; wholesome. —**sal′u tar′i ly,** *adv.*

salve (sav), *n., v.,* **salved, salv ing.** —*n.* **1** a soft, greasy substance put on wounds and sores; healing ointment. **2** something soothing; balm. —*v.t.* **1** put salve on. **2** smooth over; soothe.

sanc ti fy (sangk′tə fī), *v.t.,* **-fied, -fy ing. 1** make holy; make legitimate or binding by a religious sanction. **2** set apart as sacred; observe as holy.

san guine (sang′gwən), *adj.* **1** naturally cheerful and hopeful. **2** confident; hopeful. **3** having a healthy red color; ruddy. **4** (in old physiology) having an active circulation, a ruddy color, and a cheerful and ardent disposition. —**san′guine ly,** *adv.* [< Latin *sanguineus* < *sanguinem* blood]

sa ti ate (*v.* sā′shē āt; *adj.* sā′shē it), *v.,* **-at ed, -at ing,** *adj.* —*v.t.* **1** feed fully; satisfy fully. **2** weary or disgust with too much. —*adj.* filled to satiety; satiated. —**sa′ti a′tion,** *n.*

saun ter (sôn′tər, sän′tər), *v.i.* walk along slowly and happily; stroll. —*n.* **1** a leisurely or careless gait. **2** a stroll. [origin uncertain] —**saun′ter er,** *n.*

scath er (scath′ər), *n.* OBSOLETE. criminal; thief; murderer. [Old English *sceatha*]

scep ter (sep′tər), *n.* **1** the rod or staff carried by a ruler as a symbol of royal power or authority. **2** royal or imperial power or authority; sovereignty. Also, **sceptre.**

scin′til late (sin′tl āt), *v.i.,* **-lat ed, -lat ing.** sparkle; flash.

—**scin til lat′ing ly**, *adv.* —**scin′til la′tor**, *n.*

scotch (skoch), *v.t.* **1** inflict such hurt upon (something regarded as dangerous) that is made harmless for the time. **2** stamp on or stamp out (something dangerous); crush.

screed (skrēd), *n.* a long speech or writing.

scru ple (skrü′pəl), *n.* **1** a feeling of doubt about what one ought to do. **2** a feeling of uneasiness that keeps a person from doing something.

scru pu los i ty (skrü′pyə los′ə tē), *n., pl.* **-ties. 1** a being scrupulous; strict regard for what is right; scrupulous care. **2** an instance of this.

scru pu lous (skrü′pyə ləs), *adj.* **1** very careful to do what is right; conscientious. **2** attending thoroughly to details; very careful. —**scru′pu lous ly**, *adv.* —**scru′pu lous ness**, *n.*

scud (skud), *v.,* **scud ded, scud ding,** *n.* —*v.i.* **1** run or move swiftly. **2** (of a boat, etc.) run before a storm with little or no sail set. —*n.* **1** a scudding. **2** clouds or spray driven by the wind. [perhaps < Scandinavian (Danish) *skyde* shoot, glide]

scul lion (skul′yən), *n.* ARCHAIC. **1** servant who does the dirty, rough work in a kitchen. **2** a low, contemptible person.

scur ril i ty (skə ril′ə tē), *n., pl.* **-ties. 1** coarse joking. **2** indecent abuse. **3** an indecent or coarse remark.

scythe (sīᴛʜ), *n., v.,* **scythed, scyth ing.** —*n.* a long, thin, slightly curved blade on a long handle, for cutting grass, etc. —*v.t.* cut or mow with a scythe.

sea mew, sea gull, especially the common gull of Europe.

sear (sir), *v.t.* **1** burn or char the surface of. **2** make hard or unfeeling. **3** dry up; wither. —*v.i.* become dry, burned, or hard. —*n.* mark made by searing.

sec ond (sek′ənd), *n.* (in music) a lower tone.

sedge (sej), *n.* any of a large family of monocotyledonous herbs growing chiefly in wet places, resembling grasses but having solid, three-sided stems and small, inconspicuous flowers usually in spikes or heads. [Old English *secg*]

sem blance (sem′bləns), *n.* **1** outward appearance. **2** likeness. Also, **semblance.**

sen tient (sen′shənt), *adj.* that can feel. —**sen′tient ly**, *adv.*

sep ul cher (sep′əl kər), *n.* **1** place of burial; tomb; grave. **2** structure or recess in stone of old churches in which sacred relics were deposited. —*v.t.* bury (a dead body) in a sepulcher. Also, **sepulchre.** [< Old French < Latin *sepulcrum < sepelire* bury]

se pul chral (sə pul′krəl), *adj.* **1** of sepulchers or tombs. **2** of burial. **3** deep and gloomy; dismal; suggesting a tomb. —**se pul′chral ly**, *adv.*

se ques ter (si kwes′tər), *v.t.* **1** remove or withdraw from public use or from public view; seclude. **2** take away (property) for a time from an owner until a debt is paid or some claim is satisfied. **3** seize by authority; take and keep. [< Latin *sequestrare < sequester* trustee, mediator < *sequi* follow]

sere (sir), *adj.* ARCHAIC. dried; withered. Also, **sear.** [Old English *sēar*]

serf (sėrf), *n.* **1** (in the feudal system) a slave who could not be sold off the land, but passed from one owner to another with the land. **2** person treated almost like a slave; person who is mistreated, underpaid, etc. [< French < Latin *servus* slave] —**serf′like′**, *adj.*

se ros i ty (si ros′ə tē), *n.* a condition characterized by an effusion of fluid.

ser ous (sir′əs), *adj.* **1** of, having to do with, or producing serum. **2** like serum; watery. Tears are drops of a serous fluid.

shal lop (shal′əp), *n.* a small, light, open boat with sail or oars. [< French *chaloupe* < Dutch *sloepe*]

shard (shärd), *n.* **1** piece of broken earthenware or pottery. **2** a broken piece; fragment. Also, **sherd.** [Old English *sceard*]

shav er (shā′vər), *n.* INFORMAL. youngster; small boy.

shin gle (shing′gəl), *n.* **1** loose stones or pebbles that lie on the seashore; coarse gravel. **2** beach or other place covered with this.

shire (shīr), *n.* one of the counties into which Great Britain is divided, especially one whose name ends in *-shire.*

shoal (shōl), *n.* place in a sea, lake, or stream where the water is shallow. —*adj.* shallow. —*v.i.* become shallow.

shrift (shrift), *n.* ARCHAIC. **1** confession of one's sins to a priest, followed by the granting of forgiveness by the priest. **2** act of

shriving. [Old English *scrift < scrīfan* shrive]

shriv en (shriv′ən), *v.* ARCHAIC. a pp. of **shrive,** pardon after confessing.

a hat	i it	oi oil	ch child		a in about
ā age	ī ice	ou out	ng long		e in taken
ä far	o hot	u cup	sh she	ə =	i in pencil
e let	ō open	ù put	th thin		o in lemon
ē equal	ô order	ü rule	ᴛʜ then		u in circus
ėr term			zh measure		< = derived from

shroud (shroud), *n.* **1** cloth or garment in which a dead person is wrapped or dressed for burial. **2** something that covers, conceals, or veils: *The fog was a shroud over the city.* **3** Usually, **shrouds,** *pl.* rope from a mast to the side of a ship. Shrouds help support the mast. —*v.t.* **1** wrap or dress for burial. **2** cover; conceal; veil: *Their plans are shrouded in secrecy.* —**shroud′like′**, *adj.*

SHROUDS

shrouds (def. 3)

si dle (sī′dl), *v.,* **-dled, -dling,** *n.* —*v.i.* **1** move sideways. **2** move sideways slowly so as not to attract attention. —*n.* movement sideways. [< *sideling,* variant of *sidelong*] — **si′dling ly**, *adv.*

si mil i tude (sə mil′ə tüd, sə mil′ə tyüd), *n.* **1** a being similar; likeness; resemblance. **2** comparison drawn between two things or facts. **3** copy; image.

si ne cure (sī′nə kyùr, sin′ə kyùr), *n.* **1** an extremely easy job; position requiring little or no work and usually paying well. **2** an ecclesiastical benefice without parish duties. [< Medieval Latin *(beneficium) sine cura* (benefice) without cure (of souls)]

sin ew (sin′yü), *n.* **1** tendon. **2** strength; energy; force. **3** Often, **sinews,** *pl.* means of strength; source of power. —*v.t.* furnish with sinews. —**sin′ew less**, *adj.*

sin gu lar i ty (sing′gyə lar′ə tē), *n., pl.* **-ties. 1** condition or quality of being singular. **2** something singular; peculiarity; oddity. **3** a point that cannot be mathematically defined, especially one characterized by infinite quantities. The center of a black hole, thought to have infinite density, is often called a singularity.

sin u ous (sin′yü əs), *adj.* **1** having many curves or turns; winding. **2** indirect; devious. **3** untrustworthy. [< Latin *sinuosus < sinus* a curve] —**sin′u ous ly**, *adv.* —**sin′u ous ness**, *n.*

skir mish (skėr′mish), *n.* a brief fight between small groups of soldiers. —*v.i.* take part in a skirmish.

slake (slāk; *also* slak *for v.t.* 4, *v.i.* 1), *v.,* **slaked, slak ing.** —*v.t.* **1** satisfy (thirst, revenge, wrath, etc.). **2** cause to be less active, vigorous, intense, etc. **3** put out (a fire). **4** change (lime) to slaked lime by leaving it in the moist air or putting water on it. —*v.i.* **1** (of lime) become slaked lime. **2** become less active, vigorous, intense, etc. [Old English *slacian* slacken < *slæc* slack]

slan der (slan′dər), *n.* **1** a false statement spoken with intent to harm the reputation of another. **2** the spreading of false reports. —*v.t.* talk falsely about. —*v.i.* speak or spread slander.

slav ish (slā′vish), *adj.* **1** of or having to do with a slave or slaves. **2** like a slave; mean; base. **3** weakly submitting. **4** like that of slaves; fit for slaves. **5** lacking originality and independence.

sleight (slīt), *n.* **1** skill; dexterity. **2** a clever trick.

sloth (slôth, slōth), *n.* **1** unwillingness to work or exert oneself; laziness; idleness: *His sloth keeps him from engaging in sports.*

GLOSSARY

2 ARCHAIC. slowness. **3** any of a family of very slow-moving mammals of South and Central America that live in trees and hang upside down from tree branches. [Old English *slāwth* < *slāw* slow]

slov en ly (sluv′ən lē), *adj.*, **-li er**, **-li est**, *adv.* —*adj.* untidy, dirty, or careless in dress, appearance, habits, work, etc. —*adv.* in a slovenly manner. —**slov′en li ness**, *n.*

slum ber ous (slum′bər əs), *adj.* **1** sleepy; heavy with drowsiness. **2** causing or inducing sleep. **3** inactive or quiet. —**slum′ber ous ly**, *adv.*

smirch (smėrch), *v.t.* **1** make dirty; soil with soot, dirt, etc. **2** cast discredit upon; taint; tarnish. —*n.* **1** a dirty mark; stain. **2** blot on a person's reputation. [Middle English *smorchen* discolor]

smith y (smith′ē, smiтн′ē), *n.*, *pl.* **smith ies**, *v.*, **smith ied**, **smith y ing.** —*n.* workshop of a smith, especially a blacksmith. —*v.t.* make or shape by forging.

smit ten (smit′n), *adj.* hard hit; struck. —*v.* a pp. of **smite,** give or strike a hard blow.

soi ree or **soi rée** (swä rā′), *n.* an evening party or social gathering. [< French *soirée* < *soir* evening]

so journ (*v.* sō′jėrn′, sō jėrn′; *n.* sō′jėrn′), *v.i.* stay for a time. —*n.* a brief stay. —**so′journ′er,** *n.* [< Old French *sojorner,* ultimately < Latin *sub* under + *diurnus* of the day] —**so′journ′er,** *n.*

so lic it (sə lis′it), *v.t.* **1** ask earnestly; try to get. **2** influence to do wrong; tempt; entice. —*v.i.* make appeals or requests. \

so lic i tous (sə lis′ə təs), *adj.* **1** showing care or concern; anxious; concerned. **2** desirous; eager. [< Latin *solicitus* < *sollus* all + *ciere* arouse] —**so lic′i tous ly,** *adv.* —**so lic′i tous-ness,** *n.*

so lil o quize (sə lil′ə kwīz), *v.i.*, **-quized, -quiz ing. 1** talk to oneself. **2** speak a soliloquy. —**so lil′o quiz′er,** *n.* [< Late Latin *soliloquium* < Latin *solus* alone + *loqui* speak]

sol i tude (sol′ə tüd, sol′ə tyüd), *n.* **1** a being alone. **2** a lonely place. **3** loneliness.

som ber or **som bre** (som′bər), *adj.* **1** having deep shadows; dark; gloomy. **2** melancholy; dismal. —**som′ber ly, som′bre ly,** *adv.* [< French *sombre,* probably ultimately < Latin *sub* under + *umbra* shade]

soph ist (sof′ist), *n.* **1** a clever but misleading reasoner. **2** Often, **Sophist.** one of a class of teachers of rhetoric, philosophy, ethics, etc., in ancient Greece. [< Greek, ultimately < *sophos* clever]

sor did (sôr′did), *adj.* **1** dirty; filthy. **2** caring too much for money; meanly selfish; greedy. **3** mean; low; base; contemptible. **4** of a dull or dark color. [< Latin *sordidus* < *sordere* be dirty < *sordes* dirt] —**sor′did ly,** *adv.* —**sor′did ness,** *n.*

sot (sot), *n.* person who commonly or habitually drinks too much alcoholic liquor; confirmed drunkard. [Old English, a fool]

sov er eign (sov′rən), *n.* a former British gold coin, that was equal to 20 shillings or one pound.

span (span), *n.*, *v.*, **spanned, span ning.** —*n.* **1** part between two supports. **2** the distance between the tip of the thumb and the tip of the little finger when the hand is spread out; about 9 inches (23 centimeters). —*v.t.* **1** extend over or across. **2** measure by the hand spread out. [Old English *spann*]

spas mod ic (spaz mod′ik), *adj.* **1** having to do with, like, or characterized by a spasm or spasms. **2** occurring very irregularly; intermittent. —**spas mod′i cal ly,** *adv.*

spe cious (spē′shəs), *adj.* **1** seeming desirable, reasonable, or probable, but not really so; apparently good, but without real merit. **2** making a good outward appearance in order to deceive. [< Latin *speciosus* < *species* appearance, sort]

spec ter (spek′tər), *n.* **1** phantom or ghost, especially one of a terrifying nature or appearance. **2** thing causing terror or dread. Also, **spectre.** [< Latin *spectrum* appearance]

spin et (spin′it), *n.* **1** a compact upright piano. **2** an old-fashioned musical instrument like a small harpsichord.

splay (splā), *v.t.* **1** spread out; expand; extend. **2** make slanting; bevel. —*v.i.* **1** have or lie in a slanting direction; slope. **2** spread out; flare. —*adj.* wide and flat; turned outward.

spor tive (spôr′tiv, spōr′tiv), *adj.* playful; merry; *a sportive puppy.* —**spor′tive ly,** *adv.* —**spor′tive ness,** *n.*

sprad dle (sprad′l), *v.i.*, **-dled, -dling.** sprawl.

spright ly (sprīt′lē), *adj.*, **-li er, -li est,** *adv.* —*adj.* lively; gay. —*adv.* in a sprightly manner. Also, **spritely.** —**spright′li-ness,** *n.*

sprite (sprīt), *n.* fairy. [< Old French *esprit* spirit < Latin *spiritus*]

spurn (spėrn), *v.t.* **1** refuse with scorn; scorn. **2** strike with the foot; kick away. —*v.i.* oppose with scorn.

squall (skwôl), *n.* **1** a sudden, violent gust of wind, often with rain, snow, or sleet. **2** INFORMAL. disturbance or commotion.

squan der (skwon′dər), *v.t.* spend foolishly; waste. [origin uncertain] —**squan′der er,** *n.*

squeam ish (skwē′mish), *adj.* **1** too proper, modest, etc., easily shocked; prudish. **2** too particular; too scrupulous. **3** slightly sick at one's stomach; nauseated. —**squeam′ish ly,** *adv.*

staff (staf), *n.*, *pl.* **staves** or **staffs.** a stick, pole, or rod used as a support, as an emblem of office, as a weapon, etc.

stag nant (stag′nənt), *adj.* **1** not running or flowing. **2** foul from standing still. **3** not active; sluggish; dull.

stag nate (stag′nāt), *v.*, **-nat ed, -nat ing.** —*v.i.* be or become stagnant. —*v.t.* make stagnant. [< Latin *stagnatum* made stagnant < *stagnum* standing water] —**stag na′tion,** *n.*

stal wart (stôl′wərt), *adj.* **1** strongly built; sturdy; robust. **2** strong and brave; valiant. **3** firm; steadfast. —*n.* **1** a stalwart person. **2** a loyal supporter of a political party. [Old English *stælwierthe* serviceable < *stathol* position + *wierthe* worthy] —**stal′wart ly,** *adv.* —**stal′wart ness,** *n.*

stan dard (stan′dərd), *n.* flag, emblem, or symbol.

staves (stāvz), *n.* a pl. of **staff.**

stead fast (sted′fast′), *adj.* **1** firm of purpose; loyal and unwavering. **2** firmly fixed; not moving or changing. Also, **sted-fast.** [Old English *stedefæst* < *stede* place + *fæst* fast[1], firm] —**stead′fast′ly,** *adv.* —**stead′fast′ness,** *n.*

stealth (stelth), *n.* secret or sly action.

stealth y (stel′thē), *adj.*, **stealth i er, stealth i est.** done in a secret manner; secret; sly: —**stealth′i ly,** *adv.* —**stealth′i-ness,** *n.*

stew ard (stü′ərd, styü′ərd), *n.* **1** person who has charge of the food and table service for a club, restaurant, etc. **2** man employed on an airplane, a ship, etc., to look after passengers. **3** person who manages another's property or finances: *He is the steward of that great estate.* **4** person appointed to manage a dinner, ball, show, etc. [Old English *stigweard* < *stig* hall + *weard* keeper, ward]

sti pend (stī′pend), *n.* fixed or regular pay, especially for professional services; salary.

stip u late (stip′yə lāt), *v.*, **-lat ed, -lat ing.** —*v.t.* arrange definitely; demand as a condition of agreement. —*v.i.* make an express demand or arrangement *(for).* [< Latin *stipulatum* stipulated] —**stip′u la′tor,** *n.*

sto i cal (stō′ə kəl), *adj.* like a stoic; indifferent to pleasure and pain; self-controlled. —**sto′i cal ly,** *adv.* —**sto′i cal ness,** *n.*

stone (stōn), *n.*, *pl.* **stone.** a British unit of weight, equal to 14 pounds. [Old English *stān*]

stoup (stüp), *n.* a drinking cup; flagon; tankard.

strand (strand), *n.* shore; land bordering a sea, lake, or river.

strat a gem (strat′ə jəm), *n.* scheme or trick for deceiving an enemy; trickery. [< Greek *stratēgēma* < *stratēgein* be a general < *stratēgos* general]

strife (strīf), *n.* **1** a quarreling; fighting. **2** a quarrel; fight. [< Old French *estrif;* of Germanic origin]

strip ling (strip′ling), *n.* boy just coming into manhood; youth; lad.

sub-, *prefix.* **1** under; below: *Subnormal = below normal.* **2** down; further; again: *Subdivide = divide again.* **3** near; nearly: *Subtropical = nearly tropical.* **4** lower; subordinate: *Subcommittee = a lower or subordinate committee.* **5** resulting from further division: *Subsection = section resulting from further division of something.* **6** slightly; somewhat: *Subacid = slightly acid.* [< Latin < *sub* under, beneath]

sub lime (sə blīm′), *adj.*, *v.*, **-limed, -lim ing.** —*adj.* lofty or elevated in thought, feeling, language, etc.; noble; grand; exalted. —*n.* something that is lofty, noble, exalted, etc. —*v.t.* **1** make higher or nobler; make sublime. **2** purify or refine (a solid substance) by applying heat and condensing the vapor given off. —*v.i.* pass from a solid to a vapor or from a vapor to a solid without going through a liquid state.

sub or di na tion (sə bôrd′n ā′shən), *n.* **1** act of subordinating. **2** submission to authority; willingness to obey; obedience.

sub orn (sə bôrn′), *v.t.* **1** persuade, bribe, or cause (someone) to do an illegal or evil deed. **2** persuade or cause (a witness) to give false testimony in court. [< Latin *subornare* < *sub-* secretly + *ornare* equip] **—sub′or na′tion,** *n.* **—sub orn′er,** *n.*

sub ser vi ence (səb sėr′vē əns), *n.* **1** slavish politeness and obedience; tame submission; servility. **2** a being of use or service.

sub tile (sut′l, sub′təl), *adj.* subtle. **—sub′tile ly,** *adv.*

suc cor (suk′ər), *n.* person or thing that helps or assists; help; aid. **—v.t.** help, assist, or aid (a person, etc.). Also, **succour.**

sump tu ous (sump′chü əs), *adj.* lavish and costly; magnificent; rich. **—sump′tu ous ly,** *adv.* **—sump′tu ous ness,** *n.*

sun dry (sun′drē), *adj.* several; various: *From sundry hints, I guessed his age.* [Old English *syndrig* separate < *sundor* apart]

su per flu ous (sü pėr′flü əs), *adj.* **1** more than is needed. **2** needless; unnecessary. [< Latin *superfluus,* ultimately < *super-* over + *fluere* to flow] **—su per′flu ous ly,** *adv.* **—su per′flu ous ness,** *n.*

su per nal (sü pėr′nl), *adj.* **1** heavenly; divine. **2** lofty; exalted. [< Latin *supernus* < *super* above] **—su per′nal ly,** *adv.*

su pine (sü pīn′), *adj.* **1** lying flat on the back. **2** lazily inactive; listless. [< Latin *supinus*] **—su pine′ly,** *adv.*

sup pli cate (sup′lə kāt), *v.,* **-cat ed, -cat ing. —v.t.** beg humbly and earnestly. **—v.i.** pray humbly. [< Latin *supplicatum* bent down, suppliant < *sub-* down + *plicare* to bend] **—sup′pli ca′tor,** *n.*

sup po si tion (sup′ə zish′ən), *n.* **1** act of supposing. **2** thing supposed; belief; opinion.

sup pos i ti tious (sə poz′ə tish′əs), *adj.* **1** not genuine. **2** hypothetical.

sup pu rate (sup′yə rāt), *v.i.,* **-rat ed, -rat ing.** form pus; discharge pus; fester. [< Latin *suppuratum* festered < *sub-* under + *puris* pus]

sur cease (sėr sēs′, sơr sēs′), *n.* end; cessation.

sur feit (sėr′fit), *n.* too much; excess. **—v.t.** feed or supply to excess. **—v.i.** eat, drink, or indulge in something to excess.

sur ly (sėr′lē), *adj.,* **-li er, -li est.** bad-tempered and unfriendly; rude; gruff. [Middle English *sirly,* perhaps < *sir* lord] **—sur′li ness,** *n.*

sur mise (*v.* sơr mīz′; *n.* sơr mīz′, sėr′mīz), *v.,* **-mised, -mis ing,** *n.* **—v.t., v.i.** infer or guess. **—n.** formation of an idea with little or no evidence; a guessing.

sus pi ra tion (sus′pə rā′shən), *n.* a sigh.

sus te nance (sus′tə nəns), *n.* **1** food or provisions; nourishment. **2** means of living; support.

swain (swān), *n.* ARCHAIC. **1** lover. **2** a young man who lives in the country. [< Scandinavian (Old Icelandic) *sveinn* boy]

sward (swôrd), *n.* a grassy surface; turf. [Old English *sweard* skin]

swath (swoth, swôth), *n.* **1** space covered by a single cut of a scythe or by one cut of a mowing machine. **2** row of grass, grain, etc., cut by a scythe or mowing machine. **3** a strip. **4 cut a wide swath,** make a showy display; splurge. Also, **swathe.**

swill (swil), *n.* **1** kitchen refuse, especially when partly liquid; slops. Swill is sometimes fed to pigs. **2** a deep drink. **—v.t. 1** drink greedily. **2** fill with drink. **—v.i.** drink greedily; drink too much.

swoon (swün), *v.i.* **1** faint. **2** fade or die away gradually. **—n.** a faint. [ultimately < Old English *geswōgen* in a swoon]

syl van (sil′vən), *adj.* of, in, or having woods. Also, **silvan.** [< Latin *sylvanus, silvanus* < *silva* forest]

syn co pe (sing′kə pē), *n.* a fainting.

tab ard (tab′ərd), *n.* a coarse outer garment worn by the poor during the Middle Ages.

taff rail (taf′rāl′), *n.* a rail around a ship's stern. [< Dutch *taffereel* panel, diminutive of *tafel* table]

tag (tag), *n.* a familiar quotation.

tam-o'-shan ter (tam′ə shan′tər), *n.* a soft, woolen cap, originally of Scotland, with a flat, round crown and often with a tassel. Also, **tam.** [< *Tam o' Shanter,* the hero of a poem by Robert Burns]

tar ry (tar′ē), *v.,* **-ried, -ry ing. —v.i. 1** delay leaving; remain; stay. **2** be tardy; hesitate. **—v.t.** ARCHAIC. wait for.

a hat	i it	oi oil	ch child	
ā age	ī ice	ou out	ng long	
ä far	o hot	u cup	sh she	ə = { a in about, e in taken, i in pencil, o in lemon, u in circus
e let	ō open	ů put	th thin	
ē equal	ô order	ü rule	ŦH then	
ėr term			zh measure	< = derived from

te di ous (tē′dē əs, tē′jəs), *adj.* long and tiring; boring; wearisome. **—te′di ous ly,** *adv.* **—te′di ous ness,** *n.*

teem (tēm), *v.i.* be full (of); abound; swarm. [Old English *tēman* < *tēam* progeny]

tem per ance (tem′pər əns), *n.* **1** a being moderate in action, speech, habits, etc.; self-control. **2** a being moderate in the use of alcoholic drinks.

te na cious (ti nā′shəs), *adj.* **1** holding fast. **2** stubborn; persistent; obstinate. **3** able to remember; retentive. **4** holding fast together; not easily pulled apart. **5** sticky. [< Latin *tenacem* holding fast < *tenere* to hold] **—te na′cious ly,** *adv.* **—te na′cious ness,** *n.*

te nac i ty (ti nas′ə tē), *n.* **1** firmness in holding fast. **2** stubbornness; persistence. **3** ability to remember. **4** firmness in holding together; toughness. **5** stickiness.

ten ant less (ten′ənt lis), *adj.* not occupied; empty.

tench (tench), *n., pl.* **tench es** or **tench.** a freshwater fish of Europe, of the same family as the carp, noted for the length of time it can live out of water. [< Old French *tenche* < Late Latin *tinca*]

ten e ment (ten′ə mənt), *n.* **1** tenement house. **2** any house or building to live in; dwelling house. **3** a dwelling, or part of a dwelling, occupied by a tenant. **4** abode; habitation.

ten or (ten′ər), *n.* **1** in music: **a** the highest natural adult male voice. **b** singer with such a voice. **2** the general tendency; course. **3** the general meaning or drift; gist; purport.

ten ta tive (ten′tə tiv), *adj.* **1** done as a trial or experiment; experimental. **2** hesitating. [< Medieval Latin *tentativus* < Latin *tentare* to try] **—ten′ta tive ly,** *adv.* **—ten′ta tive ness,** *n.*

ter ma gant (tėr′mə gənt), *n.* a violent, quarreling, scolding woman. **—adj.** violent, quarreling, or scolding. [< *Termagant,* a fictitious Moslem deity in medieval plays]

tern (tėrn), *n.* any of a family of sea birds of the same order as the gulls but with a more slender body and bill and usually a long, forked tail. [< Scandinavian (Danish) *terne*]

thorpe (thôrp), *n.* ARCHAIC. village; hamlet.

thrall (thrôl), *n.* **1** person in bondage; slave or serf. **2** bondage; slavery. [< Scandinavian (Old Icelandic) *thrǣll*]

thwart (thwôrt), *v.t.* prevent from doing something, particularly by blocking the way; oppose and defeat. **—n. 1** seat across a boat, on which a rower sits. **2** brace between the gunwales of a canoe. [< Scandinavian (Old Icelandic) *thvert* across]

thwarts (def. 2)

ti dings (tī′dingz), *n., pl.* news; information.

tim brel (tim′brəl), *n.* a tambourine or similar instrument. [diminutive of Middle English *timbre* < Old French, drum]

tim or ous (tim′ər əs), *adj.* **1** easily frightened; timid. **2** characterized by or indicating fear. [< Latin *timor* fear < *timere* to fear] **—tim′or ous ly,** *adv.* **—tim′or ous ness,** *n.*

tinct (tingkt), *adj.* tinged. **—n.** tint; tinge. [< Latin *tinctus*]

tinc ture (tingk′chər), *n., v.,* **-tured, -tur ing. —n. 1** solution of medicine in alcohol. **2** trace; tinge. **3** color; tint. **—v.t. 1** give a trace or tinge to. **2** color; tint.

-tion, *suffix added to verbs to form nouns.* **1** act or process of _____ing: *Addition = act or process of adding.* **2** condition of being _____ed: *Exhaustion = condition of being exhausted.* **3** result of ____ing: *Reflection* = *result of reflecting*. [< Latin *-tionem*]

tip pet (tip′it), *n.* **1** scarf for the neck and shoulders with ends hanging down in front. **2** a long, narrow, hanging part of a hood, sleeve, or scarf. **3** band of silk or other material worn around the neck by certain clergymen.

tip ple (tip′əl), *v.*, **-pled, -pling**, *n.* —*v.t.*, *v.i.* drink (alcoholic liquor) often or too much. —*n.* an alcoholic liquor. [origin uncertain] —**tip′pler,** *n.*

tithe (tīᴛH), *n.*, *v.*, **tithed, tith ing.** —*n.* **1** one tenth. **2** one tenth of one's yearly income paid as a donation or tax for the support of the church. **3** any small tax. —*v.t.* put a tax or a levy of a tenth on. —*v.i.* give or pledge one tenth of one's income to the church or to charity.

tor rid (tôr′id, tor′id), *adj.* **1** very hot; burning; scorching. **2** exposed or subject to great heat. **3** very ardent; passionate. [< Latin *torridus* < *torrere* to parch] —**tor′rid ly,** *adv.* —**tor′rid ness,** *n.*

tra duce (trə düs′, trə dyüs′), *v.t.*, **-duced, -duc ing.** speak evil of (a person) falsely; slander. [< Latin *traducere* parade in disgrace < *trans-* across + *ducere* to lead] —**tra duce′ment,** *n.*

tram mel (tram′əl), *v.t.*, **-meled, -mel ing** or **-melled, -mel ling.** **1** hinder; restrain. **2** catch in or as if in a trammel; entangle.

tran quil (trang′kwəl), *adj.*, **-quil er, -quil est** or **-quil ler, -quil lest.** free from agitation or disturbance; calm; peaceful; quiet. —**tran′quil ly,** *adv.* —**tran′quil ness,** *n.*

tran scend ent (tran sen′dənt), *adj.* **1** surpassing ordinary limits; excelling; superior; extraordinary. **2** above and independent of the physical universe. —**tran scend′ent ly,** *adv.*

trans gress (trans gres′, tranz gres′), *v.i.* break a law, command, etc.; sin. —*v.t.* **1** go contrary to; sin against. **2** go beyond (a limit or bound). [< Latin *transgressum* gone beyond < *trans-* beyond + *gradi* to step] —**trans gres′sor,** *n.*

trans gres sion (trans gresh′ən, tranz gresh′ən), *n.* a transgressing or a being transgressed; breaking a law, command, etc.; sin.

tran si to ry (tran′sə tôr′ē, tran′sə tōr′ē), *adj.* passing soon or quickly; lasting only a short time; fleeting; transient. —**tran′si to′ri ly,** *adv.* —**tran′si to′ri ness,** *n.*

tra vail (trə vāl′, trav′āl), *n.* **1** toil; labor. **2** trouble, hardship, or suffering. **3** severe pain; agony; torture. **4** the labor and pain of childbirth. —*v.i.* **1** toil; labor. **2** suffer the pains of childbirth; be in labor. [< Old French < Late Latin *trepalium* torture device, ultimately < Latin *tri-* three + *palus* stake]

trea tise (trē′tis), *n.* a formal and systematic book or writing dealing with some subject.

tre bly (treb′lē), *adv.* three times; triply.

trem u lous (trem′yə ləs), *adj.* **1** trembling; quivering. **2** timid; fearful. **3** that wavers; shaky. [< Latin *tremulus* < *tremere* to tremble] —**trem′u lous ly,** *adv.* —**trem′u lous ness,** *n.*

trib u la tion (trib′yə lā′shən), *n.* great trouble; severe trial; affliction. [< Late Latin *tribulationem* < *tribulare* oppress, press < Latin *tribulum* threshing sledge]

trib u tar y (trib′yə ter′ē), *n.*, *pl.* **-tar ies**, *adj.* —*n.* **1** stream that flows into a larger stream or body of water. **2** person or country that pays tribute, an obligation or forced payment. —*adj.* **1** flowing into a larger stream or body of water. **2** paying tribute; required to pay tribute.

trite (trīt), *adj.*, **trit er, trit est.** worn out by use; no longer new or interesting; commonplace; hackneyed. —**trite′ly,** *adv.*

troll (trōl), *n.* (in Scandinavian folklore) an ugly dwarf or giant with supernatural powers, living underground or in caves. [< Swedish and Norwegian < Old Icelandic, giant, demon]

troth (trôth, trōth), *n.* ARCHAIC. **1** faithfulness or fidelity; loyalty. **2** promise. **3** truth. **4** betrothal. **5 plight one's troth, a** promise to marry. **b** promise to be faithful. —*v.t.* **1** promise. **2** betroth.

trun cheon (trun′chən), *n.* **1** a stick cut and shaped for use as a weapon; club. **2** staff of office or authority. —*v.t.* beat with a truncheon; club.

tu mult (tü′mult, tyü′mult), *n.* **1** noise or uproar; commotion. **2** a violent disturbance or disorder. **3** a violent disturbance of mind or feeling; confusion or excitement. [< Latin *tumultus*]

tur bid (tėr′bid), *adj.* **1** muddy; thick; not clear. **2** (of air, smoke, etc.) thick; dense; dark. **3** confused; disordered.

tur bu lent (tėr′byə lənt), *adj.* **1** causing disorder; disorderly; unruly; violent. **2** stormy; tempestuous. [< Latin *turbulentus* < *turba* turmoil] —**tur′bu lent ly,** *adv.*

twain (twān), *n.*, *adj.* ARCHAIC. two. [Old English *twēgen*]

-ty[1], *suffix added to numbers.* ____ tens; ____ times ten: *Seventy* = *seven tens, or seven times ten*. [Old English *-tig*]

-ty[2], *suffix added to adjectives to form nouns.* quality, condition, or fact of being ____: *Safety* = *condition or quality of being safe*. Also, **-ity.** [< Old French *-te, -tet* < Latin *-tas, -tatem*]

tyr an nous (tir′ə nəs), *adj.* acting like a tyrant; cruel or unjust; arbitrary; tyrannical.

ty ro (tī′rō), *n.*, *pl.* **-ros.** beginner in learning anything; novice. Also, **tiro.** [< Latin *tiro* recruit]

un-[1], *prefix.* not ____; the opposite of ____: *Unequal* = *not equal*; *the opposite of equal. Unchanged* = *not changed. Unjust* = *not just*. [Old English]

un-[2], *prefix.* do the opposite of ____; do what will reverse the act: *Unfasten* = *do the opposite of fasten. Uncover* = *do the opposite of cover*. [Old English *un-, on-*]

un al ter a ble (un ôl′tər ə bəl), *adj.* that cannot be altered; not changeable; permanent. —**un al′ter a ble ness,** *n.* —**un al′ter a bly,** *adv.*

un can ny (un kan′ē), *adj.* **1** strange and mysterious; weird. **2** so far beyond what is normal or expected as to have some special power. —**un can′ni ly,** *adv.* —**un can′ni ness,** *n.*

unc tion (ungk′shən), *n.* **1** an anointing with oil, ointment, or the like, for medical purposes or as a religious rite. **2** the oil, ointment, or the like, used for anointing. **3** something soothing or comforting. **4** fervor; earnestness. **5** affected earnestness, sentiment, etc.; smoothness and oiliness of language, manner, etc. [< Latin *unctionem* < *unguere* anoint]

up braid (up brād′), *v.t.* find fault with; blame; reprove.

ur bane (ėr′bān′), *adj.* **1** courteous, refined, or elegant. **2** smoothly polite. [< Latin *urbanus*, originally, urban. —**ur′bane′ly,** *adv.* —**ur′bane′ness,** *n.*

u sur ous (yü′zhər əs), *adj.* OBSOLETE. **1** taking extremely high or unlawful interest for the use of money. **2** of, having to do with, or of the nature of usury.

u surp (yü zėrp′, yü sėrp′), *v.t.* seize and hold (power, position, authority, etc.) by force or without right. —*v.i.* commit usurpation. —**u surp′er,** *n.*

vac il late (vas′ə lāt), *v.i.*, **-lat ed, -lat ing.** **1** waver in mind or opinion. **2** move first one way and then another; waver. [< Latin *vacillatum* wavered] —**vac′il la′tion,** *n.*

vale (vāl), *n.* valley. [< Old French *val* < Latin *vallis*]

van (van), *n.* the front part of an army, fleet, or other advancing group. [short for *vanguard*]

van quish (vang′kwish, van′kwish), *v.t.* **1** conquer, defeat, or overcome in battle or conflict. **2** overcome or subdue by other than physical means.

var let (vär′lit), *n.* a low, mean fellow; rascal.

vaunt (vônt, vänt), *v.t.* boast of. —*v.i.* brag or boast. [< Old French *vanter* < Late Latin *vanitare* be vain, boast < *vanus* vain]

ve he mence (vē′ə məns), *n.* vehement quality or nature; strong feeling; forcefulness; violence.

ve he ment (vē′ə mənt), *adj.* **1** having or showing strong feeling; caused by strong feeling; eager; passionate. **2** forceful; violent. [< Latin *vehementem* being carried away < *vehere* carry] —**ve′he ment ly,** *adv.*

vel li cate (vel′ə kāt), *v.*, **-cat ed, -cat ing.** —*v.t.* pluck. —*v.i.* twitch; move with convulsions.

ven e ra tion (ven′ə rā′shən), *n.* **1** a feeling of deep respect; reverence. **2** act of venerating. **3** condition of being venerated.

ver dur ous (vėr′jər əs), *adj.* green and fresh.

ver i ty (ver′ə tē), *n.*, *pl.* **-ties.** **1** truth. **2** a true statement or fact. **3** reality. [< Latin *veritatem* < *verus* true]

ver min (vėr′mən), *n. pl.* or *sing.* **1** small animals that are troublesome or destructive. Fleas, lice, bedbugs, rats, and mice are vermin. **2** very unpleasant or vile person or persons.

ves per (ves′pər), *n.* **1** evening. **2 Vesper,** the planet Venus, when it appears as the evening star. **3** an evening prayer, hymn, or service. **4** an evening bell. **5 vespers** or **Vespers,** *pl.* **a** a church service held in the late afternoon or in the evening; evensong. **b** the sixth of the canonical hours. —*adj.* **1** of evening. **2** Sometimes, **Vesper.** of or having to do with vespers. [< Latin]

vex (veks), *v.t.* **1** anger by trifles; annoy; provoke. **2** worry; trouble; harass. **3** disturb by commotion; agitate. [< Latin *vexare*] —**vex′ing ly,** *adv.*

vex a tion (vek sā′shən), *n.* **1** a vexing. **2** a being vexed. **3** thing that vexes.

vi al (vī′əl) *n.* a small glass or plastic bottle for holding medicines or the like; phial. [variant of *phial*]

vi car i ous (vī ker′ē əs, vi ker′ē əs), *adj.* **1** done or suffered for others: *vicarious work.* **2** felt by sharing in others' experience. **3** taking the place of another; doing the work of another. **4** delegated. —**vi car′i ous ly,** *adv.* —**vi car′i ous ness,** *n.*

vice roy (vīs′roi), *n.* person ruling a country or province as the deputy of the sovereign. [< French *vice-roi* < *vice* vice + *roi* king]

vict ual (vit′l), *n., v.,* **-ualed, -ual ing** or **-ualled, -ual ling.** —*n.* **victuals,** *pl.* food or provisions. —*v.t.* supply with food or provisions. —*v.i.* **1** take on a supply of food or provisions. **2** eat or feed. [< Latin *victualia,* plural of *victualis* of food < *victus* food, sustenance < *vivere* to live]

vie (vī), *v.i.,* **vied, vy ing.** strive for superiority; contend in rivalry; compete. [short for Middle French *envier* to wager, challenge < Latin *invitare* invite] —**vi′er,** *n.*

vin di ca tion (vin′də kā′shən), *n.* a vindicating or a being vindicated; defense; justification.

vin dic tive (vin dik′tiv), *adj.* **1** feeling a strong tendency toward revenge; bearing a grudge. **2** showing a strong tendency toward reverge. [< Latin *vindicta* revenge < *vindex* avenger] —**vin dic′tive ly,** *adv.* —**vin dic′tive ness,** *n.*

vint ner (vint′nər), *n.* dealer in wine; wine merchant.

vis age (viz′ij), *n.* **1** face. **2** appearance or aspect. [< Old French < *vis* face < Latin *visus* sight < *videre* to see]

vis cous (vis′kəs), *adj.* **1** thick like heavy syrup or glue; sticky. **2** having the property of viscosity. [< Latin *viscosus* < *viscum* birdlime] —**vis′cous ly,** *adv.* —**vis′cous ness,** *n.*

vi sion ar y (vizh′ə ner′ē), *n., pl.* **-ar ies,** *adj.* —*n.* **1** person given to imagining or dreaming; person who is not practical. **2** person who sees visions. —*adj.* **1** not practical; dreamy. **2** having visions; able to have visions. —**vi′sion ar′i ness,** *n.*

vo lup tu ous (və lup′chü əs), *adj.* **1** caring much for the pleasures of the senses. **2** giving pleasure to the senses. [< Latin *voluptuosus* < *voluptas* pleasure] —**vo lup′tu ous ly,** *adv.* —**vo lup′tu ous ness,** *n.*

wag ger y (wag′ər ē), *n., pl.* **-ger ies.** **1** act or habit of joking. **2** joke.

wan (won), *adj.,* **wan ner, wan nest.** **1** lacking natural or normal color; pale. **2** looking worn or tired; faint; weak. [Old English *wann* dark] —**wan′ly,** *adv.* —**wan′ness,** *n.*

wane (wān), *v.i.,* **waned, wan ing.** **1** lose size; become smaller gradually. **2** decline in power, influence, or importance. **3** decline in strength or intensity. **4** draw to a close.

wan ton (won′tən), *adj.* **1** reckless, heartless, or malicious. **2** without reason or excuse. **3** not moral; not chaste. **4** frolicsome; playful. **5** not restrained. —*n.* a wanton person. —*v.i.* act in a wanton manner. —*v.t.* waste foolishly; squander. [Middle English *wantowen* < Old English *wan-* not, lacking + *togen* brought up] —**wan′ton ly,** *adv.* —**wan′ton ness,** *n.*

ware (wer, war), *n.* Usually, **wares,** *pl.* a manufactured thing; article for sale: *The peddler sold his wares cheap.*

war rant (wôr′ənt, wor′ənt), *v.t.* **1** authorize. **2** justify. **3** promise; guarantee.

was sail (wos′əl, was′əl), *n.* **1** a drinking party; revelry with drinking of healths. **2** spiced ale or other liquor drunk at a wassail. [< Scandinavian (Old Icelandic) *ves heill* be healthy!]

wat tle (wot′l), *n., v.,* **-tled, -tling.** —*n.* Also, **wattles,** *pl.* sticks interwoven with twigs or branches; framework of wicker.

a hat	i it	oi oil	ch child		a in about
ā age	ī ice	ou out	ng long		e in taken
ä far	o hot	u cup	sh she	ə =	i in pencil
e let	ō open	ù put	th thin		o in lemon
ē equal	ô order	ü rule	₮H then		u in circus
ėr term			zh measure	< = derived from	

—*v.t.* make (a fence, wall, roof, hut, etc.) of wattle.

weal (wēl), *n.* well-being; prosperity. ARCHAIC. society; the state.

ween (wēn), *v.t., v.i.* ARCHAIC. think; suppose; believe; expect. [Old English *wēnan*]

wel ter (wel′tər), *n.* **1** a rolling or tumbling about. **2** a surging or confused mass. **3** confusion; commotion.

wend (wend), *v.,* **wend ed** or **went, wend ing.** —*v.t.* direct (one's way): *We wended our way home.* —*v.i.* go [Old English *wendan*]

whelk (hwelk), *n.* pimple or pustule. [Old English *hwylca*]

whet (hwet), *v.t.* **whet ted, whet ting.** **1** sharpen by rubbing. **2** make keen or eager; stimulate. **3** rub vigorously together.

whet stone (hwet′stōn′), *n.* stone for sharpening knives or tools.

whim si cal (hwim′zə kəl), *adj.* **1** full of whims; having many odd notions or fancies; capricious. **2** of or like a whim or whims; odd; fanciful. —**whim′si cal ly,** *adv.* —**whim′si cal ness,** *n.*

whin ny (hwin′ē), *n., pl.* **-nies,** *v.,* **-nied, -ny ing.** —*n.* the prolonged, quavering sound that a horse makes. —*v.i.* utter a whinny or any sound like it. —*v.t.* express with such a sound.

wight (wīt), *n.* **1** ARCHAIC. a human being; person. **2** OBSOLETE. any living being; creature. [Old English *wiht*]

wile (wīl), *n., v.,* **wiled, wil ing.** —*n.* **1** a trick to deceive; cunning way. **2** subtle trickery; slyness; craftiness. —*v.t.* coax; lure; entice.

wim ple (wim′pəl), *n., v.,* **-pled, -pling.** —*n.* cloth for the head arranged in folds about the head, cheeks, chin, and neck, worn sometimes by nuns and formerly by other women. —*v.t.* **1** cover with or as if with a wimple; veil. **2** cause to ripple. **3** ARCHAIC. lay in folds, as a veil. —*v.i.* **1** ripple. **2** ARCHAIC. lie in folds. [Old English *wimpel*]

wist (wist), *v.* ARCHAIC. pt. and pp. of **wit.**

wist ful (wist′fəl), *adj.* longing; yearning. —**wist′ful ly,** *adv.* —**wist′ful ness,** *n.*

wit (wit), *v.t., v.i.,* **wist, wit ting.** **1** ARCHAIC. know. **2 to wit,** that is to say; namely. [Old English *witan*]

with al (wi ₮Hôl′, wi thôl′), *adv.* **1** with it all; as well; besides; also. **2** ARCHAIC. in spite of all; nevertheless. **b** therewith. —*prep.* ARCHAIC. with. [Middle English < *with + all*]

wold (wōld), *n.* high, rolling country, bare of woods. [Old English *weald,* a wood]

wont ed (wun′tid, wōn′tid, wôn′tid), *adj.* accustomed; customary; usual. —**wont′ed ly,** *adv.* —**wont′ed ness,** *n.*

wretch (rech), *n.* **1** a very unfortunate or unhappy person. **2** a very bad person. [Old English *wrecca* exile]

wretch ed (rech′id), *adj.* **1** very unfortunate or unhappy. **2** very unsatisfactory; miserable. **3** very bad. —**wretch′ed ly,** *adv.* —**wretch′ed ness.** *n.*

yeo man (yō′mən), *n., pl.* **-men.** **1** (formerly, in Great Britain) a person who owned land, but not a large amount, and usually farmed it himself. **2** ARCHAIC. servant or attendant in a royal or noble household. [Middle English *yoman*]

yoke (yōk), *n.* **1** a wooden frame to fasten two work animals together. **2** something that joins or unites. **3** something that holds people in slavery or submission.

yore (yôr, yōr), *n.* **of yore, a** now long since gone; long past. **b** of long ago; formerly; in the past. —*adv.* OBSOLETE. long ago; years ago.

zeal ous (zel′əs), *adj.* full of zeal; eager; earnest; enthusiastic.

zeph yr (zef′ər), *n.* **1** the west wind. **2** any soft, gentle wind; mild breeze. [< *Zephyrus*]

INDEX OF AUTHORS AND TITLES

INDEX OF FEATURES

INDEX OF READING AND LITERATURE SKILLS

INDEX OF THINKING SKILLS

INDEX OF VOCABULARY EXERCISES

INDEX OF COMPOSITION ASSIGNMENTS

INDEX OF ENRICHMENT ACTIVITIES

INDEX OF GENRES

1014

INDEX OF THEMES

This index suggests some thematic units that might be used in teaching the selections in *England in Literature*. Selections are shown in the order in which they appear in the text. Many selections are shown under more than one theme. A few works are omitted.

★ Date of composition or (in the case of plays) first performance. Dates not asterisked are publications dates.

INDEX OF GRAPHIC AIDS

INDEX OF ARTISTS

ILLUSTRATION ACKNOWLEDGMENTS

All photographs not credited are the property of Scott, Foresman. Source abbreviations are: BL for The British Library; BM for reproduced by Courtesy of the Trustees of the British Museum; NPG for National Portrait Gallery, London; TG for The Tate Gallery, London; VA for Victoria and Albert Museum, Crown Copyright.

UNIT 1

xx (l) Roman Baths Museum, Bath. Photo by Stephen Bird; (c) Sonia Halliday Photographs; (r) BL. **1** (l) Cathedral Treasury, Aachen. Photo by Ann Münchow; (c) Werner Forman Archive, London; (r) BL. **3** Rita Bailey/Leo de Wys. **6** BL. **9** BM. **17** Michael Holford. **24** BM. **37** University Museum of National Antiquities, Oslo, Norway. Photo by Ove Holst. **43** (all) BM. **47** Werner Forman Archive, London. **50** BM. **56** The Board of Trinity College Dublin. **59** BL. **61. 65** The Board of Trinity College Dublin. **66** University Museum of National Antiquities, Oslo, Norway. Photo by Eirik Irgens Johnsen. **70** BL.

UNIT 2

76 (l) BL; (c) Michael Holford; (r) Sonia Halliday Photographs. **77** (l) BL; (c) Rare Books and Manuscripts Division, The New York Public Library, Astor, Lenox and Tilden Foundations; (r) Giraudon/Art Resource, NY. **80** Michael Holford. **83, 86** BL. **90** Detail of MS W. 219, fol. 245, ca. 1415. Walters Art Gallery, Baltimore. **92** The Burrell Collection, Glasgow Museums & Art Galleries. **95** Bodleian Library, Oxford. **96** Museum of London. **98, 99, 103, 106, 107** The Huntington Library, San Marino, California. **109** BL. **115** The Huntington Library, San Marino, California. **119** Museum of London. **124** The Huntington Library, San Marino, California. **136** BL. **139** The Metropolitan Museum of Art, The Cloisters Collection, Munsey Fund, 1932. **141** By permission of His Grace the Archbishop of Canterbury and the Trustees of Lambeth Palace Library. **143** BL. **148** The Huntington Library, San Marino, California. **153** BL.

UNIT 3

156 (l) Scala/Art Resource, NY; (c) Scottish National Portrait Gallery, National Galleries of Scotland; (r) From the Art Collection of the Folger Shakespeare Library. **157** (l, c) BM; (r) By permission of the Folger Shakespeare Library. **160** BL. **161** Thyssen-Bornemisza collection. **163** Bridgeman Art Library/Art Resource, NY. **166** Drawing of Sir Thomas Wyatt by Holbein. Windsor Castle Library, © Her Majesty Queen Elizabeth II. **167** NPG. **168** VA. **170** NPG. **173** Detail of *The Ermine Portrait of Queen Elizabeth I* by Nicholas Hilliard. By courtesy of the Marquess of Salisbury. **174** NPG. **176** Private Collection. **179** By permission of the Master and Fellows, Pembroke College, Cambridge. **180** VA. **181** NPG. **182** VA. **185** NPG. **187** Staatliche Museen Preussischer Kulturbesitz, Nationalgalerie, West Berlin. MACBETH Edition: **201** NPG, on loan from the Tate Gallery. **233** VA. **250** (l) BM. **251** Scale drawing by Irwin

Smith from *Shakespeare's Globe Playhouse: A Modern Reconstruction in Text and Scale Drawings* by Irwin Smith. Charles Scribner's Sons, New York, 1956. Hand colored by Cheryl Kucharzak. HAMLET Edition: **203** *The Ghost on the Terrace* by Eugene Delacroix, National Gallery of Art, Washington, Rosenwald Collection. **205** By permission of the Folger Shakespeare Library. **208** (l) BM. **209** Scale drawing by Irwin Smith from *Shakespeare's Globe Playhouse: A Modern Reconstruction in Text and Scale Drawings* by Irwin Smith. Charles Scribner's Sons, New York, 1956. Hand colored by Cheryl Kucharzak. **229, 249** TG. **255** Giraudon/Art Resource, NY. **265** Putative portrait of Christopher Marlowe. By permission of the Master, Fellows and Scholars of Corpus Christi College, Cambridge. **267** VA. **269** NPG. **271** Yale Center for British Art, Paul Mellon Collection. **273** By Permission of the Governors of Dulwich Picture Gallery. **274, 275,** BL. **278** NPG. **281** Detail of *Melancholy I* by Albrecht Durer, 56.947. © 1987 The Art Institute of Chicago. All Rights Reserved. **283** Conway Library, Courtauld Institute of Art. **286** Bridgeman Art Library/Art Resource. NY. **287** The Louvre, Paris. Cliché des Musées Nationaux, Paris. **288** NPG. **289** Telarci-Giraudon/Art Resource, NY. **292** NPG. **297** BM. **305** Stirling Maxwell Collection, Pollok House, Glasgow Museums & Art Galleries.

UNIT 4

312 (l) VA; (c) NPG. **313** (l) Aldo Tutino/Art Resource, NY; (c) Walker Art Gallery, Liverpool; (r) U. S. Capitol Historical Society. National Geographic Society Photograph. **317** Sheldonian Theatre, Oxford. Photo by Thomas-Photos, Oxford. **318** The Trustees of Sir John Soane's Museum. **320, 321, 324** NPG. **329** Pepys Library, by permission of the Master and Fellows, Magdalene College, Cambridge. **331** Museum of London. **333** NPG. **335** The Bettmann Archive/BBC Hulton. **339** The Mansell Collection. **347** Library of Congress. **353** The Granger Collection, New York. **358** NPG. **363** Bridgeman Art Library/Art Resource, NY. **365** NPG. **369** BM. **372** NPG. **374** BM. **376** Bodleian Library, Oxford. **389** NPG. **390** Pepys Library, by permission of the Master and Fellows, Magdalene College, Cambridge. **393** NPG. **397** Henry Fuseli, *Blind Milton Dictating to His Daughters*, 1793, oil on canvas, 118.1 × 115.6 cm, Preston O. Morton Memorial Purchase Fund for Older Paintings, 1973.303. © 1987 The Art Institute of Chicago. All Rights Reserved. **400** Scottish National Portrait Gallery, National Galleries of Scotland. Photo by Tom Scott. **403** The Granger Collection, New York. **408** NPG. **411** From *Designs by Mr. R. Bentley for Six Poems by Mr. T. Gray*, London, 1753. **413** From *The Poetical Work of Alexander Pope*, ed. R. Carruthers, Vol. I, London, Ingram, Cooke & Co., 1853. **417** Society of Antiquaries, London.

UNIT 5

420 (l) Bibliothèque Nationale, Paris; (c) BM; (r) NPG. **421** (l) Scala/Art Resource, NY: (c) Sidney Sabin Galleries, London; (r) Science Museum, London. **425** Clive House Museum, Shrewsbury. **428** NPG. **429** BM. **431** Library of Congress. **435** TG. **436** BM. **438** NPG. **439** BL. **443** The Bettmann Archive. **445** VA. **449** NPG. **451** BM. **461** Repro-

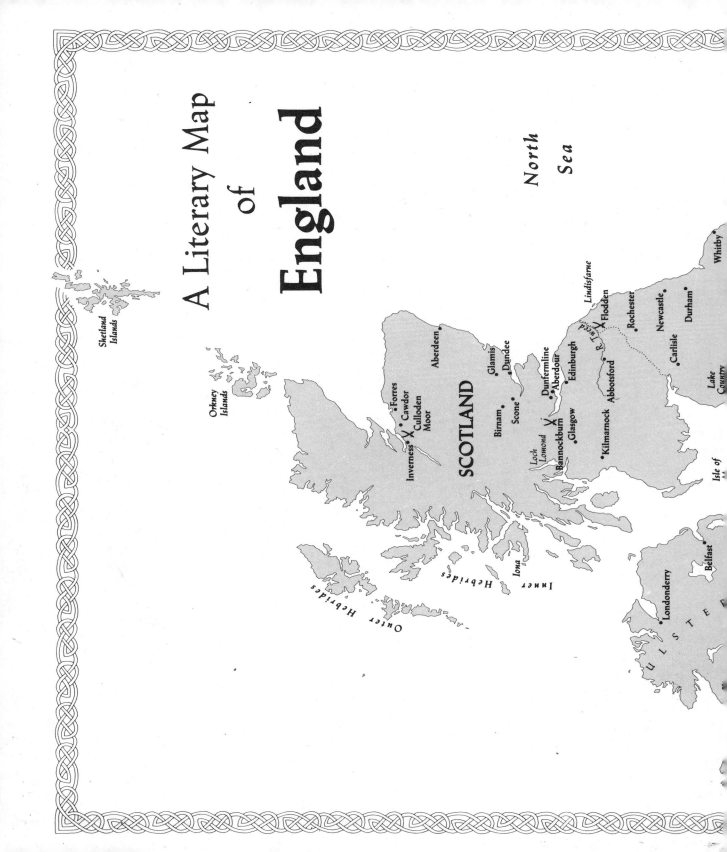

A Literary Map

of

England

North Sea

Shetland Islands

Orkney Islands

Outer Hebrides

Inner Hebrides

Iona

Aberdeen

Forres
Cawdor
Culloden Moor
Inverness

SCOTLAND

Birnam
Glamis
Scone
Dundee

Loch Lomond
Bannockburn
Glasgow

Kilmarnock

Dunfermline
Aberdour
Edinburgh
Abbotsford

Lindisfarne
Flodden
Rochester
Newcastle
Carlisle
Durham
Whitby

R. Tweed

Lake Country

Isle of

Londonderry
Belfast

ULSTER